Bart De Smet

C# 4.0

UNLEASHED

SAMS | 800 East 96th Street, Indianapolis, Indiana 46240 USA

C# 4.0 Unleashed

ISBN-13: 978-0-672-33079-7
ISBN-10: 0-672-33079-2

Library of Congress Cataloging-in-Publication Data

Smet, Bart de.
  C# 4.0 unleashed / Bart de Smet.
    p. cm.   .
  Includes index.
  ISBN 978-0-672-33079-7
  1. C# (Computer program language) I. Title.
  QA76.73.C154S63 2011
  005.13'3—dc22

                    2010050192

Printed in the United States of America

First Printing: January 2011

Editor-in-Chief
Greg Wiegand

Executive Editor
Neil Rowe

Acquisitions Editor
Brook Farling

Development Editor
Mark Renfrow

Managing Editor
Sandra Schroeder

Senior Project Editor
Tonya Simpson

Copy Editor
Keith Cline

Indexer
Larry Sweazy

Proofreader
Chrissy White

Technical Editor
Doug Holland

Publishing Coordinator
Cindy Teeters

Book Designer
Gary Adair

Compositor
Nonie Ratcliff

Trademarks

Warning and Disclaimer

Bulk Sales

Pearson offers excellent discounts on this book when ordered in quantity for bulk purchases or special sales. For more information, please contact:

U.S. Corporate and Government Sales
1-800-382-3419
corpsales@pearsontechgroup.com

For sales outside of the U.S., please contact:

International Sales
+1-317-581-3793
international@pearsontechgroup.com

Contents at a Glance

Introduction 1

Part I   Introduction

   1   Introducing the .NET Platform 5

   2   Introducing the C# Programming Language 55

   3   Getting Started with .NET Development Using C# 99

Part II   C#—The Language

   4   Language Essentials 171

   5   Expressions and Operators 247

   6   A Primer on Types and Objects 299

   7   Simple Control Flow 351

   8   Basics of Exceptions and Resource Management 409

   9   Introducing Types 463

  10   Methods 501

  11   Fields, Properties, and Indexers 545

  12   Constructors and Finalizers 579

  13   Operator Overloading and Conversions 603

  14   Object-Oriented Programming 643

  15   Generic Types and Methods 697

  16   Collection Types 753

  17   Delegates 777

  18   Events 833

  19   Language Integrated Query Essentials 901

  20   Language Integrated Query Internals 967

  21   Reflection 1047

  22   Dynamic Programming 1109

  23   Exceptions 1167

  24   Namespaces 1213

  25   Assemblies and Application Domains 1233

Part III   Working with Base Class Libraries

26   Base Class Library Essentials 1291

27   Diagnostics and Instrumentation 1363

28   Working with I/O 1391

29   Threading and Synchronization 1431

30   Task Parallelism and Data Parallelism 1501

Index 1539

Table of Contents

Introduction   **1**

Who Should Read This Book? 2
What You Need to Know Before You Read This Book 2
How This Book Is Organized 3

Part I   Introduction

1   Introducing the .NET Platform   **5**

A Historical Perspective 5
    Win32 Programming in C 6
    Raising the Abstraction Level with MFC and C++ 6
    Component-Driven Development with COM 7
    Windows Development for the Masses in Visual Basic 7
    Reaching Out to the Web with Windows DNA 8
    Reaching Out to Java with J++ 8
    Time for Lightning 8
A 10,000-Feet View of the .NET Platform 9
    The .NET Platform 9
The Common Language Infrastructure 12
The Multilanguage Aspect of .NET 14
Introducing .NET Assemblies 15
The Common Type System Explained 17
    What's Type Safety? 17
    Primitive Types 19
    Classes, Structures, and Enumerations 19
    Interfaces 20
    Delegates 21
    Members 22
    A Note on Generics 23
    The Role of the Common Language Specification 23
Executing Managed Code 24
    The Assembly Manifest 26
    IL Code 27
    Metadata 29
    Mixing Languages 30
Diving into the Common Language Runtime 32
    Bootstrapping the Runtime 33
    Assembly Loading 35

Application Domains 37
JIT Compilation 39
Native Image Generation 42
Automatic Memory Management 43
Exception Handling 46
Code Access Security 47
Interoperability Facilities 49
The Base Class Library 51
Summary 54

2   Introducing the C# Programming Language   55

The Evolution of C# 55
C# 1.0: Managed Code Development, Take One 56
C# 2.0: Enriching the Core Language Features 59
C# 3.0: Bridging the Gap Between Objects and Data 64
C# 4.0: Reaching Out to Dynamic Languages 76
A Sneak Peek at the Future 89
Multiparadigm 89
Language-Shaping Forces 91
Compiler as a Service 92
Taming the Concurrency Beast 94
Summary 97

3   Getting Started with .NET Development Using C#   99

Installing the .NET Framework 99
The .NET Framework Version Landscape 99
.NET Framework 4 103
Running the Installer 106
What Got Installed? 106
Your First Application: Take One 109
Writing the Code 110
Compiling It 111
Running It 112
Inspecting Our Assembly with .NET Reflector 112
Visual Studio 2010 116
Editions 117
Expression 119
Installing Visual Studio 2010 119
A Quick Tour Through Visual Studio 2010 120
Your First Application: Take Two 124
New Project Dialog 124
Solution Explorer 126
Project Properties 127

Code Editor 128
Build Support 130
Debugging Support 136
Object Browser 139
Code Insight 139
Integrated Help 144
Designers 144
Server Explorer 155
Database Mappers 157
Unit Testing 163
Team Development 167
Summary 169

Part II   C#—The Language

4   Language Essentials   171

The Entry Point 171
A Trivial Console Application 171
Method Signatures 172
Allowed Entry-Point Signatures 173
Running the Sample 175
Under the Hood 176
Keywords 177
Contextual Keywords 178
Syntax Highlighting in Visual Studio 179
A Primer on Types 180
Code and Data 180
Types, Objects, and Instances 182
Variables 183
Classes and Other Types 184
Built-In Types 185
Integral Types 186
Floating-Point Types 190
The Decimal Type 194
The Boolean Type 196
The String Type 197
Object 198
Dynamic Typing 201
A Word on CLS Compliance 202
A Matter of Style: Aliases or Not? 208
Local Variables 209
Declaration 209
Scope 210

Assignment 212

Constants 213

Implicitly Typed Local Variable Declarations 215

Intermezzo on Comments 220

Single-Line Comments 220

A Primer to Preprocessing Directives 221

Delimited Comments 223

Documentation Comments 224

Arrays 228

Internal Representation 228

Single-Dimensional Arrays 229

Array Initializers 231

Jagged Arrays 233

Multidimensional Arrays 235

The Null Reference 237

What's Null Really? 237

A Common Source of Bugs 239

Nullable Value Types 240

Internal Representation 242

Use in C# 242

A Type Background 244

Summary 246

5   Expressions and Operators   247

What Are Expressions? 247

Arity of Operators 248

Precedence and Associativity 248

Evaluation of Subexpressions 250

The Evaluation Stack 251

Arithmetic Operators 255

Integer Arithmetic 255

Floating-Point Arithmetic 255

Decimal Arithmetic 258

Character Arithmetic 259

Unary Plus and Minus 260

Overflow Checking 260

Arithmetic with Nullables 265

String Concatenation 266

Shift Operators 270

Relational Operators 271

Equality for Different Types 272

Lifted Operators 273

Logical Operators 273
    Integral Bitwise Logical Operators 273
    Use for Enumerations 274
    Boolean Logical Operators 275
    Nullable Boolean Logic 277
Conditional Operators 278
    Under the Hood 278
An Operator's Result Type 281
    Associativity 282
Null-Coalescing Operator 282
Assignment 285
    Decaration Versus (Simple) Assignment 285
    Compound Assignment 287
    A Gentle Introduction to Definite Assignment 290
    Postfix and Prefix Increment and Decrement Operators ... 294
Summary 297

6   A Primer on Types and Objects   299

Implicit Versus Explicit Conversions 299
    Cast Expressions 300
    The is Operator 306
    The as Operator 311
    Intermezzo: The Mythical Type Switch 315
The typeof Operator: A Sneak Peek at Reflection 317
Default Value Expression 320
Creating Objects with the new Operator 323
    Behind the Scenes of Constructors 325
    Object Initializers 328
    Collection Initializers 333
Member Access 335
    A First Look at Dynamic Typing 337
Invocation Expressions 339
    Method Invocation 339
    Delegate Invocation 341
Element Access 347
Summary 349

7   Simple Control Flow   351

What Are Statements, Anyway? 351
Expression Statements 353
    Method Calls 353
    Assignments 354
    Pre- and Post-Increment/Decrement 355

The Empty Statement 355

Blocks 356

Declarations 357

Selection Statements 358

    The if Statement 358

    The switch Statement 363

Iteration Statements 376

    The while Statement 376

    The do...while Statement 380

    The for Statement 381

    The foreach Statement 384

A Peek at Iterators 392

Loops in the Age of Concurrency 400

The goto Statement 402

The return Statement 406

Summary 408

8   Basics of Exceptions and Resource Management   409

Exception Handling 409

    Exceptions Are Objects 411

    Causes of Exceptions 412

    Throwing Exceptions 423

    Handling Exceptions 423

    The finally Clause 432

Deterministic Resource Cleanup 438

    Garbage Collection in a Nutshell 438

    Object Disposal 439

    The using Statement 441

    Implementing IDisposable 443

    (In)appropriate Use of IDisposable 446

Locking on Objects 447

    Under the Hood 449

    The lock Statement 452

    Intermezzo: Code Generation for Lock 456

    Be Careful with Locks 458

Summary 462

9   Introducing Types   463

Types Revisited 463

Classes Versus Structs 466

    References Versus Values 466

    Heap Versus Stack 470

Boxing 478
The Dangers of Mutable Value Types 483
Type Members 486
Visibility 486
Static Versus Instance 490
Partial Types 496
Summary 499

10   Methods   501

Defining Methods 501
Return Type 502
Parameters 504
Value Parameters 505
Reference Parameters 508
Output Parameters 508
Parameter Arrays 510
Optional and Named Parameters 512
Overloading 516
Defining Method Overloads 517
Method Groups 518
Overload Resolution 519
Extension Methods 522
Defining Extension Methods 524
Overload Resolution 526
Using Extension Methods 527
How the Compiler Marks and Finds Extension Methods 529
Partial Methods 532
Extern Methods 536
Refactoring 537
Code Analysis 543
Summary 544

11   Fields, Properties, and Indexers   545

Fields 545
Declaring Fields 546
Accessing Fields 546
Initializing Fields 549
Read-Only Fields 553
Constants 555
Volatile Fields 557
An Intermezzo About Enums 558
Why Enums Matter 558
Underlying Types 559

Assigning Values to Members 559
The System.Enum Type 561
Flags 564
Revisiting the switch Statement 568
Behind the Scenes 568
Properties 569
Declaring and Using Properties 569
Auto-Implemented Properties 572
How Properties Work 573
Indexers 574
Defining Indexers 575
How Indexers Are Implemented 577
Summary 578

12   Constructors and Finalizers   579

Constructors 579
Instance Constructors 579
Static Constructors 586
Destructors (Poorly Named Finalizers) 589
Defining Finalizers in C# 591
How Finalizers Are Run 591
How Finalizers Are Implemented 594
Disposal Before Collection: IDisposable 595
Summary 601

13   Operator Overloading and Conversions   603

Operators 603
Defining Operators 604
How Operators Are Found 605
Nullability and Lifted Operators 606
Which Operators Can Be Overloaded? 609
Implementing Equality Operations 615
How Operators Are Translated 626
Conversions 627
Built-In Conversions 627
User-Defined Conversions 631
Other Conversion Mechanisms 638
Summary 641

14   Object-Oriented Programming   643

The Cornerstones of Object Orientation 643
A Historical Perspective 643
Encapsulation 647

Inheritance 648
Polymorphism 654
Types in Pictures 656
Inheritance for Classes 657
Single Inheritance for Classes 661
Multiple Inheritance for Interfaces 663
Blocking Inheritance 665
Hiding Base Class Members 666
Protected Accessibility 669
Polymorphism and Virtual Members 670
Virtual Members 671
Overriding Virtual Members 673
Declaring Virtual Members 675
Sealing and Hiding: Take Two 676
How Virtual Dispatch Works 678
How Base Calls Work 682
Abstract Classes 683
Interfaces 686
Defining Interfaces 686
Some Design Recommendations 688
Implementing Interfaces 690
Summary 694

15 Generic Types and Methods   **697**
Life Without Generics 697
A Real-World Example with Collections 697
Performance Worries 699
Getting Started with Generics 699
Declaring Generic Types 703
Using Generic Types 708
Performance Intermezzo 709
Operations on Type Parameters 714
Default Values 714
Getting the Type's Reflection Info Object 716
Generic Constraints 716
Interface-Based Constraints 717
Base Class Constraints 723
Default Constructor Constraint 724
Restriction to Value Types or Reference Types 731
Generic Methods 732
Co- and Contravariance 740
Annoyances with Generic Types 740
Broken Covariance for Array Types 741

Safety Guarantees 744
Generic Co- and Contravariance 746
Under the Hood 748
Where to Use 750
Summary 751

16 Collection Types   **753**

Nongeneric Collection Types 753
ArrayList 754
Hash Tables 755
Queue 758
Stack 759
Summary 761
Generic Collection Types 762
List<T> 762
SortedDictionary<TKey, TValue>
    and SortedList<TKey, TValue> 770
Queue<T> and Stack<T> 774
Other Collection Types 775
Summary 775

17 Delegates   **777**

Functional Programming 777
Historical Perspective 778
Programming with Functions 779
What Are Delegates? 782
Delegate Types 782
Delegate Instances 787
Anonymous Function Expressions 789
Closures: Captured Outer
    Variables 790
Lambda Expressions 795
Expression Trees 797
Invoking Delegates 799
Putting It Together: An Extensible
    Calculator 803
Case Study: Delegates Used in LINQ
    to Objects 807
Asynchronous Invocation 811
Combining Delegates 824
Summary 831

18 Events   **833**

The Two Sides of Delegates 834
A Reactive Application 835
    Using Delegates 836
    Limitations on Plain Use of Delegates 839
    Using .NET Events 840
How Events Work 843
Raising Events, the Correct Way 845
Add and Remove Accessors 847
Detach Your Event Handlers 852
Recommended Event Patterns 861
    `EventHandler` and `EventArgs` 862
    `EventHandler<T>` 867
    Designing Events for Use by Derived Classes 869
Case Study: `INotifyProperty` Interfaces and
  UI Programming 871
    Events in UI Frameworks 876
Countdown, the GUI Way 882
Modern Approaches to Reactive Programming 888
    Events Revisited 890
    Pull Versus Push 894
    Dictionary Suggest Revisited 897
Summary 900

19 Language Integrated Query Essentials   **901**

Life Without LINQ 902
    In-Memory Data 902
    Relational Databases 903
    XML 907
    The Birth of LINQ 908
LINQ by Example 909
    In-Memory Data 909
    Relational Databases 911
    XML 917
Query Expression Syntax 920
    Why Query Expressions? 920
    Getting Started 922
    Source Selection Using a `from` Clause 923
    Projection Using the `Select` Clause 927
    Filtering Using a `where` Clause 933
    Ordering Using the `orderby` Keyword 935
    Grouping Using the `group by` Clause 942

Joining Using the `join` Clause 949

Continuing a Query Expression Using
the `into` Clause 955

Bindings with the `let` Clause 961

Summary 964

20 Language Integrated Query Internals   967

How LINQ to Objects Works 967

`IEnumerable<T>` and `IEnumerator<T>` Recap 968

LINQ to Objects Extension Methods 970

Iterators 974

Lazy Evaluation 981

How Iterators Work 984

Standard Query Operators 990

Source Generators 990

Restriction 992

Projection 997

Ordering 1002

Grouping and Joining 1003

Aggregation 1008

Predicates 1017

Set Theoretical and Sequencing
Operators 1018

Sequence Persistence 1020

Remote Versus Local with `AsEnumerable` 1022

The Query Pattern 1024

All About Methods 1024

Overloading Query Expression Syntax 1025

Parallel LINQ 1027

The Cost of Optimization 1028

`AsParallel` 1028

How PLINQ Works 1031

`AsOrdered` 1032

Tweaking Parallel Querying Behavior 1033

Parallel Enumeration with `ForAll` 1034

Expression Trees 1036

Query Expression Translation 1036

Homoiconicity for Dummies 1038

Expression Trees for Query
Expressions 1041

`IQueryable<T>` 1043

Summary 1046

21 Reflection   **1047**

Typing Revisited, Static and Otherwise 1048
    The Role of Metadata 1048
    The Multilanguage World 1049
    Taking Multilanguage to the Next Level 1051
    How Does All of This Relate to C# Programming? 1052
Reflection 1054
    `System.Type` 1054
    A Primer on Application Extensibility 1059
    Reflection for Methods, Properties, Events,
        and More 1070
    Custom Attributes 1075
Lightweight Code Generation 1082
    Hello LCG 1082
    A Toy Compiler for Arithmetic Expressions 1084
Expression Trees 1091
    Compiler-Generated Expression Trees 1092
    The Expression Tree API 1093
    Using the `ExpressionTreeVisitor` 1105
Summary 1107

22 Dynamic Programming   **1109**

The dynamic Keyword in C# 4.0 1109
    The `dynamic` Type 1111
    Dynamic Typing Is Contagious 1112
    Deferred Overload Resolution 1114
    No `System.Dynamic` Type 1117
    When to Use `dynamic`: Case Study
        with IronPython 1119
DLR Internals 1127
    Dynamic Call Sites and Binders 1128
    Dynamic Dispatch 1134
    Custom Dynamic Objects with `DynamicObject` 1140
    A Primer to `DynamicMetaObject` 1144
    Dynamic Operations 1147
    Overall Architecture 1148
Office and COM Interop 1150
    Essentials of COM Interop 1152
    Simplified COM Interop in .NET 4 1152
    Case Study: COM Interop with Excel and Word 1154
Summary 1165

23 Exceptions   1167

Life Without Exceptions 1167

    Win32 1168

    COM 1169

    Lessons Learned 1170

Introducing Exceptions 1170

Exception Handling 1172

    try Statements 1176

    First-Chance Exceptions 1178

    Intermezzo on Historical Debugging
       with IntelliTrace 1183

    When and What to Catch 1184

    Beyond Your Control 1187

Throwing Exceptions 1188

Defining Your Own Exception Types 1190

(In)famous Exception Types 1193

    DivideByZeroException 1193

    OverflowException 1194

    NullReferenceException 1194

    IndexOutOfRangeException 1195

    InvalidCastException 1195

    ArrayTypeMismatchException 1196

    TypeInitializationException 1196

    ObjectDisposedException 1198

    OutOfMemoryException 1200

    StackOverflowException 1202

    ExecutionEngineException 1205

    ArgumentException 1205

    ArgumentNullException 1206

    ArgumentOutOfRangeException 1207

    InvalidOperationException 1207

    NotImplementedException 1208

    NotSupportedException 1209

    FormatException 1210

    AggregateException 1211

Summary 1212

24 Namespaces   1213

Organizing Types in Namespaces 1213

    Once Upon a Time 1214

    Assemblies and Namespaces 1216

Declaring Namespaces 1219
   Naming Conventions 1221
   Visibility 1221
   Name Clashes Within Namespaces 1222
Importing Namespaces 1223
   Name Clashes Due to Imports 1225
   Using Aliases 1226
   Extern Aliases 1227
   Extension Methods 1230
Summary 1232

25   Assemblies and Application Domains   **1233**

Assemblies 1233
   Modules and Assemblies 1234
   Types of Assemblies 1236
   Assembly Properties 1237
   Naming, Versioning, and Deployment 1240
   Strong Naming 1244
   The Global Assembly Cache 1249
   Referencing Assemblies 1253
   How Assemblies Get Loaded at Runtime 1255
   Native Image Generation (NGEN) 1261
   Visibility Aspects 1265
   Embedded Resources 1268
   Type Forwarding 1270
   Reflection Flashback 1272
Application Domains 1277
   Creating Application Domains 1278
   Cross-Domain Communication 1279
   The Managed Add-In Framework 1287
Summary 1289

Part III   Working with Base Class Libraries

26   Base Class Library Essentials   **1291**

The BCL: What, Where, and How? 1293
   What Is Covered? 1293
   Default Project References 1293
   Namespaces Versus Assemblies 1294
   The `System` and `mscorlib` Assemblies 1296
   `System.Core`'s Story of Red Bits and Green Bits 1298

The Holy System Root Namespace 1301
    Primitive Value Types 1301
    Working with Arrays 1305
    The Math Class 1308
    BigInteger: Beyond 32-bit and 64-bit Integers 1310
    Complex Numbers 1312
    Generating Random Numbers 1314
    Working with Date and Time 1317
    GUID Values 1325
    Nullability Revisited Briefly 1327
    The Uri Type 1328
    Interacting with the Environment 1328
    Leave the GC Alone (Most of the Time) 1334
    Native Interop with IntPtr 1341
    Lazy Initialization Using Lazy<T> 1343
    Tuple Types 1344
Facilities to Work with Text 1346
    Formatting Text 1346
    Parsing Text to Objects 1352
    Regular Expressions 1353
    Commonly Used String Methods 1356
    The StringBuilder Class 1359
    Text Encoding 1361
Summary 1362

27   Diagnostics and Instrumentation   1363

Ensuring Code Quality 1364
    Code Analysis 1364
    Asserts and Contracts 1366
    Diagnostic Debugger Output 1371
    Controlling the Debugger 1373
    Logging Stack Traces 1375
    Measuring Performance Using StopWatch 1376
Instrumentation 1378
    Using Event Logs 1379
    Monitoring with Performance Counters 1382
    Other Manageability Frameworks 1385
Controlling Processes 1386
    Querying Process Information 1386
    Starting Processes 1387
Summary 1389

28 Working with I/O   **1391**

Files and Directories 1392
    Listing Drives 1392
    Working with Directories 1394
    Working with Paths 1397
    The `FileInfo` Class 1398
Monitoring File System Activity 1400
Readers and Writers 1401
    The `File` Class 1401
    `TextReader` and `TextWriter` 1406
Streams: The Bread and Butter of I/O 1408
    Memory Streams 1409
    Working with Files: Take Two 1410
    `BinaryReader` and `BinaryWriter` 1411
    Asynchronous Read and Write
       Operations 1413
    Streams Are Everywhere 1422
A Primer to (Named) Pipes 1423
Memory-Mapped Files in a Nutshell 1426
Overview of Other I/O Capabilities 1429
Summary 1430

29 Threading and Synchronization   **1431**

Using Threads 1432
    Explaining the Concept of Threads 1432
    The Managed Code Story 1434
    Where It All Starts: The `Thread` Class 1436
    More About a Thread's Life Cycle 1441
    Managed Thread Characteristics 1446
    Dealing with Exceptions 1451
    Thread-Specific State 1452
    Essential Threading Debugging
       Techniques 1460
Thread Pools 1463
    .NET's Thread Pool 1464
Synchronization Primitives 1471
    Atomicity (or Lack Thereof) Illustrated 1472
    Monitors and the `lock` Keyword 1474
    Mutexes 1477
    Semaphores 1480
    More Advanced Locks 1483
    Signaling with Events 1486

Interlocked Helpers 1492

More Synchronization Mechanisms 1494

BackgroundWorker 1495

Summary 1499

30 Task Parallelism and Data Parallelism   1501

Pros and Cons of Threads 1502

Cutting Costs 1502

An Ideal Number of Threads? 1502

The Task Parallel Library 1503

Architecture 1503

Declarative Versus Imperative 1504

What Are Tasks? 1507

Task Parallelism 1508

Creating and Starting Tasks 1508

Retrieving a Task's Result 1511

Dealing with Errors 1513

Continuations 1518

Cancellation of Tasks 1523

Parallel Invocation 1525

Waiting for Multiple Tasks 1525

How the Task Scheduler Works 1527

Data Parallelism 1529

Parallel For Loops 1529

Parallel Foreach Loops 1535

Summary 1537

Index   1539

About the Author

Bart J.F. De Smet is a software development engineer on Microsoft's Cloud Programmability Team, an avid blogger, and a popular speaker at various international conferences. In his current role, he's actively involved in the design and implementation of Reactive Extensions for .NET (Rx) and on an extended "LINQ to Anything" mission. You can read about Bart's technical adventures on his blog at http://blogs.bartdesmet. net/bart.

His main interests include programming languages, virtual machines and runtimes, functional programming, and all sorts of theoretical foundations. In his spare time, Bart likes to hike in the wonderful nature around Seattle, read technical books, and catch up on his game of snooker.

Before joining Microsoft in October 2007, Bart was active in the .NET community as a Microsoft Most Valuable Professional (MVP) for C#, while completing his Bachelor of Informatics, Master of Informatics, and Master of Computer Science Engineering studies at Ghent University, Belgium.

Acknowledgments

Writing this book was a huge undertaking that would have been impossible without the support of many people. I want to apologize upfront for forgetting any of you. (I'll buy you a Belgian beer if I did.)

First and foremost, I can't thank my family enough for the support they've given me over the years to pursue my dreams. I owe them complete gratitude for their support of my 6 years of university studies in Ghent and their tolerance of my regular absence to participate in the technical community. Moving halfway across the world to work at the Microsoft headquarters has also been met with their understanding. Words seem insufficient to describe how incredibly lucky I am to have their ongoing support. Thanks once more!

I wouldn't have ended up in the world of computer science if not for some of my teachers. For my first exposure to computers, I have to go back to 1993, checking sums during math class at elementary school. Thanks to "Meester Wilfried" for his MS-DOS- and GWBASIC-powered calculator that shaped my future. In high school, several people kept me on this track as well. Math teachers Paul, Geert, and Ronny had to endure endless conversations about programming languages. In a weird twist of history, I didn't actually study informatics in high school, but I nevertheless spent countless hours in the computer rooms of my school. Without the support of Hans De Four, I wouldn't be where I am today. Sorry for all the network downtime caused by my continuous experiments with ProfPass, domain controllers, and whatnot.

Looking back over the past 10 years, I'm eternally grateful to the people at the local Microsoft subsidiary in Belgium (back then called Benelux) for adopting me into the early .NET community and for giving me the chance to work on various projects. In particular, I want to thank my first contact at Microsoft, Gunther Beersaerts, for all the advice he has given me over the years. Gunther's been a true source of inspiration, causing me to take the speaker stand at various conferences. Your first presentation I ever attended (on "Windows DNA") is fondly remembered as a font of inspiration, an inspiration directly related to my own "Speaker Idol" award at TechEd EMEA 2006.

During a number of summers in the early 2000s, many Microsoft Belgium people provided a nice place for me to grow and learn while working on various exciting projects. Thanks to Chris Volckerick for taking me on board to build the (now defunct) http://www.dotnet.be website, using what was called ASP+ back then. Later, Gerd De Bruycker took me under his wing to develop the first MSDN home page for Microsoft Belux. Your passion for the developer community has always stuck with me (not just that wild community VIP party in Knokke).

A bigger project called SchoolServer was born in the summer of 2004. Christian Ramioul's faith in my technical skills needed to land this project was unbelievable. And getting to know the IT professional audience that had to work with the solution wouldn't have been possible without the wonderful collaboration I had with Ritchie Houtmeyers (remember the countless hours spent in our server room office?) and Ricardo Noulez. Big thanks go to Bart Vande Ghinste for giving me a crash course in COM+.

Over the years, I've had the honor to interact with a large number of community members at various conferences. Listing all of them would be a Herculean task, so I won't even attempt to do so. I want to mention a few, though. First of all, thanks to the Belgian developer evangelism team for their relentless support over the years. Gerd De Brucyker and Tom Mertens, you've done a great job. Today's community is in great hands with Katrien De Graeve, Hans Verbeeck, and Arlindo Alves. Hans De Smaele, you continue to be my ongoing source of debugging and bit-twiddling inspiration. Finally, and sadly enough, this list wouldn't be complete without taking a moment to remember the late David Boschmans and Patrick Tisseghem, who passed away suddenly. We miss you guys!

My Redmond-based Microsoft Corporation career started in October 2007, thanks to Scott Guthrie's mail through my blog, asking me to interview with the company. Ultimately, I ended up working on Windows Presentation Foundation's AppModel team, where I felt welcome from day one. In particular, I want to thank my first office mate, Chango Valtchev, for the countless hours he spent bringing me up to speed in the codebase, sharing tons of debugging insights, and sharing epic hikes. My first couple of managers, Grzegorz Zygmunt and Adam Smith, have been great in helping me shape my early career, while also accommodating my speaking engagements abroad.

As I began writing this book in 2009, many of my colleagues were put to the test. My office mates Mike Cook and Eric Harding had to endure the most boring stories on various language constructs, generated IL code, functional programming adventures, and ways to (ab)use the C# programming language. Benjamin Westbrook, with whom I've worked for several months, underwent a similar ordeal during lunchtimes. I have to thank Ben for sharing the things he enjoys most when reading technical books; I hope you find some of your stylistic ideas here and there throughout the book. Patrick Finnigan deserves a special mention here, too. He's a great colleague who has "had my back" with regard to work our team has been doing. He has also provided invaluable technical and stylistic feedback about this book, making it better in the process. Thanks a lot!

Thanking all the other Windows Presentation Foundation colleagues I've worked with and who gave me various technical insights would take up way too much space. Instead, here's a sampling of folks I'm very grateful to have worked with: Adam, Alik, Andre, Dwayne, Joe, Eric, Matt, Saied, Zia. Thanks so much!

While on this writing adventure, I transitioned to the Cloud Programmability Team. Thanks to Erik Meijer for taking me on board into the oasis he's created for innovative and creative ideas and for allowing me to work on one of my key passions: LINQ. My colleagues Danny Van Velzen, Jeffrey Van Gogh, Mark Shields, and Wes Dyer have been fantastic with bringing me up to speed. Endless technical discussions were a tremendous source of inspiration that contributed directly to this book's contents. This is also the right spot to thank my professor Raymond Boute. It turns out Erik and I caught the passion for functional programming from the same professor (although a few decades apart).

I can't thank the Sams team enough, in particular Neil Rowe for his incredible patience with me. Even though I always knew writing this book was going to be a huge task, lots of unexpected twists made the schedule more challenging than anticipated. Combine this with an ever-growing page count and changing table of contents, and I'm very grateful I could write the book I think is right for a C# programmer audience, with virtually no constraints. I also want to thank the technical team for leading the way through new authoring and publication software and assisting with my numerous technical requests. A special word of thanks goes to the technical reviewer, Doug Holland, and various other team members who participated in various reviews. Writing a book is not only about teaching your readers, it's also a lot about learning things yourself (including some of the English language, thanks Keith).

None of this book would exist if not for the wonderful C# language and its designers. I want to thank Anders Hejlsberg and the entire language design team for giving us the most popular .NET language out there. This big thank you also applies to the CLR team for bringing a managed runtime to a wide variety of platforms. Internal resources, in particular on our C# discussion list, have provided valuable insights.

Last but not least, I want to thank the waiters and waitresses in various downtown Bellevue restaurants for tolerating my regular book-writing presence, as I hid behind a laptop screen and asked for endless soda refills.

We Want to Hear from You!

As the reader of this book, you are our most important critic and commentator. We value your opinion and want to know what we're doing right, what we could do better, what areas you'd like to see us publish in, and any other words of wisdom you're willing to pass our way.

As an executive editor for Sams Publishing, I welcome your comments. You can email or write me directly to let me know what you did or didn't like about this book—as well as what we can do to make our books better.

Please note that I cannot help you with technical problems related to the topic of this book. We do have a User Services group, however, where I will forward specific technical questions related to the book.

When you write, please be sure to include this book's title and author as well as your name, email address, and phone number. I will carefully review your comments and share them with the author and editors who worked on the book.

Email: feedback@samspublishing.com

Mail: Neil Rowe
Executive Editor
Sams Publishing
800 East 96th Street
Indianapolis, IN 46240 USA

Reader Services

Visit our website and register this book at informit.com/register for convenient access to any updates, downloads, or errata that might be available for this book.

Introduction

Does the world need yet another book about C#? Very rightfully, you might be asking this question right now (and so did some of my colleagues when I first told them about this book project). In short, what sets this book apart from many others is its in-depth coverage of how things work. Personally, I'm a firm believer in education that stimulates the student's curiosity. That's exactly one of the things this book aims to do.

> The important thing is not to stop questioning. Curiosity has its own reason for existing. One cannot help but be in awe when he contemplates the mysteries of eternity, of life, of the marvelous structure of reality. It is enough if one tries merely to comprehend a little of this mystery every day. Never lose a holy curiosity.
>
> —Albert Einstein

Understanding how a language brings its features to life is always a good thing, which will help you on many fronts. For one thing, coming up with a proper software design requires a good insight into the "à la carte menu" of language features, so that you pick the ones best suited for the job at hand and those that won't leave you with a bitter after-taste. Also solid knowledge about the language and its caveats is invaluable while debugging your (or someone else's) code. Occasional historical perspectives interwoven throughout this book highlight why the language looks the way it does today.

A tremendous number of .NET libraries have been developed over the years, each addressing specific needs for particular applications. Doing justice to any of those by trying to reduce their coverage to a few tens of pages seems overly optimistic. Moreover, different developers have different needs: Maybe you're in charge of user interface (UI) design or web development, or maybe you specialize in service-oriented architectures or designing a data-access layer. Each of those domains has specific concepts that deserve whole books dedicated to them.

For all those reasons, this book shies away from even attempting such shallow and brief coverage of the .NET Framework. Instead, this book focuses on the common ground where all developers meet, the way they express their thoughts through programming languages. In this book, you get essential insights into the foundations of the platform and one of the most commonly used languages, C#. Armed with this knowledge, you should be able to discover and understand many technologies that build on the platform.

As a concrete example, today's libraries are built using object-oriented programming, so the capabilities of this feature are fully explored. Similarly, recent application programming interfaces (APIs), such as Language Integrated Query, have started to leverage the expressiveness of programming constructs borrowed from the functional world, such as lambda expressions, so we delve into how they work.

Finally, at the intersection of different developer audiences, there are quite a few libraries that no one can live without. Examples include primitive types, collections, parallel programming capabilities, performing I/O operations, and so on. A discussion of those libraries offers several benefits. Not only do you get a good idea about the essential toolset the .NET Framework offers, you also learn about various language features that use them. A good example is the discussion of generic types and Language Integrated Query through the lens of collections.

I sincerely hope you enjoy reading this book as much as I enjoyed writing it. I've learned a lot during the process, and I'm confident you will, too.

Homines dum docent discunt. (Latin phrase translated "Men learn while they teach.")

—Seneca, Epistolae, VII, 7

Happy coding!
Bart J.F. De Smet
Bellevue, Washington

Who Should Read This Book?

This book is for anyone who wants to learn the C# programming language in depth, understanding how language features truly work. While giving you those insights, you'll learn where and how to use the features to design various kinds of software. Essential tools and techniques to carry out tasks such as debugging are covered too.

If you've already had prior exposure to C#—maybe a previous version of the language—this book will help you grasp the new language features that have been added over the years. If you're new to the C# language and/or the .NET platform as a whole, this book will guide you through the language in a step-by-step manner.

In summary, this book not only teaches the language's capabilities, but it also looks behind the scenes to build a solid foundation that will aid you in studying other parts of the .NET platform. Because programming languages are at the heart of a developer's expressiveness, such a foundation is essential no matter what your day-to-day programming activities are.

What You Need to Know Before You Read This Book

No prior knowledge of the C# programming language is assumed, although it helps to have a basic idea of typical language constructs. Any kind of modern programming background can help here. For example, readers with a background in C, C++, or Java will feel at home with the C# syntax immediately. Those coming from C++ or Java will have no issue appreciating the power of object-oriented programming. For Visual Basic developers, the different syntax might be a hurdle to overcome, but lots of concepts will sound familiar.

Likely the most important thing to have is technical curiosity and the willingness to learn and truly understand a (new) programming language and the platform on which it's built.

How This Book Is Organized

Two writing principles have been taken as a guide in this book:

- ▶ Avoid backward references, causing mental jumps for the readers. In other words, this book tells you the story of how various language features are built on top of each other, starting from primitive constructs such as expressions and statements. Sometimes making a little jump is unavoidable due to the historical evolution the language has undergone. In such a case, I present you with the basics of the feature in question and refer to a later chapter for in-depth coverage.

- ▶ Samples of technologies are interspersed with the coverage of language features that underpin them. For example, a discussion of generics naturally leads to an overview of various collection types in the .NET Framework. Similarly, a good explanation of Language Integrated Query (LINQ) cannot take place without coverage of constructs such as extension methods and lambda expressions.

From a 10,000-feet point of view, this book consists of three core pieces:

- ▶ The first four chapters introduce the .NET platform, the tooling ecosystem, and the C# programming language. In this part, a good historical perspective is provided that will help you understand why those technologies were created and how they evolved.

- ▶ Chapters 5 through 25 cover the C# programming language itself, with immediate application of language features where applicable. A further breakdown looks as follows:

    - ▶ We start by looking at basic constructs, such as expressions, operators, and statements. These language elements should be familiar to anyone who's been programming before, allowing things such as arithmetic, control flow, and so on. Finally, we introduce the notion of exception handling.

    - ▶ Next, our attention is aimed at larger units of code. To set the scene, we start by introducing the notion of types, and then cover members such as methods and properties.

    - ▶ This naturally leads to a discussion of object-oriented programming in Chapter 14, covering the notions of objects, classes, interfaces, virtual methods, and so on.

▶ After explaining generic types and methods, we move on to orthogonal language features, such as delegates, events, and Language Integrated Query (introduced in C# 3.0). Constructs borrowed from functional programming are covered here too.

▶ Next, we revise our notions of typing and introduce runtime services, such as reflection, that allow a more dynamically typed code characteristic. This brings us to an in-depth discussion of C# 4.0's dynamic feature, including the Dynamic Language Runtime infrastructure that underpins it.

▶ To put the icing on the cake, we take a closer look at the largest units of code the programming language deals with: namespaces and assemblies. The latter of the two touches quite a few runtime concepts, such as the global assembly cache, native images, and application domains, all of which are explained here too.

▶ Finally, the last chapters give an overview of the .NET Framework libraries about which every good developer on the platform should know. Here we cover essential types in the BCL, how to perform various kinds of I/O, diagnostic capabilities, and the increasingly important domain of multithreaded and asynchronous programming.

All in all, this book takes a language-centric approach to teaching how to program rich and possibly complex applications on the .NET Framework. Activities such as API design, coming up with proper application architectures, and even debugging issues with existing code all benefit from a deep understanding of the language and runtime. That's precisely the sweet spot this book aims for.

CHAPTER 1

Introducing the .NET Platform

IN THIS CHAPTER

▶ A Historical Perspective 5

▶ A 10,000-Feet View of the .NET Platform 9

▶ The Common Language Infrastructure 12

▶ The Multilanguage Aspect of .NET 14

▶ Introducing .NET Assemblies 15

▶ The Common Type System Explained 17

▶ Executing Managed Code 24

▶ Diving into the Common Language Runtime 32

▶ The Base Class Library 51

The computer programming landscape is changing constantly to accommodate the needs of end users and to bridge the gap between modern powerful hardware and meaningful software applications. It's a great time for us developers to live, or should I say, us geeks. Personally, I remember writing my first programs in BASIC, trying to impress my teachers with computer solutions to mathematical problems. Today, I'm as excited about computer programming as I was back then: Every few years, paradigm shifts occur, old technologies vanish, and new ones are introduced. At the time of this writing, it's common to design distributed software with pieces of code running here and there, on various kinds of devices and in the cloud, inside the browser and outside, talking to databases and web services, and so on.

For developers to be successful in the jungle of software engineering today, we need solid tools and basic building blocks we can leverage to build up the solutions our customers dream of. The .NET platform is such an environment adapted to the needs of the modern software developer. In this chapter, we explore the .NET platform in all its breadth, covering its execution environment, the support for various programming languages, the libraries it comes with, and the tooling support available to develop on it. In addition, we talk about the role of C# in this picture.

A Historical Perspective

It's a general truth that you will have a better understanding of today's affairs when you appreciate the past. Total overhauls of software platforms or revolutions in the way we think about programming do not occur that often, but when they happen, the lessons learned from the past play a central role in the design of the future. The .NET platform is no exception to this rule.

Let me raise a question to start the discussion. Why is it that the the Windows boot screen has shown the year 1985 in the copyright caption for a long time? The answer is shockingly simple: because the core application programming interfaces (APIs) of the operating system go all the way back to that time, a quarter of a century ago. Obviously, ever since then that API has grown to adapt to the current state of affairs with respect to hardware and the way we write software. Backward compatibility is a great thing to ensure our applications keep working without major rewrites every time the underlying platform changes. In today's world of connected systems, that's even more true: Interoperable protocols are used to ensure things keep working the way they originally did.

Win32 Programming in C

Talking about the Windows API, what did it mean for a developer to target the platform? At that time, the use of C was the most obvious choice with which to write software, so the API was designed to align with that programming model. The result was a flat API with tons of functions spread across multiple header files, back then a well-accepted means to tame complexity. But as the API grew with the introduction of new versions of the operating system, it soon became clear that better techniques were required to keep the complexity under control.

Not only that, the use of C as the programming language of choice caused grief for many developers writing applications on top of the platform. Although C is a great language to do low-level systems programming, it lacks higher-level constructs to organize programs, and the need to deal with machine-level details such as memory management places a big burden on the developer.

Raising the Abstraction Level with MFC and C++

One significant evolution that made developers' lives easier was to raise the abstraction level by embracing the object-oriented (OO) programming techniques from the world of C++. The use of classes to group and expose platform functionality offers a more structured approach, making concrete development tasks easier. For example, using Microsoft Foundation Classes (MFCs), one can be more productive in building graphical user interface (GUI) applications because needless Win32 details such as message pumping and window subclassing can be hidden from the developer.

On the flip side, MFC isn't the solution to all problems because it doesn't abstract over all areas of Windows functionality. For instance, although MFC is well suited to do GUI programming with all the bells and whistles like network communication and multi-threading, it's not a good choice to create Windows services. And although C++ is a vast improvement over C thanks to object-oriented programming and templates, it still doesn't free the developer from difficult problems such as manual memory management.

Component-Driven Development with COM

Because larger applications were written on the Windows platform, it became apparent that a more structured approach to building software was required. This evolution originated from the world of Office, where users wanted to embed content from different Office files in other containers (for example, to display an Excel chart in a Word document). The technology that enabled this was called Object Linking and Embedding (OLE). No longer could applications be written as silos; different parts had to start working together.

In essence, one can think about software as a Lego kit: Given a number of building blocks, it should be easy to compose bigger constructs using the individual blocks. Such blocks were called components, and the Component Object Model (COM) was born. Given this infrastructure, developers can define interfaces between different pieces of functionality so that components can be built and maintained independently, potentially in different languages. By doing so, islands of code become reusable in many contexts. To make development for COM easier for C++ developers, the Active Template Library was built.

COM wasn't the silver bullet to all problems, though. Its very powerful nature can be perceived as scary to many developers, and although COM solved lots of problems, new concerns were born. For instance, the reference counting memory management approach can cause different sorts of debugging headaches, and the deployment of COM-based applications is difficult because of component registrations and versioning issues, often referred to as the dynamic-link library (DLL) hell.

This said, COM was, and still is, a success story upon which very complex software has been built, also opening up for distributed computing using Distributed COM (DCOM) and enterprise-level services such as reliable messaging, transaction management, declarative security, and object pooling with COM+.

Windows Development for the Masses in Visual Basic

Another significant shift came with the introduction of Visual Basic, bringing the popularity of the BASIC language to the Windows platform. Besides being an easy (and, for lots of developers, familiar) programming language, Visual Basic offered rich tooling support to allow for Rapid Application Development (RAD) where design of interactive user interfaces becomes very easy.

The combination of an integrated development environment (IDE) with simple and approachable abstractions over the underlying Win32 platform, easy data access mechanisms, lots of handy built-in functions, and the capability to develop reusable controls and COM components made Visual Basic a big success. Nevertheless, the heavy simplification of the view on the underlying platform made certain concepts, such as multithreading, unavailable to the masses. On the language level, Visual Basic got stuck in between its ancestors' procedural nature and the modern approach of object-oriented programming. Visual Basic remains a very popular language and has undergone many transformations since its early days, having grown out to a full-fledged OO language on the .NET Framework.

Reaching Out to the Web with Windows DNA

In the late 1990s, standalone personal computing on Windows and enterprise-scale distributed applications got a new big brother called the Internet. Obviously, the need to target the new application models that came with it became a gigantic requirement for development platforms to be successful. One early attempt to turn Windows developers into web developers was the so-called Windows Distributed interNet Applications Architecture (DNA), which tried to push the use of COM for the creation of web applications.

Unfortunately, the Web had many loosely related technologies that needed to be mingled together somehow: (D)HTML, JScript, VBScript, and Active Service Pages (ASP) jump to mind. Tools such as Visual InterDev were created to aid in the creation of web applications, but soon it became apparent that the COM-style approach didn't scale very well for various reasons.

Reaching Out to Java with J++

Around the same time, Sun Microsystems created Java. There are two aspects to the technology. From the language point of view, Java was designed to be a modern object-oriented language that did away with the complexities of C++ around memory management and bug-prone features like multiple inheritance, unhygienic macros, and so on. The other interpretation, Java as a platform, brought a runtime with a rich library to write enterprise applications that run on various platforms and target various application models both for the client and the Web.

A major downside to the Java strategy at the time was its tight coupling to a single language, making it hard to interoperate with existing code or to reuse existing programming skills in different languages while still targeting the same underlying runtime and libraries. So to make Java- programming available on the Windows platform, a product called Visual J++ was created together with a Java Virtual Machine (JVM) implementation, a port of the libraries and bridges to the world of Windows in the form of the Windows Foundation Classes (WFC).

Time for Lightning

So we've arrived in the late '90s with a bunch of languages (C, C++, Visual Basic, J++, scripting, and so on) and technologies (Win32, ATL, MFC, COM+, and so forth) that do not line up nicely for various reasons: mismatches in the type systems, incompatible interfaces requiring lots of plumbing, lack of end-to-end tooling support, and more. This, combined with the emergence of new application models such as web services, cried out for a fundamentally new platform to support the needs of modern application development.

Recognizing this problem, two camps formed within Microsoft. One camp believed in pushing COM forward to what could have become COM++, eliminating the known limitations of the platform and adding support for better web development, including web services. Another camp had the opinion that it would be better to start with a blank page, building a new runtime infrastructure from the ground up while providing interoperability capabilities to existing code like Win32 platform code and COM components.

And the rest is, as they say, history: The latter camp won, and the project code-named Lightning was started. We're now about 10 years later and shipping the fourth major release of the .NET platform, which we take a closer look at now.

A 10,000-Feet View of the .NET Platform

The .NET platform is Microsoft's development platform for Windows and the cloud. This includes support for desktop applications, smart device applications, server and database applications, web applications and services, and cloud applications deployed to Windows Azure. In addition, the technology is available in more exotic corners of computer science, ranging from operating system implementation (for example, Microsoft Research's Singularity research operating system) to gaming with the XNA framework and Microsoft Robotics Studio for robotics. Figure 1.1 gives an overview of the .NET platform from a 10,000-feet view.

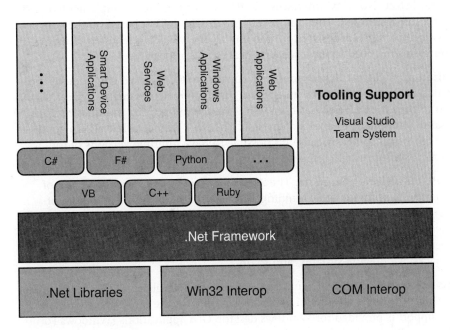

FIGURE 1.1   The .NET platform.

The .NET Platform

Before we dive into a more detailed structure of the platform and the surrounding ecosystem, let's point out the key features and advantages of the .NET platform as a whole:

▶ **Object-oriented programming:** Recognized to be the current paradigm of choice to master complexity, the platform was built around the concepts of object-oriented programming (OO). The core of languages like C# are based on the OO principles, and the OO paradigm is used as the glue that makes language interoperability possible.

▶ **Support for multiple languages:** Although COM supported multiple languages (most notably C++ and Visual Basic) in order to talk together, its cross-language capabilities were limited to implementing interfaces. In .NET, true interoperability between languages becomes possible with capabilities such as cross-language inheritance. Together with a unified type system, this makes integration between code written in different languages totally seamless. This also accommodates other programming language paradigms, ranging from a functional programming style (as seen in F#, but nowadays in certain C# and Visual Basic language features too) to dynamic languages (such as Ruby and Python).

▶ **Easy component-based development:** The art of creating components containing libraries and sharable pieces of application functionality is much simpler in .NET than it was before. No COM interfaces like IUnknown need to be implemented, and no registration is required. The unit of code sharing in .NET is based on the concept of an assembly, which carries version info and all the metadata required to use it. This eliminates the need to have separate header files and such.

▶ **Simplified application deployment:** In contrast to COM-based components, no registration is required to deploy assemblies; just "xcopy deployment" suffices. In addition to this, the DLL hell has been eliminated by supporting multiple versions of the same component to exist side by side. The .NET Framework itself is a good example of this capability, because it's possible to have multiple versions of the framework installed next to one another on the same machine.

▶ **Rich base class library support:** The .NET Framework comes with a rich set of class libraries that provide basic building blocks to build rich applications, all of which are provided in a consistent manner and designed based on OO principles. Examples of such libraries include collections, text manipulation, database access, file system manipulation, networking, XML support, rich service-oriented communication stacks, windowing systems, and so on.

▶ **Various application types:** Thanks to the rich base class library (BCL), it becomes incredibly easy to write all sorts of applications based on the same framework foundation. Support is provided for Windows desktop GUI applications (Windows Forms and Windows Presentation Foundation [WPF]), web applications (ASP.NET), web services (Windows Communication Foundation [WCF]), smart device applications (Compact Framework), browser and Windows Phone 7 applications (Silverlight), cloud applications for Windows Azure, and more.

▶ **Unified runtime infrastructure:** At the core of the .NET Framework sits the Common Language Runtime (CLR), which provides unified runtime infrastructure in the form of an intermediate language (IL) shared by all languages that run on the platform, Just-in-Time (JIT) compilation of such IL code to native code for the machine on which it's running, automatic memory management through a garbage collector (GC), assembly loading services, debugging services, threading, and so on.

▶ **Interoperability with existing code:** Although the .NET platform is meant to be a solid replacement for older technologies, it's quintessential to have good support to reuse existing software components that were written in older technologies like COM and to provide access to native operating system Win32 API functions through a mechanism called P/Invoke.

▶ **Exception handling:** Error handling in the .NET Framework is provided through a mechanism known as exception handling. This eliminates many of the worries associated with manual error checking as done in Win32 programming and COM-based APIs with so-called HRESULTs.

▶ **Improved security model:** With the advent of the Web, deployment of code becomes a severe security risk. To mitigate this, the .NET runtime has a built-in security mechanism called Code Access Security (CAS) that sandboxes code based on the code's origin, publisher evidence, and configurable policies. This security model is orthogonal to the security mechanisms provided by the operating system, such as access control lists (ACLs) and Windows security tokens.

▶ **Web services capabilities:** Right from the start of the .NET Framework, the platform has had support for web services as a modern way of performing cross-platform remote procedure calls based on Simple Object Access Protocol (SOAP) and Extensible Markup Language (XML) standards. All this is provided using programming paradigms that feel natural in the world of .NET, so developers do not require a fundamentally different mindset to deal with web services. Over the years, the web services support on the .NET Framework has grown significantly with support for the WS-* set of web services standards.

▶ **Professional tooling support:** Visual Studio 2010 is the latest version of the toolset that accompanies the .NET Framework to provide professional support for the development of various types of applications with rich designer support, unit testing frameworks, a project and build system (MSBuild), and, thanks to the unified runtime infrastructure, rich debugging support can be provided for the cross-language platform of .NET. The higher-end editions of Visual Studio, Premium and Ultimate, are aimed at team development in conjunction with a server product called Team Foundation Server (TFS) used for work-item tracking, source-control, project-reporting, and document-sharing capabilities. Starting with the 2010 release, you can also install TFS on client operating systems, which allows individual professional developers to benefit from things such as source control.

Let's take a closer look at the essential concepts and features of the .NET platform right now.

The Common Language Infrastructure

The Common Language Infrastructure (CLI) is an ECMA standard (specification 335) that specifies the runtime infrastructure required to execute so-called managed code, to allow different libraries and languages to work together seamlessly. At the time the .NET project was started at Microsoft in the late '90s, it was clear that the key to success in the space cross-language interoperability was to involve language groups both inside the company and outside (like Fujitsu to provide a COBOL implementation on the platform) to ensure the robustness of the design. As part of that initiative, Microsoft formed a team with Hewlett-Packard and Intel to work on standardizing the CLI, which took place in 2001.

One implementation of the CLI is the Common Language Runtime provided by Microsoft itself, though other implementations exist, such as Mono and DotGNU Portable.NET. Another reference implementation is provided by Microsoft, called the Shared Source CLI (SSCLI), also known as Rotor, which runs on platforms like FreeBSD. This means code written to target the .NET platform not only allows cross-language interoperability but also enables you to run code on various platforms. More recently, the Moonlight project, headed by Mono, has enabled Silverlight applications to run on UNIX-based platforms.

So what does the CLI embody? Figure 1.2 outlines the relationship between the three core elements.

Starting on the outside, the CLI defines the Virtual Execution System (VES), an execution engine or virtual machine (VM) that knows how to execute code as defined by the standard. The format of the code is called Common Intermediate Language (CIL), and metadata is used to describe information about the code. In addition, the CLI outlines the file format of assemblies to ensure cross-platform compatibility.

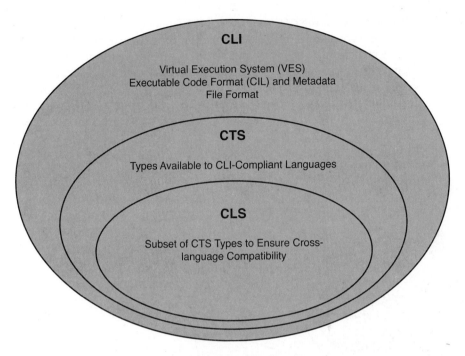

FIGURE 1.2   The Common Language Infrastructure.

Next is the Common Type System (CTS). This is one of the key parts to ensure cross-language interoperability because it unifies the representation and behavior of data types shared by those languages. For example, in the pre-.NET era, it was a common problem to match up similar types between technologies, a typical example being string types: A char* in C is different from a BSTR in COM. In today's world, a string used in C# is no different from one used in Visual Basic .NET or any other .NET language in use. To achieve this goal, the CTS defines how valid types can be created: For example, multiple inheritance is not allowed by the CLI's type system, and in the end every type must derive from the mother of all types: System.Object.

Finally, we arrive at the Common Language Specification (CLS). The CLS is a set of rules on which all .NET languages should be based to make sure no types are exposed that some languages cannot deal with. If all rules pass, a type can be marked as CLS-compliant, which means all .NET languages will be able to interact with it. A concrete example of a CLS rule is that a type should never have two public members that only differ in casing (for example, Bar and bar) because some languages, like Visual Basic, are non-case-sensitive and therefore are unable to resolve such a member name unambiguously.

The relationship between the CTS, the CLS, and a few .NET languages is shown in Figure 1.3. From this figure, you can see that .NET languages provide a superset to the CLS (for example, in C# one can create a class with members that are different only by casing, which is not CLS-compliant) but that the superset is not necessarily the same for all languages. Also, some languages offer capabilities that fall outside the CTS; for example, C++ supports multiple inheritance, but such code cannot be executed on a CLI-compliant runtime (but it can use native code, which is outside the control of the execution engine).

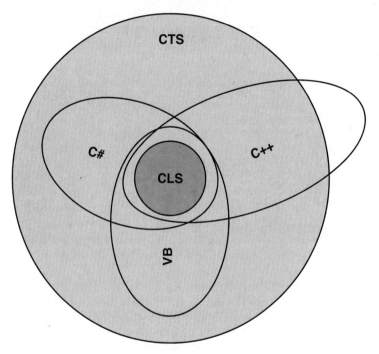

FIGURE 1.3   Relationships between the CTS, the CLS, and .NET languages.

The Base Class Library (BCL) provided by the .NET Framework is written such that CLS compliance is ensured, meaning all the rich functionality defined in it is readily available to all .NET languages.

The Multilanguage Aspect of .NET

As mentioned before, the .NET platform is a multilanguage platform, meaning different programming languages can be used to build .NET applications and class libraries. Right from the introduction of the .NET Framework, both Microsoft and external vendors offered a rich set of languages compatible with the runtime, its type system, and the CLS. At the time of this writing, more than 50 languages (according to Wikipedia) have been implemented on top of the runtime.

The core languages provided by Microsoft as part of the .NET Framework 4.0 software development kit (SDK) and the Visual Studio 2010 language family are as follows:

▶ **Visual Basic .NET:** A language immediately familiar to people who've written (classic) Visual Basic applications before, but now targeting the .NET Framework with full-fledged OO support.

▶ **C#:** The language developed in parallel with the creation of the .NET runtime and first release of the BCLs, obviously based on the OO paradigm and with a very practical nature.

▶ **C++/CLI:** Formerly known as the Managed Extensions for C++, allows C++ code to be executed on top of the .NET runtime, providing a great tool to deal with interoperability problems.

▶ **F#:** The latest addition to the core .NET language family is aimed at scientific and financial computing and combines functional programming with the richness of class libraries and OO.

Outside Microsoft, several languages have been ported to run on the .NET Framework. Examples include COBOL, Smalltalk, Delphi, APL, Pascal, and much more.

The programming language landscape is always in flux, and having a unified runtime infrastructure provides a great way to accommodate the needs of those different languages while being able to reuse libraries across languages and provide tooling support. All of this enables developers with different language preferences to work together and to choose the right tools for the job. For example, whereas C# is a great general-purpose programming language to create business applications, it's more attractive to use F# when developing scientific libraries.

Although the runtime is largely inspired by the fundamental principles that drive OO programming and static typing, other paradigms have been successfully enabled on top of the platform. Recently we've seen a resurgence of dynamic languages thanks to projects such as Ruby on Rails. A few years ago, the need to provide a common infrastructure for those dynamic languages became apparent, and work started to implement the dynamic language runtime as an extension on top of the CLR. This work is now available in the .NET Framework 4.0, where dynamic languages become primary citizens on the platform, making the cross-language vision true across statically and dynamically typed languages. Together with the development of the DLR, several dynamic languages have been implemented to run on top of it; examples include IronRuby and IronPython.

Introducing .NET Assemblies

To execute code on the CLR, it needs to be translated into a format the runtime understands, which is common to all higher-level .NET languages. This format is known as Common Intermediate Language (CIL), mostly abbreviated IL. Code executing on the CLR is known as managed code, in contrast to native code that executes directly on the machine's processor without additional runtime infrastructure. In addition to the IL instructions that catalyze the runtime to execute an application, the CLR needs metadata, which describes the structure and organization of types. The use of metadata also eliminates the need to have header files and helps various tools inspect types. Good examples of such use of metadata include Red Gate's .NET Reflector and the Visual Studio environment to provide services such as IntelliSense.

Besides their role as runtime institutes, assemblies also form the basic units of deployment on the .NET platform. Because of their self-describing nature provided through the use of metadata, assemblies can stand by themselves without requiring complicated registrations carried out by installers: Simple file copy suffices. In addition, the built-in versioning support makes it possible to have multiple versions of the same assembly on the same machine, thus reducing deployment worries even more.

> **NOTE**
>
> Assemblies do not necessary imply single files. The .NET Framework also has the notion of multifile assemblies, which are composed of individual modules. In other words, the lowest unit of deployment granularity is not an assembly but a module. The advantage of this model is the reduction of deployment cost in case common user scenarios require only parts of assemblies to be present. On the flip side, modules cannot be created using Visual Studio tools and require direct use of the command-line compilers.

Static languages like Visual Basic and C# are compiled into assemblies, which are containers for IL and metadata. Strictly speaking, code can also be compiled into modules to allow linking of many such modules at a later stage; we ignore this detail for now. Assemblies are typically stored in files with the extension .dll or .exe but can be stored in other places, too, such as databases. Although assemblies use the same extensions as native executables or DLLs, this is where the similarity ends. The execution of assemblies immediately triggers CLR to provide the necessary runtime services for the application to run, which are fundamentally different from the means to run native code or COM servers.

Dynamic languages behave a little differently because it's atypical for these types of languages to get compiled as a separate step in the development process. Instead, script files are fed into the runtime directly without prior compilation into separate assembly files. To facilitate multiple dynamic languages on the runtime, a common format is required to represent such code and translate it into CIL instructions during the execution of the program. This is achieved by having multiple language-specific binders that know how to translate script code to expression trees. Finally, those expression trees are taken in by the DLR to turn them into CIL instructions so that the CLR can take over from that point. Runtime-generated IL code is sometimes referred to as dynamic assemblies, too.

Figure 1.4 outlines the relationship between various languages, their compilation support, and the underlying runtime. In reality, the picture is a bit more complicated because static languages like C# can also target the DLR to bridge with dynamic languages. We elaborate on that quite extensively when covering dynamic programming support in C# in Chapter 22, "Dynamic Programming."

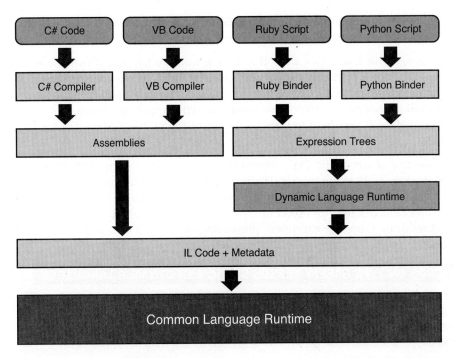

FIGURE 1.4   From code to instructions.

The Common Type System Explained

Types are the way of life in the world of the CLR. They define the way libraries and programs are organized and how interactions between components can be realized. Assemblies are containers for such types.

Let's explore the merits of types in some more detail and look at the various kinds of types supported by the runtime. Don't worry about the C# syntax for now; we cover that extensively as we move along.

What's Type Safety?

To enforce code to deal with types in a correct manner, the CLR guarantees type safety. This ensures objects can only be accessed in a manner that's consistent with the object's type contract. Types consist of two things: the data that's contained by objects of the type (for example, a customer's name and credit balance) and the operations you can perform on that data (for example, DiscountPrice on a Product).

To illustrate type-unsafe operations, assume you were able to treat an object of type Customer as if it were of type Product. Then, what would it mean to perform an operation DiscountPrice to the customer object? Maybe you'd be changing the customer's credit balance. This is clearly an unsafe thing to do. Similarly, arbitrary memory access is an unsafe thing because you might end up in the middle of some type without knowing the type of the data that resides there.

Unmanaged languages like C and C++ allow this kind of thing to happen, which opens the door to hard debugging problems and security vulnerabilities. At best, the process crashes when invalid operations are carried out (for example, because of an attempt to overwrite protected memory), but chances are good that type-unsafe operations go unnoticed for a while, making it very hard to trace the source of the problem when damage has occurred already.

To eliminate this class of errors, the CLR enforces type safety. This is done by various means, including code verification during JIT compilation and monitoring of the use of types to make sure no operations incompatible with an object's runtime type are made. Our example vulnerability where an object of type Customer was "casted" to type Product would result in a runtime exception, preventing the invalid operation from happening at all.

A FEW WORDS ON TYPE SAFETY VERSUS STATIC AND DYNAMIC LANGUAGES

Do not confuse type safety with statically typed programming languages (like C#, for the most part, and F#). Although dynamic languages (like Ruby and Python) do not require users to specify types when dynamically typed code is written, objects still have a well-defined type when the code is run. This is enough for the runtime, in this case the DLR in concert with the CLR, to detect violations against type safety.

What distinguishes statically typed languages from their dynamically typed counterparts is their potential to catch a good amount of violations early, at compile time, by enforcing various rules. Code that can statically be proven to be type safe is called verifiably type-safe code. The .NET Framework comes with a tool called PEVerify to determine whether code is verifiably type safe.

TABLE 1.1   CLS-Compliant Primitive Types

Type	C#	VB	C++/CLI	F#
System.Byte	byte	Byte	unsigned char	byte
System.Int16	short	Short	short	int16
System.Int32	int	Integer	int/long	int/int32
System.Int64	long	Long	__int64	int64
System.Single	float	Single	Float	single/float32
System.Double	double	Double	Double	double/float
System.Boolean	bool	Boolean	Bool	bool
System.Char	char	Char	wchar_t	char

TABLE 1.1   Continued

Type	C#	VB	C++/CLI	F#
System.Decimal	decimal	Decimal	Decimal	decimal
System.String	string	String	String^	string

Primitive Types

User-defined types typically contain data, and all pieces of such data should have a type by itself. Those types could be user-defined again but, obviously, at some point predefined types need to be used. One of the CTS's roles is to provide a number of such primitive data types. Various languages on top of the .NET Framework have different "friendly names" defined for those data types, but in the end they are all represented using their underlying type, which is defined in the mscorlib.dll assembly that's part of the BCL. The fact that the same built-in types are used by various languages is one of the cornerstones that allows true cross-language integration.

Table 1.1 shows primitive types that CLS-compliant languages are supposed to support. The corresponding keywords in various languages are shown, too. In addition to those types, various other non-CLS primitive types exist, such as unsigned variants for the numeric data types.

Classes, Structures, and Enumerations

Because the CLI is inspired by the principles of OO programming, it shouldn't surprise you that classes are one kind of type the CLI supports. In essence, a class is a container for data and operations that can be performed on that data. By keeping the data representation of a class private, one reaches the virtue of encapsulation, where implementation details can change as long as the public contract stays the same.

Also in true OO style, the CLI supports the creation of class hierarchies, where one type derives from another. For example, an Apple type could derive from a Fruit base class. The details of this will be explained extensively when we cover OO programming with C#.

Classes are formally known as *reference types* because they live on the heap and are used through references. An example of a built-in reference type is the String type. However, lightweight types that are stack allocated can come in handy at times, so the CLI also supports the notion of value types. Examples of value types include the numeric data types (like Int32 and Double), the DateTime type, and so on. In the world of C#, value types are declared as structs:

```
static class Calculator
{
    public static int Add(int a, int b)
    {
        return a + b;
```

```
    }
}

struct Point
{
    private readonly int _x;
    private readonly int _y;
    private readonly int _z;

    public Point(int x, int y, int z)
    {
        _x = x; _y = y; _z = z;
    }

    public int X { get { return _x; } }
    public int Y { get { return _y; } }
    public int Z { get { return _z; } }
}
```

Enumerations are a special kind of value type used to represent a limited set of possible values (for example, colors). This is quite different from named constant numeric values in that enumerations enforce strong typing. Although Color.Red might have the same numeric representation as Weekday.Monday, one cannot assign a Color value to a Weekday variable:

```
enum Color
{
    Red,
    Green,
    Blue
}
```

Interfaces

Interfaces provide the capability to define contracts that can be implemented by classes or structures. This way, the contract and the implementation of specific functionality can be decoupled from one another. For example, given the following interfaces, one can define what it means to enumerate over "something," whether that is a collection type or data received from a network socket:

```
interface IEnumerable
{
    IEnumerator GetEnumerator();
}

interface IEnumerator
```

```
{
    bool MoveNext();    object Current { get; }
    void Reset();}
```

Now code can be written to deal with anything that obeys this contract—for example, to print the results of enumerating to the screen. This way, interfaces allow polymorphic code to be written, something we look at in much more detail later on.

Delegates

The capability to pass blocks of code around for use in another place is very powerful. A typical task that requires such a setting is the creation of a new background thread, which requires the code the thread should start executing. Some platforms have solved this by providing single-method interfaces like Runnable. This is quite some plumbing just to pass a piece of code around. Another possibility is the use of function pointers, but type safety suffers in such an approach.

Delegates combine the conciseness of function pointers while preserving the type safety characteristic of single-method interfaces but without the ceremony to deal with them. An example that deals with threading is shown here:

```
var t = new Thread(delegate(object data)
    {
        // Process customer object in the background
    });
Customer customer = new Customer();
t.Start(customer);
```

This only shows delegates at the use site, where we pass a piece of code for customer data processing to a new thread. The CTS has first-class support for code to declare its own delegate types, which you can think of as statically typed method signatures that describe the input and output types of the expected code blocks:

```
/* declaration of a delegate for binary mathematical operations on two integer
values */
delegate int BinaryOperation(int a, int b);

class WorkingWithDelegates
{
    public int Calculate(BinaryOperation op, int a, int b)
    {
        // calling through the delegate
        return op(a, b);
    }
```

```
public void Sample()
{
    int three = Calculate(delegate(int a, int b) { return a + b; }, 1, 2);
}
}
```

> **NOTE**
>
> Since C# 3.0, the language supports lambda expressions, a more concise notation to pass code around without much syntactical noise. In the preceding example, the sum function we're passing to the Calculate method could be written more concisely as (a, b) => a + b.
>
> We examine lambda expressions when talking about delegates in C# and during the exploration of Language Integrated Query (LINQ), which was the main justification for putting lambda expressions in the language.

Members

Most types can contain zero or more members of the following sorts:

▶ **Fields:** Used to store data, typically hidden from the outside to establish abstraction and encapsulation.

▶ **Methods:** Define operations that can be carried out on the type or instances thereof.

▶ **Constructors:** Used to create an object instance of the containing type; in fact, constructors are special methods in disguise.

▶ **Finalizer:** A type can have one finalizer method that gets called when the garbage collector reclaims its memory. This is typically used to clean up native resources that object instances hold on to.

▶ **Properties:** Provide get and set accessors to the state of the type or instances thereof. Properties are a syntactical veneer over getter and setter methods and provide metadata describing them.

▶ **Indexers:** Special properties that allow access on an object instance as if it were an array. For example, List data can provide position-based indexing to make accessing the data stored in it easier.

▶ **Events:** Means for consumers to register event handlers that are triggered when something interesting happens. For example, UI frameworks use events to signal user interactions such as button clicks.

The CTS also defines modifiers that can be used to specify the intended behavior of a member. An example of such a modifier is the visibility of the member, which determines whether the member can be accessed by other types, by subtypes only, or from inside the defining assembly only.

A Note on Generics

The second version of the CLI introduced support for generics, a way to make types and members dependent on a certain type of parameter. In the type theory literature this is known as *parametric polymorphism*. Typical applications of generics include the definition and use of collection types:

```
var primes = new List<int> { 2, 3, 5, 7 };
int firstPrime = primes[0];
```

In the preceding example we're using a generic collection type List<T>, where T has been substituted for int. Similarly, we could construct specialized list types to contain strings, Customer objects, or whatever else we see fit (including lists of lists). The use of generics makes static typing possible in many more cases than before, resulting in better compile-time checking and various performance improvements.

In times of .NET 1.x, collection types required the use of System.Object—the mother of all types—as the element type, to be as generally applicable as possible. Dealing with nongeneric collection types always required the use of runtime type conversions, incurring a performance hit and the potential for runtime exceptions when the collection is misused:

```
ArrayList primes = new ArrayList();
primes.Add(2);
primes.Add(3);
primes.Add(5);
primes.Add(7);
primes[0] = "Bart"; // Wouldn't be valid on a List<int>
int firstPrime = (int)primes[0]; // Invalid conversion causes runtime exception
```

The Role of the Common Language Specification

The CLS defines a subset of the CTS, limiting it to types that can be understood by any .NET language on the platform. It accomplishes this by defining a set of rules that type definitions need to satisfy.

Without a doubt, the first CLS rule is the most important one because it reduces the work-load imposed on .NET developers to keep their types CLS-compliant:

> *CLS Rule 1: CLS rules apply only to those parts of a type that are accessible or visible outside of the defining assembly.*

This rule should cause a "D'oh" effect for everyone reading it. Because the CLS is about cross-language interoperability, only things that are visible to the outside world matter. Or string the reverse: Internal implementation details of assemblies can violate CLS rules at will.

THE ART OF DEFINING RULES

The design of a proper set of CLS rules wasn't a trivial exercise. On one hand, the rules should be flexible enough to allow the implementation and use of language constructs commonly used by developers. On the other, they should be restrictive enough so that a large set of languages can be implemented on the CLI.

To ensure the relevancy of the runtime design in the light of permitting different languages to run on top of it, Microsoft and its partners ran Project Seven. This project implemented a set of popular languages on the runtime while its design and implementation were in progress, to provide early feedback and to steer the CLI, CTS, and CLS in the right direction.

Today we pluck the fruits of this exercise with many languages targeting the .NET runtime, allowing true interoperability without having to worry about too restrictive or too permissive rules: The CLS strikes the right balance, and we should adore it.

Three audiences are affected by the CLS, so every rule is written from three different angles:

▶ **Frameworks** (libraries) are concerned about guaranteeing their maximum applicability across languages. For example, frameworks should avoid the use of language keywords in type or member names.

▶ **Consumers** access types defined by CLS-compliant frameworks but are not required to be able to define types themselves. For example, consumers should be able to instantiate types.

▶ **Extenders** are in between frameworks and consumers. They enable us to extend upon framework-provided types but do not necessarily allow brand new types to be defined. For example, extenders should be able to implement interfaces.

CLS rules will matter to you as a .NET developer primarily if you're building framework libraries you expect other developers to use from any .NET language they see fit. To indicate CLS compliance and to trigger the C# compiler to check your compliance claims, an assembly should have a CLSCompliant attribute applied to it:

```
[assembly: CLSCompliant(true)]
```

We return to this at a later point when you have a more solid understanding of the use of custom attributes.

Executing Managed Code

Now that you know how types can be built and how IL code and metadata can be generated, either at compile time or at runtime, we should take a closer look at the execution model for managed code.

Consider the following fragment of C# code, which implements and uses a simple Calculator class. If the language constructs used here look foreign to you, don't worry; we cover the syntax and meaning of C# programs extensively throughout the book.

```csharp
using System;

static class Program
{
    static void Main()
    {
        var random = new Random();
        int a = random.Next();
        int b = random.Next();
        var calc = new Calculator();
        int sum = calc.Add(a, b);
        Console.WriteLine("{0} + {1} = {2}", a, b, sum);
    }
}

public class Calculator
{
    public int Add(int a, int b)
    {
        return a + b;
    }
}
```

The Main method in the class Program is where the execution of the program starts. First, a random-number generator is created that is subsequently used to generate two integer values, a and b. Next, a calculator object is used to add those two numbers together, and finally the result of the calculation is printed to the screen.

The result of compiling this piece of code using the C# compiler is an executable assembly that contains all the information required for the runtime to execute the code. We explore the use the C# compiler and richer tools like Visual Studio 2010 in Chapter 2. What matters for this first exploratory exercise is the structure of the resulting assembly. To examine this, we can use the IL disassembler tool (ildasm.exe) that comes with the .NET Framework SDK, as shown in Figure 1.5. In this figure, we can identify several pieces that we'll drill into right now.

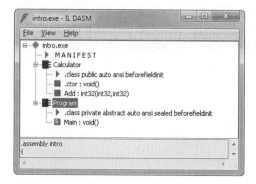

FIGURE 1.5   Use of the IL disassembler to inspect assemblies.

NOTE

If you wonder where the application icon of ILDASM comes from, try to remember the initial code name of the CLR that was mentioned earlier in this chapter.

NOTE

ILDASM has a sister tool called ILASM, the IL assembler. Instead of writing in higher-level languages like C# and VB, you could use this tool to assemble handwritten IL code. However, this is a very extreme approach to managed code development. A slightly more common use of ILASM is to use it in combination with ILDASM to do "IL round-tripping": Given an input assembly, it's disassembled into IL, tweaked by hand or with some tool, and reassembled. The ILDASM and ILASM tandem has been specifically designed to make such lossless round-tripping possible.

The Assembly Manifest

To start, there's a manifest that describes the identity of our assembly, its dependencies, and a couple of flags. For our little application, the manifest looks like this (omitting a few irrelevant details):

```
// Metadata version: v4.0.30319
.assembly extern mscorlib
{
  .publickeytoken = (B7 7A 5C 56 19 34 E0 89 )
  .ver 4:0:0:0
}
.assembly intro
{
```

```
  .hash algorithm 0x00008004
  .ver 0:0:0:0
}
.module intro.exe
.imagebase 0x00400000
.file alignment 0x00000200
.stackreserve 0x00100000
.subsystem 0x0003        // WINDOWS_CUI
.corflags 0x00000001     // ILONLY
```

From the first comment line, we can see the metadata (and hence runtime) version for which this assembly was built.

.NET FRAMEWORK VERSION HISTORY

Different versions of the CLR have been built over the first decade of the .NET platform's existence. However, not every version of the .NET Framework implies a new version of the underlying runtime. The first release of the .NET Framework came with CLR v1.0.3705 and was quickly updated to v1.1.4322 in the v1.1 release of the framework.

A major extension to the runtime, introducing generics, was on the menu for version 2 of the framework with version number v2.0.50727. If you're curious about what the big build number stands for: 2005/07/27.

The next few releases of the .NET Framework, versions 3.0 and 3.5, didn't introduce fundamental changes to the CLR but added lots of libraries such as Windows Presentation Foundation (WPF), Windows Communication Foundation (WCF), Windows Workflow Foundation (WF), and Language Integrated Query (LINQ). In other words, version 3.0 and 3.5 of the .NET Framework came with the v2.0 CLR.

Now, with the fourth version of the framework, a major update to the CLR is shipped as well, primarily improving the runtime services offered by the execution engine. The underlying IL instruction set and metadata formats are kept compatible, though, to ensure a smooth transition to the latest and greatest release of the .NET Framework with binary compatibility for assemblies. For the curious, the full .NET 4 version number is 4.0.30319.

The next entry in the manifest indicates an external assembly reference, which denotes a dependency for our assembly. This assembly, mscorlib, is one of the core parts of the BCL. Notice how version info about the referenced assembly is present; this is one of the keys to eliminating the DLL version hell that existed before the advent of .NET. Besides our own assembly's identity, general information about its characteristics (for example, the fact it's a console user interface, or CUI) is kept in the manifest.

IL Code

By now we already know the role of IL code as a language-independent format in which to express instructions. However, its generic nature extends in the other direction, too: Being an intermediate representation, it also allows decoupling from the specifics of any underlying hardware platform. The result is a very generic instruction set that's rich enough to express the needs of various languages and simple enough to be mapped onto processor instructions, as we'll see later.

Let's take a closer look at one of the methods declared in our program (the Calculator's Add method). Here's what it looks like:

```
.method public hidebysig instance int32  Add(int32 a,
                                             int32 b) cil managed
{
  .maxstack  8
  IL_0000:  ldarg.1
  IL_0001:  ldarg.2
  IL_0002:  add
  IL_0003:  ret
}
```

On the first line, the signature of the method is visible: Add is a method that takes in two 32-bit integer values and produces such a value. Besides this, metadata is present about the visibility of the method, among other things.

Inside the method body, we see a total of four IL instructions being emitted by the C# compiler. Without going into much detail about IL at this point, it's worth noticing the execution model of IL code is extremely simple. In essence, IL represents the instructions to manipulate a stack-oriented execution environment. For instance, our Add method pushes the method's two arguments, a and b, on the stack, adds them together, and subsequently returns the result. The evaluation of the method is illustrated in Figure 1.6, with inputs a = 2 and b = 3.

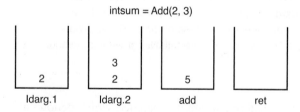

intsum = Add(2, 3)

| 2 | 3 | 5 | |
| ldarg.1 | ldarg.2 | add | ret |

FIGURE 1.6   Evaluation stack transitions during IL code execution.

As you can imagine, IL has many more constructs than the ones illustrated here. Types of instructions include arithmetic and comparison operations, branching, method calls, object allocations, and more.

PROTECTING YOUR INTELLECTUAL PROPERTY

People sometimes worry about how to protect their software's intellectual property (IP) when dealing with managed code, which is easy to inspect and even to decompile with tools like .NET Reflector. The benefits of self-describing assemblies are huge (for example, to aid in debugging scenarios), but concerns like IP are equally important to consider. Luckily, tools exist to obfuscate managed code to make reverse engineering much harder. For example, .NET Reflector itself is protected using such a technique. Visual Studio ships with a community edition of a product called Dotfuscator that's designed to do precisely this.

Metadata

The last piece in the puzzle to turn assemblies to execution is metadata. It describes all the types contained in the defined assembly in excruciating detail so that the runtime can set up the required infrastructure to make execution possible. Tools also benefit from having self-describing assemblies. The whole metadata system provided by the CLI is in fact much like a relational database of related pieces of data, which makes it possible to query various kinds of relationships. For instance, given a type, it's easy to find all its members, and the reverse relationship is equally easy to traverse. The .NET library that makes introspection of types possible at runtime is called Reflection.

As a developer, you don't have to worry much about metadata. Language compilers on the .NET platform take the responsibility of emitting the necessary metadata details about the types you as a developer define during your day-to-day programming job. However, the flexibility of metadata allows for lots of scenarios that reach beyond the metadata required to describe types. Using a feature called custom attributes, it's possible to tag various entities such as types, members, parameters, and so on with custom metadata. Such metadata can then be consumed at runtime by libraries to facilitate operations such as serialization or exposure of methods through web services.

To illustrate matters, let's take a look at the metadata describing the `Calculator` class from our example:

```
TypeDef #2 (02000003)
-------------------------------------------------------
    TypDefName: Calculator  (02000003)
    Flags     : [Public] [AutoLayout] [Class] [AnsiClass] [BeforeFieldInit]
      (00100101)
    Extends   : 01000001 [TypeRef] System.Object
    Method #1 (06000002)
    -------------------------------------------------------
        MethodName: Add (06000002)
        Flags     : [Public] [HideBySig] [ReuseSlot]  (00000086)
        RVA       : 0x0000209e
        ImplFlags : [IL] [Managed]  (00000000)
```

```
CallCnvntn: [DEFAULT]
hasThis
ReturnType: I4
2 Arguments
        Argument #1:   I4
        Argument #2:   I4
    2 Parameters
        (1) ParamToken : (08000001)
                Name : a
                flags: [none] (00000000)
        (2) ParamToken : (08000002)
                Name : b
                flags: [none] (00000000)

Method #2 (06000003)
- - - - - - - - - - - - - - - - - - - - - - - - - - - - - - - - - - - - - - - -
    MethodName: .ctor (06000003)
    Flags     : [Public] [HideBySig] [ReuseSlot] [SpecialName]
                [RTSpecialName] [.ctor]   (00001886)
    RVA       : 0x000020a3
    ImplFlags : [IL] [Managed]   (00000000)
    CallCnvntn: [DEFAULT]
    hasThis
    ReturnType: Void
    No arguments.
```

Here, you can observe the names of types and members associated with several flags (for things such as visibility, method table layouts, and so forth). In addition, notice that every piece of metadata has a unique number that allows for other pieces of metadata to cross-reference it.

Mixing Languages

In the previous discussion, you've seen how to use a single language, in our case C#, to build a complete application. This seldom is the case in a real-world environment where libraries from various sources need to be combined to provide an end-to-end solution to the problem at hand. In fact, our use of BCL types like System.Random and System.Console is a good example of such a scenario. Although those happen to be written in C# too, as most of the code in BCL is, that's not a requirement at all thanks to the cross-language capabilities provided by the CLR. However, consuming libraries is just the tip of the language interoperability iceberg. Richer capabilities, such as extending existing types in a different language than they were initially written in, is also part of the picture.

Let's explore this angle to the CLR in a more concrete fashion. Instead of compiling our Calculator class as part of an executable assembly, we'll compile it into a library with a .dll extension. As a matter of fact, the runtime cares little about the file extension to an assembly, apart from the fact that EXE files are supposed to have an entry-point method.

After we've built our calculator library, we can reference it when building a Visual Basic application to use its functionality. Or we could go one step further, extending the Calculator class using Visual Basic code. This way we achieve cross-language inheritance for types, a very powerful capability that becomes possible thanks to the unified type system. The Visual Basic code that does this is shown here:

```
Public Class FancyCalculator
    Inherits Calculator

    Public Function Multiply(a As Integer, b As Integer) As Integer
        Return a * b
    End Function

End Class
```

Obviously, this code also compiles to IL code, which looks like this:

```
.method public instance int32  Multiply(int32 a,
                                         int32 b) cil managed
{
  .maxstack  2
  IL_0000:  ldarg.1
  IL_0001:  ldarg.2
  IL_0002:  mul.ovf
  IL_0003:  ret
}
```

Nothing in this code reveals it was written in Visual Basic, and indeed exactly the same IL could originate from compiling any other .NET language that carries out a multiplication between two integer values. Figure 1.7 illustrates how the CTS supports inheritance of types across languages.

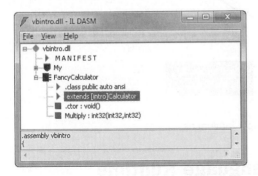

FIGURE 1.7   Cross-language inheritance.

Now, when using the `FancyCalculator` type from any .NET language, we don't know that its `Add` method was implemented in a different language than its `Multiply` method. To illustrate the seamless integration the unified type system offers, let's use our library from inside F#'s interactive console. This is shown in Figure 1.8.

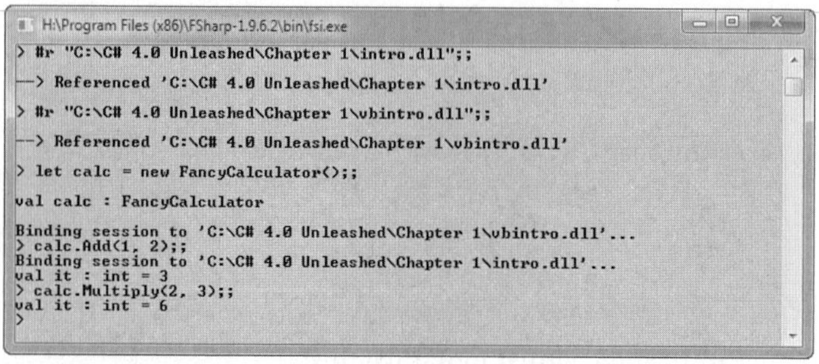

H:\Program Files (x86)\FSharp-1.9.6.2\bin\fsi.exe
> #r "C:\C# 4.0 Unleashed\Chapter 1\intro.dll";;
--> Referenced 'C:\C# 4.0 Unleashed\Chapter 1\intro.dll'
> #r "C:\C# 4.0 Unleashed\Chapter 1\vbintro.dll";;
--> Referenced 'C:\C# 4.0 Unleashed\Chapter 1\vbintro.dll'
> let calc = new FancyCalculator();;
val calc : FancyCalculator
Binding session to 'C:\C# 4.0 Unleashed\Chapter 1\vbintro.dll'...
> calc.Add(1, 2);;
Binding session to 'C:\C# 4.0 Unleashed\Chapter 1\intro.dll'...
val it : int = 3
> calc.Multiply(2, 3);;
val it : int = 6
>

FIGURE 1.8 Using our multilanguage calculator type in F#.

Figure 1.9 summarizes the development flow we've gone through to enable this scenario.

Calculator (C#)
C# Compiler (csc.exe)
Calculator.dll
Add
Fancy Calculator (VB)
VB Compiler (vbc.exe)
FancyCalculator .dll
Multiply
F# Interactive (fsi.exe)
calc.Add(1, 2)
calc.Multiply(2, 3)

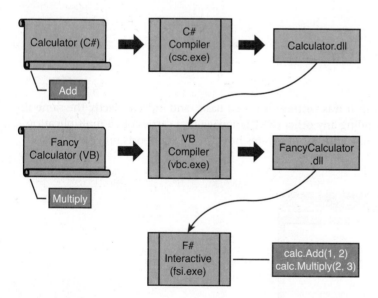

FIGURE 1.9 Developing and using code in multiple languages.

Diving into the Common Language Runtime

Now that you know how assemblies are built, the time has come to focus on the runtime infrastructure the CLR offers. Actually, the concept of a runtime wasn't groundbreaking at the time the CLR was introduced: Languages such as Visual Basic have had them for years, and so did Java with its virtual machine (JVM). What distinguishes the CLR from other runtimes, though, is the fact that it's decoupled from any particular language. Also, the generalization of metadata through custom attributes was quite an innovative feature, as you read much more about throughout this book.

Bootstrapping the Runtime

Previously you saw that executable assemblies are built as EXE files, which as we all know are loaded by the operating system to run them in a separate process. In the pre-.NET world, executable files simply contained native machine instructions that could be understood directly by the processor. Because managed code assemblies require runtime services to execute, a natural question is how the .NET runtime gets loaded when the operating system encounters a managed executable.

For the operating system's loader to recognize the executable file as a valid one, it needs to have a structure that is defined in the PE/COFF file format, which stands for Portable Executable, Common Object File Format. This file format describes the structure of executable files with regard to the code and data sections they contain, in addition to metadata structures describing things such as imported and exported functions. This standardized format is referred to in the CLI as the way to store assemblies in files.

Despite the richness of PE/COFF files, managed executables use just a tiny little bit of its functionality, enough to transfer control to the CLR as soon as the executable starts. This is achieved by emitting a tiny code section in every managed executable (at compile time) that does basically just one thing:

```
JMP _CorExeMain
```

This jump instruction transfers control to a function called _CorExeMain that lives in the mscoree.dll file under the system32 folder. From that point on, the runtime is in control.

REVEALING THE COMMON LANGUAGE RUNTIME ENTRY-POINT

The interested reader is invited to use the dumpbin.exe tool that ships with Visual Studio (and is also available in the Windows SDK) to dump the import table of any managed executable using the tool's /imports flag. This will reveal the _CorExeMain entry point being imported from mscoree.dll.

What's this mscoree.dll thing anyway? The acronym stands for Component Object Runtime Execution Engine, where the COR part is a last trace of the days when the runtime was still considered an extension to COM, adding runtime services to make developers' lives easier. Actually, the role of this DLL is very limited: It's really a very tiny shim that knows how to load an appropriate version of the CLR that's capable of executing the application being started. This facilitates side-by-side installations of multiple .NET Framework versions. The decision which runtime to load is based on the metadata embedded in the executable as well as policy configurations that live in the Registry.

> **NOTE**
>
> Beginning with Windows XP, the operating system's executable loader has some limited built-in knowledge of the common language runtime to redirect the execution of a managed executable to the runtime as early as possible. Nowadays, various built-in services, such as Windows Installer, have intrinsic knowledge about the existence of managed assemblies. Starting with Windows Vista, parts of the .NET Framework are an integral part of the operating system installation to facilitate services that depend on them.

Once the shim knows what version of the runtime to load, it goes ahead and locates the real execution engine DLL for the selected version of the runtime. The version-specific runtime components live in folders underneath the %windir%\Microsoft.NET folder. In .NET 2.0, the runtime DLL was called mscorwks.dll, which stands for Component Object Runtime Workstation, another historical naming that reflects there once were multiple flavors of the runtime. (One flavor was optimized to run on servers, while another was optimized to run on clients or workstations, the main difference being different GC behavior.) Today, this distinction is mode configurable, and no separate DLLs are required, so .NET 4.0's execution engine lives in a more logically named file, clr.dll.

> **NOTE**
>
> Keeping shims as tiny as possible is not always an easy thing to do. It sounds more than logical that no version-specific runtime functionality should live in the shim, but in practice that turns out to be a challenge. In .NET 4.0, the original shim has been trimmed down to make it more future-proof. This refactoring made mscoree.dll into a super-shim, with the remainder functionality moved to a new DLL called mscoreei.dll. This way, the need to update mscoree.dll every time an update to the .NET Framework is applied should decrease significantly.

One of the first things the runtime does after it has gained control over the execution of a managed executable is to inspect the PE/COFF headers looking for a CLR-specific header that specifies a pointer into the metadata directory of the assembly. Such a header is illustrated here:

```
clr Header:
              48 cb
            2.05 runtime version
            20AC [     304] RVA [size] of MetaData Directory
               1 flags
                 IL Only
         6000001 entry point token
```

Locating the entry point token through the metadata directories, the runtime now has all the required information to locate the application's entry point method and start executing it. Finally, your C# code gets a chance to run! How that works in practice is the subject of the next section.

The whole process of loading the CLR is summarized in Figure 1.10.

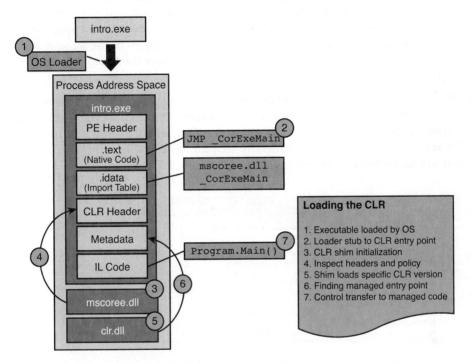

FIGURE 1.10   Loading the common language runtime.

Assembly Loading

Naturally, a key task for the runtime is to locate and load assemblies required by applications on an on-demand basis. The component responsible for this is called *fusion*. (Remember the CLR's code name?) When an assembly is requested for loading, fusion searches a set of known locations for a matching assembly.

As you might have guessed, this process is based on the name of the requested assembly. However, naming for assemblies is not always as straightforward as dealing with simple names like Calculator. To help deal with the versioning hell, assemblies can have strong names that extend beyond simple names by adding things such as version information and publisher information. This way, an application that was built to use a specific version of a library won't accidentally load a newer or older version of that library the application was never tested with (and thus avoid potential compatibility issues).

When introducing the .NET Framework, we mentioned that simplified deployment was one of the key goals of the new platform. So-called xcopy deployment is enabled by allowing an application's required assemblies to sit right next to the executable without any requirement for registrations. However, for libraries shared across multiple applications (like the framework's BCL itself), it makes sense to have a shared system location where those assemblies can be stored. This location is called the Global Assembly Cache, or GAC.

To install assemblies in the GAC, they must be "strong-named signed." Because the GAC is a machine-wide trusted location, this restriction ensures assemblies are properly signed. We talk about the process to sign assemblies in Chapter 25, "Assemblies, and Application Domains." In addition, the GAC allows multiple versions and cultures of the same assembly to live next to one another. This is a key requirement to ensure the versioning story of managed code applications works out nicely.

In reality, the GAC is a hierarchical folder structure that organizes assemblies based on the runtime they're targeting, their names, and version numbers. To hide the complexities of this folder structure and to simplify management of the GAC, a shell extension is installed by the .NET Framework to provide a user-friendly view on the assembly cache. You can find the GAC under %windir%\assembly, as shown in Figure 1.11.

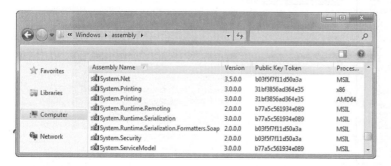

FIGURE 1.11   BCL assemblies live in the Global Assembly Cache.

BROWSING THE INTERNAL STRUCTURE OF THE GAC

To see the internals of the GAC, open a command prompt and navigate the file system to the %windir%\assembly folder. It's also possible to disable—at your own risk—the shell extension by putting a DWORD value DisableCacheViewer set to 1 under the HKLM\Software\Microsoft\Fusion Registry key. In addition, a command-line tool called gacutil.exe exists to inspect and maintain the GAC, which is the recommended and supported way to do so.

It should be noted that starting with .NET 4, the GAC has been split. While the %windir%\assembly folder contains assemblies prior to .NET 4, assemblies targeting the new version of the runtime go under %windir%\Microsoft.NET\assembly.

The loading process of assemblies deals with searching a number of paths, including the GAC, folders relative to the executing application, and configurable hint paths, trying to find a matching assembly. This process, called *assembly probing*, can be monitored for diagnostic purposes using a tool called fuslogvw.exe, the Assembly Binding Log Viewer.

Application Domains

Isolation is an important technique to increase system robustness, to establish security boundaries, and to have more granular control over execution. This well-known fact is mirrored in the design of many platforms. For example, when executables on Windows are run, the operating system executes them in separate processes to achieve isolation between them. This isolation applies to various resources such as the memory, operating system objects, and so on. By doing so, one crashing process cannot take down the whole system, and security boundaries can be established to prevent malicious code from affecting other processes (which could otherwise lead to security breaches).

The CLR has similar means of isolating groups of assemblies from one another. This is achieved by the concept of application domains (abbreviated as AppDomains), which are the units of isolation on the managed runtime. Application domains are the containers wherein assemblies get loaded and executed. In addition, configuration and security settings can be applied on individual application domains. Communication between different application domains needs to happen using dedicated mechanisms such as .NET Remoting, just like interprocess communication on Windows needs to happen using special techniques such as shared memory sections or named pipes.

> **NOTE**
>
> Assemblies by themselves cannot be unloaded. The unit of granularity for unloading on the CLR is the application domain. Therefore, application domains are typically used when loading assemblies that are untrusted and need to be sandboxed. A good example of such a scenario is the use of add-ins in a larger application.

When an application is started, the CLR creates a default application domain for the assembly with the entry point to start executing. From that point on, application domains are created on demand when the application or a library requests to do so. Typically, .NET developers won't be concerned with the manual creation of application domains; instead, libraries such as the add-in framework rely on application domains for their isolation properties while allowing developers to work with higher-level APIs that hide the complexity of application domain loading, communication, and unloading.

To reduce the memory footprint by loading common assemblies like mscorlib.dll (in which very basic data types such as string and integer live) multiple times, such assemblies can be shared across application domains. Assemblies used this way are known as domain-neutral assemblies and are highly trusted because their failure can take down the whole process. Because assemblies by themselves cannot be unloaded, and because domain-neutral assemblies always live outside the control of any real application domain, it's impossible to unload domain-neutral assemblies (other than by terminating the process). Figure 1.12 illustrates the isolation properties of application domains.

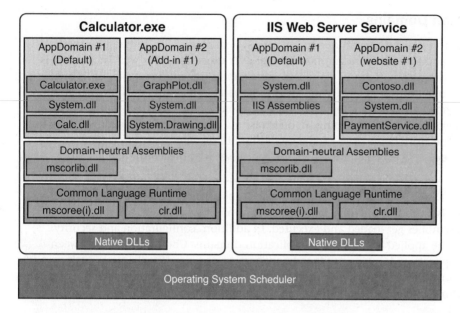

FIGURE 1.12   Processes, application domains, and assemblies.

RETHINKING THE SOFTWARE STACK

The isolation properties of application domains have been leveraged in a wide variety of scenarios, even reaching out to operating system design. Singularity is a research OS written by Microsoft Research that's almost exclusively based on managed code. The properties of type-safe managed code play a central role in the design of Singularity to isolate system services, user processes, and even drivers from each other. Software isolated processes (SIPs) form the cornerstone of this OS-level isolation and look a lot like application domains.

"Rethinking the software stack" is the design motto of Singularity and focuses on three core pillars:

▶ SIPs for improved protection of system services and processes

▶ Contract-based channels to establish communication between these SIPs

▶ Manifest-based programs to aid in verification of system properties

For more information, visit http://research.microsoft.com/singularity, where a download of the research development kit (RDK) is available if you want to experiment with this research OS.

As mentioned before, the ability to establish boundaries between logical groups of code is a great one in environments where untrusted code is to be loaded. One of the first customers of the CLR was ASP.NET, the .NET successor to classic Active Server Pages technology. In the world of web hosting, many websites need to run on the same server.

Maintaining separate processes for every website is far too heavyweight, so historically web servers like Microsoft's Internet Information Services (IIS) have had ways to run multiple websites in the same process. With the advent of ASP.NET, application domains can be leveraged to achieve this goal. Since IIS 7, the web server itself knows a good deal about managed code, and application pools have become the unit of isolation in IIS. As you might expect, those pools piggyback on application domains under the covers.

Today, managed code is running in lots of places, including in server products such as SQL Server (version 2005 and later), where uptime is one of the most essential concerns. SQL Server by itself is not a managed application, but instead it allows developers to use managed code to extend its capabilities (for example, by means of managed stored procedures). We say that SQL Server acts as a CLR host. Application domain isolation alone is not good enough for such high-demand environments in which the host wants to have much more control over what gets loaded and how the runtime behaves. For example, SQL Server has its own memory manager, and natively hosting the CLR in the service process would disturb it greatly. To answer to the needs of complex hosts, the CLR has a specialized hosting API that allows the host to have much tighter control over the CLR's behavior.

> **NOTE**
>
> Since CLR 4.0, it has become possible to host multiple versions of the runtime inside the same process side by side. At this lower level, isolation between each CLR's runtime infrastructure and the application domains living in each CLR is maintained. In other words, different applications running on different versions of the CLR in the same process cannot see each other.

JIT Compilation

As you've seen, all .NET languages compile code targeting IL as the destination code format. Today's processors do not know how to execute code written in this format, so something needs to happen to turn IL code into instructions the target processor can deal with. The runtime service that's responsible for making the mapping between IL code and native processor instructions is called the Just-in-Time compiler, often abbreviated as JIT and referred to as "the jitter."

> **NOTE**
>
> Although IL code is machine-independent, the .NET language compilers allow code to be compiled targeting a specified machine architecture, using a /platform switch. This functionality is used rather rarely but comes in handy sometimes when interoperating with native code that requires a specific machine architecture. All this flag actually does is modify a flag in the produced assembly to tell the runtime to enforce the use of a certain architecture. You can inspect this flag, and even tweak it, using an SDK tool called corflags.exe.

This trick also comes in handy when developing code on an x64 platform if you want to force your application assembly to run using x86, to inspect the runtime behavior. Typically, you don't need to do this because IL is platform-neutral, but when you run into subtle issues that reproduce only on certain architectures, this is a potential ingredient for easier debugging.

This decoupling from the runtime's abstract machine language, IL, and the destination computer's underlying instruction set reveals yet another advantage of IL code: Assemblies are independent from the target machine's architecture. In the world of assembler, C, and C++, this is fundamentally different because multiple compilations are required to target various architectures. As the processor industry continues to move from 32-bit to 64-bit processors, this is especially handy: As a .NET developer, you don't have to do anything to make your code run on a 64-bit machine.

The final compilation of IL code into native instructions opens up for extra optimization opportunities in the jitter, too. Because the runtime has intimate knowledge of the platform on which it's running, platform-specific optimizations can be made when compiling code. Other optimizations such as inlining are carried out by the jitter to improve performance. Besides compiling code into native instructions, the jitter takes on code verification and security checking tasks, too.

RUNTIME COMPILATION VERSUS INTERPRETATION

It's important to understand that .NET code ultimately gets compiled into instructions targeting the bare metal the code gets to run on. This differs fundamentally from runtimes that are based on interpretation, where intermediate code (sometimes also referred to as byte-code) is read instruction per instruction while the program runs. Although JIT compilation incurs an upfront cost for turning chunks of IL into native code, the steady-state performance of the running code is generally much higher than for runtimes based on interpretation.

But what makes this compiler deserve the status of being just in time? Assemblies might contain lots of code that's never executed during a particular run of a program. A good example of this is code that deals with error handling, which hopefully has an exceptional nature. The jitter will compile only the code that actually runs, doing this on a per-method basis.

So how does JIT compilation work? When a managed assembly is loaded, the metadata describing the structure of the types and the code contained in them becomes available. Instead of compiling every IL method body into native code right away at load time, the JIT needs to respect its "just in time" nature. To achieve this, upon entering a method the runtime detects all the types referenced by that method's code. For every type, the runtime maintains a table that associates pieces of code with the type's methods. Not surprisingly, this table is called the MethodTable. Initially, all slots in the table are filled with little pieces of code (sometimes referred to as a thunk) that call into a prestub helper.

The role of that code is to invoke the JIT compiler to turn the method's IL body into native code ready for execution on the machine's processor.

Once the JIT compiler has finished translating the method code into native instructions that now reside somewhere in an executable region of code, the prestub helper patches up the MethodTable entry for the method to call into the generated native code. From this point on, subsequent calls to the same method do not go through the prestub helper anymore but end up in native code land immediately. Figure 1.13 illustrates the working of the JIT compiler on our Calculator example.

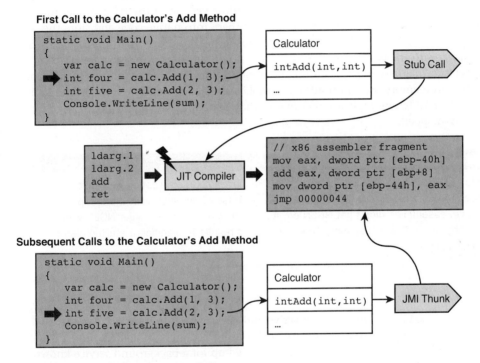

FIGURE 1.13   JIT compilation in action.

Native Image Generation

Having to pay the price to JIT-compile application code and the class library assemblies on which it depends doesn't sound like a great idea. After all, once an assembly has been deployed to a target machine, the processor architecture is certain, and all repeated JIT compilations of the code in those assemblies will result in the same corresponding native code. It seems we want a mechanism where we can still deploy IL-based assemblies (for all the benefits previously mentioned) but go through the burden of JIT compilation only once.

To counter this concern, the CLR has the concept of "native image generation," or NGEN. The simplest way to think about NGEN is as an offline version of the JIT compiler that can be invoked on whole assemblies, to translate them into native code and store the result in a central location where the assembly loader will find them. (In practice, this is a folder underneath the GAC location). From that point on, no runtime cost for JIT compilation has to be paid anymore, resulting in fast startup times for applications. In addition, a reduction in memory use can result if assemblies are loaded multiple times in the same application (in different application domains, that is) because the native code image can be memory-mapped.

GETTING TO KNOW NGEN THE HARD WAY

Users of Windows PowerShell 1.0, which is a managed code application, will have experienced the cost incurred by JIT compilations. Because of an issue with the setup package, assemblies didn't get NGEN'ed. A manual workaround to trigger NGEN was published to the PowerShell blog. This workaround results in significant startup performance improvements.

Windows PowerShell 2.0 will have proper NGEN'ing carried out by its installer.

NGEN can be used in two modes: interactive and background. In interactive mode, NGEN compilation of the specified assembly is carried out immediately. When running an NGEN task in background mode, its compilation is queued up for a background service known as the NGEN optimization service (mscorscw.exe) to do the work later. This queue is prioritized so that important assemblies can take precedence over less frequently used ones. To carry out NGEN administration tasks, a command-line utility called ngen.exe exists, although most NGEN tasks are performed by software installers (for example, to queue up background compilation jobs for the installer to finish more quickly).

All this sounds great, but there are some flip sides to NGEN. One potential issue is for assemblies and their NGEN'ed counterparts to get out of sync when updates happen. Command-line switches exist on ngen.exe to force updates when this is the case. Contrary to what you might think, the performance of an NGEN'ed assembly is potentially slower than for a JIT-compiled one. The native image compiler can't make as many assumptions about the runtime environment as its online friend, the JIT compiler. Therefore, NGEN needs to be conservative, sometimes resulting in inferior code generation compared to the JIT equivalent. Another potential performance regression comes from the potential image rebasing that needs to happen when the native image is loaded. The BCL assemblies carefully specify specific base addresses to load their NGEN'ed native image at, but calculation of suitable base addresses isn't always a trivial thing to do. This said, over the years the CLR team has spent lots of effort to make NGEN as efficient as possible. One major step forward was made in the 3.5 SP1 release.

To conclude, NGEN isn't a silver bullet, and the rule of thumb for performance optimization does apply to it: Let measurement be your guide in deciding whether NGEN is good for you!

Automatic Memory Management

Another core service provided by the runtime's execution engine is garbage collection. Historically, memory management has been a painful business for developers. Often, error-prone code results, and even the simplest code gets bloated by low-level bookkeeping code. On top of that, direct pointer manipulation isn't exactly appropriate in a world where memory safety and type safety are to be maintained.

Previous approaches to memory management were either too low-level (such as malloc/free in C and new/delete in C++), causing bugs such as dangling pointers and double frees, or reached their limits if things got too complex (such as the inability to reclaim cyclic references in the world of COM's AddRef/Release reference counting mechanism, without manual intervention to break the cycle). One of the CLR's goals was to eliminate the need for developers to deal with memory management themselves. The baked-in garbage collector (GC) realizes this goal.

> **NOTE**
>
> GCs are not a recent invention. In the late 1950s, the implementation of the LISP language already required automatic memory management mechanisms. At that time, the runtime cost of GCs was a strong argument to avoid languages that relied on them. Over the years, performance of GCs has improved drastically, making the overhead a relatively low cost to pay with lots of return on investment for developers. The CLR's GC is extremely optimized to reduce the runtime cost to an absolute minimum whenever possible.

If you were to examine the IL instruction set in detail, you'd notice the existence of an instruction called newobj to allocate object instances on the managed heap. This is the instruction that corresponds to C#'s new operator we've already encountered in our Calculator example. However, no matter how hard you try, you won't find a corresponding deallocation instruction. Enter the world of automatic memory management.

First, let's focus on the mechanism used to allocate memory on the CLR. Various instructions cause this to happen, such as newobj to create new objects and newarr to create an array. Don't be concerned if those words don't mean much yet; we discuss them extensively later. All we're concerned about for now is how memory is allocated when such requests happen. To understand this, we need to dive into the structure of the managed heap, which is the portion of memory managed by the CLR for the allocation of managed objects.

Allocations on the managed heap are extremely effective compared to allocations on different heap implementations, such as the one provided by the C++ runtime. In essence, heap allocations happen linearly, as illustrated in Figure 1.14. Here the heap already contains a couple of objects denoted by letters A, B, and C.

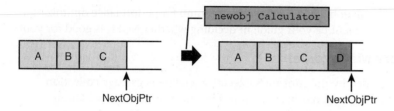

FIGURE 1.14   Allocation of a new object.

NextObjPtr is simply a pointer that indicates the first free spot following already allocated objects. Allocating object D is just a matter of reserving the necessary space from that point on and moving NextObjPtr along. Contrast this to the C runtime heap, where allocations require free list-scanning algorithms (with common strategies like first fit, best fit, or worst fit) to find an available spot that's large enough to hold an object of the requested size. Besides potentially costly allocations, such algorithms cause heap fragmentation because of unoccupied holes in the heap that are too small to hold any object.

Of course, because available memory is finite, the approach of an ever-growing linear heap can't keep working. At some point, NextObjPtr will reach the end of the heap, and something will need to happen to reclaim free space. This is where garbage collection kicks in. The basic idea is fairly straightforward. In the first phase, the GC collects so-called root objects, which are found in static variables, method arguments and local variables, thread-local storage, and CPU registers. These are special because they are directly reachable by the executing code.

Starting from the roots, references to other objects are traversed. For example, consider a root of type Order that contains references to a Customer object and a Product object. Because the Order object is reachable by the code, so are the Customer and Product objects. All it takes to get there is to follow one object reference on the Order object. This traversal is carried out exhaustively until all reachable objects are marked. Therefore, this phase is called the marking phase. Figure 1.15 illustrates the marking of reachable objects.

In this example, a garbage collection pass has been triggered because an attempt was made to allocate an object J, but the heap ran out of space, as you can see from the location of NearObjPtr. When a GC is started, the execution engine suspends (meaning the evaluation stack is frozen, among other things) so that roots can be identified and the heap can be scanned. From the identified roots, objects A, E, and I are directly reachable. Objects B, F, and G can be reached by traversing one or more object references starting from those root objects. This ends the marking phase.

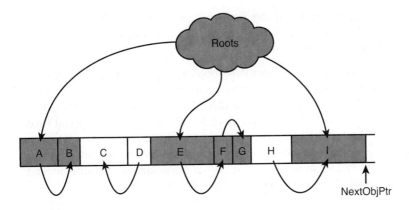

FIGURE 1.15   Finding reachable objects.

Now that reachable objects have been marked (using some bit on an object header called the SyncBlock), the GC can move on to sweep the heap. It does this by walking the memory linearly, reclaiming the space occupied by unreachable objects. In the example, those are objects C, D, and H. As part of this phase, the heap is compacted by moving objects into the space that has been freed. Figure 1.16 illustrates the result after sweeping and compacting.

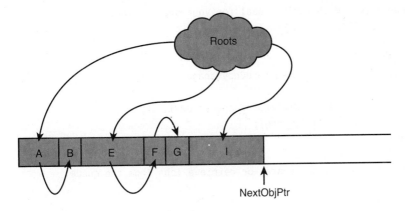

FIGURE 1.16   Result of sweeping and compacting the heap.

Notice how addresses used for object references need to be changed because of the compaction that causes objects to move. What matters most to us developers is that the heap now has plenty of free space, so our original object allocation for object J can succeed.

All of this is a gross simplification of the GC implementation in the CLR. In reality, the heap is divided into regions called generations. The idea behind generations is to reduce the number of full heap collections by splitting the heap into smaller regions. Freshly allocated objects start their lives in generation 0, the smallest region. When object allocation fails, the GC tries collecting generation 0. If this frees enough space, the allocation can succeed without collecting the rest of the managed heap. Because generation 0 is small, the pause induced by its collection is minimal.

Typical allocation patterns produce lots of short-lived objects, so most of the time generation 0 collections should suffice. Objects that survive a generation during collection get promoted to the next generation. In total, there are three such generations, numbered from 0 to 2, with an increasing size. Objects larger than 85,000 bytes deserve special treatment and are allocated on the Large Object Heap (LOH) to avoid having to move those giants around during compaction. Another complication is the existence of pinned objects, which cannot be moved because their location has been shared with unmanaged code, and the GC cannot track those references to update them.

Exception Handling

Error handling is a tricky business. Disciplined error code checking on function return has plagued developers for many years. For example, the following fragment is an excerpt from the Platform SDK documentation on a COM-based API for file transfer:

```
IBackgroundCopyManager* g_pbcm = NULL;
HRESULT hr;

// Specify the appropriate COM threading model for your application.
hr = CoInitializeEx(NULL, COINIT_APARTMENTTHREADED);
if (SUCCEEDED(hr))
{
    hr = CoCreateInstance(__uuidof(BackgroundCopyManager), NULL,
                      CLSCTX_LOCAL_SERVER,
                      __uuidof(IBackgroundCopyManager),
                      (void**) &g_pbcm);
    if (SUCCEEDED(hr))
    {
        // Use g_pbcm to create, enumerate, or retrieve jobs from the queue.
    }
}
```

This approach of error checking is tedious and greatly disrupts the flow of the code, especially because we expect errors to happen only occasionally. Also, there's little flexibility in the propagation of detailed error information; GetLastError values in Win32 and obscure HRESULT values in COM are hardly to be called descriptive. To propagate error codes to the place where the fault condition can be handled properly (for example, by retrying an operation or by showing an error message to the user), there's little room to wiggle. Function return values are the most convenient spots to signal error codes, and all the function's return data needs to be exposed through output parameters, making the code hard to write and understand.

Something needed to change to reduce the ceremony for error propagation. The solution used by the CLR is called *structured exception handling*, a technique that has been applied in various programming languages before (such as C++ and Java, to name a couple) and can leverage support provided by the operating system (called SEH).

Exceptions are simply objects that are "thrown" (some people say raised, but I like to keep that verb for another context) when an exceptional situation arises. Examples of such situations include I/O errors, detection of invalid arguments passed to a function, user authorization failures, and so on. By doing so, the contract of a function is not spoiled by the mere possibility that something bad happens. After all, almost every code can fail: Think of out-of-memory conditions for one. Here is an example of raising an exception:

```
public List<Customer> LoadCustomerData(string file)
{
    if (!File.Exists(file))
        throw new FileNotFoundException(file);

    // Read data from the file and return Customer objects
}
```

Throwing exceptions to signal error conditions is one thing. The next part of the puzzle we need to fill in is the capability to catch such an exception and act upon it. This is the second pillar of structured exception handling. To reduce the burden of manually having to propagate exceptions to callers, the runtime takes care of this by percolating the exception object up the call stack until an appropriate exception handler is found that's willing to deal with the exception. Figure 1.17 shows how the call stack is used to propagate an exception up to the point where it's caught.

The call stack is read from bottom to top: `fillGrid_Click` called into `DisplayCustomers`, which in turn called into `LoadCustomerData`. There things go terribly wrong: The specified file is not found, and an exception is thrown (step 1). Now the runtime kicks in and walks the stack looking for a protected block with an associated handler that's capable of handling the `FileNotFoundException` exception object. It finds one in `fillGrid_Click` and starts unwinding the stack in steps 2 and 3. Finally, control is transferred to the exception handler in the catch block, as shown in step 4.

Code Access Security

Another runtime service provided by the CLR is Code Access Security (CAS), which is tightly coupled to the call stack just like exceptions. At the time the CLR was designed, the Internet had become a popular means of distributing software. Unfortunately, this model also came with lots of security concerns; numerous security breaches were known to be caused by blindly executing malicious code that was downloaded from the Internet. This urgently demanded new ways to prevent malicious code from running, and that's what CAS is all about.

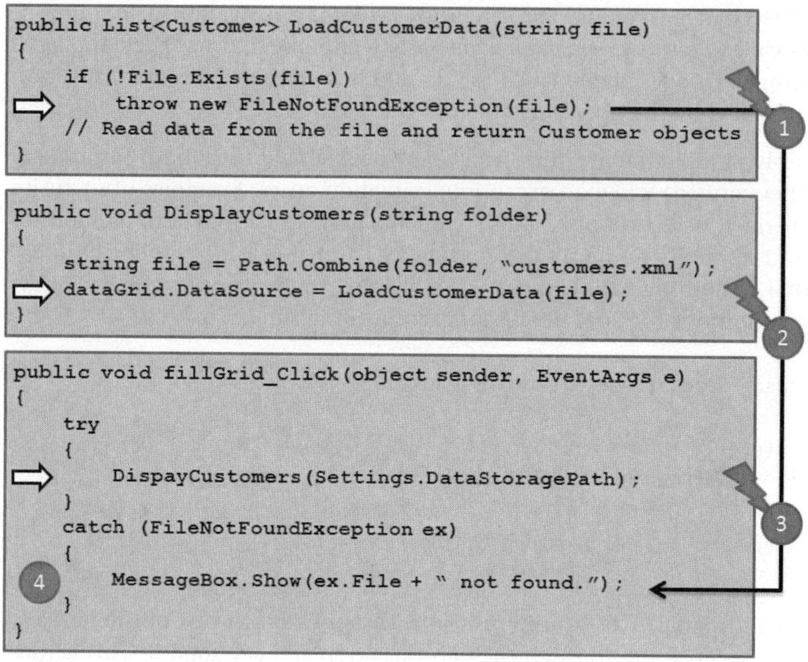

```
public List<Customer> LoadCustomerData(string file)
{
    if (!File.Exists(file))
        throw new FileNotFoundException(file);
    // Read data from the file and return Customer objects
}
```

```
public void DisplayCustomers(string folder)
{
    string file = Path.Combine(folder, "customers.xml");
    dataGrid.DataSource = LoadCustomerData(file);
}
```

```
public void fillGrid_Click(object sender, EventArgs e)
{
    try
    {
        DispayCustomers(Settings.DataStoragePath);
    }
    catch (FileNotFoundException ex)
    {
        MessageBox.Show(ex.File + " not found.");
    }
}
```

FIGURE 1.17   Exception propagation.

Up until the point the CLR was introduced, authentication and authorization mechanisms were tied to the concept of users and groups. For instance, a user authenticated to the system by providing evidence about his identity: a password, smartcard, biometrics, and so on. With the logon token, authorization can be performed to determine whether the user should be granted access to a variety of resources such as files, system management tasks, and so on. However, code run under a certain user account has the same rights as the user. What we need is a mechanism that can sandbox code.

With CAS, code comes with evidence, too: It can be digitally signed by a certain publisher, originate from a trusted location, and so on. Configurable policies relate evidence to permission sets that are granted to the code during execution. To access various APIs, certain permissions are required; for example, to interact with the file system or to call out to managed code.

At the point an API demands a certain permission to continue, the CLR takes over and performs a stack walk to make sure the assemblies in the caller chain are granted the necessary permissions. This way, assemblies that are not trusted are kept from making calls to security-sensitive APIs.

Figure 1.18 shows this stack walking in action. EvilCode.exe was downloaded from a dubious location and lacks the necessary evidence to be granted permissions to interact with the file system. In an attempt to steal or tamper with the user's data, the assembly calls out to TaxReporting.dll, a trusted assembly on the system installed by a tax-reporting tool. The code in the tax-reporting assembly calls into the File.Create method that's defined in mscorlib.dll, one of the BCL assemblies installed to the GAC, which is fully trusted. However, the `File.Create` method raises a demand for file permissions. At this point, the CLR starts the stack walk to check the granted permission set of each assembly on the call stack against the demanded permission. TaxReporting.dll passes that check, but the malicious code in EvilCode.exe doesn't. Because the demand cannot be satisfied, the CLR throws a SecurityException.

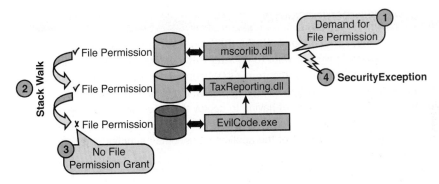

FIGURE 1.18   CAS performing a stack walk.

Interoperability Facilities

No matter how great the introduction of a new development platform and runtime environment is, the capability to interoperate with existing code is key to the success of the new technology. This is no different for the .NET Framework, so a big investment was made to ensure existing code could work together with the new platform.

One piece of the interoperability stack is called Platform Invoke, or P/Invoke, which enables calling native functions exported by DLLs. P/Invoke is typically used to call into operating system functions that haven't been exposed (yet) through the managed code libraries.

P/INVOKE FOR THE MASSES

Getting P/Invoke to work can require intimate knowledge of memory layout, conversions between different types, calling conventions, and more. This can be utterly annoying to get right. Luckily, the community of .NET developers recognized this and started an online wiki where P/Invoke signatures and mappings for structs are posted. You can find it at http://pinvoke.net.

In addition, the CLR team has built a tool called the P/Invoke Interop Assistant that you can find at http://www.codeplex.com/clrinterop.

Because a giant pile of libraries has been written in COM, it was no more than logical to have COM interop functionality in the .NET Framework too. This allows existing COM libraries to be called from managed code, as well as the opposite where managed assemblies are exposed to COM. Two tools make both directions possible; they're respectively called Type Library Importer (tblimp.exe) and Type Library Exporter (tblexp.exe). To reduce the burden of having to make such mappings for popular libraries, a set of primary interop assemblies (PIAs) are provided by Microsoft (for example, to bridge with the Office automation libraries).

NO PIA

Right after mentioning PIAs, I should point out the .NET 4.0 release provides a "no PIA" feature. An obvious question is why we want to do away with something that looks like (and is) a very powerful bridging mechanism to big COM automation libraries, like Office's. The truth is, PIAs are not disappearing completely, but their immediate use gets restricted to compile time. Instead of having to deploy the PIAs—which can be quite big—"no PIA" allows the used portions of a PIA to be linked in with the assembly that's using them. This way, deployment of the application becomes simpler, and code size is reduced significantly.

A key part of these interoperability facilities is their capability to marshal types back and forth. This process transparently maps between managed types and their native counterparts whenever required. Everyone who's dealt with COM and native code knows how much string representations exist in those worlds. By using the interoperability marshaling functionality, all of those can be exposed to the managed code world as the BCL string type (or, to be precise, the StringBuilder type if mutation is required). To guide this marshaling, custom attributes are often used to provide the necessary information about the native types that are involved.

THE COM DINOSAUR

Nobody knows how the dinosaurs came to their end. Today's question is the opposite: We don't know when (if ever) the COM dinosaur will vanish from the developer's universe.

Although rich interoperability capabilities were added to the .NET platform from day one, optimists hoped to see the use of COM decline rapidly after the new platform was introduced. Although progress has been made in this area and the number of new COM libraries has dropped, giants like the Office automation libraries will be around for the foreseeable future.

.NET 4.0 recognizes this fact and significantly reduces the number of pain points developers dealing with COM interop have been complaining about. It's funny, though, that the advent of the brand new dynamic language runtime has been one of the vehicles that makes this mission easier to achieve. COM programming has always been a dynamic experience (those familiar with COM will think of IDispatch instantaneously), and therefore the new dynamic language features introduced in C# 4.0 and Visual Basic 10 provided a great opportunity to improve part of COM interop.

Besides this, C# 4.0 has added named and optional parameters, among other features, to make dealing with COM easier than it has been for the first three releases of the language.

The Base Class Library

Obviously, having a runtime in place is an essential ingredient to the success of the .NET Framework. But far more important to application developers is the availability of a rich BCL that gives access to a wealth of functionality for applications to leverage. In that lies the success factor of various platforms: Windows with its Win32 API, Office with automation libraries, C++ with the Standard Template Library, and so on.

> ## THE MULTILANGUAGE ADVANTAGE
>
> It can't be stressed enough that the cross-language nature of the .NET Framework uniquely positions it in this picture. CLS-compliant libraries need to be written only once to be directly usable from a rich set of .NET-enabled languages. This provides a huge advantage to library writers.

The .NET Framework's BCL has grown a lot since the first version was released in the early 2000s. Today, it's nearly impossible to give complete coverage of the whole framework in one book. Instead, it's much more important to get a good idea about the basic building blocks the framework is composed of. As a reader of this book, you'll get a solid understanding of types and the members they're composed of, so that exploring the .NET Framework's BCL should be relatively straightforward. Rarely do I have the complete solution to a problem in my head when I start developing a new piece of software, but armed with those fundamentals, anything in the .NET Framework is in reach to learn about and to leverage. This said, we cover a good deal of the big pillars of the BCL in this book.

Given its enormous proportions, a good structure is invaluable to discoverability of features in the BCL. One key approach to enable this is by using a hierarchical organization of the types provided, as opposed to the flat structure seen in the Win32 API. In the world of managed code, this translates into the use of namespaces. The following are a few examples of common namespaces and the functionality they group together:

- ▶ System contains the primitive data types like Int32, Double, String, Booleans, and others.

- ▶ System.Collections provides access to convenient collection types such as lists, sets, and dictionaries.

- ▶ System.Data is the one-stop shop for data access functionality with support for online and offline data access, targeting various kinds of databases.

- ▶ System.Diagnostics allows for interacting with system services for event logs, performance counters, processes, and so on.

- ▶ System.Globalization contains classes that are used for writing globalized applications.

- ▶ System.IO provides the constructs required to do all sorts of input/output, with streams, support for files, named pipes, and such.

- ▶ System.Linq is where support for Language Integrated Query lives, enabling easier access to all sorts of data through integrated language syntax.

- ▶ System.Net contains classes for networking, supporting various well-known protocols such as TCP, UDP, and HTTP.

- ▶ System.Reflection allows runtime inspection of managed types as well as dynamic generation of IL code.

- ▶ System.Security wraps all the security-related functionality, ranging from CAS and permissions to cryptography.

- ▶ System.ServiceModel is the root namespace for the WCF APIs used in service-oriented programming.

- ▶ System.Text has several useful types for manipulation of text, support for different encoding schemes, and use of regular expressions.

- ▶ System.Web is where ASP.NET finds its home, containing various web controls, configuration APIs, support for server-side caching, and so on.

- ▶ System.Windows makes a home for various user interface technologies such as Windows Forms and the WPF.

- ▶ System.Xml obviously provides XML support of all sorts, including schema and transformation APIs, LINQ support, and more.

We take a closer look at some of those namespaces and how they relate to the use of assemblies throughout the book. For now, remember that the use of namespaces makes it much easier to find the things you're looking for, and often a simple guess or a directed keyword search within the MSDN libraries directs you to the right place.

THE SYSTEM VERSUS MICROSOFT NAMESPACES

As you'll see throughout this book, the .NET Framework contains two root namespaces: System and Microsoft. What's the distinction between them? The short answer is the latter contains types that are relevant regardless of the platform the code is run on, whereas the Microsoft namespace contains access to Microsoft-specific technologies.

For example, file access functionality lives in `System.IO` given that all supported operating systems—including UNIX variants supported by projects like Mono—have support for file access, whereas Registry access is a Microsoft Windows-specific concept and hence lives in `Microsoft.Win32`.

Other examples of Microsoft-specific APIs include MSBuild, SQL Server, SharePoint, various Visual Studio libraries, and so on.

BCL, WITH A BIG B

In the original version of the .NET Framework, nearly all the libraries that shipped with it were known collectively as the Base Class Library. It covered essentials like collection types, text manipulation, arithmetic functions, reflection, I/O functionality, and so on. Notable exceptions are Windows Forms and ASP.NET libraries, which can stand on their own, leveraging the core functionality provided in the class libraries underneath. And in fact, for a while in the early betas of the 1.0 release, ASP.NET (originally called ASP+) shipped as a separate installer. So, how to define the BCL? Everything but Windows Forms and ASP.NET? But what about things such as data access libraries? Clearly the line can be a bit blurry.

In .NET 2.0, this picture didn't change much. Functionality of various libraries was extended—with generics being a core improvement to the runtime—but no giant new libraries were introduced. With .NET 3.0, things started to change a lot. Initially called WinFX, the third release of the .NET Framework introduced a whole set of new libraries, such as Windows Presentation Foundation (WPF), Windows Communication Foundation (WCF), and Windows Workflow Foundation (WF). Apart from the fact that those libraries ship out of the box with the .NET Framework distribution and lots of applications are likely using them, they can't really be called "base" class libraries.

Personally, I don't like the BCL acronym all that much. For one thing, the types defined within the BCL are not necessarily—and more often than not, they aren't—base classes in the object-oriented sense of the word. An alternative name could have been the Fundamental Class Library, where only the bare primitives are defined, leaving other libraries outside that picture. In some sense, the BCL can be delineated by all those types that are tightly coupled with either the underlying runtime (for example, primitive types, reflection capabilities, threading support, and so forth) or require lots of bridging with native code to provide access to system-level services (for example, file access, console input and output, and so forth). Other libraries like WPF, WCF, ASP.NET, and even LINQ just happen to be bundled with the .NET Framework but shouldn't be considered part of the *Base* Class Library.

One thing is sure: Don't confuse the .NET Framework with the BCL. The .NET Framework denotes the big umbrella for the runtime, libraries, as well as various tools that ship with the redistribution. The BCL is just a tiny, though very important, part of that picture. Where to draw the line between the BCL and the rest of the libraries is much less important; all that matters is you have a lot of out-of-the-box libraries at your service.

In times of a booming blogosphere, I'd rather define the BCL in terms of the features discussed on the BCL team's blog at http://blogs.msdn.com/bclteam.

Summary

In this chapter, you learned about the .NET platform in general—its history, design goals, the cross-language interoperability story, and the core runtime services provided by the common language runtime. We even sneaked a peek at the BCL.

Now that you have a solid understanding of the platform, let's focus the C# language, our main language tool in the rest of this book. We cover the history, design trends, and core aspects of the C# language in the next chapter.

CHAPTER 2

Introducing the C# Programming Language

IN THIS CHAPTER

▸ The Evolution of C# 55

▸ A Sneak Peak at the Future 89

Loaded with a basic understanding of the .NET platform and its philosophy, we're ready to dive in to one of its core languages: C#. To set the scene, this chapter starts by looking at the evolution of the C# language throughout the first four releases of the .NET Framework. As we cover the four versions of the language, core language features and design themes will be highlighted.

Next, we take a look at the challenges that we'll face in the near future. At the end of this chapter, you'll understand the forces that have shaped the language covered in depth throughout the remainder of the book. In the next chapter, we switch gears and explore the tooling support available to develop on the .NET Framework using C#.

The Evolution of C#

In this book, we explore the .NET Framework from the C# developer's perspective, focusing on the various language features and putting them in practice with a wide range of libraries that ship in the Base Class Library (BCL) or as part of separate software development kits (SDKs). But before we do so, let's take a quick look at the various C# releases and what has shaped the language into what it is today, the .NET Framework 4. Figure 2.1 highlights the important themes that defined the evolution of C# so far.

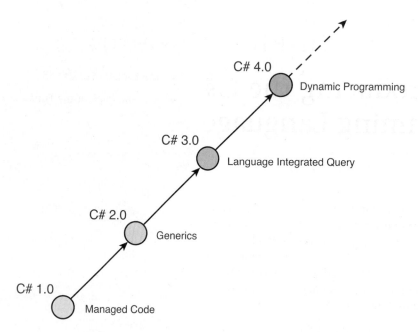

FIGURE 2.1   Main C# version themes.

C# 1.0: Managed Code Development, Take One

Creating a new runtime is one thing; providing a rich set of libraries to make the technology relevant is another thing—moreover, it's the most crucial thing developers care about when deciding whether to embrace a new platform.

This put a big task on the shoulders of Microsoft's .NET Framework BCL team, having to write code targeting a runtime that was still under development. Obviously, one of the core ingredients to make this mission successful was to have a programming language and compiler—not to mention productivity tools such as debuggers—readily available to get the development going.

Only two options were available. One was to retrofit an existing language like C++ or Visual Basic on the .NET platform. Although this was in line with the whole vision of the Common Language Infrastructure (CLI), it had its downsides. Porting languages, preserving semantics, and potentially introducing lots of backward-compatibility requirements early on didn't seem an attractive option under the pressure to get BCL development off the ground as soon as possible.

As you might have guessed by now, the second option was to come up with a brand new language. Such a language wouldn't have to care about preserving backward compatibility and could expose the richness of the Common Type System (CTS) in a no-nonsense way, mapping language features directly onto their CTS counterparts. This marked the inception of project Cool, which stood for "C-style Object-Oriented Language," later to be renamed to C# (pronounced "see sharp").

Design and implementation of C# began in late 1998, led by Anders Hejlsberg. He previously worked at Borland designing the highly successful Turbo Pascal and Delphi products and later joined Microsoft to work on J++ and Windows Foundation Classes (WFC) and, more recently, on C# and the rest of the Microsoft-managed programming languages. Other core language design members were Scott Wiltamuth, Peter Golde, Peter Sollich, and Eric Gunnerson.

THE ORIGIN OF THE NAME C#

Although Cool was a rather, let's say, cool name, marketing folks wanted a different branding for the new language. The C part in the name was a straightforward choice, given that the language embraced C-style syntax, with curly braces, types in front of names, and so on.

Because the new language was considered to allow a more modern approach to object-oriented programming with type safety as its cornerstone, having the name imply a degree of superiority to C++ (which was not designed with type safety as a central theme) was desirable. Because the name C++ comes from the post-increment ++ operator applied to regular C, one option would have been to follow along that theme. Unfortunately, C++++ is not syntactically correct (C+ = 2 would be too ridiculous), and moreover, the new language did not intend to become a superset of C++.

So some brilliant mind came up with a postfix notation that has a meaning of "higher than" but from a totally different domain: music notation. I'm not a musician myself, but my office mate (thanks, Mike) reassured me the official definition of the sharp sign (#) is to indicate "half a tone higher" on the note that precedes it. Lucky coincidence or not, the sharp sign looks a lot like two post-increment operators stacked on top of each other.

To keep typing the language's name simple, the sharp sign is not written as Unicode character U+266F (♯) but as the number sign U+0023 (#) instead. The pronunciation is "see sharp," though.

Personally, I like the name C# a lot. For one thing, it definitely sounds better than Managed C++, C++/CLI, or C++0x (no pun intended). Also, the use of the sharp sign in programming language names has become some kind of trademark of the .NET Framework, with the newborn F# language and the Spec# research project (a predecessor to code contracts in .NET 4.0). And just for the sake of it, my blog is known as B# (cheesy, I know).

References have been made to the meaning of the sharp sign in various places. At some point, there was a research project called Polyphonic C# that explored the area of concurrent programming using "chords." (I won't go into detail on this right now.) Another project was CΩ ("see omega"), which used the last letter in the Greek alphabet, omega, to indicate its rich extensive nature over C#. Technologies like LINQ in C# and Visual Basic and XML literals in Visual Basic originate from this project.

> For some unknown reason, the dynamic language folks didn't get chased by the market-ing department for choosing names with the "Iron" prefix, like IronPython and IronRuby. Maybe because the use of metals in product names has precedents (think of Silverlight) or perhaps because they did get away with the claim it stands for "I Run On .NET."

So what were the design themes of the C# language right from the start? There's no better quote than the introductory sentence of the official C# specification, which is standard-ized in ECMA 334:

> *C# is a simple, modern, object-oriented, and type-safe programming language. C# has its roots in the C family of languages and will be immediately familiar to C, C++, and Java programmers.*

Let's analyze those claims in a bit more detail:

▶ Simplicity matters. C# deliberately does away with language features that are known to cause developers headaches, such as multiple inheritance, fall-through behavior in switch statements, and nonhygienic macros.

▶ Modern is good. It means the language recognizes concepts developers are directly familiar with, such as properties, events, and more recently, data querying, even though "pure" object-oriented languages don't need those.

▶ Object-oriented programming was, and still is, a widely accepted proven technique to master complexity in worlds where tons of software components need to work together seamlessly. No wonder the CLI and C# embrace it.

▶ Type safety is a big thing in the CLI. It eliminates whole classes of bugs and security headaches that plague languages like C and C++. This said, C# still allows type-unsafe code in regions explicitly marked as such.

▶ Having roots in the C family of languages makes the learning curve to get into C# easy for developers who've been using C or any of its derivatives in the past.

With its rich feature set, great tooling support in Visual Studio .NET version 2002, and backed by the rich BCL in .NET Framework 1.0, C# programming took a jumpstart. However, the language designers were a long way from running out of ideas.

VISUAL OR NOT?

If you browse the Microsoft Developer Network (MSDN) website, you'll often see refer-ences to Visual C# rather than just C#. What's the correct name? It depends what you're talking about: The language name simply is C#, whereas the development tool Microsoft provides to develop with the language is called Visual C#, after the Visual Studio tooling family it's part of. A notable exception to this rule is Visual Basic, where both the language and the product name are the same.

C# 2.0: Enriching the Core Language Features

2.0 Shipping a first release of a brand new platform and language was key to getting the ball rolling, so sometimes decisions had to be made to cut certain features during the development of this first release. The second release of the .NET Framework allowed the opportunity to catch up with the things the design teams wanted to do but hadn't gotten a chance to in the first release.

BACKWARD COMPATIBILITY MATTERS

Making sure code written using a previous release of the language doesn't compile anymore—or worse, starts behaving differently—is an essential design criterion when evolving the language.

C# is strict about this and aims to keep new releases of the language 100% compatible with older versions. You might wonder how this is possible when introducing new language features that potentially require new keywords. The answer lies in contextual keywords.

Right from the start, C# has had contextual keywords. It simply means a certain word can be treated as a keyword in certain contexts, while it can be used as an identifier in others. A good example of such a keyword is value. In the following fragment, it's used as a keyword within the property set accessor to denote the value being set:

```
public string Name
{
    get { return _name; }
    set { _name = value; }
}
```

However, when used outside the scope of a property setter, value can be used as a regular identifier, as follows:

```
static void Main()
{
    int value = 42;
    Console.WriteLine(value);
}
```

When C# 2.0 came around, new keywords were required to enable certain features. All those newly introduced keywords were implemented to be contextual, so they can't clash with existing names used in the program. As an example, generics support the specification of constraints on generic parameters using the where keyword:

```
static void Sort<T>(List<T> items) where T : IComparable
{
    // Generic sort algorithm
}
```

In code written before C# 2.0, it was simply impossible to use where in such a context, so there's no risk of breaking something here. Also, by making the keyword contextual, it can still be used as an identifier outside this context:

```
static void Main()
{
    string where = "There";
    Console.WriteLine(where);
}
```

Later, when C# 3.0 came around (see further), query expressions were added to the language. To express a filtering clause in a query, it simply makes sense to use the where keyword (SQL, anyone?) but in another context:

```
var res = from person in db.People
          where person.Age > 25
          select person;
```

Again, contextual treatment for keywords saves the mission.

So why did C# 1.0 have contextual keywords if there was no chance of breaking existing code? Well, it's a convenience not to have to escape "common words" just because they tend to have a special meaning in certain locations. The value keyword is a great example of that, but the same holds for get and set. Sometimes I wish this were applied more aggressively, making keywords such as class contextual, too. Having developed a system for school administration in a past life, I can assure you that the use of the word *class* as an identifier was a rather natural choice to refer to an object representing, um, a class. Luckily, C# has an escape mechanism for such cases:

```
MyClass @class = new MyClass();
```

To finish this point, if you ever find a piece of code that did compile in an older version of the language but doesn't anymore, you most certainly have found a defect. Beware, though, that application programming interfaces (APIs) are a bit more relaxed when it comes to changing behavior over time. This is typically done by deprecating certain API members, making developers aware that a particular part of the API might go away in future releases. We should consider ourselves lucky that the C# language has been spared from this deprecating business thanks to careful design.

Generics

.NET Framework 2.0 came with a major update to the common language runtime, mainly to add support for generics to the type system. Generics were prototyped in a project code named Gyro run by Don Syme (later to become the creator of F#) and Andrew Kennedy, both working at Microsoft Research. Such a fundamental addition to the type system required revisions of the languages that build on top of it. Therefore, both the C# and Visual Basic .NET languages were enhanced to provide support for both declaring and consuming generic types.

To support the introdution of generics, the BCL team added various generic collection types to the System.Collections.Generic namespace, an example of which is illustrated in the code fragment here:

```
List<int> primes = new List<int>();
for (int n = 2; n <= 100; n++)
{
    bool isPrime = true;
    for (int d = 2; d <= Math.Sqrt(n); d++)
    {
        if (n % d == 0)
        {
            isPrime = false;
            break;
        }
    }

    if (isPrime)
        primes.Add(n); // statically typed to take in an integer value
};

// no performance hit to convert types when retrieving data
foreach (int prime in primes)
    Console.WriteLine(prime);
```

Generics offer better static typing, thus doing away with whole classes of code defects and various performance benefits because they eliminate the need for runtime type conversions.

Nullable Types

During the design of the first release of the CLI, a distinction had been made between value types and reference types. Value types are stack allocated, whereas reference types live on the managed heap. Therefore, reference types can have null values (conceptually comparable to null pointers in native languages), whereas value types cannot.

The lack of an orthogonal approach in the classification of types versus their nullability was seen as an oversight that was rectified in the second release of .NET Framework with the introduction of nullable value types. This proves especially handy when mapping database records to objects because nullability applies to all types in the world of (relational) databases.

The following is an example of the use of nullable types, denoted with a ? suffix:

```
int a = null; // won't compile; int is a value type and cannot be set to null
int? b = null; // valid in C# 2.0 and above
```

> **NOTE**
>
> The use of the ? suffix comes from the world of regular expressions where it is used to indicate "zero or one" occurrences of the thing preceding it. The ? operator is one of the Kleene operators used to indicate multiplicity. Other Kleene operators include * (zero or more) and + (one or more), but corresponding language features do not exist in the world of C#.
>
> The ? notation is a form of syntactic sugar, meaning it's shorthand syntax for a construct that would be tedious to type every time again. T? simply stands for Nullable<T>, a generic type, where T is required to be a value type. In the preceding example, we could have written int? as Nullable<int>, but you'll agree that's quite some typing to express such a simple concept, hence the justification to provide syntactic sugar.
>
> Oh, and by the way, contrary to popular belief, nullable value types are not just a language-level feature. Some of the runtime's instructions have been enlightened with knowledge about this type to accommodate for better integration.

Iterators

Although generics and nullable types can be seen as features to catch up with everything the design team wanted to do in .NET 1.0 but didn't get to because of the need to get the first release out of the door, C# 2.0 introduced a few language features that reduced the amount of plumbing required to express conceptually simple pieces of code. We can consider this to be the tip of the iceberg on our journey toward a more declarative style of programming.

One such feature is called an iterator and allows the creation of code blocks that produce data on demand. This introduces a form of lazy evaluation in the language. An example of an iterator declaration is shown here:

```
static IEnumerable<int> LazyPrimes()
{
    for (int n = 2; n <= int.MaxValue; n++)
    {
        bool isPrime = true;
        for (int d = 2; d <= Math.Sqrt(n); d++)
        {
            if (n % d == 0)
            {
                isPrime = false;
                break;
            }
        }

        if (isPrime)
            yield return n; // Yield primes to the caller one-by-one
    };
}
```

The use of the `yield` keyword controls the iterator's behavior. If the consumer requests an iterator to produce a value, it runs until a `yield` statement is encountered. At that point, the iterator is suspended until the consumer asks for the next value. In the preceding example, we've declared an iterator that can produce all integer primes (within the range of positive 32-bit signed integer values). How many primes are calculated is completely under the control of the consumer, as shown here:

```
foreach (int prime in LazyPrimes())
{
    Console.WriteLine(prime);

    Console.Write("Calculate next prime? [Y/N] ");
    char key = Console.ReadKey().KeyChar;
    if (char.ToLowerInvariant(key) != 'y')
        break;
    Console.WriteLine();
}
```

If the user stops requesting prime numbers, the iterator will never go through the burden of calculating more primes than were ever requested. Contrast this with an eager evaluation scheme, where a whole bunch of primes would be calculated upfront and stored in some ordered collection for return to the caller.

Manual creation of an iterator—without the `yield` keyword, that is—is an extremely painful task because of its need to support suspension and subtleties that arise with multithreading, multiple consumers, and proper cleanup of used resources. Not only that, the resulting code would look nowhere near the one we get to write with C# 2.0; the meaning of the iterator would be buried under lots of plumbing, making the code hard to understand.

C# alleviates this task by making the compiler generate all the boilerplate code required to build an iterator. This is just one example of a feature that makes the language more declarative, allowing developers to just state their intent, leaving the implementation details to the language and runtime, also reducing the risk of introducing subtle bugs.

Iterators are essential glue for the implementation of a C# 3.0 feature, LINQ to Objects. We get to that in just a minute.

> **NOTE**
>
> I consider another feature called *closures* to fall under the umbrella of "convenience features" too. Because this feature is much more obscure, I'm omitting it from this discussion, except to say that it provides essential glue to allow for seamless use of some functional programming constructs within the language.
>
> Again, the C# compiler takes responsibility over a lot of plumbing that would be imposed on the poor developer otherwise. We cover closures in detail when discussing the use of delegates and anonymous methods.

C# 3.0: Bridging the Gap Between Objects and Data

C# 3.0 In some regard, C# 3.0 was the first release where the language designers got a real chance to think deeply about the everyday problems developers face when writing real-world code. Project Clarity identified one such problem, dealing with the impedance mismatch between object-oriented programming and accessing data stores of various kinds.

Language Integrated Query

One problem developers face when dealing with data access is the wide range of data storage technologies: in-memory object graphs, relational databases, Extensible Markup Language (XML) data, and so on. Each of those stores has its own API that's different enough from the others to throw developers a learning curve each time a different type of data store is encountered. A way to unify those APIs was much desired, and that's exactly what Clarity stood for.

When this vision became real, the project was renamed Language Integrated Query, or LINQ. It enables developers to use built-in language syntax to target any data store that has a LINQ provider for it, as illustrated here:

```
var res = from product in db.Products
          where product.Price > 100
          orderby product.Name
          select new { product.Name, product.Price };
```

> **NOTE**
>
> Similar language support was added to Visual Basic 2008. Also, LINQ has more query operators than the languages surface; regular method calls can be used to take advantage of these additional query operators.

The conceptual diagram depicting the relationship between languages and underlying query providers is shown in Figure 2.2.

In addition to providing a unified query language, this approach has many additional benefits. For example, it provides strong typing over the target domain, allowing for compile-time checking of the soundness of queries. In addition, the LINQ provider libraries can make sure queries are built correctly to eliminate whole classes of errors, including security breaches such as SQL injection attacks.

This type of programming reflects the desire to move toward a more declarative style of programming, where developers yield control to the language, runtime, and libraries. By doing so, the platform as a whole can "reason" about the developer's intent and do the right thing, potentially optimizing the execution on behalf of the developer.

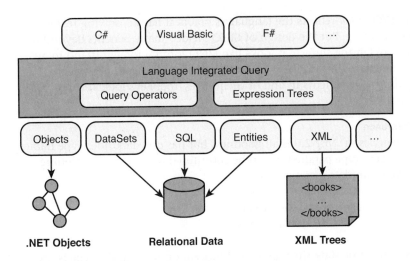

FIGURE 2.2   Language Integrated Query.

NOTE

Almost all of today's computers have multiple processor cores, allowing for true parallelism. Imperative programming techniques do not scale well to write concurrent programs for various reasons. Besides the need for low-level concurrency programming using locks and other synchronization primitives (which are very hard to deal with), we typically overspecify the solution to a problem. Instead of just expressing what we want done, we also specify—in excruciating detail—how we want it done, using a bunch of imperative constructs such as if statements, loops, and so on. By doing so, we paint the runtime out of the picture, leaving it no other choice but to execute our imperative program exactly as we've written it.

Manual parallelization of query-like constructs written in an imperative style (nested for loops with a bunch of if statements and extensive use of intermediate data structures) would be a grueling and very error-prone experience for developers. However, in the world of declarative programming, the runtime is left with enough knowledge about our intent for it to optimize the execution. Today, with LINQ, this is no longer a dream: A parallelizable version of LINQ to Objects has been created, dubbed PLINQ, which ships in .NET Framework 4. The more cores the user has in her machine, the faster the query executes. Mission accomplished.

Today, a wide variety of LINQ providers are available. Microsoft provides LINQ to Objects (to deal with in-memory data), LINQ to XML, LINQ to DataSets, LINQ to SQL, and LINQ to Entities (to deal with relational databases), and we can expect many more in the years to come. In addition, lots of third parties have developed LINQ providers that target nearly anything queryable out there: Amazon, Flickr, SharePoint, Active Directory, to name just a few.

The introduction of LINQ in C# reflects the language's practical nature, solving real-world problems developers are facing. But the design of LINQ yielded many benefits beyond the domain of querying, too. On the surface, it looks like LINQ forms a foreign island in an otherwise imperative language, but in reality it's built out of an amalgam of smaller language features that provide benefits in and of themselves, too. Let's look at those features briefly.

Local Variable Type Inference

The introduction of generics in .NET 2.0 is all goodness but has one dark side: Type names can grow arbitrarily because type parameters can be substituted for any type, including other generic types. An example concretizes this:

```
Dictionary<string, List<PhoneNumber>> whitePages =
    new Dictionary<string, List<PhoneNumber>>();
```

Wait a second: Doesn't this line state the type twice? Indeed, on the left, the type is used to declare a variable, and on the right, it's used to instantiate an instance of it. The code snippet doesn't even fit on a single line because of this duplication. With local variable type inference, you can omit the type on the left side, substituting it with the var keyword and letting the compiler figure out the type for you based on the right side:

```
var whitePages = new Dictionary<string, List<PhoneNumber>>();
```

Although we can drop the type in the declaration of the local variable, this code is still strongly typed. The compiler knows exactly what the type is, and the emitted code is exactly as if you had written out the type yourself.

By itself, local variable type inference is useful for reducing the syntactic noise that comes with the use of generic types, where it's just a nicety to have. However, in some cases, local variable type inference is required, as you'll see next.

Anonymous Types

The desire to integrate query capabilities in the language introduces the need to have an easy way to construct types on-the-fly. Projections (the select clause in a LINQ query) are the most obvious places where this need becomes apparent.

```
var res = from product in db.Products
          where product.Price > 100
          orderby product.Name
          select new { product.Name, product.Price };
```

Having to declare an explicit type for each projection would put quite some burden on developers using LINQ. In the example, the compiler synthesizes an anonymous type with properties Name and Price as specified in the projection.

The reason we call those types "anonymous" is because the compiler generates an unspeakable name for them. Because we can't refer to them, we need help from the compiler to infer their names when assigning them to local variables. In the preceding example, the result of the query was assigned to an implicitly typed local variable, letting the compiler figure out its type.

Initializer Expressions

To make the initialization of collections and objects easier, C# 3.0 introduces initialization expressions for both. Let's take a look at them.

Object initializers make the instantiation of a type followed by setting a bunch of its public properties (or public fields) easier to do, as part of one single expression. This proves particularly useful when the type you want to instantiate lacks an appropriate constructor:

```
class Product
{
    public Product(string name)
    {
        Name = name;
    }

    public string Name { get; set; }
    public decimal Price { get; set; }
}
```

In C# 2.0, you would have to write the following to create an instance of this type, with both Name and Price set:

```
Product p = new Product("Chai");
p.Price = 123.45m;
```

With object initializer syntax, this can be abbreviated as follows:

```
Product p = new Product("Chai") { Price = 123.45m };
```

> **NOTE**
>
> To be precise, the code generated for an object initializer expression is slightly different from the C# 2.0 snippet shown above it. We'll ignore this detail now and defer a more in-depth discussion until Chapter 6, "A Primer on Types and Objects."

Object initializers are typically used in the projection clause of LINQ queries, when an existing type is available (contrast this to the case where no type is available but an anonymous type can be used) but lacks an appropriate constructor:

```
var res = from product in db.Products
          where product.Price > 100
          orderby product.Name
          select new Product(product.Name) { product.Price };
```

Collection initializers bring simple initialization syntax to generic collection types. Since the very beginning of C#, it has been possible to initialize arrays simply by specifying the elements in between curly braces like this:

```
int[] primes = new int[] { 2, 3, 5, 7 };
```

However, when using generic collections like List<T> in C# 2.0, this nice syntax was no longer possible. Instead, you had to write the following:

```
List<int> primes = new List<int>();
primes.Add(2);
primes.Add(3);
primes.Add(5);
primes.Add(7);
```

With C# 3.0, you get to write this (notice the nonmandatory use of local variable type inference):

```
var primes = new List<int> { 2, 3, 5, 7 };
```

> **NOTE**
>
> Observe how collection initializers and object initializers can be combined nicely when initializing collections of rich types. Another "better together" story.

Extension Methods

Extension methods enable you to extend existing types without using inheritance and thus allow methods to be added to any kind of type. For example, suppose you want to add a Reverse method to the System.String type that comes in the BCL. The best you could do before C# 3.0 was to create a static helper method, making it rather cumbersome to use:

```
static class Helpers
{
    public static string Reverse(string s)
    {
        char[] characters = s.ToCharArray();
        Array.Reverse(characters);
        return new string(characters);
    }
}
```

```
static class Program
{
    static void Main()
    {
        string name = "Bart";
        string reverse = Helpers.Reverse(name);
        Console.WriteLine(reverse);
    }
}
```

With extension methods, we can allow the `static` method to be used as if it were an instance method:

```
string reverse = name.Reverse();
```

To enable this, the first parameter of the `Reverse` method is marked with the `this` keyword, turning it in an extension method:

```
public static string Reverse(this string s)
```

LINQ uses extension methods to add query operators to interfaces like `IEnumerable<T>` and `IQueryable<T>`.

NOTE

Extension methods allow the design and use of "fluent" APIs. A good example of a fluent API is the `System.String` type: Most of its methods return a `System.String` instance, allowing the next method to be called immediately, like so:

```
string bart = "  Bart  ";
string art  = bart.ToUpper().Trim().Substring(1); // ART
```

Without extension methods, any attempt to "chain in" another operation in the middle broke the fluency of the code:

```
string bart = "  Bart  ";
string tra  = Helpers.Reverse(bart.ToUpper().Trim()).Substring(1); // TRA
```

It takes a few reads to figure out the order of operations in the preceding code fragment. Thanks to extension methods, the preceding code can be made fluent again:

```
string bart = "  Bart  ";
string art  = bart.ToUpper().Trim().Reverse().Substring(1);
```

One great example of such a fluent API is LINQ itself, as you'll see later on.

Lambda Expressions

Although C# has been an imperative object-oriented programming since the very beginning, language paradigms have been added over the years. One such paradigm is functional programming, the ability to write programs based on the use and definition of
mathematical function.

NOTE

In fact, one of the key enablers for functional programming in C# was added in the second release of the language: closures. We won't go into details right now, except to say
that turning programming paradigms into first-class citizens in an existing language
often takes more than one feature.

Lambda expressions are simply that: definitions of functions, but in a very concise form
with little syntactical ceremony. Because the underlying platform supports delegates as a
way to pass pieces of code around, lambda expressions can leverage this infrastructure and
be converted into delegates. The following example illustrates the creation of a function
that adds two numbers together, with and without the use of lambda expressions:

```
// C# 2.0 style
Func<int, int, int> add20 = delegate (int a, int b) { return a + b; };
// C# 3.0 style
Func<int, int, int> add30 = (a, b) => a + b;
```

The Func<T1, T2, R> type used in this example (with all parameters substituted for int) is
a generic delegate for a function that takes in something of type T1 and T2 and returns
something of type R. Its definition looks like this:

```
delegate R Func<T1, T2, R>(T1 arg1, T2 arg2);
```

WHERE THE NAME LAMBDA COMES FROM

Where the heck does a fancy name like *lambda* come from? The answer lies in the
lambda calculus, a mathematical framework to reason about functions, developed in
1928 by Alonzo Church. Lambda is actually a Greek letter, λ, and happened to
be chosen to name the theory. (Other calculi named after Greek letters exist, such as
the Pi calculus, which is used in the domain of parallel computing.)

It took about 30 years for this mathematical foundation to be applied in the domain of
computer science. LISP (due to McCarthy) was created in 1958 and can be considered
the first functional programming language, although it wasn't directly based on the
λ-calculus. (Even though there was a lambda keyword, it didn't follow the rules
of the calculus strictly.) A few years later, in the early 1960s, Landin used the
λ-calculus in the design of Algol-60.

Today, lots of functional programming languages are built on top of the groundwork provided by the λ-calculus and its derivatives that mix in type theory. The interested, math-savvy reader is strongly encouraged to have a peek at those theoretical foundations: They can only make you a better programmer. Luckily, very little of this theory is required for C# developers to take advantage of lambda expressions, which you'll see as we cover them in more detail.

This evolution illustrates the continuous knowledge transfer between the domain of pure mathematics and computer science. It's a very healthy attitude for language designers to make sure the things they're doing have a strong mathematical foundation. If the mathematicians haven't figured it out yet, chances are slim that solid language features are built from loose ideas. Pretentious as it may sound, "mathematicians are always right" ought to be an axiom for programming language designers.

But why should we care about functional programming? I can come up with many good reasons, but the most prominent one nowadays is the challenge we're facing in the world of multicore processors. It turns out functional programming is one promising avenue toward effective use of multicore processors, thanks to their side-effect-free nature. The pure functional programming language Haskell uses so-called monads (yet another mathematical concept, this time from the world of category theory) to track side effects in types. It turns out C#'s LINQ feature is deeply related to monads, as we discuss later when we talk about LINQ in more depth in Chapter 19, "Language Integrated Query Essentials."

One use of lambda expressions is in LINQ queries where they're invisibly present. For example, the use of the where clause specifies a filtering condition for the records being queried. Such filters, also known as predicates, can be expressed as little functions that take in a record and produce a Boolean value indicating whether the record should be included in the result set.

To illustrate this briefly, the following two queries are equivalent, where the first one is written using built-in syntactical sugar and the latter one has "compiled away" all built-in language constructs:

```
var res1 = from product in db.Products
           where product.Price > 100
           select product;
var res2 = db.Products
           .Where(product => product.Price > 100);
```

Notice the appearance of a lambda expression in this metamorphosis. We cover this translation in much more detail when talking about LINQ.

Expression Trees

One of the more exotic language features in C# 3.0 are expression trees, which are closely related to lambda expressions. In the previous section, you saw how lambda expressions are used—potentially invisibly—in LINQ queries to represent little bits and pieces of a query, such as a filter's predicate function or a projection's mapping function. For local query execution, it makes perfect sense to compile those lambda expressions to pieces of IL code that can run on the local machine. But when the query is supposed to run remotely, say on a relational database engine, it needs to be translated into a target query language, say SQL.

LINQ providers that target external data stores therefore need a way to cross-compile the user's intended query expression—that was written using LINQ—into whatever query language they're targeting, such as SQL, XPath, and so on. Various approaches can be taken to solve this:

▶ Do not support extensibility for LINQ; instead, bake knowledge of various query languages into the C# compiler and let it do the translation. Clearly this is unacceptable from a maintenance point of view and clashes with the main goal of LINQ (that is, to provide unification of all sorts of query languages, including the ones we don't know of yet).

▶ Have LINQ providers decompile the intermediate language (IL) code that was emitted by the C# compiler and go from there to the target query language. Not only would this be far too complicated to be widely accepted by query provider writers, but it also would prevent the compiler from changing its IL emission (for example, to add more optimization, given that query providers would expect specific patterns).

▶ Instead of turning lambda expressions directly into IL code, translate them into some kind of intermediate representation with an object model that can be consumed by query providers. This sounds much more promising, and this is where expression trees come in.

So what are those expression trees? In essence, they are a way to represent code as data that can be inspected at runtime. Consider the following lambda expression:

```
(int a, int b) => a + b;
```

Two possible translations exist. The first one is to turn it into IL code that's readily available for local execution, using delegates:

```
Func<int, int, int> add = (a, b) => a + b;
int three = add(1, 2);
```

The alternative is to assign the lambda expression to an expression tree, in which case the compiler emits the code as data:

```
Expression<Func<int, int, int>> add = (a, b) => a + b;
// the code represented by add can be inspected at runtime
```

A graphical representation of the expression tree used in our previous example is shown in Figure 2.3.

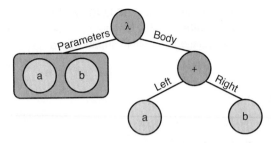

FIGURE 2.3   Graphical representation of an expression tree.

NOTE

To be absolutely precise, the compiler turns an expression tree into code that builds up a data structure representing the original code at runtime. This might sound mind-boggling, but it's not that hard. Our sample code for the add function is turned into the following:

```
var a = Expression.Parameter(typeof(int), "a");
var b = Expression.Parameter(typeof(int), "b");
var add = Expression.Lambda<Func<int, int, int>>(
            Expression.Add(a, b),
            a, b);
```

When executed, this code calls into several factory methods that build up a data structure that represents (a, b) => a + b as data. For example, on the resulting add variable, one could ask for its Body property, which would return a binary expression object that represents the addition operation with operands a and b. Such knowledge can be used by libraries like LINQ to SQL to turn the code the user wrote into efficient SQL queries.

Luckily, as a user of LINQ, you don't need to know anything about all of this, but it certainly doesn't hurt to know how things work behind the scenes.

ABOUT QUOTATIONS, META-PROGRAMMING, AND HOMO-ICONICITY

The concept of "code as data" is baked into the architecture of today's computers, which are based on the von Neumann machine. In such a machine, the memory storage for instructions and data is the same, hence the ability to treat code as data. The reverse is also true, treating data as if it were code, which is the most prominent source of security bugs (for example, buffer overruns and execution of malicious script that was downloaded with an HTML page).

However, the notion of "code as data" is far too useful to let it go. Unsurprisingly, language features exploiting this rich capability have been around since the very beginning. LISP, a language for LISt Processing created in 1958, has a mechanism called quotations to suppress direct evaluation of expressions. Two LISP expressions are shown here, both adding two numbers but the latter being quoted:

```
(+ a b)
'(+ a b)
```

It's not hard to figure out where the name "quotations" comes from, is it? LINQ expression trees actually have an expression node type named after this (constructed through the Expression.Quote factory method), and the F# language has built-in support for a similar mechanism of quoting pieces of code:

```
let add (a:int) (b:int) = a + b

let quotedAdd (a:int) (b:int) = <@ a + b @>
```

All of those quotations are similar in nature to the C# 3.0 expression:

```
Expression<Func<int, int, int>> add = (a, b) => a + b;
```

The ability to represent code as data is the cornerstone to enabling meta-programming facilities in the platform and the language. Meta-programming is the capability of code to inspect and manipulate code at runtime, which is a very rich concept. It might sound rather abstract at first, but it's real and in use today. Tools such as Reflector are one example of inspection of code. Frameworks such as the LINQ provider model illustrate the richness of runtime code inspection, too. Refactoring tools are a form of code manipulators.

Expression trees in C# 3.0 (and VB 9.0) form the tip of the iceberg of the envisioned meta-programming capabilities on the .NET platform. With the release of .NET 4.0 and the dynamic language runtime, those expression trees have grown out to full-fledged statement and declaration trees that can represent whole programs.

Finally, some trivia for true geeks. The capability to represent code written in a language by other code in that language makes that language deserve the status of being homo-iconic: homo = same, iconic = representation. Since version 3.0, C# has been homo-iconic for the expression subset of the language, thanks to the introduction of expression trees.

As you can see, expression trees are a very powerful concept to inspect code at runtime and have a reach that goes much beyond their use in LINQ. One can think of them as "reflection on steroids," and their importance will only increase in the releases to come.

Auto-Implemented Properties

One feature outside the direct realm of LINQ made it into the C# 3.0 release: automatically implemented properties. With this feature, adding trivial properties to a type definition becomes much prettier than it used to be.

What's a "trivial property," anyway? Properties are sometimes called smart fields, so one of the most common patterns is to wrap field accesses in a property, and that's it:

```
private int _age;

public int Age
{
    get { return _age; }
    set { _age = value; }
}
```

You'll agree that exposing the field directly wouldn't be a good idea because of the lack of encapsulation, a crucial technique in object-oriented programming. But why should we even have to bother defining an internal backing field if all we do with it is expose it through a property directly?

That's where auto-implemented properties come in. In C# 3.0, you simply get to write the following instead:

```csharp
public int Age
{
    get; set;
}
```

The compiler synthesizes a private hidden backing field for you, and life is good. Both a getter and a setter are required, but they support having different visibilities (for example, to create more or less immutable data structures):

```csharp
class Person
{
    public Person(string name)
    {
        Name = name;
    }

    public string Name
    {
        get; private set;
    }
}
```

If you ever want to turn the property into a nontrivial one, you can still go back to the classic syntax and manually implement a getter/setter accessor without breaking the property's consumers.

> **NOTE**
>
> Some people refer to this feature as "automatic properties." I don't like that because the word *automatic* seems to make people attribute magical runtime powers to those properties ("Hey, it's automatic...ought to be better"), even though they're nothing but a compile-time aid to reduce the amount of code a developer has to type. That alone makes them a bit magic, but solely at compile time. This said, I can understand why people want to abbreviate language feature names in spoken language; after all, terms such as *auto-implemented properties* can be quite heavy on the tongue.

C# 4.0: Reaching Out to Dynamic Languages

C#
4.0   The introduction of LINQ was a theme that drove the language evolution for both C# and Visual Basic in the .NET Framework 3.5 timeframe. This kind of scenario-driven language design formed a milestone in the history of the language and has been received very well by developers. Following this philosophy, C# 4.0 also focuses on making a key scenario that causes grief for developers much easier to deal with. Where C# 3.0 made data access easier, the fourth release of the language aims at making code access much simpler than it used to be.

A Perspective on Dynamic Languages

The capability to bridge the gap between different languages has always been a core design theme of the .NET platform, leading to its unified type system and code-execution infrastructure. However, before the advent of the DLR, there was a dark spot in the language integration gamma: dynamic languages. Despite the goal to simplify cross-language integration, little attention was paid to the domain of dynamic languages. This isn't too surprising, considering their popularity was relatively low at the time the CLI was designed, therefore making statically typed languages a much more attractive target for the platform.

Around 2005, half a decade later, the resurgence of dynamic languages was accepted as fact. Technologies like JavaScript gained attention because of AJAX web programming, interactive development experiences brought by languages like Python grew in popularity, and the meta-programming facilities of platforms like Ruby on Rails made it an attractive target for web programming. Dynamic was back, potentially stronger than ever.

THE STORY OF A GUY CALLED JIM... OR HOW THE DYNAMIC LANGUAGE RUNTIME WAS BORN

Not everyone believed that CLR would be a good fit as the underlying runtime to enable execution of dynamic languages. One such guy was Jim Huginin, who created Jython, an implementation of the Python language on the Java Virtual Machine (JVM).

But why was this perception of the CLI being an unfriendly environment for dynamic languages hanging around? Remember Project 7, the initiative run at the time of the CLI's inception to port a set of popular languages to the CLI as a sanity check for the multilanguage design of the platform. Back then, an attempt, led by ActiveState, was made to implement Python on .NET, concluding the performance of the CLI to be inadequate for dynamic language execution.

Jim wanted to figure out what made the CLR a hostile environment for dynamic languages and decided to have a go with a .NET-based Python implementation. His plan was to share his findings in a paper titled, "Why .NET Is a Terrible Platform for Dynamic Languages." In a matter of a couple of weeks, Jim had a prototype ready and came to realize it actually ran much faster than Jython. Jim became a convert to the CLR and joined Microsoft in August 2004 to become the architect of the Dynamic Language Runtime, with IronPython as the first language on top of it.

At a later stage, IronRuby was added to the family of dynamic languages targeting the DLR, and implementations of the DLR and both languages were shared with the .NET community through Microsoft's shared-source site CodePlex. Since the release of .NET 4.0, the DLR has become an integral part of the framework.

What Makes a Language Dynamic?

Often abbreviated as *dynamic languages*, we really mean to say dynamically typed languages. So the core difference between those languages and their static counterparts is in the typing. Let's explore this a little bit more to set the scene.

In a statically typed language, the compiler knows the types of all the variables, fields, and method parameters that occur in a program. Therefore, it can carry out compile-time checking to make sure operations invoked on these objects are valid based on the type information available. For example, in the following piece of code, the compiler knows that the type of variable s is System.String (because we've declared it as such), and from that it can prove that ToUpper is a valid method call because System.String has it:

```
string s = "Some text";
string u = s.ToUpper();
```

NOTE

Do not confuse local variable type inference—the var keyword introduced in C# 3.0—with dynamic typing. This feature still provides full strong and static typing; it just enables us to let the compiler figure out the type on our behalf. Nevertheless, if we attempt to carry out a nonexistent operation on an implicitly typed local variable, the compiler will still detect the problem. In other words, type checking still happens at compile time.

For example, the two declarations in the following code mean exactly the same (both variables have type System.String, which was inferred for the latter one):

```
string s1 = "Some text";
var s2 = "More text";
```

However, typing any of those variables as dynamic has a fundamentally different meaning, causing runtime lookups to happen for every operation invoked on it.

On the other hand, in a dynamically typed language, we don't need to specify any types upfront. Typically, there's no need for the developer to compile the code (often referred to as "script" in the context of dynamic languages); instead, it gets executed immediately through interpretation or by compiling the code at runtime. This allows for a very interactive experience where code can be typed and executed immediately in an interactive prompt, just like command shells. The following is an example of dynamically typed code:

```
s = "Some text"
u = s.ToUpper()
```

Only at runtime can the system determine whether ToUpper is a valid operation to be carried out on variable s because type information becomes available only at that point. If s would happen to be an integer value instead, the call to ToUpper would fail no earlier than at runtime.

WORD OF THE DAY: REPL

Interactive prompts for programming languages are called REPLs, which stands for read-eval-print-loop: Code is read from the console, evaluated by some runtime service, and the result is printed out. This interactive process keeps going until the developer quits, making it a loop.

However, lots of people believe REPLs are a luxury exclusively available to the dynamic language programmer. Nothing is further from the truth, though. Nowadays, statically typed languages like F#—and potentially C# in a future release—offer interactive prompts while preserving full static typing. It's just that those environments typically do a great deal of type inference to reduce the amount of types the user has to specify explicitly.

The "Static Versus Dynamic" War

Dynamic languages have caused quite some controversy over the years, especially in circles of believers in statically typed languages. The advantages of static languages are numerous:

▶ Robustness is perhaps the most cited benefit of static typing. The capability to catch problems early by means of static type checking enables you to uncover issues early. Or in other words, if it compiles successfully, it runs.

▶ Performance is another big advantage attributed to static typing. Because no runtime support is required to resolve members on types, the compiler can emit efficient code that doesn't beat about the bush.

▶ Rich tooling support can be realized by leveraging the type information that's statically available at development time. Popular power toys like refactoring engines and IntelliSense are just a couple of examples of this.

▶ Scalability should be called out, too. The capability to make types a means for defining strong contracts between different components has the potential of reducing the maintenance cost of complex systems as the system grows.

Nevertheless, it's wrong for statically typed languages believers to curse all the dynamic world as if it were inferior. In times when the Internet is glued together by script execution, loosely typed XML files are flying around, and large frameworks—such as Ruby on Rails—have been written based on dynamic languages, we can't close our eyes and ignore dynamic typing.

The truth is there are increasing numbers of things that are weakly typed: XML without an XSD schema, REST services, Python and Ruby libraries, even old COM APIs, and so on. Before the advent of the DLR and .NET 4.0, the dynamic landscape was rather worrisome for developers. Static language compilers refuse to emit code that's loosely typed, and therefore people have been looking for different ways to overcome this limitation through APIs. Unfortunately, there's no general approach to writing dynamic code. Each dynamic "domain" has its own APIs without any unification or consolidation between the domains whatsoever.

For example, suppose you get a .NET object from somewhere whose static type you don't know, but you happen to know the object has an Add method on it. To call it, you can't simply write the following:

```
object calculator = GetCalculatorFromSomewhere();
int three = calculator.Add(1, 2);
```

Instead, you have to go through the hoops of .NET reflection to call the method, like this:

```
object calculator = GetCalculatorFromSomewhere();
int three = (int)calculator.GetType().InvokeMember("Add",
    BindingFlags.InvokeMethod, null, new object[] { 1, 2 });
```

It almost takes a Ph.D. to come up with this kind of code, and you get lots of new worries in return: unreadable and hard-to-maintain code, potential optimization headaches, and so on.

But matters only get worse as you enter different domains. Instead of being able to reuse your knowledge about dynamic invocation techniques, you must learn new APIs. For example, the following code tries to reach out to a JavaScript calculator object through the Silverlight APIs:

```
ScriptObject calculator = GetCalculatorFromSomewhere();
int three = (int)calculator.Invoke("Add", 1, 2);
```

Similar in spirit but different in shape. This is just the tip of the iceberg; lots of other domains face similar problems, even though developers hardly think about it anymore. What about the XML you got from somewhere, without an XSD schema going with it? In times of REST-based web services, such an approach is becoming more and more popular, but consuming such an XML source gets quite painful:

```
XElement root = GetCustomerFromSomewhere();
int zip = int.Parse(root.Element("Address").Attribute("ZIP").Value);
```

This mess puts language designers at an interesting juncture: Either follow the direction of static language purity or take a turn toward a "better together" vision. Either you can make it incredibly hard for developers in static languages to reach out to dynamically typed pieces of code or data (as shown earlier), or you can open up for a smooth road to call into the dynamic world.

C# 4.0 dynamic does precisely that: makes it easy for developers to ease into various domains of dynamically typed code and data. Just like LINQ unified data access, you could see the dynamic feature unifies dynamic access. For example, the Calculator example targeting either .NET objects or JavaScript objects could be written as follows:

```
dynamic calculator = GetCalculatorFromSomewhere();
int three = calculator.Add(1, 2);
```

PRAGMATISM VERSUS PURITY

The fact that C# 4.0 embraces dynamic typing to solve real-world problems developers face emphasizes one of the core properties of the language: its pragmatic nature. This is what makes C# such a popular language in the .NET community: its sense for real problems by providing elegant solutions. LINQ is another example of this. Some may say this affects the purity of the language, but the reality is there aren't that many pure successful languages out there. At the end of the day, software developers scream for practical languages as opposed to the scientifically pure but impractical ones.

The dynamic Keyword

The only language surface for the dynamic feature is a correspondingly named keyword, as shown in the previous example. Variables, members, or parameters that are typed as dynamic will have late-bound behavior. This means whenever an operation, such as a method call or property access, is invoked on the object, its resolution gets deferred until runtime.

Let's contrast early-bound code to late-bound code. The first example is early-bound code:

```
Calculator calculator = GetCalculatorFromSomewhere();
int three = calculator.Add(1, 2);
```

Here the compiler knows precisely what the type of the calculator variable is: It's statically typed to be Calculator, so operations on it can be checked during compilation. When the compiler encounters the Add method call on the next line, it tries to find an overload that's compatible with taking in two integer values and returning an integer value. If it finds a suitable candidate, it emits IL code to call that method immediately at runtime. If no good overload is found, a compile-time error results.

In the dynamically typed code, the call to Add is resolved at runtime:

```
dynamic calculator = GetCalculatorFromSomewhere();
int three = calculator.Add(1, 2);
```

Now the compiler doesn't even bother to find an Add method at compile time because it simply doesn't know what the type of the calculator variable will be. Instead of emitting IL code to call directly into a known early-bound method, it emits code to invoke the overload resolution logic at runtime. If a good match is found, the DLR will step in to provide efficient call site code generation so that subsequent calls do not suffer from overload resolution again. If overload resolution fails, a runtime exception results.

DYNAMIC != VAR

Do not confuse the `dynamic` keyword with the `var` keyword from C# 3.0. The `var` keyword is as statically typed as it possibly can; it just enables you to omit the type and let the compiler infer it for you:

```
var languages = new List<ProgrammingLanguage>();
```

The preceding line means exactly the same as the much more verbose variant:

```
List<ProgrammingLanguage> languages = new List<ProgrammingLanguage>();
```

Trying to call a nonexistent method on the languages variable, say the misspelled Addd method, will result in a compile-time error. Or even better, the Visual Studio editor will catch the error immediately because all static type information is readily available.

In contrast, with the `dynamic` keyword, you're essentially telling the compiler not to bother attempting to infer the type, having it do overload resolution at runtime instead.

A more detailed explanation about how the C# compiler emits code that causes the DLR to kick in—allowing it to reach out to any kind of dynamically typed code—will follow in Chapter 22, "Dynamic Programming."

STATIC WHEN POSSIBLE, DYNAMIC WHEN NECESSARY

The introduction of dynamic doesn't mean you should start rewriting all your statically typed code to use dynamically typed code instead. Static typing has many advantages, and C# stays faithful to that belief. So whenever possible, use static typing—it's pure goodness.

But other than before the introduction of C# 4.0, when you absolutely need to go for dynamic typing, it's no longer a mission impossible to get it to work while keeping the code readable and maintainable. What the new dynamic feature really enables is to "gradually ease into" dynamic domains without sacrificing developer productivity.

By the way, if you don't like dynamic at all and you want to keep people from using the feature, I have good news. It's relatively straightforward to disable dynamic support simply by emitting the "C# binder" during compilation (which can be achieved through the Visual Studio 2010 IDE, for instance). I'll get back to that later when we cover dynamic end to end.

What the DLR Has to Offer

Execution of dynamically typed code relies on quite a few runtime services, such as overload resolution, code generation, and caching of acquired runtime data, to improve efficiency of calls. Let's explore what's involved in making a dynamic call.

First, the language compiler generates code to package up all the information it has about the intended call. This includes the type and name of the operation being invoked—for example, a property called `Price`, a method called `Add`, and so on—as well as information about the arguments passed in to it. To turn this information into usable information at runtime, the compiler emits code that targets helper libraries, collectively called the C# binder. Other languages targeting dynamic code have similar binders.

Next, during execution, the runtime type of the target and arguments of the call become available. Now it's up to the target domain—for example, Python, Ruby, JavaScript, regular .NET objects, COM APIs, you name it—to decide whether that call makes sense. This is the part that is involved with overload resolution and such, allowing the target domain to enforce its semantics. Each such domain has a runtime binder to carry out those tasks.

If a suitable operation target is found, the runtime binder emits expression trees that contain the code required to carry out the call. From this point on, all that keeps us from executing the code is a runtime translation of the expression trees into code that can run on the underlying execution engine, the CLR.

This last part, where expression trees get turned into real code, is the crux of the DLR. Among code generation, it also offers APIs for the expression trees it accepts, as well as runtime services to cache generated pieces of codes and provide fast paths to a call target, bypassing all runtime binder interactions after initial calls have been made. So where the CLR provided common infrastructure for statically typed languages, the DLR acts as a library on top of it, ameliorating it with support for dynamically typed languages.

NOTE

The expression *trees* used by the DLR are the natural evolution of LINQ's expression trees that were introduced in the .NET 3.5 timeframe. In the world of querying, the only required "code as data" formats required are expressions: roughly, things that evaluate to have a value (for example, predicates or projections):

```
person.Age > 25
```

Expressions are insufficient to represent complete meaningful programs. To do that, we need statements that include control flow constructs such as loops and conditions:

```
if (person.Age > 25)
    Console.WriteLine("Hello, " + person.Name);
```

The DLR needs to be able to deal with the latter format for sure because it provides a unified execution back end for dynamic languages like Ruby and Python that hand over the user's code in a tree format. Trees with the capability to express statements are called (how original) *statement trees*.

There's yet another level above statement trees: declaration trees. With these, it also becomes possible to represent entire type and member definitions in a tree format that can be consumed by the runtime and tools to generate IL code.

Confusingly, the collective set of trees is often referred to as expression trees, even though they have more expressive power than the original LINQ expression trees. What makes expression trees—*sensu lato*—an interesting topic is their role as the cornerstone in enabling "compiler as a service." To get to know what that is, read on.

The end-to-end picture of the DLR's role in enabling this full mesh between lots of front-end languages and even more dynamic target domains is shown in Figure 2.4. Some of the binders mentioned here are available out-of-the-box, while others ship with separate downloads, such as the IronRuby distribution.

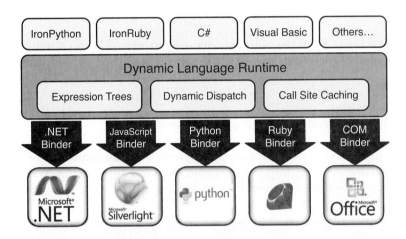

FIGURE 2.4   Dynamic language runtime architecture.

Starting with .NET 4.0, the DLR is available out of the box as part of the .NET Framework, for languages to be implemented on top of it and for others to bridge with the dynamic world.

Improving COM Interop
Despite the .NET platform's classification as a successor to COM, there are still a huge number of COM-based APIs around that developers need to integrate with. Since the earliest version of the .NET Framework, COM interop facilities have been built in to the runtime and the libraries to make this possible, mainly with regard to mapping of types back and forth and to facilitate COM calls.

At the same time, the designers of C# thought it was inappropriate for the language to support a COM style of programming where it's not uncommon to have methods that take a bunch of parameters, most of which are optional and/or passed by reference. Part of the whole .NET design mission was to make APIs more consistent and approachable, and COM wasn't always a particularly good stylistic example.

This led to an unfortunate dichotomy where Visual Basic (and Managed C++) were much more attractive languages to deal with COM interop, leaving C# developers out in the cold. Although various COM APIs have been exposed through cleaner managed APIs, the capability to talk to the bare COM metal is still required often enough to warrant the design and implementation of improved COM interop in the C# language.

One classic example of COM-based APIs is the Office automation libraries, which can be accessed in managed code through primary interop assemblies (PIAs) that are available from Microsoft. Here is an example of interop code required to create an Excel chart using C# 3.0:

```
Excel.Worksheet wks = GetWorksheet();
// ...
wks.Shapes.Add(XlChartType.Bar, Type.Missing, Type.Missing, 400, 300);
```

Notice the use of Type.Missing to fill in the holes for optional parameters? With C# 4.0, it now becomes possible to specify parameters by name, like this:

```
Excel.Worksheet wks = GetWorksheet();
// ...
wks.Shapes.Add(XlChartType.Bar, Width: 400, Height: 300);
```

The capability of APIs to declare optional parameters by supplying a default value and for consumers to skip such parameters vastly improves common COM interop scenarios. We refer to this tandem of features as *named* and *optional* parameters.

NAMED PARAMETER SYNTAX

You might wonder why the colon (:) symbol is used to specify values for parameter by name, as opposed to the more natural-looking assignment (=) symbol. The reason, once more, is backward compatibility. Although it's strongly discouraged to write code like this, it's perfectly valid to do so in C#:

```
wks.Shapes.Add(XlChartType.Bar, Width = 400, Height = 300);
```

This piece of code assigns the value 400 to something with the name Width, using the resulting value from that assignment as the second parameter to the Add method call. This is similar for the third parameter, which gets its value from a side-effecting assignment operation, too. If this syntax were to be used for named parameters, existing code that relies on this would start breaking. Although people who write this sort of code should be punished, backward compatibility means a lot to the C# team, and hence the alternative syntax with the colon was chosen.

Another feature introduced in C# 4.0 is the capability to omit the ref modifier on parameters for COM interop method calls:

```
Word.Document doc = CreateNewDocument();
// ...
string fileName = "demo.docx";
object missing = Type.Missing;
doc.SaveAs(ref fileName,
    ref missing, ref missing, ref missing,
    ref missing, ref missing, ref missing,
    ref missing, ref missing, ref missing,
```

```
    ref missing, ref missing, ref missing,
    ref missing, ref missing, ref missing);
```

No less than 15 optional parameters, all of which had to be supplied by reference! With C# 4.0, you get to write the code as it was always intended to look by the COM API:

```
Word.Document doc = CreateNewDocument();
// ...
doc.SaveAs("demo.docx");
```

This feature is known as the *optional ref modifier*.

NOTE

Optional ref modifiers are not a general language feature; this relaxation for parameter passing by reference applies only to COM interop scenarios, where this style is the default.

The need to specify the ref modifier explicitly in all other cases is pure goodness. It makes it very explicit for readers to see where arguments are passed by reference and where not:

```
    int answer = 42;

    Do(ref answer);

    // The answer might not longer be 42 as it was passed by reference.
```

Being explicit about this prevents surprises, especially because passing arguments by reference is not the default in .NET. In COM, that's different, causing lots of syntactical noise when trying to use such APIs in managed code. Therefore, it makes sense to relax the rules for those scenarios.

Although we're in the domain of method calls, another feature worth mentioning is the automatic mapping for parameter and return types from object to dynamic. Lots of COM APIs deal with `System.Object`-typed parameters and return types to allow maximum flexibility. However, to deal with those from managed code, one typically wants to cast to some interface (corresponding to a QueryInterface COM call) provided for COM interop. This gets cumbersome pretty soon, requiring lots of boilerplate code, especially when dealing with return values. This kind of experience is often referred to as "peter-out typing" because along the way you lose strong typing:

```
Workbook workbook = GetWorkbook();
Worksheet sheet = (Worksheet)workbook.Sheets["Products"];
Range range = (Range)sheet.Cells[1, 1];
// Use the selected range.
```

In the C# 3.0 code here, the return types for the indexers into the `Sheets` and `Cells` collections are statically typed to `System.Object`, so we need to cast to the appropriate interface to continue. The reality is that COM is a dynamic experience to begin with—the IDispatch interface being the ultimate example—so it makes sense to reduce this friction when dealing with COM interop. Therefore, starting from .NET 4.0, occurrences of System.Object in COM APIs are substituted by dynamic. This causes the DLR to kick in and use the COM binder to call into the underlying COM APIs:

```
Workbook workbook = GetWorkbook();
Range range = workbook.Sheets["Products"].Cells[1, 1];
// Use the selected range.
```

A final language feature that falls under the umbrella of improving COM interop is known as "no PIA." (Kind of weird for a language feature to have a negation in it, isn't it?) Historically, Microsoft has shipped so-called PIAs for popular COM libraries, containing the exported type definitions with several enhancements to make the APIs easier to consume from managed code. Although great, PIAs are typically hogs in terms of size, and in the majority of cases only very small parts of the library are used. This causes grief with regard to the size of applications—relevant for deployment—and because of the runtime cost associated with loading giant assemblies.

With "no PIA," the compiler can grab all the bits and pieces of a PIA that are used within the application's code and copy them into the application assembly being built. This eliminates the need to redistribute PIAs and reduces the load cost to a minimum.

LANGUAGE CO-EVOLUTION

Since the introduction of .NET, Microsoft has offered two mainstream managed code languages: C# and Visual Basic. Although this perfectly illustrates how the platform enables a wide variety of languages to be used for managed code development, it's been a major source of confusion for developers who have to make a language choice. Both languages more or less target the same group of developers, writing enterprise applications of various kinds.

Ideally, the main reason to prefer one language over another should simply be a matter of background and personal preference. People coming from a C++ or Java background will feel more at home in C#, whereas those who had prior exposure to Visual Basic 6 or earlier will find Visual Basic .NET more attractive.

In reality, differences in the gamma of language features offered by both languages have been a source of frustration, forcing people to choose a particular language or be left in the dark with missing features. Over the years, it became apparent this pathological situation should be dealt with, and starting from .NET 4.0, Microsoft has committed to "co-evolution" for both languages, making sure they keep on par with regard to features being added.

One can see traces of this commitment in both languages today. C# 4.0 is adding named and optional parameters, something Visual Basic has had from the start. In the opposite direction, Visual Basic 10 now supports auto-implemented properties that were in C# since version 3.0.

Covariance and Contravariance

Without a doubt, the most fancy-sounding new feature in C# 4.0 is generic interface and delegate type co- and contra-variance. I won't dive into details on the technical terminology used here, so let's just focus on what it enables instead.

A common situation people ran into when using LINQ was the following:

```
IEnumerable<Person> result = from student in db.Students
                            where student.Name.StartsWith("B")
                            select student;
```

In this piece of code, the type of the elements in the Students table is Student, which is a subtype of Person. However, to treat the resulting sequence—an IEnumerable<Student>—in a more general fashion, we'd like to assign it to a variable of type IEnumerable<Person> instead. In C# 3.0, people were surprised you couldn't do this, although it seems safe on the surface.

The reason this didn't work is because generic types were treated invariantly by the language before the introduction of C# 4.0. This means generic parameters had to match exactly for the assignment to work. However, IEnumerable<T> is safe to be used covariantly, which means an object of type IEnumerable<SubType> can be used where an IEnumerable<SuperType> is expected. Why is this safe to do? I'll omit all the gory details, but the essential point is that the generic parameter is only used in "output positions" in the interface definition:

```
interface IEnumerable<T>
{
    IEnumerator<T> GetEnumerator();
}
```

Because it's only possible to get values of type T out of the interface (through the enumerator object, that is), it's safe to treat them as less derived: "Okay, we got Student objects back, but ignore the things that make a Student special and treat them as regular Person objects instead." However, if we'd be able to feed objects in through the interface, this wouldn't be safe anymore (for example, because you'd be able to stick a Docent object into the collection while consumers expect objects to be of type Student). This would breach type safety.

A similar issue exists when generic parameters are used in input positions (for example, on the IComparer interface shown here). In C# 2.0 and 3.0, the following wouldn't compile:

```
IComparer<Person> personComp = GetPersonComparerByWeight();
IComparer<Student> strComp = personComp;
```

Intuitively, you can see this should be fine: if something can compare arbitrary Person objects, it ought to be able to compare Students, too, because every Student is a Person, at least in our type hierarchy. This case is exactly the opposite as the IEnumerable<T> case:

Now we can treat something less derived (an IComparer for Person objects) as more derived (comparing Students). We call this contravariance. Again, with C# 4.0 you're now able to do this.

Given that contravariance is the opposite of covariance, can you guess why this is safe for IComparer<T>? Because this time T is used in "input positions" only, as illustrated here:

```
interface IComparer<T>
{
    int CompareTo(T left, T right);
}
```

Typically, all you need to know about this theoretically very interesting feature is that now you can do the things you were surprised you couldn't do before. This reflects the use of covariance and contravariance. The feature is symmetrical, though, allowing developers to declare generic interface or delegate types with variance annotations on type parameters. How this has been done for the BCL types IEnumerable<T> and IComparer<T> is shown here:

```
interface IEnumerable<out T>
{
    IEnumerator<T> GetEnumerator();
}

interface IComparer<in T>
{
    int CompareTo(T left, T right);
}
```

Here the in and out keywords are used to indicate the variance treatment for the parameter. Covariance is specified using the out keyword, restricting the type parameter's use to output positions only. Likewise, contravariance is indicated using in, this time allowing the parameter to be used in input positions only. The compiler will enforce this to make sure you don't put type safety at risk.

NOTE

Covariance and contravariance are not limited to the context of generic types. In fact, since C# 3.0, the language has support for both types of variance for (nongeneric) delegate types. This proves particularly handy when dealing with event handlers. Suppose, for example, we want to have one handler both for a MouseClick event on a button and a KeyPress event on a text box. These events are defined as follows:

```
public event MouseEventHandler MouseClick;
public event KeyPressEventHandler KeyPress;
```

The delegates used to define the events look like this:

```
delegate void MouseEventHandler(object sender, MouseEventArgs e);

delegate void KeyPressEventHandler(object sender, KeyPressEventArgs e);
```

While having specialized knowledge about the events that occurred through their arguments (for example, the mouse cursor position at the time of the click), we might just be interested in the mere fact that any of those events happened without requiring additional context. In other words, we want to write the following:

```
txtAmount.KeyPress += this.LoggingHandler;

btnSave.MouseClick += this.LoggingHandler;
```

In this case, the event handler method is declared like this:

```
private void LoggingHandler(object sender, EventArgs e)
{
    // ...
}
```

See what we just did? We used the common super-type `System.EventArgs` on our general-purpose logging handler. Thanks to C#'s delegate covariance and contravariance feature, this is allowed, providing more flexibility when matching method signatures against delegate types. Parameter types are treated contravariantly, while return types are treated covariantly.

A Sneak Peek at the Future

Now that we've seen the current state of affairs of the C# language, let's talk a bit about the influences that are shaping the language's future.

Multiparadigm

Traditionally, programming languages have been classified based on the paradigms on which they're based:

▶ Imperative programming languages use statements to modify the state of a program. Those languages are very machine-oriented and reflect how the underlying hardware works, hence giving developers low-level control over the system. Writing software following this paradigm is about stating "how" execution needs to happen, not just about "what" the problem is that needs to be solved. The earliest imperative programming language was FORTRAN, and popular descendants include COBOL, BASIC, Pascal, and C.

▶ Procedural programming extends on the foundation laid by imperative languages, adding more structure to the way software is written by adding the concept of procedures. Declared once, procedures can be called many times to reuse pieces of code. This also helps to isolate state used across multiple procedures, making the program as a whole more modular. It also gets rid of excess use of GOTO to control the flow of execution.

▶ Object-oriented (OO) programming is today's most popular paradigm to tame complexity of software. Code is divided into object definitions (types) that define state and operations on that state. By keeping the internal state of an object hidden from the outside world (known as encapsulation), better modularity arises. Other techniques in the OO paradigm include polymorphism and inheritance. Languages such as Smalltalk, Eiffel, C++, Java, C#, and Visual Basic .NET can be classified as object-oriented.

▶ Declarative languages shy away from modification of machine state and take a top-down approach, starting from the problem definition (what) and hiding the execution details (how) such as control flow from the developer. This style reduces the number of side effects and is regaining attention lately because of concurrent programming.

▶ Functional programming is a subcategory of declarative programming. As the name implies, it's based on the concept of mathematical functions, avoiding mutation of state and side effects whenever possible. This makes reasoning about the program's behavior easier and has the tendency to eliminate whole classes of bugs. It also allows parallelization of execution with fewer worries than in the imperative world. Sample languages include LISP and Schema, the ML-family of languages, and its derivatives like F#, Haskell, and Erlang; but even spreadsheets can be considered functional.

▶ Logic programming is more of a niche market but is another great example of declarative programming. This paradigm tends to be popular in the development of rule engines. The idea here is that the developer expresses logical rules, after which logical questions can be asked to the program, having it figure out how to prove or disprove the correctness of the question. Probably the most notable logic programming language is Prolog.

Yet another taxonomy is established along the axis of typing, with a distinction between statically and dynamically typed languages.

Over the years, C# has become more and more of a multiparadigm language, with bits and pieces from various domains. "Pure" languages do not seem to have the reach they once had for filling in the needs for general-purpose programming tasks.

At its core, C# is an object-oriented programming language, and .NET's BCL is based on the principles of OO. Since the introduction of C# 3.0, one can argue that C# has become a functional programming language, too, with first-class functions and concise notation using lambda expressions. This happened "by accident" somewhat as a side effect of introducing LINQ, which is based on the lessons learned from the functional programming world.

> **NOTE**
>
> Categorizing C# as a functional programming language is acceptable in the broad sense of the term: the capability to program with functions. However, true functional programming makes every use of side effects explicit through so-called monads. The form of functional programming can be seen as extremist pure functional programming. Haskell is the best example of a language that falls under this category.
>
> The truth is we need side effects to do useful stuff. If everything were a pure mathematical function, we could substitute our whole program by a simple constant. Even simple tasks such as input/output (for example, from/to the screen) should be considered side effects. Requiring the developer to be explicit, in terms of types, about side effects everywhere they occur doesn't fit very well in a framework that's centered on the OO paradigm where mutation is a core feature.

With the introduction of C# 4.0, one can say C# has also become a dynamic language, though; the use of dynamic dispatch is made very explicit through the use of the new dynamic keyword.

Moving forward, you can expect more paradigms to be added to the mix. Some people argue this spoils the "purity" of the language, but in today's melting pot of cross-language interoperability—greatly stimulated by Internet programming—to be relevant, languages need to have the means to reach out to other worlds easily. This is a common theme for many languages today: Dynamic languages are adding islands of static typing, functional concepts are observed everywhere (including C++0x, the latest C++ standardization proposal), and so on

Language-Shaping Forces

To understand what to expect from the future evolution of mainstream programming languages like C#, we should first take a look at the themes that are gaining popularity and at the challenges ahead:

- ▶ Meta-programming facilities are popping up in various platforms today. Nearly every enterprise application written today contains code that has been generated somehow (for example, to wire up user interface controls, to carry out mappings like object-relational [O/R], or to consume web services through generated proxy objects). This trend is definitely calling for a more accessible object model to represent code.

- ▶ Concurrency was once a niche market given the low number of machines that could execute code in parallel. Today it's nearly impossible to purchase a new computer with just one processor core in it. Because general-purpose programming languages evolve, they'll need to provide means to structure and write code that allows for better parallelization. There are still lots of open questions in this space, with no silver bullet.

▶ Declarative programming is about yielding more control to the runtime when it comes to executing code. Today, developers tend to overspecify the solution to the programming task at hand. Our programs are embarrassingly imperative, leaving the runtime no choice but to execute the program exactly as it has been written, with little room for the runtime to be smart about how to execute the program.

▶ Domain-specific languages (DSLs) bring islands of domain specialization to the programmer toolbox. When developing software, the original problem domain often gets lost in the translation into concepts of language targeted by the programmer. Over the years, we've seen an ever-increasing number of little specialized languages being built for various domains (for example, querying). Allowing integration with general-purpose languages might be next.

The next sections sketch a couple of ideas the language teams at Microsoft are playing with as we speak. When and how those technologies will be shipped is something left open for the time being.

Compiler as a Service

As I'm writing this chapter, the managed language teams at Microsoft are working full speed to turn the C# and Visual Basic compilers into managed code for a subsequent release of the framework. This work will open the road to lots of scenarios in the field of meta-programming.

Today, Microsoft's C# and Visual Basic language compilers are black boxes: Source code goes in, and assemblies come out, but what goes on in the middle is shielded away from the users. With C# 3.0, the need to expose parts of the code representation—expression trees more specifically—became apparent as a cornerstone to allow the creation of LINQ providers. In such a setting, LINQ providers play the role of runtime extensions of the compiler, inspecting code as data and turning it to execution (for example, by generating SQL statements).

This trend of opening up the code representation has continued with the advent of the DLR, but moving forward it's desirable to have an object model for code that can be shared by various languages, including old giants like C# and Visual Basic. The port of the compilers' code bases to managed code is the first step in that direction.

NOTE

One can think of the code-as-data mantra as an extension to the reflection capabilities that have been present right from the start of .NET. The use of reflection allows code to inspect types and their structure at runtime and forms the cornerstone of dynamic code execution.

With .NET Framework 1.x, reflection was a one-way street: only loaded assemblies and their types could be inspected, but it wasn't possible to build new types on the fly. In the second release of the framework, this changed a bit with the introduction of Lightweight

Code Generation (LCG). Using LCG, code can be emitted at runtime but at a high developer cost: having to deal with IL instructions, which can be an error-prone business.

Other avenues to code generation have been explored in the past. One such technology is the Code Document Object Model (CodeDOM), which enables developers to generate source code at runtime, resulting in a source code graph that can then be consumed by CodeDOM providers to compile the code into an assembly. Providers exist for Visual Basic, C#, JScript, and F#. Although this model works for whole-type code generation, it's too coarse-grained and heavyweight for generation of small pieces of code (for example, to represent a single method with no containing type). A typical use of CodeDOM is for code generation tools, like O/R mappers.

With the development of the new generation of compilers, a unified code object model arises that can be used for various scenarios ranging from tool-driven code generation to lightweight code generation at runtime.

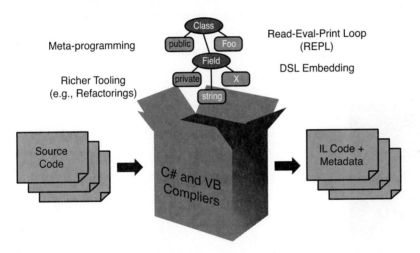

FIGURE 2.5   Compiler as a service.

This whole idea is often referred to as compiler as a service (CaaS) because the managed code compilers will become available as runtime libraries that are easy to deal with. With this infrastructure in place, the meta-programming sky becomes the limit:

▶ Code manipulation and inspection tools like refactoring engines or code verifiers like FxCop become available for anyone to write and extend.

▶ Read-Eval-Print-Loops (REPLs) come into reach for (mostly) statically typed languages like C#, allowing for an interactive development experience.

▶ Model-driven software benefits from the capability to translate a model definition into executable code at runtime.

▶ DSLs can now host islands of general-purpose code. (For example, an MSBuild file could contain C# code fragments.)

▶ Compile-time participation becomes a possibility, allowing compile-time code rewriting for purposes such as optimization or instrumentation.

When exactly all of this will happen is yet unknown, but the potential is too big to be ignored.

Taming the Concurrency Beast

Every software developer should have heard about Moore's law:

> The complexity for minimum component costs has increased at a rate of roughly a factor of two per year. Certainly over the short term this rate can be expected to continue, if not to increase. Over the longer term, the rate of increase is a bit more uncertain, although there is no reason to believe it will not remain nearly constant for at least 10 years. That means by 1975, the number of components per integrated circuit for minimum cost will be 65,000. I believe that such a large circuit can be built on a single wafer.

Gordon Moore, Electronics, Volume 38 (April 1965)

FIGURE 2.6   Gordon E. Moore, cofounder of Intel Corporation.

All the way back in 1965, Gordon Moore (cofounder of Intel) formulated his empirical law, predicting a doubling of the number of electronic components on a chip roughly once a year. In practice, this meant a steady exponential speed-up for processors, an ideal excuse for software developers to stick their heads in the sand when it comes to performance optimization: "Wait a few years, and what's slow today will be fast enough."

Although this law still holds, giving us more transistor density on chips, it no longer comes with a proportional speed-up (due to heat-dissipation issues and such). So instead of giving us higher clock speeds, processor vendors are now giving us more cores per chip. Given this, we can expect the number of cores per chip to start doubling every so often.

As an example, I started writing this book on a 4-year-old dual-core laptop, and at the time of this writing I'm as excited as an expectant parent awaiting the arrival of my recently ordered quad-core notebook. However, excited as I am, it's the depressing truth that most software written today doesn't know how to use that many cores effectively.

Up to this point, developers have been better off avoiding the use of software concurrency primitives like threads because they come with many headaches such as deadlocks, convoys, and livelocks, just to name a few. And even if threads were used by the average developer, it was most likely to work around limitations in technologies such as the single-threaded nature of user interfaces on Windows.

Today, we can no longer ignore the importance of structuring our code so that it can start taking advantage of multiple cores. Threads, being the lowest-level primitive to introduce concurrency in programs, are no longer sufficient to deal with this alone. What we need instead are higher-order primitives that open up for fine-grained concurrency: tiny bits and pieces of execution that can be done in parallel if the hardware permits it.

Over the years, many approaches to parallel programming have emerged:

- ▶ Immutability is not a technology by itself, but rather a design and coding style focusing on eliminating shared writable mutable state. If modification of data is not permitted, there's obviously no need to protect it against simultaneous modification. If data needs to be modified, new copies are made instead. The functional programming paradigm stimulates this style, and it's the default in F#.

- ▶ Software transactional memory (STM) preaches exactly the opposite of immutability. Shared writable access is permitted, but mishaps, causing the data to become inconsistent, are dealt with through transactional semantics. This allows software to continue to be written in imperative style (with little additional language surface) but requires support from either the hardware or the runtime. STM is largely a research topic at this point.

- ▶ Side-effect–free programming is like immutability in a wider context; even simple tasks like input/output are prevented unless they're made explicit through the type system. Haskell is such a language, enforcing this strictness on the developer. However, even without strict language support, a style of side-effect–free development can work. For example, filters and other clauses in LINQ queries are typically free of side effects, allowing parallelization.

- ▶ Asynchronous programming allows nonblocking calls to be made (for example, when making web requests), scheduling a piece of code (referred to as a continuation) to be called back when the call completes. Right from the start of the .NET Framework, there's been support for this programming style, but the manual wiring left up to the developer has been quite cumbersome. New features like F# asynchronous workflows hide this complexity.

These styles have obviously led to the creation of libraries, runtime extensions, and language features supporting their active use. The order in which I mention the nature of those developer tools is quite important. In most cases, it's too early for language designers to make a commitment to putting constructs in the language in support of one particular approach to concurrency. While concurrency experts figure out the best angle of attack to the problem, the language can keep itself free from potentially short-lived constructs.

This said, since the release of C# 3.0, there are plenty of language constructs library writers can piggyback on to provide a more-or-less natural integration with the existing language when trying out new approaches. A good example are the new .NET 4.0 System.Threading enhancements:

▶ Task Parallel Library (TPL) is the name for a set of primitives that allow scheduling of lightweight tasks that can be run in parallel. Such tasks can either produce values—in which case, they're often called futures—or not. Note that tasks do not map to threads in a one-on-one fashion; a user mode scheduler is used to reuse a pool of threads, to avoid costly kernel mode transitions. Use of tasks is greatly simplified by the use of lambda expressions, and even parallel control structures like loops have been built out of this:

```
Parallel.For(1, 10, i => {
    // perform computation
});
```

▶ Coordination Data Structures (CDS) are the building blocks for creating parallel algorithms, including rich concurrency-safe collection types. Other primitives offered by CDS include lightweight waits, locks, and events. Large parts of the user mode scheduler used by TPL are based on those structures, but they're also readily available for direct use by developers.

▶ Parallel LINQ (PLINQ) is a form of data parallelism, in contrast to TPL's task parallelism. In-memory queries written using LINQ expressions are ideal candidates for parallelization. Assume you're applying a filter (with the where clause) to a million records; there's nothing that prevents the runtime to be smart about the execution and run chunks of the filtering task on different cores. PLINQ exactly does that and again with minimal impact to the way code is written:

```
var res = from person in whitePages.AsParallel()
          where person.City == "Seattle"
          select person;
```

Readers interested in parallel programming—something that will only gain in importance over the years to come—are strongly encouraged to take a look at various approaches that have been researched. The .NET 4.0 System.Threading facilities are a good starting point (and we explore those in Chapter 30, "Task Parallelism and Data Parallelism"), but technologies such as F# asynchronous workflows are worth checking out, too. Other good search engine keyword searches include the Concurrency Coordination Runtime (CCR), ConcRT, and the recently released incubation project Axum (formerly known as Maestro), which is a C#-like language with first-class concepts such as agents and domains for isolation of state.

Summary

In this chapter, we took a look at the trends that have influenced—and are expected to continue to influence in the foreseeable future—the C# language. After having been born as an object-oriented language to go with the .NET Framework's initial release, more and more developer-convenient features have been added to C# (for example, to ease data access with LINQ and to bridge with dynamically typed code using the DLR's infrastructure). But we're not done with C# yet; a lot of important trends need to be addressed going forward, to simplify development of concurrent software, to make the platform a better place for meta-programming, and to accommodate for the trends in the field of modeling.

Loaded with this general understanding of the field, you're ready to start looking at the practical development of C#-based applications in the subsequent chapters. Chapter 3 starts by looking at the installation of the .NET Framework and the spectrum of tools available to develop managed code applications with it, and you write your first bare-bones application.

Getting Started with .NET Development Using C#

IN THIS CHAPTER

▶ Installing the .NET Framework 99

▶ Your First Application: Take One 109

▶ Visual Studio 2010 116

▶ Your First Application: Take Two 124

Time to set yourself up for a successful journey through the world of .NET development using C#. An obvious first thing to tackle is to install the .NET Framework and the necessary tools so that we can start running and writing code. One tool we'll pay a fair amount of attention to is Visual Studio 2010, but we cover other useful tools, too.

To get our hands dirty, we'll write a simple C# application and highlight some of the important language elements, go through the process of building it using various tools, and look at how we can debug code.

Installing the .NET Framework

The first logical step to get started with writing code targeting the .NET Framework is to install it on your development machine. At this point, we'll skip the in-depth discussion on how to deploy the .NET Framework to the machines where your application code is to run ultimately, be it a client computer, a web server, or even the cloud.

The .NET Framework Version Landscape

Over the years, various versions of the .NET Framework have been released. In this book, we cover the latest (at the time of this writing) release of the .NET Framework, version 4, which goes hand-in-hand with the Visual Studio 2010 release.

Does that mean you can't use the knowledge you gain from .NET 4 programming to target older releases of the framework? Certainly not! Although the .NET Framework has grown release after release, the core principles have remained the same, and a good part of the evolution is to be found at the level of additional application programming interfaces (APIs) that are made available through the class libraries. A similar observation of evolution obviously holds on the level of the managed languages: Features are added every time around that often require additional framework support (for example, LINQ in C# 3.0, dynamic in version 4). As you can imagine, keeping track of all those versions and their key differentiating features isn't always easy. To make things more clear, take a look at Table 3.1.

TABLE 3.1   .NET Platform Version History

Version	Codename	Visual Studio	C#	VB	Flagship Features
1.0	Lightning	2002 (7.0)	1.0	7.0	Managed code
1.1	Everett	2003 (7.1)	1.0	7.0	
2.0	Whidbey	2005 (8.0)	2.0	8.0	Generics
3.0	WinFX	2005 (8.0)	2.0	8.0	WPF, WCF, WF
3.5	Orcas	2008 (9.0)	3.0	9.0	LINQ
4.0	Dev10	2010 (10.0)	4.0	10.0	Dynamic

Notice that new releases of the .NET Framework typically go hand in hand with updates to the Visual Studio tooling support. A notable exception to this rule was the .NET 3.0 release, where Visual Studio 2005 additions were made to support the newly added features (for example, by providing designer support for Windows Presentation Foundation [WPF]). On the other hand, notice how the managed languages evolve at a slightly slower pace. It's perfectly imaginable that a future release of the .NET Framework will still be using C# 4.0 and VB.NET 10.0. History will tell.

WHAT ABOUT OPERATING SYSTEM INTEGRATION?

Being a logical extension to the Win32 API for Windows programming, it very much makes sense to have the framework components readily available together with various versions of the Windows operating system. However, Windows and the .NET Framework evolve at a different pace, so the innovation on the level of the .NET Framework is not immediately available with the operating system out there at that point in time.

One first little piece of integration with the operating system happened with Windows XP, where the image loaded was made aware of the existence of managed code, to be able to load managed executables with fewer workarounds than would be required otherwise. In the Windows Server 2003 era, the 1.1 release of the .NET Framework was brought to the operating system so that the ASP.NET web stack was available out of the box for use in web server installations.

The bigger integration story happened around Vista, driven by the WinFX vision of enhancing core system capabilities like windowing (with WPF) and communication (with WCF). For a long time during the development of Vista—known as Longhorn at the time—WinFX formed a core pillar of the next-generation operating system, and development proceeded hand in hand with the operating system. Only later was WinFX decoupled from Vista and ported back to other platforms, resulting in what became known as .NET Framework 3.0. This said, the .NET Framework 3.0 components still shipped with Windows Vista as an optional Windows component that can be turned on or off. The same holds for Windows Server 2008.

With the release of Windows 7, this tradition continues by making the .NET Framework 3.5 components available out of the box, and you shouldn't be surprised to see the .NET Framework 4 release integrated with a future release of the operating system.

This integration has several advantages, the most important of which is the decreased framework deployment cost when targeting these operating systems for managed code applications. But also for the operating system developers, this means managed code becomes an option to write new functionality in.

What Table 3.1 doesn't show is the versioning of the CLR. There's a very important point to be made about this: The CLR evolves at a much slower pace than the libraries and languages built on top of it. Slow most often has a pejorative feel to it, but for the CLR this is a good thing: The less churn made to the core of runtime, the more guarantees can be made about compatibility of existing code across different versions of the .NET Framework. This is illustrated nicely in Figure 3.1 based on the .NET Framework 3.x history.

From this figure, you can see how both .NET Framework 3.0 and .NET Framework 3.5 are built to run on top of the existing CLR 2.0 runtime bits. This means that for all the goodness that ships with those versions of the .NET Framework, no changes were required to the core execution engine, a good sign of having a solid runtime that's ready to take on a big job.

RED BITS VERSUS GREEN BITS

A concept you might sometimes hear from Microsoft people in the context of framework versioning is that of red bits and green bits. The categorization of framework assemblies in red bits and green bits was introduced in the .NET 3.x timeframe to distinguish between new assemblies (green bits) and modifications to existing ones (red bits). Although .NET 3.x mostly added new library functionality to the existing .NET 2.0 layer, some updates were required to assemblies that had already shipped. With the distinction between red bits and green bits, development teams kept track of those modifications also to minimize the changes required to red bits to reduce the risk of breaking existing applications.

What all this means in practice is that .NET 3.0 is a superset of .NET 2.0, but with some updates to the .NET 2.0 binaries, in the form of a service pack. Those service packs are also made available by themselves because they contain very valuable fixes and optimizations, and they are designed to be fully backward-compatible so as not to break existing code. Windows Update automatically deploys these service packs to machines that already have the framework installed.

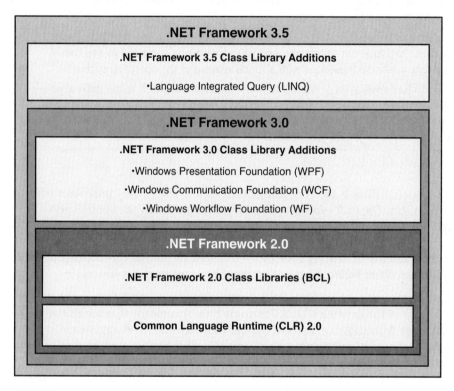

FIGURE 3.1   .NET Framework 3.x is built on CLR 2.0.

LOST IN TRANSLATION

Even more remarkable than the capability to add gigantic libraries like WPF and Windows Communication Foundation (WCF) on an already existing runtime without requiring modifications to it is the fact that very powerful language extensions have been made in .NET 3.5 with the introduction of LINQ. However, none of those new language additions required changes to the runtime or intermediate language (IL). Therefore, C# 3.0 and VB 9.0 programs can run on the .NET 2.0 CLR. Even more, it's theoretically possible to cross-compile C# 3.0 programs into C# 2.0 code with an equivalent meaning. A paper proving this claim was written by a group of language designers at Microsoft and is titled "Lost in Translation."

One caveat, though: Don't take this to mean that C# 3.0 programs can be ported blindly to .NET 2.0 because implementations of various LINQ providers ship in various .NET
3.5 assemblies.

Another advantage that comes from keeping the runtime the same across a set of framework releases is the capability to reuse existing tooling infrastructure (for example, for
debugging). With the release of Visual Studio 2008, this capability became visible to .NET
developers under the form of multitargeting support. What this feature enables is to use
Visual Studio 2008 to target .NET Framework 2.0, 3.0, and 3.5 using the same comfortable
tooling environment. And with .NET 4.0—as you'll see later in this chapter when we
explore Visual Studio 2010—multitargeting has been extended to support all releases from
.NET 2.0 to 4.0.

What about .NET Framework 1.x? Development targeting those platforms will always be
tied to the use of the releases of Visual Studio that shipped with it (that is, Visual Studio
.NET versions 2002 and 2003). Too many fundamental changes to runtime infrastructure
were made between versions 1.x and 2.0 of the CLR, making multitargeting support for
.NET 1.x unfeasible. Luckily nowadays, the use of .NET 1.x has largely been phased out. If
you still have .NET 1.x applications around, now is the time to port them to a more recent
version of the platform (preferably .NET 4.0, of course).

But why should someone care to target an older release of the .NET Framework? Most
commonly, the answer is to be found in deployment constraints within companies, web
hosting providers, and so on. Having tooling support to facilitate this multitargeting is
pure goodness and also means you can benefit from core enhancements to the Visual
Studio tools while targeting older releases of the .NET Framework.

.NET Framework 4

The particular version of the .NET Framework we target in this book is .NET 4, using
Visual Studio 2010 and C# 4.0. Other than the .NET 3.x releases, .NET 4.0 has a new
version of the CLR underneath it, and obviously—in the grand tradition—it comes with a
bunch of new class libraries that will make life easier for developers.

Two keywords about .NET 4.0 are important to point out here:

▶ **Side by side** means .NET 4.0 can be installed next to existing versions of the .NET
  Framework. What's so special about this compared to .NET 3.x? The key difference is
  updates to existing class library assemblies are no longer carried out in-place, but
  new versions are put next to the existing ones.

▶ **Backward compatible** is a core success factor to the managed code developer. In
  practice, it means that existing code that was compiled against .NET 2.0 or 3.x in the
  past can now be targeted at .NET 4.0 without requiring source-level code changes.

Figure 3.2 illustrates a machine with all the versions of the .NET Framework installed next
to one another.

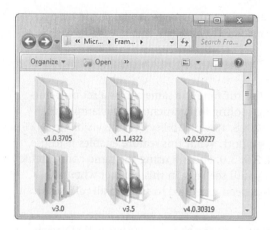

FIGURE 3.2   Side-by-side installation of .NET Framework versions.

WHAT'S UP WITH THOSE VERSION NUMBERS?

The full version numbers of the CLR and .NET Framework installations and binaries can be somewhat distracting at first sight. Where do they come from?

In the .NET Framework 1.x timeframe, the build number (the third component of the version number) was simply created incrementally. Version 1.0 released at build 3705, and version 1.1 ended up at build 4322.

With .NET 2.0, it made sense to give more meaning to the build number, and the pattern ymmdd was chosen: one digit for the year (2005), two digits for the month (July), and two for the day (27).

This approach worked very nicely until the theoretical 35th day of the 55th month of the year 2006: The metadata encoding for build numbers cannot exceed 65535, so we're out of luck using this pattern in its full glory. The result was a compromise. The month and year encodings are kept the same, but the year is now considered relative to the start of the release. For the .NET 4.0 release, the start of the release was in 2007, so from Figure 3.2, one can infer that I'm using the 2009 April 24th build at the time of this writing.

Besides having various versions of the .NET Framework, .NET 4.0 pioneers the availability of different "flavors." Around the .NET 3.5 timeframe it became apparent that the size of the .NET Framework had grown too large to enable fast friction-free installs, which are especially important for client application deployments. Significant factors for such deployments are download times and installation times.

To streamline typical deployments of the framework, a split has been made of the .NET Framework class libraries, factoring out so-called Client Profile assemblies. Inside the Client Profile bubble, one finds the Base Class Library (BCL) assemblies, things such as WPF and WCF, and C# 4.0 language support, among other assemblies relevant for client application development. The remaining part (referred to as Extended Profile) contains features like ASP.NET that client applications typically don't need.

In practice, developers target either the full framework or the client profile subset of it. Both packages have their own redistributable installers, where (obviously) the Client Profile package is the smaller of the two and installs faster. Internally, the Extended Profile package is just an increment on top of the Client Profile package, the result being a layered cake as shown in Figure 3.3. The nice thing about this organization is that it's possible to upgrade a Client Profile machine to the full framework installation.

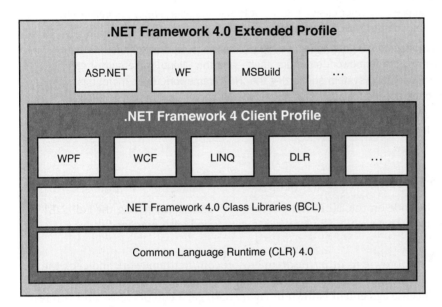

FIGURE 3.3   Client Profile subset of the .NET Framework.

FOUR POINT, OH?

The careful reader will have noticed I'm mixing the use of .NET Framework 4 and .NET 4.0. Why this distinction, and where's the .0 portion in the former? The answer is marketing: It was decided to call the fourth version of the .NET Framework simply 4, although internally assemblies have a minor version number, too. So, whenever I'm referring to the product as a whole, I'm using .NET Framework 4, whereas for the more technical reference to the current 4.x release I'm using .NET 4.0.

With this split, without a doubt you'll wonder whether you need to memorize what's available in what subset of the .NET Framework. The fortunate answer is no because Visual Studio 2010 extends its notion of multitargeting to the various "profiles" of the .NET

Framework. When the Client Profile subset is selected, Visual Studio 2010 prevents assemblies from the Full framework from being referenced.

.NET FRAMEWORK 3.5 CLIENT PROFILE

Chances are, you have heard about the .NET 3.5 Client Profile. This subset of the 3.5 version of the framework was the precursor for the idea of having different subsets of the product and was realized in the .NET 3.5 SP1 timeframe. Unfortunately, the applicability of the Client Profile 3.5 was rather limited because of architectural constraints: Only on Windows XP machines with no prior version of the framework installed could the subset be applied. In other cases, the Client Profile installer simply fell back to the installation of the complete .NET Framework.

With .NET 4.0, those constraints no longer apply—thanks to an architectural overhaul of the installer and the framework structure itself—and the Client Profile subset can be installed on any operating system supporting the .NET Framework. Even more, this exercise has been applied for other scenarios, too: On server deployments, various client-specific APIs do not make sense, so a separate refactoring has been made to lower the footprint on server installs, too.

Running the Installer

Playtime! To write code on the .NET Framework 4, let's start by installing the Full .NET Framework package. That's really all you need to get started with managed code development.

Where to get it? Just browse to http://msdn.microsoft.com/netframework and click the link to the .NET Framework 4 download. The installer itself should be straightforward to run: Accept the license agreement (shown in Figure 3.4), get a cup of coffee, and you're ready to go.

What Got Installed?

When the installation is complete, it's good to take a quick look at what was installed to familiarize yourself with where to find stuff.

The Runtime Shim

The runtime shim is really something you shouldn't care much about, but it's a convenient way to find out the latest version of the installed CLR on the machine. The purpose of the shim is to load the correct version of the CLR to execute a given application, a particularly important task if multiple versions of the runtime are installed.

You can find the shim under %windir%\system32, with the name mscoree.dll. By looking at the file properties (shown in Figure 3.5), you'll find out about the latest common language runtime version on the machine.

FIGURE 3.4 .NET Framework 4 installation.

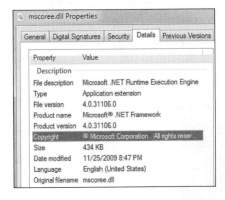

FIGURE 3.5 The version of the CLR runtime shim.

Although the file description states "Microsoft .NET Runtime Execution Engine," this is not the CLR itself, so where does the runtime itself live?

The .NET 4.0 CLR

Having a runtime shim is one thing; having the runtime itself is invaluable. All runtime installations live side by side in the %windir%\Microsoft.NET\Framework folder. On 64-bit systems, there's a parallel Framework64 folder structure. Having two "bitnesses" of the CLR and accompanying libraries is required to allow applications to run either as 32-bit (Windows On Windows, or WOW) or 64-bit.

Starting with .NET 4.0, the CLR itself is called clr.dll (previously, mscorwks.dll), as shown in Figure 3.6.

Search Results in v4.0.30319
clr
Organize
Save search
clretwrc.dll
C:\Windows\Microsoft.NET\Framework\v4.0.30319
Date modified: 3/19/2010 12:47 ...
Size: 151 KB
clr.dll
C:\Windows\Microsoft.NET\Framework\v4.0.30319
Date modified: 3/18/2010 9:16 P...
Size: 6.41 MB
clrjit.dll
C:\Windows\Microsoft.NET\Framework\v4.0.30319
Date modified: 3/18/2010 9:16 P...
Size: 376 KB

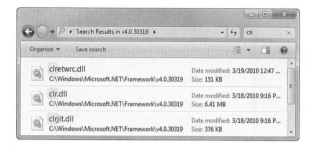

FIGURE 3.6 The common language runtime itself.

The Global Assembly Cache

The Global Assembly Cache (GAC) is where class library assemblies are loaded for use in .NET applications. You can view the GAC under %windir%\assembly, but a command-line directory listing reveals the structure of the GAC in more detail. We discuss the role of the GAC and the impact on your own applications exhaustively in Chapter 25, "Assemblies and Application Domains."

Figure 3.7 shows the structure of the .NET 4.0 GAC containing the 4.0 version of the System.dll assembly, one of the most commonly used assemblies in the world of managed code development.

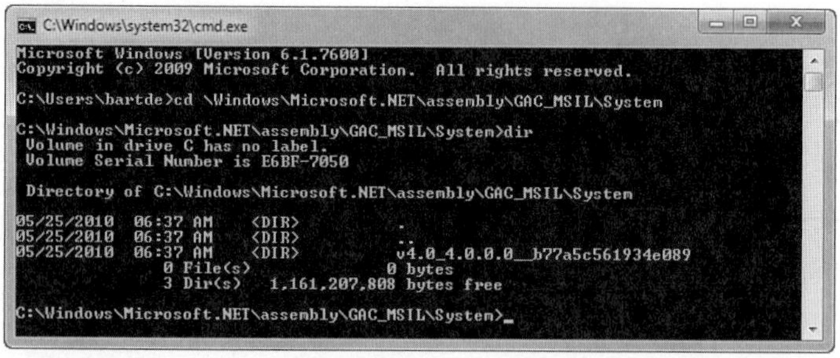

C:\Windows\system32\cmd.exe
Microsoft Windows [Version 6.1.7600]
Copyright (c) 2009 Microsoft Corporation. All rights reserved.
C:\Users\bartde>cd \Windows\Microsoft.NET\assembly\GAC_MSIL\System
C:\Windows\Microsoft.NET\assembly\GAC_MSIL\System>dir
Volume in drive C has no label.
Volume Serial Number is E6BF-7050
Directory of C:\Windows\Microsoft.NET\assembly\GAC_MSIL\System
05/25/2010 06:37 AM <DIR> .
05/25/2010 06:37 AM <DIR> ..
05/25/2010 06:37 AM <DIR> v4.0_4.0.0.0__b77a5c561934e089
0 File(s) 0 bytes
3 Dir(s) 1,161,207,808 bytes free
C:\Windows\Microsoft.NET\assembly\GAC_MSIL\System>_

FIGURE 3.7 Inside the GAC.

GAC SPLITTING

Notice the v4.0 prefix in the name of the folder containing the .NET 4.0 version of System.dll? This is an artifact of the "GAC splitting" carried out in .NET 4.0. This simple naming trick hides assemblies targeting different versions of the runtime so that a specific version of the CLR doesn't try to load an assembly that's incompatible with it. In the preceding example, CLR 2.0 will recognize only the first folder as a valid entry in the GAC, whereas CLR 4.0 recognizes only the second one. This truly shows the side-by-side nature of the different runtimes.

Tools

Besides the runtime and class library, a bunch of tools get installed to the framework-specific folder under %windir%\Microsoft.NET\Framework. Although you'll only use a fraction of those on a regular basis—also because most of those are indirectly used through the Visual Studio 2010 graphical user interface (GUI)—it's always good to know which tools you have within reach. My favorite tool is, without doubt, the C# compiler, csc.exe. Figure 3.8 shows some of the tools that ship with the .NET Framework installation.

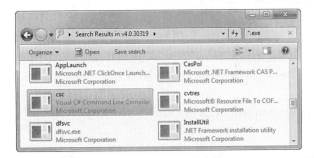

FIGURE 3.8   One of the .NET Framework tools: the C# compiler.

Other tools that can be found here include other compilers, the IL assembler, MSBuild, the NGEN native image generator tool, and so on.

We explore quite a few of the tools that come with the .NET Framework throughout this book, so make sure to add this folder to your favorites.

Your First Application: Take One

With the .NET Framework installation in place, we're ready to develop our first .NET application. But wait a minute...where are the development tools to make our lives easy? That's right, for just this once, we'll lead a life without development tools and go the hardcore route of Notepad-type editors and command-line compilation to illustrate that .NET development is not tightly bound to the use of specific tools like Visual Studio 2010. Later in this chapter, we'll get our feet back on the ground and explore the Visual Studio 2010 tooling support, which will become your habitat as a .NET developer moving forward.

THE POWER OF NOTEPAD AND THE COMMAND LINE

Personally, I'm a huge fan of coding with the bare minimum tools required. Any text editor, the good old command-line interpreter, and the C# compiler suffice to get the job done. True, colleagues think I endure a lot of unnecessary pain because of this approach, but I'm a true believer.

But why? For a couple of reasons, really. For one, it helps me memorize commonly used APIs; for the more specialized ones, I keep MSDN online open. But more important, the uncooperative editor forces me into a coding mode, where thinking precedes typing a single character.

For any decent-sized project, this approach becomes much less attractive. The ability to navigate code efficiently and use autocomplete features, source control support, an integrated debugging experience, and so on—all these make the use of a professional editor like Visual Studio 2010 invaluable.

However, I recommend everyone go back to the old-fashioned world of Notepad and the command line once in a while. One day, you might find yourself on an editor-free machine solving some hot issue, and the ability to fall back to some primitive development mode will come in handy, for sure. Anyway, that's my five cents.

So as not to complicate matters, let's stick with a simple command-line console application for now. Most likely, the majority of the applications you'll write will either be GUI applications or web applications, but console applications form a great ground for experimentation and prototyping.

Our workflow for building this first application will be as follows:

- ▶ Writing the code using Notepad
- ▶ Using the C# command-line compiler to compile it
- ▶ Running the resulting program

Writing the Code

Clichés need to be honored from time to time, so what's better than starting with a good old Hello World program? Okay, let's make it a little more complicated by making it a generalized Hello program, asking the user for a name to send a greeting to.

Open up Notepad, enter the following code, and save it to a file called Hello.cs:

```
using System;

class Program
{
    static void Main()
    {
        Console.Write("Enter your name: ");
        string name = Console.ReadLine();
        Console.WriteLine("Hello " + name);
    }
}
```

Make sure to respect the case of letters: C# is a case-sensitive language. In particular, if you come from a Java or C/C++ background, be sure to spell Main with a capital *M*. Without delving too deeply into the specifics of the language just yet, let's go over the code quickly.

On the first line, we have a using directive, used to import the System namespace. This allows us to refer to the Console type further on in the code without having to type its full name System.Console.

Next, we're declaring a class named Program. The name doesn't really matter, but it's common practice to name the class containing the entry point of the application Program. Notice the use of curly braces to mark the start and end of the class declaration.

Inside the Program class, we declare a static method called Main. This special method is recognized by the common language runtime as the entry point of the managed code program and is where execution of the program will start. Notice the method declaration is indented relative to the containing class declaration. Although C# is not a whitespace-sensitive language, it's good to be consistent about indentation.

Finally, inside the Main method we've written a couple of statements. The first one makes a method call to the Write method on the Console type, printing the string Enter your name: to the screen. In the second line, we read the user's name from the console input and assign it to a local variable called name. This variable is used in the last statement, where we concatenate it to the string "Hello " using the + operator to print it to the console by using the WriteLine method on the Console type.

Compiling It

To run the code, we must compile it because C# is a compiled language (at least in today's world without an interactive REPL loop C# tool). The act of compiling the code will result in an assembly that's ready to be executed on the .NET runtime.

Open a command prompt window and change the directory to the place where you saved the Hello.cs file. As an aside, the use of .cs as the extension is not a requirement for the C# compiler; it's just a best practice to store C# code files as such.

Because the search path doesn't contain the .NET Framework installation folder, we'll have to enter the fully qualified path to the C# compiler, csc.exe. Recall that it lives under the framework version folder in %windir%\Microsoft.NET\Framework. Just run the csc.exe command, passing in Hello.cs as the argument, as illustrated in Figure 3.9.

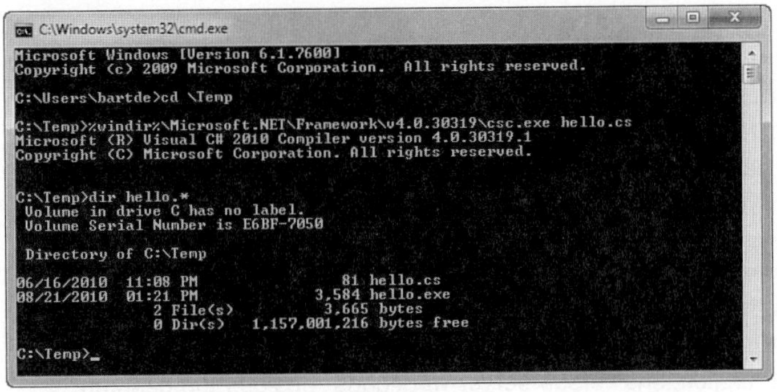

FIGURE 3.9   Running the C# compiler.

If the user has installed Visual Studio 2010, a more convenient way to invoke the compiler is from the Visual Studio 2010 command prompt. This specialized command prompt has search paths configured properly such that tools like csc.exe will be found.

MSBUILD

As we'll see later on, it happens very rarely you'll invoke the command-line compilers directly. Instead, MSBuild project files are used to drive build processes.

Running It

The result of the compilation is an executable called hello.exe, meaning we can run it immediately as a Windows application (see Figure 3.10). This is different from platforms like Java where a separate application is required to run the compiled code.

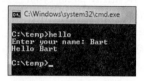

FIGURE 3.10   Our program in action.

That wasn't too hard, was it? To satisfy our technical curiosity, let's take a look at the produced assembly.

Inspecting Our Assembly with .NET Reflector

Knowing how things work will make you a better developer for sure. One great thing about the use of an intermediate language format in the .NET world is the capability to inspect compiled assemblies at any point in time without requiring the original source code.

Two commonly used tools to inspect assemblies include the .NET Framework IL disassembler tool (ildasm.exe) and .NET Reflector from Red Gate. For the time being, we'll use .NET Reflector, which you can download from the Red Gate website at www.red-gate.com/products/reflector.

When you run the tool for the first time, a dialog like the one shown in Figure 3.11 will appear. Here you can populate the initial list of assemblies displayed by .NET Reflector. The choice doesn't really matter for our purposes, but I recommend selecting the v4.0 framework version because that's the one we'll be dealing with most often in this book.

COMPACT FRAMEWORK AND SILVERLIGHT

There are more CLR flavors than you might expect. The CLR we're using for our application is known as the "desktop CLR." That one by itself has some subcategories with optimization targeting client applications versus server workloads. Besides the desktop CLR, a trimmed-down runtime exists for mobile devices targeting ARM processors, and yet another is used by Silverlight to run managed code in various browsers. (Not to mention the various other variations that exist within Microsoft for research and incubation projects.) But one thing they all have in common is support for the ECMA Common Language Infrastructure (CLI) standard.

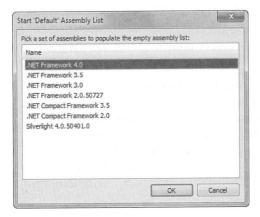

FIGURE 3.11   Populating .NET Reflector's initial assembly list.

After you've done this, you'll see a short list of commonly used .NET assemblies being loaded from the GAC ready for inspection. At this point, we're not really interested in those assemblies but want to load our own hello.exe using File, Open. This adds "hello" to the list of loaded assemblies, after which we can start to drill down into the assembly's structure as shown in Figure 3.12.

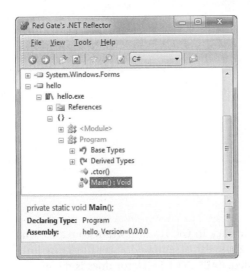

FIGURE 3.12   Inspecting the assembly structure in .NET Reflector.

Looking at this structure gives us a good opportunity to explain a few concepts briefly. As we drill down in the tree view, we start from the "hello" *assembly* we just compiled. Assemblies are just CLR concepts by themselves and don't have direct affinity to file-based storage. Indeed, it's possible to load assemblies from databases or in-memory data streams, too. Hence, the assembly's name does not contain a file extension.

In our case, the assembly has been stored on disk as a file, more specifically as a file called hello.exe. In .NET Reflector, we can observe this by the child node to our assembly, which is the hello.exe module. Assemblies can consist of one or more modules, but the most common case is to have just one module. We won't go into detail on this topic for now.

Next, we encounter a node with a {} logo. This indicates a *namespace* and is a result of .NET Reflector's decompilation intelligence, as the CLR does not know about namespaces by itself. Namespaces are a way to organize the structure of APIs by grouping types in a hierarchical tree of namespaces (for example, System.Windows.Forms). To the CLR, types are always referred to—for example, in IL code—by their fully qualified name (like System.Windows.Forms.Label). In our little hello.exe program we didn't bother to declare the Program class in a separate namespace, so .NET Reflector shows a "-" to indicate the global namespace.

Finally, we arrive at our Program type with the Main method inside it. Let's take a look at the Main method now. Select the tree node for Main and press the spacebar key. Figure 3.13 shows the result.

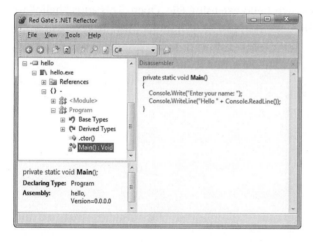

FIGURE 3.13   Disassembling the Main method.

The pane on the right shows the decompiled code back in C#. It's important to realize this didn't use the hello.cs source code file at all. The hello.exe assembly doesn't have any link back to the source files from which it was compiled. "All" .NET Reflector does is reconstruct the C# code from the IL code inside the assembly. You can clearly see that's the case because the Main method does only contain two statements according to .NET Reflector, even though we wrote it with three statements instead. .NET Reflector's view on our assembly is semantically correct, though; we could have written the code like this.

Notice the drop-down box in the toolbar at the top. Over there we can switch to other views on the disassembled code (for example, plain IL). Let's take a look at that, too, as shown in Figure 3.14.

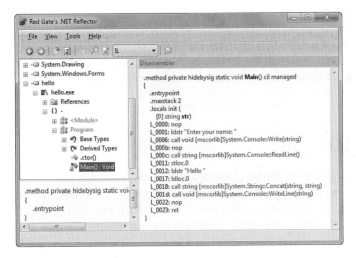

FIGURE 3.14   IL disassembler for the `Main` method.

What you're looking at now is the code as the runtime sees it to execute it. Notice a few things here:

▶ Metadata is stored with the compiled method to indicate its characteristics: `.method` tells it's a method, `private` controls visibility, `cil` reveals the use of IL code in the method code, and so on.

▶ The execution model of the CLR is based on an evaluation stack, as revealed by the `.maxstack` directive and naming of certain IL instructions (pop and push, not shown in our little example).

▶ Method calls obviously refer to the methods being called, but observe how there's no trace left of the C# using-directive namespace import and how all names of methods are fully qualified.

▶ Our local variable "name" has lost its name because the execution engine needs to know only about the existence (and type) of local variables, not their names. (The fact that it shows up as str is due to .NET Reflector's attempt to be smart.)

The attentive reader will have noticed a few strange things in the IL instructions for the `Main` method: Why are those nop (which stands for *no operation*) instructions required? The answer lies in the way we compiled our application, with optimizations turned off. This default mode causes the compiler to preserve the structure of the input code as much as possible to make debugging easier. In this particular case, the curly braces surrounding the `Main` method code body were emitted as nop instructions, which allows a breakpoint to be set on that line.

> **TIP**
>
> Explore the csc.exe command-line options (/?) to find a way to turn on optimization and recompile the application. Take a look at the disassembler again (you can press F5 in .NET Reflector to reload the assemblies from disk) and observe the nop instructions are gone.

Visual Studio 2010

Now that we've seen the hardcore way of building applications using plain old text editors and the C# command-line compiler, it's time to get more realistic by having a look at professional tooling support provided by the Visual Studio 2010 products. Figure 3.15 shows the new Visual Studio 2010 logo, reflecting the infinite possibilities of the technology.

FIGURE 3.15   The Visual Studio 2010 logo.

Since the very beginning of software development on the Microsoft platform, Visual Studio has been an invaluable tool to simplify everyday development tasks significantly. One core reason for this is its integrated development environment (IDE) concept, which is really an expansive term with an overloaded meaning today. Although it originally stood for the combination of source code editing and debugging support, today's IDE has capabilities that stretch a whole range of features such as

- ▶ **Source code editing** with built-in language support for various languages such as C#, Visual Basic, F# and C++, including things such as syntax coloring, IntelliSense autocompletion, and so on.

- ▶ **Refactoring support** is one of the powerful tools that makes manipulating code easier and allows for the restructuring of existing code with just a few clicks in a (mostly) risk-free manner.

- ▶ **Exploring code** is what developers do most of their time in the editors. Navigating between source files is just the tip of the iceberg, with the editor providing means to navigate to specific types and members.

- ▶ Visualization of project structures bridges the gap between architecture, design, and implementation of software. In the spirit of UML, **class designers and architecture explorers** are available right inside the tool.

- ▶ **Designers** come into play when code is to be generated for common tasks that benefit from a visual development approach. Typical examples include GUI design, web page layout, object/relational mappings, workflow diagrams, and so on.

- ▶ **Debugging facilities** are the bread and butter for every developer to tame the complexities of analyzing code behavior and (hopefully not too many) bugs by stepping through code and analyzing the state of execution.

- ▶ **Project management** keeps track of the various items that are part of a software development project, including source files, designer-generated files, project-level settings, and so on.

- ▶ Integrated **build support** is tightly integrated with project management features and allows immediate invocation of the build process to produce executable code and feed build errors and warnings back to the IDE.

- ▶ **Source control** and **work item tracking** are enterprise-level features for managing large-scale collaborative software development projects, providing means to check in/out code, open and close bugs, and so on.

- ▶ **Extensibility** might not be not the most visible feature of the IDE but provides a huge opportunity for third parties to provide extensions for nearly every aspect of the tooling support.

Editions

I feel like a marketing guy saying so, but to "differentiate between the needs for various software development groups," Visual Studio 2010 is available in different editions. Here's an overview:

- ▶ **Visual Studio Express Editions** are targeted at hobbyist developers and students, providing a great way to get rich tooling support to explore the .NET platform and various languages. Individual downloads for Visual C#, Visual Basic, Visual C++, and Visual Web Developer (targeting ASP.NET website development) can be found at www.microsoft.com/express. Notice there's also an Express Edition of SQL Server 2008 R2, giving access to a superb relational database engine (with a couple of enforced restrictions). To complete the family, a new Windows Phone 7 Express toolkit was added recently.

- ▶ **Visual Studio Standard Edition** is the entry-level edition for individual developers and small teams, with all the essentials for rich application development on the .NET platform, using any of the available programming languages. It has rich debugger support and project templates for Windows and web applications, but it lacks features like unit testing.

- ▶ **Visual Studio Professional Edition** is aimed at the professional developer, giving access to the various languages in the same package. It has rich tooling capabilities that stretch beyond those of the Standard Edition, including unit testing, support for Visual Studio Tools for Office (VSTO) to extend the Office products using managed code, mobile device development, SQL database project templates, and various types of application deployment projects.

▶ **Visual Studio Ultimate Edition** is the collective name for the largest editions available, targeting large-scale team development. Different flavors exist, targeting various roles within a development organization, such as developers, testers, architects, and database professionals. Unique features include source control integration, rich performance analysis tools, quality metric tools, and so on. On the server side, there's **Team Foundation Server** (TFS), which provides the necessary infrastructure for work item tracking, source control, document libraries, project metrics reporting, and so on.

TLA OF THE DAY: SKU

The different editions of Visual Studio—and similarly for other products—are often referred to as SKUs by Microsoft representatives. SKU is a TLA, a three-letter acronym that refers to *shelve-kept unit*. It comes from the days software was mostly distributed in cardboard boxes that were kept on shelves in the software store around the corner. Today, though, lots of developers get their tools through downloads, MSDN subscriptions, or enterprise agreements.

In this book, we mainly focus on language- and framework-level aspects of programming on the .NET platform, which are separate from the tooling support. However, when covering tooling support, we assume the reader has access to at least the Professional Edition of Visual Studio 2010. This said, lots of the features covered (such as debugging support to name an essential one) are available in the Express Edition, too. From time to time, we'll have a peek at Team System-level features, as well, but in a rather limited fashion.

Oh, and by the way, Visual Studio is available in different (natural) languages beyond just English. However, this book refers to the English vocabulary used in menus, dialogs, and so on.

VISUAL STUDIO SHELL

In fact, Visual Studio is a highly extensible shell for all sorts of development and management tools. An example of a tool that's built on the Visual Studio environment is the SQL Server Management Studio. To allow the use of this infrastructure for use by third-party tools, there's the so-called Visual Studio Shell. One can go even further and embed Visual Studio capabilities in a separate application by using the Visual Studio for Applications (VSTA) platform.

Expression

Applications with GUIs, either for Windows or the Web, are typically not just built by development teams. An important peer to the developer involved in GUI development is a professional designer working on the look and feel for the application's user experience.

Platform-level technologies like Windows Presentation Foundation (WPF), Silverlight, and ASP.NET are built with this fact in mind, allowing for rich styling capabilities and a separation between developer code and UI definitions (for example, in terms of XAML). This is a very powerful concept that enables developers and designers to work in parallel with one another.

Although this book focuses on the developer aspect of .NET application development, it's important to know about the Expression family of tools that can be used by your designer peers. More information about those tools can be found at www.microsoft.com/expression.

Installing Visual Studio 2010

Installation of Visual Studio 2010 should be straightforward. Assuming you are using at least the Professional Edition of the product, check boxes will appear to install managed code/native code development support (see Figure 3.16). Make sure to check the managed code option or switch the options page to the more verbose mode where individual features can be turned on or off.

FIGURE 3.16   Visual Studio 2010 Ultimate installation options.

Depending on the number of features you select (I typically do a full installation to avoid DVD or other install media hunts afterward), installation might take a while. If you don't already have those installed, various prerequisites, such as the .NET Framework, will get installed as well, potentially requiring a reboot or two. But it's more than worth the wait.

Once Visual Studio setup has completed, make sure to install the product documentation, also known as the Help Library. Although the Visual Studio help system can hook up to the online version of MSDN seamlessly, it's convenient to have the documentation installed locally if you can afford the disk space. To do so, go to the Start Menu and find the Manage Help Settings entry under the Visual Studio 2010, Visual Studio Tools folder. Figure 3.17 shows the user interface of this tool, where one can install content from the installation disk or by downloading it.

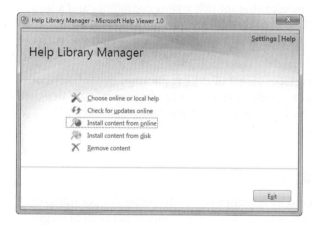

FIGURE 3.17   MSDN Library installation option.

A Quick Tour Through Visual Studio 2010

With Visual Studio 2010 installed, let's take a quick tour through the IDE you'll be spending a lot of your time as a developer in.

What Got Installed

Depending on the edition you have installed, a number of tools will have been installed in parallel with the Visual Studio 2010 editor itself. Figure 3.18 shows the Start menu entry for Visual Studio 2010 for an Ultimate Edition installation on a 64-bit machine. A few notable entries here are as follows:

▶ **Visual Studio 2010 Command Prompt** provides a command prompt window with several environment variables set, including additions to the search path to locate various tools such as the command-line compilers.

▶ **Visual Studio 2010 Remote Debugger** is one of my favorite tools when debugging services or other types of applications that run on a remote machine. It enables you to enable debugging applications over the network right from inside Visual Studio 2010.

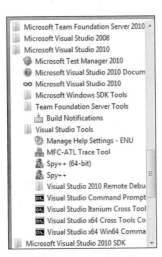

FIGURE 3.18   Visual Studio 2010 Start menu entries.

TIP

Go ahead and use the Visual Studio 2010 command prompt to recompile our first application we created earlier in this chapter. You should find that csc.exe is on the search path, so you can simply invoke it without specifying the full path.

Another tool that got installed is ildasm.exe, the IL disassembler. Go ahead and use it to inspect the hello.exe assembly, looking for the Main method's IL code. Because we'll be using this tool from time to time, it's good to know where you can launch it from.

Splash Screen and Start Page

The Visual Studio 2010 splash screen is shown in Figure 3.19. Prior to Visual Studio 2010, the splash screen used to show the different extensibility packages that were installed. Now this information is available from the Help, About menu.

New and notable packages in Visual Studio 2010 are the built-in Silverlight projects and out-of-the-box support for the F# language.

CHOOSE YOUR MOTHER TONGUE

If this is the first time you've started Visual Studio 2010, you'll be presented with a dialog to select a settings template to configure the IDE for a specific programming language. You can either stick with a general settings template or indicate your preferred language (your programming mother tongue, so to speak). If you're presented with this option, feel free to go ahead and select the C# template.

All this means is some settings will be optimized for C# projects (for example, the default language selection in the New Project dialog), but other languages are still available to you at any point in time. Hence the word *preference*.

FIGURE 3.19   Visual Studio 2010 splash screen.

The first thing you'll see in Visual Studio is the Start page shown in Figure 3.20. It provides links to various tasks (for example, to reload recently used projects). An RSS feed shows news items from the MSDN website.

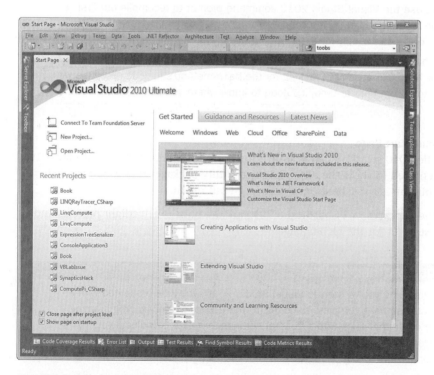

FIGURE 3.20   Visual Studio 2010 Start page.

Core UI Elements

The menu and toolbar contain a wealth of features. (We'll only cover the essential ones.) Make sure to explore the menu a bit for things that catch your eye. Because we haven't loaded a project yet, various toolbars are not visible yet.

Various collapsible panels are docked on the borders. There are several of those, but only a few are visible at this point: Toolbox, Solution Explorer, and Error List are the ones we'll interact with regularly. More panels can be enabled through the View menu, but most panels have a contextual nature and will appear spontaneously when invoking certain actions (for example, while debugging). Figure 3.21 shows how panels can be docked at various spots in the editor. The little pushpin button on the title bar of a panel can be used to prevent it from collapsing. As you get more familiar with the editor, you'll start rearranging things quite bit to adapt to your needs.

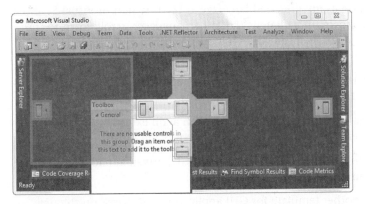

FIGURE 3.21   Customizing the look and feel by docking panels.

"INNOVATION THROUGH INTEGRATION" WITH WPF

If you've used earlier releases of Visual Studio, you no doubt have noticed the different look and feel of the IDE in the 2010 version. Starting with Visual Studio 2010, large portions of the user interface have been redesigned to use WPF technology.

This has several advantages in both the short and long term, and today we're seeing just the tip of the iceberg of capabilities this unlocks. For example, by having the code editor in WPF, whole new sets of visualizations become possible. To name just one example, imagine what it'd be like to have code comments with rich diagrams in it to illustrate some data flow or architectural design.

It's worth pointing out explicitly that Visual Studio is a hybrid managed and native (mostly for historical reasons) code application. An increasing number of components are written using managed code, and new extensibility APIs are added using the new Managed Extensibility Framework (MEF). Another great reason to use managed code!

Your First Application: Take Two

To continue our tour through Visual Studio 2010, let's make things a bit more concrete and redo our little Hello C# application inside the IDE.

New Project Dialog

The starting point to create a new application is the New Project dialog, which can be found through File, New, Project or invoked by Ctrl+Shift+N. A link is available from the Projects tab on the Start Page, too. A whole load of different project types are available, also depending on the edition used and the installation options selected. Actually, the number of available project templates has grown so much over the years that the dialog was redesigned in Visual Studio 2010 to include features such as search.

Because I've selected Visual C# as my preferred language at the first start of Visual Studio 2010, the C# templates are shown immediately. (For other languages, scroll down to the Other Languages entry on the left.) Subcategories are used to organize the various templates. Let's go over a few commonly used types of projects:

► **Console Application** is used to create command-line application executables. This is what we'll use for our Hello application.

► **Class Library** provides a way to build assemblies with a .dll extension that can be used from various other applications (for example, to provide APIs).

► **Windows Forms Application** creates a project for a GUI-driven application based on the Windows Forms technology.

► **WPF Application** is another template for GUI applications but based on the new and more powerful WPF framework.

► **ASP.NET Web Application** provides a way to create web applications and deploy them to an ASP.NET-capable web server.

We'll cover other types of templates, too, but for now those are the most important ones to be aware of. Figure 3.22 shows the New Project dialog, where you pick the project type of your choice.

Notice the NET Framework 4.0 drop-down. This is where the multitargeting support of Visual Studio comes in. In this list, you can select to target older versions of the framework, all the way back to 2.0. Give it a try and select the 2.0 version of the framework to see how the dialog filters out project types that are not supported on that version of the framework. Recall that things like WPF and WCF were added in the .NET Framework 3.0 (WinFX) timeframe, so those won't show up when .NET Framework 2.0 is selected.

For now, keep .NET Framework 4.0 selected, mark the Console Application template, and specify **Hello** as the name for the project. Notice the Create Directory for Solution check box. Stay tuned. We'll get to the concept of projects and solutions in a while. Just leave it as is for now. The result of creating the new project is shown in Figure 3.23.

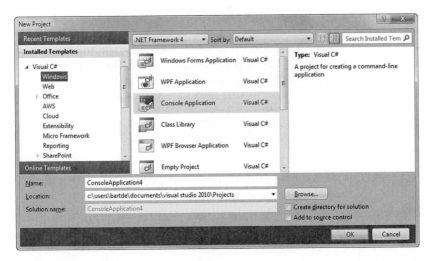

FIGURE 3.22   The New Project dialog.

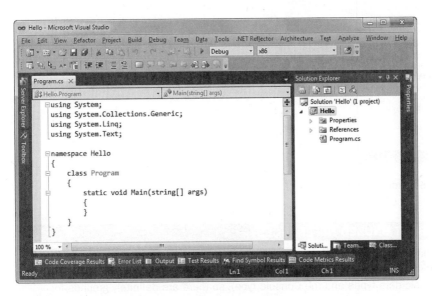

FIGURE 3.23   A new Console Application project.

Once the project has been created, it is loaded, and the first (and in this case, only) relevant file of the project shows up. In our little console application, this is the Program.cs file containing the managed code entry point.

Notice how an additional toolbar (known as the Text Editor toolbar), extra toolbar items (mainly for debugging), and menus have been made visible based on the context we're in now.

Solution Explorer

With the new project created and loaded, make the Solution Explorer (typically docked on the right side) visible, as shown in Figure 3.24. Slightly simplified, Solution Explorer is a mini file explorer that shows all the files that are part of the project. In this case, that's just Program.cs. Besides the files in the project, other nodes are shown as well:

▶ **Properties** provides access to the project-level settings (see later) and reveals a code file called AssemblyInfo.cs that contains assembly-level attributes, something we discuss in Chapter 25.

▶ **References** is a collection of assemblies the application depends on. Notice that by default quite a few references to commonly used class libraries are added to the project, also depending on the project type.

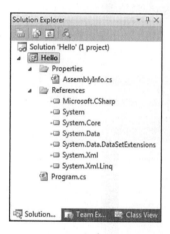

FIGURE 3.24   Solution Explorer.

WORRIED ABOUT UNUSED REFERENCES?

People sometimes freak out when they see a lot of unused references. Our simple Hello application will actually use only the System assembly (which contains things such as the basic data types and the Console type), so there are definitely grounds for such a worry. However, rest assured there's no performance impact in having unused assembly references because the CLR loads referenced assemblies only when they're actually used. As time goes on, you'll become more familiar with the role of the various assemblies that have been included by default.

So, what's the relation between a solution and a project? Fairly simple: Solutions are containers for one or more projects. In our little example, we have just a single Console Application project within its own solution. The goal of solutions is to be able to express relationships between dependent projects. For example, a Class Library project might be referred to by a Console Application in the same solution. Having them in the same solution makes it possible to build the whole set of projects all at once.

Project Properties

Although we don't need to reconfigure project properties at this point, let's take a quick look at the project configuration system. Double-click the Properties node for our Hello project in Solution Explorer (or right-click and select Properties from the context menu). Figure 3.25 shows the Build tab in the project settings.

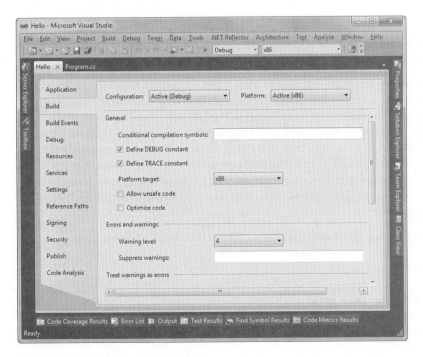

FIGURE 3.25   Project properties.

As a concrete example of some settings, I've selected the Build tab on the left, but feel free to explore the other tabs at this point. The reason I'm highlighting the Build configuration at this point is to stress the relationship between projects and build support, as will be detailed later on.

Code Editor

Time to take a look at the center of our development activities: writing code. Switch back to Program.cs and take a look at the skeleton code that has been provided:

```csharp
using System;
using System.Collections.Generic;
using System.Linq;
using System.Text;

namespace Hello
{
    class Program
    {
        static void Main(string[] args)
        {
        }
    }
}
```

There are a few differences with the code we started from when writing our little console application manually.

First of all, more namespaces with commonly used types have been imported by means of using directives. Second, a namespace declaration is generated to contain the Program class. We'll talk about namespaces in more detail in the next chapters, so don't worry about this for now. Finally, the Main entry point has a different signature: Instead of not taking in any arguments, it now does take in a string array that will be populated with command-line arguments passed to the resulting executable. Because we don't really want to use command-line arguments, this doesn't matter much to us. We discuss the possible signatures for the managed code entry point in Chapter 4, "Language Essentials," in the section, "The Entry Point."

Let's write the code for our application now. Recall the three lines we wrote earlier:

```csharp
static void Main(string[] args)
{
    Console.Write("Enter your name: ");
    string name = Console.ReadLine();
    Console.WriteLine("Hello " + name);
}
```

As you enter this code in the editor, you'll observe a couple of things. One little feature is auto-indentation, which positions the cursor inside the Main method indented a bit more to the right than the opening curly brace of the method body. This enforces good indentation practices (the behavior of which you can control through the Tools, Options dialog).

More visible is the presence of IntelliSense. As soon as you type the member lookup dot operator after the `Console` type name, a list of available members appears that filters out as you type. Figure 3.26 shows IntelliSense in action.

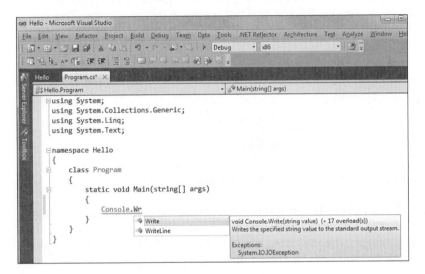

FIGURE 3.26   IntelliSense while typing code.

Once you've selected the `Write` method from the list (note you can press Enter or the spacebar as soon as the desired member is selected in the list to complete it further) and you type the left parenthesis to supply the arguments to the method call, IntelliSense pops up again showing all the available overloads of the method. You learn about overloading in Chapter 10, "Methods," so just type the `"Enter your name: "` string.

IntelliSense will help you with the next two lines of code in a similar way as it did for the first. As you type, notice different tokens get colorized differently. Built-in language keywords are marked with blue, type names (like `Console`) have a color I don't know the name of but looks kind of lighter bluish, and string literals are colored with a red-brown color. Actually, all those colors can be changed through the Tools, Options dialog.

WORRIED ABOUT UNUSED NAMESPACE IMPORTS?

Just as with unused references, people sometimes freak out when they see a lot of unused namespace imports. Again, this is not something to worry about but for a different reason this time. Namespaces are a compile-time aid only, telling the compiler where to look for types that are used throughout the code. Even though the preceding code has imported the `System.Text` namespace, you won't find a trace of it in the compiled code because we're not using any of the types defined in that namespace.

Agreed, unused namespace imports can be disturbing when reading code, so Visual Studio comes with an option to weed out unused namespace imports by right-clicking the code and selecting Organize Usings, Remove Unused Usings.

If you try this on our code, you'll see that only the System namespace import remains, and that's because we're using the Console type that resides in that namespace. This handy feature is illustrated in Figure 3.27.

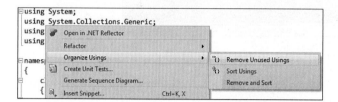

FIGURE 3.27   Reducing the clutter of excessive imported namespaces.

Another great feature about the code editor is its background compilation support. As you type, a special C# compiler is running constantly in the background to spot code defects early. Suppose we have a typo when referring to the name *variable*; it will show up almost immediately, marked by red squiggles, as shown in Figure 3.28.

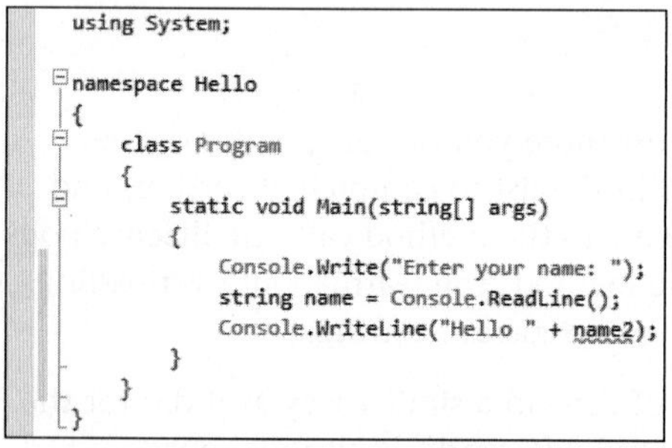

```
using System;

namespace Hello
{
    class Program
    {
        static void Main(string[] args)
        {
            Console.Write("Enter your name: ");
            string name = Console.ReadLine();
            Console.WriteLine("Hello " + name2);
        }
    }
}
```

FIGURE 3.28   The background compiler detecting a typo.

If you're wondering what the yellow border on the left side means, it simply indicates the lines of code you've changed since the file was opened and last saved. If you press Ctrl+S to save the file now, you'll see the lines marked green. This feature helps you find code you've touched in a file during a coding session by providing a visual clue, which is quite handy if you're dealing with large code files.

Build Support

As software complexity grows, so does the build process: Besides the use of large numbers of source files, extra tools are used to generate code during a build, references to dependencies need to be taken care of, resulting assemblies must be signed, and so on. You probably don't need further convincing that having integrated build support right inside the IDE is a great thing.

In Visual Studio, build is integrated tightly with the project system because that's ultimately the place where source files live, references are added, and properties are set. To invoke a build process, either use the Build menu (see Figure 3.29) or right-click the solution or a specific project node in Solution Explorer. A shortcut to invoke a build for the entire solution is F6.

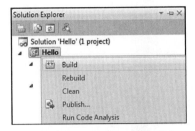

FIGURE 3.29   Starting a build from the project node context menu.

TIP

Although launching a build after every few lines of code you write might be tempting, I recommend against such a practice. For large projects, this is not feasible because build times might be quite long (though C# code compilation is relatively fast); but more important, this style has the dangerous potential of making developers think less about the code they write.

Personally, I try to challenge myself to write code that compiles immediately without errors or even warnings. The background compilation support introduced for C# since Visual Studio 2008 SP1 helps greatly to achieve this goal, catching silly typos early, leaving the more fundamental code flaws something to worry about.

Behind the scenes, this build process figures out which files need to compile, which additional tasks need to be run, and so on. Ultimately, calls are made to various tools such as the C# compiler. This is not a one-way process: Warnings and errors produced by the underlying tools are bubbled up through the build system into the IDE, allowing for a truly interactive development experience. Figure 3.30 shows the Error List pane in Visual Studio 2010.

Starting with Visual Studio 2005, the build system is based on a .NET Framework technology known as MSBuild. One of the rationales for this integration is to decouple the concept of project files from exclusive use in Visual Studio. To accomplish this, the project file (for C#, that is a file with a .csproj extension) serves two goals: It's natively recognized by MSBuild to drive build processes for the project, and Visual Studio uses it to keep track of the project configuration and all the files contained in it.

To illustrate the project system, right-click the project node in Solution Explorer and choose Unload Project. Next, select Edit Hello.csproj from the same context menu (see Figure 3.31).

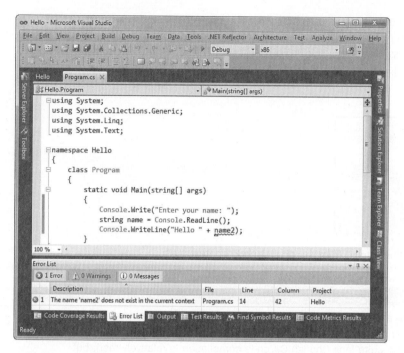

FIGURE 3.30   The Error List pane showing a build error.

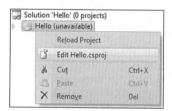

FIGURE 3.31   Showing the project definition file.

In Figure 3.32, I've collapsed a few XML nodes in the XML editor that is built into Visual Studio. As you can see, the IDE is aware of many file formats. Also notice the additional menus and toolbar buttons that have been enabled as we've opened an XML file.

From this, we can see that MSBuild projects are XML files that describe the structure of the project being built: what the source files are, required dependencies, and so forth. Visual Studio uses MSBuild files to store a project's structure and to drive its build. Notable entries in this file include the following:

▶ The **Project** tag specifies the tool version (in this case, version 4.0 of the .NET Framework tools, including MSBuild itself), among other build settings.

▶ **PropertyGroups** are used to define name-value pairs with various project-level configuration settings.

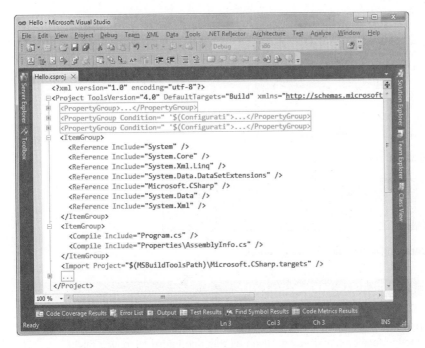

FIGURE 3.32   Project file in the XML editor.

▶ **ItemGroups** contain a variety of items, such as references to other assemblies and the files included in the project.

▶ Using an **Import** element, a target file is specified that contains the description of how to build certain types of files (for example, using the C# compiler).

You'll rarely touch up project files directly using the XML editor. However, for advanced scenarios, it's good to know it's there.

Now that you know how to inspect the MSBuild project file, go ahead and choose Reload Project from the project's node context menu in Solution Explorer. Assuming a successful build (correct the silly typo illustrated before), where can the resulting binaries be found? Have a look at the project's folder, where you'll find a subfolder called bin. Underneath this one, different build flavors have their own subfolder. The Debug build output is shown in Figure 3.33.

For now, we've just built one particular build flavor: Debug. Two build flavors, more officially known as solution configurations, are available by default. In Debug mode, symbol files with additional debugging information are built. In Release mode, that's not the case, and optimizations are turned on, too. This is just the default configuration, though: You can tweak settings and even create custom configurations altogether. Figure 3.34 shows the drop-down list where the active project build flavor can be selected.

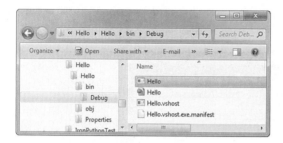

FIGURE 3.33 Build output folder.

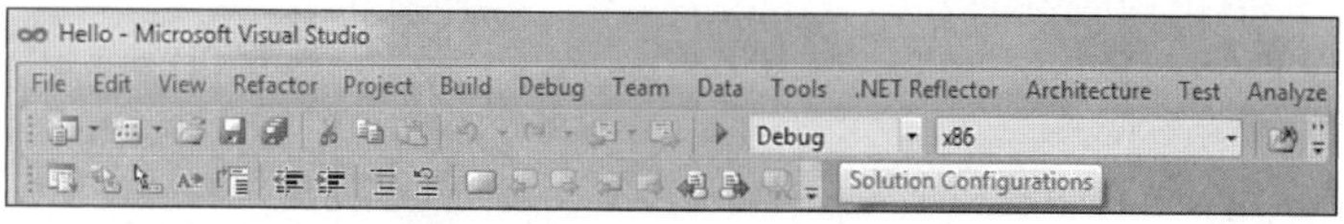

FIGURE 3.34 Changing the solution configuration.

THE ROLE OF PDB FILES IN MANAGED CODE

In the introductory chapters on the CLR and managed code, we stressed the important role metadata plays, accommodating various capabilities such a IntelliSense, rich type information, reflection facilities, and so on. Given all this rich information, you might wonder how much more information is required to support full-fledged debugging support. The mere fact that managed code assemblies still have PDB files (Program Database files) reveals there's a need for additional "debugging symbols." One such use is to map compiled code back to lines in the sources. Another one is to keep track of names of local variable names, something the common language runtime doesn't provide metadata storage for.

One of the biggest advantages of the MSBuild technology is that a build can be done without the use of Visual Studio or other tools. In fact, MSBuild ships with the .NET Framework itself. Therefore, you can take any Visual Studio project (since version 2005, to be precise) and run MSBuild directly on it. That's right: Visual Studio doesn't even need to be installed. Not only does this allow you to share your projects with others who might not have the IDE installed, but it also makes automated build processes possible (for example, by Team Foundation Server [TFS]). Because you can install Team Foundation Server on client systems nowadays, automated (that is, nightly) build of personal projects becomes available for individual professional developers, too.

In fact, MSBuild is nothing more than a generic build task execution platform that has built-in notions of dependency tracking and timestamp checking to see what parts of an existing build are out of date (to facilitate incremental, and hence faster, builds). The fact it can invoke tools such as the C# compiler is because the right configuration files, so-called target files, are present that declare how to run the compiler. Being written in managed code, MSBuild can also be extended easily. See the MSDN documentation on the subject for more information.

To see a command-line build in action, open a Visual Studio 2010 command prompt from the Start menu, change the directory to the location of the Hello.csproj file, and invoke msbuild.exe (see Figure 3.35). The fact there's only one recognized project file extension will cause MSBuild to invoke the build of that particular project file.

FIGURE 3.35   MSBuild invoked from the command line.

Because we already invoked a build through Visual Studio for the project before, all targets are up to date, and the incremental build support will avoid rebuilding the project altogether.

TIP

Want to see a more substantial build in action? First clean the project's build output by invoking msbuild /target:clean. Next, you can simply rebuild by issuing the msbuild command again.

To convince yourself the C# compiler got invoked behind the scenes, turn on verbose logging by running msbuild /verbosity:detailed. This will cause a spew of output to be emitted to the console, in which you'll find an invocation of csc.exe with a bunch of parameters.

Debugging Support

One of the first features that found a home under the big umbrella of the IDE concept was integrated debugging support on top of the editor. This is obviously no different in Visual Studio 2010, with fabulous debugging support facilities that you'll live and breathe on a day-to-day basis as a professional developer on the .NET Framework.

The most commonly used debugging technique is to run the code with breakpoints set at various places of interest, as shown in Figure 3.36. Doing so right inside a source code file is easy by putting the cursor on the line of interest and pressing F9. Alternative approaches include clicking in the gray margin on the left or using any of the toolbar or menu item options to set breakpoints.

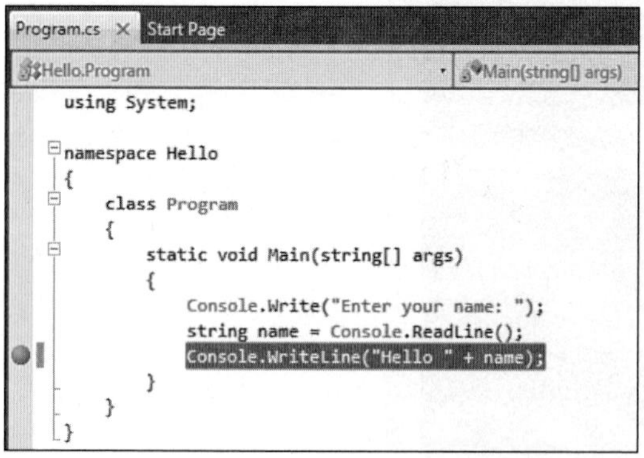
Program.cs
Start Page
Hello.Program
Main(string[] args)
using System;
namespace Hello
{
class Program
{
static void Main(string[] args)
{
Console.Write("Enter your name: ");
string name = Console.ReadLine();
Console.WriteLine("Hello " + name);
}
}
}

FIGURE 3.36 Code editor with a breakpoint set.

To start a debugging session, press F5 or click the button with the VCR Play icon. (Luckily, Visual Studio is easier to program than such an antique and overly complicated device.) Code will run until a breakpoint is encountered, at which point you'll break in the debugger. This is illustrated in Figure 3.37.

Notice a couple of the debugging facilities that have become available as we entered the debugging mode:

- The **Call Stack pane** shows where we are in the execution of the application code. In this simple example, there's only one stack frame for the `Main` method, but in typical debugging sessions, call stacks get much deeper. By double-clicking entries in the call stack list, you can switch back and forth between different stack frames to inspect the state of the program.

- The **Locals pane** shows all the local variables that are in scope, together with their values. More complex object types will result in more advanced visualizations and the ability to drill down into the internal structure of the object kept in a local variable. Also, when hovering over a local variable in the editor, its current value is shown to make inspection of program state much easier.

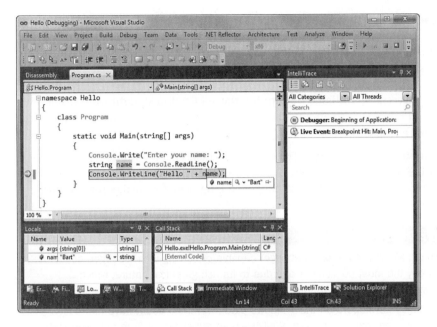

FIGURE 3.37   Hitting a breakpoint in the debugger.

▶ The **Debug toolbar** has become visible, providing options to continue or stop execution and step through code in various ways: one line at a time, stepping into or over methods calls, and so on.

More advanced uses of the debugger are sprinkled throughout this book, but nevertheless let's highlight a few from a 10,000-foot view:

▶ The **Immediate** window enables you to evaluate expressions, little snippets of code. This way, you can inspect more complex program state that might not be immediately apparent from looking at individual variables. For example, you could execute a method to find out about state in another part of the system.

▶ The **Breakpoints** window simply displays all breakpoints currently set and provides options for breakpoint management: the ability to remove breakpoints or enable/disable them.

▶ The **Memory** window and **Registers** window are more advanced means of looking at the precise state of the machine by inspecting memory or processor registers. In the world of managed code, you won't use those very often.

▶ The **Disassembly** window can be used to show the processor instructions executed by the program. Again, in the world of managed code this is less relevant (recall the role of the JIT compiler), but all in all the Visual Studio debugger is usable for both managed and native code debugging.

▶ The **Threads** window shows all the threads executing in a multithreaded application. Since .NET Framework 4, new concurrency libraries have been added to System.Threading and new **Parallel Stacks** and **Parallel Tasks** windows have been added to assist in debugging those, too.

Debugging is not necessarily initiated by running the application straight from inside the editor. Instead, you can attach to an already running process, even on a remote machine, using the Remote Debugger.

New in Visual Studio 2010 is the IntelliTrace feature, which enables a time-travel mechanism to inspect the program's state at an earlier point in the execution (for example, to find out about some state corruption that happened long before a breakpoint was hit).

ALTERNATIVE DEBUGGERS

The Visual Studio IDE is not the only debugger capable of dealing with managed code, although it's likely the most convenient one due to its rich graphical nature, which allows direct visual inspection of various pieces of state and such.

Command-line savvy developers on the Windows platform will no doubt have heard about CDB and its graphical counterpart, WinDbg. Both are available from the Microsoft website as separate downloads, known as the Debugger Tools for Windows.

Although the original target audience for CDB and WinDbg consists of Win32 native code developers and driver writers, an extension for managed code ships right with the .NET Framework. This debugger extension is known as SOS, which stands for Son of Strike, with Strike being an old code name for the CLR. You can find it under the framework installation folder in a file called sos.dll. We take a look at the use of SOS sporadically—for example, in Chapter 18, "Events," to debug a memory leak in the sidebar called "Using SOS to Trace Leaks."

Besides SOS, there's also a purely managed code debugger called MDbg, which stands for Managed Debugger. This one, too, comes as a command-line debugger. Originally meant as an example to illustrate the use of the CLR debugger APIs, I find it a useful tool from time to time when I don't have Visual Studio installed.

Given the typical mix of technologies and tools applications are written with nowadays, it's all important to be able to flawlessly step through various types of code during the same debugging session. In the world of managed code, one natural interpretation of this is the ability to step through pieces of code written in different managed languages, such as C# and Visual Basic. But Visual Studio goes even further by providing the capability to step through other pieces of code: T-SQL database stored procedures, workflow code in Windows Workflow Foundation (WF), JavaScript code in the browser, and so on. Core pillars enabling this are the capability to debug different processes simultaneously (for example, a web service in some web server process, the SQL Server database process, the web browser process running JavaScript) and the potential for setting up remote debugging sessions.

Object Browser

With the .NET Framework class libraries ever growing and lots of other libraries being used in managed code applications, the ability to browse through available libraries becomes quite important. We've already seen IntelliSense as a way to show available types and their available members, but for more global searches, different visualizations are desirable. Visual Studio's built-in Object Browser is one such tool (see Figure 3.38).

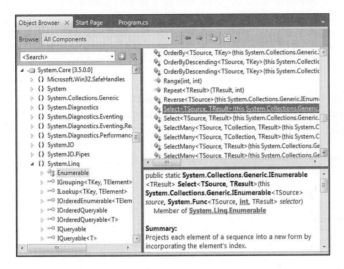

FIGURE 3.38   Object Browser visualizing the System.Core assembly.

This tool feels a lot like .NET Reflector, with the ability to add assemblies for inspection, browse namespaces, types, and members, and a way to search across all of those. It doesn't have decompilation support, though.

.NET FRAMEWORK SOURCE CODE

Want to see the .NET Framework source code itself? This has been a longstanding request from the community to help boost the understanding of framework functionality and, in answer to this request, Microsoft has started to make parts of the source code for the .NET Framework available through a shared source program starting from.NET 3.5. Even more so, Visual Studio has been enhanced to be able to step through .NET Framework source code available from the Microsoft servers.

You can find more information on the Microsoft Shared Source Initiative for the .NET Framework site at http://referencesource.microsoft.com/netframework.aspx.

Code Insight

An all-important set of features that form an integral part of IDE functionality today is what we can refer to collectively as "code insight" features. No matter how attractive the act of writing code may look—because that's what we, developers, are so excited about, aren't we?—the reality is we spend much more time reading existing code in an attempt to understand it, debug it, or extend it. Therefore, the ability to look at the code from different angles is an invaluable asset to modern IDEs.

NOTE

For the examples that follow, we shy away from our simple Hello application because its simplicity does not allow us to illustrate more complex software projects. Instead, we use one of the sample applications that ships with Visual Studio 2010 in the Microsoft Visual Studio 10.0\Samples\1033\CSharpSamples.zip compressed file, under LinqSamples\SampleQueries.

To start with, three closely related features are directly integrated with the code editor through the context menu, shown in Figure 3.39. These enable navigating through source code in a very exploratory fashion.

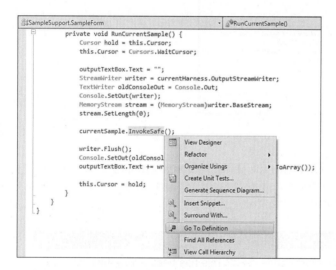

FIGURE 3.39   Code navigation options.

Go To Definition simply navigates to the place where the highlighted "item" is defined. This could be a method, field, local variable, and so on. We'll talk about the meaning of those terms in the next few chapters.

Find All References is similar in nature but performs the opposite operation: Instead of finding the definition site for the selection, it looks for all use sites of it. For example, when considering changing the implementation of some method, you better find out who's using it and what the impact of any change might be.

View Call Hierarchy is new in Visual Studio 2010 and somewhat extends upon the previous two in that it presents the user with a hierarchical representation of outgoing and incoming calls for a selected member. Figure 3.40 shows navigation through some call hierarchy.

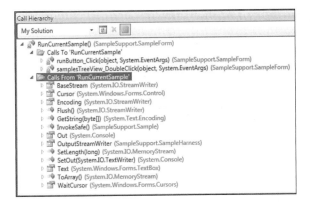

FIGURE 3.40   Call Hierarchy analyzing some code.

So far, we've been looking at code with a fairly local view: hopping between definitions, tracing references, and drilling into a hierarchy of calls. Often, one wants to get a more global view of the code to understand the bigger picture. Let's zoom out gradually and explore more code exploration features that make this task possible.

One first addition to Visual Studio 2010 is the support for sequence diagrams, which can be generated using Generate Sequence Diagram from the context menu in the code editor. People familiar with UML notation will immediately recognize the visualization of sequence diagrams. They enable you to get an ordered idea of calls being made between different components in the system, visualizing the sequencing of such an exchange.

Notice that the sequence diagrams in Visual Studio are not passive visualizations. Instead, you can interact with them to navigate to the corresponding code if you want to drill down into an aspect of the implementation. This is different from classic UML tools where the diagrams are not tightly integrated with an IDE. Figure 3.41 shows a sequence diagram of calls between components.

To look at a software project from a more macroscopic scale, you can use the Class Diagram feature in Visual Studio, available since version 2008. To generate such a diagram, right-click the project node in Solution Explorer and select View Class Diagram. The Class Diagram feature provides a graphical veneer on top of the project's code, representing the defined types and their members, as well as the relationships between those types (such as object-oriented inheritance relationships, as discussed in Chapter 14, "Object-Oriented Programming").

Once more, this diagram visualization is interactive, which differentiates it from classical approaches to diagramming of software systems. In particular, the visualization of the various types and their members is kept in sync with the underlying source code so that documentation never diverges from the actual implementation. But there's more. Besides visualization of existing code, the Class Diagram feature can be used to extend existing code or even to define whole new types and their members. Using Class Diagrams you can do fast prototyping of rich object models using a graphical designer. Types generated by the designer will have stub implementations of methods and such, waiting for code to be supplied by the developer at a later stage. Figure 3.42 shows the look-and-feel of the Class Diagram feature.

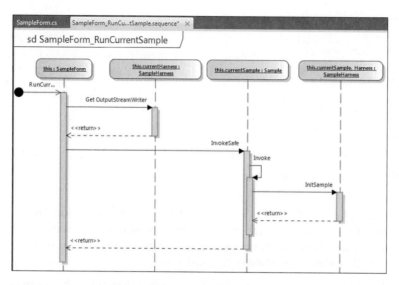

FIGURE 3.41   A simple sequence diagram.

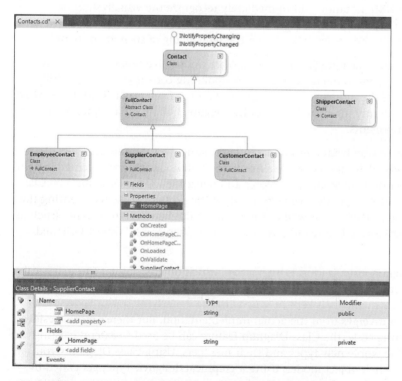

FIGURE 3.42   A class diagram for a simple type hierarchy.

Other ways of visualizing the types in a project exist. We've already seen the Object Browser as a way to inspect arbitrary assemblies and search for types and their members. In addition to this, there's the Class View window that restricts the view to the projects in the current solution. A key difference is this tool's noninteractive nature: It's a one-way visualization of types.

Finally, to approach a solution from a high-level view, there's the Architecture Explorer (illustrated in Figure 3.43), also new in Visual Studio 2010. This one can show the various projects in a solution and the project items they contain, and you can drill down deeper into the structure of those items (for example, types and members). By now, it should come as no surprise this view on the world is kept in sync with the underlying implementation, and the designer can be used to navigate to the various items depicted. What makes this tool unique is its rich analysis capabilities, such as the ability to detect and highlight circular references, unused references, and so on.

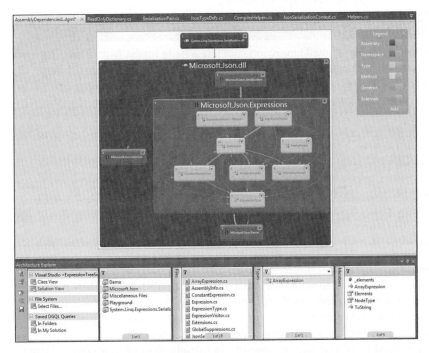

FIGURE 3.43   Graph view for the solution, project, a code file item, and some types.

IT'S AN ML WORLD: DGML

Designer tools are typically layered on top of some markup language (ML); for example, web designers visualize HTML, and in WPF and WF, they use XAML. This is no different for the Architecture Explorer's designer, which is based on a new format called DGML, for Directed Graph Markup Language. In essence, it describes a graph structure based on nodes and links and hence can be used for a variety of tools that require such graph representations/visualizations.

Integrated Help

During the installation of Visual Studio 2010, I suggested that you install the full MSDN documentation locally using the Manage Help Settings utility. Although this is not a requirement, it's convenient to have a wealth of documentation about the tools, framework libraries, and languages at your side at all times.

Although you can launch the MSDN library directly from the Start menu by clicking the Microsoft Visual Studio 2010 Documentation entry, more regularly you'll invoke it through the Help menu in Visual Studio or by means of the context-sensitive integrated help functionality. Places where help is readily available from the context (by pressing F1) include the Error List (to get information on compiler errors and warnings) and the code editor itself (for lookup of API documentation). Notice that starting with Visual Studio 2010, documentation is provided through the browser rather than a standalone application. This mirrors the online MSDN help very closely.

COMMUNITY CONTENT

Online MSDN documentation at msdn.microsoft.com has a more recent feature addition, allowing users to contribute content in some kind of wiki style. For example, if the use of a certain API is not as straightforward as you might expect, chances are good that some other user has figured it out and shared it with the world over there.

Designers

Since the introduction of Visual Basic 1.0 (as early as 1991), Rapid Application Development (RAD) has been a core theme of the Microsoft tools for developers. Rich designers for user interface development are huge time savers over a coding approach to accomplish the same task. This was true in the world of pure Win32 programming and still is today, with new UI frameworks benefiting from designer support. But as we shall see, designers are also used for a variety of other tasks outside the realm of UI programming.

Windows Forms

In .NET 1.0, Windows Forms (WinForms) was introduced as an abstraction layer over the Win32 APIs for windowing and the common controls available in the operating system. By nicely wrapping those old dragons in the System.Windows.Forms class library, the creation of user interfaces became much easier. And this is not just because of the object-oriented veneer provided by it, but also because of the introduction of new controls (such as the often-used DataGrid control) and additional concepts, such as data binding to bridge between data and representation.

Figure 3.44 shows the Windows Forms designer in the midst of designing a user interface for a simple greetings program. On the left, the Toolbox window shows all the available controls we can drag and drop onto the designer surface. When we select a control, the Properties window on the right shows all the properties that can be set to control the control's appearance and behavior.

To hook up code to respond to various user actions, event handlers can be created through that same Properties window by clicking the "lightning" icon on the toolbar.

Sample events include Click for a button, TextChanged for a text box, and so on. And the most common event for each control can be wired up by simply double-clicking the control. For example, double-clicking the selected button produces an event handler for a click on Say Hello. Now we find ourselves in the world of C# code again, as shown in Figure 3.45.

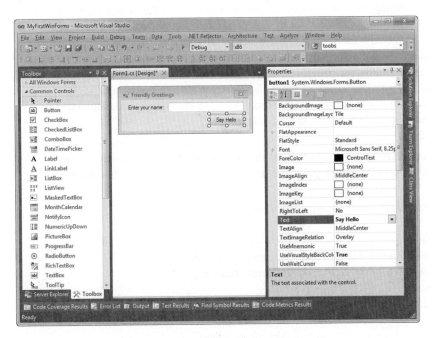

FIGURE 3.44   The Windows Forms designer.

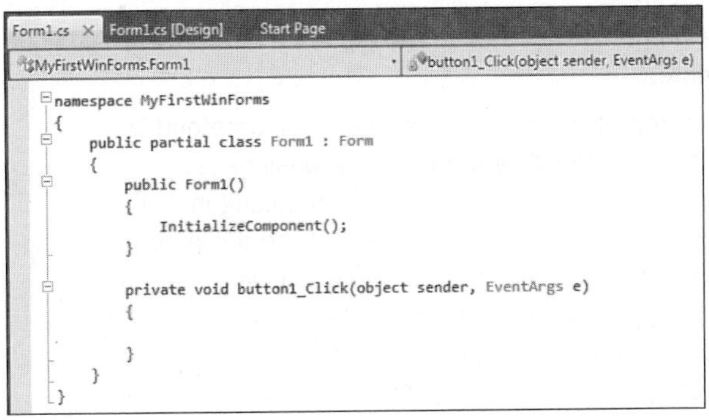

FIGURE 3.45   An empty event handler ready for implementation.

The straightforward workflow introduced by Windows Forms turned it into a gigantic success right from the introduction of the .NET Framework. Although we now have the Windows Presentation Foundation (WPF) as a new and more modern approach to UI development, there are still lots of Windows Forms applications out there. (So it's in your interest to know a bit about it.)

CODE GENERATION AND THE C# LANGUAGE

You might be wondering how the UI definition for the previous WinForms application is stored. Is there a special on-disk format to describe graphical interfaces, or what? In the world of classic Visual Basic, this was the case with .frm and .frx files. With WinForms, though, the answer is no: The UI definition is simply stored as generated C# (or VB) code, using the System.Windows.Forms types, just as you'd do yourself if you were to define a UI without the use of the designer. Actually, the designer is a live instance of your UI but with certain interactions rewired to the designer's functionality (for example, when clicking a button, it gets selected).

So where does this code live? In the screenshot with the event handler method; notice the call to InitializeComponent in the constructor of the Form class. When you right-click the call and Go to Definition, you'll see another code file opens with the extension .designer.cs:

```
#region Windows Form Designer generated code

/// <summary>
/// Required method for Designer support - do not modify
/// the contents of this method with the code editor.
/// </summary>
private void InitializeComponent()
{
    this.label1 = new System.Windows.Forms.Label();
    this.button1 = new System.Windows.Forms.Button();
    this.textBox1 = new System.Windows.Forms.TextBox();
```

Here you'll find code that sets all the properties on the controls, adds them to the form, wires up event handlers, and more.

Notice the XML document comment on top of the InitializeComponent method saying not to modify this code as it gets generated by the graphical designer and changes will get overridden (at best) or might confuse the designer resulting in weird behavior. Why is this important to point out? Well, the first release of the designer in .NET 1.0 had to use the first version of the C# language. Nothing wrong with that, of course, except for the fact that the generated code had to be emitted to the same file as the one containing the event handlers' code. Although technically challenging to ensure the user's code is not tampered with when updating the generated code, there was a bigger flaw. Developers, curious as they are, felt tempted to tweak the generated code from time to time, despite the warning comment on top of it, sometimes with disastrous results. As a way to mitigate this (partly), code was emitted inside a #region preprocessor directive to collapse it in the code editor, hiding it from the developer by default.

A better way to deal with this situation was highly desirable, and the solution came online in the .NET Framework 2.0 with the introduction of C# 2.0's *partial classes*. In essence, a partial class allows the definition of a class to be spread across multiple files. Windows Forms was one of the first tools to take advantage of this by emitting generated code to a separate file (with a .designer.cs extension) while keeping user-written code elsewhere. In this regard, notice the *partial keyword* on the *class* definition shown in Figure 3.45. As an implication, the designer can always rewrite the entire generated file, and the generated code file can be hidden from the user more efficiently. Actually, just for that reason, by default Solution Explorer doesn't show this file.

With this, we finish our discussion of Windows Forms for now and redirect our attention to its modern successor: WPF.

Windows Presentation Foundation

With the release of the .NET Framework 3.0 (formerly known as WinFX), a new UI platform was introduced: Windows Presentation Foundation. WPF solves a number of problems:

▶ Mixed use of **various UI technologies**, such as media, rich text, controls, vector graphics, and so on, was too hard to combine in the past, requiring mixed use of GDI+, DirectX, and more.

▶ **Resolution independence** is important to make applications that scale well on different form factors.

▶ Decoupled **styling** from the UI definition allows you to change the look and feel of an application on the fly without having to rewrite the core UI definition.

▶ A streamlined **designer-developer interaction** is key to delivering compelling user experiences because most developers are not very UI-savvy and want to focus on the code rather than the layout.

▶ **Rich graphics and effects** allow for all sorts of UI enrichments, making applications more intuitive to use.

One key ingredient to achieve these goals—in particular the collaboration between designers and developers—is the use of XAML, the Extensible Markup Language. In essence, XAML is a way to use XML for creating object instances (for example, to represent a user interface definition). The use of such a markup language allows true decoupling of the look and feel of an application from the user's code. As you can probably guess by now, Visual Studio has an integrated designer (code named Cider) for WPF (see Figure 3.46).

As in the Windows Forms designer, three core panes are visible: the Toolbox window containing controls, the Properties window with configuration options for controls and the ability to hook up event handlers, and the designer sandwiched in between.

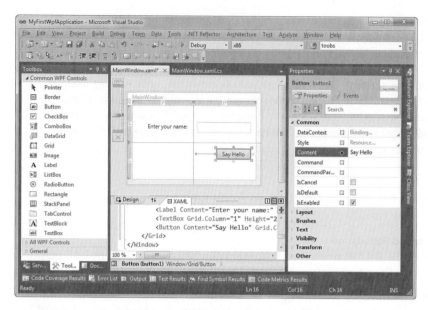

FIGURE 3.46   The integrated WPF designer.

One key difference is in the functionality exposed by the designer. First of all, observe the zoom slider on the left, reflecting WPF's resolution-independence capabilities. A more substantial difference lies in the separation between the designer surface and the XAML view at the bottom. With XAML, no typical code generation is involved at design type. Instead, XAML truly describes the UI definition in all its glory.

Based on this architecture, it's possible to design different tools (such as Expression Blend) that allow refinement of the UI without having to share out C# code. The integrated designer therefore provides only the essential UI definition capabilities, decoupling more-involved design tasks from Visual Studio by delegating those to the more-specialized Expression Blend tool for use by professional graphical designers.

Again, double-clicking the button control generates the template code for writing an event handler to respond to the user clicking it. Although the *signature* of the event handler method differs slightly, the idea is the same. Figure 3.47 shows the generated empty event handler for a WPF event.

Notice, though, there's still a call to InitializeComponent in theWindow1 class's constructor. But didn't I just say there's no code generation involved in WPF? That's almost true, and the code generated here does not contain the UI definition by itself. Instead, it contains the plumbing required to load the XAML file at runtime, to build up the UI. At the same time, it contains *fields* for all the controls that were added to the user interface for you to be able to address them in code. This generated code lives in a *partial class* definition stored in a file with a .g.i.cs extension, which is illustrated in Figure 3.48. To see this generated code file, toggle the Show All Files option in Solution Explorer.

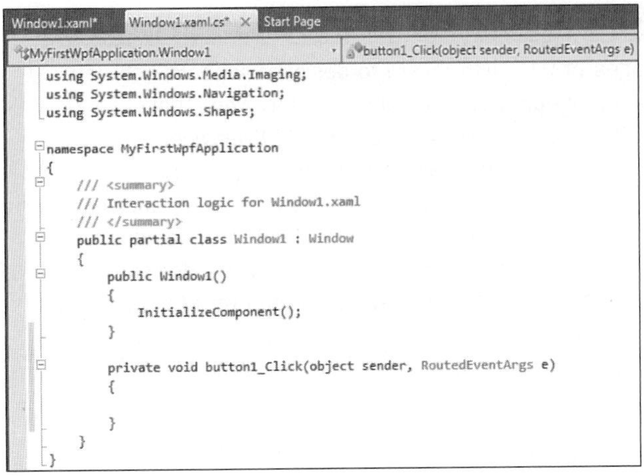

```
Window1.xaml*    Window1.xaml.cs*  ×   Start Page

MyFirstWpfApplication.Window1                    button1_Click(object sender, RoutedEventArgs e)

    using System.Windows.Media.Imaging;
    using System.Windows.Navigation;
    using System.Windows.Shapes;

  namespace MyFirstWpfApplication
  {
      /// <summary>
      /// Interaction logic for Window1.xaml
      /// </summary>
      public partial class Window1 : Window
      {
          public Window1()
          {
              InitializeComponent();
          }

          private void button1_Click(object sender, RoutedEventArgs e)
          {

          }
      }
  }
```

FIGURE 3.47   Code skeleton for an event handler in WPF.

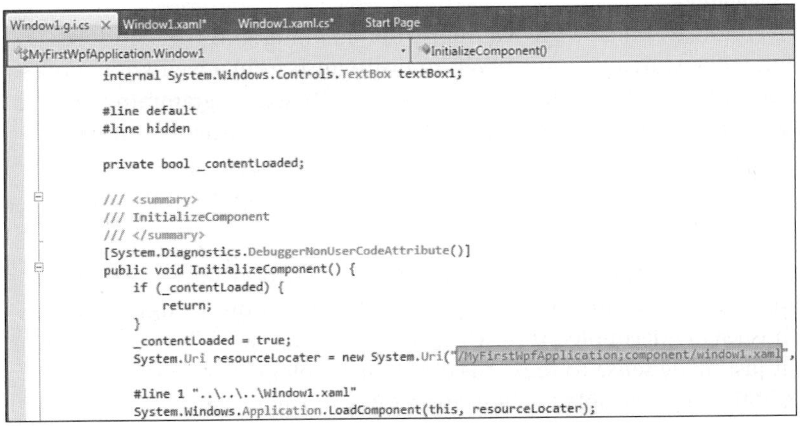

```
Window1.g.i.cs  ×  Window1.xaml*    Window1.xaml.cs*    Start Page

MyFirstWpfApplication.Window1                    InitializeComponent()

        internal System.Windows.Controls.TextBox textBox1;

        #line default
        #line hidden

        private bool _contentLoaded;

        /// <summary>
        /// InitializeComponent
        /// </summary>
        [System.Diagnostics.DebuggerNonUserCodeAttribute()]
        public void InitializeComponent() {
            if (_contentLoaded) {
                return;
            }
            _contentLoaded = true;
            System.Uri resourceLocater = new System.Uri("/MyFirstWpfApplication;component/window1.xaml",

        #line 1 "..\..\..\Window1.xaml"
            System.Windows.Application.LoadComponent(this, resourceLocater);
```

FIGURE 3.48   Generated code for a WPF window definition.

Notice how the XAML file (which gets compiled into the application's assembly in a binary format called BAML) is loaded through the generated code. From that point on, the XAML is used to instantiate the user interface definition, ready for it to be displayed by WPF's rendering engine.

As an aside, you can actually create WPF applications without using XAML at all by creating instances of the window and control types yourself. In other words, there's nothing secretive about XAML; it's just a huge convenience not to have to go through the burden of defining objects by hand.

LIGHTING UP THE WEB WITH SILVERLIGHT

There's no reason why the advantages of WPF with regard to designer support, rich and graphics layout capabilities, and so on should not be extended to the Web. That's precisely what Silverlight is about. Originally dubbed WPF/E, for WPF Everywhere, Silverlight is a cross-platform (Windows, Mac, Linux) and cross-browser (Internet Explorer, Firefox, Safari) subset of the CLR and .NET Framework class libraries (including WPF) that can be used to create rich Web experiences. In the field of UI design, it shares a lot of the WPF concepts, including the use of XAML to establish a designer-developer collaboration foundation. Given all of this, it's very straightforward for WPF developers to leverage Silverlight and vice versa.

Since Visual Studio 2010, Silverlight project support has been added to the IDE, requiring only additional installation of the Silverlight SDK.

A little tidbit for geeks: The main Silverlight in-process browser DLL is called agcore, as a subtle hint to the chemical symbol for silver. I'll leave it to the reader's imagination to figure out what was first: agcore or the public Silverlight name.

Windows Workflow Foundation

A more specialized technology, outside the realm of UI programming, is the Windows Workflow Foundation (abbreviated WF, not WWF, to distinguish from a well-known organization for the conservation of the environment). Workflow-based programming enables the definition and execution of business processes, such as order management, using graphical tools. The nice thing about workflows is they have various runtime services to support transaction management, long-running operations (that can stretch multiple hours, day, weeks or even years), and so on.

The reason I'm mentioning WF right after WPF is the technology they have in common: XAML. In fact, XAML is a generic language to express object definitions using an XML-based format, which is totally decoupled from UI specifics. Because workflow has a similar declarative nature, it just made sense to reuse the XAML technology in WF, as well (formerly dubbed XOML, for Extensible Orchestration Markup Language).

Figure 3.49 shows the designer of WF used to define a sequential workflow.

The golden triad (Toolbox, Properties, and designer) is back again. This time in the Toolbox you don't see controls but so-called activities with different tasks, such as control flow, transaction management, sending and receiving data, invoking external components (such as PowerShell), and so on. Again, the Properties window is used to configure the selected item. In this simple example, we receive data from an operation called AskUserName, bind it to the variable called name, and feed it in to a WriteLine activity called SayHello. The red bullet next to SayHello is a breakpoint set on the activity for interactive debugging, illustrating the truly integrated nature of the workflow designer with the rest of the Visual Studio tooling support.

For such a simple application it's obviously overkill to use workflow, but you get the idea. A typical example of a workflow-driven application is order management, where orders might need (potentially long-delay) confirmation steps, interactions with credit card payment services, sending out notifications to the shipping facilities, and so on. Workflow provides the necessary services to maintain this stateful long-running operation, carrying out suspend and resume actions with state (de)hydration when required.

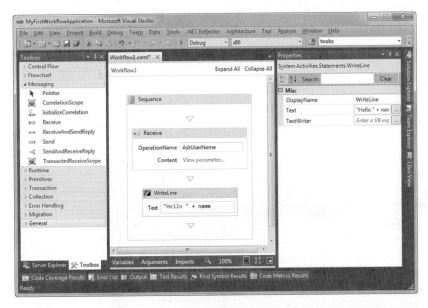

FIGURE 3.49   A simple sequential workflow.

WPF STRIKES AGAIN

Not only is Visual Studio 2010 presented using WPF technology, the new workflow designer is too. This clearly illustrates the richness that WPF can provide. Actually, the workflow designer can be rehosted in custom applications, too.

ASP.NET

Also introduced right from the inception of the .NET Framework is ASP.NET, the server-side web technology successor to classic Active Server Pages (ASP). Core differences between the old and the new worlds in web programming with ASP-based technologies include the following:

▶ Support for rich **.NET languages**, leveraging foundations of object-oriented programming, eliminating the use of server-side script as with VBScript in classic ASP.

▶ First-class notion of **controls** that wrap the HTML and script aspects of client-side execution.

▶ Related to control support is the use of an **event-driven** approach to control interactions with the user, hiding the complexities of HTTP postbacks or AJAX script to make callbacks to the server.

▶ Various **aspects**, such as login facilities, user profiles, website navigation, and so on, have been given built-in library support to eliminate the need for users to reinvent the wheel for well-understood tasks. An example is the membership provider taking care of safe password storage, providing login and password reset controls, and so on.

▶ **Easy deployment** due to the .NET's xcopy vision. For instance, when requiring a class library to be deployed to the server, there's no need to perform server-side registrations in the world of .NET.

▶ A rich **declarative configuration** system makes deployment of web applications easier, having settings stored in a file that's deployed with the rest of the application over any upload mechanism of choice.

From the Visual Studio point of view, ASP.NET has rich project support with a built-in designer and deployment facilities. Figure 3.50 shows ASP.NET's page designer.

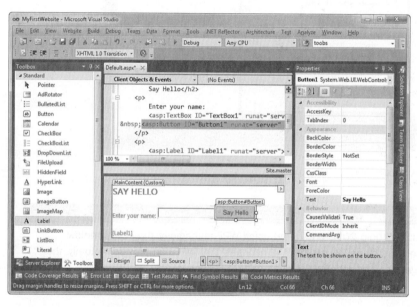

FIGURE 3.50   ASP.NET's page designer.

By now, designers should start to look very familiar. This time around, the markup is stored in HTML, containing various ASP.NET controls with an asp: prefix. The runat attribute set to server reveals the server-side processing involved, turning those controls into browser-compatible markup:

```
<asp:Button ID="Button1" runat="server" Text="Say Hello" />
```

Again, the Toolbox contains a wealth of usable controls available for web development, and the Properties window joins the party to assist in configuring the controls with respect to appearance, behavior, data binding, and more. The designer surface is put in Split mode, to show both the HTML and ASP.NET source, together with the Designer view. Both are kept in sync with regard to updates and selections.

The designer is quite powerful, actually. Take a look at the various menus and toolbars that have been added for formatting, tables, the use of Cascading Style Sheets (CSS), and more. This said, for more complex web design, another Expression family tool exists: Expression Web. In a similar way as WPF with Expression Blend, this tandem of tools facilitates collaboration between developers and designers.

Hooking up event handlers is easy once more (testified by Figure 3.51's generated event handler code). What goes on behind the scenes is much more involved. Although you still write managed code, ASP.NET wires up event handlers through postback mechanisms at runtime. With the introduction of AJAX, various postback operations can be made asynchronous as well. By doing so, no whole page refreshes have to be triggered by postback operations, improving the user experience a lot.

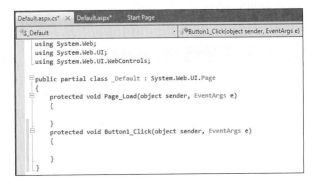

FIGURE 3.51   Event handler code in ASP.NET.

To simplify testing ASP.NET applications, a built-in ASP.NET Development Server comes with Visual Studio 2010, eliminating the need to install Internet Information Services (IIS) on development machines. The Development Server serves two goals. One is to facilitate debugging, and the other is to provide the site configuration web interface. Figure 3.52 shows the Development Server being launched in response to starting a debugging session (by a press of F5, for example).

FIGURE 3.52   The Development Server has started.

Debugging ASP.NET applications is as simple as debugging any regular kind of application, despite the more complex interactions that happen under the covers. In the latest releases of Visual Studio, support has been added for richer JavaScript debugging as well, making the debugging experience for web applications truly end to end.

Visual Studio Tools for Office

Office programming has always been an area of interest to lots of developers. With the widespread use of Office tools, tight integration with those applications provides an ideal interface to the world for business applications. Originally shipped as a separate product, Visual Studio Tools for Office (VSTO) is now integrated with Visual Studio and has support to create add-ins for the Office 2007 versions of Word, Excel, Outlook, PowerPoint, Visio, and InfoPath. Support for SharePoint development has been added, as well, significantly simplifying tasks like deployment, too.

One of the designer-related innovations in Visual Studio 2010 is built-in support to create Office 2007 ribbon extensions, as shown in Figure 3.53.

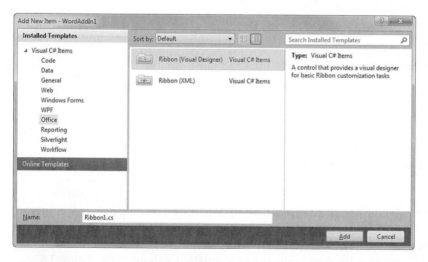

FIGURE 3.53   Ribbon designer support in Visual Studio 2010.

C# 4.0 DYNAMIC IN THE WORLD OF VSTO

Visual Studio 2010 and .NET Framework 4.0 are great releases for developers who target Office. With the underlying Office APIs written in COM, use from inside C# has always been quite painful due to the lack of optional and named parameters, the required use of "by ref" passing for all sorts of parameters, and the loose typing of the Office APIs. Because of all this, C# code targeting the Office APIs has always looked quite cumbersome.

C# 4.0 eliminates all those problems, making the code look as it was intended to in the world of the Office COM-based APIs. In addition, one of the core features that makes this possible—dynamic typing—proves useful in lots of other domains, too.

Furthermore, there's the concept of No PIA (primary interop assembly), significantly improving the deployment story for managed Office add-ins. PIAs contain wrappers for the Office APIs but can be quite large (in the order of several megabytes). Previously, those needed to be deployed together with the application and were loaded into memory as a whole at runtime. With the No PIA feature, the used portions of the PIAs can be linked in to the application's assembly, eliminating the deployment burden and reducing the memory footprint.

Server Explorer

Modern software is rarely ever disconnected from other systems. Database-driven applications are found everywhere, and so are an increasing number of service-oriented applications. Server Explorer is one of the means to connect to a server, explore aspects of it, and build software components that are used to interact with the system in question. Figure 3.54 shows one view of Server Explorer, when dealing with database connections. Adding a Component file to the project, one gets an empty design surface ready for drag and drop of different types of server objects.

FIGURE 3.54   Server Explorer with an active database connection.

Server Explorer has built-in support for a variety of commonly used server-side technologies, including the following:

▶ A variety of **database technologies**, with support for SQL Server, Access, Oracle, OLEDB, and ODBC. Connecting to a database visualizes things such as tables and stored procedures.

▶ **Event logs** are useful from a management perspective both for inspection and the emission of diagnostic information during execution of the program. .NET has rich support to deal with logging infrastructure.

▶ Management Classes and Events are two faces for the **Windows Management Instrumentation** (WMI) technology, allowing for thorough querying and modification of the system's configuration.

▶ **Message queues** enable reliable, possibly offline, communication between machines using the Microsoft Message Queuing (MSMQ) technology. To send and receive data to and from a queue, a mapping object can be made.

▶ **Performance counters** are another cornerstone of application manageability, providing the capability to emit diagnostic performance information to counters in the system (for example, the number of requests served per second by a service).

▶ The Services node provides a gateway to management of **Windows Services**, such as querying of installed services, their states, and configuration and to control them. In fact, C# can even be used to write managed code OS services.

For example, in Figure 3.55, a component designer was used to create a management component containing management objects for a Windows server, a performance counter, and an event log. No code had to be written manually thanks to the drag-and-drop support from the Server Explorer onto the designer surface. The Properties window can be used to tweak settings for the generated objects.

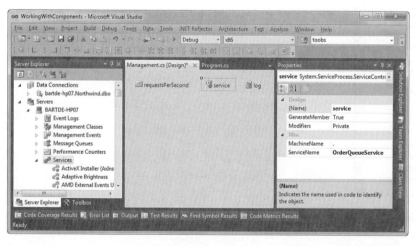

FIGURE 3.55   Component designer surface with management objects.

WHAT'S A COMPONENT?

The term *component* is probably one of the most overloaded words in the world of software design. In the context of Visual Studio's Component project item, it refers to a subtype of the Component base class found in the System.ServiceModel namespace. What precisely makes up such a component is discussed in Chapter 27, "Diagnostics and Instrumentation," where components are used quite often. In essence, components make it possible to share code, access it remotely, manage memory correctly, and so on. And on top of that, the notion of designer support is closely tied to the component model, too.

Server Explorer is not only involved in the creation of management-focused components. In various other contexts, Server Explorer can be used to drive the design of a piece of software. One such common use is in the creation of database mappings, something so common we dedicate the whole next section to it.

Database Mappers

Almost no application today can live without some kind of data store. An obvious choice is the use of relational databases, ranging from simple Access files to full-fledged client/server database systems such as SQL Server or Oracle. While having library support for communicating with the database is a key facility present in the .NET Framework through the System.Data namespaces, there's more to it.

One of the biggest challenges of database technologies is what's known as *impedance mismatch* between code and data. Where databases consist of tables that potentially participate in relationships between one another, .NET is based on object-oriented programming; therefore, a need exists to establish a two-way mapping between relational data and objects. In this context, *two-way* means it should be possible to construct objects out of database records, while having the ability to feed changes back from the objects to the database.

To facilitate this, various mapping mechanisms have been created over the years, each with its own characteristics, making them applicable in different contexts. At first, this might seem a bit messy, but let's take a look at them in chronological order. We won't go into detail on them: Whole books have been written explaining all of them in much detail. For now, let's just deal with databases in .NET programming.

DataSet

.NET Framework 1.0 started coloring the database mapping landscape by providing a means for offline data access. This was envisioned by the concept of occasionally connected clients. The core idea is as follows.

First, parts of a database are queried and mapped onto rich .NET objects, reflecting the structure of the database records with familiar managed types. Next, those objects can be used for visualization in user interfaces through mechanisms like data binding in ASP.NET and Windows Forms. In addition, objects can be directly updated in-memory, either directly through code or through data-binding mechanisms. An example of a popular control used in data binding is a DataGrid, which presents the data in a tabular form, just like Excel and Access do.

Visualizing and updating in-memory objects that originate from a database is just one piece of the puzzle. What about tracking the changes made by the user and feeding those back to the database? That's precisely one of the roles of the offline mapping established through a DataSet, in collaboration with so-called data adapters that know how to feed changes back when requested (for example, by emitting UPDATE statements in SQL).

A DataSet can be used in two ways. The most interesting one is to create a strongly typed mapping where database schema information is used to map types and create full-fidelity .NET objects. For example, a record in a Products table gets turned into a `Product` object with properties corresponding to the columns, each with a corresponding .NET type.

To create a strongly typed DataSet, Visual Studio provides a designer that can interact with Server Explorer. This makes it incredibly easy to generate a mapping just by carrying out a few drag-and-drop operations. Figure 3.56 shows the result of creating such a mapping.

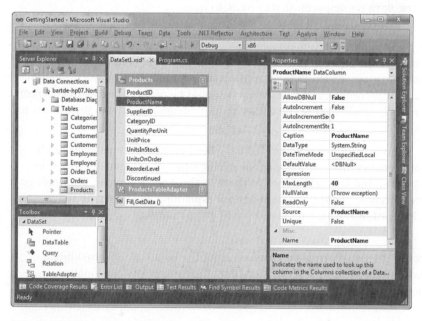

FIGURE 3.56   DataSet designer.

THE FUTURE OF DATASET

Some people believe that the use of DataSet has become redundant since LINQ's introduction in .NET 3.5 and its new mapping mechanisms. Nothing is further from the truth. As a matter of fact, there's even a LINQ to DataSet provider in the .NET Framework class libraries.

DataSet is still a convenient way to represent tabular data, regardless of the type of underlying data store. The reason this works is because DataSet was intentionally designed to be decoupled from a particular database provider and to serve as a generic data container mechanism.

One of the key advantages of DataSet is its direct support for XML-based serialization. In fact, the extension of a strongly typed DataSet is .xsd, revealing this relationship. When generating mappings from database schemas, you're actually creating an XML schema capturing type definitions and their mutual relationship. The command-line tool xsd.exe that ships with the .NET Framework developer tools can be used to generate C# or VB code from such a schema, just like the integrated designer does.

LINQ to SQL

After the relatively calm .NET 2.0 and 3.0 releases on the field of database mapping technologies, Language Integrated Query (LINQ) was introduced in .NET 3.5. As discussed in Chapter 2 (and detailed in Chapters 18 and 19), LINQ provides rich syntax extensions to both C# and VB, to simplify data querying regardless of its shape or origin. Besides LINQ providers used to query in-memory object graphs or XML data, a provider targeting SQL Server database queries shipped with .NET Framework 3.5.

In a similar way to the DataSet designer, LINQ to SQL comes with tooling support to map a database schema onto an object model definition. Figure 3.57 shows the result of such a mapping using the Northwind sample database. One core difference with DataSet lies in the SQL-specific mapping support, as opposed to a more generic approach. This means the LINQ to SQL provider has intimate knowledge of SQL's capabilities required to generate SQL statements for querying and create/update/delete (CRUD) operations at runtime.

Similar to the DataSet designer, Server Explorer can be used to drag and drop tables (among other database items) onto the designer surface, triggering the generation of a mapping. Notice how relationships between tables are detected, as well, and turned into intuitive mappings in the object model.

Once this mapping is established, it's possible to query the database using LINQ syntax against the database context object. This context object is responsible for connection maintenance and change tracking so that changes can be fed back to the database.

It's interesting to understand how the designer generates code for the mapping object model. Most designers use some kind of markup language to represent the thing being designed. ASP.NET takes an HTML-centered approach, WPF uses XAML, and DataSet is based on XSD. For LINQ to SQL, an XML file is used containing a database mapping definition, hence the extension .dbml.

FIGURE 3.57   LINQ to SQL designer.

To turn this markup file into code, a so-called single file generator is hooked up in Visual Studio, producing a .cs or .vb file, depending on the project language. Figure 3.58 shows the code generation tool configured for .dbml files used by LINQ to SQL. The generated code lives in the file with .designer.cs extension. Other file formats, such as .diagram and .layout, are purely used for the look and feel of the mapping when displayed in the designer. Those do not affect the meaning of the mapping in any way.

Not surprisingly, the emitted code leverages the partial class feature from C# 2.0 once more. This allows for additional code to be added to the generated types in a separate file. But there's more: A C# 3.0 feature is lurking around the corner, too. Notice the Extensibility Method Definitions collapsed region in Figure 3.59?

You'll see such a region in the various generated types, containing *partial method* definitions. In the data context type in Figure 3.59, one such partial method is OnCreated:

```
public partial class NorthwindDataContext : System.Data.Linq.DataContext
{
    #region Extensibility Method Definitions
    partial void OnCreated();
    #endregion

    public NorthwindDataContext(string connection)
        : base(connection, mappingSource)
    {
        OnCreated();
    }
}
```

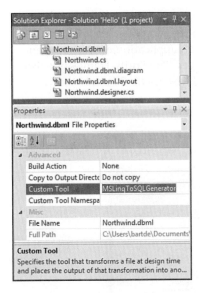

FIGURE 3.58   How the DBML file turns into C# code.

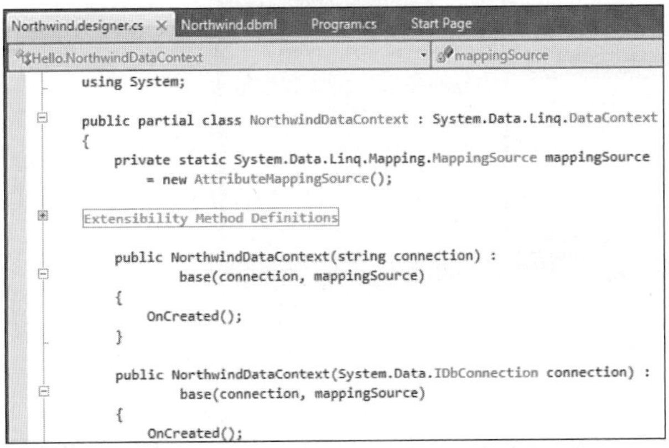

```
using System;

public partial class NorthwindDataContext : System.Data.Linq.DataContext
{
    private static System.Data.Linq.Mapping.MappingSource mappingSource
        = new AttributeMappingSource();

    Extensibility Method Definitions

    public NorthwindDataContext(string connection) :
            base(connection, mappingSource)
    {
        OnCreated();
    }

    public NorthwindDataContext(System.Data.IDbConnection connection) :
            base(connection, mappingSource)
    {
        OnCreated();
```

FIGURE 3.59   Generated LINQ to SQL mapping code.

The idea of partial methods is to provide a means of extending the functionality of the autogenerated code efficiently. In this particular example, the code generator has emitted a call to an undefined OnCreated method. By doing so, an extensibility point has been created for developers to leverage. If it's desirable to take some action when the data context is created, an implementation for OnCreated can be provided in the sister file for the partial class definition. This separates the generated code from the code written by the developer, which allows for risk-free regeneration of the generated code at all times.

ADO.NET Entity Framework

Finally, we've arrived at the latest of database mapping technologies available in the .NET Framework: the Entity Framework. Introduced in .NET 3.5 SP1, the Entity Framework provides more flexibility than its predecessors. It does this by providing a few key concepts, effectively decoupling a conceptual model from the mapping onto the database storage. This makes it possible to have different pieces of an application evolve independent of each other, even when the database schema changes. The Entity Framework also benefits from rich integration with the WCF services stack, especially OData-based WCF Data Services.

Figure 3.60 presents an architectural overview.

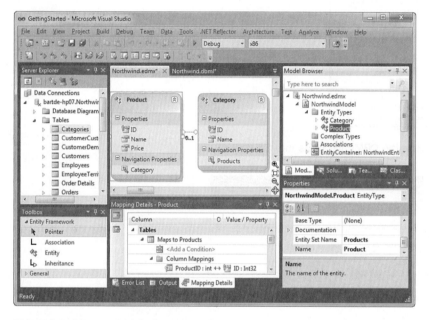

FIGURE 3.60   Entity Framework overview.

On the right is the execution architecture, a topic we'll save for later. The most important takeaway from it is the ability to use LINQ syntax to query a data source exposed through the Entity Framework. In return for such a query, familiar .NET objects come back. That's what mapping is all about.

Under the covers, the data source has an Entity Client Data Provider that understands three things:

▶ The **conceptual model** captures the intent of the developer and how the data is exposed to the rest of the code. Here entities and relationships are defined that get mapped into an object model.

▶ The **storage model** is tied to database specifics and defines the underlying storage for the data, as well as aspects of the configuration. Things such as table definitions, indexes, and so on belong here.

▶ **Mappings** play the role of glue in this picture, connecting entities and relationships from the conceptual model with their database-level storage as specified in the storage model.

To define both models and the mapping between the two, Visual Studio 2010 has built-in designers and wizards for the ADO.NET Entity Framework, as shown in Figure 3.61.

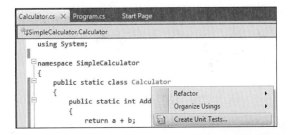

FIGURE 3.61   ADO.NET Entity Framework designer.

WHAT'S IN A NAME? ADO.NET

ADO.NET was introduced in .NET Framework 1.0 as the successor to the popular ADO technology available for COM developers, including the Visual Basic classic community. ADO stands for ActiveX Data Objects and was by itself a successor to other database access technologies such as RDO and DAO. Luckily, all of that belongs to the past, and in fact the only relevant thing ADO.NET shares with its predecessor is its name. All concepts in ADO.NET fit seamlessly in the bigger picture of managed code and an object-oriented programming style.

Unit Testing

A proven technique to catch bugs and regressions early is to use unit tests that exercise various parts of the system by feeding in different combinations of input and checking the expected output. Various unit testing frameworks for .NET have been created over the years (NUnit being one of the most popular ones), and for the past few releases Visual Studio has built-in support for unit testing.

To set the scene, consider a very simple `Calculator` class definition, as shown here:

```
public static class Calculator
{
    public static int Add(int a, int b)
    {
        return a + b;
    }

    public static int Subtract(int a, int b)
    {
```

```
        return a - b;
    }

    public static int Multiply(int a, int b)
    {
        return a * b;
    }

    public static int Divide(int a, int b)
    {
        return a / b;
    }
}
```

To verify the behavior of our `Calculator` class, we want to call the calculator's various methods with different inputs, exercising regular operation as well as boundary conditions. This is a trivial example, but you get the idea.

Unit tests in Visual Studio are kept in a separate type of project that's hooked up to a test execution harness, reporting results back to the user. This underlying test execution infrastructure can also be used outside Visual Studio (for example, to run tests centrally on some source control server). Different types of test projects exist. Unit tests are by far the most common, allowing for automated testing of a bunch of application types. Manual tests describe a set of manual steps to be carried out to verify the behavior of a software component. Other types of test projects include website testing, performance testing, and so on.

To create a unit test project, you can simply right-click types or members in the code editor and select Create Unit Tests (see Figure 3.62).

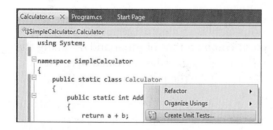

FIGURE 3.62   Creating unit tests.

Next, you select types and members to be tested (see Figure 3.63).

This generates a series of test methods with some skeleton code, ready for the developer to plug in specific test code. Obviously, additional test methods can be added if necessary.

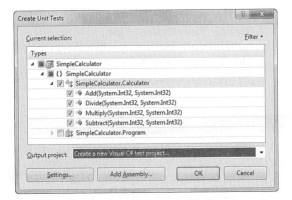

FIGURE 3.63   Selecting types and members to be tested.

The following is an illustration of such a generated test method:

```
[TestMethod()]
public void AddTest()
{
    int a = 0; // TODO: Initialize to an appropriate value
    int b = 0; // TODO: Initialize to an appropriate value
    int expected = 0; // TODO: Initialize to an appropriate value
    int actual;
    actual = Calculator.Add(a, b);
    Assert.AreEqual(expected, actual);
    Assert.Inconclusive("Verify the correctness of this test method.");
}
```

The task for the developer is now to fill in the placeholders with interesting inputs and outputs to be tested for. A much too simplistic example is shown here:

```
[TestMethod()]
public void AddTest()
{
    int a = 28;
    int b = 14;
    int expected = 42;
    int actual;
    actual = Calculator.Add(a, b);
    Assert.AreEqual(expected, actual);
}
```

Notice the removal of the `Assert.Inconclusive` call at the end. If the test harness hits such a method call, the run for the test is indicated as "inconclusive," meaning the result is neither right nor wrong. To write a more meaningful unit test, use another `Assert` method to check an expected condition. For example, the `Assert.AreEqual` test checks for equality of the supplied arguments.

TEST GENERATION WITH PEX

From the preceding example, it's clear that Visual Studio 2010 does not possess magical powers to understand your code and to thus generate a series of unit tests by itself. This does not mean such a thing is impossible to achieve, though.

By analyzing code carefully, specialized tools can infer lots of valid test cases that hit interesting conditions. In the preceding example, we haven't written a test that deals with overflow situations when the two arguments to the Add method are too big for their sum to be represented as a 32-bit integer. Tools could infer such cases by looking at the types being used.

Another appealing property of automated test generation is the capability to ensure high numbers of code coverage. Assume you have some code with a bunch of conditional branches, leading to an explosion in the possible execution paths. Flow analysis tools can generate different sets of input values so that various code paths in the unit being tested are hit.

If all of this sounds like a wonderful dream, wake up now. With Pex, Microsoft Research has created such a toolkit that plugs in to Visual Studio. Pex stands for Program Exploration, reflecting its automated test case generation powers based on reasoning about the program. If you care about test coverage (you should!), Pex is definitely something to check out. Visit http://research.microsoft.com/Pex for more information.

The nice thing about using Pex with .NET 4.0 is its synergy with managed code contracts, something we'll talk about later. An example of a contract is constraining the range of an input value, a so-called precondition. Contracts not only serve documentation purposes, they're also used to enforce correctness by means of theorem provers or runtime checks. But combining the information captured in contracts with Pex is even more exciting. Pex can use this wealth of information to come up with more test cases that check violations of contracts and such.

Does all of this mean you should no longer write unit tests yourself? No. Although Pex can take over the burden of generating various types of tests, there's still lots of value in writing more complex test cases that exercise various concrete scenarios your software component needs to deal with. In other words, Pex enables you to focus more on the more involved test cases while relieving you from the creation of slightly more boring (but nevertheless important) test cases.

Once unit tests are written, they're ready to be compiled and executed in the test harness. This is something you'll start to do regularly to catch regressions in code when making changes. Figure 3.64 shows a sample test run result.

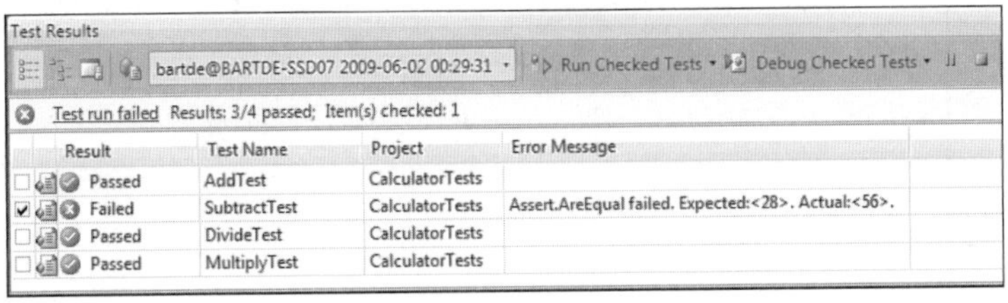

FIGURE 3.64   Test results.

Turns out I introduced some error in the Subtract method code, as caught by the unit test. Or the test could be wrong. Regardless, a failed test case screams for immediate attention to track down the problem. Notice you can also debug through tests cases, just like regular program code.

Tightly integrated with unit testing is the ability to analyze code coverage. It's always a worthy goal to keep code coverage numbers high (90% as a bare minimum is a good goal, preferably more) so that you can be confident about the thoroughness of your test cases. Visual Studio actually has built-in code highlighting to contrast the pieces of code that were hit during testing from those that weren't.

Team Development

To finish off our in-depth exploration of Visual Studio 2010 tooling support, we take a brief look at support for developing software in a team context. Today's enterprise applications are rarely ever written by a single developer or even by a handful of developers. For example, the .NET Framework itself has hundreds of developers and testers working on it on a day-to-day basis.

Team System and Team Foundation Server

To deal with the complexities of such an organization, Visual Studio Team System (VSTS) provides development teams with a rich set of tools. Besides work item and bug tracking, project status reporting, and centralized document libraries, source control is likely the most visible aspect of team development.

The entry point for the use of Team Foundation Server (TFS) is the Team Explorer window integrated in Visual Studio 2010 (see Figure 3.65).

Here is a quick overview of the different nodes in the Team Explorer tree view:

▶ The root node represents the **TFS server** we're connected to. One of the nice things about TFS is its use of HTTP(S) web services (so there is no hassle with port configurations). Underneath the server, different **team projects** are displayed.

▶ **Work Items** is the collective name for bug descriptions and tasks assigned to members of the team. Queries can be defined to search on different fields in the database. Via the Work Items view, bugs can be opened, resolved, and so on.

FIGURE 3.65   Team Explorer in Visual Studio 2010.

▶ **Documents** displays all sorts of documentation—Word documents, Visio diagrams, plain old text files, and such—that accompany the project. Those are also available through a SharePoint web interface.

▶ **Reports** leverages the SQL Server Reporting Services technology to display information about various aspects of the project to monitor its state. Examples include bug counts, code statistics, and so on.

▶ **Builds** allows developers to set up build definitions that can be used for product builds, either locally or remotely. It's a good practice for team development to have a healthy product build at all times. Automated build facilities allow configuration of daily builds and such.

▶ **Source Control** is where source code is managed through various operations to streamline the process of multiple developers working on the code simultaneously. This is further integrated with Solution Explorer.

Source Control

Source control stores source code centrally on a server and provides services to manage simultaneous updates by developers. When a code file requires modification, it's checked out to allow for local editing. After making (and testing) the changes, the opposite operation of checking in is used to send updates to the source database. If a conflicting edit is detected, tools assist in resolving that conflict by merging changes.

Figure 3.66 shows the presence of source control in Visual Studio 2010, including rich context menus in Solution Explorer and the Source Control Explorer window.

Other capabilities of source control include rich source code versioning (enabling going back in time), shelving edits for code review by peer developers, correlation of check-ins to resolved bugs, and the creation of branches in the source tree to give different feature crews their own playgrounds.

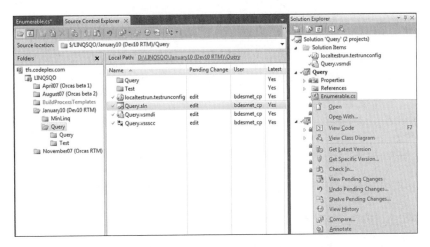

FIGURE 3.66   Source control integrated in Visual Studio 2010.

CODEPLEX

In Figure 3.65 and Figure 3.66, I've been connecting to a team project stored on the CodePlex website. CodePlex is an opensource project community provided by Microsoft and based on Team Foundation Server as the back-end technology. The project I'm using here is LINQ SQO (for Standard Query Operators) at http://linqsqo.codeplex.com. It contains a custom implementation of LINQ to Objects, something we'll talk about much more in later chapters.

Summary

In this chapter, we installed the .NET Framework 4 and went through the motions of building our first trivial but illustrative C# console application. While doing so, we focused on the development process of writing and compiling code, and then we took a look at how to inspect it using .NET Reflector. Because it's unrealistic today to build software without decent tooling support, we explored various aspects of the Visual Studio 2010 family. We covered integrated source exploration, build and debugging support, and took a peek at the various project types and associated tools available.

In the next chapter, we leave the realm of extensive tooling for a while and learn about the core fundamentals of the C# language.

CHAPTER 4

Language Essentials

IN THIS CHAPTER

▶ The Entry Point 171

▶ Keywords 177

▶ A Primer on Types 180

▶ Built-In Types 185

▶ Local Variables 209

▶ Intermezzo on Comments 220

▶ Arrays 228

▶ The Null Reference 237

▶ Nullable Value Types 240

Essentials are important. This is no different with programming languages, so we start by focusing on the essences of the C# programming language: built-in types, variables, expressions and statements, control flow, methods, and so on.

The Entry Point

To keep things simple, we'll make exclusive use of console applications in the language-oriented chapters. Doing so allows us to concentrate on the essentials of the programming language without getting distracted by user interface definitions and so on.

One thing to consider first is the managed code entry point, which is where execution of the program starts. Different types of applications have such an entry point, including console applications and GUI applications built with Windows Forms or Windows Presentation Foundation (WPF). Other technologies, such as ASP.NET web applications, start execution of managed code in a different way, but let's not go there now.

A Trivial Console Application

By far the simplest managed code application that can be written in C# is one that doesn't do anything useful. The following is only of academic interest, yes, but we have to start somewhere:

```
class Program
{
    static void Main()
    {
    }
}
```

Main is the managed code entry-point method for our application. Its body, delimited by curly braces, contains the statements that get executed by the application. In this case, our method body is empty.

CASE SENSITIVITY

Notice the casing of the Main method, with its first character uppercase. C# is a case-sensitive language, just like other C derivatives such as C++ and Java. In other words, method names that differ only in case denote different methods; so main and Main are not the same. C# requires the managed code entry point to be styled exactly as shown in the previous fragment.

Case sensitivity applies not only to method names. Keywords, names for types and their members, namespaces—they all are subject to case-sensitive treatment.

Let's point out an important point immediately. For an assembly to be Common Language Specification (CLS)-compliant, no publicly visible type or member should differ only in case as compared to one of its peers. If this were the situation, non-case-sensitive languages like Visual Basic would be in trouble, resolving the name unambiguously.

C# doesn't have the notion of global methods, meaning that all methods (and other sorts of members, as you will see) need to be contained in a type definition. In our example, the type is a class called Program. In the next chapter, we look at the distinction between types and classes, so ignore this detail for now.

Method Signatures

Methods also have a signature, which you could see as the recipe that describes how the method is to be called. The important parts of a method signature include the method name, the return type, and the parameters. It also contains modifiers that are used to "modify" the behavior of the method.

Let's decipher our Main method signature shown in Figure 4.1 with regard to these concepts:

▶ One modifier, the *static* keyword, is applied to the method. This means the method does not operate on a specific instance of the containing type. To explain this further, we first have to learn about types and object-oriented programming, which is subject of Chapter 14, "Object-Oriented Programming." Stay tuned.

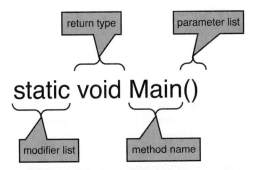

FIGURE 4.1   Decomposing the Main method signature.

▶ The return type of the method is void. As the name implies, this means the method returns nothing, making it a *procedure*. If the method were to return something, we would call it a *function*. Languages such as Visual Basic make this difference explicit by declaring procedures with a Sub keyword and functions with a Function keyword. C# doesn't make this distinction: void indicates a procedure.

▶ As we already know, Main is the name of the method. This name is used to *call* the method (for example, from other places in the program or from other libraries). Main is a bit different, being the entry point called by the CLR directly.

▶ Our entry point has an empty parameter list surrounded by parentheses, meaning the caller can't supply input for it when making a call. You'll see in just a minute that different signatures for the entry point are accepted to deal with command-line arguments. Even when empty, this pair of parentheses cannot be omitted.

We refine the definition of a method signature in Chapter 10, "Methods," when talking about visibility and generic methods.

IS VOID A FIRST-CLASS TYPE?

Although we haven't learned about types just yet, the curious reader will no doubt wonder whether void, something used to denote nothing, is a true type. Slightly disappointing, the answer is no. You'll see later why such a first-class treatment could be useful, but to be honest it's not a big deal.

Allowed Entry-Point Signatures

As we all know, invocation of programs in operating systems supports passing in command-line parameters. In addition, executables can provide an exit code upon termination, indicating the result of the invocation, with a zero value typically denoting a success state. To enable those scenarios, four different signatures for the Main method are permitted:

```
static void Main()
static int Main()
static void Main(string[] args)
static int Main(string[] args)
```

Those are essentially the four combinations formed by the following:

► Returning an integer-valued exit code or none at all

► Accepting an array of command-line arguments or none at all

Only one entry point can be defined per executable assembly, so a choice must be made. The default one chosen by Visual Studio is the third, taking in an array of command-line arguments but returning no exit code. In practice, this means the CLR supplies a zero-valued exit code on behalf of the developer, indicating a successful invocation and execution.

WINDOWS POWERSHELL

The next-generation command-line, scripting, and automation environment on the Microsoft platform is Windows PowerShell. One of the things it does fundamentally different from the classic Windows command-line interpreter involves its treatment of commands.

In Windows PowerShell, commands are replaced by cmdlets (pronounced "commandlets") that all have very specialized tasks and can be combined easily by building a pipeline out of them. The following is an example of such a pipeline:

```
dir ¦ where { $_.WorkingSet64 -gt 10MB } ¦ format-table
```

Input and output from those cmdlets is no longer based on string arguments and exit codes but instead consists of full-fledged .NET objects. Because of this fundamentally different approach, cmdlets are not written as managed executables but as classes defined in a managed class library.

In the meantime, I silently hope for the day to come when a Windows PowerShell cmdlet project template is provided by default in Visual Studio.

To illustrate a slightly more meaningful console application, taking advantage of the richest entry-point signature available, take a look at the following piece of code:

```
using System;

class Program
{
    static int Main(string[] args)
    {
        foreach (string arg in args)
        {
            Console.WriteLine(arg);
        }

        return args.Length;
    }
}
```

Here we've added quite a bit of stuff, but don't worry. By the end of the chapter, you'll be familiar with all of it. Can you guess what the program does now? It takes in an array of command-line arguments, iterates over it using a `foreach` loop, and calls the `Console.WriteLine` method to print each argument on a separate line. Finally, it returns the value of the `Length` property of the array.

WHERE'S THE EXECUTABLE NAME?

In contrast to C's main entry point, the command-line arguments array in C# does not contain the program's executable filename. In fact, this is more logical because the user is invoking the program with some arguments, and clearly the program name is not an argument to itself. However, it makes sense to get the name of the program in various contexts. A typical example is to print a command-line usage note on the screen in case invalid arguments are specified, something like this:

```
Usage: myapp.exe -U:<username> -P:<password>
```

One way to get to the executable's name in managed code is by means of the reflection application programming interfaces (APIs), something we discuss in Chapter 21, "Reflection." Another solution is to get the full command line by calling the `Environment.GetCommandLineArgs` method. This returns a string array with the first element set to the executable filename.

Running the Sample

Based on the example in Chapter 3, you should be able to write our trivial console application's code in an editor of choice, compile it, and run it. To illustrate matters one more time, we'll go through the motions of compiling the application from the command line and show its use. Figure 4.2 shows the use of the little application we've written and compiled.

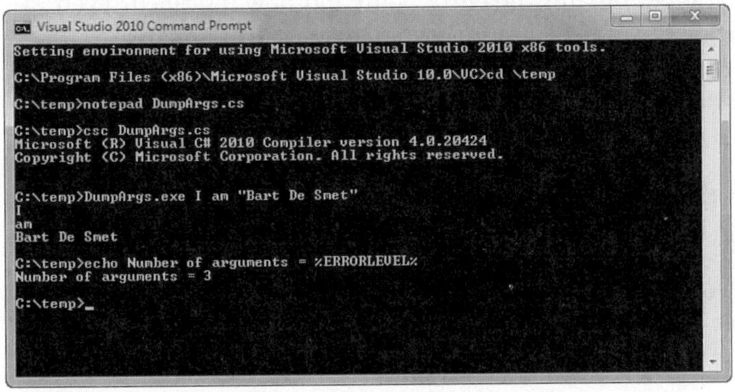

FIGURE 4.2   Compiling and running the application.

After having written the code in Notepad, saving it to a file with a .cs extension (a convention, not a requirement), we called the C# command-line compiler csc.exe on it. Next, we invoked the resulting executable passing in three command-line arguments, which are subsequently written to the screen. Finally, we use the ERRORLEVEL environment variable to print the exit code of the last command invocation. This corresponds to the value returned from the entry-point method, in our case the length of the arguments array.

Notice the double quotes around the last argument used in the preceding example. Those are processed by the command-line interpreter as a delimiter for a single argument, so the managed code application receives only three arguments in this case. If we had omitted the quotes, five distinct arguments would be observed.

TIP

Try misspelling the entry point's name (for example, by using invalid casing) or specifying more than one entry-point method and observe the compiler's error reporting on the matter. The fact that the C# compiler expects to find a suitable entry-point method is because we're compiling as a console application. This is because we've omitted the /target:<type> compiler switch, defaulting to an exe type. Try omitting the entry-point method and compile using /target:library to see the compiler ignoring the lack of an entry point when building a class library assembly with .dll extension instead.

When you look at the C# command-line compiler options for /target, you see another type called winexe. What's the difference between it and the (default) .exe type? The answer lies in the window provided by the OS loader. For an .exe type, a console user interface (CUI) is provided to the application, resulting in the typical black background command-line interpreter look and feel. For winexe, a graphical user interface (GUI) window is provided (for example, for use by applications based on Windows Forms or WPF).

Under the Hood

How does the CLR know what type contains the entry point and how it's called? Even though we didn't explicitly state this, the containing type's name doesn't matter. In line with Visual Studio's choice, we used Program, but that's not mandatory. So the idea of the CLR having hard-coded knowledge about looking for a method called Main on a type called Program falls apart.

It turns out the CLR doesn't care about the name of the method or its containing type at all; instead, the answer lies in metadata used to keep track of the entry-point method within the defining assembly. You can see this using ildasm.exe when looking at the code for the entry-point method. From a Visual Studio 2010 command prompt, run ildasm on the executable file and double-click the Main method in the Program class. Figure 4.3 shows what you see.

So why does C# require the entry point to be called Main if the CLR doesn't care? Just a matter of convenience, really. For one thing, looking for a method called Main in a source base immediately points you to the starting point of the application because only one entry point can be defined per assembly. Also if another name were to be allowed, developers would need some way to specify the entry-point method, either through a compiler switch or by means of a specialized keyword. Clearly overkill, so a naming convention in line with other C-style languages was chosen, with Main being the obvious choice.

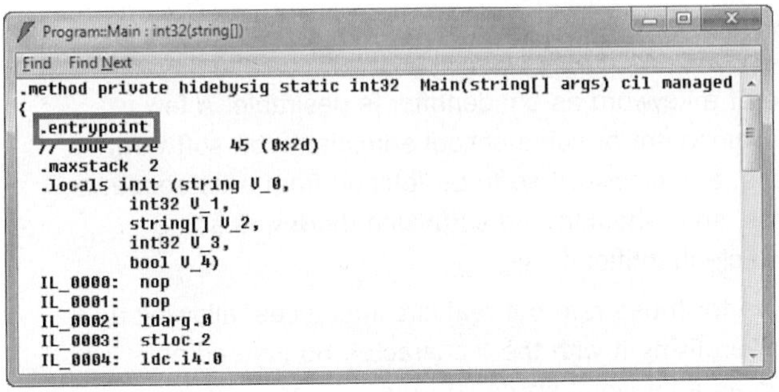

FIGURE 4.3   The .entrypoint metadata token in IL.

THE STATHREAD FOSSIL

In some older versions of Visual Studio, the generated entry-point method for a console application was decorated with a custom attribute, like this:

```
[STAThread]
static void Main()
{
}
```

As a matter of fact, the generated entry-point methods for Windows Forms and WPF applications still (and likely always will) have this STAThread attribute applied. What's its purpose? The answer lies in the COM roots that are deeply entangled in the operating system foundation. STA stands for single-threaded apartment, the most common mode of operation for various COM components. A good example of its use is in user interface programming on Windows.

Luckily, the managed code developer rarely needs to know about this unless dealing with COM interop directly. And if the attribute is omitted in, say, a WPF application, an exception will be thrown indicating to the developer to put it back.

Keywords

In our little example, we've already seen various keywords. Keywords source code character sequences reserved by the language for some special meaning, and therefore they cannot be used as identifiers in the user's code.

So far, the keywords we've seen are class, foreach, in, int, return, static, string, using, and void. At the time of this writing, C# has 78 reserved keywords. This sounds like an incredibly large number, but by the end of this chapter you'll already have seen about half of them.

@

Under rare circumstances, the use of a keyword as an identifier is desirable. A few years ago, I was involved in the development of some school administration software. Information about students, courses, and classes had to be fetched from a database. The singular form of *classes* is *class*, so it shouldn't be surprising there was some desire to use class as a local variable identifier.

Luckily, C# provides an escape valve for those rare but real circumstances, allowing a reserved keyword to be escaped by prefixing it with the @ character. So instead of writing class, which would be seen as a keyword, we could write @class.

Notice that the @ doesn't become part of the identifier string; it's just a way to escape the keyword meaning during the lexing phase of compilation. This means if such an identifier is to be exposed on the surface of some type (for example, by means of a method argument), it reads as if the In the light of CLS compliance, it's strongly discouraged to expose names that could have a reserved meaning to the outside world because other languages might not be able to deal with proper escaping. So if you use the @ trick, limit yourself to local variables or internal state.

Contextual Keywords

A language with too many reserved keywords can definitely be annoying to developers because of the need to escape keywords all over the place. Especially because keywords are typically based on the English language, clashes with identifiers are a very real risk. Imagine what would happen if value were a reserved keyword:

```
int @value = discount.Value;
```

As a matter of fact, value has a reserved meaning in C# but only in certain contexts. This combines the best of both worlds, using natural-sounding English words to represent programming language features while leaving the word available for use as an identifier in certain contexts. You can refer to those identifiers with occasional special meaning as *contextual keywords*, although this is not an official term used in the C# language specification.

Here is the illustration of the use of the value contextual keywords in a property set accessor:

```
private int _age;

public int Age
{
    get { return _age; }
    set { _age = value; }
}
```

You'll learn more about properties in subsequent chapters. Actually, the get and set keywords used in declaring property accessors are treated in a context-sensitive manner, too.

Similarly, the value identifier has a specialized meaning in the context of indexers and events. Thanks to this contextual treatment, the use of value is not reserved elsewhere, so you can just write the following:

```
int value = discount.Value;
```

ON BACKWARD COMPATIBILITY AND KEYWORD REUSE

Backward compatibility is a big deal to the C# programming language. Every time a new version is released, it's key to ensure existing code keeps compiling fine. Contextual keywords are one way to ensure this. When new keywords are required to raise the expressiveness of the language required for new language features, they're made into keywords only in certain contexts.

Even though C# 1.0 didn't have compatibility issues to worry about, contextual keywords were used to reduce the number of reserved words that are commonly used in English lingo, such as value, get, and set. In C# 2.0, new contextual keywords were added (for example, the where keyword used for generic constraints).

Going even further with this, certain keywords are reused in different contexts where they have a different meaning. This might sound confusing, but actually it's not that bad. For example, given that the where keyword was already used in C# 2.0 and version 3 wanted to add query comprehension syntax, what would be the obvious choice to express a filter? Right, where strikes again.

Syntax Highlighting in Visual Studio

Keywords, including ones that have a contextual characteristic, are highlighted in the Visual Studio code editor. Assuming a default color scheme, sequences of characters that have a special meaning in a given context are blue.

For Figure 4.4, I've changed the default setting to make keywords appear bold. Settings to control the code editor's look and feel can be found under Tools, Options, Environment, Fonts and Colors. Select Keyword under Display items to control this setting for (contextual) keywords. Notice how the background compiler for C# recognizes the contextual use of the value keyword, asking the code editor to format it appropriately only in that particular context.

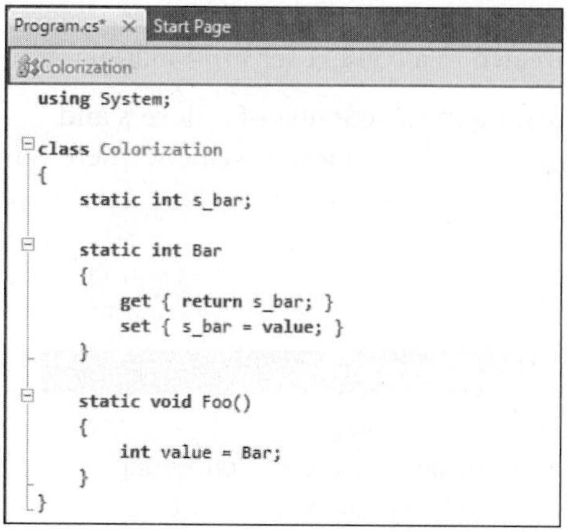

```
Program.cs*  ×   Start Page
Colorization
  using System;

  class Colorization
  {
      static int s_bar;

      static int Bar
      {
          get { return s_bar; }
          set { s_bar = value; }
      }

      static void Foo()
      {
          int value = Bar;
      }
  }
```

FIGURE 4.4   Syntax highlighting in Visual Studio.

A Primer on Types

Types are the bread and butter for managed code developers. Without going into too much detail at this point—because we'll dedicate whole chapters to in-depth exploration of types—it's good to have some basic understanding about what comprises a type.

Code and Data

Think of types as entities containing code and/or data. You can consider data to be the most important part here, based on object-oriented considerations and whatnot. Given a set of primitive types, as you'll see in just a minute, new types can be defined. On the field of data, defining a type can be seen as an act of composition.

For example, to represent a person object, you could define a Person class type containing fields to hold the relevant data:

```
class Person
{
    private string _name;
    private int _age;

    public Person(string name, int age)
    {
        _name = name;
        _age = age;
    }

    public void Print()
    {
```

```
        Console.WriteLine(_name + " is " + _age + " years young");
    }
}
```

In this example, the fields are called _name and _age. The private keyword is a modifier used to define the visibility for each field.

Fields are members that define the data the enclosing type consists of. Other members deal with the code associated with the type. Code in this context is not in the sense of source code, but executable instructions that can operate on data. Samples of such members include methods, properties, indexers, events, and so on.

A CRISP LINE BETWEEN CODE AND DATA?

The line between code and data might be bit blurry at times. For example, properties provide a means to access the data contained in an object, but strictly speaking they consist of a pair of getter and setter methods. Methods should be categorized as code (obviously).

Properties, as you will see in Chapter 11, "Fields, Properties, and Indexers," are most commonly used as smart fields, giving them a very data-centric feeling. In the context of this section, however, we think about data in a representational fashion: To represent a person object, a string is required for the name, and an integer value is used for the person's age.

The Person class example contains two pieces of code, both of which are methods. One method prints the person's name and age to the screen. The other one is a special kind of method, called a *constructor*. It's used to create instances of the type, as discussed in the next section.

Code and data aspects of a class called Person are contrasted in Figure 4.5.

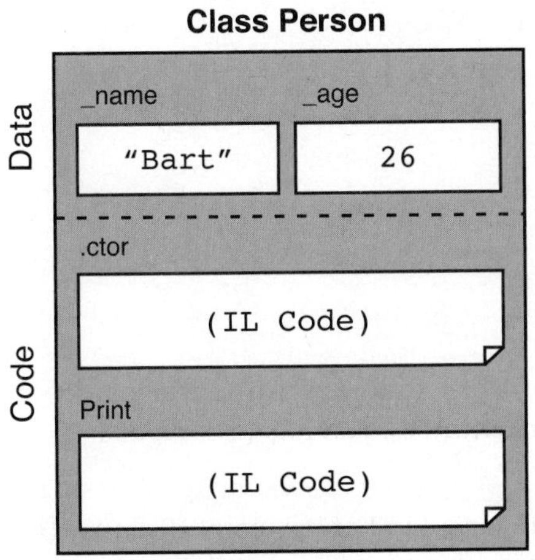

FIGURE 4.5   Code and data.

Alternative terms for code and data are, respectively, *actions* and *state*, as used in the C# language specification. Other languages use yet different terms. Just be consistent.

Types, Objects, and Instances

You've seen how types are containers for data and/or code. While some types may just contain data, others may solely consist of code. That's just a first order approximation; further refinement is desirable. Notice how I've carefully used two terms from the preceding section: person *class* versus person *object*. So what's the distinction between the two?

Types are just blueprints that describe the shape of an object in terms of data contained in it and code operating on it. By themselves, types are just a way to classify different sorts of things our program needs to deal with in a safe manner. A thorough discussion of type safety is deferred until Chapter 11. An example of a type is Person, with a capital P, as we declared the class as such.

Objects are concrete *instances* of such types. Concrete things that can be used at runtime, that is. In our example, a person called Bart, aged 26, can be represented as an instance of type Person.

A logical question is how to go from a type to an instance of it. This operation is required to create a concrete object to work with (for example, representing some person). Here constructors enter the picture. Think of a constructor as some kind of factory that knows how to produce concrete objects from type blueprints.

Figure 4.6 illustrates this concept in an abstract way. Given a type T, which just defines the shape of an object (as indicated with dashed lines), the constructor for T acts as a factory producing a concrete object (as indicated with the solid block).

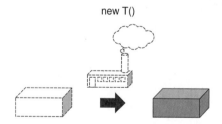

new T()

FIGURE 4.6   Abstract representation of a constructor.

In C#, constructors are invoked by using the new keyword, followed by the type name and a (possibly empty) set of parameters between parentheses, just like with regular method calls.

For our Person type, you could look at the factory as some kind of passport office that produces person objects from a given name and age, as shown in Figure 4.7. (Yes, I know, birthday would be more accurate.)

new Person("Bart", 26)

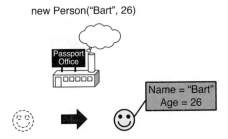

FIGURE 4.7   Creating an object of type `Person`.

FACTORY METHODS

The use of the word *factory* in this context is very appropriate, but in the world of code design patterns it's been overloaded. A design pattern called *factory method* exists to create object instances in a different way, avoiding direct use of constructors. In an object-oriented setting, this technique can be useful for returning an object of a specific subclass, depending on the input to the method. More information on object-oriented programming appears in Chapter 14.

Variables

To store data, we need storage cells. Those are called *variables* and always have an associated type. A type-safe language like C# guarantees the values stored in such a variable have the appropriate type. If this weren't the case, it would be possible to look at a `Person` instance as if it were a `Fruit` instance, something that doesn't make sense and clearly indicates a code defect.

Variables can occur in various places. Actually, we've seen most of them already. The first one is as a *local variable*:

```
int value = discount.Value;
```

This declares a variable of type `int` and immediately assigns it some value by retrieving the `Value` property (or field, if bad coding style is used) from another variable called `discount`.

Where did this `discount` variable come from? It could be a local variable by itself but could equally well be passed in as a parameter to a method:

```
public void ApplyDiscount(Cart cart, Discount discount)
{
    int value = discount.Value;
    // ...
}
```

The second line of the shown method body is a single-line comment. We'll look at commenting styles separately at a later point. I'm just using it to indicate omitted code you can fantasize about wildly.

Another variable category is found with fields, actually subdivided into two subcategories: static and instance ones. For this distinction, see Chapter 9, "Introducing Types," in the section, "Static Versus Instance." Here is an example of two instance variables, for the _age and _name fields.

```
class Person
{
    private string _name;
    private int _age;

    // ...
}
```

Other variable categories include array elements and output parameters, as you'll see later. For now, remember that variables are storage cells. What precisely they contain is explained in the next section.

Classes and Other Types

So far, we've not made the distinction between a class and a type concrete. The CLR supports multiple sorts of types (not to say "types of types"), but one big top-level distinction can be made, as follows:

- ▶ Variables of a **value type** immediately contain the data. When assigned to another variable (for example, also when passing to a method parameter), the contents are copied by value. So value types are passed by value (by default).

- ▶ Variables of a **reference type** store a reference to the data. This means multiple variables can refer to the same object, a principle called aliasing. So reference types are passed by reference.

The definition of a reference type is called a *class*, whereas that of a value type is called a *struct*. Corresponding keywords exist in C# to build self-defined types.

Ignore further implementation details for now; we discuss them in Chapter 9. To illustrate matters, analyze Figures 4.8 and 4.9 carefully.

Notice how the type tag in Figure 4.8 contains System.Int32 as opposed to int. Those are synonymous in C#, as you'll see when we discuss built-in types. What really matters in this figure is the fact that the assignment of x1 to x2 copied the value between cells. We have not aliased 42 by having two references to it; instead, we have two copies of the same value that live independently from each other.

On the other hand, with reference types, aliasing occurs as shown in Figure 4.9. For example, when manipulating the person object through either of the two variables that refer to it, the change becomes visible to both. Both variables refer to the same data, and no copies of that data are made. Also notice how the _name field has a reference type, causing a similar referencing situation. One thing we've omitted from this discussion for now is the concept of the null literal.

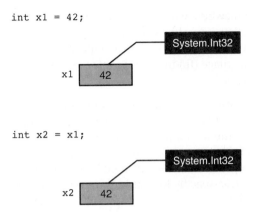

```
int x1 = 42;
```

```
int x2 = x1;
```

FIGURE 4.8   Value types are copied and passed by value.

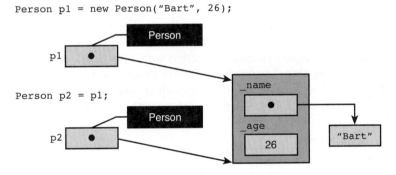

```
Person p1 = new Person("Bart", 26);
```

```
Person p2 = p1;
```

FIGURE 4.9   Reference types cause aliasing.

Besides classes, other sorts of reference types exist in the world of managed code. Interfaces, delegates, and arrays are examples of reference types. Under the umbrella of value types, we find things such as enumerations and nullable types. Enumerations are discussed in Chapter 11 in the section, "An Intermezzo on Enums." More information on nullable types appears during the discussion of expressions and operators in Chapter 5, "Expressions and Operators." For now, let's take a look at some of the primitive types.

Built-In Types

Classes and structs can be used to define new reference or value types, respectively, by defining fields for data storage. As you saw previously, fields are classified as variables, and all variables have a type. Guess what? We just spotted a recursive definition: Value types and reference types are composed of other types.

Clearly, this recursive definition needs to stop somewhere with a base case. In other words, some primitive types should be available that cannot be decomposed any further by means of fields. One way to determine such types is by looking at the types the CLR natively knows about in terms of intermediate language (IL) instructions (for example, for addition of two integers of floating-point numbers).

Actually, there are three views on the world of built-in types. First, at the lowest level there's the CLR representation of a type, consisting of bit patterns. One level up, we find ourselves in the Base Class Library (BCL)'s view of the world, where convenient types are defined to cover up the low-level details. An example is `System.Int32` to represent a 32-bit integer value as represented by the CLR. Those types add convenient members that make life easier for developers. Finally, there's the language-specific look at built-in types, where keywords are defined as aliases for the underlying BCL types. For example, in C# in stands for `System.Int32`.

Integral Types

Integral types are one category of built-in value types. They have an integral numeric value represented by a number of bits (not surprisingly in powers of two) and can either be signed or unsigned.

The u prefix is typically used as a prefix in the C# reserved word for those types to denote unsigned integral types. A notable exception is byte, which is unsigned, where an s prefix is used to indicate the signed variant. This aligns with what developers spontaneously think of when you say "byte" (range 0x00 to 0xFF to say it in hex). And the English pronunciation of "ubyte" didn't sound too appealing either! Table 4.1 summarizes the integral types with their C# and BCL names, along with their ranges.

TABLE 4.1   Integral Types

C#	BCL Type	Range
sbyte	System.SByte	−128 to 127
byte	System.Byte	0 to 255
short	System.Int16	−32,768 to 32,767
ushort	System.UInt16	0 to 65,535
int	System.Int32	−2,147,483,648 to 2,147,483,647
uint	System.UInt32	0 to 4,294,967,295
long	System.Int64	−9,223,372,036,854,775,808 to 9,223,372,036,854,775,807
ulong	System.UInt64	0 to 18,446,744,073,709,551,615
char	System.Char	0 to 65,535 (U+0000 to U+ffff)

Notice this aliasing of BCL types with C# reserved words is a constant mapping, independent from the machine hardware the programs run on. It's the Just-in-Time (JIT) compiler's job to ensure a variable's precision is respected exactly on the platform where the code is run.

HOW TO CALCULATE INTEGRAL TYPE PRECISION

If you're wondering where the range of integral types comes from, it's simply determined by the number of bits available. Given n bits, the range for unsigned values goes from 0 to $2^n - 1$. For signed values, the range stretches from $-2^{(n-1)}$ to $2^{(n-1)}$ $- 1$. Luckily, you don't need to know this because the BCL types have each two properties called `MinValue` and `MaxValue` to get this very information.

WHAT ABOUT ARBITRARY PRECISION ARITHMETIC?

Even though the range of 64-bit numbers might seem astonishingly large, it often does not suffice for scientific computations. This limitation reflects the machine-oriented nature of the CLR, where arithmetic IL instructions ultimately get JIT compiled into efficient CPU instructions.

Part of the appeal of functional languages to the scientific community is their large integer support. This is no different with F#, which introduced a bigint type. Similarly, dynamic languages on the DLR introduced their own big integer number types. To consolidate those types, .NET 4.0 introduced a `BigInteger` type with arbitrary precision in the `System.Numerics` namespace.

Clearly, register-based processors can't cope with arbitrary long numbers because they can't fit in the available registers for the ALU (arithmetic logical unit) to carry out computations. Therefore, `BigInteger` numbers are represented as an *array* of 32-bit integers, with parts of the arithmetic operations defined in managed code. This has a cost associated with it, but rest assured the type has been optimized to withstand the toughest calculations efficiently.

At the time of this writing, C# doesn't have a reserved word to alias the `BigInteger` type. Personally, I find this a good thing because C#'s numeric types have always had a machine-like performance profile. Adding `bigint` would disturb this and pose a potential pitfall for the unaware developer who thinks "arbitrary" is always better than "fixed."

Integral Literals

The ability to declare variables of integral types is one thing; the ability to assign values to them is a necessity. *Literals* are representations of values in source code that are readily understood by the compiler and turned into the correct representation at compile time.

Being integral numbers, an obvious choice for literals is to allow users to write them as is, without culture-specific notation, that is (for example, not using thousands separator characters). The following are a few examples:

```
byte b = 123;
short s = -234;
uint i = 1000000;
```

Literals do not necessarily appear is local variable assignments. For example, they can equally appear as parameters to a method.

As an alternative to decimal notation, C# also supports hexadecimal notation by use of the 0x of 0X prefix in a literal. Valid characters to follow this prefix include the 0–9 digits as well as the characters a–f (either uppercase or lowercase). For example:

```
byte b = 0x7B;
short s = 0xF15;
uint i = 0x989680;
```

NO OCTAL OR BINARY?

C# supports neither octal nor binary notation for integral literals. Those tend to be used much less than decimal and hexadecimal, but there's also a practical reason for it. Octal literals have been historically written down in various languages (such as C) using a 0 character as the prefix. However, it's not unlikely for developers to pad integral values with 0s in the front to nicely align source code. Or to write down flight number 047 as an integral value. It's highly unlikely the user meant octal in such a case. Therefore, C# chose to prevent this kind of mistake from happening.

Besides prefixes for hexadecimal, suffixes exist, too. But they serve a very different goal: to specify the desired precision. Why do we need this at all? For starters, the following code simply works as you expect it to:

```
long l = 42;
```

Even though the value 42 fits in an sbyte or byte, the fact the variable is declared to be a long means it has 64 bits of signed precision. However, in other cases, you might need to force a literal to have a certain precision for other things to work. Such a case exists when multiple method *overloads* exist (that is, methods with the same name but different signatures). For example, the System.Math class has overloads for the Abs (absolute value) method that take in different numeric types, such as int and long:

```
int Abs(int value);
long Abs(long value);
// ...
```

Now, suppose you need to take the absolute value of –2,147,483,648. Okay, I know, because this a mathematically pure function we could just calculate it upfront if we were using only a constant input value anyway. But I'm just setting the scene with the simplest possible example, so bear with me:

```
long res = Math.Abs(-2147483648);
```

If we look at the table with integral type precisions, we see that the absolute value doesn't fit in an int, so we need a uint or some long instead. Therefore, we assign the result to a long, to pick one. However, the compiler types the literal passed in as a parameter to be an int, and hence the first method is chosen:

```
int Abs(int value);
```

Because this method does not know how to represent the value 2,147,483,648 as an int required by the return type, it blows up with a runtime exception, effectively terminating our program forcefully.

What we need here is a way to tell the compiler to treat the literal not as an int but as a long, for it to pick the other overload. Different workarounds exist, ranging from using an intermediate local variable to the use of a *conversion* (see further). However, the use of an integer type suffix is more appropriate here. Three such suffixes exist: u, l, and ul (all of which can be written using any casing you want). The first one, u, indicates to treat the literal as unsigned. Next, l, means to treat it as a long. And finally, ul means to treat it as an unsigned long.

Here's our fixed example using an integer type suffix:

```
long res = Math.Abs(-2147483648L);
```

For the precise rules for determining the type of an integral literal, refer to the official C# specification, section 2.4.4.2.

NON-CASE-SENSITIVE SUFFIXES

Why are those type suffixes not case-sensitive, while C# is a case-sensitive language? Every keyword being lowercased, the natural choice would be to only allow this natural feeling style for suffix characters. However, a problem exists for the lowercase letter l looking similar to numeral 1 in lots of fonts. It is clearer to write L to avoid this confusion. To allow this and keep the typical style of lowercase, characters occurring in integral literals (including 0x and the hexadecimal letters) are not case-sensitive. This makes more sense than having one exception to the lowercase rule (just for an L).

Character Literals

The char type is used to represent a single Unicode character. Character literals consist of single quotes containing the character to be represented, or an *escape sequence*. A few examples not involving the use of escapes are shown here:

```
char c1 = 'A';
char c2 = 'b';
char c3 = ' ';
char c4 = '#';
```

Some characters need escaping using the backslash character as a prefix. Those are \' (single quote), \" (double quote), \\ (backslash), \0 (null character), '\a' (alert, beeping the system speaker), '\b' (backspace), '\f' (form feed), '\n' (new line), '\r' (carriage return), '\t' (horizontal tab) and '\v' (vertical tab). Some of these are old treasures you'll rarely ever use. Memorizing quotes and newline and horizontal tab characters should suffice for day-to-day programming activities.

Escape sequences also permit the use of a character's hexadecimal representation by prefixing it with \x. One to four hexadecimal digits can be specified, with the letters being not case sensitive. Examples of the use of escapes are shown here:

```
char c5 = '\t';
char c6 = '\n';
char c7 = '\x20';     // a space
char c8 = '\x2260';   // "not equal to" symbol
```

Floating-Point Types

You might remember the different types of numbers from grade school. Natural numbers correspond to unsigned integral values, but where are the real numbers (not to mention fractional numbers)? In the world of computer science, the answer is twofold, with a significant difference with regard to precision. As humans, we've embraced the decimal system, likely directly related to the number of fingers we're born with. Computers work with binary representation, though. This poses a problem with real numbers, some of which can't be represented exactly in binary. Let's give it a try:

```
0.30  <  1/2         = 0.5
0.30  >  1/4         = 0.25
0.30  <  1/4 + 1/8   = 0.375
0.30  <  1/4 + 1/16  = 0.3125
0.30  >  1/4 + 1/32  = 0.28125
```

We can continue refining this sum of base-2 fractions to get closer and closer to 0.30, but we cannot reach it precisely using binary representation. This is one of the things that makes the use of real numbers on computers hard.

The approach shown in Table 4.2 is a simplification of the concept of floating-point numbers, as you will see in just a minute. An alternative exists that avoids the use of those fractions and is called *decimal numbers*. Those are the topic of the next section. But first, what are the floating-point types supported in C#?

TABLE 4.2   Floating-Point Types

C#	BCL Type	Approximate Range	Precision
float	System.Single	$\pm 1.5 \times 10^{-45}$ to $\pm 3.4 \times 10^{38}$	7 digits
double	System.Double	$\pm 5.0 \times 10^{-324}$ to $\pm 1.7 \times 10^{308}$	15–16 digits

Why those strange ranges, and why are they approximate? And what's up with the number of digits precision? The answer lies in the *floating* part. Stay tuned.

Internal Representation

A float is represented using 32 bits; a double uses 64 bits. The meaning of those bits does not simply correspond to a fixed binary position, though. If it did, we would have to draw the line between positions before and after the comma somewhere. What's wrong with that? One observation about the use of real numbers is this: Both big numbers (for example, the light speed in meters per seconds has quite an impressive value) and small numbers (for example, the size of an electron in meters is embarrassingly small) are popular. For the one, we need bits as high (or large) as we can get. For the others, we need bits as low (or small) as we can get. This is clearly conflicting.

To accommodate both situations, floating-point numbers are used. As the name implies, the position of the point (decimal separator) is not fixed; instead, it floats. To achieve this, the bit representation of floating numbers is divided into three parts:

▸ One single bit is used for the **sign**, indicating a positive (0) or negative (1) number.

▸ A number of bits (8 for single precision, 11 for double precision) is used to represent an **exponent** (or coefficient).

▸ The remaining bits (23 for single precision, 52 for double precision) indicate the **mantissa** (or significand).

The exponent itself is offset relative to a so-called **bias**, which has value the 127 for single precision and 1023 for double precision. All of this might sound frightening, but it's not that hard to understand using a picture (see Figure 4.10).

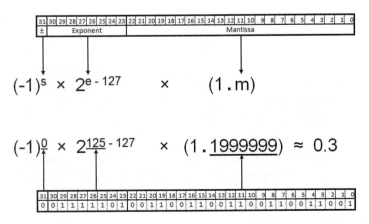

FIGURE 4.10   32-bit floating-point representation of 0.3.

IEEE-754

Floating points are a well-specified concept implemented by many platforms. The standard implemented by the CLR (and hence C# and other managed code languages) is the popular IEEE-754 standard for floating-point numbers. There's more to it than just the formula discussed here, however. The standard also defines the results of operations like division by zero and calculation with infinities.

As you can see from the figure, some fractional numbers, like 0.3, can be approximated very well but can't be represented exactly. In lots of applications, this is not a huge problem, but it's good to be aware of this because it can lead to rounding errors in calculations, and errors may accumulate. So don't be surprised if a float or a double doesn't contain exactly what you expect it to.

It's important to remember that this is not a language- or runtime-specific limitation, but a fundamental one. All platforms using floating-point numbers suffer from those restrictions. If this is not desirable, other types with precise decimal representations need to be used, as discussed next. Typical examples include banking applications, where every penny matters.

Intermezzo Behind the Scenes

For the curious readers, let's dig a little deeper and see this imprecision for real using the Visual Studio 2010 debugger. But first, let's write a little piece of code that uses a real literal, which we discuss in the next section:

```
static void Main()
{
    double d = 0.3;
}
```

Notice that I'm omitting the necessary class declaration surrounding the method, but by now you should be able to reconstruct this. When compiling, you'll see a warning about the fact we're only assigning to local variable d but never using it. For now, it's fine to ignore this, but in general this indicates you have some dead code to take a closer look at for cleanup.

Set a breakpoint (using F9, for example) on the closing curly brace of the Main method and start the debugger (F5). When the breakpoint is hit, open a Memory window through Debug, Windows, Memory. In the address box of the window, enter d as the name of the local variable we want to take a look at in raw memory. Using the context menu, the display can be set to 64-bit floating-point numbers.

Repeat the same steps to bring up another Memory window, again looking at variable d's memory contents. This time, leave the display settings alone. The result should look like Figure 4.11.

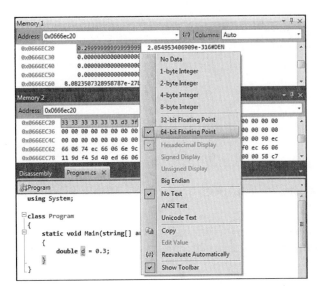

FIGURE 4.11   Looking at the memory for a floating-point number.

First of all, observe how the Memory window displays the floating-point number as 0.299... rather than 0.300..., illustrating the imprecision we're talking about. In the hexadecimal window, take a look at the byte pattern. Actually, it's shown in reverse due to the "endianness" of the platform. It really says 3FD3333333333333. Based on the floating-point formula shown earlier, you can reconstruct the decimal value as a little exercise. (Notice we're in the 64-bit "double-precision" situation now.) For those of you running Windows 7, the new Calculator has a great programmers mode to look at bit representations of numbers (see Figure 4.12).

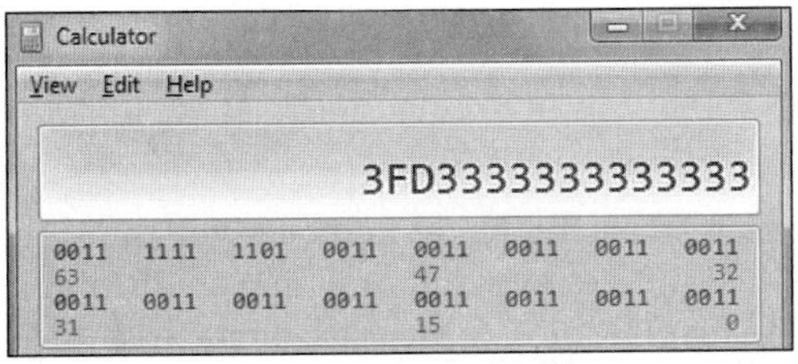

FIGURE 4.12   Looking at the bits of the floating-point number.

Along the same lines, you may also wonder how the floating-point number gets loaded at runtime. Was it the C# compiler that made the conversion into the right IEEE-754 representation, or what? The answer is yes, as you can observe from running ildasm. In Figure 4.13, I've turned on the View, Show Bytes option.

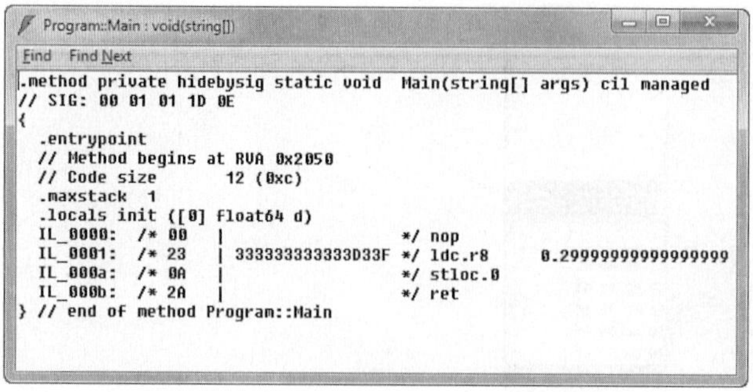

FIGURE 4.13   Loading a floating-point constant in IL.

Here, the ldc.r8 instruction is used to load a floating-point constant of the specified value. Feel free to go back to disassemble some program using integral types to see the instructions used there (ldc.i4 and so on).

Real Literals

Just like with integral values and characters, we want a way to be able to write real values right inside source code. That's what *real literals* are for. One difference compared to integral literals relates to the use of a decimal separator character, for which the dot is used:

```
double half = .5;
double pi = 3.14159265358979323846; // also available as Math.PI
```

A second difference lies in the use of scientific notation to specify an exponent part, using either e or E as a separator character. Exponents can be positive or negative and represent a power 10-based factor:

```
double mole = 6.02214179e23;
double planck = 6.62606896e-34;
```

Notice that the use of the character e doesn't clash with hexadecimal notation because such notation is not permitted in the context of real literals anyway.

Finally, there's the use of *real type suffixes* to explicitly specify the desired real type the developer wants a real literal to be treated as. Three suffixes exist, all of which are flexible in casing (just like the integral type suffixes). The first is f or F, to treat the literal as a 32-bit single-precision float. Using d or D, a 64-bit double-precision treatment can be enforced. The third one, m or M, is discussed in the next section and is used for decimal values.

The Decimal Type

In the category of real types, you've learned about floating-point types so far. Despite their wide range, the imprecision that comes with them may sometimes be problematic, especially in the context of financial calculations. To provide an answer to this, the BCL offers a System.Decimal type that is surfaced in C# through the decimal keyword.

`Decimal` is a 128-bit value with a smaller range than the floating-point numbers but with higher precision due to exact decimal representations. These two properties apply very well in the world of financial computing: Scales over a decimal order of magnitude of 300 (as with double) are ridiculously high, and the ability to represent simple values like 0.30 (for example, to denote 30 cents) precisely is much more valuable.

To keep primitive type definitions "tabled," Table 4.3 presents `decimal`'s scorecard.

TABLE 4.3   Decimal Type

C#	BCL Type	Approximate Range	Precision
decimal	System.Decimal	$\pm 1.0 \times 10^{\wedge}\text{-}28$ to $\pm 7.9 \times 10^{\wedge}28$	28–29 digits

The representation of a decimal value is rather straightforward: 96 bits are used for the coefficient and the remaining 32 bits contain flags for the sign and the scale, which should be a value between 0 and 28 (inclusive bounds). The scale is where the difference lies with floating-point types, being 10-based to guarantee (what's in a name?) decimal precision.

$$(-1)^s \times c \times 10^e$$

What about the limitation in the number of digits? Suppose you have a literal that exceeds that number, as the one that follows here has 30 digits in it, whereas only 29 are permitted. A similar situation arises beyond the use of literals when computations such as averages result in values that cannot be represented exactly anymore:

```
decimal x = 0.12345678901234567890123456789M;
```

The answer is *banker's rounding*, named after a claim that it is used by bankers. Its idea is based on balancing rounding up and down nicely to avoid a bias toward one of the two, possibly accumulating over time. In essence—contradictory as this might sound—it's meant to be a rounding that's as precise as possible.

So what's the rounding based on? Simple: If the fractional part that exceeds the available precision is over one half, round up. Otherwise, round down. And precisely in the middle, round toward the nearest even integer. Figure 4.14 shows a few examples.

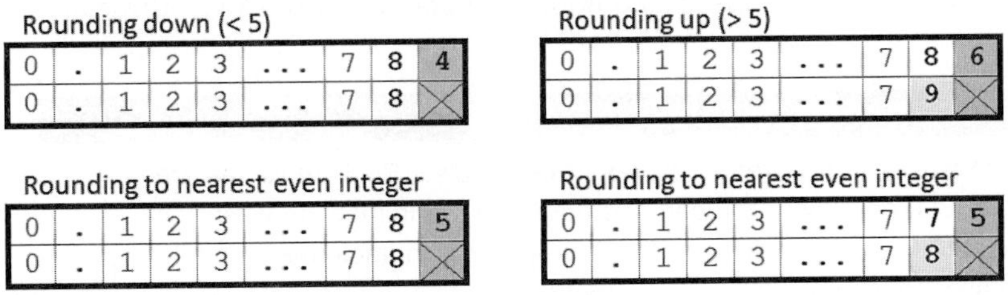

FIGURE 4.14   Banker's rounding.

Decimal Literals

The format of decimal literals is the same as that of real literals: the decimal separator character, the optional use of an exponent. As we've seen before, the real type suffix for decimal is m or M.

There's an interesting thing to notice about the use of this prefix in the context of decimals. When no real type suffix is used on a real literal, the value is considered to be treated as a floating point. As you know, floating-point numbers have precision issues, and allowing an implicit conversion of those into decimals (with a higher precision characteristic) would therefore pose a hidden data loss. For this reason, you should explicitly state that a real literal should be treated as decimal using the m suffix:

```
decimal price = 79.95m;
```

However, because an integral literal can implicitly be converted to a decimal without risk of information loss, it's valid to assign an integral literal to a decimal variable:

```
decimal price = 99;
```

WHY THE M SUFFIX?

Two stories describe the origin of the m suffix for decimal literals. The first one has a precise nature and trims down the number of possible suffixes by elimination. Starting from the word *decimal*, clearly d couldn't be used because it's already used for the double suffix. E is used for scientific notation, and c has a potential hexadecimal interpretation. For i, the story goes it would be good to keep it free for a possible (but rather unlikely) introduction of imaginary numbers or maybe to avoid font confusion with 1. That brings us to m as the first applicable character. And a and l are no good either, for reasons of hexadecimal and use for long, respectively.

Version two of the origin story is much simpler: With decimal's target audience being the financial industry, why not use m for money?

The Boolean Type

Boolean values, named after George Boole, are used to denote logical truth values. Named System.Boolean in the BCL, the type surfaces with the bool alias in C#. Only two Boolean values exist, both of which have an associated Boolean literal. Unsurprisingly, those are true and false.

MEMORY REPRESENTATION AND USE

Although only 1 bit would be required to express true or false, Boolean values are represented by the CLR as 1 byte. You can see this from the Immediate window by evaluating the sizeof(bool) expression. This is really just an implementation detail, reflecting the smallest addressable unit of memory.

But from a typing perspective, there are really only two semantic values for the Boolean type: An all-zero pattern represents false, while a byte with any bit set represents true.

In contrast to C and C++, C# is very strict about the use of Boolean values where truth value semantics are required. For example, the `if` statement's condition requires a Boolean expression be supplied and nothing else (like a pointer or any integral value in C).

The String Type

The built-in types we've seen so far are all value types. `System.String`, on the other hand, is a reference type. To understand why this is the case, we first need to know about the memory layout and its implications (the subject of Chapter 9, where we talk about the heap and the stack).

SYSTEM.STRING VERSUS THE STRING RESERVED WORD

Don't forget that the C# reserved words for built-in types are simply aliases for the underlying BCL types. In the case of C#'s string, that is `System.String`. Both can be used in source code, and when the `System` namespace is imported, the latter one can be abbreviated to `String`, with a capital S.

This casing doesn't change the characteristics of the type. String is, and always is, a reference type. People with different programming backgrounds sometimes get this wrong. For example, in Java there's quite a difference between `int` and `Integer`, while there's only `String` and no string.

To state the obvious, the `string` type is used to represent textual data, based on Unicode characters. One thing is a bit special about it: Strings in .NET are *immutable*. Once created, you can't change the contents of a string or grow or shrink it. Instead, you create a new (modified) one. You'll see some interesting implications about this in Chapter 5, in the section, "String Concatenation."

String Literals

String literals are formed by putting sequences of characters between double quotes ("). The characters supported in a string literal are the same as the ones used in character literals, including the use of escape sequences:

```
string a = "Hello world!";
string b = "Bart says \"Hello C#!\"";
string c = "\\\\bartde-dev07\\c$\\Windows\\Microsoft.NET\\Framework";
```

Having to escape backslashes all over the place can be quite cumbersome when dealing with paths, as illustrated here. To make this easier, C# supports *verbatim string literals*. By prefixing a string literal with @, characters are not escaped within the string:

```
string c = @"\\bartde-dev07\c$\Windows\Microsoft.NET\Framework ";
```

When a double quote is required in a literal string, it needs to be doubled because there's no way to escape it using \ anymore:

```
string b = @"Bart says ""Hello C#!""";
```

Verbatim string literals can also stretch multiple lines:

```
string e = @"<Products>
                <Product Name=""Chai"" Price=""49.95"" />
            </Products>";
```

Notice not only that the newlines are included in this multiline string but also that the whitespace is preserved as it appears in the source code.

One final remark: Be wary about the use of \x hexadecimal Unicode character representations. Because \x can be followed by one to four hexadecimals, the subsequent character can cause confusion if it's a hexadecimal by itself. For example, assume you want a space (hexadecimal \x20) followed by the character 1:

```
string wrong = "\x201";
```

This won't do the right thing because 201 is interpreted as the hexadecimal for one single character (which looks anything but the intended space). To avoid this kind of mistake, use fully expanded hexadecimals with all four digits:

```
string right = "\x00201";
```

ESCAPING FROM ESCAPING ESCAPES

One design rationale for adding verbatim string literals to the language was not so much file paths, but regular expressions. Paths are better off being stored in configuration files anyway; and to concatenate paths, BCL support is available through System.IO.Path.

However, regular expressions are typically burned into a program's source code and can be quite hard on the eye. Because they also use the backslash character as an escape mechanism, writing such a regular expression down in C# code without verbatim string literals would mean to "escape the escapes." This would turn into a mess quickly, so verbatim string literals come to the rescue.

As for all built-in types, we discuss the operations you can carry out with strings in Chapter 5.

Object

We kept one of the most interesting types for the last: System.Object, otherwise known as object in C#. What's so special about this one? Recall that the .NET Framework is based on the principles of object-oriented programming (OOP). In this setting, types form a hierarchy; we pay much more attention to OOP in later chapters.

Every type in .NET, except for System.Object, has a base type from which it inherits code as well as data. This sentence already gives it away. Because System.Object doesn't have a base type, it should necessarily be the (only) root of the type hierarchy. Although this may sound of interest only for theoretical purposes, it has a very practical side to it: unifying the type system across value and reference types.

Figure 4.15 shows the .NET Framework type hierarchy, constrasting the concept of value types and reference types.

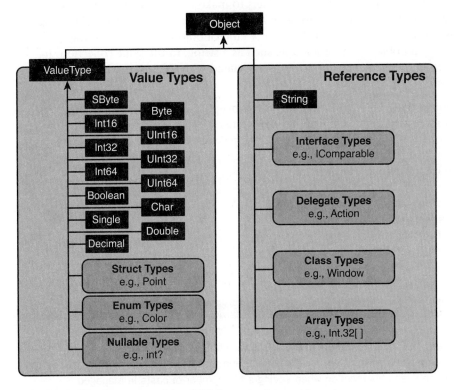

FIGURE 4.15   The roots of the .NET Framework type hierarchy.

All of this means you can write very generic code, for example, in some algorithm or data structure that can deal with objects of any type. In the first release of the .NET Framework, collection types like ArrayList were built based on this principle, making them usable as containers for data of any type:

```
ArrayList primes = new ArrayList { 2, 3, 5, 7, 11 };
int two = (int)primes[0];
primes.Add("thirtheen");
int thirteen = (int)primes[5]; // runtime error!
```

NOTE

In the preceding code snippet, I'm using a bunch of language features we haven't looked at yet. In particular, on the first line you can see a collection initializer. Line two contains a cast expression and use of an indexer, and line three makes a method call. Don't worry, we cover all of these in quite some detail as we move forward.

Earlier, I used the word *generic* in a rather ad hoc fashion. The use of System.Object for collection types wasn't ideal for various reasons that will become apparent later, but the biggest stumbling block is the potential for users to make silly mistakes (as illustrated in the code fragment). Suppose you're using an ArrayList to store integer values. Because ArrayList is defined to be able to deal with any kind of object, however, nothing prevents you from storing an object of another type, such as a string, in the same collection. In addition, there are performance implications associated with this approach (due to *boxing*, as you will see).

C# 2.0 To address that, .NET 2.0 introduced the concept of *generic types*, which we pay much more attention to in Chapter 15, "Generic Types and Methods." One of the key properties of generic types is that they make excessive use of System.Object go away, essentially improving static typing and reducing typical silly mistakes that would otherwise be caught only at runtime:

```
List<int> primes = new List<int> { 2, 3, 5, 7, 11 };
int two = primes[0];
primes.Add("thirtheen"); // compile-time error!
int thirteen = primes[5];
```

BANNING SYSTEM.OBJECT?

A colleague of mine—the ultimate native code and COM geek—told me about his first encounter with the .NET Framework in the 1.0 days. Although new runtimes like the CLR promised heaven on earth for type-safe code and promoted the use of static typing, you can guess his reaction when seeing a big number of casts in managed code. When I asked about the nature of that code, he recollected the everywhere use of collection types. That explained his original surprise, which resulted from the lack of generics in the early days of the CLR.

As time goes on, the number of scenarios requiring direct use of System.Object keeps decreasing. And by direct use I mean explicit declaration of variables of type object. With .NET 2.0, generics were introduced to improve static typing, and in .NET 4.0 a new dynamic type was introduced to deal with dynamic typing in a more explicit fashion than plain use of System.Object.

In today's world, whenever I see such direct use of System.Object in freshly written code, I get a bit nervous. As you get to know generics and dynamic better in the following chapters, you should start feeling the same way. I think the time has come to consider System.Object more of an implementation detail of the CLR type system rather than a type amenable for direct use.

Declaring objects with the System.Object type is just one side of the coin, though. An equally important perspective is that of using the operations defined on System.Object. All types inherit those commonly used *methods* whose role we discuss in more detail in Chapter 13, "Operator Overloading and Conversions." Here they are to set the scene:

▶ Equals compares the instance against another object for equality.

▶ GetHashCode calculates a hash code for the instance. Hash codes are used to store and retrieve objects efficiently in certain collection types.

▶ ToString provides a string representation of the instance.

Note that these three methods are all *virtual*, meaning derived types can (and often do) override them to provide a specialized meaning. We discuss what these terms mean when we cover OOP in Chapter 14.

All things being equal, should you still care about System.Object that much? It's without a doubt a good thing to know about its role in the type hierarchy and to see it as an ultimate resort for generic programming if—for some very rare reason—generics don't apply in some circumstance. But nowadays, the most common use of System.Object should likely be in the use of methods like ToString and Equals.

Dynamic Typing

Starting with .NET 4.0, C# supports *dynamic typing*. Variables typed as *dynamic* are used in a *late-bound* fashion, meaning that operations applied to them are resolved at runtime rather than at compile time. This is useful when dealing with an object that cannot be typed statically in a comfortable manner. Samples include XML documents without an XSD schema or objects from dynamic languages such as Python, Ruby, or JavaScript.

Other than the built-in types we've seen so far, there's no direct mapping between the C# reserved word dynamic and an underlying BCL type. Instead, dynamic is a special alias for System.Object, but with some additional metadata sprinkled on top of it to tell the compiler to emit late-bound code. This makes a lot of sense actually: The "minimal" static type in the CLR is System.Object; you can't sink lower. By typing it as dynamic, you're essentially saying this: *Dear compiler. Trust me, I'm confident that the operations I carry out will make sense at runtime. So don't waste your time trying to verify those statically at compile time.*

```
object o = GetSomething();
o.DoSomething(); // compile-time error; System.Object does not have DoSomething

dynamic d = GetSomething();
d.DoSomething(); // check for the presence of DoSomething at runtime
```

Compile Time Type Versus Runtime Type

To make things a bit more concrete, assume a PetShop object defines a method called GetPromotionOfTheDay whose return type is Animal. Different subtypes exist for Animal, such as GoldFish and Canary. There can even be more structure with intermediate types, such as Fish and Bird. We'll look at OOP in the later chapters, but you get the idea.

Statically (a compile-time thing), all we know about GetPromotionOfTheDay is that it returns an animal. Before driving to the shop to get the animal (a runtime thing), we can't know what we'll get back, assuming we didn't hear about the type of the promotion in any way. At this point, we can make a few assumptions about the things we'll be able to do with the animal. Walk (a method call) won't apply very well if we get back with a fish, and it's way too dangerous trying to Bathe (another method call) a cat. Maybe the only thing we can be sure about is to Watch it.

Dynamically (a runtime thing), though, the animal we get back will have a concrete type. It might be a dog, a goldfish, or whatnot. Now it makes sense to Walk the dog or to Bathe the goldfish and so on. But there's no way we could have known before obtaining the animal. We're using dynamic knowledge obtained in the act of getting the shop's promotion of the day.

Now let's assume through some magical powers you happen to know that the PetShop's GetPromotionOfTheDay always returns a mammal (and doesn't have the space to have a whale in stock). As far as I know, all mammals except for whales can walk (but I'm not an expert), so it will always be safe to call Walk on our purchased animal. From a *statically* typed perspective, we can't know this (a compile-time error), but given the additional information we got somehow, we can treat the animal *dynamically* and call Walk on it anyway. Figure 4.16 contrasts static and dynamic typing.

I detail the innards of dynamic typing and how to use and extend it in Chapter 22, "Dynamic Programming." With this, we conclude our journey through built-in types the C# language knows about by means of reserved words.

A Word on CLS Compliance

Chapter 1, "Introducing the .NET Platform," stressed the importance of cross-language interoperability in the vision statement of .NET. One key criterion for success in this space is ensuring that types created in one language can be used or extended from another language. This is where the Common Language Specification (CLS) comes into play.

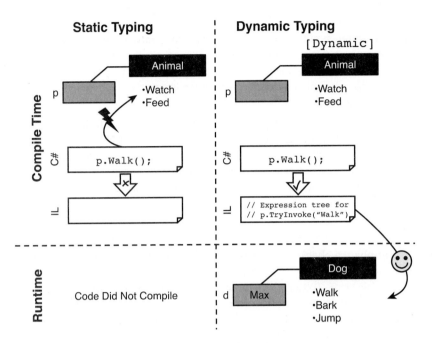

FIGURE 4.16 Static typing versus dynamic typing.

Before delving any deeper, let's revisit the first rule of the CLS:

> *CLS Rule 1: CLS rules apply only to those parts of a type that are accessible or visible outside of the defining assembly.*

We haven't talked about visibility yet, but the idea is rather simple. *Assemblies* contain *types*, some of which can be exposed to the outside world. A similar observation holds for types in relation to their members. Some members, such as fields or methods, are for exclusive use by the type's code, whereas others are part of the type's contract and hence exposed to others.

The first CLS rule states an obvious fact: To be cross-language–compatible, *only those parts of a type that are accessible or visible outside the defining assembly matter*. In other words: Do whatever you like on the inside, but stand still for a few seconds when you touch the outside.

SHOULD I CARE?

Applications are often written by separating out certain functionality into helper libraries, with the idea of code sharing in mind or for architectural cleanliness. It's sometimes tempting to say you will always be the only one using that library, and you'll always use C# for the job at hand. So why should you care about making the assembly CLS-compliant?

This naive assumption can pose a serious risk when the unexpected happens, requiring you or someone else to reach out to the non-CLS-compliant library. Maybe a new developer has been hired who's fluent in another .NET language, or your firm has decided to jump on the bandwagon of functional languages. Or you find yourself in a situation where you want to call some of your library functionality from an interactive prompt of some dynamic language.

For all those reasons, the first thing I do for 99% of my projects is to turn on CLS-compliance checking. By doing so, I avoid trying to tweak a library into becoming CLS-compliant and thus potentially breaking others that already rely on some of the noncompliant public APIs. In general, I find the act of ensuring CLS compliance not something that disturbs development workflow, and when a CLS compliance warning is raised, I've learned something new about the platform. A win-win situation, if you ask me.

How to turn on CLS compliance checking? In essence, you just state that you ensure the assembly is CLS-compliant, causing the C# compiler to carry out CLS-specific checks when dealing with publicly visible stuff. To declare an assembly CLS compliant, an assembly-level attribute is used. In Visual Studio, you can find those declared in a file called AssemblyInfo.cs under the Properties node for the project in Solution Explorer. Figure 4.17 shows where to find the AssemblyInfo.cs file.

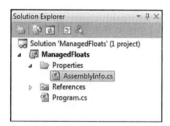

FIGURE 4.17   Locating the AssermblyInfo.cs file in a C# project.

Open this file and browse around a bit to get a feeling about what information an assembly can carry. Hover over the various attributes to see a brief explanation of their goals. Most of those can be configured through the user interface, as you will see later. To make the assembly CLS-compliant and to have the compiler check this claim, add the following line somewhere in the file (at the bottom will do):

```
[assembly: CLSCompliant(true)]
```

The square bracket syntax is used for *attributes*, pieces of metadata that can be sprinkled on top of various program entities. For example, to make a type serializable for storage on disk, you can decorate the type with [Serializable]. Or to have the runtime carry out security checks when calling a method, various permission attributes can be applied to it. In this particular case, we're targeting the CLSCompliant attribute at the whole assembly and use the C# reserved word assembly to denote that.

In fact, attributes are defined by classes that *derive* from System.Attribute. The convention is to suffix their name with Attribute, but C# (among other languages) allows us to omit that suffix when referring to the type as an attribute (that is, between the square bracket pair). So although we wrote CLSCompliant, its real name is CLSCompliantAttribute.

You'll learn more about attributes and how to create our own custom attributes later when we discuss the reflection capabilities of the platform in Chapter 21, in the section, "Custom Attributes."

A TALE OF NAMING

To ensure consistency when using types in the .NET Framework, naming conventions have been established. Without going into much detail right now, one of those rules is to use Pascal casing for everything externally visible, except for parameters.

Pascal-casing advocates the use of capital letters at the beginning of a word and for every concatenated word in a name (for example, ToString, AsEnumerable, PayCheck). When acronyms are involved, two-letter acronyms stay completely capitalized (as in DBConnection), whereas anything longer keeps only its first letter capitalized, like HtmlDocument.

The CLSCompliantAttribute class was introduced nearly from day one of the development of the .NET Framework, when those rules weren't established formally yet. According to the rules, the name should have been ClsCompliantAttribute instead. This little mishap was never corrected, and it would be a breaking change to tweak it now.

The CLSCompliant attribute lives in the System namespace, so you either have to specify the full name (System.CLSCompliant) or import the namespace by means of inserting a using directive:

```
using System;
```

The Visual Studio editor makes those tasks really easy by means of a "smart tag" that appears as soon as we write the unresolved name. You can open the little menu by using the mouse or by pressing Ctrl+. (use the . key on the central part of the keyboard, not on the numeric pad). Any of the first two options listed will resolve the name. I prefer the first one as a matter of style. Figure 4.18 shows the addition of the CLS compliance attribute to the assembly's metadata information.

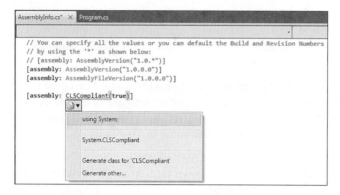

FIGURE 4.18   Adding **CLSCompliant** to the assembly.

To see CLS-compliance enforcement in action, we need to violate some rules first. Because we're discussing built-in types at this point, let's use a non-CLS-compliant type on a public member to illustrate matters. Built-in types that lack CLS compliance are UInt16, UInt32, UInt64, and SByte.

Switch back to any of your C# code files (typically Program.cs) and add a type definition to it:

```
public class Numbers
{
    public ulong Large { get; set; }
}
```

A few things are essential here. First of all, the type's modifier list sets the visibility to public. This makes the type visible outside the defining assembly. Second, the same applies to the automatically implemented property Large, causing it to be visible for users of the containing Numbers class.

Because ulong is an alias for the non-CLS-compliant UInt64 type, we'll get a CLS-compliance violation warning when compiling the code (see Figure 4.19).

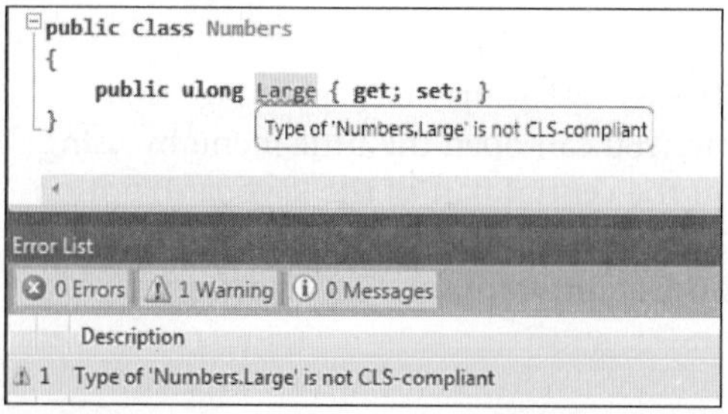

```
public class Numbers
{
    public ulong Large { get; set; }
}
                         Type of 'Numbers.Large' is not CLS-compliant
```

```
Error List
  ⊗ 0 Errors   ⚠ 1 Warning   ⓘ 0 Messages
      Description
  ⚠ 1   Type of 'Numbers.Large' is not CLS-compliant
```

FIGURE 4.19   The C# compiler catching a CLS-compliance violation.

> **NOTE**
>
> The ability to declare multiple types in the same code file (or *compilation unit* to be precise) illustrates a point of flexibility of the C# language. Some other languages are more pesky about this and enforce one type per file. In fact, this flexibility goes beyond the definition of types. Because types can be organized in hierarchical namespaces, you might think the source code folder structure needs to reflect this organization; for example, System.IO.Stream would live in System\IO\Stream.cs. This is not the case, and you can get as messy as you want.
>
> Even though this flexibility can come in handy at times, it's a good practice to limit the number of types per file and name files after the (typically one) type they define. It's also good to have the folder structure reflect the namespace organization. You'll be thankful you did when you search for a code file in the absence of a rich editor with source-exploration capabilities like Visual Studio.
>
> We detail the distinction between assemblies and namespaces, and how they contain types, in subsequent chapters.

Notice that the MSDN Library documentation points out non-CLS-compliant types with recommendations about how to solve the issue, as shown in Figure 4.20.

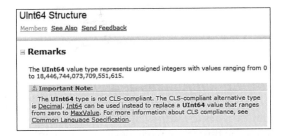

FIGURE 4.20   CLS compliance remarks in the MSDN documentation.

Sometimes changing the type to a CLS-compliant one is not an option, so you want to suppress the type, acknowledging the fact it might not be available to all .NET languages, but you can live with this restriction. To do so, you can explicitly opt out from CLS compliance for individual types or members. Typically, you want to narrow the island of non-CLS-compliance as much as possible, so a member-level suppression is preferred over a type-level one (unless the lack of a specific member's usability renders the whole containing type useless).

```
public class Numbers
{
    [CLSCompliant(false)]
    public ulong Large { get; set; }
}
```

WHAT ABOUT DYNAMIC?

Recently I had a discussion about adding a public member whose type is dynamic to the .NET class libraries. Recall that dynamic is some kind of pseudo-type, effectively standing for System.Object but with additional metadata instructing the compiler to emit late-bound calls against the object.

What if a language doesn't support late-bound code? Doesn't that render the object useless? This is definitely a blurry line; dynamic is not strictly more powerful than System.Object; it's merely a hint to a consuming compiler to emit special code. The CLS was created at a point where statically typed languages were the main concern in the world of managed code. Applying some of the CLS rules to dynamically typed code is therefore a bit unnatural.

We ultimately concluded to consider it CLS compliant in the strict sense of the word because the CLS cares primarily about static typing. From that perspective, dynamic is simply System.Object, and sure enough that particular type is CLS compliant. Luckily, in practice, the mainstream languages like C# and VB, as well as the DLR languages, offer first-class support for dynamic types starting from version 4.0.

TIP

As an exercise, experiment a bit with other CLS rules you can find in the MSDN documentation. It's good to get a feeling about what's compliant and what's not. There'll be quite a few that sound like Chinese at this point, but rules on case sensitivity and such should be easy to play with, and you'll readily see the compile-time effects in case of violations.

A Matter of Style: Aliases or Not?

As stated earlier, the C# reserved words for built-in types are simply aliases for the corresponding underlying BCL types. There's no semantic difference whatsoever, so you can use either one.

Sometimes people start long-winded discussions on what's the preferred style. I deliberately don't participate in such discussion but have one rule of thumb: consistency. Mixing aliases and raw BCL type names can yield only more confusion. But, objectively, both have their merits.

▶ The **BCL type names** clearly indicate the range of numeric types in terms of bit width but in a decimal-centric world that doesn't tell the whole story at a glimpse. And for types like decimal or byte, this argument doesn't hold: You just need to know the raw facts about precision, ranges, rounding, and so on anyway.

▶ On the other hand, the **C# aliases** tend to be shorter and reduce the number of eye-catching types in your code: Editors like Visual Studio color built-in types as keywords, whereas others are colored like types. Personally, I like to be able to skim a piece of code, looking for specific type references without the noise of all the built-in ones.

A better argument to make is the amount of code out there that's written in one style or the other. As a personal observation, I think it's safe to say the C# style has found its way into the hearts of many more developers. So if you stick with raw BCL type names, you'll still have to know about the C# aliases to read and understand other people's code from various sources.

Local Variables

We've already talked about the many places where variables can occur: as locals within a code block, as field members, as parameters, and so on. Let's focus on local variables for a second.

Declaration

A first aspect of local variables is their declaration and the scope in which they are available. *Declaring* a local variable happens in C style, with the type preceding the name:

```
int a;
long b;
string c;
```

Using a comma separator, different variables of the same type can be declared on the same line:

```
int x, y, z;
```

NAMING STYLE

Although nothing in the language cares about or mandates the naming pattern used for local variables, there are some useful recommendations to ensure code readability. The short answer is camel casing, where the first letter of a variable's name is lowercase and subsequent starting letters of concatenated words are uppercase. For example, `firstName` and `htmlDocument` are both valid camel-case identifiers.

Camel casing gets its name from the appearance of identifiers written in this style: The uppercase characters stick out of the surface at the top, making it look like a camel (either the one-humped or two-humped variety).

What about Hungarian notation, where variables get prefixed with a type hint, such as `dwSize` (for DWORD) and `pDbConnection` (for pointer)? This style is not recommended in managed code. Good variable names should carry enough meaning for you to infer the type from the context.

Scope

Scope determines the region of program text (that is, lexical scoping) in which it's valid to refer to a name of some entity without requiring further qualification. Scopes can be nested, too. For example, when declaring a class, a scope is introduced for its members. Some kinds of members, like methods, introduce a new scope:

```
class ScopeSample
{
    private int x = 42;

    public void InnerScope()
    {
        int x = 53;
        int y = x; // refers to the local variable x
        // ...
    }

    public void OuterScope()
    {
        int y = x; // refers to the field x
        // ...
    }
}
```

The InnerScope method in the preceding sample declares a local variable called x, hiding the class's instance field that's also called x. It's actually possible to refer to x in the outer scope by qualifying it as follows:

```
int y = this.x; // refers to the field x
```

The this keyword is used to refer to the current object instance, a notion detailed in Chapter 9 and Chapter 14. Also within the scope of a member's code block (for example, within a method), new scopes can be established:

```
public static void PrintAbs(int x)
{
    if (x >= 0)
    {
        int y = x;
        Print(y);
    }
    else if (x < 0)
    {
        int y = -x;
        Print(y);
    }
}
```

There are lots of other ways to write this code, but I'm merely illustrating the point of new scopes being introduced by the if statements used in the code. Both branches introduce a new scope, in which a variable y is declared. They don't conflict because they are declared in parallel with one another: Both y variables are distinct.

However, hiding a variable in the outer scope of the same code block is illegal:

```
public static void PrintAbs(int x)
{
    int y = x;

    if (x >= 0)
    {
        Print(y);
    }
    else if (x < 0)
    {
        // Error: A local variable named 'y' cannot be declared in this
        //        scope because it would give a different meaning to 'y',
        //        which is already used in a 'parent or current' scope to
        //        denote something else.
        int y = -x; // error: hiding y in outer scope
        Print(y);
    }
}
```

Not only does this reduce potential confusion, it also eliminates the need for a way to disambiguate both variables using some keyword. Think about it what would happen if you have a bunch of nested scopes, each hiding variables from the outer scope, and you want to refer to such a hidden variable declared "three scopes up."

Similarly, it's not allowed to reuse a variable name in an outer scope after it has been used in a child scope:

```
private static void PrintInt(int x)
{
    if (x >= 0)
    {
        int y = x;
        Print(y);
        return;
    }

    // Error: A local variable named 'y' cannot be declared in this scope
    //        because it would give a different meaning to 'y', which is
    //        already used in a 'child' scope to denote something else.
    int y = -x;
    Print(y);
}
```

And obviously, as you could have guessed by now, it's invalid to declare a variable with the same name but a different type in the same scope. In some other typeless languages, this is possible but often a major source of confusion.

```
int x = 5;

// Error: A local variable named 'x' is already defined in this scope.
string x = "Five";
```

Assignment

Besides declaration of local variables, there's also the need to initialize them before they can be used. C# is very strict about not permitting the use of uninitialized variables because that's a very common source of errors found in other languages. For this very reason, the following fragment won't compile:

```
int x;

// Error: Use of unassigned local variable 'x'.
Console.WriteLine(x);
```

To ensure variables are properly assigned before they get used, C# has several rules on definite assignment, based on static program flow analysis. I won't go into detail about those, but I'll sometimes mention some of the rules in passing.

Assignment is the act of substituting the contents of the storage cell associated with the variable with some value or reference, depending on the type. For this to work, types need to match. The assignment operator is =, where the left side (lhs) is the name of the variable and the right side (rhs) is an expression to be evaluated:

```
int x;
x = 42;
```

Here, 42 is simply a constant expression consisting of an integer literal that gets assigned to the variable with name x. The types line up nicely, so the compiler is happy. If you violate the type, an error results:

```
int x;

// Error: Cannot implicitly convert type 'string' to 'int'.
x = "Oops";
```

The distinction between implicit and explicit conversions is discussed in Chapter 13, "Operator Overloading and Conversions." In the previous examples, there was no reason not to declare and initialize the variable as part of the same statement:

```
int x = 42;
```

Similarly, multiple variables can be assigned on the same line:

```
int x = 0, y = 1, z = 2;
```

So far, we've discussed simple assignment. After we've studied binary operators, we'll take a look at compound assignment. The following is an example in which you can predict the behavior:

```
int x = 0;
x += 1;
```

Constants

Variables are, not surprisingly, variable. They can be written to many times, causing the contents of the cell to get replaced. Constants, on the other hand, cannot be changed after their initialization, which needs to happen at the point the constant is declared. To declare a local constant, use the const keyword:

```
const int x = 42;

// Error: The left-hand side of an assignment must be a variable, property or
indexer.
x = 43;
```

Constants are subject to restrictions on what they can be initialized to: The value needs to be computable at compile time. In practice, this means the integral and real number, character, string, and Boolean types are allowed, as well as reference types when the null literal is used.

It's educational to see what's happening here behind the scenes. Because the value is computed at compile time, there's no need to store it in some local variable (in IL-speak). It can simply be inlined everywhere it's used, as a constant.

Consider the following piece of code:

```
int x = 42;
const int y = 42;

Console.WriteLine(x);
Console.WriteLine(y);
```

Carry out the typical compile and disassemble steps to take a look at the generated IL code for the containing method. Figure 4.21 shows the result.

Notice the IL directive for declaration of local variables:

```
.locals init ([0] int32 x)
```

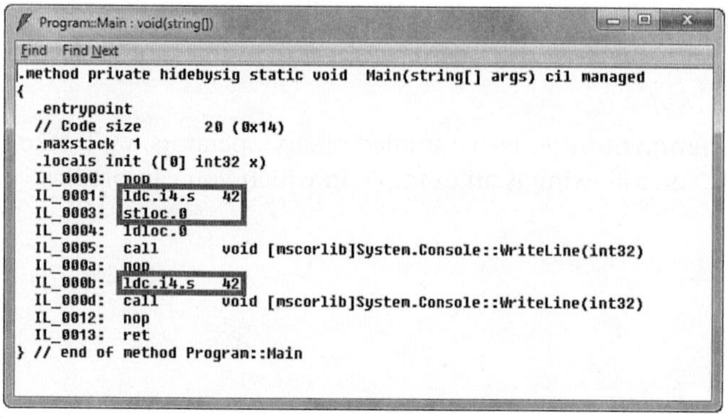

FIGURE 4.21   Variables versus constants behind the scenes.

This declares that one local variable is needed to execute the code, and it has type int32 (the CLR intrinsic type corresponding to C#'s int and the BCL's System.Int32). No such entry exists for the constant y. This already gives away the different treatment local constants deserve.

> **NOTE**
>
> Depending on whether you built in Debug or Release mode, the local variable x will pre-serve its name through the glasses of ILDASM. The reason is ILDASM looks for a PDB symbol file next to the assembly being disassembled to get more information, such as the names for local variables. To the CLR, names of variables don't matter, so they get compiled away. If you don't have a PDB file—the default behavior in Release mode— you'll see the local variable named V_0, a name generated by the disassembler for cos-metic purposes.

Inside the IL code, you can see the constant 42 getting loaded using the ldc.i4.s instruc-tion, which stands for "load constant integer 4 bytes signed," and being stored to the local variable slot using stloc.0 for "store to local slot 0." This is indicated by the first rectangle. On the subsequent couple of lines, that variable is loaded again to be fed in to the method call for Console.WriteLine.

For the constant y, no local variable slot is reserved, and every occurrence of y in the source code was substituted for the constant value. The second rectangle illustrates this. If we had multiple uses of y within the scope, each of those would see an ldc.i4.s instruc-tion for its constant value 42. On the other hand, multiple uses of x within the scope would each result in the use of ldloc.0, to read from the local variable slot.

Besides constants, there are also readonly fields, something we explore and compare to constants in Chapter 11.

Implicitly Typed Local Variable Declarations

 In the previous sections, you've seen a syntax used to declare and initialize local variables: specify the type, give the variable a name (lhs), and assign it some expression (rhs).

```
string name = "Bart";
```

Expressions, as you will see, always have a type. This means we have specified some redundant information to the compiler. On the left side, we called out a type explicitly, while the compiler could infer that information from the right side. In this case, the literal "Bart" is of type System.String. So why do we need to specify that type explicitly on the left?

The var Keyword

Until version 2.0 of the C# language, the answer was just this: That's the way it is; live with it. But starting with version 3.0, it's possible to omit the type on the left for a local variable declaration, making it implicitly typed:

```
var name = "Bart";
```

Here, the var keyword instructs the compiler to infer the type for the variable based on the expression found on the right side of the assignment symbol.

Don't confuse this with dynamic or System.Object in any way. The variable is still statically typed at compile time: The compiler knows precisely what we mean. In fact, the emitted IL code is instruction-by-instruction equivalent to that for the original fragment. To prove this, use Visual Studio and take a look at IntelliSense and ToolTips, as shown in Figure 4.22.

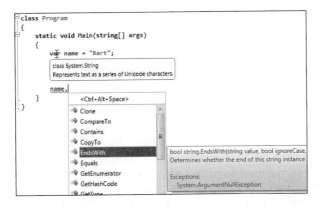

FIGURE 4.22   Implicitly typed local variables are statically typed.

If var stood for System.Object, we wouldn't see any meaningful IntelliSense for a string object (other than the triad of Equals, GetHashCode, and ToString). And if it stood for dynamic, we would see no IntelliSense at all because operations would be dispatched at runtime. To conclude, var is statically typed.

Rationale

But why would you use it? For local variables with types as simple as string or int, it doesn't pay you much. Well, on the contrary, you might find code harder to read because you have to infer the type yourself. There should be a better reason this feature was introduced. Despite the language's original code name, the C# language design team doesn't just add features because they are "cool."

 We haven't discussed generic types yet, but they're kind of simple to grasp. In essence, they allow types to be parameterized by other types. A concrete example will make things clearer:

```
Dictionary<string, List<int>> lotteryNumbers
    = new Dictionary<string, List<int>>();
```

Here I've declared a local variable called lotteryNumbers that contains a dictionary mapping each string key onto lists of integer values. Both Dictionary and List are generic types for which we've specified type parameters. Don't worry too much about the details for now; what's more important in the context of this discussion is how the code looks.

TIPS ON READING CODE

Programming languages need to be pronounceable. Not just for discussions in late-night clubs for geeks, but even more so in the context of courses and such. For example, how do you pronounce generic types? The required English glue words are *of* and *and*. In the preceding example, we've declared a local variable of type Dictionary of string and List of int.

Some languages are more syntactically terse than others. C# definitely is quite terse with short keywords, curly-brace block syntax, and symbolic operators as opposed to even more keywords. Visual Basic is closer to English and has many more keywords. Yes, it seemingly takes more time to write the code (although good editors like Visual Studio's help tremendously with autocompletion support), but on the other hand, it's easier to read. For instance, our generic type in Visual Basic looks like this:

```
Dictionary(Of String, List(Of Integer))
```

Sound familiar?

Did you see it? Yes, we had to specify that excessively long type name twice to declare a local variable of the particular type. On the left side, we pleased the compiler by telling the type for the variable. On the right side, we used *constructor* syntax to create an *instance* of the dictionary type. What constructors are precisely doesn't matter at this point, but the crux here is that the type of the expression on the right side is precisely what we've specified on the left.

In .NET 1.0, before the advent of generic types, this wasn't too much of a problem: Type names could not grow arbitrarily long when being used. However, because generic types are parameterized on other types by their very nature, you can mix and match all sorts of types together to build up a new one:

```
List<HashSet<Dictionary<string,Tuple<int,int>>>>
```

Having to specify such long type names repeatedly is not only tedious, it also reduces code readability significantly. Starting from C# 3.0, type inference for local variables can be used to shorten code:

```
var lotteryNumbers = new Dictionary<string, List<int>>();
```

Now it fits again on a single line, reducing the syntactical noise a lot.

ABOUT SEMICOLONS AND UNEMPLOYED UNDERSCORES

If it wasn't clear yet, C# allows code to be split across multiple lines. The end of a statement is indicated by the use of a semicolon character, as is common in C-style languages. Other languages, such as Visual Basic, initially chose an opposite approach: To split a code line, use a line continuation marker. In Visual Basic's case, that was the underscore character. I'm using the past tense here because the need for a line continuation has been removed almost completely in Visual Basic 10. In tough economic times, to assist the unemployed underscores in finding their next challenge, a website was created for them: www.unemployedunderscores.com.

But there's more. Although the usage simplification for generic types is a very convenient effect that comes from introducing this form of type inference, it's not a requirement. You could live perfectly without it (although maybe just a little annoyed). However, in C# 3.0, another feature was introduced as part of the LINQ mission: *anonymous types*. We defer exhaustive coverage of this feature until Chapter 19, "Language Integrated Query Essentials," in the section, "Anonymous Types and Object Initializers," but here's a sample:

```
var person = new { Name = "Bart", Age = 26 };
```

This creates an instance of a type with two properties called Name and Age, of type string and int, respectively, initialized with the specified data. What's special about the code is the fact that we didn't specify a type name at all. Instead, we let the compiler bake a type on the fly, with the desired "shape" to hold the contained data. But if the compiler generated a type for us, of which we can't know the name because we didn't have to specify it, how can we refer to it? The rescue lies in the use of var to let the compiler insert the type name on our behalf.

To see this in action, type the preceding code in some C# project and observe the IntelliSense in Visual Studio once more, as shown in Figure 4.23. As you can see, the tool knows precisely what we're talking about; we haven't lost any of the type information.

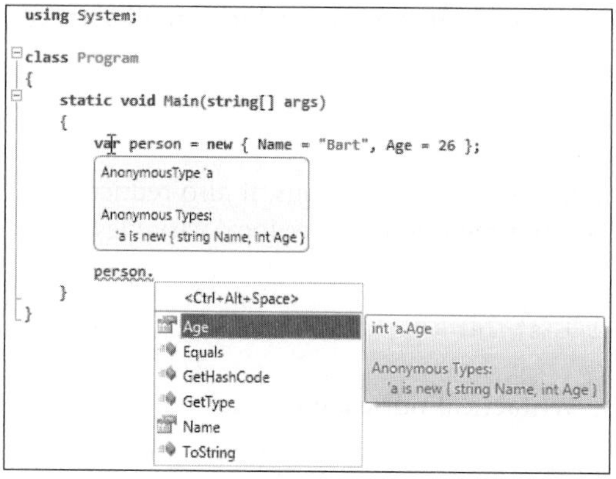

```
using System;

class Program
{
    static void Main(string[] args)
    {
        var person = new { Name = "Bart", Age = 26 };
        AnonymousType 'a

        Anonymous Types:
            'a is new { string Name, int Age }

        person.
                    <Ctrl+Alt+Space>
            🔲 Age              int 'a.Age
            🔷 Equals
            🔷 GetHashCode      Anonymous Types:
            🔷 GetType              'a is new { string Name, int Age }
            🔲 Name
            🔷 ToString
    }
}
```

FIGURE 4.23   Type inference at work for an anonymous type.

Anonymous types were introduced as a prerequisite for writing down LINQ query expressions, in particular projection and grouping clauses:

```
var expensive = from p in products
                where p.Price > 100
                select new { p.Name, p.Price };
```

To learn what the inferred type is for the expensive variable, you'll have to wait until we cover LINQ in depth in Chapter 19.

When to Use It

The appropriate use cases for this language feature have been the topic of long-winded online and offline discussion group debates. Opinions stretch the whole spectrum of possibilities:

▶ The conservative wing doesn't feel at ease with the apparent lack of static typing, even though they realize (hopefully) the use of var doesn't change the statically typed nature of the language at all. Some would go as far as banning the use of var altogether.

▶ Realists form the middle camp and acknowledge var is unavoidable in some cases, with the use of anonymous types more specifically, and beneficial in other cases (for example, to reduce the need for lengthy generic type names).

▶ Extremists would use var everywhere possible. This borders on the edge of laziness and can make code even more unreadable than it was to begin with: Type names are a good source of documentation right inside the code (especially so when the right side of the assignment contains a complicated expression).

Personally, I prefer the middle ground here. Always put yourself in the shoes of the person reading the code. If the type of the variable is not immediately apparent from the right side, don't use implicit typing using var. Examples include the following:

```
// Required
var person = new { Name = "Bart", Age = 26 };
var expensive = from p in products
                where p.Price > 100
                select new { p.Name, p.Price };


// Good
var lotteryNumbers = new Dictionary<string, List<int>>();
var name = person.ToString();


// Bad
var mystery = GetSomething();  // what's the return type of GetSomething?
var x = 2159940436;            // answer immediately: int or long?
```

PHILOSOPHICAL NOTE

C-style languages have traditionally been writing types in front of identifiers: int x, string y, List<Person> z. Personally, I can't think of many good reasons this approach was chosen, but it's all said and done now.

Although the type is quintessential, it's more convenient to find the declaration site of a variable easily by its name and see what its type is next. By having variable-length type names in front of identifiers, there's no alignment of the names. This causes what I call "Brownian eye motion" (after the name for the physical phenomenon of random movement of particles in a fluid) when reading code:

```
int x = 42;
string y = "Hello";
List<Person> z = new List<Person>();
```

Other languages have taken a different approach and write the type after the name. Samples include Visual Basic with its Dim... Because... syntax and various functional languages such as Haskell, ML, and F#:

```
' Visual Basic
Dim x As Integer = 42
Dim y As String = "Hello"
Dim z As New List(Of Person)

(* F# *)
let x : int = 42
let y : string = "Hello"
let z : Person list = []
```

Turns out with var you can reach a similar effect. But ideally, you still want to see the type, don't you? That's what the whole argument for some people is all about. Turns out you sort of can force the type in there if you really want:

```
var x = (int)42;
var y = (string)"Hello";
var z = new List<Person>();
```

Now I don't recommend this practice. That's why this sidebar is titled a "philosophical note." Turns out there are hidden caveats. Runtime costs, not really. But assume you have a complex expression as the right side of an assignment and you inserted the wrong cast. *Casts* are about stating you somehow know more than the compiler, telling it to try a conversion between types at runtime (as discussed in Chapter 6, A Primer on Types and Objects," in the section, "Cast Expressions"). Chances are that your code compiles just fine but blows up at runtime. This is definitely worse than what we started from.

Intermezzo on Comments

So far, we've dealt with some of the program text the compiler cares about the most. If you make mistakes with regard to syntax or more involved rules, you'll be punished and prompted to correct the error. As valuable as source code itself are comments to document the code. Even though good source code should be self-explanatory for the most part— because of the use of meaningful identifier names and so on—correct use of comments is invaluable, too.

Being a C-style language, C# inherits a few of its commenting styles from that group of languages. Let's take a look.

Single-Line Comments

A single-line comment starts with two consecutive forward slashes and stretches until the end of the source line. You've seen numerous examples of this style already:

```
// Bad
var mystery = GetSomething();   // what's the return type of GetSomething?
var x = 2159940436;             // answer immediately: int or long?
```

As you can see, the comment doesn't necessarily need to stand on its own in a line of code; it can also be used just at the end of a line after some meaningful source code. But it can't be used in the middle of a line of code because there's no way to terminate the run of comment text.

This style of commenting has a technical advantage: There are no worries about nesting of comments, which—as you will see in the next section—can be problematic. For this reason, Visual Studio provides tooling support for this commenting style, typically used to "comment out" a bunch of source code, as shown in Figure 4.24.

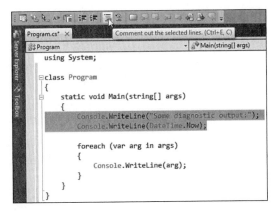

FIGURE 4.24   Single-line commenting a block of code in Visual Studio.

TIP

Don't leave large chunks of commented-out source code behind in code files; most people find it very distracting when reading code. Even though you've deleted a large portion of code because you found a better way to approach the problem, the old code might still be of value for archeological purposes. A better way to keep track of those changes is to use a decent source control system from which you can consult the history of source code files. Or if you really want to drop a hint in the source code, leave just the essence of the original problem behind to help others avoid repeating the same mistakes.

The Visual Studio editor uses a different colorization scheme for comments in source text. The default color is green, but you can change that.

A Primer to Preprocessing Directives

Use the Visual Studio feature to comment out blocks of code while evolving the code at development time. If you find yourself doing this quite often (for example, to enable or disable some diagnostic code), you're likely better off with conditional compilation using an #if preprocessing directive. We won't detail the preprocessing capabilities (which is really a misnomer in the world of C# because there's no separate preprocessor stage in compilation) right now, but here's the crux of it.

Using the #define directive, a symbol can be defined for further use in conditional preprocessing directives like #if. Blocks of code surrounded by #if and #endif are conditionally included in the source code analyzed by the compiler, based on whether the conditioning symbol is defined:

```
using System;

class Program
{
    static void Main(string[] args)
    {
#if DEBUG
        Console.WriteLine("Some diagnostic output:");
        Console.WriteLine(DateTime.Now);
#endif

        foreach (string arg in args)
        {
            Console.WriteLine(arg);
        }
    }
}
```

The DEBUG symbol I'm using in the preceding fragment is automatically set when using the Debug mode in Visual Studio. In Release mode, it isn't. You can define your own symbols using #define in the source text or by specifying the symbols to be set to a compiler flag. The Project Properties dialog's Build tab provides easy access to this setting, illustrated in Figure 4.25.

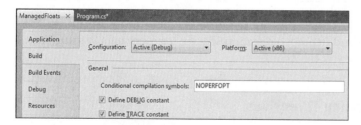

FIGURE 4.25   Defining symbols for conditional compilation.

TIP

Conditional compilation is a very powerful beast to maintain different build flavors of the same source code. For example, large portions of the BCL are compiled for the "desktop CLR" as well as for Silverlight. To accommodate for the slight differences required here and there, conditional compilation is used.

Delimited Comments

You might have expected multiline comments here, but the more significant distinguishing factor between different commenting styles is how a comment is terminated. For single-line comments, this means the comment runs until the end of the line. For delimited comments, a special character sequence is used to indicate the end of a comment.

Delimited comments are precisely that: They start with a /* sequence and end when the first */ sequence is encountered. They're especially useful for longer comments, eliminating the tedious repetition of //. In addition, you'll find them often used to provide a heading in source files, containing information about the file's reason for existence, its author, copyright information, and so on:

```
/* Program.cs
 *
 * Synopsis: Contains the managed entry-point of the application.
 * Author:   bartde
 *
 * Change history:
 * 06/07/2009 - Initial creation
 */

using System;

class Program
{
```

The use of asterisk characters in front of the lines that make up the delimited comment is not mandatory; they're just a matter of style. In fact, Visual Studio provides them by default when you add a new line to a delimited comment block.

Another place where delimited comments come in handy is to document parameters to methods at a call site in an inline manner:

```
file.Save("test.txt", /* overrideExisting = */ false);
```

In the preceding fragment, the false Boolean literal doesn't reveal its meaning from the context immediately. Instead of using local variables with an indicative name, delimited comments can be used to clarify meaning. Starting from C# 4.0, an alternative to this style exists in the form of *named parameters*, as you'll see later.

As mentioned before, one problem with delimited comments is the fact that they don't nest well. Recall my earlier definition: "They start with a /* sequence and end when the first */ sequence is encountered." So blindly surrounding a large piece of code with /* and */ is not a formula for guaranteed success. Visual Studio's choice to use single-line commenting style to comment out selected code is a direct reflection of this limitation.

As an example, consider the following piece of code:

```
/*
int x = 5;

/* Long comment starts here
 * ...
 */

Console.WriteLine("Some diagnostic output:");
Console.WriteLine(DateTime.Now);
*/
```

Here, the last `*/` isn't paired up with a starting `/*` sequence, causing a compilation error. In Visual Studio, because of correct colorization, you'll see this immediately.

Documentation Comments

The first goal of API writers obviously is to deliver a binary with the desired library functionality. But without decent documentation, it's often of little use for the consumers of it. No matter how good the naming of types and public members is, additional information on the intended behavior, caveats, and so on is invaluable, too.

To stimulate this practice and provide a structured approach for dealing with it, the C# specification defines the concept of documentation comments. They're only defined meaningfully when applied to user-defined types or members, where the compiler knows how to export them into a documentation file.

Documentation comments are based on XML to structure the different parts of documentation required. Two styles can be used to write them down, either by starting with a sequence of three forward slashes (`///`) or by using an extended version of delimited comments with an additional asterisk (`/**`). The former is preferred because Visual Studio helps you a lot. Third-party tools exist that help with the generation of comments as well. One sample is GhostDoc, which can be found through the Visual Studio Gallery of add-ins on MSDN.

For example, assume we've written a little Calculator class (cheesy, I know):

```
public static class Calculator
{
    public static int Add(int a, int b)
    {
        return a + b;
    }
}
```

Don't worry about the use of various modifiers such as static, which will become clear pretty soon. Suffice it to say I'm using best practices here by defining a stateless class as a static class.

Parts of the code that will benefit from documentation comments are the class itself, its public methods, and the parameters and the returned data. In this case, it's fairly obvious what the meaning is, but you can imagine much more involved definitions.

In Visual Studio, you can make the editor generate a template for required documentation by typing the /// sequence on the line in front of the entity to be documented. In Figure 4.26, I've done this for both the class and its Add method.

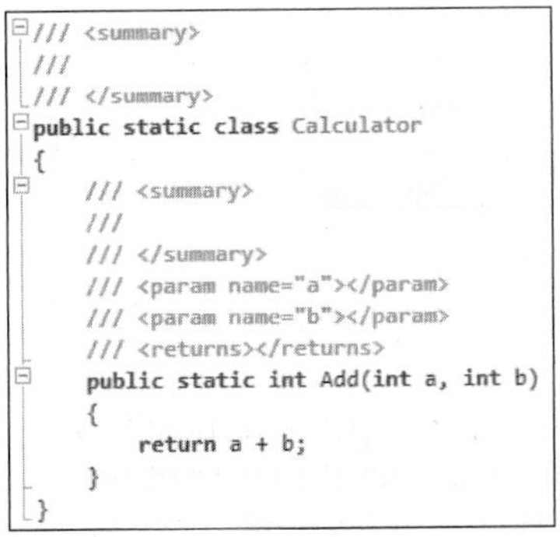

```
/// <summary>
///
/// </summary>
public static class Calculator
{
    /// <summary>
    ///
    /// </summary>
    /// <param name="a"></param>
    /// <param name="b"></param>
    /// <returns></returns>
    public static int Add(int a, int b)
    {
        return a + b;
    }
}
```

FIGURE 4.26   Generating documentation comments.

All you have to do now is supply some meaningful documentation. To make documentation as structured as possible, different tags are available, one of which appears Figure 4.27.

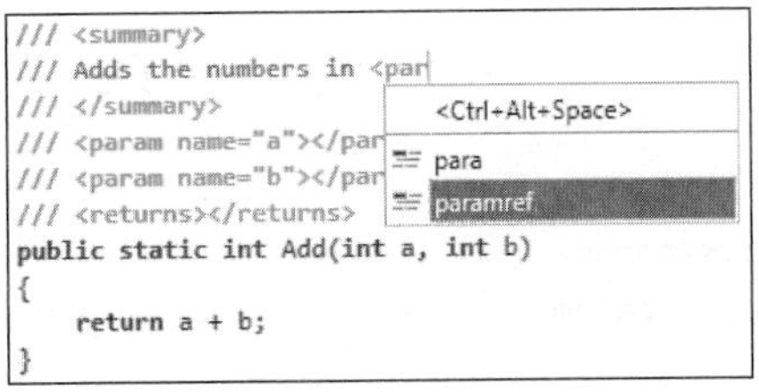

```
/// <summary>
/// Adds the numbers in <par
/// </summary>                    <Ctrl+Alt+Space>
/// <param name="a"></par
/// <param name="b"></par     ≡≡ para
/// <returns></returns>        ≡≡ paramref
public static int Add(int a, int b)
{
    return a + b;
}
```

FIGURE 4.27   IntelliSense for different tags is available.

Rich documentation on writing documentation comments is available in the MSDN library. The logical next question is how this documentation is emitted. First off, you need to tell the compiler to generate a documentation file. In Visual Studio, the one-stop shop for all such settings is the project's Properties window.

The setting that controls the documentation file generation lives under Build, Output. Notice you can tweak settings on a per-configuration basis: In Figure 4.28, I'm changing only the documentation file setting for the active Release configuration.

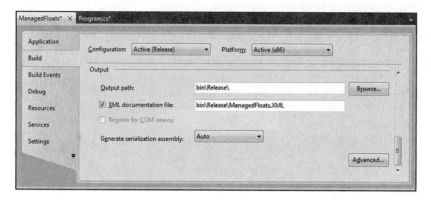

FIGURE 4.28   Enabling generation of the XML documentation file.

From this point on, the compiler will make sure all publicly visible types and members have (complete) documentation to go with them, generating warnings if that's not the case. An XML file will be emitted to the specified location. Here is an example of rich XML documentation commenting:

```
/// <summary>
/// Provides simple calculator functionality.
/// </summary>
public static class Calculator
{
    /// <summary>
    /// Adds the integer numbers <paramref name="a"/>
    /// and <paramref name="b"/> together.
    /// </summary>
    /// <param name="a">First integer term to add.</param>
    /// <param name="b">Second integer term to add.</param>
    /// <returns>
    /// Sum of the integer numbers <paramref name="a"/>
    /// and <paramref name="b"/>
    /// </returns>
    /// <exception cref="System.OverflowException">
    /// Thrown when the computed sum does not fit in the precision of
    /// System.Int32.
    /// </exception>
    /// <example>
```

```
/// <code>int res = Add(1, 2); // produces value 3</code>
/// </example>
public static int Add(int a, int b)
{
    return a + b;
}
}
```

Notice I've added more documentation about *exceptions* and provided a sample use. A whole chapter is dedicated to exceptions (see Chapter 8, "Basics of Exceptions and Resource Management"), and we also discuss the particular OverflowException later in Chapter 5, in the section, "Overflow Checking."

Take a look at the generated XML file next, shown in Figure 4.29.

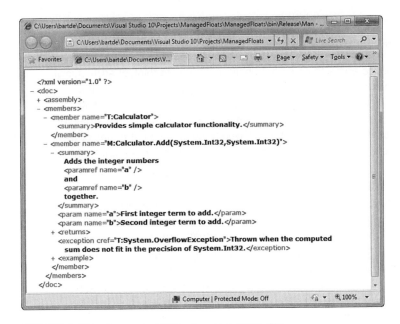

FIGURE 4.29   Generated XML documentation file.

SANDCASTLE

The XML documentation file is not ready for immediate consumption by end users; it deserves some formatting. Being XML, techniques such as XSLT can be used to put a nice face on the documentation. Various XSLT transforms for XML documentation can be found online.

But often people want more. What about tight integration with the MSDN documentation, for instance? This is possible too. To generalize the idea of XML documentation transformation, Microsoft has created a project code named Sandcastle, which is available at http://sandcastle.codeplex.com. This is highly recommended if you're looking for a professional way to generate rich documentation with indexes, search capabilities, and more.

Arrays

Now that we've covered the built-in types in quite some detail and know from a few examples it's possible to define our own types, we can delve a bit deeper. What about types of types? This might sound a bit "meta" at first, but the concept is very usable nevertheless. One such construct that allows the creation of types out of existing ones is called arrays.

A THEORETICAL UNDERTONE

Most books don't introduce arrays this way, but I believe it helps to think of such crucial concepts in a more structured manner. In particular, what we're talking about in this context are *type constructors*. Don't confuse this with *instance constructors* or *static constructors*, which both are proper C# language terms. Type constructors are a theoretical concept that expresses the capability of a new type to be created out of one or more existing ones, without the need to write down a separate definition for the new type.

Array types, *nullable types*, and *generic types* all fall under this theoretical umbrella. To focus on arrays, it's possible to take any type whatsoever and construct an array type out of it, without someone having to declare the array type explicitly. Suppose you've written a Person type. Wouldn't it be ridiculous and tedious if you had to define a Person[] array type yourself for users to be able to use that? I'm sure you agree.

Type constructors are precisely about that: Given an existing type, the runtime understands what it means to construct a more complex type over it. From a Person type, you can readily define a Person[] array or even a Person[][] array of arrays. Similar observations hold for nullable types and generic types, as you will see.

Internal Representation

Arrays provide storage for a number of variables that share a common type. Each element can be indexed by an integral number, both to retrieve it and then replace it. This index is zero-based. To create an array, a length needs to be specified to allocate memory for the contained variables. Note, too, that arrays are reference types, so they're passed by reference, and different variables can refer to the same array.

To illustrate how arrays are laid out in memory, take a look at Figure 4.30. Notice how the array variable acts as a reference to some other piece of memory containing the elements of the array.

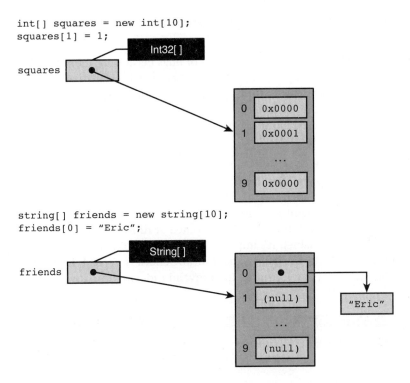

```
int[] squares = new int[10];
squares[1] = 1;
```

```
string[] friends = new string[10];
friends[0] = "Eric";
```

FIGURE 4.30   Arrays of value types and reference types.

Arrays can be created for value type or reference type elements. Upon creation, the CLR ensures the memory for the array is zeroed out and doesn't contain any garbage, as would be the case in some other languages and runtimes. For value types, this means retrieving an element from a newly allocated array will result in a zero value; for reference types, you'll get back a null reference. We discuss this later in the section, "The Null Reference."

Single-Dimensional Arrays

Let's start by having a look at single-dimensional arrays:

```
int[] squares = new int[10];
```

This code creates an instance of an integer array of length 10. To set and get elements in the array, indices between 0 and 9 (inclusive bounds) can be used:

```
squares[3] = 9;
// ...
Console.WriteLine(squares[3]); // prints 9
```

You'll see more structured ways to get or set all elements in an array later, using loops and eventually using LINQ.

Historically, arrays have been a source of lots of bugs because of the lack of bounds checking. In C and C++, for example, the length of an array is typically passed together with the array (or in lower-level terms for those languages, a pointer) for the recipient to do proper bounds checking. Bugs come from indexing too far into the array, ending up in unknown memory territory. Notorious security vulnerabilities, such as buffer overruns, come precisely from this.

To eliminate this class of bugs, arrays on the CLR are bounds-checked all the time. A little performance penalty applies, yes, but with a huge return on investment. If code violates the bounds of an array somehow, an IndexOutOfRangeException is thrown at runtime. Why at runtime? Indexing into an array does not need to happen using a constant index value; more often than not, the index is computed at runtime (for example, squares[i], where i is an integer variable). It's impossible for the compile to know the range of such a computed value in all circumstances, so a runtime check is needed. Figure 4.31 shows an IndexOutOfRangeException occurring upon invalid indexing into an array.

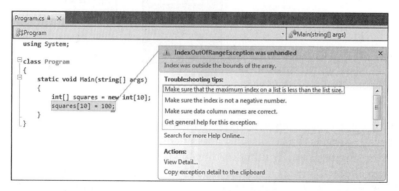

FIGURE 4.31   Invalid indexing of an array triggering an exception.

Bounds-checked omissions or violations indicate severe bugs in your code. Either you have to sanitize (user) input that resulted in the computation of an invalid index, or you need proper bounds checking somewhere nearby. To retrieve the length of an array from which you can compute the bounds, use the Length (get-only) property:

```
for (int i = 0; i < squares.Length; i++)
{
    squares[i] = i * i;
}
```

Here we're using a for loop, where the loop condition checks that the index variable falls within the range of the array's boundaries. We discuss the precise structure of this loop construct later, but it should be fairly understandable on the face of it.

Notice we need to use a strict less-than comparison because array indices in C# are zero based. Some other languages, such as Visual Basic, allow us to control the base of arrays (in Visual Basic's case using the Option Base statement); C# doesn't.

Array Initializers

Sometimes arrays have to be prepopulated with elements. To make this easier, a different form of array creation expression exists:

```
int[] squares = new int[] { 0, 1, 4, 9, 16, 25, 36, 49, 64, 81 };
```

Here the length of the array is inferred from the number of expressions in the initializer list. If you specify the length between the square brackets, the number of elements that are provided must match.

 In fact, the syntax can be abbreviated. Notice the redundancy in saying the type of the elements multiple times here. A shorter notation, using an implicitly typed array creation expression, is as follows:

```
int[] squares = new [] { 0, 1, 4, 9, 16, 25, 36, 49, 64, 81 };
```

Or even

```
int[] squares = { 0, 1, 4, 9, 16, 25, 36, 49, 64, 81 };
```

And the icing on the cake, using an implicitly typed local variable:

```
var squares = new [] { 0, 1, 4, 9, 16, 25, 36, 49, 64, 81 };
```

When the type of the array elements is left unspecified, as shown here, the best common type of the elements in the initializer list is used as the type for the array. We talk more about this concept when you have a better understanding of types and inheritance hierarchies.

Behind the Scenes

Those of you interested in the machinery for initializing arrays likely wonder about the performance of this. Is the preceding code really syntactical sugar for a bunch of store operations into an array, which would cause excessive offset calculations and bounds checking? Luckily, the answer is no.

Take a look at the disassembled code for the following fragment and compare it to the resulting IL code shown in Figure 4.32:

```
int[] squares = { 0, 1, 4, 9, 16, 25, 36, 49, 64, 81 };
Console.WriteLine(squares[5]);
```

The first two instructions here are used to create a new array (newarr instruction) with element type System.Int32 and size for 10 elements. In the last few instructions of the method, you can observe the indexing operation to retrieve the element at index 5, using the ldelem instruction.

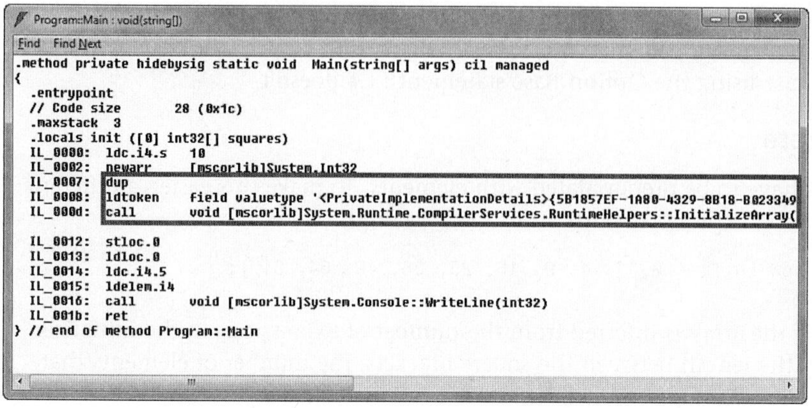

Program::Main : void(string[])
Find Find Next
.method private hidebysig static void Main(string[] args) cil managed
{
.entrypoint
// Code size 28 (0x1c)
.maxstack 3
.locals init ([0] int32[] squares)
IL_0000: ldc.i4.s 10
IL_0002: newarr [mscorlib]System.Int32
IL_0007: dup
IL_0008: ldtoken field valuetype '<PrivateImplementationDetails>{5B1857EF-1A80-4329-8B18-B023349
IL_000d: call void [mscorlib]System.Runtime.CompilerServices.RuntimeHelpers::InitializeArray(
IL_0012: stloc.0
IL_0013: ldloc.0
IL_0014: ldc.i4.5
IL_0015: ldelem.i4
IL_0016: call void [mscorlib]System.Console::WriteLine(int32)
IL_001b: ret
} // end of method Program::Main

FIGURE 4.32 Initialization of an array.

The instructions in the rectangle are of particular interest with regard to the array's initialization code. Here a method called `InitializeArray` is called, passing in the newly created array instance and a token. This token is where the magic lives.

If you scan through the name of the token provided to the ldtoken instruction, you'll see `__StaticArrayInitTypeSize=40`, indicating a total byte size of 40 bytes. Recall that `Int32` takes up 32 bits or 4 bytes, and we have 10 elements.

But where's the data itself? In the main window of ILDASM, you'll see a helper class next to the `Program` class, as shown in Figure 4.33. Here, I've highlighted a field, ready for you to double-click it. Don't be shocked by the random numbers generated by the compiler; it needs to enforce uniqueness:

```
.field static assembly valuetype '<PrivateImplementationDetails>{5B1857EF-1A80-4329-
8B18-B023349B2AC2}'/'__StaticArrayInitTypeSize=40' '$$method0x6000001-1' at
I_00002050
```

ManagedFloats.exe - IL DASM
File View Help
ManagedFloats.exe
MANIFEST
<PrivateImplementationDetails>{5B1857EF-1A80-4329-8B18-B023349B2AC2}
.class private auto ansi
.custom instance void [mscorlib]System.Runtime.CompilerServices.Compiler
__StaticArrayInitTypeSize=40
$$method0x6000001-1 : static assembly valuetype '<PrivateImplementatio
Program
.class private auto ansi beforefieldinit
.ctor : void()
Main : void(string[])
.assembly ManagedFloats
{

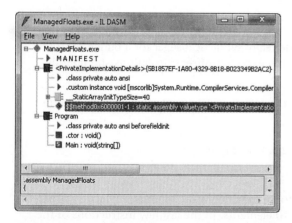

FIGURE 4.33 The field pointing at the array's initialization data.

The last line, with the at IL keyword, is of interest. This number is an offset into a section of the generated assembly file (which gets stored in the standard executable format known as Portable Executable or PE), relative to the base for the executable image. If you're a real geek, read on; otherwise, just remember this: The compiler has turned our array initializer into a blob of binary data that's being loaded as a whole in a very efficient way.

If you want to dig deeper from this point on, you'll need a tool called dumpbin.exe, which gets installed with Visual Studio 2010 in the Visual C++ binaries folder. Your Visual Studio 2010 command prompt should have it on the search path by default. If you run `dumpbin.exe /all`, passing in the name of your assembly, you'll see a bunch of data flying over the screen. This is the binary dump of the assembly.

First you need to find the base address, which is found near the top in the Optional Header Values section. It's called "image base" and should have (assuming default settings) a value of 400000. Previously, we found an offset of 00002050 through the IL disassembly. This number can be different, so double-check it. Either way, add up the two numbers, and you've found the raw address where the array's initialization data lives (in my case, that's 402050).

If you scroll down farther in the dumpbin output, you'll find a section Raw Data #1. This is where you'll take a look next. Locate the address found previously in the left column (for example, 402050). At this point, you'll see the ten 4-byte values in hexadecimal.

Jagged Arrays

As you learned earlier, arrays have a *type constructor* nature, meaning any existing type can be used to create another array type (a recursive definition, that is). So what about arrays of arrays? Sure enough, that works:

```
int[][] vectors = new int[3][];
```

An array with elements that are arrays by themselves is called a *jagged array*.

In the preceding example, we're creating an array of integer arrays and specifying the number of such arrays we want. The vectors array contains arrays by itself, which are reference types. So right after the creation of the jagged array, it contains null references for the elements. Next, we can initialize those elements as follows:

```
vectors[0] = new int[4];
vectors[1] = new int[2];
vectors[2] = new int[3];
```

Notice how the dimensions of the jagged array's element arrays do not need to match; this is where the name *jagged arrays* comes from. Notice the jagged line on the right in Figure 4.34 where we illustrate this concept.

```
int[][] vectors = new int[3][];
vectors[0] = new int[4];
vectors[1] = new int[2];
vectors[2] = new int[3];
```

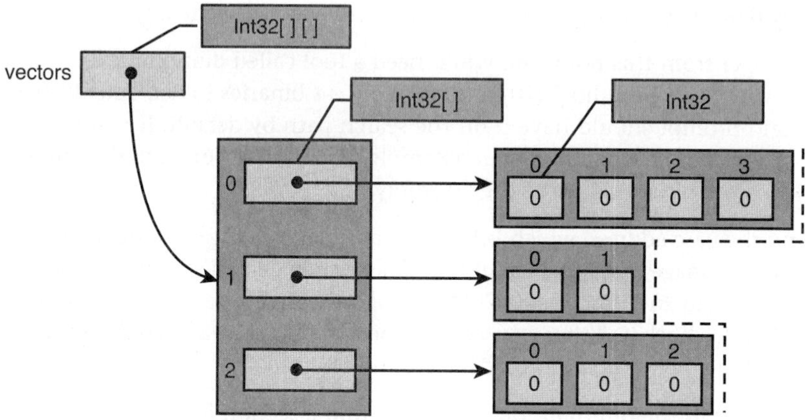

FIGURE 4.34   Jagged arrays.

More than two dimensions can be used, too. The number of dimensions is known as the *rank* of the array, which can be retrieved using the Rank *property*. Referring to elements in the array happens through consecutive indexing operations:

```
int[][][] moreVectors = new int[3][][];
// ...
moreVectors[0][1][2] = 15;
```

Having to initialize the jagged arrays one by one can be very tedious. If you already know the entire shape of the array, you can once more leverage the power of array initialization expressions:

```
var jagged = new [] {
    new [] {
        new [] { 1, 2, 3 },
        new [] { 4, 5 }
    },
    new [] {
        new [] { 6 },
        new [] { 7, 8, 9 }
    },
};
```

Multidimensional Arrays

Jagged arrays do not need to (but can) have a rectangular shape, which is what makes them jagged in the first place. In some situations, arrays have a more regular shape, making them amenable to the use of multidimensional arrays. A typical example is a Sudoku challenge, which has nine rows and nine columns:

```
byte[,] sudoku = new byte[9,9];
```

The number of dimensions is indicated by writing commas between the square brackets of the array type. When initializing the array, the size of the dimensions is specified. In this particular case, we have two dimensions, but more dimensions are allowed (creating cubes or hypercubes).

DON'T WASTE SPACE

In Chapter 27, "Diagnostics and Instrumentation," we discuss code analysis (otherwise known as FxCop) to examine how code quality can be guarded by a set of analysis rules that are run during build. Multidimensional arrays trigger a warning in the category performance because they tend to be misused from time to time, leading to a waste of space. This puts additional pressure on the garbage collector and can negatively impact performance.

As a rule of thumb, if the array you're dealing with is sparse—that is, contains a lot of empty or zero-valued cells—you're better off with jagged arrays.

Indexing into a multidimensional array is done by comma-separating the indices:

```
int topLeft = boardGame[0,0];
boardGame[3,3] = 1;
```

Internally, the indices are used to compute the offset in the consecutive range of memory storing the array. Figure 4.35 illustrates a multidimensional array.

To initialize the array, different syntaxes are allowed once more, but the most convenient one is likely the following:

```
int[,] boardGame = {
    { 0, 1, 2, 3 },
    { 1, 2, 3, 4 },
    { 2, 3, 0, 1 },
    { 3, 0, 1, 2 },
};
```

```
byte[,] boardGame = new byte[4, 4];
```

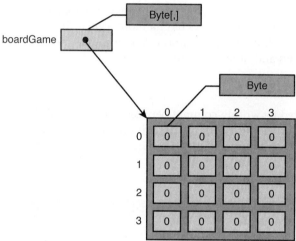

FIGURE 4.35   Multidimensional arrays have a cubic shape.

If any of the "rows" is not initialized with a sufficient number of "columns," the compiler will trigger an error.

CODING STYLE

Notice the comma at the end of the fifth line? This one is optional, but the language allows it as a matter of style. There are some other places where this is the case, such as in the definition of enumerations. So don't be surprised if you see someone writing this; the code will compile fine.

Multidimensional arrays are not a C# thing only. Write the following piece of code:

```
int topLeft = boardGame[0,0];
boardGame[3,3] = 1;
```

This assumes you have a boardGame array initialized as shown before. Now take a look at the IL code for the set operation, for example. From this, you can see how multidimensional arrays are known at a fairly low level:

```
ldloc.0    // array:            boardGame[
ldc.i4.3   // row:              3,
ldc.i4.3   // column:           3] =
ldc.i4.1   // value to be set: 1
call       instance void int32[0...,0...]::Set(int32, int32, int32)
```

The Null Reference

So as not to complicate the discussion prematurely, I've not yet introduced a special citizen in the world of reference types: null. Recall that reference types refer to some data that lives somewhere in memory. Multiple variables of that reference type can refer to the same data simultaneously, causing aliasing. However, it's equally valid for a variable of a reference type to refer to nothing. This is known as the *null reference*. Think of it as a special "value" every reference type has available, readily provided by the runtime. In C#, the null literal can be used to write down a null reference. For example:

```
string name = null;
```

Notice the null literal by and in itself doesn't have a type. More specifically, it's one of the few expressions that are typeless. Why this matters will become apparent later when we discuss method overload resolution in Chapter 10, for example. One implication that's of immediate relevance is the fact that you can't use the null literal in the context of an implicitly typed local variable:

```
var unknown = null; // Error: Cannot assign null to an implicitly-typed local.
```

NULL, NOTHING, NADA

If you ever need to read or write Visual Basic code, the null literal there is written as Nothing. It's a little unfortunate the NullReferenceException is mirrored after the C# nomenclature for null references. If we had first-class typedef support in the system, it would make sense to define a NothingReferenceException alias for Visual Basic users.

Although conceptually related, null reference exceptions are not the same as access violations, which occur in native code when a zero pointer is dereferenced. In the context of null references, we're talking about managed code references: They boil down to memory locations ultimately but are subject to garbage collection and carry rich type information for use by the CLR.

Figure 4.36 contrasts a null reference with a reference to an existing object in memory, known as the heap.

What's Null Really?

Nullability can be quite an artificial concept to think about. When something is null, is it undefined or what? Consider the example of a phone book. Given a name, you can look up a phone number. But what if you don't find an entry? Does it mean the person doesn't exist at all, or does it mean that person doesn't have a phone? Not to mention private numbers that are unlisted!

```
string name = null;
```

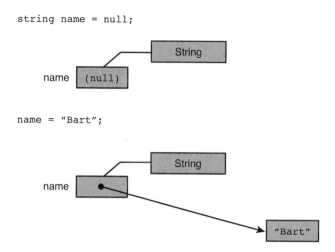

```
name = "Bart";
```

FIGURE 4.36   The null reference.

Unfortunately, opinions vary. Some say null indicates no value has been set; however, the answer is that there's no answer. Others overload the meaning to indicate situations where no value can be found or computed: It's impossible to formulate an answer. In my opinion, the latter interpretation should be avoided. Why? Null is simply not a good way to indicate errors. Better ways exist, such as returning a success/failure Boolean indicator or throwing exceptions. The absence of a value—which is what null is really about—may indicate an error, but it can equally be a valid situation.

Go back to the phone book example. Two fundamentally different conditions exist: Either the specified name can't be found or a blank entry exists. In the first case, we've caught an error; either input was invalid, or the phone book is incomplete. The second case did produce an answer, though; a user was found but no phone number is known. If null were returned in both cases, how would the caller distinguish what has happened? And consider what would happen when empty entries were initially not allowed in our phone book but we want to change that: All callers would have to be rewritten to account for the two possible interpretation of null.

This follows the idea of null as a proper value within the domain of a type.

NOTE

System.Collections.Generic.Dictionary<TKey,TElement> is a generic collection type that supports our desired phone book semantics. Two methods exist to retrieve the value for a given key: Either an exception is thrown if the key is not found or a Boolean is returned to signal this condition to the user. Notice that the use of null doesn't appear in this picture at all, keeping it available as a proper value for use within the dictionary. We discuss collections extensively in Chapter 16, "Collection Types."

A Common Source of Bugs

When an operation has to be invoked on an instance of such a reference type, a dereferencing operation occurs. It's invalid, though, to dereference the null reference, causing an exception to occur. Figure 4.37 shows such a NullReferenceException.

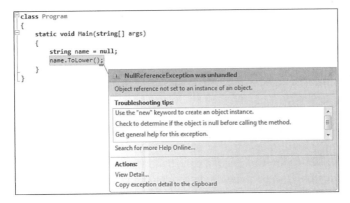

FIGURE 4.37   A bad encounter with a null reference.

Null references that are unaccounted for are probably the number one source of bugs in managed code programming. Rigorous checking for null references is an important pattern everyone should master. Obviously, the question is where such checks need to be applied.

When designing a new library, it's essential to specify the intended treatment of null references coming in: Are they allowed or not? If not, how does the system protect against them? Equally so for the output: Under what circumstances can the caller expect a null reference to be returned? Essentially, you should crisply delineate the boundaries where null references are allowed.

Although we talk much more about this, here's a typical trick to protect against null references. Assume we've defined some method—a process we discuss in Chapter 10—accepting a parameter that's potentially null:

```
public void ChargeAccount(Account account, decimal amount)
{
    if (account == null)
        throw new ArgumentNullException("account");

    // Account processing code goes here...
}
```

Here we've protected a public method against a null reference coming in—assuming no meaningful behavior can be defined in the face of such an input—by *throwing* an exception if case of a detected violation. This ensures we don't blow up much deeper in the code, potentially leaving things in a broken state and making it much harder to trace the source of the problem.

Different exception types are used to indicate different kinds of failures or in this case violations. ArgumentNullException—as the name implies—indicates an unexpected (hence exceptional) null reference for the specified parameter. When other types of violations occur, such as an argument that has an expected value outside a normal range of operation, exceptions of a different type are *thrown*. A commonly used one is ArgumentException.

ASSERTIONS AND CONTRACTS

Throwing exceptions is just one technique to guard against incoming data violating some contract. Exceptions are particularly useful to harden a public API surface where you can't trust the call to do the right thing. However, internally in your code it's common to have invariants that you want to hold true at all times, as well as pre- and post-conditions. In essence, all of those are truth-valued conditions that indicate the validity of some state. An invariant holds at all times; a precondition holds at the beginning of some block (like a method), a post-condition at the end.

In sufficiently tested code, preferably in an automated fashion, assertions for such checks suffice at development time. When the code is stressed under various conditions, the assertions should never fail. This is where the typical use of *debug asserts* come in. Not only do they check the health of the code, they also provide a great source of documentation right inside the code.

Code contracts extend on this idea of asserts, having checks for valid states right inside the code. Other than debug asserts, contracts can both be enforced at runtime and checked at compile time. The runtime aspects of contracts consists of running code that performs the required checks and throws an exception upon detection of a violation. At compile time, a theorem prover is used to derive conditions that cause contracts to be violated.

You can think of code contracts as asserts on steroids, providing much richer information about the conditions under which the code can operate and what's expected from callers. It also helps a lot with maintenance of software as contracts provide rich information and have the ability to catch violations early. You're only just starting to see what's possible with .NET 4.0 code contracts.

Nullable Value Types

So far, we've examined nullability only in the context of reference types. If this book had been written in the .NET 1.0 time frame, a reference types context would have been the only valid context to discuss the concept. Let's recap value and reference types first. Their main characteristic lies in the way instances of the type are passed. Value types pass their data by value, whereas reference types just copy a reference to the data, which means sharing can occur.

The fact that null was supported only for reference types was unfortunate, exposing to the surface something that should really have been an implementation detail. Whether a type supports null as a possible value should be decoupled from the type's physical representation.

For example, think of databases where an integer-valued column can contain null values. If you don't know the shoe size of a customer (and your database schema permits this situation), leave it empty. Whether shoe sizes are represented as values or references into some table is totally irrelevant in this discussion. Either way, they should have the right to be null.

One way to circumvent this problem in the .NET 1.0 time frame was to store a Boolean-valued "nullness" indicator next to the value-typed data:

```
class Person
{
    private int _shoeSize;
    private bool _hasKnownShoeSize;
}
```

This is definitely a cumbersome pattern in a world where null is already a well-established concept. To rectify this situation, .NET 2.0 introduced the concept of nullable value types.

UNION TYPES

Types are like sets that define all the permitted "values" instances can have. In fact, the analogy between type theory and set theory is well defined in academia. This is nothing you should really need to know to write code in C#, but some other languages make this correspondence very visible.

F# is such an example, where nullability is expressed in the form of *option types*. An option type is constructed over an underlying type, extending its value domain with an additional None value. For example, consider the int type, which does not have None as a valid value:

```
let a : int = 1
let b : int = None          (* invalid *)
```

In other words, the type is not nullable. To give the type nullability support, an option type is created:

```
let c : int option = Some(1)
let d : int option = None    (* valid *)
```

The option type is a sample of a *discriminated union*: The set of values it supports consists of the union of other sets. With the option type, this is the union of the underlying type's domain (here, int) and the singleton None value.

Internal Representation

Not surprisingly, given the existing physical representation of value types and reference types, nullable value types are represented precisely as an *encapsulation* of this pattern (but one both the runtime and various languages such as C# know about).

Let's start on the lowest level with the runtime. Given a value type, which intrinsically can't accommodate for the null value, how do we create its nullable counterpart? The answer is Nullable<T>, a generic type where T is the type parameter that accepts a value type. Figure 4.38 dissects a nullable value in terms of a Boolean flag and an optional value of type T.

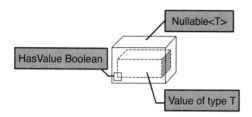

FIGURE 4.38   Representation of a Nullable<T>.

Compare this type to a box, which can either contain something or nothing (Value), as revealed by a label (HasValue) on the outside. If the box is empty according to HasValue, the Value is meaningless. In reality, some value will sit in memory (because the underlying value type is not nullable), but it's garbage that's unavailable to the user.

The whole Nullable<T> by itself is a value type—which provides benefits in terms of memory management, as you will see in Chapter 9, in the section, "Heap Versus Stack"— and maintains a Boolean flag indicating whether a value has been set.

Use in C#

Let's take a look at an example:

```
int a = 42;
int b = null; // doesn't compile

Nullable<int> c = 42;
Nullable<int> d = null; // this is valid
```

Having to write Nullable<int> every time you need a nullable integer can be quite tedious. For that reason, C# has created a shorthand syntax for nullables, suffixing the (value) type name with a question mark:

```
int? c = 42;
int? d = null; // this is valid
```

KLEENE CLOSURES

Readers who are familiar with regular expressions or formal means to express grammar and such might have heard about the Kleene closure operators. And even if you haven't, you'll have used wildcards in some command prompt environment. Three essential suffix operators exist, denoting different multiplicities. Given some kind of token, suffixing it with the * operator means zero or more instances, as in `dir *.exe` (where the asterisk means any number of permitted characters). The + operator doesn't allow for empty productions and hence means one or more instances. Finally, ? stands for zero or none.

It should be no surprise that the ? notation in C# resembles the corresponding Kleene operator, which essentially expresses the concept of nullability.

Being able to assign the `null` literal to a nullable value type is nice, but what about testing for `null`? Sure enough, C# permits this, too, to reduce friction as much as possible. Nullable value types just look like reference types in their use:

```
double? number = GetNumber();
if (number != null)
{
    // Do something
}
```

Nullable value types being value types themselves cannot have a null value on the level of the CLR though. Recall that this is where this whole exercise of making value types support null values started.

What you're looking at in the preceding code fragment is syntactical sugar: The C# language makes the code look straightforward, but internally more complex machinery is put into action. This is a good thing, relieving the developer from having to know details that hinder productivity and spoil code readability. In fact, the preceding fragment is equivalent to the following form, where the `HasValue` property is used:

```
double? number = GetNumber();
if (number.HasValue)
{
    // Do something
}
```

Curious readers can see this from ILDASM (see Figure 4.39). Many more places where syntactical sugar is applied will become apparent as we proceed. If you're curious about how things work, as I am, you'll find it irresistible to put shortcuts to ILDASM in all sorts of prominent places.

```
Program::Main : void(string[])

Find   Find Next

.method private hidebysig static void  Main(string[] args) cil managed
{
  .entrypoint
  // Code size       15 (0xF)
  .maxstack  1
  .locals init ([0] valuetype [mscorlib]System.Nullable`1<float64> number)
  IL_0000:  call       valuetype [mscorlib]System.Nullable`1<float64> Program::GetNumber()
  IL_0005:  stloc.0
  IL_0006:  ldloca.s   number
  IL_0008:  call       instance bool valuetype [mscorlib]System.Nullable`1<float64>:: get_HasValue()
  IL_000d:  pop
  IL_000e:  ret
} // end of method Program::Main
```

FIGURE 4.39   Null-checks against nullable value types are syntactical sugar.

DOES THE COMMON LANGUAGE RUNTIME KNOW?

Because nullable value types have syntactical sugar support in languages such as C# and Visual Basic, a popular misconception exists about their nature. Although they're mostly just an ordinary generic value type, they get special treatment in a few places in the CLR. Boxing, a memory-related concept covered in the next chapter, is one place where the CLR has built-in notions about Nullable<T>.

Nowadays, it's fair to say the CLR's type system in conjunction with nice language support approaches nullability and the distinction between value and reference types as two orthogonal concepts, rectifying the 1.0 situation.

A Type Background

From a type perspective, you can draw the parallel to array types and generic types as *type constructors*. Given a type, another type can be constructed thanks to out-of-the-box runtime and language facilities. For nullable value types, that's the case, too, but with some restrictions. As the name implies, they're only supported over value types, but it's also impossible to "nest" them, as in int?? or Nullable<Nullable<int>>.

The top part of Figure 4.40 shows the principle of a type constructor. Given any type T, as indicated by the dotted-lined box, a more complex type can be created. In this example, it's a Nullable<T> type that provides a box around the original type with the HasValue and Value properties on it. At the bottom, concrete instances of a Nullable<Block>—or Block? in C# lingo—are shown. The label on the box represents the HasValue property, which is either set to true or false. On the left, there's a null-valued block; on the right, a blue Lego block has been wrapped inside a nullable Block? type.

Of course, this assumes a Block would be meaningfully represented as a value type, which is done purely for illustration purposes here. Agreed, this is a bit dubious: I've rarely seen children play with blocks in a value-passing style because that would involve taking a copy of a block every time it's handed out.

Type Constructor

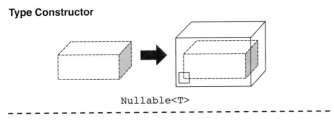

Nullable<T>

- -

Block? Objects

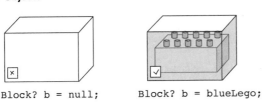

Block? b = null;   Block? b = blueLego;

FIGURE 4.40   Nullable<T> from an abstract viewpoint.

LIFE WITHOUT NULL?

Let's be clear about one thing first: An orthogonal approach for nullability versus the distinction between value and reference types is absolutely a good thing. It should be every type's right to support null as a proper value if it chooses to do so. However, the attentive reader will spot another missing piece from the puzzle. With the inception of nullable value types, null was brought to the world of value types. This aligns well with modern society: Adding capabilities is always seen as a good thing. But what about the opposite? Maybe I want to define a type for which null cannot be defined meaningfully.

So here we are with a new asymmetry. For value types, we can *opt in* to nullability if we want to support null values. But for reference types, we can't *opt out* from nullability if we don't want to support null values. This proves to be a common source of errors as people miss out on null checks.

A farfetched idea? Not really. Some languages (for example, Eiffel) have built-in support for non-null types (also known as *nonvoid* types in Eiffel). Another sample is Spec#, a research language created by Microsoft Research, based on C#. Spec#'s notation for a non-null type used the exclamation mark, as in string! for a non-null string. F# strikes a middle by embracing nullability for existing .NET types but promotes non-null types by making them the standard for newly defined types. When null is required, regardless of the underlying type representation, an option type is used.

Why are non-null types not in the mainstream languages and CLR at this point then? One answer is to be found in the complications it brings to existing languages. Where nullability extends the domain of a type, non-null types restrict it. For nullable value types, if a language doesn't support syntax for it (like int? in C#), the type is still usable (although its use will become a bit more cumbersome). However, when taking away values, the language needs to have rules to ensure no nullable values are assigned in non-nullable positions. In a multilanguage world, this would be a very invasive change.

All is not lost, though. With .NET 4.0 code contracts, a library approach is taken to provide non-null contracts on variables. The underlying type doesn't change, and no syntax has to be added to languages, so the impact on existing languages and tools is minimal. Because contracts get compiled into IL code, common tools can be provided to check non-null constraints regardless of the used language:

```
public void ContractSample(string input)
{
    Contract.Requires(input != null);
    // ...
}
```

Think of this as an extension to the method signature that can be used by tools to reason about the code, prove potential violations against the contract, emit rich documentation for users of the API, and so on. Contracts can either be compiled into the code, resulting in runtime checks, or compiled away when automated tools are used to prove or disprove the contract's validity by means of static code analysis. By having it as a library, all languages can benefit from it.

Summary

By exploring the entry point of a program, we put ourselves in a position to experiment with language essentials in this and the chapters to come. In this chapter, you learned a good deal about the role types play in programs and what the built-in types are. Concepts such as types, objects, instances, variables, assignment, arrays, and nullable value types should hold no secrets for you anymore.

In the next chapter, we continue on our merry way through the C# language by starting to write code that really does something. Expressions will be used to compute values, and statements will drive the program's execution through mechanisms such as control flow.

CHAPTER 5

Expressions and Operators

IN THIS CHAPTER

▶ What Are Expressions? 247

▶ The Evaluation Stack 251

▶ Arithmetic Operators 255

▶ String Concatenation 266

▶ Shift Operators 270

▶ Relational Operators 271

▶ Logical Operators 273

▶ Conditional Operators 278

▶ An Operator's Result Type 281

▶ Null-Coalescing Operator 282

▶ Assignment 285

Continuing our journey through language essentials, we've arrived at the point where we focus on blocks of code. One thing we need is the ability to compute values based on existing ones, using expressions. Besides this, there's a need for control flow structures, sequencing of instructions, and so on, which is provided through statements. In this chapter, we start by looking at expressions. In the next chapter we continue our journey through expressions related to working with objects. Statements are covered in the chapters following our discussion of expressions.

What Are Expressions?

A key ingredient to every programming language's expressiveness stems from the use of expressions. In fact, some languages are (almost) entirely based on this concept. C# isn't that extreme though. But what are expressions? According to the language specification:

An expression is a sequence of operators and operands.

First, it's important to notice expressions typically denote a value by means of some computation. This is achieved by having operators operate on one or more operands, carrying out the desired computation. Because expressions represent a value, they also do have a type.

Examples of operators include arithmetic operators, comparison operators, and so on. Operands can be variables, literals, or even other expressions. This gives rise to a tree structure, as illustrated in Figure 5.1.

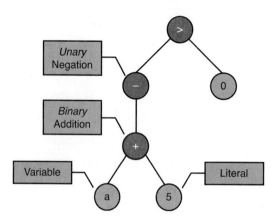

FIGURE 5.1 Operators and operands in an expression.

Arity of Operators

Operators have an *arity*, indicating the number of operands on which they operate. For example, negating an integer value takes just one operand and is said to be a *unary operator*. Other operations, such as addition or Boolean conjunction, require two operands and are therefore classified as *binary operators*. The maximum number of operands in any operator in the C# language is three, making those operators *ternary operators*.

Precedence and Associativity

Operators also have a precedence relative to one another. The use of parentheses can be used to circumvent those precedence rules. It's often clearer to add some gratuitous pairs of parentheses than to assume every reader of the code is intimately familiar with the precedence of operators used in an expression.

Everyone knows examples from high school mathematics:

```
a + b * c
```

The preceding evaluates b times c before carrying out the addition with a. Adding parentheses—here really redundant as every self-respecting developer should know those basic math rules, at least in my opinion—makes this ordering explicit:

```
a + (b * c)
```

Obviously, if you want to multiply the sum of a and b with c, precedence needs to be overridden by adding a required pair of parentheses:

```
(a + b) * c
```

Alternatively, intermediate results could be stored in temporary local variables, which is a good idea in case expressions become too large.

Table 5.1 showcases all available operators.

TABLE 5.1   Operator Precedence

Category	Operators
Primary	x.y f(x) a[x] x++ x— new typeof default checked unchecked delegate
Unary	+ , ! ~ ++x —x (T)x
Multiplicative	* / %
Additive	+ -
Shift	<< >>
Relational, type test	< > <= >= is as
Equality	== !=
Logical AND	&
Logical XOR	^
Logical OR		
Conditional AND	&&
Conditional OR	||
Null coalescing	??
Conditional	?:
Assignment, lambda	= *= /= %= += -= <<= >>= &= ^= |= =>

TIP

Come back to this table after you've reached the end of this chapter. You should be able to name all operators flawlessly, illustrate them with examples, and reason about their resulting types.

Besides precedence, associativity is an important concept when talking about evaluation of expressions. Assuming an operand (for example, the variable b) sandwiched between two operators (for example, the integer addition operator +), what's the order for the operations performed? In other words, does this operand associate with the operator on the left first or the one on the right first? For example:

```
a + b + c
```

Here, operand b is precisely in this situation. Two options exist: When treated in a left-associative manner, a + b is evaluated first. In a right-associative setting, b + c goes first. In this case, as for most binary operators, left associativity is used:

```
(a + b) + c
```

As an example of right-associativity, consider the following assignment:

```
a = b = c
```

Here, c will get evaluated first, after which it's assigned to b. The result of the assignment is then assigned to a. Yes, this means an assignment operation has a value, as you will see later:

```
a = (b = c)
```

Evaluation of Subexpressions

Precedence and *associativity* define the order in which operators are applied to their operands. This is only part of the story, though. Another question is when the operands are turned into values that the operators can deal with. One of the reasons this is important is because of the potential side effects that occur during evaluation. Having a deterministic ordering for those is a welcome feature.

Let's set the scene by tweaking our preceding example just a tiny little bit:

```
int res = a() + b() * c();
```

Now a, b, and c are *methods* (or *delegates*, as discussed later) that get invoked. Ultimately, those return some value that's used for the operands of the various operators in this expression. Recall that the multiplication operator does bind stronger than the addition operator, so we already know the result of calling b and the result of calling c are going to feed in to the multiplication. We haven't said anything about the order in which these operands are evaluated, though.

To see why this matters, make a little transformation to the code, introducing temporary local variables for the evaluation results of the calls to a, b, and c:

```
int ta = a();
int tb = b();
int tc = c();

int res = ta + tb * tc;
```

From this, you can see that we've ordered the calls to a, b, and c in a left-to-right order. This is how the C# language specifies ordering for evaluation of subexpressions. Notice six orderings are possible in the preceding sample, but the left-to-right one is strictly enforced.

As mentioned before, this matters in the face of side effects. In this example, we've left those totally unspecified, but you could imagine a, b, and c printing something to the screen during evaluation. Thankfully, the order of those side effects is defined now.

The Evaluation Stack

To get a feeling about the way code executes on the .NET platform and to be able to analyze fragments of intermediate language (IL) code, it's important to know the concept of the evaluation stack. IL is a stack-based language, meaning various operations pop their operands or arguments from the stack to carry out evaluation. When evaluation completes and a result is produced, it gets pushed on the stack.

To illustrate this, consider our running example again:

```
int a = 1;
int b = 2;
int c = 3;

int res = a + b * c;
```

To simplify matters, I'm using constant values for the three local variables. Everyone knows the result here is 7, so we could have hard-coded the value, but what matters to us is to see how the calculation is carried out.

You can guess the answer lies in ILDASM once more. Compile the preceding code into a simple console application and take a look at the resulting code. It should look like the one shown in Figure 5.2, assuming you've built in Debug mode.

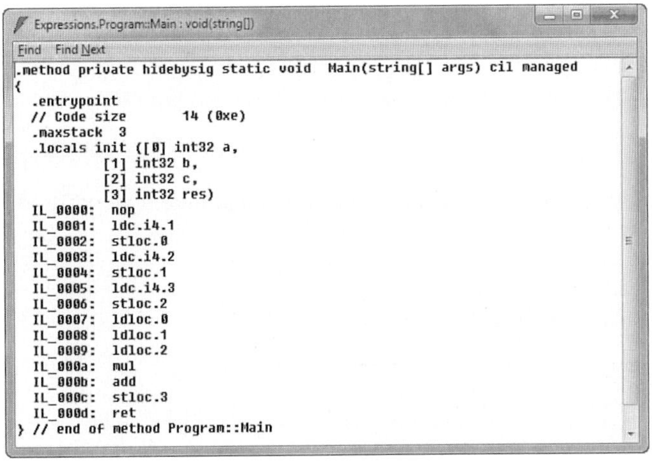

```
Expressions.Program::Main : void(string[])

Find  Find Next
.method private hidebysig static void  Main(string[] args) cil managed
{
  .entrypoint
  // Code size       14 (0xe)
  .maxstack  3
  .locals init ([0] int32 a,
           [1] int32 b,
           [2] int32 c,
           [3] int32 res)
  IL_0000:  nop
  IL_0001:  ldc.i4.1
  IL_0002:  stloc.0
  IL_0003:  ldc.i4.2
  IL_0004:  stloc.1
  IL_0005:  ldc.i4.3
  IL_0006:  stloc.2
  IL_0007:  ldloc.0
  IL_0008:  ldloc.1
  IL_0009:  ldloc.2
  IL_000a:  mul
  IL_000b:  add
  IL_000c:  stloc.3
  IL_000d:  ret
} // end of method Program::Main
```

FIGURE 5.2   Inspecting evaluation of expressions.

First, notice our four local variables are preserved and have the appropriate type. No surprise here. But let's take a closer look at the evaluation order.

OPTIMIZATION?

Couldn't the compiler have optimized the preceding code to just the constant value 7? After all, none of the operands involved in the expression are known at compile time. Sure, in this case this would be completely safe to do (and in fact, some functional languages would), but in the general case, this is not safe.

The reason doesn't lie in the operands, but in the operators. As discussed later, operators can be overloaded so that custom types can define their own meaning for operators. If those operators do not behave as a pure function—that is, side effects can occur—it's not safe to change any of the runtime behavior.

In case of Int32 operands, it just happens the compiler can know all the behavior statically. But even that is a bit brittle in relation to arithmetic overflow behavior. We'll come back to that later in this chapter.

All in all, C# is an imperative language, and this kind of nontrivial compile-time evaluation is avoided. One exception is the use of literals: If you were to write 1 + 2 * 3 in your source code, it would get evaluated at compile time and substituted with an integer value 7.

The first couple of lines of IL are fairly straightforward; they just deal with assigning constant 32-bit integer values to our local variables a, b, and c:

```
IL_0000:   nop
IL_0001:   ldc.i4.1
IL_0002:   stloc.0
IL_0003:   ldc.i4.2
IL_0004:   stloc.1
IL_0005:   ldc.i4.3
IL_0006:   stloc.2
```

However, we can already illustrate the essentials of the evaluation stack here. I've omitted the res variable from Figure 5.3, as well as the third assignment (for c).

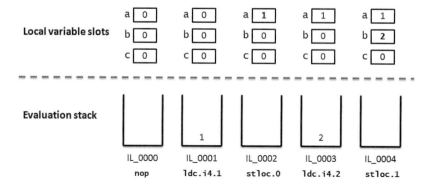

FIGURE 5.3   Evaluation stack transitions for assigning constants to variables.

The nop instruction is simply a debug build artifact that corresponds to the opening curly brace in the code. This allows developers to set a breakpoint on that line. Following this, you'll see three pairs of `ldc` and `stloc` instructions. Those correspond to the assignment statements for a, b, and c. Their stack behavior is of particular interest:

▶ `ldc` loads a constant by pushing it onto the stack.

▶ `stloc` pops the top value from the stack and stores it in a local variable slot.

At the start of the method, the stack is empty. At the end of the method, it should be, too, to keep the evaluation stack balanced. Also observe how local variable slots are zeroed out upon entrance of the method.

So far, so good. You've seen how the constants get assigned to local variables. On to the evaluation of the expression now:

```
IL_0007:   ldloc.0
IL_0008:   ldloc.1
IL_0009:   ldloc.2
IL_000a:   mul
IL_000b:   add
```

As you can guess, `ldloc` loads local variable slots and pushes the value onto the stack. The arithmetic instructions `mul` and `add` will pop two values from the stack, carry out the operation, and push the result, as shown in Figure 5.4.

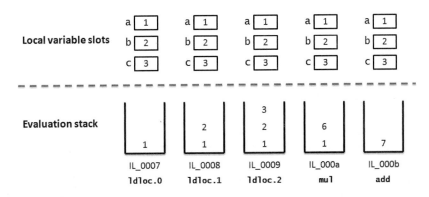

FIGURE 5.4   Evaluation stack transitions for arithmetic operations.

ABOUT REVERSE POLISH NOTATION AND HP CALCULATORS

Stack-driven evaluation as just described corresponds to postfix or reverse Polish notation, where the operator is written after its operands. For example, the infix a + b * c expression is turned into a b c * +. First a, b, and c are pushed on some stack, and then * reduces the top two values b and c by multiplying them, and finally + is performed over that result and a.

This approach has been very popular for use in desktop calculators (for example, the HP-10C series). With such calculators, you first enter operands (enter the digits, and then press Enter), and then carry out an operation (for example, by pressing +).

It's no coincidence that the CLR uses such a stack-based evaluation mechanism. Very machine-oriented in nature, it still provides enough abstraction over the way modern processors work. In reality—a reality that becomes true after Just-in-Time (JIT) compilation of IL code to x86 or x64 instructions—processors want operands in certain registers (like EAX and EBX) to carry out arithmetic operations on them. Similar arguments hold for calling conventions that use registers for efficiency. In IL, no affinity is taken to a particular machine architecture, thanks to the stack-based operation abstraction of the virtual machine.

Notice how the order of evaluation with regard to the *precedence* of the used arithmetic operators is respected. Finally, we're left with the result of the evaluation on the stack (that is, the value 7) and are ready to assign it to the res variable:

```
IL_000c:  stloc.3
```

This puts our evaluation stack in an empty state again. The remaining instruction is a return. Although the containing method was declared as a procedure (void-returning, if you will), a ret instruction is required. This transfers control to the caller (in the case of the entry point, that's the CLR infrastructure itself) to gracefully terminate the executing process.

```
IL_000d:  ret
```

MANY STACKS

What we've talked about here is only the *evaluation stack*. IL instructions directly deal with this stack by pushing and popping values onto and from it. Think of it as a structured scratchpad.

Another stack is the *call stack*, which deals with maintaining (nested) method calls. Each method call has state associated with it in a so-called *frame*. This state includes things such as parameters, local variables used within the method, a return address, and space to return a value to the caller if desired. The call stack also serves a role in security enforcement with Code Access Security (CAS). During *stack walks* the call stack is used to make sure the right permissions are in place to make certain method calls.

In reality, those stacks are tightly related to one another, and together they make up the *CLR stack*. This should be considered just an implementation detail, though; it generally helps to think about both stacks separately because they serve different goals.

Arithmetic Operators

Time to take a look at the various operators in C#. One popular category consists of arithmetic operators, including +, -, *, /, and %. I bet you can guess the role of most, if not all, of them: + is used for addition, - for subtraction and negation, * for multiplication, / for division, and % for remainder after division.

Integer Arithmetic

Obviously, the arithmetic operators can operate on integral values, including int, uint, long, and ulong. A few examples are shown here:

```
int a = 6;
int b = 7;

int mul = a * b;     // 42
int add = mul + a;   // 48
int div = add / b;   // 6
int sub = mul - div; // 36
int rem = sub % b;   // 1
```

All of this should be self-explanatory, except perhaps for the division and remainder operations. Integral division produces an integral result, rounding toward zero. For example, 3 / 2 will produce 1, and -3 / 2 will produce -1. If you want fractional results, at least one fractional number will have to be involved in the operation.

For the remainder operator, an invariant holds in relation to the subtraction, multiplication, and addition operators. More specifically (in mathematical syntax):

```
x % y = x - (x / y) * y
```

What about division by zero? An *exception* of type DivideByZeroException results, as shown in Figure 5.5, so be careful to check for a potential division-by-zero condition where required. Although you'll learn how to *catch* exceptions, this particular one typically indicates a bug in your application (for example, because of the lack of input validation).

Floating-Point Arithmetic

Float and double types cause floating-point arithmetic, as specified in the IEEE 754 standard. What's so special about this? Well, recall the inherent imprecision that exists in floating-point arithmetic. For most applications, that's fine, but scientific or monetary computation might be better off with different numeric types (such as decimal).

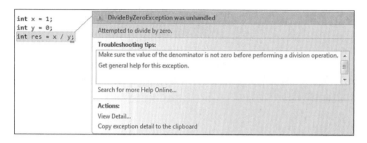

FIGURE 5.5   A `DivideByZeroException` should be avoided by checking the denominator.

But there's more: Floating-point numbers have a series of special values to deal with infinities and mathematical nonsense also known as NaN (not a number). The C# specification contains tables to indicate the behavior of all arithmetic operators for all possible combinations of input. If the result of a computation is too large to be represented as a floating-point number, the result is an infinity (because there's both a positive and negative one). In a similar way, zero is special in the world of floating-point numbers: If the result of a computation is too small to fit the precision available, it's substituted for zero. There's even a positive and negative zero.

NaN is used to represent—what's in a name?—something that's not a number. Operations involving such an animal result in NaN, too.

Table 5.2 shows division behavior when using floating-point arithmetic.

TABLE 5.2   Floating-Point Arithmetic for Division

	+x	-x	+0	-0	+∞	-∞	NaN
+x	+z	-z	+∞	-∞	+0	-0	NaN
-x	-z	+z	-∞	+∞	-0	+0	NaN
+0	+0	-0	NaN	NaN	+0	-0	NaN
-0	-0	+0	NaN	NaN	-0	+0	NaN
+∞	+∞	-∞	+∞	-∞	NaN	NaN	NaN
-∞	-∞	+∞	-∞	+∞	NaN	NaN	NaN
NaN	NaN	NaN	NaN	NaN	NaN	NaN	NaN

EPSILON

Readers with a mathematical background, more specifically in calculus, might have heard about epsilon-delta definitions. In summary, those symbolic values represent values that are made arbitrarily small—that is, taking the limit going to zero—to approach some point and are used to define theorems about limits and continuity of functions. Why should you care?

In the world of imprecision caused by floating-point arithmetic, epsilon finds a place, too. If you take a look at the static fields on any of the floating-point types, you'll find one called `Epsilon` described as "defining the smallest positive value that can be represented by the floating-point type." This is especially important when comparing two floating-point numbers for equality, to establish a margin of error. Instead of writing `a == b`, you would write `Math.Abs(a, b) <= epsilon`, essentially to express the numbers should be close enough to one another.

Unfortunately, the public `Epsilon` fields on `Single` and `Double` are not directly usable for such *approximately equals* comparisons. Explaining why that is would be quite a detour into all the oddities of floating-point arithmetic. If you want to learn more about floating-point precision, search the Internet for more detailed information.

Where do those special values actually live? For one thing, C# doesn't have literals for things such as infinity and NaN: These are (hopefully) not your everyday values. To check whether the result of a computation is any of those, *static constant fields* are available on the floating-point types, as shown in Figure 5.6.

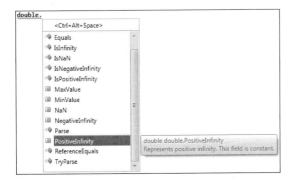

FIGURE 5.6   `System.Double` fields for special floating-point values.

The reason I chose to illustrate the division table as an example is to point out an important observation: Division by zero is allowed and returns an Infinity value. This is shown in Figure 5.7 by looking at a Watch window to display the res variable.

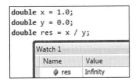

FIGURE 5.7   Floating-point division by zero.

This behavior conforms with the IEEE standard for floating-point arithmetic.

Decimal Arithmetic

Being a numeric type as well, decimal defines the same arithmetic operators as the integral and floating-point types. The main difference lies in the way rounding is done, as you saw Chapter 4. Based on the scales of the operands, the scale for the result is determined. For example, if you're adding two decimal values with different precision, what does the resulting precision look like? For addition, the larger of the two precisions is used, numbers are added, and then rounding is applied.

One more thing on the subject of rounding: In Chapter 4, you saw how the banker's rounding approach is used in the implementation of System.Decimal. One characteristic of this is that it minimizes rounding errors. It doesn't eliminate the need for rounding, though. The following shows a typical example:

```
decimal res = (1m / 3m) * 3m;
```

Recall that the m suffix denotes a decimal literal. Although mathematically you would expect the preceding example to evaluate to 1.0, the result is 0.9999999999999999999999999999. The reason for this is the fixed precision available to represent the one-third decimal division result. The successive multiplication by 3 doesn't see anything but the number of digits available, resulting in the shown decimal. In other words, decimal is not a rational number (which would mean keeping divisor and dividend for numbers).

If you're wondering, the arithmetic operations on System.Decimal are not implemented by the CLR directly. Instead, most of the logic is defined in the BCL using operator overloads. This is proven in Figure 5.8 using .NET Reflector.

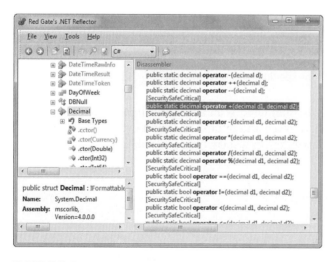

FIGURE 5.8   Implementation of decimal arithmetic.

Character Arithmetic

Strictly speaking, we've already covered arithmetic with the character type because it involves integral arithmetic. I want to take a look at it separately, though, because syntactically it might look a bit weird at first. Here is an example of some operations:

```
int numberOfLetters = 'z' - 'a' + 1;
char e = (char)('a' + 4);
```

On the first line, two character literals are being subtracted. How does this work? Recall that characters are represented in 2 bytes to be able to represent Unicode characters. In fact, C# doesn't directly specify arithmetic operations for integral types with a precision of less than 4 bytes. That's why our discussion about integral arithmetic only mentioned int, uint, long, and ulong types.

What's happening here is an *implicit widening conversion*, from the System.Char type to a System.Int32, before the subtraction is carried out. Notice that I'm using associativity rules here: 'z' - 'a' is carried out first, before the addition to 1 (which is an int literal). In other words, 'z' becomes a System.Int32 value (122, its ASCII value, that is), and so does 'a'. The subtraction then results in 25, and finally we add 1 to end up with 26. We discuss widening and narrowing conversions later, but it should be easy to see where the naming comes from. Going from a System.Char, which is 2 bytes long, to a System.Int32, which is 4 bytes long, clearly widens the representation.

The second line illustrates a *cast expression*, as we discuss later. Ignoring the cast, the same rules of widening conversion apply: 'a' turns into a System.Int32, and 4 is added. The result of this is by itself a System.Int32, which is represented as 4 bytes. However, we were interested in getting a character back. To accomplish this, we need a *narrowing conversion*, which can be carried out using an explicit cast expression. Because this can result in loss of information (if the 4-byte value doesn't fit in the desired 2-byte representation, that is), C# doesn't want to do this implicitly and forces the user to be aware of this by requiring an explicit cast.

A handy trick to see where those implicit conversions lurk is to leverage local variable type inference. Figure 5.9 shows the type inferred for arithmetic with character values.

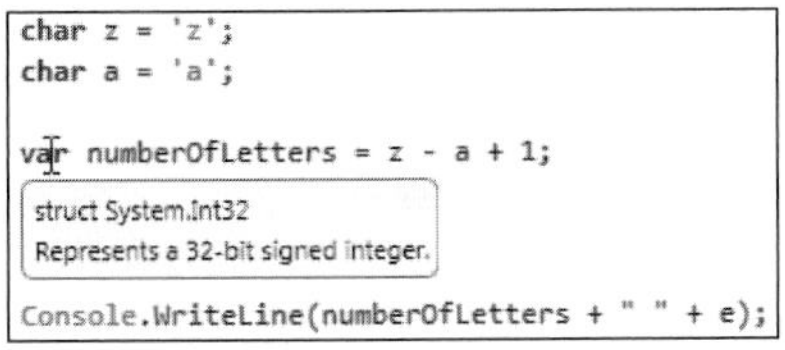

```
char z = 'z';
char a = 'a';

var numberOfLetters = z - a + 1;
    struct System.Int32
    Represents a 32-bit signed integer.

Console.WriteLine(numberOfLetters + " " + e);
```

FIGURE 5.9   Local variable type inference revealing arithmetic result types.

Unary Plus and Minus

You've seen the + and - tokens being used for binary addition and subtraction already, but they can also be used in a unary context, with one operand. In that setting, they are used—not surprisingly—for unary plus and minus:

```
int x = 42;
int y = -x;
```

Overflow Checking

So far, we've omitted an all-important detail from this discussion: overflow checking. Due to the limited precision offered by the built-in types—ignoring the new .NET 4.0 BigInteger type—there will be places where things go wrong. For example, take the biggest 32-bit integer value and add 1 to it. What's the result going to look like? To see what's going on, let's take a look at the bit representation for int.MaxValue. To do this, Visual Studio can help again, as illustrated in Figure 5.10.

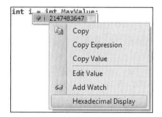

FIGURE 5.10   Hexadecimal display for variables.

The result will be 0x7fffffff, from which we can easily get to bit representation. Notice the first bit indicates the sign: 7 in binary is 0111, where 0 indicates the number is positive. Now add 1, whose representation is 0x00000001 (again with the very first bit to indicate the sign, again positive). Figure 5.11 shows addition at the bit level.

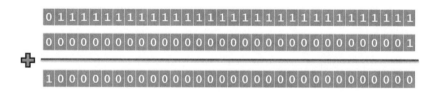

FIGURE 5.11   Addition on the binary level.

Applying elementary calculation with carrying over (1 + 1 = 0 with 1 carried over), we end up with 0x80000000 (remember that 1000 in binary corresponds to 8 in hexadecimal), whose sign bit clearly is 1, and hence the number is negative. This bit pattern actually represents the most negative signed 32-bit integer value, which is int.MinValue. If it looks like -0 to you, browse the Web for 2-complement representation to learn how negative numbers are encoded. Either way, we've just observed an overflow during calculation.

Other situations that give rise to overflow exist. Obviously, other binary operations such as multiplication can cause an overflow, but unary negation can too. Negating the smallest integer value (-2147483648 for 32-bit signed integers) results in nothing less than that number itself. Hard to believe? Just the wonders of 2-complement arithmetic.

By default, arithmetic operations in C# are *unchecked*, meaning overflow conditions don't crash the program. For most (business) applications, this is fine because the range of numbers is typically not employed in its entirety. For example, a loop such as the following is highly unlikely to cope with an array that exceeds int.MaxValue elements (swiping memory allocation issues under the rug, as well):

```
for (int i = 0; i < array.Length; i++)
{
    // Do something
}
```

Cleaner ways to enumerate an array exist using the foreach loop, which we cover when talking about control flow statements in Chapter 7, "Simple Control Flow."

ARIANE-5

Overflow conditions have given rise to notorious bugs. Arguably, the most famous one is the Ariane-5 rocket crash. The software to control the trajectory calculation for the rocket was written in Ada, with overflow trapping disabled for some reason. When positive numbers controlling velocity or acceleration all of a sudden become negative, you can guess the result, and your rocket will be back to earth earlier than expected.

Note that C# chooses the "dangerous" overflow treatment by default, in contrast to Visual Basic, where overflow checking is enabled by default. Overflow checking comes at a cost, though, and given the intended audience for the language (that is, not for scientific computing and such), it was chosen to go with unchecked arithmetic by default. I sometimes regret this choice, but we have to live with it.

So suppose you care about overflow conditions and want the program to crash in case such a dangerous situation arises. How do you turn unchecked arithmetic into checked? To do this, C# has two keywords to control the behavior: checked and unchecked. These keywords are used to establish a context that affects arithmetic instructions emitted by the compiler. The CLR has checked and unchecked variants of arithmetic instructions that can cause overflow, as we'll prove now using some experiments.

As the running example, consider the following code:

```
int max = int.MaxValue;
int res = max + 1;

Console.WriteLine(res);
```

We already know this overflows results in -2147483648. Take a look at the IL code in Figure 5.12 to see what's going on here.

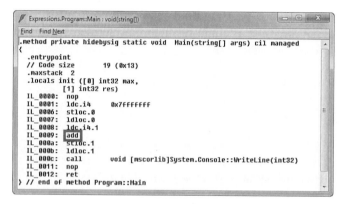

FIGURE 5.12   The add instruction doesn't protect against overflow.

The resulting add instruction allows overflow conditions, causing the observed behavior. Various options exist to turn on overflow checking. The first one is to use the `checked` keyword as a unary expression:

```
int max = int.MaxValue;
int res = checked(max + 1);

Console.WriteLine(res);
```

Here, only the arithmetic operations in the expression surrounded by the `checked(...)` syntax are subject to overflow checking. To accomplish this, the compiler has emitted different code for the addition using the `add.ovf` instruction instead, as shown next. But first, let's see what the runtime behavior of the code is now. Figure 5.13 shows the result of running this code in the Visual Studio debugger.

The result is an *exception* that, if left unhandled, results in program termination. We discuss exceptions thoroughly, but the `OverflowException` is likely something you want to leave unhandled. If you opted in to arithmetic overflow checking, it's likely because you wanted to avoid disaster in case of an overflow, and you'll be better off having the program terminate on the spot instead of trying to recover from it. Overflow should be considered a serious bug, and likely you need higher precision or a scientific number type such as `BigInteger`.

class Program
{
static void Main(string[] args)
{
int max = int.MaxValue;
int res = checked(max + 1);
Console.WriteLine(res);
}
}
OverflowException was unhandled
Arithmetic operation resulted in an overflow.
Troubleshooting tips:
Make sure you are not dividing by zero.
Get general help for this exception.
Search for more Help Online...
Actions:
View Detail...
Copy exception detail to the clipboard

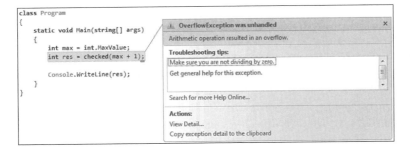

FIGURE 5.13 Arithmetic overflow causing an `OverflowException`.

What's up with the IL that causes this behavior? As you can see in Figure 5.14, the resulting code uses the `add.ovf` instruction instead.

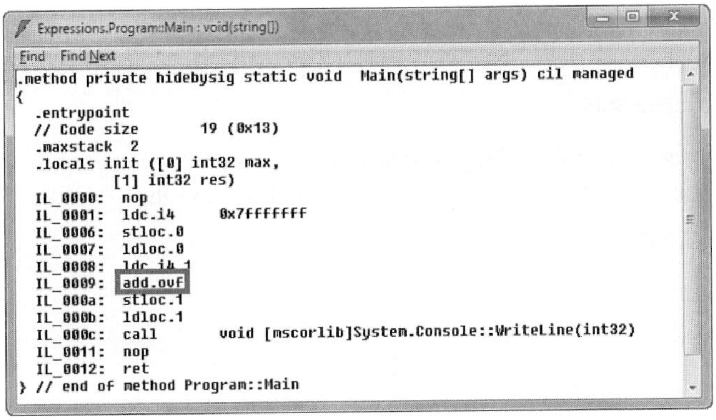

Expressions.Program::Main : void(string[])
Find Find Next
.method private hidebysig static void Main(string[] args) cil managed
{
.entrypoint
// Code size 19 (0x13)
.maxstack 2
.locals init ([0] int32 max,
[1] int32 res)
IL_0000: nop
IL_0001: ldc.i4 0x7fffffff
IL_0006: stloc.0
IL_0007: ldloc.0
IL_0008: ldc.i4.1
IL_0009: add.ovf
IL_000a: stloc.1
IL_000b: ldloc.1
IL_000c: call void [mscorlib]System.Console::WriteLine(int32)
IL_0011: nop
IL_0012: ret
} // end of method Program::Main

FIGURE 5.14 The `add.ovf` instruction throws an OverflowException in case of overflow.

Having to type checked around every expression can become very tedious. To avoid that, you can define whole blocks to be checked as follows:

```
checked
{
    int max = int.MaxValue;
    int res = max + 1;

    Console.WriteLine(res);
}
```

Now every arithmetic instruction subject to overflow within the code block (delimited by the curly braces) is checked. In this particular example, there's only our addition operation, so this code is equivalent to our previous snippet.

UNCHECKED AND HRESULT

You might wonder what the role of the unchecked keyword is and where it comes in handy. For one thing, it's possible to turn on overflow checking for a whole program, so unchecked gives you an option to opt-out of overflow checking in some part of the code.

Another place where unchecked proves useful is when dealing with interop code that needs to check for HRESULTs. Based on bit-level flags, HRESULTs have a high bit of 1, which corresponds to the severity bit. A bit value of 1 indicates failure, making it very popular in code that rigorously needs to check for failure conditions. As an example, take a look at E_FAIL's definition. If you have the Windows SDK installed, you'll find this in a file called WinError.h; otherwise, just take my word for it:

```
#define E_FAIL _HRESULT_TYPEDEF_(0x80004005L)
```

When dealing with such HRESULTs in C#, you typically want to declare symbolic constants for them to make code more readable. You also want to make them signed integers so that a Succeeded function can simply check for positive values and a Failed function for negative ones:

```
const int E_FAIL = (int)0x80004005;
```

However, the compiler will complain that you're trying to assign a hexadecimal (positive) literal within the uint range to a variable typed as int. Figure 5.15 illustrates the compiler's objection against such code.

```
const int E_FAIL = 0x80004005;
                   struct System.UInt32
                   Represents a 32-bit unsigned integer.

                   Error:
                   Cannot implicitly convert type 'uint' to 'int'. An explicit conversion exists (are you missing a cast?)
```

FIGURE 5.15   Unsigned integer values don't convert to signed integers implicitly.

To prevent this, the unchecked keyword comes in handy, used as an expression:

```
const int E_FAIL = unchecked((int)0x80004005);
```

Now the compiler will be fine with it, treating the hexadecimal as-is and just stuffing its value in the E_FAIL variable.

But what if you want to protect your whole application against overflow conditions? Requiring the use of the checked keyword everywhere is way too intrusive, so a compiler flag exists to turn it on for the whole assembly. Not surprisingly, the flag is called /checked, and it can also be enabled through the Visual Studio UI for the project settings. Go to the project properties, open the Build tab, and click the Advanced button. An

Advanced Built Settings dialog box opens, in which you'll find a check box to turn on overflow checking (see Figure 5.16).

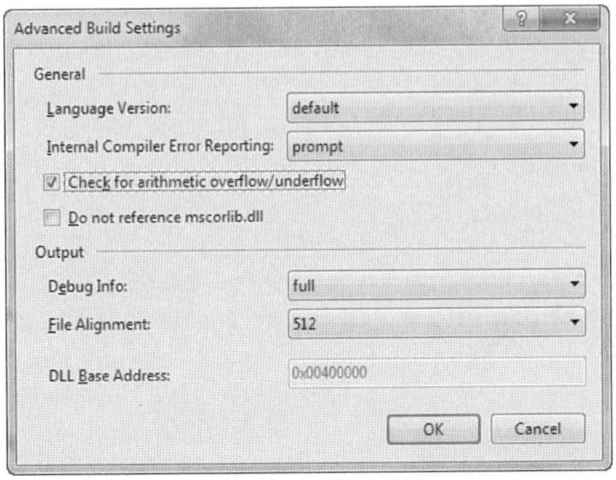

FIGURE 5.16   Whole-project overflow checking.

Notice that a performance penalty might be associated with this. But as usual with performance, don't judge before you consider the user scenarios you care about. Premature optimization is never a good idea. Personally, I tend to turn on checked arithmetic for most, if not all, of my new projects. Unfortunately, making this the default in a future release would be a breaking change (although programs relying on overflowing behavior likely have a bug in them anyway).

Arithmetic with Nullables

What about nullable value types? How does arithmetic deal with the magical null value? The answer lies in the concept of *lifted operators*, which are operators that "lift" the use of operators that normally deal with non-nullable types to use with nullables:

```
+   ++  -   --   !   ~
+   -   *   /   %   &   |   ^   <<  >>
==  !=  <   >   <=  >=
```

Don't worry about operators that don't look familiar yet; we'll get to those soon. The specification of lifted operators defines what it means to apply the operator to a number of null values. For example, for the binary arithmetic operations, the result is null if any of the operands was null:

```
int? a = null;
int b = 5;
int? res = a + b;
```

Let's not go into too much detail on this subject because things can get quite involved. You can find more information in the official C# language specification.

String Concatenation

Syntactically closely related to arithmetic operations is string concatenation, reusing the + operator notation. The following is an example:

```
Console.Write("Enter your name: ");
string name = Console.ReadLine();

string message = "Hello " + name;
Console.WriteLine(message);
```

The way concatenation works internally is by calling into any of the String.Concat *static methods*, as shown in Figure 5.17.

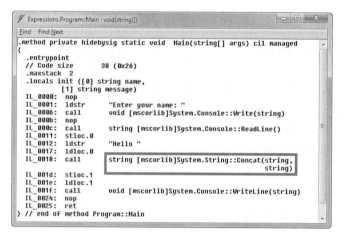

```
Expressions.Program::Main : void(string[])
Find   Find Next
.method private hidebysig static void   Main(string[] args) cil managed
{
  .entrypoint
  // Code size       38 (0x26)
  .maxstack  2
  .locals init ([0] string name,
           [1] string message)
  IL_0000:  nop
  IL_0001:  ldstr      "Enter your name: "
  IL_0006:  call       void [mscorlib]System.Console::Write(string)
  IL_000b:  nop
  IL_000c:  call       string [mscorlib]System.Console::ReadLine()
  IL_0011:  stloc.0
  IL_0012:  ldstr      "Hello "
  IL_0017:  ldloc.0
  IL_0018:  call       string [mscorlib]System.String::Concat(string,
                                                              string)
  IL_001d:  stloc.1
  IL_001e:  ldloc.1
  IL_001f:  call       void [mscorlib]System.Console::WriteLine(string)
  IL_0024:  nop
  IL_0025:  ret
} // end of method Program::Main
```

FIGURE 5.17   String concatenation under the hood.

String concatenation is available not only between two string types but also between a string and any object (System.Object). In that case, ToString is invoked on the object before carrying out the concatenation. For example:

```
string res = "The answer is " + 42;
```

When any of the operands to string concatenation are null, it gets substituted for the empty string ("," or string.Empty). It's quite popular for the empty string and the null reference to be treated interchangeably in quite some cases, hence this choice. In fact, the BCL has an IsNullOrEmpty method on System.String to check for either of those cases:

```
if (string.IsNullOrEmpty(s))
{
    // Do something
}
```

Concatenation of string literals or constants doesn't result in runtime concatenation because the compiler can just append the two strings. This can be useful to clarify code:

```
const string VER = "1.0.0.0";
Console.WriteLine("Sample version " + VER);
```

It would actually be better to get the version number at runtime by means of *reflection*, but consider this just as an illustrative fragment. The preceding code compiles into this:

```
ldstr      "Sample version 1.0.0.0"
call       void [mscorlib]System.Console::WriteLine(string)
```

The `ldstr` instruction just loads a string token from the executable's binary, which is already mapped into memory, making this more efficient than runtime concatenation. There's actually quite a bit to be said about performance in the light of string concatenation. Concatenation doesn't replace any of the operands with the new string because strings in .NET are immutable. With *compound assignment*, you can write the following:

```
string people = "";
foreach (string name in names)
{
    people += name + ", ";
}
```

The compound assignment in the loop body is something we discuss later in this chapter, in the section "Compound Assignment," but it desugars (as in removing *syntactic sugar*) into the following form:

```
people = people + name + ", ";
```

What we want to achieve here is a comma-separated string containing all the person names in some collection called names. In other words, we're aggregating a sequence of strings into a single one.

STRING.JOIN AND LINQ'S AGGREGATE OPERATOR

The preceding code fragment suffers from having a trailing comma-space pair at the end, which we probably don't want. Better ways exist to do such an aggregation, allowing us to avoid those trailing characters. One is `string.Join`:

```
string people = string.Join(", ", names);
```

In fact, aggregating data is such a common pattern it's been generalized in LINQ by means of a generic Aggregate operator that can deal with aggregation of any data type:

```
int[] numbers = new [] { 1, 2, 3, 4, 5 };
int sum = numbers.Aggregate(0, (acc, n) => acc + n);
```

This uses functional programming concepts like lambda expressions, which we discuss extensively when covering LINQ in Chapter 19, "Language Integrated Query Essentials."

To build up the aggregated string, we really want to mutate an existing string and append things at the end during every visit through the loop. Although we're not interested in the intermediate stages, we're allocating a new string in every iteration:

```
" "
"Bart, "
"Bart, John, "
...
```

This creates memory pressure, which will result in a performance degradation. The allocated strings always grow, lots of memory copies have to be created during every concatenation, and so on. To illustrate this, set a breakpoint at the end of the loop body (you can set a breakpoint on the closing curly brace) and inspect the location of the people variable in memory, illustrated in Figure 5.18. It will change after every iteration.

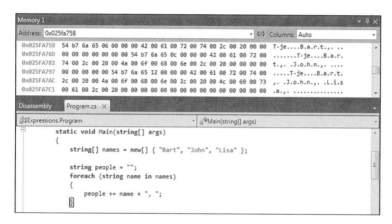

FIGURE 5.18   Watching intermediate strings getting allocated in memory.

In the text display on the right, you can clearly see intermediate strings being allocated.

NOTE

After every iteration, the previous string object is orphaned; there's no way to get back to it, anyway. After all, we're replacing the reference in the people variable with a reference to the newly allocated string. Remember that strings are reference types, so the reference is replaced to point to some other location in memory containing the new (slightly more aggregated) string. In summary, this means that after every previous string object, an unreachable object remains in memory that's under control of the garbage collector.

In the preceding sample, you need to be a little lucky not to induce a garbage collection (which is the source of potential performance bottlenecks) during this excessive string concatenation. If this happens, the memory display will change.

Does this mean you should avoid string concatenation at all costs? No. A good rule of thumb is that if you know the number of concatenations statically at compile time (for example, because you do something like first + " " + last), string concatenation is fine. However, if dynamic behavior (such as loops over collections of unknown size) is involved, string concatenation can bite you.

Of course, you're wondering what the better approach for such excessive string creation patterns is. The solution is `System.Text.StringBuilder`:

```
using System;
using System.Text;

class Program
{
    static void Main(string[] args)
    {
        string[] names = new[] { "Bart", "John", "Lisa" };

        var peopleList = new StringBuilder();
        foreach (string name in names)
        {
            peopleList.Append(name);
            peopleList.Append(", ");
        }

        string people = peopleList.ToString();
        // More code...
```

`StringBuilder` provides a buffer for in-place string manipulation operations such as concatenation, replace operations, and so on. It grows dynamically (in a smart way, to provide additional space for subsequent operations) as more space is required and creates less memory pressure than naive string concatenation.

ON STRING INTERNING AND THE STRINGBUILDER'S ROLE IN INTEROP

`StringBuilder` also plays a role in interoperability. When calling into unmanaged code through the P/Invoke mechanism, the signature of the method used to make the call needs to contain types that are *marshalable*. `System.String` is marshalable, but its immutable nature makes it unsuitable when the unmanaged application programming interface (API) needs to mutate the string. In such a case, it's better to use the `StringBuilder` type.

Why? Immutability for strings is baked into the runtime for various reasons. It helps to eliminate nasty types of bugs in multithreaded code, it has nice security characteristics, and so on. During P/Invoke, what you're effectively doing is handing out a memory location to unmanaged code. That code can then violate the immutability by scribbling in the memory of the CLR string. One place where this really breaks functionality in an observable way is with string interning.

String interning is a mechanism that reuses memory storage for strings if their contents are the same. For example, if a string containing "Bart" is loaded twice, the CLR can decide to allocate the string once and return the same reference to both users. The reason this is safe to do is because strings are deemed immutable: No other user can tweak the string, which would be visible to the other user. However, during interop with unmanaged code, the CLR has no control over memory manipulations, and changes to interned string can be made. For example:

```
string me = "Bart";
string he = "Bart";
SomeInteropMethod(ref me, me.Length);
Console.WriteLine(he);
```

Because both he and me have the same contents, the CLR can intern them: The same memory containing the Unicode representation of "Bart" will be referenced by both he and me. Assuming that SomeInteropMethod writes to the memory referenced by the supplied first argument, the change will become visible in both he and me!

Interop can be tricky. For example, when using a StringBuilder to provide room for the unmanaged API's output, you'll have to make sure the StringBuilder has a sufficiently large capacity. The StringBuilder constructor has an overload that accepts an initial capacity that can be used for this purpose.

We discuss the essentials of interop in Chapter 22, "Dynamic Programming." One recommendation in the meantime is to avoid it whenever possible. But when you absolutely need it because none of the Framework APIs exposes the unmanaged code functionality you're looking for, browse the Web to see whether someone else has already created a P/Invoke signature for you. A site to add to your favorites is http://pinvoke.net.

Shift Operators

Far less commonly used than arithmetic operators are the operators that are tightly bound to the underlying bit representation of integral types. One such category consists of shift operators >> and <<, respectively known as left shift and right shift. Shift operators are defined for the int, uint, long, and ulong types but can also be used with other integral types because of implicit conversions.

The following are examples of shift operations:

```
int left = 3;
int lres = left << 5; // 96

int right = 42;
int rres = right >> 3; // 5
```

Both operators take two operands. The one on the left takes the expression that needs to be shifted, and the one on the right specifies the number of bits to shift (specified as an int). The operation of both shift operations is illustrated in Figure 5.19.

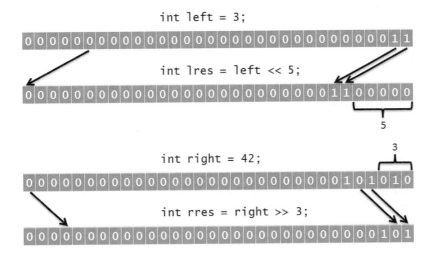

FIGURE 5.19   Shift operations illustrated.

As you can see in the figure, zero bits are shifted to the right in case of a left-shift, and to the left in case of a right-shift. In both cases, bits get lost because they shift outside the available bit positions.

Relational Operators

Another category of operators consists of relational operators, used to perform equality checks or comparisons. The meaning of the following operators should be easy to guess:

`==   !=   <   <=   >   >=`

Built-in types, like the numeric types, support these operators, each of which returns a Boolean value to indicate the result of the check. All of those operators can be overloaded by types, as well, as you will see in Chapter 13, "Operator Overloading and Conversions."

FLOATING-POINT NUMBERS

Floating-point numbers have some weird values, such as NaN, infinities, and positive- and negative-zero representations. In compliance with IEEE 754, the CLR implements the meaning for relational checks on floating-point numbers based on the following ordering:

    –∞ < –max < ... < –min < –0.0 == +0.0 < +min < ... < +max < +∞

You can find more information about this and the treatment of NaN values in the C# language specification.

Equality for Different Types

Equality checks are of particular interest. For reference types, the default behavior of == and != is to check equality and inequality of the references. In other words, do both the left and right sides of the operator refer to the same object in memory? Often this behavior is not desirable, and operator overloading is used to redefine the meaning of equality, typically based on the underlying data contained by the type. A good example is System.String, where == checks that both strings have the same length and contain the same characters.

In the context of reference types and nullable value types, the equality checks against the null literal should also be considered. For reference types, this is based on checking for the null reference. For nullable value types, a call to HasValue is emitted.

NULL IN DIFFERENT WORLDS

As you've already seen in previous chapters, null can be bewilderingly strange at times. The fact that other technologies and platforms sometimes have other definitions of null doesn't help for sure. Here are a couple of examples:

- ▶ In the world of relational databases and the SQL language, null is never equal to null. Reasoning: If two pieces of data are undefined, what right do we have to state they are equal?

- ▶ The situation is different for managed code developers: Two null references are always considered the same.

Such differences can pose interesting challenges when bridging both worlds. A good example is LINQ, where true C# syntax is used to formulate queries against any kind of data source, including SQL. Does the use of == in a query expression need to match the CLR semantics or the SQL semantics? Because LINQ abstracts over all kinds of data sources, it's desirable to implement source language semantics, and that's exactly what's done.

For value types, unless overloaded, the == operator returns true if both operand values are equal. In practice, that means equality of the bit pattern.

Object.ReferenceEquals, Equals, and ==

Equality is, perhaps surprisingly, a fairly complicated concept. There are three main players that are closely related to one another.

Object.ReferenceEquals is a *static method* that can compare two objects for referential equality. (That is, do they refer to the same data?) This corresponds to the default notion of equality for reference types. We'll delay the discussion of value types in this respect until you've learned about *boxing*.

System.Object also has a *virtual method* called Equals. Virtual methods can be overridden by subtypes to redefine the implementation of the method. Because Equals is available on System.Object, it's a popular method that gets called in a variety of places in the framework to check for object equality (for example, for use in collections). As an example, think of a set collection type that needs to enforce that all elements contained in the set are different from one another.

Finally, there's the == operator, which is merely provided for syntactical convenience and is easier on the eye to most people.

After we discuss defining our own types, we'll turn our attention to defining the meaning of equality for our custom types.

Lifted Operators

For nullable value types, the relational operators are also lifted. Comparison of a non-null value to null always results in false, except when inequality is checked:

```
int? a = 5;
int? b = null;

bool gt = a >  b;  // false
bool le = a <= b;  // false
bool eq = a == b;  // false
bool ne = a != b;  // true
```

Nullable logic can be surprising. For example, if you thought the result of >= and < would always be exact opposites when applied to the same operands, you can clearly see this doesn't hold any longer when null is in play.

Logical Operators

Logical operators are defined for integral types, Booleans, and enumerations.

Integral Bitwise Logical Operators

The available operators that deal with integral values—as usual defined for int, uint, long, and ulong—include the following:

```
&  |  ^  ~
```

These, respectively, correspond to the bitwise AND, OR, XOR (exclusive OR), and complement operations. The following are a few examples:

```
int x = 5;
int y = 3;

int and   = x & y; // 1
int or    = x | y; // 7
int xor   = x ^ y; // 6
int compX = ~x;    // -6
```

Figure 5.20 illustrates the operation of those operators (restricting myself to 4-bit representations to save space).

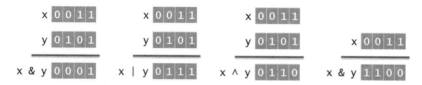

FIGURE 5.20   Integral bitwise operations.

Use for Enumerations

Enumerations provide a way to define symbolic constants that belong together in a logical fashion. Two different uses exist. One is to represent constants that represent distinct values, such as values DayOfWeek.Monday through DayOfWeek.Sunday. It doesn't make sense to try to combine two such values into a new one.

The second use is with flags, where values can be combined meaningfully. As an example, consider file I/O access modes FileAccess.Read and FileAccess.Write, which are very useful when combined to open a file for read and write.

Where logical operators come into play is with *flag-based enums*. Enumerations have an underlying integral type, and each member of the enumeration has a value of that type. By declaring those as powers of two, bit mask operations can be used to see whether a certain flag is set, and flags can be meaningfully combined:

```
[Flags]
public enum FileShare
{
    None      = 0x0,
    Read      = 0x1,
    Write     = 0x2,
    ReadWrite = Read + Write, // has value 0x3
```

```
    Delete      = 0x4,
    Inheritable = 0x10,
}
```

The preceding example is actually taken from the System.IO namespace. Ignore the jump for the value used for Inheritable; this is likely chosen to make interop with Win32 APIs easier. The important part is that every "basic flag value" has a unique bit associated with it. Convenience values can be defined in terms of others by making a sum, as done for ReadWrite.

Now the logical operators can be used to combine flags. For example:

```
FileShare flags = FileShare.Read ¦ FileShare.Write ¦ FileShare.Delete;
```

At another point in the code, we might need to check what flags are set, which can be done by masking the input with the desired flag's value. The way this works at the bit level is depicted in Figure 5.21:

```
if ((flags & FileShare.Read) != 0)
{
    // FileShare.Read was set, can proceed to read
}
```

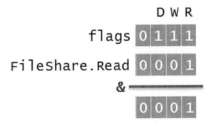

FIGURE 5.21   Checking whether an enumeration flag has been set.

Boolean Logical Operators

A lof of readers will have thought of Boolean values by now in the context of our discussion of logical operators. Yet I've kept Boolean logical operators for the last for a good reason: short-circuiting variants exist, also known as the conditional logical operators.

But first, the regular non-short-circuiting ones. No surprises here: Standard Boolean logic applies for AND, OR, XOR, and NOT, which are written as follows, respectively:

```
&  ¦  ^  !
```

Obviously, the result of those Boolean operators is a Boolean itself. However, from the truth tables of the AND and OR operators, you might recall some important properties of those operators: They can be short-circuited. To refresh your memory on this subject, take a look at Figure 5.22.

AND	false	true
false	false	false
true	false	true

OR	false	true
false	false	true
true	true	true

FIGURE 5.22   Boolean logic truth tables for AND and OR.

Observe the first row for AND and the second for OR. Once the first truth value is known, the result is already fully defined. Operators with short-circuiting behavior exist for AND and OR:

```
&&  ||
```

Recall that expressions can be formed from subexpressions, so the left and right operands to the C# Boolean operators can be any Boolean-typed expression:

```
if (CheckPermissions(user) & !UserBlackListed(user))
{
    // Perform sensitive operation
}
```

In this particular case, if CheckPermissions returns false, there's no point in even checking the UserBlackListed result value (which could be a costly operation; for example, hitting a directory service on the network). So we can use the short-circuiting variant of the & operator instead, which is written as &&:

```
if (CheckPermissions(user) && !UserBlackListed(user))
{
    // Perform sensitive operation
}
```

A similar operator exists to short-circuit the ¦ operator and is written as ¦¦. If the first operand is true, the second one won't be evaluated.

WHEN SIDE EFFECTS MATTER...SIGH

Modifying code to use short-circuiting behavior in an imperative language like C#—where side effects are (unfortunately?) a way of life—can be a breaking change. For example, in the preceding example, the UserBlackListed method might have the side effect of writing to a log file that's analyzed by some automated tools. Some of those tools may depend on finding paired entries for CheckPermission operations followed by UserBlackListed operations. By changing the code to short-circuit, the side effect of writing to the log will also be gone in the negative case. Farfetched? Not really. Know your side effects!

As an aside, these short-circuiting operators can be indirectly overridden by means of their regular counterparts (& and ¦) and two other operators called true and false. That's right: true and false also have operators associated with them that get used when a custom type needs to be evaluated for a truth value. That can be mind-boggling and is very rarely used, but be aware of the fact that the language supports this kind of overloading. If you're wondering, && and ¦¦ are defined in terms of those underlying operators as follows (with T standing for the type that overloads the operators):

```
x && y = T.false(x) ? x : T.&(x, y)
x ¦¦ y = T.true(x)  ? x : T.¦(x, y)
```

The ?: conditional operator used here is the subject of the next section. An example of this kind of overloading could be a TrafficLight type, where drive/stop conditions can be modeled as truth values.

Nullable Boolean Logic

Logic involving nullable Boolean values is three valued and mirrored after the SQL behavior. The idea is pretty much based on the short-circuiting observation: For AND, if any of the operands are false, the whole result ought to be false (similar for OR, but with the true value). In other words, we don't care if the other operand is null in such a case; the result is well defined. Figure 5.23 summarizes nullable Boolean logic.

&	false	true	null
false	false	false	false
true	false	true	null
null	false	null	null

¦	false	true	null
false	false	true	null
true	true	true	true
null	null	true	null

FIGURE 5.23   Truth tables for nullable Boolean logic.

Personally, I try to avoid nullable Booleans in decision logic wherever possible. Even though everything seems "logical," basic laws of logic become very counterintuitive in a nullable setting.

Conditional Operators

The conditional operator is the only ternary operator in the C# language, meaning it has three operands. Some people like to refer to it as *the* ternary operator. I dislike this particular wording because nothing prevents the language designers from adding another ternary operator at some point. So the conditional operator it is.

Being an expression, the conditional operator produces a value from its operands. In essence, it's a decision operator that computes and produces either the second or third operand's value, based on the outcome of the first operand's truth value. An example will make this clear:

```
int absOfX = x >= 0 ? x : -x;
```

In the preceding example, first the Boolean-valued relational expression x > 0 gets evaluated. If the result is true, the operand between the ? and : characters is evaluated and becomes the operator's result. In the other case, the last operand following the : is evaluated and returned. We can rewrite the preceding code as follows:

```
int absOfX;
if (x >= 0)
    absOfX = x;
else
    absOfX = -x;
```

The statement-centric approach has the same effect but is much more verbose. What sets the conditional operator apart is the fact that it's an expression, so it can be used wherever an expression is expected:

```
DoSomethingWithPositiveValue(x >= 0 ? x : -x);
```

Without the conditional operator, you would have to declare a temporary variable to hold the result of the conditional evaluation before feeding it into the place where the value is needed.

Under the Hood

The conditional operator is implemented using branching similar to the `if` statement. The code shown in Figure 5.24 is the result of an optimized Release build because the Debug code is a bit more involved with temporary compiler-generated variables. Yes, that's right. The C# compiler knows to optimize code to some extent.

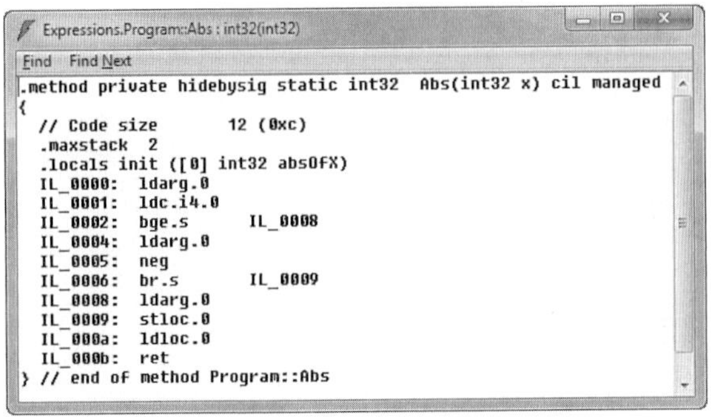


```
.method private hidebysig static int32  Abs(int32 x) cil managed
{
  // Code size       12 (0xc)
  .maxstack  2
  .locals init ([0] int32 absOFX)
  IL_0000:  ldarg.0
  IL_0001:  ldc.i4.0
  IL_0002:  bge.s      IL_0008
  IL_0004:  ldarg.0
  IL_0005:  neg
  IL_0006:  br.s       IL_0009
  IL_0008:  ldarg.0
  IL_0009:  stloc.0
  IL_000a:  ldloc.0
  IL_000b:  ret
} // end of method Program::Abs
```

FIGURE 5.24 The conditional operator behind the scenes.

A WORD ON OPTIMIZATION

People sometimes freak out when IL code doesn't look as optimized as they expect it to. The general approach taken by managed code compilers it to limit optimizations and leave some of the potential further optimizations to the JIT compiler. This has an important advantage of having a language-independent place to carry out optimizations.

So what's up with this IL code fragment? As you see, it's the code for an `Abs` method that takes in an `int` and produces its absolute value. The `ldarg.0` instruction is used to retrieve the first argument passed in and push it onto the stack. We already know what `ret` does; namely, it pops the value on top of the stack and returns it to the caller. What goes in between is what's of real interest to us.

A way to approach this code fragment is by means of basic block analysis. That is, we look at the branch instructions (such as `bge`, meaning "branch if greater than or equal") and split the code in blocks that end with such a branch instruction or start with a label that's the target of a branch instruction. Finally, we draw arrows between the block based on the branch targets and dotted arrows between consecutive blocks to indicate the case of "fallthrough." The result of this analysis is shown in Figure 5.25.

Solid arrows indicate the jump taken in case the branch instruction evaluated positively; for example, bge of x and 0 saying "yes" causes a branch to IL_0008. Dotted arrows indicate fallthrough, either because the block ends with no jump or because of a negative branch condition result.

But why all this buzz? There's something very important to be observed here: The conditional operator evaluates only one of the value-producing operands. In the preceding case, either `-x` is computed (using the `neg` instruction, for negate) or `x` is (which is a trivial operation). Again, this is very important in terms of side effects:

```
bool success = systemsOk ? LaunchRocket() : SendMaintenance();
```

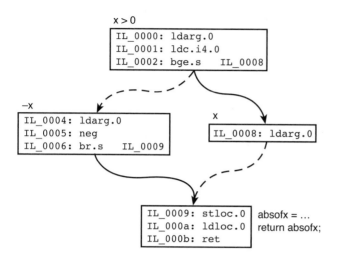

FIGURE 5.25   Deciphering a conditional operator's use.

If both method-call expressions were evaluated regardless of the systemsOk value, disastrous results would follow. This might seem logical, but I've seen people believe the conditional operator can be rewritten as follows (where a generic parameter T is used to make the "operator-alike method" work on any type):

```
T GetConditionalValue<T>(bool condition, T positiveValue, T negativeValue)
{
    if (condition)
        return positiveValue;
    else
        return negativeValue;
}
```

We explore generics in Chapter 15, "Generic Types and Methods." What's wrong with this? The answer lies in the way method calls are processed, in a *call-by-value* manner:

```
bool success = GetConditionalValue(
                systemsOk, LaunchRocket(), SendMaintenance());
```

This means that all arguments to the method call are evaluated first in a left-to-right manner, pushed onto the stack, and finally the method is called. As you can see, this would mean both LaunchRocket and SendMaintenance are called first, even though the method will use only one of the two arguments (but the caller can't know that).

IMMEDIATE IF

The problem with mimicking the conditional operator using a method is historically grounded. Visual Basic had no conditional operator until very recently. Instead, there was the "immediate if" function `Iif`, which basically implements like our `GetConditionalValue` in the preceding example. The new `If` operator, on the other hand, provides short-circuiting behavior just like the conditional operator in C# does.

Lack of a true conditional operator has bitten many people in the past. You can wonder whether this problematic circumstance Visual Basic found itself in is due to the lack of the operator or due to the way function calls are evaluated in most modern languages today. After all, why do we need to evaluate all arguments to a method call (which can be a potentially expensive operation) if the method may just use some (or even none) of them in certain circumstances? This is the nature of call-by-value semantics.

Alternative call semantics exist that prevent this problem, such as Haskell's call-by-need semantics, where function parameters are lifted into "thunks" that get evaluated at the point of their use. You'll see those semantics can be simulated in .NET using delegates and the new `Lazy<T>` type that was introduced in .NET 4.0.

An Operator's Result Type

What about the type produced by the operator? Because either the second or third operand can deliver the operator's result, there needs to be some kind of compatibility between them. When both have the exact same type, there's no question at all. But what if they don't line up? Then the answer lies in *implicit conversions*. For example:

```
condition ? 42 : 123L
```

The resulting type of this conditional operator use will be long because it's possible to convert implicitly from int to long (without loss of data, that is). Obviously, the rule holds symmetrically if the second and third arguments are swapped:

```
!condition ? 123L : 42
```

However, in the face of type hierarchies, the operator does not look for the "least common supertype" as some people expect. Although we don't know yet how type hierarchies are formed, you can apply your gut feeling here. Both Apple and Kiwi are subtypes of Fruit, so we could attempt to write the following:

```
Fruit forLunch = hasSpoon ? basket.GetKiwi() : basket.GetApple();
```

After all, Kiwi and Apple have a common supertype Fruit, right? Some think it would be a good thing if the language would figure this out and infer the resulting type to be Fruit. Others say no because of the Fruit type appearing out of nowhere. Languages that do a lot of type inferencing tend to produce rather cryptic error messages. Consider the case where the conditional operator is used as an argument to a method call:

```
AddToLunchPacket(hasSpoon ? basket.GetKiwi() : basket.GetApple());
```

Assume the compiler infers the type of the conditional to be Fruit, but the method does not have an *overload* taking in a Fruit but only has one taking in a Vegetable. The error message would read something like "No overload is found that accepts a Fruit," even though you haven't written or used the Fruit type directly. This can be confusing, especially if deep type hierarchies come into play and the determined least common supertype is totally nonobvious. Therefore, C# errs on the safe side and doesn't permit this:

```
Type of conditional expression cannot be determined because there is no implicit
conversion between 'Kiwi' and 'Apple'.
```

If you really want the conditional operator to produce a Fruit, an artificial cast will have to be inserted to clarify your intent, as follows:

```
hasSpoon ? (Fruit)basket.GetKiwi() : basket.GetApple()
```

Either of the result operands will do because an implicit conversion exists between a type and one of its supertypes, such as Kiwi to Fruit or Apple to Fruit. Now if you get an error message about some Fruit not lining up, at least you can see where it's coming from.

Associativity

A relatively minor remark to conclude the discussion of the conditional operator is its right-associative behavior:

```
condition1 ? a : condition2 ? c : d
```

The preceding means the same as the following:

```
condition1 ? a : (condition2 ? c : d)
```

However, nested conditional operators tend to produce unreadable code quickly (partly due to the terse ?: syntax), so I generally recommend avoiding such use.

Null-Coalescing Operator

Closely related to the conditional operator is the well-sounding null-coalescing operator, which was introduced in C# 2.0 as part of the whole nullability straightening mission. When dealing with reference types or nullable value types, it sometimes makes sense to be able to supply a default value as a substitute for null. That's precisely what the null-coalescing operator provides:

```
int? deposit = GetDeposit(user);
AddToAccount(user, deposit ?? 0);
```

Written as an infix ?? operator, the null-coalescing operator first evaluates the left operand. If it results in the null reference (for a reference type) or a nullable value with no value set (HasValue is false), the right operand is evaluated to produce the result; otherwise, the left operand's value becomes the result. Let's analyze the preceding example:

```
deposit ?? 0
```

It actually behaves like this:

```
deposit.HasValue ? deposit.Value : 0
```

As you can see, the nullable's value gets *unwrapped* if not null. For reference types, no unwrapping is needed. Assume that name is of type string in the fragment here:

```
name ?? "Person X"
```

Then this is shorthand for the following:

```
name != null ? name : "Person X"
```

Notice that the operator is lazy just like the conditional one, meaning the right default value operand is evaluated only when needed:

```
name ?? GetDefaultValue()
```

If name is non-null, the GetDefaultValue method will not be called. Similar remarks about types hold: Implicit conversions are permitted, but the language refuses to chase after a least common supertype:

```
GetApple() ?? new Jonagold() // this is fine, a Jonagold is an Apple
GetApple() ?? new Kiwi() // this isn't, no magical inference to Fruit supertype
```

The null-coalescing operator is also right-associative:

```
data ?? GetDefault() ?? GetAlternativeDefault()
```

This is the same as the following:

```
data ?? (GetDefault() ?? GetAlternativeDefault())
```

In other words, if data is null, we're chasing for a default value. First we attempt GetDefault(), but if that results in null, GetAlternativeDefault() is tried. But again, this coding style is quite brittle, so it's better to avoid it. Others may write it, though, so it's good to know how the language defines its meaning.

THE MYTHICAL NULL-PROPAGATING DOT

With null being a common source of frustration—creative minds don't want to spend their days writing null checks—people often ask for more constructs to deal with null. One such common request is the null-propagating dot. The dot operator is used for member lookup of various sorts, as shown here:

```
decimal discount = person.GetAccount(AccountLevel.Gold).Discount;
```

But what if the person doesn't have a Gold account? Suppose the GetAccount method returns null in such a case, requiring the caller to check for null:

```
Account account = person.GetAccount(AccountLevel.Gold);
decimal discount = account != null ? account.Discount : 0m;
```

This illustrates how intrusive null checking can become, especially if you "dot-chain" a lot of lookups together. With the mythical null-propagating dot, this code could look like the following:

```
decimal? discount = person.GetAccount(AccountLevel.Gold)?.Discount;
```

Here, ?. stands for "peter out at this point if the left side is null; otherwise, continue." Although this looks nice, a few complications can arise.

Notice how nullability becomes contagious to the whole expression. The result no longer is of type decimal but of type decimal?. So introducing null propagation in the middle of some existing code will start breaking other things because the type has changed. Maybe such code breakage is a good thing because you're most likely working on eliminating a NullReferenceException. To fix such an issue, some code churn should be acceptable. And sure enough, you could add a null-coalescing operation at the end:

```
decimal discount = person.GetAccount(AccountLevel.Gold)?.Discount ?? 0m;
```

You can approach the situation with the null-propagating dot also from a different angle. It might well lead to bad coding practices where nonignorable null values are swept under the rug in an almost invisible way. What if the maintainer of the example were overly eager and did the following:

```
decimal discount = person?.GetAccount(AccountLevel.Gold)?.Discount ?? 0m;
```

Did you see the difference at a glance? Likely not. It's not unreasonable to believe this code wants to deal with the person object in some other place (for example, in the middle of a shopping cart checkout line). Having a null reference for person is definitely not a good thing in such a case. With the null-propagating behavior, it becomes easy to ignore this important "detail," causing code to crash much later, where it might be less obvious where the null value comes from. Of course, it all boils down to coding discipline.

One last thing on this subject is the fact people tend to forget other operations on objects exist that would benefit equally well from such a feature. Indexers and delegate invocations jump to mind. Syntax becomes quite terse here:

```
vector?["x"]
calculator.Add?(1, 2) // where Add is a property of type Func<int, int, int>
```

Don't worry too much about indexers and delegates just yet; we cover them exhaustively in Chapter 11, "Fields, Properties, and Indexers," and Chapter 17, "Delegates," respectively. It remains to be seen whether such null-propagating operators will make it into the language at some point. Maybe support for non-null types would be a much better value proposition to reduce null-centric bugs.

Assignment

We've used assignment repeatedly already. It's simply a way to assign a value to a variable (or property, indexer or event, to be precise). For example:

```
// Assigning to a local variable, declared elsewhere.
person = new Person("Bart", 26);

// Assigning to a property through a setter.
person.DayOfBirth = new DateTime(1983, 2, 11);
```

Decaration Versus (Simple) Assignment

It's important to realize the fundamental difference between declaring variables and assigning to them. *Declaring* a variable simply introduces a symbolic name (specified using an identifier) in the containing scope, also specifying its type. *Assignment* is the act of setting a value for the variable, which can be done multiple times as long as the variable is in scope (unless the variable is declared as constant, that is). The following piece of code

```
int x = 42;
```

can be decomposed into two separate discrete steps:

```
int x;
x = 42;
```

The latter one is what we're talking about here. It's called a *simple assignment* that has the form lhs = rhs. After evaluating the right side (rhs), it gets assigned to the left side (lhs).

Those of you who've been paying attention will remember that expressions have a value. The fact that we're covering assignment during our discussion of expressions reveals that an assignment yields a value as a result. Here's the language specification:

> The result of a simple assignment expression is the value assigned to the left operand.

We've already used this property of assignment in passing, when talking about the as operator, where we wrote a multiway branch for type checking:

```
if ((f = item as Fruit) != null)
{
    return IsFreshFruit(f);
}
else if ((v = item as Vegetable) != null)
{
    return IsFreshVegetable(v);
}
```

Here we're assigning the result of the as operator expression to f or v and use the same value to carry out a null check subsequently. Essentially, we're using assignment for its side effect of modifying a local variable's value while also carrying out a null check for the essential type check.

This kind of code should not be used excessively, though, because keeping track of the many things happening on one line can be quite difficult. In this case, I'm convinced it's fine to do, but the use of assignment in all sorts of random places can make code very subtle in no time:

```
DoSomething(a, a = 5, b = a + c)
```

There's one other place where this property of assignment as an expression comes in handy, multiple assignments:

```
x = y = z = 0
```

Simple assignment is a right-associative operation, so the preceding snippet is written as follows in its parenthesized form:

```
x = (y = (z = 0))
```

SUBTLE BUT PRECISE

Language specifications need to be precise, but in being so they can get quite subtle, too. Believe it or not, the specification of the assignment operation is a place that gives rise to subtleties. Let's rephrase what the specification states:

The result of a simple assignment expression is the value assigned to the left operand.

Now an example to illustrate this. What's the equivalent to the code here?

```
bar.Foo = foo.Bar = a + b;
```

We already know this can be rewritten as follows by using the property of right associativity:

```
bar.Foo = (foo.Bar = a + b);
```

This already defines order unambiguously. To assign to bar.Foo, we need to evaluate the right side first. So we end up with the following sequencing:

```
foo.Bar = a + b;
bar.Foo = ...;
```

But what do we replace the ellipsis with? What about a + b? That would clearly be a waste of computation resources, but not only that. Undesirable but possible, a + b could be implemented using an operator overload that has a side effect; for example, it may print to the screen for some reason. By reevaluating a + b, we would cause that side effect to happen twice.

What about using foo.Bar on the ellipsis? This isn't any better: bar.Foo may be a property, and calling its getter may carry out additional operations besides just getting the value. Or in a more contrived scenario, the property might even not have a getter but only a setter. What really happens here is the following:

```
var __temp = a + b;
foo.Bar = __temp;
bar.Foo = __temp;
```

In fact, some other languages define assignment in a different way: subtlety at the fundamental level.

Compound Assignment

Beside simple assignment, the language also supports *compound assignment*. This form of assignment allows the use of a binary operator to be combined with assignment at one time and has the following general form (where *op* stands for a binary operator):

```
x op= y
```

In the simplest case, it's the equivalent to the more verbose form:

```
x = x op y
```

The reason I'm saying this is the simplest case is because rules exist that permit a conversion to take place before assigning the result to x. Here are a few examples to illustrate the use of compound assignments of various sorts:

```
int a = 42;
a += 6; // a = 48
a /= 8; // a = 6

char c = 'z';
c -= (char)2; // c = 'x'
```

Notice the explicit conversion of the integer literal 2 to a char on the last line. This is required because of a relatively simple rule that states types should line up. Intuitively, for the form x *op=* y to work, it should be possible to assign y to x. If you omit the conversion syntax, a very actionable compile-time error will result:

```
Constant value '2' cannot be converted to a 'char'
```

COMPOUND ASSIGNMENT: AN EXPRESSION TOO...

I wondered whether it was a good idea to mention this explicitly but ultimately decided in favor of it: Compound assignment is an expression. Expressions are things that produce a value. So they can be used wherever a value is expected:

```
bar.Foo(x += 5)
```

But don't do this unless you want to explode your coworkers' (or your own) heads.

Notice that compound assignment can be used on yet-to-be-discussed properties and indexers, as well:

```
vector["x"] += 2;
account.Balance *= 1.05m;
```

Properties and indexers are methods in disguise: One is used to retrieve the value (the getter); the other is used to change it (the setter). For compound assignment to work, both a (visible) getter and setter need to be in place. The preceding forms translate into the following:

```
vector["x"]     /* set */ = vector["x"]     /* get */ + 2;
account.Balance /* set */ = account.Balance /* get */ * 1.05m;
```

Although my examples used only some of the arithmetic operators, be aware that others work equally well: &=, |=, <<=, >>=, and so on.

When operator overloading is in play, compound assignment works, too. In fact, overload resolution for the binary operator proceeds just as if you had written the long form instead. The best overload for the operator is chosen. An example can be found for DateTime and TimeSpan, their sum being a DateTime. For example, to increment a DateTime object with five days, you could write this:

```
DateTime d = DateTime.Now;
d += TimeSpan.FromDays(5);
```

For strings, += works as well, but with the big caveat of string concatenation being a memory-intensive operation due to the immutable characteristic of .NET strings. The following code is worrisome for that very reason:

```
string alphabet = "";
for (char c = 'a'; c <= 'z'; c++)
{
    alphabet += c;
}
```

Every concatenation through the += compound assignment abandons the existing string object and creates a new one. In total, we'll have allocated no fewer than 26 intermediate string objects (including the empty string, although that one should be interned). It's much better to write this kind of code using the StringBuilder object:

```
var sb = new StringBuilder(26 /* capacity hint for higher efficiency */);
for (char c = 'a'; c <= 'z'; c++)
{
    sb.Append(c);
}

string alphabet = sb.ToString();
```

Alternatively, you could create an array of characters and use one of the String type's constructors to create a string out of it:

```
var ch = new char[26];
for (int i = 0; i < 26; i++)
{
    ch[i] = (char)('a' + i);
}

string alphabet = new string(ch);
```

ANOTHER USE OF += AND -=

The += and -= compound assignments are used in a different context, as well: to hook or unhook *event handlers* for an *event*. We discuss this thoroughly when talking about delegates and events in Chapter 17, "Delegates," and Chapter 18, "Events," but let's whet your appetite a bit by means of an example:

```
// Assume payCheck is a button control (for example, in WinForms, WPF or
ASP.NET),
// then the code below hooks up an event handler method to the Click event.
payCheck.Click += payCheck_Click;
```

```
void payCheck_Click(object sender, EventArgs e)
{
    // This code will execute when the button is clicked.
}
```

As you might expect, to remove an event handler from an event, the dual -= syntax is used.

In the context of UI development, those event handlers are set up by code emitted through the UI designer tools. Events are useful in other contexts too, though, where a pure code-driven approach will be required to hook up the handlers.

A Gentle Introduction to Definite Assignment

A significant part of the language specification deals with rules of *definite assignment*, in short to ensure a variable is not used before it has been assigned to. Use of unassigned variables has been a historical source of many bugs, and C# wants to avoid these kinds of mishaps.

Let's set the scene by looking at some simple native C/C++ code. What will the following code print to the screen?

```
void main()
{
    int x;
    printfn("%d\n", x);
}
```

Before answering, notice the code will compile fine. In fact, some C/C++ compilers (for example, Microsoft's) will raise a red flag by emitting a warning:

```
warning C4700: uninitialized local variable 'x' used
```

But warnings can be ignored. As you will see, in C# this code would not compile because the language treats this condition as an *error* instead. You can see why from the result of executing the preceding C/C++ code, as shown in Figure 5.26.

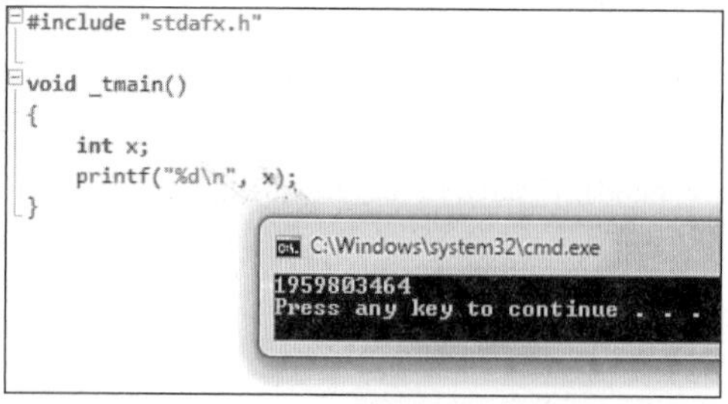

FIGURE 5.26   An uninitialized variable exposing garbage.

The result? Garbage. To understand why this is the case, you should know about memory management in the operating system, which does not guarantee zeroing out acquired pieces of memory. In this case, the variable that's allocated on the stack contains some random data in it, and results can and will vary.

You'll wonder whether it would be better to have memory zeroed out to begin with. That certainly has its merits, eliminating the nondeterministic behavior that results from random data. And in fact, the common language runtime guarantees that memory is zeroed out before it's exposed to code: Allocating a new object (using newobj) makes sure the allocated memory consists of all-zero data and similar local variable slots are initialized with zero data. To illustrate this, we can really go hardcore by writing—for this one time, I promise—plain IL code in some text file:

```
.assembly extern mscorlib {}
.assembly Zero {}

.class Zero
{
  .method static void Main()
  {
    .entrypoint
    .locals init (int32 x)
    ldloc.0
    call        void [mscorlib]System.Console::WriteLine(int32)
    ret
  }
}
```

Feels a bit like C#, doesn't it? Believe me, IL isn't hard at all. Either way, the preceding code defines an assembly called Zero with a Main entry-point method that has one 32-bit integer local variable called x. The code itself simply loads the local variable (ldloc.0) and then calls the Console.WriteLine method on it. Don't worry about mscorlib; this simply indicates the assembly in which the System.Console class is defined. For the same reason, the very first line adds a reference to the mscorlib external assembly, so the runtime knows it should be prepared to load that one when required by the code.

Save this code in a file with an .il extension and call ILASM (for IL assembler, the opposite of the disassembler) on it to produce an assembly. You'll see the assembler doesn't complain about uninitialized data because the common language runtime guarantees it will be initialized to zero as proven in Figure 5.27.

Notice the executable simply prints 0 because the local variable slot on the stack was allocated with zero memory. Reason for euphoria? Maybe, maybe not.

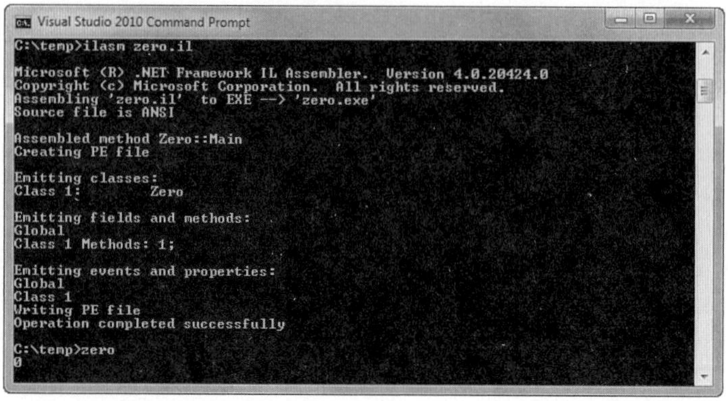

FIGURE 5.27   The CLR's clean slate with regard to memory management.

On the level of the runtime, this guarantee is nice to have. But in higher-level languages, it's better for the user to be explicit about things. Zero (or the null reference) might be a good default value, but it might not be. For that reason, the seemingly equivalent C# code does not compile, resulting in the error shown in Figure 5.28:

```
using System;


class Zero
{
    static void Main()
    {
        int x;
        Console.WriteLine(x);
    }
}
```

To make the preceding code compile fine, you need to write the following where the intent is unambiguously expressed by the user:

```
using System;


class Zero
{
    static void Main()
    {
        int x = 0; // Or, in case the original code had a bug, another value...
        Console.WriteLine(x);
    }
}
```

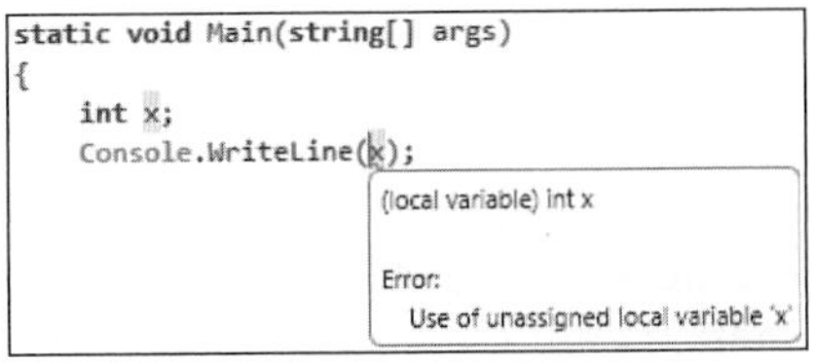

```
static void Main(string[] args)
{
    int x;
    Console.WriteLine(x);
```

(local variable) int x

Error:
    Use of unassigned local variable 'x'

FIGURE 5.28   Use of an unassigned local variable is an error in C#.

NO REDUNDANT ASSIGNMENTS

It's not because C# forces the user to explicitly assign zero (if that's the intended value) that it needs to emit such an assignment in the produced IL code. The C# compiler knows about the common language runtime guaranteeing zero initialization, so in the preceding fragment it won't emit redundant `ldc.i4.0` and `stloc` instructions to initialize x to 0.

The rules for definite assignment make sure a variable cannot be used before it has been assigned to, unless it's considered *initially assigned*. (For example, array elements or parameters to a method start their life as initially assigned.) To ensure this, the compiler uses static flow analysis to make sure every code path leading to the use of a variable guarantees it has been assigned. There are a few language constructs that guarantee a variable is assigned to. One is the use of a simple assignment; another is the use of the variable for an output parameter of a method, discussed in Chapter 10, "Methods."

Let's consider static code flow analysis for the following fragment to illustrate matters:

```
static int Abs(int x)
{
    int res;
    if (x < 0)
    {
        Console.WriteLine("Negative");
        res = -x;
    }
    else
    {
        Console.WriteLine("Positive");
    }

    return res;
}
```

The compiler rightfully complains about res not being assigned on the last line with the return statement. It has inferred this by considering all paths of execution that could lead to that line. In this case, there are two if statement branches, of which the latter doesn't guarantee definite assignment for res. The compiler has caught a bug for you; for if default assignment of zero were implicitly allowed, our code would return zero for every positive value passed to this function. Figure 5.29 illustrates definite assignment analysis for our little piece of sample code.

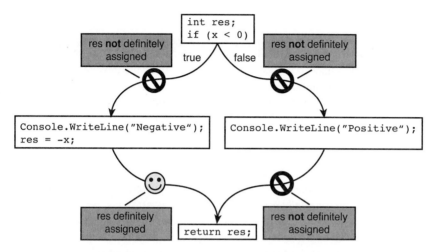

FIGURE 5.29   Definite assignment checking through static flow analysis.

Postfix and Prefix Increment and Decrement Operators

Conceptually closely related to compound assignment with the + and - binary operators are the postfix and prefix increment and decrement operators. In essence, they abbreviate simple operators as "plus one" and "minus one" into succinct syntax, respectively as ++ and --. One common use can be found in the context of for loops, which are discussed in the Chapter 7, "Simple Control Flow." Here is the typical pattern to create a loop that will execute the loop body 10 times:

```
for (int i = 0; i < 10; i++)
{
    // Use integer value i if desired.
}
```

A for loop consists of four parts: an initializer (here int i = 0), a condition (i < 10), an iterator (i++), and a loop body (the part in between curly braces). After initialization, the loop runs until the condition evaluates false. At the end of every iteration, the iterator executes. The loop that goes in reverse is written using a unary decrement operator, as shown here:

```
for (int i = 9; i >= 0; i--)
{
    // Use integer value i if desired.
}
```

MANUAL ARRAY INDEXING OR FOREACH?

Given the length of an array and the fact that indexing is zero-based, the typical loop structure shown earlier is a popular technique to iterate over the elements of an array. However, enumeration over collections—including arrays—is such a common thing that the BCL defines IEnumerable and IEnumerator interfaces for such tasks. Languages such as C# and VB provide for-each loop constructs that build on top of that. So unless you need the index for elements, a foreach loop will yield cleaner code.

The iterator part is where a postfix increment operator is used, effectively increasing the integer variable i with 1. In effect, we're only using the postfix increment operator for this side effect in the preceding example. However, being expressions, those operators produce a value that can be used any place expressions can occur. The difference between postfix and prefix behavior lies in what the resulting value is.

▶ Prefix operators perform the increment or decrement operation first and produces the resulting value.

▶ Postfix operators produce the value before the increment or decrement operation is carried out.

PRE, POST, IN

To make sure everyone is on the same page, a short explanation of vocabulary is in order here. *Pre* stands for before or "in front of." Examples include !b, -i, ~f, and ++x, where the operator appears before its operand. *Post* is the opposite, meaning "after," as in x++, where the operator appears behind the operand. Finally, *in* means "in between," as with a + b and other binary operators in C#.

Prefix and postfix notation are not limited to unary operators; you can think of + a b and a b + as valid syntaxes for addition. In fact, LISP prefers the use of prefix syntax, whereas evaluators typically like postfix notation. (For example, in the stack-driven world of IL, an operator appears *after* the operands are pushed onto the evaluation stack.)

A few examples will clarify this behavior, starting with the postfix case:

```
int x = 0;

// The value before the increment is assigned, so y will be set to 0.
int y = x++;
```

```
// At this point, x will have been incremented to 1.
Console.WriteLine(x);
```

In the prefix case, things are a bit different:

```
int x = 0;
```

```
// The value after the increment is assigned, so y will be set to 1.
int y = ++x;
```

```
// At this point, x will have been incremented to 1.
Console.WriteLine(x);
```

Decrement operators work in a similar fashion. To test your understanding, what does the following code correspond to? No, I'm not advocating that you write this kind of code; I just want to make sure evaluation order is clear in case you encounter such code.

```
int x = 0;
int y = (x += 1);
Console.WriteLine("X = " + x);
Console.WriteLine("Y = " + y);
```

FUN WITH SIDE EFFECTS

This should be nothing more than a pop quiz, but the combination of the behavior of different operators can yield interesting results. At your next visit to a programmer's nightclub, try to distinguish C developers from C# developers by having them evaluate the following:

```
int x = 0;
x += x++;
```

Even blogs have been subtitled with this fun expression. (If you don't believe me, take a look at http://blogs.msdn.com/lucabol.)

It should be clear that all arithmetic operations, including the ones discussed here, are subject to overflow checking only when they appear in a checked context. Therefore, the following code will run forever when it doesn't appear in a checked context because the value of x will overflow:

```
for (int x = 0; true; x++)
{
    Console.WriteLine(x);
}
```

The discussed increment and decrement operators can also be applied to properties and indexers if both getters and setters are available:

```
vector["x"]--;
person.Age++;
```

Summary

In this chapter, we explored one of the key sources of expressiveness in the C# programming language no developer can live without: expressions. After covering the role of expressions and the runtime's evaluation stack, we covered one particular set of expressions; namely, operators.

The discussion of operators brought you to arithmetic operators and aspects of overflow checking using the checked and unchecked keywords. Use of floating-point arithmetic was explained as well, focusing on implications of limited precision. Next, you looked at other kinds of operators, such as relation and logical ones. The conditional operator (commonly referred to as the ternary operator) was covered too, pointing out its lazy evaluation of operands. You also learned various aspects of working with null and nullable value types, including the null-coalescing operator.

Finally, you learned various forms of asignment, ranging from simple to compound. This also allowed you to learn increment and decrement operators, as commonly seen in for loops to update an index variable.

Chapter 6, "A Primer on Types and Objects," focuses on the concept of types from an expression angle. More specifically, you learn how you can check for types, create new object instances, access members on objects, and so on.

A Primer on Types and Objects

IN THIS CHAPTER

▶ Implicit Versus Explicit Conversions 299

▶ The **typeof** Operator: A Sneak Peek at Reflection 317

▶ Default Value Expression 320

▶ Creating Objects with the **new** Operator 323

▶ Member Access 335

▶ Invocation Expressions 339

▶ Element Access 347

I have to admit, and colleagues will second, that I live and breathe type systems. Static typing is a great thing because you get feedback on invalid use of objects early on during compilation.

With the CLR type system centered on object-oriented programming concepts such as subtyping and virtual dispatch, you have a powerful tool at hand to deal with typing in a rich manner. When correctly used (especially since the advent of generics in .NET 2.0), the need for runtime type checks or conversions between types should be quite rare. Rare, but not nonexistent.

This chapter focuses on various aspects of dealing with types and objects. First, we discuss conversions and casts, type checks, and operators such as typeof. Next, we briefly explore the concept of dynamic types in C# 4.0. Finally, our discussion focuses on the use of expressions to access members, invoke methods, and so on.

Implicit Versus Explicit Conversions

Simply stated, conversions are a way to treat an expression as being of a specified type. This gives rise to two different situations: Either the conversion is statically known by the compiler to be safe (no data loss can occur) or such guarantees do not exist.

In the former case, *implicit conversions* are permitted by the compiler. Primitive types form a good playground to illustrate this. For example, given an int variable, it's possible to treat it as if it were a `long` because all `Int32` values definitely fit in the range of the `Int64` type. This particular conversion is a representation-changing conversion that needs runtime assistance because we're stuffing a 4-byte value in an 8-byte one:

```
long Add(long a, long b)
{
    return a + b;
}
```

```
Add(1, 2); // providing int literals that get converted to long implicitly
```

Implicit conversions can also occur without change of representation (for example, in case of a conversion between a subtype and a supertype):

```
void PrintObject(object o)
{
    Console.WriteLine(o);
}
```

```
PrintObject("Bart"); // System.String is a subtype of System.Object
```

There are some hidden caveats with regard to a mechanism called "boxing" that occurs when a value type is treated as a `System.Object`. We'll delay discussion of this subtlety until Chapter 9, "Introducing Types."

Explicit conversions are conversions that are not permitted to go unnoticed because they can potentially fail at runtime. The compiler doesn't have enough evidence you know what you're doing, so you need to express your intent explicitly by means of a *cast expression*. All implicit conversions can be written down explicitly, though (for example, as a way to make code self-documenting):

```
PrintObject((object)"Bart");
```

An example of an explicit conversion between built-in types is one that goes from `long` to `int`, where the potential for loss of information exists as `int` is less precise than `long`:

```
long x = 42;
int y = (int)x;
```

Both implicit and explicit conversions can be defined by custom types, as you will see in Chapter 13, "Operator Overloading and Conversions."

Cast Expressions

Cast expressions are a way to carry out explicit conversions at runtime. In essence, you're telling the compiler you know more about the type of an object than it can possibly know. Don't worry, the compiler is hardened against this type of insult.

The syntax for a cast expression looks like this (where type is the name of a type):

```
(type) unary-expression
```

An example where this is used on a regular basis is while dealing with a weakly typed API. To be maximally applicable, some APIs use the root of the type hierarchy, System.Object, to deal with any kind of object imaginable. A good example can be found in the old, nongeneric collection types in the System.Collections namespace:

```
var list = new ArrayList();
list.Add("Bart");
list.Add("John");
list.Add("Lisa");
string bartIsBack = (string)list[0];
```

On the last line, we're using *indexer* syntax to retrieve the list's element in the first position (in a zero-based world, that is). For ArrayList to be able to cope with any kind of element type, it has been typed to take in and give out objects of type System.Object. Because we know this particular use of the ArrayList contains only string elements, it's safe to use a cast expression to convert the result of the indexer operation to the string type. But the compiler can't know this from the statically available type information, so it has to take your word for it. An *explicit* word, that is.

CAST SYNTAX

The cast syntax using the two parentheses is not exclusively used for runtime conversions. For one thing, implicit conversions can be written out explicitly, too:

```
string s = "Bart";
object o = (object)s; // (object) part can be omitted
```

This redundant "cast" does not imply any representational change at runtime: System.String and System.Object are both reference types, and references (but not the data they're referring to!) all have the same size. And it's also safe to do so from a typing perspective because System.Object is a supertype of System.String. In effect, you're losing type information here, so you'll only be able to perform a subset of the string functionality.

But there's also the case of runtime conversions on literals, which is changing representations. Only they happen at compile time, not at runtime. For example, the widening conversion of an int literal to a long can be written as follows:

```
long a = (long)42;
```

In essence, you started with a literal that fits in 4 bytes and asked the compiler to widen it into 8 bytes because for some reason you need a long. Of course, you could have used the L suffix for long literals, but I'm merely illustrating a point here: Cast syntax does not imply runtime operations.

So how does a cast work? It depends. In the less-common case, a user-defined conversion is available, and a plain call to the underlying conversion method results. The more typical scenario of casting from some type (like System.Object) to a more specific type (like System.String) involves a baked-in instruction of the IL instruction set.

Let's take a quick look at this. Consider a simplified version of the preceding code fragment where only Bart is added to an ArrayList and read back using the indexer notation:

```
var list = new ArrayList();
list.Add("Bart");
string bartIsBack = (string)list[0];
```

Let's pay specific attention to the last line. Notice that for this code to compile you must import the System.Collections namespace by means of a using directive:

```
using System.Collections;
```

ILDASM reveals the code shown in Figure 6.1, where I've highlighted the instruction that carries out the casting job.

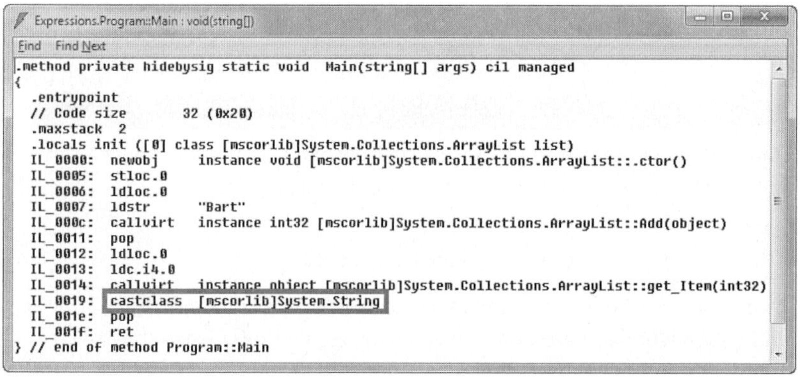

```
Expressions.Program::Main : void(string[])

Find  Find Next

.method private hidebysig static void  Main(string[] args) cil managed
{
  .entrypoint
  // Code size       32 (0x20)
  .maxstack  2
  .locals init ([0] class [mscorlib]System.Collections.ArrayList list)
  IL_0000:  newobj     instance void [mscorlib]System.Collections.ArrayList::.ctor()
  IL_0005:  stloc.0
  IL_0006:  ldloc.0
  IL_0007:  ldstr      "Bart"
  IL_000c:  callvirt   instance int32 [mscorlib]System.Collections.ArrayList::Add(object)
  IL_0011:  pop
  IL_0012:  ldloc.0
  IL_0013:  ldc.i4.0
  IL_0014:  callvirt   instance object [mscorlib]System.Collections.ArrayList::get_Item(int32)
  IL_0019:  castclass   [mscorlib]System.String
  IL_001e:  pop
  IL_001f:  ret
} // end of method Program::Main
```

FIGURE 6.1   Casting under the hood.

In the previous instruction, the call to the indexer was made (internally corresponding to a method call to get_Item, as you will see later), which resulted in pushing the System.Object-typed return value on the stack. Subsequently, the castclass instruction pops that object from the stack and attempts to convert it into an object of the specified type, in our case System.String.

> **NOTE**
>
> Although my examples always go between System.Object and its immediate subtype System.String, casting can be done between any two types. For example, you may have a FruitStore object that returns Fruit instances, but through unexplainable powers you know that FruitStore sells only apples. In such a case, you would cast Fruit to Apple.

Notice how I said it *attempts* the conversion. Recall that explicit conversions are about forcing your will onto the compiler so that it faithfully emits a cast instruction to the type of your choice even though it has no clue whether that call will succeed at runtime. In this particular example, we do know that we only add string objects to the collection, so we can only get objects of that type out.

But the fact the C# compiler is willing to believe you doesn't mean the runtime has to. Actually, if you would be able to cast an object to an incompatible type, you're breaching type safety. Treating a Kiwi object as an Apple to be fed into a Bakery will not yield the right kind of AppleCakes in return. Clearly, that's undesirable. To protect against such dangerous situations, the runtime checks that the cast operation is sound.

As an example, the following code fragment will compile fine:

```
object o = 5;
string s = (string)o;
```

Here we attempt to treat a System.Int32 object as a System.String. This illustrates a very important difference between compile-time types and runtime types. What the compiler deals with is static knowledge. In the preceding code, we've stated o to be of type System.Object, and nothing more specific than that. And even though we assigned it a System.Int32 object, that doesn't affect the compiler's view of the world. To make this even clearer, consider the variable o was not assigned anywhere near but came in through a formal parameter on some method:

```
private void DoSomething(object o)
{
    // Dear compiler, I know o ought to be a string:
    string s = (string)o;

    // Do something useful
}
```

Now we clearly don't know what the runtime type of o will be. All we can know from static analysis is that it ought to be System.Object or any of its derived types. But suppose we know that callers to this method will only ever pass in System.String instances; in this scenario, it's fine for us to use a cast inside the method body to do a runtime conversion.

You might be wondering why we would actually ever type a parameter of a method to be less specific than what we know it should be. In the preceding case, why didn't we type the parameter to be System.String? There are various reasons this situation can arise, actually: *Interfaces* and *delegates* are common sources of such seemingly pathological cases. You'll see why later.

Anyway, back to our fragment:

```
object o = 5;
string s = (string)o;
```

Clearly, this is not going to work: A number is not a string. Yes, we could turn a number into a textual string somehow (by calling ToString), but from a typing perspective numbers aren't strings. If they were, operations such as ToUpper would have to be defined on numbers, which is clearly nonsense.

The runtime responds to this attempt at violating type safety by means of an InvalidCastException, as shown in Figure 6.2.

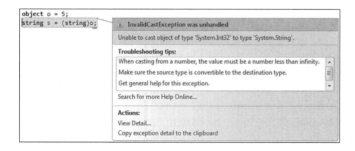

FIGURE 6.2   InvalidCastExceptions signal runtime type violations due to casts.

GENERIC TYPES

System.Object is the weakest strong type available in the framework. It's obviously very "generic" but rarely usable because you've lost any further knowledge about the object's type. Since .NET 2.0, generics can be used to achieve similar effects while still preserving full-fledged type information. Therefore, various places that used to be typed using System.Object can now be typed generically by use of a *type parameter*. List<T> is such a type, where T indicates the element type of the collection, which is used for the Add method's input parameter and for the indexer's type. This eliminates the need for casts, has positive performance impact, and prevents certain classes of errors because types get checked early (at compile time).

This doesn't mean, though, that `System.Object`-typed variables or members will vanish completely. One of the restrictions of generics is the need to fully specify all type parameters (resulting in a so-called *closed type*). The mere desire to treat some member generically brings on the burden to add a type parameter to the containing type. For example, in Windows Presentation Foundation (WPF), controls can have a `Content` property that can be set to the data that needs to be visualized by the control. Because every type of data should be allowed, two options exist: `System.Object` or a generic parameter. The latter would definitely be handy because reading from the property would yield data of a statically known type:

```
// Using a hypothetical generic Label<T> type
Label<Customer> businessCard = new Label<Customer>();
businessCard.Content = customers.GetByName("Bart");
Customer bart = businessCard.Content;
```

On the other hand, do you really want to bring on the need for developers to state the `Content` type every time a control is used? Maybe `Content` is not used at all or is only set. And what about designer tools? Is it reasonable to prompt the user for a type every time a drag-and-drop operation of a content-enabled control is carried out? Given all those observations, it's probably better to use `System.Object`, and indeed that's what WPF does in this case:

```
// Using the realistic non-generic Label type
Label businessCardReal = new Label();
businessCardReal.Content = customers.GetByName("Bart");
Customer bart = (Customer)businessCardReal.Content;
```

In summary, generics where possible; `System.Object` where necessary.

Does this mean the compiler doesn't do any checking at all and blindly emits a cast instruction whenever you write code of this form? Despite the dynamic nature of casts, there are still cases that are statically known to be impossible. For example, given that Kiwi and Apple are both subtypes of Fruit, we know them to be siblings in the type hierarchy. Such a relationship can never yield an "is a" relationship at runtime: There's enough information to determine this as compile-time nonsense, which is illustrated in Figure 6.3.

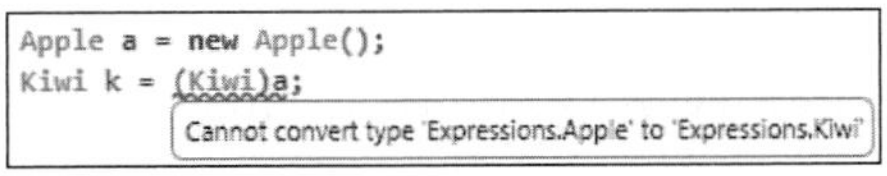

```
Apple a = new Apple();
Kiwi k = (Kiwi)a;
        Cannot convert type 'Expressions.Apple' to 'Expressions.Kiwi'
```

FIGURE 6.3   A cast that can be proven never to succeed results in a compile-time error.

The knowledge of a static type establishes a minimum for the runtime type. If we know variable "a" to be of type Apple, it can still turn out to be a Jonagold or another other type of apple, but it can't ever turn out to be a Kiwi (unless type safety is broken). If, on the other hand, you would have typed variable a as System.Object, the compiler would not complain. Now all that's known at compile time is that a can't be anything less than System.Object. It could well be a Kiwi, and hence the compiler trusts the judgment of the developer. To put it another way, if no evidence is found against the user's claim, the compiler goes with it as is.

The is Operator

Casts, as described previously, should be used only if you're absolutely sure that the object can be converted to the specified type. If it can't, a runtime exception occurs. In effect, think about this exception as the absolute latest time where a typing error can be caught: Face it, you have a bug.

So what if we're just interested in knowing whether an object has a particular runtime type? In other words, we want to make a *runtime type check*, essentially resulting in a Boolean truth value. This is what the is operator is all about:

```
object o = "Bart";

bool isString = o is string; // true
bool isInt = o is int; // false
```

The is operator is concerned only with types and considers type hierarchies as part of its operation. For example, assuming Apple derives from Fruit:

```
// The jonagold variable represents an instance of Jonagold, a subtype of Apple
bool jonagoldIfFruit = jonagold is Fruit; // true
```

> **NOTE**
>
> What the is operator does not consider are user-defined conversions. Languages emit calls to such methods when the user requests a conversion. But to the runtime, that's the end of it: A method by itself doesn't define relationships between types.

Although in general the is operator requires a runtime type check, sometimes it can be degenerate if enough information is known at compile time. For example, the following is a tautology, meaning it always evaluates true:

```
bool IsAppleFruit(Apple a)
{
    return a is Fruit; // true: I don't know any apple that isn't fruit
}
```

It's statically known that every apple is a fruit because `Apple` is a subtype of `Fruit`. The opposite case exists when the compiler knows for sure a typing relationship cannot possibly hold:

```
bool IsAppleKiwi(Apple a)
{
    return a is Kiwi; // false: can never hold
}
```

The interesting case is obviously when the compiler doesn't have any clue about the expressed type check, in which case the decision is left to the runtime:

```
bool IsItFruit(object it)
{
    return it is Fruit; // who knows?
}
```

Internally, the `is` operator doesn't look very exciting. Or does it? Let's take a look anyway. Turns out the CLR has a seemingly simple `isinst` instruction that pops the object from the top of the stack, checks it against the given type, and pushes some result onto the stack. But what's the result? A Boolean? Not really... As usual, boil down the sample to its essence and look at the generated code in Figure 6.4:

```
object o = "Bart";
// compiler can't judge the following because o is typed as System.Object...
bool isString = o is string;
```

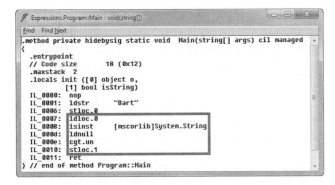

FIGURE 6.4   The `is` operator exposed.

What's up here? On the first line of the marked block, the local variable is pushed onto the stack. Next, `isinst` plays the runtime judge to decide whether the object is a string. However, the result on top of the stack is not a Boolean; it's the original object casted as a string in case it turned out to be a string and null otherwise.

SOFT AND HARD CASTS

Casts come in many flavors. Languages such as C and C++ are notorious for the many forms of casting they offer. The CLR's view of the world is simpler but also different. C and C++ have casts that permit low-level bit reinterpretation, an operation that's not type safe in any way. In managed code, two casts exist merely as a way to either fail immediately (`castclass`) or let the caller decide what to do in case of failure (`isinst`). You could say `castclass` is "hard" and `isinst` is "soft" based on that behavior.

This explains the next two instructions, where the null reference is pushed onto the stack using `ldnull`, followed by a comparison operation. It's this comparison that ultimately produces the desired Boolean value.

Now the ultimate question: Why would you use the `is` operator? People typically use it as a means to do type-based dispatch: If an object is of type X, do this; if it's of type Y, do that; and so on. However, better ways to code up such a pattern often exist: *virtual methods*. Because we cover this concept in Chapter 14, "Object-Oriented Programming," I'm keeping the explanation brief here.

Suppose you have a type hierarchy for food products sold by some store. The root of the hierarchy is Food with immediate subtypes like Vegetable and Fruit that have further subtypes of their own, like Tomato and Apple. Now, given any Food object, you need to assess its freshness. The object-oriented approach to this is to have a virtual method defined on Food and have subtypes override it to specialize its meaning. For example, Tomato could define it in terms of the skin color, while Apple could key off freshness estimation based on wrinkles on the skin or signs of rotten spots. Cookies, you say? Just look at the "best before" date on the package. Figure 6.5 illustrates the notion of a virtual method using a type hierarchy.

Given any Food instance, calling the IsFresh method on it will dispatch to the implementation for the runtime type. If the Food passed in is actually an Apple, it will call Apple's IsFresh override:

```
public void EnsureFreshness()
{
    foreach (Food item in stock)
    {
        if (!item.IsFresh())
        {
            store.TossOut(item);
        }
    }
}
```

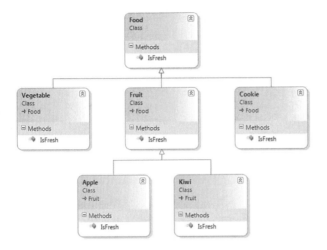

FIGURE 6.5   A type hierarchy with an `IsFresh` virtual method.

All is good and well if you control the `Food` type and its descendants: Add the `IsFresh` virtual method, implement it for each type that needs specialized treatment, and just call the virtual method where required. The runtime will take care of making sure the right method is called for you.

But when you're dealing with an existing set of types you can't extend, how do you go ahead and implement a similar `EnsureFreshness` procedure? The answer lies in type checks: For each food item you're scanning, you'll check the type and take the appropriate action based on that outcome. A potential approach—which we refine in the next section—looks like this:

```
public void EnsureFreshness()
{
    foreach (Food item in stock)
    {
        if (!IsFresh(item))
        {
            store.TossOut(item);
        }
    }
}


private bool IsFresh(Food item)
{
    if (item is Fruit)
    {
```

```
        return IsFreshFruit((Fruit)item);
    }
    else if (item is Vegetable)
    {
        return IsFreshVegetable((Vegetable)item);
    }
    else
    {
        throw new InvalidOperationException("Unknown food type.");
    }
}
```

And further down, you would have methods like `IsFreshFruit` and `IsFreshVegetable` that check for known subtypes, all the way to a point where freshness can be judged correctly. The pattern put into practice here is known as a (simple) visitor.

Clearly, this is a lot more boilerplate code than leveraging virtual methods, which essentially perform a similar operation at runtime but baked in to the runtime and the type system. For this very reason, you should use type checks only sparingly.

DYNAMIC

The use of dynamic typing, available since C# 4.0, is another way to tackle this problem. Actually, it's all about gradations of typing. Let's explore this a bit further...

Even the very first approach using virtual methods has some dynamism to it: The runtime gets to choose what method will be invoked based on the actual runtime type. However, the compiler statically knows such a method will be available, so you're assured there won't be a failure to "resolve the target method."

Then there's the visitor-based approach, where we specify type checks and casts in excruciating detail. If type checks and casts are paired up correctly, we can be confident of avoiding trouble at runtime: The type check guarantees we can carry out a runtime cast, and ultimately we perform operations against the casted object in a statically typed fashion.

Finally, there's the dynamic newborn in C# 4.0. Instead of doing all sorts of type checks, we could just say, "But I know there's a method called `IsFresh` on all those objects, so don't bother to find it at compile time." In this particular example, there should be no reason at all to use this approach. However, if you're handed in objects from outer space (like a dynamic language), it will be your only reasonable way to proceed.

We discuss dynamic in Chapter 22, "Dynamic Programming." It's just important to realize that C# provides you with all the tools to tackle a wide range of scenarios. Personally, I favor trying to use static typing wherever possible (virtual methods included, that is), but when absolutely necessary, I know I can rely on type checks or dynamic to make my life easier.

The as Operator

You might wonder why I made all that fuss about the underlying implementation of the is operator. Well, as you've seen, the is operator actually performs a cast underneath the covers and checks the result against null to determine whether the cast succeeded. Contrast this with the behavior of the cast expression that throws an InvalidCastException in case of a failed cast. Clearly, both cast mechanisms are useful.

This brings us to the as operator, which is the gentle equivalent to the cast expression: Instead of throwing an exception on failure to cast, it simply returns null. In the previous example where we dispatched types using the is operator, we actually did things rather inefficiently. First we carried out a type check:

```
if (item is Fruit)
```

Although internally this already has produced the casted object in case of success, we ask the compiler to check for null immediately and throw away the intermediate result of the isinst cast instruction. And if the is operator evaluates to true, we cast again, this time preserving the result:

```
return IsFreshFruit((Fruit)item);
```

INEFFICIENT OR NOT?

The inefficiency discussed here has to be taken with a grain of salt. First, you should consider something inefficient only if realistic user scenarios are hurt by it. Chances are the runtime's JIT compiler does a good job of making things better under the hood. What likely matters most is whether the code you wrote passes all sorts of tests with regard to readability and maintainability.

Either way, it's a good excuse to talk about Code Analysis tools and whatnot.

In fact, this inefficiency can be caught by code analysis tools in Visual Studio. While we're at it, let's take a peek at this. Under the project's Properties, you'll spot a tab called Code Analysis, illustrated in Figure 6.6. Use the first check box to enable code analysis during build and choose the Microsoft All Rules rule set to turn on the most verbose checking. This includes checks for performance issues resulting from bad coding practices.

Now write some code that follows the pattern described before. Check an object for some type using the is operator and cast it subsequently in an if statement:

```
object o = "Bart";

if (o is string)
{
```

```
    string s = (string)o;
    Console.WriteLine(s);
}
```

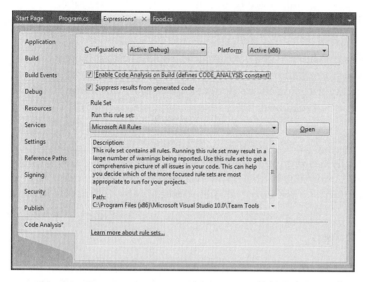

FIGURE 6.6   Enabling Code Analysis in Visual Studio 2010.

Now build the project and watch the Error List. It should show something like Figure 6.7. You might have more warnings; just ignore those for now.

Notice how it even mentions the underlying redundant instruction in the emitted IL code: castclass. By now, you should be able to puzzle together the pieces of the code the compiler has emitted. The is operator uses results in an isinst instruction, and the cast expression (using the parentheses syntax) uses castclass, while isinst already produced a result. The tools even suggest a fix: Use as.

So that's what we're going to do:

```
object o = "Bart";

string s = o as string;
if (s != null)
{
    Console.WriteLine(s);
}
```

And away goes the Code Analysis warning. Now we're caching the result of the "soft" cast for both purposes of type checking and using the resulting object, avoiding the redundant cast instruction.

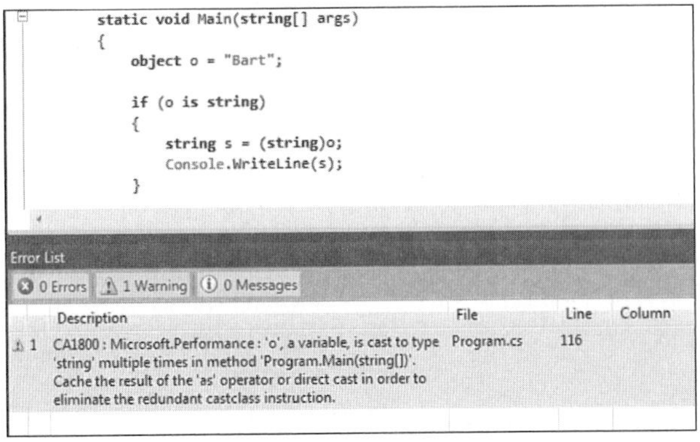

```
       static void Main(string[] args)
       {
            object o = "Bart";

            if (o is string)
            {
                string s = (string)o;
                Console.WriteLine(s);
            }
```

Error List

🚫 0 Errors ⚠ 1 Warning ⓘ 0 Messages

Description	File	Line	Column
⚠ 1 CA1800 : Microsoft.Performance : 'o', a variable, is cast to type 'string' multiple times in method 'Program.Main(string[])'. Cache the result of the 'as' operator or direct cast in order to eliminate the redundant castclass instruction.	Program.cs	116	

FIGURE 6.7   Code Analysis catching a potential performance issue.

Obviously, more often than not we want to check for a variety of possible types and take action for either of the known types. To illustrate how to do this, let's try to rewrite our IsFresh method from before:

```
private bool IsFresh(Food item)
{
    Fruit f = item as Fruit;
    Vegetable v = item as Vegetable;

    if (f != null)
    {
        return IsFreshFruit(f);
    }
    else if (v != null)
    {
        return IsFreshVegetable(v);
    }
    else
    {
        throw new InvalidOperationException("Unknown food type.");
    }
}
```

Clearly this is wasteful because we don't need to attempt all casts to know what type of object we're faced with. It would be better to write the code as follows instead:

```
private bool IsFresh(Food item)
{
    Fruit f = item as Fruit;
    if (f != null)
    {
```

```
        return IsFreshFruit(f);
    }
    else
    {
        Vegetable v = item as Vegetable;
        if (v != null)
        {
            return IsFreshVegetable(v);
        }
        else
        {
            throw new InvalidOperationException("Unknown food type.");
        }
    }
}
```

But now our nice flat decision structure is lost. As stated before, it would be much better to avoid having to write this kind of code altogether because better approaches are available, but in some cases we don't have a choice. So, can we make the code look better while still avoiding the potential performance issues we saw before?

```
private bool IsFresh(Food item)
{
    Fruit f;
    Vegetable v;

    if ((f = item as Fruit) != null)
    {
        return IsFreshFruit(f);
    }
    else if ((v = item as Vegetable) != null)
    {
        return IsFreshVegetable(v);
    }
    else
    {
        throw new InvalidOperationException("Unknown food type.");
    }
}
```

This gets a little subtle and combines assignment with null checking. Some colleagues will likely curse me for writing this style of code, but I think it's acceptable. We take a look at the nuts and bolts of assignment in a few moments, so the preceding code should become crystal clear.

EXCESSIVE USE OF AS CONSIDERED HARMFUL

Overuse of the as operator is not a good idea. Use it for what it's designed for, the means of combining use of the is operator and a regular cast expression. This means as should be seen as a type check in the first place, with the casted result as a free gift.

Code that uses as but omits a null check almost certainly has a bug in it. If you know for sure the object should be of a well-known target type, use a regular cast; otherwise, you're effectively trading the much-telling `InvalidCastException` for a `NullReferenceException` down the road. An example of a case where you know the type for sure but you're losing it because of a weakly typed API is the use of the threading APIs:

```
// A delegate is used as the parameter to the Thread constructor.
// Essentially we're passing a reference to the method to run on the thread.
// The delegate used here requires the parameter to be of type System.Object.
var thread = new Thread(BackgroundWork);
thread.Start("Hello" /* this becomes the parameter to the method */);

void BackgroundWork(object parameter)
{
    // But here we know for sure we'll always pass in a string message.
    var message = (string)parameter;
    // Do background processing for the message.
}
```

There's a second reason the use of as might not be ideal: It doesn't enable you to distinguish between a null value originating from a failed cast and one that comes from the input being null in the first place. So if null is to be considered a proper value for the type under consideration, you'll be better off with a regular cast expression.

Also notice that the as operator does work only with types that are nullable: reference types and nullable value types. The is operator, on the other hand, works with all types. This gives rise to a situation where the pattern of is followed by a regular cast expression is still required.

Intermezzo: The Mythical Type Switch

The switch statement is a convenient way to express multiway branches that would normally get written using tons of if statements. Switches typically operate based on compile-time constant values, and that's no different in C#:

```
switch (card.Type)
{
    case CardType.Credit:
        // Do something.
        break;
```

```
case CardType.Debit:
    // Do something else.
    break;
default:
    // Other type of card. Do yet something else.
    break;
}
```

We talk extensively about the switch statement in Chapter 7, "Simple Control Flow," but I wanted to point out one thing here: C#'s switch statement does not support "switch on type."

There are various reasons for this. First, the order of case labels in a switch statement is irrelevant to the switch's operation. This works because the object we're switching on gets compared to the constants for equality. Because all constants used in case labels need to be unique, only one case can apply to the object. With types, the situation is different because they comprise a hierarchy. For example, assume you're switching a piece of food on its type and specify cases for Fruit and Apple. For a Kiwi this is fine; the Fruit case will fire. However, what about an Apple? Order of evaluation starts to matter: Does the object's type get checked for Fruit first or for Apple? Both apply. Different syntax would be desirable to stress the fact that evaluation order matters.

But there's another reason: If you decide to go through the burden of designing, implementing, testing, and shipping a full-fledged language feature, it better be a good one that's widely usable. As mentioned throughout the text, switching on type can be avoided in quite a few cases by taking advantage of runtime features such as virtual method dispatch. But that doesn't help you if switching on type is really the only option available.

In the light of good language design, it's also important to take a look at the big picture. Other languages are helpful with regard to providing possible approaches to a given problem. With switching on types, that's definitely the case. Languages such as ML (and F# as a derivative of it) offer a bigger feature than just type-based switching. It's called *pattern matching*. Basically, the observation is made that besides switching on types, one typically wants to extract data from the object at the same time:

```
match card with
| CreditCard(account, expiration) -> (* do something *)
| DebitCard(account, balance) -> (* do something else *)
| _ -> (* do yet something else *)
```

Here, the card object is checked against various types, and when a match is found data is extracted from it and bound to local variables. Pattern matching doesn't operate only on regular objects; it can also be used to match over different types such as lists (extracting the head element and tail list) or tuples (extracting the elements at the different positions in the tuple).

It's not clear whether C# will ever get a full-fledged pattern matching operator. But it would definitely seem to be the better feature compared to simple type switching and may provide more value. In the meantime, if you're designing an API that needs to be friendly toward type switching and the use of virtual methods doesn't give you what you want, there are workarounds.

For example, the expression tree APIs in `System.Linq.Expressions`—which we explore during our discussion of reflection in Chapter 21, "Reflection"—provide a tree-based object model for expressions and statements. It's a convenient way to represent code as data so that code can be inspected at runtime (for example, for interpretation, optimization, and translation). It's common for consumers of such an API to have to switch on types corresponding to nodes in the tree. For example, a + operation will be represented as a `BinaryExpression`, whereas a ! operation is done using a `UnaryExpression`. Not to mention other types of expressions like method calls and such.

Instead of requiring consuming languages to have a type switch or pattern matching capabilities, the expression tree APIs define a `NodeType` enumeration to facilitate any switching requirements:

```
switch (expression.NodeType)
{
    case ExpressionType.Add:
        var add = (BinaryExpression)expression;
        // Do something.
        break;
    case ExpressionType.Not:
        var not = (UnaryExpression)expression;
        // Do something else.
        break;
    /* other cases */
    default:
        throw new InvalidOperationException(
            "Unknown node type: " + expression.NodeType);
}
```

Doesn't look too bad after all. And in this particular case, it's even advantageous to have such an enumeration because it's more fine-grained than the different types that are used to represent expression tree nodes. There's one `BinaryExpression` that's used for all binary expressions such as +, -, *, /, &, ¦, and so on. So while switching, you already get more information than from a bare-bones type check.

The `typeof` Operator: A Sneak Peek at Reflection

One of the big advantages of having metadata baked in to the runtime is the capability to provide reflection capabilities. Tools can use metadata to provide designer experiences by providing property grids to configure items that need configuration (for example, UI controls). Via reflection, that metadata is readily available at runtime.

The most common starting point for use of reflection is at the type level. Suppose we want to know all the properties a type exposes. For example, a `Button` control could have a `Width` and `Height` of type `double` and a `Text` of type `string`. Or the built-in `DateTime` type has properties like `Day`, `Month`, `Year`, and so on. So what we need is a runtime representation of a type.

Now there are two popular routes to bring us to this information, depending on what we have. Suppose we have an object somewhere that is an instance of a particular type. Using the `System.Object GetType` method, we can simply ask every object, "Hey dude, what's your type?" The result of making such a call is a `System.Type` object describing the type you were asking for. Do you see the meta-factor here? To describe a type at runtime, an object of type `System.Type` is used. How nice can it get?

```
DateTime now = DateTime.Now;
Type t = now.GetType();
// Reflect on it...
```

It's important to distinguish a couple of concepts here:

- ▶ A type describes the shape of and operations on an object; for example, `DateTime` has storage for day, month, and year (among others) and provides operations to access those (in this case, properties).

- ▶ Instances of a type represent something concrete; for example, the current time is an instance of `DateTime` and similarly the moment Einstein was born can be represented as an instance of this type.

- ▶ `System.Type` is a type that describes a type—for example, providing information about the properties, methods, fields, events, and so on that are available on the type. To do so, it provides operations like `GetProperties`.

- ▶ An instance of `System.Type` represents a specific type; for example, the type `DateTime`. By calling operations on the object you can find out about the type's properties (for example, `Day`, `Month`, and `Year`).

The first way to get to a `System.Type` object is shown in Figure 6.8, illustrating the relationship between a type, an instance thereof, and the result of calling `GetType`.

So given such an instance of `System.Type`, what can we do with it? Let's not go into details just yet because we'll talk extensively about reflection in Chapter 21, but let's just illustrate a very simple use to display a type's properties:

```
DateTime now = DateTime.Now;

Type t = now.GetType();
foreach (var prop in t.GetProperties())
{
    Console.WriteLine(prop.Name);
}
```

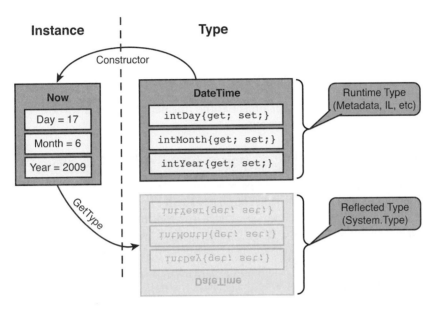

FIGURE 6.8   Retrieving reflection information from an instance of a type.

In this code fragment, the type of `prop` is inferred using an implicitly typed local variable (remember the `var` keyword?), not to reveal the reflection types yet: Can you guess how a type describing a property would be called? Doesn't really matter much; the bigger picture is much more important. Not only types, but also the bits and pieces they're composed of (like properties, methods, and so forth) have a runtime representation in the world of `System.Reflection`. And from that, you can delve even deeper, asking questions like, "What are the types of a method's parameters?" This is a very powerful concept.

The result of running the previous code snippet is shown in Figure 6.9.

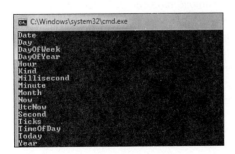

FIGURE 6.9   Properties on `System.DateTime`.

But what if you don't have (or want to have) an instance of a type to call `GetType` on? How do you get to the type information in that case? Assuming you know the type's name, the `typeof` operator comes to the rescue:

```
Type t = typeof(DateTime);
```

This produces exactly the same `System.Type` object as the fragment before but without the need to have an instance of the type lying around.

WHAT ABOUT GENERIC TYPES?

As stated before, generic types are a form of *type constructors*. Types like `List<T>` are *open* in a sense they have type parameters that are not set to a specific type. In case of `List<T>`, T is such a type parameter. From open types, you can create a *closed* one by supplying a type name for all type parameters (for example, `List<int>` or `List<string>`).

Both open and closed generic types can be referred to using the `typeof` operator. The closed ones are predictable; you can just write things like `typeof(List<int>)` to get the `System.Type` object back that represents that type. In there, you'll find things such as an Add method with an `int`-typed parameter, just as if there were a specialized `List` type that operates on integer numbers.

To deal with an open type in reflection, one more thing matters: the *arity* of the generic type. The arity is simply the number of generic parameters on a type. It's perfectly valid to have multiple generic types with the same name but a different number of type parameters. The `Tuple` types are a good example of this: `Tuple<T1,T2>` exists and so does `Tuple<T1,T2,T3>` and so on. So to refer to an open type using `typeof`, you must specify the arity somehow. This is simply done by omitting names for the type parameters but leaving the commas in: `typeof(Tuple<,>)` refers to the one with two type parameters.

Why would you want to refer to an open generic type? Reflection is about true dynamic behavior, where tasks that normally would be done at compile time can be deferred until runtime. One such task is dynamic construction of a closed generic type, starting from an open one. Suppose you want to create a `Tuple<T1,T2>` where the type parameters are not known until runtime for some obscure reason. In other words, the "values" for T1 and T2 are supplied at runtime in the form of `System.Type` instances. With reflection, it becomes possible to construct such a generic type completely at runtime. Not that I expect most readers will ever have to do this, but just in case, you now know it's possible.

Default Value Expression

As you've seen repeatedly, the introduction of generics in .NET 2.0 took away a bunch of limitations that came from the mandatory use of `System.Object` in generic code, resulting in weaker typing than desired. With generics, it's possible to use *type parameters* and write code in a fashion as generic as possible.

However, sometimes one needs to synthesize a special "default value" for a type parameter without knowing the type of the parameter until runtime. All that matters to set the scene is that we are defining a generic type with a type parameter T. In the definition of that type, we don't know anything about T. It could be an int, a string, a Customer, whatever. The generic type can use T anywhere as if it were a known type:

```
class Sample<T>
{
    private T _data;

    // ...

    public void Reset()
    {
        // How can we set _data to the default value for type T?
    }
}
```

For example, in this case we're defining a field of type T. All is good and well, our code is very generic as we intended it to be. But what if we need to check that _data against a default value? (For example, if T were a reference type, that would be a null check?) Or say you need to reinitialize the field to go back to its default value? Clearly, we need something here to express "default value of T," for whatever T may be. That's where the default value expression comes in:

```
class Sample<T>
{
    private T _data;

    // ...

    public void Reset()
    {
        _data = default(T);
    }
}
```

Talking about generic parameters gives us a good opportunity to take a little look behind the scenes and get a feel for how generics work. The essential idea is simple: *Open generic types* are types with holes in them. Every type parameter creates such a hole whose size is unknown. For example, if it's set to an Int32, 4 bytes of storage will be required, but for a DateTime more space will be needed. Think of the act of defining a generic type roughly as operating a perforator that leaves holes for every occurrence of a type parameter. This analogy is depicted in Figure 6.10.

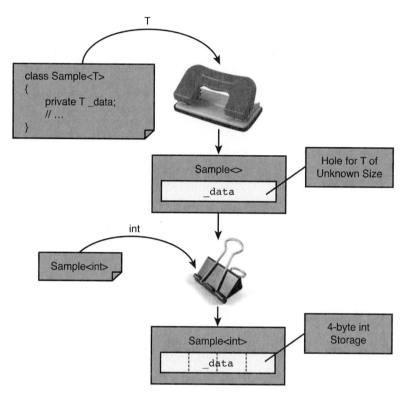

FIGURE 6.10   Generic types in a nutshell.

To use a generic type, the holes need to be filled with some type, resulting in a *closed generic type*. In office equipment terms, you can think of this operation as using a binder to combine the open generic type with the supplied type parameters and bundle everything up. Now the runtime knows how to lay out things in memory; it knows about the holes and what needs to be put inside them.

In ILDASM, a generic type definition reveals the holes that originate from the use of generic type parameters. You'll find references to those holes in the various places where type parameters can appear in the source code, such as fields, parameters, and so on. Figure 6.11 shows a generic type through the lenses of ILDASM.

I'll leave it to you to inspect the Reset method and see how default(T) is translated. Suffice to say, the IL code needs a way to refer to the type parameter so that the runtime can substitute it for the type that's used. This results in types getting cooked up at runtime that are statically typed in an end-to-end fashion, just as if you had written the specialized type yourself. A little tidbit about performance is that closed generic types that share the same underlying representation will be reused by the runtime. (For example, Sample<T> will have one representation for all uses where T is a reference type.)

FIGURE 6.11   A generic type with a field of type T gives rise to a "hole."

Notice the default value expression doesn't just work with type parameters; it can be used with any type. For reference types, `default` will produce a null reference; for value types, it will produce the default value (everything "zeroed out" essentially):

```
int zero = default(int);
string nothing = default(string);
DateTime longAgo = default(DateTime); // 01/01/0001 12:00:00 AM
```

Creating Objects with the new Operator

We already know a couple of ways to create instances of types: the use of literals and default value expressions. And because expressions *evaluate* to produce something of a certain type, they can be used in all places where objects are expected.

However, so far we've yet to discuss one of the most common ways of creating object instances: the use of *constructors*. Constructors are nothing but regular methods that are defined on a type but are known to serve a special goal: They return an instance of the containing type. Every type can have different constructors that take in different arguments, as a matter of friendliness toward the consumer of the type. This is facilitated by means of *method overloading*, discussed in Chapter 10, "Methods."

Because we are deferring the discussion of defining our own types with constructors until later, let's take a look at an existing type from the BCL: `System.TimeSpan`, the representation of a difference between two times. To inspect the type while being able to peek under the hood, we can use .NET Reflector. You can find a type by using the search option or by drilling down through the tree view on the left (in this case, by following mscorlib, CommonLanguageRuntime, System, TimeSpan). Figure 6.12 highlights the constructors of `TimeSpan` as seen through .NET Reflector.

The most familiar way for a C# developer to spot the constructors is to look at the right side where the decompiled C# code is shown. Constructors look like methods but don't have a return type and are named after the type itself. In this particular case, four overloads have been defined:

```
public TimeSpan(long ticks);
public TimeSpan(int hours, int minutes, int seconds);
public TimeSpan(int days, int hours, int minutes, int seconds);
public TimeSpan(int days, int hours, int minutes, int seconds,
                int milliseconds);
```

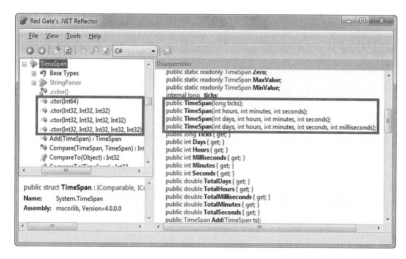

FIGURE 6.12   Looking at the constructors for `System.TimeSpan`.

On the left side, in the tree view, the internal representation is shown. In reality, constructors are defined as methods with the name `.ctor`. Because of their special status as creators for object instances, they deserve special syntactical treatment in the language. That's what the new operator is about.

To create an instance of the `TimeSpan` type, you use the new operator followed by the type name and a (possibly empty) set of parameters:

```
var oneHourAndAHalf = new TimeSpan(1, 30, 0);
```

Because the type already appears on the right side of the assignment, it's perfectly fine to omit the type on the left side and use type inference by means of the var keyword.

CONCRETE OR NOT?

Constructors can be called only for *concrete types*, but what does that mean? Let's go the opposite direction: Something concrete is not abstract. *Abstract types* are types that lack parts of their implementation.

Interfaces are an example of this: They just describe what an object is capable of doing (for example, `IEnumerable` says an object can be enumerated over, for example to retrieve elements in a collection), rather than saying how it is done. So it doesn't make sense to create an instance of just `IEnumerable`; we need something that *implements* the interface instead (like `ArrayList`).

We discuss the role and use of abstract classes and interfaces when talking about object-oriented programming techniques in Chapter 14.

Constructors can also be used on generic types. One common use is to instantiate a *closed generic type*, meaning all generic parameters are supplied. For example, to create a list collection for integer values, you can write the following:

```
var numbers = new List<int>();
```

Notice the use of an empty parameter list here. The constructor taking in no arguments is also known as the *default constructor*. Types are not required to have a default constructor, as you saw with the TimeSpan type.

Behind the Scenes of Constructors

To satisfy our technical curiosity, we would like to know how constructors are called when writing code as shown earlier. As you already know, constructors are special methods that cannot be called directly. Their special treatment reaches beyond the managed code language compilers, though. The runtime also needs to treat them specially because they are tightly coupled with memory-allocation mechanisms and such.

Let's illustrate matters by using the ILDASM for the TimeSpan constructor call, as shown in Figure 6.13.

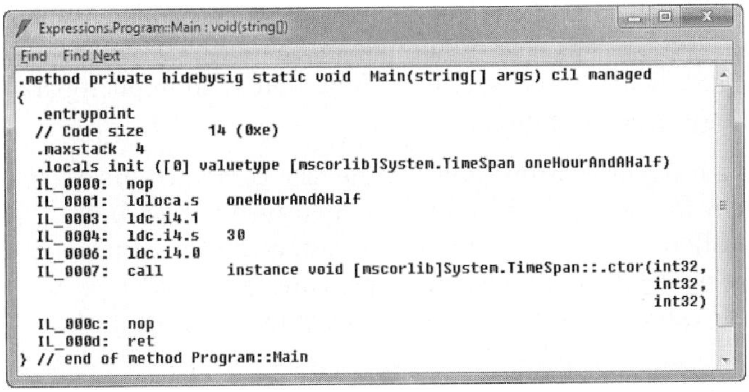


```
.method private hidebysig static void  Main(string[] args) cil managed
{
  .entrypoint
  // Code size       14 (0xe)
  .maxstack  4
  .locals init ([0] valuetype [mscorlib]System.TimeSpan oneHourAndAHalf)
  IL_0000:  nop
  IL_0001:  ldloca.s   oneHourAndAHalf
  IL_0003:  ldc.i4.1
  IL_0004:  ldc.i4.s   30
  IL_0006:  ldc.i4.0
  IL_0007:  call       instance void [mscorlib]System.TimeSpan::.ctor(int32,
                                                                      int32,
                                                                      int32)
  IL_000c:  nop
  IL_000d:  ret
} // end of method Program::Main
```

FIGURE 6.13 A constructor call for a value type unraveled.

In fact, a few different cases for constructor calls exist. In our example, we're creating an instance of a value type and assigning it to a local variable. Upon entry of the method, this local variable is already filled with all-zero bytes in memory. All the constructor has to do is fill that memory with something more useful. Figure 6.14 illustrates the initialization process of a value.

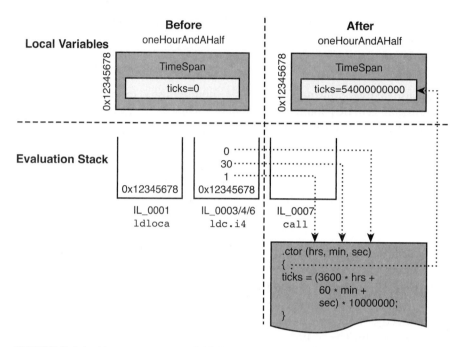

FIGURE 6.14   How a constructor initializes a value type object.

First, the memory address of the local variable is retrieved using the `ldloca` instruction, which stands for "load a local's address." In addition to the address being pushed on the stack, the arguments to the constructor are pushed, too. For our example, there are three: 1 for hours, 30 for minutes, and 0 for seconds. Finally, a call is made to the constructor method. The address where the data being initialized lives can be seen as an implicit parameter to the runtime to call the constructor method.

With reference types, things go a little differently. Room for the data contained in a reference type is allocated dynamically in another portion of memory (called the *heap*). In-depth coverage of memory allocation in the CLR would lead us astray at this point, so let's ignore the nitty-gritty details for now. Just recall reference types consist of a reference to data that lives elsewhere. Aliasing can occur, causing multiple references to exist to the same piece of data.

The prototypical example of a reference type is `System.String`, which has a few constructors defined that allow us to illustrate how instances of reference types are created:

```
var tenStars = new string('*', 10);
```

This constructor takes in a `char` parameter and an integer one, producing a string that consists of the repetition of the specified character as many types as specified by the integer parameter. In the preceding example, 10 asterisks result.

What the CLR needs to carry out here consists of a few tasks. First, it needs to allocate memory where the string object can live. Next, it has to call the constructor to initialize the data. This by itself may result in other allocations elsewhere in memory; in the preceding example, that's the case because it will be the constructor that figures out the total length of the string (10 times a character takes 20 bytes due to Unicode). Finally, once the constructor has run, a reference to the initialized object is returned. In terms of IL code, this looks like Figure 6.15.

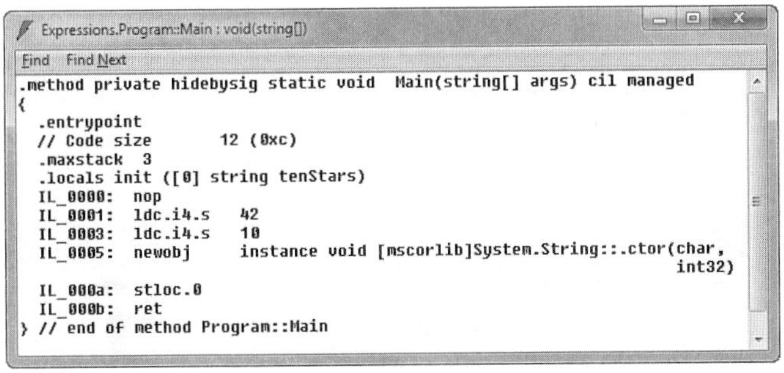

```
Expressions.Program::Main : void(string[])

Find   Find Next
.method private hidebysig static void  Main(string[] args) cil managed
{
  .entrypoint
  // Code size       12 (0xc)
  .maxstack  3
  .locals init ([0] string tenStars)
  IL_0000:  nop
  IL_0001:  ldc.i4.s    42
  IL_0003:  ldc.i4.s    10
  IL_0005:  newobj      instance void [mscorlib]System.String::.ctor(char,
                                                                     int32)

  IL_000a:  stloc.0
  IL_000b:  ret
} // end of method Program::Main
```

FIGURE 6.15   Instantiating a reference type using the newobj instruction.

The key instruction here is newobj. It's this instruction that's responsible for allocating memory for the object's data, calling the constructor to initialize the freshly allocated memory using the arguments supplied on the stack, and finally pushing a reference onto the stack. On the last significant line of IL, this reference is stored in the local variable slot for tenStars.

Notice that once an instance of an object is created using the newobj instruction, it's under control of the garbage collector. So don't confuse a reference with a memory address or pointer. Pointers are something physical, whereas references are a logical concept in managed code. Although a reference internally consists of a pointer, users typically don't have any need to know what that pointer's value is, nor can they control it. That's merely an implementation detail the CLR is concerned with. Why? Because the pointer is not stable; the garbage collector can move objects freely in memory whenever it sees fit. In Figure 6.16, the string object can move through the cloud at any time.

PINNING

Strictly speaking, it's possible to hand out a raw pointer to a managed object. But to do so, you effectively need to the tell the CLR the object should not be moved in memory while something (for example, a native code component used in interop) holds on to the pointer. The task of doing this is called pinning and is a specialized concept typically used only in interop scenarios.

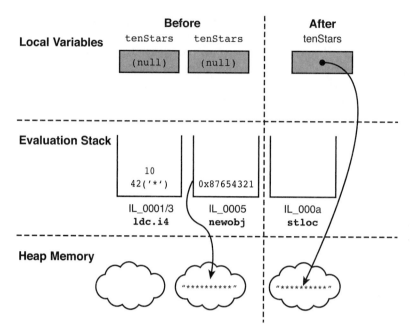

FIGURE 6.16   How a constructor creates a reference type object.

Object Initializers

Calling constructors is an essential mechanism for creating new instances of objects, but sometimes it doesn't suffice. A common problem with constructors is the number of overloads they have to accommodate for various scenarios. For example, the TimeSpan type has no fewer than four constructor overloads for developer convenience. Internally, a TimeSpan simply consists of a tick count, but as you've seen, more handy overloads exist that allow us to supply hours, minutes, and seconds (for example).

It turns out TimeSpan is a type that leads to a good developer experience: The most useful overloads are available, so while browsing the list of overloads, you'll most certainly want something that's close enough to what you want. In our previous example, we had to express 1.5 hours, for which we used the overload taking in hours, minutes, and seconds. Although seconds are of no interest to us, it doesn't hurt much to have to specify a zero value for that parameter.

Unfortunately, lots of other types exist that lack convenient constructors that suit everyone's needs. This problem ultimately boils down to an explosion of possible combinations of the discrete pieces of data to be initialized. Assume you have a Person type that contains 20 fields for name, date of birth, address, and so on. Maybe a few fields are required, but others aren't. So how many constructors do you provide to make everyone happy? Not only would you go nuts trying to come up with all combinations, think of the poor API user browsing the list of overloads in search of the right constructor. Figure 6.17 pinpoints this issue by looking at constructor overloads in the code editor.

FIGURE 6.17   Constructor overloads? Brain overload!

If scanning a bunch of overloads yields no suitable overload, this can be quite a frustrating experience. Object initializer expressions can help alleviate this. To illustrate this, let's first create the simplest type possible:

```
class Person
{
    public Person(string name)
    {
        Name = name;
    }

    public string Name { get; set; }
    public int Age { get; set; }
}
```

IntelliSense will show exactly one overload for this Person type, which for some reason doesn't provide an overload that also accepts an age. But still we want to initialize both the Name and Age (automatically implemented, as discussed in Chapter 11, "Fields, Properties, and Indexers") properties. Before the C# 3.0 release, you had to write two statements to do this:

```
Person me = new Person("Bart");
me.Age = 26;
```

For creation of a new instance, this is a bit verbose, but it gets even worse if you just want to pass a Person object to a method because you need an intermediate variable:

```
Person he = new Person("John");
he.Age = 62;
LogEntry(he /* why can't I create the Person object inline? */, DateTime.Now);
```

Object initializer expressions combine calling a constructor with assignment to fields or properties, like this (also using type inference for the variable using C# 3.0 var):

```
var me = new Person("Bart") { Age = 26 };
```

and

```
LogEntry(new Person("John") { Age = 62 }, DateTime.Now);
```

THE LINQ LANGUAGE FEATURE BAG

The introduction of object initializer expressions in C# 3.0 was a positive side effect of the design of LINQ. In query expressions, it's common to project data onto rich objects using a projection clause with the `select` keyword:

```
from p in db.People select new Person(p.Name) { Age = p.Age }
```

Because a query expression is, well, an expression, it's desirable for all its clauses to be expressible using expressions themselves. Initialization of objects using multiple statements (recognized by sequencing using semicolons) does not fit in this picture (hence the need for an expression to do rich object initialization). Without this, imagine if you had to write something like this:

```
from p in db.People
select { Person res = new Person(p.Name); res.Age = p.Age; return res; }
```

Yuck.

A little tidbit: When a default (parameterless, that is) constructor overload exists, you can omit the empty pair of parentheses when using an object initializer:

```
var product = new Product /* optional () */ { Name = "Chai", Price = 12.34m };
```

One of the academically interesting properties of C# 3.0 is that it can be compiled into a C# 2.0 equivalent. In other words, to show how C# 3.0 features are implemented, we can simply show a piece of C# 2.0 code instead of having to resort to IL code. Because of this, C# 3.0 features are often referred to as *syntactical sugar* (a good thing!). This applies to this feature, too, so what's the C# 2.0 equivalent of the code that initializes the me variable? It might be a bit surprising to see two local variables being used for this:

```
Person me = new Person("Bart") { Age = 26 };
```

The preceding translates into this:

```
Person __temp = new Person("Bart");
__temp.Age = 26;
Person me = __temp;
```

The reason for this is that expressions are a means to express some kind of computation that results in an object of some type. Once this computation is carried out, the result is fed in to the place of use (for example, an assignment or a method call or whatever). Notice we're mentioning just one object here, being the result of the expression's evaluation. In the case of the preceding assignment, the whole expression's result is to be used as the right-side object in the assignment.

This treatment has the nice property of atomic assignment. If you're initializing a publicly visible object (for example, exposed through a property on some type), either the fully initialized object becomes visible or the previous one remains visible (but nothing in between). Here's an example:

```
class Sample
{
    public Person Visible { get; set; }

    // More meaningful members.

    private void Update()
    {
        // Bad.
        Visible = new Person("Bart");
        Visible.Age = 26;

        // Good.
        Visible = new Person("Bart") { Age = 26 };
    }
}
```

This is of utmost importance in a concurrently executing context: One thread could be executing the Update method while another is reading the Visible property. In the case marked Bad, your thread may see the state between the constructor assignment and the Age property setter call. This would result in you seeing a person called Bart of zero age.

On the other hand, in the Good case, there's no such risk: A temporary (invisible to the outside world) variable will be fully initialized first before it gets assigned to the Visible property.

NAMED PARAMETERS TO THE RESCUE?

The constructor overloading paradox I sketched before can be really annoying in practice. I find myself searching for the best overload that suits my need quite often. Object initializers help but only after the fact. Why? Follow me through it.

I know I need an instance of type X, setting properties A, B, and C. During my scan of the overload list, I encounter constructors accepting, say, A, C, A+B, B+C, and A+C. But none of that takes in all three. Sigh. The next step is to go through the overload list again, knowing there's no ideal match but now scanning for the best match. I decide to choose A+B and use an object initializer to set C:

```
new X(someA, someB) { C = someC }
```

The case of too-specific constructors can also be annoying. Suppose I just need to initialize B in the preceding case, but there's no overload that takes in just B. I would need to search for an overload with the fewest redundant parameters and supply a default value for it:

```
new X(null, someB)
```

With C# 4.0, there's a new API design option due to *named parameters*: provide just one constructor that accepts all possible parameters. Wait a minute, doesn't that mean the user has to specify all of them even if only a few may be of interest? Not if the nonmandatory parameters are given default values:

```
class X
{
    public X(A a = null, B b = null, C c = null)
    {
        // Initialization logic goes here.
    }
}
```

Now the consumer of the type can write the following to initialize just B:

```
new X(b: someB)
```

Better or worse than object initializers? A hard call. For one thing, object initializers require the properties used in the initializer list to have public setters. This is in distinct contrast with the desire to promote immutable types in a world of concurrency (more about that later). Named and optional parameters have their disadvantages, too: Not all languages support them, and there are various subtleties around default values, as you will see. So, suffice to say, this new approach is an option to consider in API design, if nothing more.

What about Visual Studio support for object initializer expressions? Rest assured, IntelliSense knows about it (proven in Figure 6.18) and tries to make your life as easy as possible by showing the properties (or fields) that can be initialized while gradually reducing the number of items in list as you go along.

FIGURE 6.18   IntelliSense for an object initializer's initializer list.

PROPERTIES VERSUS FIELDS

Object initializers can deal with two sorts of members: properties and fields. Which one is better to use in APIs is discussed in Chapter 11, but suffice to say properties are recommended. In lots of cases, properties just play the role of smart fields, being simple wrappers around an underlying field for storage. The thing that distinguishes them from fields is that data access is carried out using getter and setter methods. This has the advantage that internal representation for a type is kept hidden to the consumers. By doing so, internals can change without breaking the external use.

Collection Initializers

 When arrays were introduced in Chapter 4, "Language Essentials," you saw the use of array initializer expressions to create an array and initialize its elements in one operation:

```
int[] primes = new int[4] { 2, 3, 5, 7 };
```

Recall that various kinds of type inference can be used to simplify the preceding declaration and initialization, even all the way down to the following:

```
var primes = new [] { 2, 3, 5, 7 };
```

What's of more relevance here is the use of an initializer list delineated by curly braces to supply the array's elements. You'll agree that's way more handy than having to write the following:

```
int[] primes = new int[4];
primes[0] = 2;
primes[1] = 3;
primes[2] = 5;
primes[3] = 7;
```

Although arrays are very useful constructs, they're of limited use in various scenarios. Often you need dynamically growing collection types instead, the ability to insert elements at some location, or ordering properties, and so on. The System.Collections namespace contains richer types with those capabilities. With the advent of generic collection types underneath System.Collections.Generic in .NET 2.0, things only improved.

But one thing has been lacking on collection types: a similarly easy way to create a collection type instance and initialize it in one go. So to do the same as the preceding code but with a generic List<int> type, you would have to write this:

```
List<int> primes = new List<int>();
primes[0] = 2;
primes[1] = 3;
primes[2] = 5;
primes[3] = 7;
```

This is using convenient indexer access provided by the List<T> type, which makes it look like an array. The same code could be rewritten as follows:

```
List<int> primes = new List<int>();
primes.Add(2);
primes.Add(3);
primes.Add(5);
primes.Add(7);
```

With C# 3.0, this kind of code can be replaced by a collection initializer expression, as follows (also using local variable type inference with var):

```
var primes = new List<int> { 2, 3, 5, 7 };
```

The way this feature is specified is by requiring a suitable Add method to be available on the collection type being used in the initialization. Every element specified in the curly braces is fed to such an Add method. In a way similar to object initializer expressions, a temporary variable is used to initialize the collection before it gets assigned to its target or used elsewhere (like a method parameter):

```
var __temp = new List<int>();
__temp.Add(2);
__temp.Add(3);
__temp.Add(5);
__temp.Add(7);
var primes = __temp;
```

As mentioned before, this has positive effects for multithreaded code. Some may worry about performance: "What, another local variable?" Because a reference type is used here, no copying of the whole data is needed. A simple copy of a reference is all that's happening on the last line, which is a very lightweight operation.

THE LINQ CATALYST, AGAIN

Just like object initializer expressions, the introduction of collection initializer expressions was directly motivated by LINQ as a way to have expression syntax for complex initialization tasks in the context of a query.

Collection initializers can be used for types that have more complicated Add methods, too. The generic Dictionary<TKey,TElement> type is such a case:

```
var ages = new Dictionary<string, int> { { "Bart", 26 }, { "John", 62 } };
```

Here key/value pairs are supplied, which results in an Add method with two parameters being called:

```
var __temp = new Dictionary<string, int>();
__temp.Add("Bart", 26);
__temp.Add("John", 62);
var ages = __temp;
```

DUCK TYPING

Where does the language require the Add method to come from? Answer: No place special. When translating the comma-separated list of elements in the initializer list into Add method calls, regular *overload resolution* is used to find a suitable Add method. This approach is called *duck typing*: "If it walks and quacks like a duck, it ought to be one."

However, just requiring an Add method to exist may give rise to weird uses. For example, a Calculator type is likely to have an Add method, and writing something like the following seems like nonsense:

```
var calc = new Calculator { 2, 3 };
```

With this, you create a Calculator instance, invoke the Add method on it, and throw away the invocation result and end up with just the Calculator instance being assigned. Clearly, not very useful.

To counter this weird use, the language wants to have a clue about the type being used as a collection. The most general interface used by all collection types is IEnumerable. Together with the Add method use, our duck type analog boils down to "if you can enumerate over its contents, and it supports adding objects, it ought to be a collection."

The IEnumerable interface doesn't have an Add method, though. Just finding "an" Add method, wherever it comes from, suffices for usability with the collection initializer syntax. And actually this is a good thing because collections, like a dictionary, don't have their Add methods defined on any interface.

Member Access

One thing we've been dealing with all the time without giving it explicit attention is the concept of *member access*, indicated by the period (.) token:

```
Console.WriteLine("Hello");
person.Age = 26;
placeOrder.Click += placeOrder_Click;
```

Here we're respectively looking up a method, a property, and an event using the member access. Members are what types consist of and are accessible either through the type itself (as in the first case, called a *static* method) or through a type's instances (as in the latter two cases). Fields can be accessed in a similar way.

GENERICS

Sometimes member access is paired with the specification of *type arguments* in the context of *generics*. A method itself may need a type argument, which is specified in between < and > tokens:

```
var result = Activator.CreateInstance<MyType>();
```

We discuss this aspect when covering generics in Chapter 15, "Generic Types and Methods."

Member access is one of the places where IntelliSense can make a developer's life much easier (at least when statically typed objects are in place because the code editor can leverage the type information to provide a list of available members to access, as shown in Figure 6.19).

FIGURE 6.19   IntelliSense showing a list of instance members.

Icons are used to differentiate between various kinds of supported members:

▶ Events show up with a lightning bolt, indicating they can be "fired" (or *raised*).

▶ Properties get a little hand pointing at a key/value entry on a card.

▶ Methods have the dynamism of invocation represented by displacement lines.

▶ Extension methods get sprinkled on an existing type, as indicated by an arrow.

▶ Fields are indicated by a blue cube for some reason.

Notice how members from base types (just plain old `System.Object` in the example) and implemented interfaces (none in the example) show up in the IntelliSense list.

In the preceding example, only *instance members* show up. As the name implies, those are associated with instances of a type. In addition, a type can have *static members*, which are not tied to instances but live on the type itself. We discuss this distinction when defining our own types in Chapter 9. Figure 6.20 shows static members on a type.

FIGURE 6.20   IntelliSense showing a list of static members.

IntelliSense capabilities are one of the great merits of static typing. We say that member access is *early bound* when the compiler exactly knows the member being targeted by the code. The IL code reflects this knowledge because it contains metadata tokens that unambiguously refer to the selected member. Consider the following code:

```
string s = "Bart";
Console.WriteLine(s.ToUpper());
```

And take a look at the corresponding IL code in Figure 6.21.

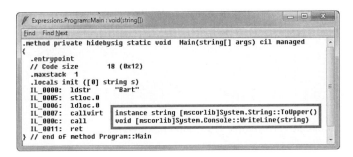

FIGURE 6.21   Metadata tokens revealing early bound statically typed code.

A First Look at Dynamic Typing

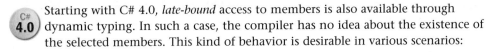

Starting with C# 4.0, *late-bound* access to members is also available through dynamic typing. In such a case, the compiler has no idea about the existence of the selected members. This kind of behavior is desirable in various scenarios:

▶ Objects may be totally typeless because they come from some dynamic language like Ruby or Python.

▶ Data representations may not have a schema, like with XML documents with no corresponding XSD schema.

▶ You received some object back using the static System.Object type but have no more specific type in reach to cast it to.

Historically, interacting with "loosely typed" objects from C# has been very painful, leading to lots of boilerplate code that hides the intent of the program. Because there is an ever-increasing number of dynamically typed objects out there, the C# language designers thought it would be a good idea to make such access easy.

To track the places—read: member accesses—where late-bound operations are required, C# introduces a dynamic type:

```
dynamic misterX = GetUntypedPerson();
string name = misterX.Name;
Console.WriteLine(name);
```

Can you spot the dynamically dispatched late-bound member access in the preceding fragment? Let's walk through the code. On the first line, we get a person object that has no static type. Maybe it comes from Python or script. Who knows? Instead of declaring the misterX variable as System.Object (which every object can be typed as because it's the mother type for everything), we use dynamic. This tells the compiler to emit code that does discovery of member accesses at runtime instead. In this particular case, the Name property getter access will be deferred until runtime.

The code editor in Visual Studio knows about dynamic typing in the sense it clearly admits it can't provide any meaningful IntelliSense because of the dynamic nature of the code. Figure 6.22 illustrates how missing type information manifests itself.

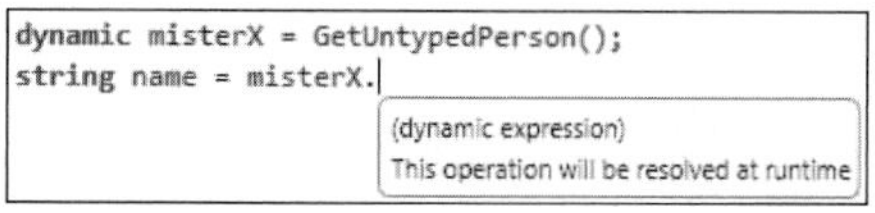

FIGURE 6.22   No IntelliSense is available for dynamic late-bound operations.

To avoid exploding brains, we won't examine the IL code. Instead, we can use a version of .NET Reflector that's not aware of C# 4.0 features, which should look like Figure 6.23.

> **NOTE**
>
> As of this writing, the latest version of .NET Reflector still succeeded in meeting this goal, but I expect a newer release of .NET Reflector will be able to fully decompile C# 4.0 code; at that point, the nitty-gritty details shown here will vanish.

What you're looking at here are C#-specific binders that represent the late-bound operations we want to carry out. Highlighted in the figure is the member binder to a member called Name. All the plumbing with call-site objects allows the Dynamic Language Runtime (DLR) to kick in and dispatch the call efficiently. We go into detail about this subject in Chapter 22.

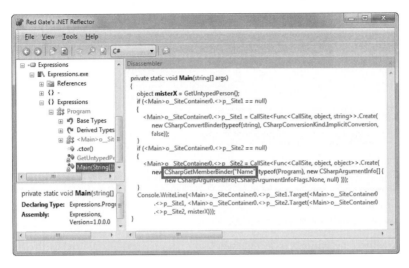

FIGURE 6.23   A dynamic call site behind the scenes.

Invocation Expressions

Invocation is the act of calling another piece of code, possibly passing in arguments to influence the code's execution. Invocation mechanisms other than method calls exist due to the concept of delegates.

Method Invocation

Keeping the best for the (almost) last: invocation expressions. Methods being the main containers for code—and in fact, properties and indexers are methods in disguise—the most meaningful operation to carry out with them is invocation.

Methods can be called directly or indirectly, the latter case referring to the use of delegates. Either way, invocation syntax has the same shape: an expression followed by a (potentially empty) comma-separated list of arguments between parentheses. You've already seen numerous examples:

```
Console.WriteLine("Hello");
string s = person.ToString();
int three = calc.Add(1, 2);
```

All the preceding examples are regular method invocations. A call instruction targeting the method is emitted in the IL code, as shown in Figure 6.24.

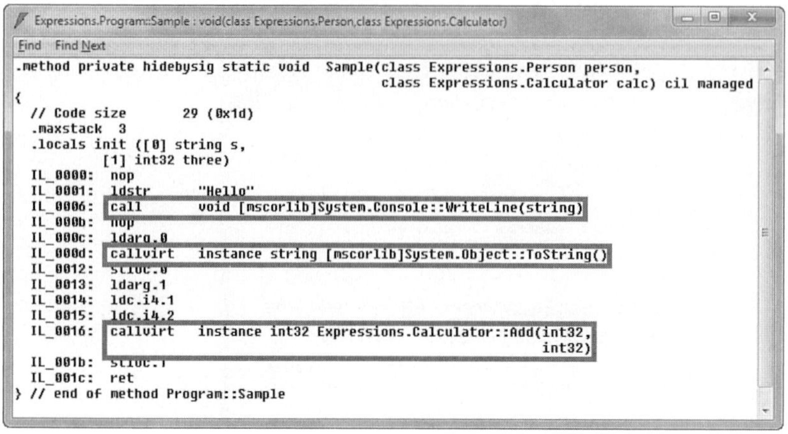

```
Expressions.Program::Sample : void(class Expressions.Person,class Expressions.Calculator)
Find  Find Next
.method private hidebysig static void  Sample(class Expressions.Person person,
                                             class Expressions.Calculator calc) cil managed
{
  // Code size       29 (0x1d)
  .maxstack  3
  .locals init ([0] string s,
           [1] int32 three)
  IL_0000:  nop
  IL_0001:  ldstr       "Hello"
  IL_0006:  call        void [mscorlib]System.Console::WriteLine(string)
  IL_000b:  nop
  IL_000c:  ldarg.0
  IL_000d:  callvirt    instance string [mscorlib]System.Object::ToString()
  IL_0012:  stloc.0
  IL_0013:  ldarg.1
  IL_0014:  ldc.i4.1
  IL_0015:  ldc.i4.2
  IL_0016:  callvirt    instance int32 Expressions.Calculator::Add(int32,
                                                                   int32)
  IL_001b:  stloc.1
  IL_001c:  ret
} // end of method Program::Sample
```

FIGURE 6.24 Direct method invocations at the IL level.

CALL VERSUS CALLVIRT

The CLR has two different IL opcodes for method invocation: call and callvirt. But what's the difference? As the name implies, callvirt can call *virtual methods*. In the preceding example, the ToString method we're calling is defined on System.Object. By making a virtual method call, the most specific override of that method is called: If our Person type has redefined ToString, that implementation will execute; if not, System.Object's default implementation will get called. We discuss virtual methods in more detail in Chapter 14.

The call instruction, on the other hand, doesn't do this virtual dispatching and calls the target method as specified. A typical example of its use is when calling static methods such as Console.WriteLine in our example.

But what about the Add method on Calculator? Let's take a look at the definition of that type as used in the preceding example:

```
class Calculator
{
    public int Add(int a, int b) { return a + b; }
}
```

This method is not declared using the virtual modifier, making it not a virtual method, yet the resulting IL code uses a callvirt instruction. Why? Besides its virtual dispatch properties, callvirt has another useful property: It throws a NullReferenceException if the object used as the target of the invocation is a null reference. For that reason, the C# compiler emits callvirt even when a simple call will suffice if the null case can be ignored.

Delegate Invocation

Another form of invocation is what I call *indirect invocation*. This is where delegates come in: Instead of knowing the precise target of an invocation, you know how the target looks in terms of the method signature. In essence, *delegates* are a way to pass methods around as objects. They form a kind of contract between two parties: a consumer and a provider. An example will clarify things, but we defer more thorough discussion until Chapter 17, "Delegates."

Let's consider a "modest" calculator as a trivial (and honestly, contrived) example. What the heck is a modest calculator? It's one that knows about all commonsense arithmetic operations but also admits it can't know everything. So it enables the user of the calculator to supply (code for) custom operations while it provides a simple-to-use user interface for all operations, whether they're built in or provided by the user. Consider the self-confident part of the calculator first, defining the operations it knows out of the box:

```
class Calculator
{
    public int Add(int a, int b) { return a + b; }
    public int Sub(int a, int b) { return a - b; }
    public int Mul(int a, int b) { return a * b; }
    public int Div(int a, int b) { return a / b; }
}
```

Imagine it being a bit more extended than just this: The calculator may have a user interface, a way to accept input from the user in a natural way (click 1, +, 2 and press = to cause a call to the Add method underneath). So there could be some internal tables that associate programmed buttons (with a nice-looking caption) with methods.

Now on to the part that allows the calculator to be extended with custom operations. Again ignoring lots of practical aspects on how to extend the user interface, we just focus on the core essence: How can the user supply the calculator with a custom (binary) operation for it to use? The answer lies in a delegate, which is essentially a contract stating the connection between inputs and output from a typing point of view. Without further ado, here's what a delegate declaration for a binary operation on integral numbers looks like:

```
delegate int BinOp(int a, int b);
```

Pretend the delegate keyword isn't there and the BinOp identifier and you end up with a method signature that says "given two integer values, I'll produce an integer value as the result." How it does this is intentionally left unspecified.

Now we can extend the calculator with a method that not only takes in two operands for an arithmetic operation but also the custom-defined operation itself by means of a delegate:

```
public int Ext(BinOp op, int a, int b)
{
    if (op == null)
```

```
        throw new ArgumentNullException("op");

    return op(a, b);
}
```

I agree that this example is a bit contrived because all we're doing with the delegate is making a single call on it. In reality, the act of setting up a custom operation in our calculator may be much more involved: A DefineOperation method could take in a BinOp, together with a string for the programmable button's caption, and wire up that button to the BinOp instance.

The last line of the Ext method is where the delegate invocation happens: op is a variable of type BinOp, and we use exactly the same syntax for invocation as if it were a (compile-time) well-known method. So we're calling a method *through* the delegate.

CODE IS DATA

Today's computers follow the von Neumann machine model, where code and data live side by side in the same memory. Delegates are a direct proof of this capability: They are a means to pass code (a custom binary operation implementation) around as if it were data (the op variable).

Delegate Invocation Behind the Scenes

So how does a delegate invocation work behind the scenes? You might be surprised to see it's a plain old method call to some Invoke method on a Delegate object. The instance of the delegate is where the reference is made to the method to be called. This is conceptually similar to a function pointer in languages such as C and C++, but with much more infrastructure around it to ensure type safety, to allow for garbage collection (meaning the address of where the code lives in memory can change over time), to enforce security rules, and so on. To illustrate the implementation, I've omitted the null-check code for brevity in Figure 6.25.

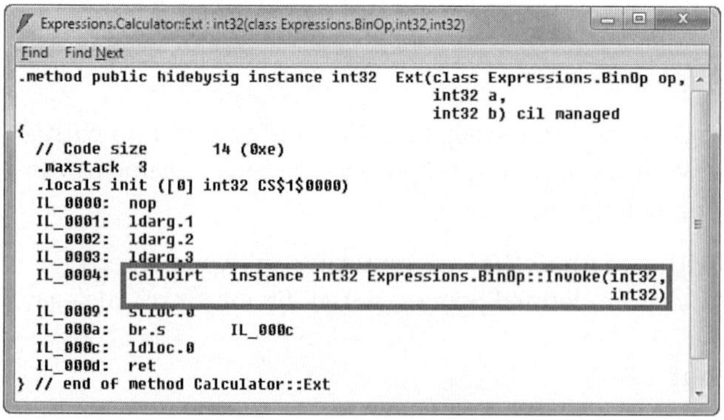

```
Expressions.Calculator::Ext : int32(class Expressions.BinOp,int32,int32)

Find   Find Next
.method public hidebysig instance int32   Ext(class Expressions.BinOp op,
                                              int32 a,
                                              int32 b) cil managed
{
  // Code size       14 (0xe)
  .maxstack  3
  .locals init ([0] int32 CS$1$0000)
  IL_0000:  nop
  IL_0001:  ldarg.1
  IL_0002:  ldarg.2
  IL_0003:  ldarg.3
  IL_0004:  callvirt    instance int32 Expressions.BinOp::Invoke(int32,
                                                                 int32)
  IL_0009:  stloc.0
  IL_000a:  br.s        IL_000c
  IL_000c:  ldloc.0
  IL_000d:  ret
} // end of method Calculator::Ext
```

FIGURE 6.25   Calling through a delegate.

Creating Delegate Instances

So far, you've seen how to consume a delegate, which is what the calculator does by calling through it. Equally important is how to create a delegate instance. Delegate instances are created by using the new keyword, this time specifying the name of a method to be passed on:

```
static void Main()
{
    var calc = new Calculator();
    Console.WriteLine(calc.Ext(new BinOp(Hypotenuse), 3, 4));
}

static int Hypotenuse(int a, int b)
{
    return (int)Math.Sqrt(a * a + b * b);
}
```

The cast used in the Hypotenuse method carries out a narrowing conversion as Math.Sqrt produces a double-typed result, but our calculator works only with integer numbers. It's a trivial exercise for you to change the calculator to work with double values instead, allowing the cast to disappear. What's of more interest to us is how the delegate instance is created:

```
new BinOp(Hypotenuse)
```

This is how things can be done since C# 1.0, but since then things have been simplified. We take a look at this in just a second, but first look at the plumbing at the IL level (see Figure 6.26). It's clear the runtime somehow needs to capture a reference to the Hypotenuse method and store it inside the delegate instance.

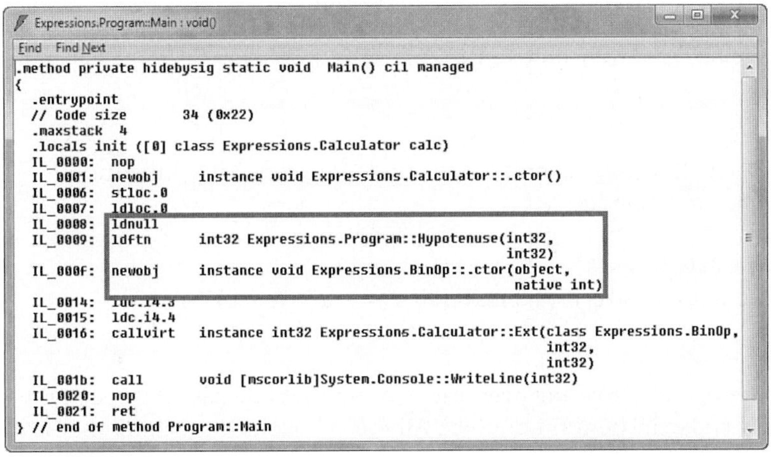

FIGURE 6.26   Creating a delegate instance through the lenses of IL.

The `ldftn`, for load function, instruction is where the magic happens. This instruction produces a "native int," essentially an address for the requested reference. The native part means the address length of the CPU we're running on will be used because IL code is machine agnostic. In addition to a reference to the method to be called, there's a reference to the object on which the method needs to be called. Because we're dealing with a static method here, `null` is specified as the target.

DEFINITELY MORE THAN FUNCTION POINTERS

The fact delegates support an invocation target object makes them quite different from function pointers. The use of function pointers in native code also requires calling conventions to line up precisely. When invoking a method on an object, the address of the object needs to be passed along, as well, which typically happens as the first argument. This makes up a "`this-call`," where `this` stands for the target object. Invoking a static method, on the other hand, doesn't have such a hidden parameter. In the world of the CLR such details are completely abstracted away through the concept of delegates.

You'll agree that the code required to create a delegate instance is quite verbose: calling some artificial constructor, having to define a separate method to form the delegate's target even if that method is almost trivial in some cases, and so on. One simplification allows us to drop the new expression because the compiler knows the first argument to Ext needs to be of type `BinOp`:

```
Console.WriteLine(calc.Ext(Hypotenuse, 3, 4));
```

This is a little better but nothing to write home about just yet. In some cases, the target method can be quite long (for example, when using a delegate for execution on a background thread), so it's fine and even desirable to declare a separate method for it. But in our case, the `Hypotenuse` implementation is just a one-liner. How the method is called is something the runtime doesn't care about: All it needs is a reference to some code to wrap a reference to inside the delegate. Welcome to C# 2.0.

Anonymous Methods

 Anonymous methods allow us to abbreviate the preceding code by writing the `Hypotenuse` implementation inline:

```
Console.WriteLine(calc.Ext(
    delegate (int a, int b) { return (int)Math.Sqrt(a * a + b * b); },
    3, 4));
```

Actually, this saves us from code-browsing overhead because the code passed through the delegate is immediately apparent from the context. All the compiler does behind the scenes is create a method with a random name (unknown to us and hence the *anonymous* characteristic) to pass on through the delegate.

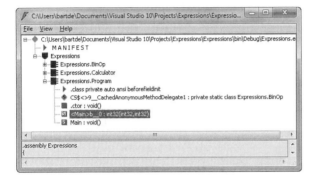

FIGURE 6.27   To the runtime, an anonymous method has a name.

!@#$%

What's up with the generated names for anonymous methods? They're intentionally created to be unspeakable, meaning it's impossible for the developer to write valid C# code that refers to them. For example, our <Main>b__0 method contains the < and > characters, which are invalid for use in an identifier.

One thing the compiler does is capture some context in the generated name. In our case, we can trace back the anonymous method to be defined in the Main method. This brings up an argument I had a while ago with a colleague who didn't like anonymous methods because they make stack traces in exceptions more cumbersome. For example, assume we've built with overflow checking on, and someone crashed our calculator by calling the programmed Hypotenuse button with overly large inputs. Figure 6.28 illustrates the error message printed due to the exception occurring.

FIGURE 6.28   Anonymous method names may reduce debuggability.

If we're running outside a debugger and face such a call stack, it might not be immediately apparent where the crash happened. Okay, this might be a little annoying at first, but it's really easy in the world of .NET to trace it back using tools such as .NET Reflector or ILDASM.

Also as the language evolves, the role of the compiler has increasingly shifted toward plumbing code generation to take this burden from the shoulders of the developer. A good example of this is LINQ, where query expressions are composed of lots of little functions to do things such as filtering, key selection for sorting, and so forth. Anonymous methods are the glue that drives such code generation.

That said, I have some sympathy for this concern. Use of anonymous methods that are way too big (like a background thread's entry-point method) is best avoided. The likelihood of something going wrong is definitely higher as code complexity increases. Getting faced with weird call stacks (with compiler-generated names) may get too common in such a case, making debugging harder. But also in terms of coding style, writing a long method inline of another one doesn't help readability of the containing method (in fact, the contrary).

Anonymous methods also support *closures*, a fairly key concept in functional programming. Because anonymous methods appear in the body of another containing method, they can capture outer variables:

```
var calc = new Calculator();
int x = GetDivOfTheDay();
int res = calc.Ext(delegate (int a, int b) { return (a + b) / x; }, 3, 4));
```

In this example, the anonymous method is capturing the outer variable x. In Chapter 17, we take a look at how this works, what the semantics and use cases are, and the potential caveats.

Lambda Expressions

 You can argue the syntactical overhead to pass the Hypotenuse function is still quite high despite (or due to?) the use of anonymous methods. Just look at the number of keywords required:

```
delegate (int a, int b) { return (int)Math.Sqrt(a * a + b * b); }
```

In fact, the compiler can know most of this from the context: We're using this as the first argument to Ext, which is of type BinOp. A BinOp is a delegate, so why do we need the delegate keyword? It takes in two integer values, so why do we need to state the obvious types for a and b? Obviously, we're going to return something, too, so the return keyword also seems redundant. *Lambda expressions* take all those observations into account and allow us to reduce the code to the following:

```
Console.WriteLine(calc.Ext((a, b) => (int)Math.Sqrt(a * a + b * b), 3, 4));
```

The => lambda arrow can be read as "goes to," so the preceding line merely states that we're passing in a function that takes arguments a and b (of types inferred from the context but still statically known) to the square root of the sum of their products. Concise, very readable, and desirable properties to promote a more functional style of programming.

WHY "LAMBDA"?

Lambda is a Greek letter (written as λ) referring to the so-called lambda calculus, which is the theory underlying functional programming concepts. Lambda calculus was developed by Alonzo Church in the late 1920s. The theory-savvy reader is encouraged to search the Web for a paper called "History of Lambda-Calculus and Combinatory Logic" by Cardone and Hindley to learn more about this calculus (and a story on the origin for the use of the letter lambda).

TWO REPRESENTATIONS

Lambda expressions do not have a type by themselves. Together with the null literal, they make up the only kinds of expressions that are typeless in and of themselves, meaning you can't use local variable type inference on them:

```
var sum = (int a, int b) => a + b;
```

Even though it seems the compiler could infer this ought to be a delegate with two int parameters and an int return type, that's not what causes ambiguity around the type. The key thing to know here is that lambda expressions can be represented either as delegates (meaning readily executable code) or as expression trees. Expression trees allow you to view the code that makes up the lambda, at runtime, through the eyes of an object model. This allows libraries to take in a code-as-data representation and manipulate it at runtime (for example, to cross-compile it into some other language). Remote LINQ query execution (for instance, on a SQL database) is based on this principle, as you will see when we discuss LINQ in depth in Chapter 20, "Language Integrated Query Internals."

Element Access

The concept of member access has a finite feeling to it: If a member doesn't exist, you can't call it. Whether finding a member is done by means of static typing at compile time or using dynamic typing at runtime is mostly orthogonal to this. In some other settings, though, it makes sense to have syntax to index into an object as a way to query for runtime state in a friendly fashion.

Sound quite theoretical? In fact, you've already seen an example of this before when we talked about arrays in Chapter 4. Consisting of elements, an operation to retrieve or replace an element is desirable. This is achieved by means of square-bracket syntax:

```
int[] primes = new int[] { 2, 3, 5, 7 };
int five = primes[2];
```

There's no "member-driven" way to access elements in an array. In fact, the array type itself doesn't know about the array's arity (recall, the number of dimensions) and size of the dimensions. Element access, therefore, has a dynamic feel to it, and validity of access is enforced at runtime.

DEPENDENT TYPES

The concept of a type depending on a value (for example, an array type depending on the array's size) does actually exist in type theory. It's called dependent types but hasn't made it to mainstream platforms or languages. Using such a construct, it's possible to check more aspects of code at compile time (for example, to protect against invalid array accesses). But even though the kind of typing isn't baked into either the runtime or the languages, theorem provers can be used to spot some cases of invalid accesses.

Because array element access has such a concise and natural notation, it was deemed useful to allow types to define their own indexed access operations by means of so-called *indexers*. Typical examples can be found in collection types:

```
var primes = new List<int> { 2, 3, 5, 7 };
```

```
// Index-based access just as with arrays. Lists are flexible arrays after all.
int five = primes[2];
```

```
var ages = new Dictionary<string, int> { { "Bart", 26 }, { "John", 62 } };
```

```
// Indexers can also use a different type.
// Dictionary<K,T> uses an index of type K, for the dictionary's key type.
int bartAge = ages["Bart"];
```

```
// We can add or replace key/value pairs in the dictionary as follows.
// This uses a setter method underneath.
ages["Lisa"] = 8;
```

Another example is with indexing into a Vector object, where indices 0, 1, and 2 are used to indicate a dimension. It's even possible to provide different overloads for the indexer so that x, y, and z are also allowed.

Indexers are essentially default properties that benefit from the concise square-bracket access notation. They have two sides (each of which is optional): one to retrieve an "element" (the getter) and one to replace an "element" (the setter). Ultimately, code that uses an indexer results in calls to the underlying methods:

```
var primes = new List<int> { 2, 3, 5, 7 };
```

```
// Index-based access just as with arrays. Lists are flexible arrays after all.
int five = primes[2];
```

Here, the indexer access results in the following IL code:

```
// Indexer's argument.
ldc.i4.2

// get_Item is the indexer getter method.
callvirt instance !0 class [mscorlib] List`1<int32>::get_Item(int32)

// Store in slot for "five" variable.
stloc.1
```

You'll read more about indexers and learn how to define them on your own types in Chapter 11.

Summary

In this chapter, we continued our exploration of expressions, this time focused on types and objects. First, we focused on different ways to carry out type checks, convert between types, and so on.

After learning about the creation of object instances, we explored how to access members, call methods, and delegates and perform element accesses. Delegates will receive much more attention in Chapter 17, so we skimmed over some of the details. Nonetheless, you have become familiar with different syntaxes to create delegates, including anonymous methods and lambda expressions.

Expressions are all about computing values. But a life of computation is not sufficient for the imperative code programmer; control flow mechanisms, such as conditional branching and loops, are important items in the developer's toolbox. The next chapter examines those concepts, commonly referred to as *statements*.

IN THIS CHAPTER

▶ What Are Statements, Anyway? 351

▶ Expression Statements 353

▶ The Empty Statement 355

▶ Blocks 356

▶ Declarations 357

▶ Selection Statements 358

▶ Iteration Statements 376

▶ A Peak at Iterators 392

▶ Loops in the Age of Concurrency 400

▶ The goto Statement 402

▶ The return Statement 406

CHAPTER 7

Simple Control Flow

After our thorough exploration of expressions, we've arrived in the domain of statements. Programmers with a background in any of the well-known imperative languages will feel immediately at home with C#'s statements that facilitate things such as branching and looping.

What Are Statements, Anyway?

Where expressions are used to drive computation, statements are the main drivers for a program's flow of execution. Simply stated, they define the actions a program takes under various circumstances.

C# supports a variety of statements that make up a taxonomy like this:

▶ **Expression statements** allow a subset of the expressions supported by the language to appear by themselves typically because they have useful side effects besides producing a value. A few examples include various forms of assignment, the increment and decrement prefix/postfix notation, but also method invocations.

▶ **Blocks** by themselves—roughly speaking, regions of code delimited by curly braces—are a way to group multiple statements together. They also play a role in scoping of variables.

▶ **Declaration statements** are used to declare local variables or constants by associating a name with an identifier. They're closely related to blocks due to scoping rules.

▶ **Selection statements** provide the tools to branch the execution flow based on the result of an expression's evaluation. Flow can be switched in a table-driven manner based on that result, or Boolean conditions can be used to go one direction or another.

▶ **Iteration statements** are commonly referred to as loops; they execute the contained statement a number of times based on some condition or to execute a given piece of code for every element in a data sequence.

▶ **Jump statements** are a way to transfer control explicitly, which can mean various things: You can go to the next iteration of a loop or break out of the loop altogether, return from a method, throw an exception, and so on. Even the notorious goto statement is available as a supported jump statement.

▶ **Exception handling** is done in a block-driven manner, where a region of code—called a *protected block*—has associated exception handler blocks for the types of exceptions it's willing to handle. Besides the act of catching exceptions, a block can be specified that runs regardless of the outcome of the protected block (*finally*).

▶ **Resource management** ensures proper disposal of used resources no matter what happens during execution of the code. C#'s using statement provides a means to take a structured approach when dealing with resources by scoping a resource's use to a block, guaranteeing the resource gets cleaned up no matter how control leaves that block.

▶ **Locks** are one (rather low-level) way to coordinate execution of concurrent code. By performing operations on an object by acquiring a lock, it's ensured no other code can execute as long as the lock is held. This allows you to serialize execution of operations that touch the object, preventing inconsistent states.

▶ **Checked and unchecked contexts** to control arithmetic overflow behavior are also categorized as statements. We discussed checked versus unchecked arithmetic extensively in Chapter 5, "Expressions and Operators," where you saw both the expression syntax and the block-based statement syntax.

We take a look at all of those throughout the chapter, deferring detailed explanations on exception handling, resource management, and locks until later. By the end of this chapter, you should be fluent in all sorts of control flow.

ON SIDE EFFECTS AND EVALUATION ORDER

Statements also have an operation-sequencing nature; they define the order in which things happen, denoted by semicolons and block syntax in C#. Expressions, on the other hand, could be treated in a more flexible manner to improve efficiency of the code. For example, expr1 * expr2 is a commutative operation, so the subexpressions expr1 and expr2 could be reordered. Or they could even be evaluated in parallel.

So much for theory. Libraries written with many side-effecting operations in them (like the Base Class Library, BCL), which are typically consumed from imperative languages (like C#), give rise to nondeterministic behavior if the compiler (or runtime) would be free to rearrange evaluation order. This is clearly not a very desirable property, and therefore C# defines order of evaluation unambiguously. Refer to Chapter 5 to learn more about this left-to-right evaluation of subexpressions.

(Pure) functional languages ban side effects—or more accurately, track them carefully through the type system—to allow (among other reasons) this kind of flexibility in the evaluation of expressions.

Expression Statements

Go to Chapter 5, copy and paste. It's *almost* as simple as this. C# being an imperative language doesn't shy away from side-effecting operations in its core language definition.

Method Calls

Methods are the main way of performing operations. While method calls embody a type of expression, they're often used without caring about the return value (if any). That's a typical case of using an expression as a statement.

Side Effects Everywhere?
One concrete proof of this lies in the existence of the void type that can be used as the return type of a method. Clearly, calling such a method is useful only for the side effects it exposes, not for some value it returns:

```
Console.WriteLine("Hello World");
```

We're lucky we have those side effects at our service. How would we print to the screen otherwise? The preceding code line actually is a statement formed out of an invocation expression, the sole difference being the occurrence of a semicolon at the end of the line. The presence of side effects is so deeply rooted in the platform that calling a method and discarding its result is permitted:

```
static void Main()
{
    // Wasteful computation, ignoring the result.
    Math.Sin(Math.PI / 2);
}
```

`Math.Sin` being a pure function with no side effects, the preceding code effectively throws away the result of a computation. But to the compiler, it could equally well be the case that the called method exposes interesting behavior, so it's impossible to prune out the whole call site. In other words, the compiler needs to be conservative.

Do Not Ignore Method Results
As a good rule, avoid ignoring method results. They exist for good reasons, sometimes to indicate success or failure either directly (through a Boolean value) or indirectly (by means of a null-valued result or another result object with error state inside it).

In fact, the Visual Studio built-in Code Analysis feature has a warning for known cases in which lacking checks for return values is a guaranteed formula for disaster. Let's illustrate with an example:

```
static int AddOne(string number)
{
    int num;
    int.TryParse(number, out num);
    return num + 1;
}
```

Here we're using the TryParse method with an output parameter, as explained when we discuss methods in Chapter 10, "Methods," to return the integer value for the parsed string. However, TryParse also returns a Boolean, indicating whether the input was a valid string representation of an integer number. Because we're not checking for the failure condition, the preceding code is probably buggy.

If you've turned on Code Analysis for your project (through the project's Properties window, Code Analysis tab), the preceding code will yield the warning shown in Figure 7.1.

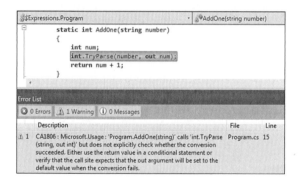

FIGURE 7.1   The dangers of ignoring method results.

Assignments

Assignments are generally considered to be statements in the first place, even though we discussed them in the context of expressions before. In 99 percent of cases, assignments will take a statement form:

```
name = "Bart";
age = 25;
age += 1;
```

In Chapter 5 you saw how assignment expressions take on the value that is assigned to the left side. Although this is definitely a nice property, it should be used sparingly. One of the few legitimate uses I can think of is the type switch mentioned in Chapter 6, "A Primer on Types and Objects," the section, "Intermezzo: The Mythical Type Switch."

```
if ((f = item as Fruit) != null)
{
    // Do something with the juicy piece of fruit...
}
```

Because you already know everything about assignments, there's no need to repeat that here.

Pre- and Post-Increment/Decrement

The increment and decrement operators are similar to assignments with regard to their usual treatment as statements. Useful for their side effects, they're typically used in loop constructs, as you will see later. Let's revisit the example from Chapter 5.

```
for (int i = 0; i < array.Length; i++)
{
    // Do something
}
```

In fact, in such a setting it doesn't matter whether prefix or postfix syntax is used for those operators because the only difference lies in the value that gets returned and not in the side effect they're causing. You'll see both styles used interchangeably, with some (ancient) C/C++ developers slightly preferring the prefix notation for its performance benefit over the postfix one.

The Empty Statement

To ease into the subject of statements gradually, let's start with the most mind-blowing of all: the empty statement. Written as a simple semicolon by itself, it's rarely useful. One of the only cases where this comes in handy is when you're writing some kind of "message pump," a loop that calls some processing method until it returns false to indicate no further messages are to be handled:

```
while (ProcessMessage())
    ;
```

I predict most readers won't ever have to write such a loop anymore—we're well beyond the manual message pumping required in classic Win32—but it's good to know about its existence in case you encounter this kind of code. In fact, you could eliminate the use of the preceding empty statement by using an empty block instead:

```
while (ProcessMessage())
{
}
```

In this particular case, either an empty block or an empty statement is fine. In most other contexts, the use of the empty statement most certainly indicates an error, and the compiler will warn you about this, as shown in Figure 7.2.

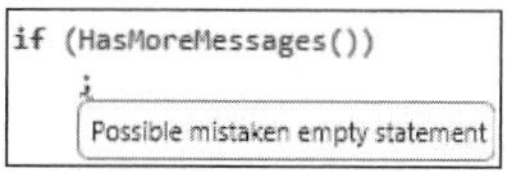

FIGURE 7.2   Possible mistaken empty statement.

Blocks

Blocks provide a way to combine multiple statements and treat them as if they were just one statement, as the language may expect in some places. At the same time, blocks establish a scope for local variables. (See Chapter 4, "Language Essentials," for more information.) An example of a typical use for blocks is found in various other statements, like the if statement:

```
if (condition)
    statement-if-true
else
    statement-if-false
```

Notice that the if statement by itself doesn't prescribe the use of curly braces for its embedded statements. With blocks, we can provide multiple statements in those places:

```
if (user.Age >= 18)
{
    session.User = user;
    NavigateToHomepage(user.Homepage);
}
else
{
    LogInvalidAccessAttempt();
    ShowAccessDeniedPage();
}
```

Blocks also have a code-stylistic property because they promote indentation to reflect a code's structure. Visual Studio will automatically indent when starting a new line after an opening curly brace. To make browsing code easier, matching curly braces are highlighted when moving the cursor around (see Figure 7.3).

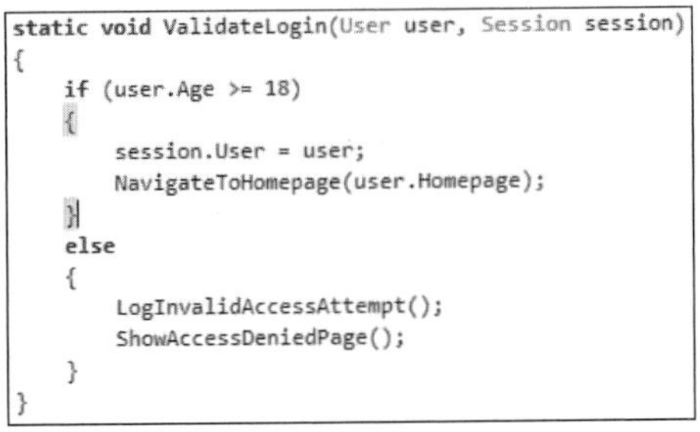

```
static void ValidateLogin(User user, Session session)
{
    if (user.Age >= 18)
    {
        session.User = user;
        NavigateToHomepage(user.Homepage);
    }
    else
    {
        LogInvalidAccessAttempt();
        ShowAccessDeniedPage();
    }
}
```

FIGURE 7.3   Matching curly braces highlighted in Visual Studio.

Declarations

To wrap up the discussion about well-known statements, we should consider declarations, too. The declaration of a local variable consists of a type and a name specified using an identifier:

```
int age;
```

Initial assignment can be carried out at the same time but is optional. All that's required for a declaration is a name and a type, unless local variable type inference (var) is used. In that case, the compiler needs to see a right-side expression from which to infer the type:

```
var name; // This is invalid.
var name = "Bart"; // Here we can infer System.String.
```

It can't be stressed enough that local variable type inference is just that: inference. The variable is still completely statically typed; we just reduce the amount of physical keyboard-driven typing we have to do. Figure 7.4 shows evidence of static typing in a type-inferred context by means of IntelliSense.

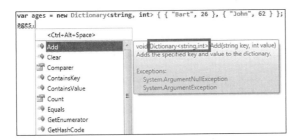

FIGURE 7.4   Local variable type inference? Still statically typed!

For local constant declarations, the `const` keyword is used:

```
const int triangleSideCount = 3;
```

As you already know from Chapter 4, it's invalid to try to reassign to a constant; otherwise, what would be the point in calling it a constant?

NAMING MATTERS

Naming of identifiers is a relevant concern. Consistency and clarity can greatly help you understand the meaning of variables. Some people prefer casing conventions for constants, too, writing them all uppercase. Feel free to do so if it helps you.

Selection Statements

No meaningful program can operate without conditional execution. Depending on runtime state, different groups of statements are executed. C# has two constructs that enable this style: the `if` statement and the `switch` statement.

The `if` Statement

Starting by evaluating a Boolean expression, the `if` statement can conditionally execute an embedded statement. Two forms exist, depending on whether you want to handle the negative case:

```
// Ignore when condition evaluates false.
if (condition)
    statement-if-true


// Also handle the false case.
if (condition)
    statement-if-true
else
    statement-if-false
```

Let's look at an example that uses both branches:

```
static void Main()
{
    var rand = new Random();
    int n = rand.Next(0, 100);
    PrintEvenOrNot(n);
}


static void PrintEvenOrNot(int n)
{
```

```
if (n % 2 == 0)
{
    Console.WriteLine("Even");
}
else
{
    Console.WriteLine("Odd");
}
}
```

In the `Main` method, we're using a random number generator to select a number between 0 (inclusive) and 100 (exclusive). We pass it as a parameter to a method called `PrintEvenOrNot`, where we use an `if` statement to check for even versus odd. Such a check is typically carried out by taking the remainder after integral division, comparing it against zero to identify an even number. In fact, this code could be simplified quite a bit by using the conditional "ternary" operator to select the "Even" or "Odd" message based on the condition. It's clear such an approach works only for trivial cases where a value (here a string) is selected in a conditional manner:

```
static void PrintEvenOrNot(int n)
{
    Console.WriteLine(n % 2 == 0 ? "Even" : "Odd");
}
```

This remark aside, let's focus on the job at hand: the use of an `if` statement. First, notice the condition needs to be a Boolean-valued expression (or to be precise, implicitly convertible to `System.Boolean`). This is different from C and C++, where it's common to check for a nonzero value without using any relational operator at all. An often-seen pattern is null checking:

```
// How one would check a string for null in C or C++.
int ManipulateString(LPWSTR str)
{
    if (!str)
    {
        // Passed-in string was NULL. Return error condition.
        return -1;
    }

    // Do core processing here.
    return 0;
}
```

C# is much more strict about typing and therefore requires zero checks or null checks to be stated explicitly. A typical case is argument checking, as shown here:

```
void ManipulateString(StringBuilder str)
{
    if (str == null)
        throw new ArgumentNullException("str");

    // Do core processing here.
}
```

Notice how I've omitted the curly braces surrounding the if's embedded statement. Do this sparingly because it can lead to confusion. Why? One problem is the so-called dangling else, as illustrated here:

```
if (condition1)
    if (condition2)
        // condition1 == true and condition2 == true
else
    // ???
```

Question of the day: What does the else "associate" with? Does it go with the outer or inner if? The preceding fragment is deceptive due to its outlining; it makes you believe it goes with the outer if statement, which isn't the case. The code is treated as follows:

```
if (condition1)
{
    if (condition2)
    {
        // condition1 == true and condition2 == true
    }
    else
    {
        // ??? means condition1 == true and condition2 == false
    }
}
```

With curly braces, you can completely avoid this kind of confusion. Another reason to avoid the omission of block syntax is code diff tools, as used in source control systems. If an if statement starts its life with a single line in one of its branches but lines get added, you end up with more noise in code version comparison tools. A little annoyance you might say, but still a very real one.

WHITESPACE SENSITIVITY... A RELIGION?

Remember that C# isn't whitespace-sensitive, so you can't change behavior by alignment only. This makes me think of a little story about a colleague.

Being a language freak, I tend to speak highly about various languages at lunch or in other chats with my colleagues. One such language is F#, with its #light mode, which essentially makes the language—in true ML language family style—whitespace-sensitive. What's the initial reaction of some of my imperatively trained colleagues? Yes, right (as their stomachs turn). Today, it's interesting to see how some of these colleagues have been converted to the whitespace-sensitive camp after exposure to languages like Python and F#.

Conclusion? Whitespace-sensitive languages are not necessarily a bad idea; it's more a matter of getting used to them than anything else. Personally, I like a few aspects whitespace sensitivity brings with it: Outlining reveals part of the meaning of your code (for example, the dangling else problem gets resolved by the width of the indentation, no possibility for deception), and it makes the code look cleaner overall. And the fact no curly braces or End keywords are needed is another plus, reducing the code size.

Personally, I omit the curly braces only in argument validation code that's nothing more but "test invalid condition and throw exception," as shown in the preceding example, while still keeping the two-line style:

```
if (str == null)
    throw new ArgumentNullException("str");
```

I won't debate whether the opening curly brace belongs at the end of the first line of the statement or on a line by its own. Choose whatever you feel most comfortable with and let Visual Studio know through Tools, Options, Text Editor, C#, Formatting, Indentation, New Line Options for Braces (see Figure 7.5).

Those settings are used when typing code and when asking the editor to format a selection or a whole document, options you can find in the Edit, Advanced menu. A handy shortcut that's baked in my genes is Ctrl+K,D, which formats the whole document (source file) you're currently editing. How much you actually appreciate those features directly correlates with how much of a style freak you are. As you can guess, I am! Oh, and I like the defaults in Visual Studio, but—as promised—let's not be fanatical about one particular style versus another. *De gustibus non est disputandum* ("no disputes about tastes").

COPPERS AHEAD! FXCOP AND STYLECOP

FxCop is the fancy name for the technology underlying the Code Analysis feature in Visual Studio. It's a collection of rules that perform static analysis on the intermediate language (IL) level to spot potential code defects or inefficiencies. You've seen examples of this already, such as the detection of ignored method results.

StyleCop, on the other hand, operates on the C# source file level and is currently not included with Visual Studio. It's a free download from http://code.msdn.microsoft.com/sourceanalysis. Its role is to enforce coding style guidelines to aid code readability.

As usual, cop kinds of tools work best when applied right from the start of a project and when turned on in the build system from day one. Running such tools on existing large projects can be a great source of frustration in seeing how many potential issues are found.

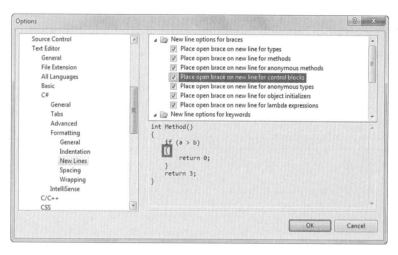

FIGURE 7.5   Code formatting options in Visual Studio.

Internally, control flow is implemented by branching instructions. Plain old goto, if you will. Figure 7.6 shows an illustration of the innards of the PrintEvenOrNot method.

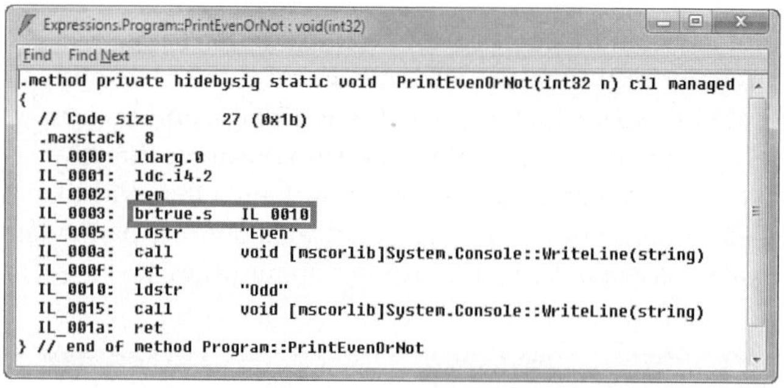

FIGURE 7.6   Branching operations fueling an if statement.

This (optimized Release build) code is fairly easy to understand. The first three lines take the remainder after division by zero. On the fourth line, the branching itself takes place. Notice that on the IL level the `brtrue` (for branch when true) instruction can operate on an integer value, where `true` stands for nonzero. In C#, to avoid mistakes, this is not allowed: Conditions need to be expressed as a logical Boolean value. Conditional branch instructions like `brtrue` cause either control to be transferred to the target label or control to fall through to the next instruction.

WHAT DOES THE .S SUFFIX IN IL STAND FOR?

The answer is simple: short. Internally, branches are represented as offsets in the code: Branch to the instruction x bytes away relative to the end of the current instruction in the code. Jumps can go in either direction (for example, a loop will jump backward), so offsets are encoded using signed integral values. When this distance is sufficiently small (as it often is), a short instruction can be used that takes its operand as a 1-byte (signed) value rather than a 4-byte one. This means short jumps can bridge a distance of at most 128 bytes back or 127 bytes forward. The result of all this is smaller code size because of more efficient encoding for short jumps.

Another geeky tidbit: The labels in the IL reflect the byte positions of the instructions in the code. Notice how IL_0003 jumps to IL_0005, meaning two bytes are used for the branch instruction: one for the opcode (brtrue.s = 0x2D) and one for the (short 1-byte) offset (which is 0x0B in our case). Those details can be revealed by turning on the Show Bytes option from the View menu in the main ILDASM window. A quick calculation proves the theory: The first byte following the branch instruction is at 0x05, and the offset is 0x0B. Guess what? The sum is 0x10, which is where the "Odd" case code lives.

The `switch` Statement

It's a tradition to introduce the `switch` statement using the `if` statement first. Consider the following fragment:

```
Image GetBackgroundForColorScheme(Color color)
{
    if (color == Color.Red)
        return Image.FromFile("Roses.png");
    else if (color == Color.Green)
        return Image.FromFile("Grass.png");
    else if (color == Color.Blue)
        return Image.FromFile("Sky.png");
    else
        throw new InvalidOperationException("Expected primary color.");
}
```

I'm using some `System.Drawing` types such as `Color` and `Image` in the preceding fragment, but ignore this detail for just a second and focus on what makes this fragment tick.

Programmers often refer to this if statement pattern as a multiway branch. In fact, here we're using the ability to omit the curly braces around an embedded statement. I'll leave it to you to expand the fragment with curly braces everywhere and observe the "shape" of the resulting code. It won't look flat anymore.

Anyway, there are lots of cases where a multiway branch is based on the same three fixed properties for the comparisons in the conditions:

- The **same expression** is used in every condition.

- **Equality** is tested.

- Comparison with a **constant**.

To be absolutely precise, the expression used will typically be a side-effect free one; if we were to reevaluate the expression in every if statement, we would replicate side effects. So a local variable is usually used as the basis for comparison.

This pattern of an expression's comparison against different constant values is simplified in the switch statement. In essence, it "switches" the execution of the code based on constant comparisons, executing the code associated with the positive comparison *case*.

To delve a little deeper into the working of a switch statement, let's simplify the fragment a bit more by peeling off the System.Drawing aspect and defining our own Color type using an enumeration. Although we discuss enumerations later, suffice to say, they are named constants that are grouped together to form a (value) type of their own.

```
enum Color
{
    Red,
    Green,
    Blue
}
```

Using the switch statement, the preceding code can be rewritten as follows, now using the custom defined enum for Color:

```
Image GetBackgroundForColorScheme(Color color)
{
    switch (color)
    {
        case Color.Red:
            return Image.Fromfile("Roses.png");
        case Color.Green:
            return Image.Fromfile("Grass.png");
        case Color.Blue:
            return Image.Fromfile("Sky.png");
```

```
    default:
        throw new InvalidOperationException("Expected primary color.");
    }
}
```

On the first line, we state our intent to switch on the value of color. Inside the `switch` statement's body, multiple case labels are defined, each specifying a constant value to compare against. If the equality check passes, the code associated with the label is executed. The default label takes care of the values that didn't match any of the case labels' constants.

FACTORY METHODS

The code shown here uses the `System.Drawing` application programming interfaces (APIs) to match a color with a known value and return an Image instance for it. Notice how the `Image` instance gets created—not by calling a constructor but by calling a *static method*, a method associated with the type itself rather than a particular instance. Its signature looks like this:

```
    public static Image FromFile(string filename);
```

This pattern for object instantiation is known as a *factory method*: a static method defined on a certain type (here `Image`), returning an instance of the containing type. But why was this pattern chosen over a regular constructor?

The answer lies in object-oriented programming, where Image is the base type for different more-specific image representations, such as a bitmap (for example, a .bmp file) versus a metafile (for example, an .emf file). By using a factory method, the caller doesn't need to know which particular subtype to instantiate. Instead, the factory method takes on the task of determining the desired type of the object based on its arguments. In this particular example, it would open the file and analyze a header to decide the best object type to represent the image.

To eliminate the `Image` type dependency, we'll change our method to print a message to the screen using the familiar `Console` type:

```
void PrintMessageForColor(Color color)
{
    switch (color)
    {
        case Color.Red:
            Console.WriteLine("Red roses.");
            break;
        case Color.Green:
            Console.WriteLine("Green grass.");
            break;
```

```
        case Color.Blue:
            Console.WriteLine("Blue skies.");
            break;
        default:
            throw new InvalidOperationException("Expected primary color.");
    }
}
```

This also gives us the opportunity to highlight another important property of the switch statement in C#: Control is not permitted to *fall through* from one case to another, unlike in C and C++, where this is a common source of bugs. Instead, C# requires each section to end with a break statement. An exception to the rule is when there's another guarantee that a section is quit, such as returning from the containing method (our first example) or throwing an exception (the default case in both examples).

Executing the break statement causes control to transfer to the line immediately following the entire switch statement. Notice that the default case is optional; if it's left unspecified, execution simply resumes after the switch statement as if nothing happened. It's also possible to handle different cases with the same piece of code:

```
switch (color)
 {
    case Color.Red:
    case Color.Green:
    case Color.Blue:
        Console.WriteLine("Saw a primary color!");
        break;
 }
```

JUMP BETWEEN CASES?

You can think of the case labels as jump labels, usable in goto statements (see the section, "The goto Statement"). If a "basic block" of code does not end with a jump statement, control falls through to the next line. It's based on this observation: C and C++ allowed this to happen between switch statement sections (accidentally, it seems).

Sometimes it makes sense to have one section execute other sections, as well, though this occurs rarely. Because C# seems to enforce a break statement at the end of each section, it looks like this wouldn't be possible. Not true. A goto statement can be used to jump between switch sections:

```
switch (color)
 {
    case Color.Red:
        Console.WriteLine("Red roses.");
        goto case Color.Blue;
```

```
        case Color.Green:
            Console.WriteLine("Green grass.");
            break;
        case Color.Blue:
            Console.WriteLine("Saw a primary color!");
            break;
    }
```

Personally, I use this sparingly, if at all. Code can get quite unreadable in a matter of seconds, and you might end up spending many hours tracing through code that jumps all over the place. Try to avoid it.

What types of expressions (in this context, referred to as the *governing type*) can be switched on? Any of the integral types (sbyte, byte, short, ushort, int, uint, long, ulong), bool (why would you do that?), char, and enumeration types. If the expression that's being switched on doesn't have any of those types, an implicit conversion is attempted, but if that attempt doesn't work either, a compile-time error occurs.

The case labels need to have compile-time constant values, which are all distinct:

```
string john = "John";

switch (name)
{
    case "Bart": // OK.
        // ...
        break;
    case john: // Not OK, unless you would use const string john = "John" instead.
        // ...
        break;
    case "Bart": // Not OK, already have "Bart" case covered.
        // ...
        break;
}
```

One of the properties of the switch statement in C# is that ordering of the case labels doesn't matter. (In C and C++, it does matter because fallthrough is permitted.) This also helps explain why compile-time constants are required: If case label values could be the same at runtime and the order of evaluation for case labels is left unspecified, in what order will code execute? In addition, think about what would happen with regard to ordering of side effects if case labels were expressions that need evaluation. If you need to check for nonconstant values or want to enforce ordering, the if statement is your friend.

When using an enumeration for the governing type, the possible values are well defined. Because of this, the code editor can be made more intelligent. To switch on an enumeration value with cases for every possible enumeration value, a code snippet can be used (see Figure 7.7).

1. IntelliSense for Switch Snippet

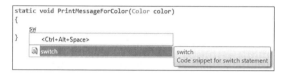

2. Press Tab Twice and Type Color

3. Press Enter

```
static void PrintMessageForColor(Color color)
{
    switch (color)
    {
        case Color.Red:
            break;
        case Color.Green:
            break;
        case Color.Blue:
            break;
        default:
            break;
    }
}
```

FIGURE 7.7   Code snippet for switch on enumeration value.

A "COMPLETE" SWITCH

Enumerations denote a finite set of known constant values that belong to the same domain. For example, we've defined three colors, and that's it. So in essence, the switch illustrated here is "complete" because it stretches the whole range of possible values. Or is it?

First, why would we bother about a switch having the property of being complete? Here's why: Suppose you want to write a function that returns some value for every potential case, as shown here:

```
string ToDutchString(Color color)
{
    switch (color)
    {
        case Color.Red:
            return "rood";
```

```
        case Color.Green:
            return "groen";
        case Color.Blue:
            return "blauw";
    }
}
```

Unfortunately, the preceding code doesn't compile because the C# compiler doesn't realize (for a good reason, read on) we're exhaustively testing for what appear to be all values in the domain of the `Color` enumeration. Because of this, it sees a code path exists that doesn't guarantee a string is returned from the method. Either we need to supply a default case or return some dummy value at the end of the method. Or we return in a forceful way by throwing an exception:

```
default:
    throw new InvalidOperationException("Unknown color.");
```

This can be particularly annoying if you're working on code coverage because it seems impossible to hit the default case. Wouldn't it be nice we could tell the compiler that `switch` is "complete" (or let it infer that)? It would, if enumeration types would really establish finite domains. But they don't.

You already know this from one use of enumerations, with flags. In Chapter 5, we looked at bit-level mask operations to test for flags. An enumeration for `FileMode` can have `Read` and `Write` values defined as powers of two, allowing the user to combine them into a `ReadWrite` by using the bitwise ¦ operator. We've just created a value that's also a valid `FileMode` but hasn't necessarily been declared explicitly in the enumeration.

But also without the use of flags, enumerations are just integral numbers in disguise. In our `Color` definition, the enumeration is really an `int` with some symbolic constants defined using compiler-generated numbers (Red = 0, Green = 1, and Blue = 2). Because the integral representation is handy as a storage mechanism (as opposed to storing a new as a string), you can convert back and forth between an enumeration and its underlying type:

```
var unknownColor = (Color)4;
```

Here's how an unknown enumeration value can be born, a little unfortunately.

From a stylistic point of view, an often-recurring question is whether a `switch` statement's embedded statements should be wrapped in a pair of curly braces. Remember, blocks can be used for scoping purposes, so the use of curly braces can be beneficial in case you need local state and don't want to spoil the outer scope:

```
static int Eval(Expression ex)
{
    switch (ex.NodeType)
    {
```

```
        case ExpressionType.Constant:
        {
            var ce = (ConstantExpression)ex;
            if (!(ce.Value is int))
                throw new InvalidOperationException("Only int supported.");
            return (int)ce.Value;
        }
        case ExpressionType.Add:
        {
            var be = (BinaryExpression)ex;
            return Eval(be.Left) + Eval(be.Right);
        }
        case ExpressionType.Multiply:
        {
            var be = (BinaryExpression)ex;
            return Eval(be.Left) * Eval(be.Right);
        }
        // Other binary operations.
        default:
            throw new NotSupportedException("Can't evaluate " + ex + ".");
    }
}
```

This code uses expression trees from the System.Linq.Expressions namespace to define a recursive expression evaluator for mathematical expressions. The mechanics of this are irrelevant for the scope of this discussion (and a real evaluator would be more complex, for sure). What matters is the use of blocks underneath the case labels, allowing us to reuse variable names in different cases and such. Although this style of coding works, I don't like it very much.

Consider this: The preceding switch statement will likely have many more cases (subtract, divide, remainder, checked counterparts, unary operators, and so forth), resulting in the containing method growing really big. This hurts not only code readability, but it also hampers "psychic debugging." Your IT colleague walks into the office with an exception stack trace scribbled down on a Post-It note (or sends an email if you're in a modern company). It reads Eval, Eval, Eval, Eval, Eval. Can you tell where the code went wrong? If you're lucky, there'll be some more immediately apparent state (as shown in Figure 7.8, the ex parameter's ToString is shown by the debugger), but having more meaningful method names can help a lot.

Personally, I like to break down the code into succinct methods, so the use of blocks in switch statements decreases significantly:

```
static int Eval(Expression ex)
{
    switch (ex.NodeType)
    {
```

```
        case ExpressionType.Constant:
            return EvalConstant((ConstantExpression)ex);
        case ExpressionType.Add:
            return EvalBinary((BinaryExpression)ex, (a, b) => a + b);
        case ExpressionType.Multiply:
            return EvalBinary((BinaryExpression)ex, (a, b) => a * b);
        // Other binary operations.
        default:
            throw new NotSupportedException("Can't evaluate " + ex + ".");
    }
}
```

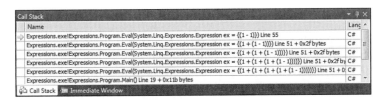

FIGURE 7.8   Obfuscated call stack due to excessive use of switch blocks.

I couldn't resist, though, using a little lambda expression in EvalBinary to simplify the binary operator case. You'll see more on the use of lambdas Chapter 17, "Delegates," and when covering LINQ in Chapter 19, "Language Integrated Query Essentials," and Chapter 20, "Language Integrated Query Internals."

Also notice the self-confident use of cast expressions rather than the fail-safe as keyword. In this case, we know for sure that an expression whose type is, say, Add needs to be a BinaryExpression. If you know it for sure, use a cast!

ROBUST EVALUATORS

The approach taken to write an evaluator in the preceding snippet is quite standard. It's called "recursive descent" because we're descending the expression tree recursively. One potential issue with such an approach is its call stack behavior; it's not unimaginable for very complicated expressions to exhaust the call stack space resulting in a StackOverflowException. Alternatives exist but are beyond the scope of this book. So if you ever need to write a recursive evaluator that should be resilient against deeply nested input, be sure to test for this potential issue.

Internally, the switch statement is implemented with direct assistance from the IL instruction set. To keep things simple, let's just use an int-based switch for illustration purposes only:

```
static string ToDutchBinaryString(int x)
{
    switch (x)
    {
        case 0:
            return "nul";
        case 1:
            return "een";
        default:
            throw new InvalidOperationException("Not a binary digit.");
    }
}
```

The switch instruction is table-driven, basically specifying target labels for integral values 0, 1, 2, and so on. If gaps occur in the case labels (such as only having 0 and 2 above), switch will transfer control to the default label for the missing ones (1, that would be). All the ones that don't belong to the "covered range" would fall through the switch instruction, where control is transferred to the default label, too.

In Figure 7.9, switch looks at the parameter value x and transfers control to label IL_0012 in case the value was equal to 0, and IL_0018 in case of 1. Otherwise, control falls through where an unconditional jump is made to IL_001e where the default case lives.

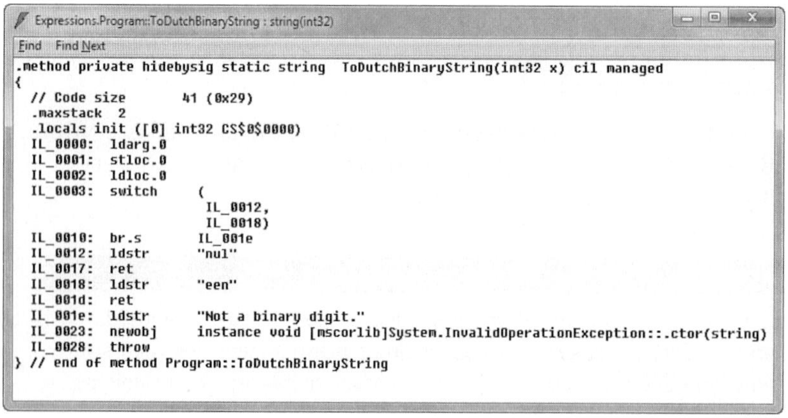

```
 Expressions.Program::ToDutchBinaryString : string(int32)                    _ □ x
 Find   Find Next
.method private hidebysig static string  ToDutchBinaryString(int32 x) cil managed
{
  // Code size       41 (0x29)
  .maxstack  2
  .locals init ([0] int32 CS$0$0000)
  IL_0000:  ldarg.0
  IL_0001:  stloc.0
  IL_0002:  ldloc.0
  IL_0003:  switch     (
                        IL_0012,
                        IL_0018)
  IL_0010:  br.s       IL_001e
  IL_0012:  ldstr      "nul"
  IL_0017:  ret
  IL_0018:  ldstr      "een"
  IL_001d:  ret
  IL_001e:  ldstr      "Not a binary digit."
  IL_0023:  newobj     instance void [mscorlib]System.InvalidOperationException::.ctor(string)
  IL_0028:  throw
} // end of method Program::ToDutchBinaryString
```

FIGURE 7.9   A switch label specifies jump targets.

Because the switch instruction knows about values 0, 1, 2, and so on for its consecutive set of target labels, the compiler does some elementary math to fit code on this behavior. For example, if you switch with cases for values 10 and 11, the compiler would subtract 10 before doing the switch, which is then based on 0 again. An example of this is shown here, also leaving a gap in the range of values:

```
switch (x)
    {
        case 11:
            return "elf";
        case 13:
            return "dertien";
        default:
            throw new InvalidOperationException("Unexpected value.");
    }
```

Instead of switching on x, the code will switch on x, 11. Notice this is safe to do because the subtraction operator used here is well known to the compiler for not having side effects because only the built-in integral types are supported. The 11-case will correspond to the first switch label, the nonexisting 12-case will be patched up to correspond to a jump to default, and the 13-case will end up in its appropriate spot. The rest fall through. Figure 7.10 illustrates this and also shows the bytes for the instructions and their operands.

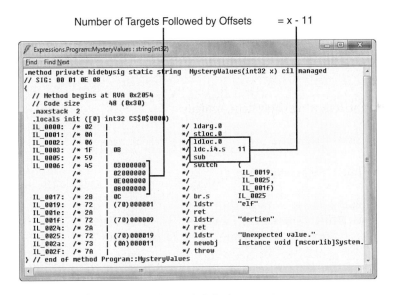

FIGURE 7.10   More-complex switch logic.

If the range of values used in the switch is too fragmented to be normalized to a more or less consecutive range, the compiler will resort to emitting code as if a regular multiway if statement were written instead.

Notice that the zero-based nature of the switch instruction makes it ideally suited for enumeration values because (in the standard case) those comprise a zero-based set of values. For example, our Color enumeration has values 0 to 2 for Red through Blue because we haven't vetoed the default values chosen by the compiler (more on that later).

For string-based switches, the code is treated as if it were a multiway if statement comparing the string against the supplied values using the == operator defined on the System. String type. This performs a case-sensitive character-by-character equality check. If the number of cases grows too big (today's threshold being six or more, but that can change at any time)—and because ordering shouldn't matter to the developer—the compiler emits more efficient code that uses a Dictionary<string, int> internally. This collection type uses a technique called *hashing* to speed up lookup operations, as you will see when we discuss collections in Chapter 16, "Collection Types."

For example:

```
static string DutchDecimalDigitToEnglish(string s)
{
    switch (s)
    {
        case "nul":  return "zero";
        case "een":  return "one";
        case "twee": return "two";
        // Enough additional cases here.
        default:
            throw new InvalidOperationException("Not a decimal digit.");
    }
}
```

This code gets compiled to the following equivalent, roughly:

```
static Dictionary<string, int> s_switchHelper; // really a random name

static string DutchDecimalDigitToEnglish(string s)
{
    if (s_switchHelper == null)
        s_switchHelper = new Dictionary<string, int>
            { { "nul", 0 }, { "een", 1 }, { "twee", 2 }, /* more cases */ };

    int __num;
    if (s_switchHelper.TryGetValue(s, out __num))
        switch (__num) {
            case 0: return "zero";
            case 1: return "one";
            case 2: return "two";
            default: goto __default;
        }
```

```
__default:
    throw new InvalidOperationException("Not a decimal digit.");
}
```

The real code is slightly more complicated to accommodate multithreaded execution, but the core of the idea is to turn a string-based switch into an int-based one natively supported by the runtime. This mapping is based on a dictionary that is instantiated on first use.

But why all this fuss? Actually, I wanted to bring up a hidden message by using this particular example: Table-driven execution is a very useful technique. Obviously, your case labels' embedded statements could be much more involved and do much more than just establish some mapping. But the next time you write a switch to encode some kind of mapping, think about the possibility to use a table instead. Our example could be completely rewritten as follows:

```
static Dictionary<string, string> s_dutchToEnglish;

static string DutchDecimalDigitToEnglish(string s)
{
    if (s_dutchToEnglish == null)
    {
        s_dutchToEnglish = new Dictionary<string, string>
            { { "nul", "zero" }, { "een", "one" }, /* more mappings */ };
    }

    string english;
    if (!s_dutchToEnglish.TryGetValue(s, out english))
        throw new InvalidOperationException("Not a decimal digit.");

    return english;
}
```

FOREIGN LANGUAGES IN A NUTSHELL: SELECT CASE AND MATCH

Although this book talks about C#, in the world of .NET you might have to face code written in another language at some point. So I want to point out more-or-less corresponding features to switch in other languages.

Visual Basic has Select Case, which can be used for the things we've done with switch in C# but also a bit more, such as checks for ranges (Case 1 to 10) and inequalities (Case > 1).

F# has a matching construct that goes way beyond what C#'s switch and Visual Basic's Select Case can do. It allows for full-fledged pattern matching of tuples, lists, discriminated unions, and types. An example defining a function to calculate a shape's surface is shown here:

```
let surface shape =
    match shape with
    | Rectangle(w, h) -> w * h
    | Circle(r) -> PI * r * r
```

Notice how match in F# is an expression rather than a statement because it produces a value as the result of its evaluation.

Iteration Statements

Another quite fundamental technique in the context of imperative style of programming is iteration, the repetition of execution of a certain piece of code. Time to cover C#'s four loop constructs: while, do, for, and foreach.

The while Statement

To continue executing an embedded statement as long as a certain condition holds true, the while statement is the ideal choice. Its shape is as follows:

```
while (condition)
    embedded-statement
```

Just as with the if statement, the condition is a Boolean-valued expression, or to be completely accurate, something implicitly convertible to a Boolean. Once more, this means null checks or nonzero checks need to be made explicit, as opposed to C and C++, where it's not uncommon to write code like this:

```
// How one would copy a string in C or C++.
while (*cpy++ = *str++)
    ;
```

Side-effecting assignment, treatment of a character as a truth value, and other wackiness with pointer arithmetic—no way in C#. (For the curious, the preceding code is a popular string-copy pattern.)

A sample use of the while statement is shown here:

```
int i = 1;
while (i <= 10)
{
    Console.WriteLine(new string('*', i));
    i++;
}
```

Here we count from 1 to 10 using a local variable and print a number of asterisks to the screen on every loop iteration. The block syntax is used to make have the loop body contain two statements, though I recommend using curly braces even for single statement loop bodies. Readers proficient with the post-increment operator—and by now everyone should be—will notice this code can be abbreviated as follows:

```
int i = 1;
while (i <= 10)
    Console.WriteLine(new string('*', i++));
```

True, it's shorter but not more readable. Avoid this in production code. Next, someone comes around and adds an if statement to the loop body, causing the increment of i to be conditional. Chances are the loop gets in a state where i isn't incremented and the condition never evaluates false: a runaway loop!

Sometimes it makes sense to write an infinite loop (for example, to create a message processor that's the driver of a service). Its task is to accept messages and dispatch them to some worker that does the real processing. Don't be surprised if you sometimes see code like this:

```
while (true)
{
    // Do something.
}
```

Your next logical question should be how the loop is terminated. This is a topic on its own and highly depends on context. Sometimes exceptions are used for this purpose, sometimes a Boolean flag is set (but it might not have an immediate effect because the loop might be blocked while waiting for messages to come in), but yet other techniques exist. While we're at it, this is the ideal place to discuss how a loop's iteration behavior can be modified.

break

The break statement can be used to break out of a loop. It transfers control to the statement immediately following the loop. For example:

```
var rand = new Random();
while (true)
{
    var num = rand.Next();
    if (num % 2 == 0)
        break;
    Console.WriteLine(num);
}
```

An odd-number lottery if you will. As soon as an even random number is found, we break out of the loop. Break is one of those statements that justify the omission of curly braces when used as the embedded statement for an if statement.

BREAKING... ONE LEVEL AT A TIME

In contrast to some other languages, C#'s break statement only allows us to break out of the closest loop or switch statement. That is, if you have nesting going on—such as loops inside loops or a switch inside a loop—you can only break out of the inner-most construct.

Why doesn't C#'s break account for that? There are probably a few reasons: Perhaps it's historically rooted; perhaps it's because C and C++, the spiritual parents of C#, don't supply such a multilevel break either. Or perhaps it's because such multilevel breaks are not common, so there's no reason to bloat the language.

"Too weak arguments," you say. So what about this? Refactoring. Assume a multilevel break is done by labeling loops and specifying the label as an "argument" to the break statement, as shown here:

```
// Warning: this is not a valid C# program.
outer:
while (conditionOuter)
{
    // Do stuff.
    while (conditionInner)
    {
        // Some inner loop code.
        break outer;
    }
    // Do more stuff.
}
```

When the inner loop grows too big, it'll be a good idea to have the refactoring function-ality in Visual Studio do its thing and extract a method for it. But in the presence of labeled breaks, the code to be refactored is dependent on code much higher up, making straightforward refactoring impossible. Obviously, this problem also exists when using regular (much to be avoided) goto statements. Using labeled breaks, we've essentially brought back part of the goto hell. In fact, you can explicitly use C#'s goto statement to achieve this break effect if you *really* want.

One last argument I can bring up against labeled breaks is the fact that they don't improve code readability, requiring scrolling to find labels. With some flag-based plumb-ing—as you will see—you can follow the break path one level at a time. You can think of alternatives to labeled breaks, but they are at best cumbersome, too. For example, specifying the nesting level to break out of (0 for current loop, 1 for outer one, and so forth) is error-prone in the face of making updates to the code. Changing the nesting levels requires us to patch up all break statements that depend on it.

If you need to break at another level, some plumbing will be required. It's clear you need to break out of the innermost one and percolate the break up to the desired point. A common technique is to set a Boolean flag and check for that flag immediately after the inner construct to see whether another break is needed. A little example will make this clear:

```
while (conditionOuter)
{
    bool breakOuter = false;
    // Do stuff.
    while (conditionInner)
    {
        // Some inner loop code.
        breakOuter = true;
        break;
    }
    if (breakOuter)
        break;
    // Do more stuff.
}
```

This might not be as sexy as labeled breaks and whatnot, but it's easy enough to trace the flow of the code one level at a time. And it's refactoring friendly: If you attempt to refactor the inner loop into a separate method, breakOuter will become the return value for that method.

continue

Whereas the break statement enables you to jump out of the loop and continue execution with the statement following it, the continue statement enables you to go to the next iteration. Figure 7.11 provides a conceptual overview by showing both next to each other.

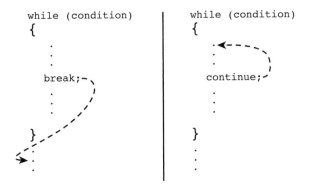

FIGURE 7.11   The break and continue statements compared.

I deliberately chose to make the continue control flow arrow point at the closing curly brace as opposed to the first ellipsis inside the loop body. As you'll see, other loop constructs put some end-of-iteration logic at the bottom of the loop, nearly behind the closing curly brace, if you will. But the more important part here is the fact the condition is reevaluated when control is transferred using the continue statement. As with the break statement, you can only continue the current loop.

LOOPS? GOTO IN DISGUISE, ONLY A BIT HARDER...

Under the hood, loops are implemented using branch instructions. Branches are plain old goto statements on the IL level. That said, there are some subtleties in the implementation for control transfer with loops, break statements, and continue statements in managed code.

The source of those complicates lies in exception handling, which we discuss extensively in Chapter 8, "Basics of Exceptions and Resource Management," largely dedicated to the topic. For example, a break statement occurring in a *protected block* inside a loop's body is more complicated than a simple goto because a special instruction is required to *leave* a protected block. This instruction, appropriately called leave, tells the runtime to ensure all the guarantees the exception handling code provides are met (see further to learn what those are).

The do...while Statement

The while statement evaluates its condition before entering the loop body on every iteration. If evaluation of the condition at the end of the loop is desired, the do statement is your choice:

```
do
    embedded statement
while (condition);
```

(Don't forget the semicolon at the end of the last line.) An implication of this loop structure is that the body of the loop runs at least once. Control simply falls into the loop at the start, and when the condition at the end evaluates positively, control is transferred to the beginning of the loop body again.

As with the while statement, the break and continue statements can be used in a do statement's embedded statement, too.

CODE MAINTENANCE CAVEAT

Because I once spent a couple of minutes staring at code that caused an infinite loop, I thought I would share this little caveat with you. At some point, I decided to change a do-while loop into a while loop: Code for the first iteration got somehow conditioned inside the loop but could be pulled out of it, and all of a sudden there was no reason anymore to keep the loop as a do-while. The condition got tweaked a little bit, too. But for some unknown reason (at least at first), the code got stuck. Here's what the code looked like:

```
while (newCondition)
{
    // Quite a bit of refactored code here.
    // Next line not within the scroll area of the editor.
} while (oldCondition);
```

In my enthusiasm, I forgot to pull out the trailing while part of the do-while loop. The result was my new loop ran flawlessly (as expected), but immediately thereafter the remainder while part got turned into a new loop:

```
while (oldCondition)
    ;
```

The oldCondition expression always evaluated true, and there's the infinite loop. I considered myself lucky that the oldCondition was probably always going to evaluate to true at the end of the loop, so I caught the problem immediately. If oldCondition would have been false during the first testing, I know for sure it would have turned out to be true the first time when demonstrating the project, making the whole thing hang. Yes, Murphy was lurking, but this time he didn't get me (believe me, he has on numerous other occasions).

Personally, I rarely use the do statement. Most problems lend themselves to solving via the while statement or for style loops, as you see in the next few sections.

The for Statement

Besides a condition and a body, lots of loops require an initialization phase as a preamble to the execution of the loop. In addition to this, it's common to have an update phase that gets executed at the end of each iteration. The for statement is what enables cleaner syntax for this scenario:

```
for (initializer; condition; iterator)
    embedded-statement
```

As usual, the embedded statement has an optional pair of curly braces surrounding it. (The usual remarks apply.)

The `for` statement can be seen as shorthand syntax for the following equivalent `while` statement:

```
{
    initializer;
    while (condition)
    {
        embedded-statement;
        iterator;
    }
}
```

Notice the outer pair of curly braces establishing a scope for variables that may get introduced in the initializer phase. This allows those variables to be reused across multiple `for` statements, which is commonly seen for index variables such as i, j, and k:

```
var primes = new [] { 2, 3, 5, 7 };

// Forward loop over the array.
for (int i = 0; i < primes.Length; i++)
{
    Console.WriteLine(primes[i]);
}

// Backwards loop over the array.
for (int i = primes.Length - 1; i >= 0; i—)
{
    Console.WriteLine(primes[i]);
}
```

Unless you need the index values, there's a cleaner way to iterate over an array (or any collection for that matter) using the `foreach` statement, as you see in the next section. Either way, `for` statements are most commonly used for loops that need some kind of index.

The initializer and iterator parts are comma-separated lists of *expression statements*, though the typical use consists of a declaration in the initializer and some compound assignment or pre- or post-increment/-decrement operation in the iterator. The following example prints a list of powers of two:

```
for (int exp = 0, pow = 1; exp <= 10; exp++, pow *= 2)
{
    Console.WriteLine("2^{0} = {1}", exp, pow); // Using a string formatter.
}
```

Ignore the use of the string formatter for now. Intuitively, you should be able to see what {0} and {1} stand for.

Break and continue statements are available for for loops just as they are for other kinds of loops. The following is an example of the use of a break statement in the context of a for loop:

```
static void PrintPrimes(int max)
{
    for (int num = 2; num < max; num++)
    {
        bool foundDiv = false;

        for (int div = 2; div <= Math.Sqrt(num); div++)
        {
            if (num % div == 0)
            {
                foundDiv = true;
                break;
            }
        }

        if (!foundDiv)
        {
            Console.WriteLine(num);
        }
    }
}
```

Be aware that this algorithm for finding prime numbers is not the most intelligent one and is meant only to illustrate nested loops and the use of the break statement. Notice that in the condition for the inner for statement a comparison is done between an integer value and a floating-point number resulting from the Math.Sqrt call. This works because an implicit conversion from int to double is available.

Finally, although some people prefer while (true) as the most appropriate way to write an infinite loop, others believe they can make more of a statement using an obscure for loop. I disagree with the latter group but leave the judgment to you (you agree!):

```
for (;;)
{
    // Do something for"ever"; the (;;) above doesn't really read like "ever".
}
```

The `foreach` Statement

One of the most common sources of loop constructs enumerating over a collection of some sort and executing some code for all the elements found. Welcome the `foreach` statement, which provides you with this functionality.

Before we delve into details, let's take a look at a few examples. The simplest collection type is the array. Instead of writing a `for` loop that goes over a range of indices using the array's `Length` property as an exclusive upper bound, we can write the following:

```
int[] primes = new int[] { 2, 3, 5, 7 };
foreach (int prime in primes)
{
    Console.WriteLine(prime);
}
```

The `foreach` statement breaks down into the following pieces:

```
foreach (type identifier in expression)
    embedded-statement
```

Here, *expression represents the source of the loop. You'll see in just a minute what expressions can be used for enumeration. In front of the* `in` keyword, a local variable—referred to as the iteration variable—is introduced. For every iteration, it will take on the value of an element found in the source.

Another example can be found with the collection types. I'm using the generic ones from the `System.Collections.Generic` namespace here:

```
var primes = new List<int> { 2, 3, 5, 7 };
foreach (int prime in primes)
{
    Console.WriteLine(prime);
}

var ages = new Dictionary<string, int> { { "Bart", 26 }, { "John", 62 } };
foreach (string name in ages.Keys)
{
    Console.WriteLine("{0} is {1}", name, ages[name]);
}
```

The first example should be self-explanatory. In the last one, we're using the `Keys` property of the `Dictionary<K,T>` generic type to get all the keys back that appear in the dictionary. Inside the loop, we index into the collection based on that key to retrieve the age. This is just one technique:

```
foreach (KeyValuePair<string, int> item in ages)
{
    Console.WriteLine("{0} is {1}", item.Key, item.Value);
}
```

Here, we're enumerating over the dictionary itself as a sequence of (generic) KeyValuePair objects, each of which has a Key (of type string in the preceding example) and a Value (of type int here). Having to type the long generic type name can be tedious, so consider yourself lucky that an implicitly typed local variable can be used here, too. To learn where the compiler infers the type from, read on. Figure 7.12 shows IntelliSense for the KeyValuePair object. Inferring the type using the var keyword should result in the same IntelliSense auto-completion.

```
foreach (var item in ages)
{
    Console.WriteLine("{0} is {1}", item.Key, item.Value);
}
```

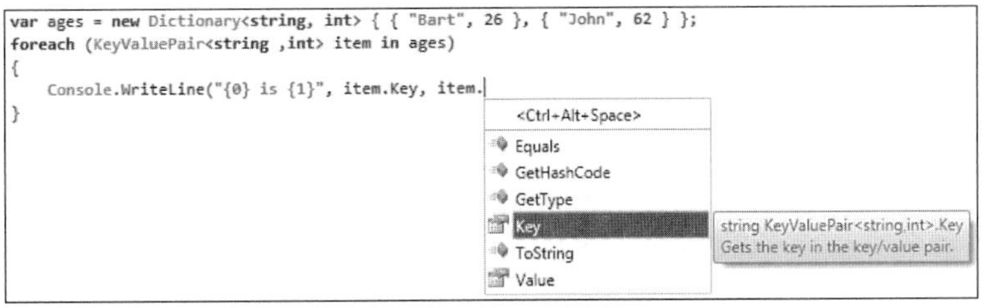

FIGURE 7.12   Using the explicitly typed iteration variable.

To conclude our exploration of possible uses of the foreach statement—and to continue down the road of type inference—here's a sneak peek of the use of LINQ to query in-memory data:

```
const int MB = 1024 * 1024;
var memHungry = from proc in Process.GetProcesses()
                where proc.WorkingSet64 > 50 * MB
                select new { proc.ProcessName, MB = proc.WorkingSet64 / MB };
```

To run this example, you must import the System.Diagnostics namespace, where the Process type is defined. Recall that importing a namespace is done by means of a using directive at the top of the file. The code editor can assist you in putting the right directive in place: As soon as you've typed the unresolved type name, a little tip lights up underneath the name. You can either click this or press Ctrl+. (that is, the period key [or "dot"] on the letters part of the keyboard) to select the namespace to import. Figure 7.13 shows the smart tag that shows the option for importing the missing namespace.

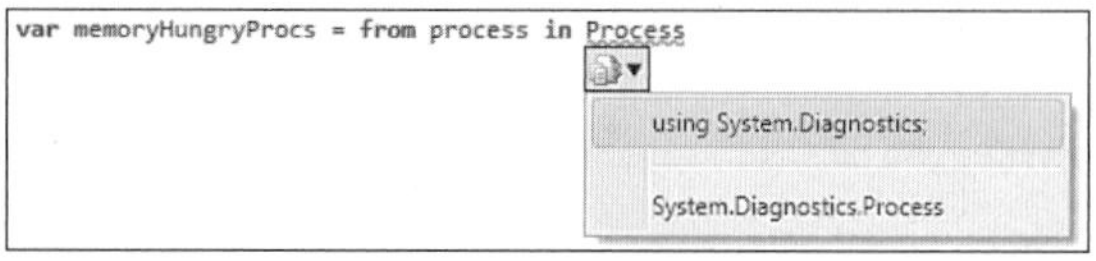

```
var memoryHungryProcs = from process in Process
                          [icon]▼
                              using System.Diagnostics;

                              System.Diagnostics.Process
```

FIGURE 7.13   Importing namespaces made easy.

It should be pretty clear what this query does: It finds all the processes running on the machine with a working set larger than 50MB. The 64 in the WorkingSet64 property name reflects the precision of the value (long, or Int64). Another 32-bit property called WorkingSet exists, which is now marked obsolete due to its insufficient range to deal with 64-bit processes that can have a working set that doesn't fit in a 32-bit value.

Where the need for implicitly typed local variables comes in is due to the select clause, in which we're using an *anonymous type* to project out only the pieces of data we're interested in: the process name and the working set in megabytes. We cover anonymous types when talking about LINQ more extensively in Chapters 19 and 20, but your gut feeling is right: If a type doesn't have a name (at least not pronounceable by the developer because the compiler has generated a name behind the scenes anyway), how can we refer to it? The answer is to have the compiler infer the type:

It's clear the type used in the select "projection" clause is used to shape our resulting objects, so it should appear somewhere on the surface of our query. This is illustrated in Figure 7.14. In fact, I'm temporarily driving attention away from the enumeration aspect that comes with a query: Before we can enumerate over elements, the foreach statement requires us to state the type somehow. Here we can't do anything but have the compiler infer it for us:

```
foreach (var memoryHungryProcess in memHungry)
{
    Console.WriteLine(memoryHungryProcess);
}
```

FIGURE 7.14   The anonymous type used in the select clause propagates to the result.

Figure 7.15 shows the result of running the query by means of iteration using the foreach loop construct.

Notice that anonymous types have a ToString override in place that prints their property names and values in a comma-separated string. Handy.

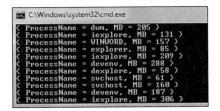

FIGURE 7.15   The result of the memory hungry processes query.

IEnumerables Are the foreach Loop's Best Friends

Time to take a look at how the foreach statement works. Although a little more complicated than that, the foreach statement is intimately related to the IEnumerable interface in the System.Collections namespace and its generic friend IEnumerable<T>. Essentially, this means that foreach can deal with everything that's "enumerable."

ENUMERATIONS VERSUS ENUMERABLES

Don't confuse enumerations with enumerables. It's an unfortunate naming conflict that's historically rooted. Enumerations are value types that define a number of symbolic constants, as you saw with Color during our discussion about the switch statement. Enumerables, on the other hand, are objects that support being enumerated over, named after the corresponding interfaces in the BCL. It should be clear from context what's meant if we use the word *enumeration*, either as a noun (for example, Color) or as a verb (the act of enumerating over an enumerable (for example, with foreach).

To see how enumeration is formalized through the IEnumerable and IEnumerable<T> interfaces, let's take a look at them in Figure 7.16.

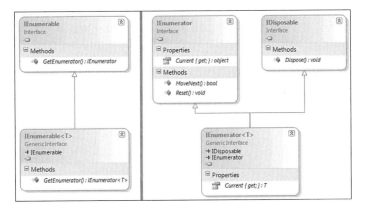

FIGURE 7.16   IEnumerable interfaces and friends.

At the bottom is the new (post .NET 2.0) world, with generic types. Because we'll be dealing mostly with those, our journey begins there.

First there's IEnumerable<T>, providing a way to get an enumerator. In essence, an enumerable only states it can be enumerated over, but the act of doing so is separated out into a different enumerator type. This allows us to keep enumeration state on a per-enumeration basis, so multiple iterations can be carried out simultaneously.

This brings us to the IEnumerator<T> type that gets returned by calling GetEnumerator on the IEnumerable<T> object. Think of the enumerator as a cursor-driven way to retrieve elements in a sequential fashion. A call to MoveNext advances the cursor and returns a Boolean indicating whether a next element was found. If so, the get-only Current property can be used to retrieve that element. Mix in a loop and you end up with a nice pattern for enumeration: "while MoveNext returns true get the Current element," as illustrated here:

```
List<int> primes = new List<int> { 2, 3, 5, 7 };
IEnumerator<int> enumerator = primes.GetEnumerator();
while (enumerator.MoveNext())
{
    int prime = enumerator.Current;
    Console.WriteLine(prime);
}
```

And indeed, this is *almost* what the foreach statement compiles into *in this case*. Those with an eye for detail will have spotted another interface in the previous diagram: IDisposable. Enumerators implement this interface to provide proper resource cleanup, something discussed in more detail in Chapter 8. Nevertheless, the IDisposable interface is easy enough to explain in one line. Types implementing it establish a contract with their consumers that states "if you're done with an instance of mine, call the Dispose method for me to clean up after you."

Why do we need resource cleanup for enumeration? The short answer is to enumerate over collections for no particular reason. But enumeration could also be provided over things such as the contents of a text file in a line-by-line manner. No matter how iteration is finished—by reaching the end, by breaking out of the loop, or because an unhandled exception forcefully terminated the loop—we need to release resources that may be held. A more accurate translation for the preceding iteration looks like this:

```
IEnumerator<int> enumerator = primes.GetEnumerator();
try
{
    while (enumerator.MoveNext())
    {
        int prime = enumerator.Current;
        Console.WriteLine(prime);
    }
```

```
}
finally
{
    if (enumerator != null)
        enumerator.Dispose();
}
```

You'll see the meaning of the try and finally keywords later, but the essence is this: The code underneath try makes up a *protected block*. Exception handlers (using the catch keyword) can be associated with such a block, as well as a finally block. The exception-handling system guarantees the finally block is called no matter how control leaves the protected block it's associated with. In other words, in the preceding code, we're guaranteed to clean up the enumerator's state even if—for some reason—the code in the enumeration blows up.

As you might expect by now, the collection types we've been using implement the IEnumerable<T> interface, for some T. Typically, the *generic parameter* T is simply carried over from the defining type; for example, a List<T> obviously can enumerate over elements of type T, no matter what type is substituted for T. For a dictionary though, the type parameter to IEnumerable<T> is more complex, as revealed in Figure 7.17 using a Visual Studio Class Diagram.

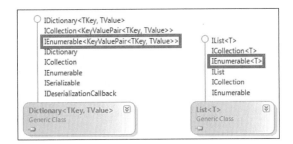

FIGURE 7.17   A few commonly used collection types.

Can you see how the generic parameter on IEnumerable<T> ultimately ends up as the type for the iteration variable? From IEnumerable<T>, we get an IEnumerator<T> whose Current property is typed to be of type T. Because the generic Dictionary type implements the IEnumerable<KeyValuePair<TKey, TValue>>, the iteration variable will be of type KeyValuePair<TKey, TValue>.

INTERFACES IN A NUTSHELL

In this whole discussion, we've met no less than five interfaces: the generic and non-generic IEnumerable and IEnumerator ones, as well as IDisposable. Interfaces establish a contract between two parties. One party says, "As long as you provide such and such operations, I can work with you." An example of such a party is the `foreach` statement, requiring someone to *implement* what it means to perform an enumeration. The other side says, "I'll obey the rules of the contract so that others can work with me to carry out a specific task." The obvious example of that side is the collection types that have gone through the burden of implementing an `IEnumerable` interface. Oh, for the record, the I prefix stands for "interface" and not the first person in the English language as in "Look mom, *I* can enumerate."

How It Really Works

Even though the `IEnumerable<T>` and `IEnumerable` interfaces are great ways to express the ability to enumerate over something, the `foreach` statement is a bit looser in its consideration of what's "enumerable." In fact, all the `foreach` statement cares about is having the enumeration pattern available:

▶ Can I ask the source expression for an enumerator by means of some method called `GetEnumerator`?

▶ Does the resulting enumerator have a `MoveNext` method returning a Boolean to indicate the success state of advancing the cursor?

▶ Is it possible to ask that same enumerator object for the current element we're at in the iteration, using a property `Current` with a getter?

▶ And—this is optional—if there's a disposable pattern on the enumerator object, I'll call it faithfully.

In addition to this, the type used to declare the iteration variable can be used in a hidden cast expression. This has historical grounds because .NET 1.x only had the nongeneric `IEnumerable` interface, whose enumerator was `IEnumerator`. Because enumeration should work for all collections with any element type imaginable, the logical choice was made to type the `Current` property as `System.Object`. An example is `ArrayList`, as shown here (using plain old C# 1.0 syntax to put us in a pre-generics mood):

```
ArrayList primes = new ArrayList();
primes.Add(2);
primes.Add(3);
primes.Add(5);
primes.Add(7);

foreach (int prime in primes)
{
    Console.WriteLine(prime);
}
```

Even though the elements appear as `System.Object` to the `foreach` loop's innards, C# allows the user to specify a more specific type for the iteration variable. Internally, a cast is carried out. Obviously, if the (nongeneric) source collection contains something of a type incompatible with the iteration variable's type, an `InvalidCastException` will occur. But typically that indicates you have a bug in the first place because most collections are meant to be containers for elements of the same type (or at least something more specific than `System.Object`; for example, `Fruit`). One more caveat is the hidden cost of boxing and unboxing (explained in Chapter 9, "Introducing Types," in the section, "Boxing") associated with nongeneric collections containing value typed objects. And the use of nongeneric collection types in the post .NET 1.x era should be less common than it used to be.

DUCK TYPING

The fact that the `foreach` statement doesn't strictly depend on interfaces but rather can deal with patterns that look "okay" for the task at hand is a form of duck typing in the language. Some shiver at the thought of this, but let's be honest: What are the chances that an object that has a `GetEnumerator` method that returns an object with `MoveNext` and `Current` is not meant to be enumerated over?

More Trivia

The `foreach` statement was arguably the most complex statement in C# 1.0 in terms of its behavior and implementation. One more characteristic it has is the read-only treatment of the iteration variable. The `IEnumerable` pattern is a one-direction retrieval-only mechanism, so there's no way to stuff items back in. In fact, the enumerator's contract is that it requires only a getter for the `Current` property. Therefore, every attempt to assign to the iteration variable (either directly or indirectly; for example, using the ++ operator) will result in a compile-time error. Figure 7.18 shows an error message originating from an attempt to mutate the iteration variable.

```
var primes = new List<int> { 2, 3, 5, 7 };
foreach (int prime in primes)
{
    prime++;
}   Cannot assign to 'prime' because it is a 'foreach iteration variable'
```

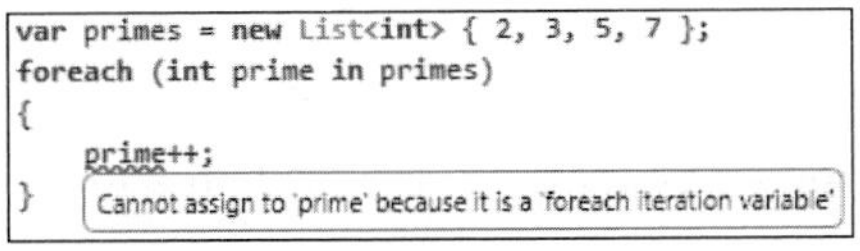

FIGURE 7.18   Read-only treatment of the iteration variable.

Notice that the read-only property is a shallow concept. Although you can't replace the element itself, you can change its content when dealing with a reference type. Assume you have some `Account` class that keeps the balance of a banking account and you want to pay out interest (ignoring lots of complications around transactions):

```
foreach (var account in bank.GetAccounts())
{
    account.Balance *= 1.05m;
}
```

In addition to this, various collection types enforce rules that make it impossible to change a collection's contents while enumeration is in progress. Such conditions are checked at runtime, causing an exception to be thrown when a violation is detected. Figure 7.19 shows the runtime exception occurring from the loop when the underlying collection has been tampered with during iteration.

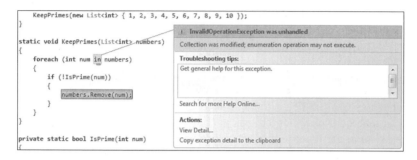

FIGURE 7.19   Don't modify collections while enumerating over them.

A Peek at Iterators

Now that you've learned about iteration constructs in general and the `foreach` loop's capability to deal with `IEnumerable` objects, we're in an ideal position to introduce the concept of iterators. So far, all enumeration sources we've seen are collections of some sort. But what about creating our own sources to provide *sequences* of data consumable through enumeration?

Observe the true nature of the `foreach` loop first. In its true essence, it pulls data from some sequence of elements by querying that sequence using the `MoveNext` and `Current` members. Nothing requires the data returned to be available before the iteration starts; what about computing it as we go? Here we enter the domain of *lazy evaluation*.

An example of a lazy computation is to ask prime numbers one by one rather than have a persistent collection of them in memory. For this sequence of data to be consumable through the `foreach` loop, it needs to expose the iteration pattern explained in the previous section.

So let's give it a try to make up such a lazy computation by hand. Rest assured that the feature discussed here, iterators, will make the following code much easier to write. I merely want to point out what a royal pain writing such a thing by hand can be. First, we define a class that will act as the entry point to the computation. Here the enumeration pattern starts by providing a `GetEnumerator` method:

```
class PrimeGenerator
{
    public PrimeEnumerator GetEnumerator()
    {
        return new PrimeEnumerator();
    }
}
```

We detail the mechanics of declaring classes and their members in Chapter 9, but as you can see, there isn't much to it. Ultimately, we want to be able to use an instance of this type as the source for a `foreach` statement:

```
foreach (int prime in new PrimeGenerator())
{
    Console.WriteLine(prime);

    Console.Write("Want More? ");
    if (!Console.ReadLine().ToLower().StartsWith("y"))
        break;
}
```

Notice we're using the flexibility of the `foreach` statement because we're not implementing any of the `IEnumerable` interfaces. There's no reason not to implement those, but to keep it simple I chose to omit details on interface implementation for now.

Next up is the enumerator itself. Here, we need to have two members: One is the `MoveNext` method; the other is the `Current` property with a *get accessor* available on it. Don't worry too much about the details for now but concentrate on how our nice algorithm now needs to maintain state across `MoveNext` calls. A call to `MoveNext` signals that the consumer—in our case, the `foreach` statement—is asking us for the next element. At that point, we need to know what the last prime was we yielded back to the caller and start our search for the next one. When we find one, we need to break from the loop, assign to the _current field (which is used in the `Current` property to return a value to the caller) and return from `MoveNext` saying we found one:

```
class PrimeEnumerator
{
    private int _current = 1;

    public bool MoveNext()
    {
        for (int num = _current + 1; num < int.MaxValue; num++)
        {
            bool foundDiv = false;

            for (int div = 2; div <= Math.Sqrt(num); div++)
            {
                if (num % div == 0)
                {
                    foundDiv = true;
                    break;
                }
            }
```

```
            if (!foundDiv)
            {
                _current = num;
                return true;
            }
        }

        return false;
    }

    public int Current
    {
        get { return _current; }
    }
}
```

Notice how I've bound the outer loop to `int.MaxValue` to avoid overflow conditions, which would put us in the land of negative integers where prime numbers are ill defined (and worse, our algorithm would choke on it). Figure 7.20 illustrates lazy computation of prime numbers using an iterator in practice.

FIGURE 7.20   Computing prime numbers on request.

As you can see, creating an iterator by hand is doable but not very appealing. And here we're not even dealing with resource deallocation (through `IDisposable`) or more complex control flow inside the iterator. Starting with C# 2.0, iterators can be used to make writing such a beast much easier. In fact, the LINQ to Objects implementation is almost completely based on this feature (as you will see in Chapter 20).

Recall our PrintPrimes example? If not, browse back to the section "The `for` Loop" and commit it to memory. Now look at the following code and search for the few differences:

```
static IEnumerable<int> GetPrimes(int max)
{
    for (int num = 2; num < max; num++)
    {
        bool foundDiv = false;

        for (int div = 2; div <= Math.Sqrt(num); div++)
        {
            if (num % div == 0)
            {
                foundDiv = true;
                break;
            }
        }

        if (!foundDiv)
        {
            yield return num;
        }
    }
}
```

To make things easy, I've highlighted the differences in bold:

▶ The return type of the method has become IEnumerable<int>. This has the potential of turning the whole method body into an iterator if the feature mentioned in the next point is used.

▶ Instead of returning from the method using the plain-vanilla return keyword, we yield objects back to the caller on a one-by-one basis using the yield return keywords instead.

Internally, iterators do precisely what we've done by hand: They build up a state machine that keeps track of the point in execution where control was yielded so that a subsequent MoveNext call can resume in a state where the previous call left off. In addition, the generator iterator code ensures proper cleanup of resources that are used within the iterator's code. It also deals with multithreaded access so that multiple iterations can be in flight simultaneously. Without going into detail, let's just glance at the macroscopic structure of the generated code. Figure 7.21 shows the complexity of an iterator through the glasses of ILDASM.

FIGURE 7.21   Generated code for an iterator.

All we have to do now is patch up our consuming code:

```
foreach (int prime in GetPrimes(int.MaxValue))
{
    Console.WriteLine(prime);

    Console.Write("Want More? ");
    if (!Console.ReadLine().ToLower().StartsWith("y"))
        break;
}
```

The most important property of an iterator is without doubt the fact it keeps the code readable, as it was intended to look in the first place. Everyone knows return; now you simply use yield return and don't have to worry with all the bookkeeping around suspending and resuming the iterator's execution. All such plumbing is taken care of by the compiler.

To whet your appetite about LINQ, let's give away the implementation of one of its query operators: Where (a method, hence with a capital letter). We've already used the where clause (a keyword, hence a lowercase letter) in a previous example to filter out those processes whose memory footprint is larger than 50MB:

```
const int MB = 1024 * 1024;
var memHungry = from proc in Process.GetProcesses()
                where proc.WorkingSet64 > 50 * MB
                select new { proc.ProcessName, MB = proc.WorkingSet64 / MB };
```

The where keyword is just syntactical sugar over a call to a Where method, which in this context is referred to as a *query operator*. We detail this translation of query expressions into method calls in more detail during our coverage of LINQ in Chapter 19, but here's what the query expression in the preceding code "desugars" into:

```
var memHungry =
    Process.GetProcesses()
        .Where(proc => proc.WorkingSet64 > 50 * MB)
        .Select(proc => new { proc.ProcessName, MB = proc.WorkingSet64 / MB });
```

LINQ to Object's Where operator is implemented as follows:

```
public static IEnumerable<T> Where<T>(this IEnumerable<T> source,
                                      Func<T, bool> predicate)
{
    foreach (T item in source)
    {
        if (predicate(item))
        {
            yield return item;
        }
    }
}
```

I've omitted some details here around parameter validation, which you'll see later. More important to understand is how this iterator works. First, notice it's a generic method that can deal with any IEnumerable<T> as its input. The fact the first parameter has the this modifier on it makes it an *extension method*. This allows slightly different and more natural calling syntax by allowing that argument to appear as the left side:

```
result = src.Where(predicate);
```

The preceding code is the same as the following:

```
result = Enumerable.Where(src, predicate);
```

Enumerable is the name of the class in which this Where method is implemented; its namespace is System.Linq, as you will see later. Either way, the first calling syntax definitely feels more natural because you can read it from left to right: Take the src and apply the Where operator, giving it a predicate. In fact, in our example, Select is another such query operator. Without extension methods, the whole query (expressed as method calls) would look like this:

```
var memHungry =
    Enumerable.Select(
        Enumerable.Where(
            Process.GetProcesses(),
            proc => proc.WorkingSet64 > 50 * MB
        ), proc => new { proc.ProcessName, MB = proc.WorkingSet64 / MB }
    );
```

Do you still recognize the original query with a simple glance? No. Although extension methods are purely cosmetic, they serve a very important goal: code clarity (would that be the reason LINQ's original code name was Clarity?).

Back to our Where operator implementation. By now you should have enough intellectual baggage to understand the essence of it:

```
foreach (T item in source)
    {
        if (predicate(item))
        {
            yield return item;
        }
    }
```

On the outer level, we loop over a sequence "source" of type IEnumerable<T>, so the elements are of type T, whatever that may be. That's the essence of programming with generics: You end up with an abstraction over "any type" by using a type parameter. Inside the loop, we use delegate invocation to call through the predicate delegate. Its type is Func<T, bool>, a generic type that's defined as follows:

```
delegate TResult Func<T, TResult>(T arg0);
```

So this Func generic type of arity 2 (meaning it has two generic type parameters) can represent any unary function: Given one argument of type T, it produces an answer of type TResult. Here are a few examples to make the use of this function delegate type clear:

```
Func<int, int> twice = x => x * 2;
Func<string, int> length = s => s.Length;
```

Here we're using lambda expressions (introduced and briefly discussed earlier in this chapter). Notice how the same Func<,> delegate type can be used with different generic type arguments to denote functions operating on different types. Generics once again.

In the context of our Where query operator, we're describing a function that goes from type T to System.Boolean. That's what a predicate is all about: asking whether an element should be included in the resulting sequence. And that's precisely what happens in the `if` statement. If the predicate says yes, the element is yielded to the caller. And all of this is done in a lazy fashion: When the caller stops pulling out elements from the query, no more elements are analyzed, and the loop terminates. Fascinating, isn't it?

LINQ enables us to arbitrarily chain together several operators. For filtering, `Where` is used; it takes in a sequence and produces a new one. In our sample query, we fed the output of this filtering operation into the projection done by `Select`, producing yet another sequence. And we can continue doing so, with operations like sorting, grouping, aggregation, and so on. This concept is illustrated graphically in Figure 7.22.

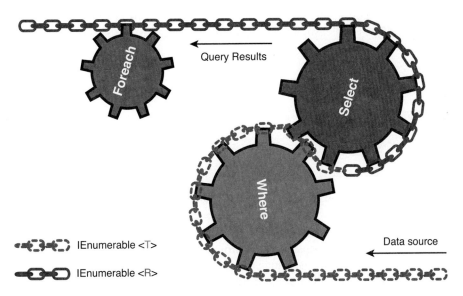

FIGURE 7.22   Interaction between different iterators in a query.

This use of wheels and chains precisely illustrates the point. The `foreach` statement essentially pulls the chain, causing the `Select` wheel to move. Internally, this one uses a `foreach` statement to suck data out of the results of the `Where` query operator. And that one ultimately consumes data from the data source; in our case, `Process.GetProcesses()`. As soon as the consuming `foreach` statement stops running (for example, because of a break statement), the iterators connected through the chain stop ticking, too.

We discuss LINQ in much more detail later on, but I want you to remember one thing right now. If you're writing loop constructs to process data, LINQ might be a better choice. For one thing, it leads to a dramatic improvement in code readability, and laziness can be an advantage to avoid needless computation.

As a little exercise, try to rewrite the process-filtering example in terms of typical loop constructs. I'm sure you'll come to realize the intent of the code gets buried underneath the imperative style of code. And we're not yet doing more fancy query operations like sorting, grouping, and so on.

Loops in the Age of Concurrency

Looked at from a different perspective, loop constructors are essentially a source of tasks. If every iteration of a loop is independent from another iteration's state, there's no reason the individual iterations can't be run in parallel. In the age of multicore processors on every desk, better ways to unleash the hardware's power are a much-searched-for treasure. The new System.Threading namespace additions in .NET 4.0 provide for this in various ways, one of which is the concept of parallel loop constructs. We look at this in more detail in Chapter 30, "Task Parallelism and Data Parallelism." Figure 7.23 shows the Parallel class's static methods.

FIGURE 7.23   The System.Threading.Parallel type's parallel loop constructs.

It's important to realize that those constructs are provided by libraries as opposed to any of the managed code languages. This is a huge advantage because all languages immediately benefit from this addition while not committing to new language syntax just yet. They may slip into the language at some point, however, but only if those constructs become popular. However, because C# has become expressive enough due to the introduction of lambda expressions in version 3.0, the use of those constructs feels quite natural:

```
Parallel.For(1, 100, i =>
{
    // Loop body code goes here.
});
```

To make parallel loops worthwhile, the work they do inside their loop bodies should be sufficiently heavy to exceed the overhead of setting up the multithreaded infrastructure required. One place where those conditions are met is when dealing with data-intensive operations, as in LINQ. For example, when filtering a huge set of data, it's possible to partition the input data and let every processor core handle a part of it. Figure 7.24 shows parallel execution of filtering.

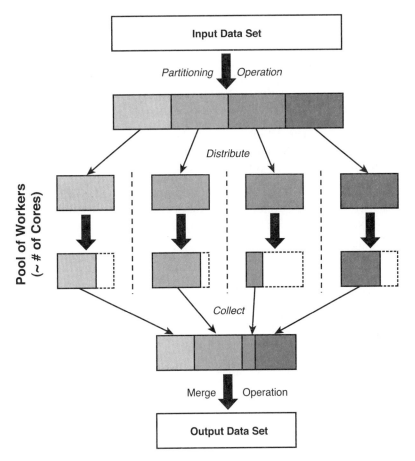

FIGURE 7.24   Data filtering lends itself to parallelization.

PLINQ, for Parallel LINQ, is an implementation of the query operators that allow for parallel execution, leveraging the new System.Threading.Tasks namespace in .NET 4.0. For an input set as small as the processes on your machine, this won't be worth it. For larger input sets, however, this can make a significant difference. The change required to make a query parallel is easy:

```
var memHungry = from proc in Process.GetProcesses().AsParallel()
                where proc.WorkingSet64 > 50 * MB
                select new { proc.ProcessName, MB = proc.WorkingSet64 / MB };
```

The `goto` Statement

In true C and C++ style, C# provides a goto statement to perform unconditional control transfer to a point in the code marked by a label. The greatest computer scientists have debated the use of goto for years:

▶ Edsger Dijkstra, a Dutch computer scientist, published his infamous paper "Go To Statement Considered Harmful" in 1968. At that time, structured programming (if, while, and so on) was gaining popularity, and most typical cases of goto got eliminated by it. And true, use of goto all over the place quickly results in spaghetti code.

▶ Donald Knuth, known for his "The Art of Computer Programming" series, stated this viewpoint is too extreme and argued that in some cases use of the goto statement still makes sense. He did so in his "Structured Programming with go to Statements" paper a few years later in 1974.

The goto statement has often been used, even in the world of structured programming, for error propagation (for example, in the world of COM with its success-reporting through HRESULTs):

```
// Dealing with HRESULT return codes in C or C++.
HRESULT InitDownloadManager()
{
    IBackgroundCopyManager* g_pbcm = NULL;
    HRESULT hr;

    hr = CoInitializeEx(NULL, COINIT_APARTMENTTHREADED);
    if (FAILED(hr))
        goto Exit;

    hr = CoCreateInstance(__uuidof(BackgroundCopyManager), NULL,
                    CLSCTX_LOCAL_SERVER,
                    __uuidof(IBackgroundCopyManager),
                    (void**) &g_pbcm);
    if (FAILED(hr))
        goto Exit;

    // More code here.

Exit:
    // More cleanup here.

    if (g_pbcm)
    {
```

```
        g_pbcm->Release();
        g_pbcm = NULL;
    }

    return hr;
}
```

To make matters worse, the check-for-FAILED-and-jump pattern is sometimes obfuscated using a CKHR macro. Nevertheless, without a better error condition propagation system, it can be argued this style of coding is the best one can use to propagate errors.

However, in the world of the common language runtime and C#, we have a full-fledged exception-handling mechanism (as explained later), so error propagation is no longer an argument to justify the use of the goto statement. Personally, I haven't had the honor (?) of using a goto statement in C# for a long time. One place where it can come in handy is to jump out of nested loops, which is only supported through the use of the goto statement in C#. But that, too, I haven't had to do for an equally long time.

No matter how unlikely the need for a goto statement is nowadays, it isn't fair to omit it from the discussion. The crux of it? A labeled target and a goto statement:

```
        // Code here.
Target:
        // More code here.
        goto Target;

        // Even more code here.
```

Internally, the goto statement is as straightforward as an unconditional jump in IL code. Notice that branching is a core concept in the world of IL, providing the fuel that makes various statements run. If statements and switch statements typically jump forward to the place where the code to be executed lives. Loops, on the other hand, jump backward to reexecute a code block over and over again as long as a condition holds. So, yes, IL is spaghetti code but at an appropriate level. The real concerns about misuse of goto are about use in higher-level languages.

COMEFROM

Goto has become so infamous that some (not-so-useful) languages have introduced the dual concept of "come from" as a joke. In fact, this idea is not as stupid as it sounds and is used in flow analysis mechanisms inside compilers and such. But useful as a real control flow mechanism? Not so much.

The careful reader will have noticed something weird about the preceding piece of code: How can control ever reach the comment stating "Even more code here" if there's an

unconditional jump in front of it? Similar situations exist for loops that run forever or
return right inside their body, leaving the code following the loop unreachable:

```
while (true)
{
    // Act busy.
}


Console.WriteLine("Done.");
```

One task the compiler carries out is reachability analysis to find dead pieces of code; those
typically indicate leftovers of some refactoring or reveal a bug where the developer still
thinks some piece of code executes sometimes but in fact never can. In the code editor,
unreachable code is marked as a green squiggly warning (see Figure 7.25).

FIGURE 7.25   Unreachable code analysis raising a warning.

This brings up the point of warnings versus errors. Most of the time, warnings raise valid
concerns that the developer should address. To avoid sloppiness, you can turn on the
Treat Warnings as Errors mode in the project configuration. Also make sure the warning
level is set to the highest available (see Figure 7.26).

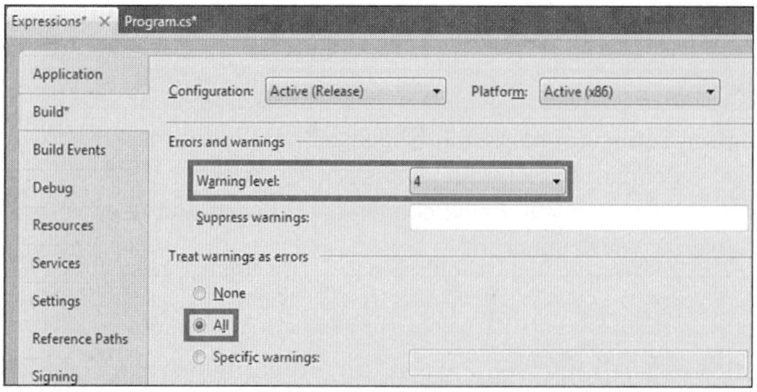

FIGURE 7.26   Configuring levels for and treatment of warnings.

But what if you encounter a warning that you think is safe to ignore? In that case, you can suppress it, either at the project level using the Suppress Warnings list, where you enter a comma-separated list of warning numbers, or in line with the code. The first thing to know, though, is the warning's number, which you can find in the Output window, as shown in Figure 7.27.

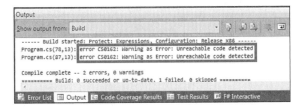

FIGURE 7.27   Finding warning numbers through the Output window entries for the build.

Suppressing this particular warning can (should!) be seen as complete nonsense, but I am just illustrating the point that—as a last resort, after you've convinced yourself repeatedly—warnings can be suppressed. To do this inside the code, use a #pragma *directive* (an abbreviation for pragmatic, also an inheritance from C and C++). Figure 7.28 shows a #pragma directive in the code editor.

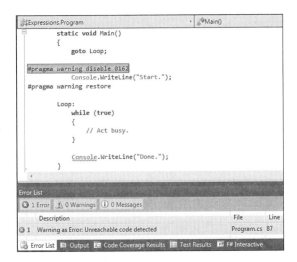

FIGURE 7.28   Use of a #pragma directive to suppress a warning.

The 0162 number is what we found inside the Output window as the warning number. Also be sure to restore the suppression as a best practice to avoid covering up potential other occurrences of the same warning that you didn't want to suppress. If you really think a certain warning should be suppressed for the whole project, you can do so in the project's Build configuration, as pointed out before.

The `return` Statement

In a world where method calls are one of the most essential ways to structure code, we need two core concepts: One is to call a method, using invocation syntax, as you saw when we discussed expressions; the other is a way to return from a method, transferring control back to the caller. Intimately related to this is the concept of a call stack as a means to keep track of who's called what. Figure 7.29 shows the transitions of the call stack when making a method call and returning a result.

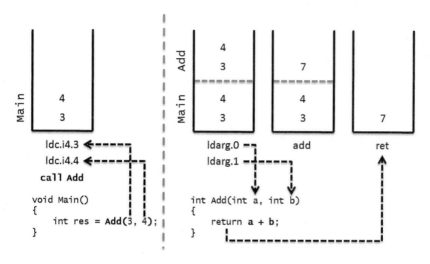

FIGURE 7.29   Illustrating the call stack.

The `return` statement has two forms. When used in a procedure—a method that returns the magical void type—it takes no operand and simply means to transfer control back to the caller before reaching the end of the current method:

```
void PrintName(string name)
{
    if (name == null)
        return;

    Console.WriteLine(name);
}
```

Depending on the structure of the code, this might be cleaner than using opposite logic where the end of the method is used as the one and only place where control is transferred to the caller. Such a style tends to yield quite some indentation typically and decreases code readability:

```
void PrintName(string name)
{
    if (name != null)
    {
        // Imagine this code is much,
        // much
        // longer...
        Console.WriteLine(name);
    }
}
```

The second case is where a method has a *return type*, requiring the return statement to specify an expression as its operand. That expression should be implicitly convertible to the return type of the containing method:

```
void Add(int a, int b)
{
    return a + b;
}
```

All possible execution paths through the code should eventually lead to a point where a return occurs (modulo edge cases like having an infinite loop). If this condition is not met, the compiler will complain (see Figure 7.30).

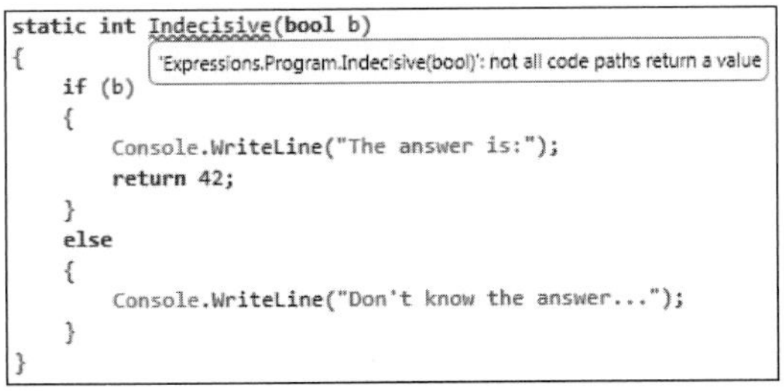

```
static int Indecisive(bool b)
{                   'Expressions.Program.Indecisive(bool)': not all code paths return a value
    if (b)
    {
        Console.WriteLine("The answer is:");
        return 42;
    }
    else
    {
        Console.WriteLine("Don't know the answer...");
    }
}
```

FIGURE 7.30   All code paths should return a value.

With a void-returning method, it's fine to just fall out of the current method upon reaching the end of the method. There's no value to return anyway.

Summary

In this chapter's primer to statements, we started by looking at treating expressions as statements, and then explored blocks and declarations to set the scene. Next, the bare-essential control flow mechanisms, such as selection and loop statements, were explored. You even got a peek at iterators, which are the essential glue that binds LINQ to Objects, as you will see later.

To further understand control flow, we looked at the (mostly) evil `goto` statement and `return` statements. There's more to be told about more advanced control flow with regard to exceptions and mechanisms to ensure proper resource clean-up, which are part of the next chapter.

IN THIS CHAPTER

▶ Exception Handling 409

▶ Deterministic Resource
Cleanup 438

▶ Locking on Objects 447

CHAPTER 8

Basics of Exceptions and Resource Management

Continuing our exploration of statements in the C# programming language, we now look at concepts such as exceptions, locks, and proper resource disposal. Later chapters detail many of those aspects. For now, it's essential for you to have a good understanding of the breadth of statements.

Exception Handling

One strength of managed code lies in the structured approach to error handling using exceptions. Recall our native code fragment in the context of the goto statement's discussion in Chapter 7, "Simple Control Flow," in the section, "The goto Statement?" Let's refresh our minds and highlight a few aspects of it:

```
// Dealing with HRESULT return codes in C or C++.
HRESULT InitDownloadManager()
{
    IBackgroundCopyManager* g_pbcm = NULL;
    HRESULT hr;

    hr = CoInitializeEx(NULL, COINIT_APARTMENTTHREADED);
    if (FAILED(hr))
        goto Exit;

    hr =
CoCreateInstance(__uuidof(BackgroundCopyManager), NULL,
                CLSCTX_LOCAL_SERVER,
                    __uuidof(IBackgroundCopyManager),
                    (void**) &g_pbcm);
```

```
    if (FAILED(hr))
        goto Exit;

    // More code here.

Exit:
    // More cleanup here.

    if (g_pbcm)
    {
        g_pbcm->Release();
        g_pbcm = NULL;
    }

    return hr;
}
```

Our observations are as follows:

▸ Methods typically return an error code, whether it's a plain old int (as seen in Win32 APIs) or something more advanced like an HRESULT (as practiced in the world of COM). This monopolizes one of the most useful pieces of a method signature, the return type, leaving no space for a real return value. And numeric error codes don't tell anything; one needs to have a header file or some gigantic table on the side to look up the meaning of an error code.

▸ This approach reflects itself onto the caller. First, callers need to be disciplined enough to check the return value for every single call to make sure execution succeeded. But that's not the only thing: Because the return type is not used to return the true result of the call, output parameters need to be wired up by passing addresses to local variables.

▸ Cleanup logic is tedious, as well, making sure no cases are missed regardless of how the method executes (success or failure). The most convenient way to organize this is by means of an unconditional jump to clean up logic near the end of the method body. However, this decentralizes the use of a resource from the place where it gets released. During code inspection, this can be rather annoying because it distracts you from the real intent of the code.

▸ Errors need to be propagated manually if the code is not willing to deal with certain error cases itself, hoping someone will not ignore it upstream. All it takes to end up in a nasty situation is one sloppy method on the call stack that ignores the error code. You can hope for the best but nothing more.

In short, exceptions provide a means for detailed error propagation that doesn't interfere with the method signatures (highly reduced need for the use of output parameters) and allows for a structured way to catch errors and handle them.

Exceptions Are Objects

One question is how errors are represented in the world of exceptions. Given that the CLR is an object-oriented platform, the answer is pretty obvious: objects. We won't look at how to define exception types of our own just yet but will instead focus on the essence of such a type and look at how exceptions can be *thrown* and *caught*.

Exceptions are subtypes of a class called `System.Exception`, which defines the following useful members (see Figure 8.1). (I've omitted a few irrelevant details for now.)

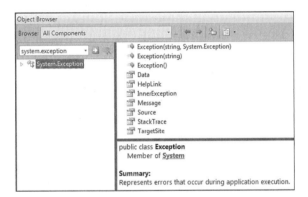

FIGURE 8.1   Most relevant members of the `Exception` base type.

One key piece of information about an exception lies outside its members: the type name of the exception itself. For example, an error signaling a missing file will be represented as a `FileNotFoundException`, deriving from the `System.Exception` type in one way or another. Compare this to the meaningless integral value 2 used in the Win32 API to represent such a condition. (To verify this for yourself, you can print the corresponding message at the command line by running net helpmsg 2.)

A second piece of information is found in the `Message` property, which contains a string explaining the problem. This can be shown to the user but is useful during debugging, too. One string message can be worth a thousand cryptic error codes. HelpLink is sometimes populated with a URI to available help information.

Other more-technical error details can be retrieved through the `StackTrace` property, which dumps information about the location where the error happened in terms of the call stack. This highlights a key aspect of the exception mechanism in the CLR: Errors propagate automatically through the call stack as long as they're not caught. Contrast this with the manual and error-prone propagation of error codes.

Causes of Exceptions

Different situations give rise to exceptions:

- ▶ Code defects, such as forgetting null checks causing NullReferenceExceptions or passing invalid arguments to some method that signals the defect using an ArgumentException or variation thereof.

- ▶ Runtime disasters that prevent the CLR's execution engine from continuing execution; for example, due to insufficient memory (OutOfMemoryException) or a stack overflow.

- ▶ Error conditions in the environment where the code is operating, such as a missing configuration file, failure to connect to a web service or a database, or an external component failing.

- ▶ Rarely ever recommended, exceptions can sometimes be (mis)used to drive certain aspects of code execution. An example is the runtime's use of ThreadAbortException to signal to a thread that it should terminate.

The developer's course of action depends on the category under which an exception type falls (which, admittedly is an ill-defined concept)—an exploration.

Code Defects and Input Validation

Failure to check for null in a case where it's not permitted is inexcusable and a bug in your code, for sure. On the other hand, failure to pass in a valid argument to some method could be a bug or not, depending on where the input comes from. For example:

```
int[] numbers = new [] { 2, 3, 5, 7 };
for (int i = 0; i <= numbers.Length; i++)
{
    Console.WriteLine(numbers[i]);
}
```

Do you see the problem? We're not using the right range of indices to retrieve elements from the array because of an off-by-one error; the less-than operation should be noninclusive. This is a bug, for sure, causing an IndexOutOfRangeException.

But what if the input to some API comes from the user? It really depends. Some APIs provide a means for you to validate input before calling the method that does the real work. Others provide a "safe" function that won't throw an exception in case of an error but will instead signal it using a Boolean or such. Let's start by showing an example of an API that throws in case of invalid input:

```
Console.Write("What's your age? ");
string age = Console.ReadLine();
int yearOfBirth = DateTime.Now.Year - int.Parse(age);
Console.WriteLine("I bet you were born around " + yearOfBirth + ".");
```

Here we ask the user for an age, which should be a numeric value. The `ReadLine` method returns a string, so we need a way to convert from a string to an integer, which can be done using the static `Parse` method on `System.Int32` (here using the C# keyword). But what if the user writes something non-numeric or something that doesn't fit in the precision of a 32-bit signed integer? Right, `int.Parse` will throw an exception (see Figure 8.2).

FIGURE 8.2   An unhandled exception causes the program to terminate.

From this, you can see how unhandled exceptions will crash the program. Depending on the computer's configuration, this will either result in a dialog where the user can choose to attach a debugger or a Watson crash memory dump that can be used for post-mortem debugging. Obviously, your code should protect against such a program crash for these kinds of exceptions because they're within your control.

For example, to harden the integer-parsing code shown previously, you could handle the `FormatException`. However, APIs that require exceptions to be handled for a reasonable scenario are not well designed. Code gets more obscure, and there's a significant performance hit incurred by throwing and catching an exception. Notice this performance penalty is irrelevant if exceptions are kept for true exceptions cases: If the bottleneck for execution speed of your program lies in exception handling, you have a much more serious issue to tackle first. But let's show what handling the exception would look like:

```
Console.Write("What's your age? ");
string age = Console.ReadLine();
try
{
    int yearOfBirth = DateTime.Now.Year - int.Parse(age);
    Console.WriteLine("I bet you were born around " + yearOfBirth + ".");
}
catch (FormatException)
```

```
{
    Console.WriteLine("Invalid age specified.");
}
```

We explore the details of the exception-handling syntax later, but the idea is fairly easy: The code within the try block is "tried" for execution. If an exception occurs somewhere in there, the runtime searches for handlers that can deal with the exception type at hand. If one is found in a catch block, the exception is caught, and control is transferred to the handler's block.

Notice that we could have restricted the contents of the try block to just the int.Parse call because that's the one that can throw a FormatException. Although restricting the protected region is a good idea in many cases, doing so in this example would cause the code to change even more by introducing another local variable for the int.Parse result. Feel free to try this at home.

As an exercise, try to build some retry logic around this using a loop and observe how much more obfuscated the code gets because it needs to deal with an error condition for the perfectly valid scenario of the user entering dumb input.

One good thing to keep in mind when dealing with input to an API is to make sure input is properly validated, especially when the input is under your control. In this case, however, the user can specify every possible string, and there's no way of knowing upfront whether that string represents a valid integer. The way to do that is to use Parse, which throws an exception if the input is invalid. We're in a circular argument here. In this case, there's a "safe" API called TryParse that will signal validity of input using a Boolean:

```
Console.Write("What's your age? ");
string ageString = Console.ReadLine();
int age;
if (int.TryParse(ageString, out age))
{
    int yearOfBirth = DateTime.Now.Year - age;
    Console.WriteLine("I bet you were born around " + yearOfBirth + ".");
}
```

Notice TryParse is using a feature we didn't quite explore yet, *output parameters*, to allow a method to return other values besides the method return value itself. We take a closer look at this feature after we discuss parameter-passing styles such as by reference and by value.

Again as an exercise, try to create a retry loop around this using a loop. Tip: The do statement will work very well in this case, allowing you to ask for an age until a valid integral number is specified that causes TryParse to succeed.

IMPROVING APPLICATION PROGRAMMING INTERFACES

In the previous sections, you've actually read about lessons learned in API design directly inside the BCL itself. The .NET 1.x libraries lacked "safe" Try variants for parsing methods on various basic types, requiring users to catch a FormatException to validate input for a required type. This API shortcoming was addressed in .NET 2.0 with the introduction of the Try variants illustrated here.

At the time of the introduction of the first version of the .NET Framework, not all API design guidelines were perfectly tuned yet. This whole new way to deal with error conditions is like a new toy that could easily be overused when older approaches are more suitable. int.TryParse is a good example of this. Error reporting through return values definitely feels like the old-fashioned Win32 or COM style, but the difference here is the use of a Boolean rather than a meaningless integral value.

Runtime Disasters

You can't protect against some exception types, and you shouldn't try, either. Those are the real disastrous types that should cause the execution engine to shut down (because it can, and most likely will, become unstable).

One such type I hope you never see pop up is the ExecutionEngineException. It signals that the virtual machine has encountered an internal error. More commonly seen are exceptions that signal a lack of much-required resources, such as call stack space (StackOverflowException) or heap memory (OutOfMemoryException). The latter one will occur if, after the bravest attempts of the garbage collector, not enough space is found in the process's virtual memory address space to provide room for a requested object allocation. But let's focus on the former one; it's much easier to reproduce for illustration purposes.

The call stack is a finite resource. With every method call, the stack depth grows until that method returns. One really interesting aspect of the use of a call stack is the capability to write recursive algorithms, where a method calls itself (most likely with different arguments). A typical example is crawling tree structures to visit every node. If the tree depth is too large and/or the number of methods called for every node visit is substantially big, you'll overflow the stack. Lots of things live on this stack, such as method arguments and local variables, also contributing to memory pressure.

That said, call stacks typically have enough space to accommodate a program's needs, so hitting a StackOverflowException is most likely the result of a bug in the user's code:

```
static void Main()
{
    Main();
}
```

A little contrived, true, but it's always possible to have some silly typo somewhere causing a cycle in methods that call each other. If this goes on forever, your program is trapped in infinite recursion, but you'll learn soon enough through this exception shown in Figure 8.3.

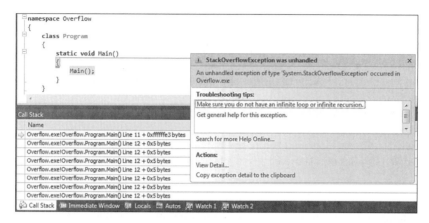

FIGURE 8.3   Overflowing the call stack.

THE CASE OF MY SILLY TYPO (AND NAMING CONVENTIONS)

I had the honor of plowing through a stack overflow because of a silly typo. Using XML serialization APIs, object instances can be created from an XML file: <Student> maps on the Student type; you get the idea. Attributes of XML elements are mapped onto properties, and nesting can occur. Life was good until I hit this weird stack overflow exception. XML being hierarchical, my immediate thought was an issue with the deserializer API implementation getting stuck in infinite recursion. Always blame others first, right?

Because I couldn't pinpoint the issue from looking at the call stack, I started peeling off complexity from my objects. Each object, representing a Student or whatnot, had many properties. In an attempt to prove my theory of the serializer being at fault, I took away half of the properties until the code ran and put them back gradually until it failed again. Here's the property I narrowed the problem down to:

```
private string name;

public string Name
{
    get { return name; }
    set { Name = value; }
}
```

Do you see the flaw? No? Look again and remember that letter case matters in C#. The deserializer needs to set properties based on attributes. It does so by calling the property set accessors. Because this code was written before C# 3.0's introduction of *auto-implemented properties* (discussed later), I had to create storage fields myself for every property. The standard pattern is to create trivial getter and setter accessors around those in corresponding properties.

However, I used the wrong letter case on the name of the field in the setter: Instead of writing name, I wrote Name, which is the name of the property itself. That's the source of the unbounded recursion. Assigning to a property calls its setter, and we're doing this from the setter itself. The reason I didn't run into this problem outside the deserializer's case was because my types had constructors defined for use elsewhere, which directly assigned to the underlying fields:

```
public Student(string name)
{
    this.name = name;
}
```

Three lessons learned here are as follows:

- ▶ Be sure to have high code coverage with unit tests, even for things that seem as trivial as property setters.
- ▶ Naming conventions can help reduce the likelihood of introducing problems. Ever since, I prefix my fields with an underscore.
- ▶ Don't blame others blindly, especially when talking about framework code that's highly tested. That blame will bounce back at you quickly.

So the next time you see a stack overflow and you haven't intentionally written a deeply recursive algorithm, you can be quite sure you have some bug somewhere in your code.

Notice that the runtime doesn't enable you to catch disastrous exception types. No matter how hard you try, the runtime will give up all hope and terminate the process to avoid risking instabilities, data corruption, and so on.

TIDBIT FOR HARDCORE DEBUGGERS

Sometimes when people get deep into debugging managed code application crashes using advanced debuggers like WinDbg with SOS (more on that later), they get misled by the presence of an OutOfMemoryException object that you can find on the heap. Figure 8.4 uses SOS to prove the existence of this instance on the managed heap. For some reason, this sometimes leads novices to conclude an out-of-memory condition caused the program to fail. Chip vendors have probably benefited from this as developers recommended buying more RAM, but this is a completely wrong conclusion for reasons we're explaining here.

OutOfMemoryException doesn't necessarily (and usually doesn't) mean there's not enough physical memory in the machine. All it means is there's insufficient address space left in the executing process for the garbage collector to allocate additional space for the managed object heap. An in-depth discussion about virtual memory and address space is beyond the scope of this book, but you'll find such information in every self-respecting book on operating systems.

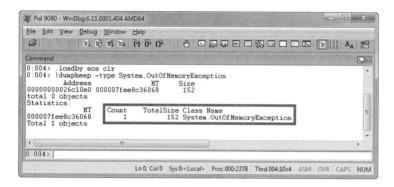

FIGURE 8.4   The pre-allocated `OutOfMemoryException` for managed code.

So you might wonder why there's an `OutOfMemoryException` to be found on the man-aged object heap at all times. Think about it and you'll see it's quite logical. Exceptions are classes, whose instances get allocated on the heap. If this particular exception type is used to indicate the inability to get more heap space for object allocations, how would you allocate space for the exception object itself when the condition arises? Right, you can't. So, early during the startup of the runtime, it allocates an instance of the `OutOfMemoryException` to have it ready in case it needs to be thrown.

Environment Error Conditions

Besides bugs such as null dereferences and out-of-bounds indexing or runtime disasters, there's also the situation of error conditions in the environment the code is operating under. For example, our code might rely on the existence of a file or expect to be able to create a network connection to another machine (for example, to access a database). It's outside the control of our code to ensure the environment is in a good condition. However, we can (and typically should) make our code robust against such failures to signal issues to the user or at least to terminate gracefully. Consider the following code:

```
static void PrintFile(string path)
{
    foreach (string line in File.ReadAllLines(path))
    {
        Console.WriteLine(line);
    }
}
```

To write this code, you have to import the `System.IO` namespace that contains the `File` type we're using to read all lines from a file. But can you spot the problem? Right, the file with the specified path might not exist at the time of executing this method. One thing we can do to mitigate against this condition, at least partially, is to check whether the file exists and take appropriate action if not:

```
if (!File.Exists(path))
{
    // Handle the problematic situation.
}
```

The question is, of course, whether we can handle the problem locally or should do the check higher up, at the point we pass the path to the method. This very much depends on your domain. Maybe a fallback to defaults exists, maybe not. Documenting the error-handling behavior of a method is very desirable, as you can see. This is no different for the BCL and .NET Framework library APIs. Figure 8.5 shows the list of exceptions that can be thrown from `File.ReadAllLines`.

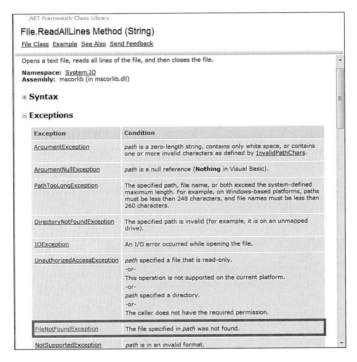

FIGURE 8.5   MSDN library documentation for `File.ReadAllLines` exceptions.

Notice how many other error conditions exist for this `System.IO` method. I've just selected one as the topic for discussion, but others are equally valid for consideration here. Some simply indicate bugs, such as `ArgumentNullException`, whereas lots of others indicate problems encountered during the core execution.

MORE TYPING?

Exceptions signaling silly bugs should be regarded as deferred code checks, to compensate for issues that can't be caught at compile time. Being a type system freak, I like to point out that some classes of errors could really be checked at compile time when enhancements to the type system are implemented. One case is the cruel null value, which could be avoided if non-null (non-void in Eiffel lingo) types were introduced. Range checks (for example, an integer needs to be a number between 1 and 10) could be avoided if it were possible to create a dedicated type with just that range.

Some of those ideas are actually getting implemented today. Non-null types can be mimicked (to enough of an extent that compile-time checking can be done) in the world of .NET 4.0 code contracts, as you will see later. Some other type systems allow type such as "int where value >= 1 && value <= 10."

However, even if we check for the file's existence upfront, we've only partially mitigated the problem. Between the time the check is carried out and the file is opened, there might have been a context switch that caused another program to delete, rename, move, lock, or secure the file. Perhaps the particular circumstances under which your code is running make this an unlikely situation, but it's important to realize the potential for problems here. Other factors are the amount of code that runs between when the check is carried out and the file operation is attempted and the location of the file (for example, a file share accessible to lots of users or machines).

Either way, if the file doesn't exist at the point ReadAllLines tries to open it to read its contents, a FileNotFoundException occurs (see Figure 8.6).

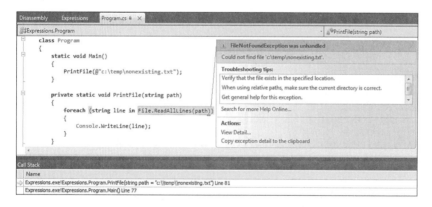

FIGURE 8.6   An unhandled FileNotFoundException showing up in the debugger.

In contrast to the preceding two categories of exceptions—the ones that originate from bugs and the ones that indicate truly fatal runtime circumstances—this sort of exception is fine to be caught in case a meaningful action can be defined in case of failure or maybe just to log the condition and terminate a unit of work. (For example, failure to handle a request should not bring down the whole server.) Let's take a look at how this can be done:

```
static void Main(string[] args)
{
    if (args.Length != 1)
    {
        string executable = Environment.GetCommandLineArgs()[0];
        string executableFileName = Path.GetFileName(executable);
        Console.WriteLine("Usage: {0} <file>", executableFileName);
        return;
    }

    string path = args[0];
    try
    {
        PrintFile(path);
    }
    catch (FileNotFoundException ex)
    {
        Console.ForegroundColor = ConsoleColor.Red;
        Console.WriteLine(ex.Message);
        Console.ResetColor();
    }
}
```

You run this example under the Visual Studio debugger by pressing F5, and you'll have to specify the command-line arguments. This can be done through the project properties, illustrated in Figure 8.7.

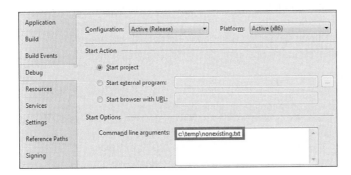

FIGURE 8.7   Specifying command-line arguments for the debugger.

In writing a little ad hoc tool, the use of File.Exists is likely acceptable, too. But there are lots of other exceptions we might want to mitigate, such as the

UnauthorizedException. Even the ArgumentException might need treatment in this case because it's not unimaginable for the user to specify an invalid path. As an exercise, implement a few other exception handlers and take a look at the properties available on the various exception types.

WHERE ARE THE CHECKED EXCEPTIONS?

Some other programming languages have the concept of checked exceptions by which a method declares the exceptions it may throw, forcing the caller either to catch the exception or propagate it to its caller:

```
string[] ReadAllLines(string path) throws FileNotFoundException /* and more */
```

Although this is a nice way to ensure proper exception handling, there are a couple of practical issues.

First, using checked exceptions on interface declarations is rather fragile. A practical implementation of the interface may require other exceptions to be thrown. For example, a GetUser interface method may be implemented based on file access (IOException being a reasonable error condition) or based on database access (where a SqlException may occur). And changing the interface after its initial release is a big no-no because you'll break everything that depends on it: Adding an exception type to a throws clause requires callers to handle or propagate it, so you end up breaking everything that already used the interface. You have a version issue at this point:

```
interface IUserManagementService
{
    User GetUser(string username) throws UserNotFoundException;
}
```

Second, use of checked exceptions can be very annoying because the compiler starts complaining about unhandled exception types all the time. In lots of cases, you find yourself in a project phase where you want to throw something together quickly, in a mindset of "I'll patch parts up later." The simplest way to get around excessive compiler warnings is either to catch and swallow exceptions on the spot ("oh, this will never happen") or propagate all of them by adding a throws Exception clause (that is, throwing the mother type of all exceptions accommodating for everything inside):

```
void Foo() throws Exception
{
    // Every checked exception is propagate unnoticed here.
}
```

You've effectively just suppressed the whole feature. Exceptions are unfortunately something you have to think about all the time, severely impairing your development productivity at times. It's not clear whether checked exceptions are worth the trouble because of those hidden rat holes. Therefore, C# (and many CLR languages) go for a more minimalist approach without checked exceptions.

Throwing Exceptions

Time for a more structured look at working with exceptions. We'll start with the act of throwing exceptions to signal an error condition. Not surprisingly, throwing an exception is done using the throw keyword, specifying an instance of an exception type. For example:

```
void DisplayUserProfile(string user)
{
    if (user == null)
        throw new ArgumentNullException("user");

    if (user == "")
        throw new ArgumentException("exception");

    if (!Profiles.Exists(user))
        throw new UserNotFoundException(user);

    // Do real work here.
}
```

The third exception type used here is a custom exception type, something we explore later. What matters here is the syntax of the throw statement, which is, as you can see, very straightforward. That said, I sometimes make the silly mistake of thinking throw also creates an instance:

```
throw /* don't forget new here */ ArgumentException("user")
```

So you might be getting your exception instance from elsewhere rather than by using a new expression in conjunction with the throw statement. This instance could be instantiated upfront (like OutOfMemoryException's single instance is in the runtime) or be retrieved by calling some method. The latter technique is often handy when exception messages have to be localized, which can be taken care of by custom logic in the exception creator method.

Handling Exceptions

Handling exceptions is done by protecting a certain block of code using try and having an exception handler associated with it using catch. You saw examples of this earlier, but let's take a closer look:

```
try
{
    PrintFile(path);
}
catch (FileNotFoundException ex)
{
```

```
Console.ForegroundColor = ConsoleColor.Red;
Console.WriteLine(ex.Message);
Console.ResetColor();
}
```

Here we're protecting the call to `PrintFile` against the `FileNotFoundException`. Of course, the protected block of code (following the `try` keyword) can consist of more than one line of code, but it's a good practice not to protect too much code if you're only after catching an exception from a specific call somewhere in there.

CURLY BRACES REQUIRED

Sometimes there are those unexplainable asymmetries in languages. Even though statements such as `if`, `while`, `for`, and so on enable you to omit curly braces if the embedded statement is just a one liner, `try` and its friends don't. Because I love curly braces (because the C# language lacks whitespace sensitivity), I'm not offended by this asymmetry.

Notice in the preceding code that the `PrintFile` method doesn't throw `FileNotFoundException` itself; instead, one of the methods it calls, `ReadAllLines`, does. This illustrates the intimate coupling that exists between exception propagation and the call stack. Contrast this to manual `HRESULT`-checking code, where it's the user's responsibility to propagate errors by hand all over the place.

In fact, it's not even the `ReadAllLines` method that executes the `throw` statement for this exception type. Internally, the `ReadAllLines` method calls into many more helper methods, and one of those will detect the problem and throw the exception. To illustrate this, first disable the Just My Code feature via Tools, Options, Debugging, General, as shown in Figure 8.8.

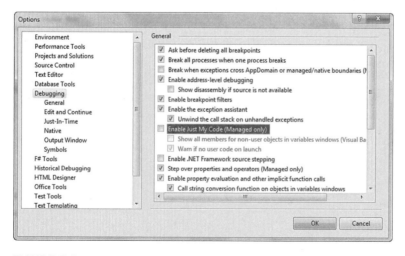

FIGURE 8.8   Disabling Just My Code.

Just My Code hides code you haven't written from various places like the Call Stack window. Because we're already handling the exception, simply executing the code won't enable us to observe the point where the exception is thrown. One way to get to see this is by inspecting the stack trace through the exception object's StackTrace property. You can try this by setting a breakpoint inside the exception-handler block and inspecting the ex local variable when the breakpoint is hit. Visual Studio also has an exception helper tool that can show you the exception that was caught (see Figure 8.9). After opening the exception helper, click View Detail to inspect the exception object.

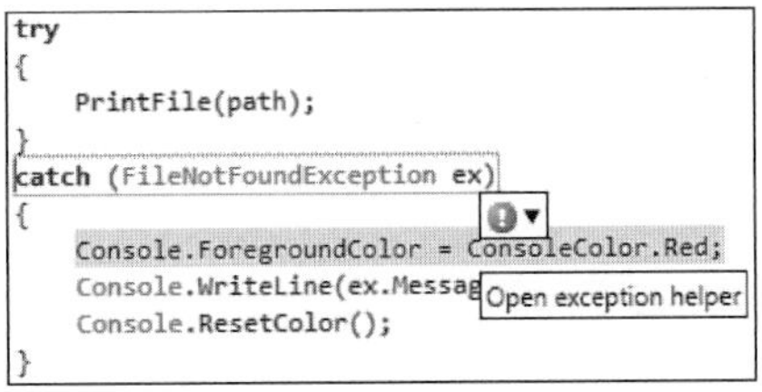

```
try
{
    PrintFile(path);
}
catch (FileNotFoundException ex)
{
    Console.ForegroundColor = ConsoleColor.Red;
    Console.WriteLine(ex.Messag Open exception helper
    Console.ResetColor();
}
```

FIGURE 8.9   The exception helper in the debugger.

There's another way for you to see precisely where an exception occurred, even though it's caught by the code. From the time an exception is thrown until its caught (or not, depending on the situation), lots of things happen. The whole exception system in the runtime is quite complicated, but in essence there are different phases:

▶ When the exception is thrown, a first-chance exception notification is sent out. This can be seen in a debugger, as you see shortly.

▶ Next, the runtime walks the call stack looking for a protected block that has an associated handler willing to handle the exception based on its type.

▶ The next thing on the runtime's checklist is to unwind the stack until it finds an exception handler or all the way back to the entry point if no handler exists.

▶ Finally, control is transferred to the found handler, supplying the exception object to the handler's catch block.

To observe an exception as it gets raised, you can enable first-chance exception notifications under the debugger. In Visual Studio, you can do so through a dialog under Debug, Exceptions, as shown in Figure 8.10.

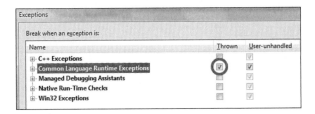

FIGURE 8.10   Enabling first-chance exceptions.

Now if you run the application again with an invalid file path, you'll see the debugger break at the point the exception is thrown, as shown in Figure 8.11. That is, at the point where it starts to pop up in our own code because the real origin is deep in the stomach of the BCL code.

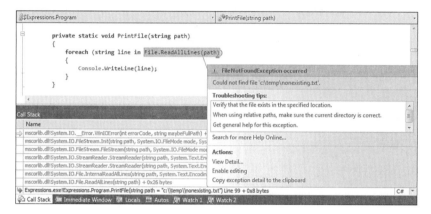

FIGURE 8.11   A first-chance exception notification.

Notice the Call Stack window now that the Just My Code option is disabled. The exception was really thrown by some helper method called __Error.WinIOError in a response to initialization of a FileStream object through the use of a StreamReader. This illustrates where the exception starts its life and how it bubbles up the call stack to a point where it can get handled. Figure 8.12 shows a stack walk carried out by the runtime to find an exception handler.

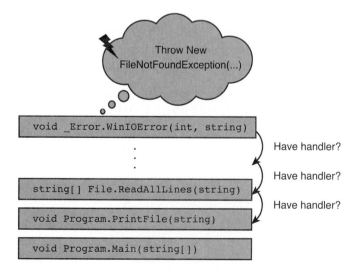

FIGURE 8.12   Walking the stack to find an appropriate handler.

The same code block can be protected by declaring handlers for different exception types. In fact, this is shorthand for nested `try` statements:

```
try
{
    PrintFile(path);
}
catch (FileNotFoundException ex)
{
    PrintException(ex);
}
catch (UnauthorizedAccessException ex)
{
    PrintException(ex);
}
```

Under the covers, protected regions of code are kept track of by means of offsets and lengths within the instruction stream of a method. This is carefully hidden, and even tools like ILDASM reflect the readable block structure (see Figure 8.13). Notice the use of the leave instruction to jump outside a protected region or a handler, which is a requirement so the runtime can do the necessary bookkeeping.

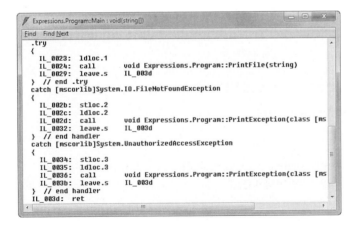

FIGURE 8.13   Exception handling from an IL perspective.

Back in C# world now: Because exception types form a hierarchy—the root being `System.Exception`—the order of handlers matters. For illustration purposes, assume you have a `BadFoodException` from which a `RottenAppleException` is derived. The following code handles exceptions to avoid bad food being processed in some production chain:

```
try
{
    AddToPackage(fruit);
}
catch (BadFoodException)
{
    TossAway(fruit, RecycleBins.GeneralGarbage);
}
catch (RottenAppleException)
{
    TossAway(fruit, RecycleBins.Compost);
}
```

Notice in the preceding fragment that you don't need to specify a variable name for an exception object in a catch block. Anyway, because RottenAppleException derives from BadFoodException, the former will never execute. The compiler will actually prevent you from writing this kind of code. Figure 8.14 shows the error message produced by the compiler when it detects a meaningless ordering of exception handlers.

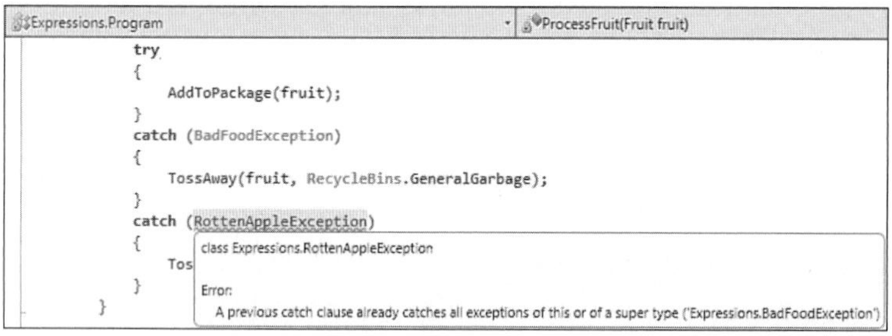

FIGURE 8.14   Ordering of catch clauses matters.

Don't Catch All Exceptions

It might be tempting in some cases to write a catch-all handler by using either the root type System.Exception or by simply omitting a type:

```
try
{
    // Do something here.
}
catch /* or with (Exception ex) */
{
    // Catches all exceptions.
}
```

In general, this is highly discouraged. There will be exceptions you can't handle properly, so there's no point in even attempting to catch those. Because lots of people actually wrote this kind of code—causing certain fatal runtime exception types to be caught even though the process was in an instable state—the .NET 4.0 CLR has classified some of its own exception types as uncatchable.

In some rare cases, catching all exceptions is a valid thing to do. For example, the crash of a single worker thread should perhaps not bring the whole process down. In such a case, it might be worth it to wrap the contents of the worker thread's method in a catch-all try statement. Other than for such scenarios, be responsible in the way you handle exceptions.

RUNTIMEWRAPPEDEXCEPTION

At the level of IL, it's possible to throw any kind of object, even if it's of a type that doesn't derive from System.Exception. This support was put in place to accommodate other languages, such as C++, where this is a perfectly valid thing to do. However, this poses a problem for other languages interoperating with such code because it causes a distinction between catch and catch (Exception), where only the former would be able to catch the exception object. But even if you did so, you couldn't get to the object because it's invalid to write the following:

```
catch (object o)
```

To resolve this nasty situation, the CLR wraps such exception objects in a special exception type called RuntimeWrappedException so that catch (Exception) handlers will catch it, too. Its WrappedException property exposes the object that was originally thrown.

Rethrow

Sometimes you come to the conclusion you can't really handle an exception even though you've caught it inside a catch clause. You may conclude so by inspecting the exception object's properties or maybe because some other condition holds true at the time the exception is caught. In such a case, you want to propagate the caught exception further up the call stack, a technique known as rethrow:

```
try
{
    motor.Start();
}
catch (MotorFailureException ex)
{
    if (ex.Component != EngineComponent.Transfer)
        throw;

    // Handle transfer component failure.
}
```

You can either rethrow by writing a throw ex statement, where ex stands for the caught exception object, or by simply writing throw, which rethrows the exception object being handled currently. Obviously, the naked `throw` statement will work only in the context of a `catch` clause.

THE MYTHICAL DIFFERENCE BETWEEN THROW AND RETHROW

At the IL code level, there are two different throw instructions. One is `throw`, specifying an object to be thrown on top of the stack. The other is `rethrow`, which rethrows the exception currently being handled. The C# compiler actually translates the "naked throw" to a `rethrow` instruction, whereas one specifying an exception object gets encoded using a `throw` instruction. Figure 8.15 shows the `rethrow` instruction for the following piece of C# code:

```
try
{
    Do2();
}
catch
{
    throw;
}
```

Also notice how a catch-all without any exception type specified gets encoded as a `catch` clause using the `System.Object` type.

But is there any difference in the behavior of `throw` versus `rethrow`? Unfortunately, at the moment, because of a common language runtime implementation quirk, the answer is no. The goal of `rethrow` was to preserve the stack trace of the original exception's location, whereas `throw` would reset it. So a `rethrow` would be completely transparent with regard to any intermediate handlers that intercepted it.

Unfortunately, in the current CLR implementation, the stack trace also gets reset on `rethrow`, so you lose the original context. In the preceding example, you really want to see `Do2` on the stack trace, but that information gets lost. Instead, you'll see `Do` on top of the stack trace.

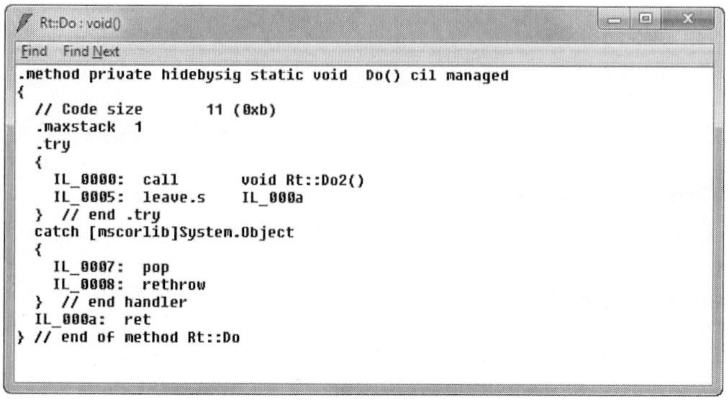


```
.method private hidebysig static void  Do() cil managed
{
  // Code size       11 (0xb)
  .maxstack  1
  .try
  {
    IL_0000:  call       void Rt::Do2()
    IL_0005:  leave.s    IL_000a
  }  // end .try
  catch [mscorlib]System.Object
  {
    IL_0007:  pop
    IL_0008:  rethrow
  }  // end handler
  IL_000a:  ret
} // end of method Rt::Do
```

FIGURE 8.15 The `rethrow` IL instruction for a throw statement in C#.

In the preceding example, the need for an `if` statement inside a `catch` clause can be questioned if we own the exception types ourselves. It would have been better to avoid this altogether by introducing a hierarchy for exception types instead so that we could catch a more specific type. Unfortunately, you don't always control exception types, or conditions may be more complex, giving rise to the use of a rethrow instead.

Filters, but Not at the Language Level

In fact, the CLR supports another exception-handling feature called filters, which allow you to specify a predicate to go with a catch clause. When an exception is about to be caught based on its type, the CLR first transfers control to the filter to decide whether it needs to be caught. If the filter evaluates to true, control is transferred to the handler; otherwise, the exception mechanism keeps looking for another handler.

Filters execute in the context of the first phase of exception handling (first-chance exceptions, as we've seen before), where the stack is walked in a search for a suitable handler. Things can get nasty when a filter by itself throws. Although they can be useful at times, C# omits filters from the language altogether. Some other languages like Visual Basic have them, though:

```
Try
    motor.Start()
Catch ex As MotorFailureException When ex.Component = EngineComponent.Transfer
    // Handle transfer component failure.
End Try
```

Some framework libraries actually provide means to hook up filters from any language, despite the fact C# doesn't have them. One such example is WPF's Dispatcher, which has an `UnhandledExceptionFilter` event that allows users to hook up a filter (see Figure 8.16).

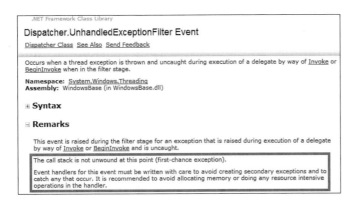

FIGURE 8.16   Filters are sometimes provided through framework library means.

Notice how the Remarks section warns against causing secondary exceptions in the context of a filter. Internally, the infrastructure for this feature is implemented using a tiny bit of Visual Basic code that gets linked in to the rest of the WindowsBase assembly, which is written in C#. So yes, there's a bit of Visual Basic in the framework here and there. It's also interesting to see how Reflector reacts to encountering a filter. Have a look at Figure 8.17 and notice the invalid C# syntax emitted by Reflector.

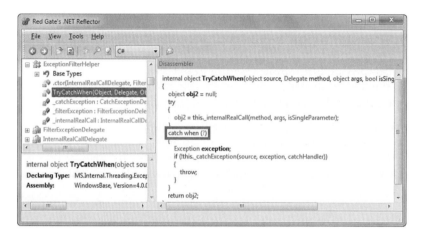

FIGURE 8.17   Filters through the eyes of .NET Reflector.

The `finally` Clause

Another aspect to exception handling is found in the `finally` clause that can be associated with a `try` statement. To illustrate its purpose, let's rewrite our `PrintFile` method using some more low-level primitives from the `System.IO` namespace:

```
static void PrintFile(string path)
{
    FileStream fs = File.OpenRead(path);
    StreamReader sr = new StreamReader(fs);

    string line;
    while ((line = sr.ReadLine()) != null)
    {
        Console.WriteLine(line);
    }
}
```

This code has severe flaws in it. Even if we succeed in opening the file on the first line, we never close the `FileStream` object, which causes leakage. Wait a minute, didn't the CLR have a garbage collector to take care of this? True, but as you will see, the garbage collector doesn't allow for deterministic "on the spot" disposal of objects. Even though we're abandoning the `FileStream` object after the method returns (in garbage collector terms, the object referred to by fs has become unreachable), it may take a considerable amount of time until the garbage collector comes around to clean it up.

Because we don't want to hold on to the resources used by the FileStream object, we want to close them as soon as we're done with it. This is what the FileStream's Close method is responsible for. The reason this is important for this particular API is because it depends on native Win32 resources (in this case, file handles). To observe this problem on your own, set a breakpoint in the Main method beyond the execution of PrintFile and try to delete the file being printed. Because a file handle is kept open by our process (assuming the GC hasn't come around to *finalize* the FileStream object yet), you won't be able to carry out this task. Figure 8.18 shows a file being locked because of improper cleanup.

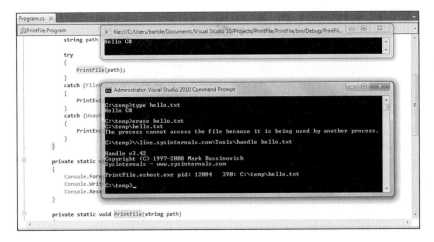

FIGURE 8.18   Failure to release native resources can lead to severe problems.

WHAT ARE HANDLE.EXE AND VSHOST.EXE?

In Figure 8.18, I'm using the Sysinternals tool handle.exe to see what process is holding on to a Win32 handle for our file. As expected, it reveals our PrintFile process that's being run under the debugger. Make sure to check out the other invaluable Sysinternal tools at the following publicly accessible share: \\live.sysinternals.com\ tools.

However, notice the process name is not PrintFile.exe (by default, the assembly file name is the project's name with .exe appended), but PrintFile.vshost.exe. Here you're seeing the effect of the Visual Studio hosting process debugging feature, which enables improved performance and expression evaluation (for example, in the Immediate Window, you can type a + b if a and b are two variables in scope when a breakpoint is hit), among other features.

It's clear we need to close down the resources held on to by some of the objects involved in the file reading operations. Looking at the IntelliSense for the FileStream and

StreamReader objects, we will see Close methods that look precisely like what we're looking for. It might be tempting to patch up the code as follows:

```
static void PrintFile(string path)
{
    FileStream fs = File.OpenRead(path);
    StreamReader sr = new StreamReader(fs);

    string line;
    while ((line = sr.ReadLine()) != null)
    {
        Console.WriteLine(line);
    }

    sr.Close();
    fs.Close();
}
```

Not too bad, but not quite okay just yet. What if an exception is thrown anywhere between opening the underlying resources and the point where we call Close? Right, the Close method calls wouldn't succeed, and we would be leaking the file handle again until the process terminates. What we actually need is a way to write a block of code that's guaranteed to execute regardless of whether an associated block ran successfully or was quit due to an exception. This is what the try statement's finally clause can be used for:

```
FileStream fs = File.OpenRead(path);
try
{
    StreamReader sr = new StreamReader(fs);
    try
    {
        string line;
        while ((line = sr.ReadLine()) != null)
        {
            Console.WriteLine(line);
        }
    }
    finally
    {
        sr.Close();
    }
}
finally
{
    fs.Close();
}
```

You see in the next section how this pattern of deterministic resource disposal can be simplified with a using statement, but it's important to understand the essence of the finally clause. No matter how control flow leaves the try block, the finally clause will execute:

```
void NothingHere()
{
    try
    {
        throw new NotImplementedException("Nothing of interest here.");
    }
/*
    catch (NotImplementedException ex)
    {
        Console.WriteLine(ex.Message);
    }
*/
    finally
    {
        Console.WriteLine("Leaving NothingHere.");
    }
}
```

The preceding fragment illustrates how the finally clause executes if the associated try block encounters an exception. The use of a finally clause can be combined with one or more catch clauses. Even if an exception gets caught (by uncommenting the catch clause in the preceding fragment), the finally clause still executes when control leaves the corresponding catch clause. Just think of this setting as consisting of nested try statements, the outer one with a finally clause and the inner one with the catch clauses.

Leaving control from a try block by means of a method return gives rise to execution of the finally clause, as well:

```
int GetNumber()
{
    try
    {
        return new Random().Next();
    }
    finally
    {
        Console.WriteLine("Leaving GetNumber.");
    }
}
```

Notice that it's impossible for the user's code to transfer control to or out of a finally clause; such control transfers are completely within the control of the runtime through the exception handling subsystem and the use of the leave instruction. So for example, it's not possible to return from a finally clause. This is quite logical if you think about it for a moment. If a finally clause gets executed because an unhandled exception terminates the containing method's execution, what would be the meaning of returning a value to the caller? And what about returning from a finally clause if it gets executed because the corresponding try block executes a return statement? Would it override the try block's return value?

FINALLY AND FAULT

The CLR's exception handling system is more complete than what most languages expose. You've already seen how filters are not available in C#, whereas Visual Basic offers them. Where filter can be seen as a sister feature to catch, finally has a sister feature, too. It's called fault.

Finally clauses always execute regardless upon leaving the associated try block, but fault clauses execute only when the associated try block is left because of an exceptional state. To mimic this functionality from C#, you could use a Boolean flag that gets set when the try block is left in a successful state. Inside the finally block, this flag can get checked to detect an exceptional exit.

Figure 8.19 illustrates different possible execution flows in a try-catch-finally setting under the absence or presence of an exception.

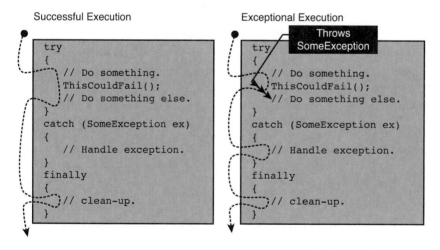

FIGURE 8.19   Execution flow with a finally clause.

What about throwing an exception from a finally clause? In general, try to avoid this wherever possible but note that it's possible to do exception handling in the context of a finally clause, too. The same holds true for a catch clause, but throwing an exception while another one is being handled will cause the first one to get lost. In other words, there can be only a single exception flowing through the exception-handling system at a time (to be precise, on a per-thread basis).

One situation where throwing from the catch clause is used regularly is when wrapping exception objects. For example, an API may fail to connect to a server because of some network exception or because the server exceeded the number of connections it can accept. In such cases, one often wants to present this kind of failure as a general "connection failure exception" (whatever the name is you chose for it) so that callers can catch that type of exception if they're interested in handling connection failure somehow (for example, by showing the user some dialog box). At the same time, though, you want to preserve the original context in a so-called inner exception:

```
try
{
    conn.Open(host, port, user);
}
catch (ServerExceededConnectionLimit ex)
{
    throw new ConnectionException("The server refused the connection.", ex);
}
catch (SocketException ex)
{
    throw new ConnectionException("Failed to open socket to the server.", ex);
}
```

Notice the second parameter passed to our ConnectionException constructor call. You'll see later how to declare your own exception type, but the typical pattern is to have a constructor that takes in a string for the exception message and an Exception instance for the inner exception. Internally, this constructor simply calls the similar constructor on the System.Exception base class. Figure 8.20 shows the correlation between this constructor parameter and the read-only property that exposes the inner exception.

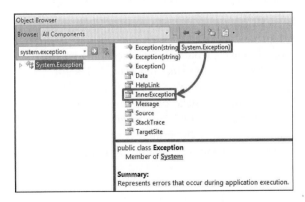

FIGURE 8.20   The inner exception object.

Deterministic Resource Cleanup

Dealing with various kinds of resources is an everyday task for most developers. This ranges from local files to remote databases or web services. To make your application well behaved, it's often important to release resources as soon as they're not needed anymore. While the .NET runtime has automatic memory management using the garbage collector, other external resources often don't. In such cases, cooperation from your code might be needed to properly close such resources.

Garbage Collection in a Nutshell

As mentioned previously, the .NET runtime features automatic memory management using a garbage collector. The advantages of the service should not be underestimated because whole classes of bugs get eliminated by it. Examples of common memory management issues that come to mind include leaking objects or freeing objects multiple times (a "double free").

Conceptually, the garbage collected memory heap gives you the illusion of an infinite memory space from which you can allocate as much as needed. Obviously, resources are limited. Not as limited as the physical memory, obviously, because today's operating systems offer memory virtualization mechanisms. But still, the party can't last forever. Instead of having to reclaim memory yourself in a disciplined way, the garbage collector will come around every so often and eliminate dead objects.

But it's not all heaven on earth. One of the fundamental properties of the garbage collector is its asynchronous background nature. You can't predict when a garbage collection will happen, so the lifetime of objects is nondeterministic. Although nondeterminism in a world as precise as computer science doesn't sound very good, it's a perfectly viable thing for automatic memory management in most cases.

To illustrate matters, take a look at the diagram in Figure 8.21.

Allocation for a new object is requested in step 1, but insufficient heap space is available. Ignore managed heap generations for now; we'll assume there's one contiguous block of memory available to comprise the entire managed object heap.

This request for object allocation triggered a collection, which is carried out in step 2. In the first phase, the collector finds all reachable objects (that is, objects code could still reference because references thereto exist in the evaluation stack) in static fields and whatnot. How this tracing and subsequent marking of live objects is carried out is of little relevance. During a second pass, the collector eliminates dead objects to make room for new ones and compacts the heap to reserve room at the end. You can envision the result of this being a move of the "high-water mark" indicating the end of contiguous space allocated by objects on the heap. Notice how much room is available after object I following the compaction phase.

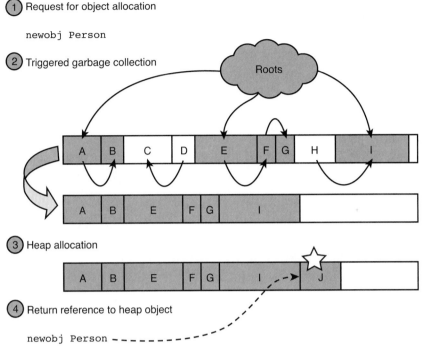

FIGURE 8.21   Garbage collection induced by new object allocations.

Now that we have enough room, step 3 can proceed with granting the request for heap space and performs the allocation. This moves the high-water mark farther, and the heap starts filling again. If at some point a collection as in step 2 can't make room for enough memory, an OutOfMemoryException is thrown.

Step 4 is trivial; the address to the newly allocated object on the heap is pushed onto the evaluation stack so that IL code can now work with the object (for example, to store it in a local or a field), call methods on it, and so on.

Object Disposal

Now I want you to look outside the reach of the garbage collection itself and focus on object C in the heap. At the point of the collection, C is not reachable anymore because there's no single path through object references that can lead to it from a root, which is a location known to be reachable. Apparently, there was an object D holding on to it, but that object by itself is not reachable anymore.

What we don't know is at what point in the past object C was allocated. It could be a few milliseconds ago, but it could also be hours or more (assuming, for instance, the application was idle waiting for user input). If C holds on to some resource that should not be kept alive needlessly (like a database connection or a file handle), we've created a problematic situation. This is the pitfall nondeterministic timing for object deallocation causes.

For objects that require a deterministic way of cleanup, it's clear we need something else. This is where the IDisposable interface kicks in, which is incredibly simple: It just contains a single Dispose method that takes no parameters and doesn't return anything (see Figure 8.22). As you can guess, the goal of that method is to be called when an object instance needs to be cleaned up on the spot:

```
void Dispose();
```

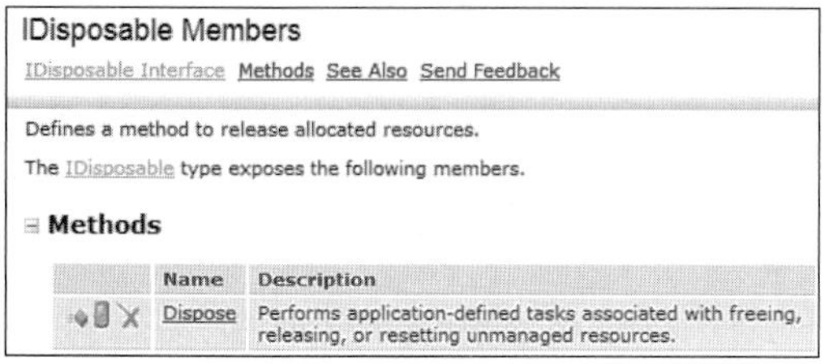

IDisposable Members

IDisposable Interface Methods See Also Send Feedback

Defines a method to release allocated resources.

The IDisposable type exposes the following members.

Methods

	Name	Description
⬧ ◨ ✕	Dispose	Performs application-defined tasks associated with freeing, releasing, or resetting unmanaged resources.

FIGURE 8.22   The IDisposable interface.

The IDisposable interface is not something the runtime knows about intrinsically. In other words, this doesn't change the way the garbage collector will ultimately reclaim the object's memory allocated on the heap. What it does, on the other hand, is provide a means for code to trigger cleanup of resources the object holds on to (for example, file handles and database connections). Notice that the documentation actually hints at this use by mentioning "unmanaged resources."

Because we shouldn't hold on to those resources when we're done with them under any circumstance, it's important to trigger this cleanup operation on every code path: normal or exceptional. Recall our discussion about the use of the finally clause to ensure proper cleanup of a FileStream and StreamReader object:

```
FileStream fs = File.OpenRead(path);
try
{
    StreamReader sr = new StreamReader(fs);
    try
    {
        string line;
        while ((line = sr.ReadLine()) != null)
        {
            Console.WriteLine(line);
        }
    }
    finally
    {
        sr.Close();
```

```
    }
}
finally
{
    fs.Close();
}
```

This gets quite clunky due to syntactical noise associated with `try` and `finally` blocks and the need for increasing indentation levels all over the place.

The `using` Statement

Step back for a moment and reflect on the preceding piece of code. We're writing down how object disposal needs to be carried out in excruciating detail. But really, all we want to say is we're *using* a certain resource and want to leave the guaranteed cleanup to the language and runtime. This is where the using statement comes in:

```
using (FileStream fs = File.OpenRead(path))
using (StreamReader sr = new StreamReader(fs))
{
    string line;
    while ((line = sr.ReadLine()) != null)
    {
        Console.WriteLine(line);
    }
}
```

This code does almost exactly the same as the original code. The using statement consists of two different parts. Between the parentheses is the *resource-acquisition expression*; it indicates the resource that will be used inside the block underneath and needs to be cleaned up no matter how the block is left. The block itself is simply the code that executes with the acquired resource in scope.

The translation carried out by the compiler is as follows. Assume the following code fragment that uses the using statement:

```
using (T resource = expression)
    embedded-statement
```

This corresponds to the following expansion:

```
{
    T resource = expression;
    try
    {
        embedded-statement
    }
```

```
    finally
    {
        if (resource != null)
            ((IDisposable)resource).Dispose();
    }
}
```

NO DUCKS HERE

Previously, you saw how the `foreach` statement allows duck typing. The objects it deals with don't need to implement `IEnumerable` and `IEnumerator`; as long as they have the required methods, things are fine. The `using` statement requires an `IDisposable` object, so just having an object that has a `Dispose` method is not sufficient to use the `using` statement.

By having the outer set of curly braces, a new scope is established for the resource variable. The null check in the `finally` clause exists only for reference type resources because value types cannot have a null value.

There are a few rules about what you can do inside the `using` block. For starters, the variable declared for the resource cannot be assigned to; after all, what would it mean to "replace" a resource you're using in the middle of using it: disposing the current resource when it gets reassigned and disposing the new resource at the end of the block? Lots of complications would arise here, so this is not allowed. Along the same lines, the resource variable cannot escape the block in a by-reference manner because that would allow it to be replaced, too. You'll learn more about by-reference argument passing later.

This is likely the most common form in which the `using` statement is used. Other forms exist where the resource-acquisition expression is not a local variable declaration but just a plain-vanilla expression of some kind. In such a case, the compiler simply infers the type of the expression and creates an unnamed local variable for you:

```
using (expression)
    embedded-statement
```

becomes

```
using (var __resource = expression)
    embedded-statement
```

To be completely honest, the example of printing a file can be simplified as follows:

```
using (StreamReader sr = File.OpenText(path))
{
    string line;
```

```
    while ((line = sr.ReadLine()) != null)
    {
        Console.WriteLine(line);
    }
}
```

The reason I kept things a bit more complicated was to show the (fairly obvious) ability to nest try-finally statements and using statements. From our previous use of nested using statements, you can see it's possible to omit curly braces around the embedded statement, which is typically done only when multiple resources are used together, and thus reduce the indentation level of the code:

```
using (FileStream fs = File.OpenRead(path))
using (StreamReader sr = new StreamReader(fs))
{
    // Two indentation levels for the price of one.
}
```

Readers paying attention to detail will have spotted a subtle difference between the original use of the finally clauses in the original PrintFile example versus the expanded forms of the using statements presented here. The using statement expands to a call to a Dispose method, whereas our original code called a Close method. For objects such as FileStream and StreamReader, it makes more sense to name the disposal method Close because that feels more natural for the domain of file I/O APIs. Similarly, objects that deal with connections may have a Disconnect method as an alias to Dispose.

In general, though, when an object implements IDisposable, it's often recommended to leverage the using statement to deal with proper cleanup. Sometimes this is not possible, for instance when the disposable object lives in an object field. In such a case, its disposal time is correlated with the lifetime or disposal time of the containing object. Calling the Dispose method or an alias thereof must be carried out manually in such a situation, in the appropriate place.

Implementing IDisposable

You haven't seen how to declare a type or implement an interface just yet, but it is very simple to understand. To create an IDisposable type, you write something like this:

```
class MyResource : IDisposable /* this means we're implementing IDisposable */
{
    // Useful members go here.

    public void Dispose()
    {
        // Do some disposal operation here.
    }
}
```

Things are a bit more complicated, though, because you typically want the underlying resources to get deallocated even if the Dispose method is not called (because of a type's user screwing up, for example). This is where the use of a *finalizer* comes in. We detail the concept of a finalizer when talking about classes, but put simply, it gets called by the garbage collector when the object is about to be cleaned up:

```
class MyResource : IDisposable /* this means we're implementing IDisposable */
{
    // Useful members go here.

    public void Dispose()
    {
        // Do some disposal operation here.
    }

    ~MyResource()
    {
        // This is the finalizer method.
    }
}
```

UNFORTUNATE SYNTAX

The use of the tilde syntax to indicate a finalizer method is a bit unfortunate because the same syntax is used in the world of C++ to indicate a destructor, which is a form of deterministic cleanup. In the world of the CLR, though, the garbage collector causes nondeterministic cleanup, and finalizers are part of that picture. In fact, under the hood, the finalizer is implemented as a Finalize method; you can verify this by looking at the generated IL code. Languages such as Visual Basic require the user to write a Finalize method instead, thus avoiding syntactical confusion.

Finalizable objects go through an additional step when the garbage collector detects they're no longer reachable and subject to deallocation. Instead of deallocating the object during the collection cycle, the object is put in a queue (sometimes referred to as the freachable queue, for finalization-reachable queue). Before deallocation happens, the finalizer methods for the objects in that queue are getting called. Finally, the object reaches a state where it can get deallocated just like any regular object. As a rule of thumb, don't implement a finalizer method unless you absolutely need it. Violating this rule will put additional stress on the garbage collector, which is strongly discouraged.

The big question now is how to relate the IDisposable pattern and the use of finalizers with one another. If a user calls the Dispose method explicitly, there's no need for the finalizer to run anymore because you've already got a chance to clean up resources onto which the object holds. On the other hand, if Dispose is never called but the object got unreachable, the finalizer is required to run and do the same cleanup as the Dispose method would have done if it were called properly by the user during the object's lifetime. So we have the same cleanup logic in both places. Those observations give rise to the following pattern:

```
class MyResource : IDisposable
{
    private bool _disposed;

    public void Dispose()
    {
        Dispose(true /* called by user directly */);
        GC.SuppressFinalize(this); // Tell the GC not to finalize this object.
    }

    void Dispose(bool disposing)
    {
        if (!_disposed)
        {
            // Clean up logic goes here.
            // Code can use "disposing" to distinguish between cases.
            _disposed = true;
        }
    }

    ~MyResource()
    {
        Dispose(false /* not called by user directly */);
    }
}
```

The _disposed field is also used in other members to check whether the object is not disposed before carrying out an operation: If a file handle is already closed, it's invalid to invoke subsequent operations on the object wrapping it. If a member is called when _disposed is already set to true, the code should throw an ObjectDisposedException:

```
public void Write(string message)
{
    if (_disposed)
        throw new ObjectDisposedException("MyResource" /* name of the resource */);

    // Do work here.
}
```

If the disposable pattern looks frightening, take a second look at it with me. The public Dispose method is what the user calls, either by calling it directly, through an alias like

Close, or by means of the using statement. Internally, it simply calls the helper Dispose method with a Boolean argument to perform the cleanup. Here we centralize all logic for both the IDisposable case and the finalizer case. The disposing parameter is used to differentiate both cases in case cleanup logic needs to be a bit different depending on the use. In addition to calling the cleanup code, Dispose also tells the garbage collector it doesn't need to bother calling the finalizer method because the user has already done the disposal explicitly.

To wrap up this preliminary discussion about disposal patterns, note that generally you'll be at the consuming side where the proper use of the using statement can save you lots of headaches. If you forget to dispose of a resource properly, issues may pop up when you least expect them, so make sure to check whether a type implements IDisposable. If so, take the appropriate action to ensure the object gets disposed at a reasonable time.

Along those lines, try to avoid having a using statement's code block exceed the time the acquired resource is needed. This keeps the resource alive for an unnecessarily long period and can lead to all sorts of contention (lock duration, pool exhaustion, and so forth) on whatever system maintains that resource. Remember, you're probably not the only one who relies on the resource or the system maintaining it.

```
/*ab*/using (resource)
{
    // Lots of resource-agnostic fluff here.

    /* Really using the resource here. */

    // And more fluff that doesn't rely on the resource.
}
```

(In)appropriate Use of IDisposable

One danger of telling people the implementation of the using statement is that they start to retrofit the pattern for purposes other than deterministic resource cleanup. In its true essence, the using statement is a try-finally statement in disguise with some method call happening nearly at the very end of the associated block. The following is a sample use of IDisposable is to implement a code execution timing facility:

```
using (new ExecutionTimer(Console.Out /* to log to */))
    // Code to be benchmarked goes here.
```

Here, the constructor of ExecutionTimer would start the timer and the Dispose method would stop it, printing the elapsed time since the constructor was called to the specified logger. Although this can be handy at times, the using statement was never intended to be a general-purpose code block decoration facility. When browsing code, seeing a using statement is meant to trigger "aha, the developer is dealing with some resource that requires cleanup" (IDisposable semantics) and not "aha, the developer is sneaking in some code at the end of the block to do whatever he sees fit."

In the preceding example, things are even a bit more subtle because the constructor hides essential logic, too. Refactoring the code to construct the object higher up and feed it in a local variable expression in the resource-acquisition part of the using statement would have very different semantics because you would be measuring a bigger code block's execution time.

What we would really need to make such scenarios of associating pieces of code with leaving and entering of a block is some kind of first-class treatment of blocks by the language. Action delegates turn out to be such a thing in disguise but still suffer from some syntactical noise:

```
ExecutionTimer.Measure(() => // using lambda expression syntax here
{
    // Code to be benchmarked goes here.
});
```

In the preceding example, the Measure method would start a timer first, then call the delegate that's passed in, and finally stop the timer and report the elapsed time at the end. Obviously, the destination logger could be fed in to the method as a parameter, too.

You could think of a way to allow this syntax to be made easier if (and this is all hand-waving amateur language design) some delegate appears as the last parameter on a method, so that "juxtaposition" of a method and a block means the same as feeding the block in to the method as a delegate:

```
ExecutionTimer.Measure(Console.Out) // The block becomes a second parameter.
{
    // Code to be benchmarked goes here.
}
```

Another concern is the fact that calling through the delegate has an additional cost that becomes truly hidden now to the user of the method. It's not clear first-class block treatment based on delegates (or any such feature at all) will hit the top of feature prioritization lists for the language in the foreseeable future.

Locking on Objects

Lots of real-world software doesn't have a single thread of execution. To execute multiple tasks at a time, threads or abstractions thereof (such as tasks in .NET 4.0) are used. It's the responsibility of the underlying operating system scheduler or a runtime facility to let units of execution get a turn at making progress. Concepts such as context switches, thread pool management, and so on directly relate to this.

What's of more interest to us in this context is the problem of different threads accessing the same resource simultaneously. This gives rise to potential issues with regard to consistency of state. To avoid going too abstract here, let's make things very concrete by presenting a Counter class that maintains a single integer value and has two operations, Increment and Decrement:

```
class Counter
{
    private int _value;

    public void Increment()
    {
        _value++;
    }

    public void Decrement()
    {
        _value−;
    }

    public int Value { get { return _value; } }
}
```

Dissecting this code, we start by observing a field called _value that stores the counter's value. The property at the end of the class definition provides a read-only means to read out the value of the counter. The Increment and Decrement methods are trivial to understand and operate on the underlying field.

Based on this, you can certainly predict the behavior of the following code:

```
const int N = 100000000;

var count = new Counter();

for (int i = 0; i < N; i++) count.Increment();
for (int i = 0; i < N; i++) count.Decrement();

Console.WriteLine(count.Value);
```

If that doesn't produce zero, things have gone really wrong. But what if the incrementing and decrementing loops are operating in parallel? To illustrate this, we could use plain old threads, but let's go for .NET 4.0's new facilities and use the Parallel class to declare our parallel invocation desire:

```
const int N = 100000000;

var count = new Counter();

Parallel.Invoke(
    () => { for (int i = 0; i < N; i++) count.Increment(); },
    () => { for (int i = 0; i < N; i++) count.Decrement(); });

Console.WriteLine(count.Value);
```

Parallel.Invoke simply takes in a series of delegates that we want to execute in parallel. The most natural way (starting from C# 3.0) to pass in such delegates is by means of lambda expression syntax: () => { /*code*/ } stands for "no arguments, (), goes to, =>, /*code*/." The result? Faster code, but truly nondeterministic (see Figure 8.23).

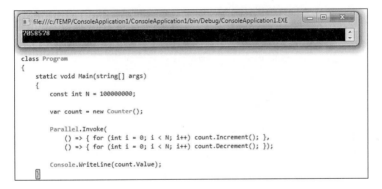

FIGURE 8.23   Parallel execution nondeterminism.

Under the Hood

You might, and actually should, wonder where this nondeterminism comes from. To understand this, we need to delve a little deeper. The crux of the problem lies in the fact Increment and Decrement are not atomic operations:

```
public void Increment()
{
    _value++;
}
```

The use of the post-increment expression (used as a statement here) really decomposes in three distinct operations that are carried out sequentially: First the value is read, then it gets incremented, and finally it gets assigned back to the field. Figure 8.24 shows the IL code corresponding to a post-increment expression.

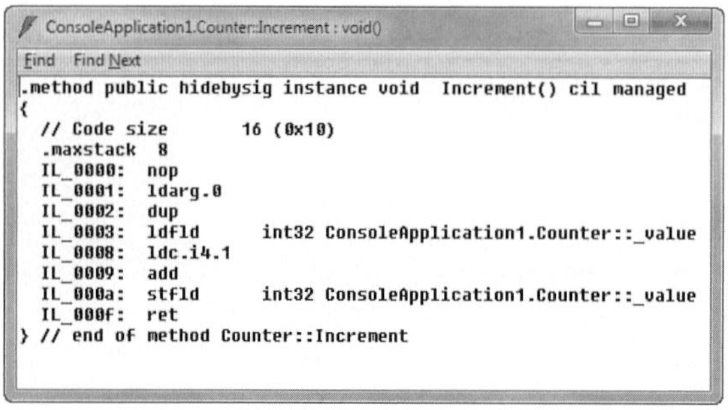

ConsoleApplication1.Counter::Increment : void()
Find Find Next
.method public hidebysig instance void Increment() cil managed
{
// Code size 16 (0x10)
.maxstack 8
IL_0000: nop
IL_0001: ldarg.0
IL_0002: dup
IL_0003: ldfld int32 ConsoleApplication1.Counter::_value
IL_0008: ldc.i4.1
IL_0009: add
IL_000a: stfld int32 ConsoleApplication1.Counter::_value
IL_000f: ret
} // end of method Counter::Increment

FIGURE 8.24 Non-atomic post-increment on a field.

It's worth the effort to try to understand this code fully. And how better than to show it with an evaluation stack transition diagram, as we've done before on various occasions (see Figure 8.25)? You'll get the hang of it soon, believe me.

Counter Object
Evaluation Stack
Counter
_value = 123
Counter
_value = 123
Counter
_value = 123
Counter
_value = 123
Counter
_value = 124
this
this
this
123
this
124
this
IL_0001
ldarg.0
IL_0002
dup
IL_0003
ldfld
IL_0008/9
ldc.i4.1
add
IL_000a
stfld

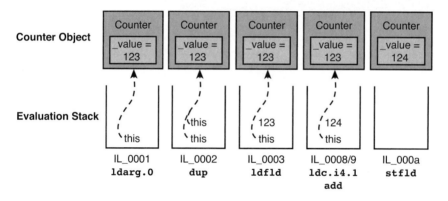

FIGURE 8.25 An "innocent" post-increment operation on a field.

The first two instructions are really setting up plumbing for what's coming afterward: `ldarg.0` loads the very first argument on the method, which is a reference to the object instance itself in case of an instance method (the `this` reference). Instructions such as `ldfld` and `stfld` (load and store field) require the instance on the top of the stack. They'll pop the instance reference from the stack and subsequently load or store from or to the field in question. Because we need to carry out both operations in the same method body, the loaded this reference is duplicated by the dup instruction. This prevents having to use `ldarg.0` twice, in favor of the dup instruction, which merely copies a few bytes holding the object reference to be duplicated on the evaluation stack.

Where the trouble in multithreaded execution comes in is with the last four instructions. Assume any number of other threads are executing operations on the same field (for example, to decrement). Any number of interleaving schemes is possible because the runtime (typically aided by the operating system underneath) is allowed to context switch threads at any point. One example is shown in Figure 8.26.

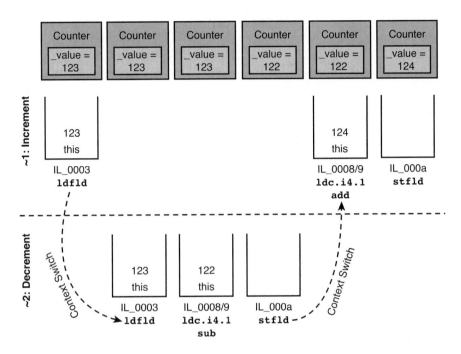

FIGURE 8.26   Interleaved execution of two threads.

Every managed thread of execution has its own evaluation stack. In the figure, right after the field is read by the first thread (~1), a context switch occurs, giving the second thread some time to execute (~2). That thread reads the field as well and subtracts and stores the resulting value. However, the first thread has a copy of the original value on its evaluation stack, and when a switch occurs back to the first thread, it proceeds under the assumption the field hasn't changed in the meantime. It increments the original value and stores the resulting value, effectively overwriting the second thread's update. In the world of database transactions, terminology such as "nonrepeatable reads" would apply to describe this circumstance.

Most likely, the time a thread gets to execute (known as a quantum at the OS level) will exceed more than four IL instructions by far. However, a context switch could occur in the middle of each thread. As such, the code is flawed, and observing this multithreading issue can take some time (likely it fails for the first time during a presentation to your manager). What we need to enforce here is atomicity of the increment and decrement operations by making sure the four instructions that read, calculate, and store are not interrupted by context switches. Or more accurately, during that *critical section*, no other thread should get a chance to touch the same state.

Actually, you can see the threads executing simultaneously by using the Parallel Stacks window found under the Debug, Windows menu (see Figure 8.27). This feature was added in addition to the Threads window in .NET 4.0, where threads got an additional abstraction level called "tasks." The Parallel Tasks and Parallel Stacks windows enable users to get a better picture of what task spawned which other tasks and so on.

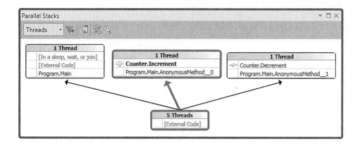

FIGURE 8.27   Parallel stacks showing simultaneous execution.

A SIMPLER FIX

Before I continue discussing multithreading and locking techniques, I have to say this particular example is so simple that we can tackle it in a very specific way to yield the correct result. Incrementing and decrementing values are such common operations that atomic variants for it exist, directly supported by the processor hardware. During a single instruction on the hardware level, it's impossible for the OS to perform a context switch, so that takes care of the problem:

```
public void Increment()
{
    Interlocked.Increment(ref _value);
}

public void Decrement()
{
    Interlocked.Decrement(ref _value);
}
```

Notice that the hardware itself has parallelization built in based on the concept of pipelining, but that stretches way beyond our scope of discussion.

The lock Statement

Since the very first version of the C# language, it was thought important to have language-level support for mutual-exclusion execution of code. The central concept here is that of a lock, which is acquired upon entrance of a block of code and released at the end of it. Lock ownership is an exclusive right; no two blocks of code should be allowed to execute simultaneously. When a lock is already held when another piece of code tries to acquire it, the latter piece of code will have to wait until the lock is released again. The idea of threads acquiring and releasing locks is shown in Figure 8.28.

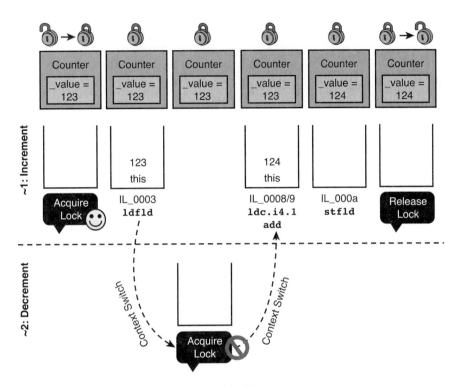

FIGURE 8.28 Mutual exclusion due to locking.

When the first thread starts its execution, it acquires the lock, which is fine because no other thread is currently holding it. The mechanics of acquiring a lock are shown later, but let's just focus on the conceptual diagram for now. Next, the thread starts its execution. Assuming a context switch occurs at the same time, as we've shown in our previous example (but that could vary, of course), the second thread gets scheduled and a context switch occurs.

Now the second thread starts by attempting to acquire the same lock as the first thread. Locks are put on resources that cannot be accessed simultaneously by different parties, so the same lock should be used by the different parties trying to access the protected resource. Because thread one already holds the lock, the request of thread two to acquire the lock fails. The second thread now enters a blocked state, and the threading infrastructure will decide to switch it off and give control to another thread. Thread two now effectively becomes "unschedulable" and won't be considered for context switches until the lock is released. Ultimately, thread one, which isn't blocked on anything, will get scheduled and can continue to run. Ultimately, it will release the lock, at which point the book-keeping for threads will indicate that thread two now is schedulable because it no longer has to wait for the lock to become available. Figure 8.29 shows how the decrementing thread runs its code inside the lock, while the first thread cannot proceed.

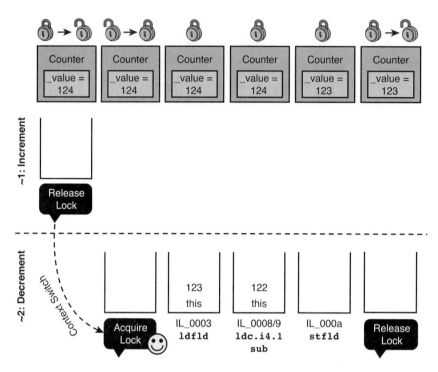

FIGURE 8.29   Mutual exclusion due to locking, continued.

PREEMPTIVE, NOT COOPERATIVE

To be precise, I should point out that the diagrams hide an important detail. The dotted lines that indicate context switches seem to be triggered by the threads themselves, which is not the case. In reality, the thread switching is controlled by the runtime in concert with the operating system, deciding when a thread switch happens and which thread gets scheduled next, based on information about blocked threads (waiting on some operation to complete) and things such as fairness rules (making sure every thread eventually gets a chance to make forward progress). The previous thread gets interrupted, which is known as preemption, hence the name *preemptive scheduling*.

Preemptive scheduling is in contrast to *cooperative scheduling*, where threads decide themselves to yield control to another thread at some point. Bookkeeping for cooperative scheduling is much harder because every thread needs to have insight as to the global picture: who's waiting for what (to avoid yielding control to a thread that will remain stuck for the rest of its days, bringing the system to a halt), how long every thread had a chance to run (to ensure fairness), and so on. This is a specialized domain that is not feasible for general-purpose runtimes and operating systems. Advanced software, such as the SQL Server database engine, employ such schemes.

So far, we've not yet considered how to acquire and release a lock from C#. The answer lies in the lock statement, which provides a simple block-based mechanism to establish mutual exclusion based on an object on which to lock. Instances of a reference type can be used to take a lock on, essentially making that object the lock protecting some resource. Here is an example of its use in the context of our Counter class:

```
class Counter
{
    private int _value;
    private object _lock = new object();

    public void Increment()
    {
        lock (_lock)
        {
            _value++;
        }
    }

    public void Decrement()
    {
        lock (_lock)
        {
            _value—;
        }
    }

    public int Value { get { return _value; } }
}
```

Upon entrance of the block used in a lock statement, the code attempts to acquire the lock that lives on the object specified in the expression between the parentheses (in the example, _lock). It's very common to use a plain-vanilla System.Object instance as an object to use as a lock; after all, it's the smallest reference type possible, and you won't typically use it for anything but the lock.

WHY NO LOCKING ON THE THIS REFERENCE?

As a rule, never lock on publicly accessible objects. The user of the Counter class could lock on an instance of it, which will upset the logic inside. You could essentially sabotage the working of the object from the outside, causing bad things such as deadlocks.

How does the lock statement work internally? It's important to make sure the lock is released under any circumstance where control leaves the critical section, so a try-finally statement will be an essential part of the picture. A remaining question is how the lock is acquired and released. The CLR doesn't have those primitives inside the IL instruction set, so BCL calls have to be used to realize this. The whole picture is shown in Figure 8.30.

```
ConsoleApplication1.Counter::Increment : void()
Find   Find Next
.method public hidebysig instance void  Increment() cil managed
{
  // Code size       44 (0x2c)
  .maxstack  3
  .locals init ([0] bool '<>s__LockTaken0',
          [1] object CS$2$0000)
  IL_0000:  ldc.i4.0
  IL_0001:  stloc.0
  .try
  {
    IL_0002:  ldarg.0
    IL_0003:  ldfld       object ConsoleApplication1.Counter::_lock
    IL_0008:  dup
    IL_0009:  stloc.1
    IL_000a:  ldloca.s    '<>s__LockTaken0'
    IL_000c:  call        void [mscorlib]System.Threading.Monitor::Enter(object,
                                                                         bool&)
    IL_0011:  ldarg.0
    IL_0012:  dup
    IL_0013:  ldfld       int32 ConsoleApplication1.Counter::_value
    IL_0018:  ldc.i4.1
    IL_0019:  add
    IL_001a:  stfld       int32 ConsoleApplication1.Counter::_value
    IL_001f:  leave.s     IL_002b
  }  // end .try
  finally
  {
    IL_0021:  ldloc.0
    IL_0022:  brfalse.s   IL_002a
    IL_0024:  ldloc.1
    IL_0025:  call        void [mscorlib]System.Threading.Monitor::Exit(object)
    IL_002a:  endfinally
  }  // end handler
  IL_002b:  ret
}  // end of method Counter::Increment
```

FIGURE 8.30   The `lock` statement unraveled.

The portion wrapped in the big curly braces is the compiled code from inside the `lock` statement's code block. The rest of the code is what the `lock` statement itself is responsible for and essentially boils down to a call to `Monitor.Enter` before executing the code and one to `Monitor.Leave` inside the `finally` clause to be guaranteed it runs for sure, even if an exception is thrown during execution of the block.

Those primitives from the `System.Threading` namespace can be called manually, as well, if you want. More `Monitor` methods exist to accommodate a variety of scenarios (for example, if you want to wait to acquire a lock only for a specified duration). If that timeout is exceeded, you could go on to do something else and attempt to acquire the lock again at some later point.

Intermezzo: Code Generation for Lock

In the last release of the C# language, code generation for the `lock` statement has been changed due to a truly fascinating story in compiler development land. Consider the following fragment:

```
lock (expression)
    embedded-statement
```

Before version 4.0, this lock statement translated into the following fragment:

```
var __lockExpression = expression;
Monitor.Enter(__lockExpression);
try
{
    embedded-statement
}
finally
{
    Monitor.Exit(__lockExpression);
}
```

It turns out, the preceding code is plagued with some very subtle issues. For starters, the lock object is stored in a temporary local variable to ensure the same lock is released as the one that was acquired. If the lock expression references a field or calls a method, it's possible (though definitely not recommended as a good practice) for the lock object to change. In such a case, other threads blocked on the original lock object would never get unblocked if the lock release weren't symmetric to the acquisition. That was easy to grasp, wasn't it?

Even more headaches come from a seemingly innocent instruction: nop, which stands for no operation and is essentially a resource-wasteful instruction because it doesn't do anything useful by itself. One place where it's used is to allow users to set a breakpoint on lexical tokens such as curly braces, so the compiler emits a nop instruction for those in debug builds. However, any instruction in the CLR can throw a thread abort exception, including this one.

Where does the problem with this fragment come from, and what does nop have to do with it? Turns out in nonoptimized builds, the compiler can emit a nop instruction between calling Monitor.Enter and entering the following try-finally statement. The reason for this is to allow the user to set a breakpoint on the try keyword itself, which doesn't result in an instruction itself (and breakpoints can be set only on instructions). However, because of this case, it's possible the lock gets acquired but never gets released if the nop instruction throws a ThreadAbortException and the protected block is not entered yet (so the finally clause never runs). As a result, we may have deadlocked the code because other threads waiting for the lock to be released will never be able to continue.

THE DREADED THREADABORTEXCEPTION

Before I proceed here, you should realize that using ThreadAbortException is almost never a good idea. Given a Thread object, calling the Abort method on it causes the CLR to throw a ThreadAbortException on that thread in an attempt to take it down. There are lots of issues with this approach: You don't know in what state the thread is at the point it gets aborted, potentially causing an inconsistent state as a result. And more horror stories exist about ThreadAbortException.

Whenever a thread (or task in the world of .NET 4.0 concurrency constructs) is meant to be able to be stopped before it naturally finishes, you should implement a graceful mechanism that allows doing so. For example, a Boolean flag could be set to signal to the thread that it needs to stop at the first moment it sees fit (and when it's safe to do so with regard to the state it manipulates).

So why does Thread.Abort even exist? Answer: Emergency situations, when an application domain (the unit of isolation for code execution on the CLR, see Chapter 25, "Assemblies, and Application Domains") needs to be terminated forcefully.

What we're pointing out in the text is merely the potential for this dreaded thread abort exception to cause troubles in the face of the lock statement implementation, without actually judging whether the use of it is a good thing (it isn't).

Starting with C# 4.0, the generated code for the lock statement has changed to be as follows, just as shown in the IL fragment earlier:

```
bool __lockTaken = false;
var  __lockExpression = expression; // assignment really happens in try block
try
{
    Monitor.Enter(__lockExpression, ref __lockTaken);
    embedded-statement
}
finally
{
    if (__lockTaken)
        Monitor.Exit(__lockExpression);
}
```

The Boolean __lockTaken flag is set by the Monitor.Enter method and is required to reflect the truth about the lock acquisition state in the face of ThreadAbortExceptions.

Be Careful with Locks

Just as with the using statement, it's highly recommended to keep the embedded block as tiny as possible. For both statements, the main motivation is contention. If a resource is used with the using statement, others might be waiting for it, or you might be putting a needless amount of stress on the resource management system underneath. In case of a lock, you'll be slowing down other threads, keeping them blocked longer than absolutely required to ensure the consistency we're in search of.

But there's another reason, too. Locking is just an essential primitive to provide for mutual exclusion between multiple threads of execution. But that's about it. The lock statement by itself doesn't give any atomicity or consistency guarantees whatsoever. An example:

```
void TransferFunds(Account from, Account to, decimal amount)
{
    lock (globalTransferLock)
    {
        from.Funds -= amount;
        to.Funds += amount;
    }
}
```

The core idea of this lock sample is simple: We don't want to see money appearing out of nowhere or see the total amount of money in the world decrease because of inconsistent transfers. This could happen in lots of cases (for example, if two threads are dealing with the same "from" account and both have read the balance to be $1,000,000 before doing the transfer). As a result, write operations will overlap, and money comes out of nowhere (assuming a positive amount):

```
Thread 1: 1,000,000 - 500,000 = 500,000
Thread 2: 1,000,000 - 250,000 = 750,000
```

Either way, whatever thread wins the battle, the result is clearly not $250,000 as would be expected.

But there are quite a few problems with the suggested solution's code. First, we seem to lock on some global lock object called transferService. All transfers in the whole bank depend on a single lock object, which is definitely very safe. (No two transactions can happen at the same time *at all*, assuming all transaction code is wrapped in such a lock statement.) On the other hand, this can be a big source of resource contention. Performance issues with locks typically stem from contention, but there's only one way to know whether it affects you: Measure it!

In fact, we should consider ourselves lucky we went for a global lock earlier for reasons of correctness. If you conclude there's too much contention going on, slowing down the whole system, you might be tempted to suggest the following fix:

```
lock (from)
{
    lock(to)
    {
        from.Funds -= amount;
        to.Funds += amount;
    }
}
```

Congratulations, you've just made matters worse than they were. But if you lock on both accounts, we should be fine, shouldn't we? Conceptually that sounds right, yes, but some caveats apply. Okay, we're locking on a publicly visible object, which is definitely not recommended, but we can argue that we're in a trusted subsystem where we're the only ones that will acquire locks on those objects, so let's dismiss that argument. The bigger issue here lies in the ordering of locking on account objects, a classic in concurrency courses. Think about what happens if another thread is attempting a transfer with the same two accounts but from and to are swapped.

In Figure 8.31, you can see what happens if context switches happen between both threads in the middle of acquiring locks. Both threads are waiting for a lock, and neither can make progress, ever: They're waiting for each other, resulting in a deadlock situation. Unless you can ensure locks on multiple objects are always acquired in the same order, you shouldn't do such a thing. Learning how to ensure a consistent lock ordering for the case of two random accounts would lead us too far. Devising a fine-grained locking scheme may even be a totally irrelevant question if the solution using a global lock doesn't pose a bottleneck.

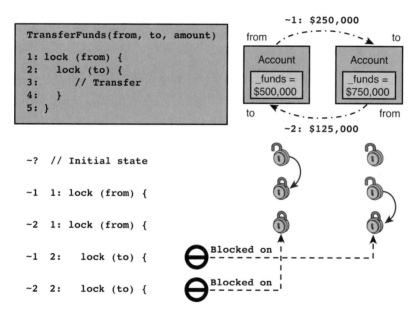

FIGURE 8.31   Inconsistent ordering of lock acquisition leads to deadlocks.

This brings us to the point we're making here: limit the amount of code that executes under a lock that's being held. Not only to reduce contention, but also because of the risk of causing exceptions while you're modifying critical state. The lock statement doesn't help with that: If an exception is thrown in the middle of touching state, changes made up to that point aren't rolled back. In the running example, it *seems* there's not much going on:

```
from.Funds -= amount;
to.Funds += amount;
```

However, this could be very deceptive. Funds is most likely implemented as a *property*, so in reality the preceding code is calling get and set accessor methods. Although it's highly recommended to make property accesses not excessively expensive (in a sense, they would trigger an amount of code of a different order of magnitude compared to accessing a field), there might be a bit of code in there. Maybe setting a property triggers a change notification to other parts of the system (for example, to synchronize the online banking view of the account). Such operations could fail and throw an exception. If that's the case and we don't protect against it in the calling code, we might have subtracted the amount from one account without adding it to the other one. Avoiding running large pieces of code mitigates such a risk.

ACID

In the world of database systems, transactions are characterized with four properties, often abbreviated as ACID for atomicity, consistency, isolation, and durability:

- ▶ Atomicity means a whole transactional operation either succeeds or rolls back as a unit. No intermediate inconsistent states are possible. In the example of accounts, that means it's impossible for one account to be debited if the other didn't get credited.

- ▶ Consistency denotes the guarantee the database will remain consistent in all circumstances. Transactions preserve the consistency property no matter whether they were committed or rolled back. For a banking system, it means no money falls off the radar or enters it out of nowhere.

- ▶ Isolation ensures intermediate states that exist during execution of a transaction are invisible to other transactions that are in flight. In the accounts example, this means no one should be able to see one account in a debited state while the other hasn't been credited yet.

- ▶ Durability is about the database system guaranteeing that as soon as the trans-action is committed, the results are persisted in such a way that they are perma-nent. If the bank suffers an electric power outage right after the user saw the transaction completed, it's guaranteed the database will get back to that completed state as soon as power is restored.

The lock statement construct doesn't really provide ACID guarantees as full-fledged database systems do. Instead, consider it just a low-level primitive that can be used to write systems that provide more guarantees but that is and stays the user's responsi-bility. It would take introducing software transactional memory (STM) to get beyond this "restriction," but when (and if) that will (ever) happen is a big unknown.

In other words, locking doesn't provide a way to perform transactional operations by itself. All the lock statement ensures is mutual exclusion and avoidance of deadlocks if an exception occurs due to the use of a try-finally protected region of code, guaranteeing release of the lock under all circumstances. This might be a good thing, but typically it isn't. Assume one thread threw an exception during modification of state, and things just got terribly inconsistent. Because of the use of the lock statement, the lock will be released through the `finally` clause underneath. This allows other threads that are waiting on the lock to continue running (well, one at a time of course, due to mutual exclusion), but they will now do *from an inconsistent state*. The key message here is this: Avoid throwing during the time a lock is held.

Summary

Congratulations. After having read this and Chapter 6, "A Primer on Types and Objects," you're pretty much an expert in procedural programming techniques now, employing the whole reach of the C# statements spectrum. In this chapter, we discussed different parts of the exception-handling system, most notably focusing on how to write code that's robust in the face of exceptions but also showing how to throw exceptions ourselves.

Next, we took a look at constructs that build on the exception-handling system, such as proper resource cleanup with the `using` statement and coordination of concurrent code using mutual exclusion provided by the `lock` statement.

In the next chapter, we continue to zoom out and look at classes, structs, and containers for them in the form of namespaces. You'll learn how to create your own types using object-oriented principles and provide typical members for them such as constructors, methods, properties, and indexers.

CHAPTER 9

Introducing Types

IN THIS CHAPTER

▶ Types Revisited 463

▶ Classes Versus Structs 466

▶ Type Members 486

Step by step, we're emerging from the cave of discrete language elements and starting to combine them into large programs. After our extensive coverage of expressions and statements, time has come to use them in a broader context. In this and the following few chapters, we lay the basis for "programming in the large," exploring classes and structs as well as the various sorts of members they support.

In this chapter, we focus on the concept of types and contrast classes and structs. The discussion of a type's members is deferred until further chapters.

Types Revisited

At the heart of managed code lies the concept of types. Defining the concept of a type is not an easy task, but put simply, it offers a means for the runtime to know *what* precisely a certain object is, and hence what the valid operations are to be performed on it. Typing is a crucial concept in the world of managed code because of the type-safety guarantees the platform offers.

Types are blueprints for objects. They describe the shape of objects that are said to have that particular type. Such a shape has two key elements:

▶ **Data** is what an object contains and operates on. It directly relates to the layout of objects in memory because storage needs to be provided for all the discrete pieces of data that make up an object.

▶ **Operations** are defined to offer functionality that operates over the data, possibly taking in and/or returning other pieces of data (which by themselves have types).

If you read carefully, you can spot a recursive nature in this definition. While a type defines the shape of an object, it does so by wrapping up pieces of data and providing operations over it. All data involved has a type by itself, too. Obviously, this needs to end somewhere. This is where primitive types enter the picture. For example, some type representing a `Person` may contain a name stored as a string as well as a date of birth stored as a `DataTime`. Notice that `DateTime` by itself can be broken down further into year, month, day, and so on. But ultimately, the `DateTime` type contains some integral values that describe a date and time unambiguously.

In addition to the code + data breakdown, types can be categorized as concrete versus abstract. Concrete types can have instances of them, whereas abstract ones can't. *Abstract types* provide a means to define proper *type hierarchies*, where parts of a type's implementation are left to extenders of a type. Interfaces are the canonical example of such abstract types, defining a set of operations as a contract for collaboration between different components: "If you *implement* this and that operation, we're in business."

The simplest way to remember the relationships in which a type participates is to think in terms of verbs. The "is a" relationship denotes a type hierarchy. Every Person is also an Object. To describe the data a type combines together, the "has a" relationship fits it all. And finally, to describe operations, "can" seems an appropriate choice.

Figure 9.1 contains more information than we've categorized so far. It states that `Person` and `Object` are *classes*, denoting the sort of type we're dealing with. After we've expanded a type definition, collapsible regions appear for the different kinds of *members* that exist: fields, properties, methods, and so on. For now, we've only characterized methods as code and fields as data but haven't classified properties yet. Conceptually, they're a way to expose data, although physically they're defined as operations (that is, code).

To be completely fair, a third element exists in this cocktail: *metadata*, which is data about the type and its members itself. Metadata has several roles. For starters, it enables the exploration of the capabilities of types at runtime using reflection, allowing questions to be asked (such as, "What are the methods on this type?") at runtime. Furthermore, certain kinds of members are fueled by metadata. For example, although properties look like a mechanism to expose data, they really consist of (pairs of) methods underneath. Using metadata, tools can explore the capabilities of types (for example, for IntelliSense) and receive guidance on how to consume the type (for example, use of a property getter corresponds to such a method call). Finally, metadata is a driver for certain runtime aspects. The canonical example is serialization, which can be turned on for a type using a *custom attribute*:

```
[Serializable]
class Person { /* ... */ }
```

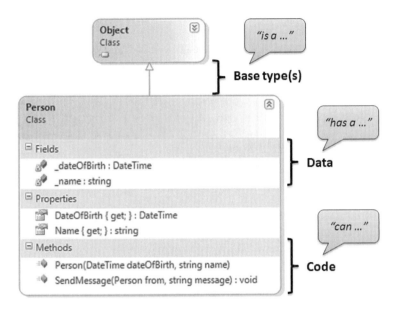

FIGURE 9.1   Decomposing a type.

Different sorts of types exist, two of which we look at in this chapter: *classes* and *structs*. Both provide containers for code and data, whereas some of the other types are exclusively focused on one aspect. For example, *delegates* and *interfaces* are all about operations you can perform, whereas *enumerations* are all about data that gets defined as named constants. Figure 9.2 illustrates where classes and structs live.

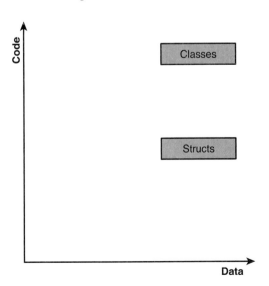

FIGURE 9.2   Where classes and structs are situated.

Classes Versus Structs

Figure 9.2 illustrates where classes and structs fit in the sea of types that are available to managed code developers. You can debate where exactly in the diagram sorts of types belong, but let's accept my choice for now.

References Versus Values

Struct is a fancy word for value type. Recall that value types are copied by value; every time an instance of a value type (sometimes abbreviated simply as value) is passed, a copy is created. This is in sheer contrast to reference types, where a reference to the object is passed along.

Let's concretize matters by considering integral numeric values. Why are those value types? There are a couple of reasons. First, values have some kind of immutable characteristic: 1 is 1 and will always be. Although immutability is not a requirement for value types, not obeying it is asking for trouble, as you will see. This doesn't mean a variable of a value type can't change (after all, isn't the point of a variable to vary?); all I'm saying is that the value itself can't change:

```
for (int i = 0; i < 10; i++)
    // Do something
```

Here, the value of variable i is changing all the time. However, the instances of the Int32 type are not changing: By incrementing 1, you're not affecting everyone who's using 1 somewhere. Even in natural language, this is reflected: When using the word one to mean a number, you're not *referring* to some magical instance of the number 1 kept in some central location (*that* one). And we deem it pretty unlikely a genius mathematician will come around anytime soon mandating a change to the number 1! Figure 9.3 contrasts the notion of a value with that of a reference.

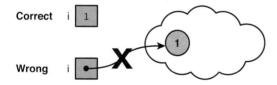

FIGURE 9.3   Integral numbers are value types.

Another canonical example of a value type is a point. A point has different coordinates, like X and Y, but those are fixed. You might wonder: But what if something needs to be moved? What's changing is not the point's data itself, but rather the location of the object being moved. This location will be of type Point, and during a move it will get a different value assigned. Imagine that Point is a reference type and the following code sets the

`Location` property for a table and a kid in two different rooms, where location is relative to some corner of the room. The table is positioned at position (10,10), and the kid is reading his Tintin book also at position (10,10), so the same instance of the `Point` type could be used for both:

```
var p = new Point(10,10); // with Point a reference type
kid.Location = p;
table.Location = p;
```

Now, what happens if the person in the first room wants to move his table to position (20,20)? Different approaches can be taken, but the aliasing property of reference types can be disadvantageous. Because the same instance of `Point` is used for both `Location` properties, changes to this very instance will affect both objects' locations:

```
p.X += 10;
p.Y += 10;
```

I'm guessing the kid won't be happy to be moved by some invisible teleportation force, as illustrated in Figure 9.4.

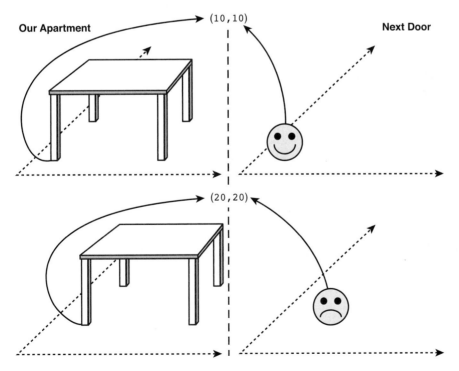

FIGURE 9.4 Point as a reference type.

Two things are really going on here. First, the fact `Point` is treated as a reference type makes aliasing possible. Second, we can assign to X and Y of the `Point` object—that is, the data is mutable. There are different ways to avoid the problem, but really the core problem lies in the fact we're using a reference type to denote something that has value characteristics. Is it really the case multiple things should be able to *refer* to the same point? Rather unlikely.

Using a value type for `Point`, things start to look quite different. Even though the same code will work, semantics are different. Upon assignment of the struct's value to the different `Location` properties, a copy is taken:

```
var p = new Point(10,10); // with Point a reference type
kid.Location = p;
table.Location = p;
```

The kid and table objects no longer refer to the same object: They simply don't *refer* to the point anymore; instead, they *store* a point *value*. The effect of changing the point's value on one of the objects is illustrated in Figure 9.5.

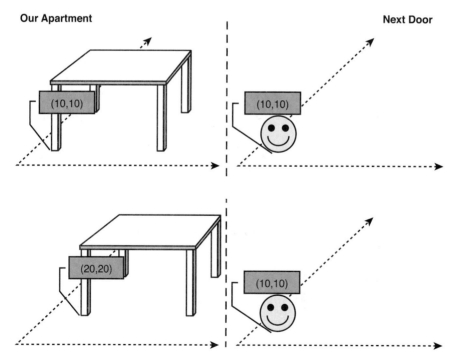

FIGURE 9.5   Point as a value type.

MUTABILITY, AN ORTHOGONAL CONCERN

The main consideration for choosing between value types versus reference types should be the desired semantics. If you naturally *refer* to some object, a reference type is appropriate so that multiple entities can refer to the same *instance* of it. On the other hand, value types represent things that are just that: values, as in quantities, coordinates, colors.

Although it typically doesn't make sense to mutate a value—and indeed, doing so is highly discouraged, as discussed later—neither the runtime nor the C# language prevents you from doing it. But quick, tell me what it would mean to you to change the number 1 or tweak the RGB representation of the color Red.

Reference types, more often than not, are written to be mutable in true imperative programming style, which gets reflected in object-oriented programming, as well (although it's not a fundamental pillar of OO). For example, calling a method for money transfer on an account will change its balance, and setting a person's age property will, uhm, change its age. However, it's perfectly doable to construct reference types that are immutable: Once created, you can't change their state anymore. The canonical example of an immutable reference type is `System.String`.

The de facto use of mutability in all sorts of circumstances is no longer an ideal practice in today's world of concurrent software. The more mutable state there is, the more synchronization is needed when objects are handed out and all sorts of components can start to mutate them. Therefore, the use of data structures that are immutable by default can be a huge advantage to aid in parallelizing software. When state is only readable, it's fine to hand out objects to different components; they can't spoil things. Simply stated, "shared mutable state = trouble."

At this point, neither the runtime nor most languages on top of it provide direct means to ensure or enforce immutability. That certainly may change in the future because the role of parallel computing is increasing. Traces of this influence can be found today in the new .NET 4.0 `System.Threading` namespace but also in the F# language where immutability is the default.

In summary, structs are value types and classes are reference types. Figure 9.6 highlights the role of structs and classes in the bigger picture of types. To declare such types, dedicated keywords are used, which unsurprisingly are called `struct` and `class`, respectively:

```
struct Point
{
    // Members go here.
}


class Person
{
    // Members go here.
}
```

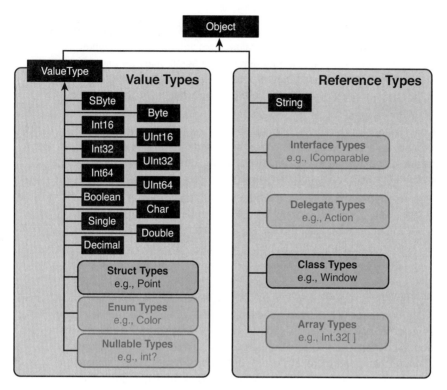

FIGURE 9.6   Structs and classes.

Heap Versus Stack

Lots of books start the discussion about reference types versus value types by pointing out their different memory-allocation characteristics. To say the least, this is a weird thing to do because this is truly an implementation detail. So the first decision factor when choosing between a reference type and a value type should concentrate on the intended semantics as opposed to potential benefits in terms of memory-allocation and -deallocation patterns.

We should pay some attention to the way things work on this level, too. Here's the deal:

- ▶ Value types (such as structs) are stack allocated.

- ▶ Reference types (such as classes) are heap allocated.

I'm actually omitting a slight detail for now (boxing), but this is the general picture. Pretty simple, isn't it?

So, what's this heap and stack thing all about? We've already seen the use of the evaluation stack when looking at some intermediate language (IL) code generated by the C# compiler. The data stored for value type instances simply lives on that stack directly (that is, without referring to some other place in memory). For example, Int32 is a value type, so in the following method, variables a and b, as well as the return value, live directly on the stack:

```
static int Add(int a, int b)
{
    return a + b;
}
```

Recall that this code basically performs four operations on the IL level, to fetch the two arguments one by one (pushing them on the stack), add them, and return to the caller:

```
ldarg.0
ldarg.1
add
ret
```

Figure 9.7 shows how this method operates, assuming it has been called from some Main method that passed in arguments 3 and 5.

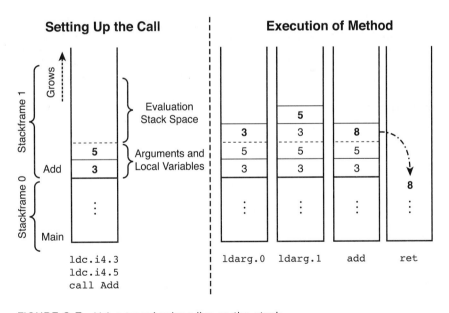

FIGURE 9.7   Value types' values live on the stack.

Strictly speaking, the runtime doesn't require all stack structures to be interwoven. In fact, we're dealing with at least two conceptual stacks:

▶ The call stack, where arguments, locals, and return values are kept

▶ The evaluation stack, where the IL code operates on as some kind of scratchpad

What's of more importance here is to observe that the values themselves are allocated on the stack. This has a couple of interesting effects with regard to memory use: A value can't outlive its stack frame. (That is, when a method returns, all its local variables and argument values are automatically deallocated.) In the last transition in Figure 9.7, this is made very clear: When Add returned, the values 3 and 5 that lived in its stack frame got lost.

THE KEY TO RECURSION

Stack-allocated arguments and return values are the key to enabling recursion where a method is permitted to call itself. In much more primitive languages, arguments to procedures were kept in statically known memory locations. As a result, only one call to a certain procedure could be in flight at the same time because there's only one place for its arguments. Making a second call would override the data in those argument slots, and similar problems exist for keeping track of the return value (and the return address, for the same reason).

Not only deallocating memory on the stack is trivial (simply by lowering the high-water mark for memory allocated on the stack), allocation is equally trivial. Just store the value on top of the stack and move the high-water mark up for subsequent allocations not to overwrite the newly allocated value. If the stack runs out of space for some reason (for example, too deep recursion), a StackOverflowException results.

The main advantage lies in the trivial deallocation, which has a performance benefit over deallocation of heap objects, as you will see. As a downside, extra care is needed when handing out references to objects on the stack. Luckily, this is something the C# language protects us against, putting very strict rules on passing stack-allocated objects "by reference." We discuss this further in Chapter 10, "Methods," but here's the idea:

```
static void ChangeIt(ref int a)
{
    a = 42;
}

static void Main()
{
    int x = 24;
    ChangeIt(ref x);
    Console.WriteLine(x); // will print 42
}
```

Notice that the use of the ref keyword to indicate a parameter is passed by reference, both at the declaration site (the ChangeIt method definition on top) and the use site (the call to it from Main). The execution of the preceding code is depicted in Figure 9.8.

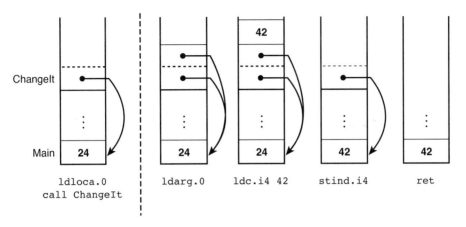

FIGURE 9.8   References to an object on the stack.

In the execution diagram that is Figure 9.8, ldloca stands for "load local address," which produces a strongly typed reference to the local variable. The stind instruction allows setting what such a reference is referring to and stands for "store indirect." Don't confuse the concept of references in managed code with pointers because the runtime has full knowledge of the type of the reference as opposed to pointers being naked memory addresses.

Passing a value by reference doesn't magically turn it into a reference type: The value still lives on a stack as it always did. But what's the protective measure required we were alluding to? Consider the following code:

```
static ref int s_badRef; // Invalid C# code!

static void Main() {
    First();
    Second();
}

static void First() {
    int x = 5;
    StoreRef(ref x);
}

static void Second() {
    double d = 3.14159;
}

static void StoreRef (ref int x) {
    s_badRef = x; // Can't do such a thing in C#.
}
```

The problem is we're storing a reference to something on the stack while that reference outlives the stack frame. Figure 9.9 shows such a potential mishap.

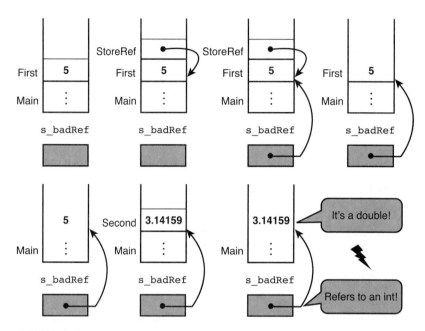

FIGURE 9.9 Hypothetical incorrect use of references into the stack.

When First is called, the local variable for the integer value 5 gets allocated on the stack. StoreRef uses the C# by-reference argument-passing feature to get a reference to the variable on the stack. Assume it were possible to store away such a reference; you would have successfully captured a reference into the stack memory that would be kept beyond the point where First returns, and hence the local variable for 5 is abandoned. A subsequent call to Second would reuse that stack memory (for example, to allocate a double). But because the stored reference is of type int32& (& being the notation of such a reference in IL terms), you could invoke operations on the data as if it were an integer, even though it is a double value. We've just broken type safety.

Correctly behaving managed code, as generated by C# programs, can't do such a thing. Although the use of the stack poses some restrictions, it provides great benefits because of the low cost involved in *deallocating* memory. No complex memory management systems are required to deal with this, as is required on the heap.

Reference types are allocated on what's known as the managed object heap, which is under control of the garbage collector. It provides a way for objects to be allocated such that their lifetime can outlive stack frames. All that can possibly live on the stack are references to the data, which is heap allocated.

Other than in the world of native code, allocating memory on the heap is simple and efficient because of the illusion of infinite memory the heap creates. Heaps for use by native code typically maintain a free list to find memory to grant allocation requests, which requires search logic and use of some fitting algorithm. The difference in the case of allocation is illustrated in Figure 9.10.

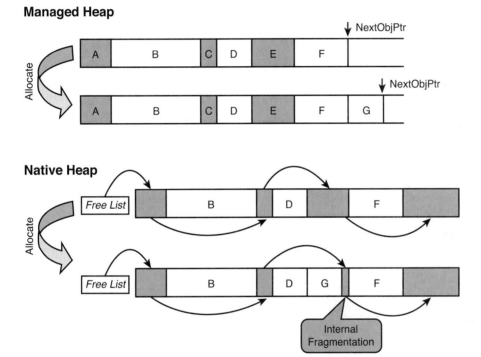

FIGURE 9.10   Heap memory allocation.

Notice how easy it is to allocate memory on the managed heap: Just see whether there's enough space left, allocate, and move the high-water mark. Looks familiar, doesn't it? Allocating memory on the managed heap is conceptually similar to stack-based allocation.

In the world of native code, more complexity is usually involved: To find available space, a free list needs to be searched. When a suitable spot is found (for example, by first-fit search), a pointer to the memory location is returned and the free list is patched up. In doing so, little regions of memory can appear that nearly no object can ever fit in. These allocate space nevertheless and are a waste of memory space. This is known as internal fragmentation, something the managed heap doesn't suffer from.

Before we explain what happens when the heap is full in both the native and managed world, let's first illustrate how deallocation happens in the native world. Managed code takes away this burden of manual memory management from the developer, but in native code it's the only way to reclaim memory (see Figure 9.11).

Native Heap

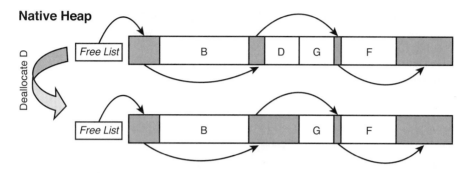

FIGURE 9.11   Heap memory deallocation in native code.

Simply stated, the freed memory is returned to the free list. Obviously, adjacent free space can be merged into one block of free space to reduce fragmentation. In managed code, there's no deterministic deallocation. Instead, memory gets reclaimed when the heap runs out of space, a task carried out by the garbage collector, as shown in Figure 9.12.

Managed Heap

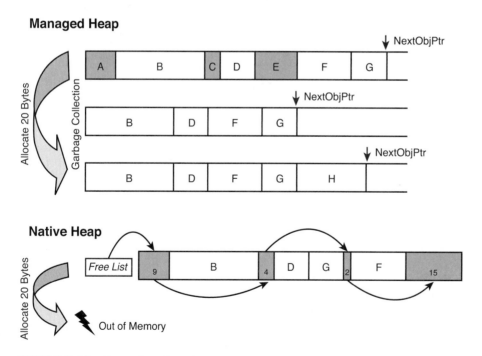

FIGURE 9.12   Heap allocation triggering garbage collection.

Notice how running out of memory in native code is possible due to the effects of internal fragmentation. Even though enough space might still be available from a global point of view, there might be no single free block that's big enough to fit the requested amount of memory. Garbage collectors deal with this problem by compacting memory to make more contiguous space available.

The garbage collector operates in a few phases:

> ► Live objects are traced recursively by following references between objects starting from known live locations: Things on the heap, in static locations, and so on are all within reach of executing code and should not be deallocated. Similarly, all objects to which they refer (either directly or by following more references) should stay alive too.

> ► After marking all the live objects, the collector sweeps the heap to free all dead objects. During this phase, objects may be detected that need finalization, complicating this a bit. But in essence, unmarked objects are dead and are subject to cleanup.

> ► Compacting moves objects together so that they make up contiguous space. During this process, references need to be patched up. If an object moves in memory, all objects referring to it need to be tweaked so that they refer to the right location in memory.

As we've seen, allocating managed objects is very cheap. The flip side is that it can trigger a garbage collection from time to time as the heaps gets populated and runs out of space. Because garbage collecting the whole heap is a costly operation, the heap is split in different generations. The idea is that lots of programs create a bunch of objects that are short-lived in nature. Many more such objects exist than the ones that remain in memory for longer durations of program execution.

This observation leads to a design where the heap is divided into three generations: Gen0, Gen1, and Gen2. Gen0 is the smallest one; when objects are allocated, they start their life in Gen0. At some point, Gen0 will run out of space. This triggers a garbage collection, which starts by cleaning up the dead objects in Gen0. Objects that survive the collection cycle—and it's expected lots of objects were short-lived, so the number of survivors is relatively low—get promoted to Gen1, which means they're starting to age and are less likely to be reclaimable anytime soon. The size of Gen1 is larger than that of Gen0.

Promotion of objects from Gen0 to Gen1 can by itself cause Gen1 to become full, at which point it gets collected, too. Because it's larger than Gen0, it will take more time to carry out this collection, but the whole theory is that Gen1 collections should be much less common than Gen0 collections. And as you can guess by now, survivors of Gen1 collections are promoted to Gen2. If Gen2 gets full, it's collected, but objects are no longer promoted to a next generation (because Gen2 is the last one). It's also the largest one, providing room for the long-lived objects of the application. Again, the idea is that Gen2 collections are much less common than Gen1 collections.

If at some point Gen2 is still full after a collection and the memory request can't be granted, the garbage collector may respond to this by asking the operating system for more memory. However, when nothing helps anymore, an `OutOfMemoryException` will be thrown, indicating the allocation failure.

LARGE OBJECT HEAP

To be completely honest, I should point out there's a fourth space on the managed heap called the large object heap (LOH). It provides space for objects that have a size of 85,000 bytes or more. Those are not subject to collection based on generations because they're deemed too expensive to move around all the time. Typical examples include images that got loaded in memory.

Boxing

One of the core design choices made for .NET's type system is to have a unified view over value types and reference types. By doing so, every type derives from the mother of all types: System.Object. Especially in the pregenerics era, this had several advantages because you could define a general-purpose data structure such as a list to hold objects of any type:

```
public class ArrayList
{
    private object[] items;
    ...
}
```

In languages such as Java, there was no such unification, requiring users to jump through seemingly artificial hoops to package up (the equivalent to) a value typed object in some "box" before it could be used where an Object-typed instance is expected:

```
// How things would look in Java, requiring explicit boxing.
Object number = new Integer(42);
```

Compared to unmanaged languages like C and C++, the .NET platform tries to abstract away from memory-centric design choices such as stack allocation and heap allocation that would have to be taken by developers using types. The allocation location of an object depends solely on its type, not its use. This is in direct contrast with, for example, C++, where one can either heap-allocate (using the new keyword) or stack-allocate objects.

In fact, it's fair to say that even the use of the stack for value type object allocations on .NET is pretty much an implementation detail. One of the biggest advantages of using the stack for value type allocation is that it makes deallocation simple. Just drop the high-water mark of the stack (for example, upon returning from a method) to deallocate objects that live at the top of it. Because no one can reference to those cells (in well-behaved and verified programs, that is; refer to Figure 9.9), it's safe to do so.

In the world of this unified type system (with regard to value versus reference types), what do you expect to be the characteristic of the root of the type inheritance hierarchy, namely System.Object? Does it have to be a reference type of a value type? There's no simple answer to this question, without going into detail about the implementation of the runtime. Suffice to say that it's more convenient to make System.Object a reference type and have value types derive from it through a System.ValueType that receives special treatment from the runtime. The following piece of code can be used to visualize the inheritance hierarchy a value type, like a `System.Int32`, is involved in:

```
int x = 42;


var int32 = x.GetType();
Console.WriteLine(int32);


var valueType = int32.BaseType;
Console.WriteLine(valueType);


var @object = valueType.BaseType;
Console.WriteLine(@object);


var nothing = @object.BaseType;
Console.WriteLine(nothing == null ? "Root of hierarchy" : "Oops");
```

REFLECTION

The preceding fragment uses a runtime facility called reflection that allows us to take a look at an object's type and all of its members, at runtime. We discuss the use of reflection later in Chapter 21, "Reflection." For now, just take a look at the return type of the GetType and BaseType calls, which is System.Type. This type acts as a descriptor for a *type*. An instance of System.Type describes a *type*. It can be compared to metadata catalog *tables* in database systems, which, for example, reflect the columns defined on a *table*.

Because `System.Object` is a reference type, receivers of such an object will want to reach out to the heap to access the encapsulated data. However, because value types derive from this base type, there seems to be an issue:

```
Bar(42);
...


void Bar(object x)
{
    // Use x one way or another
}
```

Here, the `Bar` method expects a parameter that's statically typed to be `System.Object`, so code using this object inside the `Bar` method will look out for the object on the heap. Essentially, a `System.Object` is the managed code analogy to a pointer. However, if we pass an Int32 *value* 42 to it, does that mean to look at address 42 in the heap? Clearly, something is missing to make the preceding code work. In contrast, the following fragment doesn't suffer from this problem because the receiving end sees the Int32 coming in with that particular type:

```
Foo(42);
...

void Foo(int x)
{
    // Use x one way or another
}
```

Stated otherwise, there's a convention that says value typed parameters must be located on the stack. (The caller pushes them on there, the callee finds them there.) In the first example, though, receiving a reference typed parameter would mean to look on the heap. Figure 9.13 shows how invalid treatment of a value (which is merely an opaque bit sequence) as a reference would violate memory and type safety.

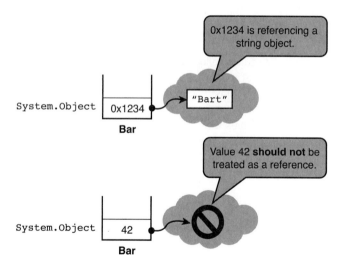

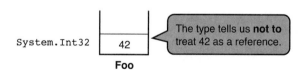

FIGURE 9.13   Treating a value type as a reference would violate type safety.

To solve this problem, the runtime has a mechanism called boxing (and the reverse operation called unboxing) to pass a value typed object in such a manner that it can safely be viewed through the lenses of a reference. To do so, it basically "boxes" the value up in a heap-allocated cell, tagged with type information. This only needs to happen when an instance of a value type is to be treated as a System.Object. To go back the other way, the contents of the cell can be transferred back to the stack to be used as a value type directly.

For illustrative purposes, compile the little Bar calling code fragment and take a look inside ILDASM. To show the unboxing as well, cast the received parameter back to an int, as shown here:

```
class Box
{
    static void Main()
    {
        Bar(42);
    }

    static void Bar(object value)
    {
        // For some mysterious reason, we know we'll always
        // get an Int32 through the value parameter.
        int a = (int)value;
    }
}
```

Figure 9.14 shows the code emitted for the Main method. As you can see, the compiler has emitted a box instruction to wrap up the int32 value in a heap-allocated object to make sure the receiving end can safely access the object.

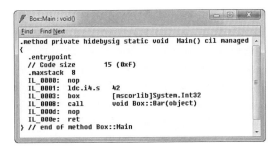

FIGURE 9.14   The value type object gets boxed before the call to Bar(object).

On the receiving end, the opposite operation happens as a result of casting the object-typed parameter up to an Int32. At this point, the integral value needs to be transferred back to the stack, which is done by the unbox operation, as shown in Figure 9.15.

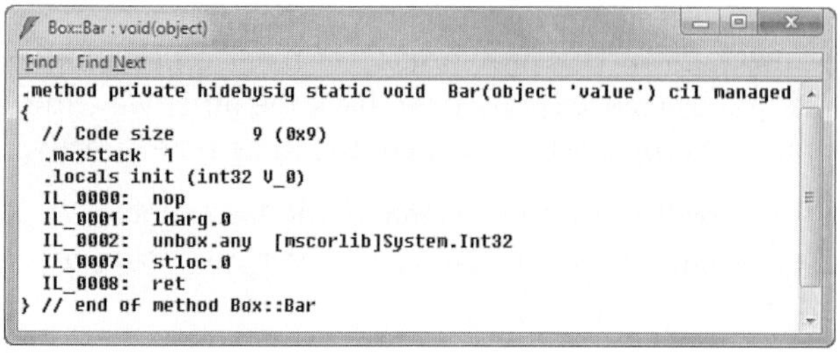

Box::Bar : void(object)
Find Find Next
.method private hidebysig static void Bar(object 'value') cil managed
{
// Code size 9 (0x9)
.maxstack 1
.locals init (int32 V_0)
IL_0000: nop
IL_0001: ldarg.0
IL_0002: unbox.any [mscorlib]System.Int32
IL_0007: stloc.0
IL_0008: ret
} // end of method Box::Bar

FIGURE 9.15 Unboxing transfers the heap-allocated box contents back to the stack.

This whole mechanism is summarized in Figure 9.16.

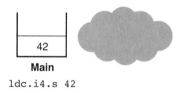

42
Main
ldc.i4.s 42
Int32
42
0x1234
Main
box Int32
Call Bar
Int32
42
value
0x1234
42
Bar
unbox Int32

FIGURE 9.16 Unboxing a value that got boxed before.

One of the most attractive aspects of boxing is also the main disadvantage. Because the whole boxing and unboxing process is transparent to the developer (module the cast, which just looks like any other ordinary cast), it's not at all clear that heap allocations are happening. In some cases, this could lead to suboptimal performance, typically when used in conjunction with large-volume nongeneric collections:

```
var lst = new ArrayList();
for (int i = 0; i < 1000000; i++)
    lst.Add(i);
```

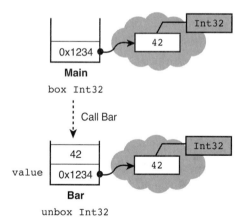

```
var sum = 0L;
foreach (int i in lst)
    sum += i;
```

Here, every call to Add causes boxing because the receiving parameter is typed to take in a System.Object. In the foreach loop, which is really syntactical sugar on top of the enumerator pattern, unboxing happens when the IEnumerator.Current property is to be assigned to the loop variable i, which is typed to be Int32.

GENERICS

The key issue with the preceding fragment is not so much about boxing and unboxing but points at a missing type system feature pre-.NET 2.0. In particular, the lack of being able to parameterize the ArrayList on an element type forces us to cast up and down all over the place, both to get elements in and out of the collection. If the elements turn out to be value types, this corresponds to boxing and unboxing.

Generics were introduced in .NET 2.0 to mitigate the omission of parameterized types. By creating a blueprint of a collection type that can hold "elements of type T, where T can be substituted for any concrete type," the runtime knows exactly what the layout of a constructed type looks like. In other words, the use of object as the escape valve is no longer needed, hence avoiding boxing. In the world of generics, we would write the earlier code as follows:

```
var lst = new List<int>();
for (int i = 0; i < 1000000; i++)
    lst.Add(i); // Now takes in an int parameter...

var sum = 0L;
foreach (int i in lst)
    sum += i;
```

No boxing or unboxing takes place for this piece of code anymore. You are invited to run some performance tests on these code fragments using the Stopwatch class. As usual, keep in mind that the value of performance tests is to be questioned, especially if you haven't set a baseline for your application's performance against which to measure. Nevertheless, having core improvements at the runtime level pays off because every user of the runtime (and the frameworks on top of it) benefits from it. Generics are such a feature.

We discuss generics in much more detail in Chapter 15, "Generic Types and Methods."

The Dangers of Mutable Value Types

Being passed by value, there are some dangers associated with the use of value types, especially when they're made mutable. In general, it's a bad idea to allow mutation of structs; instead, simply create a new value instance and substitute the original value altogether. A

good example of the problems that could arise when dealing with mutable value types is
shown here:

```csharp
using System;

class Program
{
    static void Main()
    {
        var kid = new Kid();
        Console.WriteLine(kid.Location.X + ", " + kid.Location.Y);
        kid.Location.X = 3;
        kid.Location.Y = 4;
        Console.WriteLine(kid.Location.X + ", " + kid.Location.Y);
    }
}

class Kid
{
    public Point Location { get; set; }
}

struct Point
{
    public int X { get; set; }
    public int Y { get; set; }
}
```

What would you expect the outcome to be? Let's take a look. Due to the zero initialization
of fields by the runtime, the original printout of the coordinates should be all zeros. The
interesting bit happens on lines three and four of the Main method. Because we're trying
to move the object, we're retrieving the original Location object, which is typed to be a
Point. Because this type is a struct, it's copied by value. In other words, we just got a local
copy of the (0, 0) point and will now try to mutate it:

```csharp
// How line 3 would be translated
_temp = kid.Location; // Oops, this creates a copy
_temp.X = 3;
// How line 4 would be translated
_temp = kid.Location; // Again, a copy is made
_temp.Y = 4;
```

If this code would compile fine, the kid's location wouldn't change at all because nothing
but the local copy of the point was changed. Luckily, the C# compiler prevents you from
making this mistake:

```
pt.cs(9,1): error CS1612: Cannot modify the return value of 'Kid.Location'
        because it is not a variable
pt.cs(10,1): error CS1612: Cannot modify the return value of 'Kid.Location'
        because it is not a variable
```

Instead of trying this, it's better to prevent changes to the Point object and just have the user substitute the Location property value for an entirely new Point instead:

```
using System;

class Program
{
    static void Main()
    {
        var kid = new Kid();
        Console.WriteLine(kid.Location.X + ", " + kid.Location.Y);
        kid.Location = new Point(3, 4);
        Console.WriteLine(kid.Location.X + ", " + kid.Location.Y);
    }
}

class Kid
{
    public Point Location { get; set; }
}

struct Point
{
    private int _x;
    private int _y;

    public Point(int x, int y)
    {
        _x = x;
        _y = y;
    }

    public int X { get { return _x; } }
    public int Y { get { return _y; } }
}
```

Alternatively, turn the location's type into a reference type. However, doing so blindly just to restore the mutability property usually is not a good idea. Always think about the characteristic of the type first: Does it represent a value, or is it something one wants to refer to? When the former is true, a struct is the right choice, and declaring the value type as immutable is highly recommended.

MAKING IMMUTABILITY SIMPLER

Because of a growing desire to have a simpler concurrent programming model, it is quite possible that future versions of the runtime and/or language will offer more immutability primitives.

Notice that our declaration of properties with private setters doesn't offer all the desired protection against mutation. It's still possible for code defined on the struct to mutate its fields. It would be much better to declare two read-only fields for the X and Y coordinates. A thorough discussion of fields and properties is the subject of Chapter 11, "Fields, Properties, and Indexers."

Type Members

Types have members defined on them that provide means to store state or invoke operations. Those members include methods, constructors, fields, properties, indexers, events, and a few more concepts. Before we focus on each of those, we'll cover some of the general aspects associated with members, such as visibility and the distinction between static and instance members.

Visibility

To limit access to members, accessibility modifiers exist. This functionality is intertwined with support for object-oriented programming, as you will see in Chapter 14, "Object-Oriented Programming."

Type Visibility

Visibility exists not only on the member level, but also on the type level. Let's take a look at that first. A type's visibility determines from where it can be used, in particular whether other assemblies can access it. Assemblies can be seen roughly as containers for types (as detailed in Chapter 25, "Assemblies and Application Domains"). For example, the System.String type lives in an assembly called mscorlib.dll and has been declared as "public," which means other assemblies can access it.

If you were to take a look at mscorlib.dll in tools like Reflector, you would notice quite a few types that are displayed using a gray font, indicating they're nonpublic. Those types can be used only from within the same assembly and are said to be "internal." This is the default for types if no visibility modifier is specified:

```
namespace HR
{
    class Person
    {
        public string Name { get; set; }
        public int Age { get; set; }
    }
}
```

Here, the `Person` type doesn't have an explicit access modifier specified. Assuming the type is defined directly in a namespace (which can be omitted and is discussed in Chapter 24, "Namespaces"), its visibility defaults to internal such that other types in the same assembly can access it, but types on the outside can't. Notice that you can also nest structs and classes, in which case the omission of an access modifier defaults to private:

```
class Person
{
    class Jewelry  // Only accessible to code inside the Person class
    {
    }
}
```

The same defaults hold for types other than classes, including interfaces, structs, enums, and delegates. To override those, you can specify another access modifier explicitly:

```
namespace HR
{
    public class Person
    {
        public string Name { get; set; }
        public int Age { get; set; }
    }
}
```

With the `Person` type declared as public, another assembly referencing ours can now access and use it. You learn how to structure types in assemblies and cross-reference them in Chapter 25.

For nested types, things are a bit different. Here the concept of accessibility domains comes into play. In short, an accessibility domain indicates where in a program a type or member can be referenced. Nesting of members in types but also of types in other types causes the accessibility domain not only to depend on the access modifier but also on the accessibility domain of the enclosing type. For example:

```
class Person
{
    public class Jewelry
    {
    }
}
```

Here, the `Jewelry` class is declared public, but it won't reveal the type to the outside world because the enclosing class isn't made public too. The effective accessibility for the innermost type is internal, just like its enclosing type.

LIKE ACCESS CONTROL SYSTEMS

It might help to think about accessibility domains as being similar to access control systems (for example, on the file system level). In there, you may have full access to a file (our analogy to a member), but if you don't have the rights to traverse the folder hierarchy (analogous to possibly nested types) leading to the file, you're still out of luck with regard to access to the file.

By default, it's a good practice to keep types internal to your own assembly unless you're providing a framework library or require different components of your program to depend on each other. When you make something public, you can bet that others will start to depend on the exposed functionality. This will prevent you from evolving the types in various ways without breaking others. The opposite way of starting by making things internal (the default) enables you to change your mind and expose stuff going forward.

Member Visibility

At the level of types, we've seen a number of access modifiers already. One is public, whereas another is internal (the default, hence we didn't show it). To recap, the former exposes the type to other assemblies, whereas the other restricts its access to the current assembly.

When nesting members in types or when nesting types in types, there are a few more options to pick from in the realm of accessibility. The defaults are also quite different depending on the nature of the types involved. For classes and structs, things are very similar. The default visibility for a member in those is private:

```
class Person
{
    int _age;
}

class Program
{
    static void Main()
    {
        var p = new Person();
        p._age = 27;  // Error: _age cannot be accessed; it's private to Person
    }
}
```

To avoid confusion, it's good practice to explicitly state the visibility. Especially for people coming from a C/C++ background, things may get confusing otherwise because the distinction between structs and classes is tightly coupled with visibility in those languages. An example of a mix of visibility modifiers is shown here:

```
class Person
{
    private int _age;

    public void Pay(decimal amount) { ... }
    internal void Fire() { ... }
}
```

The private access modifier restricts access to the same type only. For example, the Pay method could use the _age field to make some calculations, but no one outside the type can access the field.

When using public, the member has the potential to be seen from outside the enclosing type, in case the enclosing type has sufficient visibility by itself. This is based on the concept of accessibility domains, as discussed previously. In the preceding example, the type is internal, so Pay won't be visible outside the current assembly even though it's public.

Finally, the internal modifier exposes the member to the whole enclosing assembly, which isn't any different from Pay in the example. However, if the Person type were to be public, the Fire method would still be restricted to the current assembly only.

Two more accessibility levels exist, called protected and protected internal. Those are tightly coupled with object-oriented programming, which is discussed in Chapter 14. Because structs cannot be used in inheritance hierarchies, the use of those access modifiers is restricted to classes.

Two other type categories exist. One is the concept of an *enum*, which is much like a collection of named values. Those values act as members of the enum and are always public. Chapter 11 contains an overview of enums and their use.

```
enum Color
{
    Red,
    Blue,
    Green
}
```

For interface types, members are always public, too. Interfaces enable you to declare a contract to be implemented by a type. We discuss interfaces in Chapter 14.

```
interface IEnumerable
{
    IEnumerator GetEnumerator();
}
```

Static Versus Instance

Different types of members can be associated with instances of a type or with the type itself. This is where the static modifier comes in, allowing one to associate a member with a type rather than individual instances. Or to look at it another way, a type's static members are shared across all instances, whereas instance members can be associated with and operate on individual instances. This sharing viewpoint is, in fact, how Visual Basic surfaces static members, using a Shared keyword rather than C#'s static.

As mentioned previously, classes allow bundling together state and operations in one notion, which closely aligns with object-oriented programming principles. When looking at the concept of shared static members, both those concerns apply there, too. One place where we've already seen the use of the static keyword to denote an operation is on every single entry point to a program we've written so far:

```
class Program
{
    static void Main(string[] args)
    {
        ...
    }
}
```

CODE SNIPPETS FOR COMMON TASKS

Visual Studio has a feature called code snippets that enable templated snippets of code to be inserted by using a shortcut. Because declaring a Main method is common, snippets for different Main method definitions are included with the product. For example, to insert "static void Main," you can type svm and press Tab twice. The "sim" snippet is used to insert a Main method with an int return type.

The value of this feature is rather limited for Main method declaration; after all, the creation of an executable project includes the entry-point declaration right from the start. However, for other patterns, such as various kinds of statements or members, snippets are quite handy. For example, you can insert a constructor on a type using ctor.

Notice that the omission of an access modifier on the Main method is permitted because it gets very special treatment by the runtime. What's of key importance in our example is the fact that the Main method is shared across all instances of Program. In fact, you usually don't even create an instance of the Program class. Now let's try to add another method to the Program class and call it from Main, as follows:

```
class Program
{
    static void Main(string[] args)
    {
```

```
        if (args.Length != 1)
        {
            PrintUsage();
            return;
        }
    }

    void PrintUsage()
    {
        Console.WriteLine("Usage:  sample.exe <file>");
    }
}
```

The preceding won't compile because `PrintUsage` is not declared as static. Because of their instance-independent nature, static members cannot reach out to instance members (if no target instance is specified). Figure 9.17 pinpoints this code defect in the error list.

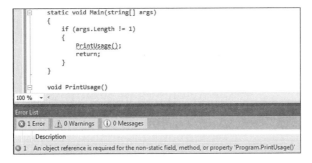

FIGURE 9.17   Static members cannot call instance members directly.

Declaring the `PrintUsage` method as static will resolve this issue. Similar remarks hold for the use of state, which is kept in so-called fields. We cover methods, fields, and other members in much more detail, but suffice to say that fields cover the data and state aspect of a type, whereas methods deal with the operational behavior. Here is an example of a singleton class that leverages a static field. This allows us to explain quite a few concepts all at once.

- ▶ Notion of class instances
- ▶ Creation of instances using constructors
- ▶ Recap of visibility aspects on members
- ▶ Use of static members and fields

Because this example serves merely to set the stage for further exploration, we'll not delve too deeply into the object-oriented concepts (which are covered in Chapter 14).

```
sealed class PaymentService
{
    private static PaymentService s_service;
    private Queue<Payment> _payments;

    private PaymentService()
    {
        // This is a private constructor; therefore it can only
        // be called from inside the PaymentService type.
        _payments = new Queue<Payment>();
    }

    public static PaymentService Service
    {
        get
        {
            // Create service the first time it's requested. For
            // the remainder of the program's lifetime we'll be
            // using this singleton instance.
            if (s_service == null)
            {
                s_service = new PaymentService();
            }

            return s_service;
        }
    }

    public void SchedulePayment(int fromAccount, int toAccount, decimal amount)
    {
        _payments.Enqueue(new Payment(fromAccount, toAccount, amount));
    }
}
```

The idea of this PaymentService is to be a singleton, meaning only a single instance of it can exist in the program. In a slightly more flexible setting, you might want to control the number of instances of a given type that can be created. The first thing you must do to avoid creation of arbitrary instances of the class is to make sure no one can call the constructor. Instance constructors are a means of creating an instance of a class; you'll see later that static constructors exist, too, allowing you to initialize static state.

```
private PaymentService()
{
    // This is a private constructor; therefore it can only
    // be called from inside the PaymentService type.
    _payments = new Queue<Payment>();
}
```

They look like methods but lack a name or a return type, depending on your point of view. One way to look at it is as a method whose name is the same as the containing class's. Alternatively, you could say it doesn't have a name and the return type is the containing class.

Because there's no static keyword on the preceding constructor, it's an instance constructor, which can be called using the new keyword, as we see in the Service property. Because it's declared with the private access modifier, the only valid place for it to be called is from inside the same class. Notice that the constructor does initialize per-instance state that's kept in the _payments field. The underscore-prefixed notation is a widely used pattern to recognize the use of fields rather than, say, local variables or parameters.

```
private Queue<Payment> _payments;
```

The Service property is declared as public and static, hence the way to call it will be as follows, "dotting into the type":

```
PaymentService theOneAndOnlyInstance = PaymentService.Service;
```

On the inside, this property checks whether there's already a single instance of the type created by checking the static s_service field. Across all instances of the type, there'll be only one such field, which is exactly what allows us to enforce the singleton policy:

```
public static PaymentService Service
{
    get
    {
        // Create service the first time it's requested. For
        // the remainder of the program's lifetime we'll be
        // using this singleton instance.
        if (s_service == null)
        {
            s_service = new PaymentService();
        }

        return s_service;
    }
}
```

Again, the use of the s_ prefix to denote a static field is purely a convention that you can either take or leave (but if you take it, be consistent about it across your codebase).

From a user's point of view, dealing with the singleton and invoking SchedulePayment now looks like this:

```
// Static members are called with the type (name) as the left-hand side.
var service = PaymentService.Service;

// Instance members are called with an instance as the left-hand side.
service.SchedulePayment(123, 321, 456.78m);
```

After we've created our single authoritative payment service instance by calling the Service property, we can call instance members such as the method shown here:

```
public void SchedulePayment(int fromAccount, int toAccount, decimal amount)
{
    _payments.Enqueue(new Payment(fromAccount, toAccount, amount));
}
```

This one now operates on instance data (in this particular case, the _payments field). In every single instance of PaymentService (in our case, carefully controlled to be just a single one), such a piece of _payments data exists.

Almost all types of members can be used either on a static level or an instance level. In the preceding example, we saw an instance constructor and an instance method, together with a static property.

WHY BOTHER WITH SINGLETONS?

You might wonder why you would want to bother with a singleton instance if you could make all the operations and state static anyway. For example, in our code, we could have created a static SchedulePayment method that uses a static field for payments internally. Although this is true, there are cases where the use of a singleton leads to a cleaner overall design. One case is where you want the returned singleton object to obey a certain interface contract, which exists only for instance members. So in such a situation, you must have an instance.

Related to this is the factory pattern, where you want to create a static method to construct an object of a given type. However, thanks to object-oriented principles, you can return an instance of a subtype from inside the factory method:

```
static Animal CreateAnimal(int legs, ...)
{
    if (legs == 0 && ...)  return new Fish();
    else ...
}
```

In this example, CreateAnimal could return a Fish or a Mammal based on different inputs. The decision what to return could be based on the number of legs or other characteristic properties of an animal that got passed to the factory method.

Another example of the use of static is shown here. It basically keeps a counter for the number of instances created, on a per-type basis. If this state were to be kept on each instance, it clearly couldn't be a "shared" counter.

```
class Person
{
    private static int s_population;

    public Person()
    {
        s_population++;
    }
}
```

STATIC ISN'T YOUR MAIN APPLICATION INGREDIENT

The brilliance of cooks with a flagship cuisine lies in their intimate knowledge of which flavors and ingredients work and don't work for their masterpiece dishes. In the world of programming, the same truth holds.

As object-oriented as C# (and, in fact, the CLR) is, seldom should you see static members be dominant in your code base. In fact, use of static members on all possible occasions comes very close to procedural programming. By using static everywhere, you can't take advantage of core object-oriented principles such as virtual methods and polymorphism. Those concepts are discussed in Chapter 14.

Beginning programmers in C-style object-oriented languages sometimes miss out on the object-oriented constructs and spread the use of "static" throughout the code in a contagious manner. Perhaps the fix vaguely suggested by Figure 9.17's error (that is, "I don't seem to have an instance, let's make it static") encourages this.

Either way, the core question to ask for each member is whether you want it to operate on a per-type basis or a per-instance basis. For example, the notion of opening a database connection likely has most meaning when applied to some instance of a Connection object.

To summarize our discussion, the distinction between static and instance state is illustrated in Figure 9.18.

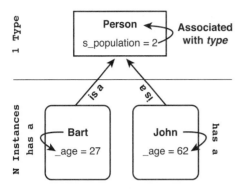

FIGURE 9.18   Static versus instance state.

Partial Types

C# 2.0 Although at this point we're focusing on members that live in types such as structs and classes, this is a good time to introduce the concept of *partial definitions*. To set the scene, we have to discuss the physical structure of a development project in terms of files and the types they define.

It's typical and considered good style to define types in a file that has the same name as the type itself. For example, a class Person would be defined in a file called Person.cs. Although this is not required by the compiler or the runtime (in contrast to, say, Java, where folders and files play a role in type lookup), it has various advantages when browsing code.

During prototyping or experimentation, though, it's often handy to put multiple types in the same file. Sometimes it also makes sense to put (little) types that belong together close to each other in one file, too. As you will see later, types are structured in namespaces, which are typically reflected in a folder structure in a project. Again, this is not required by the runtime. It's up to you to apply good judgment when making decisions about physical file organization in a project, but seriously consider these hints.

PROJECT FOLDERS AND "USAGE-FIRST" DEVELOPMENT

Some features in Visual Studio apply the guidance mentioned here when organizing the structure of a project and when generating types. For example, the creation of folders inside a project will reflect itself in the namespace chosen for new files that get added to that folder. If the project's default namespace is Contoso.Cashflow and a folder is called Services\Payment, a new file added to that folder will get a namespace declaration for Contoso.Cashflow.Services.Payment, containing a type reflecting the filename. All this can be modified by the developer, but there are good reasons to follow such a convention. Clarity and consistency of project file organizations is invaluable.

Starting with Visual Studio 2010, you can also let the IDE generate types and their members based on "usage-first" development. Before actually defining a class called Person, you can start writing code that will reflect its use:

```
var p = new Person("Bart", 27);
```

Right-clicking `Person` will give an option to generate a type of choice (either a class or a struct), which will be placed in a file called Person.cs. Again, disciplined use of well-defined folder and file organization is encouraged.

Now that you've learned how a single code file can contain multiple type definitions, the opposite question can be asked: Can the definition of a type be stretched across different files? Starting with C# 2.0, the answer is yes, thanks to the feature of partial classes (structs and interfaces). Although this feature is useful by itself to group various aspects of a type's implementation in distinct files, resulting in faster code browsing, the feature's main reason for existence stems from code-generating tools. A good example can be found in the Windows Forms designer, which emits code that defines the layout of controls on a form. This autogenerated code is not meant to be touched by developers directly because it gets regenerated when using the designer, possibly overwriting changes made by developers. Before C# 2.0, this code got emitted to a (collapsed) "region" in the form's code file:

```
class LoginForm : Form
{
    #region Windows Form Designer generated code
    ...
    #endregion

    //
    // Developer code goes here...
    //
}
```

The `#region` directive enables sections of code to be collapsed in code editors such as Visual Studio. Obviously, having this generated code section in the same code file where developers had to add code for various event handlers (which obviously cannot be generated by the designer because you want custom code in there) piqued developers' curiosity. By accident or not, and despite warnings discouraging people from changing the generated code, this code got tweaked by users from time to time, sometimes even rendering the designer broken as it choked on unknown code.

XAML TO THE RESCUE?

Although code generation works just fine, it's often a source of headaches, too. One of the main flaws of automatic code generation is the difficulty for tools to regain intelligence about the code's intent. For example, the Windows Forms designer must execute the designer-generated code to figure out how the controls are laid out. Furthermore, the ability for developers to mess with generated code can cause quite a bit of grief as well. Changes can get overwritten by tools, causing developer frustration. Tweaked generated code can also cause designers to freak out due to unexpected behavior caused by the foreign code inserted by the developer (for example, exceptions may occur).

Even though code is usually required to execute items, it's not the ideal medium for sharing across different tools and even people. In some sense, the use of code is "one bridge too far," going directly to details of the implementation rather than expressing the domain-specific notions (such as nesting of UI controls). For example, the code that gets generated by the Windows Forms designer isn't well suited for use by tools other than Visual Studio's, which may be a worthy goal when professional (human) designers enter the picture.

XAML is a markup language used by WPF to express the declaration of a UI in a way that it can be shared easily between different tools such as Visual Studio and Expression Blend. To make the XAML markup executable, it ultimately is turned into code during compilation, but the original declarations remain available (and are generally safe to be tweaked manually by designers and developers). This is basically what allows the "designer-developer" collaboration food chain that's a key design goal for Windows Presentation Foundation (WPF) and Silverlight.

To avoid those issues, C# 2.0 introduced the notion of partial classes, such that the generated code can be separated from the code that's written by the developer. When looking in Visual Studio 2010, you'll clearly see two files for a Windows Forms form that was added to the project, as shown in Figure 9.19.

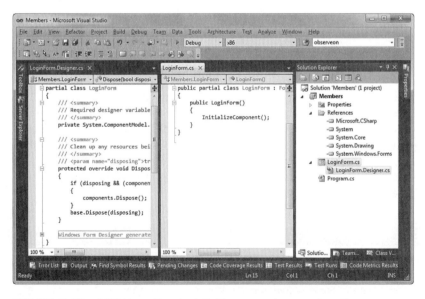

FIGURE 9.19   A Windows Form's definition spread across two files.

Notice how simple the code on the right (which is the developer's playground to add custom logic to the form) looks, in contrast to what it would have looked like before C# 2.0. In practice, you almost never have to inspect the generated code that appears on the left and is stored in a .Designer.cs file.

The key essence of this feature lies in the fact that a class's (or struct's or interface's) members can be spread across multiple files. To use it, you just prefix the class, struct, or interface keyword with *partial*. One or more partial definitions of the type can now occur throughout all the files that get compiled. During compilation, it's the compiler's job to paste together all the fragments that make up the same type.

PARTIAL METHODS

C# 3.0 introduced another "partial definition" feature, called partial methods. We take a look at them in Chapter 10. The common theme between all those features is to aid in code-generation scenarios where a code generator takes responsibility for one part of a type definition and the developer takes care of the other parts.

Summary

Types are the containers for state and operations. Although we haven't talked about object-oriented programming yet, we've learned about various essential features of types. First, we constrasted classes and structs, discussing concepts of references and values. Related to this, we learned about memory management provided by the runtime, in particular the stack and the heap. Finally, the concept of boxing was explained.

In preparation for the next few chapters, we also talked about common aspects of a type's members. This includes the notion of visibility and the difference between static- and instance-level members. To wrap up our discussion of members, we also learned how to use partial types to split the definition of a type's members across different code files.

Now that we've learned about types as containers of members, we're ready to look into them in more detail. The next chapters discuss the code aspect of types being methods, followed by an exploration of the data aspect exposed through fields, properties, and indexers. Constructors and finalizers are covered as well.

IN THIS CHAPTER

▶ Defining Methods 501

▶ Return Type 502

▶ Parameters 504

▶ Overloading 516

▶ Extension Methods 522

▶ Partial Methods 532

▶ Extern Methods 536

▶ Refactoring 537

▶ Code Analysis 543

After having introduced the notion of types in Chapter 9, we're now ready to zoom into a type's members one by one. In this chapter, we focus on methods. Classes and structs act as containers for both data and operations. As you'll see, all the available members emphasize one of those aspects. For methods, we're clearly in the latter camp because they consist of code bodies. Users of the type can invoke those methods to carry out certain tasks that can modify state.

We also learn how to declare methods, dealing with concepts such as signatures, parameters, and overloading. Furthermore, our attention will reach out to method-related language features such as partial methods, extern methods, and extension methods.

Special kinds of methods, such as constructors or property getters and setters, are discussed in later chapters. For now, we focus on "plain old" methods only.

Defining Methods

A method can be defined as either a static or an instance member, which influences what state is available to it. You've seen the use of a special static method plenty of times, namely an application's entry point Main method:

```
class Program
{
    static void Main(string[] args)
    {
        ...
    }
}
```

Of the modifiers available on a method declaration, we've only used the static one. Many other modifiers exist to specify things such as visibility (public, private, internal, and the OO-related protected and protected internal access modifiers). You'll see more of those modifiers in Chapter 14, "Object-Oriented Programming," including abstract, virtual, override, sealed, and new.

The declaration of a method consists of two parts: a method header and an optional implementation code block (referred to as the method body). Don't worry about the fact that the implementation is optional for now; it will become clear in the next chapter.

Figure 10.1 illustrates what makes up the method header. The required parts include the method name, return type, and parameter list.

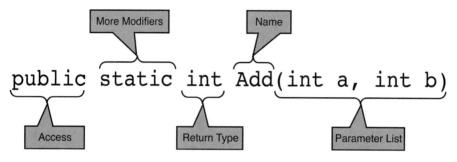

FIGURE 10.1   Method header.

GENERIC METHODS

From the illustration in Figure 10.1, we omitted two more optional parts that deal with generics: type parameters and generic constraints. Because a whole chapter is devoted to generics (Chapter 15, "Generic Types and Methods"), we don't discuss them here.

Return Type

The return type of a method can be either a type or void. This indicates what a caller of the method will get (under normal circumstances) in return for calling the method. When a type is specified, all execution paths through the method's body should reach a point where the return keyword is used to hand back a result to the caller. As you see later, it's also possible for a method to throw an exception. For example:

```
public static int Div(int n, int d)
{
    if (d == 0)
        throw new ArgumentOutOfRangeException("d");

    return n / d;
}
```

In the preceding example, the expression n / d results in an int value that can be returned to the caller by using the return keyword. If the denominator is zero, an exception will terminate the method without the need to reach a return statement. It's invalid to have any code path that doesn't return a value that's compatible with the return type. This is shown in Figure 10.2. In this particular example, the compiler reasons that the last if statement's condition might not be evaluated as true, so we would fall through to the end of the method without returning a value.

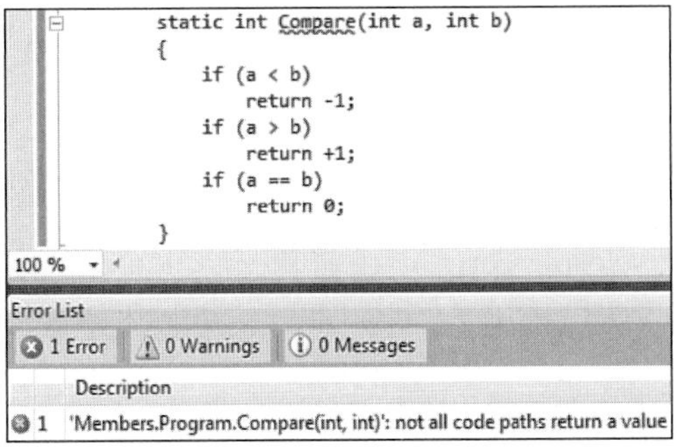

```
static int Compare(int a, int b)
{
    if (a < b)
        return -1;
    if (a > b)
        return +1;
    if (a == b)
        return 0;
}
```

100 %

Error List

⊗ 1 Error   ⚠ 0 Warnings   ⓘ 0 Messages

Description

⊗ 1 'Members.Program.Compare(int, int)': not all code paths return a value

FIGURE 10.2   Every code path should return a value of the specified return type.

Notice that the compiler doesn't apply type-specific "domain reasoning" to be smarter about certain branching logic. With our human reasoning, we could figure out we cannot reach the end of the method without returning correctly because two integers are either less than, greater than, or equal to each other. A correct fix would be to restructure the code as follows:

```
static int Compare(int a, int b)
{
    if (a < b)
        return -1;
    else if (a > b)
        return +1;
    else
        return 0;
}
```

Alternatively, you could leave out the last if statement and simply return zero when the execution reaches that point. Or if the contract of Compare is to return a negative number when a is smaller than b, zero when they are equal, and a positive number if a is greater than b, the following code would be much simpler:

```
static int Compare(int a, int b)
{
    return a - b;
}
```

Besides the use of exceptions, one other case where you don't need to return from a method is when the compiler can prove you got an infinite loop going on. In that case, you simply can't return from the method anyway, short of throwing an exception:

```
static int Forever()
{
    while (true) { ... }
}
```

If the return type is declared to be void, no return statements are necessary. It's valid to use them to quit the method before reaching the closing curly brace of the method body if no expression is specified. (That is, you can't return "something" from a "void"-returning method.) For example:

```
static void Main(string[] args)
{
    if (args.Length == 0)
    {
        Console.WriteLine("Usage: echo <name>");
        return;
    }

    Console.WriteLine("Hello {0}", args[0]);
}
```

As you can see, the use of return is not needed at the end of the method, and we can simply fall "through the bottom of the method" to exit and return to the caller. To exit the method before reaching the end, the return statement can be used to simplify logic inside the method body. (For example, in the preceding example it saves us from an else case.)

Parameters

A method can accept zero or more parameters, which mainly act as inputs to a method, in particular to communicate additional state to it. When no parameters are required, an empty pair of parentheses is still required:

```
static void PrintUsage()
{
    Console.WriteLine("Usage:  echo <name>");
}
```

If one or more parameters are required, the parameter list is a comma-separated list of distinctly named parameters, prefixed with a type and optional modifiers.

PARAMETER OR ARGUMENT?

Terms that are often confused and incorrectly used interchangeably are *parameter* and *argument*. The distinction is quite simple, though. Parameters live on a declaration site (for example, in the parameter list of a method), whereas arguments are specified in a call site (for example, when invoking a method). Depending on the angle you approach them, they're very similar: One makes up the receiving end; the other makes up the sending end.

Here are a couple of valid method headers with a different numbers of parameters and some modifiers:

```
string Concat(string str0, string str1, string str2)
bool TryParse(string s, out int result)
int Exchange(ref int location1, int value)
void WriteLine(string format, params object[] arg)
```

Except for the first method, all methods show a different parameter modifier in action. We now discuss all those modifiers in more detail.

Value Parameters

One type of parameter is known as a value parameter. Basically, it's a parameter that doesn't have special modifiers. But why is it called a *value* parameter? Basically, such a parameter receives its input (the *argument* on the call site) *by value*. Notice that this has nothing to do with value or reference types but is simply an aspect of the invocation of a method. Passing a parameter by value means that one can simply assign to the parameter inside the method without affecting the call-site argument.

In more technical terms, the receiving method has a separate storage location for each value parameter that is not shared with the call site at all. To make this clearer, take a look at Figure 10.3, which illustrates passing an argument by value.

When Foo mutates the received parameter value, it's really mutating a local copy that was made during the call. When the call returns, the assigned value isn't propagated to the caller.

The same holds true for a reference-typed object that's passed to a value parameter. When the callee assigns to the received parameter, the assignment doesn't affect the caller. However, changes to the object instance itself will be visible to the caller. It might help to think in terms of what gets copied (just the reference, not what it refers to) and where the accessed data lives. Figure 10.4 shows the effects of a method mutating a reference-typed object instance.

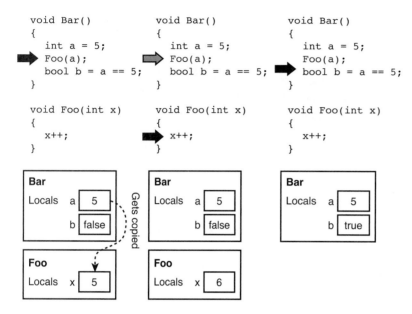

FIGURE 10.3 Passing an argument to a value parameter.

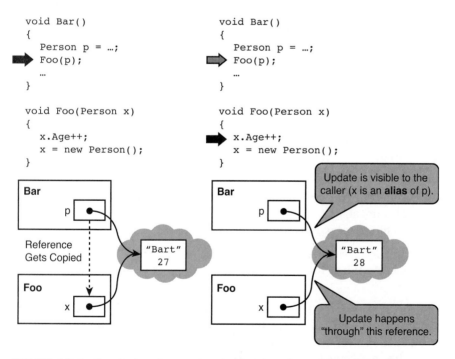

FIGURE 10.4 Passing a reference-typed object by value causes aliasing.

ASSIGNING TO VALUE PARAMETERS CAN BE CONFUSING

From these examples, it should be clear that assigning to a value parameter results in possibly confusing code. I prefer to use an extra local variable when the input of a method needs to be manipulated locally. This also helps debugging because the parameter value will always reveal what was originally received.

What happens here is that the reference gets copied *by value* when making the call from Bar to Foo, passing p as an argument to *value* parameter x. Once the call is made, both p and x now refer to the same object that lives on the .NET heap. In other words, those two variables act as aliases, both referring to the same object. A change through one of the references will become apparent to subsequent accesses made through one of the aliases.

However, when the callee assigns to its local variable x, it effectively puts a reference to another object in the cell, which is invisible to the caller. You are invited to draw the state transitions (similar to the last transition shown later in Figure 10.5) caused by the following line in Figure 10.4:

```
x = new Person();
```

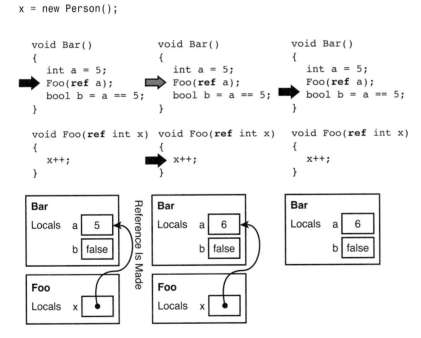

FIGURE 10.5   Passing an argument to a reference parameter.

A reference or value type simply indicates where instances of the type get allocated and what gets copied upon passing such an object *by value*. Value-typed objects are copied wholesale, whereas for reference-typed objects the reference to the target instance is copied, causing aliasing (multiple references referring to the same instance). When using value parameters, the receiving end holds such a local "copy" of the object. Any assignment to that local cell is invisible to the caller, but modifications made through a reference will be visible to the caller due to aliasing.

Reference Parameters

Although assignment to a value parameter is visible only to the current method and not to its caller, reference parameters can circumvent this. Instead of making a copy of the object (whatever that means is dependent on the value- or reference-type characteristic of the object, as you learned in Chapter 9, "Introducing Types"), a reference is made to the local variable held by the caller. Figure 10.5 illustrates the use of the ref modifier to create a reference parameter. Contrast the diagram with that shown earlier in Figure 10.3 to see the difference.

Now inside the Foo method we have a reference to the local variable held in the context of the calling Bar method. Any assignment to the reference parameter will happen to the original location that was passed.

Notice that the use of the ref keyword is mandatory both on the declaration of the parameter and when passing the argument. The latter requirement was introduced to make it obvious what's going on when reading the code of the call site. Whenever you see an argument being passed *by reference*, you can expect the variable that's passed to be replaced wholesale by the method being called.

REF MANDATORY, MOST OF THE TIME

Starting in C# 4.0, ref is not mandatory when used *for interop with COM only*. This is discussed later in Chapter 22, "Dynamic Programming."

Output Parameters

Closely related to reference parameters are output parameters. Conceptually, they serve as additions to the single "return channel" provided by a method's return type. By using the out modifier, such a method can be created:

```
static bool TrySqrt(int input, out double root)
{
    root = 0.0;  // Will learn in while why this is needed

    if (input < 0)
        return false;

    root = Math.Sqrt(input);
    return true;
}
```

In this example, we use the return type to denote success or failure, while the output parameter will receive the result in case of success. This is a common pattern for various Base Class Library (BCL) types such as numeric value types that have a TryParse method:

```
Console.Write("Enter your age: ");
string input = Console.ReadLine();

int age;
if (!int.TryParse(input, out age))
    // Print error message, maybe let the user retry
else
    // We got a valid age
```

Prior to .NET 2.0, such methods didn't exist, and Parse methods had to be used instead. The difference between TryParse and Parse is what happens upon passing invalid input to the method. Parse throws an exception, whereas TryParse doesn't. Because exceptions are expensive and an invalid numeric string is not an exceptional case when dealing with user input, TryParse makes much more sense because it communicates success or failure through a Boolean value that can be checked easily.

Notice again how the out keyword has to be used at both the declaration site and the call site. Similar to reference parameters, this clarifies to the reader of the code what's going on at the method's call site.

Internally, ref and out are implemented both as ref. In fact, the common language runtime does not have a notion of output parameters. Figure 10.6 shows the method header for the following declaration, which uses both ref and out:

```
void Bar(int a, ref int b, out int c)
```

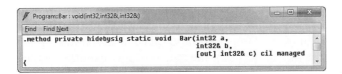

FIGURE 10.6 Reference and output parameters use the **&** suffix.

Basically, output parameters are implemented as reference parameters with an extra piece of metadata stuck on them. The use of this metadata allows compilers to give reference and output parameters different treatment.

So what's the key difference between both parameter types from a C# programmer's point of view? The answer lies in "definite assignment rules" both at the side of the caller and of the callee. For a variable to be passed to a reference parameter, it must be assigned first. For output parameters, the responsibility for assignment is with the method being called, which should guarantee that every code path ensures the output parameter to get assigned to. Figure 10.7 shows violations of both rules.

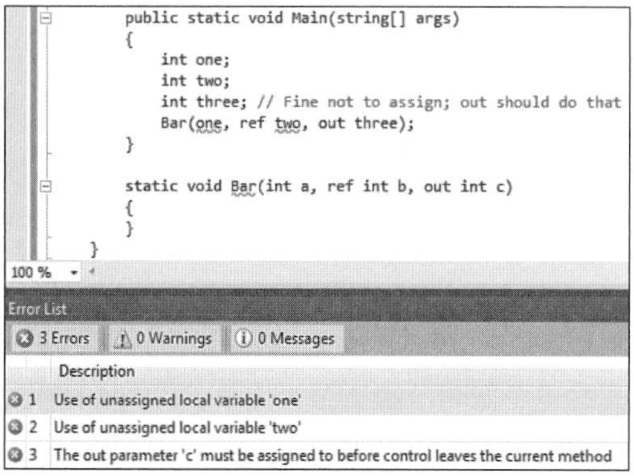

```
public static void Main(string[] args)
{
    int one;
    int two;
    int three; // Fine not to assign; out should do that
    Bar(one, ref two, out three);
}

static void Bar(int a, ref int b, out int c)
{
}
```

100 %

Error List

❌ 3 Errors	⚠ 0 Warnings	ⓘ 0 Messages

	Description
❌ 1	Use of unassigned local variable 'one'
❌ 2	Use of unassigned local variable 'two'
❌ 3	The out parameter 'c' must be assigned to before control leaves the current method

FIGURE 10.7   Definite assignment enforcement for reference and output parameters.

DON'T USE TOO MUCH

Use of output parameters can seem tempting to return multiple results from a method but is rather sticky in the call site because a separate local variable must be declared upfront and the out keyword is required. When you start returning a lot of data, consider wrapping it in some specialized return type. Also starting from .NET 4, you can use the System.Tuple generic types to package objects.

Parameter Arrays

Some methods can benefit from having an unbounded number of arguments passed to them. So far, we've seen an example of this in passing, namely the Console.WriteLine method. Because the first argument can be used to provide a so-called format string, which is a string with placeholders for variant portions, the remainder arguments to fill in those gaps depends on the string itself. For example:

```
Console.WriteLine("{0} + {1} = {2}", a, b, a + b);
```

The use of format strings comes in handy when dealing with quite a bit of formatting, where string concatenation would become very ugly and unreadable:

```
Console.WriteLine(a + " + " + b + " = " + (a + b));
```

In addition to this, it allows for a clean way to localize strings, such as error messages, where the position of the variant portions will be language-dependent:

```
Could not find file {0}.
Het bestand {0} werd niet gevonden.
```

It's clear that the last arguments passed to Console.WriteLine can be plentiful. To allow for a natural calling syntax, it should be possible for the user to pass any number of arguments in a comma-separated manner. But how should the other side (being the method implementation) receive those arguments? This is precisely what parameter arrays enable. They're simply parameters of some array type that appear at the end of the parameter list and are prefixed with the params keyword. The receiving end simply sees them as arrays, but the calling side can omit the array creation code and simply pass arguments comma-separated as if they were corresponding to separate parameters. For example:

```
static int Sum(params int[] numbers)
{
    int sum = 0;
    foreach (var n in numbers)
        sum += n;
    return sum;
}
```

This method can be called either by passing an array or by using the more convenient comma-separated notation:

```
int six = Sum(new[] { 1, 2, 3 });
int ten = Sum(1, 2, 3, 4);
```

The last call basically gets turned into a form like the one here, where an array gets allocated on the user's behalf.

Only one parameter array can appear in a method header, and if it does, it should be the last parameter of the list. Because methods can have overloads (discussed in the "Overloading" section in this chapter), overload resolution might have to pick between a parameter array and a regular method. For example:

```
static int Sum(params int[] numbers)
{ ... }

static int Sum(int a, int b)
{ ... }

static int Sum(int a, int b, int c)
{ ... }
```

The definition of additional low-parameter-count regular methods in addition to one that takes a parameter array is a common practice to reduce excessive heap allocations for arrays passed to every single method call. When calling the Sum method with two or three arguments, the regular methods will take precedence over the parameter array one. This technique is also applied to Console.WriteLine, as shown in Figure 10.8.

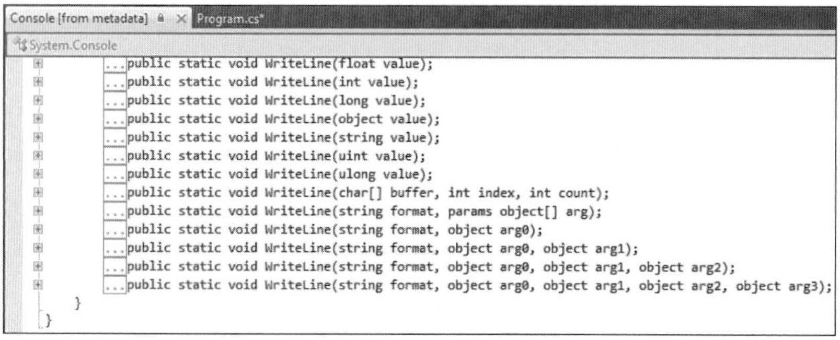

FIGURE 10.8   Use of parameter arrays for methods with high argument count.

Optional and Named Parameters

To aid with COM interoperability scenarios, C# 4.0 introduced optional and named parameters. Although we discuss those interoperability features in more detail when talking about dynamic programming, this is the right place to discuss optional and named parameters.

Methods can have overloads. Basically, that means that different method headers can exist that all share the same name but differ in the number of parameters or the type those parameters have. Often, one wants to provide "convenience overloads" for methods that take a bunch of parameters, supplying default values for more advanced parameters.

A good example is the file-creation application programming interface (API) that exists in the System.IO namespace. One of the most specialized overloads looks like this:

```
public static FileStream Create(string path, int bufferSize,
                                FileOptions options)
```

Two other overloads exist that gradually peel off parameters to reduce the burden put on the user of the API when default values make sense:

```
public static FileStream Create(string path)
{
    return Create(path, 0x1000, FileOptions.None);
}

public static FileStream Create(string path, int bufferSize)
{
    return Create(path, bufferSize, FileOptions.None);
}
```

Those simply supply default values for the omitted parameters and call into the most specific overload that will do all the heavy lifting. Although this works just fine, there's a

lot of overhead associated with the declaration and wiring up of all the different overloads. In addition, the API writer must sense which parameters are going to be most
popular and which ones users will usually want to omit. In this example, the designers of
System.IO thought there was no need for the following overload:

```
public static FileStream Create(string path, FileOptions options)
```

With optional parameters, you can take an alternative approach for defining those
methods. Instead of having more overloads, parameters can specify a default value that's
put in place when the parameter is omitted in a method call. In this example, the API
could be redefined as follows:

```
public static FileStream Create(string path, int bufferSize = 0x1000,
                        FileOptions fileOptions = FileOptions.None)
```

After specifying the parameter type and name, a default value is supplied using what looks
like an assignment. Optional parameters have to go after all required parameters. Valid
default values include constants such as numerals, Boolean values, strings, enums, and the
null reference.

Looking in ILDASM, we see that those parameters got some additional metadata that indicates their optional nature, as well as the default values. Figure 10.9 illustrates this. In
particular, notice that no overloads get generated. Just a single method is defined, with
extra information about the optional parameters.

FIGURE 10.9   Representation of optional parameters uses [opt] and .param metadata.

When calling the method, you can omit any of the optional parameters:

```
Create(\temp\test.txt")
Create(\temp\test.txt", 1024)
Create(\temp\test.txt", 1024, FileOptions.RandomAccess)
```

Figure 10.10 shows how the IntelliSense in Visual Studio communicates the default values
for optional parameters when targeting a certain method. The square bracket notation is
commonly used to indicate something that's optional.

```
public static void Main(string[] args)
{
    Create(
    ┌─────────────────────────────────────────────────────────────────────────────┐
 1. │ FileStream Program.Create(string path, [int bufferSize = 0x1000], [FileOptions fileOptions = FileOptions.None]) │
    └─────────────────────────────────────────────────────────────────────────────┘
    private static FileStream Create(string path, int bufferSize = 0x1000, FileOptions fileOptions
    {
```

FIGURE 10.10   Optional parameter default values showing up in IntelliSense.

If an optional parameter is omitted, the compiler inserts its default value in the call site (indicated in bold), so the preceding examples are turned into these:

```
Create(\temp\test.txt", 4096, FileOptions.None)
Create(\temp\test.txt", 1024, FileOptions.None)
Create(\temp\test.txt", 1024, FileOptions.RandomAccess)
```

BE SURE DEFAULT VALUES ARE TRULY CONSTANT

The mechanism of burning the default values for optional parameters in the call site has advantages and disadvantages. On the positive side, the runtime doesn't have to perform checks to somehow determine which parameters have been left out during a call, inserting default values at runtime. An alternative implementation by which the compiler would generate overloads could have worked, too, but it wouldn't interoperate with existing languages that support optional parameters (such as Visual Basic).

On the flip side, you might be surprised by the fact that the compiler copies default values into the call sites where an argument corresponding to the optional parameter was omitted. In particular, suppose you have multiple assemblies, one of which has a public method with optional parameters defined. Now another assembly calls this method and omits an optional parameter, causing the compiler to copy the default value into your assembly's call site. In this scenario, it no longer suffices to update the default value in the assembly that declares the method because the value got copied to all assemblies using the method. All clients need to be recompiled to pick up the new default.

For this reason, it's strongly encouraged to use optional parameters only when you're absolutely sure the defaults will remain as is, for eternity. If this is not the case, you're better off with classic overloads.

In contrast to a fixed set of overloads, you can now mix and match which parameters to supply to a method call by using the C# 4.0 named parameter feature. The idea is simply to specify an argument value for a parameter by writing down the name rather than matching argument values to parameters by their positions. Suppose you want to override the default value for the FileOptions flag but leave the default bufferSize alone. Using named parameters, you can write the following:

```
Create(\temp\test.txt", fileOptions: FileOptions.RandomAccess)
```

Figure 10.11 shows the IntelliSense experience showing the availability of a certain parameter by its name.

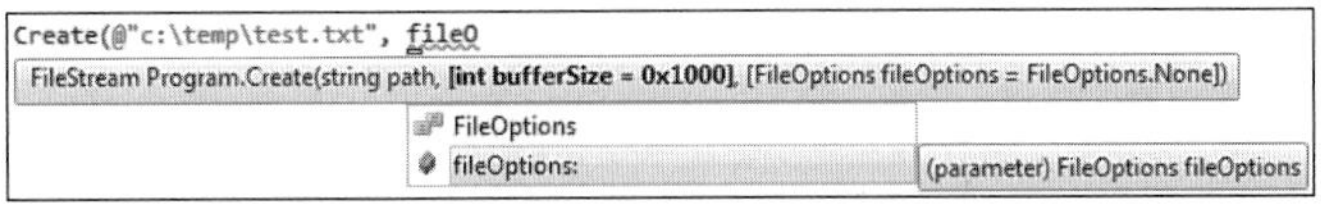

```
Create(@"c:\temp\test.txt", fileO
  FileStream Program.Create(string path, [int bufferSize = 0x1000], [FileOptions fileOptions = FileOptions.None])
                              FileOptions
                            fileOptions:                              (parameter) FileOptions fileOptions
```

FIGURE 10.11   Named parameters showing up in IntelliSense.

Named parameters are independent from optional parameters in that they can be used to specify any parameter by its name. For example, you could even call a method like int.TryParse as follows, using the parameter names:

```
int res;
if (int.TryParse(result: out res, s: "Hello"))
    ...
```

No matter how you specify arguments, the C# compiler will always check whether you're calling an existing method overload. For example, if you were to omit the s parameter just given (which is not declared as optional on TryParse), the compiler would complain that it can't find a suitable overload. Also once you start specifying parameters by name in a method call, subsequent parameters should be specified by name, too; otherwise, the following would be very cryptic and likely ambiguous. Think about it...which parameter should the string literal be assigned to?

```
Create(fileOptions: FileOptions.RandomAccess, @"c:\temp\test.txt")
```

DON'T MESS WITH NAMES!

Because languages can specify parameters by name, you should never rename a public method's parameters after you've shipped your library for the very first time. If you do so, a recompile of client code using your library may fail because it can't find a renamed parameter anymore. For example, if the File.Create API were to change the fileOptions parameter to be called fileOption, some of our sample calls would no longer compile. Notice, however, that clients will continue to work fine as long as the code doesn't get recompiled. Resolving named parameters is a compile-time only job.

Note that that the order in which arguments are evaluated is always left to right, also when named parameters are involved. Consider the following code:

```
public static void Main(string[] args)
{
    Console.WriteLine(Add(b: AskInt("b"), a: AskInt("a")));
}

private static int AskInt(string name)
{
```

```
    Console.Write(name + ": ");
    return int.Parse(Console.ReadLine());
}

private static int Add(int a, int b)
{
    return a + b;
}
```

The call to Add specifies for some bizarre (but valid) reason both its parameters by name, in reverse order. Let's simplify the code first to illustrate what the compiler does when it encounters named parameters. Suppose you write the following expression:

```
Add(b: 5, a: 3)
```

Lookup of named parameters is a task performed by the compiler, not the runtime. In other words, every call to Add in the resulting assembly expects argument values for parameters a and b to be specified in that order. As a result, the compiler will rewrite the preceding expression code to the following call at runtime:

```
Add(3, 5)
```

However, it's a bit more subtle than this. If the evaluation of the expressions for the argument values would have a certain side effect, this would change the meaning of the program compared to what people will expect. Consider our sample call:

```
Add(b: AskInt("b"), a: AskInt("a"))
```

AskInt reads an integer value from the console. If the preceding call were to get reordered as follows, the order of the prompts would be different from the lexical left-to-right order in which the calls to AskInt appear in the code:

```
Add(AskInt("a"), AskInt("b"))
```

To restore the expected behavior and have consistent left-to-right evaluation order, the compiler generates the following code instead:

```
int __t1 = AskInt("b");
int __t2 = AskInt("a");
Console.WriteLine(Add(__t2, __t1));
```

Overloading

Within the same struct, class, or interface, different methods with the same name can exist, as long as they differ in their signatures. The concept of a signature goes beyond just methods; instance constructors, indexers, and operators have them, too. For a method, a signature roughly corresponds to the method's header, as illustrated earlier in Figure 10.1. One notable difference is the fact that a signature doesn't include the return type as part of its formal definition. Although other differences exist that can be studied by specification lovers, this description suffices for our purposes.

Defining Method Overloads

To define overloads for a method with a given name, you just define all the overloads as part of the same containing type. Where you put the method in the file (or files, in case partial classes are used) doesn't matter, though keeping overloads of a method lexically together helps when browsing the code.

A WORD ON NAMING CONVENTIONS FOR METHODS

Talking about method naming as the grouping key for a set of overloads, it's good to say a word or two on the conventions in use for method names. Basically, they follow the so-called Pascal naming convention, where they start with an uppercase letter and each word starts with a capital too. For example, `TryParse` and `WriteLine` are conventional names, whereas `tryParse` or `Writeline` are not.

In fact, Visual Studio 2010's IntelliSense actually has intrinsic knowledge about this naming convention and allows you to autocomplete a method name simply by specifying the uppercase letters that appear in it. The same holds for type names that follow the same convention. Figure 10.12 shows this new IntelliSense feature put into practice.

FIGURE 10.12   IntelliSense got smarter in Visual Studio 2010.

As usual with conventions, they're just that: conventions. For consistency in API design, it's good to follow them, though neither compilers nor the runtime do check conformance. Other tools, such as FxCop and StyleCop, can be used to perform such checks as part of your development process.

As you've seen in the rough definition of signatures, the return type doesn't get included, so one cannot overload solely by return type. Therefore, the following code is invalid because both methods have the same parameter types but differ only in their return type:

```
static int Add(int a, int b) { ... }
static long Add(int a, int b) { ... }  // Oops: only differs in return type
```

However, if the second method were to differ from the first in more than just the return type (for example, taking two long parameters instead), things would be fine.

```
static int Add(int a, int b) { ... }
static long Add(long a, long b) { ... }  // Oops: only differs in return type
```

Another part of a signature that cannot be the sole difference across different overloads are the ref and out modifiers. Readers with an eye for detail will remember that out and ref are implemented using the same calling mechanism at the runtime level and differ only by an additional piece of metadata for the compiler to inspect. Because the runtime cannot differentiate between out and ref (well, without going through metadata hoops, which would be rather inefficient in today's world), it isn't possible to compile the following:

```
static bool TryParse(string s, out int result) { ... }
static bool TryParse(string s, ref int result) { ... }
```

Method Groups

Closely related to method overloads are method groups, which are typically used with delegates, as you will see later in Chapter 17, "Delegates." Basically, a method group is a set of overloaded methods that's classified as an expression and is created by using a member lookup operation. For example, the following are method groups:

```
Console.WriteLine
name.Substring
```

In a nutshell, delegates are a means to refer to a method such that it can be passed along as an object. For example, one piece of code might need "a method that will be able to take an object and return a Boolean to indicate whether it passes a condition." To express this, it can take in a delegate that basically captures the signature of such a helper method it needs to carry out its task. For example:

```
delegate bool Filter(int number);
```

Delegates are types and hence can have instances. To create an instance of the Filter type, you can declare a variable and assign a method group to it. Given the following method, which has the appropriate signature, a Filter object can be created as shown on the last line:

```
static class Predicates
{
    static bool IsEven(int number)
    {
        return number % 2 == 0;
    }
}
...
Filter filter = Predicates.IsEven;   // Using a method group
```

Creation of a delegate by use of a method group carries out some overload resolution to check whether the set of overloads represented by the method group contains a method that's compatible with the delegate's signature. For example, we could have multiple IsEven overloads that differ in the input parameters they accept. When the group gets assigned to a Filter delegate that expects an int input parameter, it's the job of the compiler to figure out the best match for the delegate object to refer to.

Delegates can be invoked just as if they were regular methods. By doing so, the target methods captured by the delegate instance will be invoked. Essentially, delegates are a means to introduce one level of indirection to call a method. With our Filter delegate in place, a general-purpose filtering method can be created:

```
static int[] Where(int[] numbers, Filter predicate)
{
    // In fact, a more general-purpose Where method exists in LINQ.
    // It uses a generic delegate to filter elements of a generic collection.
    // For a thorough explanation, see the chapter on LINQ.

    var results = new List<int>();
    foreach (int n in numbers)
        if (predicate(n))  // delegate invocation
            results.Add(n);

    return results.ToArray();
}
```

We discuss delegates in much more detail in Chapter 17 and put them into practice in Chapter 18, "Events" (events use delegates under the covers).

Overload Resolution

When multiple overloads for a method with a given name exist, one of the compiler's duties is to figure out which method is to be called given a certain argument list. A whole set of rules exists to figure out the "best target." Those rules largely correspond to common sense and what developers would expect to be the best match. A simple example can be given using the Math.Abs method, which has seven overloads:

```
public static decimal Abs(decimal value);
public static double Abs(double value);
public static float Abs(float value);
public static int Abs(int value);
public static long Abs(long value);
public static sbyte Abs(sbyte value);
public static short Abs(short value);
```

Most, if not all, readers will agree on the overload that has to be called in the following piece of code using Math.Abs:

```
int x = int.Parse(Console.ReadLine());
Console.WriteLine("Abs({0}) = {1}", x, Math.Abs(x));
```

Because there's an exact match of a method signature in the set of available overloads, it shouldn't be a surprise that the Math.Abs(int) candidate is chosen. If no exact match is found, other rules kick in to find the best possible match:

```
uint x = uint.Parse(Console.ReadLine());
Console.WriteLine("Abs({0}) = {1}", x, Math.Abs(x));
```

Although taking the absolute number of a positive unsigned integer doesn't make much sense, it illustrates the point of overload resolution quite well. Because there's no exact match taking in a uint as the sole parameter, implicit conversions (see Chapter 13, "Operator Overloading and Conversions") are considered. In this case, it's possible to convert the uint argument to a long *implicitly* (that is, without the user specifying it explicitly), that overload is used as shown in Figure 10.13. The reason this implicit conversion from a uint to a long exists is because every 32-bit unsigned integer fits, without any loss of precision, in a 64-bit (long) signed integer.

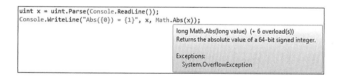

FIGURE 10.13   An implicit conversion bridges the gap between argument and parameter.

Many more rules exist to define overload resolution in a more formal manner in the C# language specification. I won't digress; if you're interested, see the specification. All you need to know for practical purposes is the fact the compiler (not the runtime) is in charge of finding a good overload. If the chosen target is not the expected one (which shouldn't happen too often), it's always possible to influence the decision by adding more casts. This is also the way to guide the compiler in a certain direction if no best match can be found and the call is ambiguous:

```
public static void Main(string[] args)
{
    Bar("Which one", "will  you pick?");
}

public static void Bar(object a, string b) { ... }
public static void Bar(string a, object b) { ... }
```

Because both overloads of Bar are equally suited (since every string is an object and can be treated as such), the compiler cannot make up its mind (luckily) and raises an error signaling the ambiguity, as shown in Figure 10.14. One way to solve this is to specify the intended parameter types explicitly:

```
public static void Main(string[] args)
{
    Bar((object)"Pick the", "first one");
    Bar("Pick the", (object)"second one");
}
```

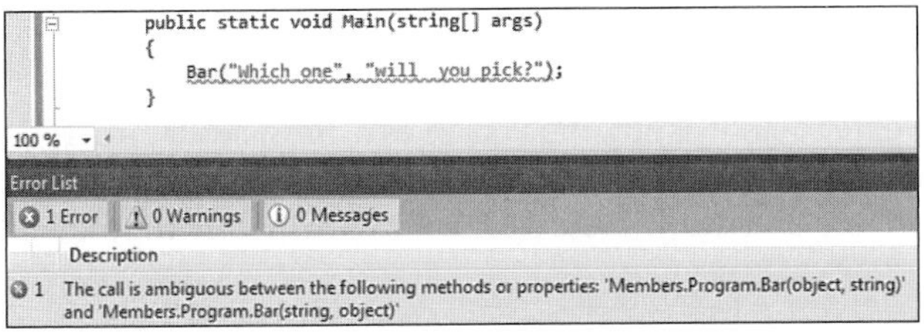

FIGURE 10.14   Ambiguities found during overload resolution prompt for manual resolution.

CHALLENGES WITH GENERICS

Generics, which are the subject of Chapter15, pose extra challenges in relation to overload resolution. Basically, generics enable you to abstract over types used as parameters to types or methods:

```
public static void Main(string[] args)
{
    Bar<int, string>(1, "2"); // This is fine...
    Bar<int, int>(1, 2);      // ...but what's meant here?
}

public static void Bar<TFirst, TSecond>(TFirst f, TSecond s) { ... }
public static void Bar<TFirst, TSecond>(TSecond s, TFirst f) { ... }
```

When type parameters are inferred from the generic method's usage, some tie-breaker rules exist that will prefer nongeneric parameters that provide a good match over going down the generic road. For example:

```
public static void Main(string[] args)
{
    Foo(1, 2); // second one is used as "int" is better than "TSecond"
}

public static void Foo<TFirst, TSecond>(TFirst f, TSecond s) { ... }
public static void Foo<TFirst>(TFirst f, int n) { ... }
```

When designing generic-rich APIs, it's always a good idea to think about cases where the substitution for generic type parameters could result in ambiguities as the ones shown here. Whenever possible, try to avoid putting disambiguation challenges on the API user because they can be quite tricky to resolve.

The best way to get a good feeling about overload resolution is to play with it in the context of .NET Framework APIs and such. Overloads are used quite extensively to provide developer convenience, so you'll encounter them frequently.

Extension Methods

Introduced in C# 3.0 as part of the LINQ-enabling language feature set, extension methods provide a means to extend an existing type (such as a class, struct, interface, enum, delegate) with additional methods that can be invoked as if they were instance methods. Basically, they provide user convenience for calling helper methods.

Prior to .NET 3.5 (which carried C# 3.0 and VB 9.0, both with extension methods as a language feature), it was rather cumbersome to define additional functionality on an existing type if you didn't own that type. For example, assume you got some urgent need for a method to reverse a string. Wouldn't it be great to be able to write the next piece of code to do so?

```
var input = Console.ReadLine();
Console.WriteLine(input.Reverse());
```

Unfortunately, the framework designer didn't feel like introducing a Reverse method on the System.String type, so the preceding code can't be written. Extending the string type isn't a feasible option to resolve this issue because you want to have the Reverse method on every string object, not on just some specialized subtype thereof. (Besides that, the string type in the BCL is sealed, and therefore you cannot derive from it, as you learn in Chapter 14.) The only way you can introduce a Reverse operation is to define a helper method like the following:

```
static class StringExtensions
{
    public static string Reverse(string s)
    {
        var chars = s.ToCharArray();
        Array.Reverse(chars);
        return new string(chars);
    }
}
```

Because strings are immutable in .NET, you cannot modify them in place, and therefore you need to create a new string with the reversed character sequence to achieve this task. Using the preceding helper, you can now write the following code:

```
var input = Console.ReadLine();
Console.WriteLine(StringExtensions.Reverse(input));
```

Unfortunately, this breaks the "fluency" of the code quite a bit. In particular, it's not possible to "chain together" a set of method calls that transform the string. For example:

```
var input = Console.ReadLine();
Console.WriteLine(input.ToUpper().Reverse().ToLower());
```

Whether such excessive chaining is a good thing can be debated. Because every intermediate method call could return null or throw an exception, it can become quite hard to track down a point of failure. In addition, no local variables hold the intermediate results, which could be handy for debugging. Nonetheless, the need for helper methods breaks fluency and left-to-right reading of code in a lot of cases:

```
var input = Console.ReadLine();
Console.WriteLine(StringExtensions.Reverse(input.ToUpper()).ToLower());
```

One concrete API where the fluent pattern is very attractive to have is LINQ. We discuss this in much more detail later (see Chapter 19, "Language Integrated Query Essentials"), but for now contrast the following two sample queries from a syntactical point of view. I'm sure you'll agree the first one is more readable and communicates the order of operations much better:

```
var resNew = new[] { 1, 2, 3 }
            .Where(x => x % 2 == 0)
            .Select(x => x.ToString());

var resOld = Enumerable.Select(
                Enumerable.Where(
                    new[] { 1, 2, 3 },
                    x => x % 2 == 0
                ),
                x => x.ToString()
            );
```

In fact, the first fragment is turned into the second at compile time by means of the extension methods language feature. Ignore the weird-looking arrow syntax for now; those are lambda expressions, which are discussed in Chapter 17. If you want to read the code aloud, pronounce the fat arrow as "goes to," and you should be able to get a feel for what those lambda expressions stand for.

Defining Extension Methods

Back to our string reversal example to show how we can enable the instance-method-looking invocation syntax for our extension to the `System.String` type. Compared to the original helper class and method code we wrote before, the only difference is to put a `this` modifier on the first parameter of the method:

```
static class StringExtensions
{
    public static string Reverse(this string s)
    {
        var chars = s.ToCharArray();
        Array.Reverse(chars);
        return new string(chars);
    }
}
```

In C#, the `this` keyword is used in no fewer than four different places, most of which we still have to discuss. Here's an overview:

▶ To refer to the current instance of an object. This can be used to refer to all sorts of members, such as `this._age` to refer to a field. An extra example is an instance method `Bar` calling another instance method `Foo` on the same object by writing `this.Foo(arguments)`. The `this` keyword can be omitted in those cases but is often included for clarity.

▶ To call one instance constructor overload from another one. You'll see this in Chapter 12, "Constructors and Finalizers."

▶ As the keyword to denote an indexer, which is a special kind of property that can be defined on a type. For example, a `Vector` type could define an indexer allowing users to write `vector[0]` or `vector["x"]` to refer to a component of a vector instance. You'll learn about indexers later in this chapter.

▶ For the declaration of extension methods (as you have seen just now).

Now that we've turned our helper method in an extension method, we can write the code to reverse a string in a much nicer form:

```
var input = Console.ReadLine();
Console.WriteLine(input.Reverse());
```

In the IntelliSense list, extension methods show up with an extra adorner on top of the method icon, as shown in Figure 10.15.

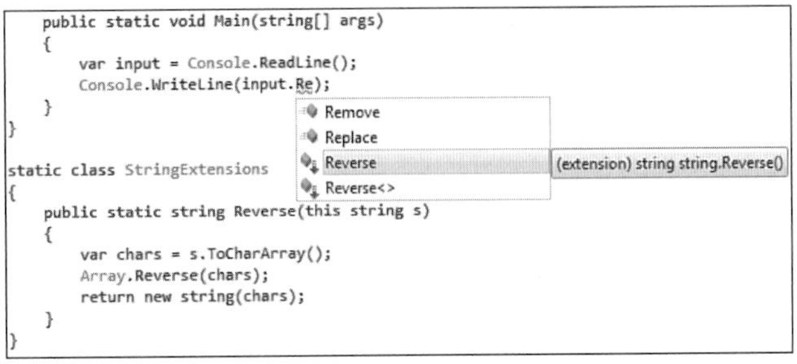

```
public static void Main(string[] args)
{
    var input = Console.ReadLine();
    Console.WriteLine(input.Re);
}                              Remove
}                              Replace
static class StringExtensions  Reverse          (extension) string string.Reverse()
{                              Reverse<>
    public static string Reverse(this string s)
    {
        var chars = s.ToCharArray();
        Array.Reverse(chars);
        return new string(chars);
    }
}
```

FIGURE 10.15   An extension method showing up in IntelliSense.

Notice that another `Reverse` extension method seems to exist on `System.String`. In fact, this is an extension method on the generic `IEnumerable<T>` interface type, which is defined as part of the Standard Query Operators of LINQ. Every string is a sequence of characters. and hence `System.String` implements the `IEnumerable<char>` interface. The `Reverse` operator in LINQ can operate on every sequence (of any type T) and return the sequence in reverse.

STATIC CLASSES

Notice extension methods are defined in static classes, which is a requirement enforced by the compiler. Static classes were introduced in C# 2.0 to guard against creation of unusable classes that result from forgetting to mark a method as static. Before C# 2.0, to declare a class with only static utility methods, the following pattern was used:

```
class Helpers
{
    private Helpers() {}
    public static void Bar() { ... }
    ...
}
```

By defining a private instance constructor (see Chapter 12), no one can ever create an instance of the helper class, which is clearly the right thing to do because all methods on the class are static and hence don't need an instance to operate on. However, mistakes in definitions of such types weren't caught, in particular when someone added a method and forgot to mark it as static:

```
class Helpers
{
    private Helpers() {}
    public static void Bar() { ... }
    public void Foo() { ... }          // Oops, forgot to mark as static
    ...
}
```

Now nobody can ever call this method (without playing dirty tricks using reflection APIs, that is) because no instance can be created to invoke the method on. By marking the class as static, the compiler enforces that only static members are defined.

Overload Resolution

Actually, the fact that two `Reverse` extension methods show up illustrates how overload resolution applies to extension methods, too. When we write the following code, the compiler considers the extension method on string to be a better match than the one that's defined on `IEnumerable<T>`, with `T` substituted for `char`:

```
var input = Console.ReadLine();
Console.WriteLine(input.Reverse());
```

Hence, our method will take precedence over the one defined by the LINQ APIs. Also, extension methods are considered only when no suitable instance method is found. In other words, they are performed as a "last-chance lookup" operation after all attempts to find instance methods fail:

```
static class StringExtensions
{
    public static string Substring(this string s, int startIndex)
    {
```

Although it's valid to define an extension method like the preceding one, you won't be able to call it through "instance invocation syntax" because `System.String` already has a `Substring` method that takes in an `int` parameter:

```
var art = "Bart".Substring(1);
```

Because an instance method is found, the compiler doesn't have to go and look for some extension method that takes a string as the first parameter and accepts an integer after it. If we still want to call our extension method, we can do so by using static method invocation syntax:

```
var art = StringExtensions.Substring("Bart", 1);
```

Notice that because of this order of overload resolution, only attempting to use extension methods after all instance method lookups fail, an extension method cannot be called because it's a "better match than" an instance method. For example:

```
static class StringExtensions
{
    public static string Substring(this string s, byte startIndex)
    {
```

The preceding extension method could be somehow defined as an efficient substring that takes advantage of taking in a byte-sized `startIndex` as opposed to a 32-bit integer. So if we write a substring with an index typed to be a byte, the compiler will first hunt for a suitable instance method. Because a byte is implicitly convertible to an int, it will pick the `Substring` method defined on `System.String`, never considering our "overload":

```
var art = "Bart".Substring( (byte)1);  // Calls System.String.Substring
```

This might be surprising at first, but it's one of the measures put in place to ensure that C# 2.0 code continues to work as it did before, even after being recompiled in C# 3.0.

VERSIONING STORY

Extension methods have a poor versioning story due to the overload resolution rules explained earlier. As soon as the this parameter's type introduces an instance method with the same name, it will be considered first upon recompiling code that used an extension method with the same name. For example, if .NET 4+x introduces a `Reverse` instance method without any parameters on `System.String`, that one will be picked up when you recompile the code targeting that new platform. If this method has different behavior than our own extension method, it can lead to unexpected changes.

Nonetheless, it's always possible to switch back to invoking the extension method by using a static method call instead, once such a regression is spotted. It's also not unimaginable for tools to help detect such versioning issues when code is upgraded to use a newer version of a library or framework that might have brought new and conflicting instance methods with it.

Using Extension Methods

You've already seen how to use an extension method simply by using the first parameter as the left side (mimicking instance method invocation syntax), but another question is how those extension methods become available. The answer is to be found in the use of namespaces, which are covered in Chapter 24, "Namespaces." In short, a namespace provides a means to group types in a hierarchical manner. For example, the `System.Text` namespace contains types like `StringBuilder`, while `System.IO` contains types that deal with files, streams, and so on. Instead of having to specify full type names all over the place, you can import a namespace using the `using` keyword in C#:

```
using System;

class Program
{
    static void Main()
    {
        // Same as writing System.Console.WriteLine("Hello");
        Console.WriteLine("Hello");
    }
}
```

Starting from C# 3.0, the using keyword is also used to import extension methods that are defined in public static classes within the imported namespaces. For example, the following complete program defines two namespaces, one of which contains extension methods. As long as that namespace is not imported for the code defined in the other, the extension method is not visible. Figure 10.16 proves this point by looking through the lenses of IntelliSense. Also notice that because of the lack of an import of System.Linq, the Reverse method defined on IEnumerable<T> doesn't show up:

```
namespace Fabrikam.Utilities
{
    using Contoso.CashFlow;   // This is required to "see" the Reverse method.

    public class Program
    {
        public static void Main(string[] args)
        {
            var traB = "Bart".Reverse();
        }
    }
}


namespace Contoso.CashFlow
{
    static class StringExtensions
    {
        public static string Reverse(this string s) { ... }
    }
}
```

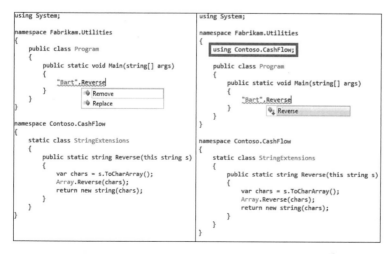

FIGURE 10.16   Extension methods come and go with namespace imports.

How the Compiler Marks and Finds Extension Methods

Two more questions can be raised about the implementation of extension methods at the level of the compiler. Both those questions relate to the bookkeeping done to mark extension methods and find them during overload resolution.

As with most post-C# 2.0 language features, extension methods are syntactical sugar on top of runtime primitives, introduced to provide more developer convenience. To implement those features, the runtime didn't have to change at all. This can be seen clearly in the code emitted for our Reverse extension method call:

```
var input = Console.ReadLine();
Console.WriteLine(input.Reverse());
```

The preceding code is turned into this:

```
var input = Console.ReadLine();
Console.WriteLine(StringExtensions.Reverse(input));
```

To the runtime, an extension method simply looks like a static method call. Extension methods enable developers to make the code look better, favoring instance method call resemblance over plain static method calls. For the compilers of languages that support extension methods (such as C# and Visual Basic) to recognize an extension method as a special kind of static method, an attribute is applied on the method as a piece of metadata. This ExtensionAttribute is defined in the System.Runtime.CompilerServices namespace. In our case, the Reverse method definition is really equivalent to the following:

```
static class StringExtensions
{
    [Extension]
    public static string Reverse(string s) { ... }
}
```

Because this is merely an implementation detail, the compiler requires you to use the this keyword instead of using the attribute directly (even though the Visual Basic language publicly documents to use the ExtensionAttribute to declare an extension method in Visual Basic). Figure 10.17 proves this attribute is recognized and used by the compiler.

To find extension methods suitable for use during overload resolution, the compiler searches for visible methods marked with ExtensionAttribute across all static classes in types defined in imported namespaces for all the referenced assemblies. Using the reflection APIs, you can write a similar extension method dumper for a given interface. The use of reflection and the LINQ syntax that follows is explained in Chapter 21, "Reflection," and Chapter 19, "Language Integrated Query Essentials," respectively:

```
var res = from t in typeof(Enumerable).Assembly.GetTypes()
          let n = t.Namespace
```

```
        where n != null && n.StartsWith("System.Linq") // "using System.Linq"
        from m in t.GetMethods(BindingFlags.Public ¦ BindingFlags.Static)
        where Attribute.IsDefined(m, typeof(ExtensionAttribute))
        select m;

foreach (var m in res)
    Console.WriteLine(m);
```

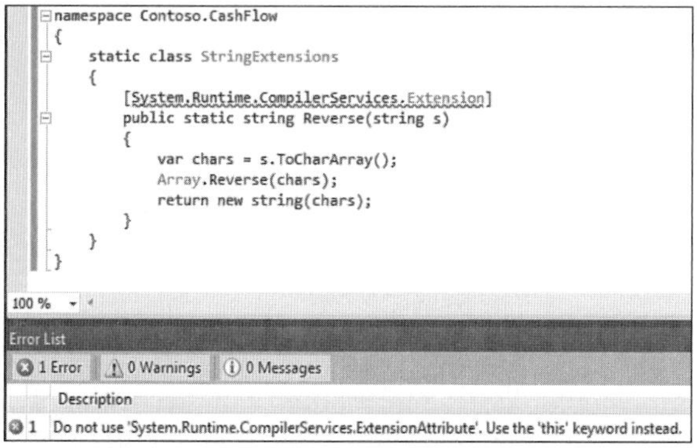

```
namespace Contoso.CashFlow
{
    static class StringExtensions
    {
        [System.Runtime.CompilerServices.Extension]
        public static string Reverse(string s)
        {
            var chars = s.ToCharArray();
            Array.Reverse(chars);
            return new string(chars);
        }
    }
}
```

```
100 %  ▼
Error List
❌ 1 Error   ⚠ 0 Warnings   ⓘ 0 Messages
    Description
❌ 1   Do not use 'System.Runtime.CompilerServices.ExtensionAttribute'. Use the 'this' keyword instead.
```

FIGURE 10.17   Use of the ExtensionAttribute happens behind the scenes.

EXTENSION PROPERTIES, EVENTS, INDEXERS, FIELDS, AND SO ON

Typically, language features are quite broad, treating different types of members on the same footage. For historical reasons, extension methods haven't been generalized into "extension members." After all, to enable LINQ with fluent chaining of query operators, only extension methods were needed.

The lack of the generalized concept of extension members has given rise to many feature requests for things such as extension properties. Those even made it to the tentative feature list for C# 4.0 but fell off the list mainly due to design difficulties. In particular, there's no convenient place on today's syntax for properties to put the this parameter. Different approaches were considered, ranging from adding some notion of indexable properties to pattern-based recognition of properties:

```
public static int Size[this FileInfo file]
{
    get { ... } set { ... }
}

// Another possibility
public static int get_Size(this FileInfo file) { ... }
public static int set_Size(this FileInfo file) { ... }
```

Both have major drawbacks. First, although the concept of indexed properties exists at the runtime level, having such a language feature could cause confusion because expressions such as `x.Bar[0]` could either mean retrieving a collection from property Bar and index into it or calling the indexed property Bar with argument 0. Also assignments to such an indexed property feel a little weird (agreed, this is a subjective thing as with most language features).

The second approach of using `get` and `set` prefixes (which follow internal naming convention used for compiler-code generated for properties) is unprecedented in the language and doesn't look like a regular property at all.

Furthermore, the first proposed syntax isn't well suited to enable for auto-implemented properties (see Chapter 11, "Fields, Properties and Indexers") where getter and setter blocks are omitted. The difficulty with those is how to store the data get and set by the property in some location associated to the object instance targeted by use of the property. This would have to be some kind of global dictionary, which introduces global state and poses challenges for the garbage collection of extension property data when a target instance goes away.

Other extension members have their own difficulties with regards to a clean syntax that fits a model following the design of extension properties. Yet another approach would be to define the concept of an "extension class" that has the this parameter implicitly available in all the members that become extension members:

```
class StringExtensions extends String  // not "extends" as in Java
{
    public string Reverse() { /* use this as if we were a string ourselves */ }
    public int Size { get { ... } set { ... } }
}
```

One drawback is that it would result in quite a few such extension classes when used to extend generics. For example, some of LINQ's query operators are defined on the generic `IEnumerable<T>`. Other LINQ operators (such as Sum, Min and Max) target specific sequence types such as `IEnumerable<int>` or `IEnumerable<long>`. Besides the explosion in the number of "extension types," it also introduces yet another way to do extension methods alongside the existing this syntax.

EXTENSION MEMBERS, UNLIKE EXPANDOS

Dynamic languages use a concept called *expandos* to be able to add members to existing objects. Extension methods, though, use a different compile-time approach to create the illusion of being able to extend *types* with an additional method. One difference between both concepts lies in the fact that an expando can extend a particular object instance with additional members, whereas extension methods are associated with a type instead.

Starting with C# 4.0, the concept of an expando can be implemented, as well, thanks to the dynamic keyword and the DLR infrastructure. (See Chapter 22 for more information.) The ExpandoObject type defined in System.Dynamic enables scenarios like bags that gain members at runtime:

```
dynamic person = new ExpandoObject();
person.Name = "Bart";
person.Age = 27;

Console.WriteLine("{0} is {1}", person.Name, person.Age);
```

Although it seems that the object gains a property called Name and one called Age, it really acquires some more data stored in it. Basically, the Expando provides some dictionary that associates Bart to Name and 27 to Age, while dynamic lookup using property syntax provides access to this storage.

Extension properties would be quite different because you would be able to define a new property associated with a type and have custom code inside it. Some dynamic languages offer such abilities, as well; for example, Windows PowerShell with its extensible type system (exposing notions like script properties). However, being a statically typed language at its core, the concept of extension members in C# would likely have to be a statically typed notion.

Partial Methods

C# 3.0 Closely related to partial classes are partial methods, which were introduced as part of the LINQ language features wave in .NET 3.5 and C# 3.0. As with all "partial" features, this you must do with code-generation scenarios, too. The original use case for the feature serves as a good illustration of its purpose. Enter LINQ to SQL.

LINQ to SQL has a designer to create classes corresponding to tables in a database (a form of object-relational mapping). To try this out for yourself, add a new LINQ to SQL Classes file to your project using the Add New Item dialog. An example of a mapping created in the designer is shown in Figure 10.18. A thorough discussion about how to define a LINQ to SQL mapping is irrelevant for our discussion, but one essential configuration task for this example is to have one property declared as a primary key (which will influence the code generation). Setting properties on the mapping's properties can be done using the Properties pane in Visual Studio.

Although the mapping file is stored as an XML file with extension .dbml (to be used and regenerated by the designer), a single file generator registered in Visual Studio turns this markup into a generated .designer.cs file, which can be seen in Solution Explorer. Let's take a look at the code that was generated for our simple mapping, which is found in the .designer.cs file (not the regular .cs file).

FIGURE 10.18   Generated files for a LINQ to SQL mapping.

One trimmed-down fragment of the generated code for the Person class looks like this:

```
public partial class Person : INotifyPropertyChanging, INotifyPropertyChanged
{
    private int _ID;
    private string _Name;
    private int _Age;

#region Extensibility Method Definitions
partial void OnNameChanging(string value);
partial void OnNameChanged();
...
#endregion

    public string Name {
        get {
            return this._Name;
        }

        set {
            if ((this._Name != value)) {
                this.OnNameChanging(value);
                this.SendPropertyChanging();
                this._Name = value;
                this.SendPropertyChanged("Name");
                this.OnNameChanged();
            }
        }
    }
    ...
}
```

Notice the highlighted portions of code while inspecting the example. At the bottom of the generated class, we find a property for the person's name. As you will see later, a property has a getter and setter that are invoked when the property is read or written to, respectively. The generated setter code adds quite a bit of logic to track changes made to the object, such that the LINQ to SQL data context can be used to submit changes to the database in the form of a T-SQL UPDATE statement. To facilitate this, it uses the INotifyProperty interfaces that are part of the BCL. People familiar with SQL DML statements will likely already know why a primary key was needed in our mapping because the generated T-SQL UPDATE statement will select the record targeted for update by specifying a filtering T-SQL WHERE clause based on the primary key value of the object. All this plumbing results in easy-to-use object-relational mapping.

Two lines of code in the setter are of particular interest and are highlighted in bold in the preceding code snippet. Calls to OnNameChanging and OnNameChanged were emitted by the code generator as *extensibility points* for the generated code. If we follow those method calls to the target method definition, we end in a region containing methods that are declared as *partial*:

```
#region Extensibility Method Definitions
partial void OnNameChanging(string value);
partial void OnNameChanged();
...
#endregion
```

Also notice how the generated Person class is marked as partial itself. The goal of the partial methods is for developers to provide custom logic in other parts of the partial class definition. Figure 10.19 shows us typing the partial keyword in the Person class in another (nongenerated) .cs file to specify logic for any of the partial methods.

FIGURE 10.19   Implementing partial methods of our choice.

An example of an implementation for one of the property change methods is to reject invalid input by means of throwing an exception. Yet another use is to perform some kind of logging whenever changes happen. What's quintessential about the `partial` methods feature is that it cleanly separates generated code from customizable code, while both kinds of code belong to the same type definition:

```
partial class Person
{
    partial void OnAgeChanging(int value)
    {
        if (value <= 0)
            throw new ArgumentOutOfRangeException("value");
    }

    partial void OnCreated()
    {
        Console.WriteLine("New Person created.");
    }
}
```

When no implementation is given for a `partial` method, the whole call site (typically in the generated portion of the class definition) simply disappears. For example, for the preceding code, the setter for `Age` will really look like this:

```
if ((this._Age != value)) {
    this.OnAgeChanging(value);
    this.SendPropertyChanging();
    this._Age = value;
    this.SendPropertyChanged("Age");
    // This code gets dropped as no implementation is given:
    // this.OnAgeChanged();
}
```

It's easy to verify this claim using tools like Reflector or ILDASM. As a result of this technique, partial methods can only be void-returning and cannot have any output parameters. If that weren't the case, it would be unclear what those resulting output values for the method call would have to be if no implementation is given.

Also, partial methods can only be private (and for that reason no access modifier is allowed). If they were public and someone were to try to call them without having the guarantee an implementation exists, things would go terribly wrong. Along the same lines, it's impossible for a delegate to refer to a partial method because it might not exist.

In summary, the use of partial methods is usually related to code-generation scenarios where the code generator wants to provide "extensibility points" to the developer. By doing so, a clean separation between custom logic and generated code can be achieved. At the runtime level, there is no such thing as partial classes or partial methods; those are purely compile-time illusions.

Extern Methods

One other type of method declaration supported by C# is an extern method. Basically, it enables you to specify a method whose definition lives somewhere else. This sounds rather vague, and indeed it is, as the runtime has to come in to help and find the target implementation for the method. Basically, the only directly applicable scenario for end users is the technique of P/Invoke, where one bridges to a method defined in unmanaged code (for example, in a Win32 API). The following piece of code shows this in practice:

```csharp
public static void Main(string[] args)
{
    int size = 0;
    var user = new StringBuilder(size);
    if (!GetUserName(user, ref size))
    {
        var error = Marshal.GetLastWin32Error();
        if (error != ERROR_INSUFFICIENT_BUFFER)
        {
            Console.WriteLine("Unexpected error: " + error);
            return;
        }

        user = new StringBuilder(size);
        if (!GetUserName(user, ref size))
        {
            error = Marshal.GetLastWin32Error();
            Console.WriteLine("Unexpected error: " + error);
            return;
        }
    }

    Console.WriteLine("Welcome, {0}", user.ToString());
}

const int ERROR_INSUFFICIENT_BUFFER = 122;

[DllImport("Advapi32.dll", SetLastError = true)]
static extern bool GetUserName(StringBuilder lpBuffer, ref int nSize);
```

Interop plumbing can be quite challenging because you need to take care of a lot of things. One key thing is to make sure the interop signature is correct in terms of data types and input/output behavior of parameters. The www.pinvoke.net community site can be a good help to find interop signatures for Win32 APIs, and in fact the DllImport shown here was taken from that site.

Although we could have allocated a buffer that's large enough to begin with (the current maximum length of a username, in Windows 7, is set to 256 and is defined in the UNLEN #define inside the LMCons.h header file in the SDK), we went for a coding approach that's more illustrative of typical excessive error checking and handling when dealing with P/Invoke. The parameters on the DllImport attribute applied to the extern method indicate where the function is defined as well as certain aspects of its behavior, such as error code communication and marshaling of strings (of which there are many different kinds in the unmanaged world). Here, we're using a function GetUserName that's defined in the Advapi32.dll Win32 system binary. The signature corresponds to the one of the native function (see MSDN for more information):

```
[DllImport("Advapi32.dll", SetLastError = true)]
static extern bool GetUserName(StringBuilder lpBuffer, ref int nSize);
```

The use of SetLastError indicates whether the Win32 GetLastError way of storing error codes is used by the function. In essence, this tells the interop infrastructure of the CLR to call GetLastError upon returning from the P/Invoke call, such that the managed code can access the last Win32 error code (another set of cryptic constants that are documented in MSDN documentation) through Marshal.GetLastWin32Error.

From a language point of view, an extern method is indicated with the extern keyword, cannot have an implementation body (notice the trailing semicolon is required), and must have a custom attribute applied to it. From the runtime's point of view, how the method gets found depends on the attribute that's applied to the method. DllImport is one such attribute the runtime knows about, triggering the P/Invoke infrastructure to be looped in when a method call needs to be dispatched.

Other attributes for extern methods exist, though they're not directly accessible to users of the framework. One example is MethodImpl, which can be used to make internal calls to runtime infrastructure methods. An example is the System.Object.GetType method, whose implementation lives deep inside the runtime. Figure 10.20 shows the use of the extern modifier on its definition through the eyes of Reflector.

Refactoring

Methods are at the center of a type's operational behavior. They often acquire quite a bit of logic to carry out the task at hand. To tame this complexity, it's essential to have a proper code structure where common tasks are factored out in utilities. By making each method carry out a well-described specialized task, it should become easier to compose and reuse bits and pieces of functionality. On a larger scale, object-oriented programming techniques (which are discussed in Chapter 14) are very useful to separate concerns.

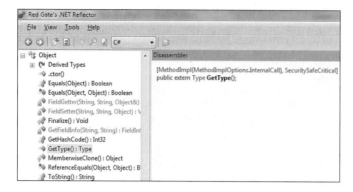

FIGURE 10.20   An internal runtime call used for the extern GetType method on Object.

Refactoring is the label applied to a set of techniques that involve continuous attention to keeping a program's code readable, maintainable, and sound for ease of extensibility in the future. One way to achieve this is to reduce the complexity and entanglement of different pieces or components in the system. Although methods and other operational aspects of code are typical targets for refactoring, similar techniques apply to the data-intensive portions of a program. For example, although it might be meaningful to have a Person object contain a street, city, and ZIP code, integration of the program with some online map service may steer toward a design where a Person has an Address object.

Various metrics can be used to quantify the complexity and maintainability of a piece of code. A good developer tends to recognize the need for refactoring while operating on autopilot, though various tools may be of help to spot possible code-maintenance nightmares. Visual Studio has a Code Metrics feature that can help spot possible issues, as shown in Figures 10.21 and 10.22.

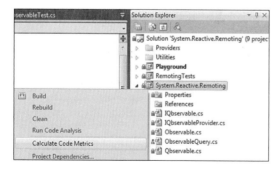

FIGURE 10.21   Calculating code metrics for a project.

Code Metrics Results						
Filter: None		Min.		Max.		
Hierarchy	Maintainability Index	Cyclomatic Complexity	Depth of Inheritance	Class Coupling	Lines of Code
System.Reactive.Remoting (Debug)		76	1,329	2	116	3,862
{} System		100	3	0	4	0
{} System.Joins		75	79	2	37	197
{} System.Linq		72	1,247	2	102	3,665
ObservableEx		76	4	1	7	8
ObservableQuery		96	3	1	1	3
ObservableQuery<TSource>		74	9	2	14	20
ObservableQuery<TSource>.ObservableRewriter		54	44	2	31	113
ObservableQueryProvider		75	16	1	25	22
Qbservable		58	1,171	1	77	3,499

Error List Output Find Symbol Results Pending Changes Code Coverage Results Test Results Test Runs Code Metrics Results

FIGURE 10.22 A project with good maintainability.

The Code Metrics feature includes a set of different metrics computed from the compiled project. A full explanation of those metrics goes beyond the scope of this book, but you want to try keeping the maintainability index high while reducing both class coupling (the more types are coupled through calls, parameters, and so on, the harder it is to reuse) and cyclomatic complexity (number of distinct code paths makes testing harder).

Although refactoring is a noble goal, never lose sight of correctness of the code. In fact, the idea of refactoring techniques is never to change the functionality of the software. In essence, every refactoring should be nothing but a mechanical rewrite of code such that all original properties are maintained. This can prove quite tricky in an imperative programming language that's full of side effects. For example, elimination of common subexpressions doesn't always preserve semantics:

```
// Before: will ask input twice and concatenate it
Console.WriteLine(Console.ReadLine() + Console.ReadLine());

// After: will ask input once and duplicate it
string x = Console.ReadLine();
Console.WriteLine(x + x);
```

Visual Studio contains some refactoring techniques that can be carried out through the code editor. Figure 10.23 shows where to find those. Third-party extensions often come with more-sophisticated refractoriness that can become quite addictive once you get the hang of refactoring-assisted development.

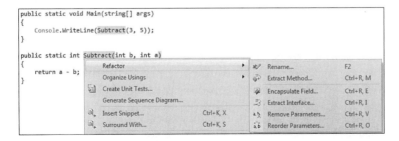

FIGURE 10.23 The Refactor context menu hosts a few simple refactoring techniques.

In the example shown in Figure 10.23, you can think about three possible explanations for the weird definition of Subtract that performs the subtraction operation out of order compared to the method parameters. Maybe it's a bug, perhaps it's an artifact of the code's evolution (unlikely given the simplicity of the example), or maybe it's just some unexplainable strange convention (or oversight) introduced by the original author. In all but the first case, reordering of parameters may be a good idea to make the code look better and behave more predictably. Figure 10.24 shows this refactoring in action, first allowing the user to pick the new order of parameters.

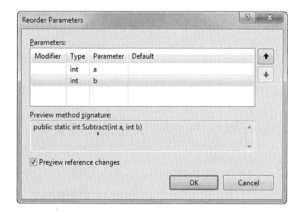

FIGURE 10.24   Preview of a new method signature after parameter reordering.

Once we have found a suitable ordering, we can confirm the refactoring and preview the changes. Visual Studio will propose the following refectories code. Notice how all call sites to the refectories method are changed, as well.

```
public static void Main(string[] args) {
    Console.WriteLine(Subtract(3, 5));
}

public static int Subtract(int a, int b) {
    return a - b;
}
```

BEHAVIOR MAINTAINED?

Even those simple refactorings tend not to preserve semantics in more advanced scenarios. For example, reorder parameters will reorder arguments in each call site. But if evaluation of an argument is based on an expression that has possible side effects, those effects will be swapped as well because of C#'s left-to-right evaluation of subexpressions. Whether you should write such code to begin with is another matter.

Perhaps the most useful refactoring is the one to extract methods. Performing this can be triggered by a number of motivations. One is when you notice a method growing too large and a certain portion of it can be factored out as a piece of functionality that can stand on its own (and potentially be reused). Another related one is based on spotting common helper methods being used in different places throughout your source code base.

An example of the extract methods refactoring is shown here. Don't worry too much about the APIs used by this piece of code; all the magic will become clear in Chapter 21. Suffice to say, the code to determine a table name based on some entity type is quite involved and has little to do with the surrounding code. One place where such code would be written is in a LINQ provider's query translation code. It's also not uncommon for such utilities to be useful in different places, so extracting a common helper method is a good practice:

```
public static void Main()
{
    string query = TranslateQuery(typeof(Person) /* more args omitted */);
    Console.WriteLine(query);
}


public static string TranslateQuery(Type entity /* more params omitted */)
{
    string tableName;
    if (Attribute.IsDefined(entity, typeof(TableAttribute)))
    {
        object[] attributes = entity.GetCustomAttributes(
                                  typeof(TableAttribute), false);
        TableAttribute table = (TableAttribute)attributes[0];
        tableName = table.Name;
    }
    else
    {
        tableName = entity.Name;
    }

    //
    // Much more (nicely factored) code here...
    //
    string projection = TranslateProjection(/* args omitted */);
    string filter = TranslateFilter(/* args omitted */);

    return "SELECT " + projection + " FROM " + tableName + " WHERE " + filter;
}
```

Instead of having the if-else branch right inside TranslateQuery, we would like to have a separate method that will return a table name for further use. In fact, the code that's responsible for translating the projection and filter clauses is already nicely factored out in helpers, as you can see. Figure 10.25 shows the extract code dialog with the proposed resulting method signature for the selected piece of code.

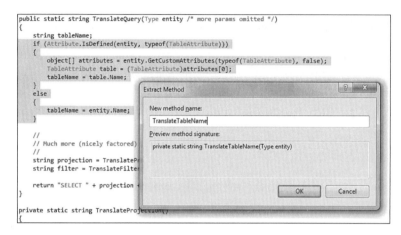

FIGURE 10.25   Extract Method has inferred a suitable signature based on the code.

The resulting code now looks like this, after a little bit of additional cleanup to eliminate some excessive local variables (in favor of redirect return statements):

```
public static string TranslateQuery(Type entity /* more params omitted */)
{
    string tableName = TranslateTableName(entity);
    ...
}

private static string TranslateTableName(Type entity)
{
    if (Attribute.IsDefined(entity, typeof(TableAttribute)))
    {
        object[] attributes = entity.GetCustomAttributes(
                                typeof(TableAttribute), false);
        return ((TableAttribute)attributes[0]).Name;
    }
    else
    {
        return entity.Name;
    }
}
```

In fact, further refactoring could be done to extract a helper method whose sole purpose is to obtain the single custom attribute applied to a Type object. This would hide the complexity of GetCustomAttribute, casts, and indexing. We leave such an experimental cleanup to you.

Code Analysis

Running Code Analysis (available through the project's context menu) typically yields quite a few warnings related to methods. Figure 10.26 shows the result of running the analysis (with all rules enabled in the project's settings) for a simple program. All the warnings should be understood by now, and fixes should be obvious.

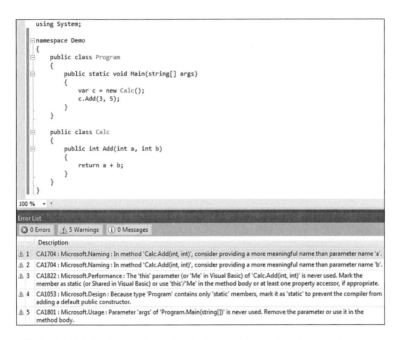

FIGURE 10.26   Some Code Analysis warnings related to methods.

Warnings can be suppressed if you have some good reason for it. Using the rule sets feature available through the project's configuration settings, each project can decide what level of strictness to apply with regard to various rules. For example, the naming of parameters may be something you don't care much about. That said, keep in mind that publicly visible methods can be called with parameters specified by name. Once you ship with certain names, you must keep it that way to avoid breaking client code.

Two rules deserve a bit more explanation. CA1822 warns about instance methods that do not access instance state. In this particular case, there's no reason we can't mark the Add method as static. If we do so, we'll see CA1053 for `Calc` as well because the class contains only static methods. For utility classes like this one, it does make a lot of sense to mark the whole class as static, as discussed earlier in this chapter. Although some rules produce a lot of noise, these two show useful design improvement suggestions.

Summary

Right at the center of the code aspect of types are methods. While you learned how to invoke methods while covering C# expressions, this chapter went into the aspect of declaring methods in various ways.

First, you learned about method parameters and various ways they can be passed. This includes input-only parameters as well as parameters that are passed by reference or act as an output for the method. You also learned about parameter arrays and the C# 4.0 features of named and optional parameters.

Next, the discussion led you to the notion of signatures and the ability to overload methods. Overloading methods comes in handy quite often to increase an API's flexibility. Resolution of calls based on method groups and overloads finished off the coverage of this concept.

Special kinds of methods were discussed as well. Introduced in C# 3.0, extension methods provide a means to define a static method that can be applied to an object as if it were an instance method. Partial methods (introduced in C# 2.0) aid with code generation tools, and extern methods allow for interoperability scenarios.

Finally, you learned a few things about refactoring and code analysis aspects of working with methods. In the next chapter, you learn about the data aspect of types, embodied by fields, as well as members to expose the data: properties and indexers.

IN THIS CHAPTER

▶ Fields 545

▶ An Intermezzo About
  Enums 558

▶ Properties 569

▶ Indexers 574

Having covered the code aspect of types by looking at methods in Chapter 10, we can now move on to the data aspect of types. Fields are containers for data that's part of a type or its instances. We now discuss how to declare and use fields.

After an intermezzo about enum types—which merely are very data-centric types with symbolic names for special values—we continue our exploration with properties and indexers. Those members are closely related to the data aspect of types in that they usually provide code-based accessors to an object's start.

Fields

Whereas methods delineate the far-left end of the code-data spectrum, fields are on the far-right end. Fields serve as the data storage associated with a class or a struct (static fields) or instances thereof (instance fields).

Fields are variables that are declared within a class or struct definition and can have access modifiers controlling their access. Typically, fields are declared as private or protected as a matter of encapsulation, an object-oriented technique explained in Chapter 14, "Object-Oriented Programming." By doing so, it's possible to evolve the internal data structure of a class or struct without breaking users of the type. Properties can be used as a convenient way to access fields, while retaining the ability to change the underlying storage of data.

Declaring Fields

To declare a field, you must specify at least a type and a field name. Multiple fields with the same type can be put on a single line in a comma-separated manner, just like you can do for variables within a code block. Here, some instance and static fields are declared on a Person class:

```
class Person
{
    private static int s_population;
    private string _name;
    private int _age;
}
```

By default, fields are private, regardless of whether the containing type is a struct or a class. This is different from C++, where classes and structs don't relate to the allocation location of objects but instead determine the default visibility of members. It's deemed good style to be explicit about visibility, though.

NAMING CONVENTIONS

The naming guidelines for fields differ based on visibility. Pascal casing (starting with an uppercase) is used for public and protected fields, but as mentioned previously, nonprivate visibility is discouraged. Camel casing is used for private fields (that is, starting with a lowercase and capitalizing subsequent "words" in the name).

For private fields, another convention is often used, derived from MFC. Instead of just starting with a lowercase, you prefix the name with s_ for static fields and with m_ (likely from member) for instance fields. Sometimes, the m is dropped for the latter category of fields.

It is quite convenient to be able to distinguish local variables from fields. Also in constructors, as you'll see later, the name of a field is often identical to a parameter that's used to initialize the corresponding field. This avoids the need to qualify the field with the this keyword. I prefer the use of s_ and _ as prefixes to field names. But as usual, be consistent with conventions.

Accessing Fields

Depending on whether the field is declared as static or as an instance field, it can be accessed in a different manner. For instance fields, you must qualify the lookup by specifying the target instance. To access a field from within the declaring type, you can omit the target instance qualification or use this:

```
class Person
{
    private string _name;
    private int _age;
```

```
    public override string ToString()
    {
        return _name + " is " + this._age;
    }
}
```

You'll learn what the override modifier on a method means in Chapter 14. It's also essential to realize that the private access modifier doesn't prevent you from accessing another instance's private fields as long as that access happens within code defined on the type. To clarify this, consider the following code, which implements an equality check operation for Person instances:

```
class Person
{
    private string _name;
    private int _age;

    public override bool Equals(object obj)
    {
        if (obj == null ¦¦ obj.GetType() != this.GetType())
            return false;

        var other = (Person)obj;
        return other._name == this._name && other._age == this._age;
    }
}
```

Implementing a correct Equals override is discussed in Chapter 13, "Operator Overloading and Conversions," when we discuss operator overloading. The essence is quite simple, though. First we make sure the object passed to us for comparison is of the same type. Instead of using is or as (which produce a positive result when subtyping is involved), we perform an exact match on the System.Type returned by GetType. In addition, we also have to make sure we're not asked to compare with the null reference because null is never equal to an instance. When we know we're comparing existent apples to apples (well, in this case, people), we simply compare the fields pairwise. This illustrates that code declared within the Person type can access the private members of any instance of that Person type.

Static fields are qualified by the type of the containing type. Except for static read-only fields (covered later in this chapter), it shouldn't be the case that such fields are being accessed from outside the containing type. If that holds true, type qualification can be omitted:

```
class Person
{
    private static int s_population;
    private string _name;
    private int _age;
```

```csharp
    public Person(string name, int age)
    {
        s_population++;
        _name = name;
        _age = age;
    }
}
```

This piece of code defines an instance constructor that will initialize the _name and _age fields on the current instance. In addition, it increments the population counter, which is kept in a static field (and hence shared across all instances). Notice that the population count will never go down, even though Person objects can become garbage and get collected. You'll see later how we could achieve such a decrement effect using destructors (and why you shouldn't do it that way).

Because the s_population field is declared as private, we can access it only from within the declaring Person type. Because outsiders might be interested in this information, you'll want to expose it. Instead of marking it public (which would imply everyone can mess with it), we provide an accessor get-only property:

```csharp
class Person
{
    private static int s_population;

    public static int Population
    {
        get { return s_population; }
    }
}
```

Notice that we've marked the property (another member type that is discussed later in this chapter) as static, and therefore we can access it as follows from the outside:

```csharp
class Universe
{
    public static void PrintStatistics()
    {
        Console.WriteLine("Number of citizens: {0}", Person.Population);
    }
}
```

Static fields can be accessed from within instance members, as you saw already when we incremented the s_population value from within an instance constructor. On the outside, static members don't show up on instances. Figure 11.1 shows a compilation error shown for an invalid attempt to access a static field through an instance.

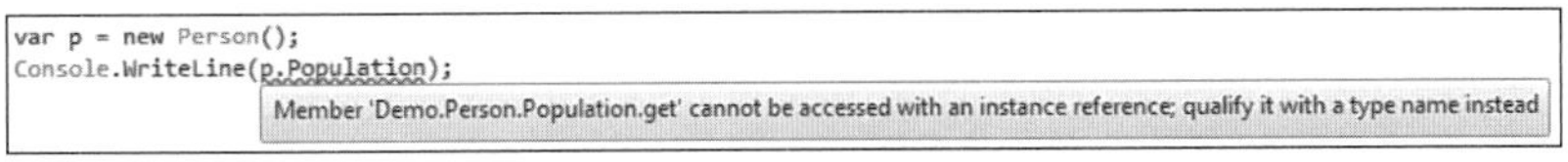

```
var p = new Person();
Console.WriteLine(p.Population);
                   Member 'Demo.Person.Population.get' cannot be accessed with an instance reference; qualify it with a type name instead
```

FIGURE 11.1   Static members cannot be accessed using an instance reference.

Although the language could support this, code tends to be cleaner if it's apparent from a member's use whether that member is static or an instance.

Because static members are shared across instances, you can access them from within an instance member (without the need for qualification by type name). However, because a particular instance's state is not accessible when no target instance is specified, you cannot access instance members from within static members. An example of a mistake against this rule is shown in Figure 11.2. Because the expanded form of this particular field reference would be this._age, it should be clear why this can't work. There is no such thing as a current this reference in a static member.

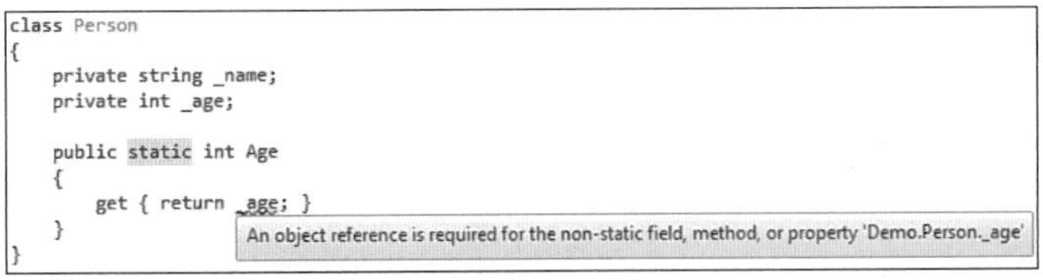

```
class Person
{
    private string _name;
    private int _age;

    public static int Age
    {
        get { return _age; }
    }                 An object reference is required for the non-static field, method, or property 'Demo.Person._age'
}
```

FIGURE 11.2   Static members can't provide an implicit this instance reference.

Finally, notice how a static member can access (private) instance members as long as an instance is specified:

```
class Person
{
    ...

    public static bool IsYounger(Person x, Person y)
    {
        // Don't forget to add null-checks!
        return x._age < y._age;
    }
}
```

Initializing Fields

The common language runtime (CLR) ensures that fields (as well as other kinds of variables) get zero-initialized when their memory is allocated. In practice, this means that reference typed fields will have a default value of null. For value types, all the object's fields will recursively get zero-initialized. Primitive value types receive their default values; for example, an int will be set to 0. Consider the following example:

```
class Basis
{
    private Vector _direction1;
    private Vector _direction2;
}

class Vector
{
    private Point _start;
    private Point _end;
}

struct Point
{
    private int _x;
    private int _y;
}
```

Creation of a new Basis instance will result in both direction fields to be set to null. For each new Vector instance, we'll receive zero-initialized Points in both _start and _end. Such a zero-initialized Point will have both _x and _y set to a zero 32-bit integer. This default initialization is revealed in Figure 11.3, where the compiler has detected the fields are never being assigned to.

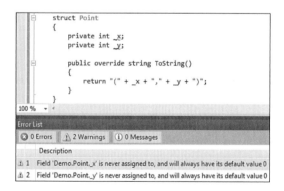

FIGURE 11.3   Default values are automatically assigned to fields.

Notice that the compiler doesn't enforce that fields must be assigned to before they are used. This is in contrast to local variables that do need assignment prior to use:

```
static void Bar()
{
    int a;
    Console.WriteLine(a);   // Error!
}
```

It's not atypical for certain fields to keep their default value for certain construction modes. One constructor may set three fields, another convenience constructor might set only two, leaving the third to its default value. This can be said to be pretty intentional, while reaching the use of a local variable that didn't get assigned to yet (determined based on control flow analysis within the method) can be said to be more dubious. For this reason, leaving fields uninitialized (or should we say, default-initialized) is valid, whereas use of unassigned locals is not.

Besides using default initialization values for fields, you can also initialize them manually (for example, if a nondefault value is required as the initial state). For example, if you would like a Point to start off with 3, 5 as the x and y coordinates, you could write this:

```
class Point
{
    private int _x = 3;
    private int _y = 5;
}
```

Field initializers can be defined only on a class, not on a struct. The reason behind this is related to the ease of struct allocation on the stack, such that no code has to run. As you'll see right now, field initializers translate into constructor code. If structs were to have parameterless constructors that guarantee field initialization, parts of their design would start to fall apart.

The code for the preceding class is turned roughly into the following:

```
class Point
{
    private int _x;
    private int _y;

    public Point()
    {
        _x = 3;
        _y = 5;
    }
}
```

I'm saying "roughly" because there's a subtle difference in the order in which the object's state is initialized and the base class's constructor (in this case, System.Object's) is called. Figure 11.4 shows the code generated for the field initializer code.

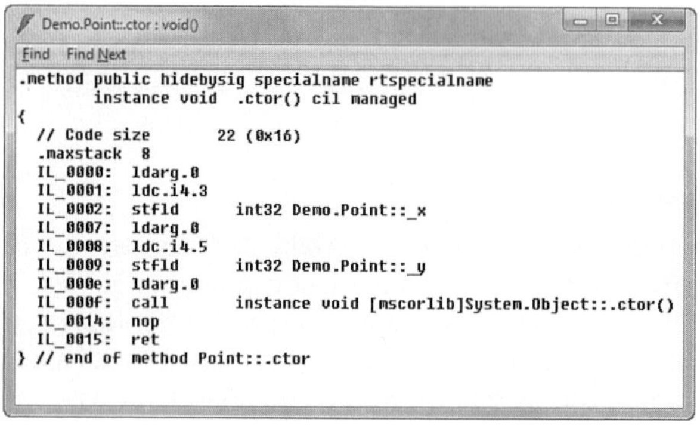

```
 Demo.Point::ctor : void()                                   _ □ x
 Find  Find Next
.method public hidebysig specialname rtspecialname
        instance void  .ctor() cil managed
{
  // Code size       22 (0x16)
  .maxstack  8
  IL_0000:  ldarg.0
  IL_0001:  ldc.i4.3
  IL_0002:  stfld        int32 Demo.Point::_x
  IL_0007:  ldarg.0
  IL_0008:  ldc.i4.5
  IL_0009:  stfld        int32 Demo.Point::_y
  IL_000e:  ldarg.0
  IL_000f:  call         instance void [mscorlib]System.Object::.ctor()
  IL_0014:  nop
  IL_0015:  ret
} // end of method Point::.ctor
```

FIGURE 11.4   Field initializers run in the constructor before calling the base constructor.

Field initializers can contain more code than just constant expressions. Just to illustrate an extreme use of this feature, consider the following code:

```
class Person
{
    private string _name = Console.ReadLine();
}
```

Creating an instance of Person will now trigger a Console.ReadLine call whose output will be assigned to the new instance's _name field. Obviously, such a side effect that gets triggered by object construction is usually not desired. More appropriate uses of the feature include initialization of fields to results of some computation (for example, using Math methods or using string operations). In fact, field initializers are simply run in the textual order in which they appear in the source code. Although it's important for the language to have a strict definition of what's expected, it's discouraged to rely on this order because it can result in subtle and brittle code because just reordering the fields could cause different results:

```
class Person
{
    private string _first = Console.ReadLine();  // Gets asked first
    private string _last  = Console.ReadLine();  // Gets asked second
}
```

Basically, the this reference is not available for any use during field initialization. For this reason, it's also not allowed to reach out to any of the object's instance members (other than the fields being initialized) from inside field initialization expressions. The following piece of code is invalid, and (believe me) you even don't want to think about what it would mean if it were allowed:

```csharp
class Person
{
    // Error CS0027 will result, indicating the "this" keyword cannot be used here.
    private string _name = this.ToString();

    public override string ToString()
    {
        return _name;
    }
}
```

In a constructor, though, you can call methods (including virtual ones, which are explained in Chapter 14). Be careful when you do so because the order of initialization will matter quite a bit.

Similar initialization options are available for static fields. One difference is that you can, in fact, call static methods during the initialization. But just because you can doesn't mean you should. In general, use initializers for (relatively) simple and straightforward initialization tasks.

Read-Only Fields

Read-only fields can be initialized only from inside the constructor or through a field initializer. Basically, this stimulates the use of immutability as it protects against further modification of the field after the containing object's (or type's) initialization. The following code illustrates correct use of a read-only field that's initialized within a constructor:

```csharp
class Person
{
    private static int s_population;
    private readonly int _id;

    public Person()
    {
        _id = s_population++;
    }

    public int ID
    {
        get { return _id; }
    }
}
```

Figure 11.5 shows a violation against the read-only field assignment requirements. As you will see later, the use of auto-implemented properties does not (sadly) provide for the use of read-only fields.

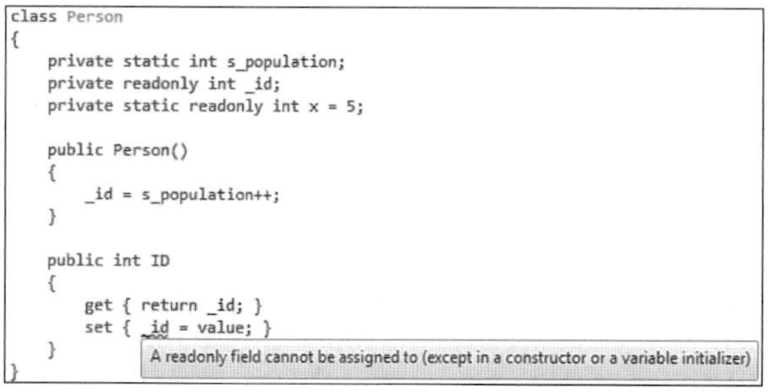

```
class Person
{
    private static int s_population;
    private readonly int _id;
    private static readonly int x = 5;

    public Person()
    {
        _id = s_population++;
    }

    public int ID
    {
        get { return _id; }
        set { _id = value; }
    }                    A readonly field cannot be assigned to (except in a constructor or a variable initializer)
}
```

FIGURE 11.5   Read-only fields should not be initialized after the object's construction.

Notice it's also not allowed to pass read-only fields by reference or supply them to an output parameter of a method beyond the point of initialization. We illustrate this by showing how read-only fields can be used with ref and out, but only in a valid context for their initialization.

For example, the following doesn't work because _id is assigned from a method that could be called from a place other than a constructor. If InitializeId were to be called from a place other than a constructor or field initializer, the read-only property would be violated.

```
class Person
{
    private static int s_population;
    private readonly int _id;

    public Person()
    {
        InitializeId();
    }

    private void InitializeId()
    {
        _id = s_population++;
    }
}
```

However, you can pass the read-only field by reference or as the target of an output parameter as a workaround because the compiler can prove _id will be modified only from within the constructor:

```
class Person
{
    private static int s_population;
    private readonly int _id;

    public Person()
    {
        InitializeId(out _id);   // This is valid in this context.
    }

    private void InitializeId(out int id)
    {
        id = s_population++;
    }
}
```

If you try to feed _id to InitializeId elsewhere, the compiler will complain again.

Constants

Similar to, yet different from, read-only fields are constants. Constants aren't fields but deserve treatment in this context because of their similar syntax and to point out some of the fundamental differences.

The goal of constants is to provide a way to declare values that will never change both during the duration of the program until eternity. Examples of constants include e (2.71828...) and Pi (3.14159...). Things that seem constant but deceptively are not include values such as tax percentages.

For example, System.Math defines a couple of public constants:

```
public static class Math
{
    public const double PI = 3.1415926535897931;
    public const double E = 2.7182818284590451;
    ...
}
```

Constants can be computed at compile time and are stored in the metadata associated with the containing type. Figure 11.6 shows how Math.E looks in ILDASM.

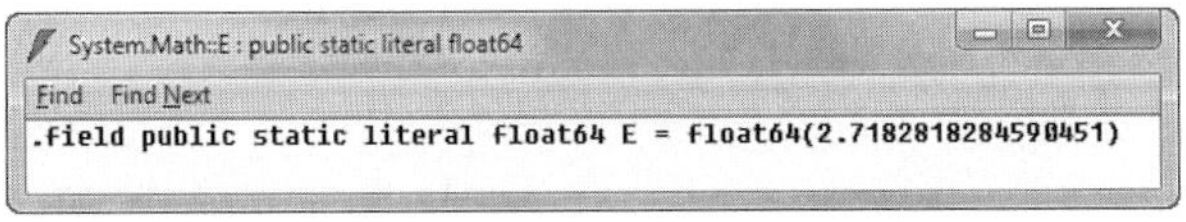

FIGURE 11.6   A constant turns into a "literal" in IL code.

The declaration of a constant uses the `const` keyword and cannot include the `static` keyword. The value supplied to the constant should permit to be fully evaluated at compile time. This includes primitive types like numbers and Booleans, string literals, and null references for reference types. Calling a constructor (or another other kind of method) is not permitted because it would involve runtime execution of code.

When using a constant, the compiler copies its value verbatim to the use site. For example, consider the following piece of code used to calculate the surface of a circle:

```
class Circle
{
    private double _radius;

    public Circle(double radius)
    {
        _radius = radius;
    }

    public double Surface()
    {
        return Math.PI * _radius * _radius;
    }
}
```

Looking in `Reflector` for the `Surface` method, we see no trace whatsoever of `Math.PI`. Figure 11.7 shows how the constant got burned into the use site at compile time.

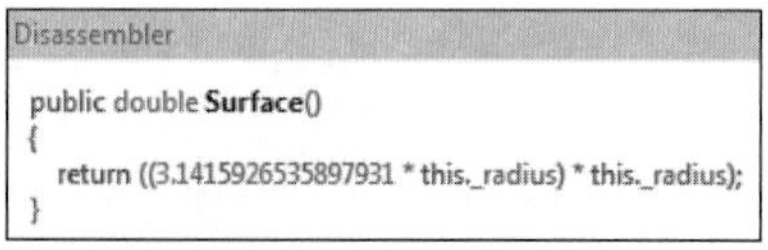

```
Disassembler
public double Surface()
{
    return ((3.1415926535897931 * this._radius) * this._radius);
}
```

FIGURE 11.7   Constant values get copied wherever they are used.

Because constants are copied to places where they're used, you cannot change a constant after it's been exposed. For example, if the .NET Framework developers were to change the value of Pi (and no, they don't have such a mandate, contrary to the stories about American states trying to legislate the value of Pi in the late 1800s), every application that picked up the original value would have to be recompiled. This is in contrast to (static) read-only fields, which are accessed at runtime:

```
class IndianaMath
{
    public static readonly double PI = 3.2;
}
```

Figure 11.8 shows `Reflector` when using `IndianaMath.PI` from the `Surface` method.

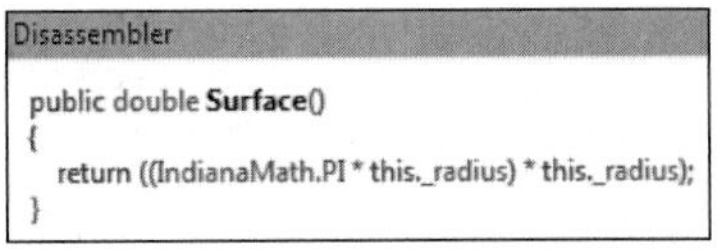

```
Disassembler
public double Surface()
{
    return ((IndianaMath.PI * this._radius) * this._radius);
}
```

FIGURE 11.8   Read-only fields are looked up at runtime.

Despite the fact that constants are computed at compile time, that doesn't prevent you from making them dependent on one another, as long as there's no cyclic dependency:

```
class Naturals
{
    public const int ZERO = ONE - 1;
    public const int ONE  = ZERO + 1;
    public const int TWO  = ONE + ONE;
}
```

In the preceding code, `ZERO` and `ONE` are mutually dependent, so the compilation will fail; however, if we assign 0 to `ZERO`, the preceding code will compile fine. Also you shouldn't use expressions that cause arithmetic overflow at compile time unless you explicitly wrap them in an `unchecked(...)` expression:

```
class Naturals
{
    // CS0220: The operation overflows at compile time in checked mode
    public const int LARGERTHANLARGE = int.MaxValue + 1;
}
```

With regard to naming, both read-only fields and constants are typically spelled using all-uppercase words.

In summary, read-only fields and properties differ in two aspects:

▶ Read-only fields can be computed at runtime by running code, whereas constants need to be fully evaluated at compile time.

▶ Constants have a nonexistent versioning story because their value gets burned into use sites, whereas read-only fields are looked up at runtime.

Volatile Fields

Multithreaded programming is notoriously hard, especially when optimizations are carried out by the compiler, runtime, or even the hardware. In particular, reads and writes to memory can sometimes be reordered to improve execution efficiency. In such a case, fields can be declared as volatile to ensure reads and writes to the field are not moved relative to surrounding code. Because this is a very specialized subject, refer to online documentation detailing the CLR memory model and practical uses of the volatile keyword.

An Intermezzo About Enums

Related to constants are enums, which are value types that contain for their members a set of named constants. A typical example of an enum is `Color`, as shown here:

```
enum Color
{
    Red,
    Green,
    Blue,
}
```

Right inside the framework you can find quite a few enums, as well; for example, to indicate a "file open mode" when using `System.IO` APIs. Just like other value types, you can apply an access modifier to the type.

(TRAILING) COMMAS

Notice that an enum's members are comma separated and not semicolon separated. Basically, they denote a list of symbolic values. A trailing comma is allowed after the last member, which is often put there so that the addition of new members to the enum doesn't show up while comparing old and new versions of a file.

Why Enums Matter

One key difference with constants defined on (and exposed by) some type is the fact an enum puts all related constant values under a common umbrella. Because of this, stronger typing ensues, (partly) avoiding invalid assignments. The use of our `Color` enum is shown here on the first line; the second line is invalid:

```
Color red = Color.Red;
Color blue = 17;  // Invalid assignment.
```

Notice that we've stated that invalid assignment to an enum-typed variable is only partly mitigated because an explicit conversion from the underlying type to an enum exists. This allows for easy serialization scenarios where an enum's value is stored away and put back in after deserialization. As you will see later, enums can also be used for "flag masks," in which case values may be assigned that represent a combination of flags. In such a case, protection against invalid values would become slightly harder:

```
Color red = Color.Red;
Color blue = (Color)17;  // This works.
```

Underlying Types

Because we've mentioned the word *constant* quite a bit, you might be wondering where enum members get their values. Moreover, what's the type of those constant values? To answer those questions, we must introduce the notion of an underlying type that's associated with an enum's definition. The underlying type indicates the domain for the constants declared within the enum. If left unspecified, an enum's underlying type is a 32-bit integer. You can specify the underlying type explicitly as shown here:

```
enum Color : long
{
    Red,
    Green,
    Blue,
}
```

You'll see this colon "derives from" syntax recurring quite a bit in Chapter 14 when we discuss inheritance. Permitted underlying types are integral numeric types such as byte, short, int, and long, together with their unsigned variants.

Assigning Values to Members

What we haven't explained yet is where the (constant) values for the enum's members come from. Because we didn't specify any values here, the enum will automatically get consecutive constant values for its members, starting from zero. So the definition of our Color enum is equivalent to the following:

```
enum Color
{
    Red = 0,
    Green = Red + 1,
    Blue = Green + 1,
}
```

You can see those values by casting an enum value to the underlying type. Notice that calling ToString on an enum will actually print the symbolic name corresponding to the enum member:

```
Color red = Color.Red;
Console.WriteLine(red);      // Prints "Red".
Console.WriteLine((int)red); // Prints "0".
```

Instead of relying on the automatic numbering, you might want to supply values yourself, as shown here. This provides several advantages because you might want to use some relevant integral values that make sense in the target domain of the enum:

```
enum Color : uint
{
    Red = 0xFF0000,
    Green = 0x00FF00,
    Blue = 0x0000FF,
}
```

BEWARE OF CONSTANTS

Being containers for constant values, enums exhibit the properties similar to those for regular constants. In particular, a constant's value gets copied into use sites, which means versioning of an enum needs some careful treatment.

For one thing, changing explicitly assigned constant values will obviously break users that rely on those values, and because of the copying behavior they won't notice the change until a recompilation of their code happens. Also, when some storage system is using an enum's underlying values, changes will get persisted data and actual enum definitions out of sync, resulting in disasters.

Another caveat to be aware of is that the order of members in an enum matters when values are implicitly assigned in a sequential manner. So reordering values in an enum is not a good idea. If you need to add new values in a next release, add them at the end (rather than, say, sorting them alphabetically).

Those remarks hold especially if enum values are externally visible, either through some persistence mechanism or through a public access modifier that will cause clients to clone the values into their code.

Within an enum definition, it's possible to have different members with the same value, which can be useful if two aliases are desired for a same underlying value. In the following code, we're using both English and Dutch names for the colors, just for illustration purposes:

```
enum Color : uint
{
    Red = 0xFF0000,
    Rood = Red,
    Green = 0x00FF00,
    Groen = Green,
    Blue = 0x0000FF,
    Blauw = Blue,
}
```

It's also possible to use automatic numbering for some members and explicit values for others. When no value is specified for an enum member, it gets its value by adding one to the enum member preceding it.

The `System.Enum` Type

Consider the example shown in the previous section. Now think about what you would expect to happen when using a `ToString` operation on, say, the `Color.Red` value. Recall that this operation provides a symbolic name for the enum value in question. However, because there are two enum members with the same value, only one of both symbolic names will be returned. Which one it will be? You can't tell.

This brings us to another discussion about the use of metadata within the platform. Because the runtime representation of an enum value is nothing but its underlying numeric (integral) value, associating it back to a friendly member name is a bit of an unnatural act that requires the `ToString` operation to reach into metadata associated with the enum type. The code that enables this lives in the `System.Enum` type and leverages the reflection subsystem (which is discussed in Chapter 21, "Reflection").

Every enum type derives from `System.Enum`, as illustrated later in the "Behind the Scenes" section. Although this doesn't buy us much at the instance member level (except for a method called `HasFlag`, which is explained in a minute), the Enum type has some handy static members defined on it.

Three Different Ways to Get a String Representation

The capability to turn an enum value into a string representation with a friendly name proves to be useful quite often. Besides the instance `ToString` method, you might want to get the string representation of an enum's underlying type value. Such a value may be retrieved from some external storage where the numeric value is kept rather than a string representation.

For example, assume we got our `Color` enum, this time without the Dutch aliases for the contained members:

```
enum Color : uint
{
    Red = 0xFF0000,
    Green = 0x00FF00,
    Blue = 0x0000FF,
}
```

Next we got the raw constant value for, say, Red. This value might have been retrieved from a database, the Registry, a configuration file, or whatnot. To turn it into a friendly string representation, we can do a couple of things. One possibility is to cast the value back to the enum and perform `ToString` on it:

```
uint value = 0xFF0000;

Color c = (Color)value;
Console.WriteLine(c.ToString("G"));  // "G" is the default and can be omitted.
Console.WriteLine(c.ToString("D"));
Console.WriteLine(c.ToString("X"));
```

Three format strings are available on Enum methods that turn an enum value into a string. The default, G, prints the friendly name associated with the constant. To get the decimal or hexadecimal value, respectively, use D or X. Alternatively, we can use the *System.Type of the enum type and leverage the Format method:

```
Console.WriteLine(Enum.Format(typeof(Color), value, "D"));
Console.WriteLine(Enum.Format(typeof(Color), value, "X"));
Console.WriteLine(Enum.Format(typeof(Color), value, "G"));
```

Yet another possibility is to use Enum.GetName, as follows:

```
Console.WriteLine(Enum.GetName(typeof(Color), value));
```

Enumerating an Enum

Being an "enumerated series" of named constants, you might want to get all of an enum's defined members. Both GetNames and GetValues allow you to do so. Both will return an array with results, ordered by the binary values of the corresponding constants. If no aliases with the same value exist, both arrays will have equal length. The following code is used to print all the names and values available in an enum:

```
foreach (string member in Enum.GetNames(typeof(Color)))
    Console.WriteLine(member);

foreach (uint member in Enum.GetValues(typeof(Color)))
    Console.WriteLine(member);
```

Notice that the output of the preceding code will be Blue, Green, Red because of the value used for each of the enum constants. Because it's common to think of colors in terms of RGB values, it makes sense to list them in that order, despite their common hexadecimal representations growing in the opposite order.

If no duplicates exist, the following examples with LINQ's Zip operator can be used to get name/value pairs for an enum's members. The Zip and Cast methods used here are discussed in detail when we cover LINQ in Chapter 19, "Language Integrated Query Essentials."

```
var res = Enum.GetNames(typeof(Color)).Zip(
    Enum.GetValues(typeof(Color)).Cast<uint>(),
    (name, value) => new { Name = name, Value = value }
);

// { Name = Blue, Value = 255 }
// { Name = Green, Value = 65280 }
// { Name = Red, Value = 16711680 }
foreach (var member in res)
    Console.WriteLine(member);
```

Converting Integral Values to Enum Values

You learned how to turn an integral value back into an enum value, simply by using an explicit conversion. However, what happens if that integral value isn't defined on the target enum type? Such a situation is likely to arise when such a value is retrieved from some persistent external storage (for example, the Registry, which can be tweaked by some administrator):

```
uint value = 0xFF0001;
Color c = (Color)value;
Console.WriteLine(c);
```

The preceding code will just work fine and print the decimal representation of the color even though no enum member exists with the given value. When talking about flags enums, we see this may come in handy. However, if an enum defines a "discrete" domain of values (either this *or* that but not a combination of those), stricter checking might be desirable. Enter the IsDefined method of System.Enum that enables precisely this scenario:

```
static void Main()
{
    PrintColor(0xFF0000);
    PrintColor(0xFF0001);   // Oops...
}

static void PrintColor(uint color)
{
    if (!Enum.IsDefined(typeof(Color), color))
        throw new ArgumentOutOfRangeException();

    Color c = (Color)color;
    Console.WriteLine(c);
}
```

Use of exceptions is the subject of Chapter 23, "Exceptions." All you must remember from this example is the behavior of the IsDefined method, returning false if the specified value is not defined on the enum.

Converting Strings to Enum Values

One final type of conversion is to start from a string representation like "Red" and go back to a corresponding enum value. Ignoring localization scenarios, this may be used to allow a user to enter a color "by name" while code wants to use the corresponding enum value on Color. Other uses include persistence based on a name rather than a value (which would allow enum values to change across versions of an application, though that's still not recommended, especially if the enum type is publicly visible).

Both the Parse and TryParse methods can be used to achieve such a conversion. The latter method was introduced in .NET 4. Whereas the former method throws an exception if the string is not found as any of the enum's member names, the latter uses an output parameter and returns false if conversion fails. For flagged enums, which are discussed next, you can also pass in a comma-separated list of enum members that will make up the enum's value:

```
Console.Write("Enter a color name: ");
var colorName = Console.ReadLine();

Color color;
if (!Enum.TryParse(colorName, /*ignoreCase*/ true, out color))
    Console.WriteLine("Color {0} doesn't exist.", colorName);
else
    Console.WriteLine(color);
```

Use of `TryParse` is recommended over `Parse` because invalid input is not too uncommon, and the expense (both in terms of processor cycles as well as code bloat) of exception handling to detect such input is high. Also because the `TryParse` method was introduced post-.NET 2.0, it can leverage generics to return the enum value in a strongly typed manner (rather than the `System.Object` return type on `Enum.Parse`).

Flags

Besides their use for discrete named constants, enums can also be used to describe flags. For example, `System.IO` defines the `FileOpen` enum as follows:

```
public enum FileMode
{
    CreateNew = 1,
    Create = 2,
    Open = 3,
    OpenOrCreate = 4,
    Truncate = 5,
    Append = 6,
}
```

This nonflags enum is passed to APIs like `File.Open` to specify which mode to open the file with. Basically, this enum corresponds to Win32 constants passed to `CreateFile`. In fact, the values used for the different `FileMode` members directly map onto those used on the Win32 API being called. It's clear that something like `FileMode` describes a set of discrete values that are mutually exclusive. You can only "open" the file in any of the six available modes. Combining things such as `Append` with `CreateNew` doesn't make sense.

A similar nonflags enum is `System.ConsoleKey`, which contains key codes. Because it excludes values for modifier keys like Shift, Ctrl, and Alt, there's no meaning to combining multiple enum values. After all, you can't press A and B exactly at the same time;

instead, your program will get to see each value one at a time in the order they were delivered by the input subsystem. Other examples include System.DayOfWeek because clearly it can't be both Monday and Wednesday at the same time (and place).

However, for lots of other enums, it makes sense to combine values. For example, the FileShare enum in the System.IO namespace does this. Can you tell the difference compared to the FileMode enum declaration?

```
[Flags]
public enum FileShare
{
    None = 0,
    Read = 1,
    Write = 2,
    ReadWrite = Read | Write,
    Delete = 4,
    Inheritable = 16,
}
```

By putting the Flags attribute on top of the enum, it becomes known as a flags enum whose values can be combined, typically using the | bitwise OR operator. For example, the ReadWrite entry in the preceding enum is built out of the combination of Read and Write. Its decimal value is 3, obtained from the bitwise OR (which coincides with the sum of the two values).

Defining Flags Enums

Values of a flags enum are typically powers of two, except for auxiliary entries such as ReadWrite that associate a friendly name to a combination of flags. Wherever a flags enum is used, a combination of flags can be passed in by using the | operator. Whether certain combinations are meaningful for the target API is another question that should be addressed by providing proper documentation. For more information about the use of FileShare, refer to the MSDN documentation.

An equivalent way of looking at those flags enum values is to regard them as "values with exactly 1 bit set to 1" (which are powers of two). Each bit on the underlying type represents exactly one flag, and there's no interference between flags in terms of the bits they use. This also shows why the underling type may be of importance to you. For flags enums, it's no longer the range of an integral value type that matters (such as the large range for uint, stretching from 0 to 4,294,967,295). Instead, the number of bits in the number matters (32 for a uint or int) and determines the maximum number of distinct flags that can be set by an enum value.

Use of a flags enum is often preferred over APIs that take a bunch of Boolean values as parameters to determine a modus operandi. For example, File.Open takes three enums, one of which is the FileShare flags enum:

```
public static FileStream Open(
    string path,
    FileMode mode,
    FileAccess access,
    FileShare share
) { ... }
```

Imagine what it would look like if `FileShare` were expanded into four Boolean parameters that stand for Read, Write, Delete, and Inheritable, respectively. Use of the method would involve passing four Booleans that have little meaning to the reader. Writing down a series of flags immediately conveys the message to the reader:

```
File.Open("c:\\boot.ini", FileMode.Open, FileAccess.Read,
                    FileShare.Read ¦ FileShare.Write);
```

NAMED PARAMETERS: A VIABLE ALTERNATIVE?

Some readers might object to the statement that an API with a bunch of Boolean parameters is less desirable, in favor of flags enums. Because C# 4.0 now enables you to specify parameters by name, such an API could be defined with default false values for every parameter. The ones to be set could be passed by name:

```
File.Open(..., read: true, write: true);
```

Although this is a great observation, parameter passing is just one place where enums are used. What if your method takes in a set of flags but needs to store those flags somewhere? Do you now declare a whole bunch of fields (each of which will take up 32 bits by themselves, the size of a Boolean)? Also, do you want to pass those flags on to other methods all over the place? Likely, the answer to both questions is no, so you'll agree that flags are a better idea.

Checking for Flags

So far, we've explored how a flags enum value can be constructed simply by using the bitwise OR operator. What we haven't explained yet is how the receiving end can find out about the flags that are set on a value. Arithmetic-savvy readers will immediately get some ideas about how to check whether a certain bit in a value is set. In essence, what you're going to do is apply a bit mask to perform the check. Figure 11.9 illustrates this.

The bitwise AND operator comes to the rescue to check whether a flag is set. As an example, the following code takes in a `FileShare` enum and checks whether the Read flag is set. The use of `TryParse` (and `Parse`) enables users to specify flags in a comma-separated manner. Try entering things such as `Read`, `Read, Write`, and `Delete` to see the behavior. Because `FileShare` lives in the `System.IO` namespace, you'll have to add a `using System.IO;` directive at the start of the file:

```
Console.Write("Enter FileShare flags: ");
var input = Console.ReadLine();

FileShare fileShare;
if (!Enum.TryParse(input, /*ignoreCase*/ true, out fileShare))
{
    Console.WriteLine("Invalid flags specified.");
    return;
}

if ((fileShare & FileShare.Read) == FileShare.Read)
    Console.WriteLine("Read flag set.");
```

Declaration

```
enum FileShare
{
  None = 0,   // 0 0 0 0
  Read = 1,   // 0 0 0 1
  Write = 2,  // 0 0 1 0
  Delete = 4, // 0 1 0 0
}
```

Constructing a value

```
  FileShare.Read    0 0 0 1
| FileShare.Write   0 0 1 0
----------------------------
-> value            0 0 1 1
```

Checking a flag

```
   value              0 0 1 1
&  FileShare.Write    0 0 1 0
-----------------------------
== FileShare.Write    0 0 1 0

   value              0 0 1 1
&  FileShare.Read     0 0 0 1
-----------------------------
== FileShare.Read     0 0 0 1

   value              0 0 1 1
&  FileShare.Delete   0 1 0 0
-----------------------------
== FileShare.Delete   0 0 0 0
```

FIGURE 11.9   Read-only fields are looked up at runtime.

Instead of using the bitwise AND operator, you can also use the `HasFlag` method that's introduced as an instance method on `System.Enum` starting from .NET 4:

```
if (fileShare.HasFlag(FileShare.Read))
    Console.WriteLine("Read flag set.");
```

From these examples, you can already see various operators are supported on enum values. We use bitwise AND and bitwise OR, as well as the == equality operator. Other supported operators include all comparison operators (such as <), the addition and subtraction operators, more bitwise operations (^ for XOR and ~ for inversion), and the increment and decrement operations (++ and --).

Revisiting the `switch` Statement

Code often has to dispatch to certain logic based on an enum value. One of the best candidate statements to carry out this task is the `switch` statement. In fact, the code editor in Visual Studio has a handy feature for generating a full `switch` statement for all of an enum's members. Here's the way to do it: Given a variable of an enum type, type **switch** and press Tab twice. Now enter the variable name and press Enter. For our `Color` type, this technique is illustrated in Figure 11.10.

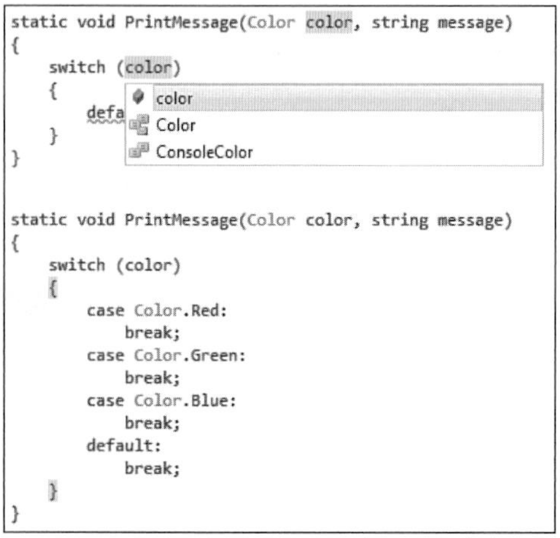

```
static void PrintMessage(Color color, string message)
{
    switch (color)
    {
                color
        defa    Color
    }           ConsoleColor
}


static void PrintMessage(Color color, string message)
{
    switch (color)
    {
        case Color.Red:
            break;
        case Color.Green:
            break;
        case Color.Blue:
            break;
        default:
            break;
    }
}
```

FIGURE 11.10   Generating a `switch` statement for an enum.

Although it might seem tempting to get rid of the default branch, this isn't a good idea because enums can carry undefined values, as discussed previously. Put some proper code in there that raises a runtime exception to guard against unknown values. Also, if your code is to return something based on an enum value, you won't get away with omitting the default branch due to the language's definite assignment rules ("all code paths need to return a value").

You can also use regular `if` statements to carry out specific actions based on an enum's value. However, when there are a lot of cases to look for, the `switch` statement is almost certainly the better choice, both for code readability and efficiency of execution.

Behind the Scenes

To wrap up our discussion about enums, let's take a quick peek behind the scenes. Even though the use of the colon syntax to specify an underlying type makes it seem like the enum type derives from the underlying type, this is not the case. All enum types derive from the `System.Enum` base type that's supplied by the runtime. Each member defined on the enum turns into a constant field. An instance of the enum contains a single field holding the value that's being used. Figure 11.11 shows what an enum definition looks like in ILDASM.

FIGURE 11.11   Under the hood, an enum contains both instance and static members.

If you're somehow interested in the underlying type for an enum type, there's a handy static method called `GetUnderlyingType` on `System.Enum`. On an enum value, you can invoke the instance method called `GetTypeCode` to get a `TypeCode` enum that denotes the underlying type.

Despite an enum being classified as a value type, each enum type's base class derives from `System.ValueType`, which is a class. Don't worry about this oddity at the runtime level. What you get is a value type with all the copying semantics discussed before; how it's implemented internally should be the least of your concerns.

Properties

With knowledge of the cornerstones of a type's operations and state under our belts, we can proceed with our exploration of other members available on classes and structs. Properties are a mix between state and operations. On the one hand, they're like fields providing get and set access to a piece of state; on the other hand, they're like methods because those get and set operations can contain code. For those reasons, properties are sometimes said to be *smart fields*.

Declaring and Using Properties

Like most other members, properties can have access modifiers, can be associated with the type (static) or an instance thereof, and can support other object-oriented modifiers that are discussed in Chapter 14. Their characteristic syntactic surface consists of one or two accessors, which are code blocks that deal with get or set operations:

```
class Person
{
    private string _name;
    private int _age;

    public string Name
    {
        get { return _name; }
```

```
        set { _name = value; }
    }

    public int Age
    {
        get { return _age; }
        set { _age = value; }
    }
}
```

In the preceding example, both Name and Age are properties. Each of those properties has a get and a set accessor, both of which are publicly visible. Properties can also be made read-only or write-only by omitting a getter or setter. It's quite uncommon to have write-only properties, but read-only properties are common.

Using the properties on our Person class looks like this:

```
var person = new Person();
person.Name = "Bart";
person.Age = 27;
Console.WriteLine(person.Name + " is " + person.Age);
```

The second and third lines call the property set accessors, which receive the object to the right of the assignment operator through the contextual value keyword. Outside property (and indexer) setters, value can be used as a regular identifier. This was one of the first contextual keywords to appear in C#, all the way back to C# 1.0. On the fourth line, both properties' get accessors are invoked to obtain the property's value. Getters are like methods that have to return an object of a type compatible with the property's return type.

Alternatively, the preceding code could be written using an object initializer expression, which was introduced in C# 3.0:

```
var person = new Person {
    Name = "Bart",
    Age = 27
};
Console.WriteLine(person.Name + " is " + person.Age);
```

One subtle difference lies in the use of an intermediate local variable used to construct the object and set its properties, prior to final assignment to the person variable. This is required to make sure no one can see the object in an intermediate initialization stage:

```
var __t = new Person();
__t.Name = "Bart";
__t.Age = 27;
var person = __t;
```

Accessors can also differ in accessibility, as long as it's strictly more restrictive than the property they're defined in. For example, our `Age` property could be declared as public, making both getter and setter publicly accessible. To restrict access to the set accessor, that one could be declared as private:

```
public int Age
{
    get { return _age; }
    private set { _age = value; }
}
```

Making an accessor more accessible than its containing property is not allowed. Although use of a private setter in combination with a public getter is a possible approach to limit access, it doesn't protect against mutation of the object. All members inside the type can call the setter. Use of read-only fields is recommended if the data is meant to be set only once during construction. In such a setting, you can't have property setters because those would have to assign to the "backing field," which isn't allowed:

```
class Person
{
    private readonly string _name;
    private readonly int _age;

    public Person(string name, int age)
    {
        _name = name;
        _age = age;
    }

    public string Name
    {
        get { return _name; }
    }

    public int Age
    {
        get { return _age; }
    }
}
```

The code inside accessors shouldn't be heavyweight and typically doesn't do much more than access some local state kept in a field or so. Some exceptions to this rule apply (such as .NET 4's `Lazy<T>.Value` property), but in most cases users expect a property to be merely a *smart field*.

Use of properties is recommended over publicly accessible fields because use of fields limits a type's capability to evolve the internal storage structure without breaking the type's users. Properties provide you with a level of indirection (*encapsulation*) when accessing fields (or small computations derived from it).

Concerning exceptions, it's fine for property accessors to throw exceptions. The most common case where this is used is to validate the `value` coming in to a property set method, which is just like any other public input that should be validated:

```
public string Name
{
    get { return _name; }
    set
    {
        if (string.IsNullOrEmpty(value))
            throw new ArgumentNullException("value");

        _name = value;
    }
}
```

"CONSTITUENT TYPES" AND VISIBILITY

Although we've discussed accessibility in various contexts already, we haven't told the whole story yet. A member's constituent types are the set of types that appear in that member's declaration, such as a property type or a method's return types and its parameter types.

It's not permitted to have constituent types that are less accessible than the declaring member itself. For example, a public method cannot take in an object of a type that's not publicly accessible. If it were to, how could a user invoke the method? As an exercise, try to expose an internal Address type through a property's return type and observe the compiler error that ensues.

Auto-Implemented Properties

C# 3.0 introduced a feature called auto-implemented properties to reduce the "syntactic ceremony" involved in creating "simple properties" that are nothing but smart fields. Instead of having to declare the backing field and a property accessing that field manually, the following syntax takes care of it all:

```
class Person
{
    public string Name { get; set; }
    public int Age { get; set; }
}
```

The preceding code is turned into this equivalent:

```
class Person
{
    private string <Name>k__BackingField;
    private int <Age>k__BackingField;

    public string Name
    {
        get { return <Name>k__BackingField; }
        set { <Name>k__BackingField = value; }
    }

    public int Age
    {
        get { return <Age>k__BackingField; }
        set { <Age>k__BackingField = value; }
    }
}
```

Although the accessibility of the generated get and set accessor can be specified, it's not possible to declare the backing fields as read-only. I hope that this little feature omission gets rectified in a future release of the language, maybe as part of larger immutability crusades undertaken by the language designers. Auto-implemented properties can easily be inserted in Visual Studio by using the prop snippet. Type **prop** and press Tab twice, as shown in Figure 11.12.

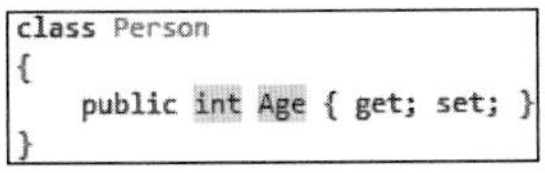

```
class Person
{
    public int Age { get; set; }
}
```

FIGURE 11.12   Auto-implemented property snippet in Visual Studio 2010.

How Properties Work

Properties are nothing but one or two accessor *methods* that are grouped together by a piece of metadata. This allows code editors and runtime services like reflection to see them as a unique kind of member. Some other languages don't have such a first-class treatment for concepts like properties (and indexers, and events, and so on) and rely on some naming convention instead:

```
class Person
{
    public string getName() { ... }
    public void setName(string name) { ... }
}
```

Although this works just fine, it makes tooling harder, and (what ought to be) properties are clustered together in the method list. Because get and set accessor pairs are such an established concept, .NET made them first-class metadata citizens.

Figure 11.13 shows a property definition in our much beloved ILDASM tool. As you can see, there are methods for the accessors that use get_ and set_ prefixes. In addition, a property acts as a piece of metadata that bundles those two methods together. Code that uses a property's getter or setter uses a direct method call to the respective methods. The metadata is simply there for tooling and services like serialization.

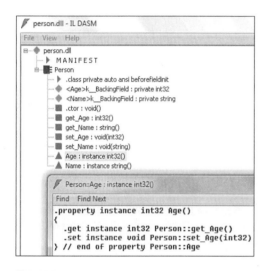

FIGURE 11.13   Dissection of a property.

Indexers

Closely related to properties are indexers. Both classes and structs can contain just one indexer, which is best described as a parameterized property that can be invoked by using an indexing expression. The stereotypical example of an indexer is on a vector object or a dictionary collection. Let's first show how the latter is used on the generic `Dictionary` type defined in `System.Collections.Generic` and then move on to defining our own `Vector` type with an indexer:

```
var phoneBook = new Dictionary<string, int>();
phoneBook["Bart"] = 51662;
phoneBook["John"] = 96207;
Console.WriteLine("Bart's phone number is: " + phoneBook["Bart"]);
```

The second and third lines add entries to the dictionary by passing the intended key as a parameter to the indexing expression and by assigning to it. On the fourth line, we read an entry from the dictionary. Notice with C# 3.0 collection initializers, you can initialize the dictionary as follows:

```
var phoneBook = new Dictionary<string, int> {
    { "Bart", 51662 },
    { "John", 96207 }
};
```

This doesn't use the indexer but invokes the dictionary's Add method two times, once for each element initialization entry.

"EVERYTHING SHOULD BE A DICTIONARY"

In some dynamic languages, the art of indexing is indistinguishable from regular member access. For example, accessing element 0 in an array xs could be xs.0 (not permitted in C#), accessing a member could either be pt.X or pt["X"], and you could simply add members by assigning to a yet-undefined member.

Starting from C# 4.0, this can be enabled through the use of dynamic and the ExpandoObject type in the System.Dynamic namespace. However, it's my (and my manager's) opinion that static typing should be preferred over dynamic typing whenever possible. You learn more about dynamic later in Chapter 22, "Dynamic Programming."

Defining Indexers

To define an indexer, you use the this keyword in yet another context. Take a moment to think back about all the allowed uses of this you've seen so far. To see why the this keyword is used in this context, take a closer look at the following code:

```
Vector victor = new Vector(1, 2, 3);
Console.WriteLine("X = " + victor[0]);
// We're leaving the implementation of an indexer with a string-typed parameter
// as an exercise for the reader. (See the next code fragment.)
Console.WriteLine("Y = " + victor["y"]);
Console.WriteLine("Z = " + victor[2]);
```

Because indexing operates on the object directly, there's no member name involved. In fact, from the receiving end's point of view, the left side of the indexing operation is nothing but the object itself, hence this. To define the first indexers taking in an integer parameter, you therefore write the following:

```
class Vector
{
    private int _x, _y, _z;

    public Vector(int x, int y, int z)
```

```
    {
        _x = x; _y = y; _z = z;
    }

    public int this[int index]
    {
        get
        {
            if (index == 0) return _x;
            else if (index == 1) return _y;
            else if (index == 2) return _z;
            else throw new ArgumentOutOfRangeException();
        }
    }
    // Insert the implementation of an indexer with a string-typed parameter
    // here, allowing the user to write things like vector["x"] or vector["Y"].
}
```

There are different ways to look at it. One is to see the indexer as a property with this as its name, taking in *one or more* parameters specified between square brackets rather than parentheses. Inside both accessors, those parameters' values are available for use; in the setter, the contextual value keyword receives the incoming object.

For the most part, indexers and properties are similar. One notable difference is that indexers cannot be defined as static members. Also notice that because indexers require at least one parameter (none of which can be ref or out) to be specified at the use site, putting a default value on the first parameter isn't allowed:

```
class Vector
{
    ...
    public int this[int index = 0] { ... }
```

If this were permitted, you could write the following, which could be interpreted as quite confusing (compared to array-creation expressions):

```
Vector v;
int x = v[];
```

I leave it as an exercise for you to define a set accessor on the preceding indexer and to implement the setter that takes in a string parameter that specifies the axis using letters x, y, or z.

How Indexers Are Implemented

Even though the CLR has the notion of indexed properties, which are properties that accept parameters, C# doesn't fully expose this feature. Only in COM interop scenarios (the subject of Chapter 22) and starting from C# 4.0, indexed properties can be consumed in limited scenarios. One key problem with generalized use of indexed properties is the multiple meanings the following piece of code could have:

```
employees.Numbers["Bart"];
```

Does this mean we can obtain an object called numbers that we subsequently are indexing into, or does it mean that there's an indexed property called Numbers that does accept a string as its parameter?

Indexers as they're known in C# are a special indexed property of which only a single one can be defined on a type. The way this is realized is by means of giving it a fixed name called Item and applying a DefaultMember custom attribute to the class or struct containing it. Figure 11.14 shows this whole setup.

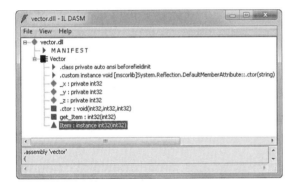

FIGURE 11.14   Indexers are indexed properties called Item, declared as a default member.

Languages know that default members deserve special treatment in a way that they don't require the property name to be used to access them. So indexing into one of our Vector object's x coordinate using an index of zero is turned into the following code. However, it's not permitted to use the Item name to access an indexer in C#.

```
victor.Item[0] = 42;
```

An artifact of this implementation mechanism is that you can't declare both a property called Item and an indexer in a class or struct in C#. Even though the DefaultMember attribute could refer to something other than Item, the compiler doesn't rename an indexer to disambiguate this scenario. Figure 11.15 shows the (rather unexplainable, at least to people who didn't read this) error message that results.

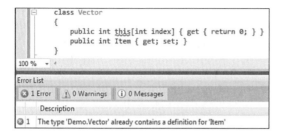

FIGURE 11.15   Properties named `Item` will clash with indexers.

Summary

After our coverage of the code aspects of types in Chapter 10, "Methods," we aimed our discussion at their data aspect in this chapter. Both aspects are quintessential in the definition of types. Nonetheless, some members of types don't fall in just one category; for example, properties and indexers.

First, you explored the extreme end of a type's state spectrum by covering fields, which act as containers for state associated with a type or an instance of a type. You learned how to declare and initialize fields, also covering the notion of read-only fields that are immutable outside what's known as the constructor. At first sight, constants are similar to read-only fields, so you learned about some important differences.

After talking about fields, you explored properties and indexers. Both of those types of members are quite "stateful" but can have logic associated with retrieval (`get`) and assignment (`set`) operations. Properties are sometimes called smart fields for this very reason. You also learned about the C# 3.0 feature of auto-implemented properties.

In Chapter 12, "Constructors and Finalizers," you look at another place where code and data meet on the level of types. Constructors act as members responsible for initializing a type's or an instance's state. Finalizers can be used to clean up state upon destruction of an object.

IN THIS CHAPTER

▶ Constructors 579

▶ Static Constructors 586

▶ Destructors (Poorly Named Finalizers) 589

After having covered the code and data aspects of types by exploring methods, fields, properties and indexers, we're now ready to discuss where both aspects clearly meet. This includes logic to initialize a type (by means of a static constructor) and its instances (by means of an instance constructor). Furthermore, sometimes it's needed to perform certain clean-up actions upon destruction of an object instance. As you'll see, this use of so-called finalizers can be reduced to a minimum due to the presence of garbage collection. In some cases though, use of finalizers is required to ensure proper clean-up of native resources held on to by an object.

Constructors

Constructors serve the goal of carrying out initialization tasks that are required for new class instances or for the initialization of a type. The first type of constructor is called an instance constructor; the latter is called a static constructor (or initializer in terms of CLR lingo).

Instance Constructors

During the creation of a new instance of a class, one often wants to run some code to initialize the state associated with the instance being created. Examples include setting fields or running other initialization tasks.

As such, constructors are special kinds of methods that cannot be called directly but are invoked through the use of the new operator. Parameters can be used on a constructor definition to pass data to the newly created object. To declare such an instance constructor, you define what looks like a method but has the name of the class and omits a return type:

```
class Person
{
    private readonly string _name;
    private readonly int _age;

    public Person(string name, int age)
    {
        _name = name;
        _age = age;
    }
}
```

The constructor shown here will be called when you write the following piece of code that creates a new Person object:

```
var bart = new Person("Bart", 27);
```

It's best to think about constructors as just a special kind of method. This means that all the following similarities apply:

▶ Constructors can have an access modifier.

▶ Multiple overloads can be defined.

▶ The constructor's body can contain all constructs allowed in a method.

▶ Starting from C# 4.0, default parameter values can be present.

Despite these similarities, it's recommended to keep a couple of best practices in mind for a constructor's design. For one thing, it's best to make constructors basically a way to set a series of fields with minimal work. Avoid doing long-running computation as part of construction; instead, factory methods or initialization methods may be used.

Behind the Scenes
To convince you about this resemblance to regular methods, let's inspect the definition of a class with a constructor. Figure 12.1 shows that a constructor is nothing but a method with a special .ctor name. Notice how certain pieces of metadata applied to the method indicate this "special name" nature.

The creation of a new object instance using the new keyword will trigger a call to the constructor. It's pretty much like a method call in terms of evaluation stack behavior except for the use of a different newobj instruction. This is where the runtime gets in control to allocate the (zero-initialized) heap memory needed for the instance. When everything is set up to run custom code, the constructor method is invoked. Figure 12.2 illustrates the newobj instruction.

p.dll - IL DASM
File View Help
p.dll
MANIFEST
Person
.class private auto ansi beforefieldinit
_age : private int32
_name : private string
.ctor : void(string,int32)
Pay : void(valuetype [mscorlib]System.Decimal)
Person::.ctor : void(string,int32)
Find Find Next
.method public hidebysig specialname rtspecialname
instance void .ctor(string name,
int32 age) cil managed

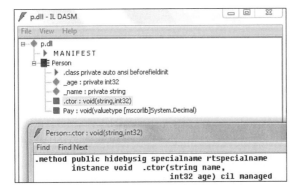

FIGURE 12.1 Constructors are methods with a special name.

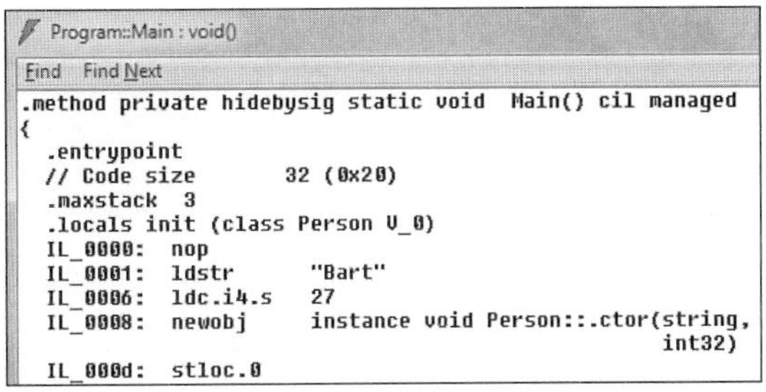

Program::Main : void()
Find Find Next
.method private hidebysig static void Main() cil managed
{
.entrypoint
// Code size 32 (0x20)
.maxstack 3
.locals init (class Person V_0)
IL_0000: nop
IL_0001: ldstr "Bart"
IL_0006: ldc.i4.s 27
IL_0008: newobj instance void Person::.ctor(string,
int32)
IL_000d: stloc.0

FIGURE 12.2 Constructors are invoked through a `newobj` instruction.

Default Constructors

If no constructors are defined explicitly, a default parameterless constructor will be created for you. Because a newly allocated object will be guaranteed to have all of its fields zero-initialized, this shouldn't pose any problem.

```
class Person
{
    private string _name;
    private int _age;

    public string Name
    {
        get { return _name; }
        set { _name = value; }
    }

    public int Age
    {
        get { return _age; }
```

```
        set { _age = value; }
    }
}
```

In the preceding example, a new `Person` instance will have a `Name` property that returns `null` and an `Age` property that returns zero. Because the act of initializing an object by setting a bunch of properties is quite tedious (even a bit with C# 3.0's object initializer syntax), it's recommended to have a way to initialize state using constructors. Also, the use of constructors enables you to declare fields as read-only and limit the initialization of those fields to constructors.

After a constructor with parameters is defined, the default constructor is no longer emitted automatically. If it still makes sense to have a default constructor, you can put it in manually:

```
class Person
{
    private string _name;
    private int _age;

    public Person()
    {
        // Does anything meaningful go in here?
    }

    public Person(string name, int age)
    {
        _name = name;
        _age = age;
    }
}
```

In design patterns like factory methods, a default publicly visible constructor is not desired because a static method will take over the externally visible job of construction. In such a case, you can hide the default constructor by explicitly adding a private one:

```
class Ticket
{
    private readonly int _id;

    private Ticket(int id)
    {
        _id = id;
    }
```

```
public static Ticket PurchaseTicket()
{
    // A long-running task may be needed to purchase a ticket, ultimately
    // returning one that can only be constructed here:
    return new Ticket(321);
}
}
```

What About Structs?

Up to this point, we've only mentioned classes during our constructor discussion. This raises the question of whether structs can have constructors. The answer is yes, except for parameter-free "default" ones.

One of the main reasons why nondefault parameter-free constructors on structs are considered harmful (and are disallowed by C# for that reason) is the cost that would be associated with creating arrays of a struct type. For each element in such an array, the runtime would have to run the default constructor. Notice that this isn't the case when you initialize an array of reference types because all elements will be set to null.

Also, if you implement a constructor on a struct, you need to make sure all fields are explicitly assigned to. The reason for this is that your struct's constructor is taking over initialization tasks. In fact, no newobj instruction is used to allocate a new struct value because such a value lives on the stack. Basically, your constructor gets to operate on a piece of reserved stack space and needs to initialize all of it. For example:

```
struct Point
{
    private readonly int _x;
    private readonly int _y;

    public Point(int x, int y)
    {
        _x = x;
        _y = y;
    }
}
```

To initialize a Point value, you can either invoke the constructor using the new operator or invoke the default constructor, which cannot be hidden on structs. The rationale for this is pretty simple. Because the default way to create a new struct value is by returning all-zero memory (and this is used for arrays, too), it makes little sense to block that off. And if such a hiding operation were permitted, what would it mean to create an array of a value type? Is the runtime somehow allowed to call your private default constructor?

The following code fragment shows two ways to initialize a new Point value:

```
var p1 = new Point(3, 5);
var p2 = new Point();
```

HEAP VERSUS STACK, ONCE MORE

In contrast to languages such as C++, the use of the new operator does not imply heap allocation. Where an object gets allocated solely depends on its type: Value types go on the stack, reference types go on the heap. Sometimes the use of an object also affects where it goes (cf. boxing).

This piece of code gets translated into what's shown in Figure 12.3, assuming the code was compiled without optimizations turned on.

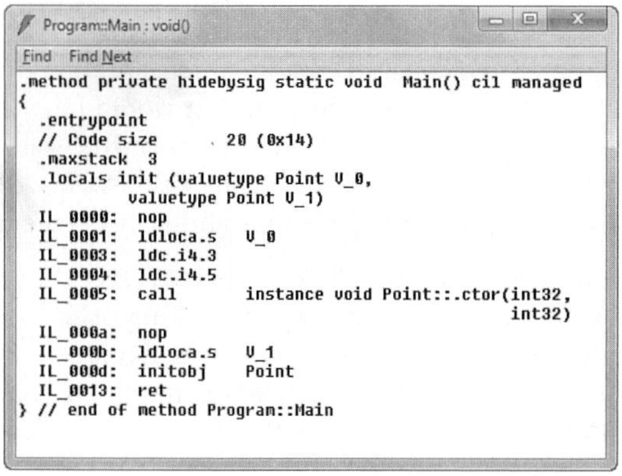

FIGURE 12.3   Constructors for structs operate on allocated stack space.

One thing to observe here is the lack of newobj calls. Instead, the address of the (stack-allocated) local variable is passed to the constructor method to operate on. The code in the constructor is then responsible for properly initializing all fields contained in that piece of memory. If this is not done, the compiler complains in the way depicted in Figure 12.4. When using the default constructor, the initialization of the local variable is carried out by the initobj instructions.

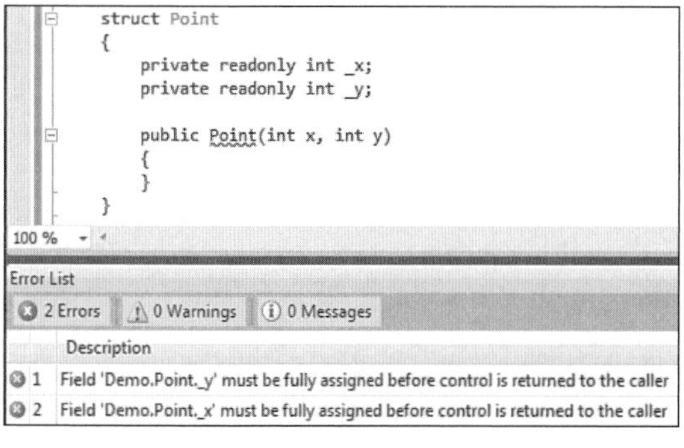

FIGURE 12.4   All fields of a struct must be fully assigned by code run in the constructor.

To invoke the default initialization behavior (for example, if your struct's constructor wants to set only a couple of fields), you can write the following, which is discussed next:

```
struct Point
{
    private readonly int _x;
    private readonly int _y;

    public Point(int x) : this()  // Will set _y = 0
    {
        _x = x;
    }
}
```

ZERO: HARDER THAN YOU EXPECT

Zero-initialization is a seemingly simple topic but has quite a few complications, especially when the runtime wants to make guarantees. Memory that hasn't been zeroed-out could pose severe security and reliability risks. It's one of the most common programming errors in unmanaged code.

For more information about all aspects of zero-initialization and which guarantees can be made by the runtime (or why not), the interested reader is most welcome to take a look at the Common Language Infrastructure (CLI) specification. Luckily, there's no need to worry about it all.

Constructor Initializers

In the earlier example of the struct, I introduced some syntax you haven't encountered yet. For our constructor to call the default one (which is always present on a struct), we wrote the following:

```
public Point(int x) : this()
```

Use of the this keyword to invoke a constructor from another one is known as a constructor initializer. In Chapter 14, "Object-Oriented Programming," you'll see there's also the base keyword that can be used to invoke a base class constructor. This feature permits "overloading for constructors" and is usually used to avoid code duplication across different constructors. For example, a Point might have some default initialization for certain fields if they are omitted from the constructor argument list:

```
struct Point
{
    private readonly int _x, _y, _z;
    private readonly DateTime _t;
```

```
    public Point(int x, int y, int z, DateTime t)
    {
        _x = x; _y = y; _z = z; _t = t;
    }

    public Point(int x, int y, int z)
        : this(x, y, z, DateTime.Now)
    {
    }

    public Point(int x, int y)
        : this(x, y, 0, DateTime.Now)
    {
    }
}
```

Inside the call to this, all the constructor's parameters are in scope. Fields of the object under construction obviously are not available yet. In contrast to default parameter values in C# 4.0, the default arguments passed from one constructor to another can include any expression (such as DateTime.Now, which isn't constant).

CALLS TO THIS AND BASE MUST COME FIRST

Different languages have different orders for initialization. C++ objects suffer from an identity crisis when they're being created (due to vtable changes), Java has the additional complexity of instance initializers, and so on. One thing Java and C# have in common is the restriction to call initializers, using this or base (or super in Java), only on a constructor's first line. C# enforces this through the colon-based syntax, whereas Java allows a call to this to appear on the first line of the constructor body only.

Static Constructors

Where instance constructors take on the task of initializing a new object instance, the role of static constructors (sometimes referred to as type initializers) is to initialize a type's static state. Although the runtime provides type initializers for more than just classes and structs, C# restricts their declaration to those categories of types (mainly because of their limited use of other types).

A static constructor looks like an instance constructor but is declaring using the static keyword, doesn't have an access modifier, and can't take any parameters. Just like any other static member, it can only access other static members and is primarily used to assign the type's static fields. In fact, static field initializers become part of the code run by the static constructor. For example:

```
class PaymentService
{
    private static PaymentServiceProxy _proxy;
    private static Logger _logger;

    static PaymentService()
    {
        _proxy = new PaymentServiceProxy();
        _logger = new Logger("log" + _proxy.Timestamp + ".txt");
    }

    ...

}
```

Static constructors can't be invoked by the user directly. Instead, it's the runtime's task to ensure a static constructor has run any time before static members on the containing type are used or an instance of a class is created.

To illustrate this, consider the following struct definition containing a static member and a static constructor. Per the rules described earlier, the static constructor will be run only when the static B method is called. For a class, things are bit a different, and the static constructor will also be run prior to any instance creation. In either case, a static constructor is run only once per application domain. This concept is explained later; for now, it suffices to simplify this statement to "once in an application's lifetime":

```
struct A
{
    static A()
    {
        Console.WriteLine("In A::.cctor");
    }

    public static void B() { /* ... */ }
}
```

For the preceding example, the following code illustrates the behavior of when the static constructor is triggered by the runtime for a struct:

```
//
// None of those lines will trigger the static constructor.
//
A a = new A();
Console.WriteLine(a.ToString());
```

```
//
// However, this will.
//
A.B();
```

Also try to turn the struct into a class and observe the differences. From all of this, there's one key takeaway: You don't directly control when a static constructor is run and therefore you shouldn't rely on it. The only guarantee made by the runtime is that the execution of the code happens "early enough" such that subsequent uses of the type will see static state in a fully initialized shape.

Because static constructors get run at a time that might not be obvious to the user of a type, it's highly recommended not to throw exceptions from this code unless things get really, really bad. Instead, it's better to have a static initialization method that could be wrapped in an exception handler if things can be expected to fail. Establishing database connections, opening files, and so on are all tasks that can go wrong. If an exception occurs from a static constructor, it will surface wrapped in a TypeInitializationException:

```
static void Main()
{
    A a = null;
    try {
        a = new A();
    }
    catch (TypeInitializationException ex) {
        Console.WriteLine(ex.InnerException.Message);
    }
    Console.WriteLine(a.ToString());
}

class A
{
    static A(){
        throw new Exception("Oops!");
    }

    public A(){
        Console.WriteLine("Will never get here!");
    }
}
```

Even though the preceding code will catch the exception, this should be considered a very lucky coincidence. In general, your code won't scale if you have to wrap every single instance creation or static member access in a handler protecting against the possibility you're triggering a type initializer to run. Furthermore, even if you feel brave and try to make this happen, what about field initializers, which can't be wrapped in try-catch blocks?

Also, things get unreliable in no time because the preceding code won't succeed in creating the requested new instance of class A. As a rule of thumb, consider the app domain to be crashed if a type initializer fails. One way to do some final cleanup in response to any exception that's taking down the application domain is to use the following code with an event handler on the AppDomain object. You'll learn about event handlers in Chapter 18, "Events," and the lambda expression syntax in Chapter 17, "Delegates," to specify a delegate.

```
AppDomain.CurrentDomain.UnhandledException += (o, e) =>
{
    // Could inspect e.ExceptionObject in here.
};
```

Finally, Figure 12.5 shows how a static constructor is surfaced in IL code, with the .cctor special name.

FIGURE 12.5   Static constructors are just methods with special names and treatment.

Destructors (Poorly Named Finalizers)

Besides constructors, C# has the notion of destructors. Before going any further, let's start with the mandatory warning. In the world of garbage collection, destructors only share their name with the concept known from C++. That is, they are totally different in behavior, despite their common syntax. To put this straight, consider the following piece of C++ code. Readers unfamiliar with C++ can skip the following example.

```c++
#include <stdio.h>

class Destruct
{
public:
    Destruct() {
        printf("Constructing\n");
    }

    ~Destruct() {
        printf("Destructing\n");
    }
};

void Stack() {
    printf("Stack - begin\n");
    Destruct d;
    printf("Stack - end\n");
}

void Heap() {
    printf("Heap - begin\n");
    Destruct *d = new Destruct();
    delete d;
    printf("Heap - end\n");
}

int main() {
    Stack();
    Heap();
}
```

One key difference is the fact that C++ classes and structs can be allocated either on the stack or the heap, depending on their use. Just declaring a local variable of the type will cause it to be stack-allocated, whereas use of the new operator results in heap allocation. Let's start with the stack-allocated case, which prints this:

```
Stack - begin
Constructing
Stack - end
Destructing
```

At the point we declare the local variable of type `Destruct`, the default constructor is called, causing `Constructing` to be printed. At the point the method is quit, the code compiled for the method ensures the stack-allocated object is destructed by a call to the destructor. This is a form of *deterministic cleanup*.

For the heap-allocated example, the output differs slightly. Here the responsibility of deleting the object is upon the user by using the `delete` operator. At that very point in time, the destructor will be called:

```
Heap - begin
Constructing
Destructing
Heap - end
```

This, again, is a form of *deterministic cleanup*. In both cases, it's either lexical scoping or manual user intervention that causes the destructor to be called. In none of the cases does a runtime service kick in to call the destructor's code.

Defining Finalizers in C#

Before discussing their behavior in full detail, also contrasting it to the C++ behavior shown earlier, we first show how to declare a finalizer in C#. Because they share the C++ syntax, the language specification calls them destructors, but to avoid confusion with any of your C++ programmer friends, let's call them finalizers.

Here's a finalizer defined in C#, using the class's name prefixed with a ~ character:

```
class A
{
    ~A()
    {
        Console.WriteLine("Destructing instance of A");
    }
}
```

Finalizers cannot have an access modifier, nor can they have any parameters. They cannot be called explicitly by the user (so it doesn't make sense to pass parameters), as you will see.

How Finalizers Are Run

Now let's move on to the discussion about their behavior and best practices associated with the use of finalizers. In contrast to C++, finalizers are called by the runtime when the object instance is no longer accessible by user code. The runtime service in charge of their invocation is the garbage collector that's responsible for releasing memory held by heap-allocated objects at a point after they've become unreachable by code. Earlier we discussed the mark-and-sweep mechanism employed by the garbage collector to scan memory, mark objects that are still alive, and collect the ones that cannot be used any longer.

When an object gets garbage collected and it implements a finalizer, that method will be scheduled to be run by the garbage collector before the final reclamation of the memory held by the object. Because of how the garbage collector works, finalizers put additional stress on the runtime. Here's why.

During garbage collection, the runtime's execution of managed code is suspended because memory is being manipulated and references are temporarily inconsistent. If code were allowed to run at this time, this would pose a breach in type safety because following a managed reference could lead you into no-man's land. As a result, code in finalizers cannot be run while the collection is in progress. Instead, the object that has become eligible for finalization (determined by the implementation of a custom finalizer) is put in a queue to be processed later when the execution engine is restarted after the garbage collection that was in-flight.

Because of this behavior, use of an empty finalizer is the worst possible thing you can put an object through because you simply postpone its death for no good reason. You'll soon learn how the use of a finalizer can and should be avoided whenever possible. But first, let's show a finalizer being called:

```
static void Main()
{
    A a = new A();

    // Won't collect before the application quits.
    Console.ReadLine();
}

class A
{
    ~A()
    {
        Console.WriteLine("Destructing instance of A");
    }
}
```

Unless something totally unexpected happens, causing the garbage collector to kick in for the preceding fragment, the finalizer for the instance of A won't get called until the very last point in time when the application quits. There's simply not enough stress on the managed heap to warrant a collection in the preceding example. To truly illustrate the nondeterministic behavior of finalization, let's show a more contrived example of excessive allocation, resulting in collection:

```
while (true)
{
    A a = new A();
}
```

A new object is allocated on the heap for every iteration through the loop. This causes the heap to grow until generation 0 becomes full. At that point, the garbage collector will kick in to collect objects that are no longer reachable. In fact, all objects allocated by prior iterations are unreachable because we overwrote the local variable in which their reference was kept. To show which objects get allocated and which ones get finalized, we'll add some counting mechanism to A:

```
class A
{
    private static int s_id;
    private int _id;

    public A()
    {
        _id = s_id++;
        Console.WriteLine("Allocated instance " + _id);
    }

    ~A()
    {
        Console.WriteLine("Finalized instance " + _id);
    }
}
```

When executing this code, results will likely vary from computer to computer and from run to run because of the parameters the garbage collector takes into account (such as the system's overall memory pressure). However, you should see objects being allocated for a long while until the very first collection kicks in and removes orphaned instances:

```
Allocated instance 8338
Allocated instance 8339
Allocated instance 8340
Allocated instance 8341
Finalized instance 8331
Allocated instance 8342
Allocated instance 8343
Finalized instance 6
Finalized instance 7
```

The order in which those objects get finalized is totally nondeterministic. You could also monitor collection count to see when a gen0 collection happens:

```
int gen0 = 0;
while (true)
{
    A a = new A();
    var new0 = GC.CollectionCount(0);
    if (gen0 != new0)
    {
        Console.WriteLine("Gen0 collection triggered");
        gen0 = new0;
    }
}
```

How Finalizers Are Implemented

To justify our naming of finalizers over destructors, take a look in ILDASM at the generated code, as shown in Figure 12.6. As you can see, C# destructors get turned into methods that override the Finalize method, which is defined on System.Object. The user's custom logic and a call to the base class's finalizer live inside this method. Although we still have to learn about inheritance, the idea is simple. When a class derives from another one to specialize its behavior, it's essential for the base class's cleanup logic to run as part of finalization. The code in our finalizer will be equivalent to the following:

```
~A()
{
    try {
        Console.WriteLine("Finalized instance " + _id);
    }
    finally {
        base.Finalize();  // Calls System.Object's Finalize method.
    }
}
```

Even though destructors turn into Finalize methods, C# disallows direct use of this method (for example, using the override keyword). Visual Basic, on the other hand, doesn't add destructor syntax and lets users override the Finalize method.

NOT FOR STRUCTS

Finalizers can only be defined on classes. The bookkeeping to determine when a struct's finalizer has to run would seriously hamper their lightweight nature.

FIGURE 12.6   Destructors override the `Finalize` method.

Disposal Before Collection: `IDisposable`

Finalizers are typically implemented to ensure resources that are beyond the garbage collector's domain of responsibility get cleaned up properly. A good example is when you must deal with unmanaged resources (for example, in Win32 interop scenarios requiring manual release of object using calls to `CloseHandle`). Although lots of Win32 APIs have been wrapped in the .NET Framework, you might sometimes need to P/Invoke some other APIs manually. As an example, consider the `CreateJobObject` Win32 function, which allows for the creation of jobs, which are groups of processes. A managed code wrapper could look like this:

```
public class Job
{
    [DllImport("kernel32.dll", CharSet = CharSet.Unicode, SetLastError = true)]
    static extern IntPtr CreateJobObject(SECURITY_ATTRIBUTES att, string name);

    [DllImport("kernel32.dll", SetLastError = true)]
    static extern bool AssignProcessToJobObject(IntPtr job, IntPtr process);

    [DllImport("kernel32.dll", SetLastError = true)]
    static extern bool TerminateJobObject(IntPtr job, uint exitCode);

    private IntPtr _handle;

    private Job(IntPtr handle)
    {
        _handle = handle;
    }

    public static Job CreateOrOpen(string name)
    {   // Notice a "null" name is allowed by the Win32 function.
        var res = CreateJobObject(null, name);
```

```
        if (res == IntPtr.Zero)
            throw new Win32Exception(); // Will use the last Win32 error.
        return new Job(res);
    }

    public void AddProcess(Process process)
    {   // Omitted required null-check!
        if (!AssignProcessToJobObject(_handle, process.Handle))
            throw new Win32Exception(); // Will use the last Win32 error.
    }

    public void Terminate(uint exitCode)
    {
        if (!TerminateJobObject(_handle, exitCode))
            throw new Win32Exception(); // Will use the last Win32 error.
    }
}
```

Don't worry too much about the P/Invoke signatures, which are a subject on their own.
Adam Nathan's great book on interop (*.NET and COM: The Complete Interoperability Guide*,
Sams Publishing) is the ultimate resource if you want to become an interoperability wizard
on .NET. Here are some essential facts:

▸ The return value of various functions often determines success or failures in the
  world of Win32. Here, checks for NULL and Boolean false are carried out.

▸ Win32 errors are often communicated through a last error slot, which can be
  accessed through GetLastError. The Win32Exception method will capture this code
  automatically, as long as we set SetLastError to true.

▸ Marshaling of strings requires proper configuration depending on the target API.
  Here we marshal the string using Unicode.

▸ More essential to our discussion is the storage of the IntPtr handle in a field on the
  Job wrapper object.

For completeness, here's the security attributes wrapper used by the CreateJobObject
method. Use of the StructLayout attribute makes sure the receiving end (Win32) will see
the fields in the intended order. If this attribute is omitted, the CLR is free to pick the best
layout for the fields to reduce memory occupation and/or word alignment:

```
[StructLayout(LayoutKind.Sequential)]
internal class SECURITY_ATTRIBUTES
{
    public int nLength;
    public IntPtr lpSecurityDescriptor;
    public int bInheritHandle;
}
```

Using this type is shown in the following code. It creates five instances of Notepad, puts them in the same Win32 job object, and then terminates all of them in one go upon user request. Jobs have more capabilities beyond process termination. The interested reader could regard this as a great P/Invoke exercise to port other job object functions (see MSDN) to our wrapper class:

```
var job = Job.CreateOrOpen("Demo");


for (int i = 0; i < 5; i++)
{
    using (var proc = Process.Start("notepad.exe"))
        job.AddProcess(proc);
}

Console.WriteLine("Press ENTER to terminate job...");
Console.ReadLine();

job.Terminate(0);
```

Unfortunately, our wrapper code is flawed in one fundamental way: We're leaking the handle returned by CreateJobObject. This isn't cool, and even though the operating system will close the handles automatically upon the owning process's termination, it forms a potentially critical leak when lots of Job wrappers are created. In fact, notice how we wrapped the creation of a new Process object in a using block as well:

```
using (var proc = Process.Start("notepad.exe"))
    job.AddProcess(proc);
```

Recall that the using block is merely syntactical convenience for the following equivalent code (ignoring the introduction of a surrounding scope to limit use of the proc variable):

```
Process proc;
try
{
    proc = Process.Start("notepad.exe");
    job.AddProcess(proc);
}
finally
{
    if (proc != null)
        proc.Dispose();
}
```

Enter the IDisposable interface, which we're going to bring to our Job object next. The call to Dispose realizes a form of *deterministic cleanup*, such that the resource kept by the wrapper class (in this example, Process) can be released on the spot. Notice closing a handle for a Win32 process object doesn't terminate that process; it merely releases the "reference" we hold to that process.

Providing a way to do deterministic cleanup is preferred over the use of finalizers. Or better, as you will see, it's used in conjunction with finalizers. But let's not skip ahead and ameliorate our Job object with an IDisposable implementation:

```
public class Job : IDisposable
{
    ...
    [DllImport("kernel32.dll", SetLastError = true)]
    static extern bool CloseHandle(IntPtr obj);

    private IntPtr _handle;

    ...

    public void Dispose()
    {
        CloseHandle(_handle);
    }
}
```

This is a good first attempt, which will allow the user to wrap the Job object in a using block for the kept handle to be disposed:

```
using (var job = Job.CreateOrOpen("Demo"))
{
    for (int i = 0; i < 5; i++)
        using (var proc = Process.Start("notepad.exe"))
            job.AddProcess(proc);

    Console.WriteLine("Press ENTER to terminate job...");
    Console.ReadLine();

    job.Terminate(0);
}
```

However, there are a couple of issues left. First, what happens if the user doesn't take the using block route and calls Dispose manually? At first sight, there's no issue with that, but the disposed object can still be used after the Dispose call. Now we have an already closed _handle field, but the instance methods can still use it:

```
...
job.Dispose();
job.Terminate(0);
```

In this code fragment, the call to `Terminate` will fail because the handle is no longer valid, which will be surfaced as a `Win32Exception` with a proper message. To prevent such mishaps, you'll want to keep some disposal flag around and reject method calls other than `Dispose` after disposal:

```
public class Job : IDisposable
{
    ...
    private bool _disposed;

    public void AddProcess(Process process)
    {
        if (_disposed)
            throw new ObjectDisposedException("job");
        ...
    }

    ...

    public void Dispose()
    {
        if (!_disposed)
        {
            CloseHandle(_handle);
            _disposed = true;
        }
    }
}
```

REPEATED DISPOSAL SHOULD BE ALLOWED

It's a good practice to allow multiple `Dispose` calls because there may be multiple code paths that double, triple, and so on release an object. Every `Dispose` call beyond the first one should be a no-op. Such a `Dispose` method is said to be "idempotent."

Although this is already better, we're still in trouble. No matter how much you believe in the goodwill of mankind, there will be developers who forget to dispose the `Job` object. In such a case, you still don't want to leak the acquired handle if the object is no longer reachable by code. To accommodate for this eventuality, you want to put a finalized in place, too. The pattern to be used here looks like this:

```
public void Dispose()
{
    Dispose(true);
    GC.SuppressFinalize(this);
}

protected virtual void Dispose(bool disposing)
{
    if (!_disposed)
    {
        if (disposing)
        {
            // We were called by the Dispose method.
            // Release managed resources (like other IDisposables) here.
        }
        // Also null out reference type fields here.
        CloseHandle(_handle);
        _disposed = true;
    }

    // If there were a base class that's IDisposable, call that one too.
    // base.Dispose(disposing);
}

~Job()
{
    Dispose(false);
}
```

That's quite a bit of code but a recurring pattern. In the user calls Dispose manually, we call the Dispose helper method with a true flag, such that the code in there can do some additional work to release other managed resources (such as Component objects, which do have a Dispose method themselves). No matter what case we're in, we'll also release the unmanaged resource (which is the only resource in our case). If the finalizer gets invoked, we'll get into that same helper method, but passing another flag to reduce work since other managed resources will be taken care of.

A few other things should be noted. First, the act of making the Dispose helper method protected and virtual will allow a subclass to call the base class's corresponding Dispose helper method to perform further cleanup. Alternatively, we could prevent users from deriving from our class by marking it sealed, as discussed in Chapter 14.

Finally, and not without significant importance, notice how the Dispose method adds a call to the SuppressFinalize static method on the GC class. This basically tells the GC not to bother calling our finalizer because the user has already triggered deterministic cleanup and the finalizer doesn't have any work left to do anymore. By doing so, you avoid the extra object death ceremony involving the finalizer queue:

```
public void Dispose()
{
    Dispose(true);
    GC.SuppressFinalize(this);
}
```

With all of this in place, we should never leak the job object handle anymore. To verify this claim, you can use Task Manager and observe the Handles column decrementing by 1 after the call to Dispose. Figure 12.7 shows this experiment. If the Dispose method isn't called, it will take some garbage collector cycles before the object disappears.

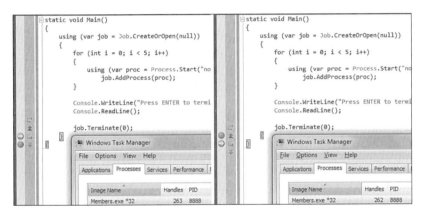

FIGURE 12.7   Proper handle release triggered by a call to Dispose.

SAFEHANDLE

Dealing with handles and providing a manual implementation of IDisposable and a finalizer is tricky business. To simplify this task, .NET 2.0 introduced the concept of SafeHandle objects, which are recommended to be used when dealing with some typical types of handles (see MSDN). The Microsoft.Win32.SafeHandles namespace contains base classes for a series of handle types.

Summary

Initialization logic for newly created object instances or even types themselves is what constructors are about. In this chapter, you learned how to declare constructors that deal with such initialization of state. You saw how to chain constructor calls and learned about implications of having type initialization logic in static constructors.

Finalizers (sometimes referred to as destructors) deal with cleanup logic that's executed upon destruction of an object. Although not necessary for pure managed code, the use of finalizers is important when native resources need to be released because they are beyond the control of the garbage collector. To enable the user to clean up an object prior to its automatic destruction by the garbage collector, the IDisposable interface can be implemented.

In Chapter 13, you look at a last set of members that can be declared on a type. In particular, you explore the concept of operator overloading and user-defined conversions between objects of different types.

Operator Overloading and Conversions

IN THIS CHAPTER

▶ Operators 603

▶ Conversions 627

One set of members declared on a type is left to be discussed: operator overloads and user-defined conversions. All of those types of members are defined as a special kind of static methods that can be invoked through various built-in language constructs.

Operator overloading comes in handy when defining types that have natural meanings for operations such as addition, logical operators, and whatnot. A good example is a Vector type. User-defined conversions are typically related to objects that represent some kind of value. In such a case, it might make sense to define conversions between different types of values—that is, from an angle in degrees to one in radians.

Operators

We're almost at the end of our journey through the world of class and struct members. Possibly the most powerful member type (but not quite as powerful as the same notion in languages such as C++) are operator overloads. Basically, operator overloads are special static methods that can be invoked as a result of using operator syntax such as +, && (a very special one consisting of two operator invocations, as you will see), ==, and so on.

Using this feature, it becomes possible to provide more natural-looking and convenient syntax for various operators a type can support on its instances. Vectors are a great example of this:

```
Vector v1 = new Vector(1, 2, 3);
Vector v2 = new Vector(3, 2, 1);
Vector allFour = v1 + v2;   // (4, 4, 4)
Vector larger  = v1 * 4;    // (4, 8, 12)
int dotProduct = v1 * v2;   // 10
```

POWERFUL TOOLS ARE WEAPONS, TOO

A powerful tool's main drawback is its potential to be used as a weapon. Overloading of operators is one of those tools. Although physicists will drool at the sight of operator overloading, it might not be obvious to people reading your code what's meant by the nonstandard use of an operator. Even the simple `Vector` sample shown in this section can be interpreted ambiguously: Does * mean dot product or cross product (recall that you can't overload by return type)?

Defining Operators

The definition of an operator looks like a public static method that uses the `operator` keyword to indicate its specialized nature. Unary operators should take exactly one single parameter, whereas binary ones should take two. None of the parameters can be passed by reference or as an output parameter. The return type does have restrictions for certain operators, too.

As an example, consider the `Vector` class again. This time we'll define a set of useful operators:

```
class Vector
{
    private int _x, _y, _z;
    ...

    // Whitespace is allowed between "operator" and "-".
    public static Vector operator -(Vector vector)
    {
        return new Vector(-vector._x, -vector._y, -vector._z);
    }

    public static Vector operator +(Vector left, Vector right)
    {
        return new Vector(
            left._x + right._x, left._y + right._y, left._z + right._z);
    }
```

```
    // We choose the dot product to show a different return type.
    public static int operator *(Vector left, Vector right)
    {
        return left._x * right._x + left._y * right._y + left._z * right._z;
    }


    // For a scalar product, just one of the operands has to be a Vector.
    public static Vector operator *(Vector vector, int scale)
    {
        return new Vector(
            vector._x * scale, vector._y * scale, vector._z * scale);
    }
}
```

Notice that with the unary arithmetic negation operator and the binary arithmetic addition operator it's not yet possible to do binary arithmetic subtraction unless you write the following:

```
Vector difference = v1 + -v2;
```

To enable proper subtraction as a single-step operation, you'll want to define such an operator, too.

How Operators Are Found

For an operator to be valid, at least one of its parameters should be the same as the declaring type (or, for structs, the nullable variant of it). This requirement is related to the way operators are searched for by the compiler, scanning static methods defined on operand types that participate in the operator's signature. Note that none of the operators have certain fixed properties such as "commutativity" (for example, where a + b and b + a always yield the same result). As a result, our overload of multiplication of a Vector with an integer value works only one way:

```
Vector okay = v1 * 4;
Vector fail = 4 * v1;
```

Because the compiler can't find a binary arithmetic addition operator accepting the two specified operand types on either System.Int32 or Vector, it bails out. To enable the second use, you must define a second operator that accepts the operands in the order that's desired. Obviously, the operator's implementation can invoke another's:

```
public static Vector operator *(int scale, Vector vector)
{
    return vector * scale;
}
```

The act of locating the best possible candidate operator follows principles similar to method overload resolution. In particular, operators defined on more-derived types will be better candidates than ones defined on less-derived types. This is illustrated here with the (limitedly useful) unary plus operator:

```
class Bar
{
    public static Bar operator +(Bar b)
    {
        return b;
    }
}

class Foo : Bar
{
    public static Foo operator +(Foo f)
    {
        return f;
    }
}
```

The first line of the following example will call Bar's operator, while the second line is turned into a call to Foo's operator. As you can see, the operator on the most derived type wins in that case. Hovering over the + token in Visual Studio will, in fact, reveal which operator is picked:

```
Bar b = +new Bar();
Foo f = +new Foo();
```

Nullability and Lifted Operators

 Introduced in .NET 2.0, nullability allows for the use of struct values in conjunction with a null value. As a short recap, the ? suffix can be appended to a value type name to create the nullable variant of it. This enables you to write code like this:

```
int? a = 42;
if (a != null)  // Really a.HasValue
    Console.WriteLine("Value = " + a /* .Value */);

int? b = null;
if (b == null)
    Console.WriteLine("Null");
```

As with most changes that touch the type system of the runtime (and hence languages taking advantage of its features), nullability had quite an impact on the language. In the context of operators, the concept of lifted operators was introduced. The idea is this: Instead of requiring predefined and user-defined operators to operate both on value type parameters as well as their nullable forms, it suffices to define such operators for the plain value types only. By means of the concept of lifting, operators like these become readily available on the nullable forms.

For example, the binary arithmetic addition operator can operate on two int operands but is available on nullable int operands, as well, through lifting. If any of the operands are null values, the result will be null, too. If both are non-null, their contained values are unwrapped, added together, and wrapped back into a nullable int:

```
int? a = 3, b = 5, c = null;


// Will print 8. The type of a + b is by itself an int?.
Console.WriteLine(a + b);

// All of those will simply print an empty line since the results are null.
Console.WriteLine(a + c);
Console.WriteLine(c + b);
Console.WriteLine(c + c);
```

Lifted operators include unary operators +, -, ~, !, ++, and --; binary operators +, -, *, /, %, <<, >>, &, ¦, and ^; as well as relational and equality operators <, <=, >, >=, ==, and !=.

Most of the unary and binary lifted operators return null if (one of their) operands is null, with the exception of ¦ and &, which follow three-valued logic principles. (For example, use of ¦ on true and null will produce null.)

The relational operators return false if any of the operands is null. Equality operators consider null to be equal to null. This is aligned with the behavior for reference types where two null references are equal.

Because of the lifted operator feature, the following struct's user-defined operators can be used on the struct's nullable form, as well:

```
struct Vector
{
    private int _x, _y;

    public Vector(int x, int y)
    {
        _x = x; _y = y;
    }

    public static Vector operator +(Vector left, Vector right)
    {
        return new Vector(left._x + right._x, left._y + right._y);
```

```
    }

    public override string ToString()
    {
        return string.Format("(X = {0}, Y = {1})", _x, _y);
    }
}
```

If `Vector` were to be defined as a class, the + operator obviously will simply accept null references. However, because the parameters on the + operator overload are not declared to be nullable, there's no way for those to receive null values. Instead, the language lifts the use of the + operator on nullable arguments:

```
Vector? v1 = new Vector(3, 4);
Vector? v2 = new Vector(2, 1);
Vector? v3 = null;

// Will print (5, 5). The type of v1 + v2 is by itself an Vector?.
Console.WriteLine(v1 + v2);

// All of those will simply print an empty line since the results are null.
Console.WriteLine(v1 + v3);
Console.WriteLine(v3 + v2);
Console.WriteLine(v3 + v3);
```

It's also possible for just one operand to be nullable. In that case, the non-nullable one will be converted to a nullable one, prior to invoking the operator.

To illustrate how the lifted + operator is implemented in terms of the nonlifted custom one, consider the following code:

```
static Vector? Add(Vector? v1, Vector? v2)
{
    return v1 + v2;
}
```

This code gets turned into the following equivalent piece of code. In reality, there are some slight differences, which are irrelevant to our discussion.

```
static Vector? Add(Vector? v1, Vector? v2)
{
    if (v1.HasValue && v2.HasValue)
        return v1.Value + v2.Value;   // Call our operator definition.
    return null;
}
```

Instead of relying on the lifted operator behavior, it's also possible to take control over dealing with null values. To do so, define an operator overload that operates on the value type's nullable form. An example is shown here, where we consider a vector that's null to be the same as a zero-length vector:

```
public static Vector? operator +(Vector? left, Vector? right)
{
    if (left == null & right == null)
        return null;

    if (left == null)
        return right;
    if (right == null)
        return left;

    return left.Value + right.Value;
}
```

Make sure not to write "left + right" on the last line because you would be calling the operator itself over and over again, ultimately causing stack overflow. Our example now produces different results:

```
Vector? v1 = new Vector(3, 4);
Vector? v2 = new Vector(2, 1);
Vector? v3 = null;

// Will print (5, 5). The type of v1 + v2 is by itself an Vector?.
Console.WriteLine(v1 + v2);

// Print (3, 4) and (2, 1).
Console.WriteLine(v1 + v3);
Console.WriteLine(v3 + v2);

// Prints an empty line since the result is null.
Console.WriteLine(v3 + v3);
```

The right design decision will vary from case to case. First, it's important to make sure the use of a struct is appropriate, as discussed before. If that's the case, figure out whether null is a value that needs special treatment. If so, take control by defining specialized operators.

Which Operators Can Be Overloaded?

Lots of operators support being overloaded by the developer of classes and structs. Although I could show examples of all of them, I'll limit myself to illustrating a couple of special ones. We also discuss in this section how certain expressions that use operators are turned into uses of custom operators.

A Mandatory Listing

An exhaustive list of all the operators that can be overloaded is shown here. All but a few should look pretty straightforward. The others are the subject of further discussion in the following sections.

- ▶ Unary operators: +, -, ~, !, ++, --, true, false
- ▶ Binary operators: +, -, *, /, %, <<, >>, |, ^, <, <=, >, >=, ==, !=

Some operators are implemented in terms of the others. Examples include &&, ||, and the ternary conditional operator.

Increment and Decrement, Pre and Post

The first two operators we take a look at are ++ and --. Because we all know from our discussion of expressions in Chapter 5, those operators can appear in two positions, as shown here. The result of running this code is that all variables will have a final value of 1.

```
int i = 0;

// j will be assigned i's value prior to incrementing it, hence it will be 0.
// After this post-increment, i's value will be equal to 1.
int j = i++;

// j will be pre-incremented before its updated value is used, and becomes 1.
// k gets this updated value of j, resulting in a value of 1.
int k = ++j;
```

When defining our own ++ (or --) operator, we can't control the behavior depending on the position in which the operator appears. For both uses, our operator's code will be called. All that's different is when this call happens. Another restriction on ++ and -- operators is that their return type should be the same as the defining type's or a subclass thereof.

As an example, let's define a cursor class with a ++ operator on it. The definition of the class is trivial, containing one position field and an overload for ToString used for pretty printing. What's of more interest to us is the operator's definition:

```
public static Cursor operator ++(Cursor c)
{
    // The definition of Cursor is left as an exercise. A simple implementation
    // could just encapsulate an integer value. More advanced examples of a
    // cursor include a "caret" rendered in some custom textbox control, where
    // increment means moving the "caret" to the right.

    // Just return a new cursor that has advanced one position.
    // Contrast to C++'s overloading for this operator, one isn't asked to
    // change the incoming Cursor's position in place.
    return new Cursor(c._pos + 1);
}
```

With this in place, let's analyze how the operator gets invoked for the pre-increment and the post-increment uses of it. There should be no big surprises about this, and the output of the following code should be predictable:

```
var c = new Cursor(42);
Console.WriteLine("Before: " + c);
Console.WriteLine("During: " + c++);
Console.WriteLine("After:  " + c);

var d = new Cursor(42);
Console.WriteLine("Before: " + d);
Console.WriteLine("During: " + ++d);
Console.WriteLine("After:  " + d);
```

Got your solution ready? Here are the results. The first use, the post-increment one, will print 42 twice and 43 once. That is, the increment operator call for c happens after c's value has been used to compute the string concatenation that's put on the screen. For the second pre-increment example, the outcome is 42 once and 43 twice.

Compound Assignment

The use of compound assignment (for example, +=) also supports user-defined operators. With a few simplifications around conversions and cases where complex expressions are used (requiring constituent expressions of the left side to be evaluated only once), the form a += b is turned into a = a + b. For the binary + operator, user-defined operators and lifted operators can be taken into consideration.

Reusing our vector example, the following fragment will use our operator definition:

```
Vector v1 = new Vector(3, 4);
Vector v2 = new Vector(2, 1);

// Turns into v1 = v1 + v2;
v1 += v2;

Console.WriteLine(v1);
```

Compound assignment can be used with all the overloadable binary operators that were listed before.

Short-Circuiting Logical Operators and the Conditional Operator

Looking at the list of overloadable unary operators, two weird-looking operators catch the eye immediately. Aren't true and false just Boolean *literals* rather than *operators*? Obviously, the answer is no. The true and false unary operators play an important role in defining both of the short-circuiting && and || operators. It also helps out for the definition of the conditional operator.

To understand this, let's recap the behavior of those operators. What makes them so special? The short answer is that not all the expressions that are used as operands on the operator have to be evaluated in certain cases. Here is a code fragment that proves this point by means of side effects:

```
static bool PromptBool(string s)
{
    Console.Write(s);
    return bool.Parse(Console.ReadLine());
}

static int Get(string s)
{
    Console.WriteLine(s);
    return 42;
}

static void Main()
{
    bool and     = PromptBool("l: ") &  PromptBool("r: ");
    Console.WriteLine("&  -> " + and);

    bool andAlso = PromptBool("l: ") && PromptBool("r: ");
    Console.WriteLine("&& -> " + andAlso);

    bool or      = PromptBool("l: ") ¦  PromptBool("r: ");
    Console.WriteLine("¦  -> " + or);

    bool orElse  = PromptBool("l: ") ¦¦ PromptBool("r: ");
    Console.WriteLine("¦¦ -> " + orElse);

    int res = PromptBool("condition: ") ? Get("true") : Get("false");
    Console.WriteLine("?: -> " + res);
}
```

By entering true or false at the prompts, you can easily illustrate the fact that some of the operators short-circuit evaluation as soon as the result can be determined.

For example, while the evaluation for and will always ask for a left and right operand value, the evaluation for andAlso won't. If the left operand value is false, there's no way the Boolean AND operation can still produce true. Because of this, the prompt for a right operand will never be displayed. A similar behavior exists for the Boolean OR operator's short-circuiting ¦¦ variant: When the left operand evaluates to true, there's no point in evaluating the right operand anymore.

This is where the true and false operators come in. To define the short-circuiting && and ¦¦ operators in terms of the & and ¦ operators, the language specification says the following:

```
x && y   is evaluated as   T.false(x) ? x : T.&(x, y)
x ¦¦ y   is evaluated as   T.true(x)  ? x : T.¦(x, y)
```

Because this is quite terse syntax, some further elaboration is most welcome. First, T here stands for the type defining the binary operator that got picked by resolution rules. In the syntax used for the language specification, calling an operator defined on a type simply looks like a static method invocation.

To evaluate a short-circuiting version of a binary logical operator, the first question the resulting code has to ask is whether the outcome of the operation can be determined by just looking at the first operand. This is precisely what true and false unary operators do. They ask this question: Hey, are you semantically equivalent to true (or false)? If that is not the case, the underlying binary operator is called.

SYNTAX VERSUS SEMANTICS

The C# specification (like most other languages) quite intensively uses the English language to describe the semantics of various constructs. Although this works relatively well in practice, you must memorize lots of remarks to fully grasp some of the evaluation rules that are applied.

For example, in the excerpt for the definition of && and ¦¦ in terms of &, ¦, true, and false shown earlier, there's a bit of imprecision because this literal transformation has different behavior than what's intended. Extra English-written clauses document that the expression for x will get evaluated only once and that this result will be reused for every appearance of x in the conditional operator.

In more-formal language specifications (of which I only know academic language examples), the semantics would shine through the (more mathematically dense) notation.

For example, with regard to overloading the binary logical & operator and enabling it for use in a short-circuited form, consider the following FilterBool struct. Such a type can come in handy for scenarios of scientific computing or bridging between C# code and some evaluation engine (like a database performing filter operations using Boolean logic):

```
struct FilterBool
{
    public static FilterBool operator &(FilterBool left, FilterBool right) {
        // Carry out the evaluation.
    }
```

```
public static bool operator true(FilterBool value) {
    return value.Evaluate();
}

public static bool operator false(FilterBool value) {
    return !value.Evaluate();
}

...
}
```

Here, we've omitted the Evaluate method and some additional state that's likely to be kept by a FilterBool value. Such state may be a string that's sent to an evaluation engine (such as a symbolic mathematics package), an expression tree data structure, or whatnot. Either way, the Evaluate method gets called by both the unary true and false operators (which need to be defined in pairs) to tell the caller whether the FilterBool value is semantically equivalent to true or false. This enables short-circuiting. Both those unary operators need to return a regular System.Boolean. The binary operator itself will only work for short-circuiting if the return type corresponds to the operand types. From the user's point of view, consider the following code:

```
FilterBool a = ...;
FilterBool b = ...;
FilterBool and = a & b;
FilterBool andAlso = a && b;
```

For the evaluation of and, our & operator will simply be called, without any use of the true and false operators whatsoever. However, in evaluating andAlso, we first see a call to the false operator, passing in a. If that one returns true (acknowledging that a is semantically equivalent to false), b never gets evaluated. In the other case of the false operator returning false (denying that a is false), the & operator will get called to make the final call on the result of the logical AND.

Yeah, I know, that's a whole lot of juggling with true and false in sentences. To see how those operators really work, it's best to step through the evaluation of && or ¦¦ using the debugger.

DID YOU KNOW... THERE ARE NON-SHORT-CIRCUITING LOGICAL OPERATORS?

Some people using C#-like languages have forgotten (or never knew) about the existence of the & and ¦ non-short-circuiting operators. Even more so, some people believe those are just there for bitwise operations. Most likely, excessive use of the short-circuiting operators in documentation and examples is the reason for this. Admittedly, the virtues of those operators justify their use in most cases.

However, when defining your own type with Boolean logic binary operators on it, people might be surprised when your type isn't enabled for short-circuiting operator use. From your perspective, this means no `true` and `false` operators were defined. There are two ways to put people at ease. The best, of course, is if you can provide a meaningful implementation for the `true` and `false` operators, triggering some kind of evaluation on the spot. However, even if that's not the case, you could play a little trick and enable the short-circuiting syntax nonetheless. Just implement both the `true` and `false` unary operators to return `false`. If you look back at the language specification for the short-circuiting operators, you'll see that this will cause the underlying & or ¦ operator to be called in any case, due to the way the conditional operator works:

```
our special   x && y   is evaluated as   false ? x : T.&(x, y)
our special   x ¦¦ y   is evaluated as   false ? x : T.¦(x, y)
```

Yes, you're overloading the semantics of the short-circuiting operators to be non-short-circuiting in any case, but it may be justifiable for user convenience.

Finally, using the conditional "ternary" operator with a non-Boolean condition operand also leverages the unary true operator (unless an implicit conversion, discussed at the end of this chapter, can turn the condition operand type into a Boolean). For example, the following piece of code will be allowed using our `FilterBool` type:

```
FilterBool condition = ...
int result = condition ? 42 : 31;
```

The result of this fragment's compilation will be as follows (using pseudo-syntax), invoking the unary `true` operator to have a Boolean value for the condition:

```
FilterBool condition = ...
int result = FilterBool.true(condition) ? 42 : 31;
```

Pairwise Declaration for Relational and Equality Operators

When specifying user-defined relational or equality operators, the language enforces proper pairwise declaration such that essential (Boolean logic) manipulations can be applied on any applicable expression. Therefore, it's not possible to overload the == operator without having a != operator in place, too. Similarly, < and > operators need to be declared in pairs and so do <= and >=. Figure 13.1 shows the compilation errors resulting from omitting a paired operator where needed. Notice that the return type of those operators can differ from Boolean.

Implementing Equality Operations

One of the most commonly overloaded operators is == (and its != sister operator). To ensure expected behavior for those operators, a few guidelines exist. In particular, we have to explain the relationship between the operators and the `System.Object Equals` methods that are available.

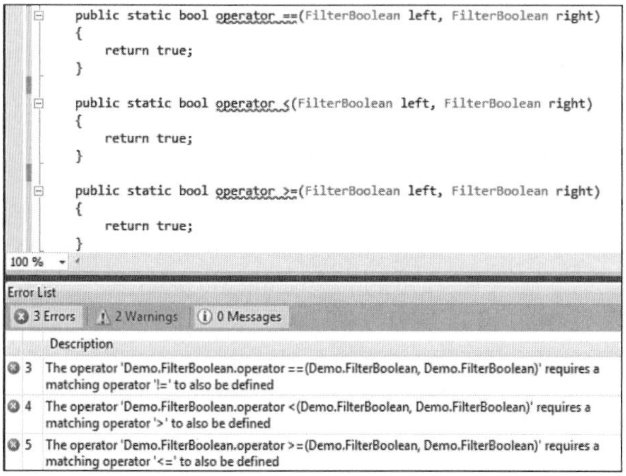

FIGURE 13.1   Pairwise operator declaration enforcement.

The Role of `System.Object`'s Instance Equals Method

Defined on `System.Object`, the "mother type of all types", the `Equals` instance method is used to compare whether two objects are "equal," whatever that means for the types of the target object and the one being compared.

```
class Object
{
    ...
    public virtual bool Equals(object obj) { /* default implementation */ }
}
```

As you learn in Chapter 14, "Object-Oriented Programming," virtual methods can be overridden by deriving types. It's typical for types to do so for `System.Object`'s virtual methods, which include `Equals`, `GetHashCode`, and `ToString`. Before we get into overriding the `Equals` method, let's discuss its default behavior.

For reference types, the default `Equals` method implementation performs a reference equality, checking whether both references refer to the same object. For value types, a bitwise equality is carried out, checking whether both values carry the same data. This is illustrated in Figure 13.2, where public fields are used to keep things simple.

WHAT ABOUT BOXING?

Because reference types get compared by reference equality and boxed value types are a form of reference types, you might wonder about the outcome of the following code (with `Point` declared as a struct):

```
var p1 = new Point { X = 3, Y = 5 };
var p2 = new Point { X = 3, Y = 5 };
Console.WriteLine(p1.Equals(p2));
```

```
object o1 = p1;
object o2 = p2;
Console.WriteLine(o1.Equals(o2));
```

The first result, comparing p1 and p2, which consist of the same bit sequence for their representation, should be a straightforward `true`. Based on the previous discussion, you might think the second result, comparing the boxed values, will print `false` because clearly the two boxes will be at different locations on the heap, such that o1 and o2 will hold different references.

Luckily, the `Equals` method for a `System.ValueType` (which is the base type for all structs, especially important for boxing) has been overridden to do the right thing, namely comparison of the boxed values in a bitwise manner. So the output of the second equality check is `true`, too.

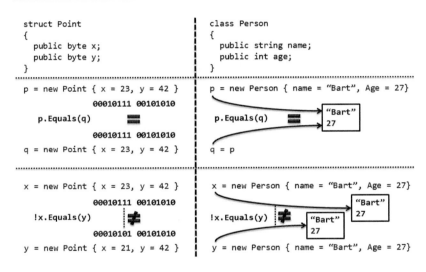

FIGURE 13.2   Default implementation of `Object.Equals`.

Overriding the Equals Method

In some cases, it might make sense to override the default equality behavior for either a value type or a reference type. The most common scenario is to customize this for a class, to do a (partial) field-by-field equality check. An example is to treat two `Person` objects as equal if they have an equal identifier, which is considered to be unique for each living person our application cares about:

```
class Person
{
    public int Id { get; set; }
    public string Name { get; set; }
    public int Age { get; set; }
```

```
    public override bool Equals(object obj)
    {
        // Implementation goes here.
    }
}
```

For this chapter, don't worry about the override modifier on the Equals method, which is explained thoroughly in Chapter 14. It simply indicates we're specializing the base class's Equals method.

So what's the right way to implement the Equals method? Because Equals is weakly typed, taking in another System.Object instance, we might be comparing objects that have different types (for example, comparing apples to lemons). To take care of this case, we need to include an *exact type check* first. Use of is or as would also pass if we're comparing a Person object with a subtype thereof (see Chapter 14, "Object-Oriented Programming"). Also, the input object could be null in either case. Clearly, comparing an instance (being ourselves, one that the Equals method is being called) to the null reference has to return false, too. Putting all those pieces together, we end up with the following implementation that will only allow two Person objects to be compared. In other scenarios, it might be possible to compare objects of two different types, resulting in more type checks:

```
public override bool Equals(object obj)
{
    if (obj == null ¦¦ obj.GetType() != this.GetType())
        return false;
    var other = (Person)obj;
    return this.Id == other.Id;
}
```

For this implementation, we only compare both Person object's Id properties because that's what we consider to be unique about a person. Obviously, more properties could be subject to comparison in other scenarios.

Notice how we used the == operator for the Id properties, assuming it does the right thing for that property's type. (It does because it's an int.) When carrying out field-by-field equality checks, it's good to use == or the static Object.Equals method (which we look at next). One particular reason that's the case is that use of the instance Equals method would need more care:

```
public override bool Equals(object obj)
{
    ...
    // Assume each Person has a unique Name, and that's what we compare.
    return this.Name.Equals(other.Name);
}
```

What would happen if this.Name is somehow set to null? When using the == operator or the static Object.Equals method, you don't run into that problem because those take in both objects to be compared and should do the right thing in the face of null references.

Required Properties for the Equals Instance Method

Each implementation of an Equals method override is assumed to exhibit a set of fixed properties on which all users can rely. Those properties include the following:

▶ Commutativity, such that x.Equals(y) is the same as y.Equals(x).

▶ Transititivity, such that x.Equals(y) and y.Equals(z), if and only if x.Equals(z).

▶ Reflexivity, such that x.Equals(x) always holds (except for cases where floating-point arithmetic is involved, offering a bit more relaxation).

▶ Successive x.Equals(y) calls return the same result if x and y aren't modified.

▶ Don't throw exceptions for an Equals method.

▶ No instance is equal to null; that is, x.Equals(null) returns false if x is not null.

When to Override the Equals Method

Overriding the Equals method is recommended for reference types that do have some property that warrants different instances (hence resulting in different instances) to be treated as equal. Our Person example does precisely this based on some unique identifier property each instance of the type carries.

For value types, the default implementation often suffices, but overriding it manually can cause considerable speed-ups. If the performance of value type comparison tends to be a bottleneck in your application, providing a manual override would be a good thing to check out.

As you see later, recommendations for overloading the == operator differ slightly from the advice to override the Equals method. In particular, doing so for structs is wholeheartedly recommended, whereas it should be less common for classes.

The Importance of GetHashCode Consistency with Equals

If we just override the Equals method without also overriding the GetHashCode virtual method that's defined on System.Object, the compiler will emit a warning, as shown in Figure 13.3.

The GetHashCode method is essential for certain collection types (such as Hashtable) that create element lookup structures based on each object's hash code. When searching for an element in the collection, the search scope first gets narrowed by finding the "bucket" to which the object belongs. This is based on the hash code. After that bucket is found, and if it contains more than one element, the Equals method is used to figure out whether the object is present in the collection.

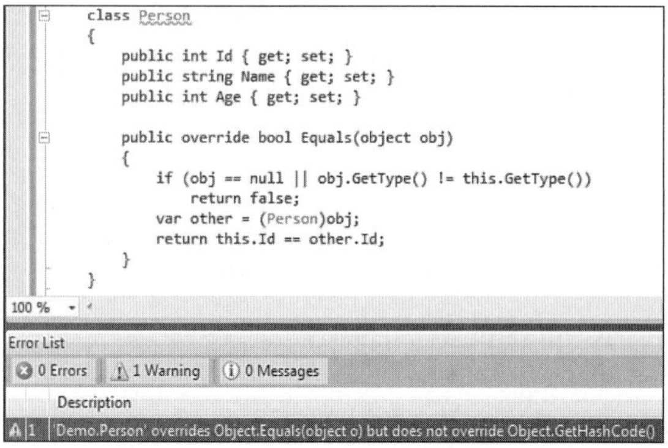

FIGURE 13.3   You should pair overrides for `Equals` with overrides for `GetHashCode`.

If two objects are said to be equal according to the result of `Equals`, they should also return the same hash code. Conversely, if two objects have the same hash code, they do not necessarily need to be equal. The reason why the latter isn't a requirement is quite fundamental. Notice that the return type of `GetHashCode` is an `int`:

```
class Object
{
    ...
    public virtual int GetHashCode() { /* default implementation */ }
}
```

If the hash code for every distinct instance of a certain type had to be unique, that type could never support more than 2 power 32 instances, which is determined by the range of a 32-bit integer. Also, ensuring unique numbering for all instances would likely involve complicated bookkeeping and state maintenance for the type implementer. Instead, a good hash code exhibits the property that the likelihood for the hash code computed for two different instances of a type is different, too. The better a hash code is, the better collection types containing objects of that type will perform.

Implementing `GetHashCode` is usually not that hard. You simply want to return an integral value based on the object's fields that contribute to its equality. In our example for a `Person` type, the only field that participates in the equality check is `Id`, and therefore our implementation could look like this:

```
public override int GetHashCode(object obj)
{
    return this.Id.GetHashCode();
}
```

Typically, you want to delegate to each (non-null) field's `GetHashCode` to provide the constituent parts of your own object's hash code. If multiple fields are involved, use of the bitwise XOR operator is extremely handy to put hash codes together:

```
public override int GetHashCode(object obj)
{
    // Assume each Person has a unique Id and Name.
    // The Equals method should use those fields for equality checking.
    return this.Id.GetHashCode()
        ^ (this.Name != null ? this.Name.GetHashCode() : 0);
}
```

The implementation of `GetHashCode` should not return an exception and should keep returning the same value for an object as long as it doesn't change. There's no need to ensure that hash codes for equal objects stay the same across different executions of the program; as long as equal objects have the same hash code during one run of the code, that's fine. As a result, a hash code should not be used for persistence purposes. Finally, computing a hash code should take little time.

To wrap up our discussion about hash codes, Figure 13.4 illustrates the inner workings of a hashtable-based collection type while evaluating a Contains inquiry for an element. In this example, both Bart and John share the same hash code. When looking for Bart, the first very efficient lookup operation is to find the bucket corresponding with his hash code. When the bucket is found, a linear search is needed to check whether any of the objects in the bucket equals the input. This illustrates that the more distributed the hash codes are, the better the lookup will perform (because buckets will contain fewer elements).

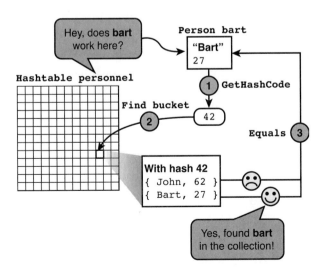

FIGURE 13.4   How a Hashtable collection uses `GetHashCode` and `Equals` methods.

IEQUALITYCOMPARER<T>

Starting from .NET 2.0, a generic interface has been introduced to provide a new means to perform equality checks and hash code retrieval. This interface, called IEqualityComparer<T>, is discussed in Chapter 16, "Collection Types."

For implementing the interface, all the remarks for overriding System.Object's Equals and GetHashCode methods hold for the corresponding methods that live on the interface. An abstract base class called EqualityComparer<T> can be used to implement the interface in a robust manner. A related IEquatable<T> interface was added to the mix as a means to perform equality checks in a strongly typed manner. Instead of taking in a weakly typed object to the Equals method, it takes in an instance of the generic type parameter T, hence comparing objects of compatible types. Refer to MSDN for more background information about this particular interface and when to use it.

The Static Equals and ReferenceEquals Methods on System.Object

Besides an instance-level Equals virtual method, System.Object also defines two static equality check methods. One is called Equals and provides a means to compare any two objects. It basically performs a couple of null checks before dispatching into the first object's instance Equals method:

```
class Object
{
    ...
    public static bool Equals(object objA, object objB)
    {
        return objA == objB
            || objA != null && objB != null && objA.Equals(objB);
    }
}
```

First, it checks whether both objects are the same based on a reference equality check carried out by the IL code generated for the == operator applied between two objects. This particular use of the == operator on System.Object operands will always result in a reference equality check, which is also what the ReferenceEquals static method does:

```
class Object
{
    ...
    public static bool ReferenceEquals(object objA, object objB)
    {
        return objA == objB;
    }
}
```

If objA and objB are not the same reference, Equals makes a second attempt dispatch to the virtual Equals method on the first parameter, if none of the parameters are null.

(If both are null, the == operator will have returned already.) The most specialized `Equals` method override will now take responsibility in determining the equality.

OPERATORS ARE NOT DISPATCHED

It's important to realize this `Equals` method is as weakly typed as it can be. Because operators are static methods that are resolved at compile time, the == operator has to be found on the either of the operand types, in this case `System.Object`. No special == operator overload is defined on `System.Object` though; instead, a simple IL instruction is used to implement this equality check.

Because operators are static methods, there's no virtual dispatch happening based on the dynamic types of the operands at runtime. Suppose `Object.Equals` were called with two `Person` objects; the == operator in the preceding code would still use the `System.Object` default == behavior, even if `Person` has a more specialized == operator defined. In short, operators are resolved entirely at compile time (well, if we ignore C# 4.0's dynamic typing feature). We discuss virtual dispatch in Chapter 14.

It's important to emphasize that `Equals` method implementations should obey the law of commutativity with respect to both parameters. If this isn't the case, executing the static `Equals` method with the arguments swapped will produce different results. Because of this, you should never implement equality between one of your types and a type whose implementation you don't control. For example, consider a `Person` type that returns true when applying `Equals` between a `Person` instance and a string corresponding to the name of the person:

```
bool returnsTrue = new Person { Name = "Bart" }.Equals("Bart");
```

Although this particular direction of comparison can work perfectly, there's no way for you to ensure commutativity will be realized. For the following piece of code to work, the `Equals` method on `System.String` would have to know about your type:

```
bool returnsFalse = "Bart".Equals(new Person { Name = "Bart" });
```

Because `Object.Equals` calls the virtual `Equals` instance methods of the first argument, the broken commutativity will surface there, too:

```
bool returnsTrue  = Object.Equals(new Person { Name = "Bart" }, "Bart");
bool returnsFalse = Object.Equals("Bart", new Person { Name = "Bart" });
```

So performing type checks inside an `Equals` override is fine as long as you control the implementation of the `Equals` operator on all the types involved. All of them should know which types of objects can be compared for equality.

It's better to avoid such contrived equality checks because there's a good risk of missing out on a particular case, causing hard-to-debug problems. For instance, if a collection type once compares two elements a and b using a.`Equals(b)` and another time (because of another element traversal order) using b.Equals(a), things will likely go terribly wrong. And typically with such problems, the issue will crop up only after the code has run a long time.

Overloading the == Operator

Finally, after some mandatory detours through the world of System.Object's methods, we've arrived at our final goal of overloading the == operator. Doing so is encouraged if the type carries value semantics, meaning two instances are really the same. A good example is a complex number type, which may be implemented as a class or a struct. If no value semantics are present, it's best to omit a == operator definition in favor of just an Equals override (if needed).

One first thing to realize is that no default == operator is present for types, in contrast to the availability of a default Equals implementation. For example, the following won't work:

```
struct Point { public int X; public int Y; }
...
var p = new Point { X = 1, Y = 2 };
var q = p;

Console.WriteLine(p == q);   // Fails since no == operator is found.
```

For classes, things are a bit different because the use of a == operator will be allowed, as shown here. However, there's no default *type-specific* implementation for == as there is for Equals. Instead, == applied to any two reference typed objects will return the result of a reference-equality check:

```
class Person { public string Name; public int Age; }
...
var p = new Person { Name = "Bart", Age = 27 };
var q = p;

Console.WriteLine(p == q);   // Returns true due to reference equality.
```

Following the guidelines, we won't overload == for our Person class because you can barely claim a person to be a value. In that case, just overriding Equals suffices. For value types, though, if you override Equals, you *must* also implement an == operator:

```
struct Point
{
    private readonly int _x, _y;

    public Point(int x, int y)
    {
        _x = x; _y = y;
    }
```

```
public override bool Equals(object obj)
{
    if (obj == null || obj.GetType() != this.GetType())
        return false;

    var other = (Point)obj;
    return this == other;
}

public override int GetHashCode()
{
    return _x.GetHashCode() ^ _y.GetHashCode();
}

public static bool operator ==(Point p1, Point p2)
{
    return p1._x == p2._x && p1._y == p2._y;
}

public static bool operator !=(Point p1, Point p2)
{
    return !(p1 == p2);
}
}
```

Notice how we avoided any redundancy in equality checking code by calling into our operator overload from the Equals method. Also, the mandatory paired != operator uses the == implementation to determine its result.

Make sure to test all uses to catch any possible cyclic reference that causes some infinite recursion. It's any easy trap to fall into. For the preceding code, the next series of tests do a decent job at checking some properties:

```
var p1 = new Point(1, 2);
var p2 = new Point(2, 3);
var p3 = new Point(1, 2);
var s = "Other";

// False
Console.WriteLine(p1.Equals(p2));        Console.WriteLine(p2.Equals(p1));
Console.WriteLine(p1 == p2);             Console.WriteLine(p2 == p1);
Console.WriteLine(p1.Equals(s));         Console.WriteLine(s.Equals(p1));
Console.WriteLine(p1.Equals(null));   // Console.WriteLine(null.Equals(p1));

// Shouldn't compile as there's no == operator between Point and string
//Console.WriteLine(p1 == s);            Console.WriteLine(s == p1);
```

```
// True
Console.WriteLine(p1.Equals(p3));       Console.WriteLine(p3.Equals(p1));
Console.WriteLine(p1 == p3);            Console.WriteLine(p3 == p1);
```

Based on our discussion about both of Object's Equals methods and the discussion about == operator overloading, none of the results shown earlier should come as a surprise.

STRING INTERNING AND EQUALITY

Strings are interesting objects for a number of reasons. They're immutable, are implemented as reference types, but have value semantics. Adding all of those properties together, we have something rather exotic. Matters get even fancier since the runtime knows a great deal about string objects. One thing it does is so-called interning, allowing strings with the same contents to be reused, which is possible thanks to immutability. The following code shows some of this behavior:

```
var s1 = "Hello";
var s2 = "Hel"; s2 += "lo";   // Runtime concatenation to avoid compiler smarts
var s3 = string.Intern(s2);   // Memory used for s1 will be found to equal s2
Console.WriteLine(s1 == s2);        // Value equality on string contents -> true
Console.WriteLine(s1 == s3);        // Same deal
Console.WriteLine(s1.Equals(s2));   // Value equality again
Console.WriteLine(s1.Equals(s3));   // Same deal
Console.WriteLine(Object.ReferenceEquals(s1, s2));   // Not the same!
Console.WriteLine(Object.ReferenceEquals(s1, s3));   // But those are...
```

The second-to-last call returns false because s1 and s2 are different references; however, using interning s3 will have the same reference as s1.

How Operators Are Translated

To conclude our discussion about user-defined operators, we take a quick peek at the way their definition gets implemented. As revealed by the static modifier, operators are associated with the type on which they're defined, rather than with an instance. This has some advantages in terms of compile-time resolution of operators but also limits their expressiveness in terms of runtime dynamism. It's also not possible to create interfaces that require an implementing type to support certain operators, which is precisely what the mythical INumeric interface would be about ("can Add, Multiply, and so on"). This is a bit of an unfortunate implication of the design of operators.

Operators' operational nature makes their most natural implementation to be regular (static) methods. No metadata is associated with them to declare their "operatorness." Instead, a simple naming convention was introduced such that languages that support user-defined operators can search for them. In particular, each operator has an English noun (such as Equality for ==). An op_ prefix indicates the method is an operator. Some languages that don't support direct use of operators in terms of syntax can still make operators available as regular method calls. Language documentation on MSDN provides those names for all supported operators, in case you're interested.

Figure 13.5 shows the methods available on our Vector type, reflecting the various operators we've defined.

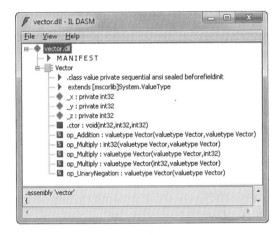

FIGURE 13.5   Implementation of operators in terms of methods with an op_ prefix.

Conversions

The final member type discussed in this chapter is the conversion operator. *Conversions* enable an object of one type to be turned into an object of another type, either in an implicit manner (where simple assignment suffices) or an explicit manner (where explicit "cast" syntax must be used).

Built-In Conversions

Both the CLR and C# support a number of built-in conversions that can be used with primitive types and some special types like enumerations and delegates. To start our discussion about conversions, and the user-defined ones more specifically, let's get in the right mindset by looking at some of the built-in ones first.

Numeric Conversions

A large number of numeric conversions exist. Some of those conversions don't require cast syntax to be used and are called *implicit*. This means that wherever a number of a specific type is expected, you can supply one of a type that's implicitly convertible into the expected type. Support for implicit conversions on numbers typically corresponds with those conversions that will not lose precision (a few floating-point cases set aside) through the conversion. An example is assignment of a 32-bit integer to a 64-bit long:

```
int i = 123;
long l = i;   // Can hold the int.
```

Some other languages, such as Visual Basic, also introduce the related notion of widening versus narrowing conversion. Widening conversions go from a type with a smaller range to one with a larger range (but including the first's range entirely). The preceding example of int to long falls under this category because every int can be held by a long, too. Such widening conversions can be done implicitly, whereas the narrowing ones (that may lose information or fail at runtime) must usually be carried out explicitly.

Back to the world of C#, one of the explicit conversion examples is exactly the opposite of the one shown earlier. Instead of going from an int to a long, we could try exactly the other way around. In that case, the compiler won't allow you to do this implicitly because the conversion may lose information. Not every 64-bit long fits in a 32-bit int:

```
long l = 123;
int i = (int)l;  // Dear compiler: believe me, I know what I'm doing!
```

Recall from our coverage of expressions that the checked keyword can be used to turn on overflow checking as part of an expression's evaluation. This can be used for such explicit conversions, too, triggering an OverflowException if the conversion fails. The following will actually do so:

```
long l = 2L << 32;  // Notice the use of L to calculate 2^32 as a long
int i = checked((int)l);  // This will throw an OverflowException.
```

Enumeration Conversions

As you learned in Chapter 11, "Fields, Properties, and Indexers," enumerations are nothing but numeric value types in disguise. The underlying type is what determines all of an enum's values' representation. Only one implicit conversion exists, from the literal 0 to a value of the enum's type. This allows default-value initialization of enum values. It's assumed that the zero value of an enum provides a meaningful default. Often, it is named None for precisely that reason:

```
ConsoleColor color = 0;  // Will be the same as ConsoleColor.Black.
FileShare share = 0;  // Will be the same as FileShare.None.
FileMode mode = 0;  // Meaningless, since there's no 0 value in the enum.
```

Explicit conversions requiring a cast exist between the enum type and its underlying type (but in fact also to other numeric types), in both directions:

```
ConsoleColor red = (ConsoleColor)12;
int twelve = (int)red;
```

Nullable Conversions

Intended to be a natural extension to the use of regular value types, their nullable forms support a series of conversions that are much expected. For example, you can always go from an underlying type to its nullable form in an implicit manner. Furthermore, all the implicit numeric conversions apply to nullable forms, too:

```
int i = 42;
int? ni = i;    // int  -> int?
long? nl1 = i;  // int  -> long?
long? nl2 = ni; // int? -> long?
```

When converting between values of different nullable types, a null-value represented by a HasValue property retuning false will simply result in a null value of the target type. If the value isn't null, the underlying value will be converted and wrapped in a value of the target type.

On the explicit conversion side, nullables support the lifted form of the underlying type's explicit conversions. In addition, you can also go from a nullable value to its non-nullable type. In such a case, an exception will be thrown if the original value is the null value:

```
long? l = 123;
int? i = (int?)l;
int? n = null;
int j = (int)n;  // Will throw an InvalidOperationException
```

Reference Conversions

For reference types, a wide range of conversions exist, most of which require a further discussion about object-oriented programming principles, which are covered in Chapter 14. For completeness, we simply mention the supported conversions here and illustrate them with a couple of examples.

Implicit conversions exist between an object of a certain reference type and any of its base types or interfaces it implements. As a result, every object of a reference type can be converted to an object of type System.Object:

```
List<int> xs = new List<int> { 1, 2, 3 };
IList<int> list = xs; // Every List<T> implements IList<T>.
IEnumerable<int> sequence = list;  // Every IList<T> is an IEnumerable<T>.

Student s = new Student("Bart", 27, Grade.Third);
Person p = s;  // Every Student is a Person.

string s = "Hello";
object o = s;  // Every string is an object.
```

Arrays support covariant conversion, which is discussed as part of our coverage of generics in Chapter 15, "Generic Types and Methods," which simply means you can assign an array of a more derived type to one of a less derived type. For example, an array of strings can be assigned to an array of objects:

```
string[] names = new[] { "Bart", "John" };
object[] objects = names;  // Because every string is an object...
```

BROKEN ARRAY COVARIANCE

As you learn in Chapter 15, covariance for arrays poses an issue concerning type safety, which is mitigated by runtime type checks. The history of this broken form of variance lies in the CLI's intent to support a whole range of programming languages, including some that have broken variance in their type system. As you'll see, with generics, things are much better nowadays.

One more implicit conversion that's often used when dealing with reference types is the use of the null literal, which can be converted into any reference type. In fact, the null literal doesn't have a type of its own; instead, it's flexible in that it lends itself to be used with any reference type (or nullable value type):

```
string s = null;
```

Furthermore, there are a few implicit reference type conversions to special base types that are provided by the runtime. Every delegate can be assigned to System.Delegate and every array to a System.Array. You might recall that every enumeration value can also be assigned to a System.Enum, which is in fact not a reference conversion because the original type isn't a reference type to begin with. This causes what's known as a boxing conversion, which is discussed in the next section.

For the explicit conversions supported on reference types, you can always attempt to cast upward, from a less-derived type to any of its deriving types. For example, because an object *may be* a string, attempting such a conversion is permitted. However, because there's no guarantee it works, an InvalidCastException can result if the given object turns out to be something other than a string. If an explicit conversion can be proven not to work, ever, the compiler won't permit it to be written:

```
object o = "Hello";
string s = (string)o;  // An object could be a string.

Person p = new Student("Bart", 27, Grade.Third);
Student s = p;  // A Person could be a Student.

object q = new Person("John", 62);
string t = (string)q;  // Throws an InvalidCastException.

Animal a = new Giraffe();
Person x = a;  // Will fail to compile: an Animal is never a Person.
```

Similar explicit conversions are permitted using interfaces: An IEnumerable<int> could be List<int>, but it could well be of another collection type. So the conversion may fail at runtime.

THE IS AND AS KEYWORDS

Type checks using the is and as keywords can be used to mitigate runtime exceptions that result from attempts to cast objects. Whereas is returns a Boolean as the result of comparing an object with a type (roughly indicating whether it will be possible to assign the object to a variable of that type), as will attempt the conversion and return null if it's invalid. Therefore, as cannot be used if a null reference is permitted for the operand object because disambiguation of a failed conversion and a null reference cannot be achieved.

Boxing and Unboxing Conversions

As you learned before, assignment of a value type to a reference type invokes a runtime-level mechanism called *boxing*. The opposite direction invokes the reverse operation known as *unboxing*. Those operations are directly associated with the CLR's memory layout, going between stack and heap allocation. Although flexible and allowing for a unified view on types, boxing puts additional stress on the garbage collector. With the advent of generics, boxing largely can be avoided.

The following code fragment shows an implicit boxing conversion and an explicit one that performs unboxing thereafter:

```
int i = 42;
object o = i;  // Boxing is happening here
int j = (int)o;  // Unboxing is happening here.
```

Other implicit boxing conversions include going from an enum to System.Enum, going from a value type to System.ValueType, and going from a value type to an interface it implements. Support for dealing with nullable types exist, too.

The explicit unboxing conversions pretty much go the opposite way as the ones that were described previously for implicit boxing.

User-Defined Conversions

Now that you have a sense of various supported built-in conversions, you can learn how you can define both implicit and explicit conversions on user-defined types. Although conversions can be handy, it's recommended to keep a few design best practices in mind. The most important one involves implicit conversions, which should never lose any information, nor should they ever throw an exception as part of their operation. The reason for those recommendations is straightforward: Because an implicit conversion can be injected silently by the compiler, it might not be obvious at all what's going on with the code.

Implicit conversions are considered by the compiler when an expected type (for example, for the target of an assignment to a field or a parameter) does not match the type of the object that's available. In such a case, the compiler will start a hunt for an applicable implicit conversion and pick the best match subject to a set of rules. A compilation error is raised if no such operator can be found (or more than one is equally well applicable).

To illustrate user-defined conversion operators, we start by defining an explicit one that operates on a Point type. Points can have multiple representations depending on the coordinate system that's picked. For illustration purposes, we'll consider points in two dimensions, which can be represented using Cartesian (x, y) coordinates but also using polar coordinates. Figure 13.6 shows those coordinate systems for a given point, including conversions back and forth.

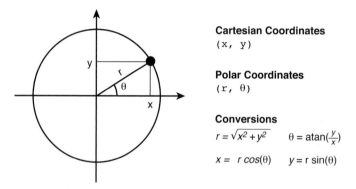

Cartesian Coordinates
(x, y)

Polar Coordinates
(r, θ)

Conversions

$$r = \sqrt{x^2 + y^2} \qquad \theta = \text{atan}\left(\frac{y}{x}\right)$$

$$x = r\,cos(\theta) \qquad y = r\,sin(\theta)$$

FIGURE 13.6   A point represented in Cartesian and polar coordinates.

For each coordinate system, we'll define a representation using a struct type that will simply contain two fields for the coordinates. We'll pick double for the representation of those coordinates and consider the angle theta to be represented in radians. To allow users to make use of the point values in APIs that support either of the two coordinate systems, we'll define an explicit conversion between the two.

The reason we're going with an explicit conversion is rather obvious. Because the conversion involves possible loss of precision, due to the use of floating-point numbers, we should not go for an implicit conversion. Going back and forth between coordinate systems might not result in exactly the same original point due to rounding errors. The following code implements both structs and the conversions:

```
struct CartesianPoint
{
    private readonly double _x, _y;

    public CartesianPoint(double x, double y)
    {
```

```
        _x = x; _y = y;
    }

    // Add get-only properties and ToString overload.

    public static explicit operator PolarPoint(CartesianPoint p)
    {
        // Math.Atan could be used below as well, feeding in p._y / p._x. This
        // will still work fine, even if _x is zero, due to the use of floating
        // point PositiveInfinity or NegativeInfinity for the division-by-zero.
        return new PolarPoint(
            Math.Sqrt(p._x * p._x + p._y * p._y),
            Math.Atan2(p._y, p._x)
        );
    }
}

struct PolarPoint
{
    private readonly double _radius, _theta;

    public PolarPoint(double radius, double theta)
    {
        _radius = radius; _theta = theta;
    }

    // Add get-only properties and ToString overload.

    public static explicit operator CartesianPoint(PolarPoint p)
    {
        return new CartesianPoint(
            p._radius * Math.Cos(p._theta),
            p._radius * Math.Sin(p._theta)
        );
    }
}
```

Notice how we use the same operator keyword as we did for user-defined operators, with the sole difference being the presence of the explicit (or implicit, as you will see further) keyword to denote we're defining a conversion. Conversion operators are unary operators that either take in or return an object of the containing type. The order of the keywords and the return type is also determined strictly: first "explicit operator," then the return type, and then the single-parameter list.

With this code in place, we can write the following user code, invoking the explicit operator by means of cast syntax. This code assumes we have a decent `ToString` defined on the two types such that we can inspect the result easily.

```
var pt = new CartesianPoint(1, 1);
Console.WriteLine(pt);
Console.WriteLine((PolarPoint)pt);
Console.WriteLine((CartesianPoint)(PolarPoint)pt);
```

Try substituting the Cartesian coordinates on the first line with some other values to see the round-tripping behavior of the first line. For quite a few values, you'll see the original value being printed to the screen again. However, because of rounding errors, you might see slight differences from time to time (for example, for a Cartesian point with (0, 1) as its coordinates):

```
(0, 1)
(1, 1.5707963267949)
(6.12303176911189E-17, 1)
```

This is nothing but floating-point imprecision, where the X-coordinate of the result really is a zero value, hidden by some incredibly small noise. However, it illustrates nicely why we shouldn't have used an implicit conversion here. Figure 13.7 shows a user-defined conversion to be nothing but a special op_Explicit (or op_Implicit) method.

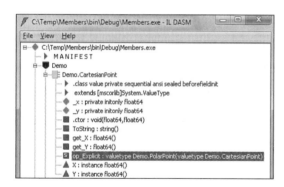

FIGURE 13.7   An explicit conversion gets implemented as an `op_Explicit` method.

Use of implicit conversions is less generally applicable and is restricted to some more specialized scenarios. One is where a type acts as a wrapper around a value of another type (for example, a `FilterBoolean` that has some special semantics implemented behind custom-defined operator s), but whose representation can always be turned into a regular CLR Boolean (or maybe a nullable form thereof). The opposite direction for the conversion is often also applicable:

```
struct FilterBoolean
{
    private readonly bool _value;

    public FilterBoolean(bool value)
    {
        _value = value;
    }

    // Other members from previous examples could go here.

    public static implicit operator bool(FilterBoolean b)
    {
        return b._value;
    }

    public static implicit operator FilterBoolean(bool b)
    {
        return new FilterBoolean(b);
    }
}
```

With the preceding definition, it becomes incredibly easy for users to supply one of those FilterBoolean values where a regular Boolean is expected and vice versa. For example:

```
static void Main()
{
    PrintIfTrue(new FilterBoolean(true), "Hello");
}

static void PrintIfTrue(bool value, string s)
{
    if (value)
        Console.WriteLine(s);
}
```

Implicit conversions are considered only if a better overload match isn't found. That is, if a PrintIfTrue overload would exist taking in a FilterBoolean, that one would be taken over the one requiring an implicit conversion for the first argument value.

Also, multiple user-defined implicit conversions cannot be used on a single expression. The following example illustrates such a case:

```
struct FilterInteger
{
    // Field, constructor, etc. omitted
```

```
    public static implicit operator SpecialInteger(FilterInteger i)
    {
        return new SpecialInteger(i._value);
    }
}

struct SpecialInteger
{
    // Field, constructor, etc. omitted

    public static implicit operator int(SpecialInteger i)
    {
        return i._value;
    }
}
```

Given this, it's not possible to write the following, even though you could go from FilterInteger to SpecialInteger and then to a System.Int32, all implicitly. Only a single implicit conversion step with a user-defined conversion is allowed.

```
int i = new FilterInteger(42);
```

When built-in conversions are involved, you've got one more shot, so to speak. In this example, you could take a SpecialInteger and assign it to a long. This will first go to an Int32 using the user-defined conversion and be widened into a long afterward:

```
long l = new SpecialInteger(42);
```

Figure 13.8 shows the implicit conversion from SpecialInteger to Int32 taking place through the invocation of the op_Implicit method. Once we've arrived at the Int32, one more instruction takes care of the built-in conversion to a long (that is, conv.i8, where the 8 stands for the number of bytes making up the integer).

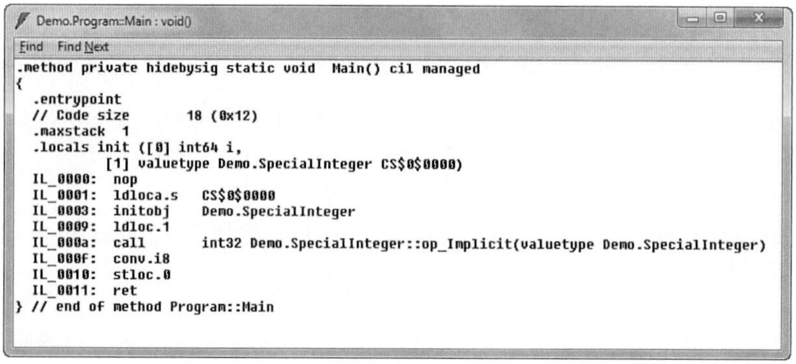

```
 Demo.Program::Main : void()

 Find   Find Next
.method private hidebysig static void  Main() cil managed
{
  .entrypoint
  // Code size       18 (0x12)
  .maxstack  1
  .locals init ([0] int64 i,
           [1] valuetype Demo.SpecialInteger CS$0$0000)
  IL_0000:  nop
  IL_0001:  ldloca.s   CS$0$0000
  IL_0003:  initobj    Demo.SpecialInteger
  IL_0009:  ldloc.1
  IL_000a:  call       int32 Demo.SpecialInteger::op_Implicit(valuetype Demo.SpecialInteger)
  IL_000f:  conv.i8
  IL_0010:  stloc.0
  IL_0011:  ret
} // end of method Program::Main
```

FIGURE 13.8   An implicit conversion followed by a conversion of an Int32 to an Int64.

To emphasize the danger of ill-behaved implicit conversion operators, consider the case where an exception would appear on a seemingly innocent assignment statement as the one shown in the last code fragment. It won't at all be obvious to people reading (or debugging) the code why this exception appears out of nowhere.

```
struct BadInteger
{
    public static implicit operator int(SpecialInteger i)
    {
        throw new Exception();
    }
}

...

var bad = new BadInteger();
int val = bad; // Throws here?!
```

When defined on value types, conversions also participate in null-value lifting, as you've seen for other operators, too. In our running example, a nullable FilterInteger or a non-nullable FilterInteger could be converted into a nullable Int32:

```
int? i = new SpecialInteger();
int? j = default(SpecialInteger?);
```

SYSTEM.NUMERICS

One of the best examples of valid uses of user-defined operators and conversions can be found in the .NET 4 System.Numerics namespace, containing types like BigInteger and Complex. Both of those types implement a bunch of conversions that allow primitive typed values to be turned into those special ones, thus reducing the friction that would exist to create new instances of those types. Implicit ones are used to take primitive types to BigInteger, and explicit ones are used to leave that world again (because not every BigInteger will fit in, for instance, an Int32):

```
BigInteger x = int.MaxValue;  // Implicit conversion from Int32.
BigInteger y = x + 1;  // BigInteger arithmetic.
BigInteger z = (int)y;  // Will throw an exception since it doesn't fit.
```

The Complex type also has a bunch of conversions, mostly implicit ones that can be used to turn a numeric value of a built-in type into a Complex number (which will use the input value for the real part). Explicit ones aren't provided to leave the world of a complex number. This would have little use because for every number with an imaginary part, the conversion would fail. Instead, users can access the real and imaginary parts using properties named as such.

Other Conversion Mechanisms

Conversion is such an important concept that history has yielded many shapes and forms of conversion mechanisms. We briefly touch on those here, but refer to MSDN documentation for a more thorough discussion.

System.Convert, Your One-Stop Conversion Shop

The first version of the .NET Framework introduced a (static) Convert class in the System namespace to help out people with all sorts of conversions involving primitive types supported by the runtime and the framework. Although some of the methods on the class do have a corresponding method elsewhere, the overall intent of Convert is to bundle all sorts of conversions together.

Most methods start with To, followed by a primitive type name, such as Int32, Char, Boolean, String, and so on. All of those methods have a whole series of overloads that accept 19 or so different parameter types. As a result, one gets a "full mesh" of from-to type pairs, the *from* part encoded in the parameter type and the *to* part encoded in the method name. For example, the ToInt32 method can be used in a variety of ways:

```
int five = Convert.ToInt32(5);  // Essentially a no-op.
int nine = Convert.ToInt32("9");  // Much like int.Parse.
int four = Convert.ToInt32((byte)4);  // Much like an implicit cast.
int zero = Convert.ToInt32(false);  // Cannot be achieved using a cast.
int oops = Convert.ToInt32(DateTime.Now);  // InvalidCastException.
```

The second of those example uses also accepts an additional format provider argument that allows to influence the behavior of the parse operation carried out on the string (for example, for globalization purposes).

Except for a few handy methods like FromBase64String, ToBase64String, and some of the numeric conversion method operators accepting a numeric base (as 2 for binary), I have seldom used the Convert class. Be prepared, though, to encounter code that uses this type excessively; some people really like it.

IConvertible

Closely related to the System.Convert class, the IConvertible interface provides all the To* conversion methods supported through System.Convert. When a type chooses to implement this interface, it readily becomes through System.Convert methods that take in a System.Object as the argument. For example:

```
var pt = new Point(3, 4);
var s = Convert.ToString(pt, null /* format provider */);
```

If Point were to decide to implement IConvertible, it could provide a ToString method that comes from the IConvertible interface, providing a meaningful conversion. However, other than the primitive types in the System namespace, little types do implement this interface. Unless your type supports a lot of conversions to the 16 primitive types that have conversion methods defined on IConvertible, and you really want to enable the use of the `Convert` class with your type, there's little incentive to bother providing an implementation.

TypeConverter

A generalization on top of type conversion is provided by the `TypeConvert` class that's defined in the `System.ComponentModel` namespace. Its goal is to provide a means for both designers and runtime libraries to deal with conversions. This is usually used in conjunction with UI frameworks like WPF, where the concept of a conversion is known to the XAML language. For example, to specify a `Point`, you can write `"3,4"` as a string, which is turned into a `Point` whose X- and Y-coordinates are 3 and 4, respectively.

The `TypeConverter` base type provides a set of virtual methods one can override. Those methods include `CanConvertFrom`, `CanConvertTo`, `ConvertFrom`, and `ConvertTo`, as well as a couple of other ones that are infrequently overridden. An example of a type converter for a `Point` type is shown here:

```
class PointConverter : TypeConverter
{
    public override bool CanConvertFrom(ITypeDescriptorContext context,
        Type sourceType)
    {
        if (sourceType == typeof(string))
            return true;
        return base.CanConvertFrom(context, sourceType);
    }

    public override bool CanConvertTo(ITypeDescriptorContext context,
        Type destinationType)
    {
        if (destinationType == typeof(string))
            return true;
        return base.CanConvertTo(context, destinationType);
    }

    public override object ConvertFrom(ITypeDescriptorContext context,
        System.Globalization.CultureInfo culture, object value)
    {
        if (value == null)
            throw base.GetConvertFromException(value);

        var s = value as string;
        if (s != null)
        {
            double x, y;
            string[] parts = s.Split(',');
```

```
            if (   parts.Length != 2 ¦¦ !double.TryParse(parts[0], out x)
                 ¦¦ !double.TryParse(parts[1], out y))
                throw base.GetConvertFromException(value);
            return new Point(x, y);
        }
        return base.ConvertFrom(context, culture, value);
    }
    public override object ConvertTo(ITypeDescriptorContext context,
        System.Globalization.CultureInfo culture, object value,
        Type destinationType)
    {
        if (value is Point && destinationType == typeof(string))
            return ((Point)value).ToString();

        return base.ConvertTo(context, culture, value, destinationType);
    }
}
```

To enable the type convertor for our `Point` type, we have to register it by using a custom attribute:

```
[TypeConverter(typeof(PointConverter))]
struct Point
{
    ...
}
```

By putting this attribute in place, (UI) designers will be able to find a converter that can be used to convert user input into a `Point` type and vice versa. An implementation like ours exists for the `Point` type defined in WPF's `System.Windows` namespace (as well as for the `Point` in `System.Drawing` used by Windows Forms). Figure 13.9 shows the use of another converter type that deals with brushes, allowing them to be specified using a string. A brush is an abstraction over a way to paint some surface, which can be a solid color, as shown here.

FIGURE 13.9   Specification of a Label's brush using a string that gets converted.

Summary

This chapter wrapped up the discussion of a type's set of members by looking at operator overloading and user-defined conversions. Care should be taken when deciding on the definition of any of those: It might not be immediately obvious what code means if primitive language operators get a totally different meaning due to excessive overloading. However, there are quite a few cases where overloading operators and providing conversions between types (typically values) is beneficial. Typical samples include mathematical constructs such as a Vector.

Extra care should be taken also when overloading equality operators. More information about this appears in Chapter 14, when you learn about virtual methods, such as `System.Object`'s `Equals` method.

Now that you've learned about all members supported on classes and structs, you're ready to explore the notion of object-oriented programming in the next chapter.

CHAPTER 14

Object-Oriented Programming

IN THIS CHAPTER

▶ The Cornerstones of Object Orientation 643

▶ Inheritance for Classes 657

▶ Protected Accessibility 669

▶ Polymorphism and Virtual Members 670

▶ Abstract Classes 683

▶ Interfaces 686

Because you've familiarized yourself with the various members that make up classes and structs, you're now ready to step up one more level and establish relationships between classes. This is one of the various aspects that object-oriented programming embodies.

Before delving into the language-specifics of object-orientation, you start by learning the three big pillars of this programming paradigm: encapsulation, inheritance, and polymorphism. After you've familiarized yourself with those concepts, you take a look at a series of language and runtime features that enable them, including virtual methods (and v-tables), keywords such as override, new, protected, and abstract. Finally, you examine different ways to establish contracts for a type's functionality in terms of abstract classes and interfaces.

The Cornerstones of Object Orientation

Object-oriented programming is largely built on three core pillars, which we discuss in just a minute. But first, why should you care? Or, better, what types of problems does object-oriented programming (OOP) aim to solve?

A Historical Perspective

As the art of programming has continually and increasingly tried to move away from bare-bones down-to-the-metal machine instruction sequences, more-structured programming approaches have entered the programmer's toolbox.

It should be clear that low-level manipulation of machine state in terms of registers, manual memory management, valid instruction ordering, and so on is not the most appealing way to program enterprise-level applications (or, in fact, anything beyond the lowest levels of kernel or driver primitives).

One of the first advances made in democratizing programming was the introduction of textual symbolic languages, moving away from raw byte sequences. Although assembler languages were an obvious first target, higher-level structured programming concepts had even more appeal. Instead of dealing with branch statements (à la goto), why can't we have statements and abstract away branching logic? Figure 14.1 illustrates an overlay of C code with its corresponding assembler, emphasizing some of the low-level maintenance tasks that are abstracted away.

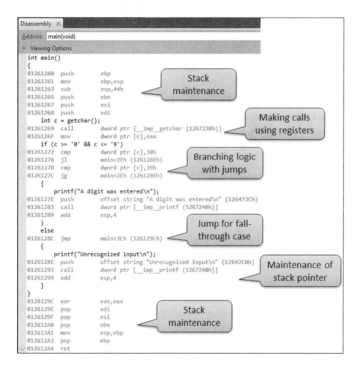

FIGURE 14.1   Control flow and stack maintenance abstractions in C.

Another common source of programmer pain was the fact that low-level languages were tied to a particular machine's architecture. You had to know a whole bunch of details of the instruction set, registers, and so on to write good code. Besides hindering portability of code to other machines, things were very error-prone. Also, the slightest change to the intended logic could cause a huge impact on the rest of the code. For example, adding a single parameter to a routine can require spilling registers into stack allocations. The need for procedural programming became obvious. This notion roughly corresponds to the C# and CLR notions of methods and method calls. Extra layers of indirection are put in place such that intermediate language (IL) code has instructions to deal with any number of arguments, regardless of the target machine architecture. The Just-in-Time (JIT) compiler will do the rest to make sure the code gets executed in an efficient manner, leveraging CPU registers wherever possible.

We've made quite a leap here, omitting intermediate stages of evolution, but concepts such as blocks, variables, scope, and so on all contributed to those first generations of languages. These concepts enabled structuring programs in terms of reusable routines, but one big thing was still lacking: how to manage state used by all those little routines. In particular, it's extremely useful to have a way to deal with state beyond a single invocation of a procedure. One of the features in C is the capability to declare a local variable as static, which will cause its contents to stay alive across invocations:

```c
void Inc() {
    static int i = 0;
    printf("%d\n", ++i);
}

int main() {
    Inc();  // Prints 1
    Inc();  // Prints 2
}
```

In this example, the C/C++ compiler has allocated a memory location for static variable i, away from the stack frame tied to a particular invocation of Bar. In other words, we've created some kind of global state that is visible only from inside Bar methods. What makes it global is the fact it isn't local (another shocker). Looking at it from a different angle, you could also say that Bar is no longer a "pure function" because it relies on state that's not coming in through any of its parameters.

Although the preceding sometimes comes in handy, it lacks the capability to share state across different functions, unless all such state is always threaded through the code by means of explicit parameter passing. For example, how would we define counter functionality with increment and decrement options? One solution is to introduce *really global* state:

```c
static int i = 0;

void Inc() {
    printf("%d\n", ++i);
}

void Dec() {
    printf("%d\n", —i);
}
```

Although this will work fine, we've just opened a big hole in our application because code other than Inc and Dec could manipulate the shared integer global variable.

And this has brought us pretty close to one of the pillars of object orientation, namely the capability to encapsulate state and operations in logical units, referred to as classes. In fact, the preceding code suffers from more issues than just the exposure of the global state variable. Because it's global (and static), there cannot be two or more counters that operate on their own counter values. This introduces the need for instances of those classes. In C++, one of the first truly mainstream industrial-strength object-oriented languages, we would write the following:

```cpp
class Counter {
    int id, i;
public:
    Counter();
    void Inc();
    void Dec();
};

Counter::Counter() {
    static int n = 0;
    id = n++;
    i = 0;
}

void Counter::Inc() {
    printf("%d -> %d\n", id, ++i);
}

void Counter::Dec() {
    printf("%d -> %d\n", id, -i);
}

void main() {
    Counter *c1 = new Counter();
    Counter *c2 = new Counter();
    c1->Inc();  // 1
    c2->Dec();          // -1
    c2->Inc();          // 0
    c1->Inc();  // 2
    c1->Dec();  // 1
    c2->Inc();          // 1
}
```

Ignore the separation between the class definition and the implementation of the class's members, which is one of the intricacies of C++ (typically used in conjunction with the concept of headers). What matters more is that each `Counter` has instance-level state for its identifier (a unique number for each counter, maintained by the constructor), as well as the current counter's value. This state no longer leaks outside the boundaries of the containing class instance, which realizes encapsulation. Also, the operations for the counter are no longer global functions but have turned into methods associated with the class.

Encapsulation

Even though the previous discussion has pretty much introduced this concept already, let's bring it over to the world of C# first. Encapsulation enables members (including fields for state, as well as all the other members discussed in Chapters 11, 12, and 13) to be associated with a type. In fact, C# doesn't allow global members that are defined outside a type (even though the CLR does). In this world, our counter looks like this:

```
class Counter {
    private int _id, _i;
    private static int s_n;

    public Counter() {
       _id = s_n++;
    }

    public void Increment() {
       Console.WriteLine("{0} -> {1}", _id, ++_i);
    }

    public void Decrement() {
       Console.WriteLine("{0} -> {1}", _id, −_i);
    }

    public int Count
    {
        get { return _i; }
    }
}
```

We already know from Chapter 10, "Methods," what keywords such as `static` and `public` mean. All we're emphasizing here is the fact that you put members in types, which will be restricted to classes (and interfaces) in this chapter. To use our counter type, we can construct instances by using the `new` keyword, which shouldn't be new either:

```
Counter c1 = new Counter();
Counter c2 = new Counter();
c1.Increment();  // 1
c2.Decrement();      // -1
c2.Increment();      // 0
```

```
c1.Increment();  // 2
c1.Decrement();  // 1
c2.Increment();        // 1
```

Of incredible importance to the technique of encapsulation is the capability to declare an accessibility level on members. This serves a couple of goals, one of which is to make sure no outsiders can touch state in a manner that's inconsistent with the consistency intended for (instances of) the type. In our case, it should never be possible for the counter to experience a lapse in values if no Inc or Dec commands were issued.

Even if the outside world is well intentioned with exposed writable state, other dangers are lurking. For example, private state may not be secure to be exposed. Also, exposing implementation details of a type hinders the type's owner in evolving the way the type works. This is the main reason to never expose fields directly but to instead provide get/set accessors through properties, as discussed in Chapter 11, "Fields, Properties, and Indexers."

Inheritance

The next pillar of OOP is inheritance. Now that we have nice encapsulation of functionality in a (class) type, what about reusing it for other types? There are two ways to do this. One is to wrap the use of one type in another one. For example, a customer tracking system may *use* a counter to keep track of the number of current visitors in an online store.

However, this containment mechanism is not very different from any other use of a counter elsewhere in the code. In fact, our customer-tracking system (implemented as another class) encapsulates a counter and may expose some of the counter's operations to the outside world. For example, our counter could have a Count get-only property that may simply be exposed on the customer-tracking system:

```
class Tracking
{
    private Counter _activeVisitors = new Counter();

    public User Logon(string user, string password)
    {
        // Authenticate and authorize. Throw on failure.
        _activeVisitors.Increment();
        // Code to return a User object.
    }

    public void Logoff(User user)
    {
        // Some plumbing...
        _activeVisitors.Decrement();
    }
```

```
    public int CurrentVisitorCount
    {
        get { return _activeVisitors.Count; }
    }
}
```

Another scenario for reuse of a counter is to create a *specialized* counter. Given the bare-bones functionality that our `Counter` class defines, we could create a new kind of counter that exposes more operations or specializes the existing operations. To do so, we want to create a *subclass* of `Counter` that shares the same contract to the outside world. This establishes three important properties:

▶ **Reuse:** Someone has already invested in creating a solid counter; why can't we leverage those operations if we want to create an advanced counter?

▶ **Extend:** In addition to reusing the existing operations on a counter, a subtype of a counter could add more operations, possibly using the existing ones.

▶ **Modification:** By overriding some of the counter base type's members, those could be tweaked to provide specialized behavior.

Let's take a look at all of those now. Starting from a slightly modified `Counter` class, we want to create specialized counter subtypes. One will guard against negative values, while another will count by increments and decrements larger than 1. Yet another one will extend the counter with a `Reset` operation.

Don't worry too much about a whole set of concepts and related keywords that are introduced here; they all get in-depth treatment later in the chapter. Just go with the flow to get some basic notions wired up in your brain. To make our class a bit more useful, we'll redefine it somewhat to get rid of a counter identifier and the printing behavior and to expose the `Count` value:

```
class Counter {
    public int Increment() {
        return ++Count;
    }

    public int Decrement() {
        return —Count;
    }

    public int Count { get; private set; }
}
```

Notice we're using an auto-implemented property to keep the counter value, with only public accessibility for the `get` operation. Such a property saves us from declaring a backing field and trivial `get` and `set` accessors, which is fine because we don't need the field to be declared as read-only (as explained in Chapter 11).

The first thing we have to do is permit our Counter for inheritance, basically allowing other classes to *derive* from it. This is enabled by default (that is, if no sealed keyword is used on the class definition):

```
/* I am not "sealed" */ class Counter
{
    ...
}
```

At this point, we can already extend the class by declaring a subclass. To do so, we just declare another class and specify Counter in its inheritance list, which appears after the colon token:

```
class ResettableCounter : Counter
{
}
```

Just doing this will allow us to use the ResettableCounter with exactly the same members as Counter exposed on it (with the exception of constructors, as you will see later). We say that the subtype has inherited the base type's members:

```
var counter = new ResettableCounter();
Console.WriteLine(counter.Increment());
```

Obviously, we want to add more to operations to this specialized counter; in particular we promised the user the capability to reset it to zero. One way to do this is by defining a Reset method that will count down until the counter reaches zero:

```
class ResettableCounter : Counter
{
    public void Reset()
    {
        if (Count < 0)
            while (Count < 0)
                Increment();
        if (Count > 0)
            while (Count > 0)
                Decrement();
    }
}
```

> **A NOTE ON THREAD SAFETY**
>
> In our discussion about the `Counter` class and its subtypes, we consider a type that doesn't make any promises of thread safety. If multiple users are dealing with the counter at the same time, from different threads, invariants may get broken. It's the user's responsibility to prevent simultaneous use of the counter.

To say the least, this code is an annoying and inefficient way to get back to zero. Nonetheless, it shows we've inherited the `Increment` and `Decrement` operations from the base class and can use those perfectly well from inside the derived class. To make things nicer, the base class could allow subclasses to access other base class members by declaring those as *protected*:

```
class Counter {

    ...

    public int Count { get; protected set; }
}
```

This means that the `Count` property is accessible to the code defined on the class itself (that is, just like private accessibility) but also to derived types. It isn't available to the others outside the inheritance hierarchy. As a result, our `ResettableCounter` can write the following:

```
class ResettableCounter : Counter
{
    public void Reset()
    {
        Count = 0;  // The setter is accessible to us, a derived class.
    }
}
```

You will agree this code is much easier on the eye and arguably more efficient.

So far, you've seen how to derive from a base class and extend it with additional members. This leaves us with the modification promise made earlier. How can we tweak the behavior of, say, `Decrement` to throw an exception if the counter is about to drop below zero? The answer is twofold. First, the base class needs to give the green light for such modification. It does so by marking a member overridable using the `virtual` keyword:

```
class Counter {
    public virtual int Increment() {
        return ++Count;
    }
```

```
    public virtual int Decrement() {
        return —Count;
    }

    public int Count { get; protected set; }
}
```

DIFFERENT LANGUAGES, DIFFERENT DEFAULTS

In a true fundamentalist object-oriented spirit, some languages declare members as virtual by default, requiring the user to block the capability to override it explicitly using keywords like final (or sealed in C# terms). Although this seems desirable, it causes nightmares in terms of maintainability of framework libraries because it isn't possible to disable overridability after it has been exposed as such. Doing so would break existing subclasses. For that very reason, the default in C# is to have nonvirtual members, requiring explicit use of the virtual keyword if desired.

Notice that C# has a hybrid set of defaults. For members, the default is sealed. For classes, the default is to allow inheritance (that is, nonsealed). Whether this inconsistency is a good thing can be debated. I tend to mark classes as sealed by default, whereas my boss defends the C# default.

With virtual members in place, subclasses can use the override keyword to specialize a member's behavior. Typically, you'll want to call the base class's functionality as part of the specialized implementation, which is done using the base keyword:

```
class NonNegativeCounter : Counter
{
    public override int Decrement()
    {
        if (Count == 0)
            throw new InvalidOperationException("Can't count below zero.");

        return base.Decrement();
    }
}
```

Another counter built by extending and modifying the base class's behavior through inheritance is shown here:

```
class StepCounter : Counter
{
    private int _step;

    public StepCounter(int step)
```

```
    {
        _step = step;
    }

    public override int Increment()
    {
        Count += _step;   // Remember the setter is protected!
        return Count;
    }

    public override int Decrement()
    {
        Count -= _step;   // Remember the setter is protected!
        return Count;
    }
}
```

Besides inheritance from classes, you can also "inherit from" an interface, which more commonly is referred to as *implementing* an interface. Interfaces provide a contract between two parties: an implementer and a consumer. They are related to *abstract* classes in that they don't provide a default implementation of their members. We'll look at this in more detail in the section "Abstract Classes," later in this chapter. It's the task of the deriving or implementing type to do so:

```
// Contract: "I can compare myself to somebody else of type T"
interface IComparable<T>
{
    int CompareTo(T other);
}
```

Our counter could implement this (generic) interface. You see how implementing an interface is handy for use through polymorphism in just a minute:

```
class Counter : IComparable<Counter> {

    ...

    public int CompareTo(Counter other)
    {
        // Negative if "this < other", positive if "this > other", zero if equal
        return this.Count - other.Count;
    }
}
```

Polymorphism

The final pillar of object-oriented programming is known as polymorphism, from the Greek word that stands for "many shapes." In fact, when talking about inheritance, we have already seen most of the polymorphic principles illustrated at the level of member declarations. More specifically, the virtual and override keywords are at the heart of the principle of polymorphism. What we haven't talked about yet is the different uses it allows. So far, we've used virtual and override to be able to specialize a class:

```
class NonNegativeCounter : Counter
{
    public override int Decrement()
    {
        if (Count == 0)
            throw new InvalidOperationException("Can't count below zero.");

        return base.Decrement();
    }
}
```

To use this counter, we could simply write the following:

```
NonNegativeCounter counter = new NonNegativeCounter();
counter.Increment();
counter.Decrement();
counter.Decrement();   // Will throw an exception.
```

However, in addition to this, the principle of polymorphism enables you to use all types of counters through their base class type. That is, where a Counter is expected, you can use an object of any type derived from Counter, as well:

```
Counter counter = new NonNegativeCounter();
counter.Increment();
counter.Decrement();
counter.Decrement();   // Will throw an exception.
```

Despite the static type of the variable counter to be different from NonNegativeCounter, we'll still see the specialized counter's behavior being triggered by calls to the methods Increment and Decrement. The mechanism enabling this is virtual dispatch, which is discussed in more detail later.

Essentially, calls to virtual methods loop in the CLR to take care of a virtual dispatch operation that depends on the runtime type of the object involved. In the preceding example, the static type (that is, the type known to the compiler for the variable slot) of counter is Counter, while the runtime type of the object held in that variable happens to be the more specialized NonNegativeCounter. Calls to virtual methods are routed to the most specific implementation, which is found by looking at the runtime type.

The reason for the name *polymorphism* should be more or less apparent. For a single type, multiple different shapes can exist, which are defined by subtypes. All of those share common parts. For example, each Shape object can have a bounding rectangle and a color, whereas a more specialized Circle will have additional properties like radius, while yet another subtype Polygon will have a count of sides, too. To UI frameworks, it won't matter which Shape object you give it, as long as all of them have some virtual Draw method available.

Polymorphism is applicable everywhere objects are passed or held. For example, you can have collection types that are declared to hold Shape objects, but every object of a type derived from Shape will be allowed to get in there, as well:

```
List<Shape> shapes = new List<Shape>();
shapes.Add(new Rectangle(3, 4));
shapes.Add(new Circle(5));
```

Places where objects are passed are equally important in polymorphic code. Often, you will see constructors, methods, or other members expecting objects of a certain type that support a set of required operations. The runtime type of the object passed in will determine the final behavior:

```
class Graphics
{
    public void Paint(Shape shape)
    {
        // Code could query the shape for its dimensions and finally
        // call some virtual Draw method to ask the objects to draw
        // itself at calculated coordinates x and y:
        int x = ...; int y = ...;
        shape.Draw(this, x, y);
    }
}
```

All of this enables an open-world model where different parties can contribute to an application by deriving from classes, overriding behavior where needed. In our running example of a UI framework, third parties can contribute their own controls, as long as they implement the required operations for things such as rendering.

During our further discussion about polymorphism and inheritance, we'll describe a series of language constructs that are related:

▶ Establishing type hierarchies by deriving classes using the : syntax

▶ Declaring virtual members using the virtual keyword

- ▶ Overriding base class members using the `override` keyword

- ▶ Blocking member overrides using the `sealed` keyword

- ▶ Dispatching to a base class member using the `base` keyword

- ▶ Hiding base class members using the `new` keyword

- ▶ Abstracting base classes using the `abstract` keyword

- ▶ Notes on single inheritance, interfaces, and extension methods

But first, we examine the various relationships between types.

Types in Pictures

Because there's quite a bit of vocab associated with OOP, it's worth taking a moment and putting all of it together in a picture. Follow Figure 14.2 while reading the following few paragraphs.

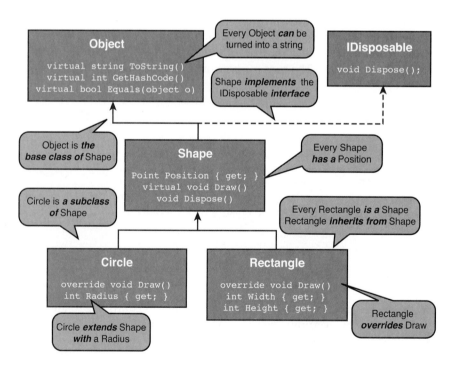

FIGURE 14.2   Object-oriented concepts for classes and interfaces.

The CLR, and hence C#, supports single *inheritance* for classes and multiple inheritance for interfaces. This means that every class has a single *base class* (which by default is `System.Object`, the mother of all types). Alternatively, we could say that a class is a *subclass* of its base class. Each class can *implement* zero or more interfaces, which means providing an implementation for the interface's members. At this point, the class supports or exposes the interface. Classes have members that are inherited from the base class or are introduced by the class itself.

As a result of inheritance, we end up with a type hierarchy. Notice that the "subclass of" relationship is transitive. That is, if D is a subtype of a subtype of a type B, we also consider D to be a subtype of B. An implication of this is that every type is a subtype of the System.Object mother type, which acts as the root to any type hierarchy (and is often omitted because it's implied). Subtypes are different from the base type, which denotes the (single) immediate parent of a type.

Inheritance for Classes

The first thing we want to look at is how to derive a class from another one. C# uses a single syntax for inheritance both from a class or a set of interfaces, which is different from languages like Java, in which two keywords, extends and implements, are used. In the following example, we explicitly derive a class from System.Object:

```
class Person : Object
{
    public Person(string name, int age)
    {
        Name = name;
        Age = age;
    }

    public string Name { get; private set; }
    public int Age { get; private set; }
}
```

The preceding code is no different from omitting the colon and base type altogether because Object is the default base type if left unspecified:

```
class Person
{
    public Person(string name, int age)
    {
        Name = name;
        Age = age;
    }

    public string Name { get; private set; }
    public int Age { get; private set; }
}
```

Where things get more interesting is when we specify another nontrivial base class, as shown here. In this scenario, Student is declared as a subclass of Person:

```
class Student : Person
{
}
```

There are a few interesting things to be discussed about the preceding code. First and foremost, the preceding code doesn't compile. The reason for this is that the base class's members are inherited and hence available on the subclass, with the exception of constructors. Because the base class has declared a nondefault constructor, what would it mean from an initialization point of view if we were to create a new instance of Student? How does the base class constructor ever get invoked?

```
var student = new Student();
Console.WriteLine(student.Name + " is " + student.Age);   // What should it be?
```

Figure 14.3 shows the error message produced by the compiler when this situation is detected. To convince yourself that constructors are not inherited from the base class, try writing the following piece of code:

```
var student = new Student("Bart", 27);
Console.WriteLine(student.Name + " is " + student.Age);
```

FIGURE 14.3   Constructors are not inherited.

To resolve this issue, we have to provide an instance constructor on the subclass. Let's try it by adding a default constructor first:

```
class Student : Person
{
    public Student() { }
}
```

Again, the compiler will complain, this time pointing out that Person does not contain a constructor that takes zero arguments. It's simply not possible to initialize Person without calling any of its constructors (low-level mechanisms in the CLR serialization stack set aside), so the subclass cannot escape its responsibility to loop one of the base class's constructors when creating an instance of its own. Here is a valid way to get out of this situation:

```
class Student : Person
{
    public Student(string name, int age)
        : base(name, age)
    { }
}
```

The base keyword is used here to refer to the immediate base class, in this case to call a constructor. Figure 14.4 shows the IntelliSense provided upon invoking the base class constructor, which is possible only in the context of a constructor using the colon-prefixed syntax (symmetric to the declaration of a subclass).

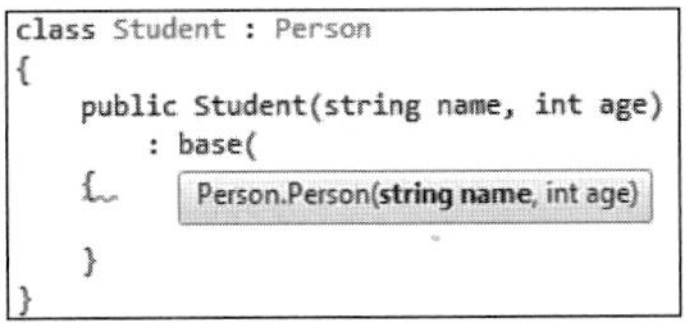

FIGURE 14.4   Calling a base class constructor.

Now it's no longer possible to create a Student instance without specifying a name and an age, which will be set on the members inherited from the base class:

```
var student = new Student("Bart", 27);
Console.WriteLine(student.Name + " is " + student.Age);
```

Figure 14.5 proves that the Name property was inherited from the base class: IntelliSense mentions the base class Person in the tooltip for the selected Name property. Notice members from the base class's base class also show up. In this case, this is System.Object.

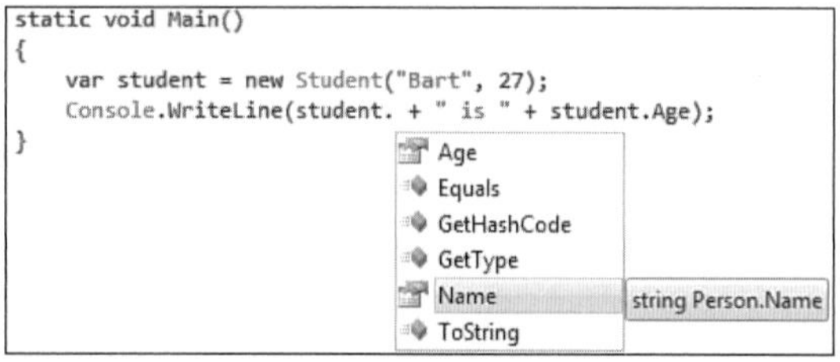

```
static void Main()
{
    var student = new Student("Bart", 27);
    Console.WriteLine(student. + " is " + student.Age);
}
```

FIGURE 14.5   Members are inherited from base classes.

Typically, just creating a subclass without further specialization is not very useful. In the next parts of the chapter, you learn how to override behavior, but for now let's just focus on extending a class with new members. For example, let's extend a student with a new College property:

```
class Student : Person
{
    public Student(string name, int age, string college)
        : base(name, age)
    {
        College = college;
    }

    public string College { get; private set; }
}
```

Notice how we use the base class constructor to initialize the inherited state, while we add more code to the constructor to initialize the state that's specific to the subclass. As you saw before, constructors can also be chained within the current class, using the this keyword. This still works in the context of subtyping, as long as the constructor calls ultimately result in a proper call to a base class constructor:

```
class Student : Person
{
    public Student(string name, int age)
        : base(name, age)
    { }

    public Student(string name, int age, string college)
        : this(name, age)
    {
        College = college;
    }

    public string College { get; private set; }
}
```

In this example, it's possible to create a new Student object without specifying a college parameter (if that were desirable). Either way, we ultimately have to initialize the base class's inherited state by calling a base class constructor.

OUTSMARTING THE COMPILER... OR NOT?

If you have a hacker's mind like I do, you'll find it challenging to try to work around restrictions imposed by the compiler, like the one shown in Figure 14.3. In fact, you can, with very limited success. If you create a cycle in constructor chains using the this keyword, the compiler won't notice you've never called a base constructor. However, all you've done is create a set of mutually recursive constructors that will result in a stack overflow exception at runtime.

Single Inheritance for Classes

The CLR, the C# programming language, as well as other Common Language Infrastructure (CLI) languages support only *single inheritance* for classes. In other words, only a single base class can be used for any given class. When omitted, that base class is System.Object. In the example shown in Figure 14.6, we try to declare a class Tomato, which is both a Fruit and a Vegetable.

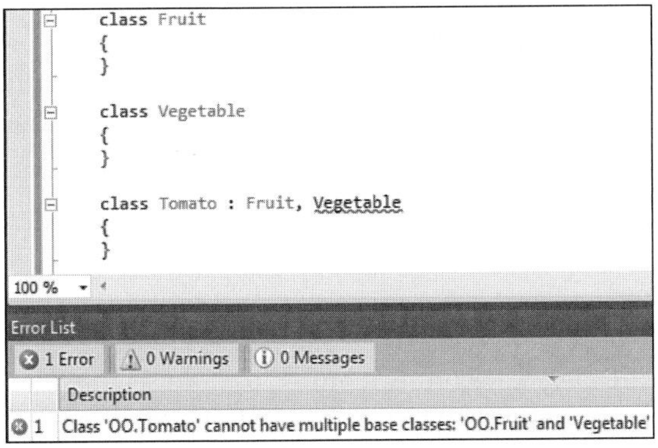

```
class Fruit
{
}

class Vegetable
{
}

class Tomato : Fruit, Vegetable
{
}
```

100 %   ▾   ◂

Error List

❌ 1 Error   ⚠ 0 Warnings   ⓘ 0 Messages

	Description
❌ 1	Class 'OO.Tomato' cannot have multiple base classes: 'OO.Fruit' and 'Vegetable'

FIGURE 14.6   No multiple-class inheritance allowed.

THE DIAMOND PROBLEM

One of the main reasons for not supporting multiple-class inheritance in the CLR comes from the well-known problems and complexities that arise from multiple inheritance, as seen in languages like C++. One such problem is known as the *diamond problem*.

Named after the shape of a type hierarchy where a class D derives from both B and C, both of which derive from A, the diamond problem pinpoints complexities that arise in this setting. Suppose A has a member called Bar and both B and C override it. Which of the two overrides should be called when code in D calls the equivalent of base.Bar() in C#? This introduces the need for virtual base classes, which complicate programming quite a bit.

Less-invasive forms of multiple inheritance have been suggested here and there, the most notable of which include traits and mixins. In fact, those aren't really forms of multiple inheritance but allow certain sets of functionality to be adopted by classes, thus reducing the need for duplication of code. Approaches such as those have their problems, too.

As you will see, the CLR supports multiple inheritance for interfaces, which doesn't suffer from those problems but is of limited use to overcome some of the scenarios where multiple inheritance proves handy. However, extension methods can be used to mimic "interfaces with default implementations" to some extent.

Because of single inheritance for classes, the base class of any class is defined in an unambiguous manner. Therefore, to refer to a base class's members explicitly, you can use the single keyword called base. Where this refers to the current instance (of the containing type), base refers to the immediate base class. In most cases, the use of the base keyword is optional:

```
class Student : Person
{
    // Constructors shown earlier.

    public string College { get; private set; }

    public override string ToString()
    {
        return   base.Name + " is " + base.Age
                + " and studies at " + this.College;
    }
}
```

Later you'll see one case where the use of the base keyword is required to disambiguate between a subclass's member and a base class's member with the same name. We discuss this scenario when talking about hiding members in the section, "Sealing and Hiding: Take Two."

INHERITANCE OR CONTAINMENT?

Here's another story for you. A long while ago, in the .NET 1.0 days, I was explaining OOP and inheritance. It turned out my explanation was unnecessary for a reason I'll explain here.

Some of my friends were working on a user interface application that had to display a Windows Forms tree view control to visualize an organization chart. If the user clicked a node in the tree, details for the selected node should have been displayed in another pane to the right (much like Windows Explorer). The obvious question was how to associate the rich business object representing an entry in the organization hierarchical structure with the TreeNode object used in the UI.

Knowing the art of OOP, my choice was quite obvious: Let's derive a subclass from
TreeNode, add a property to it to contain the business object, and that's it. Windows
Forms will still work fine with our custom TreeNode object (polymorphism), and we have
a spot to put the business object.

However, explaining this object-oriented technique turned out to be challenging because
my friends didn't have such a background. Exploring the API surface of TreeNode a bit
more, I soon discovered a Tag property on the Windows Forms Control type, allowing
an arbitrary object to be associated with a control. Instead of inheritance, this uses the
technique of containment. The only drawback is the weakly typed nature of it, having to
cast back from Tag's object type to the business object type. Ultimately, we settled for
this approach.

Yet another option is to have an external collection that associates the (regular)
TreeNode objects with the business objects (for example, using some kind of dictionary collection type). This, however, leads to memory-management concerns: Upon
removal of a tree node, you should clean the auxiliary data structure, too.

Multiple Inheritance for Interfaces

Each class (or struct) can implement multiple interfaces. Interfaces are covered at the end
of this chapter, but you can roughly regard them as contracts that do not have an implementation of their own. When implementing an interface, you basically promise to obey
the contract specified by the interface. One example is IDisposable, which we talked
about in Chapter 12, "Constructors and Finalizers."

```
public interface IDisposable
{
    void Dispose();
}
```

Implementing an interface is allowed to coexist with derivation from a base class or implementation of zero or more interfaces. In the class base specification, which is the part of
the class declaration after the colon, the base class (if any is specified) has to come before
the list of interfaces implemented by the class. All of those are comma-separated:

```
class Stream : MarshalByRefObject, IDisposable
{
    ...

    public void Dispose()
    {
        // I promised to implement IDisposable. Here it is.
    }
}
```

The Base Class Library (BCL) is full of types that implement multiple interfaces. Some notable ones are all the numeric primitive types that derive from System.ValueType and implement a bunch of interfaces allowing for comparison, equality checks, formatting, and so on. This is illustrated in Figure 14.7 by means of inspection through .NET Reflector.

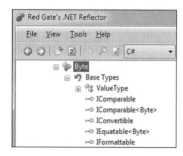

FIGURE 14.7   Multiple inheritance for interfaces.

INHERITANCE FOR STRUCTS: WHY (NOT)?

In the example shown in Figure 14.7, you might notice how Byte derives from the System.ValueType class, even though the Byte type itself is a struct. This is one of the implementation details of the CLR unified type system, facilitating things such as boxing.

Beyond inheriting from System.ValueType, there's no subtyping possible for value types, other than the implementation of interfaces. By implication, there's also no means to do polymorphism with structs. The reason this is the case is a rather fundamental one. Recall that value types get allocated on the stack by default. If we were to allow subtyping for structs, you could have a Point2D variable on the stack and assign it a subtype of type Point3D:

```
static double Distance(Point2D first, Point2D second)
{ ... }

static void Main()
{
    var point1 = new Point3D(1, 2, 3);
    var point2 = new Point3D(4, 5, 6);
    Console.WriteLine(Distance(point1, point2));
}
```

Assume in the preceding example that both Point2D and Point3D are structs and the latter is a subtype of the former (hypothetically). Implementation of the Distance method using stack allocation for the parameters has just become incredibly hard because the size of the parameters is no longer fixed. Where a Point2D may have two fields of type Int32 (hence causing a total of 8 bytes to allocate the object), any subtype may add an arbitrary amount of data to it.

Because of this, the `Distance` method could not be written with a fixed layout in terms of stack-allocated memory. The way to get out of this issue is to put the parameters elsewhere, for example by storing the parameters on the managed heap. But wait a second, why did we have structs in the first place then? Indeed, one of the major strengths of structs is their lightweight stack-allocated fixed-size nature. Allowing subtyping would defeat this.

Therefore, the following will fail to compile, pointing out that `Point2D` in the interface list is not an interface:

```
struct Point2D
{
    int x, y;
}

struct Point3D : Point2D
{
    int z;
}
```

The nomenclature for the part after the colon differs for classes and structs. In the first case, it's called the "class base specification." In the latter case, it's referred to as the "interface list" because the word *base* has no meaning in this context, as explained earlier.

Blocking Inheritance

Allowing inheritance yields a great amount of flexibility with regard to application programming interface (API) design. At the same time, it comes as a big responsibility for the designers of the base classes. If the behavior of a base class method changes, it might break subtypes. This is especially true if virtual methods are used, as you will see later.

To avoid such responsibilities, you can mark a class as noninheritable by means of the `sealed` keyword. Doing so prevents anyone from inheriting from the class:

```
sealed class Student : Person
{
    ...
}

class GraduateStudent : Student   // fails to compile
{
}
```

Figure 14.8 shows the error emitted by the compiler in this case. Later you see how you can apply the `sealed` keyword to a member.

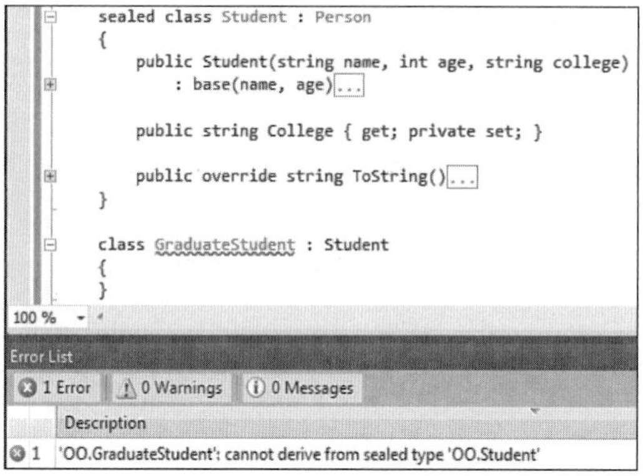

FIGURE 14.8   Multiple inheritance for interfaces.

A BALANCING ACT

Deciding to use the `sealed` keyword on classes is a bit of a balancing act. If you do it, you escape some responsibility for future compatibility guarantees. At the same time, you limit flexibility for the type's users.

Hiding Base Class Members

Sometimes it's useful to hide a base class member by introducing a member with the same name of a subclass. After all, when defining a subclass, you don't control the names chosen by the author of the base class. If it turns out the best name for the new member to be introduced on the subclass clashes with a member's name on the base, hiding can be used. Later, in the section called "Interfaces," you see how a similar situation can arise when an interface is being implemented.

The following example illustrates what we're talking about for both instance and static members. Although we're only showing methods here, the same applies for other member types.

```
class Bar
{
    public void Foo() { Console.WriteLine("Bar.Foo"); }
    public static void Qux() { Console.WriteLine("Bar::Qux"); }
}

class Baz : Bar
{
    public void Foo() { Console.WriteLine("Baz.Foo"); }
    public static void Qux() { Console.WriteLine("Baz::Qux"); }
}
```

To see what happens in the preceding code, consider the following piece of code:

```
Bar bar = new Bar();
bar.Foo();
Baz baz = new Baz();
baz.Foo();
Bar bazAsBar = baz;
bazAsBar.Foo();
```

This code will print `Bar.Foo`, `Baz.Foo`, and `Bar.Foo`. Both the second and third outputs are of interest. Depending on the static type of the variable, a different `Foo` method is called. In fact, the compiler has chosen which method to call based on that type. You'll see how this is different when the virtual modifier is used, resulting in virtual dispatch.

Notice how we're using `bazAsBar` as an illustration of the polymorphic property of OOP. Here, we're assigning an object of a more-derived type to a variable of a less-derived type. That is, everywhere a `Bar` is expected, we can also pass a more-specialized `Baz`.

When looking at Baz's declaration, it might not be immediately apparent `Foo` indeed is hiding a base class member. Code within Baz's implementation may also call `Foo` in the belief it will result in a call to the base class member. But as soon as someone puts a new `Foo` method on the type, hiding the inherited one, the meaning of that code will start to change. To prevent such mishaps, the compiler emits a warning telling you about the naming clash introduced. Figure 14.9 shows this, suggesting a solution (use of the new keyword as a modifier on the method):

```
class Baz : Bar
{
    public new void Foo() { Console.WriteLine("Baz.Foo"); }
    public new static void Qux() { Console.WriteLine("Baz::Qux"); }
}
```

```
class Bar
{
    public void Foo() { Console.WriteLine("Bar.Foo"); }
    public static void Qux() { Console.WriteLine("Bar::Qux"); }
}

class Baz : Bar
{
    public void Foo() { Console.WriteLine("Baz.Foo"); }
    public static void Qux() { Console.WriteLine("Baz::Qux"); }
}
```
100 %

Error List

🔴 0 Errors   ⚠ 2 Warnings   ⓘ 0 Messages

	Description
⚠ 2	'OO.Baz.Qux()' hides inherited member 'OO.Bar.Qux()'. Use the new keyword if hiding was intended.
⚠ 1	'OO.Baz.Foo()' hides inherited member 'OO.Bar.Foo()'. Use the new keyword if hiding was intended.

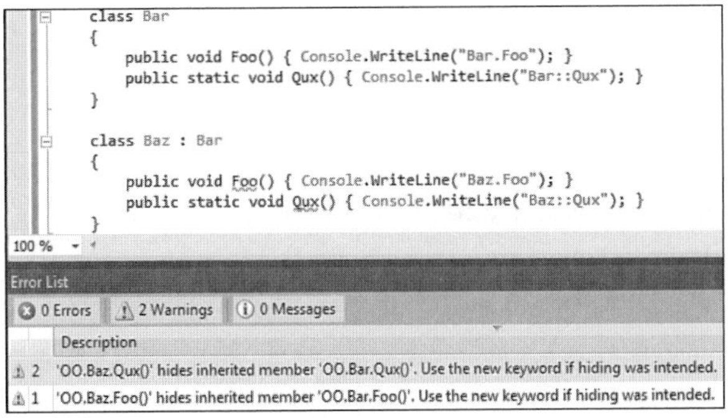

FIGURE 14.9   The C# compiler warning about possibly unintentional hiding taking place.

THREE MEANINGS OF THE NEW KEYWORD

Since C# 2.0, the new keyword can be used in three places. The most well-known one is in an expression context to create a new instance of a given type, typically invoking a constructor. (For delegates, things are a bit more complex.) The second use site for the new keyword is hiding, which was available in C# 1.0, too. Here, the new keyword is used as a modifier.

With the introduction of generics in C# 2.0, the new keyword was reused to allow decla-ration of a generic constraint. We take a look at generics and constraints later, but here's a code fragment to whet your appetite:

```
class Factory<T> where T : new()
{
    // Code is allowed to do new T()
}
```

Here, the generic type Factory<T> cannot be constructed with a type parameter for a type that doesn't have a default constructor defined.

The new modifier is simply used to declare intent and acknowledge the subtleties that may arise by writing code this way. To call the base class member from the inside, you can use the base keyword. For static members, qualification with the type name is used to indicate the target member:

```
class Bar
{
    public void Foo() { Console.WriteLine("Bar.Foo"); }
    public static void Qux() { Console.WriteLine("Bar::Qux"); }
}

class Baz : Bar
{
    public void Foo() { base.Foo(); Console.WriteLine("Baz.Foo"); }
    public static void Qux() { Bar.Qux(); Console.WriteLine("Baz::Qux"); }
}
```

From the outside, you can use casts to indicate which static type to operate on, causing the compiler to pick the intended method:

```
static void Main()
{
    Baz baz = new Baz();
    baz.Foo();
```

```
    ((Bar)baz).Foo();   // calls base one

    Bar bazAsBar = baz;
    bazAsBar.Foo();
    ((Baz)bazAsBar).Foo();   // calls derived one
}
```

When we discuss virtual methods in the section, "Polymorphism and Virtual Members," you learn how the new and override modifiers are mutually exclusive.

Protected Accessibility

So far, we've dealt with publicly accessible members during our explanation of inheritance. However, a more granular accessibility level, called *protected*, exists for use in combination with inheritance and OOP.

Whereas public members are visible to the world, both inside and outside the assembly, private members are visible only within the declaring type (including nested types). Because type hierarchies establish "families of types," a corresponding accessibility level seems attractive. This is what protected does: It allows access to the member to code in the declaring type as well as code in derived types. You've seen such an example with our introductory Counter exploration:

```
public class Counter
{
    public int Count { get; protected set; }
}
```

In this example, the Count property is available to be read from anywhere (public), whereas the setter is only available to code in Counter or any subclass:

```
public class ResettableCounter : Counter
{
    public void Reset()
    {
        base.Count = 0;   // base can be omitted
    }
}
```

Figure 14.10 shows accessibility with arrows indicating "is accessible to" relationships. The internal accessibility level is explained when we cover assemblies in Chapter 25, "Assemblies and Application Domains."

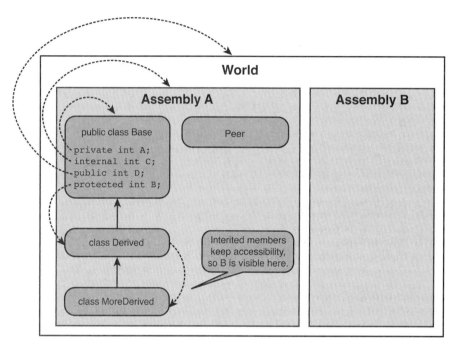

FIGURE 14.10   Accessibility in pictures.

THE MYTHICAL PROTERNAL AND INTECTED MODIFIERS

One accessibility level that hasn't been covered in Figure 14.10 is spelled out as "protected internal" or "internal protected" in C#. Both orders of the modifiers mean the same: The member is available to other types within the same assembly *and* available to types in the inheritance hierarchy.

Although the CLR supports an *or* interpretation for the combination of both modifiers (that is, accessibly to derived types but only in the same assembly), C# doesn't. This is sometimes referred to by the C# team as the "proternal" or "intected" feature request, mainly because it's not at all clear what the modifier would look like.

Polymorphism and Virtual Members

Now that you know how to derive a class and call members on the base class, we're ready to introduce another pillar of OOP: polymorphism. In passing, we've already seen how an instance of a subclass can be used in a place where a less-derived type is expected. This enables code such as that shown here:

```
string s = "Hello";
object o = s;
```

Because every string *is* an object, we can do this assignment. Where things get interesting is when we try to invoke a method on o. In particular, what should happen if we call, say, the ToString method:

```
Console.WriteLine(o.ToString());
```

Who's responsible for creating a suitable ToString method that will provide meaningful output? In this particular case, we happen to know that o really contains a string, so we expect the ToString result on a string to be... well, that very same string. However, if we look at what the compiler knows about o, it cannot emit code that does immediately invoke a System.String-specific method. After all, we've typed o to be of type System.Object, *and nothing more*. This becomes more obvious when we increase the "distance" between the definition and use of the Console.WriteLine parameter:

```
static void Main()
{
    Print("Hello");
    Print(5);
}

static void Print(object o)
{
    Console.WriteLine(o);  // Console.WriteLine will call ToString on o.
}
```

Clearly, the compiled code for neither Print nor Console.WriteLine can anticipate what the runtime type will be for the input parameter. In other words, the compile-time static type knowledge is reduced to what we've told the compiler: Print takes an object, and that's it.

So how can the ToString call on the object passed in (ultimately happening in the depths of the Console.WriteLine implementation) ever *defer* the decision on the final behavior to the object's best ToString method available? Obviously, we must define what we mean by "best available," but you get the idea. The System.Object default ToString implementation won't cut it because it would print just the object's type name:

```
System.String
System.Int32
```

This observation brings us to virtual members and virtual dispatch.

Virtual Members

Methods, properties, indexers, and events can be declared as virtual members using the virtual keyword used as a modifier on the member declaration. Virtual members can be *overridden* in a derived class to specialize their behavior. The simplest example can be found on the System.Object type itself, which is roughly defined as follows (omitting a bunch of irrelevant custom attributes and members):

```
public class Object
{
    public virtual bool Equals(object obj) { /* default implementation */ }
    public virtual int GetHashCode() { /* default implementation */ }
    public virtual string ToString() { /* default implementation */ }
    public Type GetType() { /* the one and only implementation */ }
    ...
}
```

Notice how three methods have been declared as virtual by the .NET Framework team. Although those methods have default implementations, a common developer task is to override them with specialized behavior to account for the specific semantics of the derived type. You see how in just a moment.

Notice how the GetType method is not declared as virtual. All this means is that the method's implementation cannot be overridden by a derived type, and only the built-in implementation can be used. After all, how could one provide a meaningful override for this low-level primitive? If you call GetType on an instance, you always expect to get back the runtime type of that object. The CLR exactly knows how to do this, and therefore there's no role for subtypes to specialize this behavior.

As you saw before, the mere act of deriving from a class causes the members of the base class to be inherited. To be precise, not all of those may be accessible in the subclass; for example, a private member won't be available to the subclass. In other words, all the System.Object methods shown earlier, including GetType, are readily available on any subtype:

```
Person bart = new Student("Bart", 27, "C# Academy");
Person lisa = new Student("Lisa", 23, "VB Academy");

Console.WriteLine(bart.ToString());     // OO.Student (the full type name)
Console.WriteLine(bart.Equals(lisa));   // false (no reference equality)
Console.WriteLine(lisa.GetHashCode());  // Some 32-bit integer value
Console.WriteLine(lisa.GetType());      // OO.Student (ToString of Type object)
```

At this point, we haven't done anything but inherit the base class's default behavior, ultimately going all the way back to System.Object: Student derives from Person, and Person derives from Object. None of our custom Student and Person types has defined custom specialized behavior for any of the virtual methods shown earlier.

In the following section, we take a look at how to override virtual members based on the example with System.Object virtual methods shown earlier.

Overriding Virtual Members

Overriding a virtual member is done by means of the `override` keyword. When you type the keyword in the Visual Studio IDE, IntelliSense provides a list of members that can be overridden, as shown in Figure 14.11.

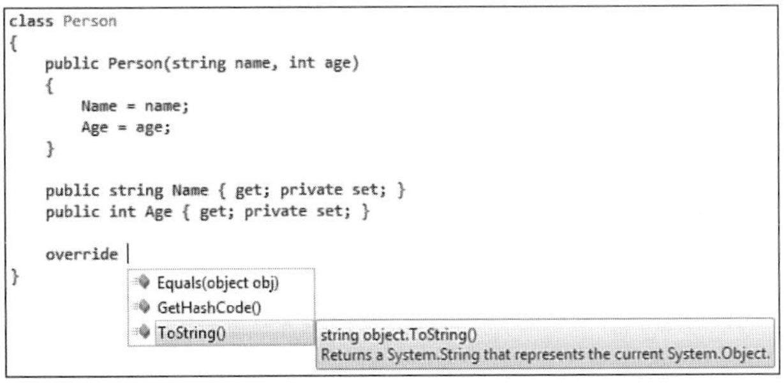

```
class Person
{
    public Person(string name, int age)
    {
        Name = name;
        Age = age;
    }

    public string Name { get; private set; }
    public int Age { get; private set; }

    override |
}                    Equals(object obj)
                     GetHashCode()
                     ToString()        string object.ToString()
                                       Returns a System.String that represents the current System.Object.
```

FIGURE 14.11   Use of the `override` keyword.

As soon as we pick a member from the list presented to us, Visual Studio generates a default implementation that does nothing but defer execution to the base class implementation, as shown in Figure 14.12.

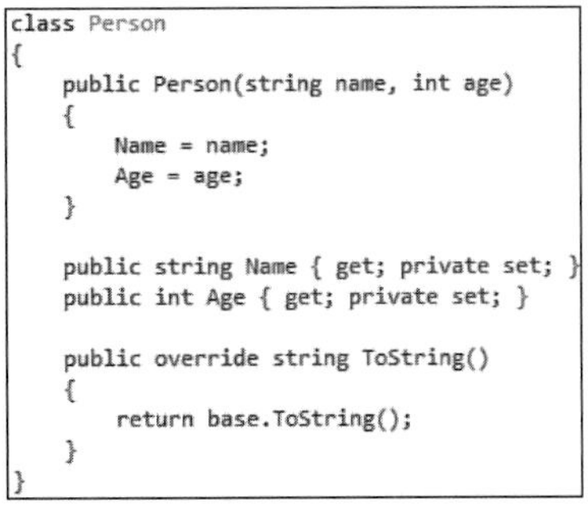

```
class Person
{
    public Person(string name, int age)
    {
        Name = name;
        Age = age;
    }

    public string Name { get; private set; }
    public int Age { get; private set; }

    public override string ToString()
    {
        return base.ToString();
    }
}
```

FIGURE 14.12   Default implementation for an overridden method.

Obviously, you'll usually want to substitute this code for something more meaningful. However, in some cases, you'll still be using a call to the base method to assist in your implementation's logic. You'll see this in a moment. First, let's override `ToString` for our `Person` type, simply to print the name and age of the person:

```
public override string ToString()
{
    return Name + " is " + Age;
}
```

Even though we haven't talked about virtual dispatch yet, this suffices to illustrate the behavior of calling ToString in two different ways. One time we call ToString simply on a variable that's declared to be of type Person. Things get more interesting in the second example, where we call ToString on a variable whose static type is object:

```
Person bart = new Person("Bart", 27);
Console.WriteLine(bart.ToString());
object him = bart;
Console.WriteLine(him.ToString());
```

Both calls to ToString result in the same output, calling into our implementation with the specialized Person-specific behavior. Figure 14.13 proves this behavior through the lenses of the debugger. This is, as you will see, virtual dispatch at work.

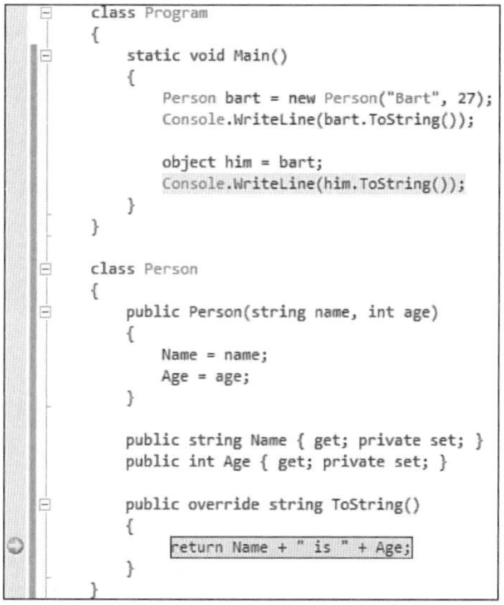

```
class Program
{
    static void Main()
    {
        Person bart = new Person("Bart", 27);
        Console.WriteLine(bart.ToString());

        object him = bart;
        Console.WriteLine(him.ToString());
    }
}

class Person
{
    public Person(string name, int age)
    {
        Name = name;
        Age = age;
    }

    public string Name { get; private set; }
    public int Age { get; private set; }

    public override string ToString()
    {
        return Name + " is " + Age;
    }
}
```

FIGURE 14.13   Virtual dispatch of ToString in action.

Given that we've overridden ToString on Person and given that a subtype inherits its base type's members, what you would expect the ToString operation on Student to print? Right, our Person's ToString implementation will be invoked, once more illustrated in the presence of polymorphic code (as we treat bart as object):

```
object bart = new Student("Bart", 27, "C# Academy");
Console.WriteLine(bart.ToString());
```

Obviously, we can now also override the ToString method on the Student class. Here it becomes useful to invoke the base class's ToString method simply to append the subclass's additional information to it:

```
public override string ToString()
{
    return base.ToString() + " and attends " + College;
}
```

As soon as we do this, the call to ToString in the preceding sample code dispatches to the ToString implementation on the more-derived Student type.

Declaring Virtual Members

To illustrate the concept of virtual members from a different angle, let's define another type hierarchy in which we declare virtual members ourselves (rather than overriding the ones from System.Object). A good example is the concept of a Shape that can be queried for its area and circumference. Depending on the subclass of Shape, calculation of those values will differ:

```
class Shape
{
    public virtual double Area
    {
        get { return 0.0; }
    }

    public virtual double Circumference
    {
        get { return 0.0; }
    }
}
```

For the time being, we use default implementations for those virtual property getters, which don't look as if they produce very meaningful values. Later on, after you've learned about abstract classes and members, we discuss how to omit such an implementation altogether.

Now let's define a couple of subclasses, Circle and Square, both of which have pretty simple computations for both metrics. We define those computations by means of overriding:

```
class Circle : Shape
{
    public Circle(double radius)
    {
        Radius = radius;
    }
```

```csharp
    public double Radius { get; private set; }

    public override double Area
    {
        get { return Math.PI * Radius * Radius; }
    }

    public override double Circumference
    {
        get { return Math.PI * 2 * Radius; }
    }
}

class Square : Shape
{
    public Square(double side)
    {
        Side = side;
    }

    public double Side { get; private set; }

    public override double Area
    {
        get { return Side * Side; }
    }

    public override double Circumference
    {
        get { return 4 * Side; }
    }
}
```

As we enter this code, IntelliSense will help us by suggesting the members that can still be overridden. With this code in place, we can write polymorphic code:

```csharp
Shape s1 = new Circle(2.0);
Console.WriteLine(s1.Area);
Shape s2 = new Square(3.0);
Console.WriteLine(s2.Circumference);
```

Sealing and Hiding: Take Two

As previously mentioned, the sealed keyword prevents a class from being derived any further. We can also apply such specialization prevention at a more granular level of members, too. For example, while we may leave our Square type unsealed (the default), we can prevent people from overriding the virtual properties we've defined:

```
class Square : Shape
{
    public Square(double side)
    {
        Side = side;
    }

    public double Side { get; private set; }

    public sealed override double Area
    {
        get { return Side * Side; }
    }

    public sealed override double Circumference
    {
        get { return 4 * Side; }
    }
}
```

Now if someone comes in and defines a subclass of Square, say ColoredSquare, it's no longer possible to override the computation properties Area or Circumference.

With regard to hiding using the new modifier, it's possible to hide an inherited member, including virtual ones, but the combination of override and new doesn't make sense. After all, what would it mean to state that you're hiding a base member and at the same time insist on overriding a base member? First you ask to define a different member altogether, and next you want to override the base member. Those are clearly conflicting requirements stated by the developer:

```
class Bar
{
    public new string ToString()
    {
        return "Hi there!";
    }
}
```

Considering the preceding code, try to predict the output of the following:

```
Bar b = new Bar();
Console.WriteLine(b.ToString());
Console.WriteLine(b);
```

Here, the first call to Console.WriteLine involves calling ToString on a variable that's statically typed to be Bar. The compiler will find a ToString method on the Bar type that hides the inherited member, so it chooses that one. As a result, the first call will print "Hi there!"

The second call, however, uses the WriteLine overload that accepts System.Object as its argument. Inside WriteLine, ToString will be invoked without any compile-time knowledge of the type passed in, other than the fact it is a System.Object. A virtual call results. Because we didn't override ToString but have hidden it, the default ToString method, inherited from System.Object, is called, hence printing Bar's type name.

If we were to do things polymorphically by assigning the newly created Bar instance to a variable of type System.Object, things are different, too:

```
object o = b;
Console.WriteLine(o.ToString());
Console.WriteLine(o);
```

Now, both calls to ToString, once explicitly and once by Console.WriteLine's code, result in a virtual call. Because Bar hasn't overridden the ToString method, both calls print the type name of Bar.

How Virtual Dispatch Works

At first sight, virtual dispatch might look like a bit of magic. The compiler did know about a static type, yet a virtual method override on the runtime type is considered for execution. How does that work? The answer lies in the runtime facilities provided for method calls. A set of different instructions exist to call methods, two of which are used by the C# compiler. One is call, the other is callvirt. From the name, you can already infer the task of the second (although the C# compiler uses it for other purposes, as you will see).

Consider the following piece of code, given our Shape and Circle classes we defined earlier. Observe how the call to Radius involves a nonvirtual member, whereas the call to Area should be carried out using virtual dispatch.

```
Circle c = new Circle(3.0);
Console.WriteLine(c.Radius);

Shape s = c;
Console.WriteLine(s.Area);
```

Figure 14.14 shows the IL code corresponding to the preceding fragment. A few things should be pointed out. First, notice how all calls to the static WriteLine method overloads are carried out using the call instruction. Because static methods can never be virtual (after all, you call them by specifying a *type name*), this is expected. However, both calls for the Radius and Area property getters are done using callvirt. When looking at the code for Shape and Circle, you would expect only the get_Area call to use callvirt. The reason both use callvirt is a difference in behavior with regard to null checks: callvirt will properly throw a NullReferenceException as soon as it sees the target is a null reference.

The call instruction, on the other hand, might not do so if the method does not touch any instance state on the target.

Other than the little IL reading caveat pointed out earlier, the callvirt instruction will quite rapidly figure out the method is in fact nonvirtual and work just as call would. Now that we've highlighted the existence of two different instructions, we can take a close look at both of them and how virtual dispatch works.

The first thing to point out is that virtual dispatch works at the method level from a CLR's point of view. Despite the fact it's valid to use the virtual modifier on other member types in languages such as C#, it really is a method-level construct. For example, for a property, it's a characteristic of the getter/setter methods.

Now take a look at the code generated for our code, as shown in Figure 14.14. Notice the types on which the method being called is defined. No surprises should exist for the static WriteLine methods. The calls to property getters are based on the information available about static types at compile time. For Radius, the compiler knew that the target was of type OO.Circle. Where things get interesting is for virtual methods that are being targeted. In such a case, the least derived type declaring the virtual method will be used. For our example, OO.Shape's get_Area method is targeted. But even if we were to write the following code, this particular method would be used:

```
Circle c = new Circle(3.0);
Console.WriteLine(c.Area);
```

```
OO.Program::Main : void()

Find  Find Next
.method private hidebysig static void  Main() cil managed
{
  .entrypoint
  // Code size       40 (0x28)
  .maxstack  2
  .locals init (class OO.Circle V_0,
           class OO.Shape V_1)
  IL_0000:  ldc.r8     3.
  IL_0009:  newobj     instance void OO.Circle::.ctor(float64)
  IL_000e:  stloc.0
  IL_000f:  ldloc.0
  IL_0010:  callvirt   instance float64 OO.Circle::get_Radius()
  IL_0015:  call       void [mscorlib]System.Console::WriteLine(float64)
  IL_001a:  ldloc.0
  IL_001b:  stloc.1
  IL_001c:  ldloc.1
  IL_001d:  callvirt   instance float64 OO.Shape::get_Area()
  IL_0022:  call       void [mscorlib]System.Console::WriteLine(float64)
  IL_0027:  ret
} // end of method Program::Main
```

FIGURE 14.14   IL code containing both virtual and nonvirtual calls.

Despite the fact we're calling Area on something that's statically known to be Circle, a virtual call to Shape's Area getter will be emitted. From this point on, the runtime is in control to dispatch the call to the most specific implementation it can find.

The way this virtual dispatch mechanism works at runtime is quite involved, but we'll do our best to boil it down to its essence. At runtime, when loading types, the CLR builds a so-called v-table, which stands for *virtual dispatch table*. This table contains a mapping from virtual methods to their code location. Given an object instance, it's an easy step to get to the object type's v-table, simply by computing some offset in memory. When the `callvirt` instruction is used, the runtime finds the v-table, grabs the entry at the offset corresponding to the virtual method, and invokes the code at the location the entry points at.

Essentially, from an object, we can find its type information, and from that we can find the v-table (which is like a telephone book) from which we can find the method target to be called (which is like an address for a given name in a telephone book). Figure 14.15 shows the v-table for the `Circle`, `Shape`, and `Object` types. The dark gray areas indicate virtual method slots. Notice that the order is preserved through subtyping. When a call is made to the `get_Area` property getter defined on `Shape`, the runtime looks at v-table slot 4 on the target object. That slot will always point at the code that takes up the role of executing the virtual method. For a `Circle` object, `get_Area` will refer to the code we wrote on the `Circle` class, using the `override` keyword to specialize the `Area` getter defined on the `Shape` base class.

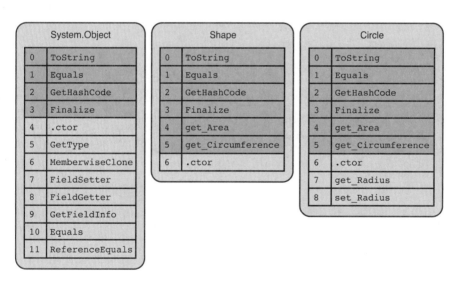

FIGURE 14.15   v-tables for different types, related through subtyping.

Because we didn't override `ToString`, `Equals`, or `GetHashCode`, however, entries in those slots will refer to the implementation defined by `System.Object`. If `Shape` were to have an override for, say, `ToString`, the v-table slot for `ToString` on `Circle` would refer to that implementation because it's the "best one" available.

Figure 14.16 shows how the v-table is laid out for our `Person` class where we override the `ToString` method but leave the `Equals`, `GetHashCode`, and `Finalize` methods in place by simply inheriting them from System.Object. Recall that the Finalize method is used for destructors in C#.

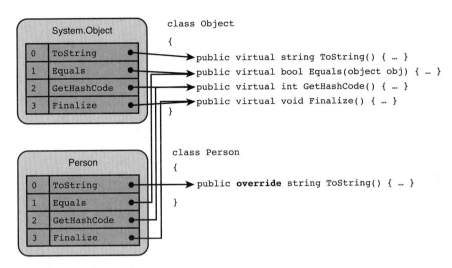

FIGURE 14.16   How override influences a v-table.

When a call is made to System.Object::ToString on an object whose runtime type is Person, the v-table slot at position 0 will be consulted, referring to the ToString method override defined on the class Person. On the other hand, if someone is comparing a Person object to another object by calling the System.Object::Equals virtual method, the v-table slot corresponding to Equals will refer to the implementation that Person inherited from the System.Object base class:

```
object o = new Person("Bart", 27);
// IL code for the call here:
// ldloc.0                                  // local variable containing o
// ldstr       "Hello"                      // pushes a string reference
// callvirt    System.Object::Equals(object) // causes v-table lookup at slot 1
bool equal = o.Equals("Hello");
```

One simple trick to remember v-tables is the telephony network. Some numbers like yours and mine are fixed: Calling them from anywhere in the country will place a call to the outlet in the wall. However, some numbers that seem fixed, such as emergency lines (for example, 911 in the United States) really relay to a response center that's "not too far away." Those numbers can be considered virtual and are overridden at more granular levels of the phone network. Nonetheless, callers always use the same emergency number, despite the fact that routing may occur to deliver the call to the "closest response unit." In this setting, a region can be seen as a subclass of a bigger region, which can override the "implementation of" certain numbers.

How Base Calls Work

Now that you know how virtual calls are made, one remaining question is how a base call avoids getting trapped in some kind of endless recursion. Consider the following code we wrote for Student:

```
class Student : Person
{
    public override string ToString()
    {
        return base.ToString() + " and attends " + College;
    }
}
```

Assume the base call for ToString would be handled in a virtual manner using a callvirt instruction for System.Object::ToString. The innards of virtual dispatch would inspect the v-table of the runtime type of the object (that is, a Student). In the slot for ToString, a reference would be found to the Student's ToString code, as shown in the preceding code. So we end up where we started, resulting in an endless recursion. Clearly, the implementation of the base call should be different. And indeed it is, as shown in Figure 14.17.

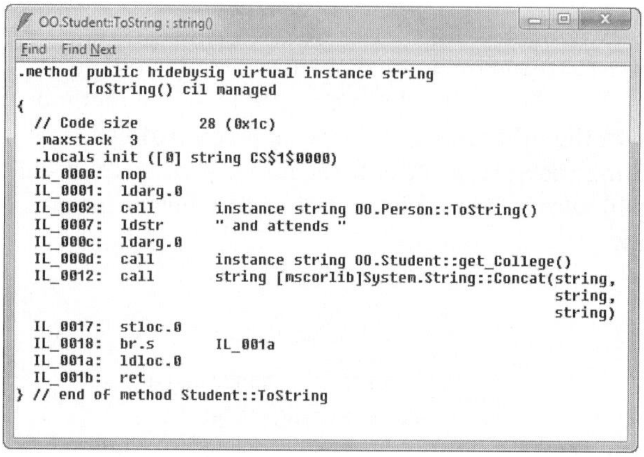

```
OO.Student::ToString : string()
Find  Find Next
.method public hidebysig virtual instance string
        ToString() cil managed
{
    // Code size       28 (0x1c)
    .maxstack  3
    .locals init ([0] string CS$1$0000)
    IL_0000:  nop
    IL_0001:  ldarg.0
    IL_0002:  call       instance string OO.Person::ToString()
    IL_0007:  ldstr      " and attends "
    IL_000c:  ldarg.0
    IL_000d:  call       instance string OO.Student::get_College()
    IL_0012:  call       string [mscorlib]System.String::Concat(string,
                                                                string,
                                                                string)
    IL_0017:  stloc.0
    IL_0018:  br.s       IL_001a
    IL_001a:  ldloc.0
    IL_001b:  ret
} // end of method Student::ToString
```

FIGURE 14.17   Base calls use the call instruction.

As you can see on line IL_0002, the base call gave rise to the use of a call instruction, which results in a direct call into the target method, bypassing any runtime intelligence for virtual dispatch.

Abstract Classes

Recall our definition of the Shape class. One remark we made when defining its two virtual properties was the fact we had to provide default implementations that didn't really have much meaning:

```
class Shape
{
    public virtual double Area
    {
        get { return 0.0; }
    }

    public virtual double Circumference
    {
        get { return 0.0; }
    }
}
```

Although 0.0 might seem like a good default value, wouldn't it be much better not to have to specify a value at all? Moreover, does it even mean to create an instance of the Shape object? Isn't a shape something very *abstract* that needs to be concretized to help someone draw a mental picture? Although Square and Circle are very *concrete*, the concept of a Shape definitely isn't. The following use of Shape looks weird for that very reason:

```
Shape someShape = new Shape();
// So you tell me: what can we do with it?
```

This brings us to the concept of abstract classes, which are classes that do not permit instantiation and are meant to be inherited from. Subclasses can continue to be abstract or can be concrete if they've filled in all the "abstract holes." To declare an abstract class, we use the abstract keyword on the class's declaration itself:

```
abstract class Shape
{
    public virtual double Area
    {
        get { return 0.0; }
    }

    public virtual double Circumference
    {
        get { return 0.0; }
    }
}
```

At this point, it's no longer possible to instantiate an object of type Shape:

```
Shape someShape = new Shape();
// The problem is gone: the above simply doesn't compile anymore.
```

But we can do a better job, getting rid of the bogus default implementations for Area and Circumference by declaring those properties as abstract members, again using the same abstract modifier:

```
abstract class Shape
{
    public abstract double Area
    {
        get;
    }

    // Same for Circumference
}
```

At this point, we can no longer use the virtual modifier because every abstract member will be virtual per definition: It takes some subclass to override it before it's possible to use the member at all. Also, it's not allowed to have any implementation whatsoever on a virtual member, hence the use of a semicolon to indicate the absence of a code block implementing the member's behavior. Figure 14.18 shows typical compiler errors raised when those rules are disobeyed.

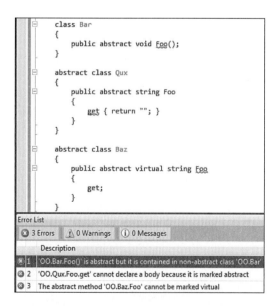

FIGURE 14.18   Some errors made in the definition of abstract classes and members.

When deriving from an abstract class, you can choose to provide implementations for all the abstract members or to leave certain members abstract. In the latter case, the derived class should also be marked as abstract. Thus, abstract classes allow for gradual specialization until a point where the resulting most derived class can be marked concrete (that is, without abstract specified on it).

Implementation of abstract members uses the override modifier, just as if the member were not abstract:

```
class Circle : Shape
{
    ...

    public override double Area
    {
        get { return Math.PI * Radius * Radius; }
    }

    public override double Circumference
    {
        get { return Math.PI * 2 * Radius; }
    }
}
```

Abstract classes can have constructors, which even can be declared as public, for use by subclasses. Because only subclasses should use them, the only correct accessibility level should really be protected (without the internal part). If no constructor is put in place, C# automatically puts a protected default constructor in place.

One good example of an abstract class that ships in the .NET Framework is the Stream class in System.IO, which has many derived concrete types, such as FileStream. The part of Stream that's abstract includes various Write and Read methods, as well as things such as Seek, properties for CanRead and CanWrite, and so on. It's up to a subclass to override those abstract members (for example, by implementing them in terms of Win32 file I/O APIs).

AVOID A LARGE BURDEN ON THE IMPLEMENTORS

Good use of abstract classes often provides a base implementation with a whole bunch of members but limiting the abstract portions to a minimum. For example, while an abstract class may provide a large set of overloads for some methods, it's good to mark only the most specific (that is, with the highest parameter count) overload as abstract. This way, implementors need to override just one method and get all the overloads, including argument checking, for free.

As usual when multiple parties are involved, the key to success is to give people a good return on investment: Implement a handful of members, and you'll get a rich concrete class in return. One of the most demotivating experiences is to face an abstract class with a gazillion abstract members on the to-do list.

Interfaces

Although some framework designers disagree with the statement, I (and the C# specification) sincerely think that interfaces denote contracts. In some respects, the concept of an interface is similar to that of an abstract class. First, you cannot create instances of an interface, which therefore can be considered to be "abstract." Second, the syntax of declaring members on an interface is pretty similar to abstract members on an abstract class. As you will see, this is pretty much where analogies end. Figure 14.19 illustrates the role of interfaces in terms of a contract shared between two parties: the implementor and the consumer.

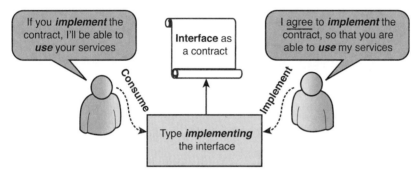

FIGURE 14.19   Interfaces are contracts between implementors and consumers.

Defining Interfaces

To declare an interface, you use the `interface` keyword rather than `class` or `struct`. In the interface body, zero or more members can be specified, without any implementation provided. For example:

```
public interface IDisposable
{
    void Dispose();
}
```

All this says is that a type implementing this interface promises to support the disposal operation by providing an implementation for the `Dispose` method.

CONTRACTS OR NOT?

Where some people disagree with the idea of interfaces as contracts is that they do not really specify a "complete contract" beyond a series of signatures that are merely a syntactic concern. For example, what's a type supporting `IDisposable` supposed to do if `Dispose` is called multiple times? Or what does implementing `IDisposable` mean for other operations on the type if `Dispose` has been called? The answer to those questions lies in documentation.

It's also possible to have interfaces derive from one or more other interfaces. An example in the BCL is the IList<T> generic interface, which defines positional access over an ICollection<T> object, using an indexer and a pair of methods:

```
public interface IList<T> : ICollection<T>
{
    T this[int index] { get; set; }
    void Insert(int index, T item);
    void RemoveAt(int index);
}
```

In fact, ICollection<T> by itself derives from another base interface, IEnumerable<T>:

```
public interface ICollection<T> : IEnumerable<T>
{
    int Count { get; }
    bool IsReadOnly { get; }
    void Add(T item);
    void Clear();
    bool Contains(T item);
    void CopyTo(T[] array, int arrayIndex);
    bool Remove(T item);
}
```

Finally, the IEnumerable<T> interface has the nongeneric variant as its base interface:

```
public interface IEnumerable<out T> : IEnumerable
{
    IEnumerator<T> GetEnumerator();
}
```

The out modifier specified on generic type parameter T is explained in Chapter 15, "Generic Types and Methods," and is used to indicate so-called contravariance. You can ignore it for the time being.

A few more remarks are called for. Notice how none of the members on interfaces have an accessibility modifier. Members of an interface are always considered to be public because they can be called *through* the interface contract with no restrictions:

```
FileStream fs = File.OpenRead(...);


// Can be done everywhere if we can put our hands on fs.
((IDisposable)fs).Dispose();
```

You see later, in the "Implementing Interfaces" section, why the cast may be necessary sometimes. In the preceding example, we're just making the call through the interface *explicit* using this syntax.

Furthermore, it's invalid to specify any modifier on an interface's members. They're always abstract and virtual, and it's an error to state this explicitly. No accessibility is allowed, and things such as override or static don't make sense. The last statement might be surprising, but there's no such thing as static interfaces.

Some Design Recommendations

Contracts are sensitive matters. This is no different for interfaces, so some design recommendations are in order to ensure you don't paint yourself in a corner when defining interfaces or abstract base classes.

Versioning

Interfaces are particularly weak in the context of versioning of code. Once an interface has shipped and customers are implementing it, it's a breaking change to add members to the interface in subsequent releases. Because of this, it's never a good idea to define interfaces that do a bunch of unrelated things, as their "dumping ground" for a potpourri of members will last for only a single release. Instead, make sure an interface does one thing well.

Or Should I Use a Class?

Because of the versioning troubles that interfaces can bring, it's sometimes better to use a class. Adding members to a class is not a breaking change, whereas adding abstract members would be. If new members can have a decent default implementation and can be marked as virtual such that derived types can override it, use of a class may be a good thing.

On the other hand, classes support only a single inheritance axis, whereas interfaces support multiple inheritance. For that reason, be wary about giving away the one shot you've got at class inheritance. As an example, if the only way to get a type to be disposable were to derive from a Disposable base class, no single customer would be able to design a class hierarchy of her own because the Disposable base class monopolizes the single spot for a base class.

During an object-oriented design challenge, I like to ask myself what a type's relationship to a base class or interface should be. If the best fit is the "is a" relationship, an abstract class is the best choice. An example includes Stream because every specialized stream clearly "is a" Stream. If the answer is the "supports" or "can" relationship, interfaces should be a better choice. For example, IDisposable means that every implementing type "can" dispose.

Finally, interfaces can be used on structs, whereas abstract base "structs" don't exist.

Single-Method and Zero-Method Interfaces

Interfaces with zero or one methods are interesting beasts that could have different reasons for existence. Depending on the reason, it might or might not be good idea to use an interface at all.

One case is the first-class object characteristic of an interface. An object implementing an interface can be passed using the interface type. If the sole goal of passing such an object is to wrap a single method, a delegate is usually a better choice. In languages like Java that lack delegates, the only way to achieve this is by providing a single-method interface like Runnable. However, in .NET you can do better by declaring a delegate à la ThreadStart. You'll learn about delegates later, including how a delegate can wrap addition state thanks to closures.

Another case occurs when an interface is simply used as a marker to declare that a type supports some kind of usage. A good example is to communicate the capability to expose a class through a web service. Instead of using a zero-member marker interface, the use of custom attributes is often better and reduces clutter:

```
[WebService(/* parameters can be specified here */)]
class PaymentService /* rather than : IWebService */
{ ... }
```

The preceding example stems from the .NET 1.x days with classic web services supported in ASP.NET. In today's world, Windows Communication Foundation is preferred, which also uses attributes to denote things such as contracts, even on interfaces themselves:

```
[OperationContract]
public interface IPaymentService
{
    void TransferBalance(int from, int to, decimal amount);
}
```

REENFORCING THE INTERFACES AS CONTRACTS PHILOSOPHY

Windows Communication Foundation (WCF) takes the idea of interfaces as contracts one step further and maps the idea onto a distributed setting of services. The idea is to separate the contract from implementations, allowing an interface to be shared across tiers as the single authoritative contract. Such exchange of contracts can be exposed through various formats as well, including WSDL and the Metadata Exchange specification for web services. Either way, what denotes the contract in the world of CLR services and clients is the interface, annotated with custom attributes to provide more parameterization of intent.

If an interface is to be implemented on an object to add some aspect or "ability" to it, the use of an interface is recommended. An example includes IDisposable, where it suffices to implement a single method to turn on the "ability of disposing."

Contracts: Take Two

Because interfaces can be regarded as contracts between different parties, it's important to provide good documentation stating what the different members should do. A good example is the `IDisposable` interface where multiple calls to `Dispose` should have no further effect beyond the first call (the property of idempotency) and where no further interactions with the object should be possible after it has been disposed (by throwing an `ObjectDisposedException`).

One example of an interface contract gone bad is `ICloneable`, which is used to indicate that instances of a type can be cloned. However, the designers never specified whether a shallow clone (just copying a reference for reference typed members) or a deep clone (recursively cloning reference-typed members) is desired. As a result, the interface has a limited value:

```
public interface ICloneable {
    object Clone();
}
```

Implementing Interfaces

To implement an interface, you specify the interface name on the class or struct definition after the colon:

```
class Resource : IDisposable
{
    public void Dispose() { ... }
}
```

When doing so, provide implementations for the interface's members or mark them as abstract, deferring to a subclass. Two ways to implement interface members are available. The one shown in the preceding snippet is sometimes referred to as *implicit interface implementation*. When defining the `Dispose` method, we didn't state we're going to satisfy the contract provided by `IDisposable`. As a result, we can call the interface method in a variety of ways:

```
Resource res = new Resource();
res.Dispose();
((IDisposable)res).Dispose();
```

In the second case, we're using virtual dispatch mechanisms to deliver the call through the interface contract. The runtime facilities to materialize the call are similar to the ones we saw before but involve an additional concept of "interface maps," which are beyond the scope of this book. For the first call to `Dispose`, we're invoking the method as it is exposed on the `Resource` type's public "interface." You learn later how we can hide the method from an implementing type's public interface.

Notice how the accessibility of the `Dispose` method provided for the implicit interface implementation is declared to be public. This is a requirement because every interface member should be accessible through the interface wherever it is used. Figure 14.20 shows an error against this rule.

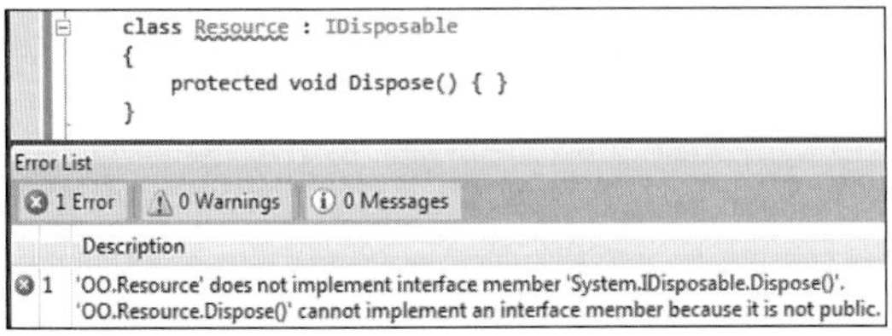

FIGURE 14.20   Implementations for interface members should be public.

Modifiers allowed on interface members include abstract and virtual. The latter can be used to allow subclasses to override the interface member's implementation.

Because multiple interfaces can be implemented by a single class or struct, it's obvious that naming clashes can occur. For example, assume we're implementing both IBar and IBaz, which have a member with the same name and signature:

```
interface IBar
{
    void Foo();
}

interface IBaz
{
    void Foo();
}

class Qux : IBar, IBaz
{
    // How can we have two Foo methods here?
}
```

To satisfy the implementation needs, we somehow need to get out of the naming clash. The answer lies in explicit interface implementation. Figure 14.21 shows the two options Visual Studio provides when adding an interface to the declaration of the struct or class.

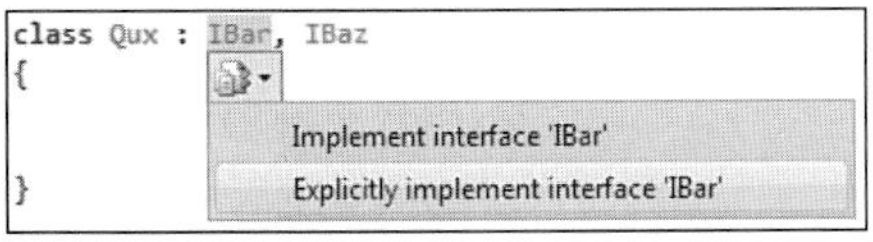

FIGURE 14.21   Implicit or explicit?

If you click the option to explicitly implement the interface, the following code is generated:

```
class Qux : IBar, IBaz
{
    #region IBar Members

    void IBar.Foo()
    {
        throw new NotImplementedException();
    }

    #endregion
}
```

Observe the name of the generated Foo method, prefixed with the IBar interface name. Also notice the lack of an accessibility modifier. In fact, you're not permitted to specify an accessibility modifier on the member. The result of the preceding code is we've declared a Foo method that doesn't appear on the public interface of the containing Qux class and can be invoked only through the interface:

```
Qux qux = new Qux();
qux.Foo();  // Doesn't exist
((IBar)qux).Foo();  // But this works
```

Obviously, we still need to implement the Foo method for IBaz. We can do so either in an explicit manner as well or implement it implicitly, thus making its Foo method appear on the public interface of Qux. For example:

```
class Qux : IBar, IBaz
{
    void IBar.Foo()
    {
        Console.WriteLine("IBar.Foo");
    }

    public void Foo()
    {
        Console.WriteLine("IBaz.Foo");
    }
}
```

I'll leave it to you to call both methods in a variety of ways, through their respective interfaces and in a public manner where applicable.

Besides their help in resolving name clashes, explicit interface implementations can also be used to reduce clutter on a class's or struct's public interface. This technique also comes in handy to provide a friendlier name for an interface's functionality:

```
class Resource : IDisposable
{
    void IDisposable.Dispose() { ... }

    // May be a name users expect, rather than Dispose.
    public void Close()
    {
        ((IDisposable)this).Dispose();
    }
}
```

Notice that the preceding implementation of IDisposable is still usable through the using block feature in C#:

```
using (var res = new Resource())  // Will call ((IDisposable)res).Dispose
{ ... }
```

One example where the use of explicit interface implementation is unavoidable is the use of the generic IEnumerable<T> interface, which derives from the legacy nongeneric IEnumerable variant. As soon as you hit Visual Studio's smart tag's option to implement the interface *implicitly*, you'll see an explicit part being emitted, as well:

```
class Trie<T> : IEnumerable<T>
{
    public IEnumerator<T> GetEnumerator()
    {
        throw new NotImplementedException();
    }

    IEnumerator IEnumerable.GetEnumerator()
    {
        throw new NotImplementedException();
    }
}
```

Because both IEnumerable<T> and IEnumerable contain a method called GetEnumerator with the same signature (recall that the return type isn't part of a signature), one or both implementations have to be done explicitly. Because both implementations will expose the same enumerator (every IEnumerator<T> is also a nongeneric IEnumerator), you can avoid duplication by wiring the nongeneric GetEnumerator to its generic brother:

```
IEnumerator IEnumerable.GetEnumerator()
{
    return GetEnumerator();   // This does not recurse infinitely!
}
```

Because the GetEnumerator call is not decorated with a specific interface type (by means of a cast, as you saw before for our Resource type's Close method), it does correctly call the implicit implementation method, thus not causing endless recursion as one might first think.

ITERATORS

IEnumerable<T> is one of my most beloved interfaces in the entire BCL. It's the interface that fuels the LINQ to Objects implementation, providing very rich querying capabilities over in-memory collections.

All the LINQ operators over such in-memory sequences are implemented to return IEnumerable<T> return sequences. However, to implement them, iterators were used. *Iterators* are methods that return IEnumerable<T> or IEnumerator<T> and use the yield keyword to return the sequence's elements to the caller upon a call to MoveNext. You learn more about those later when we discuss LINQ in Chapter 20, "Language Integrated Query Internals."

This concludes our discussion about interfaces. In general, if you're writing code where you want some other party or component to provide a specialized implementation of some operations, you can use interfaces to formalize such a contract.

Summary

In this chapter, you explored the breadth and depth of object-oriented programming in both the C# programming language and the CLR. First you learned three fundamental pillars of the object-oriented paradigm:

▶ Encapsulation, to hide implementation details and bundle members together in logical units such as classes.

▶ Inheritance, providing the capability for subtypes to inherit base type members and extend upon them.

▶ Polymorphism, allowing use of a more-derived type where a less-derived type is expected. Virtual dispatch allows for polymorphic use of objects.

After covering those pillars, we mapped them onto several concepts as exposed by the C# programming language. First, we familiarized ourselves with the syntax used to perform inheritance of a single base class or multiple interfaces. Inheritance is limited to interfaces for structs, whereas a class can have a single base class, which by default is `System.Object` if left unspecified.

Packed with essential knowledge of inheritance, we moved on to a discussion about base member calls, how constructors are not inherited, and the protected accessibility level that restricts member access to the declaring class and any of its subclasses. You also saw how inheritance can be blocked at the class level and at the member level and how inherited members can be hidden by other members.

Next, we discussed the concept of polymorphism, which is surfaced through the C# language in terms of keywords such as virtual and override. To explain those concepts, we related them to inheritance first, followed by several observations of the way virtual methods are dispatched. This led to a brief exploration of v-tables in the CLR.

Finally, we covered the concept of nonconcrete types, materialized through abstract classes and interfaces in the CLR and C#. Both those kinds of types omit (some or all of) the implementations of members and defer providing such implementations to derived types. Although both represent some kind of contract between two parties, both have their advantages and disadvantages around, most notably, versioning (interfaces) and the impact on inheritance hierarchies (abstract classes).

CHAPTER 15

Generic Types and Methods

IN THIS CHAPTER

▶ Life Without Generics 697

▶ Getting Started with
  Generics 699

▶ Declaring Generic Types 703

▶ Using Generic Types 708

▶ Performance Intermezzo 709

▶ Operations on Type
  Parameters 714

▶ Generic Constraints 716

▶ Generic Methods 732

▶ Co- and Contravariance 740

The second release of the .NET Framework and the CLR added support for generic types, which provide a way to parameterize types on...types. This allows for the creation of more generally applicable types while preserving static type information. In this chapter, we study the language-level and runtime-level constructs exposing this feature. Besides this, we also see how to design and build our own generic types, using rich features like constraints and the new generic co- and contravariance annotations added in .NET 4.

Life Without Generics

In the first release of the .NET Framework, the declaration of a type had to be *closed*, meaning all the information of a type's layout with regard to its fields and members had to be filled in. This posed an important limitation upon framework designers who wanted to keep their types as generally applicable as possible. A typical example can be found in the realm of collection types.

A Real-World Example with Collections

Suppose you're writing an implementation of a list data structure, which maintains a sequential ordering of elements and allows index-based access to its elements. Our collection type provides an improvement over arrays because it allows for the underlying storage to grow when needed. Internally, the most obvious way to implement this is by using an array to store the elements and copy elements to a larger array when storage space is exceeded. So what's the problem?

Well, with a regular array, you can statically type the array so that it can contain elements of only a certain type:

```
int[] xs = new int[] { 1, 2, 3 };
```

This is very convenient as the type is dragged along throughout the code, preventing the user from making silly mistakes:

```
xs[0] = "Should not be here";
```

Now our framework developer in charge of creating a list collection object comes along and wants to make arrays better by providing dynamic growing capabilities and various other interesting features. To make it work with any element type, the underlying storage, an array, has to be typed such that it can contain objects of any type. Before .NET 2.0, the only way to do so was by looking at the type hierarchy and generalizing along that axis by using a common supertype. What's the least common supertype of all objects? Right, System.Object:

```
class ArrayList {
    private object[] _elements;
    ...
    public object this[int i] {
        get { return _elements[i]; }
        set { _elements[i] = value; }
    }

    public void Add(object o) {
        // Add to array, dynamically growing as necessary.
    }
    ...
}
```

However, typing the internal storage as an object-array causes a cascading effect of this very general type to appear everywhere on the public surface of the type. Because users of the list typically want a homogeneous list of elements with regard to their types, this is highly undesirable and causes trouble:

```
ArrayList xs = new ArrayList();
xs.Add(1);
xs.Add(2);
xs.Add(3);

// An evil guy messing with the collection...
xs[0] = "Should not be here";

// This cast causes an InvalidCastException to be thrown...
int first = (int)xs[0];
```

Not only do users have to use an excessive amount of casts to work with the application programming interface (API), the compiler doesn't catch any violations against any implicit contract with regard to the (by the human) expected types fed in to the collection.

In the preceding example, the evil guy can just go ahead and stuff a string in our collection: It's a System.Object anyway, so the compiler is fine with it. However, when getting it out we're still working under the assumption only integer values could have been added to the collection, so we're casting the result of an indexer operation back to int. The only way for the CLR to guarantee type safety is to check types dynamically at runtime (which is the case for casts in general) and throw an exception if a violation is detected. The preceding example dies pathetically with an InvalidCastException, as shown in Figure 15.1

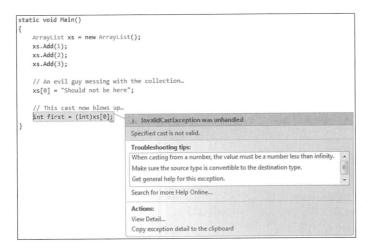

FIGURE 15.1   Without generics, typing needs to be enforced at runtime.

Performance Worries

Use of System.Object as the escape valve to make things as general as possible doesn't only have bad characteristics with regard to compile-time safety; things are getting very suboptimal on the field of performance, as well. Not only do runtime checks' needed cast instructions induce additional cost, keeping a value type object as a System.Object causes boxing. Recall how boxing involves wrapping a value in a heap-allocated box, therefore adding pressure to the garbage collector. And when the value needs to be retrieved with its original type, the symmetric unboxing operation occurs. Figure 15.2 illustrates boxing and unboxing.

Getting Started with Generics

Generics allow developers to define types and methods that are parameterized with *type parameters*. Those parameters are ultimately filled in when such types or methods are used. Let's concentrate on generic types for the time being, deferring treatment of methods until later.

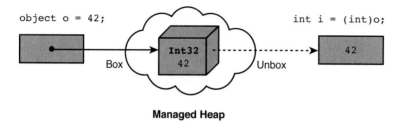

object o = 42;   int i = (int)o;

Int32
42

Box   Unbox

42

Managed Heap

FIGURE 15.2   Boxing and unboxing.

When creating a generic type, whether it's a class, struct, interface, or delegate, you're adding one or more type parameters to the type declaration. On the other side of the picture, a user of the type can specify types for those parameters. Let's take a look at an example to set the scene:

```
class List<T> {
    private T[] _elements;
    ...
    public T this[int i] {
        get { return _elements[i]; }
        set { _elements[i] = value; }
    }

    public void Add(T o) {
        // Add to array, dynamically growing as necessary.
    }
    ...
}
```

In the preceding example, we're defining a generic type called List, with one type parameter that listens to the symbolic name of T. Or, if you prefer it shorter, we've created a List of T. When using this type to store elements of a certain type, T gets substituted for something more tangible (for example, int or string):

```
List<int> xs = new List<int> { 1, 2, 3 };
List<string> names = new List<string> { "Bart", "John" };
```

In fact, the generic type shown here is already implemented for us in the BCL, under the System.Collections.Generic namespace, where a bunch of other generic collection types reside. We take a closer look at those later in this chapter because collections are one of the main motivators for this feature.

A generic type that's "instantiated" with its type parameters carries type information that makes things much stronger typed, as shown in Figure 15.3.

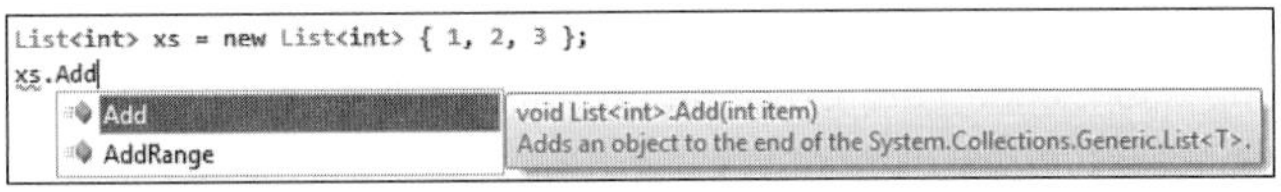

FIGURE 15.3   Generics improve static type checking.

Notice in Figure 15.3 how the List<T>'s Add method that takes in an argument of generic type parameter T gets surfaced, *at compile time*, as a method that takes in an int value. Trying to specify an object with an incompatible type now causes compile-time errors as opposed to failed runtime checks that get surfaced as exceptions:

```
List<int> xs = new List<int> { 1, 2, 3 };


// An evil guy trying to mess with the collection...
xs[0] = "Should not be here";


// No need to cast here anymore...
int first = xs[0];
```

The second line of code now fails to compile, as shown in Figure 15.4. This is a good example of failure being a positive thing because intractable runtime errors are now prevented entirely.

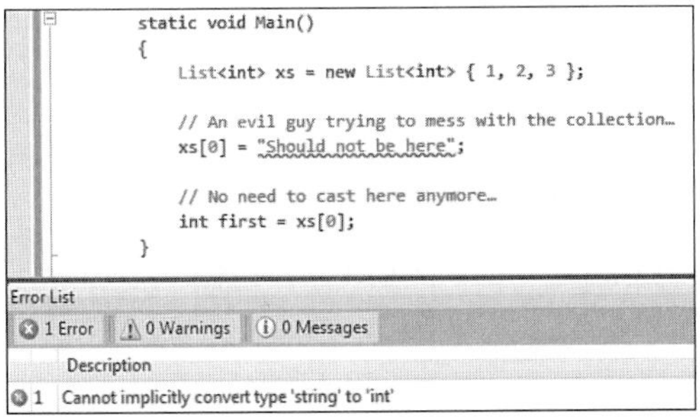

FIGURE 15.4   Better compile-time checking facilitated by the use of generic types.

COLLECTION INITIALIZERS

In the previous examples, we've used a C# 3.0 feature called collection initializers, which enables us to initialize a collection's elements using the curly brace syntax familiar from arrays:

```
int[] xsArray = new int[] { 1, 2, 3 };
List<int> xs = new List<int> { 1, 2, 3 };
```

This feature is enabled for types that implement the IEnumerable<T> type and have an Add method available. Under the hood, code gets generated that calls this Add method for all the elements specified in the initializer list.

For more information about the rationale of this feature with regard to LINQ, refer to our earlier discussion about object initializers in Chapter 6, "A Primer on Types and Objects."

Conceptually, you can compare the declaration of a generic type with a *blueprint* from which other types can be formed. In a more formal setting, those blueprints are known as *unbound generic types*, where the unbound adjective qualifies the presence of type arguments that haven't been applied yet.

With some goodwill, you can draw a parallel between object instantiation and the use of generics to instantiate types. Although in the former case one constructs bigger objects out of smaller ones (for example, a Person consisting of a name and an age), the latter uses types to create types out of. Also on the syntactical level, there's a little analogy, where object constructors use regular parentheses to take in object parameters, whereas generic types use angle brackets to take in type parameters.

Figure 15.5 compares construction of objects with construction of types.

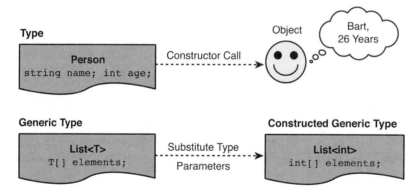

FIGURE 15.5   Analogies between constructing objects and constructing generic types.

POLYMORPHISM, UNIVERSAL QUANTIFICATION AND GYRO

Whenever something can take on multiple shapes or forms, it can be said to be polymorphic. Generics are no exception to this rule and are in fact a form of type-level polymorphism: For every substitution of its type parameters, another flavor of the original type is created.

In the preceding paragraph, I subtly used the phrase *for every*. Readers familiar with predicate logic will recognize the "for all" quantifier in the informal language used over here. Type theoreticians have recognized the same similarity (well, sort of, as types were invented before programming languages were) and called the theoretical foundation of generic types *universal quantification*.

Rich type systems have always inspired computer scientists to do better, trying to catch more and more errors at compile time in favor of runtime checks. The way generics came along in the CLR is no different. In the early .NET 1.0 era, it was widely recognized within Microsoft that an extension to the type system would be very desirable to allow parameterized types. A little later, two researchers of Microsoft Research, Don Syme and Andrew Kennedy, improved the CLR with generic types originally code named Gyro. The rest is history, and today you can harvest this great type system-level feature addition.

Declaring Generic Types

Let's take a closer look at how generic types are declared. We've already seen the syntax used, using angle brackets < and > to specify a comma-separated list of type parameters. For example, here's another generic collection type with two type parameters:

```
class Dictionary<TKey, TValue>
```

VISUAL BASIC SYNTAX

When talking about generic types, use the word *of* to separate the name of the type from its type parameters, as denoted by angle brackets in C#. Visual Basic sounds like plain English language and uses the Of keyword to make this explicit:

```
Class List(Of T)
    '...
End Class
```

To construct a type out of the generic type, the same of keyword is used, followed by the type to be substituted for the type parameter in that position—for example, List(Of Integer).

Stylistically, generic type parameters are prefixed with a capital T, followed by a description of the parameter. This pretty much mirrors the naming convention used with interfaces, where an I prefix is used. Sometimes, especially when there's only a single type parameter, a single letter is used, although style best practices do not recommend this.

Obviously, the names of type parameters need to be unique to avoid name clashes, just as is the case for variable names within a method. Within the declared generic type, its type parameters can be used in places where a type is expected (for example, when declaring fields, for method parameters, to declare variables).

Let's continue our investigation of generic type declaration by taking a look at the way they get represented under the hood. For illustration purposes, consider the following fairly empty List<T> implementation:

```
class List<T> {
    private T[] _elements;
}
```

TRAIN YOUR KNOWLEDGE ON DATA STRUCTURES!

I leave it as an exercise for you to implement an efficient generic list type with Add and Insert methods, as well as indexer accessors to get and set the list's elements. To get inspiration about what a real List<T> implementation might look like from a usage point of view, take a look at System.Collections.Generic. Obviously, you won't want to create your own List<T> implementation (after all, the BCL folks have already done it for you), but it's still a fun little exercise!

Looking at the resulting assembly through the eyes of ILDASM, you'll see something along the lines of Figure 15.6.

FIGURE 15.6   A generic type seen in ILDASM.

First, notice the weird-looking name of the resulting type at this level: List`1<T>. After the back-tick, the compiler has encoded the type's arity, indicating the number of type parameters it takes. Fair enough, but what's up with the _element array's type? We recognize the square bracket syntax that denotes an array type, but what about the !0 part that goes in front of it? That's nothing less than a "hole" caused by the occurrence of the T type parameter in that spot, referring to it by its index in the type parameter list. The exclamation symbol indicates that a reference to a hole follows, and 0 refers to the first type parameter, which is T. If you double-click the _elements entry, you'll see the following:

```
.field private !T[] _elements
```

Here ILDASM is so kind to resolve this !0 business down to the original parameter name for readability purposes. So, in their true essence, generic types are types with holes punched in them. Figure 15.7 shows List<T> with its single generic parameter.

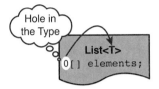

FIGURE 15.7   Generic types are blueprints with placeholders, or holes.

UNLIKE TEMPLATES

Generics should not be confused with C++ templates. Although they serve similar purposes, templates are a compile-time technique, whereas generics survive until runtime, as seen through our IL code inspection. This results in several advantages, such as the capability to declare a generic type in one language and use it from another one, which is one of the main features of .NET.

Not only classes support generics. Structs and interfaces do, too, as illustrated by the IEnumerable<T> and IEnumerator<T> interfaces in System.Collections.Generic:

```
public interface IEnumerable<out T> : IEnumerable {
    IEnumerator<T> GetEnumerator();
}

public interface IEnumerator<out T> : IDisposable, IEnumerator {
    T Current { get; }
}
```

WHAT'S THE OUT MODIFIER USED FOR?

Don't freak out about the out modifier used on the declaration of the type parameter T in the preceding fragment. Later in this chapter, in the section "Co- and Contravariance," you read in great detail about this feature called *generic covariance*, introduced in C# 4.0.

It's not uncommon for generic interfaces to have their nongeneric counterparts in the implementation list, so that nongeneric usage is still possible when such a need arises for one reason or another.

Type parameters on the declaring type can be used as type parameters on other generic types. For example, in the IEnumerable<T> interface, the GetEnumerator method returns an IEnumerator<T>. All this says is that whenever IEnumerable<T> is instantiated with a type for its type parameter T, that same type will be used to instantiate the IEnumerator<T> returned by GetEnumerator.

How about implementing this interface? Different possibilities exist, one of which is to carry on the type parameter to the implementing type, which will become generic by itself in that case. List<T> is a good example because it implements IEnumerable<T>:

```
public class List<T> : ..., IEnumerable<T> {
    ...
}
```

Notice that the choice of the name for a type parameter is not tied to the declaring type. For example, when implementing to IEnumerable<T>, you are not required to use T as the name for the type parameter on the implementing type. In other words, at the use site, you can choose a different name:

```
public class List<TElement> : ..., IEnumerable<TElement> {
    ...
}
```

In fact, Visual Studio will show you the mapping between the type parameter names at the declaration site and use site. Figure 15.8 shows IntelliSense revealing parameter names and their mapping.

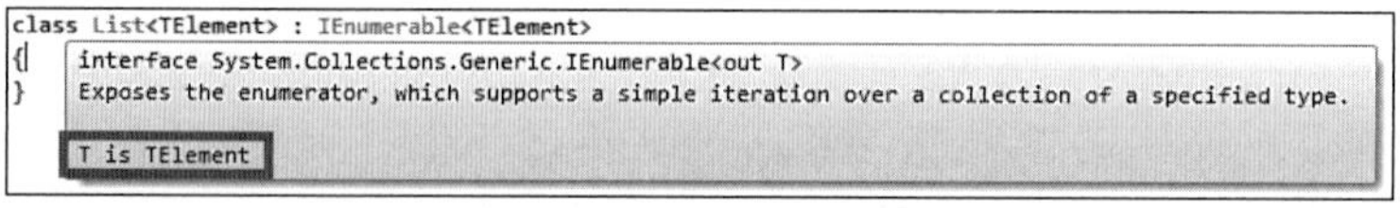

```
class List<TElement> : IEnumerable<TElement>
{|    interface System.Collections.Generic.IEnumerable<out T>
}    Exposes the enumerator, which supports a simple iteration over a collection of a specified type.

   T is TElement
```

FIGURE 15.8   Naming of type parameters is flexible.

Instead of propagating type parameters, you can also implement a generic interface by supplying any of its type parameters:

```
class Numbers : IEnumerable<int> {
    public IEnumerator<int> GetEnumerator() {
        ...
    }

    ...
}
```

Because a type parameter can be substituted for any type (though, as you see later, this can be restricted by use of *constraints*), it can be filled in with a generic type by itself, too. A good example is found on IDictionary<TKey, TValue>, a generic interface of arity two, meaning it has two type parameters:

```
public interface IDictionary<TKey, TValue> : ...,
                    IEnumerable<KeyValuePair<TKey, TValue>> {
    ...
}
```

Here, notice how the IEnumerable<T> interface is getting implemented with another generic type in its T type parameter position. KeyValuePair<TKey, TValue> by itself is a generic struct of arity two (the arity is the number of parameters):

```
public struct KeyValuePair<TKey, TValue> {
    public KeyValuePair(TKey key, TValue value);

    public TKey Key { get; }
    public TValue Value { get; }
}
```

Let's concretize this a little bit by performing a mental substitution of IDictionary's type parameters. Suppose we're implementing a phonebook where the key is a person's name (represented as a string) and the value is used to contain that person's phone number (for sake of argument represented as a simple int). This phonebook can be enumerated over, producing a sequence of key/value pairs that tie together a string (for the person name) with an int (for the phone number). An example is shown here:

```
var numbers = new Dictionary<string, int> {
    { "Bart", 911 },
    { "John", 119 }
};

foreach (KeyValuePair<string, int> entry in numbers) {
    // Do something...
}
```

In the preceding code, we're using C# 3.0's collection initializers once more to populate the created dictionary object. This corresponds to the following code (using variables with a double underscore prefix to indicate their compiler-generated nature in case collection initializers are used):

```
var __temp = new Dictionary<string, int>();
__temp.Add("Bart", 911);
__temp.Add("John", 119);
var numbers = __temp;
```

The Add methods being called are defined on Dictionary<TKey, TValue> with the following signature, again using the type parameterization introduced by the containing type:

```
void Add(TKey key, TValue value);
```

This should give you a good initial idea about where type parameters can be used to make a type as *generic* as possible with regard to the objects it operates on, without losing any of the rich type information at compile time.

Using Generic Types

In our discussion about generic types, you learned how a generic type is used repeatedly. Let's concentrate on the phonebook example a bit more:

```
var numbers = new Dictionary<string, int> {
    { "Bart", 911 },
    { "John", 119 }
};
```

In the preceding code, we're making a *constructed generic type* by substituting the TKey type parameter for string and the TValue type parameter for int. As you expect from a great development environment, Visual Studio provides IntelliSense when supplying types for generic type parameters, as shown in Figure 15.9.

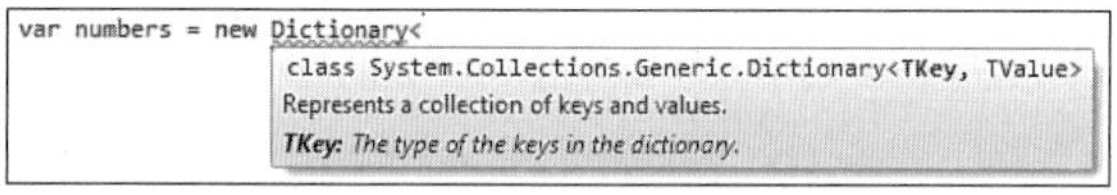

```
var numbers = new Dictionary<
                class System.Collections.Generic.Dictionary<TKey, TValue>
                Represents a collection of keys and values.
                TKey: The type of the keys in the dictionary.
```

FIGURE 15.9   Creating a constructed generic type with help from Visual Studio.

Behind the scenes, the type parameterization specified while creating a constructed generic type survives in the intermediate language (IL) code. Looking at it from a different angle, it's the CLR that's responsible for dealing with the creation of the ultimate type, rather than the front-end language compiler. As mentioned before, this is quite different from the way C++ templates work.

The role of the CLR—and in particular the Just-in-Time (JIT) compiler—is to come up with concrete memory layouts for all the constructed generic types it comes across at runtime. This effectively constitutes substitution of the holes created by type parameters, as you saw earlier during our discussion about the declaration of generic types. Ultimately, the result is just as if someone created a specialized nongeneric class with the parameter types baked into the appropriate positions, as shown in Figure 15.10.

NO ERASURE

Another platform that provides a way to parameterize types is Java. Despite sharing the name generics, the way it's implemented differs from the CLR's approach. Generic types in Java are more of a compile-time illusion, allowing the runtime to remain the same and even to target existing nongeneric collection types. All the compiler does is make sure the constructed generic types are used correctly, but in the end the type parameters are *erased* away.

To realize a true cross-language interop story and to eliminate inefficiencies like boxing of value types, the .NET folks chose to bake generics into the CLR type system instead.

Hole in the Type
List<T>
0[] elements;
List<int>
int[] elements;
List<string>
string[] elements;
Hole Got Filled Up

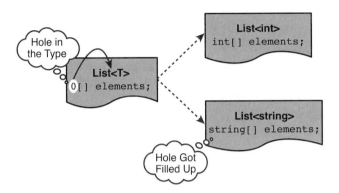

FIGURE 15.10 Creating a constructed generic type fills up the holes in the type definition.

Figure 15.11 shows the creation of a constructed generic type through the lenses of the ILDASM tool once more. Don't worry too much about the details, but observe how the full type information about the generic type's parameterization is preserved.

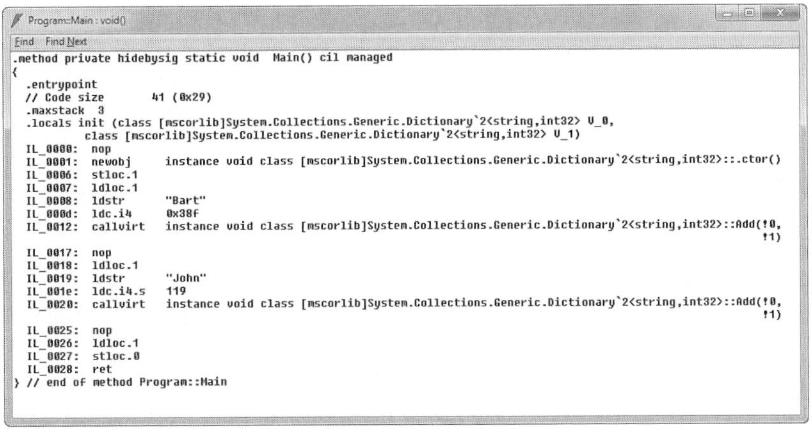

Program::Main : void()
Find Find Next
.method private hidebysig static void Main() cil managed
{
.entrypoint
// Code size 41 (0x29)
.maxstack 3
.locals init (class [mscorlib]System.Collections.Generic.Dictionary`2<string,int32> V_0,
class [mscorlib]System.Collections.Generic.Dictionary`2<string,int32> V_1)
IL_0000: nop
IL_0001: newobj instance void class [mscorlib]System.Collections.Generic.Dictionary`2<string,int32>::.ctor()
IL_0006: stloc.1
IL_0007: ldloc.1
IL_0008: ldstr "Bart"
IL_000d: ldc.i4 0x38f
IL_0012: callvirt instance void class [mscorlib]System.Collections.Generic.Dictionary`2<string,int32>::Add(!0, !1)
IL_0017: nop
IL_0018: ldloc.1
IL_0019: ldstr "John"
IL_001e: ldc.i4.s 119
IL_0020: callvirt instance void class [mscorlib]System.Collections.Generic.Dictionary`2<string,int32>::Add(!0, !1)
IL_0025: nop
IL_0026: ldloc.1
IL_0027: stloc.0
IL_0028: ret
} // end of method Program::Main

FIGURE 15.11 Constructing a generic type from an IL perspective.

Performance Intermezzo

As mentioned at the beginning of this chapter, one benefit of generic types is their allegedly better performance profile. An underlying problem also mentioned earlier in this chapter is the excessive boxing that occurs when storing value types using the most applicable type in .NET: System.Object.

WHAT ABOUT BOXING IN OTHER PLATFORMS?

.NET's capability to treat value types and reference types in the same manner is a side effect of its unified type system design philosophy. It allows all languages to think in terms of a single type hierarchy, abstracting away seemingly irrelevant differences between various kinds of types: Everything is a `System.Object` in the end.

Other platforms, such as Java, did not go that far and maintained some differentiation between values and references. In particular, primitive types could not be used in places where an `object` type was expected. Instead, wrapper classes (which are reference types) were created to bridge the gap. For example, an `int` value has a counterpart called `Integer`. In fact, this is nothing but manual boxing.

One positive implication of the Java approach is the fact that heap allocations get more visible because users must manually new up a wrapper object when adding it to a collection. However, it came at the cost of true unification of types, and with the advent of generics in this platform, things have gotten more implicit, too.

Going back to our sequential list example, we can ask ourselves what the most efficient collection type will be: `ArrayList` or its generic counterpart `List<T>`. As a reference for any measurements, we also consider a plain old array. Of course, we first need to define how we're going to test matters.

The only thing we're concerned about here is the cost of boxing: Is it really that bad? Because in this analysis we don't really care about dynamically growing collections, we'll fix the number of elements upfront. For an array, that's easy to do when creating the new array instance. And for the collection types, we can do so by specifying an initial capacity as a constructor argument. Internally, both `ArrayList` and `List<T>` use an array for the underlying storage, so effectively this corresponds to an array size specification:

```
const int N = 10000000; // 10 million elements
```

```
var array   = new int[N];
var arrList = new ArrayList(N);
var genList = new List<int>(N);
```

Because `ArrayList` is object based, the array that will keep the integer values inside of it will be an `object[]`. This is where we expect the costly boxing to kick in, as shown in Figure 15.12. Obviously, an array with element type `Int32` is the most efficient representation for the data, being a consecutive range of memory to keep the elements in. Because of the way generics work, we expect the `List<int>` to correspond to such an array internally.

Nevertheless, we shouldn't expect the generic `List<int>` to be as efficient as the plain old int array because the collection type has to do a little more work. On every insert into the list, it must check whether there's sufficient space left to store the value in the backing array storage. If not, it has to grow the array. We've avoided the condition of having to grow the array by setting an initial capacity, but the cost of checking against the current array size remains for every insert.

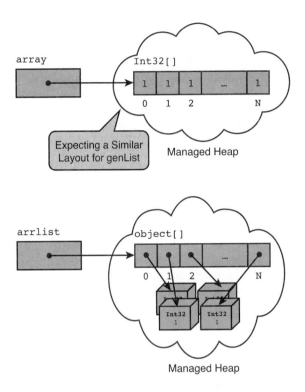

FIGURE 15.12   Storing `Int32` values in an object array causes boxing.

Based on this observation, we expect `List<int>` to be a bit slower than `int[]`. However, the use of an `ArrayList` to store `int` values is expected to be quite painful due to the cost of having to box up the values when storing them in the array, as well as the inverse when retrieving a boxed value and casting it back to the value type.

In addition, we expect the excessive use of boxing behind the scenes to add pressure to the garbage collector (observe the huge managed heap cloud in Figure 15.12), so the number of garbage collections will provide an idea about the cost, too. So let's put things to the test and write some code. First, here's a helper method:

```
static void Measure(string message, Action a) {
    var sw = new Stopwatch();
    sw.Start();
    a();
    sw.Stop();
    Console.WriteLine(message, sw.Elapsed);
}
```

`Measure` takes in a message to be printed in the form of a format string with a `{0}` hole where the elapsed time will be stuffed in. The second parameter is a delegate of type

`Action`, something we examine in excruciating detail in Chapter 17, "Delegates." Think of it as a way to pass a piece of code in, which will get invoked on the third line.

MEASURE, MEASURE, MEASURE... BUT DO IT RIGHT!

Performance is a verb: to measure. Keep in mind this experiment is merely to prove a point about generic types. In the real world, you should spend your valuable time hunting down performance bottlenecks that impact your application's performance. But to know whether there's an impact, you first need to establish a min-bar against which to *measure* your performance. For example: "the time to respond to the user should be under a certain threshold." In summary, optimize what matters. But at the same time, it doesn't hurt to have some basic idea what to look for, like boxing.

One word of advice can't be omitted: If you measure (and you *should* if you want to assess your app's performance), do it right! The `StopWatch` class in `System.Diagnostics` is your best friend whenever you want to do performance measurements. Don't use subtraction of `DateTime.Now` values because those don't have a large enough time resolution to be useful or trustworthy for purposes of performance measurements. `StopWatch`, on the other hand, uses low-level Windows primitives to perform the measurement based on a higher-resolution timer.

The key takeaway is this: Avoid premature optimizations, set a min-bar, measure against it, and save your valuable time for things that really matter.

Given our little measurement helper method, we'll kick off six tests: reading from and writing to each of the three collection types. In addition, we'll print out the number of garbage collections as we go along. First, here's our `ArrayList`:

```
Measure("Write ArrayList: {0}", () => {
    for (int i = 0; i < N; i++)
        arrList.Add(1); // Expected: BOXING!
});
Measure("Read ArrayList:  {0}", () => {
    int sum = 0;
    for (int i = 0; i < N; i++)
        sum += (int)arrList[i]; // Expected: UNBOXING!
});
PrintGCStats();
```

Don't worry about the syntax used to pass the `Action` delegate as the second argument to the `Measure` method calls. This syntax, called lambda expression syntax, will become clear to you in Chapter 17, "Delegates." Until then, read it as an inline method declaration taking no arguments (hence the empty pair of parentheses) and that *goes to* (the fat arrow token =>) a method body containing the code to execute (between curly braces).

In the preceding code, we expect that storing elements in the `ArrayList` will cause boxing because the underlying storage type is an object array (and in fact, it occurs much earlier as we're passing the constant value 1 *as an object* to the Add method). When reading from the list using indexer syntax, we must cast the retrieved object back to the Int32 value type, something we expect to cause unboxing.

The PrintGCStats method uses the System.GC class to query the garbage collector for statistics about the number of collections carried out so far during the runtime of the program, on a per-generation basis. (See earlier chapters in this book for more information about this.)

```
static void PrintGCStats() {
    Console.WriteLine("Gen 0: {0}, Gen 1: {1}, Gen 2: {2}\n",
        GC.CollectionCount(1), GC.CollectionCount(2), GC.CollectionCount(3));
}
```

Next, we do the same for the generic List<int> type. For this case, we expect things to be better because the storage array will get strongly typed at runtime when the CLR creates a specialized constructed generic type:

```
Measure("Write List<int>: {0}", () => {
    for (int i = 0; i < N; i++)
        genList.Add(1); // Expected: capacity check
});
Measure("Read List<int>:  {0}", () => {
    int sum = 0;
    for (int i = 0; i < N; i++)
        sum += genList[i];
});
PrintGCStats();
```

Notice how the read loop no longer needs a cast expression because the indexer on the generic list object will be statically typed to produce an int value.

Finally, to establish a basis for comparisons, we apply the same tests to a plain int array, which we expect to get the best performance across the board. After all, each of the collection types we're testing encapsulates an array:

```
Measure("Write int array: {0}", () => {
    for (int i = 0; i < N; i++)
        array[i] = 1;
});
Measure("Read int array:  {0}", () => {
    int sum = 0;
    for (int i = 0; i < N; i++)
        sum += array[i];
});
PrintGCStats();
```

Again, no boxing is expected because the array is statically typed to have Int32 elements, and getting elements out of it is a statically typed operation, too, requiring no casts. Time to run all of our tests! Figure 15.13 shows my results.

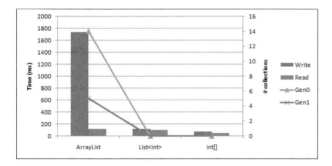

FIGURE 15.13   Execution time and the number of garbage collections.

From this, you can clearly see how the ArrayList has put significant pressure on the heap due to the excessive boxing for the 10 million elements stored in it. In fact, this has triggered no less than 14 gen0 collections and even a handful of gen1 collections, which are more expensive. No wonder the performance of ArrayList is quite terrible compared to raw array accesses.

Use of generics, on the other hand, makes things much better. First, we didn't cause any more garbage collections, and performance got very close to raw arrays. Although there's still a minor performance difference compared to raw arrays, don't forget about the additional value added by generic collections (for example, the capability to dynamically expand the collection when needed).

Operations on Type Parameters

Let's ask ourselves a quick question: Given a type parameter T, what kind of operations can we carry out over it? Because the type parameter T can be substituted for *anything*, our generic code can't deal with *specifics* of a certain type. Nevertheless, a few basic operations can be meaningfully defined.

Default Values

One operation is to retrieve a default value for a type parameter. For a reference type, the default value is always the null reference, whereas for value types it's a value with all-zero content. This is something the CLR can meaningfully provide as an operation that makes sense for any type parameter used. In C# terms, this is realized using the default keyword:

```
int      zero = default(int);
string   @null = default(string);
T        @default = default(T); // could be null, could be all-zero
```

One place that comes to mind where this can be put to handy use is inside constructors for generic types, initializing fields of a generic parameter type. This is a bit far-fetched, though, because the default behavior is to provide all fields in their default state upon object construction (a hard guarantee made by the runtime). A better example is when we need to clear a field of type generic parameter type T outside the constructor (for example, when writing a generic cache mechanism):

```
class Cache<T> {
    private bool _invalidated;
    private T _value;

    // Provide a way to recompute the value, for example, using a delegate.
    // In fact, the BCL has a similar construct called Lazy<T>.

    public void Reset() {
        _invalidated = true;
        _value = default(T);
    }
}
```

Here, we need to reset the cached value by setting the stored value back to its default value. By doing so, for a reference type, the stored object is no longer referenced and can hence be reclaimed by the garbage collector.

WEAK REFERENCES

In fact, the framework provides a more fundamental mechanism to deal with the situation where an object is handy to have but an application can live with it being collected by the garbage collector (for example, because it can be recomputed if needed). This mechanism is called a weak reference and is exposed through a type in the BCL called (how surprising) WeakReference.

In fact, the garbage collector knows about this special type and knows to give it special treatment. Inside the WeakReference lives a System.Object-typed object that can be accessed through a Target property. A property called IsAlive can be checked to see whether the target object is still there or has been reclaimed because the garbage collector thought there was a better use of memory on the system.

For more information, take a look at the MSDN documentation on the topic.

Let's take a quick look at how the default(T) expression gets realized in IL. In essence, the initobj instruction can deal with any type specified as its operand, turning the referenced location into the type's default value. The first two nontrivial lines of the code take the address of the this._value field, which is then used as an input to initobj to zero out the contents, resulting in either a null reference or an all-zero value type. Figure 15.14 shows the inner workings of default(T).

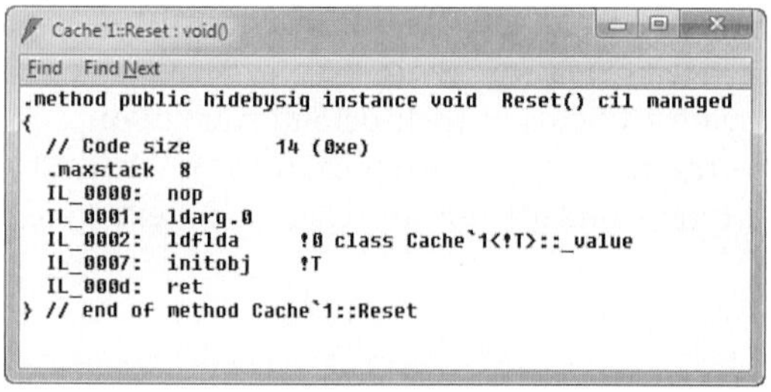

FIGURE 15.14   `Default(T)` relies on `initobj` to get its behavior.

Getting the Type's Reflection Info Object

The other operation that's meaningfully defined on a generic parameter T is the `typeof` expression that gets the `System.Type` object describing, at runtime, the type that was supplied for the type parameter T:

```
Type t = typeof(T);
var methods = t.GetMethods();
```

Because you'll be reading a whole chapter about reflection (Chapter 21, "Reflection"), we defer further discussion about `System.Type` until later. Practically speaking, you should rarely have to use the `typeof(T)` trick.

Generic Constraints

So far, you've learned how to declare a generic type and how to use it. Although the latter operation will be your main point of contact with the world of generics, you'll sometimes want to write your own generic type. However, up to this point, we haven't been able to do much with a generic type parameter inside the type definition. Let's take a look from an abstract point of view first. Consider the following piece of code:

```
class Foo<T> {
    public void Bar(T input) {
        // What can be do with T?
    }
}
```

The main question is what we can do with the input received as a parameter on `Bar`. For one thing, we can take the object and store it somewhere (for example, in a private field). That's precisely what a `List<T>` does, sticking the received elements in an array with element type T. For example:

```
class Foo<T> {
    private T _field;

    public void Bar(T input) {
        _field = input;
    }
}
```

Similarly, we could read from a field typed a T and give the object back through some means like a method, a property, or an indexer. But maybe we also want to perform certain actions on an object of the parameter type T. Let's see in Visual Studio what IntelliSense suggests in Figure 15.15.

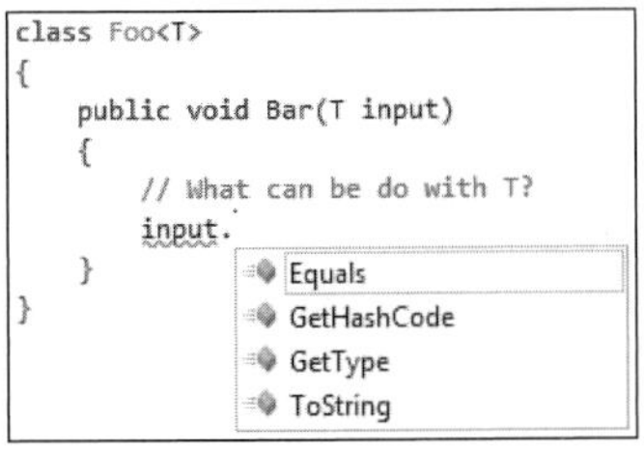

FIGURE 15.15   The compiler doesn't know about T other than it should be an object. D'oh!

What we're seeing here is nothing more than the IntelliSense for the instance members on System.Object. This really makes sense because T can be substituted for everything, an int, a string, another generic type, whatever. And all of those have nothing in common except that they all derive from System.Object at some point.

So can't we do anything but those operations on an object declared to be of a generic parameter? Luckily, the answer is no. By putting constraints on type parameters, we can enrich the number of operations we can perform. That sounds a little contradictory at first, so let's examine this further. You'll see this is nothing but a world of give and take.

Generic constraints are a way to restrict the constructed types that can be created from a generic type definition. In other words, what gets *constrained* is the use site of the generic type. As a result, the declaration site gets more *guarantees* about operations it can perform with objects typed to be of the constrained type parameter. So by *giving* more guarantees about the type parameter to the generic type using it, we're taking away some of the flexibility as to which constructed generic types can be defined out of it.

Interface-Based Constraints

An example is in order. Suppose we want to create a collection that can keep elements sorted. To make the collection maximally applicable, we want to declare it as a generic type. However, just creating an OrderedList<T> is too permissive because not every type is suitable for sorting purposes. So we want to constrain the flexibility on the type parameter

T by saying we only allow "types T that are orderable." What makes a type orderable? That starts to smell like a *contract*, something that can be enforced by the implementation of a certain interface. IComparable<T> comes to mind:

```
public interface IComparable<in T> {
    int CompareTo(T other);
}
```

If we can compare any two objects of type T, we can keep things sorted. Lots of types in the .NET Framework, especially the primitive types, implement IComparable<T>:

```
public struct Int32 : ..., IComparable<Int32> {
    public int CompareTo(Int32 value) {
        return this - value; // if this < value, the result is negative; etc
    }
}
```

The semantics of IComparable<T>'s CompareTo method should be easy to understand: If the current object (this) is less than the specified object of the same type (value parameter), the return value is negative; if it's equal, the result is zero; if it's greater, we get a positive value back.

The remaining question is how to make our OrderedList<T> constrained to accept only types T that implement IComparable<T>. The answer lies in the where keyword:

```
class OrderedList<T> where T : IComparable<T> {
    // Now we can use the CompareTo method on objects of type T...
}
```

In this particular case, we're saying that OrderedList<T> can only accept, for its type parameter T, types that implement (the colon syntax) IComparable<T>. Let's see what this adds to the things we can do *inside* the generic type first. Assume we're using a List<T> as the internal storage for an OrderedList<T> so that we don't have to worry about dynamically growing array-based storage. Now we have the task to implement an Add method that will insert the object in the right spot based on comparisons made to the existing elements:

```
class OrderedList<T> where T : IComparable<T> {
    private List<T> _elements = new List<T>();

    public void Add(T value) {
        int i = 0;
        while (i < _elements.Count) {
            if (_elements[i].CompareTo(value) >= 0)
                break;
            i++;
```

```
        }
        _elements.Insert(i, value);
    }}
```

This algorithm is naively simple, and much better ways exist to keep a sorted collection using tree structures and whatnot, but what matters to us here is how the constraint now allows us to rely on the CompareTo method on objects of type T. In this particular case, the compiler knows that List<T>'s indexer will return an object of type T. Because the value argument passed to Add is also of type T, it's possible to resolve the CompareTo method call correctly as proven in Figure 15.16.

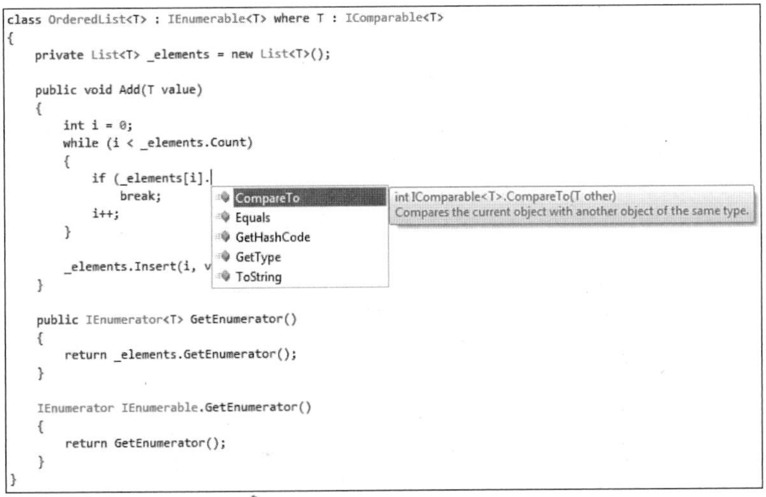

```
class OrderedList<T> : IEnumerable<T> where T : IComparable<T>
{
    private List<T> _elements = new List<T>();

    public void Add(T value)
    {
        int i = 0;
        while (i < _elements.Count)
        {
            if (_elements[i].|
                break;                CompareTo          int IComparable<T>.CompareTo(T other)
            i++;                     Equals             Compares the current object with another object of the same type.
        }                            GetHashCode
                                     GetType
        _elements.Insert(i, v        ToString
    }

    public IEnumerator<T> GetEnumerator()
    {
        return _elements.GetEnumerator();
    }

    IEnumerator IEnumerable.GetEnumerator()
    {
        return GetEnumerator();
    }
}
```

FIGURE 15.16   IntelliSense knows about the generic constraints.

To convince yourself this algorithm works (and to get an idea about how suboptimal this choice of algorithm is), you can use the following code:

```
var ordered = new OrderedList<int>();
var rand = new Random();
for (int i = 0; i < 10000; i++)
    ordered.Add(rand.Next(100));

bool faulty = false;
int prev = -1;

// Note: don't forget to implement GetEnumerator methods as shown in Figure 15.16.
foreach (var n in ordered) {
    if (prev > n) {
        faulty = true;
```

```
        break;
    }
}
Console.WriteLine(!faulty);
```

The reason this code compiles fine is because the OrderedList<T> type is given a type parameter, int, that obeys to the constraint of being IComparable<T>. However, if we try to construct a generic OrderedList type given a type that doesn't implement this interface, the compiler will complain (see Figure 15.17).

FIGURE 15.17   Generic constraints are enforced at compile time.

MORE FUN WITH DATA STRUCTURES

The data-structure-savvy reader might find it an interesting exercise to implement a more efficient OrderedList<T> type based on binary search trees. As you will see, the BCL has such data structures out of the box, so consider this exercise a brainteaser rather than a necessity.

As soon as we implement the IComparable<T> interface on Person, this code will start to compile fine. This emphasizes how powerful generics are: We've essentially written what it means to keep a list ordered just once, and it automatically works for every type that supports comparison. For example, we could make a Person orderable by Age:

```
class Person : IComparable<Person> {
    public Person(string name, int age) {
        Name = name;
        Age = age;
    }
```

```
    public string Name { get; private set; }
    public int Age { get; private set; }

    public int CompareTo(Person other) {
        return this.Age - other.Age;
    }
}
```

A DIFFERENT LOOK AT ORDERING

Our SortedList<T> follows the ordering semantics implemented on T by means of an
IComparable<T> implementation. For types like Person, it's highly unlikely to see an
implementation of IComparable<T> because it would require to "prefer" a certain
ordering key over another. In the preceding example, we chose the Age property for the
natural order of Person objects, but there isn't really a "natural" ordering defined here.
IComparable<T> usually makes much more sense for value types.

With LINQ, as you'll see in Chapter 19, "Language Integrated Query Essentials," query
operators will be layered on top of IEnumerable<T>, allowing arbitrary ordering keys to
be specified by the user, rather than the person who implemented (or forgot to do so)
the IComparable<T> interface on the objects in the collection to be sorted.

As you've seen in this example, the use of interfaces as constraints on type parameters is a
very useful feature. Once more, I want to emphasize the importance of the IL-level representation because it provides the essential glue required to work with generic types across
multiple languages, without losing any of its expressive power. After all, if you define a
constrained generic type, you don't want users of any language in the .NET arsenal to be
able to violate that constraint. So let's see how the generic type carries along its
constraints by looking in ILDASM in Figure 15.18.

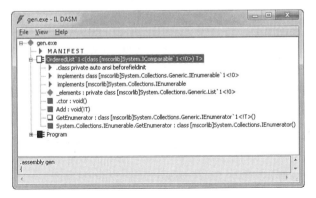

FIGURE 15.18   Generic constraints survive in IL, making them work cross-language.

It goes almost without saying that multiple constraints are allowed on a single generic type parameter, just like a type can implement multiple interfaces. To express this, use a comma-separated list of constraints on the same parameter:

```
class OrderedList<T> where T : IComparable<T>, ISerializable {
    ...
}
```

When dealing with multiple type parameters, each of those can have its own set of constraints, requiring multiple uses of the where keyword:

```
class OrderedDictionary<K, T>
    where K : IComparable<K>
    where T : IComparable<T> {
    ...
}
```

In addition, it's possible to express generic constraints that establish a relationship between multiple type parameters (sometimes called a *naked type constraint*):

```
class Bar<TDerived, TBase> where TDerived : TBase {
    ...
}
```

This is much less common in practice than simple interface-based constraints, but it's good to know about the expressiveness of generic constraints.

HOW I WISH THERE WERE AN INTERFACE FOR...

Being able to express generic constraints based on interface types is one thing; having enough widely used interfaces around is another. One place where the lack of an interface-driven design tends to be problematic is when dealing with operator overloading.

As you've seen before, operator overloading on the .NET Framework is realized by using static methods. As opposed to implementing operators by using some interface, this allows a null reference as the left side for an operator. Also, the flexibility to overload operators based on types makes a naïve interface-driven approach like the one shown here not very appealing:

```
interface IMultiply<T> {
    T Add(T left, T right);
}
```

For example, vector multiplication has various forms, allowing for multiplication with a scalar but also between two vectors. In addition, the return type can also vary depending on the use of a dot product or a cross-product.

Generic constraints are not expressive enough to express the requirement of an operator to be present on a generic type parameter. If we were to have interfaces as containers for operator contracts, generic constraints based on interfaces could be used.

The ability to constrain based on operators has been a longstanding request, but the fear is this could turn into a black hole where the number of different constraint mechanisms keeps growing release after release. Only the future will tell whether there will ever be enough motivation to design, implement, test, and document such a feature. If you have a definite need for this, raise your voice loud and clear and make sure the .NET language teams can hear it. In the meantime, make sure to look at F# as well, where numeric data types get a somewhat different treatment, especially if you find yourself back in the domain of scientific computing.

Base Class Constraints

Not just interfaces can be used to constrain a type parameter to only those types that implement it; base classes can also be used to enforce a similar relationship. You can constrain a type parameter such that only subclasses of a specified base class can be used to instantiate the parameter:

```
class FruitMixer<T> where T : Fruit {
    private T[] _ingredients;
    public FruitMixer(params T[] ingredients) {
        _ingredients = ingredients;
    }
}
```

Enforcement of the constraint is similar to what we've seen with interfaces. The following will work fine, for the obvious reason that every Jonagold is an Apple:

```
var appleMixer = new FruitMixer<Apple>(new Jonagold());
```

Notice that generics go hand in hand with the well-known capability to pass in an object of a more-specific type where a less-specific type is expected. Even though the constructor used to create the FruitMixer<Apple> instance will be typed to take in a params array of Apples, we can put in elements of a more derived type, like Jonagold. However, when you try to construct the generic type using a type that doesn't derive from Fruit, you'll get into trouble at compile time:

```
var cementMixer = new CementMixer<Cement>();
```

Adding a constraint to the users of the generic type provides more guarantees for the party declaring the generic type. Because we're guaranteed to get only Fruit-derived types, we can rely on the methods defined on the type Fruit:

```
class FruitMixer<T> where T : Fruit {
    private T[] _ingredients;

    public FruitMixer(params T[] ingredients) {
        _ingredients = ingredients;
    }

    public Juice MakeJuice() {
        var juice = new Juice();

        foreach (T ingredient in _ingredients)
            juice += ingredient.Squeeze();

        return juice;
    }
}
```

Default Constructor Constraint

Besides generic constraints expressed based on interfaces or base classes, a few other techniques are available. One is the new constraint, expressing the requirement to have a default constructor available for a certain type parameter:

```
class Factory<T> where T : new() {
    ...

    public T CreateInstance() {
        return new T();
    }
}
```

Obviously, the preceding Factory<T> type's CreateInstance method doesn't provide any value over direct instantiation of an object from the outside. It's merely a way to show how the expected constructor syntax can be used in conjunction with a type parameter as long as that parameter is properly constrained. From the outside, this type would be used as follows:

```
var factory = new Factory<int>();
var zero = factory.CreateInstance();
```

It turns out the Int32 type has a default constructor (returning the default value 0), so this works fine. In contrast, a type that doesn't have a default constructor gets rejected for use in place of the generic parameter T. Figure 15.19 shows the compile-time error that results in that case.

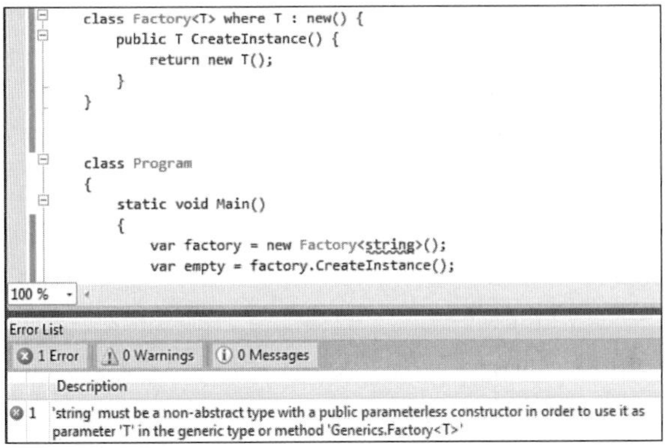

FIGURE 15.19   Violation against a default constructor constraint.

A place where a *default constructor constraint* comes in handy is when you need a way to instantiate an object of a parameter type (for example, to provide default storage or to reset items in some kind of storage). Consider a service object pool as an example of such a situation. On the essential level, a pool could look like this:

```
class ServicePool<T> : IService where T : IService, new() {
    private List<T> _objects;

    public ServicePool(int min, int max) { /* TODO */ }
}

// Any IService interface would do, so we just give a simple example here.
interface IService
{
    void TransferFunds(string sourceAccount, string targetAccount, decimal amount);
}
```

At the type level, a ServicePool<T> implements a certain service interface, exposing that functionality to the outside world. To provide this service, it delegates all requests to worker objects that implement the same interface. This explains the type definition and its constraint:

```
class ServicePool<T>
    : IService            // expose the service to the outside
    where T : IService,   // need to be able to delegate to a worker
              new()       // need to be able to instantiate workers as needed
```

The pool is responsible for making sure a certain minimum number of workers are on standby at any time. It does so by creating instances of the worker type, as specified through the type parameter T, leveraging the default constructor constraint.

Whenever a request on the pool's service interface arrives, the request is forwarded to one of the available workers, also marking that worker as occupied somehow. This implies that a different, preferably thread-safe, data structure will have to be used to keep track of workers who are either occupied or available (free). When the request finishes, the worker can be returned to the free list, ready to serve other requests. Figure 15.20 shows an interaction sequence with a service pool.

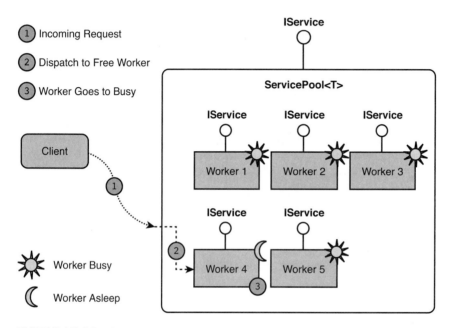

FIGURE 15.20   Service pool interaction sequence.

It might be the case that a request arrives when no free workers are available. If the threshold on the maximum number of workers hasn't been reached yet, the pool can choose to create more worker instances, again using the default constructor constraint. This on-demand instantiation of workers is shown in Figure 15.21.

Other mechanisms can be implemented to keep the pool as efficient as possible (for example, by dropping workers from the pool if the workload on the service pool drops). This could be beneficial to reduce resource consumption (for example, when workers keep a connection open to another machine serving requests). And by making a (reference typed) object unreachable, it can be reclaimed from the managed heap, too.

IMPACT OF GENERICS ON THE CLS

The Common Language Specification (CLS) is the key to .NET's true cross-language interoperability story. By having multiple languages adhere to a set of rules, it becomes possible to get full-fidelity integration with regard to types and their use.

When the CLS was introduced back in the early .NET 1.0 days, a lot of languages implemented the "CLS roles" (refer to Chapter 1, "Introducing the .NET Platform," for more information about this). To make generics in .NET 2.0 and beyond stand out as a first-class .NET Framework feature, the CLS had to be extended with extra rules to ensure cross-language interoperability when dealing with such types.

Given the huge benefit that generics provide, having to put an additional burden on language implementers was considered a good tradeoff. Hooray!

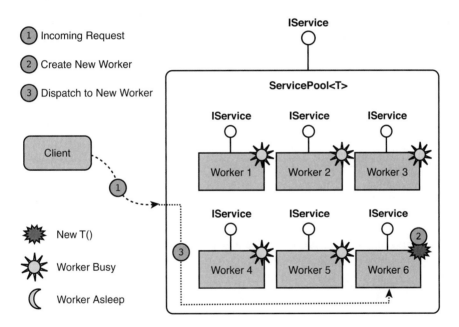

FIGURE 15.21   Service pool interaction sequence.

Obviously, we all wonder how the new T() call is realized under the hood. First, notice the generic constraint mechanism is enabled for cross-language use. This is shown in Figure 15.22, where the .ctor T part reveals the constraint made it through the compilation all the way into metadata for other languages to inspect.

More interesting things go on at the place the new T() is compiled. In fact, my choice to present a Factory<T> with a CreateInstance method wasn't arbitrary because it acts as a great starting point for our discussion of *generic methods* in a moment. Let's take a look at what's going on inside CreateInstance, shown in Figure 15.23.

gen.exe - IL DASM
File View Help
gen.exe
MANIFEST
Factory`1<.ctor T>
.class private auto ansi beforefieldinit
.ctor : void()
CreateInstance : !T()
OrderedList`1<(class [mscorlib]System.IComparable`1<!0>) T>
Program
.assembly gen
{

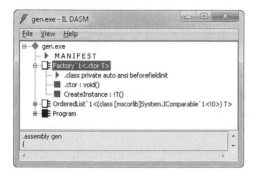

FIGURE 15.22 The default constructor constraint works cross-language.

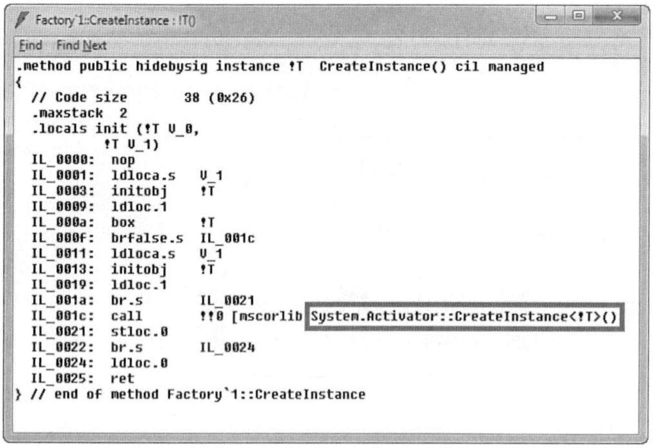

Factory`1::CreateInstance : !T()
Find Find Next
.method public hidebysig instance !T CreateInstance() cil managed
{
// Code size 38 (0x26)
.maxstack 2
.locals init (!T V_0,
!T V_1)
IL_0000: nop
IL_0001: ldloca.s V_1
IL_0003: initobj !T
IL_0009: ldloc.1
IL_000a: box !T
IL_000f: brfalse.s IL_001c
IL_0011: ldloca.s V_1
IL_0013: initobj !T
IL_0019: ldloc.1
IL_001a: br.s IL_0021
IL_001c: call !!0 [mscorlib]System.Activator::CreateInstance<!T>()
IL_0021: stloc.0
IL_0022: br.s IL_0024
IL_0024: ldloc.0
IL_0025: ret
} // end of method Factory`1::CreateInstance

FIGURE 15.23 `Activator.CreateInstance<T>` is a generic factory method in the BCL.

Don't worry too much about the boilerplate code in here, emitted to provide different treatment for reference type and value type parameters. What's more worthwhile to take a look at is how the `new T()` call ultimately results in a call to a BCL method on a type called `Activator`, shown in Figure 15.24. Its role is to provide a one-stop shop for all imaginable sorts of *object activation* calls, ultimately leading to the construction of an object of a given type. Most overloads use reflection primitives, such as `System.Type`, as you learn Chapter 21.

In .NET 2.0, a static generic method called `CreateInstance<T>` was added. We take a look at generic methods shortly, but the essence is simply this: Methods by themselves can have a list of type parameters, independent of the type in which they're contained. In the case of `System.Activator`, the class type itself is not generic, whereas `CreateInstance` is:

```
class Activator {
    public static T CreateInstance<T>() {
        ...
    }
}
```

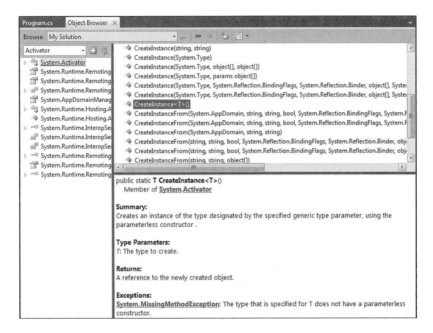

FIGURE 15.24   A look at System.Activator.

How CreateInstance performs its magic by calling into the depths of the CLR is beyond the scope of this book. Nevertheless, full disclosure requires that I mention that the machinery required to discover a default constructor dynamically at runtime is more expensive than cases where the compiler knows statically what constructor to call. Constructors are just methods at the IL level, and methods contain the name of the type on which they are defined. Obviously, in case of a generic parameter, this information is missing at the place where the new T() call is made, as T can be substituted for everything.

This requires the CLR's reflection system to be used to discover the default constructor at runtime. As the fourth frame in the call stack in Figure 15.25 reveals, reflection can put us on a slower execution path. If you don't see the gray-highlighted methods in the Call Stack window, just right-click a line in the window and choose Show External Code.

Notice that, despite dynamic constructor discovery at runtime, languages understanding generic constraints will prevent the generic type from being constructed using a type parameter that violates the constraint. Or to put it another way, in languages such as C# we're *statically* guaranteed that this *dynamic* discovery will succeed at runtime.

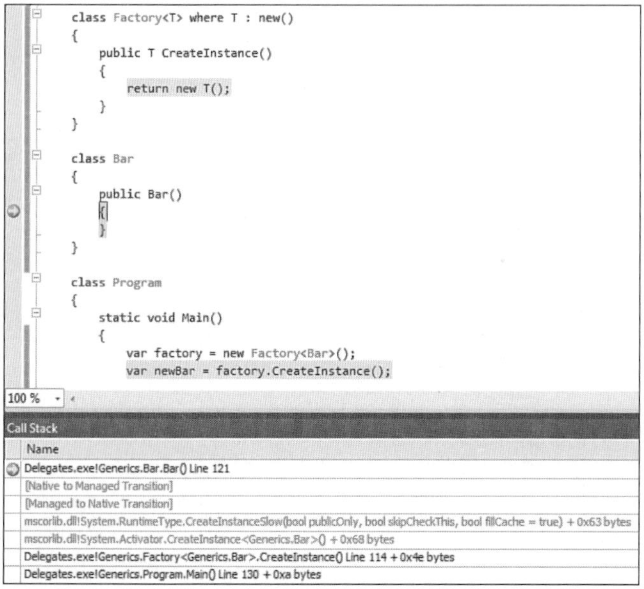

```
class Factory<T> where T : new()
{
    public T CreateInstance()
    {
        return new T();
    }
}

class Bar
{
    public Bar()
    {
    |
    }
}

class Program
{
    static void Main()
    {
        var factory = new Factory<Bar>();
        var newBar = factory.CreateInstance();
```

100 % ▾ ◂

Call Stack

Name
Delegates.exe!Generics.Bar.Bar() Line 121
[Native to Managed Transition]
[Managed to Native Transition]
mscorlib.dll!System.RuntimeType.CreateInstanceSlow(bool publicOnly, bool skipCheckThis, bool fillCache = true) + 0x63 bytes
mscorlib.dll!System.Activator.CreateInstance<Generics.Bar>() + 0x68 bytes
Delegates.exe!Generics.Factory<Generics.Bar>.CreateInstance() Line 114 + 0x4e bytes
Delegates.exe!Generics.Program.Main() Line 130 + 0xa bytes

FIGURE 15.25   `CreateInstance` invokes CLR machinery to discover a default constructor.

EVERYTHING IS RELATIVE...

Even though we've pointed out this little caveat on the hidden use of reflection-based mechanisms, the chance of this becoming your application's performance bottleneck is rather slim. As usual with performance, establish a baseline and measure against it. Use of generics often simplifies code significantly, which is definitely a more valuable thing in the long run compared to wasting your time on premature optimizations. Enhanced code readability reduces code maintenance costs. Unfortunately, code readability is overseen as a potentially huge cost-saver way too often.

Taking a step back and looking at this alleged pitfall from a different angle, we can make another conclusion: If `CreateInstance` becomes a real bottleneck due to the rate at which it gets called, you likely are going to have other problems too. Don't forget you're instantiating objects and hence allocating memory. This is usually a cheap operation on the managed heap unless you're doing it so excessively that garbage collection is triggered. Everything is relative.

While we're at it, you might wonder whether the same caveat applies for interface-based constraints: Do those result in reflection-based method lookups, as well? Lucky for us, the answer is no. This is because calls on the target object can be made through the interface, relying on low-level machinery in the CLR to dispatch the call efficiently. If you were to analyze the Add method of our OrderedList<T> class in more depth at the IL level, you would see something like this:

```
ldloca.s   V_1     // fetching array element "_elements[i]"
ldarg.1            // the method's "value" parameter to compare to
constrained. !T
callvirt   instance int32 class System.IComparable`1<!T>::CompareTo(!0)
ldc.i4.0           // load the constant 0
clt                // and compare the CompareTo result was less than 0
```

On the fourth line, you can clearly see a method call made to the CompareTo method on
the interface, using the callvirt IL instruction. The constrained prefix on the line above
it was added to the IL instruction set in .NET 2.0 to allow compilers to simplify the code
emitted for method calls, regardless of whether the target object is a value type or a reference type. This became very desirable in the face of generic types because type parameters
can be filled up with either value types or reference types.

Restriction to Value Types or Reference Types

Talking about different treatment for value types and reference types, one more way to
constrain a generic type exists. Using the class and struct keywords, a type parameter can
be constrained to accept only reference types or value types, respectively:

```
class HasRef<T> where T : class {
    private T _reference;
}
class HasVal<T> where T : struct {
    private T _value;
}
```

For the reference type constraint, using the class keyword, any reference type can be
used, including classes, interfaces, and delegates. For value types, using the struct
keyword, you can use all value types but no nullable types.

Notice that based on the constraint, the compiler again rejects certain uses both at the
declaration site and use site. Compile-time checks carried out at the use site are
predictable: If you use a value type where a class constraint is used, the compiler will
complain (similarly in the other direction for a struct constraint). At the declaration site,
a struct constraint will reject uses of null references. For example:

```
class HasVal<T> where T : struct {
    private T _value;

    public bool IsNull() {
        return _value == null; // Fails to compile
    }
}
```

REUSE OF KEYWORDS

Ever since the beginning, the C# language has reused keywords in various places, often to mean fundamentally different things. Although the meaning should be clear from the context in which the keyword occurs, sometimes this can cause a bit of confusion. A few examples (omitting quite a few other examples) follow:

▶ In C# 1.0, the `this` keyword is used to refer to the current instance from within a class or struct, to call one constructor from another, or to write an indexer.

▶ In C# 2.0, generic type declarations reuse the `new`, `class`, and `struct` keywords to express generic constraints, as explained earlier.

▶ In C# 3.0, the `this` keyword gets reused for extension methods, the `in` keyword appears in LINQ queries, and so does the `where` keyword for query filters.

▶ In C# 4.0, generic co- and contravariance (which is discussed in the section "Co- and Contravariance," later in this chapter) reuse the keywords `in` and `out`.

Being able to enumerate all the uses of a keyword is a good check of your language skills.

One example where the restriction to value types is used inside the framework itself is the definition of `Nullable<T>`:

```
public struct Nullable<T> where T : struct {
    public bool HasValue { get { /* definition omitted */ } }
    public T Value { get { /* definition omitted */ } }

    public T GetValueOrDefault() { /* definition omitted */ }
    public T GetValueOrDefault(T defaultValue) { /* definition omitted */ }

    ...
}
```

Generic Methods

Classes, structs, interfaces, and delegates (see Chapter 17) are not the only things that can be declared using generics. Methods can make use of generics, too. A generic method is simply a method that has one or more type parameters that can be used for its parameter types or return type.

Syntactically, the type parameter list is put between angle brackets in between the name of the method and the parameter list. A great source for generic method examples is in the LINQ extension methods defined on the `Enumerable` type defined in the `System.Collection.Generic` namespace. For example, here's the `Where` method:

```
static class Enumerable {
    public static IEnumerable<T> Where<T>(this IEnumerable<T> source,
                                          Func<T, bool> predicate) {
        // See the chapter on LINQ to understand how this works inside
        throw new NotImplementedException();
    }
}
```

The method signature states that given a sequence of any element type T and a *function delegate* from T to Boolean (to be explained in more detail in Chapter 17) the method can give back a filtered sequence of that same element type T. Substitute the type parameter T for any type that comes to mind to concretize this example.

Let's take a sequence of integral numbers using the Int32 type. Given this sequence and a function that says for each Int32 in the sequence whether it should pass the filter (that is, the function defines a *predicate*), the result will be a filtered sequence of Int32 objects. The following shows how to call this method, using simple static method invocation syntax:

```
IEnumerable<int> evens = Enumerable.Where<int>(new int[] { 1, 2, 3 },
                                               (int x) => x % 2 == 0);
```

Ignore the second argument for the time being, which is a lambda expression that takes any object in the input sequence to a Boolean expression denoting the filter's result (in our case expressing whether an integer value is even). To call the method, we've specified a type parameter, which immediately shows up in the editor, as shown in Figure 15.26.

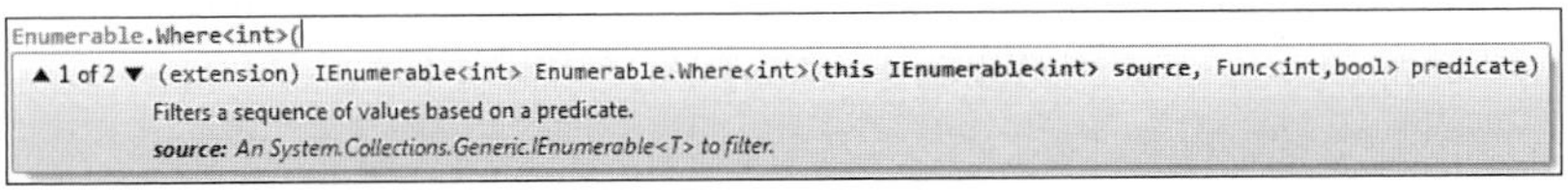

```
Enumerable.Where<int>(
▲ 1 of 2 ▼ (extension) IEnumerable<int> Enumerable.Where<int>(this IEnumerable<int> source, Func<int,bool> predicate)
           Filters a sequence of values based on a predicate.
           source: An System.Collections.Generic.IEnumerable<T> to filter.
```

FIGURE 15.26   Calling a generic method.

All occurrences of the type parameter T in the signature have been substituted for int, just as if we had a specialized method at hand that was statically typed to take in both an IEnumerable<int> sequence and a Func<int, bool> delegate, returning a sequence of the same type as the input one.

However, there's quite some redundancy in specifying the type for our generic method call. We've said int no fewer than four times in the whole assignment statement:

```
IEnumerable<int> evens = Enumerable.Where<int>(new int[] { 1, 2, 3 },
                                               (int x) => x % 2 == 0);
```

Can't we reach the same effect with less noise? In fact, there's plenty of opportunity for the compiler to *infer* what we mean. Let's start on the right, where we can take away the type on the parameter to the lambda expression, something you'll have to believe my word for until you've read Chapter 17:

```
IEnumerable<int> evens = Enumerable.Where<int>(new int[] { 1, 2, 3 },
                                       x => x % 2 == 0);
```

The preceding code is still full of redundancy. Up until now, we've stated we want to call a generic method Where specifying the type parameter explicitly. However, if the type of the first parameter is known to be an IEnumerable of *something*, that same something ought to be the generic parameter type of the method. Let's see what happens if we try the following:

```
IEnumerable<int> evens = Enumerable.Where(new int[] { 1, 2, 3 },
                                  x => x % 2 == 0);
```

If you try to compile the preceding code, you'll see it still succeeds. Here, we're omitting the generic type parameter altogether and leave it to the compiler to go and figure it out for us. So whoever says that type inference is new to C# 3.0 and later is seriously mistaken: This is a form of type inference starting from C# 2.0!

Starting with C# 3.0, we can go further, though. First, we can make the compiler infer the type of the array for us based on the most common supertype of its elements, also known as the implicitly typed array initializer feature:

```
IEnumerable<int> evens = Enumerable.Where(new[] { 1, 2, 3 }, x => x % 2 == 0);
```

We're back to one single line now, and the compiler still knows precisely what we're talking about. Let's prove this by hovering over the x parameter used in the lambda expression. This is what we expect the compiler to have figured out: Because the array contains elements of type Int32, and such an array implements IEnumerable<Int32>, the generic type parameter to Where ought to be Int32. Hence, the second argument has to be of type Func<Int32, bool>. Finally, x is used as the argument of that function, which is of type Int32. Guess what, Figure 15.27 shows the compiler found this out, too.

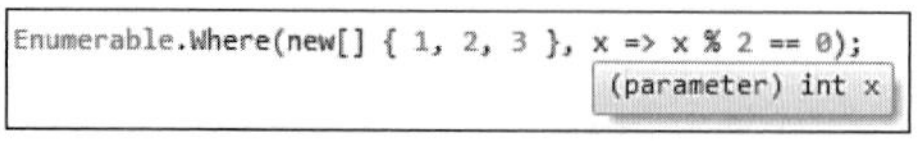

```
Enumerable.Where(new[] { 1, 2, 3 }, x => x % 2 == 0);
                                    (parameter) int x
```

FIGURE 15.27   Type inference at work.

Finally, local variable type inference, also introduced in C# 3.0, can be used to get rid of the evens variable's type, although that might start to become too unreadable for some programmers:

```
var evens = Enumerable.Where(new[] { 1, 2, 3 }, x => x % 2 == 0);
```

Alternatively, but this is beyond the scope of generics, we can call the method in the following way as it has been defined as an *extension method*. Internally, this translates back to exactly the form shown earlier:

```
var evens = new[] { 1, 2, 3 }.Where(x => x % 2 == 0);
```

And to finish off our translation battle, the preceding code is exactly the same as the following LINQ query expression, as you also see later:

```
var evens = from x in new[] { 1, 2, 3 }
            where x % 2 == 0
            select x;
```

Multiple type parameters can be used for generic methods, too. An example is the Select method from LINQ:

```
static class Enumerable {
    public static IEnumerable<R> Select<T, R>(this IEnumerable<T> source,
                                              Func<T, R> project) {
        // See the chapter on LINQ to understand how this works inside
        throw new NotImplementedException();     }
}
```

A fully explicitly typed example is shown here, projecting a sequence of integer values (hence T is of type Int32) to a sequence of string objects (making R of type String):

```
IEnumerable<string> numbers = Enumerable.Select<int, string>(
                              new int[] { 1, 2, 3 },
                              (int x) => x.ToString());
```

This should be intuitively fairly straightforward to understand: Given the integer numbers 1 through 3, each of those gets fed into a function that *goes to* the string representing that number, obtained through a ToString call. All the results of those projections make up the resulting sequence, which clearly consists of string-typed elements. The idea of this query operator is illustrated in Figure 15.28.

Again, we can simplify things based on what the compiler already knows. The input array can be implicitly typed, the lambda expression argument's type can be inferred, and from the array's element type T can be *identified* with the type Int32. So far, so good—but there's more! Based on the ToString return value in the lambda expression's body, R can be determined to be of type String. In other words, T and R can be left out without the compiler complaining because it can infer the type on its own:

```
IEnumerable<string> numbers = Enumerable.Select(new[] { 1, 2, 3 },
                              x => x.ToString());
```

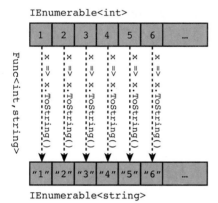

FIGURE 15.28   **S**elect<int, string> applied to an input sequence an a projection function.

You can't always omit the type parameters, though, for various reasons. For one thing, there might not be enough type information around to do inference on. Suppose we have a generic method defined like this:

```
T Identity<T>(T input) {
    return input;
}
```

This isn't useful at all, apart from wasting CPU cycles, but it is enough to show that no magic happens when this is given a typeless expression like the null literal. Figure 15.29 shows the compile-time error that occurs when type inference fails.

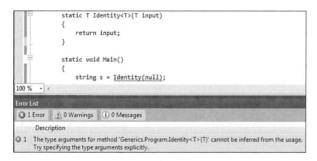

FIGURE 15.29   When type inference can't figure it out.

Notice from this example how the type does not flow from the left side to the right side. Given a null argument is all that matters for the compiler to decide it can't find a type for type parameter T.

Another case where inference of generic method type parameters is not possible is when things get ambiguous. An example is LINQ's `Concat` method, which is defined as follows:

```
static class Enumerable {
    public static IEnumerable<T> Concat<T>(this IEnumerable<T> first,
                                           IEnumerable<T> second) {
        // See the chapter on LINQ to understand how this works inside
        throw new NotImplementedException();
    }
}
```

Given two sequences with the same element type, `Concat` returns a sequence with both input sequence's elements. For example, given sequences { 1, 2, 3 } and { 4, 5, 6 }, the result will be a sequence that *yields* the numbers 1 through 6.

Now consider a simple class hierarchy with `Fruit`, `Apple`, and `Lemon`, using those types in the following piece of code (using extension method syntax):

```
var fruits = new Apple[] { ... }.Concat(new Lemon[] { ... });
```

The concrete apple and lemon objects in both arrays do not matter for our discussion; all that matters are the types of both sequences. For the "first" parameter, the compiler can infer T to be `Apple`, whereas the "second" parameter T seems to be `Lemon`. Even though both have a common supertype of `Fruit`, the compiler does not turn T into `Fruit`.

TAMING TYPE INFERENCE

This might seem odd but is a limitation introduced by well-intentioned design. Because every two types have `System.Object` as a common supertype, silly mistakes would be left unnoticed if the compiler were to decide on a type by walking the type hierarchy.

Also, constructed generic types can appear in error messages. When types get inferred with seemingly flexible rules as the hypothetical one we're discussing here, you will start to see types appearing out of nowhere when analyzing error messages. For example, consider the following code:

```
PrintAnimals(new Apple[] { ... }.Concat(new Lemon[] { ... }));
```

Assume for a moment the `Concat` method call expression's return type has been inferred as `IEnumerable<Fruit>` and `PrintAnimals` takes an `IEnumerable<Animal>`. Clearly, overload resolution is going to fail, producing an error that may mention the fact an `IEnumerable<Fruit>` was given while an `IEnumerable<Animal>` was expected. Looking at the code, you don't see any mention of `Fruit` at all.

In general, languages that rely heavily on type inference tend to produce very cryptic error messages mentioning types coming out of nowhere. Typical examples include functional languages such as Haskell and ML. With rules that seemingly take away flexibility, the C# language tries to keep things more sane.

WHY SYNTACTICAL ORDERING MATTERS

Writing out generic methods that use one of their type parameters in the method's return type got a little messy in conjunction with existing IntelliSense engines. In some sense, they didn't *intelligently sense* the intent of the user. Because the generic method's type parameter list isn't seen until it gets written, the editor tries to provide meaningful IntelliSense as soon as the following is typed:

```
public static IEnumerable<T
```

In Visual Studio 2008, this resulted in the suggested IntelliSense shown in Figure 15.30.

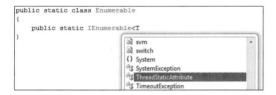

FIGURE 15.30   Eager auto-completion by IntelliSense in Visual Studio 2008.

If you were in a hurry and just continued typing, you got the following in return:

```
public static IEnumerable<ThreadStaticAttribute>
```

In Visual Studio 2010, the IntelliSense engine has gotten a lot smarter about the use patterns with generics and makes a very reasonable guess of what you mean. Because IEnumerable< indicates the user wants to write a generic type, and because that type is defined with a type parameter T, that may be a good fit (see Figure 15.31).

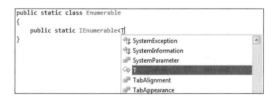

FIGURE 15.31   Visual Studio 2010's IntelliSense is smarter about generics.

Beware of the wording in the last section: *may* be a good fit; after all, the user might want to use a different name for a type parameter. You've seen an example where this is the case: The Select<T,R> query operator returns an IEnumerable<R>.

The bigger problem actually results from the syntactical order of type parameters in relation to the return type. And the position of the return type is an inheritance from the C-style language family. It's not until the type parameters have been seen that sense can be made of the return type if type parameters are used in there. In contrast, Visual Basic has always put the return type at the end, which makes things better.

```
Function Where(Of T)(source As IEnumerable(Of T), ...) As IEnumerable(Of T)
```

So the next time you design a language, consider syntactical order!

Notice that sometimes type inference for type parameters is necessary when dealing with anonymous types (for example, as commonly done with LINQ's Select method):

```
var res = people.Select(p => new { p.Name, p.Age});
```

Here, we're projecting all persons in the people collection to an anonymous object containing their Name and Age properties. This anonymous type gets used for the type parameter R on the Select method call. Besides the inference at the level of generic type parameters, to refer to the projection's result type, you must use local variable type inference, too. Here the type of res will be inferred based on the result of inferring type parameter R (that is, as IEnumerable<R> with R our anonymous type). Figure 15.32 shows how the definition of an anonymous type shows up in IntelliSense when revealing generic parameter mappings.

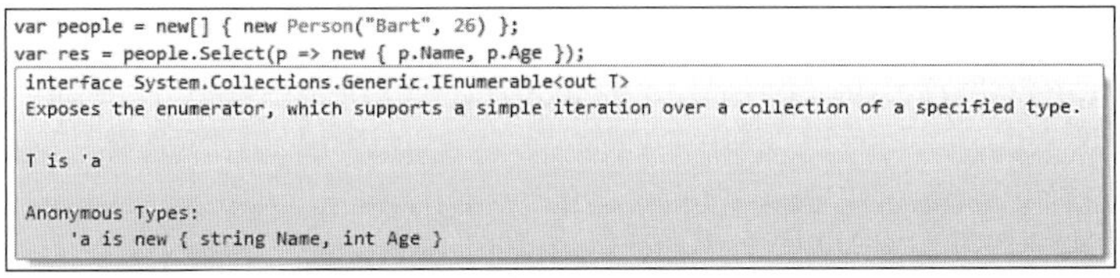

```
var people = new[] { new Person("Bart", 26) };
var res = people.Select(p => new { p.Name, p.Age });
interface System.Collections.Generic.IEnumerable<out T>
Exposes the enumerator, which supports a simple iteration over a collection of a specified type.

T is 'a

Anonymous Types:
    'a is new { string Name, int Age }
```

FIGURE 15.32   Anonymous types work fine with generics.

MUMBLE MUMBLE

Inference for generic type parameters is an all-or-nothing feature. If the compiler can't figure out any of the type parameters on its own, you'll have to specify *all* of them yourself. The hypothetical language feature of being able to have partial inference of type parameters is sometimes referred to as *mumble types*. In essence, you would give the compiler some hints about certain parameters, whereas the others can be inferred:

```
Bar<int, *, string>(...) // the * makes a mumbling sound
Bar<int, var, string>(...) // or the var keyword could be reused
```

Such a feature never made it into the language and would be useful only in rare circumstances.

Finally, we have to mention that generic methods can use the same set of constraints put on type parameters, using the same where keyword.

Co- and Contravariance

While most of the C# 4.0 set of language features deals with dynamic typing and simplifying interoperability scenarios, one other feature made it in to the language. Generic co- and contravariance is a powerful feature with a scary name. Luckily, you won't have to deal with it directly that often. Instead, this new feature makes working with certain generic interfaces and delegates easier. Let's have a look.

Annoyances with Generic Types

The mainstream .NET languages, C# and VB, introduced the concept of generic co- and contravariance as part of the .NET 4 release. Even though the CLR has supported those concepts ever since the introduction of generics, they never were exposed through the various languages. However, with the advent of LINQ in .NET 3.5, the need became much more apparent. Before explaining those concepts, let's take a look at one of the little annoyances that pop up when using LINQ:

```
IEnumerable<Apple> apples = ...;
var juice = MakeJuice(from apple in apples
                      where apple.Color == Color.Red
                      select apple);
```

In the preceding code, the query expression passed to MakeJuice will be inferred to be of type IEnumerable<Apple>. Based on the translation of the query expression (which will be explained later in Chapter 19, in the section, "Query Expression Syntax") and your knowledge of generic methods, this should be relatively easy to figure out:

```
IEnumerable<Apple> apples = ...;
var query = apples.Where<Apple>(apple => apple.Color == Color.Red);
var juice = MakeJuice(query);
```

Refer to the signature of the Where method discussed earlier in this chapter; you see that the return type is IEnumerable<T>, where T was substituted for Apple.

So, what's the problem with this? Up until this point, nothing really. But what if the query object gets passed to a MakeJuice method defined like this?

```
Juice MakeJuice(IEnumerable<Fruit> fruits) {
    var juice = new Juice();

    foreach (var fruit in _ fruits)
        juice += fruit.Squeeze();

    return juice;
}
```

Notice we're passing an `IEnumerable<Apple>` object where `IEnumerable<Fruit>` is expected. Intuitively, you might say this should be fine because every Apple is a Fruit. It turns out that this is safe, but before .NET 4, the compiler would reject this code because it treated `IEnumerable<T>` as *invariant*. What this means will become clear in a just a moment. For now, just take a look at Figure 15.33.

```
class Program
{
    static void Main(string[] args)
    {
        IEnumerable<Apple> apples = PluckApples();
        var juice = MakeJuice(from apple in apples
                              where apple.Color == Color.Red
                              select apple);
    }

    static Juice MakeJuice(IEnumerable<Fruit> fruits)
    {
```

Error List

⊗ 2 Errors   ⚠ 0 Warnings   ⓘ 0 Messages

	Description
⊗ 1	The best overloaded method match for 'LotsOfArgs.Program.MakeJuice (System.Collections.Generic.IEnumerable<LotsOfArgs.Fruit>)' has some invalid arguments
⊗ 2	Argument '1': cannot convert from 'System.Collections.Generic.IEnumerable<LotsOfArgs.Apple>' to 'System.Collections.Generic.IEnumerable<LotsOfArgs.Fruit>'

FIGURE 15.33   Before .NET 4, `IEnumerable<T>` was invariant in T.

To understand why this code got rejected before C# 4.0, we need to take a tour through the wonderful world of *variance*. While variance is deeply rooted in (scary sounding) category theory and type theory, it has become an everyday concept now in the world of .NET programming. This is not only the case for generic types but also for delegates, as you will see during our coverage of delegates in Chapter 17.

In a nutshell, generic variance annotations relate subtyping on constructed types with subtyping on the type arguments used to construct the type. For example, if we know that every Apple is a Fruit, can we also say that every `IEnumerable` of Apple objects can be treated *safely* as an `IEnumerable` of Fruit? The word *safety* is essential in this definition because type safety is at stake. (The following section illustrates the dangers that come from broken variance treatment.)

Broken Covariance for Array Types

Since the .NET Framework was released, arrays have been covariant. Going back to our definition of variance annotations, there was a mention of "constructed types." Array types are such animals because any element type can be used to construct an array type. For example, given the type `int`, we can construct an array that can hold integer values (that is, which is of type `int[]`). And this by itself is a new type we can create an array type out of, namely a jagged `int[][]` array.

Our next duty is to express a subtyping relationship between array types based on the knowledge of a subtyping relationship between the element types. For example, if we know that every `Apple` is a `Fruit`, can we treat every `Apple[]` as a `Fruit[]`? It turns out we can because of .NET's covariant treatment for arrays. This relationship between element types and constructed array types is graphically illustrated in Figure 15.34.

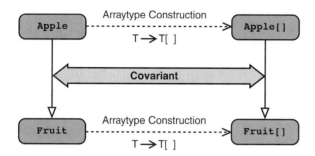

FIGURE 15.34   Arrays are covariant in .NET.

Intuitively, when drawing a diagram as the one shown here, if the subtyping arrows on both sides go in the same direction, we discuss *covariance*. In other words, when the type construction (in here the use of [ ] on a type to construct an array type over it) preserves the subtyping relationship, it is covariant. You can guess what contravariance will look like, but ignore that for now.

But there's a problem with the covariant treatment for array types. Do you recall the title of this section? It implies somehow that array covariance is broken. What does this mean? In short, there's no compile-time safety when treating arrays as covariant, so the runtime must introduce additional checks to ensure type safety. If it's unsafe, the obvious concern is where things can go wrong. Let's see:

```
Apple[] apples = new Apple[] { apple1, apple2, apple3 };


// Because of array type covariance we can write the following.
Fruit[] fruits = apples;


// We're putting a Coconut, which is a Fruit, in a Fruit array. This is fine.
fruits[2] = new Coconut();
```

The preceding code looks pretty innocent at first glance, but nothing is further from the truth. In fact, we're in an ideal position here to break type safety. First, let's make a drawing of how things look like in memory so far (see Figure 15.35). The key observation to make here is that the `fruits` array is simply a reference that's *aliasing* the original `apples` array.

```
Apple[] apples = new Apple[] { apple1, apple2, apple3 };
Fruit[] fruits = apples;
```

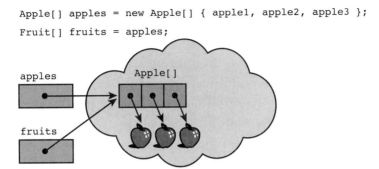

```
fruits[2] = new Coconut();
```

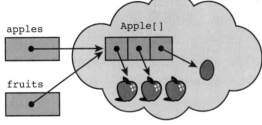

FIGURE 15.35   Not-so-innocent uses of array covariance.

Can you see what the problem is already? If not, here's a hint. Look at the third element of the array through the apples variable:

```
Apple[] apples = new Apple[] { apple1, apple2, apple3 };


// Because of array type covariance we can write the following.
Fruit[] fruits = apples;

// We're putting a Coconut, which is a Fruit, in a Fruit-array. This is fine.
fruits[2] = new Coconut();
// An element of an Apple[] should be an Apple, right?
apples[2].Peel();
```

When obtaining the third element of the array on the last line, we're getting it back as if it were an Apple. The compiler is right about this because the apples array is typed with the Apple type as the array's element type. However, in reality, we got back a Coconut instance. If we now call the Apple-specific Peel method, things will go wrong: Being able to call a method on an object that doesn't have that method available is a breach in the type safety of the system. You don't want to try to peel a coconut!

Where's the problem? It seems that, at every step, the compiler was making the right conclusions. The fundamental problem here is in allowing array types to be treated covariantly, as seen on the second line. Does this mean the CLR can be tricked to break type safety? Luckily, no, because the designers were aware of this very problem and introduced runtime checks to protect against it. The result is that the third line of code throws an ArrayTypeMismatchException, as shown in Figure 15.36.

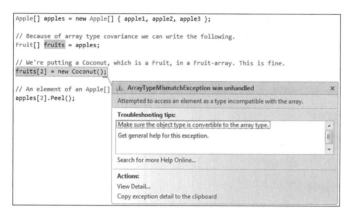

FIGURE 15.36   The CLR guards arrays against insertion of improperly typed elements.

SO THEY KNEW?

If the designers knew about array covariance being an unsafe operation, why did they permit it in the first place? As usual, knowing some history helps provide a good explanation. Recall how the CLR was invented with cross-language interoperability in mind. One popular language at the time of the creation of the CLR was Java, where broken array covariance has been allowed for ages. To make it possible to run Java code on the CLR (for example, using J#) without compile-time errors, it was decided to make arrays covariant.

As you can imagine, this broken-by-design choice was a hot topic of debate within the design groups, but in the end, the cross-language interoperability goal was deemed important enough to motivate the introduction of array covariance. Luckily, generics do much better on the variance front, as you see next.

Safety Guarantees

Co- and contravariance are means to add flexibility to the type system, ideally while making sure type safety cannot be violated. The flexibility part is clear: being able to treat an array of Apples as an array of Coconuts is more powerful than not being able to do so.

But why is this example of array covariance unsafe? The true answer lies in the writable characteristic of an array:

```
// We're putting a Coconut, which is a Fruit, in a Fruit-array. This is
// actually not fine if the underlying array has a more specific element type.
fruits[2] = new Coconut();
```

If the fruits variable is referencing an array with an element type that's more specific than Fruit, the preceding code is not fine. The reason is someone might be looking at the same array using a more specific element type (in our case, Apple), observing an object of an incompatible type that has been *put in*. Covariance and input are enemies.

Assuming we have arrays from which we can only read elements (we don't), covariance could be permitted in a safe manner:

```
Apple[] apples = new Apple[] { apple1, apple2, apple3 };

// Because of array type covariance we can write the following.
readonly /* hypothetical keyword use */ Fruit[] fruits = apples;

// Reading from the array is a safe operation.
Fruit fruit1 = fruits[0];

// This wouldn't compile anymore, because the array is read-only!
fruits[2] = new Coconut();
```

In fact, the ability to use covariance for arrays is not all bad. Think of the case where you want to print an array of Fruit objects. If the user wouldn't be able to hand you an array of Apple objects, the well-intentioned method is not very useful. The reason this method can be implemented safely is because it would only read from the input array. As you will see, the use of IEnumerable<Fruit> as the argument type would be a better choice though because this interface is safe for covariance.

Covariance is conceptually similar to the ability to treat the *output* of a function as a less-derived type. For example, even though Console.ReadLine gives me back a string, it's fine for me to *look at it* as if it were nothing more than an object:

```
object input = Console.WriteLine();
```

Staying in the domain of method calls for a tiny bit longer, we can ask ourselves what contravariance corresponds to. Intuitively, you can already guess it ought to be related to *input* arguments. When a method expects an object of a certain type, it's fine for you to give it an object of a more-derived type. For example, a method taking in two Fruit objects can safely be given an Apple and a Coconut:

```
Yogurt appleAndCocunut = CreateFruitYogurt(apple, coconut); // Yum?
```

Generic Co- and Contravariance

Let's take a closer look at co- and contravariance on generic interface types. At the start of this chapter, you saw how the next piece of code didn't compile in .NET 3.5, with the assumption that MakeJuice takes in an IEnumerable<Fruit>:

```
IEnumerable<Apple> apples = ...;
var juice = MakeJuice(from apple in apples
                      where apple.Color == Color.Red
                      select apple);
```

The reason is that IEnumerable<T> was invariant in its type parameter T. Invariance simply means that no typing relationship between the types IEnumerable<Base> and IEnumerable<Derived> is established. They're treated as unrelated to one another.

In .NET 4, IEnumerable<T> has been marked as covariant by putting the out keyword on the type parameter T:

```
public interface IEnumerable<out T> : IEnumerable {
    IEnumerator<T> GetEnumerator();
}
```

By using the out keyword, you promise the compiler to use the generic parameter only in output positions. Using IEnumerable<T> as our example, this is the case because T is used only in the return type of GetEnumerator. On its turn, IEnumerator<T> needs to be declared as covariant:

```
public interface IEnumerator<out T> : IDisposable, IEnumerator {
    T Current { get; }
}
```

Again, T occurs only in an output position, as the return type of a get-only property. On the side of the users of the interface, the means IEnumerable<Derived> can be safely assigned to an IEnumerable<Base>. For example, with Apples and Coconuts:

```
IEnumerable<Apple> apples = new Apple[] { apple1, apple2, apple3 };


// Because of IEnumerable<T>'s covariance we can write the following.
IEnumerable<Fruit> fruits = apples;


// There is no way to put a Coconut in an IEnumerable<Fruit>, hence this does
// not work anymore:    fruits[2] = new Coconut();
```

If you mark a type parameter as covariant but use it in an input position like a method parameter or for a property that's not get-only, the compiler will complain (see Figure 15.37 for the variance violation error message):

```
interface IArray<out T> {
    T this[int index] {
        get; // This is fine
        set; // Having a setter is not fine!
    }
}
```

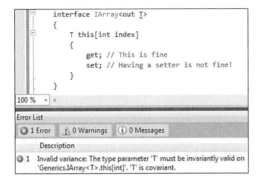

FIGURE 15.37   Violation against covariant-safe use of a generic type parameter.

Contravariance is exactly the opposite of covariance but turns out to be less intuitive to most people. Where a covariant type parameter can be used only in output positions, a contravariant one can be used only in input positions, as indicated by the in keyword. A good example can be found on the IComparer<T> interface:

```
public interface IComparable<in T> {
    int CompareTo(T other);
}
```

Here, T is used only as an input parameter on the CompareTo method. From a user's perspective, contravariance allows the following to be written:

```
IComparable<Fruit> compareFruits = new CompareFruitBySize();
IComparable<Apple> compareApples = compareFruits;
```

If an object can compare two Fruit objects, it can be used where two Apple objects have to be compared. Sure, we won't be using any specific properties of an Apple to make the comparison, but it's safe to treat an Apple as a Fruit for comparison purposes. This is completely analogous to what would be possible if a Fruit-based Compare method were called with two Apple objects:

```
public int Compare(Fruit first, Fruit last) {
    return first.Size - second.Size;
}
...
int res = Compare(apple1, apple2); // Fine for method overload resolution
```

When marking a type parameter as contravariant, it's a mistake to use it in an output position, and the compiler will prevent you from making this mistake.

WHY VARIANCE ISN'T INFERRED AUTOMATICALLY

You might wonder why variance annotations using the in and out keywords have to be provided explicitly when defining a generic interface or delegate type. (Variance is not supported except for those two generic types.) After all, it seems the compiler would be able to figure this out by itself: If a generic parameter is used only in input positions, it becomes contravariant (in), and when it only occurs in output positions, it becomes covaraint (out).

The reason for this is that the generic type might still be evolving during development, while other code may start to depend on the capability to use objects of the type in a co- or contravariant manner. Once the type gets extended (for example, a method is being added to an interface), the variance annotation may disappear silently because a type parameter is now also used in an "opposite" position, making the type invariant. This would cause code depending on the previously inferred variance to start to break. For this reason, the language requires you to be explicit about the intended variance annotation. If no variance modifier is present, the type parameter will be treated as invariant (just as it was before C# 4.0).

A schematic overview of the relationship between the apparent subtyping and the use of co- and contravariance are shown in Figure 15.38.

Under the Hood

Co- and contravariance for interface and delegate types has been supported by the CLR since the introduction of generics back in the .NET 2.0 days. And being supported at the runtime and IL level makes it amenable for cross-language support once more. Given the following two types, let's take a look under the hood:

```
interface IReadOnly<out T> {
    T Give();
}

interface IWriteOnly<in T> {
    void Take(T input);
}
```

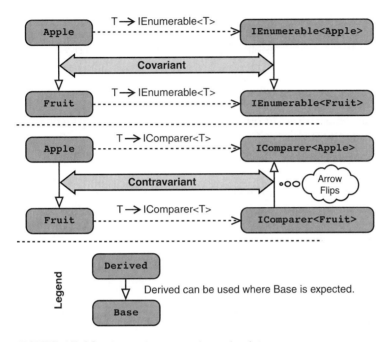

FIGURE 15.38   Co- and contravariance in pictures.

At the assembly-level as shown in Figure 15.39, covariance is indicated with a + symbol in front of a type parameter, while contravariance is denoted with -.

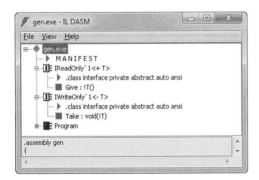

FIGURE 15.39   Co- and contravariance behind the scenes.

Different syntactical notations have been considered for C# 4.0, but ultimately the in and out modifiers were chosen because they seem to capture the meaning in a natural manner, reflecting the restrictions on how a type parameter can be used within the type. One more time: in means the type parameter can occur only in input positions, which causes contravariant treatment; whereas out restricts use of the type parameter to output positions only, leading to covariant treatment. From the perspective of the type's consumer, out means you're getting something back, so you can treat it less derived; whereas in indicates you're putting something in, so it's possible to give it something more derived.

Where to Use

The most important characteristic of co- and contravariance for generic interface and delegate types is its *definition site* characteristic. In other words, as a user of such a generic type you don't have to do anything to get more (safe) flexibility in return. We've already seen how a LINQ query can now be assigned to a variable of a more general IEnumerable<T> type, where it couldn't before.

In .NET 4, generic interfaces and delegates in the BCL have been improved by adding variance modifiers where applicable. The most important types are shown here:

```
// Used on collections and in LINQ.
interface IEnumerable<out T>;
interface IEnumerator<out T>;
interface IQueryable<out T>;

// New Reactive Framework interfaces (see next chapter).
interface IObservable<out T>;
interface IObserver<in T>;

// Comparer interfaces.
interface IComparer<in T>;
interface IEqualityComparer<in T>;

// Delegates (see next chapter); read intuitively as method signatures.
delegate void Action<in T>(T arg);
delegate void Action<in T1, in T2>(T1 arg1, T2 arg2);
...
delegate R Func<out R>();
delegate R Func<in T, out R>(T arg);
...
```

For an example of an interface that can't have its type parameter marked with either variance modifier, take a look at ICollection<T>:

```
public interface ICollection<T> : IEnumerable<T> {
    int Count { get; }
    bool IsReadOnly { get; }

    void Add(T item);
    void Clear();
    bool Contains(T item);
```

```
    void CopyTo(T[] array, int arrayIndex);
    bool Remove(T item);
}
```

Although the `IEnumerable<T>` interface is contravariant in `T`, the derived interface can't be because it adds methods that use `T` in input positions.

Summary

Generics brought a great addition to the CLR's type system, allowing for improved compile-time type checking and for easier creation of highly reusable code. The core idea is to parameterize types such as interfaces, classes, structs, and delegates (as well as individual methods) on type parameters. As a result, the generically written code is applicable regardless of the types supplied for the parameters.

In this chapter, we discussed how generics are exposed in the C# programming language. First, we familiarized ourselves with the syntax used for generics at the declaration and use sites for classes and methods. Next, we learned about the (limited set of) constraint mechanisms available for generic type parameters. Finally, we discussed the new C# 4.0 co- and contravariance features.

In the next chapter, we put the theory to practice with exhaustive coverage of the various collection types in the .NET Framework's BCL, including many of the related interfaces.

CHAPTER 16

Collection Types

IN THIS CHAPTER

▶ Nongeneric Collection
  Types 753

▶ Generic Collection Types 762

▶ Other Collection Types 775

No discussion of generic types is complete without a journey through the BCL's built-in collection types. Prior to the introduction of generic in .NET 2.0, collection types had to be defined using `System.Object` for element types and whatnot. This caused quite a bit of grief and a poor development experience.

In this chapter, we look at the various collection types that come with the .NET Framework's BCL, driving home the points about generics made in the previous chapter. Having a solid understanding of those collection types is invaluable for every C# programmer.

Nongeneric Collection Types

Before delving into the generic collection types, it's useful to get an idea of the legacy collection types out there in the `System.Collections` namespace. As you learned in the "Life Without Generics" section in Chapter 15, "Generic Types and Methods," the only way you could create maximally applicable types in the past was to use `System.Object`, the mother type of all types, somewhere. The nongeneric collection types do so for their storage and hence bubble up `System.Object` to the type's surface on methods like `Add`, `Remove`, and so on. The main reason to learn about those types is for survival purposes (when, for example, facing code that was written before the introduction of generics). For fresh code, generic collection types are the right choice.

ArrayList

An `ArrayList` provides array-like access, using indexers, while having the capability to grow dynamically as needed. The collection maintains the order in which items were added and provides the ability to insert and remove items. The following are typical operations:

```
var lst = new ArrayList();
lst.Add(1);                              // {      1 }
lst.AddRange(new[] { 2, 3, 7, 6, 5, 4 }); // {      1, 2, 3, 7, 6, 5, 4 }
lst.Insert(index: 0, value: 0);          // { 0, 1, 2, 3, 7, 6, 5, 4 }
lst.RemoveAt(index: 4);                  // { 0, 1, 2, 3,    6, 5, 4 }
lst.Remove(obj: 1);                      // { 0,    2, 3,    6, 5, 4 }
lst.RemoveRange(index: 2, count: 3);     // { 0,    2,          4 }
lst.Reverse();                           // { 4, 2, 0 }
lst.Sort();                              // { 0, 2, 4 }
bool hasTwo = lst.Contains(2);           // true
int two = (int)lst[1];                   // 2
```

From a performance point of view, `Add` is a constant time operation unless the list's capacity is reached, at which point a new storage array needs to be allocated, copying the original array's elements over. If you know upfront what the capacity of the list is going to be, use the constructor overload that allows specifying an initial capacity.

Because the internal storage is a plain array, lookup operations like `Contains` require sequential scanning of the list (but also when an element needs to be found for removal), which will pose a problem for larger collections.

Operations such as `Insert` and index-based `Remove` are linear in the size of the list as well because elements have to be moved around in the array, shifting elements either to the right for an Insert or to the left for a `Remove`.

BIG O

MSDN documentation for collections provides a Big O cost for every method. The Big O notation is used in complexity theory to indicate an upper bound on the computational resources required to execute the underlying algorithm. O(1) means constant time, O(n) means linear in the size of the collection, and similar notations are used for quadratic or logarithmic complexity in terms of the size of the collection. Obviously, constant time is the best, followed by logarithmic time. When things get linear or quadratic, you might be in for a problem if the collection size is getting high.

Let desired characteristics be your first guide when deciding what collection type to use. If you need things to have a linear ordering, use some kind of list; if you need fast lookups, a hash table is better; avoiding duplicates can be done using a set; and so on. After you've determined your needs and candidates for the collection types that have those characteristics, get some idea about the costs of the various operations.

But again, premature optimizations are typically not a good idea. Measure before you judge whether you have a problem. Just beware of large element counts, in which case an informed decision about the right type of collection is most likely a good idea to avoid too much hassle afterward. And to prepare for when you have to swap out a collection type in favor of another one, use collection interfaces whenever exposing collections to the outside world. This is a general truth in the world of object orientation (OO), but keep your public contract and implementation details separate from one another.

To iterate over a nongeneric collection, you can use the `foreach` keyword together with a type for the iteration variable that's more specific than `System.Object`:

```
foreach (int i in lst)
    ...
```

Remember that the `foreach` statement emits, if needed, a cast expression on the `Current` property getter call. The following is roughly equivalent to the preceding code:

```
var enumerator = lst.GetEnumerator();
int i;
while (enumerator.MoveNext()) {
    i = (int)enumerator.Current;
    ...
}
```

For heterogeneous nongeneric collections, this can cause an `InvalidCastException` when the target type specified on the iteration variable conflicts with an item that was retrieved by the `Current` call. And because the collection is not generic, the `var` keyword cannot be used to infer the element type (it will instead resolve to `System.Object`):

```
foreach (var i in lst)
    ...
```

Yet another reason to go for generic collections wherever possible!

Hash Tables

A hash table provides key/value pairing with support for efficient lookup by key. Being nongeneric, key and value are represented as `System.Object`. An exploratory example is shown here:

```
var tbl = new Hashtable();
tbl.Add("Bart", 26);
tbl["John"] = 62;
```

```
bool bartIsKnown = tbl.ContainsKey("Bart");
bool someIsAged62 = tbl.ContainsValue(62);
foreach (string name in tbl.Keys)
    Console.WriteLine("Age of {0} is {1}", name, tbl[name]);

tbl.Remove("Bart");
```

Internally, keys are hashed by use of the key type's GetHashCode implementation. The idea of a hash code is to provide an integer-valued identifier for an object with as good uniqueness properties as possible. Whenever an entry is requested from the table by using a key, the hash code of the supplied key gets computed. Based on that value, a fast lookup in the underlying storage can be made as opposed to a sequential scan of the key/value pairs. Characteristics of a hash code are as follows:

▶ For two objects that compare equal (by means of Object.Equals), the hash code must be the same.

▶ As long as an object does not mutate its state, the hash code must remain the same. This is important for hash tables to be able to find back an object based on its hash code-based key.

▶ The more random the distribution of a hash code across all objects of the same type, the better. For hash tables, this allows faster lookup times.

Because hash codes for different objects can be the same (preferably they are not), it's sometimes necessary to disambiguate between objects with the same hash code. This is done by using the Equals method on the conflicting objects involved. Both Equals and GetHashCode are defined on System.Object and can be overridden by your types:

```
class Person {
    // Name and Age property + a constructor

    public override bool Equals(object obj) {
        var other = obj as Person;
        if (other == null)
            return false;
        return other.Name == Name && other.Age == Age;
    }

    public override int GetHashCode() {
        return (Name ?? "").GetHashCode() ^ Age;
        }
}
```

The Equals method checks to make sure the given object is of the Person type by using the as keyword and a null check. If this is the case, all state is compared on the two instanced. For GetHashCode, we leverage the hash code of the Name string and XOR it with the Age value. With those overridden methods in place, you can empirically observe the use of GetHashCode when a Person instance is added to a Hashtable for use as a key. This experiment is shown in Figure 16.1.

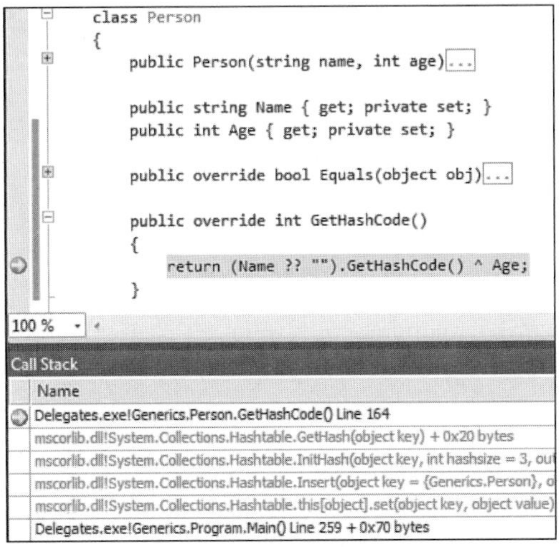

FIGURE 16.1   GetHashCode being called by the Hashtable's Insert code path.

WHAT NOT TO USE HASH CODES FOR

Hash codes are used to make object lookup more efficient but don't provide many (or any) guarantees beyond that use. For example, given two equal hash codes, you cannot conclude the two corresponding objects are equal. Don't rely on hash codes to make security decisions, as a replacement for object identity, or to find objects back in a persistent store.

The reason not to use hash codes for persistency purposes (for example, in a database) is that the default hash code implementation, as provided by System.Object, can (and will) change between different releases of the .NET Framework. All that is required from a hash code are the properties outlined earlier on, for the duration of a program's execution. More specifically, it's even valid for an application to produce different hash codes for objects across runs.

Notice how the used Person type is immutable. That's important when dealing with hash tables unless you can make sure by static code analysis that key objects do not change their state while being used in a hash table. The reason should be obvious. During insertion, the hash code of the key object is used to put the object in a certain spot in the storage. When a key is supplied for lookup (for example, through the indexer getter), the hash code is calculated to locate the object in storage. If the recomputed hash code differs, the item will not be found. Figure 16.2 shows such a case where Bart has aged and his shoe size cannot be retrieved.

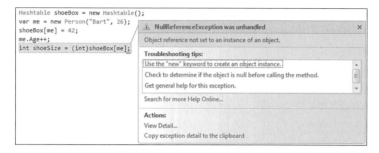

```
Hashtable shoeBox = new Hashtable();
var me = new Person("Bart", 26);
shoeBox[me] = 42;
me.Age++;
int shoeSize = (int)shoeBox[me];
```

NullReferenceException was unhandled   ×

Object reference not set to an instance of an object.

Troubleshooting tips:

Use the "new" keyword to create an object instance.

Check to determine if the object is null before calling the method.

Get general help for this exception.

Search for more Help Online...

Actions:

View Detail...

Copy exception detail to the clipboard

FIGURE 16.2   The indexer returns `null` if the key is not found.

This concludes our look at the hash table collection. All knowledge you gained in this section will be carried forward to the parallel world of generic collections, in particular the `Dictionary<TKey, TValue>` type.

Queue

A queue is a first-in, first-out (FIFO) collection. Basic operations are `Enqueue` and `Dequeue`, respectively, to add an element to the end of the queue and to retrieve the first element in the queue. Compare this to a queue in the supermarket: If you're in front, you'll be served first. Figure 16.3 illustrates the principle of a queue's operation.

FIGURE 16.3   `Dequeue`, `Peek`, and `Enqueue` operations on a queue data structure.

The following is a real-world example of a queue:

```
var postOffice = new Queue();
postOffice.Enqueue(new Person("Bart", 10));
postOffice.Enqueue(new Person("Homer", 38));
postOffice.Enqueue(new Person("Ned", 60));
var bart = (Person)postOffice.Dequeue();
var homer = (Person)postOffice.Peek(); // D'oh
int twoLeft = postOffice.Count;
```

Because all collection types implement IEnumerable, you can enumerate over a queue, as well, which will produce a head-to-tail enumeration order.

Queues are often used to queue up work items, such as order processing requests. Getting work through Dequeue is a constant time operation, whereas Enqueue is constant time unless the internal storage array has reached its capacity, at which point it becomes linear in the size of the store.

INITIAL CAPACITY AND GROW FACTOR

Specialized constructor overloads can be used to supply an initial capacity and a grow factor. The latter value, a float, is used to grow the queue's internal storage when its capacity has been reached. The more estimates you have about both the initial capacity and grow factor, the better. Of course, as usual with performance, don't start tweaking things just for the sake of it. Most other collection types have similar knobs to play with when needed.

Stack

Everyone knows a stack by now, as seen with call stacks and evaluation stacks. Stacks are last-in, first-out (LIFO) collections. Compare it to a stack of books where it's (nearly) impossible to get a book other than the one at the top without popping the books on top of it off the stack first. The basic operations are called Push and Pop, and a Peek method allows looking at the top element without popping it off. Figure 16.4 graphically depicts the operation of a stack.

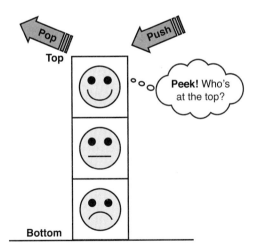

FIGURE 16.4   Operation of a stack data structure.

To illustrate the use of a stack, take a look at the following code fragment:

```
var stack = new Stack();
stack.Push(1);
stack.Push(2);
stack.Push(3);
var three = (int)stack.Pop();
var two = (int)stack.Peek();
var twoLeft = stack.Count;
```

Similar to the Queue type, Stack is implemented using an array on the inside. Pop is a constant time operation, whereas Push's behavior depends on the available capacity. If free storage is available, Push is O(1); otherwise, it gets linear due to the reallocation of the array.

BitArray

One final nongeneric collection type worth mentioning is the BitArray type, which provides an efficient bit-vector implementation. Using an array of Booleans to keep track of on/off flags for a bunch of entities in some system is not very efficient in terms of storage, requiring a full byte per Boolean (not mentioning potential 32-bit alignment caveats). If we can encode the flags on a bit basis, we're much better off. That's what the BitArray type provides for:

```
const int N = 20;

var first = new BitArray(N, false);
for (int i = 0; i < first.Length; i += 2)
    first[i] = true;

var second = new BitArray(N, false);
for (int i = 1; i < second.Length; i += 2)
    second[i] = true;

Print("First:  ", first);              // 10101010101010101010
Print("Second: ", second);             // 01010101010101010101
Print("Xor:    ", first.Xor(second));  // 11111111111111111111
```

Internally, a BitArray uses an array of integer numbers to encode the Boolean values as single bits. Logical operators like And, Or, Xor, and Not are provided, and the whole bit array can be iterated over as a sequence of Booleans:

```
private static void Print(string title, BitArray bitArray) {
    Console.Write(title);
    foreach (bool b in bitArray)
        Console.Write(b ? "1" : "0");
    Console.WriteLine();
}
```

Notice that the `BitArray` operations mutate the left side. For example, in the code shown here the "first" array will be mutated in-place to have all flags set to 1 after applying the `Xor` operations with the "second" array. This is done to make `BitArray` as efficient as possible, which is usually the goal of using this type in the first place.

Summary

An overview of all nongeneric collection types is shown in Figure 16.5. Also notice the implementation of interfaces like `ICollection` and `IEnumerable`.

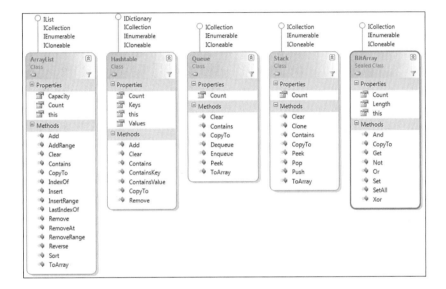

FIGURE 16.5   Nongeneric collection types (members filtered).

> **C# 3.0** Note that that the combination of `IEnumerable` and `ICollection` is enough to enable the use of the C# 3.0 collection initializer language feature:

```
var lst = new ArrayList { 1, 2, 3 };
```

The preceding code is equivalent to the following:

```
ArrayList __t = new ArrayList();
__t.Add(1);
__t.Add(2);
__t.Add(3);
ArrayList lst = __t;
```

This illustrates how new languages' features can make old APIs easier to use.

WHY ICLONEABLE IS A JOKE

Well intentioned as it was, `ICloneable` really became quite useless because of the missing specification of the intended cloning semantics. `Object.MemberwiseClone` is defined to create a *shallow* copy: All fields get copied, but references are not followed. (Just the reference is copied, but what it refers to isn't cloned.) For *deep* cloning, referenced objects would be cloned, too. `ICloneable`'s `Clone` method does not specify what type of cloning is expected, and therefore it's not usable as a solid unambiguous contract.

Generic Collection Types

Now that we've looked at nongeneric collection types, it's time to improve the static typing of collections by using the generic collections in `System.Collections.Generic`. The advantages of using generic collections were pointed out repeatedly in Chapter 15, including compile-time detection of typing errors at the level of element types as well as improved performance.

List<T>

The generic counterpart of the `ArrayList` type is the generic `List<T>` type, where the type parameter `T` stands for, unsurprisingly, the element type. Available methods on `List<T>` are pretty much the same as on `ArrayList`. We can even easily port our `ArrayList` example to `List<int>`:

```
var lst = new List<int>();
lst.Add(1);                                // {     1 }
lst.AddRange(new[] { 2, 3, 7, 6, 5, 4 });  // {     1, 2, 3, 7, 6, 5, 4 }
lst.Insert(index: 0, item: 0);             // { 0, 1, 2, 3, 7, 6, 5, 4 }
lst.RemoveAt(index: 4);                     // { 0, 1, 2, 3,    6, 5, 4 }
lst.Remove(item: 1);                        // { 0,    2, 3,    6, 5, 4 }
lst.RemoveRange(index: 2, count: 3);        // { 0,    2,             4 }
lst.Reverse();                              // { 4, 2, 0 }
lst.Sort();                                 // { 0, 2, 4 }
bool hasTwo = lst.Contains(2);              // true
int two = lst[1];                           // 2
```

NAMED PARAMETERS?

> C# 4.0
>
> You might have noticed before in the examples of nongeneric collection types that I've been using named parameters sometimes. This isn't necessary to make the preceding code compile but serves as a form of *documentation* for the meaning of used parameters. In the past, I used to document certain parameters by inline comments (using /* parameter name */) but I like named parameters better.

Also notice how certain parameter names differ from the ones on ArrayList (in particular, obj has been replaced by item) to provide more meaningful names for the API's users. Naming matters quite a bit in quality framework design!

List<T> has similar performance characteristics compared to ArrayList, based on the fact the underlying array-based storage might have to grow upon element insertion. An initial capacity can be set through a constructor overload.

Besides the familiar methods shown in the previous example, List<T> also has a wealth of methods inspired by typical functional programming techniques to deal with collections and data sequences. Most of those rely on delegates, which are covered in depth in Chapter 17, "Delegates." To illustrate those, we use lambda expression syntax, which provides a shorthand way of passing a piece of code to a method (for example, to express a filter condition):

```
var lst = new List<int> { 1, 2, 3, 4, 5, 6, 7 };

// Convert all elements and create a new list.
List<string> numbers = lst.ConvertAll(n => n.ToString());

// Condition holds for any element (Exists) or all elements (TrueForAll)?
bool hasLargerThanFive = lst.Exists(n => n > 5);            // true
bool noElementIsThirtheen = lst.TrueForAll(n => n != 13);   // true

// Find element(s) or indexes.
int firstEven = lst.Find(n => n % 2 == 0);                 // 2
int lastEven = lst.FindLast(n => n % 2 == 0);              // 6
List<int> allOdds = lst.FindAll(n => n % 2 != 0);          // { 1, 3, 5, 7 }
int indexOfFirstLargerThanThree = lst.FindIndex(n => n > 3); // 3
int indexOfLastLessThanFive = lst.FindLastIndex(n => n < 5); // 3
```

OVERLAP WITH LINQ

C# 3.0 A lot of the methods shown here were generalized in LINQ as query operators, originally referred to as *sequence operators*. The key difference is that the LINQ query operators operate on sequences (that is, IEnumerable<T> objects), which makes them more generally applicable than for List<T> alone.

However, there's more: As you will see, most LINQ query operators are *lazy*. This means the results of applying a query operator are not calculated until iteration over the result. For example, List<T>'s FindAll method iterates over all elements on the spot to produce a new list object with the filtered results, but LINQ's Where method delays computation until one iterates over the resulting IEnumerable<T>. This can be beneficial (for example, in the following case):

```
var fiveEvensLazy = lst.Where(n => n % 2 == 0).Take(5);
var fiveEvensEager = lst.FindAll(n => n % 2 == 0).Take(5);
```

In the latter case, a whole new intermediate List<int> for all even numbers gets created, whereas the former line of code is evaluated lazily. This will become much clearer when we discuss LINQ in more depth in Chapter 19, "Language Integrated Query Essentials." Once you've learned about LINQ, come back here and map the List<T> methods on their query operator equivalents. (For example, FindAll corresponds to Where.)

LinkedList<T>

LinkedList<T> is a doubly linked list, which implies navigation between consecutive elements in both directions is possible in constant time. The individual elements in a linked list are represented as LinkedListNode<T> objects, which look like the following:

```
// Illustrating the public contract of the class, omitting implementations.
public sealed class LinkedListNode<T> {
    public LinkedList<T> List { get; }
    public LinkedListNode<T> Next { get; }
    public LinkedListNode<T> Previous { get; }
    public T Value { get; set; }
}
```

Using Next and Previous, you can walk the list in both directions. For the containing list, follow the List reference. A LinkedList<T> by itself provides access to the First and Last elements:

```
// Illustrating the public contract of the class, omitting implementations.
public class LinkedList<T> {
    public LinkedListNode<T> First { get; }
    public LinkedListNode<T> Last { get; }
}
```

A schematic representation of all cross references between the list and its nodes is shown in Figure 16.6.

Common operations on LinkedList<T> include adding elements to the head or the tail of the list (using AddFirst and AndLast, respectively), inserting elements before or after a given list node, and removal of the first, last, or any element in the list. Methods to find an element in the list and return the corresponding list node are available as well and take linear time because they have to walk the list.

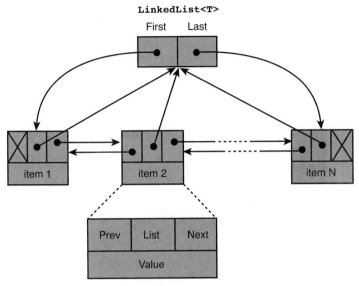

LinkedListNode<T>

FIGURE 16.6   References in LinkedList<T> and LinkedListNode<T>.

An example of creating and manipulating a list is shown here:

```
var lst = new LinkedList<string>();

var elem1 = lst.AddFirst("isn't");
var elem2 = lst.AddBefore(elem1, "This");
var elem3 = lst.AddAfter(elem1, "a");
var elem4 = lst.AddLast("list");
var elem5 = lst.AddBefore(elem4, "singly");
var elem6 = lst.AddAfter(elem5, "linked");

lst.Last.Previous.Previous.Value = "doubly";
lst.First.Next.Value = "is";

foreach (var word in lst)
    Console.Write(word + " ");

Console.WriteLine();
```

Notice all operations that manipulate the list take place through the LinkedList<T> type. This enables the list to maintain the list structure in a consistent manner, keeping all Next and Previous references in a good state. Similarly, adding an element in front of the first element requires the First reference to be updated to point at the new "head" of the list. Adding an element after the last one requires an update of the Last reference.

When walking the list manually by following Next or Previous references, be aware that the list is not circular. Null references indicate that the end or beginning of the list has been reached. In other words, First.Previous and Last.Next will always return null.

THE CASE OF THE BROKEN COLLECTION INITIALIZER

LinkedList<T> doesn't support the handy C# 3.0 collection initializer syntax. Looking at the type's interface implementation list, you might think it should; after all, it implements the ICollection interface, which has an Add method on it, right? However, this collection type implements that interface *explicitly*, thus making the Add method private on the class itself. Therefore, the compiler doesn't find an Add method to call for the collection initializer's use. The following works, though:

```
var lst = new LinkedList<string>();
((ICollection<string>)lst).Add("Hello"); // calling through the interface
```

So the duck-typed nature of collection initializers with regard to discovering an Add method sometimes (but rarely ever) works against the feature.

Dictionary<TKey, TValue>

To provide a generically typed alterative to Hashtable, the Dictionary<TKey, TValue> type was invented. Where Hashtable uses System.Object for both its keys and values, the generic dictionary allows static typing of keys and values. Let's cross-translate our original example again:

```
var tbl = new Dictionary<string, int>();
tbl.Add("Bart", 26);
tbl["John"] = 62;

bool bartIsKnown = tbl.ContainsKey("Bart");
bool someIsAged62 = tbl.ContainsValue(62);
foreach (var name in tbl.Keys)
    Console.WriteLine("Age of {0} is {1}", name, tbl[name]);

tbl.Remove("Bart");
```

The code still looks exactly the same, thanks to the mirrored API design compared to Hashtable. This makes people with prior experience using Hashtable feel at home immediately in the world of generic dictionaries. The obvious difference is you can't make any typing mistakes anymore. This is illustrated once more in Figure 16.7, also showing how IntelliSense guides you in the right direction.

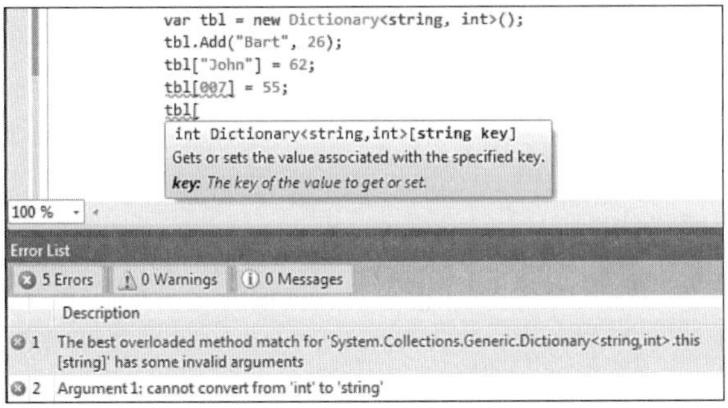

FIGURE 16.7   Stronger type checking enforced by generics.

Notice how the example uses an implicitly typed local variable for the foreach loop's iteration variable. Because all type information around generics is known at compile time, as
proven by the great IntelliSense experience, the compiler can infer statically what the loop
variable's type ought to be. This is proven by code editor inspection in Figure 16.8.

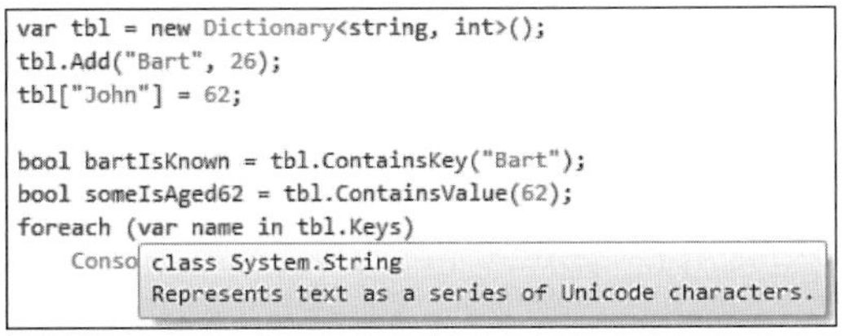

FIGURE 16.8   Rich type information available at compile time.

While we're at it, direct iteration over dictionary types (as opposed to going over keys or
values individually) is also possible. By looking at the definition of the generic type, you
can trace why this is the case:

```
public class Dictionary<TKey, TValue> : IDictionary<TKey, TValue>, ...
```

From here, we get into the IDictionary<TKey, TValue> generic interface, which in turn
leads us to an ICollection generic interface:

```
public interface IDictionary<TKey, TValue> :
    ICollection<KeyValuePair<TKey, TValue>>
```

Here things start to get more interesting: The ICollection<T> interface is parameterized
with the KeyValuePair<TKey, TValue> generic type. But first, let's finish our tracing of the
enumerable nature of a generic dictionary by following the ICollection<T> trail:

```
public interface ICollection<T> : IEnumerable<T>
```

To conclude this type-chasing exercise, we've discovered how each generic dictionary type implements IEnumerable<T>, where T is substituted for a KeyValuePair generic constructed type. KeyValuePair<TKey, TValue> is defined like this:

```
public struct KeyValuePair<TKey, TValue> {
    public KeyValuePair(TKey key, TValue value);

    public TKey Key { get; }
    public TValue Value { get; }
}
```

Based on this observation, we can also loop over our dictionary as follows, extracting the name and age values using Key and Value properties:

```
foreach (var entry in tbl)
    Console.WriteLine(entry.Key + " is " + entry.Value);
```

Once more local variable type inference knows exactly what we're talking about, as shown in Figure 16.9.

FIGURE 16.9   IDictionary<TKey, TValue> is IEnumerable<KeyValuePair<TKey, TValue>>.

IMPLICITLY TYPED LOCAL VARIABLES

Although implicitly typed local variables or local variable type inference, using the var keyword, was introduced for use mainly in conjunction with anonymous types, its use extends far beyond that. Generic (collection) types are one of the places where type inference can prove tremendously useful in reducing code clutter. With generic types, large type names can be constructed in no time:

```
Dictionary<string, List<int>> personLottoNumbers
    = new Dictionary<string, List<int>>();
```

Simple object instantiation doesn't even fit on one line anymore because the type has to be stated twice. Even though some programmers have identified the var keyword as the devil in disguise, it's hard to deny the following is cleaner:

```
var personLottoNumbers = new Dictionary<string, List<int>>();
```

Have you lost track of type information? No. Is the code cleaner? Yes. That's a win-win situation if you ask me.

One final method we should examine when talking about this collection type is the handy self-explanatory TryGetValue method:

```
int ageOfMarge;
if (tbl.TryGetValue("Marge", out ageOfMarge))
    // Code if the key was found, with ageOfMarge set to the retrieved value.
```

The generic dictionary type is, just like the Hashtable type, based on hashing to provide efficient lookup of entries by their keys. This implies the same caveats regarding providing a good hash function on the key type and ensuring immutability of key values apply.

Where the Hashtable type uses the System.Object's GetHashcode and Equals virtual methods directly for key object storage, the generic dictionary type introduces one more level of abstraction by means of an IEqualityComparer<T> interface:

```
public interface IEqualityComparer<in T> {
    bool Equals(T x, T y);
    int GetHashCode(T obj);
}
```

Although a custom equality comparer implementation can be provided to the generic dictionary constructor, one typically relies on the default EqualityComparer<T> being used. This one uses the System.Object virtual methods internally to be on par with the default behavior used by the nongeneric Hashtable collection type. Use of a custom equality comparer can come in handy to override the key type's default behavior with regard to hash code calculation and equality checking (for example, to implement non-case-sensitive key differentiation). This is already done by means of a StringComparer type in the .NET Framework:

```
var ages = new Dictionary<string, int>(StringComparer.CurrentCultureIgnoreCase)
{
    { "Homer", 38 },
    { "Bart", 10 }
};
Console.WriteLine(ages["bart"]); // different casing, still works
```

ADVANCED COLLECTION INITIALIZER SYNTAX

C#
3.0
C# 3.0 collection initializer syntax works with any Add method overload it can find on an object that implements IEnumerable. Because the generic dictionary type has an Add method that takes in arguments for the key and the value, we can have the initializer call it by writing the two arguments between curly braces. The preceding code therefore corresponds to the following:

```
var __t = new Dictionary<string, int>(StringComparer.CurrentCultureIgnoreCase);
__t.Add("Homer", 38);
__t.Add("Bart", 10);
var ages = __t;
```

This allows concise syntax to initialize a collection as an expression, and therefore it can be fed directly into a method expecting an instance of the collection type.

There's one more level of indirection in the default equality comparer: If the specified type parameter implements IEquatable<T>, it uses that implementation for its Equals method. All of this additional abstraction adds a great amount of flexibility that you might want to use on occasion. In the past, you would have had to mess around with subclassing collection types to realize such behavior.

SortedDictionary<TKey, TValue> and SortedList<TKey, TValue>

To keep a dictionary sorted by its key objects, both SortedDictionary<TKey, TValue> and SortedList<TKey, TValue> can be used. They differ in the performance profile of various operations like insertion and deletion, as well as memory consumption. Both use a binary search tree on the inside to make retrieval an O(log n) efficient operation. For more details on the precise differences between both types on the performance front, refer to the MSDN documentation.

The interface of both types is identical to that of the Dictionary<TKey, TValue> type simply because they all implement the corresponding generic dictionary interface. The only difference lies in the ordered characteristic of keys:

```
var ages = new SortedDictionary<string, int> {
    { "Homer", 38 },
    { "Bart", 10 }
};
foreach (string name in ages.Keys)
    Console.WriteLine(name + " is " + ages[name]);
```

The preceding code will print Bart first, even though Homer was inserted first. All insert and remove operations keep the keys sorted, which is visible both through key/value pair enumeration and the Keys collection directly.

Just as with the nonsorted dictionary type, abstractions are implemented to make the ordering semantics flexible through the implementation of IComparer<T>:

```
public interface IComparer<in T> {
    int Compare(T x, T y);
}
```

If a comparer object is left unspecified through the constructor, a default one is used as provided by Comparer<T>.Default. This implementation on its turn looks out for an IComparable<T> implementation, which built-in types like int and string provide:

```
public interface IComparable<in T> {
    int CompareTo(T other);
}
```

An example of a generic comparer that reverses order is shown here. It simply calls the default comparer's Compare method and negates the result. Remember that the sign of the result indicates the relative order of the two parameters, with negative for less than and positive for greater than:

```
class ReverseComparer<T> : IComparer<T> {
    public int Compare(T x, T y) {
        return -Comparer<T>.Default.Compare(x, y);
    }
}
```

As an example, consider the following code, which will result in an ordered printout of Marge, Homer, and Bart, a descending order by the string-valued keys:

```
var ages = new SortedDictionary<string, int>(new ReverseComparer<string>()) {
    { "Bart", 10 },
    { "Marge", 34 },
    { "Homer", 38 }
};
```

ONE INTERFACE TOO MUCH?

At first, you might think there's one interface too many to deal with flexible ordering. Both serve their unique goals, though. The IComparable<T> interface gets implemented on an object that wants to make itself comparable to any other object of the same type. In other words, types can provide for comparability themselves.

IComparer<T> works outside the domain of a type itself: An outsider can define what it means to compare two instances of a type T. This effectively provides a means to overrule what the type itself has defined as the meaning of comparison. That's the property collections make use of.

HashSet<T>

While we're in the mood to discuss hash codes, it's appropriate to discuss another collection type that relies on the same concept: HashSet<T>. A set is a collection that filters out duplicate entries, which is determined based on equality between elements contained in the set.

Knowing the properties of a hash code, you can already guess why the use of a hash code is beneficial for set implementation, too. Upon addition of an element to the set, its uniqueness needs to be determined in relation to the elements that are already in the set. This search can be narrowed down by use of a hash code before resorting to wholesale equality checks. Without the facility of a hash code, insertion into a set would require the new *wannabe element* to be compared for equality against *all the* set's existing elements. The conceptual internal organization of a hash-based set is shown in Figure 16.10, as used during an addition operation.

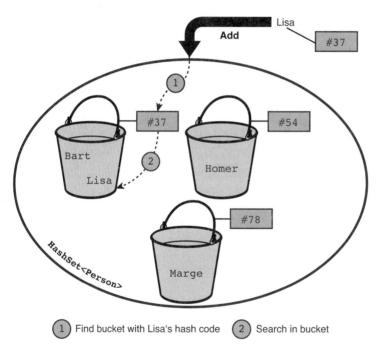

FIGURE 16.10   Operation of a HashSet<T> for an addition operation.

An example of the use of a HashSet is shown here:

```
var people = new HashSet<Person>();
people.Add(new Person("Bart", 10));
people.Add(new Person("Homer", 38));
people.Add(new Person("Lisa", 8));
people.Add(new Person("Marge", 34));
people.Add(new Person("Lisa", 8));   // Duplicate will not be added.
int four = people.Count;
```

In this example, we assume the `Person` type has an overridden implementation for both `GetHashCode` and `Equals`, as shown earlier in this chapter. The default `System.Object` implementation for those methods will result in reference equality semantics, so the two separate instances of a `Person` called Lisa with age 8 will be treated as different, resulting in five elements in the set rather than four.

Additional element-based methods are illustrated in the following example. Notice the use of the C# 3.0 collection initializer syntax once more:

```
var numbers = new HashSet<int> { 1, 2, 2, 3, 4, 5, 5 }; // { 1, 2, 3, 4, 5 }
numbers.Add(6);                                         // { 1, 2, 3, 4, 5, 6 }
numbers.Remove(3);                                      // { 1, 2,    4, 5, 6 }
numbers.RemoveWhere(n => n % 2 == 0);                   // { 1,          5 }
numbers.Clear();                                        // { }

foreach (int number in numbers)
    Console.WriteLine(number);
```

Beside methods that operate at the level of individual elements, `HashSet<T>` exposes set-level operations, too. Let's define the following sets and illustrate each of those operations using them:

```
var first = new HashSet<int> { 1, 2, 3, 5, 8, 13 };
var second = new HashSet<int> { 2, 3, 5, 7, 11 };
```

Figure 16.11 illustrates four common set-level operations graphically.

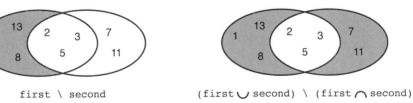

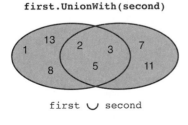

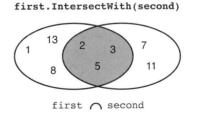

FIGURE 16.11   Set-level operations on HashSet<T>.

A darker background indicates the first set's contents after applying the operation to it. In other words, all the set-level operations mutate the first set in place.

Besides those operations, various Boolean-valued checks exist, allowing membership checks but also set-theoretic property checks such as SetEquals, Overlaps, IsSubsetOf, IsSuperSetOf, IsProperSubsetOf, and IsProperSupersetOf.

Because HashSet<T> relies on GetHashCode and Equals, flexibility has been added in the form of support for IEqualityComparer<T>, just as with the generic dictionary type we saw before.

SortedSet<T>

The sorted counterpart of the HashSet<T> is found in SortedSet<T>. Besides the set property of filtering out duplicate entries, it presents its contents in a sorted order. This order is determined by the IComparer<T> that's optionally provided to it through the constructor. When omitted, the default comparer is used in an manner analogous to the sorted dictionary types we discussed before. Not much more explanation is needed:

```
var sortedNumbers = new SortedSet<int> { 5, 2, 7, 11, 3 };

// Prints 2, 3, 5, 7, 11
foreach (int number in sortedNumbers)
    Console.WriteLine(number);
```

Not shown in the preceding code, the Add method (hidden behind the collection initializer syntax) returns a Boolean to indicate whether the element was added to the set. A false value indicates a duplicate was already present. This remarks holds for the nonsorted HashSet<T>, too. In addition, the SortedSet<T> provides a few members that deal with ordering directly. The Reverse method returns an IEnumerable<T> that walks the sorted set in reverse order. Two properties, Min and Max, are self-explanatory. And finally, a method called GetViewBetween returns a set with elements that lie between two supplied values in the original set.

Queue<T> and Stack<T>

To conclude our journey through the generic collection types, we meet again with the queue and stack collections in a generic shape. Because their use is completely analogous to the nongeneric counterparts, we'll just go for a translation of the original example, now with stronger type checking at compile time and making ugly casts go away:

```
var postOffice = new Queue<Person>();
postOffice.Enqueue(new Person("Bart", 10));
postOffice.Enqueue(new Person("Homer", 38));
postOffice.Enqueue(new Person("Ned", 60));
var bart = postOffice.Dequeue();
var homer = postOffice.Peek(); // D'oh
int twoLeft = postOffice.Count;
```

And for a stack

```
var stack = new Stack<int>();
stack.Push(1);
stack.Push(2);
stack.Push(3);
var three = stack.Pop();
var two = stack.Peek();
var twoLeft = stack.Count;
```

Other Collection Types

Collections are the bread and butter for many library or application writers. Even though the number of collection types we've already seen is quite big, even more collection types are hiding out there. Because their use is more specialized, we limit ourselves to some pointers as to where to find them:

▶ `System.Collections.Specialized` contains, as the name implies, specialized collections that aren't used very frequently and typically provide solutions to specific problems or performance challenges. Examples include a bit vector type, a hybrid dictionary, and some remains from the nongeneric ages.

▶ `System.Collections.ObjectModel` provides the `Collection<T>` base class for generic collections as well as the `ReadOnlyCollection<T>` used for read-only collections (which can be obtained from regular ones by calling `AsReadOnly`). It also contains an observable collection that raises events when elements are added, removed, inserted, and so on. You'll see that one back in Windows Presentation Foundation (WPF) later.

▶ `System.Collections.Concurrent`, covered separately when we discuss concurrent programming, provides concurrency-safe collections.

Summary

Chapter 15 introduced the notion of generics from a language point of view. One of the main motivations for the language and runtime feature's introduction in the .NET 2.0 was generic collection types. In this chapter we looked at the various collection types available in the BCL.

After starting our exploration in the nongeneric worlds, we aimed our attention at the generic collections, including stacks, queues, lists, dictionaries, and more. A solid knowledge of how any of those types work and when to use them is essential to become a successful .NET and C# developer.

CHAPTER 17

Delegates

IN THIS CHAPTER

▶ Functional Programming 777

▶ What Are Delegates? 782

▶ Delegate Types 782

▶ Delegate Instances 787

▶ Invoking Delegates 799

▶ Putting It Together: An Extensible Calculator 803

▶ Case Study: Delegates Used in LINQ to Objects 807

▶ Asynchronous Invocation 811

▶ Combining Delegates 824

In the previous chapters, you've seen how object-oriented programming provides a good paradigm to tame the complexity involved with the creation of applications. Nevertheless, object orientation is not a silver bullet that solves all problems. Different paradigms have emerged over the years to deal with other complex aspects of application development.

Functional programming is one such paradigm that got a place in the .NET Framework and its languages, too. Starting from the very first release of the .NET platform, delegates have been around as ways to treat functions as first-class citizens on the platform. On top of this, we find the everyday concept of events used around the .NET framework (for example, in UI frameworks such as Windows Forms).

This chapter covers functional programming and shows how it gets applied through use of delegates and various C# language features like anonymous methods and, more recently, lambda expressions. To illustrate matters, we look at the use of delegates through the lenses of LINQ. In Chapter 18, "Events," we continue our journey by explaining events and applying them in the realm of UI programming.

Functional Programming

Over the years, different approaches have been created to deal with complexities that arise from application development. One of the oldest paradigms is, without doubt, functional programming. We start by putting this paradigm in some historical context and then follow up with an overview of its concepts. After covering functional programming from this more theoretic angle, we apply the concept to the use of delegates in C#.

Historical Perspective

Object-oriented programming provides a means to tackle various aspects of complexity that arise during the creation and maintenance of applications. It does so through various means, such as encapsulation of state and polymorphism, stimulating reuse of existing functionality through class hierarchies.

If we go one level up from object-oriented programming, we find ourselves back in the world of procedural programming, where a different sort of complexity is dealt with. By stimulating the use of procedures (methods) to reuse blocks of code, parameterized by some inputs, excessive duplication of code is avoided.

We can continue our way up the chain, landing at structured programming, where the use of low-level goto statements is strongly discouraged, in favor of control flow primitives such as loops and conditional statements. Again, this deals with complexities that arise from the creation and maintenance of nontrivial pieces of code.

Before we go any further with our discussion, you need to understand that the paradigms mentioned are not mutually exclusive. Indeed, C# fits nicely in all of those camps. You could go as far as saying that OO-languages *derive* from procedural languages, *extending* it with the concept of classes and such. Similarly, procedural languages extend the functionality their structured parents have to offer by adding the concept of procedures.

While walking this inheritance chain of language paradigms, we've ended up close to the hardware of the underlying machine. Structured programming languages essentially provide abstractions over low-level machine primitives like branches, among others. Going back to object-oriented programming, we see layers of abstraction are added to continue to simplify the creation of applications of increasing complexity. You can compare this to the rings of an onion, around low-level assembler languages, as shown in Figure 17.1.

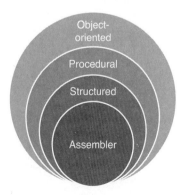

FIGURE 17.1   Dealing with complexity, bottom up from assembler languages.

This approach to dealing with complexity is not the only one that has emerged over the years. Functional programming starts from a different perspective, going all the way back to the concept of mathematical functions. Instead of adding layers of abstraction, one peels off such layers to make things executable on real-world machines. Figure 17.2 illustrates how both worlds have evolved over the years.

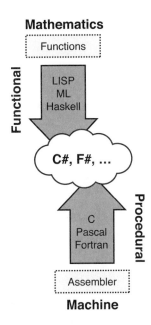

FIGURE 17.2   Language evolution in a broader perspective.

The mention of mathematics in the very first sentence introducing the concept of functional programming might make all of this sound rather scary. Believe me; it's not that bad.

Programming with Functions

So what's functional programming all about? Shockingly, it's nothing more than the concept of "programming with functions," leaving us with the task of defining what we consider to be a function. We can answer this question from different perspectives, one more practically applicable than the other. First, we take a look at the fundamentalist viewpoint, focusing on the concept of side effects. Next, we get closer to everyday reality in the world of .NET and C# development.

Pure Functions Versus Side Effects

From the fundamentalist functional programming point of view, you should think of a function in the pure mathematical sense. Rather than giving a formal definition, let's just concentrate on one of its essential properties: Every time you call a function with the same arguments, it returns the same answer:

```
add 1 2 fi 3
add 1 2 fi 3
...
```

You might think that functions are synonymous with methods, but this is not really the case. The underlying problem has to do with *side effects* that are not apparent from looking at a method's signature:

```
int Add(int a, int b)
```

Nothing in the signature tells us that the Add method will return the same answer every time it's given the same values for a and b. Furthermore, while calculating the result, side effects might result: Maybe the method writes something to a file or launches the missiles. To see why this could be a problem, consider the following fragment:

```
int res1 = Add(1,2);
// ...
int res2 = Add(1,2);
```

In the face of potential side effects, the compiler can't optimize the preceding code to avoid recomputing Add(1,2) because this might change the program's behavior:

```
int res1 = Add(1,2);
// ...
int res2 = res1;
```

Assuming for the sake of illustration that Add prints some message to the screen, the first fragment will print twice, while the second one will only print once. Clearly, the programs are not equivalent anymore.

However, if guarantees were made about the absence of side effects when evaluating a method, compilers would be able to optimize code without the risk of changing the program's meaning. This is one of the advantages *pure* functional programming has to offer. In addition, evaluation of such programs can be parallelized more effectively because you don't have to care about the order in which side effects occur.

Does this mean we should ban all side effects from our programs? Clearly, side effects are a good thing from time to time; without them, our programs wouldn't be able to communicate with the outside world! What's needed to make this work is a way to tame side effects and make them apparent through the function signature. One language that does so is Haskell.

The reality is that most mainstream languages (including C#) don't go that far and allow side effects everywhere. The future will tell whether the apparent benefits, such as simpler parallelization of code, especially important in the age of many-core processors, are considered worthwhile to overhaul languages and frameworks.

First-Class Functions

So it seems we need to take a step back and strip down our notion of functions a little bit to get to more real-world functional programming in the broadest sense, as seen in languages like C#. Here's our second, more applicable, attempt at defining functional programming languages.

In the world of functional programming, one treats functions as first-class citizens of the language. But what does this mean precisely? In essence, it means you can store and pass around functions just as you can do with other sorts of objects, such as numbers or strings.

For example, you could think of a general-purpose function that can filter a sequence of objects (for example, natural numbers) based on a certain criterion (for example, is the number even?). Instead of baking in the criterion to the filter function, we want to enable the caller to feed in the criterion as a predicate function. This way, our filter function can be reused for different sequences and criteria. Let's illustrate this:

```
int[] numbers = new [] { 1, 2, 3, 4, 5 };
// Lambda expression syntax used below will be explained later in this chapter.
// Don't worry about it for now, but it doesn't hurt to think about the meaning
// of the "=>" token. Can you come up with a pronunciation of the syntax?
var evens = numbers.Where(/* is even? */ x => x % 2 == 0); // --> { 2, 4 }
var odds  = numbers.Where(/* is odd?  */ x => x % 2 != 0); // --> { 1, 3, 5 }
```

What we want to do in the preceding code is to pass the criterion function to the Where method to apply the filter on the numbers sequence. In fact, the Where method shown is defined as one of the standard query operators in LINQ:

```
IEnumerable<T> Where<T>(this IEnumerable<T> source, Func<T, bool> predicate);
```

How this method is implemented is irrelevant for the sake of the current discussion. The essential part here is that the second argument is a function that "goes from T to bool." The .NET mechanism that allows us to represent a function as a first-class object is called a *delegate*. Notice that in the preceding example a generic delegate type is used, which works in exactly the same way as generic classes, methods, or interfaces, as we've seen before.

Don't worry about the details for now; we get into those soon. What matters as the key takeaway from this conceptual introduction is that you can pass functions around in exactly the same way you can pass objects around.

FUNCTIONS ARE DATA!

Representing functions as objects is a deeply rooted concept, not just an oddity of modern application development frameworks like .NET. A common way to speed up a function's evaluation is to implement it as a table lookup. For example, you could implement a sine function in terms of an infinite sum using Taylor series, which is quite intensive if done repeatedly. Alternatively, you could trade CPU cycles for memory storage and keep evaluated results in a table for subsequent lookups. Tables are data structures, so "functions as data" is not that far-fetched.

Unsurprisingly, this definition of functions in terms of table lookups requires the function to be pure in terms of side effects, but that's a whole different story. Just remember that functions and data are closely related concepts.

What Are Delegates?

As briefly mentioned before, delegates are the .NET concept that enables you to represent a function as an object. Because the concept of a mathematical function doesn't really exist in the world of .NET, this mechanism is implemented in terms of methods instead. At the lowest level of the CLR, delegates are objects that contain a reference to some method on some object.

This section looks at how you can declare delegate types, create instances of delegates, and use them. Besides this, you look at the language-level support provided by C#, such as anonymous methods and lambda expressions. While doing so, lots of examples are presented, ultimately showing off LINQ in .NET 3.0 as one of the most recent application programming interfaces (APIs) built around functional concepts with extensive use of delegates.

Delegate Types

As you've seen repeatedly, the CLR provides type safety, making programs more robust against errors introduced by programmers. It's no surprise that delegates are no exception to this rule. This immediately contrasts delegate types against raw function pointers as seen in languages such as C and C++:

```
int add(int a, int b) {
    return a + b;
}

void main() {
    int (*fpAdd)(int, int);
    fpAdd = &add;
    int three = fpAdd(1, 2); // calls the add function through the pointer
}
```

Although the preceding fragment is well written, lots of opportunities exist to perform unsafe operations. For example, you could trick fpAdd so that it points to a function that takes arguments of types different from int (or a different number of arguments), without any runtime protection whatsoever against this kind of mishap.

The preceding C fragment captures the essence of the function that matters to the user of the function pointer: its *signature*. On the first line of main, using quite cumbersome C syntax, a variable is created with a type that captures the target function's signature. Figure 17.3 shows a function pointer in C-style.

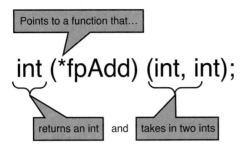

FIGURE 17.3   C-style function pointer.

Delegates in .NET are similar to this but provide a type-safe means to do so, with compile-time and runtime checking against violations. The preceding fragment would look like the following in C#:

```
delegate int BinOp(int a, int b);

static class Program
{
    static int Add(int a, int b) {
        return a + b;
    }

    static void Main() {
        BinOp add = new BinOp(Add);
        int three = add(1, 2); // calls the Add method through the delegate
    }
}
```

Notice a few differences compared to the C fragment. The use of a class, as well as static methods, should come as no surprise. More substantial differences have to do with the declaration of a *delegate type*, BinOp, and the way a *delegate instance* is created. Last but not least, there's the way to invoke the delegate.

Obviously, the preceding example is rather artificial, calling the Add method through a level of indirection by using a delegate. Stay tuned for more practical examples later in this chapter; for the time being, let's focus on the essentials.

At the top of the C# fragment, we've declared a delegate type, which is basically the description of a method signature with full type information available. Type safety will ensure the delegate object can't be used to refer to a method with a signature that's not compatible (to be explained later) with the one the delegate type is declared with.

Now, what does a delegate type consist of? Let's peek under the hood in ILDASM for a minute, as shown in Figure 17.4.

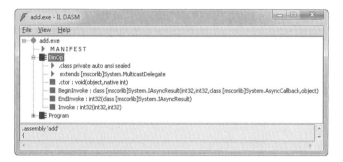

FIGURE 17.4   A delegate type under the hood.

As you can see, a delegate is just a class extending the MulticastDelegate base class, providing an Invoke method of the stated signature. It should be pretty straightforward to imagine the way a delegate is being called: Under the hood, the Invoke method will be called

```
static void Main() {
    BinOp add = new BinOp(Add);
    int three = add(1, 2); // implemented as a call to add.Invoke(1, 2)
}
```

We confirm this hypothesis when talking about delegate instances next; just believe me for the time being. Aside from the Invoke method, two other methods are generated to facilitate asynchronous invocation scenarios: BeginInvoke and EndInvoke. This goes beyond the scope of the discussion, so we ignore those two for now.

WHY MULTICASTDELEGATE?

The phrase *multicast* inside the delegate's base type name might be a little surprising. In fact, a single delegate instance can be used to refer to many methods (all with a compatible signature of course) at a time. When invoking the delegate, all the referred methods will be called after one another. You'll see that this is important to realize the concept of events where multiple handlers can be attached to the same event. In such a case, raising the event should notify all the handlers.

Another question is how an instance of this type manages to call into the methods it *refers* to. That answer can be inferred from looking at the constructor method .ctor, which takes in an object and a native int. The former of those arguments is the instance on which the target method has to be called. In our running example, this will be null because the target method, Add, is a static method. The second argument is a reference to the method that has to be called, conceptually comparable to a pointer in C.

Because I've taught you to be curious about how things work, without a doubt you'll have looked at the definition of both the .ctor and the Invoke method by now. If so, you will be slightly disappointed to see there's nothing of interest in there apart from a subtle hint that the implementation of those methods is provided by the runtime. Figure 17.5 shows the Invoke method definition from an ILDASM point of view.

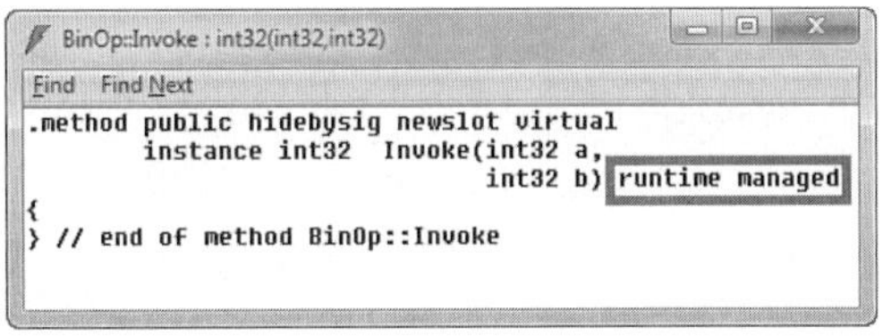

FIGURE 17.5   Low-level plumbing is the common language runtime's business.

AN ALTERNATIVE VIEW

If the concept of delegate types is a bit confusing at first, think of them slightly differently. Delegates are similar to interfaces with a single method inside them, corresponding to the Invoke method we've seen in ILDASM. In fact, platforms such as Java that have historically omitted delegates from the language specification realize similar capabilities by means of one-method interfaces such as Runnable. With this analogy in mind, creating a delegate instance is similar to implementing that single method on the interface.

Delegate type declarations are similar to method declarations in their expressive power. You can use ref and out parameters and params arrays, as shown here:

```
delegate string Foo(int a, ref double b, out long c, params DateTime[] ds);
```

The parameter list of a delegate type can be empty, and the return type of a delegate can be void. Examples of such delegates can be found in the System.Threading namespace and the System namespace:

```
delegate void ThreadStart(); // for Java folks: similar to Runnable.run
delegate void Action();
```

NOMINAL EQUIVALENCE

Delegate types in C# have so-called nominal equivalence, in contrast to so-called structural equivalence. This means that two delegate types with the same parameter list and return type are considered different. In the preceding example, Action and ThreadStart can refer to the same methods but are considered different types.

Delegate types can also be declared using generics, examples of which can be found in the System namespace in the form of the Func and Action delegate types:

```
delegate TResult Func<out TResult>();
delegate TResult Func<in T1, out TResult>(T1 t1);
...
delegate TResult Func<in T1, ..., in T16, out TResult>(T1 t1, ..., T16 t16);

delegate void Action();
delegate void Action<in T1>(T1 t1);
...
delegate void Action<in T1, ..., in T16>(T1 t1, ..., T16 t16);
```

For example, to represent a function that takes in an integer value and produces a bool, you could use the unary (that is, with one argument) generic Func delegate type; and to create an integral sum function, the binary generic Func delegate type can be used:

```
Func<int, bool> isEven = new Func<int, bool>(IsEven);
Func<int, int, int> add = new Func<int, int, int>(Add);
```

GENERIC CO- AND CONTRAVARIANCE

Notice the use of the in and out modifiers on the generic parameters on the Func and Action delegate types. During our discussion about generics, you learned about this C# 4.0 feature called generic co- and contravariance. This feature enables the following scenario that failed to compile before in C# 3.0:

```
Func<Fruit, string> printFruit = new Func<Fruit, string>(FruitPrinter);
Func<Apple, object> appleToObject = printFruit; // failed in C# 3.0
```

Before generic co- and contravariance, C# 2.0 already provided the notion of co- and contravariance for creating a delegate from a method group that doesn't have a signature that matches *exactly* with the target delegate's signature:

```
// Assume the following definition:  string PrintFruit(Fruit f);
Func<Apple, object> appleToObject = PrintFruit;
```

The compiler can prove this is safe to do because of the subtype relationships that exist between Apple and Fruit and string and object. If we pass an Apple to appleToObject, it's fine for the PrintFruit target to treat it as a Fruit. For the return type, it's safe to treat the string that came back from PrintFruit as an object.

Delegate Instances

Although delegate types provide a type-safe way to refer to methods, instances concretize this notion by referring to a particular method (optionally) on some object. In our running example, we give a first example of instantiating a delegate instance:

```
static void Main() {
    BinOp add = new BinOp(Add);
    int three = add(1, 2); // calls the Add method through the delegate
}
```

This is one possible way to create a delegate instance that has been supported since the early C# 1.0 days. As shown in Figure 17.6, Visual Studio hints at the required method signature for the delegate target.

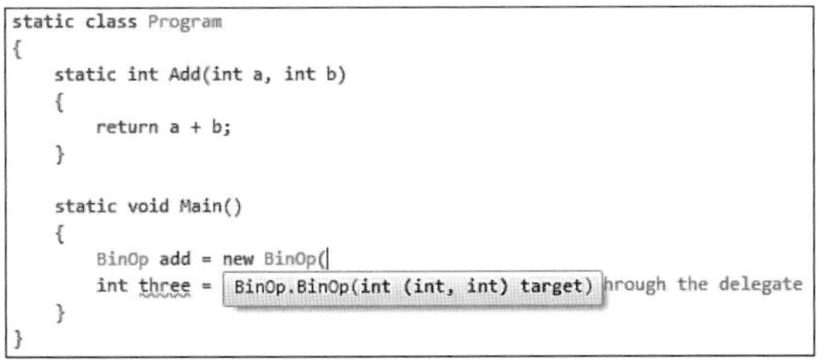

```
static class Program
{
    static int Add(int a, int b)
    {
        return a + b;
    }

    static void Main()
    {
        BinOp add = new BinOp(
        int three =  BinOp.BinOp(int (int, int) target) hrough the delegate
    }
}
```

FIGURE 17.6   IntelliSense for instantiation of a delegate type.

Since C# 2.0, the syntax for code in Figure 17.6 can be abbreviated a bit by using the so-called method group conversion. This is a rather fancy name to say that there is an implicit conversion from the name of a method to a compatible delegate type. In other words, we can simplify the preceding code as follows:

```
static void Main() {
    BinOp add = Add;
    int three = add(1, 2); // calls the Add method through the delegate
}
```

METHOD GROUPS

Why does this C# 2.0 feature contain the words *method* and *group* in its name? Take a look at what we've done in the preceding example: We assigned Add to an object of type BinOp, a delegate type. Now assume multiple Add method overloads exist. It's clear that the lexical token Add in the source code doesn't refer to a particular one of them; instead, it refers to the group of methods with that name. Method groups don't have a type by themselves: Writing something (in C# 3.0) like var add = Add could be ambiguous and can result in a compile-time error.

Method group conversion refers to the capability of the compiler to figure out from context what method from the group is meant, based on the delegate type the method group gets assigned to. For more information, refer to the C# language specification, where all rules for method group conversion are outlined.

The two previous code fragments are completely identical from an intermediate language (IL) point of view, so it's time to take a look at how delegate instantiation works behind the scenes. Figure 17.7 illustrates this.

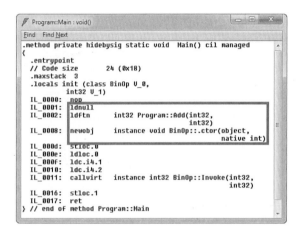

FIGURE 17.7   Delegate instantiation from an IL perspective.

You've already seen the constructor function on the delegate type in the previous section, so no surprises there. It takes two arguments, one of which denotes the object instance on which to invoke the target method. Because we're using a static method in our example, there's no instance, and hence the ldnull instruction is emitted. The way to refer to a method is observed on the line following the ldnull instruction, using ldftn, which results in a native int. It's this native int value that points at the method and allows the CLR to call into the method when requested to do so by means of delegate invocation. Notice that I didn't lie about how the delegate is getting called. Line IL_0011 clearly shows a call to Invoke being emitted for the delegate invocation.

Based on the discussion here you will have guessed delegate instances can refer to instance methods as well:

```
static void Main() {
    var calc = new Calculator(); // with an Add instance method
    BinOp add = calc.Add;
    int three = add(1, 2); // calls the Add method on calc through the delegate
}
```

EASIER THAN C-STYLE FUNCTION POINTERS

The ability to use the exact same delegate type to refer to either a static method or an instance method is a blessing. Behind the scenes, the calls to the target methods are quite different for both cases, due to the need for a "this pointer" when making an instance method call. The CLR's delegate system abstracts all those details away nicely, which is great compared to the world of C-style function pointers, where this often poses problems and frustration when calling conventions and such.

Anonymous Function Expressions

That's a good start, but the need to create a method even for the tiniest of methods to be used or passed as a delegate is quite cumbersome, too. Why do we need to create a whole Add method with the appropriate signature if we just want to express "add two numbers"? Can't we just somehow declare the method "inline" and have the compiler take care of creating a method under the hood that's referred to by the delegate? C# 2.0 introduced such a feature, called *anonymous function expressions*:

```
static void Main() {
    BinOp add = delegate (int a, int b) { return a + b; };
    int three = add(1, 2); // calls the anonymous method through the delegate
}
```

In the preceding code, we're declaring an addition method inline by reusing the delegate keyword. Under the hood, the compiler generates an anonymous method containing the return a + b part and creates an instance of the BinOp delegate referring to the generated method. This plumbing, taken care of by the compiler, is shown in Figure 17.8.

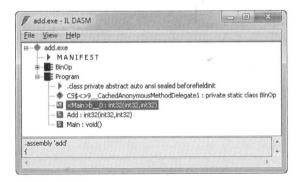

FIGURE 17.8 Anonymous function expression generated target method.

The code generated in the `Main` method to refer to the generated method roughly looks like this:

```
static void Main() {
    if (CS$<>9__CachedAnonymousMethodDelegate1 == null) {
        CS$<>9__CachedAnonymousMethodDelegate1 = new BinOp(<Main>b__0);
    }

    BinOp add = CS$<>9__CachedAnonymousMethodDelegate1;
    int three = add(1, 2); // calls the anonymous method through the delegate
}
```

Notice the little optimization by means of anonymous method delegate caching, so that subsequent calls of the containing method would not have to create a new instance of the delegate each time.

KEEP DEBUGGABILITY IN MIND

Although tool support for anonymous function expressions is great with full-fidelity source code matching under the debugger (so you can just step through the inline method declaration), things get a bit more obscure when you're faced with an exception call stack without a debugger nearby. Seeing a crash in a method like <Main>b__0 might not be incredibly helpful at first sight. Luckily, the name of the containing method is still visible, but if you end up with huge inline method declarations, it might be time to introduce a dedicated method with a proper name.

Personally, I tend to use anonymous function expressions (and lambda expressions) for short inline method declarations not exceeding a handful of statements, typically even just one single expression in case of lambdas.

Closures: Captured Outer Variables

 Because of their capability to capture local variables from the outer scope, anonymous function expressions are much more powerful than would seem to be the case at first glance. Let's take a look at an example:

```
static void Main() {
    int factor = 2;
    BinOp addAndFactor = delegate (int a, int b) { return factor * (a + b); };
    int six = addAndFactor(1, 2);
}
```

In the preceding code fragment, the local variable factor is captured inside the embedded inline method declaration. This is a powerful capability that reduces plumbing significantly. Imagine how you would communicate the factor value to a delegate if you couldn't simply use an anonymous function expression. A more real-world example is in the creation of a simple thread:

```
static void DoBackgroundWork(int nTimes, Action<int> doWork) {
    new Thread(delegate () {
        for (int i = 0; i < nTimes; i++)
            doWork(i);
    }).Start();
}
```

The preceding deserves some explanation. The Thread class in System.Threading takes in a ThreadStart delegate to pass in the method that needs to be executed on the newly created thread. Its signature has been shown earlier in this chapter: It returns void and takes in no arguments. Our anonymous function expression reflects that signature.

Now inside the anonymous function expression, we loop nTimes. Here magic happens: The nTimes variable is captured from the outer scope. Similarly, the doWork parameter (which is a delegate by itself!) is also captured from the outer scope. Without this C# 2.0 feature, also known as *closures*, you would have to write a helper class to contain all the state that has to be passed to the thread's worker function:

```
internal class MyThread {
    public MyThread(int ntimes, Action<int> doWork) {
        _nTimes = nTimes;
        _doWork = doWork;
    }

    public void Run() {
        for (int i = 0; i < _nTimes; i++)
            _doWork(i);
    }
}
```

The use of this helper type in the DoBackgroundWork method would look as follows:

```
static void DoBackgroundWork(int nTimes, Action<int> doWork) {
    new Thread(new MyThread(nTimes, doWork).Run).Start();
}
```

Quite a bit of overhead just to create a thread that accesses some local state, if you ask me. In fact, the mechanism of closures implemented by the compiler does use a similar technique to capture outer variables: They get "hoisted" into a closure object, as illustrated in Figure 17.9 for our running calculator example.

FIGURE 17.9   Capturing outer variables creates a display class.

As you can see, the compiler generates a so-called display class that contains all the captured state from the outer scope (in our example, the factor variable). Such state gets exposed on the display class through public fields (not a bad thing in this case because it's only visible to the compiler and within the outer class), which are shared between the anonymous function and the scope where they were captured.

LVAL CAPTURING

Closures in C# implement something known as lval-capturing semantics (where lval stands for "left-side value"). What this means is that the variable gets captured, not just its value at the point of the capture. For example, the following prints 2:

```
int i = 1;
Action print = delegate() { Console.WriteLine(i); };
i = 2;
print(); // print is called after i has been changed to 2
```

This has its advantages in many cases but can be the source of surprises from time to time. A Dutch saying goes, "A warned man is worth double."

WHY CLOSURES ARE HEAP ALLOCATED

People interested in the ins and outs of closures might be wondering why closures are implemented using heap-allocated display classes. That's a very good question indeed, so let's discuss this a bit more. To set the scene, assume for a minute closures could somehow capture state that lives on the stack for the delegate to use. Now consider the code fragment here:

```
static Action GetPrint(int number) {
    return delegate() { Console.WriteLine(number); };
}
```

Here, we're capturing the number variable that lives on the stack, passed as a formal parameter to the GetPrint method. Assume we would keep that variable on the stack. Recall that returning from a method can be thought of as popping stuff from the (evaluation and call) stack. Thus, when we now return from GetPrint, we would have our hands on a variable pointing at a location on the stack that no longer exists.

It's clear that's a dangerous and type-unsafe thing to do because at the point of calling the returned Action delegate, that location might already have been overridden by another stack-allocated object. Recall that you've seen a similar case when we discussed ref parameters on methods.

SCOPING OF LOOP VARIABLES

One common pitfall of closures occurs when capturing a for loop variable, as shown in the next example:

```
for (int i = 0; i < 10; i++)
    new Thread(delegate () { Console.WriteLine(i); }).Start();
```

This piece of code prints random results, depending on when the threads start to run relative to the loop spawning new threads. Unexpected as this might seem, the explanation should be obvious from the following expansion of the loop:

```
{
    int i = 0;
    while (i < 10)
    {
        new Thread(delegate () { Console.WriteLine(i); }).Start();
        i++;
    }
}
```

Only one loop variable exists, shared (and mutated) across different iterations of the loop. All the threads refer to the same variable, which is being mutated by the thread running the loop. One possible result is that all threads print value 10, which happens if all the created threads start running after the loop completed.

To fix this issue, introduce an additional scope with its own copy of the variable:

```
for (int i = 0; i < 10; i++)
{
    int j = i;
    new Thread(delegate () { Console.WriteLine(j); }).Start();
}
```

Now every anonymous delegate gets its own copy of the loop variable, which isn't shared with any other party.

BEWARE OF SPACE LEAKS

Closures are implemented by lifting captured local variables into a heap-allocated (class) object where those variables become fields. When multiple anonymous methods have overlapping sets of captured local variables, the same "display class" (refer to Figure 17.9) is used to put the anonymous methods in. This can cause managed object "space leaks" in rather arcane circumstances. Here's an example:

```
string s = "Foo";
int i = 42;

Action a = delegate () { Console.WriteLine(i); };
Action b = delegate () { Console.WriteLine(s + " " + i); };
```

You're welcome to compile this piece of code and have a look in ILDASM or .NET Reflector to see the (single) generated class containing fields for variables s and i and the two anonymous methods. This is roughly equivalent to

```
class Closure
{
    public string s;
    public int i;

    public void a() { Console.WriteLine(i); }
    public void b() { Console.WriteLine(s + " " + i); }
}

Closure __c = new Closure { s = "Foo", i = 42 };
Action a = __c.a;
Action b = __c.b;
```

After executing this code, action delegates a and b refer to the corresponding methods on the single shared display class instance. Now both delegates keep this display class instance (which in turn holds on to s and i) alive from the garbage collector's point of view. So where does the space leak come in?

Notice how the code in action a doesn't refer to s, though the code in action b does. Assume there are no outstanding references to delegate b, the sole user of string s. At this point, it seems logical that string s becomes unreachable and can be garbage collected. Unfortunately, this is not the case if delegate a is still alive. As you can see from the expanded code fragment just listed, delegate a refers to an instance method on the closure object, so the whole closure object is kept alive, including the field for string s.

This all seems pretty bad, but luckily the scenarios that give rise to this case are rather rare. Having overlapping sets of captured local variables across multiple anonymous methods is one thing. Also having fundamentally different lifetimes for the delegates makes this bad scenario less likely (but not completely unlikely). Beware of space leaks!

Lambda Expressions

 With the advent of LINQ in C# 3.0 the use of functions as arguments to higher-order query operator functions was to become a day-to-day activity for developers, having to write query expressions like the following:

```
int[] numbers = new [] { 1, 2, 3, 4, 5 };
var evens = numbers.Where(delegate (int i) { return i % 2 == 0; });
var odds  = numbers.Where(delegate (int i) { return i % 2 != 0; });
```

You will agree that the preceding code is still quite overloaded with syntactical noise that comes from the use of anonymous function expressions: delegates, returns, curly braces.

> **NOTE**
>
> Simplified query expression syntax exists in C# 3.0, reducing the need to deal with the query operator functions directly. However, in various cases, no such syntax exists, requiring users to pass functions manually as shown earlier. This makes it a worthy goal to make anonymous function expressions easier on the eye.

Lambda expressions are yet another simplification on top of delegate instantiation, also allowing inline declaration of functions (with support for closures) but in a more compact way. The two preceding calls can be simplified as follows:

```
int[] numbers = new [] { 1, 2, 3, 4, 5 };
var evens = numbers.Where((int i) => i % 2 == 0);
var odds  = numbers.Where((int i) => i % 2 != 0);
```

The lambda arrow token => can be read as "goes to." For example, "An integer value i goes to the Boolean expressing whether the integer value is dividable by 2." In fact, given the signature of Where and the type of numbers, the compiler can infer the type of the lambda argument:

```
IEnumerable<T> Where<T>(this IEnumerable<T> source, Func<T, bool> predicate);
```

Because source is an IEnumerable<int>, T has to be int, and therefore the input to the predicate has to be of the same type. This allows us to simplify the syntax even further, also dropping the parentheses around i:

```
int[] numbers = new [] { 1, 2, 3, 4, 5 };
var evens = numbers.Where(i => i % 2 == 0);
var odds  = numbers.Where(i => i % 2 != 0);
```

GOING BACK IN TIME

It's sometimes good to put things in perspective by going back to the early days of C# to see how far we've come. Imagine an implementation of LINQ on C# 1.0 (assuming we would have had generics for the sake of demonstration); what would the preceding query look like? For every single use of a Where filter (or other query operators relying on delegates as arguments), we would have to introduce yet another method to express the function. Clearly, with all of its aspects spread out across many methods, your query wouldn't be readable anymore.

Lambda expressions in C# can contain not only expression bodies (the part on the right side of the arrow token) but also statement bodies. An example is the use of lambda syntax to create a ThreadStart delegate:

```
static void DoBackgroundWork(int nTimes, Action<int> doWork) {
    new Thread(() => {
        for (int i = 0; i < nTimes; i++)
            doWork(i);
    }).Start();
}
```

The empty parentheses pair is required in case an empty parameter list is to be passed to the lambda body. What matters more in the preceding code is that we're using a statement inside the body of the lambda expression. The syntax shown here boils down to the same IL code in case we'd use C# 2.0's inline delegate syntax (using the delegate keyword instead of the => token).

FUNCTIONAL TECHNIQUES IN C#: CURRYING

Functional languages typically provide a means of applying functions partially, one argument at a time. This technique is called currying, after the mathematician Haskell Curry (after whom the Haskell programming language is named), although it really was Schonfinkel who came up with the idea.

For example, in F#, you can write an addition function as follows:

```
let add a b = a + b
```

Besides the different syntax compared to method declaration in C#, this doesn't look very special: add is a function that given a and b returns the sum of those values. (Notice the types for a, b, and the function result are *inferred* by the F#.) However, the function can be called in different ways:

```
let three = add 1 2
let addFive = add 5
let seven = addFive 2
```

The second line is what interests us: Here we're calling the add function without a second argument. The result of doing so is a *function* of a single argument that when applied to an argument will add 5 to it. This is conceptually done by simple substitution of a for 5 inside the add function's body. Therefore, the previous code is equivalent to

```
let addFive =
fun b -> 5 + b  (* lambda syntax in F# uses a fun keyword *)
let seven = addFive 2
```

In this setting of currying, every function takes one argument at a time. So the add function doesn't take a and b simultaneously but instead applies a to add first, result-ing in "a remainder function" that will eat b. For example, the following pseudo-code shows how 3 is evaluated step by step:

```
let three = (add 1) 2        (* application is left-associative *)
          = (fun b -> 1 + b) 2
          = 1 + 2 = 3
```

In other words, the signature of add in C# lingo isn't as follows:

```
delegate int BinOp(int a, int b);   // Same as Func<int, int, int>
```

Instead, it's the following, using the Func generic delegate types:

```
Func<int, Func<int, int>>
```

The outer Func<T1, TResult> delegate type has int as an input (which will corre-spond to the a parameter) and returns a Func<int, int> delegate. That will be the remainder function that takes the b parameter into the final result.

How can we write this in C#? Using nested lambda expressions:

```
Func<int, Func<int, int>> add = a => b => a + b; // same as a => (b => a + b)
var three = add(1)(2);   // add(1) returns (b => 1 + b) which gets called with 2
var addFive = add(5);    // add(5) returns (b => 5 + b)
var seven = addFive(2); // addFive(2) returns 5 + 2 = 7
```

Beautiful, but rather verbose because of the generic delegate declarations. Don't worry: Most likely, you won't ever have to write code like this.

Expression Trees

As mentioned before, lambda expressions were introduced as part of the C# 3.0 LINQ wave of languages features, but not just as a way to simplify the syntax used to create anonymous functions. One of the key promises of LINQ is the capability to express a query using the same language-integrated syntax no matter where it executes. This means the query can target in-memory object graphs (with LINQ to Objects) as well as remote data sources such as SQL databases (with LINQ to SQL or the Entity Framework).

However, databases like SQL Server cannot be approached with IL code representing the query to be executed (ignoring the concept of SQL CLR entirely here): They all speak their own query languages. For SQL Server, that's obviously T-SQL, while data sources like SharePoint use a language called CAML, and yet other data stores like Amazon would use some web service format. Quite a mess, if you ask me.

LINQ deals with this problem by providing the capability for query provider implementers to inspect a query at runtime through the concept of expression trees. By doing so, the library with the query provider can translate the LINQ expression tree, at runtime, into the target query language.

Although we don't cover expression trees in detail right here, and instead defer that discussion until we cover LINQ in more depth in Chapter 20, "Language Integrated Query Internals," it suffices to say that lambda expressions are used as the syntactical means to generate expression trees. To enable this, lambda expressions can be assigned to either a delegate type or an expression tree type. In fact, lambda expressions don't have a type by themselves, as you can see here:

```
// Error: Cannot assign lambda expression to an implicitly-typed local variable
var add = (int a, int b) => a + b;
```

Instead, the code emitted for a lambda expression depends on the type of the variable it gets assigned to. For the preceding example, two possibilities are shown here:

```
        Func<int, int, int>  addDelegate = (int a, int b) => a + b;
Expression<Func<int, int, int>> addExpr    = (int a, int b) => a + b;
```

The code generated by the compiler in the first case is already known to us; it's the same as what would get generated for a C# 2.0-style anonymous method. However, the second one gives rise to fundamentally different code:

```
ParameterExpression a = Expression.Parameter(typeof(int), "a");
ParameterExpression b = Expression.Parameter(typeof(int), "b");
Expression<Func<int, int, int>> addExpr =
    Expression.Lambda<Func<int, int, int>>(Expression.Add(a, b), // a + b
                                            a, b);                // (a, b) =>
```

All this code generates an expression tree object representing the function as a data structure that can be inspected by libraries at runtime to take whatever action they see fit (for example, to translate the expression tree into SQL statements). We take a closer look at this when talking about reflection in Chapter 21, "Reflection," dynamic programming in Chapter 22, "Dynamic Programming," and LINQ in Chapter 19, "Language Integrated Query Essentials," and Chapter 20, "Language Integrated Query Internals."

WHERE DOES THE NAME LAMBDA COME FROM?

You might wonder where all of a sudden, out of nowhere, a Greek letter is used to name a new language feature. Lambda expressions are based on the concepts from lambda calculus, a theory on mathematical computation created by Alonzo Church in the 1920s. The first language to introduce a feature named after it was LISP (in 1958), even with a LAMBDA keyword in its language to denote something similar to C#'s lambda expressions nowadays.

This once more illustrates that all good ideas come from mathematics, although it takes a while for them to appear in widely used programming languages.

Invoking Delegates

Creating delegate instances to refer to particular methods is a necessary step toward invoking those methods *through* the delegate. In passing, we've shown the way to do such invocations repeatedly: They just look like ordinary method calls. For example:

```
Func<int, int, int> add = (a, b) => a + b;
int three = add(1, 2);
```

IntelliSense in Visual Studio will obviously give the caller a hand by showing what arguments are expected. Notice that names for those arguments come from the delegate type that's being used. In the preceding example, we're using one of the generic Func types, where arguments have names like arg1 and arg2. How this looks in Visual Studio is shown in Figure 17.10.

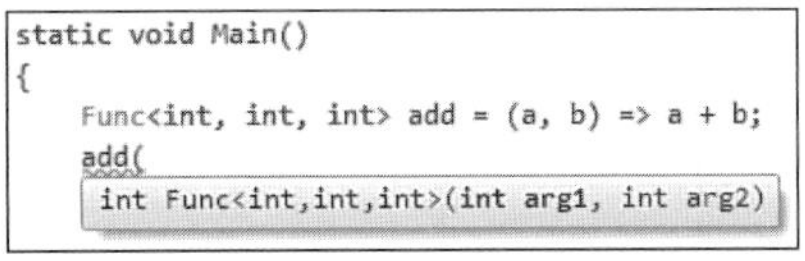

```
static void Main()
{
    Func<int, int, int> add = (a, b) => a + b;
    add(
      int Func<int,int,int>(int arg1, int arg2)
}
```

FIGURE 17.10   Invoking a delegate feels like calling a method.

When a delegate passes arguments either by reference or as outputs, the use of those modifiers is required at the call site when specifying the arguments. This is completely similar to the way such methods are invoked directly, as well:

```
// delegate string Foo(int a, ref double b, out long c, params DateTime[] ds);
Foo f = /* got it somehow */;
int a = 10;
double d = 12.34;
long c;
string res = f(a, ref d, out c, DateTime.Now);
```

C# 4.0 introduced the concept of named and optional parameters, as you saw before when we discussed methods. Both features can be used in the context of delegates, too. Let's start by looking at named parameters:

```
Func<int, int, int> add = (a, b) => a + b;
int three = add(arg2: 2, arg1: 2);
```

Again, those names come from the parameter list of the delegate and not the method to which the delegate refers. If you think about it for a while, this makes perfect sense because the compiler cannot know for sure what the target method's parameter list looks like:

```
static int Calculate(Func<int, int, int> op, int a, int b) {
    return op(a, b);
}

static void Main() {
    int three = Calculate((x, y) => x + y, 1, 2);
    int eight = Calculate((l, r) => l * r, 2, 4);
}
```

In the preceding example, the operator op argument to Calculate is supplied with two lambda expressions for an addition and a multiplication, each of which uses different names for their parameters. At the point the delegate is called, it's clear this information is not known to the compiler.

DON'T RENAME PARAMETERS IN PUBLIC APIS

Just as for regular methods, the capability to pass parameters by their names means that you shouldn't rename parameters after shipping a public API to customers. Changing the name of a parameter will break calls upon recompilation of their code: "There was a parameter named x last time around, but now it's gone."

Without recompilation, existing code will continue to work because named parameters are a compile-time-only thing. In the underlying generated IL code, parameters are passed in the order in which they are expected by the destination of the call. In other words, the runtime doesn't care about how parameters are called: Only their order matters.

Besides the use of named parameters at the invocation site of a delegate, delegates can be declared to have optional parameters using the following familiar syntax:

```
delegate void Printer(string message = "");
```

Using this, you can refer to any method that takes in a string-typed argument, but when making the call through the delegate, you can omit the message parameter, effectively causing the compiler to supply the default value for it. Figure 17.11 shows a familiar-looking tooltip when calling a delegate with an optional parameter in its signature.

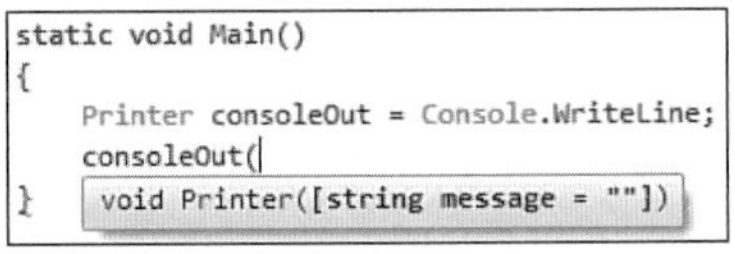

```
static void Main()
{
    Printer consoleOut = Console.WriteLine;
    consoleOut(|
}   void Printer([string message = ""])
```

FIGURE 17.11   Delegates can deal with optional parameters, too.

In the sample code, we're referring to the `Console.WriteLine` overload that takes a single `string` argument through the `Printer` delegate instance. When writing an invocation through this delegate, IntelliSense indicates the message argument can be omitted in favor of a default empty string value to be passed.

> **NOTE**
>
> Use of optional parameters on delegate types does not change the methods that can be targeted by the delegate. You might think `Printer` can be used to refer to a method with no argument because it has an optional argument. This is not the case and in fact would be an unsafe thing to implement in the language.
>
> Assume we could refer to a method with no arguments as follows:
>
> ```
> Printer p = () => Console.WriteLine();
> ```
>
> Now the delegate's user could call it, supplying a string argument as the delegate allows it to be specified:
>
> ```
> p ("Hello");
> ```
>
> Under the covers, the CLR would now try to invoke a method with an empty parameter list while handing it a string object. This will cause an imbalance of the runtime evaluation stack, which clearly is not a healthy situation.

Finally, note that exceptions thrown by the method getting called through the delegate will bubble up through the delegate invocation site:

```
Action boom = () => { throw new InvalidOperationException("Oops!"); };
try {
    boom();
}
catch (InvalidOperationException ex)  {
    // Handle exception here.
}
```

In the absence of checked exceptions (as seen in Java), it's a good practice to document the "exceptional contract" (if any is applicable) of a delegate. This allows callers to see what exceptions they should be willing to handle, while the party that instantiates a delegate should make sure to refer to a method that obeys those rules:

```
/// <summary>Implements an engine's running procedure.</summary>
/// <exception cref="OutOfFuelException">Raised when fuel ran out.</exception>
delegate void EngineRunner();
```

A generic engine controller using an EngineRunner to run the engine's procedure now knows it should be willing to handle an OutOfFuelException appropriately, while the manufacturer of an engine knows that particular exception type should be used when signaling this particular exceptional error condition.

Under the covers, invocation of a delegate involved nothing more than a call to the Invoke instance method. One particular exceptional condition that can arise from this is having a null reference for the delegate object:

```
Action ouch = null;
ouch(); // throws NullReferenceException
```

In other words, use null checks (where appropriate) to guard against such conditions unless you absolutely positively expect a non-null delegate instance to be present (for example, because of null checks earlier on).

In Figure 17.12, the delegate invocation that occurs in the following method is shown, illustrating the call to the underlying Invoke method:

```
static int Calculate(Func<int, int, int> op, int a, int b) {
    return op(a, b);
}
```

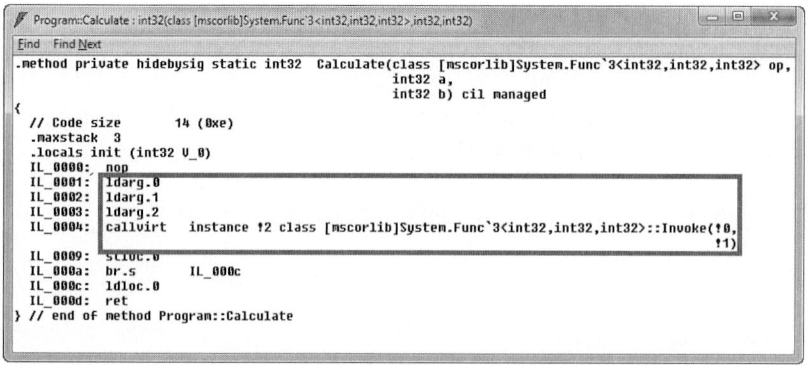

FIGURE 17.12   Delegate invocation unraveled.

USE THE GENERIC DELEGATE TYPES OR NOT?

So far, we've used handcrafted delegate types and the generic `Func` or `Action` delegate types interchangeably. This raises the question of whether you should create your own delegate types or just use the generic ones that have been in the `System` namespace since .NET Framework 3.5.

There are various ways to look at this. First, specialized delegate types can have more domain-specific documentation associated with them with regard to the semantics of arguments being passed, exceptions being raised, and so on. This can be helpful because naked method signatures don't reveal everything. This stream of thinking advocates the use of specialized delegate types as a means to help with the proper documentation of code. Nevertheless, rules such as method group conversion make delegate types less visible in the code, partially defeating this.

On the other hand, one could argue for using the generic types all over the place: People get used to the `Func` and `Action` types, and they reduce the burden of the manual declaration of delegate types. There's an additional benefit, as well: Recall that delegate types have nominal equivalence. Assume you have a `BinOp` operator and now some API needs a `Func<int, int, int>`. Although their signatures are the same, C# won't allow you to write the following:

```
BinOp op = /* got it somehow */;
Func<int, int, int> f = op; // cannot convert BinOp to Func<int, int, int>
```

To make the preceding work, you must introduce an artificial intermediate lambda expression:

```
Func<int, int, int> f = (a, b) => op(a, b);
```

Using the same generic delegate types everywhere eliminates the restrictions that arise from nominal equivalence. Nominal equivalence is deeply rooted in the CLR and extends beyond delegate types. Any two types that have the same physical representation (for example, a class with two Int32 fields) are not interchangeable. In other words, there's no accidental "type compatibility" based on structural equivalence.

In the end, it really depends on personal taste. Personally, I tend to use generic delegate types as the default, rarely ever creating my own specialized delegate type unless it's beneficial to specify the intended contract of a delegate's use in more detail using XML documentation on a handcrafted delegate type.

Putting It Together: An Extensible Calculator

To recap everything learned about delegates so far, create a calculator that can be extended by plugging in new operators. Although we don't focus on the UI aspect, take a look at Figure 17.13 to see what I have in mind.

FIGURE 17.13   An extensible calculator.

Besides typical arithmetic operations like add, subtract, multiply, divide, and modulo, four additional programmable function keys are provided. The way the programming is done is something you can dream about, but what's more interesting is how to create a generic calculator engine in which those custom operations can be plugged.

Let's try to define a Calculator class to provide the core calculator engine:

```
class Calculator {
    public int Add(int a, int b) { return a + b; }
    public int Sub(int a, int b) { return a - b; }
    public int Mul(int a, int b) { return a * b; }
    public int Div(int a, int b) { return a / b; }
    public int Mod(int a, int b) { return a % b; }
}
```

The problem with this first attempt is clear: It doesn't allow for custom functions to be plugged in, other than deriving from the Calculator class and providing methods for the additional functions you want. That by itself causes a bigger problem, though: How can the UI of the calculator discover those new operations easily?

Not only this, but given the preceding Calculator definition, how would you implement an evaluator? Suppose the user enters the following key sequence:

1, 2, +, 3, 4, =

Based on the key chosen for the operation (+ in the example), the press to the evaluate button = needs to call one of the built-in functions. In other words, you would have to use some large multiway branch to invoke the right method (for example, Add).

You can do better than this and take a more functional approach. What if you implement the calculator based on a dictionary that maps operation mnemonics (like +) onto the corresponding function implementing them?

```
class Calculator {
    private Dictionary<string, Func<int, int, int>> _ops =
                new Dictionary<string, Func<int, int, int>> {
                    { "Add", (a, b) => a + b },
                    { "Sub", (a, b) => a - b },
                    { "Mul", (a, b) => a * b },
                    { "Div", (a, b) => a / b },
                    { "Mod", (a, b) => a % b }
                };

    public int Eval(int lhs, string op, int rhs) {
        return _ops[op](lhs, rhs);
    }
}
```

The _ops field is initialized, using a collection initializer, with key/value pairs mapping the preprogrammed operators' key names onto the functions used for the computation with that operator. This table can be built very concisely using lambda expressions.

Now the Eval method becomes fairly trivial. Given the left side and right side operands, as well as the operator's friendly name, it looks up the implementation for the operator through the dictionary's indexer. After it has obtained the delegate to the implementation, it invokes it using delegate invocation syntax. Figure 17.14 illustrates the step-by-step evaluation of the delegate lookup and invocation inside Eval.

To illustrate how the UI on top of this calculator could be realized, consider the following console application code:

```
class CalculatorUI {
    public static void Main() {
        var calc = new Calculator();
        while (true) {
            Console.WriteLine("Operand 1: ");
            int lhs = int.Parse(Console.ReadLine());

            Console.WriteLine("Operator: ");
            string op = Console.ReadLine();
```

```
            Console.WriteLine("Operand 2: ");
            int rhs = int.Parse(Console.ReadLine());

            Console.WriteLine("{0}({1},{2}) = {3}", op, lhs, rhs,
                                            calc.Eval(lhs, op, rhs));
        }
    }
}
```

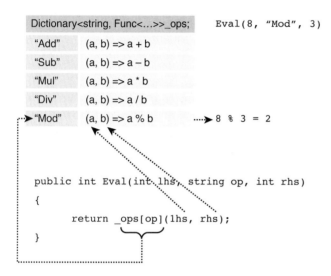

FIGURE 17.14   A table-driven lookup of operator delegate.

You are invited to make this code more bullet-proof to keep users from providing valid integer numeric strings (tip: use TryParse) or operator names (tip: expose some IsValidOperator method on Calculator, using the _ops dictionary inside).

The remaining question is how the calculator can now be easily extended from the outside by a user of the class. The answer is fairly straightforward. We just need to provide a way to add an entry to the operator's dictionary that's encapsulated inside the Calculator:

```
class Calculator {
    ...
    public void AddOperator(string name, Func<int, int, int> function) {
        _ops[name] = function;
    }
}
```

For example, the programming interface for the calculator (whatever that might look like) could allow the user to create a custom function that's bound to the F1 key:

```
Func<int, int, int> pyth = (a, b) => (int)Math.Sqrt(a * a + b * b);
calc.AddOperator("F1", pyth);
```

A call to Eval with arguments 3, F1, and 4 will now result in 5, the hypotenuse of a rectangular triangle with sides of length 3 and 4, using the Pythagorean theorem.

PHILOSPHICAL THOUGHTS ON CALCULATOR PROGRAMMING

At the start of the discussion about the extensible calculator, we mentioned an alternative design using a base type Calculator with virtual methods for the function keys F1 through F4. Customizing the calculator would then involve the creation of a derived type, supplying implementations for those virtual methods, and *compiling* the resulting type.

This technique can be compared to the use of programmable chips (such as an erasable programmable read-only memory chip or EPROM). In this setting, the manufacturer of a fancy calculator takes our generic calculator chip and extends it by programming the chip in the factory. This is an advanced task that cannot be done directly by regular end users of the fancy calculator.

On the other hand, if you allow the calculator to store pieces of executable code to realize custom functions, you no longer need to derive a custom calculator type and compile it to create an advanced calculator. Instead, you provide a means for end users of the generic calculator to extend its functionality by calling the AddOperator method.

Comparing this again with physical calculator devices, this corresponds to the use of a chip with a programmable memory and a little language in which to express custom functions. Now the end user of the calculator has all the flexibility to extend it without the hassle of dealing with EPROM chips and whatnot.

To make your little calculator really extensible *at runtime* by your end users, you would have to provide a mini-arithmetic language allowing the user to enter functions as pieces of text such as (a, b) => a * a + b * b. Given this function definition as a string, you would then go ahead and compile it at runtime into a delegate, which is much more doable than having to derive a specialized Calculator subtype on the fly. In Chapter 22, you learn how to use expression trees to generate delegates at runtime.

Case Study: Delegates Used in LINQ to Objects

Although we defer a more thorough discussion about LINQ until Chapter 19, I think it's worthwhile to spend a bit of time illustrating the use of delegates in the context of LINQ. One of the built-in "providers" for Language Integrated Query allows for querying over in-memory data sequences and is known as LINQ to Objects.

Various query operators are implemented as methods that take in an IEnumerable<T> sequence as one of their inputs, typically returning a derived sequence as a result. Such operators form the building blocks to build more complex queries from. In other words, those query operators allow for rich *composition*, in large part because of their functionally inspired nature. Let's illustrate this schematically first in Figure 17.15.

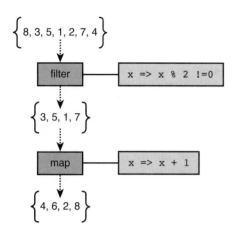

FIGURE 17.15   Composition of query operators.

Given a sequence of objects (for example, integer numbers), we want to express a query that first filters them based on a certain condition (for example, only allowing odd numbers in the result) and subsequently maps the objects onto another object (for example, adding 1 to each of them). Stated slightly differently, we want to compose the filter operator with the map operator to construct a bigger query.

In imperative-style programming, we could write this as follows:

```
var input = new List<int> { 8, 3, 5, 1, 2, 7, 4 };
var result = new List<int>();
foreach (int x in input) {
    if (x % 2 != 0) {
        result.Add(x + 1);
    }
}
```

Although this works, the intent of the code gets buried rather quickly under a heap of imperative constructs like loops and ifs. For filtering and mapping, things aren't too bad just yet, but add other requirements such as ordering and grouping to the mix, and things get messy in no time.

In the functional world, we would rather use higher-order functions that implement generic filtering and mapping algorithms by taking in a function to express the filter's predicate and the mapping's projection function. This is precisely what LINQ provides through its wealth of standard query operators. With LINQ, you can express the preceding as follows:

```
var res = input.Where(x => x % 2 != 0) // filter on predicate
               .Select(x => x + 1);    // map using projection
```

This style of programming makes code much more readable thanks to its declarative nature, while opening up for easy query operator composition. For example, if you want to sort the output sequence, you can "chain in" yet another operator:

```
var res = input.Where(x => x % 2 != 0) // filter on predicate
               .OrderBy(x => x)         // sort with key selector
               .Select(x => x + 1);     // map using projection
```

Most of those query operators take a delegate to specify the desired behavior of the operator. For example, to filter, you must provide a Boolean-valued filter function that's able to decide for each element whether it should be added to the resulting sequence. For mapping, a projection function is used to express what an element needs to be mapped to. And to realize an ordering, you must specify the key on which to order (for example, given a Person object, order by its Age property). The latter is the trivial *identity function* in our case because we're ordering integers by their raw value.

To illustrate the richness of the set of available query operators, take a quick look at Figure 17.16, where a LINQ to Objects query is used to query the operators!

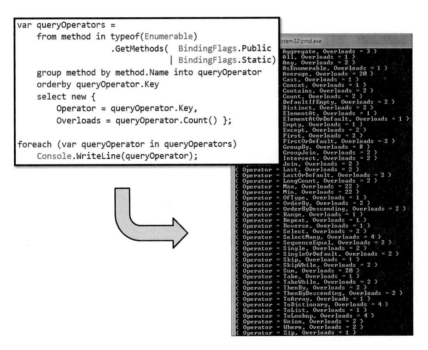

FIGURE 17.16   Querying LINQ's query operators using...LINQ itself.

THE LANGUAGE INTEGRATED PART OF LINQ

Language Integrated Query is not just about the definition of query operators and a provider model (allowing to target a whole bunch of different data sources) but also about providing first-class language integration in both C# and Visual Basic.

In the previous LINQ examples, we haven't used this syntactical language extension just yet to show off the underlying method calls and lambda expressions used to glue together the query. The C# 3.0 query expression syntax for the query shown earlier looks like this:

```
var res = from x in input
            where x % 2 != 0
            orderby x
            select x + 1;
```

This corresponds *exactly* to the form with the method calls and their lambda expression arguments we've presented so far. The main benefit of using this syntax is the fact it looks less funky and feels much more like a query because of the specialized keywords and reduced syntactical noise.

Don't worry about the query shown in this figure just yet, but the essence of it is that it uses reflection to get all the query operator methods that are defined on the Enumerable type, followed by grouping, ordering, and projection operations on it. The result is a sequence of pairs of query operator method names and the number of overloads for each one. We take a look at those operators in more detail later.

Those operators are sometimes referred to as *combinators* because they provide the capability to combine and transform input sequences into output sequences. An operator where this becomes incredibly apparent is a join operator that somehow joins two sequences.

Without going into too much detail right now, let's take a sneak peek at how some of the simplest query operators really work behind the scenes. For example, Where *takes in* a delegate to perform filtering of elements in the input sequence. How does it do that?

```
public static IEnumerable<T> Where<T>(this IEnumerable<T> source,
                                      Func<T, bool> predicate) {
   // Omitting input validation logic (trickier than you may think).

   foreach (T item in source) {
       if (predicate(item)) {
           yield return item;
       }
   }
}
```

Ignore the foreign yield keyword for the time being; we discuss this feature, known as *iterators*, in detail when talking about LINQ. The relevant bit for our discussion about delegates is where the invocation of the predicate delegate happens, inside the `foreach` loop. So for every element in the output sequence, the predicate is evaluated. If the function call returns true, the element is *yielded* to the consumer of the `Where` operator. The result of this operator definition is a generally applicable filter construct that can be used for sequences for any type of objects (due to the use of generics) and with a filter function of choice (due to the use of delegates).

The `Select` map or projection function is defined in a similar way. Follow me through the thinking for a minute. To define a maximally applicable mapping mechanism, we want to be able to consume a sequence of any type of objects, hence the input should be an `IEnumerable<T>`. Mapping of an element in the input sequence can be done by using a projection function that takes in an instance of type `T`, returning an object of some other type `R` (for example, for each integer in the source sequence, return its `ToString` representation, which is of type string). Collecting the results of the projection function calls on every element, we get a sequence of results of type `IEnumerable<R>`:

```
public static IEnumerable<R> Select<T,R>(this IEnumerable<T> source,
                               Func<T, R> project) {
    // Omitting input validation logic (trickier than you may think).

    foreach (T item in source) {
        // given an item of type T, project(item) returns something of type R
        yield return project(item);
    }
}
```

This finishes our sneak peek at LINQ for the time being. The key takeaway from this high-level overview is that the use of functions is a great way to define general-purpose query operators that can be composed easily. We detail the query expression syntax and the wealth of available operators when talking about LINQ specifically.

Asynchronous Invocation

So far, you've seen delegates that return nearly instantaneously when they are being invoked. For example:

```
Func<int, int, int> add = (a, b) => a + b;
int three = add(1, 2); // returns in nanoseconds
```

However, delegates can invoke long-running operations, too. If the method being referred to takes a long while to complete, the invocation site of the delegate will be blocked until the call returns. This is an important realization for APIs that accept as their input a delegate that gets called subsequently: The API can't know how the call will perform given certain inputs. For example, in our calculator example, we could add the following custom function:

```
calc.AddOperator("F1", (a, b) => {
    Thread.Sleep(5000);
    return a + b;
});
```

When the user of the calculator now uses the F1 function through the UI, the calculator engine will issue a call to the function that was passed to AddOperator:

```
calc.Eval(1, "F1", 2); // calls into the custom delegate
```

However, the added operator is quite evil because it will hang for five seconds before returning the sum. If we blindly invoke the delegate in the calculator engine, this might cause the user interface to appear hung. Or to say it in another way: While the custom function is doing its "work" (which could be sleeping for five seconds!), no other useful work can be done because we're blocked until the call returns.

In fact, we shouldn't even look for contrived examples like sleeping for five seconds; it's quite possible the programmed function is computing-intensive and takes a while to return when faced with specific inputs. Such an example is a very naïve implementation of a Fibonacci function based on recursion:

```
uint Fibonacci(uint n) {
    return n <= 1 ? n : Fibonacci(n - 1) + Fibonacci(n - 2);
}
```

Assume for the sake of argument that our calculator supports not just binary functions but also unary ones and uses uint (or even ulong or BigInteger) rather than int. By now, it shouldn't be a hard exercise for you to extend our Calculator class to support this.

SPEEDING UP FIBONACCI

A popular programming interview question is to ask for an implementation of an algorithm calculating Fibonacci numbers. Candidates who come up with a recursive approach tend to experience heavy sweating when the interviewer starts asking performance-related questions. Let me share a few thoughts on this subject.

The problem with the recursive algorithm is the excessive recomputation of the intermediate results. For example, take a look at the following expansion of calls:

```
Fibonacci(5) = Fibonacci(4)                    + Fibonacci(3)
             = Fibonacci(3) + Fibonacci(2) + Fibonacci(3)
             = ...
```

If you continue to expand those calls, you'll soon come to the conclusion that lots of wasteful recomputation is taking place. Although this makes this example ideal for the discussion about long-running delegate invocations, it's far from ideal in practice. You'll see how bad things get in a moment.

So how do we speed up our Fibonacci implementation? One way is to employ a technique from the world of functional programming called *memoization*. People will immediately recognize the word memory in this weird-sounding word. Indeed, memoization is a way to cache the result of a function call so that subsequent calls with the same arguments can immediately return the cached value. This poses a tradeoff: reducing CPU cycles at the expense of adding memory pressure (to keep the cache). However, it has the nice property that the Fibonacci computing algorithm can be kept in its natural-looking recursive form. More information can be found by searching the Web for this term.

An alternative, left to you as an exercise, is to create an imperative loop-based implementation.

So let's take a look at calling our `Fibonacci` method with an increasing value for the argument, measuring its performance using the `Stopwatch` class in `System.Diagnostics`:

```
for (uint n = 0; n <= 40; n++) {
    var watch = new Stopwatch();
    watch.Start();
    uint result = Fibonacci(n);
    watch.Stop();

    Console.WriteLine("Fib({0}) = {1} (in {2} ms)",
                    n, result, watch.ElapsedMilliseconds);
}
```

A fragment of the last iteration's output is shown in Figure 17.17. Notice how things start to slow down exponentially as the input gets larger. The important bit here is that we can't do any useful work while the call to `Fibonacci` is in flight because we're stuck waiting for it to return.

```
Fib(21) = 10946 (in 0 ms)
Fib(22) = 17711 (in 0 ms)
Fib(23) = 28657 (in 1 ms)
Fib(24) = 46368 (in 1 ms)
Fib(25) = 75025 (in 8 ms)
Fib(26) = 121393 (in 4 ms)
Fib(27) = 196418 (in 13 ms)
Fib(28) = 317811 (in 19 ms)
Fib(29) = 514229 (in 26 ms)
Fib(30) = 832040 (in 35 ms)
Fib(31) = 1346269 (in 56 ms)
Fib(32) = 2178309 (in 96 ms)
Fib(33) = 3524578 (in 147 ms)
Fib(34) = 5702887 (in 238 ms)
Fib(35) = 9227465 (in 359 ms)
Fib(36) = 14930352 (in 575 ms)
Fib(37) = 24157817 (in 980 ms)
Fib(38) = 39088169 (in 1557 ms)
Fib(39) = 63245986 (in 2642 ms)
Fib(40) = 102334155 (in 4149 ms)
```

FIGURE 17.17   Performance of the recursive `Fibonacci` implementation.

THE GOLDEN RATIO

The Fibonacci series are more interesting than they seem at first, at least if you start to approach them from a mathematical angle. For one thing, it can be proven that the slowdown factor between fib(n) and fib(n + 1) for large values of n will get closer and closer to (SQRT(5) + 1) / 2, which is approximately equal to 1.62. In fact, our stopwatch results for Fib(40) and Fib(39) are already getting close to this ratio: 4,149 ms divided by 2,642 ms is 1.57.

This seemingly arbitrary value is actually much more interesting than it seems at first, to such an extent it has a name: the golden ratio. But why call one particular ratio *golden*? It turns out that lots of ratios in nature (for example, the geometry of parts of the human face) approximate this ratio. This has been a source of inspiration all the way back to ancient Greece and for scientists and artists such as Pythagoras, Leonardo Da Vinci, Kepler, and many others. It's worth reading up on in your spare time!

So how can we run the expensive computation in the background, allowing us to do other useful processing in the meantime while we're waiting for the result to come back? The answer is asynchronous invocation, which deserves whole books on its own and is part of the larger domain of *reactive programming*. Let's contrast this reactive concept against its brother, known as *interactive programming*:

▶ In **interactive programming**, you actively send out requests for information to some environment surrounding you. This could be as simple as calling some method or as complex as sending a request to a web service on the other side of the globe. The essential part is you're in the driver seat and make a request, and then wait for the response to come back.

▶ In **reactive programming**, the environment calls you at some point in time with information for you to react to. Examples include the user clicking some user interface element such as a button, over events raised by the local system (for example, signaling the hard disk is almost full), or data coming in over the network. Now the environment is in control, and your application needs to react when asked to do so.

Asynchronous calls can be categorized as a reactive technique: After initiating a request we (optionally) go off and do other work until the environment signals the request has completed and a response is available. At that point, we react to that signal and use the result of the completed asynchronous computation in some way. Figure 17.18 contrasts interactive and reactive programming.

It turns out delegates provide intrinsic support for asynchronous calls based on the so-called IAsyncResult-pattern in .NET. You see other approaches for dealing with such asynchronous programming scenarios as we get into coverage of .NET Framework APIs, such as System.Threading in Chapter 29, "Threading and Synchronization," and Reactive Extensions. For now, we focus on the pattern exposed by delegates.

Interactive

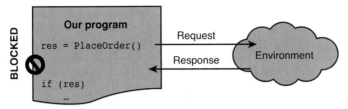

Reactive

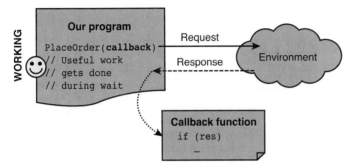

FIGURE 17.18   Interactive versus reactive programming.

In our running Fibonacci example, we want to do some useful work while computing the next number in our loop. To illustrate the essential point, we keep things simple and print dots to the screen while the computation is in flight. This should suffice to convince you we're no longer blocked while the long-running call to our terrible Fibonacci function is crunching numbers. Let's get started by creating a delegate that refers to the Fibonacci function:

```
static void CalculateFib(uint n) {
    Func<uint> fibN = () => Fibonacci(n);
    // More to follow...
}
```

The CalculateFib function we're starting to build will be responsible for calculating one Fibonacci number, printing dots to the screen in the meantime to signal to the user the application is not hanging. Notice how the fibN delegate creates a closure over the n parameter passed to the CalculateFib function. By doing so, we don't have to pass it explicitly to the fibN delegate when making the invocation. This is just a matter of taste.

With this fibN in place, we haven't solved any problem yet. Naïvely calling fibN will be a blocking call, waiting until the computation returns:

```
fibN(); // if n is big, we'll be blocked for a while
```

Discoverability of API capabilities in .NET is as simple as one keystroke: dot. Take a look at the IntelliSense for `fibN`, shown in Figure 17.19.

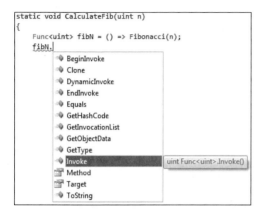

```
static void CalculateFib(uint n)
{
    Func<uint> fibN = () => Fibonacci(n);
    fibN.
           BeginInvoke
           Clone
           DynamicInvoke
           EndInvoke
           Equals
           GetHashCode
           GetInvocationList
           GetObjectData
           GetType
           Invoke          uint Func<uint>.Invoke()
           Method
           Target
           ToString
```

FIGURE 17.19   Instance members on the generic `Func<TResult>` delegate type.

We immediately recognize the `Invoke` method for which the delegate invocation syntax is simply syntactical sugar. This corresponds to the synchronous invocation mechanism for delegates, causing us to block until the target method returns. Looking a little further, we immediately observe a pair of other methods that reveal they have to do something with delegate invocation: `BeginInvoke` and `EndInvoke`. That's exactly what we need to make our delegate call in an asynchronous way. Let's see how, but first take a look at the `BeginInvoke` method signature, shown in Figure 17.20.

```
Func<uint> fibN = () => Fibonacci(n);
fibN.BeginInvoke(
  IAsyncResult Func<uint>.BeginInvoke(AsyncCallback callback, object @object)
```

FIGURE 17.20   Delegate's `BeginInvoke` method.

Two arguments are expected, the first of which is an `AsyncCallback`. This is a way to tell the `BeginInvoke` method, "Hey, if the underlying method you'll call returns, give me a call back so that I can take the result and *react* on it." What would a callback look like? Obviously, we want to react to the completion event by executing some code. I bet you can feel it coming by now: We're passing a reference to a callback method to `BeginInvoke`, which is done by means of the `AsyncCallback` delegate whose definition is revealed in Figure 17.21.

```
Func<uint> fibN = () => Fibonacci(n);
fibN.BeginInvoke(new AsyncCallback(
               AsyncCallback.AsyncCallback(void (IAsyncResult) target)
```

FIGURE 17.21   The `AsyncCallback` delegate.

The signature of the expected callback function takes in an `IAsyncResult` and returns nothing. We can declare such a method inline using an anonymous function expression or a lambda expression, as we do in Figure 17.22. Inside the body of the lambda expression, we try to satisfy our curiosity by taking a look at the members of `IAsyncResult`, as shown in the figure.

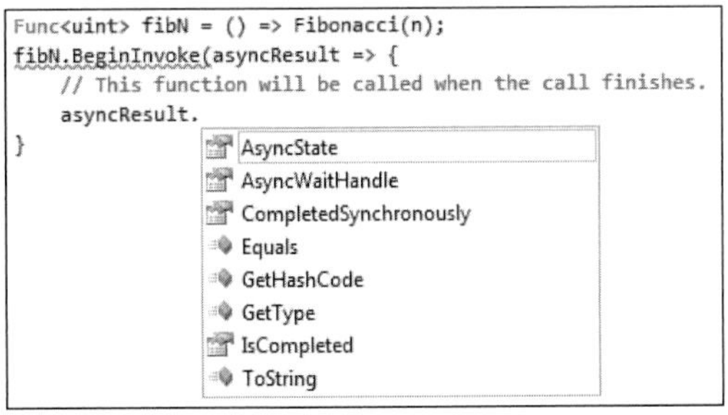

```
Func<uint> fibN = () => Fibonacci(n);
fibN.BeginInvoke(asyncResult => {
    // This function will be called when the call finishes.
    asyncResult.
}
              AsyncState
              AsyncWaitHandle
              CompletedSynchronously
              Equals
              GetHashCode
              GetType
              IsCompleted
              ToString
```

FIGURE 17.22   `IAsyncResult`'s members.

All of those members look incredibly interesting, but the most important piece of information seems to be missing: Where's the result of the completed asynchronous call? That's where `EndInvoke` comes in. In fact, an `IAsyncResult` can be compared to a ticket to hold on to an asynchronous computation during its lifetime. Look back at the `BeginInvoke` signature and observe how the `IAsyncResult` object is returned immediately from the `BeginInvoke` call. This allows us to poll the asynchronous call's state by repeatedly checking `IsCompleted` or to use a *wait handle* to wait explicitly for the call to return. The concept of wait handles is discussed in Chapter 29. For another application of asynchronous computations, refer to Chapter 28, "Working with I/O."

That still doesn't answer how `IAsyncResult` can be used to obtain the result of the call when it has completed. Surprise, surprise, but the signature of `EndInvoke` takes in this `IAsyncResult` object in return for the computation's result. Figure 17.23 shows how to call the `EndInvoke` method.

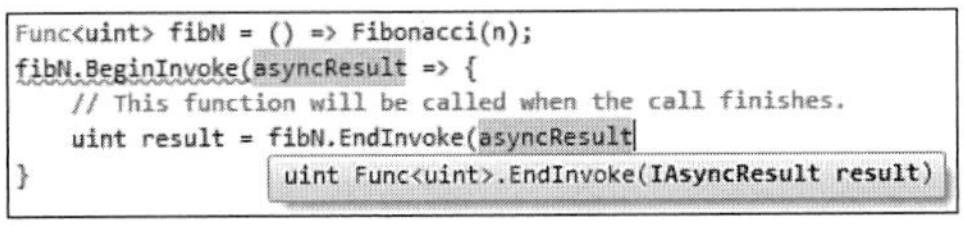

```
Func<uint> fibN = () => Fibonacci(n);
fibN.BeginInvoke(asyncResult => {
    // This function will be called when the call finishes.
    uint result = fibN.EndInvoke(asyncResult
}             uint Func<uint>.EndInvoke(IAsyncResult result)
```

FIGURE 17.23   Completing the asynchronous computation.

Gradually, one step at a time, things start to come together. So far, our code will start the computation asynchronously by means of a call to `BeginInvoke`, telling it how to proceed once the call finishes as specified by the callback function. Inside this callback function, `IAsyncResult` is used to obtain the result of the completed call through a call to `EndInvoke`. Now that we have the result, we can do whatever we want to do with it: Print it to the screen, start another call, and so on.

Let's complete the call to `BeginInvoke` first. Besides the `AsyncCallback` delegate, it also expects an object argument referred to as the "state." We can just leave that null for our purposes. If you look back at the `IAsyncResult` members, you'll see an `AsyncState` get-only property. This is where the second parameter to `BeginInvoke` ultimately ends up. In .NET 1.0, before language features such as closures, this was a convenient way to pass some state to the asynchronous callback function that had to be defined in a separate method. Today, with the use of closures, its usefulness has decreased a bit, so let's not discuss it any further.

Based on what you've learned so far, we can write something like this:

```
static void CalculateFib(uint n) {
    Func<uint> fibN = () => Fibonacci(n);

    var watch = new Stopwatch();
    watch.Start();
    fibN.BeginInvoke(asyncResult => {
        watch.Stop();
        uint result = fibN.EndInvoke(asyncResult);
        Console.WriteLine("Fib({0}) = {1} (in {2} ms)",
                        n, result, watch.ElapsedMilliseconds);
    }, null);

    Console.WriteLine("Computing Fib({0})...", n);
}
```

This code still works like a charm, but how does it illustrate we're not getting blocked upon invoking the delegate? That's what the `Console.WriteLine` call after `BeginInvoke` is for. Because `BeginInvoke` returns immediately, this console output will appear on the screen before the underlying delegate call even finishes. In other words, `BeginInvoke` doesn't block. To illustrate this, consider the following `Main` method:

```
static void Main() {
    for (uint n = 1; n <= 20; n++) {
        CalculateFib(n);
    }

    Console.ReadLine();
}
```

Because `CalculateFib` performs its heavy work asynchronously, we'll see the 20 calls to the function return immediately, heaving printed "Computing Fib(n)..." messages to the screen. In the background, the computation for the 20 asynchronous calls will be going on, each of which will eventually return by calling their callback function that will print the result to the screen. On my machine, the results looked like those shown in Figure 17.24.

FIGURE 17.24   Asynchronous computation of Fibonacci numbers.

Results might be a bit surprising at first, but the key observation here is that the messages that signal the computation of a Fibonacci number have started to cease to be printed long before the computations of Fib(13) through Fib(20) finish. Or to say it another way, we've *scheduled* the computation of 20 Fibonacci numbers asynchronously, causing our main thread not to get blocked while waiting for results to come back.

Notice a very important detail in our Main method:

```
static void Main() {
    for (uint n = 1; n <= 20; n++) {
        CalculateFib(n);
    }

    Console.ReadLine();
}
```

Did you see it? The innocent-looking Console.ReadLine call is quite important to make our example successful. Because the 20 calls to CalculateFib have returned in no time while asynchronous background work is still going on, we reach the end of the Main method very soon from the start of the program. Falling out of the bottom of Main causes the program to terminate (read: the *main thread* finishes), so we wouldn't see any results being printed as the program quits immediately.

MESSAGE PUMPS TO THE RESCUE

This problem doesn't really exist in UI applications based on Windows Forms or Windows Presentation Foundation (WPF) because those have a *message pump* that keeps the main thread occupied until an exit message is posted to the message queue. Such an exit message arrives when the program's main window is closed or programmatic calls are made.

In our example, the `Console.ReadLine` call effectively blocks the main thread, waiting for the user to press Enter to terminate the program. There are cleaner ways to deal with this problem, though, and again the `IAsyncResult` objects returned by `BeginInvoke` provide the key to success.

One of the properties on `IAsyncResult` is called `AsyncWaitHandle` and returns a so-called *wait handle* that provides a way to wait for the background work to complete. For the `Main` method to use those, we'll return the wait handle from the method:

```
static WaitHandle CalculateFib(uint n) {
    ...
    var asyncRes = fibN.BeginInvoke(asyncResult => {
        ...
        uint result = fibN.EndInvoke(asyncResult);
        ...
    }, null);
    ...
    return asyncRes.AsyncWaitHandle;
}
```

Back in `Main`, we receive all of those `WaitHandle` objects, which we can collect in an array. Based on this, we can express our desire to block until all the background work is done, as follows:

```
static void Main() {
    const int N = 20;

    var waitHandles = new WaitHandle[N];
    for (uint n = 1; n <= N; n++) {
        waitHandles[n - 1] = CalculateFib(n);
    }

    WaitHandle.WaitAll(waitHandles);
}
```

`WaitHandle.WaitAll` basically tells the CLR to block until all the background threads associated with the wait handles have finished.

> **NOTE**
>
> To be really honest, the preceding code isn't completely right just yet. Even though `WaitAll` will block and prevent the main thread from finishing until all asynchronous invocations complete, this doesn't take into account that the callback procedures (in our case, responsible for printing the result to the console) can take some time to complete. Therefore, it's still possible for the main thread to terminate before all callbacks have completed their jobs.
>
> We won't go into detail about how to fix this defect right now but defer discussion about more thread synchronization primitives and techniques until Chapter 29. Nevertheless, this proves that parallel computation isn't a simple thing to get right under all circumstances. Rest assured, APIs have improved significantly over the years as parallel, asynchronous, and reactive computing has become more and more important.

Refer to Figure 17.24 for a moment and observe some apparent oddities in the output. One thing you'll notice is that `Fib(5)` returned before `Fib(4)`. Out-of-order arrival is common when doing background processing because the runtime's and operating system's thread-scheduling mechanisms are involved. An even more extreme case is visible with `Fib(7)`'s completion message arriving after `Fib(12)`'s. Often, different background tasks have very different performance profiles (for example, because of latency experienced when making network calls and such).

For all of those reasons, you can't expect in-order arrival of asynchronous calls. Even more, every time you run the program you'll see different patterns due to differences in the "dynamics" of the system at the point the program runs. (Other threads in the OS may be competing with your application's threads.)

So what if we want to keep things in order somehow and print some progress to the screen while a number is being computed, as we promised near the beginning of this section? Using `IAsyncResult`'s `IsCompleted` property, we can also poll for the completion of an asynchronous call:

```
static void CalculateFib(uint n) {
    Func<uint> fibN = () => Fibonacci(n);

    var asyncResult = fibN.BeginInvoke(_ => { }, null);
    while (!asyncResult.IsCompleted) {
        Console.Write(".");
        Thread.Sleep(500);
    }
    Console.WriteLine();

    uint result = fibN.EndInvoke(asyncResult);
    Console.WriteLine("Fib({0}) = {1}", n, result);
}
```

This code deserves a detailed explanation. We already know how we created the fibN delegate, so let's skip that part. The first important difference is about the absence of a meaningful callback function specified to BeginInvoke. Here we're passing a funky-looking lambda expression:

```
_ => { }
```

Recall that the expected argument is an AsyncCallback delegate, which takes in one of those IAsyncResult objects and returns void. Because we don't want to use a callback procedure (we're going to *poll* for completion status later), we don't care about the argument passed in to that lambda expression. It turns out a plain underscore character is a valid identifier in C#, so it's a handy, compact way to express this: "I have a lambda expression parameter here, but I don't care about it." And obviously, to create a delegate that doesn't do anything, we specify an empty body, hence the use of { }.

> **NOTE**
>
> Quite frankly, this _ => { } trick is not required for the preceding code because BeginInvoke also accepts a null reference for its AsyncCallback argument. However, I thought it was the ideal time and place to reveal this little trick that comes in handy from time to time: _ is a valid C# identifier, and its use for a "don't care" variable name can prove useful in such situations.
>
> Nevertheless, now that you know _ is a proper identifier, you shouldn't go off and start writing code like this:
>
> ```
> (_, __, ___) => (_ + __) * ___;
> ```
>
> No matter how aesthetically pleasing this may be to the trained (ASCII-art-savvy) eye, it's just asking for nonmaintainable and unreadable code! Also keep in mind that this is nothing but a trick and not a proper language feature of its own (because you can't have multiple "don't care" arguments with the same "_" name): To the compiler, it's just another variable name that may clash with other variables already in scope.

After starting the asynchronous call, we start polling for its completion status by checking the IsCompleted property periodically in a while loop. Notice we sleep inside the loop body for half a second (an interval that can be adjusted depending on the expected performance profile of the call being polled for) before checking again. This avoids *busy waiting*, which is a bad practice that drives your CPU to full utilization with no benefit other than heating the chip. Every time we fail to see a completed status, we print an additional dot to the screen. This signals to the user we're still alive but waiting for the operation to complete.

Figure 17.25 shows the result of restructuring our code with the polled-based waiting and printing of "status dots."

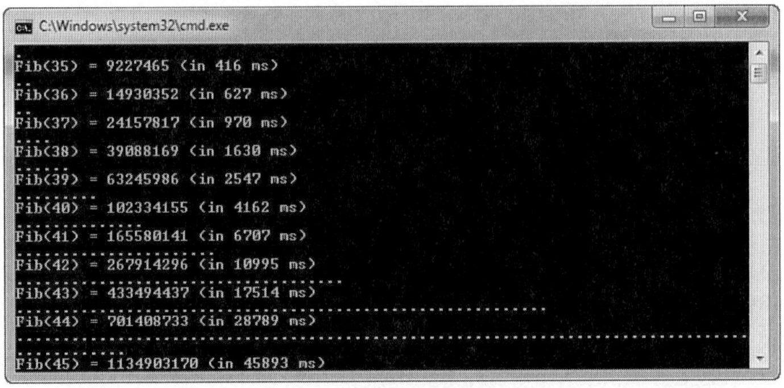

FIGURE 17.25 Asynchronous computation with status polling and reporting.

Notice that categorization of blocking versus nonblocking depends on your point of view when looking at the code. First, from CalculateFib's point of view, the call to the fibN delegate is no longer blocking due to the use of BeginInvoke. However, when looking at the CalculateFib method from Main's point of view, that one is still blocking because it doesn't return before the result of the calculation is printed to the screen (by means of the polling loop inside).

EXERCISE FOR THE READER

Figure 17.25 does not completely correspond to the code shown before because it still reports the measured time for the calculation. Extending the sample code by enabling it to report timing information accurately is left as an exercise for you.

Notice this is not as easy as it might seem at first: Because we're sleeping 500 milliseconds at a time when polling for completion status, the naïve approach of wrapping the loop in a StopWatch would always report multiples of 500 milliseconds (approximately).

One little tip: Use the BeginInvoke callback procedure to stop the StopWatch as soon as the asynchronous call finishes.

DON'T BLOCK THE MESSAGE LOOP

In reality, we would likely perform more useful work while we're waiting for an asynchronous operation to complete. If the result of the operation is not essential to continue all further processing in the system, we can start doing other work in parallel.

But even if we really depend on the value to come back before we can do more meaningful work, asynchronous computing is beneficial because we can keep the user informed about the application not being fatally hung. I bet readers have seen the scenery illustrated in Figure 17.26 far too often.

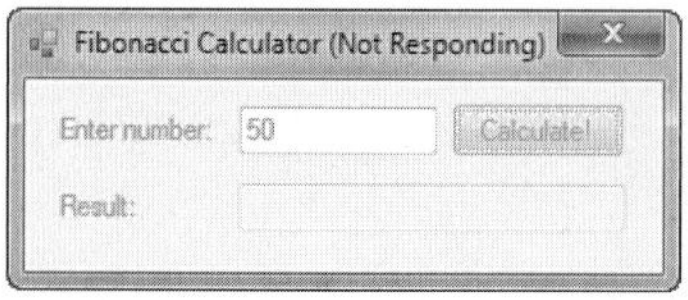

FIGURE 17.26   Windows' "Snow White effect" for hung applications.

This application is poorly written because it blocks the UI thread while doing expensive computation, thus preventing the application's message loop (which ticks on the UI thread) to process window messages. Window messages are used as a way to dispatch work to an application (for example, to process keyboard or mouse input), to restore focus, and even to repaint itself to the screen.

In Figure 17.26, the window is no longer capable of responding to the WM_PAINT message when asked by the window manager to repaint itself because it is blocked waiting for the Fibonacci number computation to come back. Windows detects the situation where an application no longer responds to window messages and indicates this state by adding the infamous "Not Responding" note to the title bar. Starting from Windows Vista, it also puts a misty cloud over the window's client region to visually indicate that the application is hung.

You'll see how to deal with long-running operations in the context of UI development frameworks like Windows Forms and WPF at a later stage. For now, just be aware of the problems that can arise from making blocking calls.

Combining Delegates

In preparation for the discussion about events in the Chapter 18, I want to mention one more thing about delegates: their capability to be used in a "multicast setting." Earlier on, you saw how delegate types in C# derive from a base class called MulticastDelegate. Looking at that type's information in Visual Studio, you see how that type by itself derives from Delegate:

```
namespace System
{
    public abstract class MulticastDelegate : Delegate
    {
        ...
```

Looking a bit further at the members of the MulticastDelegate type, you'll notice one that reveals its true essential goal, allowing multiple target methods to be called as part of the delegate's invocation call. This is hinted at in Figure 17.27

```
CombineImpl(System.Delegate)
Equals(object)
GetHashCode()
GetInvocationList()
GetMethodImpl()
GetObjectData(System.Runtime.Serialization.SerializationInfo, System.Runtime.Serializati
MulticastDelegate(System.Type, string)
MulticastDelegate(object, string)
operator !=(System.MulticastDelegate, System.MulticastDelegate)
operator ==(System.MulticastDelegate, System.MulticastDelegate)
RemoveImpl(System.Delegate)
```

```
public sealed override System.Delegate[] GetInvocationList()
   Member of System.MulticastDelegate

Summary:
Returns the invocation list of this multicast delegate, in invocation order.

Returns:
An array of delegates whose invocation lists collectively match the invocation list of
this instance.

Exceptions:
System.MemberAccessException: Cannot create an instance of an abstract class, or
this member was invoked with a late-binding mechanism.
```

FIGURE 17.27   `MulticastDelegate` objects keep a list of `Delegate` objects inside.

If a `Delegate` object can refer to one method and a `MulticastDelegate` contains an array (known as the *invocation list*) of `Delegate` objects, it's clear that a `MulticastDelegate` can refer to multiple methods. Hence, the invocation of such a delegate multicasts the arguments passed in to all methods in the invocation list.

So far, we've always created delegates that point at one method at a time. For example, the following defines three `Action<string>` delegates based on a lambda expression:

```
Action<string> sayHiEnglish = name => Console.WriteLine("Hello " + name);
Action<string> sayHiDutch   = name => Console.WriteLine("Hallo " + name);
Action<string> sayHiFrench  = name => Console.WriteLine("Allo  " + name);
```

What if we're given a name and want to call all the above to greet the incoming user in a bunch of languages? Different approaches exist. Obviously, we could invoke all three delegates one by one:

```
sayHiEnglish(name);
sayHiDutch(name);
sayHiFrench(name);
```

Code starts to get bloated if subsequently we're asked to add another language to the mix, requiring us to revisit the invocation site of those delegates. Furthermore, it might even be the case we provide a means for the users of our greeting system to plug in other delegates for different languages that we didn't anticipate. Now we can no longer have a fixed number of delegate invocations in our code.

Let's go down the route of supporting an unknown number of target methods by doing the plumbing ourselves using a handcrafted invocation list:

```
var greetings = new List<Action<string>> {
    name => Console.WriteLine("Hello " + name),
    name => Console.WriteLine("Hallo " + name),
    name => Console.WriteLine("Allo  " + name)
};
```

Now we can provide the user with some ability to add a greeting delegate to this list (obviously using all the best practices learning in object-oriented programming, not exposing this list directly) and invoke all of them by means of a loop:

```
void SendGreetings(string name) {
    foreach (var greeting in greetings) {
        greeting(name); // invokes the delegate
    }
}
```

Ignoring the trivial implementation of this method with the loop, take a look at the resulting method's signature: It takes in a string and returns nothing. In other words, it obeys the signature of an Action<string> target method. What we've effectively done here is *combine* a series of delegates into one in a rather roundabout way. Why roundabout? MulticastDelegate precisely provides for this out of the box through a static method called Combine, as shown in Figure 17.28.

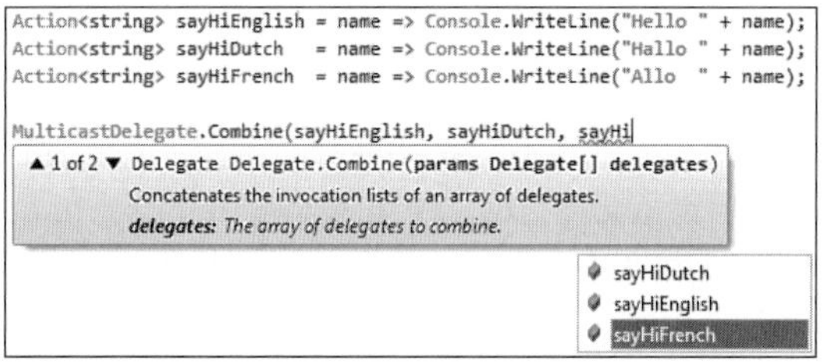

FIGURE 17.28   Combining delegates through the Delegate API.

Notice that the Combine method in fact is defined on the base type Delegate, so we could have called it on Delegate instead, too. The result of applying Combine to a set of Delegate objects is by itself a Delegate. As you might have guessed, System.Delegate is the base type for all delegate objects. To make the preceding code as strongly typed as possible, we can cast the result:

```
Action<string> sayHiEnglish = name => Console.WriteLine("Hello " + name);
Action<string> sayHiDutch   = name => Console.WriteLine("Hallo " + name);
Action<string> sayHiFrench  = name => Console.WriteLine("Allo  " + name);
```

```
var sendGreetings = (Action<string>)Delegate.Combine(sayHiEnglish, sayHiDutch,
                                                     sayHiFrench);
sendGreetings("Bart");
```

The result of invoking the resulting sendGreetings delegate is as you expect: All three greet-ing messages get printed to the screen in the order they were specified in the call to Combine.

Although the preceding works, it's a little rough on the eye due to the method call and the required cast to put us back in a more strongly typed world. In addition, there's no compile-time checking possible based on the signature of Combine and the cast:

```
Action<string> sayHiEnglish = name => Console.WriteLine("Hello " + name);
Func<int, int> twiceAsNice = x => x * 2;
ThreadStart t = (ThreadStart)Delegate.Combine(sayHiEnglish, twiceAsNice);
t();
```

Although this will compile fine, it doesn't make any sense at all because the delegates that are getting combined here are not compatible with one another. In fact, the Delegate call will fail at runtime because the incompatibility gets detected by the runtime. And even if we got this part right using two compatible delegates (for example, sayHiEnglish and sayHiDutch), the cast could fail, as well, if the target type (ThreadStart in the example) is incompatible with the resulting delegate.

Luckily, C# provides language-level support for combining delegates using the very famil-iar + operator. The sendGreetings delegate can be constructed like this:

```
Action<string> sayHiEnglish = name => Console.WriteLine("Hello " + name);
Action<string> sayHiDutch   = name => Console.WriteLine("Hallo " + name);
Action<string> sayHiFrench  = name => Console.WriteLine("Allo  " + name);

var sendGreetings = sayHiEnglish + sayHiDutch + sayHiFrench;
sendGreetings("Bart");
```

The result of doing so is statically typed, so sendGreetings is correctly inferred to be of type Action<string>, just like all the delegates from which it's composed.

Being able to use the + operator, what about compound assignment using +=? This also works:

```
var sendGreetings = sayHiEnglish + sayHiDutch;
sendGreetings += sayHiFrench;
```

WHY THIS SYNTAX MATTERS

In the discussion about events in Chapter 18, you'll see how this compound assign-ment will be used to attach event handlers to an event (although, as you can see, this feature is really defined on delegates, not just for events).

Because the compiler has all type information available about the delegate objects that are "added together," it can protect us against writing invalid combinations. Figure 17.29 shows such a mishap triggering a compile-time error.

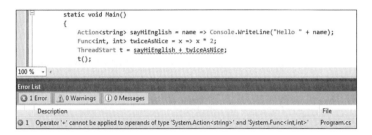

FIGURE 17.29   Compile-time checking for delegate combination.

The implementation of delegate combination using the + and += operators is no dark magic at all. We just rely on the `Delegate.Combine` method under the hood, followed by a cast to the destination type. Because of the compile-time checking for delegate compatibility, all the generated code is statically guaranteed to succeed.

What about combining delegates with a null reference? It turns out that `Combine` simply allows null references to be used without blowing up the call. Those null references simply don't end up in the invocation list and are filtered out:

```
var sendGreetings = sayHiEnglish + sayHiForeign; // assume sayHiForeign is null
sendGreetings("Bart"); // we still get here and this simply prints "Hello Bart"
```

Why does the null case matter that much? Well, there's not just an addition operation (combination, as we have called it) on multicast delegates: Removal exists, too. This is illustrated in the following example:

```
Action<string> sendGreetings = null;

sendGreetings += sayHiEnglish;
sendGreetings += sayHiDutch;
sendGreetings("Bart"); // Prints "Hello Bart" and "Hallo Bart"

sendGreetings -= sayHiEnglish;
sendGreetings += sayHiFrench;
sendGreetings("John"); // Prints "Hallo John" and "Allo John"
```

Under the covers, removal of a delegate using either the binary operator or the compound -= assignment is implemented by calling `Delegate.Remove`.

Adding and removing delegates from an invocation list is very important in the context of events, as you will see shortly. In such a setting, it's common to start off with an empty, null-valued invocation list just like sendGreetings starts its lifetime in the preceding example. Once the first delegate is added, we're really adding up a null delegate and the newly supplied delegate instance. It doesn't make sense to fail in such a case, which is why null references are allowed without causing any failure.

Also when removing all delegates from a MulticastDelegate, a null reference results, conceptually representing an empty invocation list. In a scenario where external parties can add (attach) and remove (detach) delegates, this is a common situation. That said, *invoking* a null reference delegate will result in a NullReferenceException, so we should be cautious when invoking a delegate no matter what:

```
Action<string> sendGreetings = null;
...
// external party does: sendGreetings += sayHiEnglish;
...
sendGreetings("Bart"); // Prints "Hello Bart"
...
// external party does: sendGreetings -= sayHiEnglish;
...
sendGreetings("John"); // throws NullReferenceException
```

When talking about events, we'll see that one should always check against null before *raising* the event. Raising an event technically corresponds to *invoking* a delegate.

TREASURES IN THE SYSTEM.DELEGATE ATTIC

So far, we've demonstrated only the use of multicast delegates with target methods that don't return a value. The curious reader might wonder whether it's possible to combine delegates that return a value as well. Let's give it a try:

```
Func<int, int, int> add = (a, b) => { Console.WriteLine("+"); return a + b; };
Func<int, int, int> mul = (a, b) => { Console.WriteLine("*"); return a * b; };

Func<int, int, int> all = add + mul;
Console.WriteLine(all(2, 3));        // What does it print? 5 or 6
```

The preceding works fine, maybe somewhat surprisingly. Both + and * are printed to the screen, testifying to the fact that both add and mul delegates have been called during the invocation of the combined multicast delegate. The value from the last target method invocation (that is, mul) is retained, and the printed result therefore is 6.

In practice, I never have to rely on this behavior for a useful scenario. A more common thing might be to collect the results from all the function calls and surface those results in some output sequence. There's no direct way to achieve this other than iterating over the invocation list yourself and calling the functions one by one to collect their results. I'll leave this as an exercise for you.

To conclude, let's talk a bit about exceptions raised by one of the target methods for a multi-cast delegate. If one of the target methods throws an exception, that exception will bubble up through the delegate invocation call. This is nothing special, it seems, as long as you realize that this causes the target methods following the one that blew up not to execute:

```
Action good  = () => { Console.WriteLine("OK"); };
Action boom  = () => { throw new Exception("Boom!"); };
Action never = () => { Console.WriteLine("Never printed"); };

Action all = good + boom + never;
all(); // Prints OK and throws an exception, without reaching a call to "never"
```

If, for some obscure reason, you need to reliably invoke all target methods in the face of errors, you can do so by manual iteration over the invocation list. Doing so, you never swallow all exceptions and only deal with error conditions you can deal with appropriately:

```
foreach (Action target in all.GetInvocationList()) {
    try {
        target();
    }
    catch (SomeException ex) {
        // Handle SomeException appropriately
    }
}
```

FOREACH'S HIDDEN CAST

In the preceding fragment, we're using a handy feature of the foreach statement that goes all the way back to C# 1.0 when generics weren't invented yet. Assume you're given some nongeneric collection (or a weakly typed array) and you happen to know it contains only strings. To give users easy iteration over the collection, C#'s foreach loop automatically inserted a cast from the retrieved object to the type specified on the loop variable:

```
object[] names = new string[] { "Bart", "John" };
foreach (string name in names) {
    // In reality, the enumerator's Current property returned an object,
    // so the compiler did emit code like:
    //     string name = (string)enumeratorOverNames.Current;
}
```

We're making handy use of this feature in the preceding code, as GetInvocationList returns a Delegate[], but we know the more specific type of each element in that array because add was obtained by combining Action delegates. By making Action the type for the target loop variable, we instruct the foreach loop to insert the cast on our behalf. Handy!

Summary

Delegates and events are crucial pieces that make the .NET Framework tick. Having a solid understanding of both concepts will take you a long way in discovering framework functionality and designing your own extensible APIs. This chapter looked at the concept of delegates, which form the basis for events covered in the next chapter.

Although the concept of functional programming lies, at least conceptually, at the heart of delegates, they can simply be seen as a strongly typed contract describing a single operation. One party acts as a consumer, invoking the delegate to reach out to the functionality provided from the outside. The other party hands out a piece of code that adheres to the delegate contract (its signature, if you will) by instantiating a delegate or using an anonymous function expression or lambda expression, with possible use of a closure to capture outer variables. LINQ is one of the many APIs that's designed for heavy use of delegates to pass all sorts of little functions around (predicates, projections, key selectors, and so on).

With the knowledge of delegates under our belts, we put our gained knowledge to the test by explaining events in terms of them in the next chapter. In Chapter 19, we revisit delegates from another angle, this time to unravel the innards of LINQ.

IN THIS CHAPTER

▶ The Two Sides of
Delegates 834

▶ A Reactive Application 835

▶ How Events Work 843

▶ Raising Events, the Correct
Way 845

▶ Add and Remove
Accessors 847

▶ Detach Your Event
Handlers 852

▶ Recommended Event
Patterns 861

▶ Case Study:
INotifyProperty
Interfaces and UI
Programming 871

▶ Countdown, the GUI Way 882

▶ Modern Approaches to Reactive
Programming 888

Fully loaded with a bag of knowledge about delegates, we're now in a great position to start learning about one of their direct applications: events. In Chapter 17, during our examination of asynchronous delegate invocation, we already hinted at the difference between interactive and reactive programming. Events are clearly a good fit for the latter category, where our application has to react to some event being triggered elsewhere in the system (or even far out on some server).

In this chapter, we discuss events from a C# language point of view and their first-class citizenship in the .NET Framework and the underlying runtime. As a matter of fact, without realizing it just yet, you already know almost everything there is to know about events solely by knowing how delegates work. When faced with both concepts for the first time, people tend to find things a bit confusing. To avoid such situations, our discussion will introduce events by defining them in terms of delegates, right from the start.

After you understand how events are declared and raised, we focus on typical patterns for event-driven programming and API design, putting our knowledge to the test by looking at the Windows Forms UI framework, which relies heavily on events. Finally, this chapter wouldn't be complete without a sneak peek at different approaches to writing event-driven software as seen in the WPF and Reactive Extensions (Rx).

The Two Sides of Delegates

Delegates really have two sides to them. One side defines one or more *target* methods referred to by the (multicast) delegate; the other defines a way to *invoke* those methods through the delegate. To keep things clear, let's define a little bit of vocabulary here. We'll say a target method gets *called*, whereas a delegate is getting *invoked*. With those words in place, we can sketch our current understanding of delegates as shown in Figure 18.1.

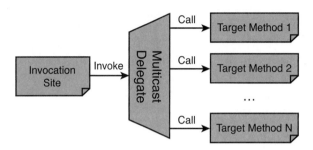

FIGURE 18.1   Invoking a delegate is an interactive act.

When we look at the picture from left to right, delegates look like very interactive beasts, where the invocation site is in the driver seat: It actively invokes the delegate, triggering the target methods to be called.

Now let's flip the figure around, keeping shapes and arrows in place but performing a few rename operations. For the verbs, to invoke becomes *to raise* and to call becomes *to handle*. For the nouns, replace *target method* with *event handler* and *invocation site* with *event source*. Now we get Figure 18.2.

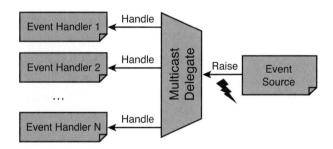

FIGURE 18.2   Event handling is a very reactive business.

Again, scanning the picture from left to right, things start to look quite different. Instead of an outgoing Invoke arrow that *interact*s with the delegate, we now see a bunch of incoming Handle arrows that allow us to *react* to an incoming event. If we follow those arrows against the flow through the delegate, we end up at the event source on the right, which *raised* an event.

All there is to understanding the fundamental principles of events is recognizing that these two figures are just each other's mirror images. So by knowing the "classic" use of delegates, you already know how events work: Congratulations! Obviously, we won't stop here; there's quite a bit to tell about the specifics of events and certain typical use patterns, so let's explore this piece-by-piece now.

A Reactive Application

Before we dive into the C# language feature called events, let's see how far the observation from the previous two figures brings us by using bare-bone delegates to create a reactive application. To keep things simple, we continue our way in the good old world of console applications to implement a countdown mechanism that's operated as follows:

- ▶ The user sets the number of seconds to count down.
- ▶ The user instructs the countdown mechanism to start.
- ▶ The countdown raises a signal for every second that has elapsed.
- ▶ The countdown raises an event when the countdown has reached zero.

By looking at the predicate of the preceding sentences, you can decide whether the described operational step is interactive or reactive. When the user does something, he or she is *interacting* with the time. Every time the countdown raises an event, the user may be *reacting* to it.

Notice how we left lots of details unspecified. We didn't say how the user sets the number of seconds, nor did we say how the countdown is started. All we've specified so far is a generic countdown *mechanism* that can be provided with many interfaces, as shown in Figure 18.3.

User's manual

1. To set, rotate the top clockwise
2. To start, release the top half
3. As time elapses, it turns counterclockwise
4. As it reaches zero, the bell rings

User's manual

1. To set, turn the knob on the top
2. To start, press the knob down
3. As time elapses, the little arrow turns
4. As it reaches zero, it stays at "60"

FIGURE 18.3 Two physical interfaces for a countdown mechanism.

Assuming both the egg timer and the chronometer are implemented using the same countdown mechanism on the inside, both the interactive parts and reactive parts are surfaced quite differently. For example, starting the timer involves releasing the egg timer's rotating top half; the chronometer needs a button press. Those actions are "interactive." We're in the driver's seat and give a signal to start the countdown mechanism.

On the reactive side, things are also different. When the countdown reaches zero, the egg timer reacts by ringing a bell. The chronometer, on the other hand, isn't really interested in this event because it doesn't provide a special notification about reaching zero to the user. Because no further time-elapsed events would be raised by the inner countdown mechanism, the little arrow will keep pointing upward to the 60 (which equals 0 in clock arithmetic, of course) indicator.

Our task is to provide a general-purpose countdown mechanism that can be embedded in both an egg timer and a chronometer. (You're invited to think about other uses.) And guess what? To realize the reactive parts, we'll use events. For now, we start by using simple delegates and refine the solution toward the use of C# events later.

Using Delegates

To realize our countdown mechanism in code, let's build a CountDown class that gets initialized with the number of seconds to countdown. This part leads to the following obvious skeleton code:

```
class CountDown {
    private uint _seconds;

    public CountDown(uint seconds) {
        _seconds = seconds;
    }
}
```

Next, we need to separate two concerns: the parts dealing with interactive user actions versus the ones that have a reactive nature. We already know how to realize interactive concepts by means of regular methods. In fact, we did so for the timer's initialization by the definition of a constructor (the method to be called to create a countdown). Besides this, we need a method to start the countdown:

```
public void Start() {
    uint n = _seconds;
    while (n > 0u) {
        // TODO: let the user know one second has ticked away
        Thread.Sleep(1000);
    }
    // TODO: let the user know we've reached zero
}
```

Ignore the "to do" notes for the time being. The preceding code realizes the core engine of the countdown as a simple whole loop. There's a problem, though: The Start method blocks upon calling it, sitting in the while loop for the duration specified by the timer. It would be more desirable for the Start call to be asynchronous, so let's introduce a background thread on which the timer will tick:

```
public void Start() {
    new Thread(() => {
        uint n = _seconds;
        while (n > 0u) {
            // TODO: let the user know one second has ticked away
            Thread.Sleep(1000);
            n--;
        }
        // TODO: let the user know we've reached zero
    }).Start();
}
```

Feel free to refactor the preceding code if you don't like the use of a lambda expression for substantial amounts of code, but that's merely a matter of taste. What's more important is that the Start method now returns immediately, with the timer ticking on a separate thread.

Now to the heart of our mission: how to fill in the gaps left by our "to do" notes, used to inform the user about certain *events*. Because we want to keep our countdown mechanism generic, we can't hard code the actions to be taken whenever an event occurs. Instead, we'll have the user supply callback procedures, or with more appropriate wording, *event handlers*, through delegates. To do so, let's introduce two more properties of a delegate type:

```
public Action<uint> Tick    { get; set; }
public Action       Finished { get; set; }
```

With the preceding in place, you can use the CountDown class as follows:

```
var countDown = new CountDown(5);


// Hook up event handlers
countDown.Tick = currentSecond => Console.WriteLine(currentSecond);
countDown.Finished = () => Console.Beep();


countDown.Start();
```

The two property assignments, later to be replaced by event handler registrations, are the means for the user to specify how a Tick event and a Finished event should be dealt with.

Inside the CountDown's background thread, we'll have to raise those events by invoking the delegates in the appropriate places, as follows:

```csharp
public void Start() {
    new Thread(() => {
        uint n = _seconds;
        while (n > 0u) {
            if (Tick != null)
                Tick(n);

            Thread.Sleep(1000);
            n-;
        }

        if (Finished != null)
            Finished();
    }).Start();
}
```

Notice the use of null checks to make the code robust against users that did not specify one or more event handler delegates. (For example, our chronometer won't care about Finished.) To be totally honest, the preceding code still has a defect with regard to how the delegates are getting invoked. You'll see why later in this chapter (hint: multithreading).

Based on the sample shown here, it's clear that the use of delegates provides a nice way to call back to the user: Raising an event is just a specialized application of invoking a delegate. The result of a sample run is shown in Figure 18.4. Because the medium of printed books doesn't permit playing a sound when looking at an image, you will have to take my word for it: Upon reaching zero, the computer produced a beep sound.

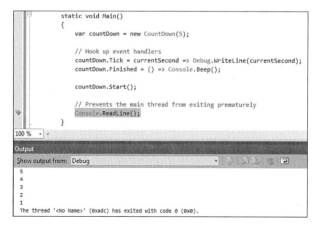

FIGURE 18.4   Use of the CountDown class with simple event handlers.

AN ACCURATE TIMER?

Our countdown mechanism is not a very accurate timer for various reasons. One reason is that the OS doesn't make guarantees about the accuracy of thread sleeps. Ultimately, many threads are competing for resources on the machine, and the thread scheduler needs to be fair to all of them. This can result in our thread being woken up later than we specified on the `Sleep` call. Improvements to this can be made using high-resolution timers, but let's not go there.

Another factor in inaccuracy is due solely to the way we wrote the code: The invocation of the `Tick` delegate inside the loop has nonzero cost. This is not just due to the fact we're invoking a delegate (which has some cost, just like every other action that burns CPU cycles), but even more so because we're calling out to event handlers we don't know the characteristic of. For example, an egg timer's mechanical subsystem may take a few milliseconds to rotate the upper half of the device. Therefore, for every call to `Tick`, we're delaying the call to `Thread.Sleep`, causing the timer to start drifting. One way to fix this deficiency is to use asynchronous delegate invocations.

A much better timer implementation exists in the `System.Threading` namespace, which is based on an OS-level timer. For any serious timing business, that one should be used rather than a home-brew loop-and-sleep-based timer.

Limitations on Plain Use of Delegates

The plain use of delegates for event-based programming seems promising, but there are a few caveats that require a slightly ameliorated approach. As usual, when more than one party is involved in making something work, there needs to be consensus as to how to do things. The exposition of raw delegates is problematic for this reason, if the user of the class does not behave politely. Let's take a look.

First, multiple parties might want to listen for an event, assuming they all have access to the type raising those events. In other words, we need a way for our users to hook up more than one event handler. That's easy. Just use multicast delegates with their handy += syntax for *combination*:

```
// Egg timer listening to the countdown
countDown.Tick     += currentSecond => TurnSpindle(6 /* degrees */);
countDown.Finished += () => Ring();

// Chronometer listening to the same countdown
countDown.Tick     += currentSecond => MoveHand(currentSecond);
```

In the preceding example, both listeners on the countdown are well behaved because they all use the += compound assignment operator to *add* their own event handlers. But because we're exposing a delegate through a settable property, nothing prevents someone from doing a plain assignment, thus replacing the whole multicast delegate. One could go as far as stating that this allows a denial-of-service attack because one client can overwrite all event handlers hooked up by other clients:

```
// Malicious chronometer overwriting the Tick delegate altogether
countDown.Tick = currentSecond => MoveHand(currentSecond);
```

This is not the only problem, though. Raising an event should really be a privileged operation that can be performed only by the event source. But by giving users a way to retrieve, through the property getter, the multicast delegate containing the hooked event handlers, everyone who can get a hold on it can raise the event:

```
// Egg timer listening to the countdown
countDown.Tick     += currentSecond => TurnSpindle(6 /* degrees */);
countDown.Finished += () => Ring();

// Evil jealous chronometer that wants to take revenge on our nice egg timer
uint n = 0;
while (true) {
    countDown.Tick(n); // Chronometer raises the event from the outside!
    n = (n + 1) % 60;
}
```

In the preceding code fragment, an evil chronometer gets a hold of the Tick delegate to which the egg timer has attached a handler. Evil as it is, it starts raising the Tick event by invoking the delegate in a tight infinite loop. A little calculation shows that at a rate of one Tick invocation every 20 nanoseconds (not unrealistic at all), our poor egg timer will start rotating at a daunting speed of 833,333 rotations per second. You don't want to be in the same room as the egg timer under attack!

Both problems outlined here are at the level of trust between two parties: the event source versus its consumers. One ill-behaved consumer can make life pretty bad for its peer consumers as well as the event source. On the technical field, we can attribute this problem to the fact we're allowing unrestricted access to the multicast delegate used for the event. In other words, our use of a property is not quite ideal.

All those reasons were among the key motivations why events were introduced as a first-class concept in .NET in general and in the C# language specifically. Let's take a look at how the CountDown code would look if we use events instead.

Using .NET Events

Events are just delegates in disguise but provide additional levels of protection against the attacks we've seen previously. Syntactically, very little has to change:

```
class CountDown {
    private uint _seconds;
```

```
    public CountDown(uint seconds) {
        _seconds = seconds;
    }

    public event Action<uint> Tick;
    public event Action       Finished;

    public void Start() {
        ...
    }
}
```

See the difference? Instead of Tick and Finished being declared as properties with a delegate type, we now use the event keyword instead and drop the get and set property accessors. (You'll see later how events have optional accessors called add and remove.)

At the use site, we can no longer write the following:

```
var countDown = new CountDown(5);


// Hook up event handlers
countDown.Tick = currentSecond => Console.WriteLine(currentSecond);
countDown.Finished = () => Console.Beep();


countDown.Start();
```

The problem is that the innocent-looking assignment operations would allow any event handler to swap out the whole existing invocation list for its own delegate, one of the problems mentioned earlier. The complaint issued by the compiler is shown in Figure 18.5 and hints at the right solution: Use += to add a handler.

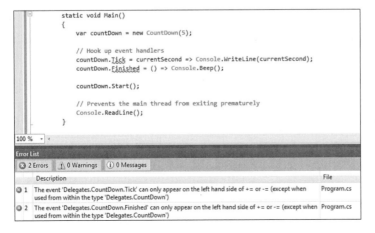

FIGURE 18.5   Event handlers need to be added or removed using the right syntax.

The corrected code, therefore, looks like this:

```
var countDown = new CountDown(5);


// Hook up event handlers
countDown.Tick += currentSecond => Console.WriteLine(currentSecond);
countDown.Finished += () => Console.Beep();


countDown.Start();
```

In addition, notice in the IntelliSense how events have a different icon to distinguish them from other sorts of members. Figure 18.6 shows how events look in IntelliSense.

FIGURE 18.6   Events appear as lightning bolts.

TO RAISE OR TO FIRE?

The lightning bolt icon refers to the phrase "to *fire* off an event." Because "to fire" sounds too pejorative (nobody wants to lose his or her job by getting fired), the phrase "to *raise* an event" is preferred. Oh, and for exceptions, you use the verb "to *throw*."

Although the required use of += protects against malicious event hander assignments, we still need to guard ourselves for external invocations. Events do so, too, allowing them to be *raised* only from within the containing type. Therefore, our existing code in the background thread's procedure still works fine using the delegate invocation syntax:

```
public void Start() {
    new Thread(() => {
        uint n = _seconds;
        while (n > 0u) {
            if (Tick != null)
                Tick(n); // doesn't change, an event is really a delegate!
    ...
}
```

However, from the outside, we won't be able to raise the event any longer. Figure 18.7 proves this in terms of a compile-time error that occurs when this rule is violated.

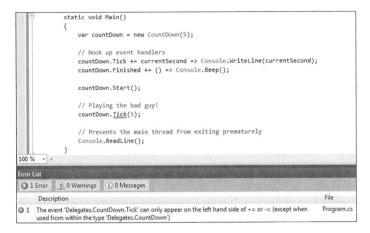

```
static void Main()
{
    var countDown = new CountDown(5);

    // Hook up event handlers
    countDown.Tick += currentSecond => Console.WriteLine(currentSecond);
    countDown.Finished += () => Console.Beep();

    countDown.Start();

    // Playing the bad guy!
    countDown.Tick(5);

    // Prevents the main thread from exiting prematurely
    Console.ReadLine();
}
```

	Description	File
1	The event 'Delegates.CountDown.Tick' can only appear on the left hand side of += or -= (except when used from within the type 'Delegates.CountDown')	Program.cs

FIGURE 18.7   Raising an event is a privileged operation.

The example is functionally still the same as our earlier attempt but is so in a much safer way. This finishes our illustration of events, putting us in a good position to take a closer look at them from the language and runtime point of view.

How Events Work

Approaching events from a C# language angle, there's not much to them. Events are declared as members of a class or a struct, with the common set of available modifiers such as the static keyword and the visibility modifiers. From a typing perspective, an event must be declared with a delegate type. For example:

```
public event Action Finished;
```

As you will see, it's a common recommended practice to use certain delegate types for events to create a common experience across the board. For now, we'll ignore this and focus on the inner workings of events for a minute or two.

What do events consist of on the inside? Let's make some informed guesses before taking a closer look with ILDASM. First, events are a different sort of member that needs to be discoverable through tools like Visual Studio's IntelliSense. This first requirement mandates metadata to be present to describe the event. Second, to prevent the problems discussed in the previous section, we can never leak the underlying multicast delegate to the outside. In other words, that delegate needs to be kept privately on the inside of the containing type. But if that's the case, adding and removing handlers using += and -= syntax should have some level of indirection. A logical choice to realize this is to create accessor methods that perform *add* and *remove* handler operations on the caller's behalf.

Given our CountDown class, Figure 18.8 illustrates how events are implemented, starting by taking a look at the metadata part.

FIGURE 18.8   Events as metadata entities.

If you double-click any of the events indicated in Figure 18.8, you'll see something along the following lines (slightly cleaned up):

```
.event Action Finished
{
    .addon instance void Delegates.CountDown::add_Finished(class Action)
    .removeon instance void Delegates.CountDown::remove_Finished(class Action)
}
```

In its bare essence, an event is nothing more than an association of a name with a type and two (compiler-generated) methods: one to add an event handler and one to remove an event handler. When using the += or -= syntax in C# to add or remove an event handler, the compiler emits a call to one of those methods:

```
countDown.Finished += () => Console.Beep();
```

```
// Compiles into...
countDown.add_Finished(() => Console.Beep);
```

From this, it's clear the multicast delegate for the event is never exposed to the users of the event. Or to say it in true object-oriented terms, encapsulation is ensured. You can already expect how those methods work on the inside: They use Delegate.Combine and Delegate.Remove, respectively, acting on a private field that keeps the invocation list as a multicast delegate. The code that gets generated for our `Finished` event looks roughly like this:

```
private Action _finished;

public void add_Finished(Action value) {
    _finished = (Action)Delegate.Combine(_finished, value);
}

public void remove_Finished(Action value) {
    _finished = (Action)Delegate.Remove(_finished, value);
}
```

MULTITHREADING IS SUBTLE

The word *roughly* in the previous paragraph is all important. In harsh reality, the generated code is slightly more complicated due to multithreading concerns. If multiple threads are adding or removing event handlers simultaneously, the door is wide open for problems.

To understand why this is the case, see how the call to `Combine` is followed by an assignment (similar for the `Remove` call). When a thread switch occurs between the call to `Combine` and the assignment, it's possible another thread messes with the multicast delegate, too. After switching back to the original thread and doing the assignment, the effects from the interrupting thread are overwritten: A *race condition* exists.

As a user of the language, you don't have to worry about this, but it's good to know this protection is in place.

Raising Events, the Correct Way

In our `CountDown` example, you've seen how to raise events using this pattern:

```
if (MyEvent != null)
    MyEvent(/* args */);
```

Looks right, doesn't it? If nobody is listening for the event, `MyEvent` is null, and we should not attempt to invoke the delegate because that will cause the runtime to yell at us with an unfriendly `NullReferenceException`.

WHY IS NULL USED ANYWAY?

It might be surprising that the empty event handlers are being presented with null references. This is really due to the way the `Combine` and `Remove` methods on `Delegate` are implemented, but that just pushes the question further out: Why not just return a `MulticastDelegate` with an empty invocation list?

If we were to do that, the compiler should make sure every event starts its lifetime with such an empty `MulticastDelegate`. In other words, all fields need to be assigned with a delegate with an empty invocation list. That's not really a problem, but think about the memory this takes, especially in frameworks that are full of events. A good example is Windows Forms, where the simplest `Button` type has no fewer than 68 events. Having multicast delegates with empty invocation lists takes up enough memory to be problematic. This is especially true because only a fraction of those events are typically handled.

Unfortunately, the preceding code isn't quite correct in the face of multithreading because the null check and invocation are not done atomically. For example, assume one thread is removing an event handler between the null check and the invocation that are done on another thread. The sequence of interactions for both threads is described in Table 18.1.

TABLE 18.1   Multithreaded Interaction with Events

	Thread 1	Thread 2	MyEvent Targets
1	`if (MyEvent != null)`		A
2		`MyEvent -= A;`	A fi null
3	`MyEvent(/* args */);`		null

On the last line, our program will crash because Thread 1 observes a null `MyEvent` delegate due to the Thread 2 interleaved execution. To avoid this problem, an intermediate assignment to a local variable can be used:

```
var evt = MyEvent;
if (evt != null)
    evt(/* args */);
```

Recall that adding or removing an event handler does not simply tweak a multicast delegate's invocation list in place; instead, the call to `Combine` or `Remove` returns a new delegate instance that contains the new invocation list. So by caching a reference to the current delegate in a local variable, we have something we can rely on to remain stable. Figure 18.9 illustrates this in more detail. Strictly speaking, this means we can lag behind a bit on the event's handlers being invoked: With the fix, the last line on the first thread will still call A even though the second thread has already unhooked it. This shouldn't usually be a big deal.

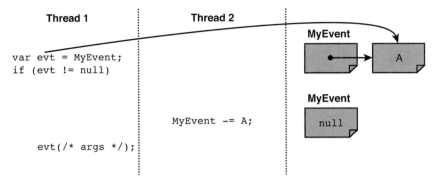

FIGURE 18.9   Safe multithreaded event handler interactions.

If you want to see the illustrated problem with your own eyes, it's pretty easy to repro using a tiny little bit of multithreaded code:

```
static event Action MyEvent;

static void Main() {
    // Thread mimicking a client attaching and detaching handlers.
    new Thread(() => {
        while (true) {
            Action a = () => Console.WriteLine("Hi!");
            MyEvent += a;
            MyEvent -= a;
        }
    }).Start();

    // Main thread raises the event with too little protection.
    while (true) {
        if (MyEvent != null)
            MyEvent();
    }
}
```

Depending on how lucky you are, the number of "Hi!" messages printed to the screen will vary. But sooner or later, the preceding code will bomb with a null reference on the main thread. The fix, as we discussed, is to copy the MyEvent reference locally.

Add and Remove Accessors

With events based on a piece of metadata pointing at two methods, it shouldn't be at all surprising that C# provides a way to customize those methods in case you want to do so.

In the context of events (and properties), we refer to those methods as accessors. For events, two accessors exist called add and remove. The syntax is predictable, being analog to get and set for properties:

```
public event Finished {
    add {
        // Called when doing +=.
    }
    remove {
        // Called when doing -=.
    }
}
```

Inside those accessors, the right side of the += and -= operator is available using the value keyword. This is similar to the way a property setter gets access to the value being assigned to it.

Once we implement add and remove accessors, the compiler no longer generates a field for the multicast delegate, leaving all plumbing to the developer. You can compare this with the use of auto-implemented properties (which create a backing storage field for you) versus manual implementation of a getter and a setter, as shown in Figure 18.10. It's quite surprising that we had to wait until C# 3.0 to get auto-implemented properties, whereas events had both "auto-implemented" and "handcrafted" variants (using explicit accessors) since the very first release of the language.

Auto-Implemented Properties

```
public int Foo { get; set; }
=
private int _foo;
public int Foo {
    get {
        return _foo;
    }
    set {
        _foo = vlaue;
    }
}
```

Events Without Accessors

```
public event Action Foo;
= (ignoring multithreading)
private Action _foo;
public event Action Foo {
    add {
        _foo += value;
    }
    remove {
        _foo -= value;
    }
}
```

FIGURE 18.10   Symmetry between properties and events.

An example where this feature comes in handy is when implementing a more memory-efficient event system. In the previous section's sidebar, I mentioned one reason null is used for multicast delegates with no target methods is to avoid heap allocations for every empty event. There's another side to this, as well: the field required for an event's multicast delegate object. For example, in 99.99% of cases, developers only handle the Click event of a button control. For Windows Form's Button, that's 1 out of 68 events on the control, which would lead to 67 null references that are a pure waste of memory. Manual implementation of our own add and remove accessors comes to the rescue here.

Before going any further, note that this manual implementation of add and remove accessors is something you'll rarely have to do unless you plan on designing systems with a very large number of events where memory footprint becomes very significant. To get an idea of the scale of frameworks we're talking about here, notice that the two concrete implementations of such an idea I am aware of are Windows Forms and Windows Presentation Foundation (WPF).

So let's give it a try and design a little efficient event management system. Instead of keeping storage fields for each multicast delegate, we're going to store an object's event handlers in a dictionary. Each available event gets represented by a unique key. The value associated with that key determines the event handler, while the absence of an entry in the dictionary indicates no handlers are present for that event. Let's keep things a bit abstract for the sake of discussion and assume we have a class like this:

```
class Bar {
    public event Action A1, A2, A3, A4, A5, A6, A7, A8;
}
```

Each instance of Bar has eight compiler-generated storage fields for Action delegates to keep the handlers for A1 through A8 in. When no event handlers are attached, that's eight wasted references. For 10 instances of Bar, that adds up to a total of 80.

With a dictionary, we get the following picture:

```
class Bar {
    static readonly object s_keyA1 = new object();
    // ...
    static readonly object s_keyA8 = new object();

    private Dictionary<object, Delegate> _handlers = /* TODO */;

    public event Action A1 {
        add    { /* TODO */ }
        remove { /* TODO */ }
    }
    // ...
    public event Action A8 {
        add    { /* TODO */ }
        remove { /* TODO */ }
    }
}
```

First, we have defined 8 symbolic constants that will act as keys in the _handlers dictionary later. These are stored as static fields, adding up to 8 references for the initial overhead. But now, for each instance we have just a single dictionary. With no single event handler attached, we just pay the price of a reference to the dictionary for each instance. For 10 instances of Bar, that's at total of 10 dictionary references on top of the 8 fixed references to the symbolic constants. That brings the total to 18, a huge saving compared to the 80 references required before.

Obviously, we've ignored the memory occupied by the dictionary's data structures, but that constant cost quickly pays off if we have enough events on the type (assuming it's common for events to remain unhooked, as is typical for UI elements).

One remaining question is how to implement the add and remove accessors with this new dictionary-driven infrastructure in place. The answer is shown here:

```
private void AddHandler(object evt, Delegate handler) {
    _handlers[evt] = Delegate.Combine(GetHandler(evt), handler);
}

private void RemoveHandler(object evt, Delegate handler) {
    var newHandler = Delegate.Remove(GetHandler(evt), handler);
    if (newHandler == null && _handlers.ContainsKey(evt))
        _handlers.Remove(evt);
    else
        _handlers[evt] = newHandler;
}

private Delegate GetHandler(object evt) {
    Delegate handler = null;
    _handlers.TryGetValue(evt, out handler);
    return handler;
}
```

Those general-purpose methods are for shared use by all accessor methods. Given an event identifier evt and a handler to attach or detach, they take care of maintaining entries in the dictionary. Adding a handler ultimately calls into Delegate.Combine, whereas removing a delegate calls Delegate.Remove but also removes the event's entry in the dictionary if no handlers are left. Notice this code is inherently unsafe for use in a multithreaded context. You are invited to think about possible solutions using appropriate synchronization schemes and whatnot.

Wiring those up for a single event is fairly straightforward. Given the event's identifier, defined as a symbolic static field constant, we can call into the two methods:

```
static object s_keyA1 = new object();

public event Action A1 {
```

```
add     { AddHandler(s_keyA1, value); }
remove { RemoveHandler(s_keyA1, value); }
}
```

One remaining question is how to raise the event. If you think it's still as easy as calling through the event's apparent delegate, you've got it wrong. Figure 18.11 illustrates this.

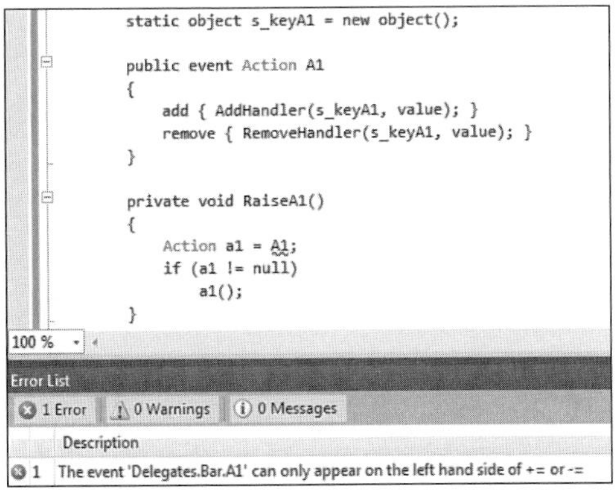

FIGURE 18.11   With custom accessors, the compiler can't know the event's delegate.

The reason should be pretty obvious. Because the compiler no longer emits a private field for the event's delegate, it doesn't know how to gain access to the delegate any longer. Ultimately, the person implementing the add and remove accessors can have left the event handler delegates anywhere, so it becomes your responsibility to implement a mechanism to raise the event by hand.

For our running dictionary-based event handler storage example, we've already added a GetHandler method, which can also be used for this purpose:

```
private void RaiseA1() {
    Action a1 = (Action)GetHandler(s_keyA1);
    if (a1 != null)
        a1();
}
```

With this, we've seen a simple end-to-end implementation of an (thread-unsafe!) event management system, conceptually just like the ones implemented in Windows Forms and WPF. When we discuss WPF in more detail, you'll see that designing a flexible event system embodies more than just a well thought-out storage mechanism. In fact, WPF has its own extension to the baseline .NET event concept, known as *routed events*.

Detach Your Event Handlers

If you would ask any number of .NET developers with a native programming background about the biggest benefits of the platform, they'll most likely bring up its automatic memory management capabilities that relieve developers of the burden of manual bookkeeping.

As good as this might sound, there are still some caveats to be aware of. In particular, event handlers tend to be common sources of memory leaks when they're not maintained correctly. What do I mean by "correct maintenance" of event handlers?

Consider the following piece of code:

```
static class SystemEvents {
    public static event Action ShuttingDown;
}

class Handlers {
    public void OnShutDown() {
        // React to system shutting down
    }

    ~Handlers() {
        Console.WriteLine("Handlers got collected.");
    }
}

class Program {
    static void Main() {
        var handlers = new Handlers();
        SystemEvents.ShuttingDown += handlers.OnShutDown;

        // Do more stuff here

        // Not interested anymore in the handlers
        handlers = null;

        // Do more stuff here; when does handlers get reclaimed?
    }
}
```

In the preceding code, we've abandoned our Handlers event sink instance by setting its reference to null. At this point, it seems that no one refers to the handlers object anymore, such that it becomes amenable for garbage collection. To prove or disprove this, we've added a finalizer to the Handlers type:

```
~Handlers() {
    Console.WriteLine("Handlers got collected.");
}
```

DESTRUCTORS

I've said it before when talking about classes, but finalizers in C# got blessed with an unfortunate syntax that mirrors the destructor syntax from C++. In fact, they even get called destructors in the language specification. However, they have a totally different behavior.

Finalizers get invoked when the object is collected by the garbage collector, which is nondeterministic concerning timing. Destructors in C++, on the other hand, are useful for determinist cleanup based on scoping of objects: When an object goes out of scope, the destructor is called on the spot.

So it's essential to keep this difference in mind. Besides that, finalizers force the garbage collector to do more bookkeeping: Before memory can be reclaimed, the object's finalizer needs to be called. This involves keeping a queue for objects that require finalization, which adds pressure to the system. Therefore, if you don't need a finalizer (as is usually the case for .NET objects that do not hold on to native resources), don't write one!

As the next part of our experiment, we'll trigger a garbage collection and wait for the finalizer to be called. To do this, add the following three lines to the end of the Main method:

```
GC.Collect();
GC.WaitForPendingFinalizers();
Console.ReadLine();
```

Use of Console.ReadLine is essential because we want to see whether the finalizer gets called *before* the application terminates. Console.ReadLine prevents the application from terminating, which would trigger finalizer runs anyway. To make things more concrete, assume there's much more relevant code after the call to GC.Collect and GC.WaitForPendingFinalizers. All we're doing is mimicking the situation in which the garbage collector comes around during the execution of the application, to observe whether the apparently abandoned handlers object is collected.

DON'T TELL THE GC WHAT TO DO

It's considered bad practice to trigger garbage collections programmatically using GC.Collect. The garbage collector is highly tuned to do the most efficient task possible on its own. Manually triggering collections can be a costly thing and should be avoided at all costs. Let the GC do its job, and stay away from calling the GC.Collect method unless you're told to do so by a CLR memory expert after extensive investigation of an application's misbehavior.

Time for the moment of truth! Run the application in its current form and observe the handlers object's finalizer doesn't get called before the application terminates. But don't jump to hasty conclusions such as "the garbage collector is broken." Let's see why.

Recall that the garbage collector is based on reachability analysis: As long as an object can be referred to by executing code (either through references on the stack, in static fields, or things such as thread-local storage), it cannot be collected. If the GC is right about our handlers object, something should be *keeping it alive* by holding on to a reference to it. What's that something? Take a look at the following line:

```
SystemEvents.ShuttingDown += handlers.OnShutDown;
```

The right side is using method group conversion for delegate types to create a delegate referring to the OnShutDown method. Where's that method located? Because it's an instance method, the handlers left side matters, too. In reality, code is getting generated that looks roughly like this:

```
System.add_ShuttingDown(new Action(&handlers, OnShutDown));
```

The preceding code doesn't compile, and is even invalid C# syntax, but illustrates the point quite well: A delegate referring to a method on an instance holds on to two things. One is information about the method being called (a method "token"), while the other refers to the instance the method has to be called on upon invoking the delegate. That's where the keepalive reference to the handlers object comes from.

How can you prevent this leak? The answer is quite straightforward: by making sure you remove an event handler when you're done with it. In our example, the act of setting the handlers reference to null does not suffice to unhook event handlers. In addition, we should make sure to get rid of the event handlers, as follows:

```
class Program {
    static void Main() {
        var handlers = new Handlers();
        SystemEvents.ShuttingDown += handlers.OnShutDown;

        // Do more stuff here

        // Not interested anymore in the handlers
        SystemEvents.ShuttingDown -= handlers.OnShutDown;
        handlers = null;

        // Do more stuff here; when does handlers get reclaimed?
    }
}
```

Because you need the reference to handlers to refer to its OnShutDown method, this can be done only as long as a reference to handlers exists. The line that removes the event handler creates a new delegate instance referring to OnShutdown on handlers, which is located in the multicast delegate's invocation list by the Delegate.Remove method. In short, don't forget to unhook your event handlers.

If all this scares you to death, don't worry too much. Although this problem exists (as our example proves), it's not all that common. The crux of the sketched problem is that we're handling the events on a separate object that does not *own* the objects that raise the events. In our case, we're even using a static event to construct a bad scenario. Why does "ownership" of event sources matter? Well, consider the case of a Windows Forms form shown here:

```
class LoginForm : Form {
    private Button login;

    public LoginForm() {
        login = new Button { Text = "Log in" };
        login.Click += login_Click;
    }

    private void login_Click(object sender, EventArgs e) { /* TODO */ }
}
```

Here, the form instance owns the login button object. The form attaches an event handler for the button's Click event, with the handler located on the form instance itself. In fact, the third line of the constructor could be read as follows:

```
login.Click += this.login_Click;
```

So the "event sink" with the event handlers (the form) is the same as the owner of the event source (the button). As soon as the form object becomes unreachable, so do all of its controls and their event handlers. As shown in Figure 18.12, this makes it possible to reclaim the form and its controls. On the other hand, the earlier example (shown at the bottom of Figure 18.12) poses a problem, as explained earlier.

USING SOS TO TRACE LEAKS

The .NET Framework comes with a low-level debugger extension called SOS (for "Son of Strike") that can be loaded inside Visual Studio for advanced debugging. One of the many things it can help with is locating the source of memory leaks.

A sample session debugging our memory leak is shown in Figure 18.13. On the first line, the SOS extension is loaded from the folder where the .NET Framework lives.

Assuming we somehow already know that a Handlers instance is being leaked, we issue the command !dumpheap to search the managed heap for objects of the specified type. We find exactly one instance of the type and wonder what keeps it alive. Given its reported address, !GCRoot does the trick.

The GCRoot command traces the path of references that keeps the object alive (that is, proves how it can still be reached by code). For our suspect Handlers object, traces look like System.Action fi Handlers. (Read the arrow as "references.")

From this, we clearly see that an Action delegate still refers to the Handlers object. In some cases, this is enough of a clue to start looking for places where the event handlers should be removed but aren't. If more information is needed, you could dump the Action delegate to see what its target method is and so forth.

Search the Web for terms *GCRoot*, *SOS*, and *event* to learn more about the use of SOS to debug object leaks like the one shown here.

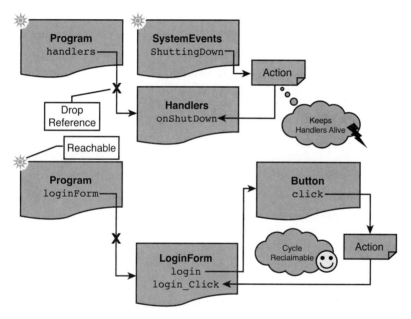

FIGURE 18.12   Ownership of event source objects can help a lot for event handler use.

Because this problem has been known as one of the main sources of memory issues in .NET applications, WPF added the pattern of "weak events." We won't elaborate on this right here, but when using WPF you may want to research this in more depth on MSDN.

Unhooking event handlers looks like a pretty straightforward business, simply using the -= operator. Although this is true, a caveat exists due to the introduction of anonymous function expressions in C# 2.0 and lambda expressions in C# 3.0. Earlier on, we've seen code like this:

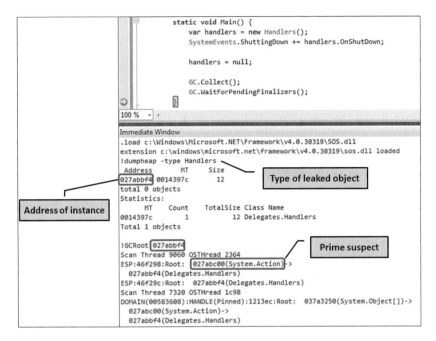

FIGURE 18.13   Analyzing a memory leak with SOS.

```
var countDown = new CountDown(5);

// Hook up event handlers, using lambda expressions
countDown.Tick += currentSecond => Console.WriteLine(currentSecond);
countDown.Finished += () => Console.Beep();

countDown.Start();
```

In the light of our discussion about event handlers, we might want to unhook the Tick and Finished event handlers as a matter of following best practices. The first question to ask is when it's appropriate to do so. Clearly, we shouldn't unhook while the events can still be raised, but we know not to expect further events after the Finished event has been raised (though such a "protocol" should really be documented by the provider of the CountDown type). This makes the code inside the Finished event handler a good place to unhook the Tick event hander as well as itself. Now the more pressing question is how to accomplish this.

To answer this accurately, let's first take a step back. Because we know that events are nothing but multicast delegates in disguise, we can use a plain multicast delegate as a petri dish for some experimentation. Take a look at the following fragment of code, where we use handy lambda expression syntax to make things concise:

```
Action evt = null;
evt += () => Console.WriteLine("Hello");
if (evt != null)
    evt();
evt -= () => Console.WriteLine("Hello");
if (evt != null)
    evt();
```

Pop quiz: How many times does it print Hello? If you say once, think twice; the answer is two times. Although it looks like we're adding and removing the same event handler on lines two and four, those are not the same object. Recall what anonymous functions compile into under the hood: compiler-generated methods containing the code specified in the anonymous function expression:

```
Action evt = null;
evt += new Action(<>__AnonymousMethod1);
if (evt != null)
    evt();
evt -= new Action(<>__AnonymousMethod2);
if (evt != null)
    evt();
```

Two anonymous function expressions result in two distinct methods being cooked up by the compiler, even though they have the same code inside them. The compiler could be smarter about this, detecting "semantically identical" anonymous function expressions and sharing the same object for them. However, this is a pretty tricky thing to implement, and the compiler writers thought there were more important matters to tackle.

Because we have two distinct methods used when adding and removing delegates, the += and -= operations do not cancel each other out. The way to fix this issue is to use an intermediate variable:

```
Action evt = null;
Action handler = () => Console.WriteLine("Hello");
evt += handler;
if (evt != null)
    evt();
evt -= handler;
if (evt != null)
    evt();
```

To be able to unhook our `CountDown` event handlers, we have to lift them into a local variable, as just shown:

```
var countDown = new CountDown(5);

// Hook up event handlers
Action<uint> tickHandler = currentSecond => Console.WriteLine(currentSecond);
Action finishedHandler = () => {
    Console.Beep();

    // Finished has been called: we can unhook both Tick and Finished now.
    countDown.Tick -= tickHandler;
    countDown.Finished -= finishedHandler;
};

countDown.Tick += tickHandler;
countDown.Finished += finishedHandler;

countDown.Start();
```

The preceding code is almost right; it just doesn't compile yet. Conceptually, everything looks right, though: We create handler delegates of type `Action` first and hook them up using regular += syntax later. Inside the event handler for `Finished`, we can unhook those again based on our knowledge of the event protocol of `CountDown`.

The remaining issue (that prevents us from compiling the preceding code) is rather subtle. Take a closer look at the `finishedHandler` lambda expression. While we're defining it, we're using it inside its own body on the last line. In more technical terms, we're defining a recursive lambda expression, which is something the language doesn't permit in this syntactical form, as illustrated in Figure 18.14.

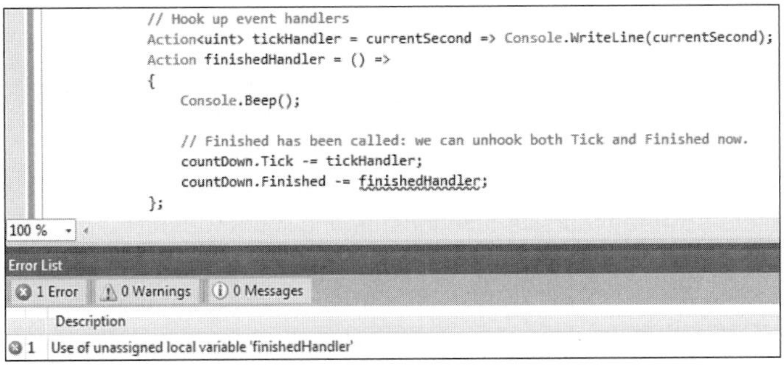

FIGURE 18.14   Recursive lambda expressions make the compiler unhappy.

The reason the compiler complains here is because a combined variable declaration and assignment decomposes into something along those lines:

```
Action finishedHandler; // this variable is unassigned!
Action __temp = () => {
    Console.Beep();

    // Finished has been called: we can unhook both Tick and Finished now.
    countDown.Tick -= tickHandler;
    countDown.Finished -= finishedHandler;
};
finishedHandler = __temp;
```

At the point the finishedHandler variable is used inside the lambda expression, it is still unassigned. I'm explicitly presenting an intermediate variable here to emphasize the fact that finishedHandler gets assigned to at the very last point in time, once the whole lambda expression has been compiled. This is always the case for an assignment: First the right side is evaluated (here, the lambda expression) before it gets assigned wholesale to the left side (here, the finishedHandler variable).

The fix for this issue is surprisingly small: manual decomposition of declaration and assignment, using an initial null reference:

```
Action finishedHandler = null; // now the variable is pre-assigned!
finishedHandler = () => {
    Console.Beep();

    // Finished has been called: we can unhook both Tick and Finished now.
    countDown.Tick -= tickHandler;
    countDown.Finished -= finishedHandler; // now the compiler is pleased...
};
```

THE WHY OF Y

There's actually a functional programming technique to help solve the problem of defining an *anonymous recursive lambda expression*: It's called a *fixed-point combinator* (or *fixpoint* for short). It allows users to write recursive functions as one-liners without requiring intermediate assignments as we've seen in C#. One such fixpoint combinator is called the Y combinator (don't ask me *why*).

For example, defining the factorial function would be done as follows, assuming the presence of a Y combinator implementation in .NET:

```
// In the argument to Y, f stands for what will ultimately become the
// recursive factorial function. Y's role is to "fix" the expression up
// so that really becomes the case. Dark magic of the highest standard!
Func<int, int> fac = Y(f => n => n == 0 ? 1 : n * f(n - 1));
```

Although I find such things incredibly fascinating, I am the first to admit it's better not to use such techniques for enterprise application development in C#. Even if *you* understand this (tip: the Internet is full of "the why and how of Y"), don't assume your co-workers will. It's definitely a good source for brainteasers.

I agree this is a very subtle point, but realistically you're rather unlikely to write such a recursive lambda expression in practice. But if you do, you know what to look out for. One word of advice, though: Although lambda expressions provide a very concise way to define delegates inline (with support for *closures*, as seen earlier), *large* lambda bodies tend to bloat the containing method quickly. As soon as you see a lambda expression with a statement body (that is, surrounded by curly braces), a bell should ring causing you to wonder whether it's time for a refactoring. Honestly, for the CountDown example, I would seriously consider doing so once I get into the tricky unhooking business we saw earlier. Doing so leads to slightly longer but arguably cleaner code:

```
private static CountDown s_countDown;

static void Main() {
    s_countDown = new CountDown(5);
    s_countDown.Tick += TickHandler;
    s_countDown.Finished += FinishedHandler;

    s_countDown.Start();
}

static void TickHandler(uint currentSecond) {
    Console.WriteLine(currentSecond);
}

static void FinishedHandler() {
    Console.Beep();
    s_countDown.Tick -= TickHandler;
    s_countDown.Finished -= FinishedHandler;
}
```

Recommended Event Patterns

To increase code maintainability and make users of your libraries feel comfortable, a few best practices for using events can be formulated.

EventHandler and EventArgs

When designing frameworks, consistency is all important to make people feel at home with new APIs quickly. For educational purposes, we've approached the concept of events from their essential property: Events are nothing but delegates in disguise. In doing so, we chose simple delegate types for our examples, as follows:

```
public event Action<uint> Tick;
public event Action        Finished;
```

In practice, it's more common to follow a certain pattern for events that makes their handlers have a consistent shape. We've already seen such a case in passing, when showing off an event handler for a button control's Click event in Windows Forms:

```
private void login_Click(object sender, EventArgs e) { /* TODO */ }
```

From this signature, you can infer the type of the event's delegate to be similar to an Action<object, EventArgs>. In reality, though, events in Windows Forms are typically using a different delegate type. For example:

```
class Control {
    public event EventHandler Click;
    public event KeyEventHandler KeyDown;
    public event MouseEventHandler MouseMove;
    // Many others
}
```

Suffixed with the word Handler, those delegates for use with events follow the pattern of taking two arguments: One specifies the sender of the event (for example, the Button instance where the Click event was triggered on), whereas the other provides event arguments (for example, the mouse cursor position at the time the MouseMove event was raised). The delegate definitions for the presented examples are shown here:

```
public delegate void EventHandler(object sender, EventArgs e);
public delegate void KeyEventHandler(object sender, KeyEventArgs e);
public delegate void MouseEventHandler(object sender, MouseEventArgs e);
```

The first question that comes to mind is this: Why do we care about a sender? After all, aren't we going to have specific event handlers on a per-object and per-event basis? Not necessarily.

So far, we've always presented multicast delegates from one point of view: They allow calling multiple targets through a single delegate invocation. That means we can have multiple handlers associated with a single event source. For instance, multiple parties may be interested in the Tick event of our CountDown so that a single instance of the countdown mechanism can be used with different displays hooked to it.

However, if you flip the picture around, it's equally valid to use the same method as the target for one or more event handlers. An example of this situation is to listen to events that signal data in a form's fields (for example, in text boxes) has changed to mark some dirty bit, which gets used to signal the user of unsaved changes when quitting the form. It makes sense to reuse that logic across all event handlers for all the controls that result in such a change. An overview of the two views on events is presented in Figure18.15.

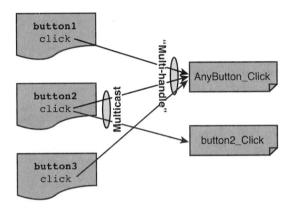

FIGURE 18.15   Multicast versus multihandle.

In the latter case, it might be useful to have the ability to distinguish between the sender of the event. This way, all the common logic can still be shared, while decisions can be made based on the sender of the event. Or if there's a common type between all the senders that share the same handler, you can correctly cast the sender argument (which is of type System.Object) to the most common supertype and use that information:

```
private void AnyButton_Click(object sender, EventArgs e) {
    MessageBox.Show(((Button)sender).Text + " was clicked!");
}
```

NAMING OF EVENT HANDLERS

A typical naming pattern for event handlers is to follow the source object's name by an underscore and the name of the event. It's so commonly used that Visual Studio's code editor has this pattern baked in, as shown in Figure 18.16.

As far as I can recall, this pattern goes back to the pre-.NET days of Visual Basic, which was one of the first mainstream languages that made events a first-class language construct.

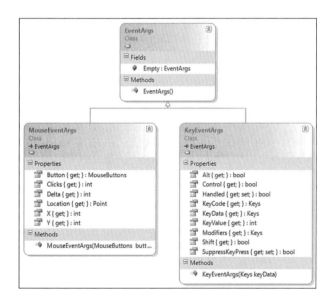

FIGURE 18.16   Auto-completion for generating and adding an event handler.

Okay, so the use of the sender parameter seems useful, so what about the EventArgs parameter? In the running example from Windows Forms, we've seen three different EventArgs types, as shown in Figure 18.17.

FIGURE 18.17   EventArgs form a class hierarchy.

As the name implies, EventArg types represent an event's arguments, which contain useful information about the event that was raised.

Notice some exposed properties are not just get-only, such as the KeyEventArgs's Handled property. This allows a handler to communicate back to the event source about further action to be taken. In case of keyboard input, this makes sense because key input is usually to be processed by only a single entity in the system.

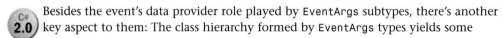

Besides the event's data provider role played by EventArgs subtypes, there's another key aspect to them: The class hierarchy formed by EventArgs types yields some interesting properties. Scary words like co- and contravariance enter the picture once more, but don't be afraid; it's easier than it sounds. Assume the scenario where you want to hook up a single event handler for different types of events. As an example, let's handle two events on a button: KeyDown and MouseMove. (Imagine the case where you want to react to any input sent to a button, either by mouse interaction or the keyboard.) First, take a look at both event declarations:

```
public event KeyEventHandler KeyDown;
public event MouseEventHandler MouseMove;
```

If we were to hook up two separate event handlers but want to share their logic, things would look like this:

```
static void Main() {
    Button sayHello = new Button { Text = "Greet me!" };
    sayHello.MouseMove += new MouseEventHandler(sayHello_MouseMove);
    sayHello.KeyDown += new KeyEventHandler(sayHello_KeyDown);
}

static void sayHello_MouseMove(object sender, MouseEventArgs e) {
    sayHello_KeyDownOrClick(sender, e);
}

static void sayHello_KeyDown(object sender, KeyEventArgs e) {
    sayHello_KeyDownOrClick(sender, e);
}

static void sayHello_KeyDownOrClick(object sender, EventArgs e) {
    // Common logic goes here, for example, using (Button)sender
}
```

See what we've done to forward the event handler calls for either MouseMove or KeyDown to a single method? Making a method call for sure, but there's one more subtle thing going on: We typed the sayHello_KeyDownOrClick's last parameter with a common subtype of both MouseEventArgs and KeyEventArgs. This is a natural rule everyone understands about regular method calls: Given an object of a certain type, you can always pass that as an argument to a method with a less specific type (that is, a supertype).

But we can do better than this. Thanks to *contravariance* for delegate parameter types, it's possible to write the following instead:

```
static void Main() {
    Button sayHello = new Button { Text = "Greet me!" };
    sayHello.MouseMove += sayHello_KeyDownOrClick;
    sayHello.KeyDown += sayHello_KeyDownOrClick;
}
```

```
static void sayHello_KeyDownOrClick(object sender, EventArgs e) {
    // Common logic goes here, for example, using (Button)sender
}
```

Here we're using the rules that relate to *method group conversion*, which take contravariance into account. All this means is that it's possible to create a delegate (here used as an event handler) referring to method that has less-derived parameter types than the types that are expected. For example, although MouseMove *expects* a delegate to a method with a second argument typed as MouseEventArgs, it's fine to pass it a delegate to a method that takes in an EventArgs in the parameter position instead. To see why this is fine, simply think of what happens when the delegate gets invoked by the event source, passing in a MouseEventArgs. Through the delegate it will be passed on to the event handler method that accepts the parameter as an EventArgs object, which is fine because every MouseEventArgs *is* an EventArgs.

Where contravariance applies to parameter types, covariance applies to the return type but is rarely used in the context of event handlers (because those typically have a void return type). Co- and contravariance for delegate return types and parameter types is depicted in Figure 18.18. It helps to keep in mind the Latin-originating meaning of the prefixes *co* (*with* the flow) and *contra* (*against* the flow) when looking at the diagrams.

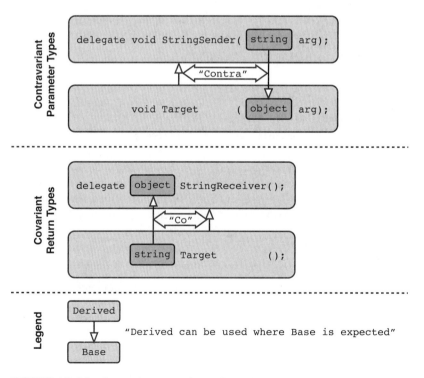

FIGURE 18.18   Co- and contravariance for delegate types.

EventHandler<T>

Requiring (or *strongly advising*, for the sake of consistency) developers to create their own EventArgs derived type is enough of a burden for them, but in the early days of .NET even that wasn't enough. One had to create a custom EventHandler delegate with the typical object sender and MyEventArgs e signature.

Since the advent of .NET 2.0, with the introduction of generics, this was simplified a bit through the introduction of EventHandler<T>:

```
public delegate void EventHandler<TEventArgs>(object sender, TEventArgs e)
    where TEventArgs : EventArgs;
```

The generic constraint put on the TEventArgs type argument enforces the correct use of the event handler pattern. By requiring the second argument to be a type derived from EventArgs, contravariance for delegate types and method group conversion keeps working across all events.

As an example, let's revamp our CountDown example by adhering to the event pattern outlined earlier. First, we define an EventArgs subtype for the Tick event because we want to provide the user with information about the time elapsed:

```
class TickEventArgs : EventArgs {
    public TickEventArgs(uint seconds) {
        this.Seconds = seconds;
    }

    public uint Seconds { get; private set; }
}
```

For the Finished event, we can simply use the EventArgs base class because we're not going to communicate any event-specific information.

Armed with our specialized EventArgs type, all that remains to be done is to change the CountDown class to use the appropriate EventHandler types for the events. A scene from the IDE when doing so is shown in Figure 18.19, illustrating the use of the generic EventHandler<TEventArgs> delegate type, with IntelliSense revealing the constraint.

The new event declarations look like this:

```
public event EventHandler<TickEventArgs> Tick;
public event EventHandler Finished;
```

Raising the event has to be changed because the signature of the delegates has changed. For the sender argument, we simply pass this. On the side of the EventArgs argument, things vary a bit, but we'll obviously use an instance of TickEventArgs in the Tick case. To reduce memory use for a plain empty EventArgs used on the Finished event, we can use the static read-only EventArgs.Empty field. All in all, the changes made to the Start method with its embedded background thread procedure are fairly small:

```
public void Start() {
    new Thread(() => {
        uint n = _seconds;
        while (n > 0u) {
            var tick = Tick;
            if (tick != null) {
                tick(this, new TickEventArgs(n));
            }
            Thread.Sleep(1000);
            n--;
        }

        var finished = Finished;
        if (finished != null) {
            finished(this, EventArgs.Empty);
        }
    }).Start();
}
```

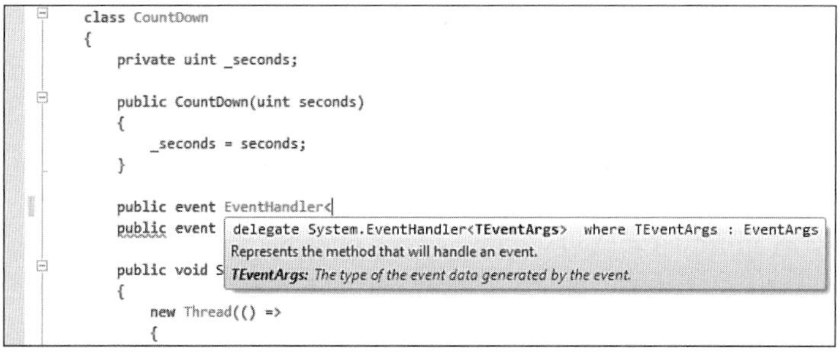

```
class CountDown
{
    private uint _seconds;

    public CountDown(uint seconds)
    {
        _seconds = seconds;
    }

    public event EventHandler
    public event     delegate System.EventHandler<TEventArgs>   where TEventArgs : EventArgs
                     Represents the method that will handle an event.
    public void S    TEventArgs: The type of the event data generated by the event.
    {
        new Thread(() =>
        {
```

FIGURE 18.19   Using EventHandler<T>.

As you should expect by now, for static events a null value for the sender argument is to be used.

Obviously, the use site needs to change, as well, to use the right signatures for the event handler methods. In the Tick event handler, we use the event arguments to obtain the number of elapsed seconds:

```
static void TickHandler(object sender, TickEventArgs e) {
    Console.WriteLine(e.Seconds);
}
```

```
static void FinishedHandler(object sender, EventArgs e) {
    Console.Beep();

    // Finished has been called: we can unhook both Tick and Finished now.
    s_countDown.Tick -= TickHandler;
    s_countDown.Finished -= FinishedHandler;
}
```

FXCOP ON NAMING

FxCop will trigger warnings if the naming for an event handler's parameters is not followed. As a matter of style, call the first argument sender and the second e. This is, in fact, one of the rare places where a single-letter identifier is officially recommended.

Designing Events for Use by Derived Classes

What about extenders of our CountDown type? Assume we've designed our countdown mechanism such that its core functionality can be overridden (for example, by marking Start as virtual) or we simply haven't sealed the class. The subtype might want to raise any of our events as part of its extension. For example, a CountDown with an EmergencyStop facility might want to call Finished before the timer reaches zero. I invite you to think about more examples.

The key question is whether a subtype can raise an event declared on its base type. A little bit of reasoning can help answer this question without having to loop in the compiler just yet. You've seen how an event declaration leads to the creation of a private field containing the multicast delegate that keeps track of the event's added event handlers. To raise the event, that private field gets fetched, followed by a delegate invocation call. All of those observations lead us to conclude that a subtype won't be able to raise the events defined on its base class because a *private* field is used.

As a confirmation, trying to compile the following code fails miserably on the line that tries to obtain the Finished event's delegate object:

```
class FancyCountDown : CountDown {
    public void EmergencyStop() {
        // Cause a stop somehow; requires more extensibility
        // provided by the base class.

        var finished = Finished; // this line fails to compile!
        if (finished != null) {
            finished(this, EventArgs.Empty);
        }
    }
}
```

Because the event itself has already been declared as public on the base class, it doesn't make sense to try marking it as protected (which would imply no visibility from the outside) in an attempt to make the underlying field protected. So what's the solution?

You should realize that the capability to raise an event is something that should be a highly privileged operation. When defining events in terms of delegate-typed events, you saw how improper exposure of the underlying delegate allows for spoofing attacks: anyone on the outside of the object can raise the event. In the face of subtyping, care should be taken, too. For this reason, you should explicitly *design* the type such that it allows an event to be raised from outside the bounds of the class itself (for example, on a subtype).

This calls for another pattern, namely the protected virtual On* method pattern. Let's take a look at how the subtype would use it to raise an event first:

```
public void EmergencyStop() {
    // Cause a stop somehow; requires more extensibility
    // provided by the base class.

    OnFinished(EventArgs.Empty);
}
```

To enable a subtype to raise an event, we've drilled a little hole in the form of a protected method that contains the logic to raise the event. By making the method protected, only derived types (and not complete external strangers) can cause the event to be raised.

Besides this, we can also make the On* methods virtual so that subtypes can override them to provide additional steps to be taken when an event is raised (for example, to do some logging). To make this useful, we need to keep ourselves honest in the base class as well. (That is, we shouldn't raise the event without making use of the On* methods.)

Adhering to those rules, our new CountDown class looks like this:

```
class CountDown {
    private uint _seconds;

    public CountDown(uint seconds) {
        _seconds = seconds;
    }

    public event EventHandler<TickEventArgs> Tick;
    public event EventHandler Finished;

    public void Start() {
        new Thread(() => {
            uint n = _seconds;
            while (n > 0u) {
                OnTick(new TickEventArgs(n));
                Thread.Sleep(1000);
```

```
            n—;
        }

        OnFinished(EventArgs.Empty);
    }).Start();
}

protected virtual void OnTick(TickEventArgs e) {
    var tick = Tick;
    if (tick != null) {
        tick(this, e);
    }
}

protected virtual void OnFinished(EventArgs e) {
    var finished = Finished;
    if (finished != null) {
        finished(this, e);
    }
}
}
```

Case Study: INotifyProperty Interfaces and UI Programming

The .NET Framework's Base Class Library (BCL) comes with two interfaces that can be used to keep track of changes to property values. Because an interface is the contract between two parties, we should ask ourselves what those parties are and why they would care. A typical example use case for those interfaces is in data binding scenarios for UI or web programming: As soon as a property changes on the bound object, the display needs to update to reflect the underlying change. In this particular case, the UI framework (for example, WPF) consumes the interface and provides auto-update services for objects that are bound to some control. To make this work, an object needs to notify the UI framework about changes to any of its properties, which it does by implementing the required interface.

Two such interfaces exist in the System.ComponentModel namespace. The first one notifies about a property that's about to change and is called INotifyPropertyChanging:

```
public interface INotifyPropertyChanging {
    event PropertyChangingEventHandler PropertyChanging;
}
```

```
public delegate void PropertyChangingEventHandler(object sender,
                                          PropertyChangingEventArgs e);

public class PropertyChangingEventArgs : EventArgs {
    public PropertyChangingEventArgs(string propertyName);

    public virtual string PropertyName { get; }
}
```

Its sister interface, INotifyPropertyChanged, is used to signal that a property's value has been changed:

```
public interface INotifyPropertyChanged {
    event PropertyChangedEventHandler PropertyChanged;
}

public delegate void PropertyChangedEventHandler(object sender,
                                          PropertyChangedEventArgs e);

public class PropertyChangedEventArgs : EventArgs {
    public PropertyChangedEventArgs(string propertyName);

    public virtual string PropertyName { get; }
}
```

Both interfaces are plain simple and specify a single event to be implemented. Most framework components only care about the latter interface that signals a property change after the fact. The former interface can sometimes be used to implement logic that guards a property against changes that violate some contract (for example, validating certain business logic rules).

For example, let's ameliorate a plain old CLR object representing a Person with change notifications:

```
class Person : INotifyPropertyChanging, INotifyPropertyChanged {
    private string _name;
    private int _age;

    public Person(string name, int age) {
        _name = name;
        _age = age;
    }

    public event PropertyChangingEventHandler PropertyChanging;
    public event PropertyChangedEventHandler PropertyChanged;
```

```
public string Name {
    get { return _name; }
    set {
        if (_name != value) {
            OnPropertyChanging("Name");
            _name = value;
            OnPropertyChanged("Name");
        }
    }
}

// Same for Age

protected virtual void OnPropertyChanging(string propertyName) {
    var propertyChanging = PropertyChanging;
    if (propertyChanging != null) {
        propertyChanging(this, new PropertyChangingEventArgs(propertyName));
    }
}

protected virtual void OnPropertyChanged(string propertyName) {
    var propertyChanged = PropertyChanged;
    if (propertyChanged != null) {
        propertyChanged(this, new PropertyChangedEventArgs(propertyName));
    }
}
}
```

From the preceding code, you can also see the benefit of having centralized On* event raising methods because it eliminates the duplication of the (thread-safe) null check and invocation calls. To avoid false negatives when setting properties to their current values, equality of the old and new value is checked in each property setter.

AUTO-IMPLEMENTED PROPERTIES

Because auto-implemented properties were added in C# 3.0, developers tend to want more and more of such features. One of the most popular feature requests in this area is the generation of INotifyProperty*-capable properties. The future will tell whether we ever get such a feature.

In the meantime, it's good to know about the handy "propfull" code snippet to generate properties with backing fields. The expansion of this snippet acts as a good start to building a "change-notifying property." Figure 18.20 illustrates how the snippet expands.

And if you always follow the same pattern for the definition of notifying properties with regard to the On* methods it calls into, you can create your own snippet (available as a Visual Studio extensibility feature) to reduce the burden of defining such properties.

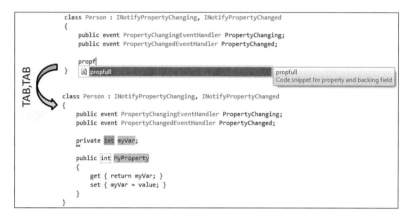

FIGURE 18.20   Using a code snippet to insert a property.

To put our new little class to the test in an easy and straightforward manner, let's create a simple Windows Forms project in Visual Studio and use a `PropertyGrid` control to visualize a `Person` object instance. In addition, drag and drop two `TextBox` and two `Label` controls to the designer surface in an arrangement that looks like the one shown in Figure 18.21. The meaning of all the controls should be straightforward.

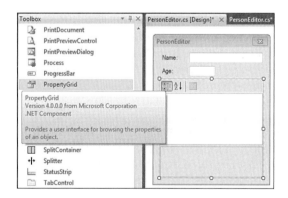

FIGURE 18.21   A simple `Person` object editor in Windows Forms.

Next, double-click an empty spot on the form to switch to the `Load` event handler for the form. In there, add the following code:

```
private void PersonEditor_Load(object sender, EventArgs e) {
    _person = new Person("Bart", 26);

    propertyGrid.DataBindings.Add("SelectedObject", _person, null);
    txtName.DataBindings.Add("Text", _person, "Name");
    txtAge.DataBindings.Add("Text", _person, "Age");
}
```

Also don't forget to add a _person field of type Person. In the preceding code, we're using the data binding feature present in Windows Forms to wire up a few things. First, the PropertyGrid control has a SelectedObject property that can be set to the object it needs to visualize. Here we're binding it to the _person instance and specifying null for the dataMember argument. This means we want to visualize the whole object and not just a specific property of it.

The next two lines establish bindings to the TextBox controls, which are named after the data members they display. This time the binding targets the Text property of the control, with the source being the Name and Age properties on _person.

RICHER DATA BINDING IN WPF

The Windows Presentation Foundation provides a data binding capability, as well, with richer capabilities than the one seen in Windows Forms. Instead of trying to explain all this in the context of a chapter on events, I refer you to a book devoted to the subject of WPF.

That said, concepts on data binding are pretty much the same across both worlds: One *declares* how things should be bound to one another, and the framework takes care of the rest. Variations on the same pattern have to do with how the bindings are declared (XAML would typically be used in case of WPF) and what the additional capabilities are (for example, WPF has value converters).

Declaring the data bindings suffices to have the framework set up all plumbing on your behalf. Data binding sources, as specified in the second parameter to the Add method, that implement INotifyPropertyChanged will cause the framework to register an event handler for the PropertyChanged event. The data binding logic reacts to this event by checking whether the changed property (matched by its name) should cause a bound control to update.

But this is only one half of the story because the established bindings are two-way. The one way described earlier covers changes to the underlying object getting mirrored in the user interface controls. However, when changes are made through the controls, those are sent to the underlying object by invoking the corresponding property setter.

Figure 18.22 shows how a change to the Name text box triggers a cascade of events:

▶ A data binding for the Text property on the text box is located and found.

▶ The target of the binding, the Name property on _person, is updated.

▶ Our Person implementation triggers a PropertyChanged event for Name.

▶ Data binding logic has subscribed to the event and looks for update targets.

▶ Because _person changed, SelectedObject on propertyGrid gets updated.

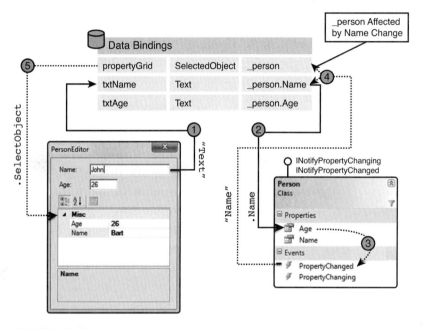

FIGURE 18.22   INotifyPropertyChanged driving updates to the UI.

The scenario illustrated here can easily be tested: Just enter a new name or age in any of the two TextBox controls and make the control lose focus (for example, using Tab). At that point, the data binding logic kicks in and the PropertyGrid control will reflect the update made. Notice all of this also works in the other direction: An update to one of the properties displayed in the PropertyGrid will make its way to the underlying object, causing a PropertyChanged event that will be picked up by the data binding layer. And that, in turn, will cause the affected TextBox control to update, too. Sweet!

Events in UI Frameworks

While we're at it, I want to emphasize the event-driven nature of UI frameworks. In the preceding example, we've subscribed to a single event (that is, the Load event of the form itself). We did so through the Windows Forms designer by double-clicking an empty region of the form, leaving all the boilerplate code being generated to the tools. Let's take a peek at how this is achieved precisely.

First, let's go after the place where events are declared in the Windows Forms designer. In Figure 18.23, spot the lightning bolt icon in the Properties window's toolbar. In fact, the control shown here in Visual Studio 2010 is the same PropertyGrid control as the one we're using inside our application, but with a few additional toolbar buttons. When the Properties window is put in the events mode by clicking the lightning bolt, events available for the selected control (or form) are displayed. As you can see, our previous double-click on the designer surface caused the Load event to be supplied.

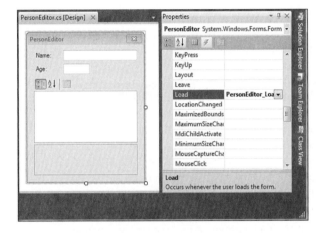

FIGURE 18.23   Events declared through the Windows Forms designer.

The drop-down button on the right can be used to display all the methods that have been defined and have a signature that's compatible (through rules of co- and contravariance for delegates and method groups) with the target event. "Default events" for a control can get handlers attached simply by double-clicking them. For a Form, this event will be Load; for a Button, it will be Click; and for a TextBox, it will be TextChanged. For all the other events a control exposes (a lot!), the events display on Properties must be used. Typically, you won't have written a handler before attaching it to an event; instead, you want to generate the handler on the spot. This can be achieved by double-clicking the empty cell next to the event name in the property grid.

To jump to an event handler defined in the code behind the form, double-click its name in the grid. Let's do that for the Load event handler. This simply puts us back in the .cs file where all the user-defined code for the form and its controls lives. Even though we've been there before, it's still worth a closer look (see Figure 18.24).

Starting at the top, the drop-down on the right provides a handy way to jump to some method defined in the current type. This is particularly handy in UI programming circumstances because there's a good chance to have a lot of event handlers.

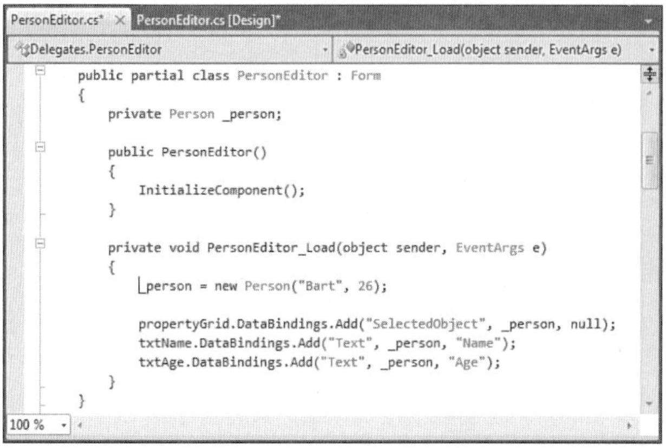

FIGURE 18.24   Event handlers for our form and its controls.

CO-EVOLUTION "AVANT LES LETTRES"

Today, co-evolution between the mainstream .NET languages, Visual Basic and C#, is a big deal. The target audiences for both languages are more or less the same, being enterprise developers, so it makes sense to provide both with very similar language features that make sense across the board. In particular, the .NET 4 wave of language innovation with C# 4.0 and Visual Basic 10.0 highlights this desire to co-evolve the languages: C# gets dynamic dispatch, VB gets things like automatic properties and statement lambda expression (and more).

However, you don't have to have .NET 4 to see co-evolution on another level, namely developer tools. Visual Basic has historically been a great tool for UI design since its very early days. That's ultimately where the *Visual* part in its name comes from. One of the biggest things in the early days of Visual Basic was the fact it abstracted away the low-level plumbing of window messages required to handle events on controls. Instead of hooking the BM_CLICK message, one would write an event handler as a procedure following some naming convention:

```
Private Sub LoginButton_Click()
    'Code goes here
End Sub
```

Navigation to event handlers was arranged through the same concept of a drop-down at the top of the code window, which later made it into a general concept to browse a class's methods.

Looking a bit further, notice some oddity on the class declaration for the form: What's that partial keyword used for? We'll get to this in a minute, but because partial classes allow for splitting parts of a class definition across multiple files, clearly something is hidden for us. A bit further, we find our event handler defined as a regular method. But where's the handler being attached to the Load event? It seems we're missing something.

That something is what the InitializeComponent call in the constructor is used for: The code generated to attach event handlers to controls (and the form) lives in a separate file hidden from the user. Put the cursor on the InitializeComponent call, right-click it, and choose Go To Definition (or press F12) to see what's going on here. The result of those steps is shown in Figure 18.25.

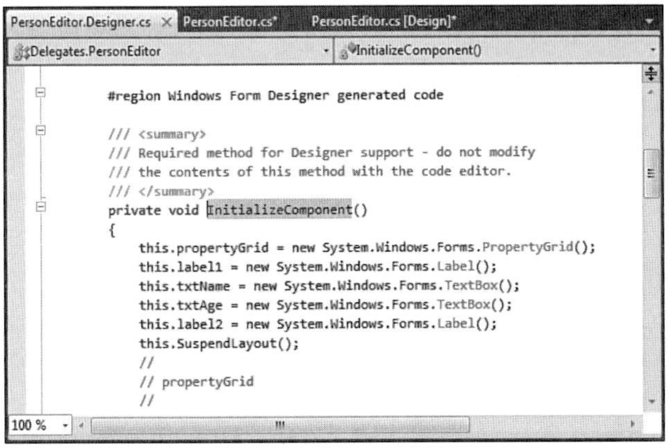

FIGURE 18.25   Code generated by the Windows Forms designer.

We find ourselves back in another file, called PersonEditor.Designer.cs, which acts as the dumping ground for code generated by the Windows Forms designer. Exploring this file a bit further, notice that it contains another part of the partial class definition for our form, defining the InitializeComponent method as well as some IDisposable stuff. It also contains the fields that contain the controls we've added to the form:

```
partial class PersonEditor {
    private TextBox txtName;
    ...

    private void InitializeComponent() {
        // Initialize controls with configured properties
        // Hook up event handlers
    }
}
```

A stripped-down view of InitializeComponent is in order here to analyze what's going on a little further:

```
#region Windows Form Designer generated code

/// <summary>
/// Required method for Designer support - do not modify
```

```
///  the contents of this method with the code editor.
///  </summary>
private void InitializeComponent() {
    // Instantiating controls
    this.txtName = new System.Windows.Forms.TextBox();
    ...

    // Setting control properties
    this.txtName.Location = new System.Drawing.Point(70, 10);
    this.txtName.Size = new System.Drawing.Size(146, 20);
    ...

    // Adding controls to form
    this.Controls.Add(this.txtName);
    ...

    // Setting form properties
    this.FormBorderStyle = System.Windows.Forms.FormBorderStyle.FixedDialog;
    ...

    // Attaching event handlers
    this.Load += new System.EventHandler(this.PersonEditor_Load);
    ...
}
...
```

```
#endregion
```

 First, notice the warning in the XML comments for `InitializeComponent` asking you not to touch the generated code. The reason is obvious: Your changes would get lost upon regeneration of the code by the designer.

This used to be more of a problem before the introduction of partial classes in C# 2.0 because the generated code had to go in the same file where the user added custom logic for event handlers and such. Not only did this make the likelihood for inappropriate edits by the user higher, it also made the job of the code-generation tools harder because they couldn't just emit a wholesale file. Instead, those tools had to recognize the piece of code they are responsible for, replacing it with the newly generated code as needed.

Before partial classes were invented, code was shielded from direct changes by the developer by putting it in a collapsible #region with the appropriate warnings added in comments. Now, with partial classes, all the generated code can go in a separate file (with "extended extension" .Designer.cs), which is somewhat hidden from the user in the IDE through the Solution Explorer's tree view. In the end, the only reason you should look at those generated files is to satisfy your technical curiosity.

Near the end of the InitializeComponent method, we find where the event handler for the Load event is registered by the generated code. No surprises there either because the already familiar += syntax is being used. In the very end, nothing is based on dark magic, and everything boils down to language primitives.

A DECLARATIVE APPROACH TO EVENT HANDLERS IN VISUAL BASIC

Visual Basic has had an intimate relationship with event handlers since the very beginning, as it targeted Rapid Application Development for, at the time, rich Win32 UI-driven applications. To make registering event handlers as friction-free as possible, it was decided to make event handler registration implicit (or, if you will, declarative) simply by defining a method with the appropriate name, following the controlName_Event pattern.

When Visual Basic .NET was designed, it was important to make people feel at home, so the underscore syntax was preserved (which also became the pattern used in C#). However, the CLR's generalization of events in terms of multicast delegates made it desirable to correlate method names with events in a more formal manner.

In C#, the += syntax was chosen because it feels kind of natural and fits nicely with the supported operations on the underlying delegates. It has one drawback, though: The place where an event handler is registered and defined is spread out. This can be observed in Windows Forms, with the registration of the handler living in the InitializeComponent method, and the handler being defined in a separate file. Other than the conventional underscore-based naming pattern, there's no way to correlate back the event handler to the event it handles.

Visual Basic chose a different approach to preserve the pre-.NET style of event handling a bit more, by introducing the Handles keyword that decorates a method with the event it handles. For example, the following code is generated for a form's Load event in Visual Basic:

```
    Private Sub Form1_Load(ByVal sender As System.Object,
                        ByVal e As System.EventArgs) Handles MyBase.Load
        'Event handler code goes here
    End Sub
```

The MyBase keyword refers to the base type of the type being defined (that is, the Form base class), just like C#'s base keyword does. An event handler for a button with name login looks like this:

```
    Private Sub login_Click(ByVal sender As System.Object,
                        ByVal e As System.EventArgs) Handles login.Click
        'Event handler code goes here
    End Sub
```

In fact, this makes the generated code for a Windows Forms application in Visual Basic easier.

THE "DEVELOPER-DESIGNER" MANTRA

The use of partial classes in Windows Forms 2.0 and later could be seen as the first split between the developer's and UI designer's orthogonal concerns. If it were possible to hand out the .Designer.cs file to a designer who could open this file in a fancy UI designer tool to stylize the look and feel, that person would never have to see the event handler code written by his colleague developer.

Unfortunately, the C# language is not an ideal way to express UI definitions, from the designer's point of view at least. Not just that, but this definition depends on the programming language chosen by the developer: In a Visual Basic project, the Windows Forms designer emits Visual Basic code for the second half of the partial class. Specialized markup languages unify UI definitions back into a single language and are perceived to be easier for use by designers. And that's where XAML in WPF come in.

Countdown, the GUI Way

To put the icing on the cake for our running countdown example, let's see what it takes to hook it up to a graphical user interface using our basic knowledge of Windows Forms.

Exploration of the various available controls is beyond the scope of this chapter, so you'll have to take my word for it that appropriate controls are being used for the task at hand. We'll keep the user interface as simple as we can, with a NumericUpDown control to select the number of seconds to countdown, a Button to start the timer, and a Label to display the current time. When the countdown has finished, a message box appears. The user interface definition is shown in Figure 18.26.

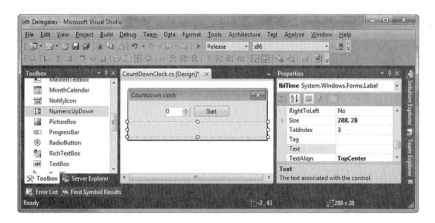

FIGURE 18.26   Countdown clock in Windows Forms.

Time to write some code! Double-click the Start button to create and attach an event handler for the button's Click event. Here, we instantiate a CountDown object, set its number of seconds to the value specified in the `NumericUpDown` control, hook up event handlers to the `CountDown`, and finally start the countdown:

```
public partial class CountDownClock : Form {
    private CountDown _countDown;

    public CountDownClock(){
        InitializeComponent();
    }

    private void btnStart_Click(object sender, EventArgs e) {
        nudSeconds.Enabled = false;
        btnStart.Enabled = false;

        _countDown = new CountDown((uint)nudSeconds.Value);
        _countDown.Tick += new EventHandler<TickEventArgs>(_countDown_Tick);
        _countDown.Finished += new EventHandler(_countDown_Finished);
        _countDown.Start();
    }

    void _countDown_Tick(object sender, TickEventArgs e) {
        lblTime.Text = string.Format("{0} seconds left", e.Seconds);
    }

    void _countDown_Finished(object sender, EventArgs e) {
        MessageBox.Show("Countdown finished!", this.Text, MessageBoxButtons.OK,
                        MessageBoxIcon.Information);

        _countDown.Tick -= _countDown_Tick;
        _countDown.Finished -= _countDown_Finished;

        lblTime.Text = "";
        nudSeconds.Enabled = true;
        btnStart.Enabled = true;
    }
}
```

HUNGARIAN NOTATION OR NOT?

Hungarian notation is a technique where an identifier is prefixed with the type of the object it contains or refers to. In the world of C and C++, this is especially handy when dealing with pointers to pointers to pointers (you can go on and on), allowing for easier reasoning about pointer dereferences and such. Because of static typing, IntelliSense, the absence of pointers, and so on, this technique is discouraged in the world of .NET.

However, as a personal matter of taste, I still find this notation useful for UI program-ming, prefixing controls with their types. For one thing, the fact that controls are declared in a separate generated code file makes it more difficult to trace back the type of a control when doing code inspections outside an IDE. Furthermore, it's not uncommon to get clashes between control names and local variables. (For example, a seconds value needs to be assigned to a seconds control's Text property.)

Now that looks easy enough, doesn't it? In the Click handler, we first disable all controls to avoid multiple countdowns being active at the same time. Next we create a CountDown instance, casting the NumericUpDown's decimal-typed Value property to uint (something we know will succeed if the NumericUpDown control is configured correctly; that is, with DecimalPlaces set to 0 and its Minimum property set to 0 or more). Two event handlers are created, with help from Visual Studio upon typing +=, which causes the two methods to be generated on the fly. Notice that the explicit delegate instance creation calls can be trimmed away if you find that style clearer:

```
_countDown.Tick += _countDown_Tick;
_countDown.Finished += _countDown_Finished;
```

Code inside the handlers looks reasonable, as well, and should be self-explanatory. As you can guess, there's a little problem lurking around the corner, which is why I'm showing this example. Let's see what the problem is by simply running the program under the debugger by pressing F5. Set the number of seconds to five or so, click Start, and watch what happens. Figure 18.27 shows the result, which might not be quite as expected.

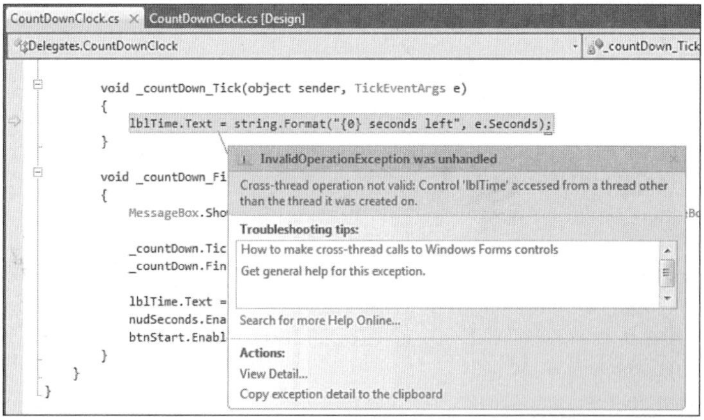

FIGURE 18.27   Cross-thread access to UI controls is troublesome.

Can you guess what's going wrong based on the message? Recall how our CountDown is implemented by using a background thread. This was done to prevent the Start call from being blocked. Raising the Tick event ultimately causes method calls to all the subscribed event handler methods, including _countDown_Tick, through the multicast delegate invocation that's going on under the covers. Those method calls happen on the background thread where our countdown is ticking.

That doesn't yet explain the problem itself, though. The bigger problem here is deeply rooted in user interface programming, where one specific thread plays an important role: The UI thread where a message pump is running to process messages coming from various sources like the window manager. Figure 18.28 illustrates the key essence of the message pump. In case you're wondering, this message pump is started from the Main method of Windows Forms application and is hidden behind the Application.Run call that lives there.

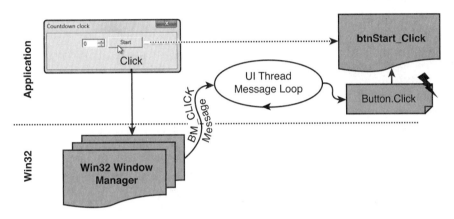

FIGURE 18.28   Window messages are dispatched through the message pump.

```
static class Program {
    [STAThread]
    static void Main() {
        Application.EnableVisualStyles();
        Application.SetCompatibleTextRenderingDefault(false);
        Application.Run(new Form1());
    }
}
```

The STAThread attribute applied to the entry-point method is also part of the single-threaded plot in UI-driven applications and means single-threaded apartment, a term that goes back to the COM days. We won't elaborate on this any further right here.

Looking at Figure 18.28, you can see that a window message is picked up by the message loop that's running on the UI thread and is getting dispatched to the button's Click event, which causes the event handler to execute. All of this action happens on the UI thread. It's typical for such event handlers to interact with UI controls (for example, by changing certain properties):

```
private void btnStart_Click(object sender, EventArgs e) {
    nudSeconds.Enabled = false;
    btnStart.Enabled = false;
```

This works like a charm and is permitted because the controls are being touched on the same thread, in particular the so-called UI thread, as where they were created. But in our setting, we're also interacting with controls from another thread (that is, the one that's making our countdown mechanism tick). The observed InvalidOperationException tells us this is a really bad idea.

Luckily, there's an escape valve to deal with this kind of situation, allowing us to run code on the UI thread. In Windows Forms, an Invoke method is provided to do so; in WPF, there's a Dispatcher type that's the central hub for operations that run on the UI thread. Because we're in Windows Forms, let's take a look at this Invoke method:

```
namespace System.Windows.Forms {
    class Control {
        ...
        /// <summary>
        /// Executes the specified delegate on the thread that owns the
        /// control's underlying window handle.
        /// </summary>
        public object Invoke(Delegate method);
        public object Invoke(Delegate method, params object[] args);
        ...
    }
}
```

The summary tells it all, with a few more Win32-specific words like *window handle*, but the important bit is we got our solution to "jump" from the countdown's thread to the UI thread to touch UI controls. And guess what, the argument is of type Delegate, something we've gotten utterly familiar with. The available overload allows for calling a delegate that expects arguments, which get specified through the params array.

Because both Tick and Finished events are raised on the background thread, we need to apply the trick of "thread jumping" in both places:

```
void _countDown_Tick(object sender, TickEventArgs e) {
    this.Invoke(new Action(() => {
        lblTime.Text = string.Format("{0} seconds left", e.Seconds);
    }));
}

void _countDown_Finished(object sender, EventArgs e) {
    this.Invoke(new Action(() => {
        MessageBox.Show("Countdown finished!", this.Text, MessageBoxButtons.OK,
                    MessageBoxIcon.Information);
```

```
        _countDown.Tick -= _countDown_Tick;
        _countDown.Finished -= _countDown_Finished;

        lblTime.Text = "";
        nudSeconds.Enabled = true;
        btnStart.Enabled = true;
    }));
}
```

The use of Invoke makes our code work correctly, with the delegates running on the UI thread. Did you see how we've made handy use of a closure in the Tick event handler, to refer to the TickEventArgs object from inside the lambda expression's body?

THE MYSTERIOUS SYSTEM.DELEGATE TYPE

In the preceding sample, we've seen how the Windows Forms folks typed the argument of the Invoke method as System.Delegate, to allow for every single delegate type. At the time of the first release of Windows Forms, with .NET 1.0, this was very beneficial because no anonymous function expressions, and hence no closures, were present in any of the languages targeting the framework. By supporting any delegate type, users could create a delegate of their taste with the needed number of arguments.

One first mystery is how such a delegate can be invoked by the framework code if the signature of the target method is totally unknown. The answer lies in the CLR's support for reflection again, with support for a DynamicInvoke method on Delegate:

```
/// <summary>
/// Dynamically invokes (late-bound) the method represented by the current
/// delegate.
/// </summary>
public object DynamicInvoke(params object[] args);
```

With that cleared up, you might ask the existential question of whether System.Delegate itself is a delegate type through the eyes of the C# language. Even though it's the base type of all delegates, method group conversions to this type are not permitted. For example:

```
Delegate d = Do;
...
void Do() { /* TODO */ }
```

The first line will fail to compile, resulting in the following message:

Cannot convert method group 'Do' to **non-delegate type 'System.Delegate'**. Did you intend to invoke the method?

That answers your question right there. An implication of this rule is that we need to instantiate a delegate object explicitly when passing an argument to Invoke.

> This is just one of the oddities of the type system in the CLR or C# with regard to base types for certain categories of types. As another example, even though System.ValueType is the base type for all value types, it's a reference type by itself.

Finally, we should mention that this common problem of *thread affinity* has given rise to built-in solutions in the .NET Framework, such as the BackgroundWorker class, which is very useful in cases where an asynchronous operation needs to report through a user interface. Once more, it's event-driven by itself, making it familiar to people who are used to event-based programming already. We cover the BackgroundWorker in Chapter 29, "Threading and Synchronization," in the section, "BackgroundWorker."

Modern Approaches to Reactive Programming

To finish off this chapter, we take a brief look at recent evolutions in the space of reactive, event-based programming. With distributed programs becoming more and more omnipresent, the importance of reactive programming is steadily increasing. Think of technologies such as AJAX, which emphasize the asynchronous nature of communications to prevent keeping the user waiting for a network operation to complete. One of the most typical AJAX examples is a dictionary suggest.

Although the concept of asynchronous distributed computing (a key part of future ways of computing with regard to "the cloud") is a great way to keep the user interface responsive, it doesn't come for free. Asynchronous programming tends to be hard, especially when events need to be combined somehow. The example shown in Figure 18.29 looks perfectly fine, but there's quite a bit of room for disaster.

Here are a few examples to illustrate the madness we're getting ourselves into by trying to be polite to our users:

- ▶ What if the result of querying the dictionary services for *re* comes back *after* the result for typing *reactive* comes back? If this happens, the results of *reactive* will get overwritten by the results of *re*. Remember from your networking courses that in-order responses to requests are not a guarantee on the Internet (it's a jungle out there, with packets getting dropped or eaten by evil monsters), so this is not very far-fetched.

- ▶ How about a network error that manifests itself during the communication with the dictionary service? Where and how will the error manifest itself as things are happening in an asynchronous manner? How do we hook the *event* of an error happening in the system to show an error message to the user or to retry the operation?

- ▶ Recall the typical difficulties that arise from dealing with asynchronous work in a UI framework context, as shown in Figure 18.27. Can't we make the mandatory "thread jumping" required to update the UI easier to get right?

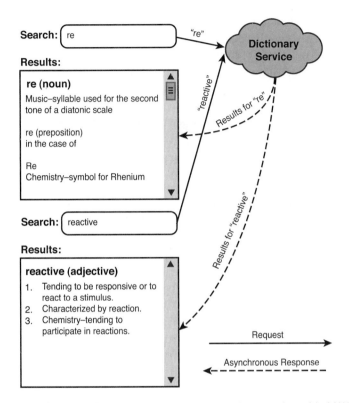

FIGURE 18.29   Asynchronous distributed computing with AJAX.

Besides this, a typical dictionary suggest implementation is full of imperative-style code that hooks events to start or cancel out asynchronous operations, spawn threads, wait for results to come back, and so on. It gets quite messy quickly. But does it have to?

Step back for a second and look at the problem again. What we're effectively trying to accomplish here is to *combine* several events and retrieve results in the end. The events getting combined are KeyPress events on the text box where the user enters the query and events signaling the response of the asynchronous dictionary request. And in the end, we're just interested in the data produced by those operations.

Based on this observation, you might wonder whether .NET events are ideally suited to provide an answer to the challenges encountered. The true answer is that you can get a long way with .NET events, but once you want to stitch together different events, things get quite tricky. One of the hardest parts of this has to do with proper unhooking of event handlers when you're done with them. And even if you succeed in getting all of this right, your code will most likely look like spaghetti, with the various event handlers spread out across the codebase.

Enter the Microsoft DevLabs project called Reactive Extensions (Rx), the source of new approaches to reactive programming on the .NET platform. In this chapter, we cover this new framework only briefly to whet your appetite for the things to come. Later, when we're talking about LINQ in Chapter 19, "Language Integrated Query Essentials," the query syntax used here will become clearer.

HOW TO GET IT?

At the time of this writing, Rx ships out of band from the .NET Framework itself, but traces of it already appear in .NET 4, more specifically the IObservable<T> interface (as you will see shortly).

To find more information about how to get it, use your favorite search engine and search for the words *Reactive Extensions* combined with *.NET* and/or *LINQ*. One of the shipping vehicles of it has been the Silverlight SDK, where it lives in an assembly called System.Reactive.dll. Nowadays it also ships with Windows Phone 7 devices, in the ROM, as a means to interact with the device's sensors (for example, GPS or accelerometers).

Where and how it will ultimately ship is not decided at this point, but rest assured it will make its way to the masses as some point.

Events Revisited

Before getting back to our example, let's reestablish the way we look at events. Recall how the typical event pattern is based on EventHandler<T> as the signature of an event and its handlers:

```
public delegate void EventHandler<TEventArgs>(object sender, TEventArgs e)
    where TEventArgs : EventArgs;
```

Every time such an event is raised, we get some *data* that travels from the event source to the listener, represented as an instance of the TEventArgs argument. In other words, it's fair to say that events are data sources. For example, in our CountDown example the event source is really a data source producing decreasing values representing the number of seconds that are left until the countdown finishes.

When someone says data they immediately think about querying (at least I do). So what would it look like to *filter* the event source for only multiples of 60 seconds remaining? This goes all the way back to our egg timer example, which so far (did you notice?) was based on seconds rather than a more conventional minute-based approach. But because we were given a great generic countdown mechanism, we need a way to filter down the second-based events into minute-based events. With classic events, you could write such a filter yourself:

```
var eggTimerCountDown = new CountDown(minutes * 60);
eggTimerCountDown.Tick += (sender, e) => {
    if (e.Seconds % 60 == 0) {
```

```
        // Update egg timer display, e.g. rotate upper half.
    }
};
```

However, this is just the tip of the iceberg. Maybe you want multiple displays to listen to the minute-based ticks. What to do then? Well, you could repeat the same filter in multiple `Tick` event handlers, which is clearly suboptimal. Instead, it would be much nicer to synthesize a new event source out of the original event source but with a filter applied to the data it produces. A conceptual diagram is shown in Figure 18.30.

FIGURE 18.30   Query operations applied to events.

Can you do such a thing by hand using plain old .NET events? You could, but things get rather messy when event handlers need to be removed. Assume the user unhooks an event handler attached to the filtered event source, shown on the right in the picture. For proper resource maintenance, this also needs to unhook the event handler that was attached to the original source (shown on the far left) by the filter "operator." To further complicate matters, the event handler hooked to the source should be unhooked only if no more event handlers are attached to the filtered event source. This kind of bookkeeping tends to get tedious and is very error-prone.

And, obviously, filters are not the only things that make sense when dealing with events; projection (for example, seconds to a string representation in hh:mm:ss format), grouping, and so much more are applicable, too. Guess what? This starts to look and feel much like Language Integrated Query, doesn't it? So what if we could write our filter from seconds to minutes as follows?

```
from n in src.Tick
where n % 60 == 0
select n
```

Now the question becomes what needs to change in the way events work for them to be usable with query expressions? The key problem with .NET events is their lack of compositionality, which makes it hard to properly unhook event handlers in a simple way. At the very essence of this problem lies the fact we need to know the event handler method not only to register it but also to unregister it:

```
src.Tick += filter.Tick;

// Lots of code can follow here, potentially calling into methods that
```

```
// don't know about (or can't access) filter.Tick to unsubscribe:
src.Tick -= filter.Tick;
```

So once we try to decouple the place of unregistering event handlers from the place where the registration happens, we get into trouble. This relates back to the concept of handler *ownership* discussed previously (for example, as in Windows Forms where handlers for events on controls live on the form object that owns these controls). From those observations, it seems it would be handier to get rid of the delegate-based deregistration of event handlers. Because the subscription phase already knows the event handler, we could hand out some kind of "cookie" that can be used to unsubscribe. In fact, this gets quite familiar to Win32 developers, where handles are used to close out a resource that has been obtained using some API call:

```
HANDLE hFile = CreateFile(L"foo.txt", ...);
// Use the file with Win32 file APIs
CloseHandle(hFile); // don't need to know "foo.txt" here anymore!
```

To close out the file, we just keep track of the handle until the point we need to feed it to CloseHandle. In other words, there's no need to remember the name of the file that was opened to close it.

To apply this principle to events, Rx introduces a new interface called IObservable<T>, which actually ships with .NET 4 in the System namespace. Its name reflects the fact that events provide the capability to *observe* data raised by them. On to the definition of the interface now:

```
public interface IObservable<out T> {
    IDisposable Subscribe(IObserver<T> observer);
}
```

Although events provide the ability to observe something, event handlers actually do observe and can therefore be called *observers*. Using the Subscribe method, you can supply an event handler that will be notified whenever the event is raised. In other words, Subscribe is Rx's counterpart to the += operator for event handler registration seen before. The key difference is that there's no unsubscribe operation. Instead, the Subscribe method returns an IDisposable object that can be used to unregister the handler as follows:

```
var srcHandler = tickSource.Subscribe(observer /* TODO */);
// Lots of code can go here, while the source is raising events and letting
// our observer know about them.
srcHandler.Dispose(); // don't need to know tickSource here anymore!
```

Whereas event handlers for classic .NET events are simply methods, those new observers are complete objects implementing some IObserver<T> interface:

```
public interface IObserver<in T> {
    void OnCompleted();
    void OnError(Exception error);
    void OnNext(T value);
}
```

The last method is the most straightforward of all to understand and corresponds to our classical notion of an event handler. Every time the event source raises an event, this method gets called. Notice the use of generics throughout the interfaces to denote the event's arguments that carry the data that's signaled by the event.

GENERIC CO- AND CONTRAVARIANCE (AGAIN)

Both the IObservable<T> and IObserver<T> interfaces use the new .NET 4 and C# 4.0 generic co- and contravariance annotations on their generic parameter T. We can try to understand the annotations in two ways.

First, the mechanical way by looking at the code just like the compiler does. For IObserver<T>, notice how T appears only in input positions, namely as an argument to OnNext. Hence, the interface can be typed contravariant, using the in keyword. For IObservable<T>, things are a bit trickier. Because IObserver<T> is used in an input position on the Subscribe method, you might think it ought to be marked as contravariant, too. This is where things start to become counterintuitive quickly. When using a contravariant type in an input position, variance flips around: T now becomes covariant on IObservable<T>. You can compare this to the double-negation rule in Boolean logic.

An intuitive approach may work out better. It's clear that data is fed into an IObservable<T> object, and therefore it makes sense to mark it contravariant because it will act as the receiver of data through input positions. An IObservable<T>, on the other hand, produces data that it will feed into the observers. Producing is an act of export or output, and therefore the type ought to be contravariant.

If all of this doesn't resonate at first, don't worry yet: Even the brightest language designer minds occasionally experience trouble when wrapping their heads around this.

The OnError method is used to signal the observer that the event source experienced some problem. This makes it much easier to handle an error occurring asynchronously (for example, when a network error occurs when talking to a web service). In the world of classic events, there was no direct channel to feed that information to the user, and things got much more cumbersome to deal with such exceptional situations.

Finally, the OnCompleted method signals that the event source won't produce any further data (for example, because the underlying operation completed). This comes in handy when you need to be sure about an event not producing anymore data (for example, to unhook observers). Classic .NET events don't raise such a notification.

Pull Versus Push

The IObservable<T> and IObserver<T> interfaces might look at little weird at first, but they are actually very closely related to the well-known System.Collections.Generic interfaces IEnumerable<T> and IEnumerator<T>. In fact, they are *mathematical duals*. It's normal you perceive this as rather abstract, but it's rather simple. Follow me.

From our discussion about statements, recall that IEnumerable<T>'s primary use is the foreach loop statement. Collections implement this interface, allowing us to retrieve their data by *pulling* it out one by one. In fact, the consumer is in control, which makes this an *interactive* mechanism. To pull data from the source, the consumer asks the enumerator for more data by calling MoveNext and Current:

```
IEnumerable<T> source = ...;
using (IEnumerator<T> sourceEnumerator = source.GetEnumerator()) {
    while (sourceEnumerator.MoveNext()) { // Do you have more?
        T item = sourceEnumerator.Current; // Give it to me!
        // Do something with the item; could break out as well...
    }
} // Calls Dispose, telling the source we're done fetching data.
```

The IEnumerable<T> and IEnumerator<T>-based approach of consuming a data source is shown in Figure 18.31.

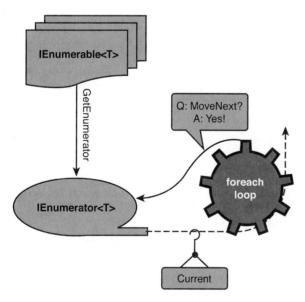

FIGURE 18.31   Enumerating a data source is based on an interactive dialog.

Event sources are exactly the opposite and are based on a *reactive* approach. Now it's the source that tells the consumer that data is available and *pushes* it to the consumer. It's the role of the event handler, the observer, to react to the event of data coming in:

```
IObservable<T> source = ...;
using (source.Subscribe(item => { /* Do something with the item */ })) {
    // While observing events, you can do other stuff.
    // Or you could call the Dispose method in a different place later.
} // Calls Dispose, telling the source we're done receiving events.
```

In the preceding code, I'm using an extension method on IObservable<T> that allows feeding in an observer's OnNext call as a lambda expression, eliminating the need to implement the IObserver<T> interface simply to register an event handler.

The IObservable<T> and Observer<T>-based approach of reacting to an event source is shown in Figure 18.32.

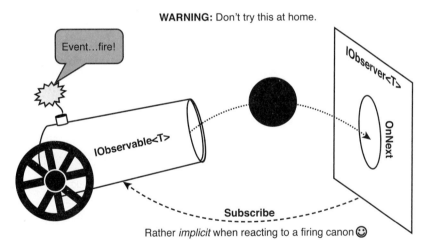

FIGURE 18.32   Observing an event source requires reaction by the observer.

To summarize, when retrieving data from an IEnumerable<T>, you actively get an enumerator object and start a conversation that goes something like this: Do you have another item for me? Yes! Please give it to me.... This is very interactive. With IObservable<T>, you're much more passive and say this: Whenever there's an item available, allow me to observe it by pushing it to me on this method.

Duality is a very deep property that yields many useful results. In mathematical terms, having certain properties on one side of the duality necessarily implies that similar properties hold on the other side of the duality. One place where this becomes apparent for the

IObservable<T> versus IEnumerable<T> relationship is in the definition of *combinators* over both domains. Simply stated, a combinator combines one or more input objects in one domain into an output object in the same domain. And you might have guessed it by now, but the standard query operators of LINQ are such combinators.

To illustrate this, consider the following LINQ to Object query operators, defined as extension methods on IEnumerable<T>. We elaborate on such operators in the chapters dedicated to LINQ, especially Chapter 20, "Language Integrated Query Internals," where there is an entire section titled "Standard Query Operators."

```
IEnumerable<T> Where<T>(this IEnumerable<T> source, Func<T, bool> predicate);
IEnumerable<R> Select<T, R>(this IEnumerable<T> source, Func<T, R> project);
```

As you can see, (most of) those operators take in an object in the IEnumerable "realm" and produce another one of those in return. With the deep duality between both worlds, we can translate the preceding signatures readily to IObservable<T>:

```
IObservable<T> Where<T>(this IObservable<T> source, Func<T, bool> predicate);
IObservable<R> Select<T, R>(this IObservable<T> source, Func<T, R> project);
```

Those make as much sense as the corresponding operators on IEnumerable<T>. For example, given an *event source* that produces items of type T, you can apply a filter using the Where operator to retrieve an *event source* with items that pass the filter's condition. In using those operators, the user doesn't have to worry about all the implementation details, including proper release of the IObserver<T> subscription.

WHERE ARE THE QUERY OPERATORS?

.NET 4 doesn't come with the query operators for IObservable<T>. Due to various release constraints, those ship out-of-band as part of Rx, which is still in a beta phase. Nevertheless, the essential IObservable<T> and IObserver<T> interfaces are in available in .NET 4 so that components can start to rely on them.

If we were to implement IObservable<uint> on our CountDown class, we could make the following mapping:

▶ The Tick event is realized by calling OnNext on subscribed observers.

▶ The Finished event corresponds to calling OnCompleted on those observers.

Once we do so, users can subscribe to the timer's events as follows (using an extension Subscribe method provided in Rx):

```
var countDown = new CountDown(5);
var unsubscribe = countDown.Subscribe(
    seconds   => { Console.WriteLine(seconds + " seconds remaining."); },
```

```
exception => { /* an error occurred */  },
()          => { Console.WriteLine("Finished!"); });
```

Thanks to the LINQ implementation over IObservable<T>, you can filter those events to get a minute-based countdown instead:

```
var countDown = new CountDown(5);
var inMinutes = from n in countDown
                where n % 60 == 0
                select n;
var unsubscribe = inMinutes.Subscribe(
    minutes   => { Console.WriteLine(minutes + " minutes remaining."); },
    exception => { /* an error occurred */  },
    ()        => { Console.WriteLine("Finished!"); });
```

Achieving the same with regular .NET events is quite difficult to get right. And with this example, we've only *observed* the tip of the iceberg.

WHAT ABOUT MY EXISTING .NET EVENTS?

You'll wonder, "What about my existing .NET events? Should I throw everything away and redo all event-providing objects using IObservable<T>?" Luckily, that's not the case because Rx provides bridges between both worlds: An existing classic .NET event can be exposed as an IObservable<T>. Similarly, other constructs in the .NET Framework, such as the IAsyncResult pattern (as you've seen with delegates), can be lifted into the world of the Rx quite easily.

At the same time, note that classic .NET events are not going away. They remain incredibly useful, and often they suffice for typical scenarios such as event handling in UIs and whatnot. Look at Rx as an extension on top of this model that takes away barriers toward richer event-driven systems without having to sacrifice existing investments made.

Dictionary Suggest Revisited

During the introduction of our discussion about reactive programming, I mentioned the typical AJAX example of dictionary suggest. In doing so, we came to the conclusion there are two event sources somehow. One is the user typing text in the Search box, causing TextChanged events to be raised. Upon every such event, we want to start an asynchronous call to a web service to get dictionary suggestions for words starting with the typed term. This can be nicely expressed in LINQ as follows:

```
// True Rx code is only slightly more complicated, due to the need to bridge .NET
// events to IObservable<T> objects first. Consult the Rx documentation for more
// information on this.
var res = from input in searchBox.TextChanged
```

```
        from suggestion in DictionaryService.Suggest(input)
        select new { suggestion.Word, suggestion.Description };
res.Subscribe(result => { /* display in Results box */ });
```

Because we haven't seen LINQ in much depth just yet, approach this query expression with your gut feeling: For every TextChanged event raised (producing a string with what the user types), fire off an asynchronous Suggest call on the dictionary service. This call will come back with suggestions that are ultimately projected onto some anonymous type exposing pairs of found words and their descriptions. Finally, we subscribe to the resulting event source to do some UI stuff where the results get shown.

This very declarative style of dealing with events is hugely beneficial because it abstracts away all the heavy lifting you would have to do manually otherwise: correctly releasing the obtained observer objects, dealing with potentially multithreading issues, and so on. This doesn't mean, though, that your grandma can write asynchronous programs now: There are still things to be aware of, most of which are intrinsic to the problem space of asynchronous computing. In fact, the preceding query has a little problem. Do you remember the first caveat I mentioned when I introduced the dictionary suggest sample? Out-of-order delivery of responses to asynchronous operations can get quite disturbing, as illustrated in Figure 18.33.

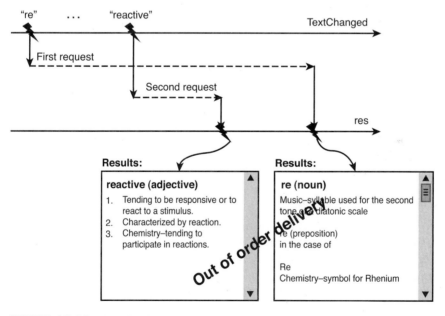

FIGURE 18.33   Out-of-order delivery of asynchronous responses.

Luckily, this problem can be tackled by using another combinator in Rx, called TakeUntil. The idea is to cancel out pending requests when a subsequent request has already responded.

```
var res = from input in searchBox.TextChanged
          from suggestion in DictionaryService.Suggest(input)
                              .TakeUntil(searchBox.TextChanged)
          select new { suggestion.Word, suggestion.Description };
res.Subscribe(result => { /* display in Results box */ });
```

In the preceding code, we're listening for the Suggest call to come back until the user types a new search key in the text box. At that point, the pending call is canceled out. Yes, you still have to put in the TakeUntil call manually (because the out-of-order behavior may be acceptable in some cases), but attempting to do the same with regular .NET events would be far from trivial with asynchronous operation cancellations and so on. The improved situation is shown in Figure 18.34.

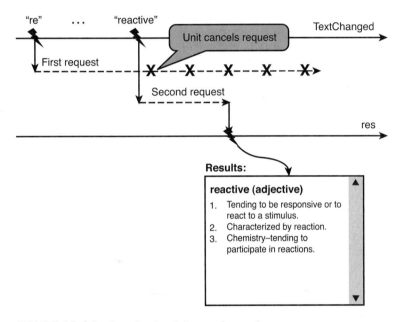

FIGURE 18.34   Out-of-order delivery of asynchronous responses.

TO BE REALLY CORRECT

There's another little hidden caveat in the code shown for our dictionary suggest query that is a bit more subtle. In fact, LINQ constructs are functional programming islands in the world of .NET, which is otherwise imperative. Sometimes those two worlds are in conflict with one another due to side effects.

The problem in the code shown here is that we're subscribing multiple times to the same event, which could cause duplication of side effects. To avoid this, it's advisable to use another Rx operator, called Publish:

```
var res = searchBox.TextChanged.Publish(textChanged =>
                from input in textChanged
                from suggestion in DictionaryService.Suggest(input)
                                            .TakeUntil(textChanged)
                select new { suggestion.Word, suggestion.Description });
    res.Subscribe(result => { /* display in Results box */ });
```

This becomes a little funky, and we'll omit further discussion about this because it gets into specialist use of Rx. Maybe someday I'll write a book on the topic. Who knows?

With this, we conclude our sneak peek at Rx, which every self-respecting .NET developer should be looking forward to because reactive programming is gaining attention every day due to the increased emphasis on distributed and cloud computing. One of the key lessons learned is the pivotal role played by LINQ in enabling this kind of scenario in a more declarative manner.

Summary

Delegates and events are crucial pieces that make the .NET Framework tick. Having a solid understanding of both concepts will take you a long way in discovering framework functionality and designing your own extensible APIs.

Although the concept of functional programming lies, at least conceptually, at the heart of delegates, they can simply be seen as a strongly typed contract describing a single operation. One party acts as a consumer, invoking the delegate to reach out to the functionality provided from the outside. The other party hands out a piece of code that adheres to the delegate contract (its signature if you will) by instantiating a delegate or using an anonymous function expression or lambda expression, with possible use of a closure to capture outer variables. LINQ is one of the many APIs that's designed for heavy use of delegates to pass all sorts of little functions around (predicates, projections, key selectors, and so on).

After covering delegates, we moved on to explain events in terms of multicast delegates. The core idea of events is to provide a way to attach event handlers to an event source in a more secure way than just exposing a delegate. This ensures that an event can be raised only from the inside of the object on which it's defined and also prevents clients from messing with the list of event handlers. Again, two parties appear, similar to the ones seen for delegates. On the one side, there's the event source, which raises the event if it wants to signal a certain condition. At the receiving end, one or more event handlers receive the event to react on it in an appropriate manner.

With the knowledge of delegates and events under our belts, we'll put our knowledge of the former concept to the test by unraveling the innards of LINQ in the next chapter.

CHAPTER 19

Language Integrated Query Essentials

IN THIS CHAPTER

▶ Life Without LINQ 902

▶ LINQ by Example 909

▶ Query Expression Syntax 920

Almost every enterprise application has to deal with data it provides to the user to interact with. This data can come from lots of different places, such as a relational database, an XML file, some other source like a web service, or in fact even just from in-memory data structures.

Before the introduction of Language Integrated Query in .NET 3.5 and languages like C# 3.0 and Visual Basic 9.0, this large variety of potential data sources was a common source of developer pain for various reasons. For each data domain, a different query language is used: Knowing how to get data out of a relational database using SQL doesn't help in querying an XML file. Besides this, queries are typically buried in strings that are opaque to the compiler, providing no compile-time checking: Writing a SQL query that compares a numeric column against a string will go unnoticed when compiling the code, resulting in a runtime exception at best.

Language Integrated Query unifies the query experience across all sorts of data domains, allowing developers to learn a single query language that's integrated with the C# programming language (and others) itself. This not only allows for code that's easier to understand, reducing lots of application programming interface (API) ceremony that was needed before, but it also makes it possible for the compiler to carry out certain checks.

In this chapter, we look at LINQ from a language point of view: what the syntax looks like, what it translates into, and how different LINQ providers plug in to this model.

Life Without LINQ

To see the benefits brought by LINQ, you must get a sense for the problems it solves. To do so, we'll demonstrate the hoops a developer has to jump through to query data from a variety of different data sources. In doing so, we'll work with different APIs and query languages, and you'll see how easy it is for people to mess up things without any compile-time feedback about query correctness.

In-Memory Data

One of the most prominent sources of data is the computer's own memory, though it's often overlooked as a true data source. In-memory collections are containers for series of objects to which you might want to apply certain operations. For the sake of discussion, let's consider an in-memory list of products stored as .NET objects in a generic list collection:

```
var products = new List<Product> {
    new Product { Name = "Chai", Price = 18.00m },
    new Product { Name = "Chang", Price = 19.00m },
    new Product { Name = "Aniseed Syrup", Price = 10.00m },
    new Product { Name = "Chef Anton's Cajun Seasoning", Price = 22.00m },
    new Product { Name = "Chef Anton's Gumbo Mix", Price = 21.35m },
    new Product { Name = "Grandma's Boysenberry Spread", Price = 25.00m },
    new Product { Name = "Uncle Bob's Organic Dried Pears", Price = 30.00m },
    new Product { Name = "Northwoods Cranberry Sauce", Price = 40.00m },
    new Product { Name = "Mishi Kobe Niku", Price = 97.00m },
    new Product { Name = "Ikura", Price = 31.00m }
};
```

Now assume we want to perform various query operations on this data to filter it, order it, group it, and so on. This turns out to be a very manual, imperative-style task, using loops, conditions, intermediate collections, and so on. Let's just show the code you could write to filter all the products with a price lower than $25:

```
var cheap = new List<Product>();
foreach (var product in products) {
    if (product.Price < 25)
        cheap.Add(product);
}
```

This code is still pretty understandable, but as we start adding more query constructs to it, things get obscure pretty quickly. For example, if we want to group products by price range in multiples of 10, we could use a hash table or dictionary to build up those groups; for example, a key of 10 means prices from 10.00 to 19.99:

```
var priceGroups = new Dictionary<int, List<Product>>();
foreach (var product in products) {
    int group = 10 * (int)(product.Price / 10);

    List<Product> productsInGroup;
    if (!priceGroups.TryGetValue(group, out productsInGroup))
        priceGroups[group] = productsInGroup = new List<Product>();

    productsInGroup.Add(product);
}
```

This code clearly doesn't reveal the grouping characteristic anymore in an obvious way. Moreover, we've only been showing one query operation at a time. "Just" adding filtering to the preceding grouping code, maybe followed by sorting on the key and retaining only the first 10 groups, clearly isn't the simplest thing to do. Knowing how to do the query operations each by themselves doesn't suffice to mix them together. In other words, composability is lacking.

Key disadvantages include the following:

- Imperative nature of the code, not revealing the intent of the user clearly
- Lots of manual plumbing needed for a seemingly simple task
- Not composable out of simple query operator primitives

Relational Databases

Relational databases serve as one of the most commonly used data sources in enterprise applications. Querying them requires the use of a different language altogether, such as the Structured Query Language (SQL). Let's assume the same data as shown earlier exists in a relational database (for example, stored in SQL Server). Figure 19.1 illustrates what the records in a Products table might look like. Notice the presence of foreign keys in other tables (for example, to *relate* a product to a category).

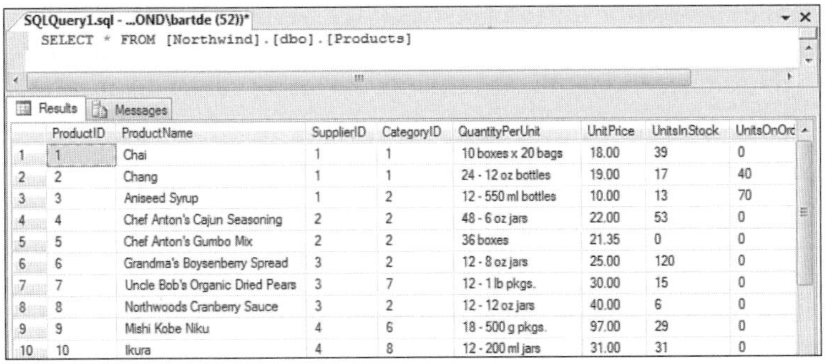

	ProductID	ProductName	SupplierID	CategoryID	QuantityPerUnit	UnitPrice	UnitsInStock	UnitsOnOrc
1	1	Chai	1	1	10 boxes x 20 bags	18.00	39	0
2	2	Chang	1	1	24 - 12 oz bottles	19.00	17	40
3	3	Aniseed Syrup	1	2	12 - 550 ml bottles	10.00	13	70
4	4	Chef Anton's Cajun Seasoning	2	2	48 - 6 oz jars	22.00	53	0
5	5	Chef Anton's Gumbo Mix	2	2	36 boxes	21.35	0	0
6	6	Grandma's Boysenberry Spread	3	2	12 - 8 oz jars	25.00	120	0
7	7	Uncle Bob's Organic Dried Pears	3	7	12 - 1 lb pkgs.	30.00	15	0
8	8	Northwoods Cranberry Sauce	3	2	12 - 12 oz jars	40.00	6	0
9	9	Mishi Kobe Niku	4	6	18 - 500 g pkgs.	97.00	29	0
10	10	Ikura	4	8	12 - 200 ml jars	31.00	31	0

FIGURE 19.1 A table in a relational database.

The command at the top of the screenshot is a SQL SELECT statement used to retrieve data from the database. This is the kind of language you must speak to the database server to get results. No matter how much API surface is being added to connect to the database and run commands, everything ultimately boils down to executing SQL statements like this. For example, to retrieve products with a price below $25, the following query can be written:

```
SELECT * FROM Products WHERE UnitPrice < 25
```

To run this command, most likely parameterized by the upper-bound price to add more flexibility, you typically uses APIs like System.Data.SqlClient that look like the following from a user's point of view:

```
var products = new List<Product>();
using (var conn = new SqlConnection(connectionString)) {
    string sql = "SELECT * FROM Products WHERE UnitPrice < 25";
    using (var cmd = new SqlCommand(sql, conn)) {
        conn.Open();
        using (var reader = cmd.ExecuteReader()) {
            while (reader.Read()) {
                string name = (string)reader["ProductName"];
                decimal price = (decimal)reader["UnitPrice"];
                products.Add(new Product { Name = name, Price = price });
            }
        }
    }
}
```

Even though the data has a structure similar to the in-memory data example, we have to go through totally different hoops to get the data out in the desired shape, applying a filter through a totally different language. In doing so, we've introduced many more opportunities for mishaps.

First, we not only need to learn a totally different language with its own syntax and semantics, we also have to know a different API. Although there is some unification in the System.Data APIs, which allows targeting different servers (for example SQL, Oracle, DB2, MySql) through various providers, there's still a significant tax to pay with regard to the learning curve of those. For example, notice the excessive use of using blocks to make sure things like connections are closed properly.

Second, the fact we've buried the SQL statement in a string is a whole problem by itself. Obviously, the compiler doesn't have any meaningful interpretation for this island of foreign code and therefore can't show IntelliSense or catch problems during the compilation of the code. Simple typos will go unnoticed until the code is run, resulting in a runtime exception signaling the server didn't understand the request. If you're lucky, a meaningful error message will be displayed, as shown in Figure 19.2, but matters can be a lot more cumbersome and unobvious when mistakes are made against types, database schemas, or when dealing with complex join operations.

```
var products = new List<Product>();
using (var conn = new SqlConnection(dsn.ToString()))
{
    string sql = "SELECT * FROM Products WHERE UnitPriice < 25";
    using (var cmd = new SqlCommand(sql, conn))
    {
        conn.Open();
        using (var reader = cmd.ExecuteReader())
        {
            while (reader.Read())
            {                        ⓘ  SqlException was unhandled
                string name = (stri  Invalid column name 'UnitPriice'.
                decimal price = (de
                products.Add(new Pr  Troubleshooting tips:
            }                        Get general help for this exception.
        }
    }
}
                                     Search for more Help Online...
```

FIGURE 19.2   No compile-time checking of query statements.

However, more problems come from using an opaque string as the input to the server. Because the query command doesn't get verified extensively before being sent to the server, it's susceptible to different types of attacks when the query string gets built improperly. A typical source of errors is in the parameterization of queries:

```
string query = "SELECT * FROM Products WHERE Name='" + name + "'";
```

If the name variable comes from an untrusted source, like the user providing direct input through some UI, several problems can arise with the preceding code. What if the name contains the following?

```
' OR TRUE --
```

This results in a query that has a WHERE clause looking like this:

```
WHERE Name='' OR TRUE --'
```

The -- is SQL's comment syntax, making the remainder of the line invisible to the query execution engine. Clearly, the preceding query will return all results instead. This just shows the tip of the iceberg of query attacks, with much more severe ones possible:

```
'; DROP DATABASE Northwind --
```

Oops, if the connection to the database server was made with an account that has the right to drop a database, the user can delete the whole database by putting well-crafted input in the "name" input field. This category of attacks is known as SQL injection attacks.

DON'T BLINDLESSLY PRINT EXCEPTION TEXT

Printing exception text in response to an error is not always a good idea. When a malicious person tries to break into the system (for example, by leveraging some SQL injection vulnerability in your code), exception text can be very helpful to explore the structure of the database. It may dump parts of the query that was sent to the server, giving the enemy more information to craft even *more malicious* input when preparing another break-in attempt.

This SQL injection attack can be mitigated by using yet different and more complex APIs to parameterize the query, obscuring the meaning of code even further:

```
string sql = "SELECT * FROM Products WHERE UnitPrice < @Price";
using (var cmd = new SqlCommand(sql, conn)) {
    var maxPrice = cmd.Parameters.Add("@Price", SqlDbType.Decimal);
    maxPrice.Value = /* get in from somewhere, e.g. user input */;
    conn.Open();
    using (var reader = cmd.ExecuteReader()) {
        while (reader.Read()) {
            string name = (string)reader["ProductName"];
            decimal price = (decimal)reader["UnitPrice"];
            products.Add(new Product { Name = name, Price = price });
        }
    }
}
```

But the list of problems goes on. Notice how the loop has to retrieve data out of the data reader object using an indexer, getting a `System.Object` back. A cast to a compatible type is needed to get the data out in a meaningful way. Solutions have been thought out for this problem, in the form of object/relational (O/R) mappings, but those don't address the querying problem directly.

.NET has some notion of O/R mapping constructs in the form of the `DataSet` type, which provides a way to map a data source onto an in-memory data structure (for example, on a per-table basis). In conjunction with so-called data adapter objects, the `DataSet` object can be used to update records in the database by manipulating the data contained in the `DataSet` and by sending out an update to the server afterward. You can export the schema of the database into a strongly typed `DataSet`, which is a form of O/R mapping. However, this has its disadvantages, too. To make updates possible, you must deal (sometimes indirectly through the use of designers) with other SQL commands for insert, update, and delete. And the typical pattern of bringing large chunks of a database into the application's memory is not always desirable because you want to leave as much of the query execution on the server as possible. That said, `DataSet` still plays an important role for use in web services and offline scenarios.

In summary, the following issues plague the use of relational databases today:

- ▶ Must learn a totally different language to address the database engine.

- ▶ Different APIs are used to address different databases.

- ▶ Lots of possibilities to mess up, including the following:

  - ▶ Syntactical errors in the target query language

  - ▶ Introducing vulnerabilities by string concatenation

  - ▶ Manual management of various objects needed to connect, and so on

  - ▶ Improper data conversions, type mismatches in the query, and so on

- ▶ Need for separate O/R mapping technologies to make things slightly better.

XML

Another popular data storage format nowadays is XML, dealing with hierarchical data structures. As you can guess by now, the story on querying this type of data source is again fundamentally different from dealing with objects or relational data. To illustrate this point, consider the following XML document for our familiar products catalog:

```
<Products>
    <Product Name="Chai" Price="18.00" />
    <Product Name="Chang" Price="19.00" />
    <Product Name="Aniseed Syrup" Price="10.00" />
    <Product Name="Chef Anton's Cajun Seasoning" Price="22.00" />
    <Product Name="Chef Anton's Gumbo Mix" Price="21.35" />
    <Product Name="Grandma's Boysenberry Spread" Price="25.00" />
    <Product Name="Uncle Bob's Organic Dried Pears" Price="30.00" />
    <Product Name="Northwoods Cranberry Sauce" Price="40.00" />
    <Product Name="Mishi Kobe Niku" Price="97.00" />
    <Product Name="Ikura" Price="31.00" />
</Products>
```

Again, focusing on our filtering query example, let's try to select the products with a price less than $25. Once more, we have to familiarize ourselves with another API, this time under the System.Xml namespace.

> ### DOM
>
> `System.Xml` is an XML Document Object Model API that isn't very easy to use. To cre-
> ate XML documents, you must write very imperative-style code that calls the methods
> `CreateElement`, `InsertAfter`, and so on. Although we'll be loading a document from a
> file in the following example, be aware of the bigger picture of the API being used. As
> you'll see later, the new `System.Xml.Linq` namespace makes the task of creating XML
> documents (or fragments) easier, too.

```
XmlDocument doc = new XmlDocument();
doc.Load(\temp\products.xml");

XmlNodeList res = doc.SelectNodes("//Product[@Price<25]");

var products = new List<Product>();
foreach (XmlNode node in res)
{
    products.Add(new Product {
        Name = node.Attributes["Name"].Value,
        Price = decimal.Parse(node.Attributes["Price"].Value) }
    );
}
```

Formulating the query takes yet another query language, this time using XPath passed as a
string to `SelectNodes`. Similar problems exist as for the relational database case, requiring
the use of foreign APIs and languages, the potential to mess up the query syntax in
various ways, the need to fight loose typing, and manual object/XML (O/X) mapping.

With XML's popularity increasing due to its use in web services and for data storage in
certain cases, we clearly need a better approach to access XML data in a friction-free
manner. The same holds for other formats (such as JSON) that are emerging; all of which
would benefit from a unified query experience where you don't have to learn entirely new
APIs or languages to be able to reach out.

The Birth of LINQ

We've looked at only three different data storage formats, but this should be sufficient to
appreciate the "jungle of data access," ranging from highly imperative code to the use of
specialized APIs with domain-specific query languages. Dealing with all of this is not just
tedious but also very error prone. Furthermore, knowledge of one data and querying
domain doesn't carry over to another. Tomorrow you'll have to get data out of some
online web service where querying is done by specialized web service methods, and again
you'll have to learn the specifics of the web service's API.

This brings us to one of the problem statements identified by language and framework
designers in the .NET 3.5, C# 3.0, and Visual Basic 9.0 time frame, which led to the

introduction of Language Integrated Query (LINQ). The core idea is to provide syntax for query expressions right inside the language, which compile down to API calls that can be targeted at various data sources. The high-level overview is shown in Figure 19.3.

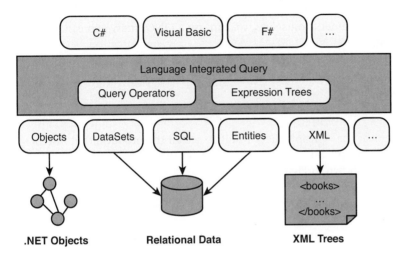

FIGURE 19.3   LINQ general overview.

LINQ by Example

Before we start investigating LINQ from a language and framework point of view, let's revisit our running example by reformulating the query in terms of LINQ for each of the three data domains. You'll see how the same syntactical language surface for query expressions can be used against different domains, abstracting away the technicalities we had to deal with manually before.

In-Memory Data

Starting from the same in-memory collection of products, we want to get rid of our imperative code that obfuscated the meaning of our query before. Here, we're using the LINQ to Objects implementation, which implements the *query pattern* for objects that implement IEnumerable<T>. Given the following data source, we want to express a query that will give us back only the products with a price less than $25:

```
var products = new List<Product> {
    new Product { Name = "Chai", Price = 18.00m },
    new Product { Name = "Chang", Price = 19.00m },
    new Product { Name = "Aniseed Syrup", Price = 10.00m },
    new Product { Name = "Chef Anton's Cajun Seasoning", Price = 22.00m },
    new Product { Name = "Chef Anton's Gumbo Mix", Price = 21.35m },
    new Product { Name = "Grandma's Boysenberry Spread", Price = 25.00m },
    new Product { Name = "Uncle Bob's Organic Dried Pears", Price = 30.00m },
```

```
        new Product { Name = "Northwoods Cranberry Sauce", Price = 40.00m },
        new Product { Name = "Mishi Kobe Niku", Price = 97.00m },
        new Product { Name = "Ikura", Price = 31.00m }
};
```

Instead of iterating over the elements ourselves, we can use a LINQ query expression and simply declare our intent:

```
var cheap = from product in products
            where product.Price < 25
            select product;
```

Now we can enumerate over the "cheap" query result to see all the products that have a price less than the specified upper bound. Notice that we get full support of IntelliSense while writing this query, as shown in Figure 19.4.

FIGURE 19.4   IntelliSense in a query expression.

We discuss this extensively in Chapter 20, "Language Integrated Query Internals," in the section, "Iterators," but there's another key difference between the use of LINQ query expressions and the imperative code we saw before. In our manual attempt to query the data, we created a new List<Product> collection in which to stick the query results. This means the query executes on the spot. However, with LINQ, it's not until you start iterating over the query expression object (cheap in the preceding code) that the query starts running. To convince yourself about this lazy behavior, write the following:

```
decimal upperPrice = 25m;
var cheap = from product in products
            where product.Price < upperPrice
            select product;

// The upperPrice variable was captured in a closure (see later), hence we
// can change it and the query expression will "see" it.
upperPrice = 100m;

// Here the query executes, and not any earlier!
foreach (var product in cheap)
    Console.WriteLine(product.Name);
```

This prints all the products with a price lower than $100 rather than $25. And if we were to change `upperPrice` later to 200 and reiterate over the cheap query result, the products with a price lower than $200 would be shown next. This shows that LINQ query expressions use *lazy evaluation*. We talk extensively about how this is realized and what the implications are in Chapter 20.

The use of lazy evaluation is great in combination with query operator composability: Given the preceding query, select just the first five results. In the imperative world, we would have to tweak the loop we created to include a counter and whatnot, but in LINQ we can just stick a `Take(5)` call on the query expression, and off we go:

```
var fiveCheap = (from product in products
                 where product.Price < upperPrice
                 select product).Take(5);
```

This code *never* persists *all* elements with a price below the specified upper bound; it just goes through the products evaluating the `where` clause, but only yielding the first five hits to the caller.

Finally, if we want to group the data by "price bucket" as we saw before, we no longer have to mess around with dictionary objects ourselves but can do so declaratively:

```
var priceGroups = from product in products
                  group product by 10m * (int)(product.Price / 10);

foreach (var priceGroup in priceGroups) {
    Console.WriteLine("From {0} to {1}", priceGroup.Key,
                                         priceGroup.Key + 9.99m);
    foreach (var product in priceGroup)
        Console.WriteLine("  {0} costs ${1}", product.Name, product.Price);
}
```

Obviously, we can do much more besides a filter and a grouping. That's where the idea of standard query operators comes in, which we look at in Chapter 20, in the section, "Standard Query Operators." What we've shown here is that any of those operators can be glued together easily, facilitating a *declarative programming style* where you simply say what you want as opposed to how it needs to be done. By using a declarative approach to querying, you also give the runtime more control over the precise mechanics of evaluating your query, potentially taking benefit of multicore processors and whatnot.

Relational Databases

Now let's try to retarget the same query to the Northwind database stored on a SQL Server database server. If LINQ delivers on its promises, we ought to be able to use the same query against the remote data source, having it take care of all the plumbing needed (such as the generation of a SQL SELECT statement under the hood).

To try this, we first create a data context in our Visual Studio 2010 project, exporting the metadata of the target database. This is the O/R part of the LINQ to SQL solution. After we've done so, we can write LINQ queries against the data source. Notice that there's also the so-called Entity Framework, which is the big brother to LINQ to SQL and the preferred way to query relational data today. We won't cover Entity Framework in this book and refer to specialized literature on the subject.

First, in Visual Studio 2010, we add a new item of type LINQ to SQL Classes to the current project, as shown in Figure 19.5.

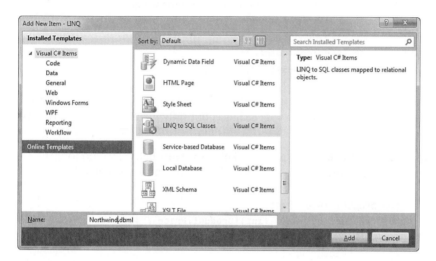

FIGURE 19.5   Object/relational mapping starts with a LINQ to SQL Classes item.

This brings up the Object Relational Designer, where we can use the Server Explorer to connect to a SQL Server database and drag and drop data sources (like tables, views, and stored procedures) to the designer surface. Doing so causes the designer to generate code that will make it easy to reach out to the database from code. Figure 19.6 shows the result after adding a few Northwind tables from the Server Explorer to the mapping surface.

REQUIREMENTS FOR LINQ TO SQL SAMPLES

To run the LINQ to SQL examples, you'll need some SQL Server installation at your service. If you don't have such a server lying around, the free Express edition can be downloaded and installed on your development computer.

For the examples, I'm using the familiar Northwind database that came with the SQL Server product until version 2000. To install it on SQL Server 2005 or 2008, search the Web for "SQL Northwind Sample" to download the database with install scripts from the Microsoft download center. The installer merely unpacks the file into a folder called SQL Server 2000 Sample Databases, leaving the rest of the installation to you. Various approaches can be taken to execute the .sql file, one of which is the use of the sqlcmd.exe tool that comes with SQL Server:

```
sqlcmd -S . -E -i Northwind.sql
```

This runs the .sql install script with Windows integrated authentication (-E) on the local server instance; the dot specified for -S means "local machine." If you need to run the script against a different server or instance, or with SQL authentication, refer to the command-line help for sqlcmd.exe.

Back in Visual Studio 2010, the Server Explorer window has a button to connect to the database, which simply prompts for the server name, credentials, and the name of the database. An expanded database connection is shown in Figure 19.6 where tables are made visible. The Server Explorer can be used to inspect the database structure, retrieve data from it, and modify settings.

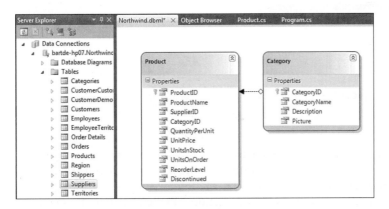

FIGURE 19.6   A simple mapping of tables to classes.

With the mapping in place, we now have a strongly typed way to talk to the database and formulate queries. Everything starts from a `DataContext` object, named after the LINQ to SQL Classes file (in our case, Northwind). From this context object, we can access the tables we exported through the designer. Let's take a look:

```
using (var ctx = new NorthwindDataContext()) {
    var cheap = from product in ctx.Products
                where product.UnitPrice < 25
                select product;

    foreach (var product in cheap)
        Console.WriteLine("{0} costs {1}", product.ProductName,
                                           product.UnitPrice);
}
```

We no longer have to deal with manual creation of a SQL SELECT statement and can use LINQ syntax to express a query over a totally foreign data domain using the generated objects. IntelliSense is present once more, as shown in Figure 19.7. Notice how we've used the LINQ to SQL Classes designer to provide aliases for various columns (through the

Property window). Instead of having to write UnitPrice, we can now write Price instead. This mapping makes the consumption of data easier and more natural-looking if columns turn out to have weird names.

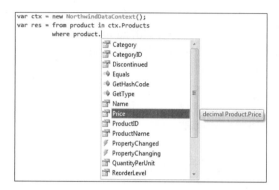

FIGURE 19.7   Static typing revealed for the generated LINQ to SQL classes.

Having statically typed objects available representing the table structure is a great improvement because mistakes against types are avoided at compile time. Internally, the query gets translated into a SQL statement at runtime by the LINQ to SQL APIs that are getting called through the LINQ syntax. How this translation is facilitated by the various language features is discussed in Chapter 20, in the section, "Expression Trees for Query Expressions," but let's take a look at what gets generated. To do so, we turn on logging on the data context object:

```
using (var ctx = new NorthwindDataContext()) {
    ctx.Log = Console.Out;
    ...
}
```

In addition, set a breakpoint on the foreach keyword to illustrate that the query doesn't get translated and executed until the point we start the iteration over the query object. Again, this proves that the query is executed lazily. Figure 19.8 shows the addition of the logging code, followed by a breakpoint on foreach, ready for the experiment to confirm laziness.

Before you press F10 twice after hitting the breakpoint, nothing will happen. Doing the two Step Over debugger actions will cause you to hit the GetEnumerator call on the cheap object, which is where the query gets translated, at runtime, into a SQL SELECT statement that's then sent to the server for execution. Figure 19.9 shows the parameterized query that was generated.

```
namespace LINQ
{
    class Program
    {
        static void Main(string[] args)
        {
            var ctx = new NorthwindDataContext();
            ctx.Log = Console.Out;
            var cheap = from product in ctx.Products
                        where product.UnitPrice < 25
                        select product;

            foreach (var product in cheap)
                Console.WriteLine("{0} costs {1}", product.ProductName, product.UnitPrice);
        }
    }
}
```

FIGURE 19.8   Using logging to show the lazy evaluation of a LINQ to SQL query.

FIGURE 19.9   The logged generated SQL SELECT statement.

WHY TRANSLATION AT RUNTIME?

You might be surprised to see LINQ query expressions get translated to the target query language at runtime as opposed to at compile time. The nice thing about LINQ is that it separates different concerns: Validating a query's structure is something that can be done by the language compiler because of the tight language integration, allowing rich type checking and such. On the other hand, it would be highly undesirable to enlighten the compiler about other languages like SQL (and the many other ones out there that might want to support LINQ). Instead, a model based on providers was put in place, allowing those runtime libraries to turn the query into any target language it sees fit.

At the heart of this feature lies the C# 3.0 expression trees feature, which we discuss in Chapter 20 when talking about IQueryable<T>. Expression trees capture a query expression's structure for the runtime library to analyze and translate (if possible) into the target language of choice (for example, SQL).

LINQ to SQL can do much more than just query a database. The mapped objects can also be used to update the database simply by changing properties to the settable properties, followed by a call to SubmitChanges on the data context object. LINQ doesn't provide syntax for insert, update, or delete statements, primarily because the mainstream scenarios involve making changes to retrieved data; for example, through some data visualization in a UI control like a data grid. Similarly, records can be inserted into or deleted from the database by manipulating the table objects through the data context:

```
ctx.Products.InsertOnSubmit(new Product() { ProductName = "Visual Studio", ... });

// Deleting an object that was retrieved before, e.g. because the user
// deleted it from a grid control.
Product chai = /* retrieved somehow through a query */;
ctx.Products.DeleteOnSubmit(chai);

// Change tracking through INotifyPropertyChanged tells the context the
// object needs to be updated upon calling SubmitChanges.
Product chang = /* retrieved somehow through a query */;
chang.UnitPrice = chang.UnitPrice * 1.2;

ctx.SubmitChanges();
```

Finally, notice how the relational nature of the database is reflected in the generated objects. You can easily write queries that traverse relationships; for example, querying products by their categories:

```
var beverages = from product in ctx.Products
                where product.Category.CategoryName == "Beverages"
                select product;
```

The query generated for the preceding code involves quite a bit of domain-specific query language knowledge on joins. Without the help of LINQ, the developer would have to figure this out herself, with opportunity for mistakes to sneak in. (For example, the preceding query would likely be parameterized on "Beverages", making plain string concatenation an obvious, but dangerous, choice because of potential SQL injection attacks.) Instead, LINQ to SQL takes care of all of this and generates the following:

```
SELECT [t0].[ProductID], [t0].[ProductName], [t0].[SupplierID],
       [t0].[CategoryID], [t0].[QuantityPerUnit], [t0].[UnitPrice],
       [t0].[UnitsInStock], [t0].[UnitsOnOrder], [t0].[ReorderLevel],
       [t0].[Discontinued]
FROM [dbo].[Products] AS [t0]
LEFT OUTER JOIN [dbo].[Categories] AS [t1]
                            ON [t1].[CategoryID] = [t0].[CategoryID]
WHERE [t1].[CategoryName] = @p0
```

Notice the use of parameterization as way to hand over query parameters like "Beverages" in a safe manner so that the database can take care of input checking.

WHAT ABOUT EFFICIENCY?

Some people raise concerns about the efficiency of the query generation and the generated queries. Let's demystify a couple of things about this.

Concerning the generation of queries at runtime, database access typically gets over-shadowed by other costs, such as setting up network connections and transport of the query and its results. The cost involved in generating the query is marginal compared to those factors, and good query providers actually cache the query they've generated for reexecution when needed. Notice how parameterization of queries also helps with this: If the `"Beverages"` parameter were stored in a local variable and got changed between two iterations over the query, the same query string can be reused, just supplying a different parameter.

What about the generated queries? Relational database vendors have spent decades figuring out how to execute queries as efficiently as possible, optimizing any query that gets thrown at their database product. I would rather trust those domain specialists to optimize generated queries than I would trust the library writers to tweak queries on behalf of the user and the server. Optimizing code is one thing, but doing so beyond the point of correctness is a big no-no. Who better knows the optimization tricks for a very specialized query language than the entity that will execute it (that is, the database engine)?

A common argument is that the use of stored procedures makes querying more efficient. Although there's some truth to this, it doesn't help when you want to run ad hoc queries, something LINQ supports in a very direct manner. And stored procedures can be used, as well, by importing them to the data context using the designer. What likely pays off (regardless of the data access technology used) is having a good database administrator who sets up indexes to optimize queries based on typical scenarios. Such optimizations will prove more effective than trying to optimize generated queries on behalf of the database engine.

Finally, notice in Figure 19.9 how the dump of the query mentions the version of the target database server. Query providers can have some awareness of the version of the server they're targeting, so newer query language constructs can be emitted when desired.

XML

Finally, we've arrived back with hierarchical data stored in the form of XML. The new `System.Xml.Linq` APIs, also known as LINQ to XML, make dealing with XML data much easier, too. In fact, LINQ to XML is LINQ to Objects in disguise, providing a way for XML data to be represented using `IEnumerable` sequences. This is achieved by providing various methods that enumerate over the XML data in different ways. For example, methods exist that go over the children of a node, others go over elements or attributes only, and yet other methods recursively visit all descendants.

Starting from the same XML document, we'll formulate some queries using LINQ to show how those methods are used to represent various enumeration strategies over the XML data:

```
<Products>
    <Product Name="Chai" Price="18.00" />
    <Product Name="Chang" Price="19.00" />
    <Product Name="Aniseed Syrup" Price="10.00" />
    <Product Name="Chef Anton's Cajun Seasoning" Price="22.00" />
    <Product Name="Chef Anton's Gumbo Mix" Price="21.35" />
    <Product Name="Grandma's Boysenberry Spread" Price="25.00" />
    <Product Name="Uncle Bob's Organic Dried Pears" Price="30.00" />
    <Product Name="Northwoods Cranberry Sauce" Price="40.00" />
    <Product Name="Mishi Kobe Niku" Price="97.00" />
    <Product Name="Ikura" Price="31.00" />
</Products>
```

Loading the document is achieved by a simple Load method on an XDocument class; LINQ to XML APIs use the X prefix rather than Xml to disambiguate from the older System.Xml DOM-based API. Once we have the document, we can start drilling into it by using methods such as Element (to select a single element with a given name) and Elements (to get all child elements of a given node):

```
var doc = XDocument.Load(\temp\Products.xml");
var products = doc.Element("Products").Elements();
var cheap = from product in products
            let name = product.Attribute("Name").Value
            let price = decimal.Parse(product.Attribute("Price").Value)
            where price < 25m
            select new Product { Name = name, Price = price };
```

Because XML documents are untyped, properties like XAttribute.Value return a string that can be turned into the expected type using the familiar Parse methods on the primitive data types. To do so, we're using a let clause in the query, which can be seen as a way to introduce a new variable that's available later in the query expression. However, the structure of the query clearly reveals the user's intent.

First we have the root element from the document, which is named "Products". From there, we retrieve all the child elements on which we expect attributes Name and Price to be present. After those attribute values have been extracted, we can start formulating rich queries. Finally, we use object initializer syntax to project the result into a Product object instance. The result of the whole query becomes an IEnumerable<Product> over which we can enumerate to visualize the results.

LINQ TO XSD

LINQ to XML remained untyped without an object/XML mapping technology next to it. When dealing with schematized XML, using XSD schemas, the experience of formulating a query could be made easier as the structure of the document is known in much detail. For example, the `Price` attribute could be surfaced as a well-typed property on a Product class. And the Products node could be retrieved from the document directly as an `IEnumerable<Product>`.

For some time during the early days of LINQ, there was an attempt to leverage XSD schemas as a way to make queries over XML data using LINQ more pleasant to write. However, this LINQ to XSD project ultimately got cancelled. Although this seemed quite attractive, there are quite a few problems. For one thing, child elements and attributes can have the same name, making the use of properties for both of them infeasible in general because of potential name clashes. Besides this, it's been a general industry trend to omit XSD schemas for lots of XML documents, sometimes in favor of using other formats, such as JSON or REST (for web services without a WSDL schema).

Finally, Visual Basic 9.0 went a slightly different direction to tackle the aesthetic problem of traversing into XML data. They added language support for so-called XML literals, together with syntax to select attributes and such (`.@`). Internally, those constructs compile into LINQ to XML API calls.

Much more complex queries can be written over XML documents, leveraging the same set of query operators as available for other data domains like SQL and objects. What should be remembered from this introductory discussion about LINQ to XML is how the technology hides lots of complexities around the use of `XPath` and certain XML data traversal patterns that would otherwise be written using imperative loop constructs.

Before concluding our first journey through the world of the LINQ to XML APIs, I want to point out that this API is also very well suited for creating new XML elements using constructor syntax:

```
var products = new XElement("Products",
    new XElement("Product",
        new XAttribute("Name", "Chai"),
        new XAttribute("Price", 18.00m)
    ),
    ...
);
```

You can write whole XML documents (or XML fragments) simply by calling nested constructors, ultimately resulting in an in-memory object tree representing the XML data.

This can then be serialized into a file or other destinations like streams. Before LINQ to XML, building up XML data by hand was a cumbersome experience using the System.XML DOM, which has a very imperative style to it.

Query Expression Syntax

In our example-driven exploration of LINQ, we've seen many query expressions. Now the time has come to take a closer look at the "syntactical surface area" for writing query expressions, as introduced in C# 3.0. During our discussion of query expressions throughout this section, we'll see examples for the various query constructs available. But first let's explain the role query expressions play in the bigger picture of LINQ.

Why Query Expressions?

LINQ is the concatenation of LIN and Q. Trivial as this might seem, it's quite important to understand those are the two core pieces of the puzzle being presented here. The latter part is clear: We want provide a way to *query* data across different domains such as in-memory, relational, and hierarchical, but also more. This mission can be separated from the former part, which has to do with *language integration* to allow more natural ways to express queries.

To set the scene, let's take a look at a totally different language: Haskell, a pure functional programming language. With a decreased emphasis on imperative-style code, programs written in a functional style tend to make more operations data driven. For example, instead of iterating over a list by obtaining an enumerator and calling some MoveNext method repeatedly, functional programmers would pattern match over the list, extracting the head element and the tail list (everything but the first element), performing some operation on the head and recursively calling itself for the tail. As an example, consider the following code, which sums a list of integers:

```
sum :: [Integer] -> Integer
sum []     = 0                -- sum of empty list is zero
sum (x:xs) = x + sum xs       -- x is the head element, xs is the tail list
```

This function can now be called to sum a list as follows:

```
sum [1, 2, 3, 4, 5]
```

That's quite neat. But now assume that we just want to sum the even numbers in the list. To realize this, we could write a filter function that takes in a function with the filter predicate and creates, recursively again, a new list that contains only elements that pass the filter function:

```
filter :: (a -> Bool) -> [a] -> [a]
filter _ []               = []              -- empty list stays empty
filter p (x:xs) ¦ p x     = x : filter p xs -- apply the filter to the head,
                ¦ otherwise = filter p xs   -- keep the head if it passes
```

Don't worry too much about this syntax (unless you want to learn Haskell as well). The core idea is that the `filter` function takes in a predicate function that's evaluated for each element. Calling this on our list introduces a bit of "ceremony," though:

```
let evens = filter (\n -> (mod n 2) == 0) nums
```

Although this clearly shows the `filter` function that's being used, it's quite verbose syntax you have to stare at for every single filter you want to apply to a list. To mitigate this, Haskell introduced list comprehension syntax, which provides a more concise way to express *the same*:

```
let evens = [ n ¦ n <- nums , (mod n 2) == 0]
```

Believe me, to a Haskell developer this looks quite sexy. But the same observation holds for LINQ: Although functions like `filter` (`Where` in LINQ) are all you need to express rich queries, it gets aesthetically unpleasant pretty quickly. Having simplified syntax helps a lot to make the code more understandable and feel more natural. Let's build a similar query in LINQ with and without the query expression syntax:

```
var nums = new List<int> { 1, 2, 3, 4, 5 };

// Without query expression syntax
var evens = nums.Where(n => n % 2 == 0);

// With query expression syntax
var evens = from n in nums
            where n % 2 == 0
            select n;
```

Although the former syntax is all you need, it looks quite funky due to the syntactical noise that comes from dots, parentheses, and lambda arrows. The latter syntax means exactly the same (and indeed, it gets compiled into the former syntax) but feels more natural thanks to specialized keywords.

This example is still too trivial to see the true advantages of LINQ. As we proceed through our exploration of query expression syntax, we'll see cases where simple-looking queries turn into quite a bit of nontrivial code underneath. Such code involves lots of lambda expressions floating around in a sea of generic operator methods being called. Doing such things by hand typically leads to queries that aren't easy to understand, whereas query expression syntax looks way more natural.

WHY DID WE MENTION HASKELL AT ALL?

You're right: We could have simply shown the C# syntax with and without query expressions to illustrate the point. Yet we decided to put Haskell in the picture for not so obvious reasons. Why?

First and foremost, Haskell's been a true source of inspiration for the design of LINQ, pushing list comprehensions to its limits in a mainstream language. Even more, LINQ went beyond what Haskell provided, and now ideas are flowing in the opposite way, with plans to ameliorate Haskell list comprehensions.

Besides this, Haskell is *the* true functional programming language on the planet today. Realizing LINQ in .NET required making functional programming more accessible by means of lambda expressions and such. By showing the definition of Haskell's filter function in the preceding discussion, you get a taste of how important functions are to build very flexible operators. This is exactly what LINQ does, too.

Getting Started

All the examples shown here are based on LINQ to Objects over in-memory data stored in collections. To make the LINQ functionality accessible, you need to make sure to have a reference to System.Core in your project (which is the case by default if you're targeting .NET Framework 3.5 or later) and to have imported the System.Linq namespace in your code file. To check whether those requirements are met, write the following piece of code:

```
using System.Linq;
...
var n = new [] { 1, 2, 3 }.Count();
```

When doing so, you should see IntelliSense come up when typing the dot preceding the call to the Count method. Figure 19.10 illustrates what you should see if everything is okay. Notice the extension method icon next to the Count method in the IntelliSense autocompletion list.

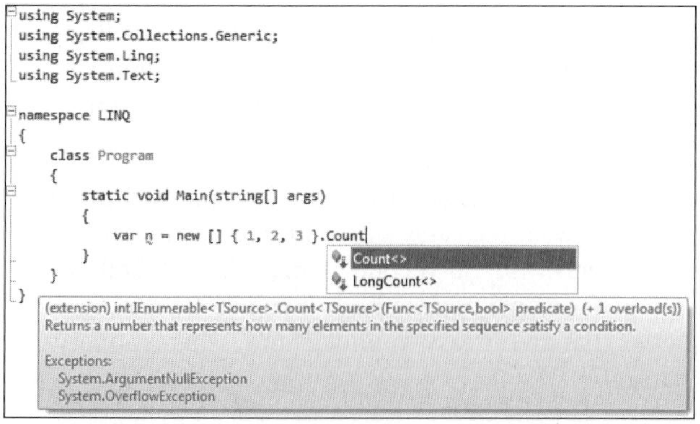

FIGURE 19.10   With the System.Linq namespace imported, the query operators appear.

Source Selection Using a `from` Clause

Query expressions start by the use of a `from` clause, which has two tasks. First, it refers to the source that's getting queried, such as an in-memory collection or a reference to an object representing a table in a database. Second, it establishes a name for the items in that source, which is used subsequently to express filters, orderings, and so on. The following is an example:

```
var nums = new List<int> { 1, 2, 3, 4, 5 };
from n in nums ...
```

Observe a few things here. On the second line, I've not assigned the query expression to a variable to emphasize it's an *expression*. You can use the whole query expression as a parameter to a method, assign it to a variable, or whatever else you're allowed to do with an expression.

Next, the `from` clause cannot stand by itself; it needs to be followed, as indicated by the ellipsis, with other query operators such as projection or grouping, among others. Those other query operators can refer to n whenever they want to express something for an element in the specified source. (In this case, nums acts as the source.)

Because the range identifier n represents an element in the nums source, it had better have the right type for use in the query expression. This type gets inferred from context, typically leveraging generics. In the preceding example, n will eventually be inferred to be of type int. Figure 19.11 shows the code editor revealing the inferred type of the range variable in our query expression.

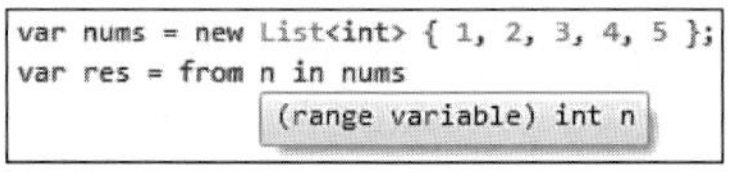

```
var nums = new List<int> { 1, 2, 3, 4, 5 };
var res = from n in nums
               (range variable) int n
```

FIGURE 19.11   The type of a range variable gets inferred.

GUESSWORK

In fact, the IntelliSense engine is merely making an informed guess here. The code illustrated here doesn't compile because the query expression isn't complete and there wouldn't be enough information for the compiler to infer the type of n just yet. So to be really precise, you shouldn't believe the compiler gets the type of the element directly from the generic type representing the source (for example, List<int>).

You'll see later in this chapter, when we discuss the translation of various query clauses into method calls, that n gets used as the parameter to lambda expressions used in the various query expression clauses. That's where the compiler infers the type from, based solely on all its method overloading knowledge. For *esoteric* query providers, the type of the range identifier can even change throughout the entire query expression. Pretend you didn't hear this because in all *practical* cases the type of the range identifier simply corresponds to the type of elements in the queried data source.

This pinpoints how IntelliSense often applies heuristics to make an informed guess about what the user is writing based on its knowledge of the typical use patterns (that make up 99.99% of all uses).

Order Matters

Readers coming from a SQL background may find the order used in query expression syntax rather weird. Why does C# choose to have the `from` clause come first, followed by operations like `select`? In SQL, you would write the following:

```
SELECT Name, Price
FROM Products
```

But in LINQ, you would write the same as follows:

```
from product in products
select new { product.Name, product.Price }
```

It turns out LINQ's design choice is better than SQL for one very important reason: IntelliSense. No matter how hard they try, SQL query editors don't have a crystal ball that can predict what table or view you're querying when you write:

```
SELECT Na
```

How is it supposed to autocomplete what you're writing when it hasn't seen the `FROM` clause (here spelled all caps because we're talking about SQL) just yet? Moreover, it doesn't make sense to write `SELECT` first because it's the last thing that happens: Tell the source, filter items, sort them, and so on. But projecting the result happens at the very end. So why does it come syntactically first? I don't know. If there's a SQL language designer reading this book, send me an email and enlighten me!

DON'T REPEAT MISTAKES

Assuming the SQL order of operations was a mistake (it is), it would be silly to repeat it in today's language design even if it were for consistency and familiarity with the SQL language people may already know. In fact, Visual Basic 9.0 was in this camp for a long while, going to great lengths to keep the `Select` clause (here using typical Visual Basic spelling of the keyword) in front, with intractable and confusing code editor jumps while typing a query. It went roughly like this, if I recall correctly:

- ▶ Type `Select` and press space; a `From` clause would be inserted below what you already typed.
- ▶ The editor jumps to the `From` clause where you specify the source and range identifier.
- ▶ When you're done with the `From` clause, as observed by the code editor upon pressing a space or Tab, you would go back to `Select`.

▶ Back in the Select clause, you can now use the range identifier introduced in the second step.

This was highly unintuitive, and the Visual Basic team eventually surrendered and made the From clause come first. The fear people would dislike it because of its difference from the already familiar SQL language has, as far as I know, never really materialized.

So, even if some SQL language designers would defend their design choices, the .NET developer audience has shown that having the From clause first is much more intuitive in the end.

Range Identifier Types

So far, we've assumed that the type of the elements in the data source can be inferred by the compiler. This is the case for most LINQ providers (like LINQ to SQL) and for generic collection types. However, you might want to use LINQ against a nongeneric collection, too. Not that many developers know this is possible as follows:

```
var nums = new ArrayList { 1, 2, 3, 4, 5 };
from int n in nums ...
```

As alluded to earlier, query expressions are simply a form of syntactical sugar over method calls. This is no different for the preceding expression, which is really the same as this:

```
from n in nums.Cast<int>() ...
```

For LINQ to Object, Cast<TSource> is defined as an extension method on the nongeneric IEnumerable interface, returning an IEnumerable<TSource>, which returns the source's elements casted to TSource. Once you've learned about iterators in Chapter 20, you see how such a query operator can be realized in C#. But to use it, you don't have to worry about its implementation, of course.

CONTEXTUAL GRAMMAR

Another nice effect that comes from putting the from clause first is the fact it helps the compiler spot where a query expression begins just by looking out for a single token from. All the way to the end of the query expression, the meaning of keywords can be treated in a purely contextual manner.

This is important for backward compatibility because all the LINQ keywords were not reserved before LINQ came around. For example, you may have a variable called select. Just switching to a newer version of the language shouldn't break that with a message stating that select has now become a reserved word. For this reason, new keywords in the language are made contextual such that they only get a special meaning in a certain context. In the case of select, the context is a query expression.

Note that this isn't anything new to C# 3.0. The same problem existed in C# 2.0, with the introduction of keywords like where (for generic constraints), which is even being reused in LINQ. Generics caused other challenges on the parser front in fact:

```
F(G<A,B>(4));
```

Because the < and > tokens were used only for comparison before, using them for generic parameters had the potential to break things. Does the preceding code mean that the user wants to call a method F with two parameters that result from comparing G and A, and B and the constant 4? That's plausible, but with generics the user may have meant to call F with the result of calling generic method G using type parameters A and B and an argument of 4. If this fascinates you, take a look at the language specification to get the answer on the language's interpretation.

foreach Analogy

If you're entirely new to LINQ, it helps to think about the from clause as if it were the same as foreach. Ultimately, queries execute with some iterative feeling, and the syntactical analogy is striking (which isn't a coincidence). For example:

```
var nums = new ArrayList { 1, 2, 3, 4, 5 };
from int n in nums ...
```

This is similar to the following:

```
var nums = new ArrayList { 1, 2, 3, 4, 5 };
foreach (int n in nums) {

    ...

}
```

From an operational point of view, this analogy holds to some extent, enough to help people reason about the query. But there are quite a few differences. The foreach loop is a statement and therefore doesn't produce a value, whereas the query expression is, well, an expression and therefore produces a value. Second, because the foreach loop is imperative, it executes on the spot, whereas a LINQ query is evaluated lazily, as explained in Chapter 20 in the section, "Iterators."

Multiple Sources

More-complex queries often require more than one data source to query from at the same time. If you reason aloud in terms of "for every element in the first source," on to "for every related element in the second source," nested from clauses are what you need. Making the comparison with the foreach statement is useful again because this looks exactly like nested loops. Here's an example:

```
from product in products
from order in product.Orders

...
```

Here we assume products is a source with Product objects, with an Orders property defined on the Products class. Orders returns a collection of Order objects. In other words, we're querying the orders for every product.

What this turns into internally is something discussed in much detail in Chapter 20 in the section, "Projection," but to convince you LINQ syntax always boils down to method calls, here's one possibility:

```
products.SelectMany(product => product.Orders, (product, order) => ...)
        ...
```

In fact, `SelectMany` is implemented using nested `foreach` loops. All that matters now is that you can have multiple sources that are being used inside the query expression. Conceptually, you can think of them as nested loops.

DIFFERENT SOURCES, DIFFERENT APPROACHES

Dealing with different data sources can be done in different ways. Maybe you want to create the Cartesian product of two sources and execute the rest of the query for each couple of elements from both sources. This is achievable through the use of multiple `from` clauses, in particular when the sources are independent:

```
from x in xs
from y in ys // ys is not dependent on x
// can use x and y here
```

Sometimes the second source depends on the element that comes out of the first one, as shown in the products and orders preceding example, which is quite different.

Finally, you might want to combine elements from two sources pair-wise. For example, if you have { 1, 2 } and { 3, 4 }, you want to get with { (1,3), (2,4) }. This can be achieved using the new .NET 4.0 standard query operator `Zip`, discussed in the next chapter in the section, "Zip."

Projection Using the `Select` Clause

Now that we've identified the query sources, we can start operating on the data they provide. Although you might think of filtering and ordering as the first kind of operations you want to perform, we'll start from the end. Every query expression in C# needs to end either by a `select` clause or a `group by` clause. The former operation is the simplest to explain so we start from there.

Identity Projection

The most trivial projection possible doesn't do any transformation on the input data and is called the identity projection, after the identity function. An example is shown here:

```
var nums = new List<int> { 1, 2, 3, 4, 5 };
var res = from n in nums
          select n;
```

This will produce a sequence with the same elements as the ones in the `nums` source and is not very useful. However, there's an observable effect in this transformation: The `nums` and `res` objects are not the same. What happens is that the preceding form gets translated into the following:

```
var res = nums.Select(n => n);
```

For LINQ to Objects, the `Select` method is defined in the `System.Linq` namespace as an extension method for `IEnumerable<T>`:

```
public static IEnumerable<R> Select<T, R>(this IEnumerable<T> source,
                                          Func<T, R> projection);
```

Notice this method returns nothing more specific than an `IEnumerable<R>`, where `R` is the type parameter corresponding to the result of the projection. In this case, `T` and `R` are the same, namely `int`, as inferred from the identity function lambda expression. You should be able to figure this out quite easily yourself: The source is a `List<int>`, hence an `IEnumerable<int>`. Thus, `T` is substituted for `int`, and therefore the input to the projection function is an `int`. The project function simply returns its input, which should be an `int` because of that. Because the output is typed as `R`, we find that `R` is also substituted for `int`. Our query is turned into the following:

```
var res = Enumerable.Select<int, int>(nums, delegate (int n) { return n; });
```

Here we've used the knowledge that `Select` is defined as an extension method using the static `Enumerable` class in `System.Linq`.

As a result, the input, which was a `List<int>`, became an `IEnumerable<int>` that hides the original source. Therefore, it's fine to hand out the result to any read-only consumer without running the risk they cast it back to `List<int>` and manipulate the elements:

```
var evil = (List<int>)res; // this fails at runtime
evil.Add(0xBAD);
```

The way the original source is hidden by the `Select` method is something that will become clear when we discuss iterators in Chapter 20, which act as the fuel for LINQ to Objects.

DIFFERENT LANGUAGES, SAME BEHAVIORS

The C# compiler doesn't "compile away" identity projections if the query doesn't consist of anything but that (a "degenerate query expression"):

```
var res = from n in nums
          select n;
```

The preceding will compile into a `Select` call that seems useless because it doesn't do anything useful, but the source-hiding property that was explained earlier is deemed important. The requirement for the user to write a `select` clause reflects this more or less. In Visual Basic, you can omit the Select clause if it's trivial, but to maintain the source-hiding property, the compiler will inject the identity projection Select call:

```
Dim res = From n In nums
```

If there's more than only a trivial select clause (for example, a filter preceding it), a trivial select clause *is* compiled away, though. The reason is that the preceding operators, like a where clause, already cause the source to get hidden:

```
var res = from n in nums
          where n % 2 == 0
          select n;
```

In C#, the user is still required to write the select clause, but this time it gets dropped at compile time, resulting in the following code:

```
var res = nums.Where(n => n % 2 == 0);
```

This illustrates how syntactical differences across C# and Visual Basic maintain the (subtle) desired behavior of trivial projections when needed.

Stand-alone identity projections are not very useful other than for their source-hiding properties. But because C# requires you to write a select clause (or a group by clause) to terminate a query expression, you'll encounter identity projections quite often:

```
var res = from n in nums
          where n % 2 == 0
          select n;
```

Nontrivial Projections

Of more interest are the nontrivial projections that really transform elements from the input sequences into some result, possibly of another type. A simple example is shown here:

```
var twice = from n in nums
            select n * 2;
```

The output of this query is an IEnumerable<int> whose produced elements contain the original elements each multiplied by two. Internally, this translates into a Select method call, as shown before, that looks like this:

```
var twice = nums.Select(n => n * 2);
```

In other words, Select takes in a function to execute on all the source's elements, giving back the output objects. The syntactical translation carried out by the compiler for a select clause is shown in Figure 19.12. We'll ignore the case where multiple range identifiers are "in scope" for the time being.

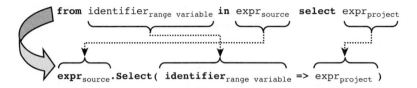

FIGURE 19.12   Translation of a `select` clause to a Standard Query Operator method call.

Projections can also emit a different result type than the source's element type. The following example illustrates a "to char" operation on numbers, translating them to ASCII characters:

```
var letters = from n in nums
              select (char)('a' + n - 1);
```

For example, a nums input sequence of { 1, 2, 2, 1 } will produce an output with the letters { 'a', 'b', 'b', 'a' }. Figure 19.13 shows the projection query operator in action for both examples shown here.

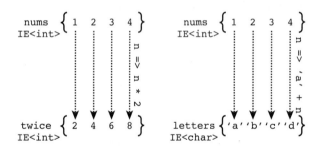

FIGURE 19.13   A few sample projections.

Anonymous Types and Object Initializers

In most concrete cases, your data source won't exist out of elements of some basic data type but rather contain entity types like a `Person` or a `Product`. Projection is usually used to select only a subset of properties (often corresponding to columns in tables in a relational database), possibly while performing some operation on any of those (for example, to multiply a product's `Price` property by a certain percentage).

An example that deals with an in-memory collection of products, selecting just a single column, is shown here:

```
var names = from product in products /* an IEnumerable<Product> */
            select product.Name;
```

Here the result will be of type `IEnumerable<string>`, assuming a `Product`'s `Name` is of type string. Knowing the signature of the underlying `Select` method reveals the output sequence's type immediately. Let's do it one more time:

```
var names = products.Select(product => product.Name);
```

Given that `products` is of type `IEnumerable<Product>` and that the lambda function returns a `Product`'s `Name` property that's typed a string, the output cannot be anything else but an `IEnumerable<string>`. In other words, `T` is inferred to be `Product`, and `R` is inferred to be `string` in the generic `Select` method being called:

```
public static IEnumerable<R> Select<T, R>(this IEnumerable<T> source,
                                    Func<T, R> projection);
```

Knowing that the underlying method call simply takes in a lambda expression means you can provide any expression for the select clause. Refer to Figure 19.12 to see how the select clause expression turns into a lambda expression body.

But we can do more than just select a single column; really, any expression will do for a select clause projection, such as plain constants, constructor or method calls, use of anonymous objects, and so on. As an exercise, infer the result type for all the following:

```
// Not incredibly useful but constants are expressions.
var oneForEveryProduct = from product in products
                         select 1;


// Using an anonymous type.
var nameAndPrice = from product in products
                   select new { product.Name, product.Price };


// Using a closure over an outer variable (refer to chapter on delegates).
decimal percent = 0.05m;
var productDiscounts = from p in products
                       select new { p.Name, Discount = p.Price * percent };


// Calling a method.
var pricingLabels = from p in products
                    select string.Format("{0} costs ${1}", p.Name, p.Price);
```

Anonymous types were a key feature introduced in C# 3.0 to make LINQ practical to use because they allow defining a type on-the-fly, while creating an instance at the same time. If every single projection would require you to create a whole type by yourself, things would start to look cumbersome quickly:

```
var nameAndPrice = from product in products
                   select new NameAndPrice(product.Name, product.Price);

...

class NameAndPrice {
    public NameAndPrice(string name, decimal price) {
        Name = name;
        Price = price;
    }

    public string Name { get; private set; }
    public decimal Price { get; private set; }
}
```

And if you really want to create a nominal type (the opposite of an anonymous type, if you will), doing so is quite easy thanks to C# 3.0's auto-implemented properties. One case where this might be necessary is when you return the result of a query to the caller of a method because anonymous types cannot "leak" the method body in a meaningful way. Figure 19.14 illustrates the inferred type for the NameAndPrice query that makes use of an anonymous type in the select clause.

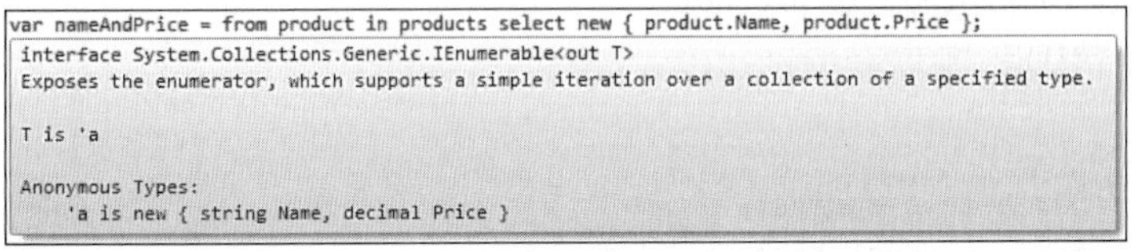

```
var nameAndPrice = from product in products select new { product.Name, product.Price };
interface System.Collections.Generic.IEnumerable<out T>
Exposes the enumerator, which supports a simple iteration over a collection of a specified type.

T is 'a

Anonymous Types:
    'a is new { string Name, decimal Price }
```

FIGURE 19.14   Inferred IEnumerable<T> type where T is an anonymous type.

If you're consuming the data immediately from the method that defines the query, the use of an anonymous type is fine. However, if you want to expose the resulting object to the outside world, you won't be able to specify the method's return type:

```
public IEnumerable</* anonymous = can't name it */> GetProductAndPrice() {
    return from product in products
           select new { product.Name, product.Price };
}
```

In this case, you must go back to a regular nominal type, which you can define by using auto-implemented properties as explained in Chapter 11, "Fields, Properties, and Indexers."

SIMPLER TYPE DECLARATIONS

It would be nice if one day we had a language feature that allows the creation of a nominal type using lightweight syntax, as shown here:

```
class NameAndPrice(string Name, decimal Price) {}
```

Such a class with a "first-class constructor" could emit a class with two read-only properties and a constructor to initialize them. In addition, overrides for `Equals`, `GetHashCode`, and `ToString` would be provided.

Alternatively (or additionally), having a refactoring to create a nominal type from an anonymous type would come in handy, too.

Vertical Partitioning

Relational databases consist of tables, which are *rectangular* blocks of data, where each element occupies a distinct row and all elements have an identical number of columns. Use of the `select` clause to carry out a projection creates a vertical partition over that data, as shown in Figure 19.15.

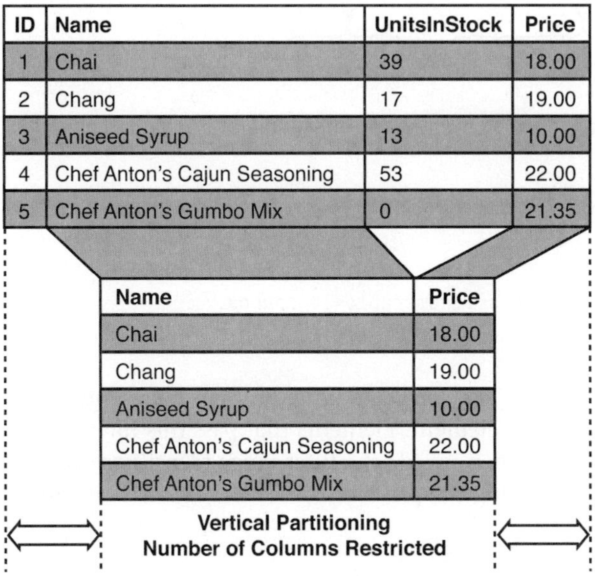

ID	Name	UnitsInStock	Price
1	Chai	39	18.00
2	Chang	17	19.00
3	Aniseed Syrup	13	10.00
4	Chef Anton's Cajun Seasoning	53	22.00
5	Chef Anton's Gumbo Mix	0	21.35

Name	Price
Chai	18.00
Chang	19.00
Aniseed Syrup	10.00
Chef Anton's Cajun Seasoning	22.00
Chef Anton's Gumbo Mix	21.35

Vertical Partitioning
Number of Columns Restricted

FIGURE 19.15 Projection is vertical partitioning.

Filtering Using a where Clause

Filtering elements of a sequence based on a predicate is one of the most common query operations performed. The query expression's `where` clause facilitates this by use of a Boolean-valued expression that's evaluated for each element in the sequence:

```
var nums = new List<int> { 1, 2, 3, 4, 5 };
var evens = from n in nums
            where n % 2 == 0
            select n;
```

Internally, the where clause translates into a class to a Where query operator method, as shown here:

```
var evens = nums.Where(n => n % 2 == 0);
```

Figure 19.16 illustrates the syntactical translation that happens here, just as we did for the select clause before. It's important to emphasize query expressions are nothing but a little syntactical veneer on top of regular method calls. You'll see in Chapter 20, in the section, "The Query Pattern," how you can implement the query pattern as a way to make objects LINQ capable (if they aren't already by means of IEnumerable<T> for instance).

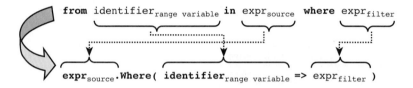

FIGURE 19.16   Translation of a where clause to a Standard Query Operator method call.

The LINQ to Objects signature for the Where method looks like this, illustrating the type of the predicate function use:

```
public static IEnumerable<T> Where<T >(this IEnumerable<T> source,
                                Func<T, bool> predicate);
```

In the nums example, T is substituted for int. The predicate function then represents the filter condition evaluated for each individual element. Elements that pass this filter end up in the resulting sequence; others are dropped. Inside the filter range identifiers can be used to express the predicate. An example using the products collection and a local variable is illustrated here:

```
// Capturing an outer local variable in the predicate expression.
decimal maxPrice = 20.00m;
var cheapProducts = from p in products
                    where p.Price < maxPrice
                    select p;
```

Figure 19.17 illustrates the execution of the where clause for the even numbers example.

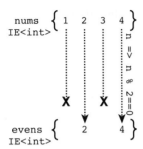

FIGURE 19.17   Execution of a filter.

Although I've made this general remark before, I should emphasize the lazy execution nature of query expressions. It's not until you start enumerating over the resulting query object that the query executes. This can be illustrated by setting a breakpoint on the where clause's predicate expression and executing the code. You won't see the breakpoint being hit before you start iterating over the result.

See Figure 19.18 for this situation illustrated for the even numbers filter. Notice how the in keyword in the foreach loop is highlighted, indicating we're executing the loop, and as a result of doing so the filter predicate gets evaluated. Hovering over n reveals the value for which the filter is currently being evaluated. A similar experiment can be conducted for a selection clause's (nontrivial) projection expression.

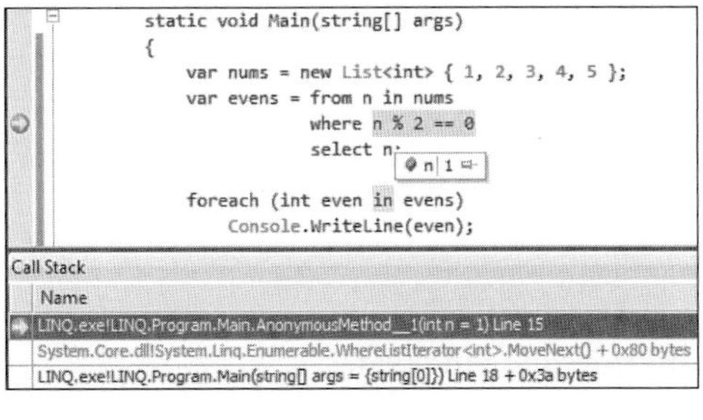

```
static void Main(string[] args)
{
    var nums = new List<int> { 1, 2, 3, 4, 5 };
    var evens = from n in nums
                where n % 2 == 0
                select n;
                       n | 1
    foreach (int even in evens)
        Console.WriteLine(even);
```

Call Stack

Name

LINQ.exe!LINQ.Program.Main.AnonymousMethod__1(int n = 1) Line 15

System.Core.dll!System.Linq.Enumerable.WhereListIterator<int>.MoveNext() + 0x80 bytes

LINQ.exe!LINQ.Program.Main(string[] args = {string[0]}) Line 18 + 0x3a bytes

FIGURE 19.18   Lazy execution of a query expression.

Horizontal Partitioning

In contrast to the select clause's vertical partitioning, the where clause's filter applies a form of horizontal partitioning, only retaining certain elements (rows) from the queried data source. Figure 19.19 shows this on our well-known products table.

Ordering Using the orderby Keyword

Sorting elements by one or more criteria is another commonly used querying action, which is supported through the orderby keyword. The basic idea is to specify a key selector function that selects an ordering key for each element in the input sequence. Upon enumerating over the query result object, the ordering key is obtained for all elements and used to sort the elements. Ordering by a key can be done either ascending (the default) or descending, using the corresponding keywords.

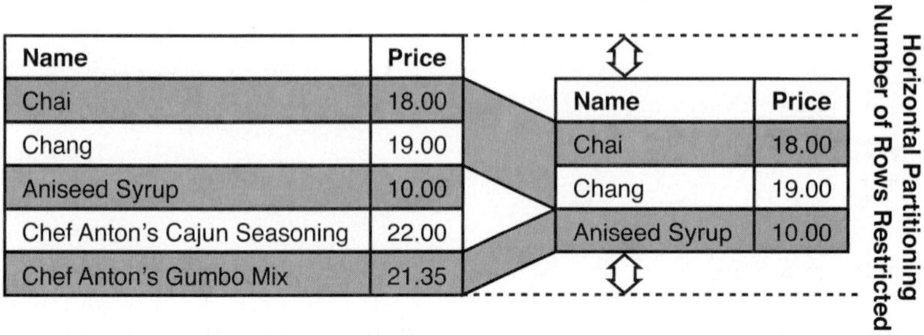

Name	Price
Chai	18.00
Chang	19.00
Aniseed Syrup	10.00
Chef Anton's Cajun Seasoning	22.00
Chef Anton's Gumbo Mix	21.35

Name	Price
Chai	18.00
Chang	19.00
Aniseed Syrup	10.00

Horizontal Partitioning
Number of Rows Restricted

FIGURE 19.19   Filtering is horizontal partitioning.

Besides doing just a single ordering (hence selecting just a single key), it's possible to specify secondary and n-ary orderings, too. For example, you might want to sort a list of products first by price in a descending fashion, followed by an ordering by name in an ascending fashion. This results in an ordering by name for all buckets of products with the same price. You'll see an example of this shortly.

The Identity Key Selector

If the elements of a sequence can be ordered by themselves (for example, because they are of some basic data type), a trivial identity key selector function can be used. For example:

```
var nums = new List<int> { 3, 5, 4, 2, 1 };
var sorted = from n in nums
                orderby n /* ascending */
                select n;
```

Use of the ascending keyword is optional. Given an element n, we simply use n itself to perform the ordering by. Internally, this turns into the following code:

```
var nums = new List<int> { 3, 5, 4, 2, 1 };
var sorted = nums.OrderBy(n => n);
```

From this, the use of the identity function becomes clear. The same identity function can be used for a descending ordering, as shown here:

```
var nums = new List<int> { 3, 5, 4, 2, 1 };
var sortedDesc = from n in nums
                    orderby n descending
                    select n;
```

This gets translated to an OrderByDescending call that looks like this:

```
var nums = new List<int> { 3, 5, 4, 2, 1 };
var sortedDesc = nums.OrderByDescending(n => n);
```

Unless specified otherwise, ordering is based, as you will see, on the default IComparer for the element type, as obtained through IComparer<T>.Default. We discuss the concept of comparers in Chapter 16, "Collection Types."

SLIGHTLY MORE EAGER

To establish an ordering, all elements from the source sequence need to be known before any element from the ordered sequence can be returned. Although the use of an ordering in a query expression still keeps the entire query lazy, the effect of requesting the first element from the resulting sequence is quite an eager operation because it "drains" the whole source sequence to establish the ordering.

Compare this to Where and Select, which just take enough elements out of the source to produce one result sequence element at a time. For Select, this is a one-to-one relationship: asking the next element from the result causes Select to fetch the next element from the source and apply the projection function. Where is a bit greedier at times because it needs to consume elements from the source until the filter function evaluates true.

OrderBy can't do anything but load all the elements in the source to perform a sort on all of them. Notice we're only talking about LINQ to Objects here, where this causes all source elements to end up in an in-memory collection suitable for performing sorting operations on. In case of remote LINQ execution (for example, using LINQ to SQL), the ordering operation will be remoted to the server and execute there.

Nontrivial Orderings

As you can already guess by now, the orderby clause simply expects a valued expression that produces the key value to order by. Any expression will do, from the absurd to the useful:

```
// Not incredibly useful but constants are expressions. Notice this doesn't
// guarantee to return the products in the input order!
var orderByConstant = from product in products
                      orderby 1
                      select product;


// Expensive to cheap requires descending sort.
var decreasingPrice = from product in products
                      orderby product.Price descending
                      select product;


// Calling a method and using a closure over a captured local variable.
DateTime from = DateTime.Now - TimeSpan.FromDays(100);
var topSellers = from p in products
                 orderby p.GetNumberOfSalesSince(from) descending
                 select p;
```

The sky (of expressions) is the limit. Just recall how the previous query expressions translate into method calls with lambda expressions for the argument as you see where this flexibility comes from. For example:

```
// Calling a method and using a closure over a captured local variable.
DateTime from = DateTime.Now - TimeSpan.FromDays(100);
var topSellers = products
            .OrderByDescending(p => p.GetNumberOfSalesSince(from));
```

Figure 19.20 illustrates this query's execution, starting with key selection at the top.

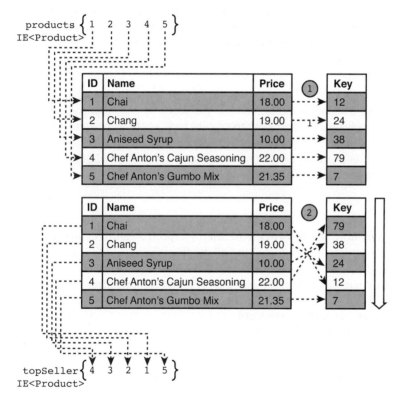

FIGURE 19.20   Execution of an ordering.

Secondary and n-ary Orderings

Use of an orderby clause with a single key selector expression creates just a primary ordering. Quite often, one wants to establish secondary and n-ary orderings on top of this, as illustrated in Figure 19.21.

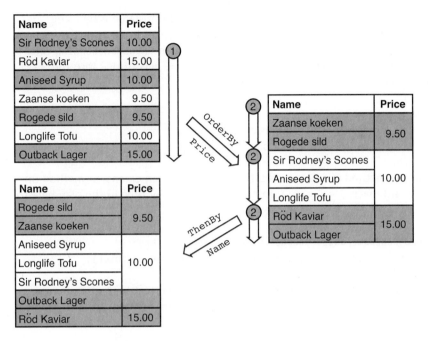

FIGURE 19.21   Establishing secondary and n-ary orderings.

Subsequent orderings are declared using a comma-separated list of key selectors, as shown here:

```
var priceThenName = from product in products
                    orderby product.Price, product.Name
                    select product;
```

Obviously, each key selector can be suffixed with either ascending (optional keyword) or descending (for example, to sort on Price descending and on Name ascending). The preceding is not the same as the following, though:

```
var priceThenName = from product in products
                    orderby product.Price
                    orderby product.Name
                    select product;
```

This will first order by Price, establishing a primary ordering, and then order on Name, reestablishing a primary ordering. This is semantically equivalent (ignoring possible side effects that would occur by running the key selector expression product.Price) to the following:

```
var priceThenName = from product in products
                    orderby product.Name
                    select product;
```

The way comma-separated key selectors in orderby clauses get translated is by using separate methods: The primary (and possibly only) ordering results in an OrderBy or OrderByDescending call, while n-ary orderings append ThenBy or ThenByDescending calls to this. For example, the Name-then-Price ordering shown here gets turned into the following equivalent code:

```
var priceThenName = products
                .OrderBy(product => product.Price)
                .ThenBy(product => product.Name);
```

Although the OrderBy method is defined for LINQ to Objects as an extension method on the IEnumerable<T> interface, ThenBy isn't. In fact, there's another type in the play here to make this work, as revealed by looking at the OrderBy signature:

```
public static IOrderedEnumerable<TSource> OrderBy<TSource, TKey>(
    this IEnumerable<TSource> source, Func<TSource, TKey> keySelector);
```

The IOrderedEnumerable<T> is nothing more than a regular IEnumerable<T>, but its type reveals a primary ordering has been established already. Extension methods on this interface are provided to establish secondary and n-ary orderings, by means of the ThenBy methods:

```
public static IOrderedEnumerable<TSource> ThenBy<TSource, TKey>(
    this IOrderedEnumerable<TSource> source, Func<TSource, TKey> keySelector);
```

Once ordered, always ordered: ThenBy starts from an IOrderedEnumerable<T> and returns one of those by itself, allowing more ThenBy calls to follow. Figure 19.22 illustrates this as a state machine of types (as nodes) and methods (as edges).

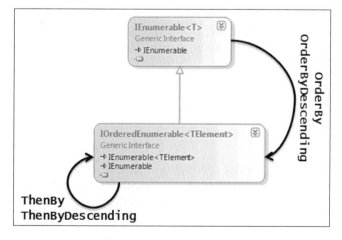

FIGURE 19.22   OrderBy and ThenBy query operators.

Query Pattern

The query expression's translation for an orderby clause with one or more ordering key selector expressions was shown in the preceding section. Let's formalize it just as we did for both the select and where clauses before, as shown in Figure 19.23. Again, lambda expressions are used as the argument to the query operator methods that get called. For descending orderings, the corresponding method with the Descending suffix is used.

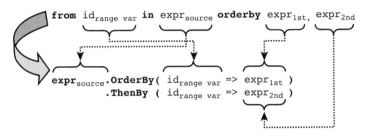

FIGURE 19.23 Translation of the orderby clause.

The number of n-ary orderings is unbounded and simply results in more ThenBy calls being added to the chain of method invocations.

Custom Orderings

The concept of ordering is formalized by means of the IComparer<T> interface that you can find in the System.Collections.Generic namespace. In some cases, it makes sense to override the default ordering behavior by implementing IComparer<T> with specialized comparison semantics.

The OrderBy and ThenBy methods (and their descending variants) provide overloads that accept an IComparer<TKey> object, where TKey stands for the key type that was used for the key selector expression's result.

```
public static IOrderedEnumerable<TSource> OrderBy<TSource, TKey>(
    this IEnumerable<TSource> source, Func<TSource, TKey> keySelector,
    IComparer<TKey> comparer
);
```

There's no query expression syntax for this method overload because it's deemed for quite specialized use, so you'll have to use method invocation syntax to use this.

QUERY SYNTAX = ALL OR NOTHING?

Some people believe query syntax is an all-or-nothing thing. This is not true. For example:

```
from product in products.OrderBy(p => p.Price) select product.Name
(from p in products where p.IsInStock select p).OrderBy(p => p.Price)
```

Query expressions are (and consist of) just expressions.

Grouping Using the group by Clause

Often data can be grouped into buckets based on certain criteria. For example, products may be grouped by category, and people may be grouped by age range (for example, based on modulo 10 division of the age). The group by clause enables you to group objects by a key, resulting in a sequence of IGrouping objects.

Partitioning

The grouping query operator is best looked at as a partitioning mechanism where items from the source sequence are grouped by matching key values. This key gets computed for all elements in the source sequence to realize this grouping. For example, we could partition a sequence of integer numbers by their remainder after division by, say, three. To put it in terms of grouping vocabulary, the *key* computed for every element is this remainder value. All elements that have the same computed key value end up in the same group: the elements that are divisible by three, the ones with a remainder of one, and the ones with a remainder of two. This is shown in Figure 19.24.

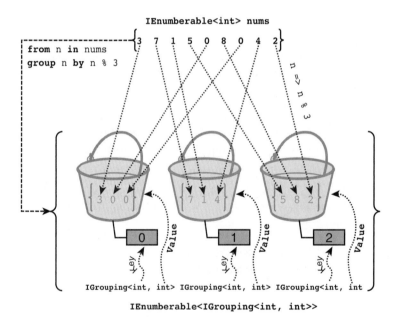

FIGURE 19.24   Partitioning of an input sequence by a grouping key.

In this example, starting from an input sequence of integer numbers, we get back a new sequence of groups that associate a key value (an integer representing the modulo three division result) with a sequence of values that belong to that group. Such a grouping is represented by an IGrouping<TKey, TValue> generic object:

```
public interface IGrouping<out TKey, out TElement> : IEnumerable<TElement> {
    TKey Key { get; }
}
```

Based on the definition shown here, let's revisit this definition of a group: The Key property, of generic parameter type TKey, indicates the key value that all the group's elements have in common. In our example, we have grouping objects with key type Int32 and values of 0, 1, and 2. Each group is a container for elements belonging to that group, as represented by the IEnumerable<TElement> interface implementation, where TElement is the generic parameter type used for the element type.

Another way to look at this is by creating a table that associates a key value with all the values that have that key in common. Each row here represents a group, which is represented by a Key property and is a sequence of its own, producing the elements in the group:

Key	Values
0	3, 0, 0
1	7, 1, 4
2	5, 8, 2

The running example can be written in LINQ syntax as follows:

```
var byMod3 = from n in new [] { 3, 7, 1, 5, 0, 8, 0, 4, 2 }
             group n by n % 3;

foreach (var remainderGroup in byMod3) {
    Console.WriteLine("Remainder = " + remainderGroup.Key);
    foreach (var number in remainderGroup) {
        Console.WriteLine("   " + number);
    }
}
```

It's good to play the type inference analysis by yourself to get an idea of how this works. Start by the source of the query, an array of integer numbers, which clearly is an IEnumerable<int>. The grouping clause now declares the key to be computed for all of those source elements (that is, n % 3). With n representing a source element of type int, the remainder after division by three, acting as the key, will also be an integer value. This results in the following type for byMod3:

```
IEnumerable<IGrouping<int, int>> byMod3 = ...;
```

You gotta love type inference, don't you? Figure 19.25 shows rich type inference.

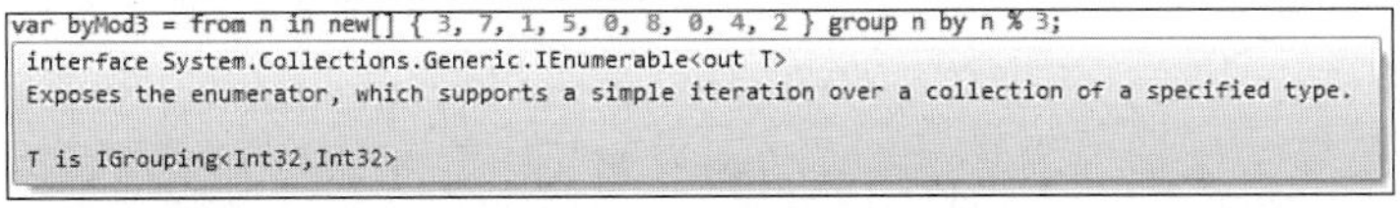

```
var byMod3 = from n in new[] { 3, 7, 1, 5, 0, 8, 0, 4, 2 } group n by n % 3;
interface System.Collections.Generic.IEnumerable<out T>
Exposes the enumerator, which supports a simple iteration over a collection of a specified type.

T is IGrouping<Int32,Int32>
```

FIGURE 19.25   Inferring the result type of a grouping operation.

What we got back is an enumerable where each element is a grouping that maps a key onto a set of values. Substituting the type parameters in the generic type definition for IGrouping results in the following:

```
public interface IGrouping</* TKey */ int, /* TElement */ int>
    : IEnumerable</* TElement */ int> {
    /* TKey */ int Key { get; }
}
```

So the result of the grouping is an enumerable sequence of such objects. The outer loop iterates over all the groups, each of which has a Key property available. Because groups can iterate over their contained elements, the inner loop can do so to print the elements in each group. Doing the type inference exercise a bit further results in the following explicitly typed code:

```
List<int> numbers = new List<int> { 1, 2, 3, 4, 5 };


IEnumerable<IGrouping<int, int>> byMod3 = from n in numbers
                                          group n by n % 3;

foreach (IGrouping<int, int> remainderGroup in byMod3) {
    Console.WriteLine("Remainder = " + remainderGroup.Key);
    foreach (int number in remainderGroup)
        Console.WriteLine("   " + number);
}
```

Figure 19.26 shows how these types flow a bit more schematically. Intuitively, all you need to know is that a foreach loop "unpacks" an IEnumerable<T> into a loop variable of type T.

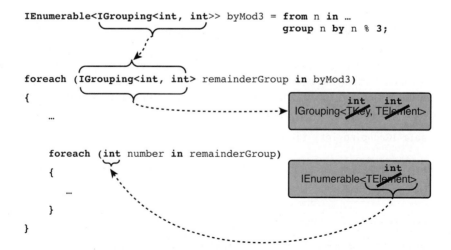

FIGURE 19.26   Type inference for foreach loops over sequences of groupings.

So far, key and element types have been the same, but shortly we'll see examples where this is no longer the case.

Computed Keys

Because the grouping key expression is just that, an expression, you can write anything in there as long as it respects the typing restrictions that are mandated by the GroupBy method signature. That is, if the key selector's parameter, representing an element from the input sequence, is used, its type has to be respected. Other than that, any sort of expression can be used (for example, selecting a property or calling a method).

For example, given all products, we might want to group those based on the first letter of the product name:

```
var byFirstLetterOfName = from product in products
                      group product by product.Name[0];
```

Here we're using an indexer expression to select the key value to group by. In this case, products Chai and Chang will end up in the same group, with 'C' as their shared key. More complex expressions can be built of course, possibly capturing an outer variable:

```
var byNthLetterOfName = from product in products
                    group product by product.Name[n] - 'a';
```

Now we're not only capturing an outer variable n (that could be a method parameter or so as well), but we're also using a subtraction to select the position of the letter in the alphabet. For example, with n equal to 1, both Chai and Chang will end up in the same group with the key being 'h', 'a', which equals 7. This example is a bit contrived and has a problem with possible index out-of-range exceptions occurring during grouping key computation. It merely illustrates the point that you can compute grouping keys with any of the expression forms supported by the language.

Simple Key Selectors

Much more common is to group by a *simple key*, typically corresponding to a single column in a table or a single property (or field) on an object. For example, assuming every product in our running example has a Category property, we could group all the products by their categories as follows:

```
var byCategory = from product in products
              group product by product.Category;
```

The result of this will be an enumerable containing a group for beverages, one for food items, and so on. In LINQ to SQL or in other LINQ providers targeting a relational database, this will typically result in the use of a groupby construct in the SQL language.

Compound Keys

Sometimes it makes sense to group by a combination of multiple keys. For example, products could be grouped by their categories and suppliers, resulting in groups for every combination of a category and a supplier that occurs in the products table. The way to put the multiple keys together into a *compound key* is by using an anonymous type, which really is just another sort of expression. Assume that every `Product` has both a `Category` and `Supplier` property so that we can write the following grouping query expression:

```
var byCategoryAndSupplier = from product in products
                       group product by new { product.Category,
                                              product.Supplier};
```

To make things a bit simpler for illustration purposes, let's create a simple in-memory table of employees, each having an `ID`, `Name`, and `Age` property. We want to group them by `Name` and `Age` so that we can throw a party for all employees with the same name and age:

```
var personnel = new[] {
    new { ID = 1, First = "Bart", Age = 26 },
    new { ID = 2, First = "John", Age = 62 },
    new { ID = 3, First = "Mike", Age = 24 },
    new { ID = 4, First = "John", Age = 53 },
    new { ID = 5, First = "Bart", Age = 26 },
    new { ID = 6, First = "Eric", Age = 26 },
    new { ID = 7, First = "John", Age = 62 },
    new { ID = 8, First = "Eric", Age = 30 },
    new { ID = 9, First = "Eric", Age = 26 },
};

var byNameAndAge = from employee in personnel
               group employee by new { employee.First,
                                       employee.Age   };

foreach (var group in byNameAndAge) {
    Console.Write(group.Key + ":  ");
    foreach (var employee in group)
        Console.Write(employee.ID + " ");
    Console.WriteLine();
}
```

This will print the following:

```
{ First = Bart, Age = 26 }:  1 5
{ First = John, Age = 62 }:  2 7
{ First = Mike, Age = 24 }:  3
{ First = John, Age = 53 }:  4
{ First = Eric, Age = 26 }:  6 9
{ First = Eric, Age = 30 }:  8
```

To understand how this works, it's advisable to take a look behind the scenes. During the query's execution, instances of the anonymous type representing the compound key with name and age will be created. To create a grouping, a data structure has to be maintained that maps key values onto all objects that share that key.

You will recall a good candidate collection type for this from our discussion about generics, namely a Dictionary<TKey, TValue>. Here, the type parameter for the key will become the anonymous type, and the value will be some collection of objects that share that key. For this to work, we should be able to check keys for equality, and to make the internal dictionary storage perform well, a good hash code is advisable. So how does this work for the anonymous type we're using for our compound key?

The short answer is that anonymous types, which are classes generated by the compiler based on the structure you specified, override the methods Equals, GetHashCode, and ToString, defined on System.Object. In the output, we've already seen what the ToString method looks like as it dumps the name-value pairs for properties:

```
// Prints { First = Bart, Age = 26 }
Console.WriteLine(new { First = "Bart", Age = 26 });
```

Figure 19.27 shows the presence of those overridden methods through ILDASM. You are invited to inspect those method implementations using more appropriate tools, such as .NET Reflector, to see how the equality check and hash code computation are done. In short, Equals uses the default equality comparer on the underlying data (in this case, both the Age integer and First string), and GetHashCode computes and combines the hash codes for the underlying data fields, mixing in a few (seemingly magical) constant numbers to ensure good hash code properties.

FIGURE 19.27   Overrides for Equals, GetHashCode, and ToString.

To conclude this example's discussion, take a look at the excessive use of type inference for local variables. Use of compound keys gives rise to anonymous types, which, as the name implies, cannot be referred to by name. Implicitly typed local variables have to be used in such a scenario, both to refer to the result and to loop over the groups:

```
var personnel = new[] {
    new { ID = 1, First = "Bart", Age = 26 },
    ...
};

var byNameAndAge = from employee in personnel
                   group employee by new { employee.First,
                                           employee.Age    };
```

Furthermore, we used an implicitly typed array containing anonymous types as the source, just for illustration purposes. It's more likely you'll have a named type for the employee objects in the personnel table. However, by using anonymous types all over the place in this example, you are in a unique position to test the understanding of grouping behavior with regard to types. As usual, the editor will guide us through this exploratory exercise.

First, let's take a look at the type inferred for the personnel array, as shown in Figure 19.28. Because the elements are instances of the same anonymous type, the type is inferred to be an array of that anonymous type.

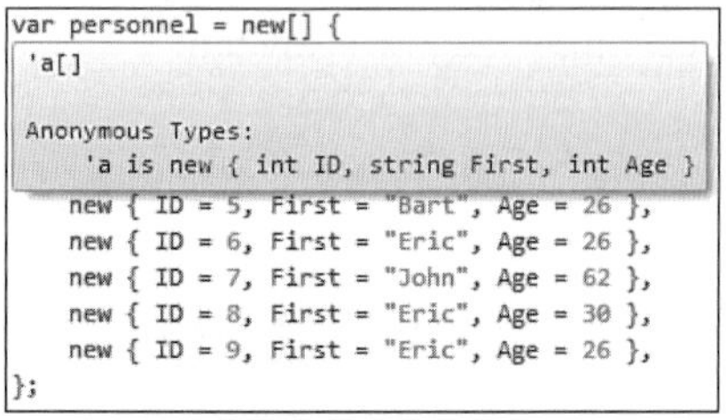

FIGURE 19.28   An implicitly typed array of anonymous type elements.

Given that the array's elements are of this anonymous type, we can already infer a part of the GroupBy resulting object's type:

```
public static IEnumerable<IGrouping<TKey, TSource>> GroupBy<TSource, TKey>(
    this IEnumerable<TSource> source, Func<TSource, TKey> keySelector);
```

Here, TSource ought to be the anonymous type used for the source elements (that is, the one shown in Figure 19.28). The key selector function takes in one of those objects and maps it onto the compound key object we've specified using another anonymous type. This allows us to infer the TKey generic type parameter. And finally, from this we can infer the resulting type of the GroupBy operation our LINQ query expression translated into. Figure 19.29 shows the resulting type.

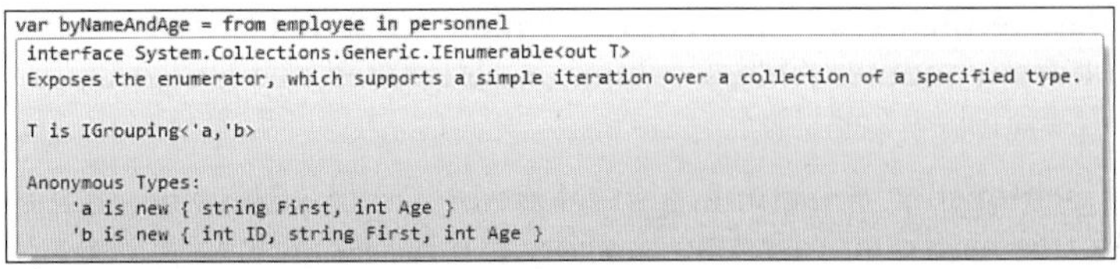

var byNameAndAge = from employee in personnel
interface System.Collections.Generic.IEnumerable<out T>
Exposes the enumerator, which supports a simple iteration over a collection of a specified type.
T is IGrouping<'a,'b>
Anonymous Types:
'a is new { string First, int Age }
'b is new { int ID, string First, int Age }

FIGURE 19.29 Resulting type from a `GroupBy` operation with a compound key.

Here, `'a` stands for the grouping's key type, which contains a `First` and `Age` property, and `'b` is exactly the same type as the one used for our source collection's elements.

Query Pattern

The `group by` clause we've seen so far can be summarized in terms of its translation that happens behind the scenes. As usual, LINQ query expression syntax turns into method calls underneath, and that's no different for `group by`. Figure 19.30 shows how this is achieved for `group by`.

from id_range in expr_source group id_range by expr_groupKey
expr_source.GroupBy(id_range => expr_groupKey)

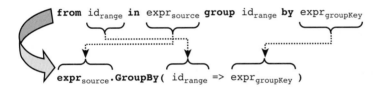

FIGURE 19.30 Query pattern translation for `group by` clause.

MORE COMPLEX GROUPING CLAUSES

The identifier specified right after the `group` and before the `by` keyword does not have to be the same as one of the range identifiers. For example, you can write things like this:

```
from product in products
group product.Price by product.Category
```

This will result in groups with a category as the key and prices inside each of the resulting groups. The translation for this form uses a different `GroupBy` overload that takes in an additional lambda expression for the "element selector."

Joining Using the `join` Clause

Data is often part of a bigger picture with many interrelated data sources, as seen in relational databases. In such a world, queries often target multiple data sources simultaneously, by joining those on a certain criterion. In relational database technologies, this is usually realized by giving data records a unique identifier, which is referred to as a *primary key*. To refer to a data record from another table, a column is designated as a *foreign key* referring to the related table's primary key.

Figure 19.31 shows such a relationship, sometimes also referred to as an *association*, in the context of LINQ to SQL. In this particular case, one category can have many products associated with it, hence the OneToMany cardinality. To go from a Product to its Category, the Parent Property is set to Category. In the opposite direction, you can get the products in a given category through the Child Property named Products. At the bottom of the Properties window, the underlying relationship is shown:

```
Category.CategoryID -> Product.CategoryID
```

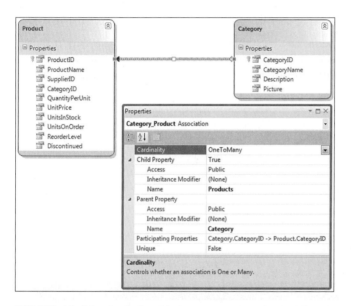

FIGURE 19.31   A relationship between two tables in LINQ to SQL.

On the left, we see the primary key that uniquely identifies a category using an ID, which is referred to on the right as a foreign key in the Product table.

Because we're currently focusing on LINQ to Objects to explain query operators and the various clauses in the query expression syntax, we leave LINQ to SQL out of the picture for the time being and cook up an example using in-memory data.

The Base Class Library (BCL) is full of interesting sources of data, and members that return a generic or nongeneric IEnumerable object are usable for querying. One such place is in the System.Diagnostic's Process class:

```
Process[] processes = Process.GetProcesses();
```

Using this method, we can get information about all the processes currently running on the machine. For example, using the query clauses we already know, we can retrieve an ordered sequence of top memory-consuming processes:

```
const int MB = 1024 * 1024;
var heavyMemoryUsers = (from p in Process.GetProcesses()
                        where p.WorkingSet64 > 100 * MB
                        orderby p.WorkingSet64 descending
                        select new { Name = p.ProcessName,
                                     Memory = p.WorkingSet64 / MB }
                       ).Take(10);

foreach (var p in heavyMemoryUsers)
    Console.WriteLine(p);
```

The call to `Take(10)` simply retrieves the first 10 objects of the query result. You'll see this and similar standard query operators in Chapter 20. On my machine, the preceding query prints the following:

```
{ Name = devenv, Memory = 552 }
{ Name = devenv, Memory = 326 }
{ Name = iexplore, Memory = 279 }
{ Name = devenv, Memory = 230 }
{ Name = devenv, Memory = 229 }
{ Name = dwm, Memory = 199 }
{ Name = iexplore, Memory = 193 }
{ Name = sqlservr, Memory = 190 }
{ Name = svchost, Memory = 173 }
{ Name = WINWORD, Memory = 169 }
```

Although this is nice, it would be nicer to have friendly names for the processes. To realize this, we can create a separate collection that maps process names on descriptions:

```
var processDescriptions = new [] {
    new { Name = "devenv", Description = "Microsoft Visual Studio" },
    new { Name = "dwm", Description = "Desktop Window Manager" },
    new { Name = "iexplore", Description = "Windows Internet Explorer" },
    new { Name = "sqlservr", Description = "Microsoft SQL Server" },
    new { Name = "svchost", Description = "Service Host" },
    new { Name = "WINWORD", Description = "Microsoft Office Word" }
};
```

Now both the collection with `Process` objects and the descriptions have something in common: the process name. What remains to be done now is to join both sources based on the equality of a *key* they have in common. This is shown in Figure 19.32.

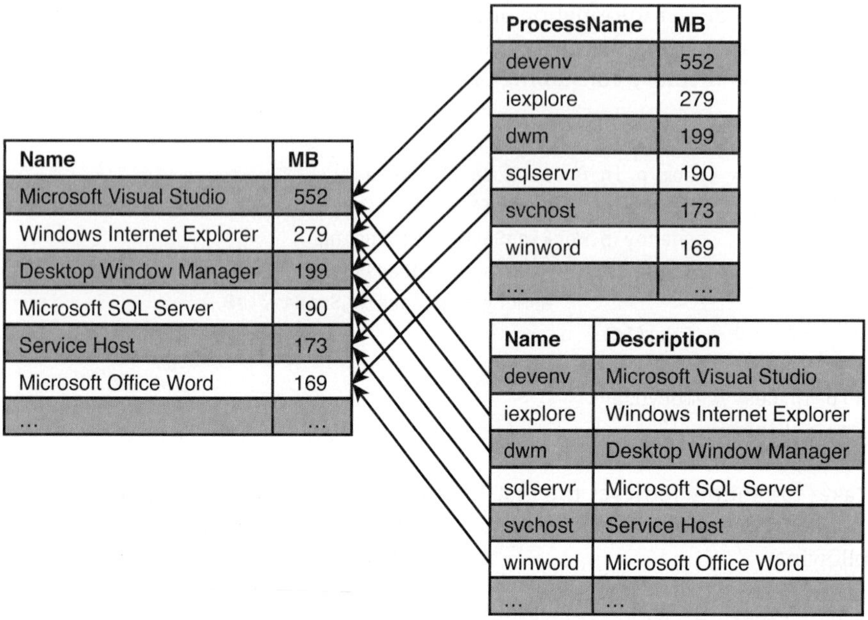

ProcessName	MB
devenv	552
iexplore	279
dwm	199
sqlservr	190
svchost	173
winword	169
...	...

Name	MB
Microsoft Visual Studio	552
Windows Internet Explorer	279
Desktop Window Manager	199
Microsoft SQL Server	190
Service Host	173
Microsoft Office Word	169
...	...

Name	Description
devenv	Microsoft Visual Studio
iexplore	Windows Internet Explorer
dwm	Desktop Window Manager
sqlservr	Microsoft SQL Server
svchost	Service Host
winword	Microsoft Office Word
...	...

FIGURE 19.32   Joining two data sources based on a common key.

To join those two (in-memory) data sources for our example, we can use the following query expression:

```
const int MB = 1024 * 1024;
var heavyMemoryUsers = (from p in Process.GetProcesses()
                        join d in processDescriptions on      p.ProcessName
                                                        equals d.Name
                        where p.WorkingSet64 > 100 * MB
                        orderby p.WorkingSet64 descending
                        select new { Name = d.Description,
                                     Memory = p.WorkingSet64 / MB }
                       ).Take(10);

foreach (var p in heavyMemoryUsers)
    Console.WriteLine(p);
```

Besides the use of the join clause to select a second source for use in the query, notice the use of range identifier d in the select clause. Once the join has been established, you can use both data sources anywhere in the query "downstream." This is similar to the use of multiple from clauses to select more than one data source, though the join clause differs in its semantics. That's what the on ... equals ... portion is responsible for, used to extract a key from both sources to match for equality.

In this particular example, we're stating that the ProcessName as it appears in the first data source, of Process objects, corresponds to the Name property in our descriptions collection used as the second data source. Once we've established this relationship, we continue with filtering operations and finally project the description of the process and the memory it consumes in the select clause.

The use of the join clause doesn't need to be paired with the from clauses that appear at the top of the query expression. We could equally well have written the following:

```
var heavyMemoryUsers = (from p in Process.GetProcesses()
                        where p.WorkingSet64 > 100 * MB
                        orderby p.WorkingSet64 descending
                        join d in processDescriptions on        p.ProcessName
                                                        equals d.Name
                        select new { Name = d.Description,
                                     Memory = p.WorkingSet64 / MB }
                       ).Take(10);
```

For LINQ to Objects scenarios, which execute in memory, reordering query operations can be beneficial from an optimization point of view. For example, instead of ordering a bunch of objects first and then filtering out only a fraction of them, you're better off filtering the first, using where, before performing an ordering operation using orderby. Similarly, joining a filtered number of objects will be less expensive than joining all objects and then filtering out specific ones.

OPTIMIZE WITH CARE AND BEWARE OF UNDESIRABLE SIDE EFFECTS

Although optimizations such as swapping filtering and sorting seem very reasonable, you should pay lots of attention while doing so. You most certainly don't want to change the semantics of your query expression by reordering operations.

The nice thing about declarative queries is that the runtime can also carry out certain optimizations on your behalf, though this is rather limited for LINQ to Objects. One of the reasons has to do with side effects that can occur in parts of the query expression:

```
from x in xs // 3, 4, 2, 1
orderby x
where x.IsEvenAndPrint() ...
```

In the preceding code, the user wrote an IsEvenAndPrint (extension) method that will check whether a number is even but will also print to the screen. If the relative order of the orderby and where operations were to be swapped by the runtime, different messages would be printed to the screen. The original query would print "1,2,3,4," whereas the optimized query (with the filter first) would print "3,4,2,1."

As a rule of thumb, avoid side effects anywhere in a query expression. They tend to be very difficult to reason about in a lazily evaluated context.

The new more user-friendly output is shown here:

```
{ Name = Microsoft Visual Studio, Memory = 552 }
{ Name = Microsoft Visual Studio, Memory = 326 }
{ Name = Windows Internet Explorer, Memory = 279 }
{ Name = Microsoft Visual Studio, Memory = 230 }
{ Name = Microsoft Visual Studio, Memory = 229 }
{ Name = Desktop Window Manager, Memory = 199 }
{ Name = Windows Internet Explorer, Memory = 193 }
{ Name = Microsoft SQL Server, Memory = 190 }
{ Name = Service Host, Memory = 173 }
{ Name = Microsoft Office Word, Memory = 169 }
```

Query Pattern

Depending on the shape of the query, the `join` clause is translated into a specific query operator method call. For an elaborate explanation of all possible translations, refer to the C# language specification. However, to give you a feeling about the kind of translation we're talking about, Figure 19.33 sketches the translation of a `join` clause immediately followed by a `select` clause.

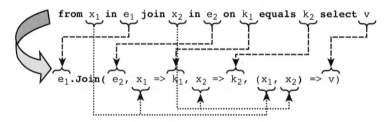

FIGURE 19.33   Query pattern translation for `join` clause.

The `select` clause was eaten by the `Join` method call and ended up in the last lambda expression parameter. This effectively eliminates the range identifiers that are involved in the query expression. However, if query expression clauses other than `select` follow the `join` clause, the range identifiers cannot be eliminated just yet:

```
var query = from p in Process.GetProcesses()
            join d in processDescriptions on p.ProcessName equals d.Name
            where p.WorkingSet64 > 100 * MB
            orderby p.WorkingSet64 descending
            select new { Name = d.Description, Memory = p.WorkingSet64 / MB };
```

Here, p and d are both continued to be used in downstream query operators like `where`, `orderby`, and `select`. When talking about the `let` clause, we see the technique carried out by the compiler to deal with multiple range identifiers, as seen in the preceding example.

Continuing a Query Expression Using the `into` Clause

Although most query expression clauses can be followed by others immediately, there are a few notable exceptions. In particular, `select` and `group by` end a query expression because of their *projective* characteristic. For example:

```
var query = from product in products
            select new { product.Name, product.Price };
```

Once the projection has happened, the query expression produces objects of the type used in the `select` clause. In this particular example, that's an anonymous type with two properties: `Name` and `Price`. At this point, we don't have an identifier anymore to refer to those objects: If `product` would still be "in scope," we could get access to properties other than the ones that have been projected out. Or to put it another way, once there's been a projection, only the projected data should be accessible downstream.

A similar scenario exists with the use of `group by`. Once a grouping has happened, the original objects have been put in groups and are not directly accessible anymore. For example, consider the following:

```
var query = from product in products
            group product by product.Category;
```

There's no point in referring to the product range identifier anymore after the grouping has occurred because they've been canned in separate groups already. What would it mean to refer to `product` after the grouping? Any product in any of the groups? If that were to be the case, you could equally well have written the additional query clause, referring to `product`, before you did the grouping. In summary, once a grouping has been made, the only things it makes sense to refer to are the groups themselves.

Sometimes you do want to continue a query expression after a projection or grouping has occurred, referring to the objects or the groups, respectively. That's where the `into` clause comes into play.

Continuation After Projection

Projection using a `select` clause has the interesting property of restricting the number of properties that are retained (vertical partitioning), but it has other useful properties too. It can alias properties by more friendly names, through the use of an anonymous type, and can transform data. Let's focus on the former aliasing example:

```
var query = from product in products
            select new { Name = product.ProductName, Price = product.UnitPrice };
```

Here, we're faced with `Product` objects given to us, but with quite ugly property names, such as `ProductName` and `UnitPrice`. To make things easier on the eye, we would like to alias those by more friendly names like `Name` and `Price`. A projection can do so by making use of an anonymous type defined on the fly. At the same time, we got rid of the properties we're not interested in querying on.

Given this new shape of data, we want to start writing query expressions over it. One way to do so is by use of an intermediate query expression. For example:

```
var products2 = from product in products
                select new { Name = product.ProductName,
                             Price = product.UnitPrice };
```

Here, products2 is of type IEnumerable<T>, where T stands for the anonymous type used in the projection. And where an enumerable sequence is available, you can use query expressions:

```
var expensiveProducts = from product in products2
                        where product.Price > 100m
                        select product;
```

Here, the range identifier product refers to the objects in products2, which are of the anonymous type created in the first query expression. You can clearly see this (as shown in Figure 19.34) in the code editor when writing the where clause.

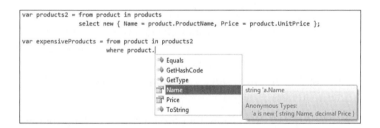

FIGURE 19.34   Chaining query expressions.

BEWARE OF LAZY EVALUATION

Keep in mind that LINQ queries are lazily evaluated; this will become much clearer once we see how various LINQ providers work.

In the preceding example, products2 hasn't been evaluated yet: only when someone starts enumerating products2 will its evaluation start to happen. In this particular example, it will be the expensiveProducts query that "pulls data out of" products2, which in its turn pulls things out of products. As a result, enumerating over the expensiveProduct query expression will cause products2 to evaluate.

This cascading effect of query expression evaluation might be surprising at first but is essential to the way LINQ works. If this weren't the case, lots of intermediate storage would be required, possibly for things that will never be asked for. As an example, consider that products2 would contain thousands of objects, while the expensiveProducts query retains only a few tens of those. If products2 were to be persisted in memory as an intermediate query result, lots of storage space is wasted for no good reason.

Having to create intermediate query expressions to declare the query we've seen before seems unnecessary. And indeed, using the into clause, this can be simplified:

```
var expensiveProducts = from product in products
                        select new { Name = product.ProductName,
                                     Price = product.UnitPrice } into product
                        where product.Price > 100m
                        select product;
```

Figure 19.35 shows the look and feel when writing this query expression in the code editor, where the new product identifier clearly refers to the anonymous typed object created in the projection clause upstream.

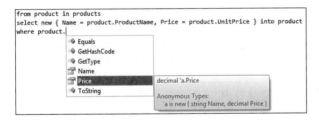

FIGURE 19.35   The new range identifier refers to objects produced by the select clause.

Here, the into clause specifies a new range identifier used to represent the objects that occur in the sequence to the left of it. We could be using a new range identifier or reuse an existing one, as we're doing here. Think about it just like you think about scopes for variables anywhere else in the language: The innermost product identifier hides the outer one, as shown in Figure 19.36.

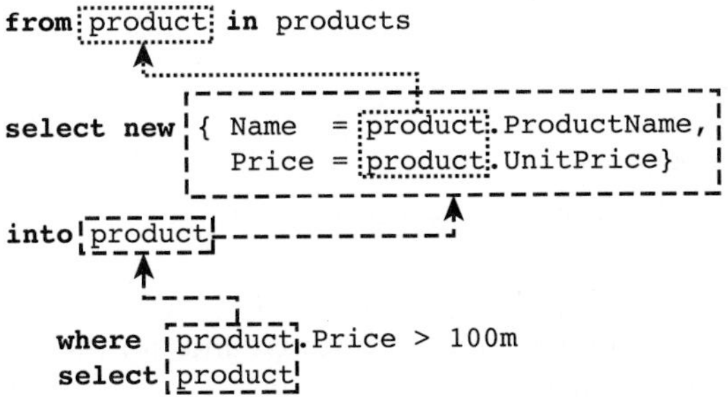

```
from product in products

select new { Name  = product.ProductName,
             Price = product.UnitPrice}

into product

     where product.Price > 100m
     select product
```

FIGURE 19.36   Use of into after a projection.

It should come as no surprise that the into clause is based on nested query expressions, just like we would do it manually by introducing our own intermediate expression. Figure 19.37 illustrates the translation carried out by the compiler when using the into clause.

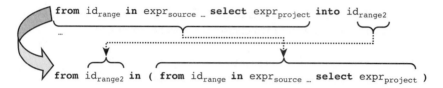

FIGURE 19.37   Translation of the into clause.

Continuation After Grouping

Grouping is often just the start of a more complex data analysis task. For example, if you're asked to create sales statistics for products on a per-category basis, grouping will be your friend. Similarly, to compute the average price of a product on a per-supplier basis, grouping is the logical first step to take.

Once you have a sequence of the available groups, you need to take it one step further, expressing operations on each of the created groups. To do so, you want to continue the query just as we've done for projection. To create a bit of a variety in the examples given, let's consider reflection information this time. Although we discuss reflection in more detail in Chapter 21, "Reflection," the essence is simple: Using reflection, you can get information about types at runtime:

```
typeof(Enumerable).GetMethods()
```

The preceding expression returns an array of MethodInfo objects describing the methods available on the Enumerable type, which lives in System.Linq. It's here all the LINQ to Objects query operators are defined as methods, as detailed in Chapter 20. Arrays are enumerable, and therefore we can write a LINQ query over them.

Because lots of query operator methods have overloads, the GetMethods call will return different MethodInfo objects with the same name, one for each overload. For example, there will be multiple entries for Where methods, corresponding to those overloads:

```
public static IEnumerable<TSource> Where<TSource>(
    this IEnumerable<TSource> source, Func<TSource, bool> predicate);
public static IEnumerable<TSource> Where<TSource>(
    this IEnumerable<TSource> source, Func<TSource, int, bool> predicate);
```

We discuss the meaning of the second overload when talking about the offering of query operators in more detail, but in short, the int parameter to the predicate stands for the index of the object being filtered in the input sequence.

Now we want to define a query over the LINQ to Objects methods, showing distinct method names together with the number of overloads they have. An obvious first step is to group them by name:

```
var query = from m in typeof(Enumerable).GetMethods()
            group m by m.Name;
```

As you know, this returns an IEnumerable<IGrouping<TKey, TValue>> object where the generic TKey type parameter will be substituted for string (because we group by the method's Name property), and TSource will correspond to MethodInfo, the type of the objects in the input sequence.

Without the into clause, our joyride would end here because we don't have an identifier to refer to each of the resulting group objects. To dump the number of overloads, we could do something like this:

```
var queryOperators = from m in typeof(Enumerable).GetMethods()
                     group m by m.Name;

foreach (var queryOperator in queryOperators) {
    int n = 0;
    foreach (var overload in queryOperator)
        n++;
    Console.WriteLine("{0} has {1} overload(s)", queryOperator.Key, n);
}
```

This gets into a quite imperative style of coding, which feels unnatural in the world of query expressions and LINQ. Counting the number of elements in a sequence is one aggregation operator that's natively supported by the query operators, allowing us to simplify the above as follows:

```
var queryOperators = from m in typeof(Enumerable).GetMethods()
                     group m by m.Name;

foreach (var queryOperator in queryOperators) {
    int n = queryOperator.Count();
    Console.WriteLine("{0} has {1} overload(s)", queryOperator.Key, n);
}
```

But we can do better. What about expressing the Count() operator call inside the query expression itself? To do so, we need to continue the existing query using into:

```
var queryOperators = from m in typeof(Enumerable).GetMethods()
                     group m by m.Name into queryOperator
                     select new { Name = queryOperator.Key,
                                  Overloads = queryOperator.Count() };
```

```
foreach (var queryOperator in queryOperators) {
    Console.WriteLine("{0} has {1} overload(s)", queryOperator.Name,
                                                 queryOperator.Overloads);
}
```

Here, the new `queryOperator` range identifier stands for the groups created for each of the operator methods (that is, `IGrouping<string, MethodInfo>` objects). Subsequently, we apply a projection to rename the `IGrouping`'s `Key` property to `Name` and to count the number of overloads using the `Count()` method, exposed through property `Overloads`. Figure 19.38 shows such a grouping object through the eyes of IntelliSense.

```
var queryOperators =
    from m in typeof(Enumerable).GetMethods()
    group m by m.Name into queryOperator
    select new {
        Name = queryOperator.Key,
        Overloads = queryOperator.Coun|
                  (range variable) IGrouping<string,System.Reflection.MethodInfo> queryOperator
                        Count<>
                        LongCount<>
```

FIGURE 19.38   The new range identifier represents a grouping object.

The reason the `Count()` method, which is defined as an extension on `IEnumerable<T>`, is available on the grouping object is because, as we've seen, every `IGrouping<K, T>` object implements `IEnumerable<T>`. This allows arbitrary nesting of query expressions over groups, too.

One of the most common operations carried out on grouping objects is aggregation, of which `Count` is just one. Other popular aggregation operators include `Min`, `Max`, `Sum`, and `Average`:

```
var categoryStats = from product in products
                    group product by product.Category into category
                    select new { Category = category.Key,
                                 AvgPrice = category.Average(p => p.Price) };
```

The `Average` aggregation extension method takes in a lambda expression to map the objects in the source on the value to compute the average over. Because the group maps a category onto the products in that category, `Average` will iterate over all the products in each of the groups, extracting the `Price` to compute the average for. As a result, the preceding query produces an `IEnumerable<T>` with `T` the anonymous type containing the category and the average price across all products in the category. Other aggregation operators are used in a similar fashion.

Because grouping objects are also sequences over their contained elements, query operators can also be used within groups (for example, using a nested query):

```
var perCategory = from product in products
                  group product by product.Category into category
                  select new { Category = category.Key,
                               Products = from p in category
                                          orderby p.Price descending
                                          select new { p.Name, p.Price } };
```

This produces a sequence of anonymous typed objects with a `Category` as well as a `Products` property of type `IEnumerable<Product>`.

Bindings with the `let` Clause

Often, you'll find it handy to carry out intermediate computations within a query expression, binding the result to an identifier within the query expression. An example is worth a thousand words:

```
var res = from i in Enumerable.Range(0, 10)
          let square = i * i
          where square % 2 == 0
          let cube = i * square
          let stars = new string('*', i)
          select new { Stars = stars, Cube = cube };
```

Starting from the source selection, we get a sequence of integral numbers 0 through 9 (the parameter `10` indicates the count) from the `Range` method on `Enumerable`. Now we're asked to compute the square of the number, filter out even square values, compute the cube, and so on.

In a typical imperative style, you would write this with intermediate variables containing the results of partial computations. Thanks to the `let` clause, you can do a similar thing in the context of a query expression. This proves particularly handy if you keep referring to the same computed expression all over the place. Instead of duplicating the computation, it simply gets stored in a `let` binding for future reference.

For example, in the preceding query, `square` is available anywhere downstream in the query expression (ignoring `into` clauses which start a whole new "scope"), including the `where` filter clause that immediately follows it, as well as other `let` bindings and other clauses. If it helps you to think about this in a more imperative style, look at the preceding example as the declarative variant of the following:

```
foreach (int i in Enumerable.Range(0, 10)) {
    int square = i * i;
    if (square % 2 == 0) {
        int cube = i * square;
        string stars = new string('*', i);
        // See further...
```

```
        // yield return new { Stars = stars, Cube = cube }
    }
}
```

The `let` clause in a LINQ query expression is another form of type inference: Based on the expression assigned, the type is inferred. But just as with `var`, the type is statically determined: Anywhere you perform operations on the object bound in a `let` clause, you'll see the compiler knows the type.

Why the use of the `let` keyword and not reusing the `var` keyword? The answer is that both are subtly different. Not from a typing point of view, as we've discussed here, but with regard to assignment. Where `var` is used for a *variable* that can be reassigned, `let` is used for a *binding* of a value to an identifier, which cannot be changed later: Bindings are not variable, and vice versa.

A Peek Behind the Scenes: Transparent Identifiers

Having seen many translation schemes for query expression clauses into query operator methods, you might wonder how the `let` clause can do its work. Ultimately, query expressions boil down to chains of method invocations, with lambda expressions used for the arguments. There are no direct local variables in use, yet with `let` it feels like there should be. How does this work?

The way to think about a LINQ query expression is like a pipeline that transforms an input sequence into an output sequence. All state involved in this transformation needs to flow through that pipeline somehow. Every clause in the query expression represents a discrete step in this transformation. Figure 19.39 shows what state is available in our sample query expression at every intermediate point.

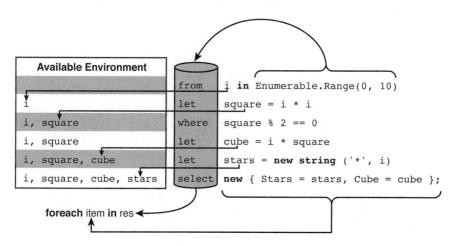

FIGURE 19.39   A query expression as a pipeline with intermediate environments.

Concerning terminology, we refer to all the available identifiers (bounds to a specific well-known static type) as the *environment*. The pipeline model of the query extends this environment whenever a new source is introduced (through from or join) or when a let clause is used. From that point on, the identifier is available later in the pipeline for query operators to refer to it.

Intuitively, you can feel that all the available identifiers and their values need to be passed between query operators, and one way to do so is by using the projection mechanism offered by Select. For example, after the from clause has selected a source, the resulting sequence contains integral values referred to by i. Next, the let clause introduces identifier square, which should be available later. This can be done by wrapping both i and square in an object that's used by the remainder part of the query expression...and so on.

This is precisely what the compiler does on your behalf. It rewrites the query to fit in a pure pipeline-based model of chained query operators, along the following lines:

```
var res = from i in Enumerable.Range(0, 10)
        select new { i, square = i * i } into __x1
        where __x1.square % 2 == 0
        select new { __x1, cube = __x1.i * __x1.square } into __x2
        select new { __x2, stars = new string('*', __x2.__x1.i) } into __x3
        select new { Stars = __x3.stars, Cube = __x3.__x2.cube };
```

Those weird-looking __x1, __x2, and __x3 identifiers are compiler-generated names known as *transparent identifiers*. (In the C# spec, an asterisk is used to denote them.) In essence, anonymous types are used to keep track of the environment, which is extended one identifier at a time. Everywhere a reference to an identifier occurs, the compiler maps it back to a path of property getter calls on those intermediate anonymous objects in a fashion transparent to the user.

EXPERIMENT: INSPECTING TRANSPARENT IDENTIFIERS

To satisfy your technical curiosity, we can call for Reflector's assistance in showing the transparent identifiers. In .NET Reflector, configure the optimization mode to .NET 2.0, through the View, Options dialog under the Disassembler section. Now navigate to the method where you wrote the preceding code and press the spacebar to disassemble it. Now we're seeing C# 3.0 LINQ code through the lens of a C# 2.0 decompiler that doesn't know about lambda expressions, LINQ, or transparent identifiers.

In Figure 19.40 you can clearly see the pipeline model that results from chaining query operators methods together as part of the query expression translation. Also notice the anonymous function syntax wherever lambda expressions were used. In this case, (other than for use in expression trees, explained in Chapter 20 in the section, "Expression Trees"), lambda expressions are semantically equivalent to C# 2.0 anonymous functions.

Feel free to explore the transparent identifier objects more thoroughly on your own; they're just anonymous types generated by the compiler.

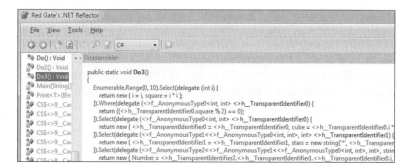

FIGURE 19.40   Pipeline model resulting from chaining query operators methods together as part of the query expression translation.

Summary

With the introduction of Language Integrated Query in .NET 3.5 (and C# 3.0), data access to a wide variety of domains has never been easier. Ranging from in-memory querying over IEnumerable<T> collections, over hierarchical XML data, to all sorts of external database formats, LINQ unifies querying over all those data domains. In doing so, it brings a lot of desirable properties to the table:

▶ Better compile-time checking of queries

▶ Object-oriented mapping of entities being queried

▶ Security advantages (for example, protections against SQL injection attacks)

▶ Rich tooling support, ranging from IntelliSense to mapping tools

▶ Support for extensibility with custom providers

▶ No need to learn a plethora of query languages with obscure syntax

After exploring the various LINQ-capable querying targets and enabling technologies such as LINQ to Objects, LINQ to XML, and LINQ to SQL, we started our study with the language integration portion, focusing on query expression syntax. Covering all the C# 3.0 keywords used in query expressions, we also learned how query expressions are nothing but syntactical sugar on top of other language constructs such as method calls, lambda expressions, and so on.

In the next chapter, we take a look behind the scenes of LINQ. We focus on the query pattern, how LINQ to Objects works using iterators, and how query expressions can be turned into expression trees for runtime translation into domain-specific query languages like SQL.

CHAPTER 20

Language Integrated Query Internals

IN THIS CHAPTER

▶ How LINQ to Objects
  Works 967

▶ Standard Query Operators 990

▶ The Query Pattern 1024

▶ Parallel LINQ 1027

▶ Expression Trees 1036

In the previous chapter, we learned how LINQ unifies the programming experience for querying various domains of data. We learned about the query expression syntax added to C# to formulate rich queries using filters, projections, joins, and so on. But how does LINQ work under the hood? This question is answered in this chapter. First, we look at LINQ to Objects, which uses C# 2.0 iterators to do its job. Next, we cover the set of Standard Query Operators present in the BCL. Finally, exploration of LINQ internals brings us to expression trees and the concept of IQueryable<T> query providers.

How LINQ to Objects Works

So far we've been looking at various query expression clauses that enable us to express queries, no matter that data domain we're targeting. Even though most of our examples assumed in-memory data collections, all those queries would have worked equally well against, say, a relational database.

Because in-memory data is common, it makes sense for us to delve a little deeper into how LINQ support for those data collections is provided. The leads us to a discussion about the IEnumerable and IEnumerator interfaces, iterators, and LINQ to Objects. From this exploration, it will become clear how query expressions are executed *lazily* and what the implications of this execution model are.

IEnumerable<T> and IEnumerator<T> Recap

To set the scene, we need to refresh our knowledge of the IEnumerable<T> interface and its little brother, IEnumerator<T>. The LINQ to Objects standard query operators are implemented as extension methods on the former interface, meaning that any query expressions can target any enumerable sequence. Because collection types implement this interface, this makes LINQ to Objects available for all of those (including arrays).

The IEnumerable<T> interface basically provides the capability to request an enumerator, which acts like a cursor over a sequence of objects of type T. Multiple enumerators can be active simultaneously, each with its own cursor into the underlying sequence:

```
interface IEnumerable<T> {
    IEnumerator<T> GetEnumerator();
}
```

Each enumerator is represented by an instance of an IEnumerator<T> interface, which keeps its own cursor. Because an enumerator may acquire resources to perform the task of enumerating over data (for example, reading data from a network connection), it implements the IDisposable interface, as well:

```
interface IEnumerator<T> : IDisposable {
    bool MoveNext();
    T Current { get; }
    void Reset();
}
```

MoveNext simply advances the cursor to the next object in the sequence, returning whether such an object is available. The get-only Current property provides a way to access the element the enumerator is currently at. Finally, the Reset method is of little use because many sources don't implement it (and neither do iterators, as discussed later).

Notice we've omitted the nongeneric interfaces from the discussion. Those are primarily important for backward-compatibility scenarios with existing code. Because most nongeneric enumerable sequences are homogenous concerning the objects they yield, a common operation is to cast all elements to a specific type. LINQ provides such an operator, called Cast<T>, as we've seen before:

```
var lst = new ArrayList { 1, 2, 3 }; // Old-fashioned List<int>


// Two equivalent ways to provide stronger typing, using Cast<T>.
IEnumerable<int> lstInts1 = lst.Cast<int>();
IEnumerable<int> lstInts2 = from int i in lst select i;
```

The important distinction between IEnumerable<T> and IEnumerator<T> is outlined in Figure 20.1. As you've seen before, the foreach statement is essentially a piece of syntactical sugar on top of both those interfaces:

```
foreach (int num in nums)
    // Do something
```

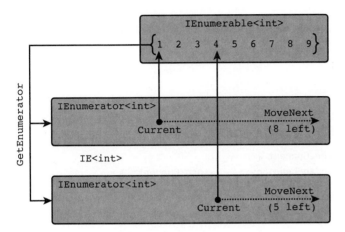

FIGURE 20.1   IEnumerable<T> versus IEnumerator<T>.

The preceding is turned into the following equivalent form:

```
using (var e = nums.GetEnumerator()) {
    while (e.MoveNext()) {
        int num = e.Current;
        // Do something
    }
}
```

An important insight is that the sequence being enumerated doesn't necessarily need to be persisted, as in a collection object. One could just implement the IEnumerator<T> interface manually, with MoveNext causing the computation of objects on the fly, which get exposed through the Current property:

```
class Integers : IEnumerable<int> {
    public IEnumerator<int> GetEnumerator() {
        return new IntegerEnumerator();
    }
```

```csharp
public IEnumerator IEnumerator.GetEnumerator() {
    return /* non-generic archeaology */ GetEnumerator();
}


class IntegerEnumerator : IEnumerator<int> {
    private int _n = 0;

    public bool MoveNext() {
        // There are always more integer values (ignoring overflow).
        return true;
    }

    public int Current {
        get { return _n++; }
    }

    public object IEnumerator.Current {
        get { /* non-generic archeaology */  return Current; }
    }

    public void Reset() {
        // Call GetEnumerator instead to start enumeration all over again.
        throw new NotSupportedException();
    }

    public void Dispose() {}
}
}
```

Enumerating over an Integer instance will go on forever (because MoveNext returns true all the time), until the consumer breaks from the loop. Multiple enumerators can be in flight at the same time, all starting with 0 as the first integer they yield to the consumer.

Writing manual implementations of IEnumerable<T> and IEnumerator<T> is a very powerful pattern but can get quite tedious. For this reason, C# 2.0 introduced *iterators*, which are discussed in the section, "Iterators." The query operator methods in LINQ to Objects are essentially implemented using iterators.

LINQ to Objects Extension Methods

From a language point of view, LINQ is nothing but the syntactical surface provided through so-called query expressions, as we've seen before. Those map onto method calls originating from the various translation schemes that we saw. For example:

```csharp
var query = from x in xs
            where x % 2 == 0
            select x + 1;
```

The preceding turns into the following:

```
xs.Where(x => x % 2 == 0).Select(x => x + 1)
```

This is all there is to LINQ from the language perspective. The methods targeted by the query expressions are collectively known as the *query pattern*. Any type that somehow exposes those methods obeys the query pattern and works with the query expression syntax integrated in languages such as C# and Visual Basic.

For LINQ to Objects, the type representing a data sequence is IEnumerable<T>, where T stands for the type of the individual data objects in the sequence. At the time of the introduction of LINQ, in .NET 3.5, this was an existing interface. Therefore, adding methods such as Where and Select was not an option because all collection types would have to reimplement the interface. Moreover, all those query operators can be expressed on their own, just *using* IEnumerable<T> functionality: If you can enumerate over data, you clearly can filter it, sort it, project it, and whatnot.

All those arguments led to the introduction of *extension methods* as a way to extend the existing IEnumerable<T> interface with query operators. This means all existing collection types simply get LINQ enabled when the extension methods are available through an import of the System.Linq namespace from the System.Core assembly:

```
using System.Linq;
```

You can readily see this from looking at the IntelliSense on any collection type object, which shows all the extension methods, illustrated in Figure 20.2. If you omit the System.Linq namespace, those methods go away.

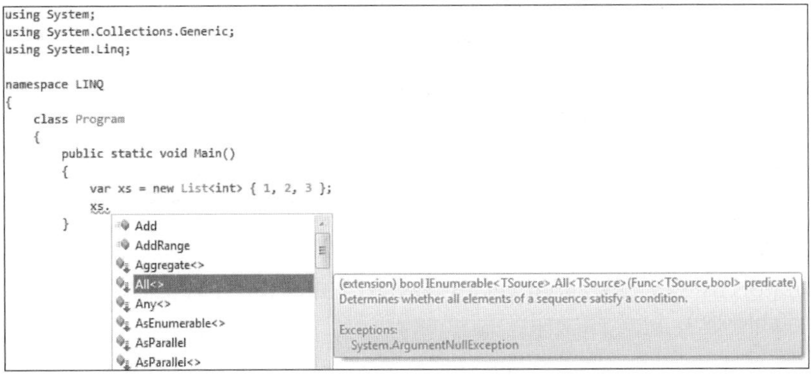

```
using System;
using System.Collections.Generic;
using System.Linq;

namespace LINQ
{
    class Program
    {
        public static void Main()
        {
            var xs = new List<int> { 1, 2, 3 };
            xs.
        }               Add
    }               AddRange
                    Aggregate<>
                    All<>            (extension) bool IEnumerable<TSource>.All<TSource>(Func<TSource,bool> predicate)
                    Any<>            Determines whether all elements of a sequence satisfy a condition.
                    AsEnumerable<>
                    AsParallel       Exceptions:
                    AsParallel<>         System.ArgumentNullException
```

FIGURE 20.2   LINQ to Objects extension methods.

All the extension methods for IEnumerable<T>, collectively referred to as LINQ to Objects, are defined in a static class called Enumerable:

```
namespace System.Linq {
    public static class Enumerable {
        ...
        public static IEnumerable<R> Select<T, R>(this IEnumerable<T> source,
                                        Func<T, R> selector);
        public static IEnumerable<T> Where<T>(this IEnumerable<T> source,
                                        Func<T, bool> predicate);

        ...
    }
}
```

One important thing about those IEnumerable<T> extension methods is the fact they take in generic Func delegate objects for certain parameters. In other words, things such as filter clauses (from where) and selectors (from select) are represented as delegates that can be invoked by the query operator to carry out certain jobs. For example, the Where method will, as you will see when talking about iterators, iterate over the source's objects and evaluate the filter function for all of those using delegate invocation.

Knowing where to look for the extension methods gives you a direct ticket to further exploration of the various query operators, simply by looking at the extension methods defined in the Enumerable static class. Or we can run our grouping example we saw earlier, to display all the Enumerable methods together with the overload count. Adding a few more clauses to only show static methods (because extension methods are always static) and to order operators alphabetically, we get to the following query:

```
var queryOperators = from m in typeof(Enumerable).GetMethods()
                     where m.IsStatic
                     group m by m.Name into queryOperator
                     orderby queryOperator.Key /* Key is method name m.Name */
                     select new { Name = queryOperator.Key,
                                  Overloads = queryOperator.Count() };
foreach (var queryOperator in queryOperators) {
    Console.WriteLine("{0} has {1} overload(s)", queryOperator.Name,
                                          queryOperator.Overloads);
}
```

Viewing LINQ operators using LINQ, can it get any better? Either way, the result of this query is shown in Table 20.1.

TABLE 20.1   LINQ to Objects Query Operator Methods

Method	#	Method	#	Method	#
Aggregate	3	GroupBy	8	SequenceEqual	2
All	1	GroupJoin	2	Single	2
Any	2	Intersect	2	SingleOrDefault	2

TABLE 20.1   LINQ to Objects Query Operator Methods

Method	#	Method	#	Method	#
AsEnumerable	1	Join	2	Skip	1
Average	20	Last	2	SkipWhile	2
Cast	1	LastOrDefault	2	Sum	20
Concat	1	LongCount	2	Take	1
Contains	2	Max	22	TakeWhile	2
Count	2	Min	22	ThenBy	2
DefaultIfEmpty	2	OfType	1	ThenByDescending	2
Distinct	2	OrderBy	2	ToArray	1
ElementAt	1	OrderByDescending	2	ToDictionary	4
ElementAtOrDefault	1	Range	1	ToList	1
Empty	1	Repeat	1	ToLookup	4
Except	2	Reverse	1	Union	2
First	2	Select	2	Where	2
FirstOrDefault	2	SelectMany	4	Zip	1

We discuss the query operator methods in more detail in the section, "Standard Query Operators," later in this chapter. First, let's get a feeling for how they are implemented in a way that makes them lazily executed.

EXTENSION METHODS PHILOSOPHY

Extension methods are not just a way to extend existing the interfaces with new members (for example, because they were omitted when the interface was created). They provide a whole new dimension to API design by themselves.

Because the CLR doesn't provide a means to have nonvirtual methods on interfaces, it becomes hard to expose common, centrally implemented functionality through an interface. One way to stick default methods on a "contract" is by using abstract classes instead. That works but is often undesirable because of the CLR's single inheritance model. You don't want to sacrifice your single base class just because you want to inherit some convenience methods that come with something that should have been an interface. Querying functionality could be exposed like this:

```
abstract class QueryableEnumerable<T> : IEnumerable<T> {
    ...
    public QueryableEnumerable<R> Select<T, R>(Func<T, R> selector) {
        /* common implementation */
```

```
    }
    public IEnumerable<T> Where<T>(Func<T, bool> predicate) {
        /* common implementation */
    }
    ...
    abstract IEnumerator<T> GetEnumerator();
}
```

Now if you want to make existing collections queryable, you would have to make them inherit from this new base type. Not only is this tedious, it's often impossible because they already have a base class for other legitimate reasons.

Extension methods effectively provide a means to layer default behavior on top of an interface without changing it or having to rely on abstract base classes. Also, the fact they can be imported through a namespace allows logical grouping of the orthogonal interface features (for example, querying, serialization, and so forth). Although the interface itself stays clean and simple, you can add centrally implemented functionality just by importing an additional namespace.

Iterators

As a precursor to the LINQ feature set, C# 2.0 introduced the concept of iterators to make the definition of IEnumerable<T> and IEnumerator<T> objects easier. You've seen before how powerful custom implementations of those interfaces can be (for example, to *yield* a sequence of numbers to a consumer, in an on-demand basis). All you need to do is respond properly to MoveNext method and Current property getter calls.

Conceptually though, your task is even simpler: You just want to hand out objects to a consumer when asked to do so. This feels quite a bit like returning data from a method, the difference being you don't just return a single object but a sequence of objects, one at a time.

Iterators precisely enable you to do this, using regular familiar control flow primitives. You just write a method from which you can produce multiple objects, which gets translated into an implementation of IEnumerator<T>. When the user calls MoveNext on the iterator, either directly or through the foreach loop, code inside it ticks until the next object is given back to the consumer.

An iterator is simply declared as a regular method, returning either IEnumerable<T> or IEnumerator<T> as indicated in its signature. However, instead of using the regular return keyword, one uses the yield return keyword. Our handcrafted Integers example can be rewritten using an iterator as follows:

```
public IEnumerable<int> GetIntegers() {
    int n = 0;
    while (true)
        yield return n++;
}
```

The execution model of an iterator is intrinsically lazy. Just calling the `GetIntegers` method returns an object that offers the *potential* to enumerate the data produced by the iterator. It's not until you start pulling data out of the iterator object by making calls to the `MoveNext` method and `Current` property that any code inside the iterator starts to execute. This can be visualized nicely under a debugger, as shown in Figure 20.3.

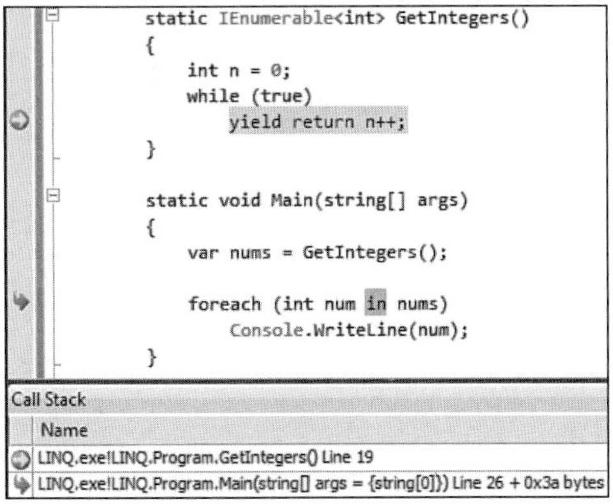

```
static IEnumerable<int> GetIntegers()
{
    int n = 0;
    while (true)
        yield return n++;
}

static void Main(string[] args)
{
    var nums = GetIntegers();

    foreach (int num in nums)
        Console.WriteLine(num);
}
```

```
Call Stack
  Name
  LINQ.exe!LINQ.Program.GetIntegers() Line 19
  LINQ.exe!LINQ.Program.Main(string[] args = {string[0]}) Line 26 + 0x3a bytes
```

FIGURE 20.3   An iterator executes piecemeal when someone enumerates over it.

If you simply step through the `Main` method, you won't see the breakpoint (or any other code) in the `GetIntegers` iterator getting triggered before the `foreach` loop starts to pull data out of the iterator.

For every call to `MoveNext`, the code in the iterator runs until the next `yield return` statement is encountered. The expression to the right of the `yield return` keywords gets computed and surfaced to the consumer through the `Current` property generated for the `IEnumerator<T>` interface implementation. In this particular case, the iterator has an infinite characteristic, never reaching the end of the iterator block. The compiler comes to this conclusion itself by means of flow analysis ("can the iterator ever reach the end of the block?"), resulting in a `MoveNext` method that always returns true to the caller.

To make this more digestible, we'll write a simpler iterator and analyze how it executes and gets turned into executable code by the compiler. Consider the following fragment:

```
public IEnumerator<int> CountDown() {
    yield return 3;
    yield return 2;
    yield return 1;
    yield return 0;
}
```

Notice we're using `IEnumerator<int>` for the return type this time. This will simplify our analysis, but both the `IEnumerable<T>` and `IEnumerator<T>` interfaces can be used for the return type of an iterator method. On the consumer side, things look like this:

```
var countDown = CountDown();
while (countDown.MoveNext())
    Console.WriteLine(countDown.Current);
```

This loop will iterate four times, with the `Current` property surfacing values 3 through 0 subsequently, which will get printed to the screen. To make the iterator's execution model more explicit, let's add diagnostic output to the iterator body itself:

```
public IEnumerator<int> CountDown() {
    Console.WriteLine("Before three");
    yield return 3;

    Console.WriteLine("After three");
    Console.WriteLine("Before two");
    yield return 2;

    Console.WriteLine("After two");
    Console.WriteLine("Before one");
    yield return 1;

    Console.WriteLine("After one");
    Console.WriteLine("Before zero");
    yield return 0;
}
```

Consuming this iterator through the `while` loop, the following gets printed to the screen:

```
Before three
3
After three
Before two
2
After two
Before one
1
After one
Before zero
0
```

The plain numeric output is produced by the consuming loop, while the textual output comes from the iterator's code body. You see that things get interleaved because the iterator runs piecemeal reacting to MoveNext calls. This is a true pull model because it's the consumer that drives the iterator's execution while *pulling out* objects from it. A picture is worth a thousand words, so take a look at Figure 20.4.

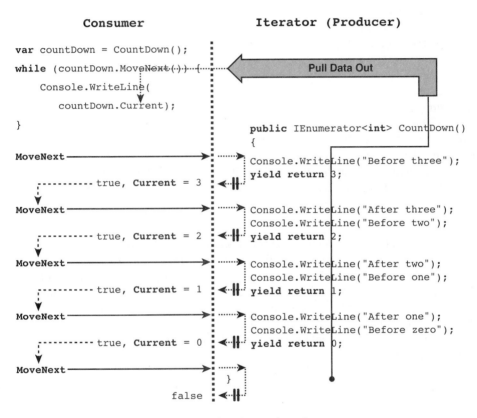

FIGURE 20.4   Piecemeal execution of an iterator's code.

The yield return statement needs to specify an object of a type compatible with the one specified in the iterator's return type. In our running example, we're creating an iterator that produces integer values, hence yield return expects an int-typed object. This is similar to a regular method's return type.

Besides yield return there's also yield break, which causes the iterator to terminate by responding false to the consumer's next call to MoveNext. This is conceptually similar to jumping to the end of the iterator block, which also causes the iterator to finish. The break keyword is intentionally chosen to mirror the consumer's capability to break out of the iterator by breaking from the loop.

By creating iterators that consume other iterators, you can realize powerful operators that apply on sequences of data. This is exactly what LINQ to Objects does with its standard query operators, as discussed in the "Standard Query Operators" section. Let's give a simple example of such an operator implementation though, to commit the core concept and execute model of iterators to your memory. The following code realizes a filter, ignoring the code to validate arguments:

```
IEnumerable<T> Filter<T>(IEnumerable<T> source, Func<T, bool> filter) {
    foreach (T item in source)
        if (filter(item))
            yield return item;
}
```

Given an enumerable of objects of type T (which can be realized using an iterator) and a filter delegate, the Filter method can produce a new enumerable of T-typed objects with only those objects that pass the filter. It's important to realize that calling the Filter method doesn't trigger any execution yet. Only when the caller starts pulling data out of the returned enumerable (iterator) object will the iterator start making progress. For example, consider the following call:

```
var evens = Filter(new [] { 2, 5, 7, 4, 1, 9, 5, 8 }, n => n % 2 == 0);
```

Once the consumer gets an enumerator and starts calling MoveNext, the loop inside the filter starts to tick. One call to MoveNext on the enumerator for evens will cause the loop to run until the first even number is found, which happens to be the first element of the input. However, the second call to MoveNext causes the inner loop to run a couple more times until the next even number, 4, is found. And the third time, it takes even a bit longer to yield an item back to the consumer, as the iterator's loop has to run until 8 is found in the input sequence. By making the filter delegate side effecting, you can see how execution takes place:

```
var evens = Filter(new [] { 2, 5, 7, 4, 1, 9, 5, 8 }, n => {
    Console.WriteLine("Filtering " + n);
    return n % 2 == 0;
});
```

On the consuming side, consider a simple foreach loop that drains the whole iterator until the very end:

```
foreach (int n in evens)
    Console.WriteLine(n);
```

This will produce the following output:

```
Filtering 2
2
Filtering 5
Filtering 7
Filtering 4
4
Filtering 1
Filtering 9
Filtering 5
Filtering 8
8
```

In other words, one MoveNext call on the resulting iterator object can cause multiple such calls to take place on the input sequence, which can be an iterator itself. In the case of a filter, the source is consulted until an object is found that passes the filter.

IENUMERABLE<T> HAS MANY FACES

The beauty of interfaces is how general-purpose they can be, by limiting the number of promises they make between the implementer and user. The IEnumerable family of interfaces is just like that, stating one should be able to enumerate over a sequence of objects somehow.

What the effects of such an enumeration are, or where the data has to come from, is left unspecified. For example, in a List<T>, the data will be persisted in memory while another implementation of the interface could consult a database on the fly, pulling one object over the wire at a time.

This sometimes makes interfaces two-edged swords: The guarantees provided to the interface's user are often very limited, while providing an immense amount of flexibility to the implementers. Only good documentation can help document how an implementer interpreted the interface with regard to various aspects.

The execution model of iterators can be summarized in a simple statement: Every call to MoveNext on an iterator's enumerator object causes the iterator to run until the next yield statement is encountered. A yield return statement will cause MoveNext to return true, with the Current property set to the specified return value, while reaching the end of the iterator or encountering yield break causes it to return false.

As an exercise, step through the following chain of iterators either using raw brainpower or with help of a debugger, assuming a consumer is iterating over it. Figure 20.5 shows the interactions between the iterators for this example.

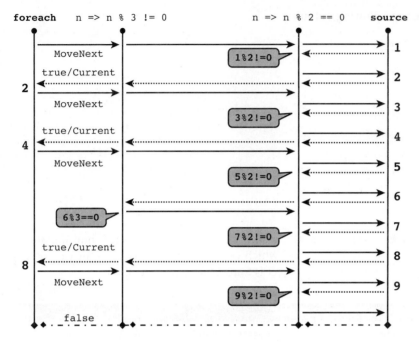

FIGURE 20.5   An iterator consuming another iterator.

```
var multiplesOfSix = Filter(
    Filter(new [] { 1, 2, 3, 4, 5, 6, 7, 8, 9 }, n => n % 2 == 0),
    n => n % 3 != 0
);
```

Filter is called Where in LINQ but is implemented essentially as shown here, modulo additional argument validation code and the fact Where is an extension method, which allows us to write the preceding example more fluently:

```
var multiplesOfSix = new [] { 1, 2, 3, 4, 5, 6, 7, 8, 9 }
    .Where(n => n % 2 == 0)
    .Where(n => n % 3 != 0);
```

Now code reads left to right, top down, which is much more natural than the deep nesting we saw before. Internally, this chain of extension method calls turns into this:

```
var multiplesOfSix = Enumerable.Where(
    Enumerable.Where(new [] { 1, 2, 3, 4, 5, 6, 7, 8, 9 }, n => n % 2 == 0),
    n => n % 3 != 0
);
```

Congratulations! You've just reverse-engineered the true essence of the query operators using knowledge of iterators, lambda expressions, and extension methods. Other query operators like `Select` are implemented in ways similar to the one shown here for the `Where` filter operator.

Lazy Evaluation

Their piecemeal on-demand evaluation characteristic makes iterators an ideal construct to express queries. Because the underlying data source can potentially change after you have declared a query expression, delaying the execution is a much desirable feature:

```
var nums = new List<int> { 2, 5, 7, 4, 1, 9 };
var evens = from n in nums
            where n % 2 == 0
            select n;

// Shows 2, 4
foreach (var n in evens)
    Console.WriteLine(n);

// Somehow the collection changes, e.g. because the user edits the data.
nums.Add(5);
nums.Add(8);

// Shows 2, 4, 8 - no need to redeclare the query
foreach (var n in evens)
    Console.WriteLine(n);
```

The query expression used here is compiled into a call to the `Where` query operator we've seen before. Because it's realized using iterators, it's only when we enumerate over the query object that execution starts to take place. Because of this, a query expression is nothing more than a *declaration of the intent of the query*.

That said, some query operators trigger immediate execution of the query, such as `ToArray` and `ToList`. Those operators essentially drain the query expression's iterator on the spot, persisting the retrieved objects in an in-memory collection:

```
var nums = new List<int> { 2, 5, 7, 4, 1, 9 };
var evens = (from n in nums
            where n % 2 == 0
            select n).ToList();

// Shows 2, 4
foreach (var n in evens)
    Console.WriteLine(n);
```

```
// Somehow the collection changes, e.g. because the user edits the data.
nums.Add(5);
nums.Add(8);

// Still shows 2, 4 since ToList caused the query to execute on the spot,
// conceptually creating a snapshot of query results at that point in time.
foreach (var n in evens)
    Console.WriteLine(n);
```

Lazy evaluation can be a little surprising for consumers of iterators. For example, the following query expression projects, using the select clause, a series of numbers on their inverse values:

```
var inverse = from n in nums
              select 1 / n;
```

If nums contains 0, you expect a DivideByZeroException to be raised. However, because of the delayed execution nature of the query expression (and hence its select clause), this exception happens no earlier than the point where iteration happens:

```
try {
    inverse = from n in nums
              select 1 / n;
}
catch (DivideByZeroException) {
    // Bug: you'll never get here.
}

// But the following line can throw, since the query executes here!
foreach (var n in inverse)
    Console.WriteLine(n);
```

To correct this code, you can do a few things. First, eliminate the 0 case (for example, by filtering out zero values using a where clause). Another possibility is to turn the select clause into a conditional, producing a dedicated value for the division-by-zero case. Finally, you could perform the exception handling in the right spot (that is, around the loop code). Keep in mind, though, that an exception raised by an iterator will terminate the query as a whole.

Also when creating your own iterators, keep in mind the lazy execution nature, especially when it comes to exception handling:

```
IEnumerable<T> Filter<T>(IEnumerable<T> source, Func<T, bool> filter) {
    if (source == null)
        throw new ArgumentNullException("source");
```

```
    if (filter == null)
        throw new ArgumentNullException("filter");

    foreach (T item in source)
        if (filter(item))
            yield return item;
}
```

Well-intentioned as this code looks, the timing of the exceptions is most likely not what you want it to be. Everything inside the iterator block is delayed until the point of the first MoveNext call. In other words, the ArgumentNullException will not be raised until the user starts enumerating over the returned iterator. Iterators are contagious to the whole method code block in which they're defined.

To solve this problem, replace the entry-point method by a regular noniterator one, calling into a separate iterator implementation:

```
IEnumerable<T> Filter<T>(IEnumerable<T> source, Func<T, bool> filter) {
    if (source == null)
        throw new ArgumentNullException("source");

    if (filter == null)
        throw new ArgumentNullException("filter");

    return FilterInternal(source, filter);
}

IEnumerable<T> FilterInternal<T>(IEnumerable<T> source, Func<T, bool> filter) {
    foreach (T item in source)
        if (filter(item))
            yield return item;
}
```

The reason this has the desired effect is because only methods with one or more yield statements inside them are turned into iterators. In our example, the Filter<T> method is a regular method, while FilterInternal<T> turns into an iterator.

NO ANONYMOUS ITERATORS

Unfortunately, C# doesn't provide a means to create anonymous iterators, which could be block-based constructs that can be used where an IEnumerable<T> or IEnumerator<T> is expected. This would make it easier to reason about the island of code that's executed lazily. For example:

```
    IEnumerable<T> Filter<T>(IEnumerable<T> source, Func<T, bool> filter) {
        if (source == null)
            throw new ArgumentNullException("source");
```

```
    if (filter == null)
        throw new ArgumentNullException("filter");

    // A hypothetical anonymous iterator (hence it won't compile!)
    return new IEnumerable<T> {
        foreach (T item in source)
            if (filter(item))
                yield return item;
    };
}
```

Such a feature would go quite nicely with object expressions or anonymous inner classes, which are in-place implementations for interfaces. For example, if you're asked to pass in an IDisposable object to an API function, you could provide an implementation of the interface in-place, potentially capturing outer local variables just as with anonymous methods closures.

How Iterators Work

To wrap up our exploration of lazy execution related to iterators, let's briefly look at how the compiler realizes iterators. We already know an iterator is a syntactical way to implement IEnumerable<T> or IEnumerator<T> automatically. The key trick is to keep track of the local state of the iterator across different calls to MoveNext.

As an example, consider the following sequence operator, which doesn't come in LINQ out of the box. Put its definition in a static class to use it on enumerable sequences:

```
public static IEnumerable<T> StartWith<T>(this IEnumerable<T> tail, T head) {
    yield return head;
    foreach (T item in tail)
        yield return item;
}
```

This operator enables you to prepend an existing sequence with a single object, much like a cons-cell in LISP does. No worries if you don't know LISP; here is a concrete example of what this does:

```
// { 0, 1, 2, 3, 4, 5, 6, 7, 8, 9 }
StartWith(
    // { 1, 2, 3, 4, 5, 6, 7, 8, 9 }
    StartWith(
        // { 2, 3, 4, 5, 6, 7, 8, 9 }
        Enumerable.Range(2, 8),
        1),
    0)
```

Using the extension method instance-method-like calling syntax, we can rewrite this as follows:

```
Enumerable.Range(2, 8).StartWith(1).StartWith(0)
```

AVOID EXTENSION METHODS ON AN UNCONSTRAINED GENERIC PARAMETER

The reason our `StartWith` method's `this` extension method parameter is not the first parameter "head," but the `IEnumerable<T>` "tail" is because it's not good practice to put an extension method on a unconstrained generic parameter:

```
static IEnumerable<T> StartWith<T>(this T head, IEnumerable<T> tail)
```

This is really the same as putting an extension method on `System.Object`, which will show up on any object there is. This gets quite noisy when looking at the IntelliSense.

The reason I chose this iterator as an illustration is because there are various states the iterator can be in. Such states can be derived from flow analysis, simply by looking at the layout of the code and where yield statements occur.

In this particular case, a first state represents the iterator hasn't started to be consumed yet. After this state, it moves on to the first `yield return` statement, outside the central loop. Yet another `MoveNext` puts us inside the loop, where iterations produce objects one at a time. Finally, we reach the end of the loop, reaching a final state where a call to `MoveNext` returns false.

What's described here is a finite state machine that conceptually keeps track of an instruction pointer in the iterator. Every time `MoveNext` is called, this state gets inspected to decide what to do next, possibly causing the state to change in preparation for the subsequent call. Figure 20.6 illustrates the states our `StartWith` iterator goes through. The numbers of the states reflect the ones used by the compiler, where the missing numbers are used to indicate intermediate states, relevant to exceptional paths and such.

Calling `StartWith` returns an `IEnumerable<T>` implementation that's in initial state -2:

```
static IEnumerable<T> StartWith<T>(this IEnumerable<T> tail, T head) {
    return new StartWithIterator(-2) {
        _tail = tail,
        _head = head
    };
}
```

The `StartWithIterator` is a compiler-generated implementation of the `IEnumerable<T>` interface, implementing the state machine shown earlier. It stores the parameters passed to the iterator as local fields. Being an `IEnumerable<T>`, it provides an implementation of the

GetEnumerator method. When called, the iterator advances to state 0. Different calls to this method can result in the creation of new iterator objects, to ensure cross-thread safety:

```
public IEnumerator<T> GetEnumerator() {
    if (   _initialThreadId == Thread.CurrentThread.ManagedThreadId
        && _state == -2) {
        // Move on to state 0.
        _state = 0;
        return this;
    }
    else {
        // Cross-thread access or not in the initial state anymore:
        // create a new iterator object that advances independently.
        return new StartWithIterator(0) {
            _tail = tail,
            _head = head
        };
    }
}
```

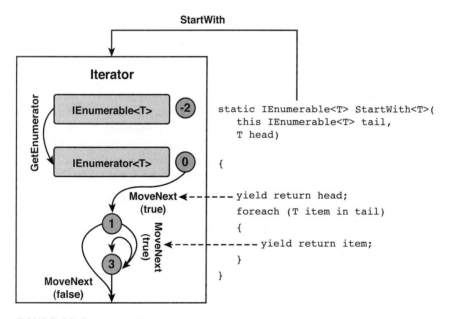

FIGURE 20.6   States the StartWith iterator goes through.

The identifier for the current thread is stored in a field called _initialThreadId, which is set by the constructor to Thread.CurrentThread.ManagedThreadId. This thread-affinity check is something we'll just skim over.

Where things get really interesting is inside the MoveNext method, which implements a switch based on the iterator's current state. The first call to MoveNext corresponds to the first line of code in the iterator, yield returning the first parameter:

```
bool MoveNext() {
    try {
        switch (_state) {
            case 0:
                _current = _head; // yield return head;
                _state = 1;
                return true;      // we got an object in Current

            ...
        }
    }
    fault {
        // If something goes wrong, the iterator cleans up all the resources
        // it has acquired. Notice the use of "fault", which is not a typo:
        // fault handlers are supported by the CLR and are transferred to when
        // the protected block has quit because of an exception. C# doesn't
        // expose this feature, but the compiler emits it in this case.
        Dispose();
    }
}
```

This corresponds to the state transition to state 1, which indicates we're about to start executing the foreach loop, which corresponds to the following while loop:

```
IEnumerator<T> e = tail.GetEnumerator();
try {
    while (e.MoveNext())
        yield return e.Current;
}
finally {
    if (e != null)
        e.Dispose();
}
```

The exception-handling logic associated with a foreach loop, to ensure proper disposal, makes the generated code quite interesting. The CLR's block-based protection mechanism for exception handling doesn't work when the code to be protected gets sprinkled around in different states of an iterator's MoveNext method. Instead, it's the job of the compiler to ensure the Dispose call happens under all circumstances that can be encountered by the iterator. The try...fault block in MoveNext is part of this.

Instead of focusing on the exceptional case, let's see how state 1 works. We're sitting in front of the foreach loop, so a next call to MoveNext has to enter that loop, potentially yielding a single object back to the caller. It's also possible the "tail" sequence is empty, which should cause the MoveNext method to return false. Here's what state 1 does:

```
bool MoveNext() {
    try {
        switch (_state) {
            case 0:
                ...
            case 1:
                _enum = _tail.GetEnumerator();
                while (_enum.MoveNext()) {
                    _current = _enum.Current; // yield return item;
                    _state = 3;
                    return true;              // we got an object in Current
// Compiler writers can use goto-labels,
// see further...
Resume:
                }
                Finally();
                break;
            ...
        }
        return false;
```

In reality, an additional state is added to the mix, but let's ignore this for sake of clarity. State 1 essentially causes the iterator to retrieve an enumerator for the tail sequence, which is stored in a field so that subsequent calls to MoveNext can reuse that same enumerator (which by itself contains a cursor in the tail sequence).

Next, the while loop simply occurs almost verbatim in the generated iterator code, to retrieve the enumerator's Current property value, which gets surfaces to the iterator's consumer through the _current field. But instead of looping until the tail sequence is at the end, the iterator is suspended by putting it in state 3 and returning true.

If the call to MoveNext on the enumerator returns false, we fall out of the switch block. This triggers a call to a helper method that ensures all the resources acquired by the iterator get properly disposed. In practice, this will cause a call to Dispose on _enum. It goes without saying that reaching the end of the tail sequence will cause the iterator to return false to the consumer, indicating it has reached the end. However, if there are yield statements after the iterator's loop, we would advance to another state:

```
static IEnumerable<T> StartWith<T>(this IEnumerable<T> tail, T head) {
    yield return head;
    foreach (T item in tail)
        yield return item;
```

```
    // If this would be here, there'd be an additional state.
    yield return default(T);
}
```

Finally, we've ended up with state 3, which should correspond to retrieving the next objects from the tail enumerator, exposing them to the iterator's consumer. This is done by a simple branch (goto) instruction jumping inside the loop from state 2:

```
bool MoveNext() {
    try {
        switch (_state) {
            case 0:
                ...
            case 1:
                _enum = _tail.GetEnumerator();
                while (_enum.MoveNext()) {
                    _current = _enum.Current; // yield return item;
                    _state = 3;
                    return true;               // we got an object in Current
Resume:
                }
                Finally();
                break;
            case 3:
                goto Resume;
        }
        return false;
```

This causes the while loop to reevaluate _enum.MoveNext(), possibly yielding a next object by means of the same logic we saw before. If the call returned false, we get to the Finally() cleanup call once more and break out of the switch statement, causing the iterator to return false to the caller.

In short, iterators are not that frightening from the inside, though the compiler has to tear apart the iterator block's code quite a bit. Luckily, you don't need to know much (or anything) about this, but it still makes sense to get a feel for the plumbing required to realize iterators because it clearly shows their execution model.

Feel free to dig a little deeper into the generated code using .NET Reflector, which you should put in .NET 2.0 decompilation mode to clearly see the plumbing. Also try to reverse-engineer a more complex iterator with more yield statements, nested loops, and so on. The key takeaway message is that every yield statement needs to cause the iterator to suspend by returning from the MoveNext method. And to resume at the proper point, there needs to be enough captured state in the iterator object. Figure 20.7 shows the innards of an iterator, where you can clearly see a switch-table to keep track of the next operations to carry out upon a MoveNext call.

FIGURE 20.7   An iterator unraveled.

Standard Query Operators

One of the core strengths of LINQ is the fact it unifies query operators across different data domains, ranging from in-memory objects to relational databases. To do so, it not only provides query syntax for mainstream languages like C# and Visual Basic, it also establishes a set of commonly used query operators.

In this section, we take a look at all the standard query operators that ship with the .NET Framework, including some of their less commonly used, but useful, overloads. Keep in mind that some of those are exposed through language integrated query syntax, whereas others aren't. For the latter set of operators, you can just use method invocation syntax to use them.

Source Generators

Source generators comprise our first big category of standard query operators. Although different source objects can be LINQ-enabled (for example, by implementing IEnumerable<T> for local query execution or by implementing IQueryable<T> for remote query execution; for example, as used in LINQ to SQL), it sometimes makes sense to create a sequence on the fly.

All the methods discussed here live on the Enumerable type and provide a means to generate a source without persisting it in memory, thanks to lazy evaluation. Obviously, you can also use array, lists, or other collection types as in-memory data sources, but with immediate memory-allocation needs.

Range

The first source generator is called `Range` and produces Int32 values starting from a given number. Its second parameter is used to specify how many numbers to yield to the consumer:

```
IEnumerable<int> firstTen = Enumerable.Range(0, 10); // { 0 .. 9 }
```

Although its use might seem limited, combined with other query operators it can produce more useful objects (for example, characters):

```
IEnumerable<char> aToz = Enumerable.Range(0, 26).Select(i => (char)('a' + i));
```

Also for simple query operator exploration, the use of `Range` provides a simple way to create a sequence to experiment with.

Repeat

Given an element, it's sometimes useful to repeat it multiple times to create a sequence with a constant value. This can be achieved using the `Repeat` operator:

```
IEnumerable<string> heyHeyHey = Enumerable.Repeat("Hey", 3);
```

Notice how the type of the resulting sequence is inferred from the element specified as the first parameter to Repeat.

Empty

In certain scenarios where an `IEnumerable<T>` is expected, you want to pass a default sequence. `Empty` produces such a statically typed sequence with no elements in it:

```
IEnumerable<int> nothing = Enumerable.Empty<int>();
```

RETURN

A missing operator in the standard set of query operators is `Return`, or Singleton, which would return a sequence with a single given element:

```
static IEnumerable<T> Return<T>(T element) {
    yield return element;
}
```

This can easily be achieved by creating a single-element array instead, which as we know implements `IEnumerable<T>`. This operator is interesting because the mathematical foundation of query operators, called *monads*, is based on two essential operators: `Bind` and `Return`. The latter was just shown and has no presence in the LINQ operators, but the former one is actually in there. It's called `SelectMany` and provides a way to combine sequences, as you will see in the "Projection" section, where we discuss this operator.

DefaultIfEmpty

Where Empty sort of plays the role of a null reference, DefaultIfEmpty plays the role of the null coalescing ?? operator. If the sequence given to this operator is empty, it yield returns a single "default" element. This default element can either be specified explicitly or inferred based on the sequence's element type:

```
var src1 = Enumerable.Empty<int>();
var res1 = src1.DefaultIfEmpty(); // { 0 }
var res2 = src1.DefaultIfEmpty(99); // { 99 }

var src2 = Enumerable.Range(1, 9);
var res3 = src2.DefaultIfEmpty(); // { 1 .. 9 }
```

This operator has quite limited use, but it's nevertheless good to know about.

Restriction

One of the most common query operations is obviously to filter out elements based on certain conditions. Those conditions can either be on a per-element basis (such as with the Where operator) or have a more global nature (as with Skip or Take). In essence, we're talking here about horizontal partitioning where a given number of objects in the input sequence are filtered down to a subset. Those restriction operators don't change the shape of the data and preserve the type of the input sequence.

Where

The first restriction operator is one we're already familiar with. The Where operator evaluates a condition for each element in the input sequence, only retaining objects for which the condition evaluated to true. Two overloads exist:

```
static IEnumerable<T> Where<T>(this IEnumerable<T> source,
                               Func<T, bool> predicate);
static IEnumerable<T> Where<T>(this IEnumerable<T> source,
                               Func<T, int, bool> predicate);
```

From our discussion about query expression syntax and iterators, we remember the first one quite well. Iterating over the source parameter, the operator feeds every object in to the predicate function. When that function evaluates to true, it yields the object into the output sequence. Any Boolean-returning expression will do, no matter how complex you make it. For illustration purposes, we keep the predicate function simple:

```
// { "Bart", "Lisa" }
var res = new [] { "Bart", "Homer", "Lisa" }.Where(s => s.Length == 4);
```

The second overload feeds an additional argument to the predicate function, standing for the zero-based index of the element in the input sequence. One example use is shown here, retaining elements at even positions:

```
// { "Zero", "Two" }
var res = new [] { "Zero", "One", "Two", "Three" }.Where((s, i) => i % 2 == 0);
```

Here, s stands for the string objects in the input sequence, while i stands for the index of the object in the input sequence. We're not using s (though we obviously could) to do the index-based filtering here.

Distinct

Sequences may contain duplicate objects, which can be undesirable. To get rid of those duplicate entries, the Distinct operator can be used. Because this deals with equality checks between objects, you can expect two overloads (one that uses the default comparer for the element type and another that allows the use of a specific equality comparer):

```
static IEnumerable<T> Distinct<T>(this IEnumerable<T> source);
static IEnumerable<T> Distinct<T>(this IEnumerable<T> source,
                                  IEqualityComparer<T> comparer);
```

Use is quite straightforward:

```
var nums = new [] { 5, 2, 1, 3, 1, 4, 5 }.Distinct(); // { 5, 2, 1, 3, 4 }
```

I leave the use of the more specialized overload to your imagination. For more information about IEqualityComparer<T>, refer to our discussion about collection types in Chapter 16, "Collection Types." A sample use is to implement a comparer for Person objects, only looking at the person's identification number to determine whether objects are equal. However, if those are the semantics for a Person object, you most likely already have an overridden Equals method in place, which will be picked up by the default equality comparer for the Person type.

Skip and SkipWhile

To skip a number of elements from the beginning of a sequence, the Skip operator can be used. Its more general-purpose SkipWhile brother can be used to skip elements as long as a given condition holds true. A few examples tell it all:

```
var res1 = Enumerable.Range(0, 10).Skip(5); // { 5, 6, 7, 8, 9 }
var res2 = Enumerable.Range(0, 10).SkipWhile(n => n < 8); // { 8, 9 }
```

If the skip count is longer than the input sequence length, or if the predicate never flips to false, the resulting sequence is empty. Notice SkipWhile is obviously not the same as a simple Where:

```
var res1 = new [] { 1, 2, 3, 4, 3, 2, 1 }.SkipWhile(n => n < 4) // { 4, 3, 2, 1 }
var res2 = new [] { 1, 2, 3, 4, 3, 2, 1 }.Where(n => n >= 4)     // { 4 }
```

It's left as an exercise for you to implement those operators by hand using your acquired knowledge of iterators. You'll find that query operators are often just a few lines of code (ignoring input validation logic).

Take and TakeWhile

The opposite of "to skip" is "to take," returning a sequence with elements from the beginning of the input sequence, either based on a count or a condition. Take simply takes a number of elements to yield, while TakeWhile expresses "yield as long as the condition holds." Examples are shown here:

```
var res1 = Enumerable.Range(0, 10).Take(5); // { 0, 1, 2, 3, 4 }
var res2 = Enumerable.Range(0, 10).TakeWhile(n => n < 8);
                                  // { 0, 1, 2, 3, 4, 5, 6, 7 }
```

Notice certain invariant properties hold. We demonstrate those in the following example using the Concat and SequenceEqual operators, which should be straightforward to understand. Both methods should return true every time:

```
bool AssertSkipTake<T>(IEnumerable<T> source, int n) {
    return source.SequenceEqual(source.Take(n).Concat(
                           source.Skip(n)));
}


bool AssertSkipTakeWhile<T>(IEnumerable<T> source, Func<T, bool> predicate) {
    return source.SequenceEqual(source.TakeWhile(predicate).Concat(
                           source.SkipWhile(predicate)));
}
```

PAGING USE SKIP AND TAKE

The combination of Skip and Take is useful for paging of data sources (for example, to show elements ten at a time):

```
// For example, page 3 = Skip(30).Take(10)
var onePageOfData = source.Skip(page * pageSize).Take(pageSize);
```

This illustrates the power of gluing together different query operators.

First and FirstOrDefault

Very restrictive restriction operators return just a single element. First is one of those operators, returning the first element of a sequence. If no element is present, it throws an InvalidOperationException. You can use the FirstOrDefault operator to return the default value for the sequence element type in case the input sequence is empty:

```
int first = new [] { 42, 24, 12, 123 }.First(); // 42
int zero  = new int[0].FirstOrDefault();
```

Predicate-based overloads exist to retrieve a sequence's first element that matches a certain criterion. If no such element is found, an `InvalidOperationException` results, which can again be mitigated by use of `FirstOrDefault`:

```
int first = new [] { 42, 24, 12, 123 }.First(n => n < 30); // 24
int zero  = new [] { 42, 24, 12, 123 }.FirstOrDefault(n => n > 999);
```

Those handy overloads are often overlooked by beginning LINQ users, causing them to use combinations of `Where` and `First` to achieve similar results.

Last and LastOrDefault

Completely analogous to `First` and `FirstOrDefault` are the `Last` and `LastOrDefault` query operators. Instead of taking the first element, possibly based on a predicate or with a default value fallback behavior, they take the last element:

```
int last = new [] { 42, 24, 12, 123 }.Last(); // 123
int zero = new int[0].LastOrDefault();
```

When a predicate is used, it gets evaluated for every element in the sequence, while remembering the last element that positively evaluated the predicate:

```
int last = new [] { 42, 24, 12, 123 }.Last(n => n < 30); // 12
int zero = new [] { 42, 24, 12, 123 }.LastOrDefault(n => n > 999);
```

Notice that infinite sequences will cause `Last` (among various other query operators) to get stuck forever. Luckily, the use of infinite sequences is quite uncommon in the world of .NET, though iterators make the creation of such sequences possible. Just watch out for such pathological cases if you rely on infinite iterators at some point.

Single and SingleOrDefault

In some cases, you expect only a single element to be present in a sequence or have only one that matches a certain criterion. In such circumstances, the `Single` operator becomes useful. Other than `First` and `Last`, it throws an `InvalidOperationException` when there's either no element or more than one element. Again, an `OrDefault` variant can be used to override the exception-throwing behavior:

```
int oneAndOnly = new [] { 42 }.Single(); // 42
int zero = new [] { 1, 2, 3 }.SingleOrDefault(); // More than one element
```

Overloads with a predicate function are self-explanatory based on the discussion about `First` and `Last`.

ElementAt and ElementAtOrDefault

The `IEnumerable<T>` and `IEnumerator<T>` interfaces lack index-based access, though their sequential natures clearly allow for such retrieval operations. `ElementAt` provides this capability, with `ArgumentOutOfRangeException` thrown if the specified index is invalid. The variant with the `OrDefault` suffix allows for an exception-free treatment once more:

```
var two = new [] { "Zero", "One", "Two", "Three" }.ElementAt(2);
```

USE ORDEFAULT OPERATORS WITH CARE

Don't use the `OrDefault` variants if you expect a first or last element to exist, the sequence to contain only a single element, or a specific index to be valid. The gratuitous use of nonexception throwing operators is a great way to obfuscate bugs in your code that would often reveal invalid assumptions. `SingleOrDefault` is especially dangerous because it would not only cover up the case where the sequence was empty but also the case where it contained too many elements than were expected.

OfType

Given a heterogeneous collection of objects, you sometimes want to filter on type, just like the query shown here:

```
// { 42, 123 }
var src = new object[] { 42, "Bart", DateTime.Now, 123 };
IEnumerable<object> res = src.Where(o => o is int);
```

Although the preceding query works just fine, it has the disadvantage of not performing a cast over all the elements that passed the type check. We would prefer a way to get all the integer values back typed as such:

```
// { 42, 123 }
IEnumerable<int> res = src.Where(o => o is int).Select(o => (int)o);
```

The `OfType` operator allows this in a much more concise manner, specifying the target type as a generic parameter to the method call:

```
static IEnumerable<T> OfType<T>(this IEnumerable source);
```

Notice this operator consumes a nongeneric `IEnumerable` for its input (for example, for use with an `ArrayList`). But every `IEnumerable<T>` is also a nongeneric `IEnumerable`, so the operator can also be used to filter based on subtypes:

```
var res = new Animal[] { elephant, ant, giraffe }.OfType<Mammal>();
```

The `OfType` operator is not, in fact, just a restriction operator; it also transforms objects in the input sequence by applying a cast. For this reason, we covered it as the last operator in the category of restrictions, adjacent to the projection operators.

Projection

To transform objects in a sequence into corresponding objects in an output sequence, projection operators are used. While those preserve the element count of the source sequence, they transform each element, potentially realizing vertical partitioning. The typical example from the database world is the *selection* of a subset of columns.

Select

The basic projection operator is `Select`, surfaced through the C# language using the `select` clause we've seen before. Two overloads exist, one of which takes in an extra integer argument to the selector delegate, representing the index of the element in the sequence. Notice that the transformative characteristic surfaces through the presence of two generic parameters (one to represent the type of the input sequence elements and one to represent the type of the output sequence elements):

```
static IEnumerable<R> Select<T,R>(this IEnumerable<T> source,
                                  Func<T, R> selector);
static IEnumerable<R> Select<T,R>(this IEnumerable<T> source,
                                  Func<T, int, R> selector);
```

Although the `Select` method can transform the type of the input objects, it's obvious this is not a required use. For example:

```
IEnumerable<int> twice = Enumerable.Range(0, 10).Select(n => n * 2);
IEnumerable<string>  s = Enumerable.Range(0, 10).Select(n => n.ToString());
```

Notice how generic type parameters are inferred from the lambda expression used as the selector function. Although this is merely a convenience most of the time, it becomes a necessity when anonymous types are used.

Finally, an example of the use of the index-supplying overload to create a numbered list of items:

```
// { "0 is Zero", "1 is One", "2 is Two", "3 is Three" }
IEnumerable<string> numbers = new [] { "Zero", "One", "Two", "Three" }
                      .Select((s, i) => i + " is " + s);
```

Cast

The `Cast` operator is fairly similar to the `OfType` operator we saw before. It transforms input elements in a similar way but doesn't drop elements that aren't compatible with the specified target type. If such an element is encountered during enumeration, it will throw an `InvalidCastException` instead:

```
foreach (int x in new object[] { 1, "2", 3 }) {
    // Will blow up on the second iteration.
}
```

You can draw the analogy between `Cast` and the typical C# cast syntax, where `OfType` is more along the lines of the C# as keyword combined with a null check.

This operator is defined on the nongeneric `IEnumerable` type for the source, just like `OfType`, and therefore produces a way to make old nongeneric collection types LINQ capable. A call to `Cast` is omitted when a query expression's range variable has a type specified explicitly:

```
from int x in new ArrayList { 1, 2, 3 } ...
```

The preceding becomes this:

```
from x in new ArrayList { 1, 2, 3 }.Cast<int>() ...
```

SelectMany

Probably the most important operator in LINQ is `SelectMany`. But why? There are two ways to answer this: One takes the theoretical route of monads, and another takes the practical route of querying. Let's start with the latter and make our way back to the former after we have a solid understanding of what the operator does.

`SelectMany` is one of the core drips of glue that exist in LINQ, in that it allows for composition of queries that span many sources of data. In fact, the following query expression with multiple `from` clauses translates in a use of the `SelectMany` operator:

```
from product in northwind.Products
from supplier in product.Suppliers
select new { product.Name, supplier.City }
```

What we're doing here is selecting all the suppliers that go with each product that's defined in the database we're querying. If you look closely, you can recognize two queries that are interwoven: one to fetch products and one to fetch suppliers for each of the products that have been retrieved. This corresponds roughly to two nested `foreach` loops, though a query can be executed remotely in its entirety and is, as you know by now, executed lazily.

To see where `SelectMany` enters the picture, you can verify through .NET Reflector (or by just reading the C# language specification) that the preceding form translates into the following:

```
northwind.Products.SelectMany(
    product => product.Suppliers,
    (product, supplier) => new { product.Name, supplier.City }
)
```

The SelectMany overload that's being used here is the following:

```
static IEnumerable<R> SelectMany<T,C,R>(
    this IEnumerable<T> source,
    Func<T, IEnumerable<C>> collectionSelector,
    Func<T, C, R> resultSelector);
```

Three generic parameters are present. One represents the element type used in the source sequence (T), while another represents the result element type (R). Right in the middle, we find C to represent the intermediate element type. In the preceding example, T will be substituted for some Product type, C stands for the Supplier type, and R stands for the projected result type (an anonymous type with two strings, one for the product name and one for the supplier's city).

Other overloads are available, such as the one shown here:

```
static IEnumerable<R> SelectMany<T,R>(
    this IEnumerable<T> source,
    Func<T, IEnumerable<R>> resultSelector);
```

This one essentially flattens sequences that are obtained by applying the result selector to the elements of the source sequence. The definition of the operator looks like this, using an iterator:

```
static IEnumerable<R> SelectMany<T,R>(this IEnumerable<T> source,
                                      Func<T, IEnumerable<R>> resultSelector)
{
    foreach (T item in source)
        foreach (R result in resultResultor(item))
            yield return result;
}
```

It's left as an exercise for you to come up with an implementation of SelectMany for the overload we've shown before. Two other overloads exist that provide integer index values to the selector functions, indicating the element's position in the sequence, analogous to similar overloads found on Where and Select.

LANGUAGE-INTEGRATED MONADS AND BIND IN DISGUISE

LINQ is based on the concept of *monads*, a term from category theory, introduced in the world of functional programming by Philip Wadler in the context of Haskell. Because of this, LINQ is not tied to querying operations alone and can be used for any type of monadic computation.

It turns out that SelectMany has the signature of the monadic bind operation, allowing for the composition of monadic computations. Because of query expressions, this mysterious monadic bind is disguised behind the use of multiple `from` clauses in a query expression, but what we really have here is language-integrated monads.

In this bigger picture, LINQ really is an implementation of a querying monad over sequences (that live locally in memory or remotely in some data store). However, other monads exist that aren't directly provided for in the BCL but could be defined easily by providing custom implementations of `SelectMany` (and other operators) over certain types. An example is the hypothetical monad for computation with nullables, where one hides the computational *aspect* of checking for nulls and propagating those, without evaluating unused values:

```
from x in (int?)null
from y in (int)Console.ReadLine() // would never get called, because...
select x + y // ...SelectMany sees x is null and returns null immediately
```

One other monad implementation leveraging LINQ are the reactive extensions to the .NET Framework, otherwise known as Rx or LINQ to Events. Using the nice syntax of query expressions, you can query observable data supplied by event sources. What the monadic computation here provides for is hiding all the complexity involving concurrency and coordination of hooking up and receiving events and data. More theoretically, Rx is the implementation of the *continuation monad*.

___

Zip

The only new query operator introduced in .NET 4 is `Zip`. It doesn't have any query expression syntactical surface (like many other operators don't), but it definitely has a place in a LINQ user's toolbox. What `Zip` does is combine two input sequences in an element-by-element pairwise way. Given two sequences (of possibly different element types) and a function used to combine elements at corresponding positions, it produces an output sequence with elements as long as both input sequences have remaining elements.

Figure 20.8 illustrates the operation of `Zip` in a shape comparable to the mechanical device used in clothing, combining the teeth of two sides of a zipper.

By now, you should be able to infer a signature for query operators by reading a textual definition as the one provided here. Two sequences of different element types, a combiner function and a resulting sequence, ought to look like this:

```
static IEnumerable<R> Zip<T1,T2,R>(
    this IEnumerable<T1> left,
    IEnumerable<T2> right,
    Func<T1, T2, R> resultSelector);
```

As soon as one of both sequences runs out of elements, the resulting sequence also terminates, in a similar way to an asymmetric zipper on your jacket. Also, when one of the inputs throws an exception, the resulting sequence will too, just like a broken tooth in a zipper spoils the zipping process and leaves you in the cold.

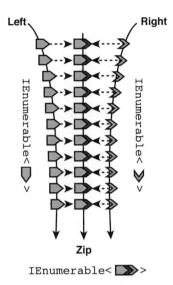

Zip

`IEnumerable< `` >`

FIGURE 20.8   Zip in action.

An example of the use of `Zip` on primitive types is shown here:

```
Enumerable.Range(0, 26).Zip(
    from i in Enumerable.Range(0, 26) select (char)(i + 'a'),
    (n, c) => "The " + n + "th character of the Latin alphabet is " + c + "."
);
```

Here, n will range over the left input (that is, the `Range` operator's output in the first line), while c will range over the right output that's provided by the embedded query expression on the second line.

NO QUERY EXPRESSION SYNTAX

Lots of standard query operators don't have a corresponding query expression syntax in C# and Visual Basic. This is often done to reduce unnecessary language surface that ages the language for less commonly used operators. Zip is one of the operators that don't have query expression syntax at the time of this writing, but it's still interesting to think about what it could look like, as it gains more insight in the type-level symmetry of the operator.

Assume C# got tuple types for a moment. *Tuples* are the generalization of pairs, triplets, and so on, wrapping up a bunch of values. A commonly used syntax for tuples is to put the values in between parentheses, in a comma-separated manner as shown here:

```
var person = ("Bart", 27);
```

The preceding could be turned into a `Tuple<string, int>`, with properties that allow you to get the respective values out (for example, `item1` and `Item2`). Syntax for those operations could be dreamed up, such as .1 and .2, and unpacking of a tuple could be done by some new form of assignment:

```
(string name, int age) = person;
```

If we now assume we have tuples in the language and allow for use of generics on them, we could write a `Zip`'s signature as follows:

```
static IEnumerable<(T1,T2)> Zip<T1,T2,R>(
    (IEnumerable<T1>,IEnumerable<T2>) sources
);
```

Observe the big symmetry between the `sources` parameter, a tuple of sequences, and the result type, a sequence of tuples. Used in a query expression, use of this syntax could yield the following form:

```
from (name, age) in (names, ages) select name + " is " + age
```

Maybe tuples will make it into C# one day, and that would be a great time to think about query expression syntax for `Zip`.

Ordering

One of the most commonly used query operations in the world of databases is applying ordering to the elements or records. Obviously, LINQ provides for this, as well:

```
var memoryHungry = from process in Process.GetProcesses()
                   orderby process.ProcessName, process.WorkingSet64 descending
                   select process;
```

The preceding query expression translates into the use of two operators, `OrderBy` and `ThenByDescending`. Their respective roles will become apparent in just a moment:

```
var memoryHungry = Process.GetProcesses()
                   .OrderBy(process => process.ProcessName)
                   .ThenByDescending(process => process.WorkingSet64);
```

OrderBy and OrderByDescending

A first set of operators start with `OrderBy` and establish a primary ordering. Within buckets with the same ordering key, secondary and n-ary orderings can be established using the `ThenBy` family of operators discussed next.

Two overloads for each of the `OrderBy` operators are available, with the most generic one allowing one to specify a comparer implementation used to investigate the relative order of elements:

```
static IEnumerable<T> OrderBy<T,K>(
    this IEnumerable<T> source,
    Func<T, K> keySelector);

static IEnumerable<T> OrderBy<T,K>(
    this IEnumerable<T> source,
    Func<T, K> keySelector,
    IComparer<K> comparer);
```

Their use should be self-explanatory. Notice, though, there's no overload that omits the use of a key selector function, but you can always use the identity function to achieve that effect:

```
// Same as   from x in new[] { 5, 2, 6, 3, 4, 1 }
//           orderby x
//           select x
var oneToSix = new[] { 5, 2, 6, 3, 4, 1 }.OrderBy(x => x) // { 1, 2, 3, 4, 5, 6 }
```

ThenBy and ThenByDescending

After establishing a primary ordering, further orderings can be established using the family of ThenBy operators. In query expressions, the commas used in the comma-separated list of ordering keys correspond to ThenBy or ThenByDescending calls.

Additional overloads with a comparer object are available, but they don't have a query expression syntax. The signatures are the same as the ones shown earlier for OrderBy operators.

Grouping and Joining

Slightly more complex query functionality exists in the family of grouping and joining operators. The number of overloads for those standard query operators may be frightening at first, so let's take a closer look.

GroupBy

To put elements in buckets with similar properties, grouping operations are used. No fewer than eight overloads exist for the GroupBy operator, which by themselves can be *grouped* into some categories. One set of overloads exposes a sequence containing IGrouping<K,T> objects, which contain the grouping key and the elements that go with it (because each grouping object is also an IEnumerable):

```
public interface IGrouping<TKey, TElement> : IEnumerable<TElement> {
    TKey Key { get; }
}
```

Another set of overloads projects the obtained groups into result objects immediately, using an extra function parameter. This proves particularly useful when performing analysis tasks such as aggregations, where the elements of the group don't matter but some sum, count, average, or another aggregation over each group's elements is what matters.

Within those categories of grouping operators, another taxonomy can be made based on the presence of additional intermediate projections over the elements. There are also overloads that provide a generic key equality comparer.

The whole set of overloads that returns grouping objects is shown here, ordered by increasing complexity:

```
static IEnumerable<IGrouping<K,T>> GroupBy<T,K>(
    this IEnumerable<T> source,
    Func<T, K> keySelector);


static IEnumerable<IGrouping<K,T>> GroupBy<T,K>(
    this IEnumerable<T> source,
    Func<T, K> keySelector,
    IEqualityComparer<K> comparer);


static IEnumerable<IGrouping<K,E>> GroupBy<T,K,E>(
    this IEnumerable<T> source,
    Func<T, K> keySelector,
    Func<T, E> elementSelector);


static IEnumerable<IGrouping<K,E>> GroupBy<T,K,E>(
    this IEnumerable<T> source,
    Func<T, K> keySelector,
    Func<T, E> elementSelector,
    IEqualityComparer<K> comparer);
```

Query expression syntax for grouping translates into the third or first overload, depending on the expression used for the computation of the grouping value:

```
// Same as   from x in new[] { 5, 2, 3, 5, 1, 1 }
//           group x by x % 2 == 0
//               ...
new[] { 5, 2, 3, 5, 1, 1 }
.GroupBy(x => x % 2 == 0) ...
```

In the preceding query, only a key selector is present, in particular a Boolean representing the odd or even characteristic of the group's values. However, we could also compute a value in one go:

```
// Same as    from x in new[] { 5, 2, 3, 5, 1, 1 }
//            group x.ToString() by x % 2 == 0
//            ...
new[] { 5, 2, 3, 5, 1, 1 }
.GroupBy(x => x % 2 == 0, x => x.ToString()) ...
```

Here we want to build groups with string elements instead of the original integers, as specified by the element selector function. Because the standard query operator creates the groups, this is the most convenient way to do such a projection *within* groups in an efficient manner, at the point the group is created. You could achieve a similar effect by using a select clause.

The set of operators that doesn't return an IGrouping object but projects the group into some related value (for example, using aggregation functions) can be derived easily from the set of overloads shown earlier. In particular, we add a function for this projection and change the return type to get rid of the IGrouping type:

```
static IEnumerable<R> GroupBy<T,K,R>(
    this IEnumerable<T> source,
    Func<T, K> keySelector,
    Func<K, IEnumerable<T>, R> resultSelector);


static IEnumerable<R> GroupBy<T,K,R>(
    this IEnumerable<T> source,
    Func<T, K> keySelector,
    IEqualityComparer<K> comparer,
    Func<K, IEnumerable<T>, R> resultSelector);


static IEnumerable<R> GroupBy<T,K,E,R>(
    this IEnumerable<T> source,
    Func<T, K> keySelector,
    Func<T, E> elementSelector,
    Func<K, IEnumerable<T>, R> resultSelector);


static IEnumerable<R> GroupBy<T,K,E,R>(
    this IEnumerable<T> source,
    Func<T, K> keySelector,
    Func<T, E> elementSelector,
    IEqualityComparer<K> comparer,
    Func<K, IEnumerable<T>, R> resultSelector);
```

GroupJoin

The use of the `join` clause in a query expression gives rise to a join operator in the generated code that calls into standard query operators. Depending on possible subsequent use of an `into` clause for a query continuation, either a `GroupJoin` operator or a plain `Join` operator is used.

When using an `into` continuation after a `join` clause, a `GroupJoin` operator call is emitted, as shown here:

```
// from product in northwind.Products
// join order in northwind.Orders on product.ID equals order.Product into g
// select product.Name + " has " + g.Count() + " orders"
northwind.Products.GroupJoin(
    northwind.Orders,
    product => product.ID,  // role of "primary key"
    order => order.Product, // role of "foreign key"
    (product, g) => product.Name + " has " + g.Count() + " orders"
)
```

If no subsequent `select` clause is used, a transparent identifier is used, as touched on briefly before. In practice, this corresponds to the use of an intermediate `Select` call, packaging up all identifiers that are "in scope" in an anonymous type object.

The reason the preceding form of joining carries grouping in its name is quite obvious: Besides joining two data sources on some common key value, the values of the inner data source (`northwind.Orders` in the preceding) are exposed as a group (g in the preceding) for use later in the query (in this case to calculate the `Count` aggregate).

Two overloads for `GroupBy` exist, one of which provides an additional comparer used in the comparison of extracted key values. The generic parameters O and I, respectively, stand for "outer" and "inner" (in reality, TOuter and TInner):

```
static IEnumerable<R> GroupJoin<O,I,K,R>(
    this IEnumerable<O> outer,
    IEnumerable<I> inner,
    Func<O, K> outerKeySelector,
    Func<I, K> innerKeySelector,
    Func<O, IEnumerable<I>, R> resultSelector);


static IEnumerable<R> GroupJoin<O,I,K,R>(
    this IEnumerable<O> outer,
    IEnumerable<I> inner,
    Func<O, K> outerKeySelector,
    Func<I, K> innerKeySelector,
    Func<O, IEnumerable<I>, R> resultSelector,
    IEqualityComparer<K> comparer);
```

The first four parameters are what entail any kind of join, specifying the sources as well as the way to extract key values from their elements. The grouping characteristic of this particular join is reflected in the presence of the `resultSelector`, which takes in the outer element with the corresponding inner elements, asking for a result value.

Join

Now that we've seen how a `GroupJoin` can combine a single outer element with all the corresponding inner elements, it's time to look at a more general kind of join that permits the combination of individual outer and inner elements that share a common key. Two overloads exist:

```
static IEnumerable<R> Join<O,I,K,R>(
    this IEnumerable<O> outer,
    IEnumerable<I> inner,
    Func<O, K> outerKeySelector,
    Func<I, K> innerKeySelector,
    Func<O, I, R> resultSelector);


static IEnumerable<R> Join<O,I,K,R>(
    this IEnumerable<O> outer,
    IEnumerable<I> inner,
    Func<O, K> outerKeySelector,
    Func<I, K> innerKeySelector,
    Func<O, I, R> resultSelector,
    IEqualityComparer<K> comparer);
```

As stated already, the key difference lies in the fifth parameter, which no longer uses the whole group of inner elements but takes in pairs of one outer and one associated inner element, based on key equality.

In terms of query expressions, this corresponds to the use of a `join` clause but without an `into` continuation following it. An example is shown here:

```
// from product in northwind.Products
// join order in northwind.Orders on product.ID equals order.Product
// select product.Name + " is ordered by " + order.Customer.Name
northwind.Products.Join(
    northwind.Orders,
    product => product.ID,  // role of "primary key"
    order => order.Product, // role of "foreign key"
    (product, order) => product.Name + " is ordered by " + order.Customer.Name
)
```

Again, immediate use of `select` results in the projection function's body to be embedded in the last parameter's selector function. As soon as other clauses follow the use of `join`, transparent identifiers enter the picture:

```
from product in northwind.Products
join order in northwind.Orders on product.ID equals order.Product
where order.Quantity >= 10
select product.Name + " is ordered by " + order.Customer.Name
```

Here, `product` and `order` will be packaged up in an anonymous type so they can be referred to (*transparently* to the user of query expression syntax) in query clauses down the query expression. The preceding roughly translates into the following:

```
northwind.Products.Join(
    northwind.Orders,
    product => product.ID,
    order => order.Product,
    (product, order) => new { product, order }
).Where(
    transparentId => transparentId.order.Quantity >= 10
).Select(
    transparentId => transparentId.product.Name + " is ordered by "
                     + transparentId.order.Customer.Name
)
```

Luckily, as a user of query expression syntax, you don't have to worry about all the hoops you must jump through to thread objects around through the query.

A comparison between `GroupJoin` and `Join` is shown in Figure 20.9.

LEFT OUTER JOINS

Sometimes people look for left outer joins, where each outer (left) element is returned, regardless of whether it has corresponding inner (right) elements. Although there's no direct operator for this, you can combine `GroupJoin` and `DefaultIfEmpty` to achieve the same effect. Search MSDN for "LINQ left outer join" for more information.

Aggregation

Analytics of information often require a reduction of data volume, computing certain statistics of the data involved. Those operations are called aggregations, which turn a collection of objects into a singleton value, representing the original information that has been combined in one form or another.

Because all aggregates are conceptually the same, we start by looking at the general-purpose `Aggregate` operator and discuss more specific aggregation operators later.

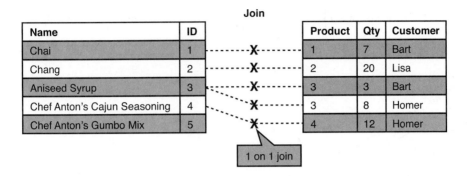

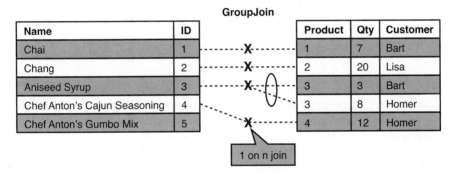

FIGURE 20.9   Types of join operations compared.

Aggregate

The `Aggregate` operator takes a sequence of elements of type `T` and turns them into a single value of another type `A`, which stands for accumulated or aggregated depending on your choice of vocab. But how can we transform any number of elements of type `T` into a single value of another type? Let's start with the simplest case where both types are the same and look at how we would create the sum of a sequence of integer values, as illustrated in Figure 20.10.

Based on this, we can see we don't need any fancy stuff to compute the sum of an unknown number of integer values: All we need is a binary function that can add two numbers. By reusing this function repeatedly, consuming one element in the input sequence at a time (in a left-to-right fashion), we can compute the sum.

So far, we've stayed in the same domain of values for our input sequence and the result of the aggregation, but in a more generalized world we want those types to differ. In fact, for a sum we might want the sum of integer values to result in a `long`, to reduce the chance of overflowing the 32-bit precision. More generally, we might want to do things like aggregating a sequence of numbers into a string concatenating them. In that case it's clear the input type (a sequence of integers) differs from the aggregated output type (a single string).

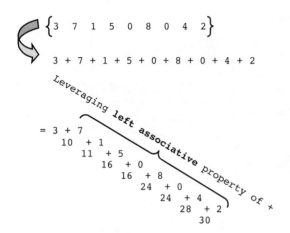

FIGURE 20.10   A sum is a simple aggregation operation.

To make this work in general, we introduce two more changes to our first attempt at an aggregation operation. In particular, we add a *seed* value to start the computation with and generalize the aggregation function to take the aggregated value so far and the next element to be aggregated. In C# terms with generics, it looks like this:

```
A Aggregate<T, A>(this IEnumerable<T> source,
                  A seed,
                  Func<A, T, A> accumulate);
```

For example, given a seed equal to the empty string " " and a function that takes a string and some element from the input, we can concatenate the aggregated string and the next element to produce the new aggregated value.

LEFT FOLD

In functional programming languages, this form of aggregation is known as a *left fold*. Given a sequence of elements, we fold them up one by one, starting from the left and making our way to the end at the right. The opposite operation, a right fold, is not available directly in LINQ; however, you can express a right fold in terms of a left fold. (Tip: The accumulation type will be a function.) In practice, though, left folds are generally more useful and have a better memory profile because one doesn't have to scan the whole input sequence first before being able to combine values from the right end.

The example illustrated in Figure 20.11 can be written as follows in C#:

```
new[] { 3, 7, 1, 5, 0, 8, 0, 4, 2 }
. Aggregate("", (s, n) => s + n.ToString())
```

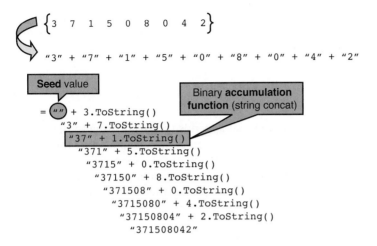

FIGURE 20.11   Aggregation with different element and accumulation types.

In summary, the general schematic representation of the Aggregate operator is shown in Figure 20.12.

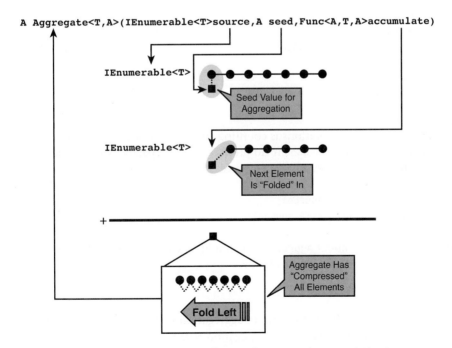

FIGURE 20.12   Aggregation with different element and accumulation types.

Notice that the string concatenation example is very inefficient due to the allocation of lots of intermediate strings for the partial results of the concatenation operation. It would be much better to use a `StringBuilder` for this, which can also be done using `Aggregate`:

```
new[] { 3, 7, 1, 5, 0, 8, 0, 4, 2 }
. Aggregate(new StringBuilder(), (sb, n) => sb.Append(n.ToString()))
```

The `StringBuilder` type has an `Append` method that appends the given string to the end of the buffer, returning the `StringBuilder` itself so one can continue appending things to it in a fluent manner. This time, the aggregation type is a `StringBuilder`, meaning the return type will be `StringBuilder`, too. Instead we likely want to transform this result into a string, which can be done by calling `ToString` on the result. Alternatively, an overload of `Aggregate` can be used to do this final transformation on the result:

```
R Aggregate<T, A, R>(this IEnumerable<T> source,
                     A seed,
                     Func<A, T, A> accumulate,
                     Func<A, R> resultSelector);
```

In our example, we can use this overload to specify the final step of turning the used `StringBuilder` into a string:

```
new[] { 3, 7, 1, 5, 0, 8, 0, 4, 2 }
. Aggregate(new StringBuilder(),
            (sb, n) => sb.Append(n.ToString()),
            sb => sb.ToString())
```

Count and LongCount

One of the simplest aggregation operations is counting the number of elements that occur in the source sequence. `Count` and `LongCount` do precisely that, respectively returning an Int32 and Int64 value. The signatures are shown here:

```
int Count<T>(this IEnumerable<T> source);
long LongCount<T>(this IEnumerable<T> source);
```

Based on the earlier discussion about `Aggregate`, it should be clear that the same effect can be achieved by relying on `Aggregate`, as follows:

```
source.Aggregate(0, (n, item) => n + 1)
```

The only slightly strange thing about this form of aggregation is that the elements from the input sequence are not being used in the aggregation result.

Some functional languages provide a don't care identifier that can be used to state that a parameter to a function will not be used. Typically, the underscore character is used. Because this is a valid identifier in C#, you can play the same trick:

```
source.Aggregate(0, (n, _) => n + 1)
```

Notice, though, an underscore is just an identifier like any other and therefore is subject to all rules that apply to identifiers, their declaration, and surrounding scopes. If multiple parameters to a function can be ignored, you won't be able to use an underscore to express the "don't care" characteristic on all of those. In functional languages, this "wildcard" syntax is really a special kind of identifier that allows such uses, but in C# it's an identifier like any other.

Additional overloads exist to compute the number of elements in a sequence that match a certain predicate:

```
int Count<T>(this IEnumerable<T> source, Func<T, bool> predicate);
long LongCount<T>(this IEnumerable<T> source, Func<T, bool> predicate);
```

Use of those overloads is merely the same as using the Where operator in conjunction with the simple form (without a predicate) of Count or LongCount.

Sum and Average

Sum and Average are closely related and compute what you expect them do. Lots of overloads exist for those aggregation operations, for all numeric primitives types and their nullable variants. Let's start by looking at Sum, illustrating the two overloads that are available for the various numeric types:

```
static int Sum(this IEnumerable<int> source);
static int Sum<TSource>(this IEnumerable<TSource> source,
                        Func<TSource, int> selector);
```

The first overload acts directly on a sequence of numeric values, whereas the latter carries out a projection first. The second form can be written in terms of Select followed by the first form of Sum, too.

When the result overflows the precision of the numeric type, an OverflowException is generated. If this is not desired, you can always use the general Aggregate operator to compute a sum manually, possibly returning a more precise type. An example to sum 32-bit integer values into a 64-bit integer, without using the checked keyword, is shown here:

```
source.Aggregate(0L, (long sum, int item) => sum + item)
```

The nullable variants implicitly coalesce null values to the default value of the numeric type being summed. This corresponds to typical database semantics for aggregation operators like Sum:

```
static int? Sum(this IEnumerable<int> source);
static int? Sum<TSource>(this IEnumerable<TSource> source,
                         Func<TSource, int?> selector);
// Sample use:
new int?[] { 1, null, 2 }.Sum() == 3
```

If this null-coalescing is not desired, you can always use Aggregate to get different behavior. For example:

```
new int?[] { 1, null, 2 }.Aggregate((int?)0, (sum, n) => sum + n) == null
```

Or if you want to throw an exception if a null value is encountered, it suffices to call the Value property on the nullable element during aggregation:

```
new int?[] { 1, null, 2 }.Aggregate((int?)0, (sum, n) => sum + n.Value)
```

This clearly illustrates the power of having a general aggregation operator acting as an escape valve if certain specialized aggregation operators don't provide desired results.

Based on our coverage of various aggregation operators so far, Average should be quite simple to understand, too. One thing to point out is that the Average operator is not the equivalent of calling Sum() and dividing by Count() on the same sequence. There are a couple of reasons this invariant doesn't hold:

▶ The null-coalescing behavior of Sum will treat null values as zeros. Count will count null values as proper elements, so null elements will be included in the denominator of the division. Average on nullable sequences will only use non-null values in the count.

▶ Using Sum and Count separately would cause two iterations over the source sequence. Because sequences are evaluated lazily, it's possible two iterations yield different results than a single iteration (for example, because of global or external state changes). Also, if the input sequence is an iterator that exposes side effects, those would get duplicated.

One final remark on the available Average overloads is that result types for averages on integral values are in the floating-point domain. For example:

```
static double Average(this IEnumerable<int> source);
```

How would you achieve a different effect by applying Aggregate manually? Based on the advice against using Count and Sum, we should think of a different way to carry out the summation and element count hand in hand. One way to do so is by making the accumulation value an anonymous type instance that has two properties for the sum and count, respectively:

```
new { 1, 2, 3 }.Aggregate(
    new { Count = 0, Sum = 0 },
    (acc, n) => new { Count = acc.Count + 1, Sum = acc.Sum + n },
    acc => acc.Sum / acc.Count /* integral division */
)
```

The preceding illustrates the expressiveness introduced in the C# language thanks to both anonymous types and lambda expressions. Notice how multiple uses of an anonymous type with the same property names and types results in compatible types within the same enclosing method. In particular, we're using the same anonymous type for both the seed and the result of the accumulation function.

STRUCTURAL TYPING

Anonymous types are a very weak form of structural typing in the language. As soon as their shape is the same in terms of property names and their types, they are compatible (within the scope of the enclosing method).

In the preceding example, the type inference on `Aggregate` has to come to conclude that the type of seed and the return type of the accumulation function are compatible with one another:

```
new { 1, 2, 3 }.Aggregate<int, <>__Anon`2, int>(...)
```

In a real structural type system (as seen in languages like Microsoft's M modeling language), the flexibility on compatibility between values would be bigger; for example, stating that { X = 1, Y = 2 } and { X = 1, Y = 2, Z = 3} participate in a subtype relationship (stating a certain compatibility between 2D and 3D points).

Min and Max

Minimum and maximum aggregations are easy to understand, too. A whole series of overloads for `Min` and `Max` provide functionality to compute numeric minimum and maximum values over a sequence. For example

```
new[] { 1, 3, 2 }.Max() == 3
```

Overloads for nullable values exist, which ignore null values in the computation of a minimum or maximum value. In addition to those, overloads that take an extra selector function are available:

```
static T Min<T, R>(this IEnumerable<T> source, Func<T, R> selector);
```

For such overloads, the default comparer on type R is used to perform the comparison. Unfortunately, no overload taking in an `IComparer<R>` is available. This non-numeric operator is also available without a selector function:

```
static T Min<T>(this IEnumerable<T> source);
```

An example use for the `Max` brother to the operator above is shown here:

```
new[] { "Bart", "Lisa", "John" }.Max() == "Lisa"
```

MINBY, MAXBY?

A relatively often requested feature for aggregation operators are `MinBy` and `MaxBy` operators that allow you to select a minimum or maximum element by specifying a key extractor function (for example, to select a person with the lowest age):

```
people.MinBy(person => person.Age).Name
```

Creation of such an operator is a bit tricky in the face of generic comparers and what-not. Although it's a good exercise, the reactive extensions to .NET will most likely ship such operators as part of the `System.Interactive` assembly. For more information, search for "DevLabs Reactive Extensions" on MSDN.

Better Together: GroupBy and Aggregations

One of the most common uses of aggregation operators is found in conjunction with the grouping operations. After grouping elements by a certain common property, one wants to calculate statistics for all the elements within each group separately. An example is shown here:

```
var procStats = from process in Process.GetProcesses()
                group process by process.ProcessName into g
                select new { Process = g.Key,
                             Count = g.Count(),
                             Memory = g.Sum(p => p.WorkingSet64) } into stat
                where stat. Memory > 100 * 1024 * 1024
                orderby stat.Memory descending
                select stat;
```

Printing those statistics will show the groups of processes that use the same executable, ordered by memory consumption in a descending manner and restricted to those that collectively consume 100MB or more. Notice how the use of the `Sum` overload with the selector function is very useful in such a scenario.

AGGREGATES IN VISUAL BASIC

The Visual Basic language has slightly more query expression exposure for standard query operators compared to C#. One field where Visual Basic has additional built-in keywords for querying operations is for aggregation:

```
From p In Process.GetProcesses()
Group p By p.ProcessName Into Memory = Sum(p.WorkingSet64), Count = Count()
Where Memory > 100 * 1024 * 1024
```

```
Order By Memory Descending
Select ProcessName, Memory
```

Other operators, such as Take, Skip, and Distinct, also have syntactical language integration in Visual Basic.

Predicates

In the world of LINQ, predicate operators express Boolean-valued truths about sequences and their elements. Operators such as Any and All should sound familiar to those who've learned basics of predicate logic. Other operators include SequenceEqual (to compare two sequences) and Contains (to ask membership questions about elements in sequences). Let's take a look at all of those.

All and Any

All and Any evaluate a predicate for each of the elements in a given sequence. If all the elements pass the predicate, All will return true. If some of the elements pass the predicate, Any will also return true:

```
static bool All<T>(this IEnumerable<T> source, Func<T, bool> predicate);
static bool Any<T>(this IEnumerable<T> source);
static bool Any<T>(this IEnumerable<T> source, Func<T, bool> predicate);
```

The extra overload for Any checks whether a sequence has any elements, returning false for an empty sequence. Some examples of the use of those operators are shown here:

```
var allEven = new[] { 2, 4, 6, 8, 10 }.All(x => x % 2 == 0); // true
var someOdd = new[] { 2, 3, 4, 5 }.Any(x => x % 2 == 1); // true
var anyElement = new int[] {}.Any(); // false, sequence empty
```

In fact, those operators also special forms of aggregation operations. For example, All can be written in terms of an aggregation using &&. One subtle difference is that the All and Any operators will stop iteration over the source sequence as soon as the result is known. All will return false as soon as an element doesn't match the predicate; Any will return true as soon as an element does match the predicate:

```
var allEven = new[] { 1, 2, 3 }.Aggregate(true,
                            (all, x) => all && x % 2 == 0);
```

Contains

As the name implies, Contains performs a membership check for a given element in a given sequence. Two overloads exist, one with and one without an equality comparer:

```
static bool Contains<T>(this IEnumerable<T> source, T value);
static bool Contains<T>(this IEnumerable<T> source, T value,
                        IEqualityComparer<T> comparer);
```

Use of this operator doesn't require further explanation. One important remark is that the operator will terminate iteration over the source sequence as soon as an element is found that matches the equality check. Also notice there's no In operator because that would create an extension method on a generic parameter T, which would appear everywhere.

SequenceEqual

To compare whether two sequences have the same elements, a check carried out by means of an equality test, the SequenceEqual operator can be used. Equality over a sequence is defined in an element-by-element pairwise equality check, also requiring that both sequences have the same number of elements:

```
static bool SequenceEqual<T>(this IEnumerable<T> first, IEnumerable<T> second);
static bool SequenceEqual<T>(this IEnumerable<T> first, IEnumerable<T> second,
                             IEqualityComparer<T> comparer);
```

A few examples illustrate the operator's behavior:

```
var f = new[] { 1, 2, 3 }.SequenceEqual(new[] { 1 }); // false
var s = new[] { 1, 2, 3 }.SequenceEqual(new[] { 2, 3, 1 }); // false
var t = new[] { 1, 2, 3 }.SequenceEqual(new[] { 1, 2, 3 }); // true
```

Set Theoretical and Sequencing Operators

So far, we've always been talking about sequences as the sources of data which LINQ operates on. Even though the use of sequences implies an ordering of elements, it doesn't preclude certain set theoretical operations, such as intersection and union, to be defined. Besides those, some operations that have an inherent affinity to sequences exist.

Intersect

The intersection of two sequences consists of all the elements that exist in both of the sequences, where an existence check is based on an equality check:

```
static IEnumerable<T> Intersect<T>(this IEnumerable<T> first,
                                   IEnumerable<T> second);
static IEnumerable<T> Intersect<T>(this IEnumerable<T> first,
                                   IEnumerable<T> second,
                                   IEqualityComparer<T> comparer);
```

Union

To merge two sequences without retaining duplicates, the Union operator can be used. Just like the Intersect operator, an equality check lies at the heart of membership tests:

```
static IEnumerable<T> Union<T>(this IEnumerable<T> first,
                               IEnumerable<T> second);
static IEnumerable<T> Union<T>(this IEnumerable<T> first,
                               IEnumerable<T> second,
                               IEqualityComparer<T> comparer);
```

Except

To retain all elements in a sequence that do not occur in another sequence, the Except operator is your workhorse. Overloads are predictable once more:

```
static IEnumerable<T> Except<T>(this IEnumerable<T> first,
                                IEnumerable<T> second);
static IEnumerable<T> Except<T>(this IEnumerable<T> first,
                                IEnumerable<T> second,
                                IEqualityComparer<T> comparer);
```

A diagram of those three operators can be found in any textbook on set theory, using Venn diagrams to represent sets.

Concat

Concatenation is a meaningful operation on any number of things that can be done in a sequential manner. Sequences obviously have a sequential nature, so it shouldn't be a surprise to see LINQ providing a Concat operator:

```
static IEnumerable<T> Concat<T>(this IEnumerable<T> first,
                                IEnumerable<T> second);
```

BEWARE OF QUADRATIC EFFECTS

Although Concat is a great operator, its current use of iterators that foreach over both sequences is a little pitfall that can come costly when lots of Concat operations are strung together.

At the heart of this problem lies the fact the iterators in C# don't provide for nested iterators, sometimes referred to as "yield foreach." Code generated for iterators is one of the most complex things emitted by the C# compiler, and so far there has been little incentive to introduce this optimization for yielding of entire sequences to the consumer of the iterator (as Concat does).

Further details are outside the scope of this book. If you're curious, however, just search for the "Iterators revisited: proof rules and implementation" paper on the Internet. Realistically, you are unlikely to face this problem unless you're using operators like Concat very heavily.

Reverse

If a sequence has an order, it has an opposite order too. To reverse the order of a sequence, you can use the Reverse operator. Be aware that this operator is very eager (as in "not lazy") because it needs to iterate over the whole sequence before it can yield the first result element, which obviously is the last element of the input sequence:

```
static IEnumerable<T> Reverse<T>(this IEnumerable<T> source);
```

QUERY OPTIMIZATION

On a related note, LINQ to Objects does provide very little query optimization intelligence for a variety of reasons. One example of an optimization one could dream of is the elimination of two Reverse calls because the net effect would be the same as retaining the original sequence. Yet other more complex optimizations could involve various properties of ordering and filtering, based on the observation that some of those query operations are seemingly commutative.

However, care must be taken in a stateful and effectful language like C#. Because sequences built on iterators could exhibit certain side effects during iteration, the slightest reordering of query logic would yield a different sequencing of those effects or even eliminate some of them.

Query optimization for in-memory queries definitely could be done, and in fact technologies like Parallel LINQ do so in a rather brute-force manner by running portions of the query in parallel, also dishonoring sequencing of possible side effects in favor of performance. More intelligent query optimization, exploiting semantic properties of query operators, could be done but is a highly specialized task. For one thing, you don't want the cost of optimizing a query at runtime to exceed the cost of just running the nonoptimized query.

Sequence Persistence

The lazy nature of iterators and query operators defined over them is a very nice property for a variety of reasons (as mentioned in passing). For example, it enables you to define a query once and execute it multiple times, yet providing possibly different results every time because the underlying data store might have changed. In addition to this, it allows for query optimization and wholesale remoting of a query expression into some domain-specific query language like SQL.

However, sometimes you just want to trigger the execution of a query on the spot, storing its results in an in-memory data structure. That's what various persistence operators such as `ToArray` and `ToList` are used for. Notice some other operators like `First`, `Last`, and `Single` also trigger execution of the query:

```
static T First<T>(this IEnumerable<T> source);
```

This becomes immediately apparent from looking at the query operator's signature, where it's clear that the sequence parameter is turned into a single object of type T, which by no means is a type that exhibits some lazy characteristic.

ToArray and ToList

The simplest persistence operators are `ToArray` and `ToList`, which simply iterate over the given sequence, putting the elements into an array or a (generic) list specifically. From that point on, iterating over the resulting collection won't trigger reexecution of the query anymore. In fact, you've just created some kind of snapshot of the query results at the point of making the call to `ToArray` or `ToList`.

Signatures of those operators are predictably easy, and their use is plain easy:

```
static TSource[] ToArray<TSource>(this IEnumerable<TSource> source);
static List<TSource> ToList<TSource>(this IEnumerable<TSource> source);
```

ToDictionary and ToLookup

Some sequences possess some key-value relationship in their elements, allowing for the creation of collections that reflect this dictionary- or lookup-alike mapping. Both `ToDictionary` and `ToLookup` can be used for such tasks. Overloads exist that take in various selector functions, to extract the key and element values, together with an optional equality comparer used for key comparisons. The richest overloads are shown here:

```
static Dictionary<K, E> ToDictionary<T, K, E>(this IEnumerable<T> source,
                               Func<T, K> keySelector,
                               Func<T, E> elementSelector,
                               IEqualityComparer<K> comparer);
```

```
static ILookup<K, E> ToLookup<T, K, E>(this IEnumerable<T> source,
                               Func<T, K> keySelector,
                               Func<T, E> elementSelector,
                               IEqualityComparer<K> comparer);
```

The difference in the return types on both families of operators lies in the shape of the returned data. A generic `Dictionary` is a well-known type by now because we covered it in Chapter 15, "Generic Types and Methods." As you'll recall, such a dictionary only provides room for one element per key. If that property exists on your source data, with applying the supplied key and element selector functions, ToDictionary is usable. However, if certain keys have multiple associated elements, you're in trouble:

```
new[] { 1, 2, 3 }.ToDictionary(x => x % 2);
```

The preceding call will fail because there are two elements, 1 and 3, that share the same key value (that is, 1). ToLookup, on the other hand, allows multiple elements per key because the ILookup interface allows for this:

```
interface ILookup<TKey, TElement> : IEnumerable<IGrouping<TKey, TElement>>
{
    int Count { get; }
    IEnumerable<TElement> this[TKey key] { get; }
    bool Contains(TKey key);
}
```

From the interfaces on ILookup, the relation of a lookup object and the grouping operators becomes clear, too. You can state that ToLookup is to GroupBy as ToList is to a regular sequence: Both To methods provide the persistent form of their corresponding data sources.

Here is an example of the use of ToLookup on a process list:

```
var procs = Process.GetProcesses().ToLookup(x => x.ProcessName);
foreach (var instance in procs["notepad"])
    Console.WriteLine(instance.Id);
```

MINLINQ AND THE ESSENCE OF LINQ

Now that we've discussed all the standard query operators, you might wonder what the essence of LINQ is. Or to state it in another way, which operators are really essential, and which ones can be derived from the core set of primitives?

I have written a blog post called "The Essence of LINQ" that elaborates on this question and provides an answer in terms of an essential implementation of LINQ called MinLINQ. For more information, see codeplex.com/LINQSQO.

Remote Versus Local with AsEnumerable

One final operator we need to take a look at is AsEnumerable. At first, it looks quite useless:

```
static IEnumerable<T> AsEnumerable<T>(this IEnumerable<T> source);
```

Looking at the implementation of the operator, this observation gets confirmed even more because it doesn't do anything but return the source parameter object. So what's its purpose? The answer is to be found in C#'s method resolution rules in the context of extension methods.

It's clear that the AsEnumerable method will be available on every object that implements the IEnumerable<T> interface (assuming the System.Linq namespace is imported, that is). One more specialized interface that's based on IEnumerable<T> is the IQueryable<T> interface, which we discuss in the "Expression Trees" section:

```
interface IQueryable<T> : IEnumerable<T>
{
    ...
}
```

Now believe me, for each query operator that's defined for IEnumerable<T>, as an extension method, a behaviorally equivalent operator is defined for IQueryable<T>. More specifically, the Queryable type contains all of those operators as extension methods:

```
static IQueryable<T> Where<T>(this IQueryable<T> source,
                              Func<T, bool> predicate);
```

Because IQueryable<T> is more specific than IEnumerable<T>, the compiler will choose the Queryable extension methods whenever you invoke a query operator on an object that implements IQueryable<T>. An example of this is the Table<T> type in LINQ to SQL, representing a table in the target database. The result of calling the IQueryable set of query operators is remoting the query into the database server for execution over there. How this works is explained in the "Expression Trees" section later in this chapter.

All of this is great until you need to use a certain query operator that's not supported on the target database server, perhaps because the underlying query language (like T-SQL) doesn't support the operator or its use. (For example, a filter predicate may contain a complex function the server doesn't know about.) Now the question is how to shake off IQueryable<T> and cause the compiler to call IEnumerable<T> extension methods, which will execute locally.

One answer is to insert a cast that tells the compiler to forget about the object's specific type and treat it as if it were nothing but an IEnumerable<T>:

```
((IEnumerable<Product>)from product in northwind.Products ... select product)
.Where(product => IsWithinMargins(product.Price))
```

Here the IsWithinMargins function is a complex function that can't be executed on the database server, so we want to execute it locally. However, the use of the cast sort of breaks the left-to-right reading order of operations: The fact we transition to local execution happens right after doing the projection remotely, yet we write this transition by inserting a cast in front. AsEnumerable allows for a fluent approach:

```
(from product in northwind.Products ... select product).AsEnumerable()
.Where(product => IsWithinMargins(product.Price))
```

In fact, we could even use query expression syntax to get rid of the explicit `Where` method call:

```
from product in
    (from product in northwind.Products ... select product).AsEnumerable()
where IsWithinMargins(product.Price)
select product
```

So all that `AsEnumerable` does is trick the compiler into emitting calls against the `Enumerable` set of extension methods because the return type of `AsEnumerable` is just an `IEnumerable<T>` (and nothing more specific).

NO HIDING

`AsEnumerable` doesn't mask its source object in any way or form. In particular

```
var xs = new[] { 1, 2, 3 };
var eq = object.ReferenceEquals(xs, xs.AsEnumerable()); // true
```

If you want to hide the identity of a sequence (for example, to prevent a user from casting it back to a more specific type [like a mutable array in the preceding example]), you can use `.Select(x => x)`. For this reason, an identity projection is not compiled away if it's the only operator in a query expression.

The Query Pattern

Now that you've seen the various standard query operators than come with LINQ and their query expression counterparts (with varying mileage in C# and Visual Basic), we can make a few more remarks about the query pattern.

The C# language specification refers to the concrete implementation of the querying operators that can be targeted by a query expression as the *query pattern*. Concretely, it means that any set of objects that happens to have (some) operators such as `SelectMany`, `Where`, `Select`, `OrderBy`, and so on can be addressed by using the query expression syntax.

All About Methods

One thing people often forget is that those query operator implementations are simply found using the typical C# method resolution rules. In particular, instance methods are considered before any extension methods are. It just so happens that the most typical LINQ implementations, such as LINQ to Objects and the `IQueryable` query providers, use extension methods on interfaces to define the query operators once and for all for all targeted data sources.

In short, you should realize that keywords such as `where`, `select`, `orderby`, `groupby`, `join`, and `let` all translate into "chains" of method calls, typically passing in lambda expressions for functional arguments such as filters, projections, key selectors, and so on. Once a query has been translated in this form, regular C# language rules for method lookup and overload resolution apply. For example:

```
from p in products
where p.UnitPrice > 100m
orderby p.UnitPrice descending
select new { Name = p.ProductName, Price = p.UnitPrice }
```

The preceding query expression is first turned into the following expression consisting of consecutive method calls using a fluent interface pattern:

```
products
.Where(p => p.UnitPrice > 100m)
.OrderByDescending(p => p.UnitPrice)
.Select(p => new { Name = p.ProductName, Price = p.UnitPrice })
```

Earlier, you saw this precise syntax-driven translation for the query operators in various figures. It's important to realize that at this point in the translation, the compiler hasn't picked any target methods yet and delays that resolution until the later phase.

Notice that besides the method calls, lambda expressions have been created out of the different clauses that occurred in the original query expression. One of the benefits of using query expression syntax is the fact you can forget about the functional concepts that are leveraged behind the scenes, which makes the code easier on the eye.

As long as the compiler is able to find good matches for the method calls with the right argument types (for example, Func delegates where the lambda expressions can be assigned), things will work just fine.

Overloading Query Expression Syntax

All of this means that you can *overload* the query expression syntax by implementing the right (sub)set of methods. For instance, if you have some type that's filterable (maybe in a more efficient manner than regular IEnumerable<T> objects), all it takes to enable the use of the where keyword is to implement a well-suited Where method. Whether that method is an instance method directly on the object being filtered or an extension method defined elsewhere doesn't matter.

This has pretty far-reaching implications, allowing quite different signatures for query operator implementations. For example, the following example shows a method that will get all the matches for a regular expression, given an input string, using the BCL support for regular expressions in System.Text.RegularExpressions:

```
static IEnumerable<Match> GetMatches(this string input, Regex regex)
{
    return regex.Matches(input).Cast<Match>();
}
```

You could argue that the preceding is a special kind of filtering operation, where the string acts as the data source and the regular expression acts as the predicate. You should feel free to disagree with this assessment, but if you're in my camp, you might like the following query expression syntax:

```
var query = from match in "Bart says \'Hallo\'"
            where new Regex(".a..")
            select match;
```

In fact, we can enable this use of the where clause simply by changing the signature of the GetMatches method a bit and by renaming it to Where:

```
static IEnumerable<Match> Where(this string input, Func<object, Regex> regex)
{
    return regex(null).Matches(input).Cast<Match>();
}
```

Notice we have to turn the second parameter into a unary function so that the first stage of the query expression compilation phase is happy. Recall how our use of the where clause results in the following chain of method calls:

```
"Bart says \'Hallo\'"
.Where(match => new Regex(".a.."))
```

Notice that the trivial identity projection doesn't remain in the translated form and is nicely compiled away in this case.

A simple Regex-typed argument is not compatible with the lambda expression that gets passed inside the translated query expression. So we apply a little (admittedly, rather dirty) trick of lifting the Regex into a function result to make the compilation pass. To make this work at runtime, we need to invoke the regex "constructor function," but we really don't care about the parameter value that's being passed to it, which is merely an artifact of the query expression translation. Therefore, we simply pass null to this regex function and out we'll get the Regex object ready to call Matches on. We've built a simple LINQ to Regular Expressions provider.

Although this is most likely a rather cumbersome LINQ provider, it illustrates the power of query expression syntax; it's not tied to enumerables or in-memory collection types whatsoever. I'll leave it to your unbounded imagination to dream up all possible uses of query syntax to express analysis over some kind of data.

STRINGS ARE IENUMERABLE

In fact, LINQ is readily available on plain string objects because every string is also an IEnumerable<char>. Because of this, you can write things such as the following:

```
var vowels = new[] { 'a', 'e', 'i', 'o', 'u' };

var stats = from c in "Bart is sitting at Joey's in Bellevue"
            where vowels.Contains(c)
            group c by c into g
            select new { Vowel = g.Key, Count = g.Count() };

foreach (var stat in stats)
    Console.WriteLine(stat);
```

Here, c is typed as char, which gets inferred through the query operator method resolution, which involves generic parameters. In particular, Where<T>'s generic parameter T gets inferred from the IEnumerable<T> source, which in this case is an IEnumerable<char> because every string implements this interface.

You might now want to decypher the query expression syntax and turn it into regular method calls, based on our discussion earlier in this chapter. Prior to Visual Studio 2010, the IEnumerable<char> based extension methods on a System.String object didn't show up for some reason, but now they do. Figure 20.13 proves this.

FIGURE 20.13   String objects are enumerables of characters.

So if you ever wonder why you see those methods on a string, remember that enumerable sequences are lurking around every corner.

Parallel LINQ

The declarative nature of LINQ queries provides us with a great opportunity to yield more control to the runtime. This is the case because we haven't buried the meaning of our querying intent under a bunch of imperative language constructs.

The Cost of Optimization

Imagine you were to write a query as follows:

```
var groups = new Dictionary<string, List<Process>>();
foreach (var proc in Process.GetProcesses())
{
    if (proc.ProcessName.StartsWith("d"))
    {
        List<Process> bucket;
        if (groups.TryGetValue(proc.ProcessName, out bucket))
            bucket.Add(proc);
        else
            groups[proc.ProcessName] = new List<Process>() { proc };
    }
}
```

It's most likely not immediately apparent to you this is carrying out a filtering operation as well as a grouping operation, let alone that the runtime would be able to see our intent from the rather complex preceding code. Also because you've prescribed the recipe to execute your algorithm very precisely, you'll most likely not want the runtime or compiler to start messing with the code in an overly smart way.

One of the main concepts exploited in imperative programming languages is the use of sequencing to control execution order or statements and elevation order of expressions. Guarantees about such orderings are made by the language, which is great if you want to reason precisely about an algorithm but hinders various forms of optimization.

However, with LINQ we do have more room for such optimizations because developers no longer overspecify the solution to the problem at hand. In the world of query expressions, you simply express your querying intent in a domain-specific language specialized for that purpose. How precisely the results are obtained at runtime is left to various runtime components, such as the query operator implementation in the BCL:

```
var query = from proc in Process.GetProcesses()
            where proc.ProcessName.StartsWith("d")
            group proc by proc.ProcessName;
```

Without the expressive nature of query expressions (or manual chaining of query operators through method calls), the user is forced into a mode where lots of decisions have to be made early. For example, in the preceding example, one picks a generic dictionary type to achieve grouping, whereas other strategies may be potentially more optimal.

AsParallel

In an age when every computer has multiple processor cores, the industry is hunting for great opportunities to keep those cores busy (to make one's computer purchase pay off by improving processing times). One of the best understood domains of concurrency is in data processing, as testified by the long history of query optimization in database management systems. For example, SQL Server can leverage huge numbers of cores because of the embarrassingly parallel domain it operates on: relational databases.

Obviously, LINQ fishes in the same pond of data and query processing, so why can't there be a way to parallelize in-memory queries, as well? Introduced in .NET 4, PLINQ, or Parallel LINQ, provides exactly this through a very simple API surface, almost entirely consisting of a single method: `AsParallel`.

Let's take a look at a data-intensive query, which may be used in a scientific context that does some kind of number crunching. More concrete examples of this include image processing, where a bitmap consists of rows and columns of pixels that can be analyzed for purposes like pixel shading and whatnot. To keep things simple, consider the next fragment of code using `Enumerable.Range` to generate a large input set:

```
var res = from x in Enumerable.Range(0, 10000)
          from y in Enumerable.Range(0, 10000)
          where x > y
          select x + y;

var sw = new Stopwatch();
sw.Start();
res.ToList();
sw.Stop();
Console.WriteLine(sw.Elapsed);
```

Two from clauses, translating into a `SelectMany` call behind the scenes, are similar to nested for loops, so from a complexity point of view the size of the input set presented to the where clause is of the order 10,000 squared. That's quite a bit of data, and it should come as no surprise that this code takes a while to execute. On my machine with two physical cores, this code took 18 seconds to run (on battery power), almost exclusively hogging a single core. Figure 20.14 shows this clearly.

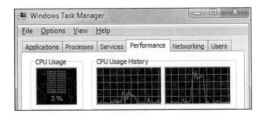

FIGURE 20.14   One core is sitting idle.

So what can we do to parallelize this code? Without LINQ, we would be in big trouble because the preceding query would have been turned into excessively imperative code:

```
var lst = new List<int>();
foreach (var x in Enumerable.Range(0, 10000))
    foreach (var y in Enumerable.Range(0, 10000))
        if (x > y)
            lst.Add(x + y);
```

Besides not being lazily evaluated, lots of issues with this code will prevent easy parallelization. Let's take a look.

One possible opportunity for parallelization is to split the input into separate partitions and run the filtering operation in parallel. On a dual-core machine, your core could process the first 5,000 values for x, while another could take care of the last half. This requires applying some partitioning policy depending on the machine capabilities. If you run the same code on a quad core, you likely want to create four partitions. Although this seems easy using `Environment.ProcessorCount`, a static partitioning with equal-size partitions might not be the right choice in general. It could be the case that the cost of applying querying operators varies from input to input, so that one partition is processed much faster than another one. In that case, the core assigned to the partition with the least cost will sit idle after a while.

Even if we come up with a good partitioning strategy, other remaining issues lurk around the corner. In the preceding code, we're adding results to an in-memory collection object, which is generally not safe for concurrency and multithreading in particular. So we need to use locks, which puts us in an error-prone situation and can cause adverse effects on our intended performance optimization. I'll leave the exercise of parallelizing this imperative piece of code to the concurrency-savvy reader. Suffice to say, things get messy immediately, and the intent of our code gets more blurry by the minute. With PLINQ, we can simply write the following:

```
var res = from x in Enumerable.Range(0, 10000).AsParallel()
          from y in Enumerable.Range(0, 10000)
          where x > y
          select x + y;
```

Now both cores are being put to work (as shown in Figure 20.15), and the total execution time went down to 10 seconds, about half of the original time. All we did to achieve this was to put the `AsParallel` call on the topmost (or outermost, depending on your mental modal) data source in the query.

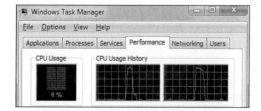

FIGURE 20.15   PLINQ puts both cores to work.

It can't be emphasized enough that measurement should be the guide to carrying out optimizations. The first question to ask is whether the original code meets a certain min-bar with regard to execution time. If it doesn't, the next step is to look out for possible optimizations.

Quantitative analysis is the key to successful evaluation of performance, especially in core data processing tasks where the raw performance matters and is not directly subject to user perception. In the world of UI programming, you most likely want to carry out user-satisfaction studies to figure out whether your application is responsive enough.

One of the big benefits of PLINQ in particular, and the .NET 4 Task Parallel Library in general, is the ease by which you can simply try to parallelize a piece of code (for example, by sticking AsParallel on a query). In imperative programming, you'd be faced with a complete overhaul of the code. Sadly, people often cross the barrier of correctness when attempting to make their code run faster. The smallest mistake can have disastrous impact on the code's meaning, sometimes going unnoticed for a long time due to the nondeterminism of parallel code execution. With technologies such as PLINQ, the cost of trying out some parallelization is low, so evaluation of a certain optimization strategy is cheap.

How PLINQ Works

We can approach the question of how PLINQ does its magic in two ways. We can look behind the scenes and study various techniques used to partition input sequences efficiently, to avoid locking when merging results together and to analyze the query wholesale to decide on certain parallelization strategies at runtime. Although all of this is incredibly interesting, we would need a whole book to cover all of this. Alternatively (and what we do here), we can ask ourselves how PLINQ gets a chance to analyze the query expression for various forms of optimization at runtime. This is immediately related to the query pattern we've seen before.

Let's start by repeating the exercise of decomposing a query expression, this time with an AsParallel call on one of its sources, into individual methods. The sample query shown earlier translates into the following:

```
var res = Enumerable.Range(0, 10000).AsParallel()
        .SelectMany(x => Enumerable.Range(0, 10000), (x, y) => new { x, y })
        .Where(_ => _.x > _.y)
        .Select(_ => _.x + _.y);
```

The precise mechanics of the SelectMany translation with transparent identifiers is irrelevant in this context. What matters more is the observation that AsParallel sits right in front of the subsequent query operator calls.

Because of this, the return type of the AsParallel call will be essential in the further resolution of the query operator methods following it. If you go to the definition of this mysterious AsParallel method (simply by pressing F12 in Visual Studio), you'll see it's defined as an extension method on IEnumerable<T>, living in ParallelEnumerable:

```
static ParallelQuery<T> AsParallel<T>(this IEnumerable<T> source);
```

The output type becomes a ParallelQuery<T>, which is defined as follows:

```
public class ParallelQuery<T> : ParallelQuery, IEnumerable<T>, IEnumerable
{
    public virtual IEnumerator<TSource> GetEnumerator();
}
```

A ParallelQuery isn't much more than a simple IEnumerable<T> with a customizable virtual GetEnumerator method, which gets implemented by the runtime to execute the query in parallel. The most important role is simply played by the identity of the type, which forces the compiler into using the query operator methods that are defined as extension methods on ParallelQuery<T>. Because ParallelQuery<T> is a better match than IEnumerable<T>, extension methods over the former will be used.

The query expression shown earlier is turned into the following form if we go all the way in expanding the extension methods into static method calls:

```
var res = ParallelQuery.Select(
            ParallelQuery.Where(
              ParallelQuery.SelectMany(
                ParallelQuery.AsParallel(Enumerable.Range(0, 10000)),
                x => Enumerable.Range(0, 10000), (x, y) => new { x, y }),
              _ => _.x > _.y),
            _ => _.x + _.y);
```

As those more specialized operators are being called, PLINQ gets to see the whole query allowing it to apply the parallelization operations at runtime.

AsOrdered

One operator that's specific to PLINQ is called AsOrdered. Although sequences have an order for the contained elements, one often doesn't care about preserving the original sequencing throughout a query. When this is the case, PLINQ can make many more optimizations than when it has to preserve the order of the original sequence.

Consider the following piece of classic LINQ to Objects code:

```
var res = from x in Enumerable.Range(0, 10000)
          where x % 2 == 0
          select x;

foreach (var x in res)
    Console.WriteLine(x);
```

This code returns the even numbers that appear in the source sequence, preserving the input order. So 0 comes before 2, 2 before 4, and so on. However, as soon as we add AsParallel to the query, this order is not guaranteed (unless we explicitly use an ordering operator such as OrderBy or OrderByDescending):

```
var res = from x in Enumerable.Range(0, 10000).AsParallel()
          where x % 2 == 0
          select x;


foreach (var x in res)
    Console.WriteLine(x);
```

Figure 20.16 illustrates an apparent artifact that can occur, caused by the introduced concurrency of PLINQ.

FIGURE 20.16   PLINQ favors speedup over preservation of input sequence ordering.

If for some reason you want to restore the original ordering while still trying to achieve a speedup, you can use the AsOrdered operator. However, realize this restricts the moving space for PLINQ's optimization logic and can result in higher memory footprint and adverse affects on performance. Again, measurement will tell:

```
var res = from x in Enumerable.Range(0, 10000).AsParallel().AsOrdered()
          where x % 2 == 0
          select x;


foreach (var x in res)
    Console.WriteLine(x);
```

Tweaking Parallel Querying Behavior

Various methods are available in PLINQ to control some aspects of the parallelization of queries. Those methods start with the With prefix and control aspects such as the following:

▶ Degree of parallelism, specifying how many parallel workers be can running during query execution

▶ Execution mode, allowing to force parallelism even if PLINQ concludes it's not worth the effort

▶ Merge options, controlling query result buffering because the parallel producers and the query consumer can move at their own paces

▶ Use of a cancellation token, allowing the executing query to be canceled without waiting for all input to be consumed

Because those operations are meant for advanced users who thoroughly understand the way the PLINQ query engine works, we forego a detailed discussion—refer to the MSDN documentation for further information. The defaults that are used when all of those options are omitted are reasonably tuned for the common PLINQ use scenarios.

Parallel Enumeration with `ForAll`

So far, we've been using a classic `foreach` loop in conjunction with a PLINQ-based query. Although this is the most obvious and natural way to consume results of a query, we can do better when we're facing concurrency. Maybe the results of the query can be consumed in parallel as well, which will allow for a higher throughput. You can see why this is the case in Figure 20.17.

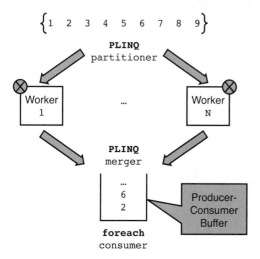

FIGURE 20.17   Buffering involved with one consumer and multiple producers.

After the input sequence is partitioned (possibly in a dynamic manner), parallel workers start executing the query (which by itself can have further decomposition in tasks). To present all information to a `foreach` loop, the results from the various workers need to be put together again in some producer-consumer collection so that the intrinsically single-thread `foreach` loop can read the results one at a time.

For example, the following piece of code will print the thread on which the WriteLine method is being called with the received result:

```
var res = from x in Enumerable.Range(0, 10).AsParallel()
          where x % 2 == 0
          select x;

foreach (var x in res)
    Console.WriteLine(Thread.CurrentThread.ManagedThreadId + " -> " + x);
```

This will always produce the same thread ID in front of the result value because foreach operates in a single-threaded manner. However, when you can reasonably consume the outputs in a parallel manner (which won't be the case if you need to update some UI, which is also intrinsically single-threaded), we can eliminate the contention caused by the serialization of query results into the producer-consumer output buffer. PLINQ's ForAll operator precisely allows for this:

```
var res = from x in Enumerable.Range(0, 10).AsParallel()
          where x % 2 == 0
          select x;

res.ForAll(x =>
    Console.WriteLine(Thread.CurrentThread.ManagedThreadId + " -> " + x)
);
```

Now the action delegate passed to ForAll takes in the received value to perform an action with. Now we'll potentially see that results are coming in on different threads, depending on how the input set was partitioned by PLINQ. Figure 20.18 illustrates a run of this code where two workers are calling the ForAll action to signal an available result.

FIGURE 20.18   Two workers are pushing results into the ForAll action.

Whether you can use the ForAll method will depend on the place where the output has to be consumed. You'll learn more about concurrency in Chapter 29, "Threading and Synchronization," and Chapter 30, "Task Parallelism and Data Parallelism."

Expression Trees

Although the availability of extension methods, lambda expressions, and object initializers seems to provide the essential building blocks for LINQ, we're still missing one big piece of the puzzle: How can we execute queries remotely? Let's take a look at this essential scenario next, enabling rich LINQ providers such as LINQ to SQL.

Query Expression Translation

To execute a query expression in a way other than in-memory processing of sequences based on iterators, as done in LINQ to Objects, you must be able to make sense of the querying intent specified by the user. While keeping unified query syntax across different data domains, LINQ must provide for a rich extensibility story that allows third parties to plug in to the query execution pipeline.

You've already seen the big-hammer approach to intercepting query expressions, simply by providing an implementation of the query pattern over any type you see fit. For example, to provide a LINQ-compatible object model over some domain-specific concept like a Table<T> (which could represent a table in a relational database), you could stick a whole set of query operator methods on that type:

```
class Table<T>
{
    public Query<T> Where(Func<T, bool> predicate) { ... }
    public Query<R> Select<R>(Func<T, R> selector) { ... }
    public OrderedQuery<T> OrderBy<K>(Func<T, K> keySelector) { ... }
    public OrderedQuery<T> OrderByDescending<K>(Func<T, K> keySelector) { ... }
    ...
}

class Query<T>
{
    public Query<T> Where(Func<T, bool> predicate) { ... }
    public Query<R> Select<R>(Func<T, R> selector) { ... }
    public OrderedQuery<T> OrderBy<K>(Func<T, K> keySelector) { ... }
    public OrderedQuery<T> OrderByDescending<K>(Func<T, K> keySelector) { ... }
    ...
}

class OrderedQuery<T> : Query<T>
{
    public OrderedQuery<T> ThenBy<K>(Func<T, K> keySelector) { ... }
    public OrderedQuery<T> ThenByDescending<K>(Func<T, K> keySelector) { ... }
}
```

As you can understand from the preceding example, to allow composition of query opera-tors ad infinitum, you have to build a carousel of related types, effectively creating a Query<T> object by acquiring one additional query clause at a time.

Although this seems feasible as a way to create a query provider over some object model, this approach suffers from many inherent limitations. First, the more query constructs are supported, the more methods you must implement on a bunch of those types. Even though the use of type hierarchies can help a lot, it still is a rather tedious process. But that's actually the least of our problems because we face much bigger issue: the various functions passed to the query operator methods.

So what's up with those functions? As you can see, they've been typed using simple generic delegate types such as Func<T, bool> and Func<T, R>. Because of this, any assign-ment to those parameters will result in the creation of a series of intermediate language (IL) instructions that directly implement the lambda expression's logic for local execution upon invocation of the delegate. Given the preceding hypothetical API, let's quickly trace through the translation of the following query expression:

```
from x in new Table<int>(/* assume there's some data */)
where x > 10
select x + 1
```

This is turned into the following equalent code, which ultimately returns a Query<int> object:

```
new Table<int>(/* assume there's some data */)
.Where(x => x > 10)
.Select(x => x + 1)
```

During the next stage of the compilation, the lambda expressions need to be assigned to the parameters of the used methods. Because those parameters are typed with delegate types, the result is equivalent to the following C# 2.0 fragment:

```
new Table<int>(/* assume there's some data */)
.Where(delegate (int x) { return x > 10; })
.Select(delegate (int x) { return x + 1; })
```

You could take it one step further and turn the anonymous methods into named ones (which is what the compiler does anyway), and it becomes clear that the functions used for predicates, projections, and whatnot get turned into IL code bodies.

For a query provider to be able to make sense of the written query expression, producing IL code is a bridge too far. Although you could dream up one way or another to decom-pile, at runtime, the query expression and all functional clauses used therein, this defi-nitely looks suboptimal. What if instead we can have the compiler generate a data structure that captures the query expression in terms of an object model? With such a capability, query providers can simply analyze this so-called expression tree to take the appropriate action to execute a query.

In such a world, the following query expression would be turned into the expression tree representation shown in Figure 20.19:

```
from x in source
where x > 10
select x + 1
```

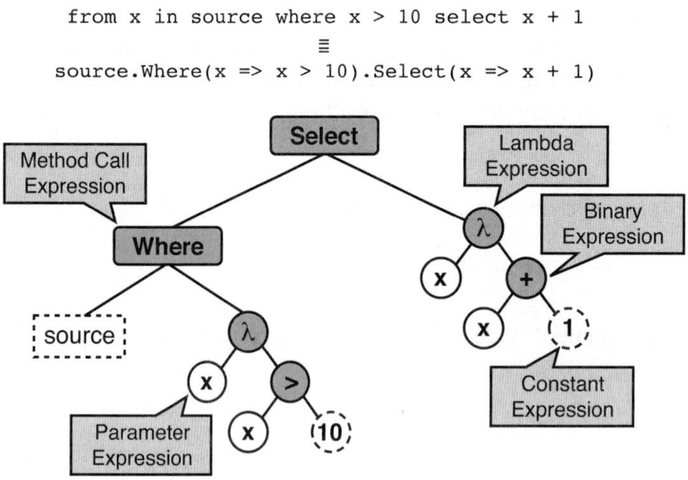

FIGURE 20.19   An expression tree representing a whole query expression.

We'll now start looking into the mechanics that cause this expression tree to be emitted by the compiler, ultimately resulting in a discussion about the IQueryable<T> interface, which is one of the typical ways to extend LINQ with new query providers. In fact, providers such as LINQ to SQL and LINQ to SharePoint are built on top of IQueryable and the expression tree APIs.

Homoiconicity for Dummies

Expression trees are a form of data. More specifically, they are the data representation of a piece of code. It's essential to see that expression trees do not contain the *result* of executing the code but capture the *shape of the code* itself. Compiler writers love and breathe such tree representations of code, starting with abstract syntax trees (ASTs).

Although expression trees are much like ASTs, they contain more information than just the syntax that lies at the origin of the expression tree. In addition, every node in an expression tree has reflective information about its data type and the operations it's representing (like the precise method overload being called or property being looked up). All of this allows for rich analysis of the code that was written by the user.

One first key question to answer, though, is how expression trees are being generated. What does the user have to do to create one of those animals? The answer is this: not much, thanks to a property of the C# programming language (starting with version 3.0) known in the literature as *homoiconicity* for lambda expressions. This property is often attributed to LISP, where one can "quote" expressions to get their data representation. All it means is that the same (homo) syntactical shape (icon) is used to capture lambda expressions either as code (IL instructions) or as a data representation (expression trees). You can't tell how the lambda expression will be translated just by looking at the following code:

```
Calculate(x => x + 1, 42)
```

To get to see what route the compiler will take in translating this lambda expression, you must peek at the type of the variable to which the lambda gets assigned. In this case, that obviously is the first parameter of the Calculate method. Two possibilities exist, the first of which should be familiar to those who have already studied delegates:

```
int Calculate(Func<int, int> op, int arg)
```

In this case, we're simply assigning the lambda expression to a delegate typed variable, causing the compiler to emit the equivalent of a C# 2.0 anonymous method:

```
Calculate(delegate (int x) { return x + 1; }, 42)
```

At the receiving end, the Calculate method can call the function by using the well-known delegate invocation syntax, like this:

```
int Calculate(Func<int, int> op, int arg)
{
    return op(arg);
}
```

However, if the assignment target for the lambda expression is not typed to be just a delegate type but an Expression<TDelegate> (where TDelegate is a delegate type), the compiler switches gears and emits an expression tree for the lambda. The following signature for Calculate will result in this situation:

```
int Calculate(Expression<Func<int, int>> op, int arg)
```

Here we're using the generic Expression type found in System.Linq.Expressions, which nowadays has a broader use than just LINQ. The dynamic language runtime also uses expression trees, as you will see in Chapter 22, "Dynamic Programming." Given this new signature, our call to the Calculate method will result in the following equivalent code being generated:

```
var x = Expression.Parameter(typeof(int), "x");
var f = Expression.Lambda<Func<int, int>>(
    Expression.Add(
        x,
        Expression.Constant(1)
    ),
    x
);
Calculate(f, 42);
```

Those factory method calls result in the creation of a data structure, at runtime, that represents the code of the lambda expression the user wrote as the first argument to the call to Calculate. In fact, this code could have been written manually in C# 2.0 (if the expression tree API would have been available in the BCL at that time), but it's clear you don't want to be involved in writing boilerplate code like this. Homoiconicity of lambda expressions allows you to generate expression trees by using exactly the same syntax for lambda expressions that can be used to create new delegate instances.

Figure 20.20 summarizes the call site effects when using lambda expressions in both their code and data form.

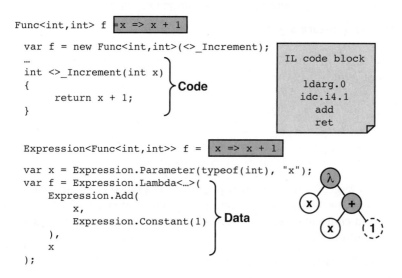

FIGURE 20.20   Lambda expressions represented as code or data.

Now that we've seen the effects of assigning a lambda expression to an expression tree type, the obvious next question is what can we do with the expression tree *object* at runtime? Because expression trees are just plain objects, we can investigate call methods on them, investigate their properties, and so on. Figure 20.21 shows the IntelliSense over the lambda expression tree node object in the expression tree received on Calculate.

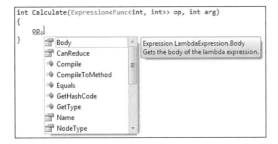

FIGURE 20.21   Investigating an expression tree by browsing its properties.

The goal of such code is to analyze what the intent of the user's code is, to turn it to execution somehow. In the calculation example, we might want to translate the expression into a specialized, highly efficient numeric processing language. In the world of LINQ, we'll take the expression tree and turn it into a domain-specific query language like SQL that we can send to the (typically out of process) database engine.

Writing a meaningful implementation of our Calculate method that operates based on a received expression tree would lead us too far. The essence of such code will be to visit all nodes of the tree recursively to turn the original tree into some target language or to execute it using interpretation. You learn more about expression trees in the context of discussing the dynamic language runtime in Chapter 22, so we'll defer further exploration until then.

Expression Trees for Query Expressions

To turn entire query expressions into some kind of remote execution, the first trick that has to be played by the LINQ providers is to get their hands on an expression tree with all the required information about the querying intent. Because you now know about the origin of expression trees, it should come as no surprise that the function arguments to a variety of query operators need to be turned into Expression<TDelegate> ones.

If we were to rewrite our hypothetical Table<T> (and Query<T>) as shown here, query expressions over the objects would trigger the generation of expression trees.

```
class Table<T>
{
    public Query<T> Where(Expression<Func<T, bool>> predicate) { ... }
    public Query<R> Select<R>(Expression<Func<T, R>> selector) { ... }
    ...
}

class Query<T>
{
    public Query<T> Where(Expression<Func<T, bool>> predicate) { ... }
```

```
        public Query<R> Select<R>(Expression<Func<T, R>> selector) { ... }
    ...
}
```

Given this new API, we can perform the translation for the following query again. This time, the Table<T> object will represent a reference to some data that can be obtained from some data source (for example, by storing the name of the underlying SQL table):

```
from x in new Table<int>(/* a reference to the data, e.g. in a SQL table */)
where x > 10
select x + 1
```

The first phrase of the translation is still the same, turning the query expression into a chain of method calls, passing in lambda expressions:

```
new Table<int>(/* a reference to the data, e.g. in a SQL table */)
.Where(x => x > 10)
.Select(x => x + 1)
```

Thanks to homoiconicity, one doesn't see any syntactical difference between the use of lambda expressions as code versus data. Now that the compiler has found the Where and Select methods, it comes to the conclusion the lambda expressions must be assigned to expression trees, and therefore it generates such code:

```
var x = Expression.Parameter(typeof(int), "x");
var f = Expression.Lambda<Func<int, bool>>(
            Expression.GreaterThan(x, Expression.Constant(10)), x);
var s = Expression.Lambda<Func<int, int>>(
            Expression.Add(x, Expression.Constant(1)), x);

new Table<int>(/* a reference to the data, e.g. in a SQL table */)
.Where(f)
.Select(s)
```

Now the Where method on Table<T> and the Select method on the returned Query<T> object get to see their parameters as expression trees, ready for translation into some target query language like SQL (for example, producing the following hypothetical code):

```
SELECT x + 1 FROM SomeTable WHERE x > 10
```

However, one remaining piece of the puzzle is missing. Even though query operator methods now get to see their functional arguments as expression trees, this is not enough. Because we want to remote the query wholesale (including the operators) and do so in a deferred manner, triggering execution at the point of enumeration, we somehow need to "stitch together" all those little expression trees. That's what IQueryable<T> is used for on query providers.

IQueryable<T>

As you've seen before, LINQ to Objects operates on plain IEnumerable<T> objects, executing the query using the magic of iterators. All of this happens in memory in the same process as where the collection object is living. The brother to IEnumerable<T> allowing for remote execution of queries is called IQueryable<T> and is based on the concept of expression trees.

Let's first take a look at the interface to set the scene. As shown here, every type that implements IQueryable<T> also implements IEnumerable<T>, which provides support to enumerate over the object. It's this enumeration that will trigger the query captured by the queryable object to be translated and executed (for example, by sending a piece of T-SQL to a database server or by making web services calls):

```
public interface IQueryable<out T> : IEnumerable<T>, IQueryable
{
}

public interface IQueryable : IEnumerable
{
    Type ElementType { get; }
    Expression Expression { get; }
    IQueryProvider Provider { get; }
}
```

The question coming up immediately when looking at this interface is where the query operators are defined. Just like IEnumerable<T> has no query operators by itself and relies on extension methods to define those, IQueryable<T> does the same and defines query operators as extension methods in a static class called Queryable:

```
public static class Queryable
{
    ...
    public static IQueryable<T> Where<T>(this IQueryable<T> source,
                                    Expression<Func<T, bool>> predicate);
    public static IQueryable<R> Select<T, R>(this IQueryable<T> source,
                                    Expression<Func<T, R>> selector);
    ...
}
```

Notice how all the functional parameters are using expression trees rather than plain old delegates, such that the code gets captured as data. A remaining question is how those methods that are implemented once and for all in the BCL cooperate with custom implementations of the IQueryable<T> interface to build up a whole query expression as an expression tree. As an example, the implementation of Queryable.Where roughly looks like this:

```
public static IQueryable<T> Where<T>(this IQueryable<T> source,
                                     Expression<Func<T, bool>> predicate)
{
    var where =
        Expression.Call(
            MethodInfo.GetCurrentMethod(), // in reality more complex
            source.Expression, // ask the source for its expression tree
            predicate
        );
    return source.Provider.CreateQuery<T>(where);
}
```

Other operators are implemented in a similar way. The essence of this code is to stitch together the expression tree that represents the source used for the operator (which by itself can be the result of a query operator call preceding it) and all the arguments passed to the operator. In this case, the only argument is a predicate lambda expression, which gets passed in from the compiled query expression code that generates an expression tree. After Queryable has stitched together all those expression trees into a bigger one, representing the method call to the operator method, it hands over the new tree to the IQueryProvider object exposed on the IQueryable source object:

```
public interface IQueryProvider
{
    IQueryable<TElement> CreateQuery<TElement>(Expression expression);

    ...
}
```

Figure 20.22 illustrates all the steps involved in constructing the expression tree for a where clause in an IQueryable-based query expression.

This process continues until all query operators have been called at the declaration site of a query. The end result is a single IQuerable object with an expression tree inside it, capturing the whole query expression with all the used operators in the right order and with information about the passed (potentially functional) arguments. Figure 20.23 illustrates the result of this runtime tree stitching on a whole query, assuming the source object is an IQueryable<T> and the Queryable extension methods are getting called as a result.

Because every IQueryable object is also IEnumerable, the GetEnumerator method used by a request to iterate over the results of the query (for example, using foreach) can inspect this big expression tree and turn it into the query language targeted by the query provider. How precisely this translation works requires deeper coverage of expression trees and is beyond the scope of this book. For more information about the subject of writing your own LINQ providers, search the Web on the topic.

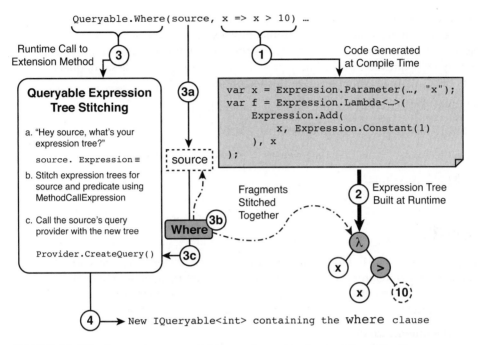

FIGURE 20.22   Expression tree stitching performed by `Queryable` methods.

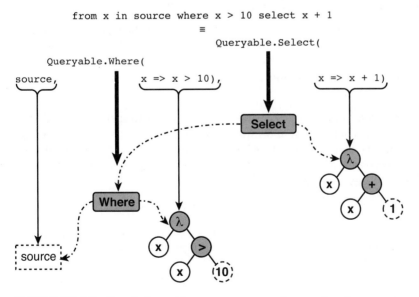

FIGURE 20.23   Translating a bigger query expression creates deeper expression trees.

Now, when you're using LINQ to SQL or other `IQueryable<T>`-based LINQ providers, think of the nice interaction between compile-time expression tree generation and the `Queryable` extension methods role in stitching those fragments together to provide a wholesale query expression to the query provider underneath. A whole set of query providers exist, many of which leverage this technique:

- ▶ LINQ to SQL, LINQ to Entities (in .NET 3.5 and later)

- ▶ LINQ to SharePoint (starting with Office 2010)

- ▶ LINQ to Amazon (the first `IQueryable<T>` provider I am aware of)

- ▶ LINQ to... Anything?

Summary

To understand how LINQ to Objects works for in-memory queries over collections, a solid knowledge of C# 2.0 iterators is required. After introducing this language feature, we put it into practice by implementing a few iterators that behave like query operators. One key takeaway from the way iterators work is the concept of lazy evaluation.

Following the intermezzo on iterators, we explored the rich set of query operators in more depth, examining the behavior of those operators. Collectively known as the standard query operators, they form the heart of LINQ queries. Query expression syntax provided by languages such as C# turns into calls to those operator methods.

Because one of the things that LINQ allows is the capability to put the runtime in control over the way queries execute, we illustrated this powerful concept in a brief detour through .NET 4's Parallel LINQ implementation. The declarative nature of LINQ not only results in more readable code, it also permits future optimizations carried out by framework writers.

Finally, because one the goals of embedded querying capabilities is to span multiple data domains, we studied the mechanics that allow queries to be translated into specialized query languages at runtime. Starting with the essentials of expression trees, we ended up in the world of `IQueryable<T>`, where query providers get to see a query expression in its entirety, ready for customized handling at runtime.

IN THIS CHAPTER

▶ Typing Revisited, Static and Otherwise 1048

▶ Reflection 1054

▶ Lightweight Code Generation 1082

▶ Expression Trees 1091

So far, we've been looking at statically typed code for the most part. In the world of static typing, it's the compiler's task to resolve information about types at the point the program is compiled. This provides various benefits related to program checks for various forms of correctness, improved tooling support thanks to IntelliSense, increased runtime performance because operations are known unambiguously, and much more.

However, such static type information is not always available. And although the benefits mentioned should be enough to convince people to get static typing wherever possible, the harsh reality is there are many dynamically typed pieces of code and data out there. In fact, we've seen an increasing trend moving away from static typing for various types of systems, such as web services (without a WSDL definition, and using REST) and data formats like XML (without XSD schema) or JSON.

In this chapter, we look at the facilities provided by the common language runtime and the .NET Framework to interoperate with objects lacking static type information. This stretches reflection and on-the-fly code generation. In the next chapter, we look at the dynamic keyword introduced in C# 4.0, which in part builds on the services explained in this chapter.

Typing Revisited, Static and Otherwise

When introducing the CLR in this book, I emphasized a series of key characteristics of the platform. One of those is the self-describing nature of assemblies and the types and members they contain, in the form of metadata. It's because of this rich metadata that describes the functionality contained in an assembly that we get rich tool support and compile-time checking of uses of the various types and members.

The Role of Metadata

Metadata plays a very important role in the world of .NET, providing both runtime and tools with a plethora of information about your assemblies, the contained types, and their members. Thanks to metadata, you have rich tooling such as IntelliSense helping you find certain functionality exposed on types in a variety of contexts (for example, with awareness of visibility). All information about what's available and how it behaves is kept in metadata.

But it goes way beyond that. Compilers leverage the same metadata to emit sound code that drives your code at runtime. For example, method calls get resolved into the right tokens in intermediate language (IL) referencing the target method. All the runtime then has to do is make sure that types are loaded when needed, that code gets compiled into efficient native code upon execution (using the JIT compiler or leveraging an NGEN native image), some type safety checks are performed, and so on. The main thing the runtime doesn't have to care about is figuring out the intent of the code, which would require it to apply overload resolution rules and whatnot. That task is mainly in the hands of the compiler, which enforces certain language-specific rules to choose and pick invocation targets.

VIRTUAL METHODS

If you know a bit about object orientation, you might have noticed that this description of compile-time resolution is a slight oversimplification, due to the existence of virtual methods and the runtime dispatch operation that goes with it.

But even in the case of virtual method calls, the runtime knows a lot about the call to be made already. In particular, it knows about the number of arguments and their types and where to find the virtual method target. All that remains to be done is to look up virtual dispatch tables at runtime to determine the ultimate receiving end of the call.

Again, it's because of the early intervention of the compiler based on available metadata that the runtime has a relatively easy job, with regard to invocation targets, that is.

As an example, consider the following few calls to `Console.WriteLine`, which use a different argument type each time:

```
Console.WriteLine(123);
Console.WriteLine("Hello metadata");
Console.WriteLine(new Foo());
```

Looking behind the scenes at the generated IL code, we recognize the static types on the parameters from looking at the method call instructions:

```
ldc.i4.s 123
call void [mscorlib]Console::WriteLine(int32)
ldstr "Hello metadata"
call void [mscorlib]Console::WriteLine(string)
newobj instance void Foo::.ctor()
call void [mscorlib]Console::WriteLine(object)
```

This illustrates how the compiler has resolved the calls based on the statically available type information for the used parameters and the available method overloads (as seen through the lenses of metadata bundled with the mscorlib assembly). Notice that the result of such overload resolution may be to use the most general System.Object type, but the result is still statically typed: There's no need for the runtime to discover which overload has to be called; all that work has been done at compile time.

The Multilanguage World

In addition to the rich metadata aspect of assemblies on the .NET platform, another key characteristic is their multilanguage usability, which explains the *common language* part in acronyms such as common language runtime (CLR) and Common Language Specification (CLS). As a result of this, the representation of type info and the use thereof had to be unified, too. This role is played by the Common Type System (CTS).

From this observation, it's clear that typing is deeply baked into the runtime, leading to great benefits in the area of cross-language interoperability, runtime performance, and so on. Even though all of this sounds great, it was recognized early on that there had to be a way to allow languages that want to live a less statically typed life on the platform. To enable such scenarios, the runtime needs to provide a set of services, which we discuss now.

An initial thing to recognize is the distinction between compile-time typing and runtime typing. The two are related but quite different at the same time. For one thing, every object has a runtime type that's known by the CLR when executing code that deals with the object. It's this type information that determines the runtime interactions that are possible and allowed with the object. Having runtime type information available is of utmost importance to a lot of runtime services such as the garbage collector (how big is the object; what fields does it have that refer to other objects?) and the JIT compiler (what's the layout of the object; how do I find methods on it?). Although the runtime type has to be known to the CLR to ensure type safety and such, the runtime type information is also available to the developer through code, by means of what's known as reflection. In particular, the System.Object base type has a GetType method that returns a System.Type object, describing the object's runtime type:

```
object o = "This is a string";
Type t = o.GetType();
Console.WriteLine(t.FullName);
```

The preceding prints System.String as the type object o. Notice how the declared type is different, though: Instead of assigning the string literal to a variable typed as a string, we assigned it to a variable of the System.Object base type. Obviously, this is perfectly fine to do because every string is an object. What this illustrates, though, is that a clear distinction exists between compile-time type information ("I tell you, dear compiler, that o is of type System.Object") and runtime type information. Although the C# compiler will verify your claim that the string literal indeed is an object, thus making the assignment a valid operation, you'll be restricted to invoking only those operations that are defined on System.Object:

```
// Fails to compile, there's no ToUpper on every System.Object.
string upper = o.ToUpper();

// Does compile fine, as every System.Object has a ToString method.
string print = o.ToString();
```

It's clear that the first line shouldn't compile because compile-time type information available for variable o states it's nothing but a System.Object. The compiler doesn't care what got assigned to o and, in fact, it might not even know where o comes from (for example, when it's a parameter or a field):

```
void DoSomething(object o)
{
    string upper = o.ToUpper(); // Oops!
    ...
}
```

In other words, the compiler doesn't make any assumptions about the type beyond what's stated in the code. Any operations it cannot prove positively to exist at runtime for all instances of the stated type get rejected. That's one of the characteristics of static typing.

Notice, however, that the absence of precise type information at compile time doesn't preclude dynamism at runtime. The use of virtual methods in object-oriented languages makes it possible to dispatch a call at runtime to a more specific implementation of the operation, based on the runtime type. One extreme case of this is the use of interfaces, where the compiler knows what operations will be available at runtime but doesn't have any clue where those are defined physically:

```
IComparable c = ...;
if (c.CompareTo(d) < 0)
    Console.WriteLine("c < d");
```

Even though there's this level of dynamism at runtime, static typing still provides firm guarantees about the availability of the CompareTo method, by making sure no object that doesn't implement that interface can be assigned to c. Although you can try to lie about an object's type by using casts, type safety at the runtime level prevents such mishaps from happening:

```
IComparable c = (IComparable)apple;
if (c.CompareTo(banana) < 0)
    Console.WriteLine("If you get here, you can compare apples with bananas?");
```

Assume that apple doesn't implement the nongeneric IComparable interface (it might implement the IComparable<Apple> interface though because it makes sense to compare apples with one another), you will get away with the compile-time upcast lie on the first line. However, at runtime the incompatibility will be detected, and an exception will be raised to prevent something bad from happening. If this weren't the case, you would be able to call a nonexistent CompareTo method on an object, pointing in no man's land in memory, which is clearly unsafe.

Taking Multilanguage to the Next Level

Although the infrastructure provided by the CLR to facilitate static typing accommodates a lot of programming languages on the platform, it doesn't suffice to satisfy the needs of dynamically typed languages like JavaScript, Python, Ruby, and so many more.

From day one, the need for discovery of operations at runtime has been recognized, so the CLR provides a variety of services that provide those facilities. At the heart of this feature set lies reflection, or the ability to discover information about types and their members at runtime. Reflection is not enough, though, to facilitate all the requirements for dynamic programming languages. Let's take a quick peek at common needs that such languages have:

▶ Discovery of type and member information at runtime, as provided by runtime services like reflection.

▶ Adding new members to types at runtime, a technique referred to as expando objects. For example, in JavaScript, every object is a bag one can tag stuff onto.

▶ Invocation of all sorts of object members, requiring runtime resolution of overloads and runtime type checking.

▶ Optimization of dynamic calls, typically by generation of dispatch code at runtime.

Over the years, the CLR and the .NET Framework have acquired more facilities that provide answers to all the above. We discuss most of those in this chapter, starting with

reflection, discussing lightweight code generation or LCG (added in .NET 2.0) and ultimately the dynamic language runtime added in .NET 4. Figure 21.1 depicts the layering of
the dynamic language runtime as a library on top of the CLR.

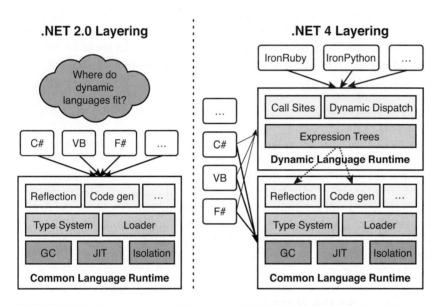

FIGURE 21.1   Layering map of languages, the DLR and the CLR.

How Does All of This Relate to C# Programming?

Notice how traditionally statically typed programming languages like C# can also
take advantage of the DLR infrastructure to reach out to the world of dynamic
typing where appropriate. This is precisely what the C# 4.0 dynamic feature is
about, which we get into later in this chapter.

When writing code as shown in the following fragment, one defers the discovery of the
member used in the method call until runtime. It should be said that this shouldn't be
regarded as a substitute for static typing, but when no static type information is within
reach, the use of dynamic makes code much more readable than it would have been if you
had to do all the member discovery and dispatching yourself:

```
dynamic d = GetCalculator(); // Could come from Python or so
int res = d.Add(1, 2);
Console.WriteLine(res);
```

As you write the fragment of code in Visual Studio 2010, it will become clear you're on
your own with regard to member selection. IntelliSense doesn't show up simply because
dynamic indicates you want to defer lookup until runtime, as no useful type information
is available at design or compile time. Figure 21.2 shows how IntelliSense on a dynamically typed variable looks.

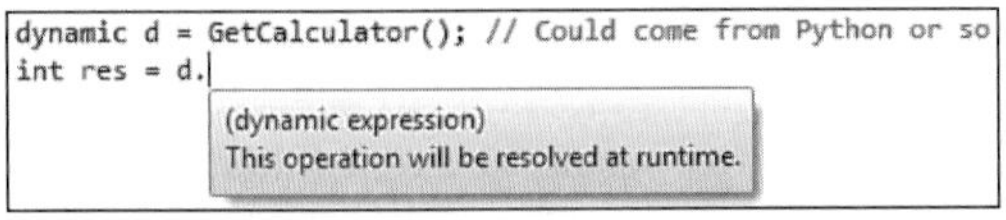

```
dynamic d = GetCalculator(); // Could come from Python or so
int res = d.|
              (dynamic expression)
              This operation will be resolved at runtime.
```

FIGURE 21.2   Dynamic expressions don't provide IntelliSense because discovery is delayed.

Since the introduction of dynamic in C# 4.0, depending on the nature of the object being targeted by the Add call, you had to write different code to achieve a dynamic call. If the object were a CLR object for which you didn't have a static type at compile time (because you loaded it dynamically from an assembly given to you at runtime or so), you had to use reflection:

```
object d = GetCalculator(); // From a dynamically loaded assembly
var res = (int)d.GetType().GetMethod("Add").Invoke(d, new object[] { 1, 2 });
Console.WriteLine(res);
```

Although you could learn the preceding plumbing techniques, it's clear code readability is hurt quite a bit by the use of reflection. Moreover, the code is prone to subtle issues such as discovery of the right method based on the name. If overloads were to exist, the preceding code would need to be bloated further to pick the right method for the call.

Assuming we get to know reflection inside out (we will later in this chapter), it still doesn't help us when we try to reach other to other object models that live outside the realm of code running directly on the CLR. We might be faced with objects coming from dynamic languages like Python, requiring us to find the invocation target method using different plumbing APIs.

In addition to this, objects may really be dynamic, meaning they can acquire and even drop members at runtime. For example, attributes on XML elements could be exposed as properties in an object model. So far so good, but during manipulation of the object new attributes could be added, so new properties have to be born at runtime. In a world where schemas are declining in popularity, simpler ways to access such kinds of dynamic data are appealing:

```
XmlElement person = GetPerson();
int age = int.Parse(person.Attributes["Age"].Value);
```

versus

```
dynamic person = GetPerson();
int age = person.Age;
```

Where LINQ unified data programming across multiple data domains, the introduction of the dynamic keyword in C# 4.0 brings unification of code invocation across multiple code domains, such as dynamic languages or untyped data models.

Reflection

At the heart of dynamic programming facilities, we find various services provided by the runtime, one of which is reflection. The goal of this service provided by the CLR and exposed through the Base Class Library (BCL) is to allow you to inspect the characteristics of types, their members, and their containers (assemblies and modules). As you will see later, reflection has additional capabilities that have to do with code generation. Figure 21.3 shows the relationship between instances, types, and the reflection data associated with a type.

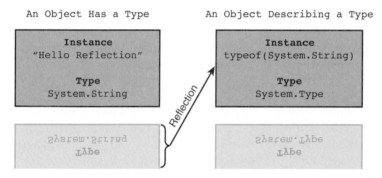

FIGURE 21.3   Reflecting on an object's type produces an object of type `System.Type`.

System.Type

One of the main entry points to the reflection data is the `System.Type` type, which can be obtained through a variety of ways, one of which is the `typeof` operator in C#:

```
var stringType = typeof(string);
var intType = typeof(int);
```

Both of those objects are of type `System.Type` (that is, you could substitute both uses of var with `Type`) and contain information about the capabilities of the said type. The uses of typeof in the preceding code translate into two instructions that map a token, which can be seen as a type name the runtime can look up in various data structure, onto the runtime object representing the type:

```
ldtoken    [mscorlib]System.Int32
call       class [mscorlib]System.Type [mscorlib]System.Type::GetTypeFromHandle(
               valuetype [mscorlib] System.RuntimeTypeHandle)
```

Reflection allows us to learn more about a type at runtime using exactly the same concepts one uses to program against any kind of object. To find out about the methods that exist on a type, you simply call `GetMethods` on the `Type` object representing it.

Reflection might seem a little weird at first, but it's a widespread concept throughout many systems. Databases, in particular today's relational ones, have had ways to describe the structure of tables for ages. The way you get to information like this is by simply writing a query over a system table (or a management view) that exposes it. Because of this, you don't have to learn different concepts to learn about the system. Reuse of the same toolbox is a great benefit.

Properties Describing Types

Types have many properties describing them. Let's take a look at most of them:

- ▶ Visibility can be inspected through various properties, such as the following:

    - ▶ IsPublic indicates whether the type was declared to be public.

    - ▶ IsNonPublic is essentially the opposite of the above.

    - ▶ IsVisible reveals whether a type can be accessed outside the assembly it's defined in. For nested types, this can differ from IsPublic.

- ▶ Types have names, which can be broken up in different ways:

    - ▶ Name is the name of the type as is was declared (for example, String).

    - ▶ Namespace tells what namespace the type is in (for example, System).

    - ▶ FullName combines the above, dot-separated (for example, System.String).

    - ▶ AssemblyQualifiedName also includes the name of the assembly in which the type lives (for example, System.String, mscorlib).

- ▶ To find out where types live, the following properties are handy:

    - ▶ Assembly reveals the assembly defining the type.

    - ▶ Module indicates the module within the type's defining assembly.

    - ▶ DeclaringType is usable for nested types, indicating the parent type. The property IsNested is related to this in an obvious manner.

- ▶ Object orientation is deeply rooted in the CLR's type system, as witnessed by the following properties:

    - ▶ BaseType, for the type's immediate base type

    - ▶ IsAbstract, indicating whether the type is abstract

    - ▶ IsInterface, identifying interface types

    - ▶ IsSealed, corresponding to the sealed keyword in C#

- Types can be classified in various categories:

  - IsPrimitive returns true for types considered primitive (such as int).

  - IsArray indicates whether you are dealing with an array type.

  - IsValueType distinguishes value types (like structs and enums).

  - IsClass, IsInterface and IsEnum should be self-explanatory.

  - IsCOMObject reveals the CLR's integration facilities to deal with types from the COM world.

  - IsPointer reveals pointer types, used in unsafe code. Notice those are not the same as reference types. For more information, read up on programming with unsafe code in languages like C#.

- Since their introduction in .NET 2.0, generics have invaded most portions of the CLR one way or another, including the reflection subsystem:

  - IsGenericType tells whether a type is generic (for example, List<int>).

  - IsGenericTypeDefinition indicates generic type definitions such as List<T>, where T is not bound (the generic parameter is left "open") to a type. In C#, you can write typeof(List<>) to obtain such a type.

  - ContainsGenericParameters will point out remaining "open" generic parameters on a type (for example, if a List<T> doesn't have its T substituted for a specific type).

  - IsGenericParameter will be true for Type objects retrieved from calls to obtain the generic parameters on a generic type, such as the T in List<T>.

  - GenericParameterPosition goes with the previous property, indicating the zero-based position of the generic parameter. For example, in Dictionary<K, T>, the Type object for T will have position index 1 while K will have a GenericParameterPosition of 0.

- Other properties are a bit more obscure, so I'll direct the interested reader to MSDN documentation on the subject.

Discovering Types

Now that you know we can query lots of properties of types, we should briefly revisit how we can obtain the Type objects themselves. There are three main ways to do so, the first of which we've already covered: use of the typeof operator in C#. Although this way is the most direct, it has little value in scenarios where you're really about to find out about type information you didn't know about at compile time:

```
var stringType = typeof(string /* you did know the type name, didn't you? */);
var intType = typeof(int /* same story here */);
```

Because every object floating around in the CLR's managed memory space has a type, it's obvious one should be able to obtain a System.Type instance from any object. Indeed, as we've seen briefly in the introduction, there's a method called GetType that does precisely this. Because it's defined on System.Object, you can use it on any object, except when you're dealing with a null reference, of course:

```
var someObject = "Reflect on me";
var someType = someObject.GetType();
```

In this particular case, we already knew the object is a System.String (as we're using a literal that results in that type), but in most scenarios requiring reflection you'll invoke this operation on an object that was statically typed to be System.Object. Later in this chapter, in the section "A Primer on Application Extensibility," you'll see an example of the use of GetType to locate a method on a dynamically loaded object.

A third common way to find out about types is to start from their containers, typically an assembly (because modules are used relatively little nowadays). Although we discuss assemblies separately in Chapter 25, "Assemblies, and Application Domains," let's briefly look at using them in the context of reflection. First, we're going to obtain a reference to the assembly defining the System.String type (that is, mscorlib) and then query it for all the types it defines by calling GetTypes. Because this method returns a collection object, we can use LINQ to write a query over it:

```
var res = from t in typeof(string).Assembly.GetTypes()
          where t.Namespace == "System" && t.IsPrimitive
          orderby t.Name
          select t;
foreach (var t in res)
    Console.WriteLine(t.Name);
```

Using the rich querying capabilities offered by LINQ, it's often possible to locate types with certain properties in a very straightforward way. If you're looking for exactly one type you got some information about, the GetType method on the Assembly type can be used, as well:

```
var int32 = typeof(string).Assembly.GetType("System.Int32");
```

Obviously, the preceding code will make more sense if the string passed to GetType is retrieved from someplace (for example, user input or a configuration file). In such a case, you'll likely want to load the containing assembly dynamically, as well, for example using a file path. We discuss such scenarios in the section, "A Primer on Application Extensibility."

Instantiating Types

Suppose you just discovered some type (for example, through the use of configuration). Although the ability to inspect the type for a variety of properties is a useful thing, you most likely want to operate on it. One common thing to do with types is to instantiate them (assuming you're not dealing with an interface or an abstract class).

To instantiate a type, a few techniques can be used. One is to obtain a constructor, also through reflection, and invoke it. You see dynamic method invocation in the section, "A Primer on Application Extensibility," so let's focus on the use of the Activator type instead. This type, living in the System namespace, is the main utility to create an instance of a type, either locally or (using .NET Remoting infrastructure) remotely. It has a couple of overloads, some of which are generic, with the following one being most applicable when we're working off a System.Type object:

```
var uri = (Uri)Activator.CreateInstance(typeof(Uri), "http://demo");
Console.WriteLine(uri);
```

In the preceding example, we're instantiating the Uri type, calling a constructor that takes one parameter. It should go without saying that the preceding code is not something you should write when all static type information is available. However, when types are discovered and loaded dynamically, this provides one way to instantiate them.

DEALING WITH GENERIC TYPES

The Activator.CreateInstance technique will work for types that can be constructed using a public constructor, given an optional (params) array of arguments. One other requirement is that the type is concrete in various senses of the word. Obviously, you can't create an instance of an interface or an abstract class.

Since .NET 2.0, there's another big category of types that are a little more complex to deal with: generics. Generic type definitions provide the blueprint for other types, which are created by substituting type parameters for "real" types. List<T> is a generic type definition, whereas List<int> is closed because no type parameters remain unbound. Only the latter types can be instantiated.

To go from a generic type definition to a generic type with its parameters substituted, you use the sharp bracket syntax in statically typed C# code. However, when dealing with dynamically loaded types, a reflection-based route has to be followed, using the MakeGenericType method on System.Type:

```
var intList = typeof(List<>).MakeGenericType(typeof(int));
var res = (IEnumerable<int>)Activator.CreateInstance(intList, new[] { 1, 3 });
foreach (var item in res)
    Console.WriteLine(item);
```

Again, the preceding should not be a substitute for cases where type information is available statically. Notice one thing, though: When dynamically instantiating types, some kind of compatibility is often expected and statically known. In the preceding code, we might have discovered the collection type dynamically, but we still know, statically, that the result should implement the IEnumerable<int> interface. This possibility to combine dynamically loaded types with static type information lies at the heart of the add-in framework, as you see next.

A Primer on Application Extensibility

Extensibility stories often add to the compelling value of an application. Seldom can an application vendor provide all the bells and whistles in an application within the constraints of the application's development cycle. Or there might be whole scenarios that cannot be envisioned today but may become the next big thing tomorrow. Having a rich extensibility model for an application can therefore significantly add value to an application. Lots of examples exist, ranging from office productivity suites and various browsers to our good friend Visual Studio.

Because we're discussing reflection and such applications typically rely on dynamic loading of extensions, this is the ideal time to bring the theory about reflection into practice with a small example of an extensible application. Notice, though, higher-level frameworks have been written to simplify this task, including the `System.Addins` namespace and the (new in .NET 4) Managed Extensibility Framework (MEF). In this chapter, we're mainly interested in the bare-bones essentials of this use of reflection. At the same time, we'll point out shortcomings of our simple approach and explain how those other frameworks provide answers to those.

Figure 21.4 illustrates the application we're about to build, called ExtensiCalc, a simple extensible calculator. For our scenario, assume we've written a great interface for a calculator, shipping with a few mathematical operations built in. However, as an application vendor, we recognize that we can't provide all operations people might want to use. To win over those people to our application, we build a rich extensibility story so that third parties can extend the calculator with custom operations.

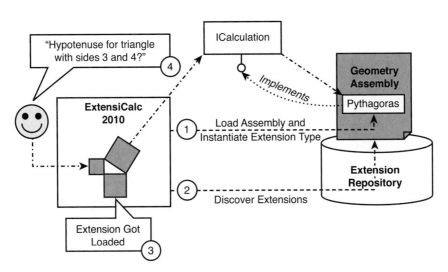

FIGURE 21.4   Loading and using extensions using reflection techniques.

In this setting, the `ICalculation` interface acts as the contract between the ExtensiCalc application and each individual extension for it. At runtime, the application searches for assemblies that implement this interface throughout some repository, which could be a folder on disk. The assemblies in there are inspected for extension implementations and get loaded into the program's memory. After adding the extension to the user interface of the calculator, the application shows up, allowing the user to select a built-in calculation or one of the extensions. When an extension is selected, the application calls into it through the common ICalculation interface.

WHAT ABOUT ISOLATION?

The preceding paragraph contains a scary statement (that we're going to load an arbitrary extension in the host application's memory). This implies that a crash of the extension will take down the whole application. Also, ways can be found (for example, using reflection) to inspect state of the host that shouldn't be seen by the extension.

In a more robust implementation of an extensible application, you will want to address such issues by leveraging other CLR features, such as application domains (which are discussed in Chapter 25). Luckily, the need for extensions by many applications has led to the creation of various frameworks that help with the proper creation of them. One example is System.Addins, where add-ins (the equivalent to what we call extensions) can be loaded into separate application domains or even in a separate "add-in host" process.

Defining the Interface

To kick off the development of ExtensiCalc with extensibility in mind, we create the interface that will be used for the communication between the host application and its extensions. To simplify matters, we'll keep the interface as simple as possible:

```
interface ICalculation
{
    int Calculate(int a, int b);
}
```

What matters more is where we define the interface. Two distinct parties will need to refer to it, one of which is the ExtensiCalc host application, of course, which uses it to make calls through it. On the other side of the curtain, we find all extension providers that need to implement it.

Although we could put the interface in the executable assembly (.exe) of the host application, this feels kind of strange because all the extension library assemblies (.dll) would have to refer to the executable. Instead, we'll do some nice refactoring and provide a separate assembly for the extensibility interfaces and possible utilities that can be of use for extension developers. For our entire example, including the host and one extension, this results in the creation of three assemblies and hence three projects in Visual Studio:

▶ The host application, an executable Console Application, containing the user interface and logic to locate and load extensions

▶ The extensibility assembly where we'll put the ICalculation interface and which could be used to provide shared utilities

▶ One extension assembly, implementing the Pythagorean theorem's formula to calculate the hypotenuse of a triangle given its two sides

The project structure is shown in Figure 21.5, using the Solution Explorer in Visual Studio. Notice the references to the Extensibility assembly in two places: the host and the Geometry extension. In reality, the Geometry package would likely live in a totally different solution on an extension developer's computer. In that case, one would make a reference to the Extensibility.dll assembly file directly, which can be found in the application's installation folder or in some SDK that could ship with ExtensiCalc.

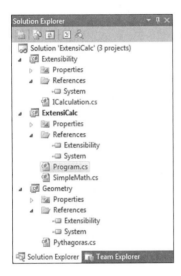

FIGURE 21.5   Project structure for an extensible application.

Built-In Operations

First, we define a couple of built-in operations and ignore the extensibility side of the picture for a moment but use the same interface as we expose for extensions. One operation is shown here; I'll leave the other three simple operations for you:

```
namespace ExtensiCalc
{
    using Extensibility;

    class Addition : ICalculation
    {
        public int Calculate(int a, int b)
        {
            return a + b;
        }
    }
}
```

Here we're already exercising the reference to the `Extensibility` assembly, which also contains the `Extensibility` namespace. We discuss the conceptual differences between assemblies and namespaces in Chapter 24, "Namespaces," and Chapter 25. In this case, the names collide as Visual Studio picks the assembly name as the default namespace for types defined in the project. Once we add the `ICalculation` interface to the `Extensibility` project, we'll be faced with a code file that looks like this:

```
namespace Extensibility
{
    public interface ICalculation
    {
        int Calculate(int a, int b); // We added this line.
    }
}
```

The User Interface

Again, to keep things simple, we're not developing a rich user interface but sticking with a straightforward console application. Here, we need to provide the user with the various supported operations, accept a selection of an operation, take parameters for the operation as user input, call into the operation implementation, and print the result on the screen.

It should be clear that the user interface, which we define in Program.cs, will be able to do all of its work given a list of `ICalculation` instances. So, we define an operation that exposes an `IEnumerable<ICalculation>` as the input to the main user interface. Given such a method, we can define the UI as follows:

```
static void Main()
{
    Console.WriteLine("ExtensiCalc - The world's best calculator");
    Console.WriteLine();
    var operations = GetOperations().ToList();

    while (true)
    {
        int i = 1;
        foreach (var op in operations)
        {
            Console.WriteLine(i++ + ". " + op.GetType().Name);
        }
        Console.WriteLine();

        int selectedOperation = -1;
        while (selectedOperation < 0 || selectedOperation > operations.Count)
        {
            selectedOperation = ReadInt("Enter selection: ");
        }
```

```
        Console.WriteLine();

        if (selectedOperation == 0)
            break;

        ICalculation operation = operations[selectedOperation - 1];
        int a = ReadInt("a: ");
        int b = ReadInt("b: ");
        Console.WriteLine("Result = " + operation.Calculate(a, b));
        Console.WriteLine();
        Console.WriteLine();
    }
}
```

Notice we're printing all operations to the screen based on the type name of the class implementing the operation. There are various ways by which we could provide more customization of operation names (for example, by adding a get-only `Name` string property to our interface). Later on, we'll see another way to associate this kind of descriptive metadata to an object, using custom attributes that are discovered through the reflection APIs, too.

In the preceding code, we're using a small `ReadInt` helper function that reads an integer value from the console, retrying as long as the user doesn't provide a valid input:

```
static int ReadInt(string prompt)
{
    int result = 0;
    bool valid = false;
    while (!valid)
    {
        Console.Write(prompt);
        valid = int.TryParse(Console.ReadLine(), out result);
    }
    return result;
}
```

If we were to stick with built-in operations online, it would suffice to provide a list of built-in operation instances from `GetOperations` (for example, as follows using an iterator):

```
static IEnumerable<ICalculation> GetOperations()
{
    yield return new Addition();
    yield return new Subtraction();
    yield return new Multiplication();
    yield return new Division();
    // You can add other built-in operations here easily...
}
```

Given this simple implementation, we already have a useful (admittedly simple) calculator, as shown in Figure 21.6.

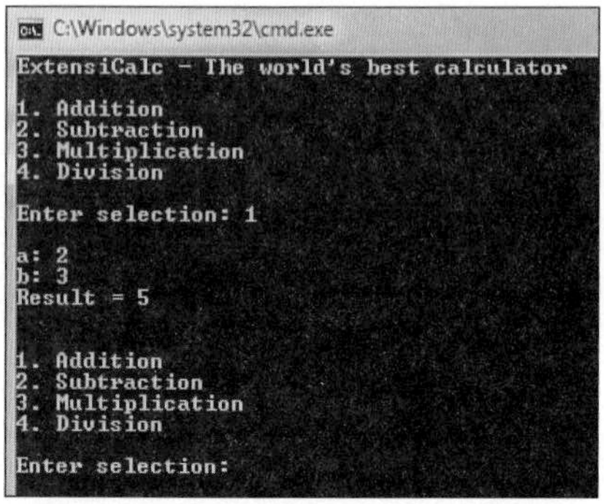

FIGURE 21.6   Our extensible calculator without any extensions loaded.

Discovery and Loading of Extensions

Besides the built-in extensions, we also want to be able to load all the extensions provided by third-party vendors. There are two contractual aspects to this: first, the requirement to implement our ICalculation interface, and second, the need to put extension assemblies in a place where the host application can find them (referred to as the "repository" in Figure 21.4). We'll assume extensions live in an Extensions folder alongside the application executable.

Using reflection, we can now discover extension types in assemblies. There are two sides to this: We first need to find all the assemblies and load them. After we've done this, we then need to scan the assemblies for types implementing ICalculation and create an instance of those. We'll assume a default constructor is required for extensions.

DISCOVERY, SAFER AND SIMPLIFIED

This discovery process is of interest to us in the scope of this example because of its use of reflection for various operations. However, a few limitations and drawbacks apply when it's implemented in the way shown here. For one thing, looking for assemblies simply by searching .dll files and trying to load them through the reflection APIs is a gross simplification of things. We might want to discover types not only based on a directory containing assemblies, but look elsewhere, too.

Second, loading those assemblies can fail for a variety of reasons. Maybe the.dll file is not an assembly but a native DLL or another kind of file that got disguised with a .dll extensions for some reason.

Finally, assemblies cannot be unloaded unless the containing application domain gets unloaded as a whole. Misbehaving assemblies or assemblies without any useful extension types will be loaded into the program's memory.

Frameworks like System.Addins and the MEF help to avoid such issues.

```
static IEnumerable<ICalculation> GetExtensions()
{
    if (Directory.Exists("Extensions"))
    {
        var icalc = typeof(ICalculation);

        foreach (var file in Directory.EnumerateFiles("Extensions", "*.dll"))
        {
            // For isolation, one will like to use AppDomains...
            var asm = Assembly.LoadFrom(file);

            // "LINQ to Reflection" to the rescue.
            var extTypes = from t in asm.GetTypes()
                           where t.GetInterfaces().Contains(icalc)
                           select t;

            foreach (var ext in extTypes)
                yield return (ICalculation)Activator.CreateInstance(ext);
        }
    }
}
```

In this piece of code, we find all .dll files in an Extension subfolder (relative to the working directory; that is, the place where the application's executable lives). After loading the files through Assembly.LoadFrom (also in the System.Reflection namespace), we use LINQ to filter the assembly's types by those that implement the ICalculation interface. To do so, we rely on the GetInterfaces method on System.Type.

Finally, after we've found all types that implement the ICalculation interface, we can instantiate each of them, using the Activator.CreateInstance method we've seen before. This assumes a default constructor is present.

Given the preceding method, we can now tweak the GetExtensions method to include both the discovered and the built-in operations (again using a LINQ operator):

```
static IEnumerable<ICalculation> GetOperations()
{
    return GetBuiltinOperations().Concat(GetExtensions());
}

static IEnumerable<ICalculation> GetBuiltinOperations()
{
    // And seen earlier...
}
```

```
static IEnumerable<ICalculation> GetExtensions()
{
    // As seen above...
}
```

THOUGHTS ON CONSTRUCTORS AND STATE

The fact we're reusing the same instance of an operation type for all calculations that use it implies those types should be careful with state. If state from one use of the calculation object sticks around and can influence subsequent operations, you may be in trouble.

Alternatively, we could create new instances of the calculation objects each time we're going to reuse them. In such a configuration, you'll still want to discover the types only once but defer the instance creation calls until the point of every use.

This brings us to a further discussion about the implicit contract of requiring a specific constructor (which cannot be captured in an interface) on extensions. Because we're taking all discovery tasks on ourselves, to the point of finding types that adhere to a certain interface contract, we're responsible for creating the instances.

Alternatively, you could think of using an interface with a single member GetExtensions that every extension assembly needs to have for discovery purposes. But all we've done then is put more burden on the extension provider, and we still need to discover this hypothetical IExtensionProvider implementation, again with the need to invoke some constructor.

Writing and Deploying an Extension

Development of an extension happens in a separate project, resulting in the creation of a separate assembly, and is usually created by a third party. The definition of such an extension should be self-explanatory, given our simple interface. For example:

```
using Extensibility;
namespace Geometry
{
    public class Pythagoras : ICalculation
    {
        public int Calculate(int a, int b)
        {
            return (int)Math.Sqrt(a * a + b * b);
        }
    }
}
```

Now we need to put the resulting file, Geometry.dll, in the Extensions subfolder where the host application is looking to discover extensions. In a real-world scenario, some installer will be used to facilitate this task when deploying extensions to end-user machines, but for demonstration (and development) purposes, we can simply copy it. The following folder structure is required:

```
ExtensiCalc
- ExtensiCalc.exe
+ Extensions
   - Geometry.dll
```

To simplify debugging of our own extensions, to be loaded by the host application, we can configure the build process in Visual Studio with a post-build step on the Geometry project. Figure 21.7 illustrates a configuration that will copy the built file to the appropriate location using some relative paths. Because we're building to the bin\Debug folder underneath the Geometry folder, we need to go three levels up so that we can take a right turn into the ExtensiCalc (host application) build folder. From here, we construct the path to the Extensions subfolder alongside the ExtensiCalc executable, again under bin\Debug (assuming you're building in Debug configuration). The $(TargetPath) variable is provided by MSBuild and contains the full path to the built assembly file. Such variables can be discovered by using the Edit Post-build button.

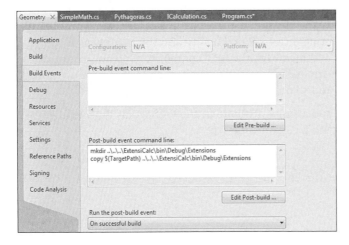

FIGURE 21.7   Configuration of a Post-build event to copy a built assembly file.

Finally, when we run the application now, we should see a Pythagoras entry appear in the operations menu, as shown in Figure 21.8.

Managed Extensibility Framework

One of the frameworks that helps with creating extensible applications on the .NET platform is MEF. Although a thorough discussion about MEF is beyond the scope of this chapter, a short introduction is warranted, especially because .NET 4 is the first version of the framework to ship this new technology out of the box.

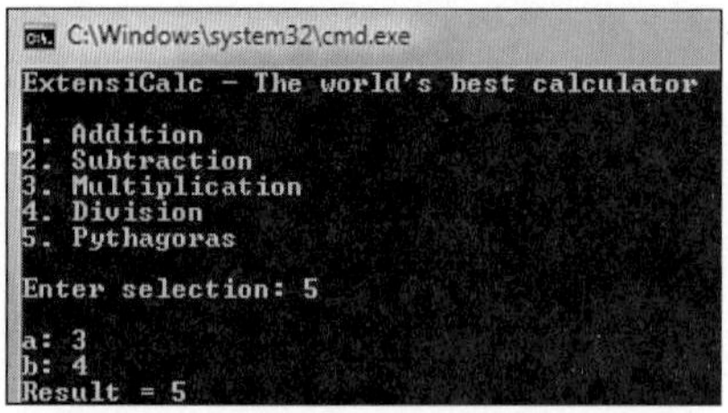

FIGURE 21.8   An extension got loaded and shows up in the menu.

MEF is centered on three core concepts, the CCC of MEF:

▶ **Contracts** are interfaces annotated with some custom attribute that enables them for use in composition.

▶ **Catalogs** act as the repositories that are searchable for extensions and abstract over the discovery aspects of extensibility.

▶ **Containers** provide the playground for composition, where host and various extensions are wired together.

In the world of composition, there are always two sides to the equation. One end acts as the provider of some functionality, and the other end wants to receive services to interoperate with. In terms of MEF, the former *exports* functionality and the latter *imports* it. By using custom attributes on types and members, the MEF composition engine can piece the puzzle together and take care of various tasks on your behalf, such as loading extensions, creating instances of extensions, and so on.

Using MEF, our extension would add a single attribute to the Pythagoras type, telling it exports functionality associated with a certain contract:

```
[Export(typeof(ICalculation))]
public class Pythagoras : ICalculation
{
    ...
}
```

On the receiving end, inside the host application's code, we want to import many of those extensions based on the same shared contract:

```
class Calculator
{
    [ImportMany(typeof(ICalculation))]
    public List<ICalculation> Operations { get; set; }
}
```

Now, if MEF finds an object that exports the ICalculation contract, it will do all the work to instantiate it and add the newly created instance to the place where the host asked to import it. You can compare the concept of composition with a bowl of soup containing various ingredients that get bound together.

The missing pieces of this puzzle are the catalog and container aspects. In other words, where does MEF find the extensions and what's the stimulus for MEF to start the task of composition. To handle discovery, various catalogs exist that perform some kind of lookup task (for example, searching a directory or an assembly for extensions). To mimic the same behavior as our manual discovery of extensions as well as the use of the built-in operations, we can write the following MEF code:

```
using (var builtIns = new AssemblyCatalog(typeof(Program).Assembly))
using (var extensions = new DirectoryCatalog("Extensions"))
using (var catalog = new AggregateCatalog(builtIns, extensions))
using (var container = new CompositionContainer(catalog))
{
    // ComposeParts is an extension method in System.ComponentModel.Composition.
    // Don't forget to import this namespace.
    container.ComposeParts(calc);
}
```

The first three lines of code deal with catalogs. Here, the first one corresponds to our iterator that yielded the instances of the built-in operations. This time, though, we're asking MEF to discover types that are amenable for composition in our own assembly. Following this catalog, we have one that searches the Extensions folder, taking over all the plumbing we had to do ourselves (with more robustness and safety). Finally, the combination of both catalogs (the analog to our use of Concat before) is achieved by using the AggregateCatalog type.

Besides the use of catalogs, the preceding fragment also reveals how composition is carried out. The CompositionContainer type acts as a "bowl of soup" in which all ingredients for the composition (known as *parts* in MEF) are thrown together. Here, calc is an instance of the Calculator type, which receives all the discovered objects that are implementing the ICalculation interface. Figure 21.9 shows how the MEF logo reflects the compositional nature of parts.

FIGURE 21.9   The MEF logo, reflecting its *compositional* nature operating on *blocks*.

LEARN MORE ABOUT MEF

Being at the heart of Visual Studio 2010 extensibility and likely many other future extensibility models, MEF is definitely worth reading up on. Whereas the extensibility examples we've shown in this chapter are pretty simple, allowing us to focus on the core technology underpinning it, typical uses are much more involved.

One particularly appealing target for composition of extensions is found in the space of UI programming, where third parties want to add functionality to the host's UI. This is precisely one of the areas where Visual Studio 2010 extensibility focuses, allowing tool vendors to add items to menus, toolbars, the code editor, and many other parts of the development environment.

Also, MEF has been developed under a shared source initiative and has gone through many publicly visible preview iterations at http://mef.codeplex.com. To learn more about MEF and to inspect the way it works, this link is a good starting point.

Reflection for Methods, Properties, Events, and More

Thus far, we've mainly focused on reflection to discover types and perform some operations based on those. Because types are containers for other concepts, we can descend the ladder of reflection to discover more about those *members*, too. Expectedly, every System.Type object exposes methods that allow you to inspect the type's methods, properties, events, constructors, and fields. For example, to retrieve all the methods on System.Int32 and make sense of the overloads by grouping them by name, we can write the following code:

```
var res = from method in typeof(int).GetMethods()
          group method by method.Name into g
          select new { Name = g.Key, Overloads = g.Count() };

foreach (var method in res)
    Console.WriteLine(method);
```

MethodInfo objects have a bunch of interesting properties, revealing more information about a method's visibility, return type, parameters, possible use of generics, and so on.

Late-Bound Invocation of Methods
Besides using reflection to learn more about their capabilities, you can also use reflection to invoke a method:

```
class Foo
{
    public void Bar(string message)
    {
        Console.WriteLine(message);
    }
}
```

```
class Program
{
    static void Main()
    {
        var f = new Foo();

        // Early-bound call
        f.Bar("Early-bound");

        // Late-bound call
        f.GetType().GetMethod("Bar").Invoke(f, new object[] { "Late-bound" });
    }
}
```

The second call locates a public instance method called Bar using reflection and makes a call to it using the Invoke method. In this example, there's no value in doing it this way because the method can be resolved statically at compile time. However, if you're dealing with an object you got from somewhere but you don't have a type to cast it to, you'll need to rely on some form of dynamic invocation. In C# 4.0, the preceding can be simplified using the new dynamic feature, as you learn in Chapter 22, "Dynamic Programming," allowing us to write the following:

```
// Late-bound call
dynamic d = f;
d.Bar("Late-bound");
```

Under the covers, this will use reflection to locate the Bar method with an appropriate number of arguments to make the call.

PERFORMANCE AND OTHER IMPLICATIONS

Late-bound calls are much slower than early-bound calls because some of the operations otherwise carried out by the compiler have to be performed at runtime.

When using plain reflection to locate a method, lots of runtime infrastructure needs to be looped in to produce the result. In addition, various optimizations cannot be performed as the runtime simply sees calls to reflection APIs where members are represented as strings like "Bar". Early bound code contains IL instructions that target members directly, allowing for optimizations such as inlining. The DLR, as used by the dynamic keyword, adds a series of optimizations such as call-site caching and code generation for "fast invocation paths," making this less of a problem. Nonetheless, you shouldn't use late binding if there's no good reason for doing so.

One other reason early binding is much more advisable than late binding is the helpful diagnostics carried out by the compiler in the former case. When relying on reflection, you're deferring all lookup operations until runtime, which can fail by throwing exceptions. In particular, using GetMethod will return a null reference if no match is found.

So let your motto be this: Static where possible, dynamic when (really) necessary.

Properties and Indexers

Because indexers are implemented as properties with parameters, both those members look the same at the level of the runtime. To access those, you can use methods such as GetProperty and GetProperties. An example is shown here that will reveal two properties on System.String:

```
foreach (var p in typeof(string).GetProperties())
    Console.WriteLine(p);
```

The results look like this:

```
Char Chars [Int32]
Int32 Length
```

The first property that's shown is called Chars and really is an indexer, recognizable by the square brackets (enclosing the indexer's parameters) in the ToString representation of the PropertyInfo instance.

Properties are nothing but metadata citizens wrapping a (possibly partial) pair of methods known as the getter and setter. Because there's only a single concept of methods at the runtime level, it shouldn't surprise you that you can get the getter and setter methods (any of which can be null) from a PropertyInfo object:

```
foreach (var p in typeof(string).GetProperties())
{
    Console.WriteLine(p.Name);

    if (p.CanRead)
        Console.WriteLine("get = " + p.GetGetMethod());
    if (p.CanWrite)
        Console.WriteLine("set = " + p.GetSetMethod());
}
```

Because both of the retrieved members on System.String are get-only, only CanRead will be true, so the output looks like this:

```
Chars
get = Char get_Chars(Int32)
Length
get = Int32 get_Length()
```

REFLECTION AS A RELATIONAL DATABASE

The metadata exposed through reflection is very much like a relational database consisting of a series of interrelated tables. For example, types can have many members, and some of those members are related to one another (for example, a getter referred to by a property).

Because of this data-intensive nature, one of the most natural ways to make sense of the data exposed by reflection is to use query expressions, as you saw earlier when learning about method overloads. When showing off LINQ to Objects, reflection is often chosen as a great in-memory data source with which to illustrate various operators.

Late-Bound Property Access

Just as with methods, if necessary for one reason or another, you can access properties in a late-bound fashion. Although the getter/setter methods could be used for this (using the Invoke method), properties provide a direct way to get and set values:

```
var f = new Foo();

// Early-bound set (assume Foo has a Bar property defined)
f.Bar = 42;

// Late-bound get
var res = (int)f.GetType().GetProperty("Bar").GetValue(f, null /* indexer */);
Console.WriteLine(res);
```

THE MYTHICAL INFOOF OPERATOR

One of the top requested features for the C# language is some infoof (read: "info of") operator, similar to the typeof operator but operating on members. Although it's significantly close to the member lookup code we've been writing earlier, it would work quite differently because it would use static type information to locate the member and emit code to get the MemberInfo object for it. One of the places where this is useful is in the creation of LINQ providers, where you must recognize certain operations carried out in expression trees to provide a meaningful translation into a target query language.

Again, starting from C# 4.0, this can be simplified using dynamic:

```
dynamic f = new Foo() { Bar = 42 /* early bound set */ };
// Late-bound get
Console.WriteLine(f.Bar);
```

Events

Just like properties, events are metadata constructs that tie together a series of methods (in this case, for add and remove accessors). System.Type methods like GetEvent(s) can be used to discover events on a given type:

```
var evt = typeof(Foo).GetEvent("Event");
Console.WriteLine(evt);
Console.WriteLine(evt.GetAddMethod());
Console.WriteLine(evt.GetRemoveMethod());

var f = new Foo();
EventHandler handler = (o, e) => { Console.WriteLine("Raised!"); };

// Early-bound add
f.Event += handler;
f.Raise(); // Prints Raised!

// Late-bound remove
evt.RemoveEventHandler(f, handler);
f.Raise(); // Doesn't print Raised! anymore
```

For this example, the following Foo type is used:

```
class Foo
{
    public event EventHandler Event;

    public void Raise()
    {
        var e = Event;
        if (e != null)
            e(this, EventArgs.Empty);
    }
}
```

Once more, if the need for dynamic discovery of an event arises due to the lack of static type information or a common interface, dynamic can be used to simplify the previous code. We examine how dynamic works and its main uses in Chapter 22.

```
// Late-bound remove
dynamic d = f;
d.Event -= handler;
f.Raise(); // Doesn't print Raised! anymore
```

Fields and Use of `BindingFlags`

Yet another type of member is a field, which can also be detected through reflection. In the following fragment, we try to find the fields on the `DateTime` struct:

```
foreach (var f in typeof(DateTime).GetFields())
    Console.WriteLine(f);
```

Although this prints a few results (the static read-only `MinValue` and `MaxValue` fields, to be precise), you might have expected more results. After all, a `DateTime` ought to store its information about date and time somewhere, shouldn't it? What we're hitting here is a restriction of visibility. By default, reflection APIs show only publicly visible things, but this can be overridden by specifying another `BindingFlags` value:

```
foreach (var f in typeof(DateTime).GetFields(  BindingFlags.NonPublic
                                             | BindingFlags.Instance))
    Console.WriteLine(f);
```

Here we're retrieving all nonpublic instance fields on `DateTime`, now revealing the following:

```
UInt64 dateData
```

The use of `BindingFlags` provides much more flexibility than we've shown here, but an exhaustive discussion about its values is beyond the scope of this chapter.

WHAT ABOUT SECURITY?

You might be a little worried when seeing the ability of reflection to get to nonpublic members and even fields. Doesn't this pose a security threat?

The answer to this question is to be found in another service provided by the CLR that controls access to certain functionality. The runtime's security subsystem deserves a book on its own, but in essence it can be used to disallow the performance of certain operations depending on the context where the code is run. Before .NET 4, the Code Access Security (CAS) model was the main way to achieve this, but starting from .NET 4, a new security transparency model has been introduced.

More information about this topic in the context of reflection can be found on MSDN in an article titled "Security Considerations for Reflection." For those familiar with the .NET security system but new to .NET 4, the "Security Changes in the .NET Framework 4" article is another recommended read.

Custom Attributes

All the reflection information we've seen so far is based on metadata that's well known to the runtime. One typical example of such metadata includes the visibility of types and members. Early on in the design of the CLR, it was clear that an extensible metadata system would be a true added value to the new runtime. This ultimately resulted in the creation of custom attributes that allow developers to define their own pieces of metadata that can be tagged onto assemblies, types, and their members.

You've seen a couple of attributes earlier in this chapter when we were discussing MEF. In the following code fragment, Export is an attribute:

```
[Export(typeof(ICalculation))]
public class Pythagoras : ICalculation
{
    ...
}
```

The goal of those attributes is to annotate runtime entities with extra data that can be inspected by tools and libraries. In the case of MEF, the composition engine uses the reflection APIs to find types and checks for the presence of the Export attribute to find out which types are marked as usable for composition.

One of the earliest uses of attributes in the .NET Framework was in the development of (classic, pre-WCF) web services. By simply sticking attributes like WebService and WebMethod onto types and methods, those could be exposed through web services protocols. Furthermore, to discover a service, an HTTP handler watches out for WSDL requests. Upon receiving such a "metadata exchange" request, it reflects on the types and members to build the XML document to hand back to the client.

In yet other places, assemblies are analyzed for the presence of certain attributes to generate other code. For example, to make a type serializable for different purposes, such as communication or persistence, you can search for attributes that guide the serialization process (such as NonSerialized on a field). Based on this information, tools could generate code that can serialize objects conform to the requirements that were specified using custom attributes on the types involved.

Defining Custom Attributes

Custom attributes are defined as classes deriving from System.Attribute and contain constructors and properties to specify the metadata they want to carry around. Because all of this data has to be embedded in the metadata storage in an assembly, restrictions on the usable types apply. Primitive types such as int, string, bool, and so on are valid, and so is the use of a Type instance.

For the attribute to be usable, you must also apply an attribute to the type, indicating what its target uses are and so on. This is done using the AttributeUsage attribute, which enables you to specify AttributeTargets flags. When using the attribute, it will be checked whether the attribute is applicable to the target to which it's applied. AttributeUsage also enables you to determine the behavior of attributes in the face of inheritance: Does the use of an attribute on a type reflect itself when querying for attributes on any of its derived types? Finally, AttributeUsage can be used to allow or disallow multiple uses of the attribute on the same target.

Let's take a look at an example of all of this:

```
[AttributeUsage(AttributeTargets.Class)]
public class ExtensionAttribute : Attribute
{
    public ExtensionAttribute(string name)
    {
        Name = name;
    }
    public string Name { get; private set; }
}
```

Different patterns for declaration of attributes exist. Because some parameters on the attribute may be optional, it's often the case that one defines a single constructor that takes all the required arguments in combination with a series of settable properties used for the optional arguments. Required arguments are also referred to as "positional" because they're specified in the order they appear in the constructor, while the optional ones are referred to as "named" because you specify them by property name.

To make the declaration of attributes easier, Visual Studio comes with a code snippet called Attribute. To insert it, enter **Attribute** and press Tab twice. The result of this operation is shown in Figure 21.10.

```
[AttributeUsage(AttributeTargets.All, Inherited = false, AllowMultiple = true)]
sealed class MyAttribute : Attribute
{
    // See the attribute guidelines at
    //  http://go.microsoft.com/fwlink/?LinkId=85236
    readonly string positionalString;

    // This is a positional argument
    public MyAttribute(string positionalString)
    {
        this.positionalString = positionalString;

        // TODO: Implement code here
        throw new NotImplementedException();
    }

    public string PositionalString
    {
        get { return positionalString; }
    }

    // This is a named argument
    public int NamedInt { get; set; }
}
```

FIGURE 21.10   Code snippet to declare a custom attribute.

Using Attributes

The use of custom attributes on applicable targets is done by using the square bracket syntax shown earlier. In between the brackets, the name of the attribute is specified, where the Attribute prefix on the type named can be omitted, followed by arguments in between parentheses. The positional arguments come first and are comma-separated, while named ones can be specified later by using the name = value syntax.

As an example, consider the `AttributeUsage` attribute itself, which shows the IntelliSense assistance in Visual Studio shown in Figure 21.11.

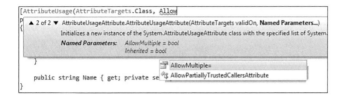

FIGURE 21.11   Use of an attribute applied to a class definition.

NAMED PARAMETERS SYNTAX

Evolving a programming language always brings up interesting challenges. One such challenge is to keep existing programs compiling under newer versions of the language. With named parameters, this is no different. First there were attributes, where the specification of optional parameters was done within parentheses using name-value pairs:

```
Bar(42, Optional = "Hi")
```

In C# 3.0, object initializer expressions were added, with slightly different syntax because the preceding form is ambiguous otherwise. (Did you mean to initialize `Optional` as a property on the `Bar` instance, or did you want to call a constructor that takes an integer and a string and assign to `Optional` as a side effect?)

```
new Foo(42) { Optional = "Hi" }
```

Finally, in C# 4.0, optional and named parameters were introduced on various forms of invocation syntax (on constructors, methods, delegates), where you could write the following if a constructor is to be called that has a parameter called `optional`:

```
new Foo(42, optional: "Hi")
```

Once more, dedicated syntax, with the colon token, is needed to disambiguate from an assignment expression that existed in previous versions of the language.

Although in hindsight it's unfortunate to have that many syntaxes for related concepts, that's what language evolution (facing a high level of compatibility requirements) brings with it.

How Are Custom Attributes Stored?

Being defined outside code blocks (which get represented as intermediate language, IL), you might wonder how and where custom attributes get stored in an assembly. Again, the answer can be found in ILDASM, also explaining some of the limitations around custom attribute data. For example, why is it that only constant expressions can be used for the data in a custom attribute? Let's take a look based on the following piece of code:

```
[My("Hello", NamedInt=42)]
class Program
{
    ...
}
```

Looking in ILDASM, the first thing you can see is how the custom attribute is hidden behind some .custom construct, as shown in Figure 21.12.

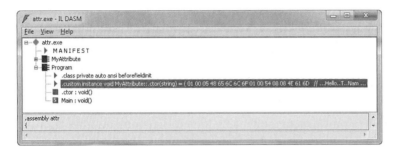

FIGURE 21.12   A custom attribute showing up in ILDASM.

What you can already see from this is how the custom attribute is represented by a sequence of bytes, which contain the constant data for it. In other words, there's no way a custom attribute can rely on the execution of code to compute its data values because all data is serialized into a byte sequence. You can dig a little deeper and go to View, MetaInfo, Show (Ctrl+M) to show type definitions and such in a textual format. In there, the type definition for Program will reveal the following attribute:

```
TypeDef #2 (02000003)
-------------------------------------------------------
  TypDefName: Program   (02000003)
  ...
  CustomAttribute #1 (0c000006)
  -------------------------------------------------------
    CustomAttribute Type: 06000001
      CustomAttributeName: MyAttribute :: instance void .ctor(class String)
    Length: 25
    Value : 01 00 05 48 65 6c 6c 6f  01 00 54 08 08 4e 61 6d ...
    ctor args: ("Hello_")
```

Discovering Custom Attributes

Although most readers will likely just have to use custom attributes to use certain pieces of the framework (like MEF, WCF, and so forth) or to use external libraries, it's useful to know how to declare and discover custom attributes. You've already seen how to declare them, but how can your code now inspect a given assembly, type, or member and figure out whether an attribute is applied? Again, the answer lies in reflection.

To put things in practice, let's extend the ExtensiCalc application by introducing the following custom attribute in the Extensibility assembly:

```
[AttributeUsage(AttributeTargets.Class)]
public class CalculationOperationAttribute : Attribute
{
    public CalculationOperationAttribute(string name, string infix)
    {
        Name = name;
        Infix = infix;
    }

    public string Name { get; private set; }
    public string Infix { get; private set; }
}
```

The goal of this attribute is to provide a friendly name for a calculation operation and provide an infix operator notation for pretty printing. For example, the Addition class could be decorated with the attribute as follows:

```
[CalculationOperation("Add", "+")]
class Addition : ICalculation
{
    public int Calculate(int a, int b)
    {
        return a + b;
    }
}
```

With this information present, the host application can now look at the type of the operation and figure out whether this custom attribute is present. If so, additional "pretty printing" can be carried out. The essence of the detection of a custom attribute and the retrieval of information defined in it is shown here:

```
var add = typeof(Addition);
var opa = (CalculationOperationAttribute)Attribute.GetCustomAttribute(
            add, typeof(CalculationOperationAttribute));
if (opa != null)
{
    Console.WriteLine("Extension: {0}", add);
    Console.WriteLine("Name: {0}", opa.Name);
    Console.WriteLine("Notation: a {0} b", opa.Infix);
}
```

Given the operation type, the second line uses the GetCustomAttribute static method on System.Attribute to detect a CalculationOperationAttribute on the add type. Alternatively, you could use the GetCustomAttributes (plural) method on System.Type (or another other reflection citizen such as MethodInfo) to detect custom attributes (again plural) of a given type. LINQ operators can be useful in such a setting again:

```
var opa = add.GetCustomAttributes(false /* inherit */)
            .OfType<CalculationOperationAttribute>()
            .SingleOrDefault();
```

Here we find all custom attributes, filter out the ones of the specified type, and finally retrieve the single one, or null if none is present. Either way, given the custom attribute object, we can now inspect its properties, namely Name and Infix in this example.

I'll leave it as an exercise for you to revamp the whole ExtensiCalc example with additional code that looks out for this custom attribute and presents a customized menu using the Name properties of the discovered operations. Figure 21.13 shows a screenshot of the output of a revamped version of the program.

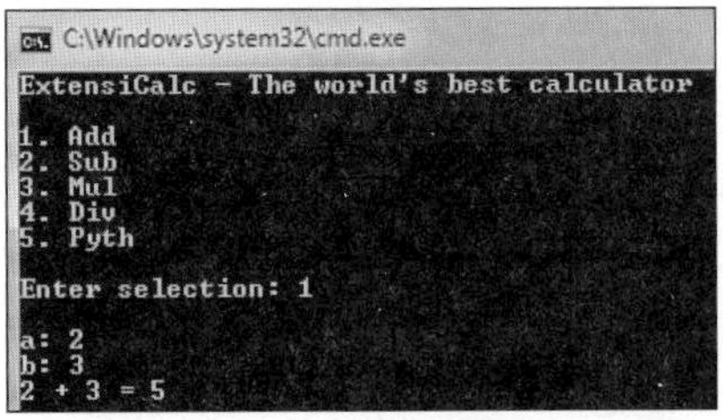

FIGURE 21.13   Custom attributes for pretty printing of operator names and infix notation.

CUSTOM ATTRIBUTES OR RICHER INTERFACES?

From the ExtensiCalc example it's clear there are various ways to expose the rich metadata associated with a class in a variety of ways. Instead of using custom attributes, we could have enriched our ICalculationOperation interface with extra properties, too. Although this would work as well, interfaces tend to create a point of tension between consumers and providers. Rich interfaces imply more work for the implementer, which might not be desirable. The use of abstract classes to get out of this issue is a possibility but poses other restrictions due to the single inheritance model.

Furthermore, custom attributes provide a richer story for metadata beyond just classes because they can be applied to various members and even whole assemblies. So ask yourself what metadata means in your particular use case, how you can deal with the absence or presence of it, and what the best solution is in the end.

Lightweight Code Generation

In the first generation of .NET, no facilities were provided to generate code at runtime, despite the fact that some portions of the runtime could take advantage of such a thing. For example, the object serialization stack has historically relied on the invocation of the C# compiler at runtime to generate some helper assemblies based on the object types that occur in the input. Although this works fine, the additional step of generating C# code and feeding it through a compiler just to obtain an assembly seems largely redundant if we have some common code representation based on IL already.

Starting with .NET 2.0, services to emit code at runtime (and save or execute it) have been added to the framework. Known as lightweight code generation, or LCG, the APIs surfacing this functionality can be found in System.Reflection.Emit. Although their use is very specialized and requires a thorough understanding of the semantics of IL code, a small discussion is in order because LCG is what expression trees and the DLR take advantage of, too.

Hello LCG

The LCG Hello World example is shown here, simply printing "Hello LCG!" to the screen based on a dynamically generated assembly:

```
// An assembly...
var asm = AppDomain.CurrentDomain.DefineDynamicAssembly(
    new AssemblyName("LCGDemo"),
    AssemblyBuilderAccess.Run);

// ...contains a module...
var mod = asm.DefineDynamicModule("MyModule");

// ...contains a type...
var tpe = mod.DefineType("Sample");

// ...contains a method...
var mtd = tpe.DefineMethod("SayHello",
                    MethodAttributes.Public | MethodAttributes.Static);

// ...contains a code body...
var gen = mtd.GetILGenerator();
gen.Emit(OpCodes.Ldstr, "Hello LCG!");
                    // The mythical infoof(Console.WriteLine(string))
gen.Emit(OpCodes.Call, typeof(Console).GetMethod("WriteLine",
                            new[] { typeof(string) }, null));
gen.Emit(OpCodes.Ret);
```

```
// Makes the code ready to execute...
var res = tpe.CreateType();
res.GetMethod("SayHello").Invoke(null /* static */, null /* args */);
```

From this code, you can see all the layering surrounding code on the CLR. On the top level, we find assemblies that are containers for one or more modules. Inside those modules, we can define types that by themselves contain members. Notice methods can also be declared outside types, as global methods, but this is not directly supported by some languages like C#. The preceding code is the equivalent to the following code compiled into an assembly called LCGDemo:

```
class Sample
{
    public static void SayHello()
    {
        System.Console.WriteLine("Hello LCG!");
    }
}
```

On the last lines of code, we concretize the type we just defined and get a Type object back, which we can reflect on (for example, to retrieve the SayHello method and invoke it through reflection once more). This infrastructure is ultimately what dynamic languages on the CLR—such as IronPython and IronRuby—use to turn the code the user wrote into execution by emitting IL code at runtime. This has various advantages over systems that are based on interpretation because all the runtime's optimizations for IL code can be used.

COLLECTIBLE ASSEMBLIES

 One extension to LCG that was introduced in .NET 4 is the concept of collectible assemblies. Prior to .NET 4, the only way to unload dynamically generated code was to unload the entire application domain in which the code was loaded.

Notice how on the first line of our example we create a dynamic assembly starting from an AppDomain object. You'll learn more about AppDomains later, but suffice to say that those are the rough equivalent to processes at the CLR level, providing various properties such as isolation of state. With the advent of dynamic languages hosted on the CLR (through the DLR), the use of dynamically generated code is increasing significantly, making the tight coupling with application domains for unload scenarios too much of a stumbling block toward achieving great performance characteristics.

To tame the memory utilization originating from the code generation of lots of little fragments that have a limited lifetime, garbage collection for generated code has been introduced in .NET 4, known as "collectible assemblies." This is yet another manifestation of the von Neumann machine architecture, where code and data are similar entities. Where data can be reclaimed using garbage collection, so can code.

Collectible assemblies are subject to a number of restrictions documented on MSDN. To enable collectible assemblies on your own manual uses of LCG, pass the `AssemblyBuilderAccess.RunAndCollect` flag to the `DefineDynamicAssembly` call.

A Toy Compiler for Arithmetic Expressions

LCG can be an endless source of fun for those who are into writing compilers (toy or otherwise). Although expression trees are the ideal abstraction for code generation nowadays (as you will see later in the "Expression Trees" section), use of raw LCG can be instructive to see the essentials of code generation starting from an object model.

In this section, we examine a very simple toy compiler for arithmetic expressions, starting from an object model for an abstract syntax tree with simple nodes such as constants, parameters, and arithmetic operators. To create a real language on top, you would have to build a lexer and a parser to turn textual input into such a tree format, which we won't do here. Figure 21.14 shows the separation between the front end and back end of a compiler, of which we'll only build the back end here.

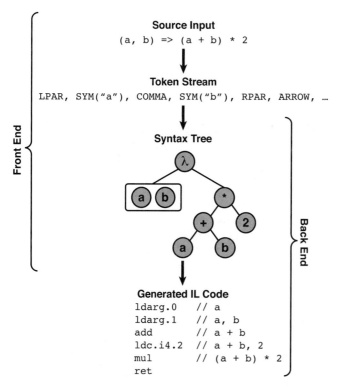

FIGURE 21.14   Front end and back end of a compiler.

An Object Model for Expression Trees

We start by creating an object model for the expression trees our compiler can turn into IL code. Later, when talking about expression trees, we'll replace them with the tree types built in to .NET 3.5 and later. To keep things simple, we support just constants, parameters, and binary operators. An abstract base type called `Expression` provides for a single virtual method that will be used for compilation:

```
abstract class Expression
{
    public abstract void Compile(ILGenerator gen, Dictionary<Param, int> env);
}
```

In a true compiler, you would separate the compilation logic from the tree representation and create a visitor over the tree object model. We'll ignore this for the sake of clarity. In the preceding code, ignore the signature for `Compile` because this will be explained later. For now, focus on the data modeled by the various `Expression` subtypes to follow. First, a parameter:

```
class Param : Expression
{
    // Implementation of Compile will be added later.
}
```

Although we could give parameters a name by adding a property, we'll omit this. In fact, at the IL level, names for parameters are irrelevant because arguments are referred to by means of a zero-based index.

Next, a constant has a slightly more complex representation as an expression tree node, also having a `Value` property:

```
class Const : Expression
{
    public int Value { get; set; }
    // Implementation of Compile will be added later.
}
```

In the entire tree object model, `Param` and `Const` form the leaf nodes. As we climb up the tree, we want ways to combine such leaf nodes into intermediate nodes. The only operations we'll allow are binary arithmetic ones, as follows:

```
class Arithmetic : Expression
{
    public Expression Left { get; set; }
    public Expression Right { get; set; }
    public Operation Operation { get; set; }
    // Implementation of Compile will be added later.
}
```

The Left and Right properties introduce a recursive structure on the type level, by which subtrees can become parts of larger trees. This allows us to define arbitrarily nested expression trees within our limited arithmetic grammar. The Operation is based on an enum, with four possible values:

```
enum Operation
{
    Add,
    Subtract,
    Multiply,
    Divide
}
```

Finally, a function acts as the root of our expression trees and has a code body together with a bunch of parameters. This node is no longer derived from Expression because a function is usable as the argument to an arithmetic operation. In fact, all the nodes in our expression trees represent a value of the same type, which will be an Int32 after compilation:

```
class Function
{
    public List<Param> Parameters { get; set; }
    public Expression Body { get; set; }
    // Implementation of Compile will be added later.
}
```

With our object model in place, we can write down the expression tree illustrated in Figure 21.14:

```
var a = new Param();
var b = new Param();
var f = new Function
{
    Body = new Arithmetic
    {
        Left = new Arithmetic
        {
            Left = a,
            Right = b,
            Operation = Operation.Add
        },
        Right = new Const
        {
            Value = 2
        },
        Operation = Operation.Multiply
```

```
        },
        Parameters = new List<Param> { a, b }
};
```

The expressiveness of C# object and collection initializers nicely reflects the structure of the tree being represented here. I leave it to you to define constructors for all the expression tree types, which would be a better design as it can enforce non-null values for all required connections in the tree.

The Compile Method Explained

On the `Expression` base class, we defined the following `Compile` method required to be overridden by all subtypes:

```
public abstract void Compile(ILGenerator gen, Dictionary<Param, int> env);
```

But what does it mean? The idea is that every node in the expression tree recursively compiles all of its children by calling this `Compile` method. For example, the tree node representing (a + b) * 2 will have to ask the subtree a + b to compile itself, and in a similar manner it should ask the (constant) subtree 2 to do the same.

All the nodes are required to emit IL code to the IL generator object that's passed in through the first parameter. One other piece of information we need to carry around during the compilation is a so-called environment, which contains information about all variables in scope. In our limited world, we only have parameters, but in a more powerful compiler, you'll also deal with local variables. In our case, the environment is a simple mapping from expression tree parameter objects onto integers for the position of the parameter in the top-level function's signature. This environment will be built up when the compilation starts, looking like this for our sample expression:

```
a --> 0
b --> 1
```

All this means is that parameter a is the first parameter and b is the second. When the recursive compilation reaches a `Param` leaf node, the `Param`'s `Compile` method will do a lookup in the environment to map the parameter onto an `ldarg` instruction:

```
class Param : Expression
{
    public override void Compile(ILGenerator gen, Dictionary<Param, int> env)
    {
        gen.Emit(OpCodes.Ldarg, env[this]); // load argument with index...
    }
}
```

In this limited language, the environment is read-only for all nodes below the top-level `Function` node. For more general compilations, this won't be the case because local variables will get declared and fall out of scope within a code block.

The compilation for the remaining leaf node is equally simple because it simply loads an integer constant value. The `ldc.i4` instruction is used for this, as shown here:

```
class Const : Expression
{
    public int Value { get; set; }

    public override void Compile(ILGenerator gen, Dictionary<Param, int> env)
    {
        gen.Emit(OpCodes.Ldc_I4, Value);
    }
}
```

Finally, we take a look at the most complicated expression, the `Arithmetic` one. Here, we need to visit the child subtrees first, in a left-to-right order, so that the code that's responsible for calculating the subexpressions gets evaluated first. Once those two calls have been made, we can emit the IL instruction corresponding to the arithmetic operation, which will, at runtime, pop the two values on the top of the stack and combine them using the arithmetic operation:

```
class Arithmetic : Expression
{
    public Expression Left { get; set; }
    public Expression Right { get; set; }
    public Operation Operation { get; set; }

    public override void Compile(ILGenerator gen, Dictionary<Param, int> env)
    {
        Left.Compile(gen, env);
        Right.Compile(gen, env);
        switch (Operation)
        {
            case Operation.Add:
                gen.Emit(OpCodes.Add);
                break;
            case Operation.Multiply:
                gen.Emit(OpCodes.Mul);
                break;
            case Operation.Subtract:
                gen.Emit(OpCodes.Sub);
                break;
            case Operation.Divide:
                gen.Emit(OpCodes.Div);
                break;
```

```
        }
    }
}
```

Now that we have all the intermediate nodes, we still need to write the entry point to this whole translation. Because the top-level construct is the Function, we provide a specialized Compile method on it with the following signature:

```
public T Compile<T>()
```

Here T is a delegate type that will be used for the result of the compilation so that the caller can make a statically typed call to the compiled function. For example, our example expression f could be compiled and executed as follows, using one of the built-in generic delegate types:

```
var res = f.Compile<Func<int, int, int>>();
Console.WriteLine(res(2, 3)); // 10 = (2 + 3) * 2
```

The top-level Compile method is relatively straightforward and contains all the plumbing to create a dynamic assembly, as we've seen before. Additional code takes care of establishing the environment data structure, based on the number of parameters specified on the Function instance:

```
public T Compile<T>()
{
    var asm = AppDomain.CurrentDomain.DefineDynamicAssembly(
        new AssemblyName("LCG"),
        AssemblyBuilderAccess.RunAndCollect);

    var mod = asm.DefineDynamicModule("Lightweight");
    var tpe = mod.DefineType("Code");
    var mtd = tpe.DefineMethod("Generation",
        MethodAttributes.Public | MethodAttributes.Static,
        // Return type
        typeof(int),
        // Every of the Parameters.Count parameters is of type int as well
        Enumerable.Repeat(typeof(int), this.Parameters.Count).ToArray()
    );

    // Establish environment; we could also use a List<T> and use IndexOf
    // in the recursive compilation code to find the parameter's index.
    var env = new Dictionary<Param, int>();
    int arg = 0;
    foreach (var par in Parameters)
        env[par] = arg++;
```

```
// Compilation is requested for the Body, and a final "ret" instruction
// is added to the IL generator.
var gen = mtd.GetILGenerator();
this.Body.Compile(gen, env);
gen.Emit(OpCodes.Ret);

var res = tpe.CreateType();

// Create a delegate of the specified type, referring to the generated
// method which we always call "Generation" (see the DefineMethod call).
return (T)(object)Delegate.CreateDelegate(typeof(T),
                                        res.GetMethod("Generation"));
}
```

Because the recursive nature of the compilation may be a bit abstract to grasp at first, some visualization can help. Figure 21.15 shows the compilation for our sample expression tree. The final step where the Compile call on Body returns is omitted from the diagram but simply appends the final return instruction to the output. It's worth tracing through the compilation code under the debugger to see this tree traversal in action, too.

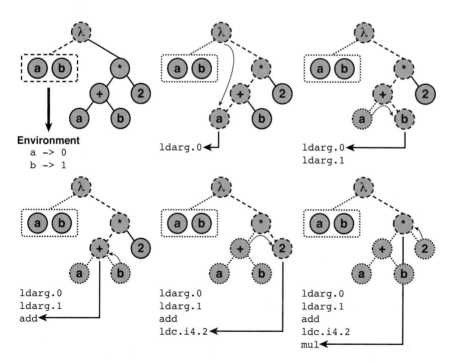

FIGURE 21.15 Compilation of our expression tree, using a depth-first traversal.

WHY BOTHER?

As mentioned before, most readers will likely never have to deal with LCG directly. However, the whole discussion earlier about the feature serves as a great basis for the understanding of expression trees, which are discussed next. In fact, the compilation feature for the built-in expression trees is based on the same technology and follows a similar tree-traversal mechanism to drive compilation into IL code.

Saving the Assembly to Disk

One final remark about LCG is that it can save the compiled assembly to disk, instead of just using it for immediate execution. This can be useful if you're writing some kind of compiler that needs to persist its results to disk:

```
var asm = AppDomain.CurrentDomain.DefineDynamicAssembly(
    new AssemblyName("LCG"), AssemblyBuilderAccess.RunAndSave);
...
asm.Save(fileName);
```

You are invited to try this out on our expression tree compiler. After the assembly has been saved to disk, add it as a reference to a Visual Studio project and call the generated method (whose name you likely want to change in the `Compile` method).

Expression Trees

In the C# 3.0 era, coinciding with the .NET Framework 3.5 release, the mission to solve the impedance mismatch between object-oriented programming and various data models required the ability to represent code as data. In Chapter20, "Language Integrated Query Internals," you saw how LINQ query expressions translate into chains of query operator method calls. For query providers to be able to make sense of the querying intent specified by the user, all information captured in the invocations of query operators needs to be available in an object model at runtime. To solve this problem, expression trees were introduced.

We now take a look at two sides spanned by expression trees. One is the generation of expression trees by the compiler, as leveraged in the translation of query expressions that target the `IQueryable<T>` interface (see Chapter20). The other is the runtime aspect of expression trees, in particular the object model and auxiliary APIs that allow you to visit the expression tree or to compile it into IL code. Finally, we also detail the evolution of those expression trees into statement trees in .NET 4, which allows them to be used as the core infrastructure for the DLR.

Compiler-Generated Expression Trees

 As mentioned in Chapter 20, lambda expressions have two representations. One is the equivalent to anonymous methods, causing the lambda expression to be translated into a piece of IL code that allows direct execution of its logic:

```
Func<int, int, int> f = (a, b) => (a + b) * 2;
```

This is the same as the following C# 2.0 fragment:

```
Func<int, int, int> f = delegate (int a, int b) { return (a + b) * 2; };
```

The preceding can be translated into a separate method that's being referred to by the delegate:

```
Func<int, int, int> f = new Func<int, int, int>(MyExpression);
...
static int MyExpression(int a, int b) { return (a + b) * 2; }
```

However, when we assign the lambda expression to an Expression<T>, where T is a delegate type, the compiler's code generation path deviates and emits IL code that will construct an expression tree representing the lambda expression at runtime. Expression tree APIs are defined in the System.Linq.Expressions namespace, revealing their first use and introduction in .NET 3.5:

```
Expression<Func<int, int, int>> f = (a, b) => (a + b) * 2;
```

Using .NET Reflector, it's easy to see the code that gets generated for the line of preceding code (assuming their decompiler doesn't become smarter in future versions):

```
ParameterExpression a, b;
Expression<Func<int, int, int>> expression =
    Expression.Lambda<Func<int, int, int>>(
        Expression.Multiply(
            Expression.Add(
                a = Expression.Parameter(typeof(int), "a"),
                b = Expression.Parameter(typeof(int), "b")),
            Expression.Constant(2, typeof(int))),
        new [] { a, b });
}
```

Expression trees are generated whenever a lambda expression gets assigned to any kind of variable (which can be a local, a parameter, or a field) that's typed as Expression<T>. Notice the use of the word *expression*. In particular, lambdas with statement bodies cannot be turned into expression trees (because they require statement trees), as shown in Figure 21.16.

FIGURE 21.16   Expression trees support only lambdas with expression bodies.

EXPRESSIONS OR STATEMENTS

As you learned earlier, expressions are valued whereas statements aren't. Because lambdas always have a value, more specifically a function that is treated as a value, they're referred to as lambda expressions. However, the lambda expression contains different language elements ranging from parameters to a body. This body can be either an expression or a statement block. The correct term to refer to the latter ones is *lambda expression with a statement body*. Those are the constructs that are not convertible to expression trees by the compiler.

In .NET 3.5, this was the end of the story. There simply was no way to create an expression tree that contained statements because the System.Linq.Expressions API had no such types in its object model. However, starting with .NET 4, the namespace also has types that can represent statements, such as conditional if statements, loops, exception handling primitives around blocks, and so on.

Although .NET 4's BCL has support for statement trees, the language compilers for C# and VB haven't been adapted to generate such code. One good reason this isn't the case is to make sure existing LINQ providers don't get to see statement nodes in the trees they're provided (though that would require users to start writing statement bodied lambdas in their query operator calls).

The extended .NET 4 API containing the statement tree node types is still called System.Linq.Expressions, which collectively are referred to as expression trees. As the arguably most useful type is LambdaExpression, which can be compiled into a delegate, it makes some sense to refer to all trees as expression trees because compilable trees will have a lambda *expression* as their root.

The Expression Tree API

The main purpose of expression trees is to allow the inspection of user-written code at runtime, through the object model provided for them in System.Linq.Expressions. In this section, we take a look at the API for those expressions.

Expression Base Class

At the root of the class hierarchy of the expression tree object model is the Expression abstract base class. From a data point of view, it has a few properties:

▶ Type indicates the runtime type represented by the node in the tree. Every node in an expression tree has a type that may be derived from its children. For example, if a and b are both Int32, the `BinaryExpression` representing the addition of a and b will also be of type Int32.

▶ `NodeType` is of type `ExpressionType`, an enum that indicates the meaning of the node in the tree. For example, for the `UnaryExpression` used to represent a Boolean negation of some operand, the node type will be `Not`. This property is usually used to switch on the node type to take some appropriate action.

▶ `CanReduce` is new in .NET 4 and is used to simplify expression trees. If this property returns true, a `Reduce` method can be called to obtain a semantically equivalent but simpler tree. This method is useful for language implementers on top of the dynamic language runtime. You can find more information about it at http://dynamic language runtime.codeplex.com.

On the operational field, the `Expression` type has two big buckets of methods. One set consists of the factory methods used to create new expression tree nodes. Inside those factory methods, checks are performed to make sure the created tree is sound from a typing and semantic point of view. For example, to create a binary expression for the addition of two expressions, the types of the operands need to be compatible so that the operation can be carried out. Therefore, the following code will throw an exception because an integer and a string cannot be added together:

```
var invalidAdd =
    Expression.Add(Expression.Constant(42), Expression.Constant("24"));
```

To make the preceding code work, you must be more specific about your intent by using other expression tree nodes. One possibility is that you mean to call `ToString` on 42 before trying a string concatenation (which requires the use of a `MethodCallExpression` because string concatenation is not an "addition" in the expression tree sense of the word). It could equally well be the case that you want to add 42 and 24 as integers, requiring a call to the `Parse` method on Int32 for the right side.

Besides the large number of factory methods, some instance methods exist:

▶ `Reduce`, `ReduceAndCheck`, and `ReduceExtensions` allow simplification of expression trees and are related to the `CanReduce` property mentioned before. We won't cover this functionality here; for more information, just read up on the dynamic language runtime documentation.

▶ `ToString` has been overridden to provide a friendly string representation of the expression represented by an expression tree. The syntax emitted is neither C# nor VB and is primarily useful for debugging and documentation in exception messages and such. You'll see other debugging enhancements in .NET 4 in Figure 21.23, too.

▶ `Accept` and `VisitChildren` are both used with the expression tree visitor that ships with .NET 4. When extending the set of expression trees with your own "extension" nodes, those methods can be overridden to participate in various operations performed over expression trees. We won't cover this extensibility feature in .NET 4 either (again, refer to DLR documentation for more information).

Expression Tree Leaf Nodes

Some nodes in an expression tree can act only as leaf nodes because they don't have any properties that can contain a subtree. Although expressions like a + b are clearly not leaf nodes (because the + operator has a left and right side), expressions representing a variable or a constant clearly are. Figure 21.17 shows the leaf types in the API.

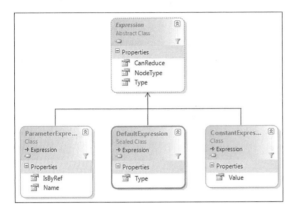

FIGURE 21.17   Leaf nodes for expression trees.

The various properties on those types (which can be set using the factory methods used to create them) should be self-explanatory. Constants have values, parameters (for lambda expressions, as you will see in the section, "Lambda Expressions, Delegate Invocation, and Quotation") have a name and either a by-value or by-reference calling behavior, and the default(T) form in C# takes in a type as parameter, so the Expression base class's Type property can be used for that purpose. An example of creating a constant expression is shown here:

```
var answer = Expression.Constant(42);
```

Unary and Binary Expressions

One way to combine different expression trees into a bigger one is the use of unary or binary operators. Because every unary operator has the same shape (one child expression tree to represent the operand) and so does every binary operator (two children for the left and right operands, respectively), one type exists for both. To discriminate between the various operators that can be represented with those types, the NodeType can be used:

▶ Binary operators include Add, And, Equal, LessThan, and so on.

▶ Unary operators include Not and unary arithmetic operations like Negate.

Figure 21.18 shows the most important properties on those expression tree node types. A few properties that have to do with nullability (IsLifted, IsLiftedToNull) and the possible use of an operator overload method (Method) have been omitted. For more information about them, refer to the MSDN documentation.

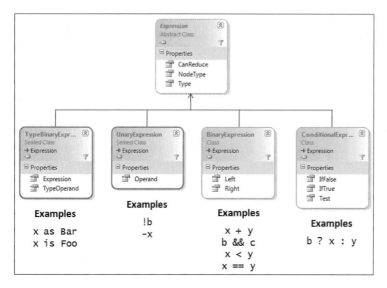

FIGURE 21.18   Some binary and unary expression tree node types.

In addition to `BinaryExpression` and `UnaryExpression`, some related node types have been included in the figure. `TypeBinaryExpression` is used for type-related operations such as the `TypeIs` (is in C#) and `TypeAs` (as in C#) node types. Conversions are represented as regular unary expression with a `Convert` or `ConvertCheck` node type, which correspond to operations like casts in C#. Finally, the `ConditionalExpression` is the equivalent to C#'s conditional operator, which really is a ternary operator.

Instantiating Objects

Another operation that can be captured in expressions is the creation of objects. C# and other languages have various ways to do this, ranging from plain constructor calls to the use of initializer expressions, including the ones targeting collections. Figure 21.19 illustrates all the expression tree nodes that fall into the category of object instantiation.

The initializer forms are slightly more complicated than other expressions because they capture additional reflection information about the members being initialized. For example, if you write the following:

```
new Foo { Bar = x }
```

In this case, you're calling the default constructor on `Foo` (but you could be calling another one, too), followed by an assignment to the `Bar` property or field, using another expression x. This `MemberInitExpression` decomposes into a `NewExpression` that captures information about the constructor call, as well as a series of bindings that each contain what expression is bound to what property. For anonymous types, things are slightly different, where the `NewExpression`'s `Members` property is used to refer to the properties that got initialized.

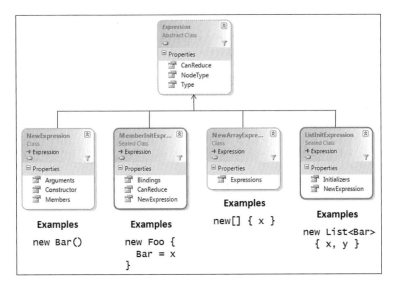

FIGURE 21.19   Instantiation of objects, arrays, and collections.

The NewArrayExpression simply contains a list of expressions for all the elements added to it, while the ListInitExpression again relies on a constructor call (captured by a NewExpression that also refers to a ConstructorInfo) but has a list of element initializer expressions to go with it.

Invoking and Accessing Members

Another big category of expression-based operations are invocation of methods and access to properties and indexers. In Figure 21.20, all the relevant expression tree nodes types are summarized. To refer to the targeted members, reflection objects are being used (such as MethodInfo).

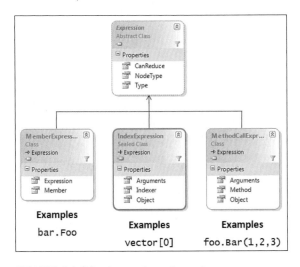

FIGURE 21.20   Invocation of members.

The Hello World example in terms of expression trees is shown here. We're using a `MethodCallExpression` for the static `Console.WriteLine` method, so we don't need to specify an expression object for the instance used in the call:

```
var hello = Expression.Call(typeof(Console).GetMethod("WriteLine",
                           new[] { typeof(string) }, null),
                Expression.Constant("Hello World!") /* first argument*/
);
```

WHAT ABOUT DYNAMIC LATE-BOUND OPERATIONS?

Because we've been dealing with early-bound statically typed operations throughout our discussion about the expression tree APIs so far, you might wonder how .NET 4 support for late-bound and dynamically typed operations fits into this picture. Part of the answer to this question is the introduction of a new expression tree node type called `DynamicExpression`. To understand this, we first need to discuss the concept of binders (which we do in Chapter 22).

Lambda Expressions, Delegate Invocation, and Quotation

One of the most important node types in the world of expression trees is the lambda expression. Those nodes act as the entry point to expression trees that can be compiled at runtime, resulting in a strongly typed delegate. In fact, the generic `Expression<TDelegate>` type derives from the `LambdaExpression` base type immediately.

Closely related to the definition of delegates it the invocation of them. Obviously, the expression tree APIs provide for such a tree node type, as well, in the form of the `InvocationExpression`.

Last but not least, there's a factory method called `Expression.Quote` that is used to create a constant expression around a given `Expression` object. What this allows is to reference an expression tree as a verbatim object (for example, if one represents a method call to some method taking in an expression tree). For more information about this node, refer to MSDN.

Figure 21.21 shows the nodes we've discussed here, also including the one used to represent a lambda expression parameter. Core properties on `LambdaExpression` are `Body` and `Parameters`, which refer to the child nodes. Other ones, such as `Name` and `TailCall` (an optimization technique used for recursive functions), have been introduced for use in the DLR in .NET 4.

Given all the tree nodes we've seen so far, we can create an expression tree for the example discussed earlier in the context of LCG. Instead of using our own expression tree object model, we can now leverage the APIs provided in the `System.Linq.Expressions` namespace. As stated earlier, the way to create new nodes is by calling the corresponding factory methods:

```
var a = Expression.Parameter(typeof(int), "a");
var b = Expression.Parameter(typeof(int), "b");
var f = Expression.Lambda<Func<int, int, int>>(
    Expression.Multiply(
        Expression.Add(a, b),
        Expression.Constant(2)
    ),
    a, b
);
```

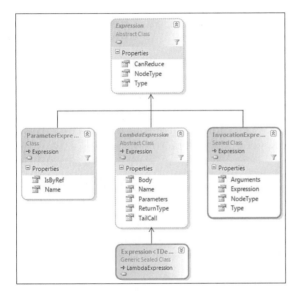

FIGURE 21.21   Lambda expressions and related expression tree node types.

Refer to the code we wrote earlier for our LCG example and notice the one-to-one correspondence between the fragments. The main difference is we're not using object initializers and constructors but instead rely on factory methods.

Although one of the most common uses of expression trees is to analyze them by means of a visitor (as you will see in just a moment), another great use exists: compilation of dynamically generated code at runtime. This is precisely why the DLR relies on those expression trees—because they nicely hide the complexities of dealing with LCG directly.

In the following code, we're compiling the LambdaExpression f by a call to Compile, which hands back a delegate of the type that was specified on the factory method used to create the lambda expression tree:

```
// Compiled at runtime (using f defined a moment ago)
var g = f.Compile();
Console.WriteLine(g(2, 3));
```

```
// Compiled at compile time
var h = new Func<int, int, int>((a, b) => (a + b) * 2);
Console.WriteLine(h(2, 3));
```

Because we recall the expression tree constructing code is the equivalent of having the compiler do the hard work (thanks to homoiconicity), the preceding code is the same as the following:

```
// Compiled at runtime
Expression<Func<int, int, int>> f = (a, b) => (a + b) * 2;
var g = f.Compile();
Console.WriteLine(g(2, 3));
```

```
// Compiled at compile time
Func<int, int, int> h =            (a, b) => (a + b) * 2;
Console.WriteLine(h(2, 3));
```

If you ever need to generate code at runtime, expression trees are your best choice today for lots of reasons: simplicity, expressiveness, performance, and so on.

WHAT ABOUT CODEDOM?

Readers who've been using .NET for a while might have heard of CodeDOM. This technology was introduced early in the .NET 1.0 days as a Document Object Model to represent code at the source code level. In particular, one object model is provided to serve a wide variety of languages that provide a CodeDOM provider, such as C#, Visual Basic, and even F#.

As with most technologies, CodeDOM has its advantages and disadvantages. First, if the output of your code generation has to be in a textual format (for example, as part of code generation in a tool or during a build process), CodeDOM is a pretty good choice. Its language-agnostic approach allows you to emit code in a variety of languages, which could be selected by the user. An example of the use of such an approach shows up in the xsd.exe tool:

```
C:\> type test.xml
<Test />
C:\> xsd /nologo test.xml
Writing file 'test.xsd'.
C:\> xsd /nologo /classes /language:CS test.xsd
Writing file 'test.cs'.
```

The generated test.cs file will now contain C# code to statically represent an XML document following the generated schema. In the header, you see this:

```
// <auto-generated>
//     This code was generated by a tool.
//     ...
// </auto-generated>
```

This is the signature of CodeDOM at work. Although still useful, CodeDOM has some limitations around the supported language features. Effectively, the technology is stuck in the .NET 2.0 time frame, so it lacks support for things such as extension methods, lambda expressions, and so on.

Statement Trees

Before moving on to the runtime analysis of expression trees, we should mention the great additions to the API in .NET 4, stimulated by the advent of the DLR. Where v3.5 expression trees supported only expression nodes, the enriched APIs now also provide for statement nodes. Exhaustive coverage of them is beyond the scope of this discussion, and unless you're writing a compiler, you won't be dealing with those directly.

DON'T FORGET ABOUT LINQ

One of the biggest advantages of LINQ is its extensibility story through various mechanisms, one of which is IQueryable<T>. When dealing with this interface to implement a custom query provider, you'll have to use expression trees to turn the user-written query expression into some target query language.

New expression tree nodes in .NET 4 used to represent statements are listed here:

- ▶ BlockExpression acts as the container for blocks that contain zero or more statements. This roughly corresponds to curly brace surrounded blocks in C#, with statements that get separated using semicolons (ignoring some corner cases where C# has an optional nature for curly braces).

- ▶ GotoExpression is used for goto statements, which jump to a given label, also represented by an expression tree node. Although it's often said that goto is an evil instrument, this is not so much the case at the level of code generation. After all, conditional statements and loops are nothing but jumps in disguise. In this respect, the expression tree APIs are closer to the runtime's language for code (IL) than to the higher-level languages (like C#, VB). This is another place where expression trees differ quite a bit from CodeDOM.

- ▶ LabelExpression goes pretty much together with GotoExpression and is used to introduce jump targets in a block of code.

- ▶ LoopExpression models a loop in its easiest form, even without a terminating condition. Essentially, this expression node type encapsulates two labels, one to break from the loop and one to continue the loop. Given those two jump targets, you can model any other loop (for example, by adding a check for a certain condition at either the beginning or the end of the loop).

- ▶ SwitchExpression is used to build the equivalent to a switch statement in C#, which is slightly more advanced than the use of a series of if statements. Next to a value expression to switch on, this node contains a series of SwitchCase objects as well as a default case.

▶ TryExpression acts as the one-stop shop for constructing exception-handling code through the expression tree API. Besides a body expression, it takes an optional fault and finally handler block, as well as an optional list of handlers (which are represented as CatchBlock objects, containing the handler code, the type of the exception to catch, and an optional filter).

WHAT ABOUT TYPES?

Wait a minute...didn't the Expression base type have a Type property? Didn't you say that expressions have a value but statements don't? So, what's the type on a statement tree node all about?

You're exactly right about this if you think inside the C# silo. However, quite a few languages (especially dynamic and functional ones) treat many more language constructs as valued expressions, including blocks. For example, in Ruby, the last statement (or should we say expression, considering this sidebar) that gets executed in a block will be used as the result value for the entire block. In case of an if statement, this basically works like the conditional ternary operator we know from C#. For loops, the value of the loop body during the last iteration will provide the valued result of the loop.

Because expression trees form an essential piece of the DLR infrastructure, it should be no surprise that this design was followed. However, this choice doesn't prevent you from capturing the C# semantics of nonvalued blocks in expression trees. The trick is to type a block as System.Void, and that's it. A pretty sweet design with generic use in mind, isn't it?

Besides the introduction of new tree node types, the ExpressionType enum has been enriched with a bunch of new values. Some of those go with the new Expression subtypes, whereas others are meant to be used together with existing stock tree nodes, such as BinaryExpression. Most new enum values have to do with all sorts of assignments such as Assign (for a = b forms), various compound assignments (like AddAssign for the a += b form), and increment or decrement operations (like PostIncrementAssign for well-known and much beloved i++ forms).

As an example, the following piece of code will print the numbers 0 through 9 using runtime generated code, taking advantage of various new expression tree features. The inline comments illustrate the corresponding C# code:

```
var i = Expression.Variable(typeof(int), "i");
var brk = Expression.Label("Break");
var a = Expression.Lambda<Action>(
    Expression.Block(
        new[] { i },
        // int i = 0;
        Expression.Assign(i, Expression.Constant(0)),
        // while (true)
```

```
      Expression.Loop(
      // {
         Expression.Block(
            // if
            Expression.IfThen(
               // (i == 10)
               Expression.Equal(i, Expression.Constant(10)),
               //    break;
               Expression.Goto(brk)
            ),
            // Console.WriteLine(i);
            Expression.Call(
               typeof(Console).GetMethod("WriteLine", new[] { typeof(int) }),
               i
            ),
            // i++;
            Expression.PostIncrementAssign(i)
         ),
         brk
      // }
      )
   )
);
var f = a.Compile();
f(); // Prints 0 to 9
```

Although all of this is quite beautiful if you need to generate code dynamically at runtime, you might wonder about debugging support. There are two answers to this. First, the factory methods will raise an exception for all semantic errors they can find, making sure your trees are well formed. Second, a new debugger visualizer has been added to .NET 4 and Visual Studio 2010 to help inspect how the expression tree looks in a more comprehensible form. This proves particularly useful if you have a bunch of code that stitches together a bigger tree. Figure 21.22 shows where the icon to open the visualizer shows up when you hover over an expression tree object.

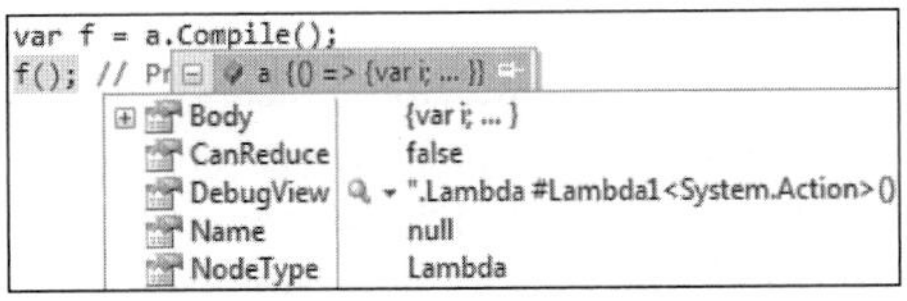

FIGURE 21.22   The magnifier icon for the debugger visualizer shows up on DebugView.

Figure 21.23 shows the visualization provided by this tool, showing a textual block-based representation of the expression tree. From this, you can see many things. First, all nodes clearly have a type; even the else branch of the If (which we never stated explicitly) has type void. Furthermore, we properly see the scoping taking place, and various expressions have a readable form.

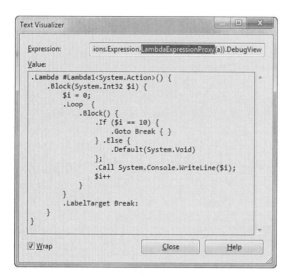

FIGURE 21.23   Our loop visualized in a more readable structure.

JEALOUS ABOUT DEBUGGER VISUALIZERS?

So you want to have a debugger visualizer on your own type? No worries, Visual Studio provides a very simple way to create debugger visualizers in managed code, simply by putting a custom attribute on the type being targeted. Alternative ways to associate a visualizer with a type exist, too. For more information, search MSDN for "debugger visualizer."

LCG OR EXPRESSION TREES? ALL OR NOTHING?

You might wonder whether LCG is no longer useful in the presence of expression tree APIs. Even though expression trees cover a lot of ground, they can't express everything yet. More specifically, they can't express declarations of whole types but focus on code blocks (and everything below) instead.

However, starting with .NET 4, there's a "better together" story that integrates nicely with LCG. Besides the Compile method on LambdaExpression we've been using here extensively, there's a new CompileToMethod method taking in a MethodBuilder from the System.Reflection.Emit LCG namespace. In other words, you can now build assemblies using LCG but leveraging the simpler model of expression trees to define methods. This effectively eliminates the nastiest part of using LCG: the generation of IL code, which required a deep understanding of the IL instruction set and various run-time behaviors.

Using the `ExpressionTreeVisitor`

As mentioned during our discussion about LINQ providers in Chapter 20, expression trees are particularly useful in scenarios where the user's intent must be interpreted at runtime; for example, to translate query expressions. To achieve this, the compiler delivers on the homoiconicity property for lambda expressions so that users don't have to write expression trees by hand.

The other stakeholder in this whole picture of runtime interpretation of expression trees is the library or application developer who wants to carry out this analysis of such an expression tree at runtime. Due to the deeply recursive nature of expression trees, this might seem like a frightening task. Luckily, however, it's a task for which standard tools can be provided quite easily. The main tool in the developer's arsenal to analyze expression trees is the `ExpressionVisitor` type introduced in .NET.

Visitors are a well-known design pattern used to implement "strategies" for visiting nodes in some data structure. In the case of `ExpressionVisitor`, a depth first traversal of the expression tree is done. Upon visiting every node, a method call is made to expose the node being visited to user code that knows how to deal with the task at hand. For example, the use of a visitor in the creation of LINQ providers will realize the translation for all the nodes into a target query language, such as SQL.

Earlier you saw traces of the built-in support for visitors, in the form of a couple of methods on the `Expression` base type: `VisitChildren` and `Accept`. For background information about those, refer to the MSDN documentation.

To create an expression tree visitor, a class is derived from the `ExpressionVisitor` base class, overriding any of the specialized `Visit` methods that the visitor wants to deal with. A simple example of a visitor is shown here, overriding `VisitBinary` to detect all uses of an addition operation in a tree:

```
class FindAdditions : ExpressionVisitor
{
    protected override Expression VisitBinary(BinaryExpression node)
    {
        if (node.NodeType == ExpressionType.Add)
            Console.WriteLine(node.Left + " added to " + node.Right);
        return base.VisitBinary(node);
    }
}
```

Notice the use of the base call, which will carry out the recursion into the subtree's left and right sides. The following piece of code runs the `FindAddtions` visitor:

```
Expression<Func<int, int, int, int>> sum = (x, y, z) => x + y + z + 1;
var fa = new FindAdditions();
fa.Visit(sum);
```

Three messages are printed to the screen. It's left as an exercise to you to figure out those messages. (Tip: Recall the associativity properties of the sum operator.)

Because visitors' `Visit` methods return an `Expression`, they can be used to transform a tree into a new tree (for example, to carry out optimizations). The default implementation of the visitor base class simply returns a node that's equivalent to the original one, while still visiting all nodes in it. A more directly useful example is a Boolean logic optimizer that tries to reduce the complexity of a Boolean expression while preserving semantics:

```
class BooleanLogicOptimizer : ExpressionVisitor
{
    protected override Expression VisitUnary(UnaryExpression node)
    {
        // If we represent a ! operator...
        if (node.NodeType == ExpressionType.Not)
        {
            // ...and the recursive visit to our operand...
            var res = base.Visit(node.Operand);
            // ...is also a ! operator...
            if (res.NodeType == ExpressionType.Not)
            {
                // ...then we can forget about the double negation:
                return ((UnaryExpression)res).Operand;
            }
        }
        return base.VisitUnary(node);
    }
}
```

In this example we've only implemented an optimizer for double negation, but we could equally well extend it with more complex rules that apply to Boolean logic (such as De Morgan's law or ways to create some normal form consisting only of AND and NOT). For the following, four redundant negations will get trimmed away:

```
Expression<Func<bool, bool>> bl = x => !!!!!x;
Console.WriteLine(bl);
var blo = new BooleanLogicOptimizer();
Console.WriteLine(blo.Visit(bl));
```

Here we're relying on the `ToString` behavior for expression trees to print them to the screen in a readable form, as shown in Figure 21.24.

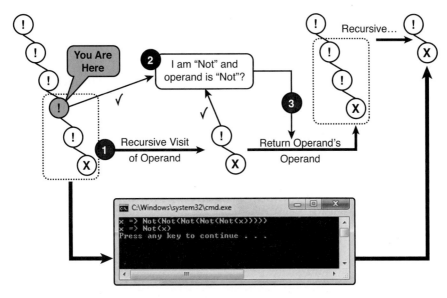

FIGURE 21.24   The Boolean expression optimizer at work.

NOT COMPLETELY RIGHT...

This optimizer is *not* completely sound. To see why, you must think of the operand types that are allowed for the ! operator. You may say the only type you're aware of is Boolean, but operator overloading is another player. It might well be the case that the double negation doesn't hold in some custom domain for which operator overloading has been used. Whether such use of operator overloading is a good thing is a discussion we'll restrain ourselves from here.

There are a variety of ways to ensure the optimizer doesn't get off track and only optimizes what's safe to optimize. One way is to check the Type of the expression tree nodes involved. Another technique that can help is to check for the Method property, which will reveal the use of operator overloading.

Summary

Static type information is not always available. Objects may be obtained without static type information, requiring discovery of type information at runtime. Exploration of options to deal with such scenarios brought us to the wonderful world of reflection provided by the common language runtime.

After a brief detour through writing extensible applications, we approached dynamic programming from the angle of dynamic code generation. Starting with the .NET 2.0 story using lightweight code generation, we gradually moved into newer APIs that facilitate this kind of metaprogramming. In particular, we looked at the expression tree APIs that originate from LINQ in .NET 3.5 and have been extended in .NET 4 with support for statement nodes.

In the next chapter, we bring all those pieces together, finding ourselves back in the world of C# 4.0 dynamic, which leverages the dynamic language runtime.

Dynamic Programming

▶ The dynamic Keyword in
  C# 4.0 1109

▶ DLR Internals 1127

▶ Office and COM Interop 1150

In Chapter 21, we learned about different facilities that can be used to deal with weakly typed scenarios. This includes the use of reflection to inspect type information at runtime, as well as different services to generate code at runtime.

Despite such services offered by the runtime, there are many more scenarios of dealing with weakly typed object that reach outside the scope of managed code. Examples include XML without schemas, JSON objects, and so on. Before the advent of .NET 4, reaching out to such dynamic worlds was quite hard and required lots of plumbing. Moreover, there was no unification whatsoever with regard to how to make dynamic calls. For example, calling .NET code using reflection requires a totally different application programming interface (API) than does reaching out to Ruby code or "dotting into" an XML document using indexer calls and whatnot.

In this chapter, we look at dynamic programming in C# before and after the introduction of the dynamic language runtime in .NET 4, paired with C# 4.0's dynamic keyword.

The dynamic Keyword in C# 4.0

One of the key features in .NET 4 is the support for reaching out to dynamically typed code (and object models representing data) from inside flagship languages such as C# and Visual Basic. The single syntactical presence of this feature in C# is the new dynamic keyword. When an object is typed as dynamic, the compiler will emit code that causes all binding and dispatch operations to be deferred until runtime, instead of statically resolving them at compile time.

So what's binding and dispatching all about? *Binding* is essentially the act of figuring out the meaning of the code with regard to intended method calls, uses of members, and so on. To make this work at runtime, enough information about the intent of the user must be communicated to whatever runtime library is involved in this binding operation. For example, a member's name, case sensitivity, parameter count, and so on are all relevant pieces of information to consider. So far, we've only been using information that's also available at compile time. Where things start to differ is where *runtime* types (in the sense of System.Type) are considered in those operations. For example, to pick a method out of a set of available overloads, the types used for parameters matter.

Different languages have different binding semantics (that is, the way they pick overloads, whether they care about casing, and so on), so each language in support of dynamic has its own set of binder types. In the world of C# 4.0, those binders live in an assembly called Microsoft.CSharp. Figure 22.1 shows this assembly in Reflector.

FIGURE 22.1   The C# 4.0 runtime binder.

Once runtime binders have performed their job and identified (or bound to) the target to be used (a method, property, indexer, operator, and so forth), the next task is to dispatch to it. Lots of optimization can go in here, in the form of caching of the discovered binding information and generation of code for specialized call sites.

The call site is where the dynamic operation occurs. Due to the dynamic nature of the operation, it's possible the same code path gets triggered for many different (runtime) types of data, so that call site needs to be willing to deal with all of those. To speed up the binding operations, call sites learn as they discover more call targets. For example:

```
void PrintName(dynamic d)
{
    Console.WriteLine(d.Name);
}
```

In the preceding, an obvious dynamic call site is the call to Name because the left side of the operation is typed to be dynamic. As you will see later, Console.WriteLine gets turned into a dynamic call as well because its argument is typed as dynamic here, too. However, it's possible to call the same method with objects of many different runtime types, such as FileInfo, DirectoryInfo, MethodInfo, Person, and so on. Because all of those types expose some Name property, the call will succeed.

Depending on the runtime type of d, a different call needs to be made, though; recall the runtime itself uses strong typing. This is what call sites keep track of. Their core role is to provide dispatching services, making sure inputs get routed to the correct call underneath. All of this happens in concert with various DLR services, as detailed later.

The dynamic Type

Now that we've identified key terminology related to dynamic operations, let's take a step back and look at the "language surface" for the feature in C# 4.0. In essence, there's just the dynamic keyword, which indicates that discovery of operations need to be deferred until runtime, relying on the (dynamic) runtime type rather than the (static) compile-time type. For example, in the following piece of code, s is statically typed to be a string:

```
string s = "Hello world";
Console.WriteLine(s.ToUpper());
```

The compiler does make sure it's impossible to assign anything other than a string (or in more general cases, anything that's not compatible with the variable's type) to s. Notice that the use of casts may result in runtime exceptions:

```
string s = (string)GetObject(); // object GetObject();
Console.WriteLine(s.ToUpper());
```

However, the invariant we stated before still holds: You should never to be able to see anything that's not a string being held by variable s. The fact the runtime prevents you from doing such an invalid thing is key to type safe and memory safety.

Because the variable is statically typed to System.String, the compiler knows precisely which ToUpper method we're talking about. This method's return type is System.String, and hence the overload of Console.WriteLine is statically determined, too. If you were to look at the generated IL code, this would be immediately apparent.

Whereas we've been using a rather specific type in the preceding example, there's another end to the static typing spectrum, where we would be using the most common supertype of all types on the platform: System.Object. Now we can't write fancy things like ToUpper anymore:

```
object s = GetObject(); // object GetObject();
Console.WriteLine(s.ToUpper() /* doesn't compile */);
```

On the static side of typing in C# (which has been the only side until the fourth version arrived), the compiler's task is to ensure operations are valid from a typing point of view. Because System.Object has no ToUpper method on it, the preceding is clearly invalid. Now, with C# 4.0, we can effectively say not to bother about this compile time proof of validity and defer all checking for operations until runtime. That's what dynamic is used for:

```
dynamic s = GetObject(); // object GetObject();
Console.WriteLine(s.ToUpper() /* does compile again */);
```

Because there's no assumption whatsoever about the type at compile time, IntelliSense won't provide any help for the dynamic operations, as shown in Figure 22.2. C# 4.0 fills in the gap in the lower-right corner where resolution of operations happens at runtime and the static compile-time type information about an object is low.

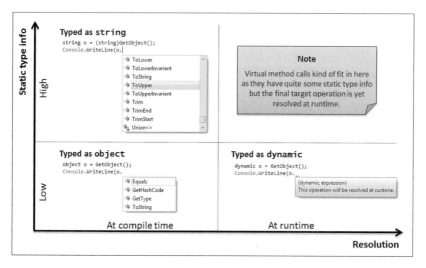

FIGURE 22.2   The typing landscape viewed through the lenses of IntelliSense.

Dynamic Typing Is Contagious

Starting from C# 4.0, dynamic is one of the types built in to the language in the form of a keyword. Everywhere other types can be used, you can use dynamic, too. For example, variables can be declared to be dynamic, and they can appear as types for members and their parameters. Yes, even generic parameters can be using dynamic.

One of the first things we should look at is the effect of using some dynamically typed expression in a larger expression. To make this more concrete, look at the following example. A multiplication of a dynamically typed object with a statically typed object is made:

```
dynamic a = 3;
int b = 5;
var c = a * b;
```

The obvious question is what the inferred static type for c will be. Recall that all var does is have the compiler infer the type from the right side of the assignment. So we're really asking what the result of multiplying a dynamic with an int is. Well, if we don't yet know the runtime type of a, how can we know how to multiply it with an int? Based on this reasoning, the answer ought to be dynamic, too. In other words, the use of dynamic inside an expression is contagious to the type of the expression as a whole. Figure 22.3 reveals this effect of dynamic typing using the Visual Studio code editor.

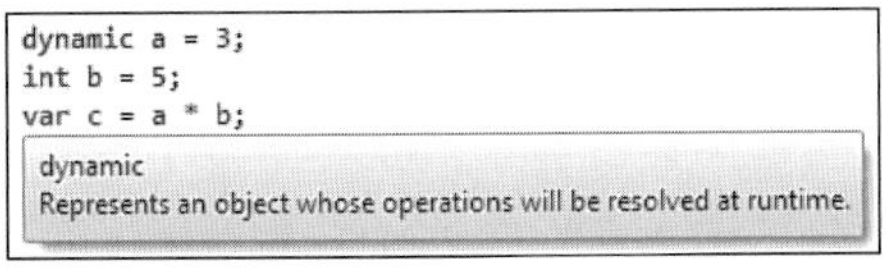

```
dynamic a = 3;
int b = 5;
var c = a * b;

dynamic
Represents an object whose operations will be resolved at runtime.
```

FIGURE 22.3   Use of dynamic inside an expression is contagious.

DIFFERENCE BETWEEN OBJECT, VAR, AND DYNAMIC

It's essential to have a solid understanding of the difference between those three concepts. The only thing they have in common is the coloring in the IDE because all of them are proper keywords in C#. Notice, though, that object is a reserved word, whereas the other two (which were introduced after the first version of the language) are contextual keywords. So if you have some piece of code with a variable named dynamic lying around, it will still compile in C# 4.0.

One key difference between the three is that only two of them are considered to be types (object and dynamic); the third one (var) is just a way to *infer* a type from the surrounding information available.

Seen from another angle, object and var are very statically typed, meaning all type information is known at compile time, whereas dynamic is (what's in a name?) dynamically typed. Use of object clearly leads to a type known at compile time because it's an alias for System.Object. And although var is very different from object, it's still statically typed because the compiler can infer the type of the variable.

Static and dynamic typing are overloaded terms in certain contexts, so sometimes it's better to discuss compile-time and runtime types. In this picture, dynamic totally relies on runtime types, whereas var is all about compile-time type information.

Another example of this contagious property is dealing with method calls on an object that's typed as dynamic or with one or more parameters that are dynamic. For example, consider the use of the Math.Max method, which has no fewer than 11 overloads for various primitive numeric types. When we use a single dynamic object as a parameter to the method, the compiler can't resolve the overload anymore because it has no static type information about that particular parameter:

```
dynamic a = 3;
int b = 5;
var c = Math.Max(a, b);
```

Again, c will be inferred to be dynamic. In all of those examples, it's been clear that a will be of type System.Int32 at runtime because the literal appears in the code snippet. Keep in mind, though, this information is not considered at all by the compiler when it looks up the type information for a. This becomes obvious in the following example, where a is retrieved from somewhere else:

```
dynamic a = ReadInput();
int b = 5;
var c = Math.Max(a, b);
```

Deferred Overload Resolution

In the preceding example, things are getting more interesting at runtime. As you will see later, a call site object is hiding behind the compiled code for the Math.Max call. Now it's totally possible this code path gets hit multiple times, with different runtime types for a. One time, a may happen to be an Int32, so Math.Max really has two Int32 inputs. The runtime magic of dynamic will figure out the best overload is Math.Max(int, int) and will cause the call to be dispatched to that target method.

When another trip through the code is made with the runtime type of a being an Int64, the call site is now faced with an Int32 and an Int64. Again, in concert with the runtime binder, it will figure out the best overload for the call and dispatch to Math.Max(long, long).

To illustrate this behavior in practice, let's cook our own Max methods and have fun with some little experiments. Suppose you have a library with the following two Max overloads:

```
static int Max(int a, int b)
{
    Console.WriteLine(MethodInfo.GetCurrentMethod());
    return a > b ? a : b;
}
```

```
static long Max(long a, long b)
{
    Console.WriteLine(MethodInfo.GetCurrentMethod());
    return a > b ? a : b;
}
```

A little bit of reflection is used to print the invoked method to reveal the method that was chosen by overload resolution. This proves especially handy for the dynamic case because the IDE won't (and can't) help us predict the outcome of a dynamic operation.

The following piece of code now contrasts static and dynamic uses of those methods. Notice the use of cast expression syntax to treat a literal as a dynamic object, simply for illustration purposes:

```
//
// Static typing - fully resolved at compile time
//
Max(3, 5);
Max(3, 5L); // the first parameter can be implicitly converted to long
Max(3L, 5L);

//
// Dynamic typing - same resolution at runtime, based on runtime types
//
Max((dynamic)3, 5);
Max(3, (dynamic)5L); // same as above, but discovered by the runtime binder
Max((dynamic)3L, (dynamic)5L);
```

Both the static and dynamic case will produce the same output, revealing the methods that were called:

```
Int32 Max(Int32, Int32)
Int64 Max(Int64, Int64)
Int64 Max(Int64, Int64)
```

From this, you can clearly see how the same decisions are made about the best match for the Max overload but being deferred until runtime in the latter case. Figure 22.4 shows the call stack (with Show External Code turned on) for a call that was dispatched dynamically. Hitting the same method through the static path will reveal an immediate call from the Main method, illustrating the compile-time resolution that took place.

From Figure 22.4, you can already see the DLR getting involved. The [Lightweight Function] entry on the call stack is in fact nothing but a function that was generated through LCG, at runtime, to create a fast call path into the targeted Max method after overload resolution took place. The frame right below this dynamically generated method stems from the generated call site code, as you learn in the "DLR Internals" section.

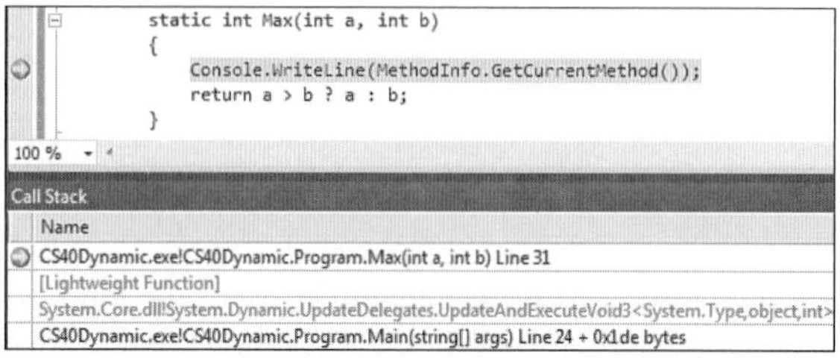

FIGURE 22.4   A dynamically dispatched call in flight.

WHY DYNAMIC IS A STATIC TYPE TOO

In fact, you can say that dynamic is a static type. Even though it has been added to C#, we can continue to say the language is statically typed at its core. When typing something as dynamic, you're really telling the compiler it has to defer all binding decisions until runtime. But in doing so, you're telling it this type information in a rather static manner. In this worldview, you are really statically typing something to be treated dynamically.

This static treatment manifests itself through various aspects of the language. As you've seen, the use of a dynamically typed object in an expression causes the whole containing expression to be typed as dynamic. And that's something the compiler is doing based on the static type information it has available: Combine something with dynamic, and you get back something else that's typed dynamic.

Again, it's probably better to discuss types known at compile time versus types known at runtime. True dynamic languages typically omit all type information at compile (or interpretation) time, so the compiler (or interpreter) doesn't have to reason about types at all. In C#, there's still compile-time reasoning about types, where dynamic now can be a type, too.

Finally, history has brought us to a point where the static and dynamic keywords in the language have fundamentally different meanings. Although static is a modifier for members and types (that stems from the C/C++ heritage), it has nothing to do with static typing. Because those keywords deal with orthogonal concerns, you can have them right next to each other, producing somewhat funny-sounding code:

```
static dynamic Foo() { ... }
```

What we have here is a static method (hence it doesn't operate on an instance, something that has little or nothing to do with typing) that returns something typed as dynamic.

Besides method calls, other expression forms can be dynamically typed. Those include access to properties and indexers (both for get and set operations), the use of fields, invocation of overloaded operators, and dealing with events. One construct that doesn't have an equivalent in the dynamic world (exposed through the C# language) is the use of the new keyword to construct an object of a type that would be dynamically discovered at runtime (based on its name). Some examples of permitted constructs are shown here:

```
dynamic d = ...;
d.Foo = d[0] * d.Bar; // Property set, indexer get, property get
d.Baz("Hello"); // Method invocation
d.WhenHappened += new EventHandler(d_WhenHappened); // Event add
```

No System.Dynamic Type

C# has a bunch of aliases for BCL types in the form of reserved words, such as int, long, bool, string, and object (among various others). You might rightfully wonder whether the new dynamic type is also an alias for some BCL type. It turns out it is, but maybe not what you expect it to be.

First, let me disappoint you. There is no such thing as a System.Dynamic type, which would be the most logical guess. To understand why this is not the way things are done to achieve the effects of the dynamic feature, you need to understand a few things:

▶ An object typed as dynamic can really be anything at runtime, so if there were a specific type for everything typed as dynamic, it would better be compatible with all types that are already supported by the runtime.

▶ Dynamic is merely an illusion created at compile time, guiding the compiler to emit code that will perform binding and dispatch logic at runtime, assisted by various runtime libraries and facilities.

▶ If there were a System.Dynamic type, what would its members look like? It's good to think for a while about what such a type could expose given it acts as a representative for all sorts of objects at runtime.

All of those points help to conclude we already have a perfectly usable type out there that can be used to represent dynamically typed objects. To the runtime (by which we mean the CLR in this context), everything derives from System.Object already, so that looks like a good candidate. When making this choice, dynamic is really nothing more than a very specialized policy for code generation carried out by various compilers that support dynamic. Instead of resolving all operations at compile time, they need to emit code that will do precisely that but deferred until runtime.

One thing is missing, though. If we were to substitute dynamic for object as the way to represent dynamically typed objects, how can we distinguish something that has been statically typed as object from something that was typed as dynamic? Once more, the extensibility story around metadata in .NET assemblies comes to the rescue. Instead of "just" typing a dynamic object as System.Object, it also gets an attribute applied to it that reveals it has to be treated as such: dynamic.

For example, consider the following piece of code where `dynamic` is used in a variety of places:

```
class Foo
{
    public dynamic Twice(dynamic arg)
    {
        throw new NotImplementedException();
    }
}
```

At the time of this writing, .NET Reflector hasn't been enlightened yet about the existence of C# 4.0 dynamic, so the decompiler simply sees the uses of `dynamic` as uses of `object` with some funky `Dynamic` attribute in the proximity. Figure 22.5 shows this.

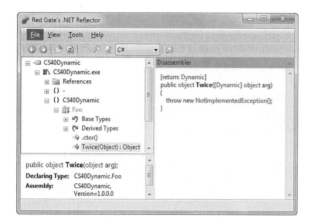

FIGURE 22.5   The dynamic type gets encoded as `System.Object` with some attribute.

CUSTOM ATTRIBUTES, TAKE TWO

When discussing custom attributes in Chapter 21, "Reflection," in the section, "Custom Attributes", we briefly mentioned how the `AttributeUsage` attribute is used to specify the applicable targets for the custom attribute. Common targets include classes and methods, but in fact most reflection entities support attributes on them.

The encoding of dynamic uses the `DynamicAttribute` applied to things such as parameters and return types. As you can see from Figure 22.5, syntax exists to apply an attribute to those. For parameters, you just put the attribute enclosed in its square brackets in front of the (type of the) parameter. When return types are targeted, the attribute is applied to the method but with a return: prefix.

Note that the manual use of this syntax for `DynamicAttribute` (which by the way lives in `System.Runtime.CompilerServices`) is not permitted by the C# compiler. Instead, you should use the dynamic keyword. In fact, what's shown here is merely an implementation detail of dynamic, which may or may not change in the future.

Besides use of the `return` keyword as a prefix to a custom attribute, other such prefixes exist. One is `assembly`, to apply an assembly-wide custom attribute. Good examples of this are found in the AssemblyInfo.cs file, which can be found by expanding the Properties node in Solution Explorer:

```
[assembly: AssemblyTitle("CS40Dynamic")]
```

You read more about assemblies in Chapter 25, "Assemblies, and Application Domains." Other attribute target specifiers include `module` (a part of an assembly), `field`, `event`, `property`, `method`, `param`, and `type` (most of which are optional and can be inferred from the context in which they occur).

When to Use `dynamic`: Case Study with IronPython

All powerful tools should be used with care, and `dynamic` is no different. By no means is `dynamic` meant to be a substitute for static typing. Use of static typing provides many benefits, such as compile-time checking, tooling advantages, a more beneficial performance profile, and so on.

The main philosophy of .NET 4 dynamic is to make reaching out to dynamically typed code and data simpler. Or to say it in another way: Why should someone be punished for embracing some piece of dynamically typed code (for example, using some Python-based library), when calling it from languages like C#? In short, C# 4.0 dynamic allows developers to "ease into" the domain of dynamic typing with minimum friction.

To this end, all examples of `dynamic` shown in this chapter so far have been violating the rule of "static where possible, dynamic where necessary," because you could have written those simple examples in a statically typed manner. With the example presented here, we use `dynamic` for what it's really meant to be used for: building bridges to the dynamic world.

Getting IronPython

In this example, we call a Python object from inside C#, leveraging the dynamic feature. Any DLR language would actually work to illustrate this kind of bridging, but Python deserves a special treatment in introductory chapters on the subject because it's the first dynamic language citizen on the DLR. This implementation of the language on the DLR is known as IronPython and is described as follows on the project's website:

> *IronPython is an open-source implementation of the Python programming language which is tightly integrated with the .NET Framework. IronPython can use the .NET Framework and Python libraries, and **other .NET languages can use Python code just as easily**.*

We illustrate both statements made in this description. One is to leverage the .NET libraries from inside Python (with something as simple as operator overloads on BCL types), and the other one, indicated in bold, is to call into Python code from C#.

The official IronPython home page is http://www.ironpython.net and provides links to downloads hosted on Microsoft's CodePlex website. The site also has an online interactive Python in the browser playground, based on Silverlight.

To run the example we show here, download and install the latest version of IronPython suited for .NET 4. After the installation has completed, you'll find an installation folder under your Program Files folder, including the binaries, an interactive console, libraries, documentation, and examples.

One great way to explore Python is by using the interactive IronPython Console, which lives in ipy.exe; a Start menu entry should have been added. This read-eval-print loop (REPL) enables you to enter little fragments of Python code and see the effects on the screen immediately. A sample run is shown in Figure 22.6.

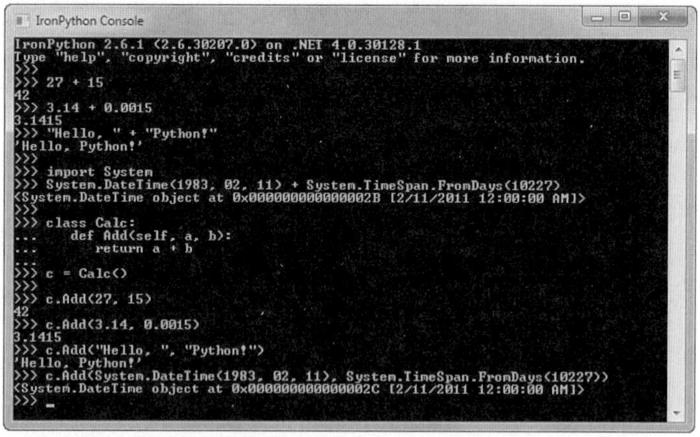

FIGURE 22.6   The IronPython Console in action.

From the interactive session shown in Figure 22.6, it's clear that IronPython is a first-class citizen on the .NET Framework, being able to utilize the BCL types. Also, the + operator is shown to be usable with quite a few operand types, which is what we have lifted into a separate Add method on a Calc type we've defined. Here, the signature of Add is totally dynamically typed because there are no static types in Python. Therefore, we can call Add with any two arguments whatsoever at the risk of hitting a pair that cannot be added together. Figure 22.7 shows this situation. Notice, though, how the type error is detected *inside* the Add method, so there was nothing keeping us from attempting to make the call. It just turned out the Add method couldn't handle the input that was given to it.

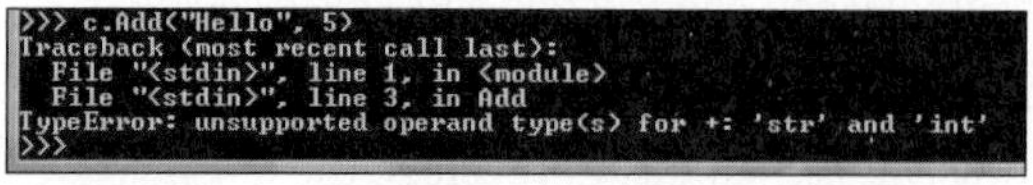

FIGURE 22.7   Strings and integers cannot be added together using +.

REPL LOOPS EVERYWHERE?

REPLs are handy tools, as you can see from the preceding example. Often, people believe, mistakenly, that REPLs exist only for dynamically typed languages. In fact, shells like PowerShell are good examples of this because they have a very dynamic characteristic, too. However, statically typed languages like F# have them too (using type inference), and in some future release, C# may get a REPL as well (thanks to the compiler-as-a-service work being done).

Hosting IronPython in C#

One of the essential capabilities of the dynamic languages (in the Iron* family with both Python and Ruby available nowadays) is their capability to be hosted inside another application through a library. Providing them the script, the library reads it at runtime (there's typically no distinct, offline, compile phase for dynamic languages), such that calls can be made to the contained functionality. In fact, the REPL loop does this one line at a time.

To get started with this hosting inside C#, we have to add references to IronPython.dll and the Microsoft.Scripting.dll assemblies that come with the IronPython installation. The former contains the language-specifics for Python, including a compiler, various modules with built-in functionality (such as mathematical functions that are part of what's considered the core library that comes with Python distributions), binders to deal with various operations, and the hosting entry point. What the Microsoft.Scripting assembly provides for is the generic functionality for scripting languages, all of which share concepts that are used to interpret and host script. In some sense, this assembly acts as the primary toolbox for dynamic scripting languages provided on the DLR.

Figure 22.8 shows the inclusion of the two required assemblies and the resulting list of required referenced assemblies, omitting the ones that aren't required. Notice we use the C# 4.0 runtime library, Microsoft.CSharp, to make use of the C# 4.0 dynamic capabilities.

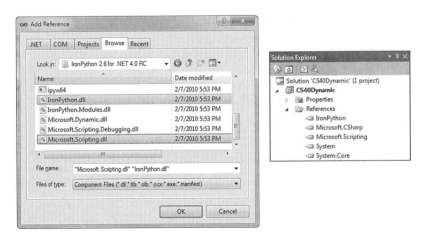

FIGURE 22.8   References needed for hosting IronPython inside a C# application.

The essential code to set up the IronPython hosting is barely one line long:

```
var py = Python.CreateEngine();
```

Alternative code paths exist depending on how many runtime facilities you want to take advantage of, but the preceding suffices for our purposes. Executing a single line of code now gets as easy as the following:

```
Console.WriteLine(py.Execute("27 + 15"));
```

If we look at the signature of Execute, we already see dynamic popping up in the return type, as shown here:

```
public dynamic Execute(string expression);
```

Other overloads exist, including one that takes a generic parameter to specify the static type of the object we expect back. If the returned object's type isn't assignable given the specified type, a runtime exception will occur:

```
Console.WriteLine(py.Execute<string>("27 + 15")); // Boom! It's not a string.
```

At this point, you already have a very powerful tool available to execute fragments of Python code. Much more can be done, including the creation of a REPL using all the shared functionality exposed in Microsoft.Scripting and auxiliary assemblies. Let's just focus on the interaction with C#, though.

A RETURN TICKET FROM STATIC TO DYNAMIC AND BACK

So far, you've mostly seen examples where we started from an object whose static type we know and turned it into a dynamically typed one. This is the least useful direction for dealing with dynamic, but it fits quite well in introductory explorations of the dynamic feature:

```
dynamic d = 15; // Gosh, we've just thrown away type information.
```

In the opposite direction (as illustrated using IronPython), objects often don't have a static type to begin with. Hence they start their life dynamically typed and enter the C# world in that manner. The Execute method's return type illustrates this point very clearly.

The billion-dollar question now is whether we can turn a dynamic object back into a statically typed one. Obviously, the answer is yes, but some caveats apply. Because dynamic is an alias for object (with some attribute stuffed on top of it), we have to do with an upcast scenario, which can fail at runtime (as it does in the following):

```
string s = d; // This may work but the runtime has the final call.
```

So simply assigning to a statically typed variable provides a way for users to break out of dynamic at any time. Casting to a static type can be used, too. Effectively, it stops the feature's contagious propagation of dynamic typing.

One alternative design considered during the creation of C# 4.0 was the use of a construct similar to the checked and unchecked keywords when used in an expression context:

```
dynamic c = dynamic(a + b); // Hypothetical C# syntax that never made it.
```

With this hypothetical language feature, every operation inside a dynamic expression would have been late bound, and one can cast back such an expression to a static type, just as we did here before. However, now the dynamic use is no longer a property of a variable or object. The language designers concluded that the design where dynamic is treated as a first-class type allows for smoother use of such objects. Contagiousness can be good, too.

Dealing with Python Types

To make our example a little more interesting than just executing single expressions, we add a script file to the project and try to call into its functionality. Here is the definition of a simple calculator in Python, as we saw before in the REPL example:

```python
class Calc:
    def Add(self, a, b):
        return a + b
def GetCalc():
    return Calc()
```

The addition of the last function will make it possible for us to create a new instance of the Calc type from inside C# because there's no syntax to instantiate objects through dynamic. In fact, we could omit the GetCalc method and invoke a little expression Calc(), which constructs a new instance, using methods like Evaluate.

Because we've obtained the calculator instance, we can invoke Add on it, with a wide range of different parameter types, as we did interactively through the REPL, as shown in Figure 22.6.

WHAT'S SELF?

In Python, instance methods on a class take a self parameter to represent the current instance, just like this does in C#. In Ruby, another dynamic language, this self parameter isn't needed to achieve this effect. In this example, we're using a separate type to illustrate the dynamic Add calls we'll be making, but we could equally well have used a plain top-level method defined outside a type. However, in typical scenarios, you'll be dealing with an existing library, where you might have to interact with existing types.

Instead of using the Evaluate method as we did before, we now carry out a two-step process by which we first import the script file and then call into it, using dynamic. The first step is shown here:

```
var py = Python.CreateEngine();
dynamic script = py.ImportModule("Calc");
```

This will try to find the specified module by doing a file lookup for Calc.py in the working folder (that is, next to the C# executable assembly). To automate the creation of a compliant folder layout, you can add a file called Calc.py to the project and configure the Build Action as Content in the Properties window. Also enable the Copy to Output Folder setting to read "Copy if newer." Those settings are shown in Figure 22.9.

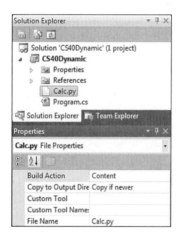

FIGURE 22.9   Build configuration for the Calc.py script file.

So what does this ImportModule method look like? From what you've seen so far on the Execute method, you might think it ought to return an object of type dynamic. This isn't the case, though, as proven by the following signature:

```
public static ScriptScope ImportModule(this ScriptEngine engine,
                                       string moduleName);
```

Even though this method returns an object of type ScriptScope, we treat it as an object typed to be dynamic. Every statically typed object can be assigned to (something typed to be) dynamic, just as you can assign every object to something of type object. The obvious question is how treating the returned ScriptScope object as dynamic helps in this particular case. Let's take a look at this type, defined in the Microsoft.Scripting assembly, so it can be shared across dynamic language implementations. The following fragment omits some irrelevant details:

```
public sealed class ScriptScope : IDynamicMetaObjectProvider
{
    public bool ContainsVariable(string name);
    public IEnumerable<KeyValuePair<string, object>> GetItems();
    public dynamic GetVariable(string name);
    public T GetVariable<T>(string name);
    public IEnumerable<string> GetVariableNames();
    public bool RemoveVariable(string name);
    public void SetVariable(string name, object value);
    public bool TryGetVariable(string name, out dynamic value);
    public bool TryGetVariable<T>(string name, out T value);
    ...
}
```

From what we've seen so far in this chapter, treating some object as dynamic doesn't give us more capabilities other than deferring lookup of operations until runtime. So does using a ScriptScope through dynamic only provide access to the methods that are shown here? Luckily, this is not the case. Because this object implements an interface called IDynamicMetaObjectProvider, it gets special treatment by the DLR in that it participates in various binding operations. You'll see how this works later in the "Custom Dynamic Objects with DynamicObject" section, but in essence it allows us to write the following code:

```
var py = Python.CreateEngine();
dynamic script = py.ImportModule("Calc");

dynamic calc = script.GetCalc();
Console.WriteLine(calc.Add(27, 15));
Console.WriteLine(calc.Add(3.14, 0.0015));
Console.WriteLine(calc.Add("Hello, ", "Python!"));
Console.WriteLine(calc.Add(new DateTime(1983, 02, 11),
                           TimeSpan.FromDays(10227)));
```

The GetCalc method clearly doesn't appear on ScriptScope. Because it's a type that can represent any "scope for script," it obviously doesn't have a crystal ball and envision all operations that might ever occur in script. Instead, when treated as a dynamic object, lots of machinery is put into action to resolve operations performed on it. The preceding code produces the expected results, as shown in Figure 22.10.

FIGURE 22.10   Calling Python script functionality from C# using dynamic.

If we didn't have dynamic here, we would have to obtain the GetCalc method in a manual way, much like classic use of .NET Reflection works. For example, the following piece of code yields the same results:

```
var py = Python.CreateEngine();
var script = py.ImportModule("Calc");

// Gets a Python function object, returned as "dynamic".
dynamic getCalc = script.GetVariable("GetCalc");
dynamic calc = getCalc();
```

Now we type the script variable statically as a ScriptScope and call the GetVariable method to obtain the defined GetCalc function. In dynamic languages, all those top-level constructs are simply treated in the same manner, so the GetCalc function can be retrieved as a variable. This GetVariable method's return type is dynamic once more (just like the Execute method we saw earlier). In this case, we make a call to the retrieved Python function object using delegate invocation syntax.

Because we've gotten rid of one layer of dynamic treatment, we're increasingly losing code clarity. All of a sudden, we need to call cryptic methods such as GetVariable, passing in strings to communicate our intent. This is precisely what dynamic helps with: reducing clutter needed to establish calls involving dynamic typing.

DYNAMIC TYPES ARE DYNAMIC: THEY CAN AND WILL CHANGE

One key aspect of dynamically typed scripting languages is that the (nonexisting) type of variables can change over time. At one point, a variable may contain an integer, and then it could be holding on to a string or even a function.

This effectively provides the same "flexibility" as typing an object using the least specific type in a statically typed system (that is, System.Object). However, in a static world, this is also the least useful type because few to no useful operations can be done on it. In dynamic languages, you can apply any operation to anything, at the cost of possible runtime errors when the lack of (or incompatibility of) an operation gets detected.

In our running example, we can show how the GetCalc top-level variable can be replaced from inside C#, using dynamic. Where the variable originally contained a PythonFunction object, we replace it with a string. Obviously, this will cause further use of the variable as if it were a function to fail because you can't "invoke a string":

```
// IronPython.Runtime.PythonFunction
Console.WriteLine(script.GetCalc.GetType());

// System.String
script.GetCalc = "Oops!";
Console.WriteLine(script.GetCalc.GetType());

// Oops! Can't invoke a string...
```

```
dynamic calc = script.GetCalc();
```

Clearly, certain developers like the flexibility of dynamic languages despite the apparent higher fragility because of errors that go unnoticed until very late during the execution of a piece of code. An accidental replacement of an object with one of a totally other "type" can cause errors at a later stage during the program's execution when the object gets used again.

That said, .NET 4.0 simply marries both camps nicely without making any value judgment about the viability of dynamic typing versus static typing. If you have dynamic code floating around, now you can bridge it in a friction-free manner.

True Cross-Language Interoperability

If you're interested in the various dynamic languages, download other DLR languages like IronRuby (http://ironruby.codeplex.com) and learn about their hosting capabilities. After you've done so, try to paste together fragments of code defined in all of those different languages.

What the CLR has traditionally enabled for cross-language interoperability between statically type languages, the DLR does for dynamically typed ones. Putting all this together with C# 4.0 and Visual Basic 10.0 support for dynamic, you can now create true interoperability stories across all of those static and dynamic languages.

One effect of this on the BCL is the introduction of auxiliary types such as `Tuple` and the `BigInteger` numeric type.

DLR Internals

Having seen the use of `dynamic` in C# 4.0, you will wonder how the dynamic dispatch is achieved at runtime. This is where the collaboration between language binders and the dynamic language runtime infrastructure enters the picture.

In this section, we look at those components. You learn how the compiler emits call site objects for every dynamic operation carried out. Those call sites act as the entry points into the DLR and as places where the language binder (in C#, this corresponds to the `Microsoft.CSharp` assembly) is looped in to help determine the right target of dynamic operation invocations.

Because the DLR generates code for specialized high-performance dynamic call sites, the existing (and extended) infrastructure around expression trees, and hence LCG, is reused.

You also learn how to develop custom dynamic objects that participate in the execution of dynamic operations. The `DynamicObject` type acts as a base type for such custom objects and relies on an interface `IDynamicMetaObject` that's well known to the DLR.

Dynamic Call Sites and Binders

Closest to the user-written code is the call site that represents a dynamic operation. For instance, if the following code is written, two call sites result:

```
static void Add(dynamic a, dynamic b)
{
    Console.WriteLine(a + b);
}
```

Why two? Because a and b are declared as dynamic, it's obvious that a + b is a dynamic operation. Multiple invocations of this method, with different arguments, can result in the use of different + operators, defined for different types. The + operation requires a first call site, as explained later.

So where's the second call site? Because a + b is a dynamic operation, its result is also typed as dynamic. This is the result of the contagious property of dynamic typing, so the Console.WriteLine call must be resolved at runtime, too. If the result of a + b is a string or some primitive type, chances are high there's a specialized overload available for the WriteLine operation.

Because runtime components now need to participate in the resolution of operations, it's quite obvious that the code generated for the call site needs to contain all information about the operation that's intended by the user. That's where the language-specific binders come into play, describing operations in terms of language primitives. For example, the first call site (for the + operation) will contain the fact we're dealing with a binary + operator; the second call site will carry information about the intent to call a method that's called WriteLine.

WHAT ABOUT DYNAMIC PARAMETERS?

Readers with eye for detail will wonder what happens if a method is called whose parameter is dynamic. For example, consider the following piece of code:

```
static void Main()
{
    dynamic d = 5;
    Do(d);
}

static void Do(dynamic d)
{
    // Something goes here.
}
```

Does this piece of code result in a direct call to Do, without a runtime-resolved call site, or does it result in the creation of a call site? The latter is true because of the simple rule that any operations containing a dynamic object will be deferred until runtime. For the preceding example, there's only one Do method, so this seems totally redundant, but consistency matters.

As an exercise, think about what happens if we call Do(5) without using an intermediate variable.

Let's look at the generated call sites right now. Figure 22.11 shows in Reflector the code generated for our simple-looking Add method.

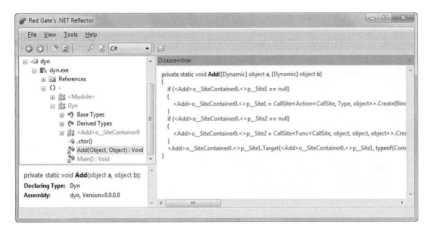

FIGURE 22.11   Code generated for dynamic call sites.

Has the C# compiler gone bananas? We can't even see a + or Console.WriteLine call in the generated code at first glance. Relax, though; this is what's expected, and we take a closer look at it right now.

Instead of staring at the screenshot, let's paste in the decompiled C# code. Notice we're relying on Reflector not decompiling dynamic call sites quite yet, so this might not continue to work for newer versions of the tool. Most likely, the View, Options menu will still provide a way to decompile based on an older version of the language, which is ideal to show how new language features got implemented:

```
private static void Add([Dynamic] object a, [Dynamic] object b)
{
    if (<Add>o__SiteContainer0.<>p__Site1 == null)
```

```
    {
        <Add>o__SiteContainer0.<>p__Site1 =
            CallSite<Action<CallSite, Type, object>>.Create(
                Binder.InvokeMember(
                    CSharpBinderFlags.ResultDiscarded,
                    "WriteLine", null, typeof(Dyn),
                    new CSharpArgumentInfo[] {
                        CSharpArgumentInfo.Create(
                            CSharpArgumentInfoFlags.IsStaticType
                            ¦ CSharpArgumentInfoFlags.UseCompileTimeType,
                            null),
                        CSharpArgumentInfo.Create(
                            CSharpArgumentInfoFlags.None, null)
                    }
                )
            );
    }
    if (<Add>o__SiteContainer0.<>p__Site2 == null)
    {
        <Add>o__SiteContainer0.<>p__Site2 =
            CallSite<Func<CallSite, object, object, object>>.Create(
                Binder.BinaryOperation(
                    CSharpBinderFlags.None,
                    ExpressionType.Add, typeof(Dyn),
                    new CSharpArgumentInfo[] {
                        CSharpArgumentInfo.Create(
                            CSharpArgumentInfoFlags.None, null),
                        CSharpArgumentInfo.Create(
                            CSharpArgumentInfoFlags.None, null)
                    }
                )
            );
    }

    <Add>o__SiteContainer0.<>p__Site1.Target(
        <Add>o__SiteContainer0.<>p__Site1, typeof(Console),
        <Add>o__SiteContainer0.<>p__Site2.Target(
            <Add>o__SiteContainer0.<>p__Site2, a, b));
}
```

That's a whole lot of code, isn't it? In the generated code, two distinct phases can be seen, the first of which creates new CallSite objects if they haven't been created yet. Those objects are kept on a generated type known as the site container. By making this object a single instance (it's a static type with a bunch of static fields on it), the call site can maintain state across method calls to the enclosing method. In our example, the Add method will reuse its call site objects that have been created during a prior invocation, which allows the call site to be *self-learning*. For example:

```
Add(27, 15); // Prints 42
Add(DateTime.Now, TimeSpan.FromDays(7)); // Prints next week's date and time
Add(15, 27); // Prints 42 again
```

In the preceding code, the same call site objects will be reused across all method calls to Add, which avoids the needs for a second discovery of how to perform a binary + operation on System.Int32 objects. During the first Add method call, it will learn how to carry this out (as discussed later), and in the third call that knowledge will be reused.

Call site containers, as illustrated in Figure 22.12, are generated on a per-method basis (whose name appears in the type name of the container).

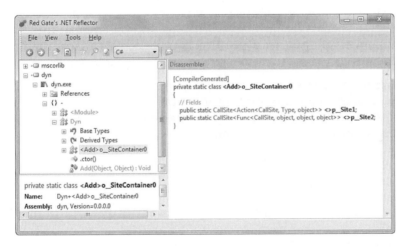

FIGURE 22.12   A generated call site container type.

Let's analyze the two call site objects that have been generated. First, what does the CallSite generic type look like?

```
public sealed class CallSite<T> : CallSite where T : class
{
    public T Target { ... }
    public T Update { get { ... } }
    public static CallSite<T> Create(CallSiteBinder binder) { ... }
}
```

This type lives in the System.Runtime.CompilerServices namespace. Its generic T parameter represents a delegate. (This restriction on bindings for T is not expressible using generic constraints, hence the use of `where T : class`, which is the strongest constraint possible here because all delegate types are classes, too.)

It should be quite obvious why this call site object is parameterized on a delegate type: After all, we're building a construct that will enable us to dispatch a dynamic call at runtime. Invocation of a delegate is an obvious choice because it will allow the runtime to provide us with a specialized (runtime-generated) function that will do the dispatch in the most optimal way possible.

In our running example, the two generated call sites are typed, as follows:

```
public static CallSite<Action<CallSite, Type, object>> <>p__Site1;
public static CallSite<Func<CallSite, object, object, object>> <>p__Site2;
```

At this level, we don't care about the use of the `dynamic` type anymore, and things were replaced by `object`. The second site object will be used to dispatch the binary + operator call, while the first one is used for `Console.WriteLine` calls. Just by looking at the types of the delegate parameters, this should become somewhat clear already. For example, the second site produces an `object` (last parameter) and takes in two such objects, too. The mystery why the `CallSite` is also passed to the delegate will become clear in a moment.

Continuing our exploration of the creation of a call site object, take another look at the generated code for Add. After checking the static field on the call site container for null (hence detecting whether the call site was already created by a prior invocation to Add), the following code runs for the first call site's creation:

```
<Add>o__SiteContainer0.<>p__Site1 =
    CallSite<Action<CallSite, Type, object>>.Create(
        Binder.InvokeMember(
            CSharpBinderFlags.ResultDiscarded,
            "WriteLine", null, typeof(Dyn),
            new CSharpArgumentInfo[] {
                CSharpArgumentInfo.Create(
                    CSharpArgumentInfoFlags.IsStaticType
                    | CSharpArgumentInfoFlags.UseCompileTimeType,
                    null),
                CSharpArgumentInfo.Create(
                    CSharpArgumentInfoFlags.None, null)
            }
        )
    );
```

The `CallSite<T>`'s `Create` factory method takes in a `CallSiteBinder` object, which is an abstract base class defined in `System.Runtime.CompilerServices`. Languages such as C# provide an implementation of such binders in their runtime libraries. The language we prefer is Microsoft.CSharp.dll. The goal of those binders is to represent the operations supported by the language and provide runtime logic to execute them.

In the code corresponding to the first call site, we were invoking the WriteLine method on a static type Console. The invocation of a member is represented by the C# runtime binder created through Binder.InvokeMember:

```
public static CallSiteBinder InvokeMember(
    CSharpBinderFlags flags,
    string name,
    IEnumerable<Type> typeArguments,
    Type context,
    IEnumerable<CSharpArgumentInfo> argumentInfo);
```

For a member invocation operation, five pieces of information are needed. First, some flags can be set to communicate intended use of the operation. In our Console.WriteLine example, the ResultDiscarded flag is set, indicating the result value is not used after the call (and therefore the binder can bind to a void-returning method).

The name parameter should be quite obvious, and so should the type arguments, which are used for generic method calls. In our case, those are WriteLine and null. (The call is not generic.) The fourth parameter captures the context in which the call is made so that the binder can make decisions around visibility if needed.

Finally, the argumentInfo parameter contains information about the arguments used on the call. Using another factory method inside the C# runtime binders library, properties of the used arguments are communicated. This includes a parameter name (if one was speci-fied) and properties such as by ref or out. Those parameters correspond to the type para-meters on the CallSite's target delegate. Figure 22.13 illustrates this mapping between the original syntax and the CallSite's target delegate generic parameters.

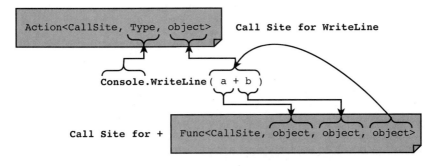

FIGURE 22.13   Mapping generic delegates used in call sites.

Sometimes the types used in call site delegates can be more specific than object—for example, if only a arguments in an operation are typed as dynamic few (or a single argu-ment, for that matter). If we had changed the type of b on Add to int, the corresponding call site delegate type would have been Func<CallSite, object, int, object>.

To wrap up our discussion about how call sites get created, let's look at the other call site that got generated for the binary addition operator:

```
<Add>o__SiteContainer0.<>p__Site2 =
    CallSite<Func<CallSite, object, object, object>>.Create(
        Binder.BinaryOperation(
            CSharpBinderFlags.None,
            ExpressionType.Add, typeof(Dyn),
            new CSharpArgumentInfo[] {
                CSharpArgumentInfo.Create(CSharpArgumentInfoFlags.None, null),
                CSharpArgumentInfo.Create(CSharpArgumentInfoFlags.None, null)
            }
        )
    );
```

From the factory method used on the C# Binder type, it's clear we're dealing with such an operation. The ExpressionType parameter should look familiar to those who've studied expression trees in Chapter 21, in the section, "Expression Trees." If we had used checked around our + operator use, we would have seen ExpressionType.AddChecked. The argument information objects are relatively boring, given no special properties are attributed to them.

By now, it should be clear that call site objects, together with the language-specific binder types, capture all information about the operation intended by the user (well, short of precise static types, that is).

Dynamic Dispatch

Once the compiler has done its duty of generating code that will construct call site objects at runtime, all remaining work is left to the runtime. We already discussed in detail how call sites are built, but we haven't yet discussed how the invocation of the dynamic operation is initiated. In the code that was generated for our running example, the dispatch can be found at the end:

```
private static void Add([Dynamic] object a, [Dynamic] object b)
{
    // Code to ensure the call site objects are instantiated.

    <Add>o__SiteContainer0.<>p__Site1.Target(
        <Add>o__SiteContainer0.<>p__Site1, typeof(Console),
        <Add>o__SiteContainer0.<>p__Site2.Target(
            <Add>o__SiteContainer0.<>p__Site2, a, b));
}
```

This code might look a little overwhelming at first, so let's abbreviate it a little by using simpler names for the call site objects retrieved from the site container. Recall that the first site corresponds to the WriteLine call, and the second takes care of the addition:

```
site1.Target(site1, typeof(Console), site2.Target(site2, a, b));
```

What's this Target business all about? Recall the definition of CallSite<T> we saw in the previous discussion:

```
public sealed class CallSite<T> : CallSite where T : class
{
    public T Target;
    public T Update { get; }
    public static CallSite<T> Create(CallSiteBinder binder);
}
```

Target clearly is a public field, typed as T, which by itself is a delegate type. So what looks like a method call to Target is really getting the delegate held by the Target field and subsequently invoking it. The type of those Target delegates is specified through the generic parameter on CallSite<T> and looks like this for both sites in our example:

```
// Call site for WriteLine:   CallSite<Action<CallSite, Type, object>>
site1.Target(site1,
    typeof(Console),

    // Call site for +:    CallSite<Func<CallSite, object, object, object>>
    site2.Target(site2,
        a, b
    )
);
```

More specifically, this Target delegate is called the Level 0 cache. (Two more cache levels exist, but we won't elaborate on them here.) In conjunction with the fact that call sites are kept in static fields across method calls, the role of this is to provide a fast dispatch path based on the history of the call site use. Once the call site has been used for, say, a + operation on two Int32 arguments, subsequent such uses will go much faster because the site has *learned* how to deal with this situation.

Thinking a bit more about this point, it should become apparent why the site is passed to the Target delegate as the first argument. Because the site has to be self-learning upon every use, the DLR needs to be able to update the Target delegate when more dispatch techniques have been learned.

POLYMORPHIC INLINE CACHE

The elite term for this caching mechanism that makes a call site self-learning and more intelligent as it's being used is *polymorphic inline cache*. First, it's polymorphic because it can have many forms depending on the runtime types of the objects involved in the dynamic operation.

Second, it's inline because the CallSite<T> object lives right at the place where the call is made and not in some arcane corner of the runtime. The in situ updates applied to the site strengthen the label of *inline*, too.

Last but not least, it's a cache that remembers how dynamic operations have to be performed, based on the runtime types of all objects involved in the operation (for example, operands or method parameters).

So how does the CallSite delegate look inside, and how does it get created or updated? As soon as a CallSite<T> object is created, its Target delegate is populated with a stub implementation that looks roughly like this (using the + call site as an example):

```
(CallSite site, object a, object b) =>
{
    return site.Update(site, a, b);
}
```

The idea is as follows. When a call is made to the call site through an invocation of the dynamic operation it represents, that call gets redirected from the Target delegate (as shown previously) to the site's Update delegate:

```
public T Update { get; }
```

Behind this delegate, code lives to call into the binders to resolve an invocation target based on all the runtime information available. For example, if we call Add with two Int32 parameters, all binding information (the fact we want to do a + binary operation) and the runtime types are communicated to the binder. We can simulate this code path by using the C# binder library directly, as shown here:

```
var add = Binder.BinaryOperation(CSharpBinderFlags.None,
    ExpressionType.Add, typeof(Program),
    new[] {
        CSharpArgumentInfo.Create(CSharpArgumentInfoFlags.None, null),
        CSharpArgumentInfo.Create(CSharpArgumentInfoFlags.None, null)
    }
);

/* A skeleton Target delegate would look like this:
    (CallSite site, object a, object b) => {
        // Different dispatch cases go here.
```

```
        Return: // jump target to return
        }
 */
var ret = Expression.Label("Return");        // Return:
var a = Expression.Parameter(typeof(object)); // object a
var b = Expression.Parameter(typeof(object)); // object b

// Let's ask the C# binder how 25 and 17 need to be added...
var res = add.Bind(
    new object[] { 25, 17 },
    new List<ParameterExpression> { a, b }.AsReadOnly(),
    ret
);

// if (a is int && b is int) { return (int)a + (int)b; }
Console.WriteLine(res);
```

This code illustrates what happens at the border between the DLR and the runtime binder for the language being used. When the Target delegate was executing, say to add two numbers together, it immediately fell through to the Update delegate, which ultimately called into the binder object's Bind method. We're mimicking this situation here by calling Bind manually using two numbers. In addition to the parameters, the Bind method takes the Target delegate's parameters, which represent where data will be coming from on subsequent calls. The return label is more of an implementation detail and will be used to return the result of the operation from the Target delegate.

What matters more for our discussion is the return type of the Bind operation. As shown before, it returns an Expression object. So what's really going on here is a dialogue between the DLR screaming for help ("I've got two Int32 objects and don't know how to add them together") and the C# runtime binder handing back an expression tree with code that does precisely this ("Relax, here's how to do it"):

```
public abstract Expression Bind(
    object[] args,
    ReadOnlyCollection<ParameterExpression> parameters,
    LabelTarget returnLabel);
```

Figure 22.14 shows what the C# binder answered to the runtime's question about how to add the two given objects, 25 and 17, together.

Now that the DLR got back a piece of code to detect and handle the case of two Int32 objects being added together, it goes ahead and "stitches" the code fragment into a new version of the Target delegate, which now is equivalent to the following:

```
(CallSite site, object a, object b) =>
{
    if (a is int && b is int)   // This is the code
```

```
        return (int)a + (int)b; // from Figure 22.14
    return site.Update(site, a, b);
}
```

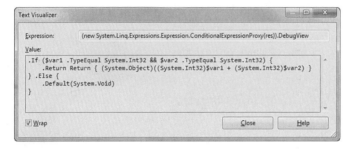

FIGURE 22.14   Code produced by the C# binder to add two Int32 objects together.

This is exactly why the call site needs to pass itself on invocation; it is the way for the DLR to get to the `Target` delegate field and substitute it for a more specialized one each time it learns more about invocation targets.

Given this new delegate, any subsequent call presenting two Int32 objects as the input will result in the specialized code fragment being executed. This short-circuits all the logic that lives in the C# binder. This logic is nontrivial; you should understand that the binder in Microsoft.CSharp.dll has knowledge of the language-specific rules for overload resolution, implicit conversions, and so on. For example, if we throw an `int` and a `long` at the binder, it will apply the C# rule that an Int32 can be implicitly converted into an Int64, so that the addition can be carried out between two Int64s:

```
if (a is long && b is int)
    return (long)a + (long)b;
```

Of course, this resolution for operations also incorporates lookups for things such as operator overloads, as shown in Figure 22.15, which shows a part of the expression tree handed back by the C# runtime binder upon seeing `DateTime` and `TimeSpan` objects.

```
var res = add.Bind(
    n  ✓ res  {IF(((Param_0 TypeEqual DateTime) AndAlso (Param_1 TypeEqual TimeSpan)), returnReturn (Conver
    n  IfTrue          {returnReturn (Convert((Convert(Param_0) + Convert(Param_1)))) }
    re      Value      {Convert((Convert(Param_0) + Convert(Param_1)))}
);          Operand    {(Convert(Param_0) + Convert(Param_1))}
                CanReduce      false
                Conversion     null
                DebugView      ☌ ▾ "(System.DateTime)$var1 + (System.TimeSpan)$var2"
                IsLifted        false
                IsLiftedToNull  false
                Left            {Convert(Param_0)}
                Method          {System.DateTime op_Addition(System.DateTime, System.TimeSpan)}
                NodeType        Add
                Right           {Convert(Param_0)}
                Type            {System.DateTime}
                Raw View
```

FIGURE 22.15   An operator overload used to add a `DateTime` and a `TimeSpan`.

From this perspective, the essence of the DLR is to provide tree-stitching services for expression tree fragments that are handed to it through language-specific binders. This also explains why the expression tree API was enhanced to support statement tree nodes—because call sites like those need conditional logic.

EXPRESSION TREES AS A NEW SWISS KNIFE

The use of expression trees is becoming more and more apparent with every release of the .NET Framework. Initially meant as a way for LINQ providers to make sense of user intent, they now act as the common back end of all sorts of compilation tasks at runtime. Languages such as IronPython and IronRuby always turn code into expression trees to execute the code efficiently through IL.

Figure 22.16 shows the states the `Target` delegate code behind our call site is going through upon invocation using different combinations of argument types. It's left as an exercise to draw the corresponding expression/statement trees that are used to represent this code before the dynamic language runtime compiles it.

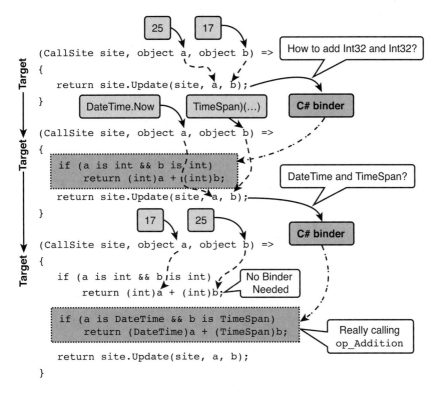

FIGURE 22.16   A call site getting updated upon feeding in new input types.

The call site for the `WriteLine` call works in a similar way. In this case, the first argument is statically determined as `typeof(Console)` because we specified this in the original C#

code (Console.WriteLine). However, because the method argument varies from a runtime typing perspective, different overloads for Console.WriteLine will be called. I leave it as an exercise for you to create a C# binder for the InvokeMember operation, based on the generated code for our running example. Hit the binder's Bind method with a variety of arguments, such as an int and a DateTime object. Generated expression trees should roughly add up to the following:

```
(CallSite site, Type t, object a) =>
{   // t will always be typeof(Console); see the CSharpArgumentInfo flags
    if (a is int)
        Console.WriteLine((int)a);
    if (a is DateTime)
        Console.WriteLine(a); // System.Object argument overload
    site.Update(site, a, b);
}
```

Custom Dynamic Objects with **DynamicObject**

So far, we haven't had a chance to control any of the binding logic that happens at runtime when invoking dynamic operations on an object. The flexible infrastructure of the DLR provides a way to create objects that participate in those operations. To achieve this, the simplest route is the use of System.Dynamic.DynamicObject, which is defined as shown in Figure 22.17.

FIGURE 22.17   A look at DynamicObject and IDynamicMetaObjectProvider.

As you can see, this base class contains `Try` methods for every dynamic operation that's supported by the DLR. The `Binder` objects passed as the first argument correspond to those operations and contain information about the performed operation, based on the code that got emitted by the front-end compiler.

When the DLR encounters an object that derives from `DynamicObject`, binding information will be passed to this object's methods first, giving it a chance to provide some nonstandard meaning to those operations. As an example, consider the concept of a bag type, which we'll see as a dictionary mapping string keys onto object values. The typical use of a dictionary object deals with strings, used on indexers. However, our bag implementation will allow us to "dot into" the object using C# syntax. The following code example contrasts both approaches:

```
// Classic dictionary
var d = new Dictionary<string, object>();
d["Name"] = "Bart";
d["Age"] = 27;
Console.WriteLine(d["Name"].ToString() + " is " + d["Age"].ToString());

// Bag using dynamic
dynamic bag = new Bag();
bag.Name = "Bart";
bag.Age = 27;
Console.WriteLine(bag.Name + " is " + bag.Age);
```

It's clear we won't provide a `Bag` object with predefined `Name` and `Age` properties on it because we want to (re)use the bag with any set of key-value pairs.

To achieve this effect, we derive `Bag` from `DynamicObject` and override a few of its members to intercept the operations performed on the bag instance. In particular, we're interested in participating in the dynamic invocation of member get and set operations, and therefore we override `TryGetMember` and `TrySetMember`:

```
class Bag : DynamicObject
{
    private Dictionary<string, object> _bag = new Dictionary<string,object>();

    public override bool TryGetMember(GetMemberBinder binder, out object res)
    {
        return _bag.TryGetValue(binder.Name, out res);
    }

    public override bool TrySetMember(SetMemberBinder binder, object value)
    {
        _bag[binder.Name] = value;
        return true;
    }
}
```

The private state of the Bag consists of a classic dictionary, to which we provide simpler access patterns. On the binder objects, we can figure out the name of the member that was targeted by the user (for example, Name or Age), as well as other information, such as case sensitivity of the language (which we ignore here). Figure 22.18 shows the call stack when TryGetMember is hit. Notice the previous frames on the stack:

▶ Program.Main is where the generated call site object is obtained from the site container and where a call is made to the Target delegate.

▶ The Target delegate by itself calls into the Update delegate pointing at a DLR function to update the call site and execute the operation. The arg0 parameter will be the reference to the Bag object.

▶ The Lightweight Function contains the type check for DynamicObject and the subsequent invocation of TryGetMember.

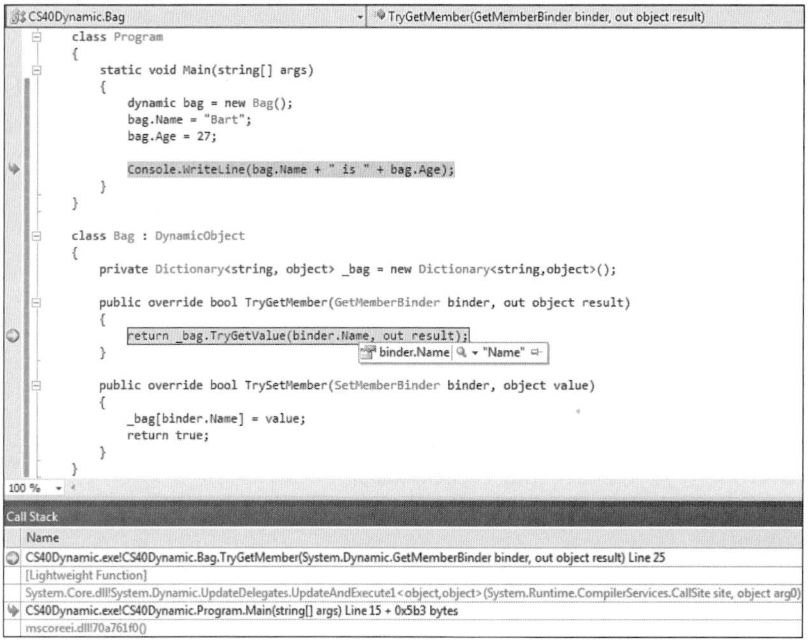

FIGURE 22.18   Invocation of TryGetMember through a DLR code path.

The Boolean return value on the various Try methods on DynamicObject is used to signal success or failure of the dynamic operation. When false is returned, fallback behavior will kick in, looping in the runtime binder (in this case, C#'s), which will look for the targeted operation on the Bag instance itself. For example:

```
public int Count { get { return _bag.Keys.Count; } }

public override bool TryGetMember(GetMemberBinder binder, out object result)
{
    // Count is never in the bag, so hand over to the C# binder (return false).
    return _bag.TryGetValue(binder.Name, out result);
}

public override bool TrySetMember(SetMemberBinder binder, object value)
{
    if (binder.Name == "Count")
        return false; // Attempt to set Count via the C# binder (will fail).
    _bag[binder.Name] = value;
    return true;
}
```

EXPANDO OBJECTS

In fact, the concept of objects that can acquire members at runtime is not very novel; after all, dynamic languages such as JavaScript rely heavily on it. In such languages, it's even the case that every single object has those capabilities.

This concept is known as expando objects because they can *expand* their surface at runtime. The Bag we just built actually exists (in a slightly more sophisticated way) in the System.Dynamic namespace, where it's called ExpandoObject. Additional functionality includes the implementation of INotifyPropertyChanged, as well as direct dictionary access because the type implements IDictionary<string, object>, so it can be used both as a dictionary (with change notification) and through the new dynamic feature:

```
var exp = new ExpandoObject();

// Use as generic dictionary
var dct = (IDictionary<string, object>)exp;
dct["Name"] = "Bart";

// Use as dynamic bag
var bag = (dynamic)exp;
bag.Age = 27;

// Use as enumerable for KeyValuePair<string, object>
foreach (var item in dct)
    Console.WriteLine(item);
```

People familiar with old-school COM programming will recognize the capabilities of the IDispatchEx interface. No wonder this interface was introduced a long time ago to support scripting languages such as VBScript and Jscript.

One common question concerns debugging of dynamic objects. In environments where static typing is the standard, you can simply see the object's members while carrying out debugging tasks. Fear not, as the GetDynamicMemberNames method is there for you to override to provide debugging information:

```
public override IEnumerable<string> GetDynamicMemberNames()
{
    return _bag.Keys;
}
```

Visual Studio 2010 has been enlightened about objects that can provide a dynamic list of member names, as shown in Figure 22.19. When expanding the list of members, a call is made to the preceding method, followed by a series of calls to gain access to the value of those members. Talking about debugging, it's even possible to use the Immediate Window to perform dynamic operations. Because of those features, debugging dynamically typed code is relatively easy.

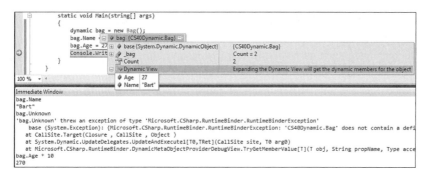

FIGURE 22.19   Some debugging features with support for C# 4.0 dynamic.

A Primer to DynamicMetaObject

As you saw earlier, the use of DynamicObject allows an object to participate in the binding process for a wide variety of operations. This is actually aligned with a general design philosophy in the DLR where objects get the first crack at defining meaning for binding operations, before language-specific binders get around to assist.

One of the core benefits of such dynamic objects is they follow a protocol that allows them to be used across different languages. Our self-written Bag object can therefore be used from languages other than C# (for example, from IronPython, as shown in Figure 22.20).

This common protocol for interoperability with dynamic objects lives at a level lower than the DynamicObject base type, though. Here the IDynamicMetaObjectProvider interface and the auxiliary DynamicMetaObject type enter the picture. The definition of those two types is shown in Figure 22.21.

FIGURE 22.20   Using our `Bag` dynamic object in IronPython.

FIGURE 22.21   Types at the heart of dynamic object interoperability.

One of the key differences between `DynamicObject` and `DynamincMetaObject` is the difference in the signature of `Bind` operations, which correspond to the family of `Try` methods in `DynamicObject`. Although those methods are also passed a `Binder` object, their arguments and return types use `DynamicMetaObject` objects.

The essential piece of information contained by a `DynamicMetaObject` instance is an expression tree that represents the code that has to be executed to compute its value. It's the DLR's role to stitch together such expression trees to make up efficient call sites that can get compiled into IL code at runtime. This is the place where the object is in total control to define the semantics of the operation that will produce its value, which enables it to emit highly efficient code.

Besides the expression tree kept in the `Expression` property, a `DynamicMetaObject` can also have a set of binding restrictions that determine when binding to the object is permitted. Such restrictions can be based on types, be written as an expression tree that will carry out some check, or restrict validity for binding to a particular instance.

When we looked at call sites earlier, in this chapter's "Dynamic Call Sites and Binders" section, we saw that the code emitted for dynamic dispatch sites have the following form:

```
(CallSite site, object a, object b) =>
{
    if (a is int && b is int)
        return (int)a + (int)b;
    if (a is DateTime && b is TimeSpan)
        return (DateTime)a + (TimeSpan)b;
    return site.Update(site, a, b);
}
```

Recall that the way this code got generated is based on the interaction between the binders and the DLR. Once a pair of two Int32 values was encountered for a and b, the DLR handed over the request to the C# runtime binder. If there would have been dynamic objects (checked based on `IDynamicMetaObjectProvider`), the request would have been handed over to the overridden `BindBinaryOperation` method. Figure 22.22 shows the relationship between binding restrictions and generated branch instructions.

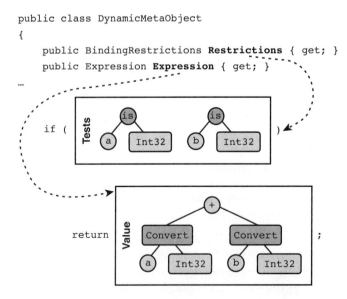

FIGURE 22.22   How restrictions and expressions relate to call sites.

No matter what path was followed, under the covers this interoperability protocol is followed, handing binding restrictions and expressions back to the DLR. In the case of the C# runtime library helping out, it gave us binding restrictions and an expression to compute the value back.

Given this information, the DLR can follow different strategies to optimize call sites, which are known as different cache levels. We don't discuss those implementation details in detail and instead defer to DLR documentation at dlr.codeplex.com. Suffice to say, manual implementation of `DynamicMetaObject` types will result in great flexibility on the code that gets run when a dynamic operation is carried out.

One example of the use of efficient code generation is caching of result values that rarely change. Immutable types form an extreme of this, where get member operations (and even instance methods that compute values based on the immutable data kept in the object) can be reduced to returning constant values. Although the first hit to operations on the object can take a while to compute the result value, immutability guarantees it won't ever change, so the emitted expression tree can simply return a constant.

Elsewhere on the mutability spectrum are objects that rarely change. For them, the same caching trick can be applied but in combination with some invalidation logic. To make this work, the `BindSetMember` override would set some flag associated with the member's name to indicate the value has been invalidated. Code emitted for the `BindGetMember` will include a check for the invalidation flag. Depending on its value, the constant-returning expression will be restricted for use. When the flag is set, a path will be triggered that recomputes the value.

Dynamic Operations

To finish off our overview of `DynamicObject` and `DynamicMetaObject`, we'll take a quick look at the various operations that can be specialized by overriding a method on those base classes. Some of those operations have a C# notation, whereas others exist in dynamic languages only.

- **Binary operations**, such as mathematical logical operators and (in)equality operators. For example, `a + b, a > b, a && b`.

- **Unary operations**, such as logical negation or complement or numeric minus or plus. For example, `-a, !a`.

- **Getting and setting members**, which correspond to properties or fields in CLR terms. For example, `a.Foo` or `a.Bar = 5`.

- **Getting and setting indexes** to index into objects such as collections, vectors, and so on. For example, `a[0]` or `vector["x"] = 1`.

- **Conversion** of objects to some specified type, either explicitly (as with cast syntax) or implicitly. For example, `(Hashtable)bag`.

- **Invocation of members**, which correspond to methods in the CLR terms (for example, `a.Print("Hello")`). Method call syntax in C# maps to this operation. In some dynamic languages, there's no such thing as invoking members, but instead all "methods" are encoded as gettable members that contain a function object. To invoke those, the direct invocation operation is used, as explained next.

▶ **Direct invocation** on objects is similar to delegate invocation in C#. For example, a(42). First-class dynamic functions can be driven by this operation.

▶ **Creating instances** in a dynamic fashion is not directly supported in C# but is in various dynamic languages. For example, dynamic new Bag.

▶ **Deleting members and indexes** is another operation that lacks some syntactic surface in C# but has been around in dynamic languages for a while. For example, in Python, you would write del bag.Name.

For example, to handle the delete member operation, you could extend our Bag dynamic object with an override for TryDeleteMember:

```
public override bool TryDeleteMember(DeleteMemberBinder binder)
{
    return _bag.Remove(binder.Name);
}
```

To show this specialized operation in action, we can use the IronPython console once more and even get into debugging by attaching the debugger to the ipy.exe process. After starting the REPL loop, go to Tools, Attach to Process in Visual Studio 2010 and set a breakpoint on the TryDeleteMember method. Now enter the following code in IronPython:

```
import sys
sys.path.append(r"c:\temp")               #wherever the Bag assembly lives

import clr
clr.AddReferenceToFile("CS40Dynamic.exe") #whatever the Bag assembly file is
from CS40Dynamic import *                 #the namespace containing Bag

person = Bag()
person.Name = "Lisa"
del person.Name
```

Figure 22.23 shows the debugger hit the breakpoint as soon as we use Python's del keyword to delete a member. This illustrates the power of the DLR's power to unify dynamic objects and dynamic operations in a cross-language manner.

Overall Architecture

To wrap up our discussion of DLR internals, let's look at an overview diagram of the infrastructure available. Figure 22.24 illustrates the DLR in the middle between languages that are enabled for dynamic and target object domains.

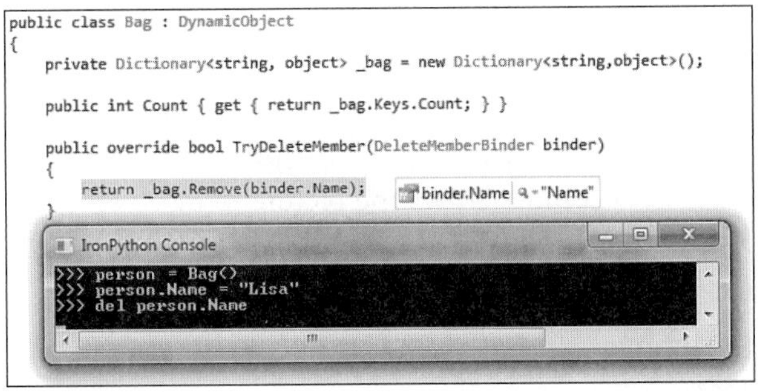

```
public class Bag : DynamicObject
{
    private Dictionary<string, object> _bag = new Dictionary<string,object>();

    public int Count { get { return _bag.Keys.Count; } }

    public override bool TryDeleteMember(DeleteMemberBinder binder)
    {
        return _bag.Remove(binder.Name);
    }
}
```

binder.Name ≈ "Name"

IronPython Console

```
>>> person = Bag()
>>> person.Name = "Lisa"
>>> del person.Name
```

FIGURE 22.23   Invoking a delete member operation from Python.

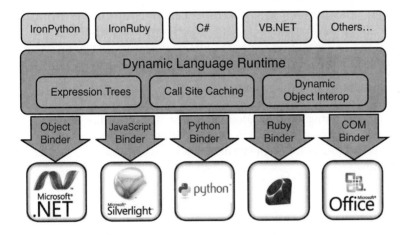

FIGURE 22.24   The DLR providing services to bridge languages and target domains.

As you've seen, it's possible to use the DLR to invoke operations on .NET objects (sometimes referred to as POCOs for plain old CLR objects), replacing the plumbing code you would have to write when dealing with the reflection APIs. Furthermore, the DLR enables us to reach out to other domains, such as JavaScript in an HTML page containing a Silverlight control, or whole Python or Ruby libraries. For the latter, the DLR also provides auxiliary services to host scripting languages. This is where the IronPython and IronRuby languages are coming in.

It's important to distinguish the front-end languages from the binders. The reason there are binders specific to languages is to help resolve operations according to required semantics for that language, with regard to things such as method overload resolution. To participate in the back end, it's possible to implement custom dynamic objects with varying degrees of complexity and flexibility, as we saw before.

Right in the middle we find the DLR, which provides a bunch of services, such as the creation and maintenance of efficient call sites based on the code object model that's provided by expression trees.

Finally, let's wrap up this chapter by taking a look at Office (and more generally COM) interop scenarios. For those scenarios, the COM binder enters the picture to resolve dynamic operations.

Office and COM Interop

No matter how revolutionary a new runtime and framework may be, there's always the "old stuff" to interoperate with. One such artifact from the old pre-CLR days is the Component Object Model (COM). At the point of its introduction in the early 1990s, the core goals of COM included the capability to deal with objects across different languages. For example, it enabled C or C++ developers to create COM components that could be used from Visual Basic and other such languages.

COM originated out of a whole set of technologies that were introduced to deal with cross-process integration scenarios, going all the way back to Dynamic Data Exchange (DDE). Out of this grew object linking and embedding (OLE), which lies at the heart of content embedding features in applications such as Office. With the use of OLE in Office, it becomes possible to, say, include an Excel spreadsheet in a Word document. The Insert Object dialog in Office, shown in Figure 22.25, is the visible side of this.

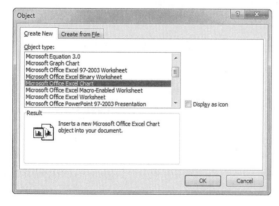

FIGURE 22.25   OLE, a precursor to COM, as a technology for the masses.

Extensions and enhancements to the OLE model were introduced in COM, with a wide range of applications emerging. Lots of components in the Windows OS are based on COM, allowing them to be used from many different languages. On the Web, ActiveX controls that get integrated with the browser are also based on the same technology. In such scenarios, it's important to allow dynamic languages such as VBScript and JScript to communicate with COM components.

Probably one of the biggest pieces of software out there that continues to have a strong affinity to COM is the Microsoft Office suite. One quite mainstream scenario for users of the suite is the ability to automate certain tasks using macros, which are written in a special version of Visual Basic called Visual Basic for Applications (VBA). To this very day, Office ships with this feature and a (somewhat ancient-looking) development environment for VBA, as shown in Figure 22.26. The technology that makes this macro scripting possible is none other than COM.

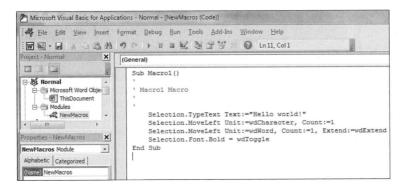

FIGURE 22.26   Visual Basic for Applications used to write a Word macro.

THE CLR, COM+, AND OTHER HISTORY

Cross-language interoperability, where did we hear that before? Indeed, the main mission of COM and the CLR is similar. The way to achieve the interoperability goal is quite different in both worlds, though.

Whereas COM is a technology centered on the concept of interfaces exposed by components and callable by other, possibly remote, components, the CLR takes the approach of defining a common instruction set (IL) with a common type and metadata information to go with it. Other core differences include the handling of errors (HRESULTs versus exception), the type system (IUnknown as the main *interface* versus System.Object as a base *class*), memory maintenance (based on ref counting versus garbage collected), component registration, and so on.

At the time the CLR project was started, two camps existed inside Microsoft. One camp believed in advancing COM by adding new functionality to it. One big advantage of that approach would have been the direct interoperability with existing technologies. The other camp believed in the creation of a completely new runtime, referred to as the Common Object Runtime (which is where the COR in mscoree and mscorlib comes from).

The CLR didn't throw away existing investments in COM, though, and provided for a rich interoperability story from day one. Not only can we call COM components from inside managed code applications, it's also possible to expose managed types as COM objects. For example, to extend Office applications, we can use managed code. To make such tasks easier, reducing the amount of plumbing code needed, libraries and tools have been created to assist in this (for example, the Visual Studio Tools for Office).

Partly in parallel with this (r)evolution, COM was extended with new services to deal with transactions, events, and so on. Commonly referred to as COM+, those new facilities are exposed in .NET under System.EnterpriseServices.

Given the large number of existing applications built on COM, you can hardly say that COM is dead. Instead, to paraphrase Don Box, COM is done, and .NET is the new programming model going forward.

Essentials of COM Interop

Interoperability with COM from inside managed code applications is based on a few essential concepts:

- **Dispatch services** to reach out to COM component operations, allowing one to make calls using (seemingly) regular .NET methods, properties, and so on. The CLR and various auxiliary libraries make this possible. For COM gurus, this includes the ability to obtain COM interfaces, deal with co-classes, and so on.

- **Marshaling services** solve the impedance mismatch between the type systems of the CLR and COM, with regard to primitive data types, in/out/ref behavior when calling methods, and so on. In addition to this, the interoperability layer also maps HRESULTs onto exceptions.

- **(Primary) Interop assemblies** provide an entry point to a COM library using managed code types that encapsulate the underlying library's functionality. For example, Office provides PIAs that .NET developers can use to reach out to Office functionality from inside any managed code language.

This concise summary is a gross simplification of the COM interop landscape that exists in .NET. In fact, the subject deserves a book of its own, as testified by Adam Nathan's book titled *.NET and COM: The Complete Interoperability Guide*, a 1,500-pager that is really recommended if you find yourself doing lots of COM interop.

Simplified COM Interop in .NET 4

 Luckily for us, C# 4.0 and .NET 4 make the use of COM from inside managed code applications much easier thanks to a lot of related features:

- **Optional and named parameters** are often used in COM APIs and have found their way into the C# programming language to simplify such scenarios. It's not uncommon for COM APIs to expose methods with a whole bunch of parameters, most of which are optional and meant to be called by specifying their names. The use of this feature is not restricted to COM interoperability, though, so one can create methods with optional parameters and call methods by specifying parameters by name.

▶ **Indexed properties** allow properties to be called with additional parameters, much like indexers work. Those are not a proper C# language feature and are restricted for use in COM interop scenarios. The main difficulty with indexed properties as a general language feature is the fact they don't distinguish the act of property retrieval and indexing into an object. For that reason, the .NET designers thought it better to leave them out for managed code APIs (and they're not part of the CLS either). In C# 4.0, they're allowed only for COM interop.

▶ **Optional ref modifier** when calling COM imported methods. Because the most common calling convention used on COM APIs methods is to pass parameters by reference, you can omit the `ref` modifier on such calls starting from C# 4.0. Again, this is not a general language feature in C# and is limited to COM interop scenarios. Recall that the philosophy of the `ref` modifier is to explicitly indicate, in the call site, the intent of passing a parameter by reference.

▶ **Mapping of object to dynamic** when importing COM APIs. Because COM is quite a dynamic experience from a typing point of view, lots of parameters and return types are typed as `IUnknown` or `IDispatch`. Those interfaces form the roots of the interface hierarchy in the world of COM and correspond roughly to .NET's `System.Object` base type. Up until .NET 4, importing COM libraries performed a mapping for such types onto `System.Object`. Now that we have `dynamic`, this mapping has changed to use the new dynamic type. This allows you to "dot into" lots of COM APIs directly.

▶ **Embedding of interop types ("no PIA")** is a tooling feature, just like the one elaborated on in the previous point. The use of interop assemblies has caused grief in the past because of difficulties with deployment with applications that are using them. One major problem with those PIAs is their size, which can go into the megabyte range for interop assemblies like Word's. Typically, you're using just a fraction of the types and functionality in the assembly, so this is a huge waste of space. In .NET 4, used portions of PIAs can be embedded into your own assembly at build time.

We now discuss those features in more detail by means of a walkthrough where we use the improved COM interop in .NET 4 to talk with Office libraries. Keep in mind that this capability is not restricted to Office but provides value for all COM interop scenarios that span a wide range of technologies (for example, lots of Windows APIs have exposure through COM).

A NECESSARY EVIL?

New language features often get widely criticized upon their introduction. This is no different with C# 4.0's improved COM interop features or `dynamic` more generally. One key question here is whether it's good to extend a language simply for interoperability enhancements.

When .NET was introduced, some people hoped for a quick disappearance of old technologies such as COM, in favor of managed code. History turned out quite different; the use of COM is still prevalent.

Smooth interoperability with such COM-based libraries has been hampered by the lack of nice managed code wrappers. PIAs typically expose the APIs they target in a verbatim manner, doing a poor job at providing a true "managed code feeling" for the APIs they interoperate with. As a result, managed code developers often don't feel at home when dealing with interoperability. This in turn has led to people technologies as a whole, solely because of poor interoperability. The goal of making such scenarios easier is definitely a good thing because "COM ain't dead."

Although every new language feature starts with a negative score (counting against the introduction of the feature to avoid bloating the language), there have been plenty of scoring points that motivate the introduction of C# 4.0 dynamic. The growing popularity of dynamic languages and untyped APIs, as well as COM interoperability senarios, were enough to go ahead and add dynamic to the language.

To limit aging the language unnecessarily, some of those features are restricted in use to COM interop scenarios only, as mentioned previously. To conclude, you could say those new features are "a necessary evil."

Case Study: COM Interop with Excel and Word

To illustrate the improvements to COM interop in .NET 4, we start in the old world of .NET 3.5 and show what the code for our scenario looked like back then. Based on this, we gradually make the code simpler while porting it to C# 4.0, while looking at the individual features that form the basis of those enhancements.

Walkthrough in .NET 3.5

The examples shown in this section assume you have a recent version of Office installed, preferably version 2007 or later. In addition, make sure to have the PIA redistributable installed, which you can find by searching the Web for "download Office PIA." If everything is correctly installed, you'll find the Office interop assemblies in the Add Reference dialog in Visual Studio, as shown in Figure 22.27. You can safely ignore the runtime version on them because PIAs don't really contain code and simply provide a set of interoperability interfaces (which can be seen as runtime neutral). Depending on the versions of Office PIAs you have installed, you'll see different entries. Office 2007 corresponds to version 12.0.0.0 and Office 2010 (selected here) version 14.0.0.0.

To illustrate the situation in .NET 3.5, we use Visual Studio 2008. Alternatively, you can use Visual Studio 2010 with the target framework of the project set to .NET Framework 3.5.

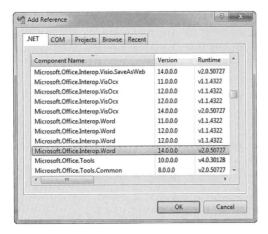

FIGURE 22.27   Importing the Office PIAs.

WHAT ABOUT THE COM TAB?

When no PIAs are available, there's always the COM tab to generate an interop assembly for a selected COM library. Alternatively, command-line tools can be used to achieve the same effect, in particular the tlbimp.exe one. TLB stands for type library.

When PIAs are available, it's recommended to use them for a variety of reasons. As the name implies, a PIA is the *primary* interop assembly for the target library provided by some vendor. When different generated interop assemblies are mixed together, problems on type identity (pre .NET 4) can occur.

Once the two interop assemblies, Microsoft.Office.Interop.Word and a similarly named one for Excel, have been referenced, we can start writing code. To avoid clashes in type names if we were to import the namespaces as is, we use an alias for abbreviation:

```
using Word  = Microsoft.Office.Interop.Word;
using Excel = Microsoft.Office.Interop.Excel;
```

The running example will be the creation of a Word document containing an Excel graph showing memory utilization for processes on the current machine. This example has been shown on various occasions introducing C# 4.0 and nicely illustrates all the applicable features.

To get started with the Office automation model, we need to instantiate an application object that serves as the entry point to an Office application such as Word or Excel. In fact, this creates an out-of-process instance of the targeted application that we communicate with cross-process through the magic of COM. In essence, our code is behind the steering wheel of an entire Office application. This activation behavior isn't the same for all COM APIs: Some run in-process; others don't.

Figure 22.28 shows how to create an instance of the Excel application. Notice we're using the new operator on an *interface type* (notice the icon next to the menu entry), which looks kind of weird. This works because the compiler detects that the interface type corresponds to a COM type. If we go to the definition of the Application interface (by using Go to Definition or by pressing F12), we see the following:

```
[Guid("000208D5-0000-0000-C000-000000000046")]
[CoClass(typeof(ApplicationClass))]
public interface Application : _Application, AppEvents_Event
{
}
```

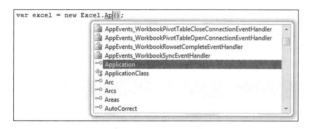

FIGURE 22.28   Instantiating an Excel application object.

The attributes used here are all defined in `System.Runtime.InteropServices`. We don't have the space to elaborate on them, but what the compiler (up until version 3.5) did with our code is turn it into a constructor call on the referred `CoClass`:

```
var excel = new Excel.ApplicationClass();
```

In C# 4.0, the generated code varies slightly, as you see later in the section called "Walkthrough in .NET 4." What matters more is we can now start writing code against the automation model of Excel. We start by making the application visible by setting the `Visible` property to true. This causes an Excel instance to show up. While we're executing code, you'll see changes getting reflected (live) in the automated application instance:

```
var excel = new Excel.Application();
excel.Visible = true;
```

Next, we ask Excel to create a new workbook. Obviously, methods exist to load an existing workbook by specifying a filename. Here we're simply creating a scratchpad on which to generate a graph, ready to be exported to Word, so we don't need any fancy calls to load an existing file:

```
// New empty workbook
excel.Workbooks.Add(Type.Missing);
```

Here things start to look a bit weird in .NET 3.5. Because C# didn't have a way to deal with optional parameters, we had to specify something for the single parameter on Add, which is defined as follows (using Go to Definition):

```
[DispId(181)]
[LCIDConversion(1)]
Workbook Add(object Template);
```

Again, ignore the custom attributes that are used to make COM interop work at runtime. The Type.Missing field is used in such scenarios to indicate the fact we're omitting a value for the corresponding parameter. You can already guess how code starts to look on methods that have a whole bunch of optional parameters.

Next, we can start emitting data to the created workbook's first sheet, using the code shown here:

```
// Column headers
Excel.Worksheet sheet = (Excel.Worksheet)excel.ActiveSheet;
sheet.get_Range("A1", Type.Missing).Value2 = "Process";
sheet.get_Range("B1", Type.Missing).Value2 = "Memory";
```

Here we're seeing two more issues with COM interop in the pre-v4 era. First, excessive casts are often needed because COM APIs tend to "peter out" into dynamic land. When we look at the definition of ActiveSheet, we see the PIA has typed this property as object because no more specific type information was available in the Excel type library:

```
[DispId(307)]
object ActiveSheet { get; }
```

The second issue with the code we had to write in .NET 3.5 is seen on the last two lines, where we have a use a method with a name that looks quite foreign in .NET. The reason we had to use a get_Range method defined in the PIA is due to the absence of indexed properties in C#. Instead, a get_ prefixed method has been generated. Also notice how optional parameters strike again.

Now that we have the headers in our sheet, we can start populating the sheet with data we can obtain through the use of LINQ to Objects run over System.Diagnostics.Process objects. No new complaints about interop are added to the pile, although the code continues to look strange because of the excessive use of Type.Missing:

```
// Populate process list with 10 most expensive processes in terms of memory
var res = (from proc in Process.GetProcesses()
           orderby proc.WorkingSet64 descending
           select new {
               Name = proc.ProcessName,
               Memory = proc.WorkingSet64 / (1024 * 1024) /* in MB */
           }
```

```
        ).Take(10);

int i = 2;
foreach (var proc in res)
{
    sheet.get_Range("A" + i, Type.Missing).Value2 = proc.Name;
    sheet.get_Range("B" + i, Type.Missing).Value2 = proc.Memory;
    i++;
}
```

Where things get really ugly is when methods have to be called where nearly all parameters are optional, but we want to specify a few of those. The ChartWizard method does precisely this, as shown here:

```
// Add new chart
Excel.Range range = sheet.get_Range("A1", Type.Missing);
Excel.Chart chart = (Excel.Chart)excel.ActiveWorkbook.Charts.Add(
    Type.Missing,
    sheet,
    Type.Missing, Type.Missing);
chart.ChartWizard(
    range.CurrentRegion, Type.Missing, Type.Missing, Type.Missing,
    Type.Missing, Type.Missing, Type.Missing,
    "Memory statistics",
    Type.Missing, Type.Missing, Type.Missing);
chart.CopyPicture(
    Excel.XlPictureAppearance.xlScreen,
    Excel.XlCopyPictureFormat.xlBitmap,
    Excel.XlPictureAppearance.xlScreen);
```

When this code has run, a bitmap will be present on the Clipboard, allowing us to paste the generated chart somewhere else. To illustrate other oddities of COM interop prior to the use of C# 4.0, we'll loop in Word as the target for our paste operation. Again, we start by creating an application instance:

```
var word = new Word.Application();
word.Visible = true;
```

Creating a new document can be done by calling the Add method on the Documents collection exposed as a property on the Word Application interface. Looking at this method, we see something else that's quite intrusive:

```
[DispId(14)]
Document Add(ref object Template, ref object NewTemplate,
            ref object DocumentType, ref object Visible);
```

More specifically, all parameters in this Word API are passed by reference. This is done in quite a few COM-based APIs and is rather tedious to use from C#. To call this method, again omitting concrete values for the parameters using Type.Missing, we have to write the following code:

```
var missing = Type.Missing;
word.Documents.Add(ref missing, ref missing, ref missing, ref missing);
```

We even need to introduce a separate local variable because Type.Missing (luckily!) is a static read-only field. Finally, we can paste the chart on our Clipboard into the Word document, using surprisingly simple code:

```
word.Selection.Paste();
```

After all this hassle, the rewarding result is shown in Figure 22.29.

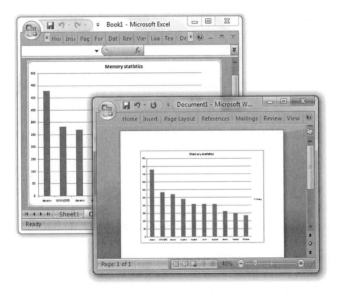

FIGURE 22.29   Result of Office automation through C# 3.0.

Walkthrough in .NET 4

Now let's go ahead and rewrite the example in .NET 4 with C# 4.0. Before we go there, it's important to note that the existing COM interop code will simply continue to work when compiled with the new tools in Visual Studio 2010. However, we can drastically simplify the code.

First, we can get rid of the Type.Missing parameters because the optional characteristic of parameters can now be leveraged from C#. Therefore, we can simply write Workbooks.Add(), omitting all parameters:

```
var excel = new Excel.Application();
excel.Visible = true;


// New empty workbook
excel.Workbooks.Add();
```

IntelliSense actually shows optional parameters with their default values, as shown in Figure 22.30.

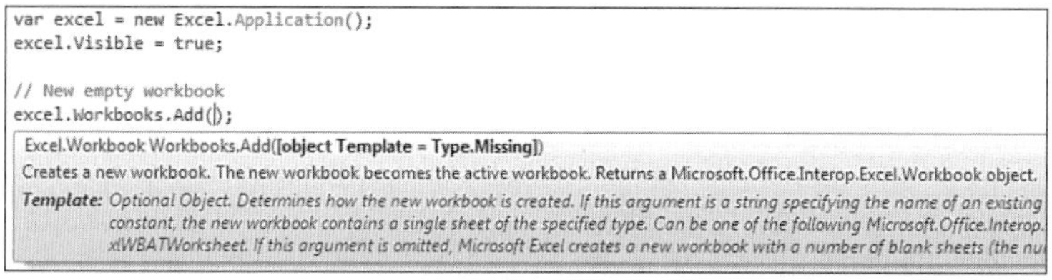

```
var excel = new Excel.Application();
excel.Visible = true;

// New empty workbook
excel.Workbooks.Add();

Excel.Workbook Workbooks.Add([object Template = Type.Missing])
Creates a new workbook. The new workbook becomes the active workbook. Returns a Microsoft.Office.Interop.Excel.Workbook object.
Template: Optional Object. Determines how the new workbook is created. If this argument is a string specifying the name of an existing
          constant, the new workbook contains a single sheet of the specified type. Can be one of the following Microsoft.Office.Interop.
          xlWBATWorksheet. If this argument is omitted, Microsoft Excel creates a new workbook with a number of blank sheets (the nu
```

FIGURE 22.30   Optional parameters on a COM interop method.

One additional change that's happening behind the scenes for the preceding code is the way the interface gets instantiated. Although the specified CoClass was instantiated before, the compiler now generates code to instantiate the object based on the specified GUID that's used for COM interop. The first line of code now translates into the following:

```
var excel = (Application)Activator.CreateInstance(
    Type.GetTypeFromCLSID(new Guid("00024500-0000-0000-C000-000000000046")));
```

You've seen Activator.CreateInstance before when talking about reflection. In this case, another helper method is used to locate the type based on a given class identifier. Later, you'll see this is related to the way PIAs get embedded in our assembly.

The next simplification involves indexed properties, as shown here. Use of indexed property syntax is limited to COM interop scenarios. There is no way for developers to declare an indexed property in C# 4.0:

```
// Column headers
Excel.Worksheet sheet = excel.ActiveSheet;
sheet.Range["A1"].Value = "Process";
sheet.Range["B1"].Value = "Memory";
```

Looking at the definition of Range, we still see it showing up as a get_ method. All the indexed property feature does is provide shorthand syntax to call such methods. If you were to look at the generated IL code, you would see a call to the get_ method.

```
[DispId(197)]
Range get_Range(object Cell1, object Cell2 = Type.Missing);
```

If setters exist (methods prefixed with set_), they can be approached using indexed property access syntax, too. The indexed property access applies only to types that were defined as COM imported types in PIAs.

Another improvement that went almost unnoticed in the preceding code is that we got away with assigning the ActiveSheet property to an Excel.Worksheet-typed object without having to perform a cast first:

```
Excel.Worksheet sheet = excel.ActiveSheet;
```

The C# 4.0 COM interop feature that fuels this is the automatic replacement of object by dynamic for types that appear in imported COM APIs. Use of Go to Definition again reveals what's going on here:

```
[DispId(307)]
dynamic ActiveSheet { get; }
```

At runtime, operations on ActiveSheet will be dispatched dynamically through the COM binder that ships with the .NET Framework 4. In our case, the assignment of the dynamically typed property to a statically typed sheet variable results in the creation of a dynamic conversion operation.

```
CallSite<Func<CallSite, object, Excel.Worksheet>>.Create(
    Binder.Convert(CSharpBinderFlags.None, typeof(WorkSheet), typeof(Program))
)
```

The code to populate the sheet based on the results of our LINQ query stays pretty much the same, also eliminating the artificial use of get_Range in favor of indexed properties:

```
// Populate process list with 10 most expensive processes in terms of memory
var res = /* same query as shown earlier */

int i = 2;
foreach (var proc in res)
{
    sheet.Range["A" + i].Value = proc.Name;
    sheet.Range["B" + i].Value = proc.Memory;
    i++;
}
```

To wrap up the Excel API usage enhancements, we can leverage optional parameters for our calls to the chart-creating functions. First, notice how `Charts.Add` again "peters out" into dynamic typing, so we can omit the cast thanks to C# 4.0:

```
// Add new chart
Excel.Range range = sheet.Range["A1"];
Excel.Chart chart = excel.ActiveWorkbook.Charts.Add(After: sheet);
```

On the method call itself, we're specifying the second parameter, `After`, by referring to it by name, as shown in Figure 22.31. Notice this parameter starts with an uppercase A, which is not uncommon as a naming pattern in some COM APIs. Although this looks unnatural to developers familiar with managed code casing conventions, it's one of the prices you have to pay for interoperability. Don't forget C# is a case-sensitive language, so you'll have to spell `After` correctly.

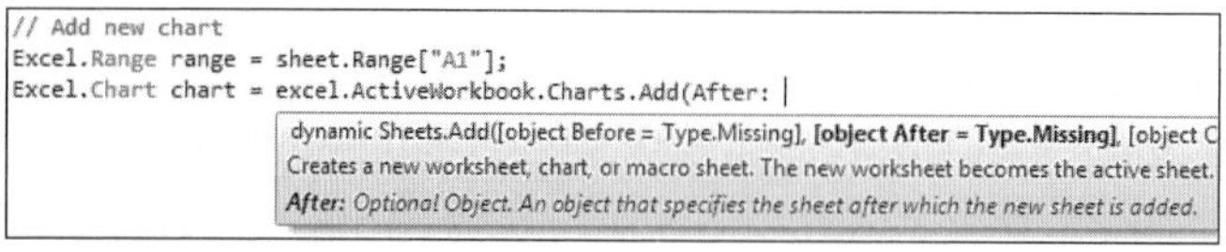

```
// Add new chart
Excel.Range range = sheet.Range["A1"];
Excel.Chart chart = excel.ActiveWorkbook.Charts.Add(After: |
```
> dynamic Sheets.Add([object Before = Type.Missing], **[object After = Type.Missing]**, [object C
> Creates a new worksheet, chart, or macro sheet. The new worksheet becomes the active sheet.
> **After:** *Optional Object. An object that specifies the sheet after which the new sheet is added.*

FIGURE 22.31   Specifying a parameter by name.

This code will ultimately compile into a call to the `Add` method specifying the default values for the unspecified parameters (that is, `Missing.Value`). In a similar manner, we can simplify the call to `ChartWizard`, specifying the `Title` parameter by name and the first parameter (referring to the range for the chart's data) just positionally. Because all the parameters on `CopyPicture` are optional and have default values, we can make this call easier on the eye as well:

```
chart.ChartWizard(range.CurrentRegion, Title: "Memory statistics");
chart.CopyPicture();
```

Finally, we can take a look at the code used to interoperate with Word. Here all the optional by-ref passing of parameters is gone, too. Although this isn't shown directly here, you can omit the `ref` modifier on COM interop methods, causing the compiler to insert them for you:

```
var word = new Word.Application();
word.Visible = true;
word.Documents.Add();
word.Selection.Paste();
```

The generated code for the `Add` method looks like this, where temporary variables are introduced for the objects (here the default values) that are passed by reference:

```
object <>r__ComRefCallLocal0 = Missing.Value;
object <>r__ComRefCallLocal1 = Missing.Value;
object <>r__ComRefCallLocal2 = Missing.Value;
object <>r__ComRefCallLocal3 = Missing.Value;
word.Documents.Add(ref <>r__ComRefCallLocal0, ref <>r__ComRefCallLocal1,
                   ref <>r__ComRefCallLocal2, ref <>r__ComRefCallLocal3);
```

Separate variables are needed because the API being called may overwrite them, which is the essential characteristic of passing them by reference.

The resulting code in .NET 4 definitely looks much more like the code was intended to look all along, reducing all sorts of clutter that was imposed on us before. And sure enough, it still produces the same results as it did before.

SOME TIPS ON APPROACHING OFFICE AUTOMATION APIS

Some readers might wonder how to discover Office automation functionality given the overwhelming number of methods and properties exposed in the APIs. The peter-out characteristic of various operations, all of a sudden ending up in an untyped world, definitely doesn't improve on this either.

Although MSDN documentation is a good starting point, it's often easier to let the system generate code for you. The support built in to Office for recording macros based on user actions can help quite a bit with this. Just mimic the creation of a sheet, document, and so on inside the Office program while recording a macro and take a look at the resulting VBA code. Apart from the syntactical differences, the code being generated can be ported quite easily to C# 4.0.

Embedding of PIAs

One tooling and compiler feature we've ignored in the previous discussion is the so-called No PIA. As mentioned during the introduction on improved COM interop, the use of PIAs has drawbacks with regard to deployment size. Even though they don't contain code, quite a bit of metadata lives on the contained interfaces and defined operations. All of that results in big assemblies, of which only a fraction of functionality is usually used by an application.

To alleviate the need for big deployments, .NET 4 provides the option to embed used interop types in your own assembly. Figure 22.32 shows where this gets enabled in the Properties window for a selected PIA reference assembly.

Under the hood, this will cause the compiler /link flag to be passed, specifying the PIA as its argument. Looking at our program's assembly after compilation, we see only the used interop types present and embedded in our own assembly. Figure 22.33 shows this embedding in action.

If you were to look at the original PIA inside .NET Reflector, you would see hundreds of types. It's clear only the used subset got embedded in our assembly. But there's more. Because COM interfaces can be quite large, lots of redundant unused operations (and the metadata defined on them) would get embedded for no good reason. The No PIA feature also operates on the level of operations inside a type, pruning out all the ones that aren't used. Figure 22.34 shows this for the Chart interface whose ChartWizard and CopyPicture methods are the only ones we've touched.

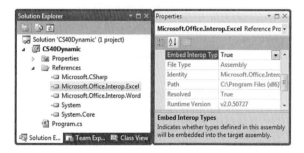

FIGURE 22.32   Enabling the No PIA feature for a reference assembly.

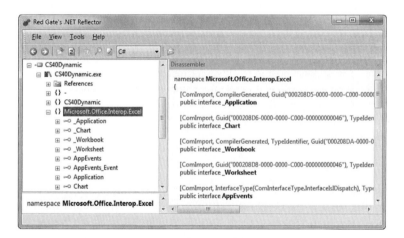

FIGURE 22.33   Embedded PIA types.

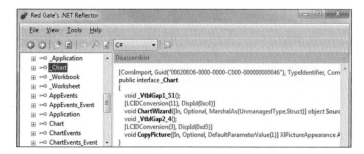

FIGURE 22.34   Reduction of operations on a COM imported interface type.

Two tricks are used to make this work correctly at runtime. Details about them are beyond the scope of this discussion, but a short overview is in order.

Vtable gap methods are inserted to maintain compatibility with the vtable used when dispatching operations. The mysterious _VtblGap methods communicate how many methods are omitted from the original interface. Calls to members on COM interfaces are implemented by invoking code that's found based on an offset computed from the start of the interface virtual function table. If we are omitting methods in the embedded interface, the runtime must be able to restore this counting, which it does based on the numbers encoded in the gap method names.

The *TypeIdentifier attribute* on the interface indicates the type participates in type equivalence relationships, in this case based on the GUID. If you have multiple assemblies that are using the same PIA using No PIA, both will have their own customized, trimmed copies of various interfaces. Because these will be different types to the CLR, there's no compatibility story for them. One may have methods A, B, and C embedded, whereas another may have B and D. Using type equivalence, the type's GUID tells the CLR the types represent the same imported (COM) type, allowing casting between them. For more information, see Type.IsEquivalentTo on MSDN.

Summary

Dynamic programming has established its position in the programming landscape for modern applications. With the increasing popularity of dynamic languages and the trend of taking weakly typed approaches to data (JSON, XML without XSD) and web services (REST), it becomes increasingly important to provide a bridge between C# and "islands" of dynamic code or data. In other words, a golden middle had to be found between the traditionally statically typed core of the C# language and the flexibility to deal with dynamically typed code and data.

In this chapter, we built on the technological foundations for dynamic programming introduced in the previous chapter. With mechanisms such as expression trees and runtime code generation all working in concert, we ended up in the world of C# 4.0 dynamic, which leverages the dynamic language runtime.

After introducing the feature, we took a look at call sites, binders, and expression tree compilation and how they relate to the C# 4.0 feature. All of this was illustrated with examples showing the dynamic feature as a replacement for reflection and in conjunction with other languages such as IronPython.

Finally, we talked about improved COM interop in .NET 4, thanks to the COM binder and a series of C# 4.0 language enhancements. Combining all the C# 4.0 features (named and optional parameters, dynamic typing, omission of ref, and so on), we learned how this results in more flexibility when dealing with various (possibly old) code models such as COM-based Office APIs.

CHAPTER 23

Exceptions

IN THIS CHAPTER

▶ Life Without Exceptions 1167

▶ Introducing Exceptions 1170

▶ Exception Handling 1172

▶ Throwing Exceptions 1188

▶ Defining Your Own Exception Types 1190

▶ (In)famous Exception Types 1193

One of the biggest frustrations of development in older styles, such as COM and Win32, was the poor support for error handling. The need to deal with error codes manually, introducing lots of checks for success states, was a grueling experience that not only led to a decrease in productivity but also caused program code to look like spaghetti. And to "improve" on that, developers relied on the ultimate C solution: macros, to deal with control flow for error-handling paths and such.

With the introduction of Structured Exception Handling (SEH) in the operating system, surfaced by language features in C++, error handling could be done in a more structured way, but retrofitting existing application programming interfaces (APIs) was hardly ever done. The .NET Framework designers were in a great position to improve on this situation by making exception handling a first-class citizen of the platform and languages built upon it.

In this chapter, we study how exceptions are thrown and caught, how they are entangled with the control flow of a program, and where it's appropriate to use them. As part of this exploration, you'll learn how to create your own exception types and how to debug in the face of exceptions using the Visual Studio 2010 debugger.

Life Without Exceptions

To give you a feeling about the poor state of things before the advent of exceptions, let's take a look at some Win32- and COM-based code with manual error handling.

Win32

In the world of Win32, integer values were used to indicate errors produced by functions. This already introduces a problem: The meaning of a plain old integer is not very clear by just looking at it. Instead, symbolic constants need to be introduced to make program code look more meaningful. Furthermore, those error codes need to be queried for manually after failed function calls using the GetLastError function. An example of such a function call, followed by error "handling," is shown here:

```
HWND hWindow = CreateWindowEx(0, g_szClassName, L"Hello Win32",
                              WS_OVERLAPPEDWINDOW, 100, 200, 300, 400,
                              NULL, NULL, hInstance, NULL);
if (NULL == hWindow) {
    dwError = GetLastError();
    // Analyze the error and handle appropriately or propagate to caller.
}
```

Combined with manual resource management, propagation of errors typically leads to the use of goto statements to jump to an epilogue in the containing function where proper release of acquired resources is done (for example, using CloseHandle and delete):

```
int ShowStartDialog() {
    int dwError = 0;

    // More code goes here

    if (NULL == hWindow) {
        dwError = GetLastError();
        // Analyze the error and handle appropriately if possible.
        goto Exit; // Too bad, couldn't handle it meaningfully...
    }

    // More code goes here

Exit:
    if (hSomeResource != NULL) {
        CloseHandle(hSomeResource);
        hSomeResource = NULL;
    }

    // Release other resources.

    return dwError;
}
```

To propagate errors, it's not atypical to sacrifice the function's return value to contain the error code, where 0 indicates success. Alternatively, in a more "natural" Win32 style, the SetLastError function can be used, too. Regardless of the technique used here, propagating errors is an act of explicit checking against error values and making an appropriate decision on the spot.

All of this leads to tedious checking against errors, introducing more complex control flow, which may then lead to missed resource deallocation and so on. And even the most innocent-looking function calls need to be checked for error conditions because low-level system failures (such as out of memory) are reported through the same means.

COM

The situation didn't get much better in the Component Object Model. Again, integral values are used to report errors, now hidden behind a typedef called HRESULT (which originally stood for handle result). One thing we should grant COM is adding a tiny little bit more structure to error handling by introducing style guidelines on the way functions should report errors. In Win32, each function had its own habits, some of which returned an error code as a return value, whereas others relied on GetLastError facilities. But guidelines are just that: guidelines. Occasionally, you will find COM APIs that don't follow those guidelines.

Because the typical COM API design is to have functions return an HRESULT, macros were introduced to make code easier on the eye (easier in the C/C++ sense of the word, that is):

```
IBackgroundCopyManager* g_pbcm = NULL;
GUID JobId;
IBackgroundCopyJob* pJob = NULL;
HRESULT hr;

hr = CoInitializeEx(NULL, COINIT_APARTMENTTHREADED);
if (SUCCEEDED(hr)) {
    hr = CoCreateInstance(__uuidof(BackgroundCopyManager), NULL,
                    CLSCTX_LOCAL_SERVER,
                    __uuidof(IBackgroundCopyManager),
                    (void**) &g_pbcm);
    if (SUCCEEDED(hr)) {
        hr = g_pbcm->CreateJob(L"MyJobName", BG_JOB_TYPE_DOWNLOAD, &JobId,
                            &pJob);
        if (SUCCEEDED(hr)) {
            // Add files to the job.
        }
    }
}
```

Sacrificing the output value of a function for error reporting purposes, the excessive use of output parameters to communicate back the result of function calls leads to less-readable code. Depending on the error-checking style, either indentation grows out of control (as seen in the preceding example, due to the repeated success checks) or the use of goto statements becomes a necessity to centralize resource cleanup:

```
if (FAILED(hr)) {
    // Maybe you can do something about it? If not...
    goto Exit;
}
```

Alternatively, one often checks for known error conditions manually:

```
if (BG_E_NETWORK_DISCONNECTED == hr) {
    // Ha! Know what to do here.
}
```

C and C++ developers have come up with more handcrafted macros to make this kind of error handling less invasive throughout their code bases:

```
#define CKHR(hr)   if (FAILED(hr)) goto Exit;
```

Although this "flattens" large blocks of code with sequential calls to various functions that may fail, it comes at the cost of introducing hidden control flow. If a new developer on the project starts using the CKHR macro shown here but omits an Exit label in the current function body, a cryptic error message will result.

Lessons Learned

Common themes can be identified between Win32 and COM, including the need for manual checking against error conditions, leading to a huge number of branches in code bases. Furthermore, error codes are based on symbolic constants that can be hard to find, often leading to forgotten cases of error handling. Mixing those disadvantages with the need for manual resource handling in both cases only makes matters worse, often sacrificing block-based structured programming in favor of goto statements to centralize resource cleanup. Improper cleanup often leads to memory problems that can be hard to track down.

Clearly, we can do better by introducing more structure to deal with exceptions. This is where structured exception handling comes in, as you see next.

Introducing Exceptions

With exceptions entering the picture, you can separate error handling from the regular flow of an application in a block-structured manner. For example, the following example illustrates the use of the System.IO .NET Framework APIs to read a file from disk:

```
IEnumerable<Customer> ReadCustomersFrom(string file) {
    try {
        using (FileStream fs = File.OpenRead(file)) {
            using (StreamReader sr = new StreamReader(fs)) {
                // Read from the file, creating Customer instances to return...
            }
        }
    }
    catch (IOException ex) {
        // If we handle this exception somehow, we can do it here.
    }
}
```

Various methods used in the preceding code can throw an exception. Instead of getting an error code back that needs to be checked on the spot, we declare an event handler using the try-catch statement. Each exception we're interested in handling can have its own catch block. If an exception is left unhandled, it simply propagates to the caller of the current method.

A structured approach to exceptions has various advantages, most of which are shown in the preceding section. First, we didn't have to sacrifice the return value of a method call in favor of error codes. Code simply reads as it was intended to behave in *regular* circumstances: If the file is found, we get a FileStream object back. Next, we can create a StreamReader and so on.

TWO RETURN VALUES AND CHECKED EXCEPTIONS

It might help to think about structured exception handling as a way to add a second return "channel" to each function. The primary return channel is used to communicate the answer of a function in response to a call and is used in *regular* circumstances. A second return channel is monitored by the runtime for reported errors that signal less-common *exceptional* circumstances.

In platforms with checked exceptions, like Java, this is made more visible by the use of a throws clause on a method signature:

```
public String readLine() throws IOException;
```

.NET doesn't have checked exceptions because they tend to lead to sloppy code where people introduce irresponsible catch-all statements. In addition, some caveats apply to versioning of code when new error conditions are introduced.

Second, propagation of exceptions that are left unhandled is a service provided by the runtime. In fact, this changes defaults: In Win32 and COM, if you don't do anything with the error code you get back, your program will continue to run. In most cases, this probably is not the right thing to do because the behavior of a program that has failed silently at some point in time is ill defined. At best, it will crash at some point in the future.

At worst, it will produce incorrect results or expose weird behavior that may go unnoticed for a long time, only making matters worse. When you use exceptions, if no one handles the exception, your program will terminate its execution.

Contradictory as it might seem, making applications crash in the face of errors that are not dealt with is a much better scenario. Although the *reliability* of a program that does sloppy exception handling is lower, it's without doubt more *robust*. Think about it this way: The most correct program is the one that doesn't do anything rather than the one that continues its merry way, producing bad results.

MORE EXCEPTION HANDLING THAN YOU MAY THINK!

In the example shown here, there's more hidden exception handling going on due to the use of the `using` statement. Recall from Chapter 8, "Basics of Exceptions and Resource Management," that the `using` block gives rise to a `try-finally` statement, ensuring proper disposal of the resource it acquired on the first line. Just as with exceptions, this results in a clear block-based structure of code, here to eliminate the need of a manual approach to resource cleanup. This is structured programming at its best.

Exception Handling

We start our journey through the world of exceptions by taking a look at the most common developer activity related to exceptions: structured handling of exceptions. The key ingredient to this is the use of the `try-catch-finally` statement. But first, we'll ensure a proper understanding of the way exceptions flow in the system. Figure 23.1 shows the execution flow depending on whether an exception occurred, which was illustrated earlier in Chapter 8, "Basics of Exceptions and Resource Management," Figure 8.19.

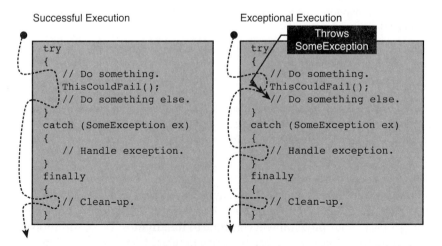

FIGURE 23.1   Flow of exceptions through a `try-catch-finally` statement.

The `try` block corresponds to a so-called *protected region* in the eyes of the CLR. A protected region simply tells the CLR to look out for exceptions within that block of code to transfer control to a potential handler or to ensure proper cleanup code gets run. Handlers are declared by means of a `catch` block, whereas the `finally` block is used to add code that's executed regardless of the outcome of the `try` block.

In Figure 23.1, two possible execution paths are illustrated. On the left, a successful pass through the code leads to the `finally` block being executed after the `try` block is left somehow. This can be due to reaching the terminating curly brace or because of the use of a `return` statement.

The runtime makes a guarantee that the `finally` block gets called no matter what happens, including the situation on the right. If an exception occurs during the `ThisCouldFail` call, a handler is looked for. Assuming there's an applicable handler associated with the protected block, control is transferred to that block of code. No matter how the handler exits (it could throw an exception by itself), the `finally` block gets called, too.

To decide whether a handler is applicable to deal with a certain exception that's raised in a protected block, the subtyping relationship is used, and handlers are scanned to find a match. This implies that the declaration order of handlers matters, as shown in Figure 23.2

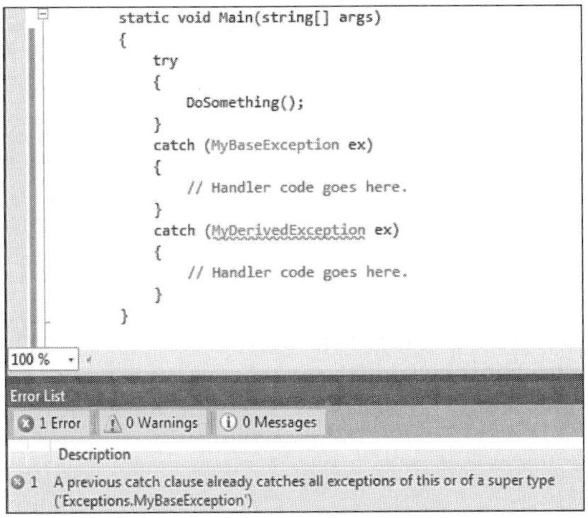

FIGURE 23.2   Order of handlers matters.

It's essential to understand the order of operations involved in locating handlers, to get a good idea about the control flow that will be observed during exception propagation. The CLR does two passes over a call stack to figure out where and in what order all the involved pieces of code need to be executed. In the first scan, the runtime searches the call stack for a protected region that has an associated handler that can deal with the exception being thrown. During this pass, filters may be executed, a feature that's not surfaced in the C# language, as explained in Chapter 8, "Basics of Exceptions and Resource Management," in the section, "Filters, but Not at the Language Level." We'll ignore this here.

The scan of the call stack for an applicable handler happens from the point where the exception was raised, making its way up the call stack. For every protected block, all handlers are scanned in the order they appear until a suitable one is found. As shown earlier, the "best" handler (in terms of subtyping) is not searched for. Instead, the first applicable handler wins.

DON'T CATCH ALL!

I'll say this many times throughout the chapter, but catching all exceptions is to be considered a crime. Whenever a catch (exception), or for that matter a catch block with no specified exception type, is found, it will be used to handle the exception. The obvious reason is that all exception types derive from this base type. Only handle exceptions you can really handle appropriately.

The first pass over the call stack is illustrated in Figure 23.3. Notice how the handler in Method1 wins over the more specific handler in Main. Not shown here is how handlers are being scanned in lexical order within a method, but that should be quite obvious. The same rule holds for nested try statements; scanning happens on an inside-out basis:

```
try {
    try {
        // Exception raised here.
    }
    catch (SomeException ex) {  /* Considered first. */ }
}
catch (OtherException ex) { /* Considered next. */ }
```

Next, the stack is unwound, executing all `finally` handlers associated with protected blocks encountered on the way out, ultimately reaching the handler that was found. The same happens if no handler was found, at which point the exception propagates all the way up to the Main method back to the point where the CLR started executing your managed code. This terminates the application. Figure 23.4 shows the continuation of the exception handling scenario of Figure 23.3.

EXCEPTIONS ARE COSTLY

All the scanning of the stack and control transfer logic is quite costly. This is not a problem if exceptions are used as intended: to deal with exceptional circumstances. Don't rely on exceptions for your program's regular flow control.

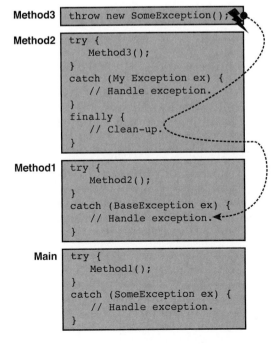

```
Method3   throw new SomeException();
Method2   try {
              Method3();
          }
          catch (My Exception ex) {
              // Handle exception.
          }
          finally {
              // Clean-up.
          }
Method1   try {
              Method2();
          }
          catch (BaseException ex) {
              // Handle exception.
          }
Main      try {
              Method1();
          }
          catch (SomeException ex) {
              // Handle exception.
          }
```

FIGURE 23.3   First pass through the stack, looking for a proper handler.

```
Method3   throw new SomeException();
Method2   try {
              Method3();
          }
          catch (My Exception ex) {
              // Handle exception.
          }
          finally {
              // Clean-up.
          }
Method1   try {
              Method2();
          }
          catch (BaseException ex) {
              // Handle exception.
          }
Main      try {
              Method1();
          }
          catch (SomeException ex) {
              // Handle exception.
          }
```

FIGURE 23.4   Unwinding the stack, executing finally blocks on the way out.

try Statements

Block-based exception handling is one of the core features of structured exception handling. The try statement in languages like C# reflects this. Associated with the try block are catch handlers and/or a single finally block. All forms shown here are valid based on those rules. First, a single handler:

```
try {
    // Protected block.
}
catch (FirstException ex) {
    // Handle the exception of the specified type.
}
```

Second, use of multiple handlers

```
try {
    // Protected block.
}
catch (FirstException ex) {
    // Handle the exception of the specified type.
}
catch (SecondException ex) {
    // Handle the exception of the specified type.
}
```

All these can have a finally block at the bottom, but that block can also be used in the absence of any catch blocks:

```
try {
    // Protected block.
}
finally {
    // This code will execute no matter how the try block is exited.
}
```

The use of a try statement with only a finally block is exactly what the using statement translates into, to guarantee a call to the Dispose method on the acquired resource occurs when the using block is left:

```
using (resource) {
    // Code using the resource; may crash.
}
```

The preceding is equivalent to this:

```
try {
    // Code using the resource; may crash.
}
finally {
    if (resource != null)
        resource.Dispose();
}
```

Because the end of the try block is not guaranteed to be reached because of possible control transfer due to exceptions, definite assignments or flow analysis may throw you off at first. The compiler is very pessimistic when it comes to flow analysis:

```
int Bar() {
    try {
        return 1;
    }
    catch (SomeException ex) {
        // Handle the exception of the specified type.
    }
    // The compiler concludes you may have ended up in the catch block.
}
```

Try statements have a much simpler form at the level of intermediate language (IL) code, where each protected block can have only catch handlers or finally blocks associated with it, but not both. More-complex try statements written in C# translate into nested try statements at the IL level, as shown here:

```
try {
    // Protected block.
}
catch (FirstException ex) {
    // Handle the exception of the specified type.
}
catch (SecondException ex) {
    // Handle the exception of the specified type.
}
finally {
    // This code will execute no matter how the try block is exited.
}
```

This gets turned into the following equivalent form for the translation to IL:

```
try {
    try {
        // Protected block.
    }
    catch (FirstException ex) {
        // Handle the exception of the specified type.
    }
    catch (SecondException ex) {
        // Handle the exception of the specified type.
    }
}
finally {
    // This code will execute no matter how the try block is exited.
}
```

You will agree the C# syntax makes this code look much nicer, eliminating the increasing number of indentation levels that would go with every nested `try` statement.

ETYMOLOGY: PROTECTED BLOCKS

It turns out the wording *protected block* fits the C# model of exception handling quite nicely because `try` statements are based on blocks delimited by curly braces (which, quite *exceptionally* for blocks, cannot be omitted on `try`, `catch`, or `finally` blocks, even if they are single line).

Nevertheless, the concept of protected blocks comes from the Common Language Infrastructure (CLI) glossary. Although IL code looks block-based, in reality it isn't. You've seen this before when we discussed various statements such as loop constructs, which really turn into branches at the IL level. Looking in ILDASM, you will see apparent blocks for exception-handling constructs, as shown in Figure 23.5.

Under the covers, things are done much more mechanically using some metadata constructs. Every method has an exception table that relates to a region of IL code (a from-to range, if you will) that's *protected* with a corresponding handler or `finally` block. In other words, curly brace blocks are a language-level illusion.

First-Chance Exceptions

Sloppy code might be swallowing exceptions improperly without decent handling. When you see source code that looks like this, you should start to shiver:

```
try {
    // Exception raised here.
}
catch (SomeException) { }
```

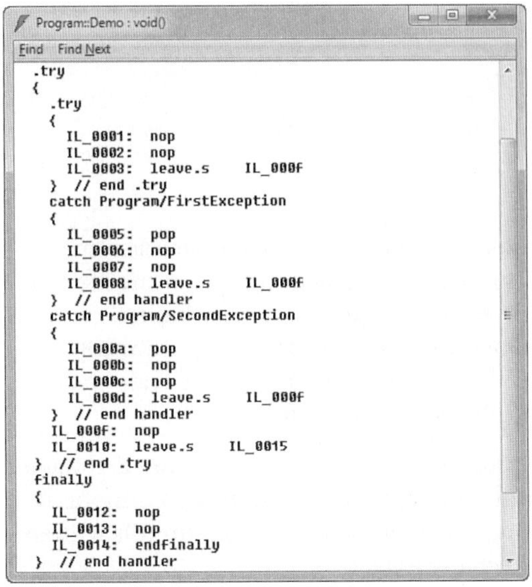

FIGURE 23.5   Block structure for exception handling in IL.

At the same time, consider yourself lucky you saw the code to begin with. Much more likely you're finding yourself back in a situation where you need to find out why the program misbehaves under certain circumstances. Assuming the preceding code lies at the heart of the observed misbehavior, the question becomes how to track it down. After all, the exception might long have been swallowed, and the program may crash in some different corner. Consider the following example:

```
static string s_Name;

static void Main() {
    B();
    A();
}

static void A() {
    Console.WriteLine(s_Name.ToUpper());
}

static void B() {
    try
    {
        C();
        s_Name = "Joe";
    }
```

```
    catch (SomeException) { }
}

static void C() {
    throw new SomeException();
}
```

This example is simple enough to spot the problem by mental debugging, but assume many more methods are involved. Let's walk through the problem first to ensure we're all on the same page. B's responsibility is to set the s_Name variable somehow but fails to do so because C threw an exception that was swallowed by the try-catch block in the B method. When A comes around, all traces of B and C are long gone, and the code crashes on a NullReferenceException when trying to call ToUpper on s_Name.

Notice that matters could be even worse without the ToUpper call. When a null argument is encountered, Console.WriteLine simply prints an empty line. This may go unnoticed for a long time. Because of sloppy error handling, no potentially critical output is written to the screen. It's hard to call the program correct any longer.

Luckily, the debugger can help figure out where things went wrong. Figure 23.6 shows the situation at the point the NullReferenceException is thrown. The Call Stack window doesn't show us much useful information because the root cause of the error has long passed. However, the Output window provides more helpful information because it logs *first-chance exceptions*. Besides the NullReferenceException that's going on right now, there's also mention of the SomeException that occurred earlier. In reality, this might be way up in the Output window, but in general, first-chance exceptions should be treated seriously.

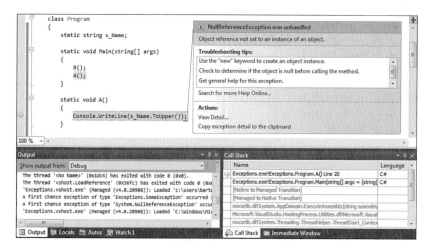

FIGURE 23.6   The Output window reveals a first-chance exception.

We can do better than look at the Output window to spot first-chance exceptions. To break the debugger as soon as an exception happens, the Debug, Exceptions menu can come in handy. If you check the Thrown check box for the Common Language Runtime Exceptions entry, the debugger will break at the point the exception gets thrown (see Figure 23.7). Feel free to explore the dialog in more detail as you can filter on exception types more granularly. In addition, other types of exceptions can be enabled for first-chance visualization, mostly from the native world. This is useful if your code calls into native APIs, especially when you're doing mixed-mode debugging.

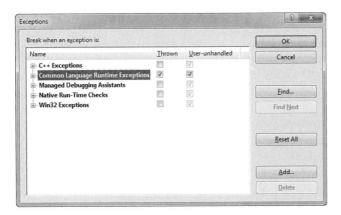

FIGURE 23.7   Enabling first-chance CLR exceptions.

MDAS

This dialog also gives access to Managed Debugging Assistants (MDAs). They can be thought of as debugger enhancements that know about various circumstances that are indicative of common programming errors in the world of managed code.

When running the program again under the debugger, we see the original exception under the debugger at the point it's thrown (see Figure 23.8). Notice the different caption of the pop-up, mentioning the exception "occurred" as opposed to the pop-up shown in Figure 23.6 that says the exception was left "unhandled."

While we're in the debugger, a handy trick to inspect the current exception object is to type $exception in any watch window. This proves particularly useful when looking at first-chance exceptions or when you're in a handler that didn't declare a variable to refer to the exception object. The result is shown in Figure 23.9.

SOS STRIKES AGAIN

SOS, the low-level native debugger extension that comes with the CLR, can deal with exceptions, too. Although most readers won't have an immediate need to use SOS for their day-to-day development jobs, it sometimes proves handy on production systems where no Visual Studio debugger is or can be installed. (I have yet to find a system administrator who allows a full Visual Studio install on every server in the data center.)

Three SOS commands to deal with managed exceptions come in handy:

▶ StopOnException, or soe, causes the debugger to break on a first-chance exception of the specified type (for example, soe MyException). A -derived flag can be used to stop on an exception of the specified type or a subclass thereof.

▶ PrintException, abbreviated pe, prints the current exception, much like the $exception trick in the Watch window. The resulting view is similar to a DumpObject (do) call on a managed object. An additional -nested flag can be supplied to show nested exceptions (that is, the situation that arises when a catch block throws an exception by itself).

▶ Threads may be the most surprising of all, but because every thread has its own evaluation stack and exceptions are closely related to the evaluation stack, this command is in a good position to show for each thread what exception object (if any) is floating around on it.

Don't worry too much about SOS if you're just starting to learn .NET development. However, if you end up outside the comfort zone of Visual Studio (for example, debugging a production system), know that the WinDbg and SOS tandem is a viable alternative.

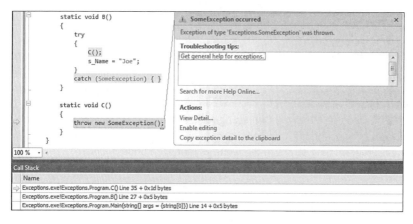

FIGURE 23.8   A first-chance exception shown in the debugger.

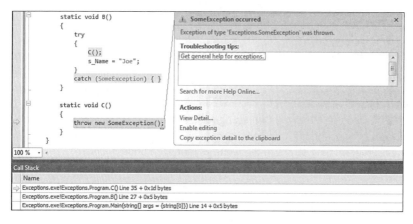

FIGURE 23.9   Using $exception to visualize the exception object.

Intermezzo on Historical Debugging with IntelliTrace

While we're in the wonderful world of debugging managed code applications, we should take a look at a new feature added to Visual Studio 2010: IntelliTrace. In the example shown in the previous section, we were dealing with an exception that was swallowed inappropriately long before the program started to fail. Wouldn't it be handy to walk the program's execution back in time to investigate the program state outside the scope of the current call stack? That's exactly what IntelliTrace enables.

To play with this exciting new feature, we need to configure it first through the Tools, Options dialog, under the IntelliTrace node in the tree view. Two modes are available; the latter one, called Diagnostic Events and Call Information, is the most powerful. Figure 23.10 shows the desired settings for the next experiment.

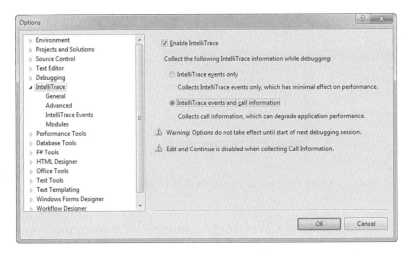

FIGURE 23.10   Configuring the new IntelliTrace feature.

Disabling first-chance exceptions for the time being, we'll execute the same program with the Historical Debugging feature properly configured. At the point we crash on the NullReference exception, make the IntelliTrace window visible (if it isn't already) through the Debug, IntelliTrace, Debug History Calls menu. This brings up the view shown in Figure 23.11.

Observe a few things here. At this point, IntelliTrace pretty much shows the same information you would see in the Call Stack window: The debugger was stopped at an exception in method A, with the Main method higher up the stack. However, from this view, we can start doing time travel. Using the buttons in the margin of the code editor, it's possible to go back to the previous event logged by the historical debugger. So far, nothing too exciting; this will just bring us back to the Main method's call to A.

Where the magic comes in is when we're back on the call to B from the Main method; now we can step into B based on the IntelliTrace information that has been collected. Not only this, but the technology enables us to debug the call to B by replaying the events that were collected. Figure 23.12 shows the different options in the margin of the code editor at the point of the call to B.

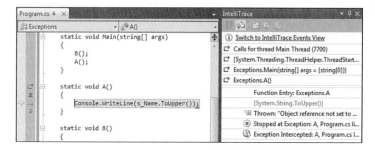

FIGURE 23.11   Debug history at the point of the crash.

FIGURE 23.12   Instead of just walking up the call stack, we can step into other paths.

This new capability comes in very handy while debugging an application when you have no clue where an invalid program state originated.

WHY LOGGING MATTERS

Using IntelliTrace should not be a reason to omit useful tracing and diagnostics in your code (for example, by writing significant events during a program's execution to a log file) because one day or another you'll face a live crash where IntelliTrace has not been enabled.

When and What to Catch

Handling exceptions correctly is a huge responsibility for framework and application developers. For that reason alone, it's important to give some guidelines on when and what to catch.

Let's start with the latter question: what exceptions to catch. You first want to know which exceptions can be thrown by the APIs being used; for this information, documentation proves invaluable. As an example, consider the System.IO.File.OpenRead API, where the following exceptions are documented:

- ► `ArgumentException`—The path is a zero-length string, contains only whitespace or contains one or more invalid characters as defined by `InvalidPathChars`.

- ► `ArgumentNullException`—The path is null.

- ► `PathTooLongException`—The specified path, filename, or both exceed the system-defined maximum length. For example, on Windows-based platforms, paths must be fewer than 248 characters, and filenames must be fewer than 260 characters.

- ► `DirectoryNotFoundException`—The specified path is invalid (for example, it is on an unmapped drive).

- ► `UnauthorizedAccessException`—The path specified a directory or the caller does not have the required permission.

- ► `FileNotFoundException`—The file specified in path was not found.

- ► `NotSupportedException`—The path is in an invalid format.

The next step is to categorize the exceptions according to various criteria. One category contains the exceptions that result from bugs in your code or improper input validation higher up the call stack. For example, an `ArgumentNullException` is something you can avoid by making sure a null reference is never fed into the relevant arguments. If the data for those arguments is provided from the outside, proper input validation at the point the data is received is the right thing to do. The execution should simply not get to this point.

Then there are the exceptions you can't provide any meaningful recovery for. In the preceding example, it's unlikely you will be able to recover from an authorized access exception because file system level settings are involved. Depending on where the call to the `OpenRead` method lives, you might want to let this exception go, present an error dialog to the user, or perform diagnostic logging.

Another category consists of exceptions you can *try* to prevent but can never eliminate completely. A good example is the `FileNotFoundException`, where the outside world will influence the outcome of the call. You may spontaneously come up with mitigations like this:

```
if (!File.Exists(file)) {
    // Preventing the FileNotFoundException by proper action here?
}

var fs = File.OpenRead(file);
```

No matter how much you check for the file's existence, you still have a race condition in the preceding code. If it disappears between the time of checking and the time of attempting to open the file, you'll still get the `FileNotFoundException`. If you're in a good position to handle the exception (for example, by informing the user), or if you have thought out a fallback scheme to look for a file in another place, that's the way to go; otherwise, let the exception bubble up to the caller and document that's the case.

Another category of exceptions has to do with situations you can't do anything about no matter how hard you try. The system might be out of memory; the call stack may overflow (which could indicate a bug in a recursive algorithm); or if things go really bad, the execution engine might be in trouble. Those exceptions should not be handled under any circumstance.

UNCATCHABLE!

The CLR contains a list of exception types it categorizes as uncatchable, meaning the user cannot handle them. Examples include the `OutOfMemoryException` and `StackOverflowException` types.

Finally, some poorly designed APIs require users to handle exceptions even for regular use. Luckily, those APIs are rare and have typically been replaced or complemented by better members. A good example is `int.Parse` in .NET 1.x:

```
int age = -1;
bool ageValid;

try {
    age = int.Parse(userAge);
    ageValid = true;
} catch (FormatException) {
    ageValid = false;
}

if (!ageValid) {
    // Take appropriate action; e.g. ask for input again.
}
```

API designers soon recognized that this was not a great way to check for valid input, so a sister method called `TryParse` was introduced:

```
int age;
if (!int.TryParse(userAge, out age)) {
    // Take appropriate action; e.g. ask for input again.
}
```

Never design APIs that require the user to catch an exception in regular circumstances; doing so will not only lead to more cumbersome code, it will also degrade performance and hinder debugging with first-chance exceptions enabled.

> **DON'T CATCH ALL (AGAIN)**
>
> Based on the discussion in the previous section, you should be discouraged from catching all exceptions already. Some simply cannot be caught, and others should be propagated to the caller to take meaningful action, if possible. Very few exceptions to this rule exist, and I won't try to define such exceptions here.

Beyond Your Control

Catching exceptions using `try` statements works only if your code appears somewhere higher up on the call stack. After all, a protected block protects only the code that runs inside it. You don't possess magical powers to stretch an exception handler around code that is not yours, somewhere in an unrelated corner of the system.

A typical source of such practical issues is in UI programming, where a dispatcher is used to run work on behalf of the user, on the right thread and with a specified right priority. The code that dispatches work items that have been scheduled is beyond your control. For example, in Windows Presentation Foundation (WPF), it's the application's `Run` method that starts the dispatcher. We talk more about the dispatcher's role when covering WPF in more detail. For now, just focus on the following little example:

```
private void crash_Click(object sender, RoutedEventArgs e) {
    Dispatcher.BeginInvoke(new Action(() => {
        throw new Exception("Oops!"); })
    );
}
```

Here we're scheduling background work through the dispatcher, allowing the event handler for the crash button to return immediately. At some point in the future, this work item will be picked up by the dispatcher, causing the delegate to be called. The call stack at the point of the crash will look roughly like this:

```
WpfApplication1.exe!WpfApplication1.MainWindow.crash_Click.AnonymousMethod__0
...
WindowsBase.dll!System.Windows.Threading.Dispatcher.Run
...
PresentationFramework.dll!System.Windows.Application.Run
WpfApplication1.exe!WpfApplication1.App.Main
```

At the top, we see our anonymous method containing the code passed to `BeginInvoke`. This was called by the dispatcher somehow, through all the machinery hidden behind the `Application.Run` call made by the application's `Main` method. There's no apparent place to handle such an exception.

One thing we can do is make sure the delegates posted through `BeginInvoke` do not crash for avoidable reasons. This is by far the best solution. However, in some cases, it makes sense to handle exceptions from the outside as a "last chance" to deal with a problem that would otherwise take down the application. To accommodate such needs, there are often global applicationwide exception-handler mechanisms. For WPF, there's the Dispatcher.UnhandledException event:

```
Dispatcher.UnhandledException += (sender, e) => {
    // The e.Exception property contains the exception object.
    // Set e.Handled to true to indicate the exception was handled; if it
    // remains false, the application will terminate.
};
```

Throwing Exceptions

As mentioned before, exceptions should be kept for exceptional circumstances where the executing piece of code cannot make any further meaningfully defined attempts to rectify a problematic situation. Big categories of exception types to keep in mind here include input validation and signaling of the inability (for various reasons) to process the call successfully.

Throwing an exception is simply done by use of the throw statement in C#, specifying an object that derives from System.Exception, specifying a meaningful message:

```
throw new InvalidOperationException("The object is in an invalid state.");
```

RUNTIMEWRAPPEDEXCEPTION

The CLR allows any managed object to be thrown as an exception, again for cross-language interoperability reasons. For instance, C++ is a language where exceptions can be any object. The only way such exceptions could be caught is by using the following code:

```
try {
    // May throw an object as an exception.
}
catch {
    // But we can't figure out what it was and we had to catch everything...
}
```

This is because C# doesn't allow a catch block to use a type that doesn't derive from System.Exception. However, this problem was recognized, and the runtime wraps them in a System.Runtime.CompilerServices.RuntimeWrappedException object. So if you're interoperating with other languages that may throw any object as an exception, be prepared to handle this exception. The original object can be retrieved from the WrappedException property.

Another way to throw an exception is available inside a `catch` block. Sometimes during exception handling, you may conclude that the caught exception cannot be dealt with properly after all. In such a case, you want to *rethrow* the current exception:

```
catch (SomeException ex) {
    if (/* some condition based on ex */)
        throw;
    ...
}
```

If the `SomeException` type is under your control, the need to write code like that shown here may indicate you need to come up with more specific exception types, allowing more granular catch handlers to be written based on the exception type.

THE GOOD, THE BAD, AND THE UGLY ABOUT FILTERS AND RETHROW

One problem with the use of rethrow, as shown in the preceding example, is that the original call stack information gets lost, as shown in the `StackTrace` property on the exception. This can hinder debugging significantly, so it's important to try to provide very specific exception types that can be used to narrow down what's caught by a catch handler.

As an alternative to rethrow, the CLR supports the exception filters, surfaced through a few managed code languages like Visual Basic. They look like this:

```
Try
    DoSomething()
Catch ex As SomeException When ex.Bar = something
    ' Handler code goes here
End Try
```

C# doesn't have filters because they can get quite hard to reason about. For reasons of backward compatibility with the Windows Structured Exception Handling (SEH), the CLR's exception-handling mechanism employs a two-pass scan of the stack. In the first pass, it looks for suitable exception handlers based on the exception type, as we've seen before. When encountering a filter, the filtering condition's code gets executed to decide whether the handler is willing to (and able to) handle the exception.

As a result of this two-pass mechanism, filter code gets run in the context of the place where the exception is thrown. In the preceding Visual Basic example, the bold expression executed at the point the `SomeException` is thrown, but because this code depends on a variable called `something`, the outcome may be surprising. The reason is that something might have changed from the point the `try` block was entered. In other words, it becomes hard to reason about filters on a purely lexical basis.

In the absence of checked exceptions, documentation is essential to ensure that users of your API can properly catch exceptions they can handle in a meaningful manner. If they don't know what to look out for, it's impossible to be prepared:

```
/// <summary>Logs a message to the log file.</summary>
/// <exception cref="ArgumentNullException">
/// <paramref name="message"/> is null.
/// </exception>
public void LogMessage(string message) {
    if (message == null)
        throw new ArgumentNullException("message");
    ...
}
```

Defining Your Own Exception Types

To signal application- or framework-specific error conditions, you should define your own specialized exception types. Among the most important advantages of using exceptions for error reporting and handling is their nominal nature: The type name contains invaluable information about the kind of error that occurred. Besides this, an exception object can carry any information it wants, which distinguishes it significantly from the Win32 and COM approaches taken in the past. So you can provide much more context that travels on the back of the exception object, ready for the handler to inspect.

Because it's important for users of the .NET Framework to feel at home with any kind of exception, guidelines have been created for the shape of an exception type. To ease into these gradually, let's take a look at the System.Exception base class first, shown in Figure 23.13.

Notice the different constructors available here. Besides a default constructor, two overloads exist that take in a message and (optionally) an inner exception. The use of an inner exception can prove useful when rethrowing exception objects, providing more context about the original point of failure. Various methods are present to support the use of serialization, when an exception needs to travel between application domains or across different machines. This is quite important when an API gets used in the context of a distributed system because you don't want to lose information about the exception when it gets transmitted to the caller over the wire.

The different properties are worth taking a closer look at, as well:

▶ Data provides a nongeneric dictionary to keep name/value pairs in with more information about the exception. This property should be used with care because its contents can be modified by catch blocks that catch and rethrow the exception. At the same time, this provides a way for catch blocks to provide contextual information about their handling of an exception. In subtypes, you typically want to add more contextual information by means of get-only properties.

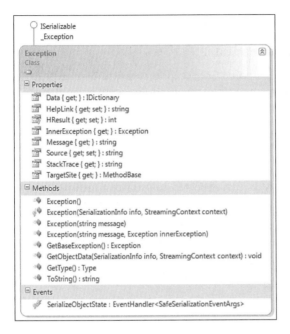

FIGURE 23.13   The `System.Exception` base class.

- ▶ HelpLink is used to specify a URI where additional information can be found about the exception. We need to emphasize this is an instance property, and therefore it can provide a different URI for each instance of an exception type. After all, for information about the exception type, XML documentation should be around somewhere. An example of a HelpLink use is for a ParserException that supplies a different HelpLink for different parse failures (for example, pointing to documentation about the specific grammar rule that was violated).

- ▶ HResult is important when the managed code component that's throwing the exception is used from a COM-based client. An example where this is the case is when writing Office add-ins. The managed exception can then be converted into an HRESULT for the COM client to detect. In the opposite direction, a failure originating from a COM component gets surfaced as an exception that contains the HRESULT of the failed call.

- ▶ InnerException allows wrapping exceptions into one another. When defining a contract between multiple components in the system (for example, using interfaces), you likely want to surface a whole set of known failures as one single exception type. At the same time, different root causes may lie at the heart of the failure. This is where InnerException comes in, providing a way to capture detailed exception information.

- ▶ Message is easy to understand: It provides a message about what went wrong. Internationalized applications should localize this property because it's meant to be used as a way to display meaningful information to the end user of an application.

▶ Source can be set to identify where an exception is coming from (for example, using an identifier for an application component or an object). If not set, the name of the assembly where the exception was raised is used.

▶ StackTrace contains the call stack at the point the exception was thrown and can be used to debug an error condition even when no debugger is attached at the time of the failure. In debug builds with a symbol file available, additional information such as line numbers may be shown, too.

▶ TargetSite provides the reflection MethodBase object indicating the place where the exception was thrown.

When defining your own exception type, it's at least expected to provide a meaningful Message property and an InnerException if that makes sense. In addition, serialization support is highly desirable.

To help developers write correct exception types that conform to those requirements, a code snippet exists in Visual Studio to generate the customizable template code. This snippet is called Exception and can be inserted, like all code snippets, by typing its name followed by two Tab keystrokes (see Figure 23.14).

```
namespace Exceptions
{
    [global::System.Serializable]
    public class MyException : Exception
    {
        public MyException() { }
        public MyException(string message) : base(message) { }
        public MyException(string message, Exception inner) : base(message, inner) { }
        protected MyException(
            System.Runtime.Serialization.SerializationInfo info,
            System.Runtime.Serialization.StreamingContext context)
            : base(info, context) { }
    }
}
```

FIGURE 23.14   The Exception snippet expanded.

Points of customization include the name of the exception, as a prefix to the common suffix Exception, and the base class. Notice how support for serialization is provided out of the box by means of the Serializable attribute and the protected constructor. For more information about serialization, take a look at the MSDN documentation that you can find starting from the System.Exception base class.

THE KEY TO WRITING GOOD CODE SNIPPETS

Good code snippets work correctly whenever they are inserted in appropriate places. The Exception snippet was clearly designed with this guideline in mind: Namespaces are expanded completely, and the global keyword is used to ensure the Serializable custom attribute is found from the global namespace. Unfortunately, this increases clutter that's often irrelevant in the context where the snippet is inserted. I typically clean up the code emitted by the snippet insertion. Feel free to do the same whenever it's safe to do so (for example, if there are no namespace clashes).

Custom exception types have value for various reasons. Not only does the type-based matching when locating applicable catch blocks provide an ideal way to do granular exception handling, it also enables you to evolve the exception types over time either by adding more properties to them or even by introducing new subtypes. Later we take a closer look at various built-in exception types that are useful for reuse, but if you want to describe an application- or library-specific error condition, it's considered a best practice to define your own custom exception types.

OVERENGINEERING FROM THE TRENCHES: APPLICATIONEXCEPTION

When exceptions were first designed, it was thought that introducing a separate class hierarchy for CLR exceptions and application-defined exceptions was a good idea. This gave rise to the definition of two classes derived from Exception. One is called SystemException and is reserved for the CLR and core framework components to signal an error condition. The other one, ApplicationException, was meant to be used as the base class for application-defined exceptions.

This well-intentioned idea didn't turn out to add much value, and because deriving from Exception directly was not prevented, lots of applications and frameworks started to use that as their base class of choice. It quickly turned into a design guideline to derive directly from Exception and forget about ApplicationException. So the code snippet is right to derive from Exception directly.

(In)famous Exception Types

The Base Class Library (BCL) comes with many exception types predefined. We now take a look at the most important ones everyone should be aware of (not only to be prepared to handle any of those, when it's appropriate to do so, but also to throw them when they're meant to be used by applications directly).

DivideByZeroException

This exception occurs when a division by zero is carried out for integral or decimal values and can be avoided by the application checking for a zero denominator upfront. Recall that floating-point types have infinity and Not a Number (NaN) values defined that will be used for the result of division-by-zero attempts.

The second and third lines here give rise to this exception, regardless of the use of a checked context; the same holds for the other integral and decimal data types:

```
int n = 1, d = 0;
int div = n / d;
int rem = n % d;
```

OverflowException

Still in the domain of arithmetic, we find `OverflowException`, which occurs in a checked context whenever an arithmetic operation, cast, or conversion overflows. For more information about the checked context, see Chapter 5, "Expressions."

Use of checked contexts is intended to make the application more robust against overflow conditions that will produce incorrect results. By default, C# programs compile with unchecked arithmetic, cast, and conversion operations. Visual Basic reverses this default, which has the potential to negatively impact performance.

It's not uncommon to leave this exception type unhandled when no overflow conditions are expected, but checked contexts are used regardless to guard against incorrect results if overflow ever occurs. This is typically the case in financial or scientific computing, though it's not uncommon to use different types (like `BigInteger`) altogether to remove limitations on the precision and range of numeric values.

A few examples of overflows are shown here:

```
checked {
    int tooHigh = int.MaxValue + 1; // add.ovf
    int tooLow = int.MinValue - 1;  // sub.ovf
    byte b = 200;
    sbyte s = (sbyte)b;             // conv.ovf
}
```

NullReferenceException

For people coming from the native code land, `NullReferenceException` is your modern access violation counterpart in the managed world. If your background lies somewhere else, just remember this exception is something you never want to see in *your* code.

It's too bad reference types by default permit the null reference, making this exception far too common in improperly tested code. Failure to return a proper object is often signaled by means of a null reference, giving callers a great opportunity to shoot themselves in the foot by omitting a null check. So don't fall into this trap yourself. Instead, check against null values wherever necessary:

```
string s = GetStringMaybeNull();
string oops = s.ToUpper();
```

Another common source of `NullReferenceException` errors is the improper use of the as keyword where a regular cast is more desirable:

```
object o = GetSomeObject();
string s = o as string;      // No null check? Cast!
string oops = s.ToUpper();
```

If you know o ought to be string, use a regular cast instead of an as expression. This will result in an `InvalidCastException`, which gives you a better clue about what went wrong. In other cases, where you're legitimately using the as keyword, you should expect to see a null check to check the result of the operation.

In an expression context, different ways of dealing with null references exist, as discussed previously. One is the null-coalescing ?? operator, which enables you to provide a default value to replace a null reference; another one is the use of the conditional operator with a null check for the condition:

```
string s = GetStringMaybeNull();
string okay = s ?? "(empty)";
string fine = s != null ? s.ToUpper() : "(empty)";
```

Computer scientist Tony Hoare recently called the introduction of null references in ALGOL (back in 1965) "his billion dollar mistake." Don't let them come and get *you*!

IndexOutOfRangeException

Another exception in the category of silly bug revealers is `IndexOutOfRangeException`, which indicates an array is accessed outside its boundaries. "Off-by-one" errors are a typical source of this exception:

```
int[] nums = new[] { 1, 2, 3 };
for (int i = 0; i <= nums.Length; i++)
    nums[i]++;
```

Bounds checks have been a historical source of bugs, which often went unnoticed in the world of native code, causing random program crashes because of memory corruption. Consider yourself lucky that the CLR catches this class of problems using runtime checks (to avoid its memory and type safety), but don't write such bugs in the first place! Off-by-one errors can be subtle, but with a little bit of extra thought, you should be able to avoid seeing this exception ever again.

InvalidCastException

Being able to cast an object to an incompatible type would lead to a breach in the type safety of the system, which clearly is to be avoided. `InvalidCastException` is the CLR's way to block every such attempt.

Nowadays, after the introduction of generic types, the use of casts should have become much rarer than it used to be. Every time you have to cast an object to a more specific type, ask yourself how you ended up in this situation in the first place. Maybe it has something to do with generics. And if you find yourself performing a type-based switch using is or as, perhaps using object-oriented virtual dispatch facilities is more appropriate.

Either way, if you do a cast, you had better darn well know what the target type ought to be. In essence, you're telling the compiler to believe you about the real type of an object, something it seemingly can't figure out on its own. If you don't know the type yourself, using casts is nothing but kamikaze programming, and you should instead use type checks. For this reason, running into an InvalidCastException is inexcusable:

```
object o = 42;
string s = (string)o;
```

ArrayTypeMismatchException

Sometimes it's not the developer's fault. Instead, perhaps the runtime or framework designers are to blame. Luckily, this doesn't happen very often, but ArrayTypeMismatchException shows that it does happen.

The introduction of covariant arrays, as discussed in Chapter 9, "Generics and Collections," was an unfortunate choice made in the early .NET 1.0 days (for very good reasons back then). This exception catches a mishap in using covariant arrays at runtime that should have instead been caught at compile time:

```
int[] nums = new[] { 1, 2, 3 };
object[] numsInDisguise = nums;
numsInDisguise[1] = "two"; // Ow!
```

To see why this is a problem and how this issue is avoided for generic types, refer to Chapter 9. Luckily, arrays aren't used often in this unsafe manner, and the problem disappears when making use of generic collection types like List<T>.

TypeInitializationException

Throwing an exception from a static constructor is not considered good practice because the exception can surface in totally unexpected places where the CLR decides to run the static constructor. Keep in mind that static field initialization code ends up in the static constructor as well, providing another potential source of exceptions.

The problem of a static constructor throwing an exception is illustrated in the following example, and Figure 23.15 shows the result of running the code:

```
class Program {
    static void Main(){
        Console.WriteLine(StaticBoom.X);
    }
}
```

```
static class StaticBoom {
    static int x = 0;
    static int y = 1 / x;

    public static int X { get { return x; } }
}
```

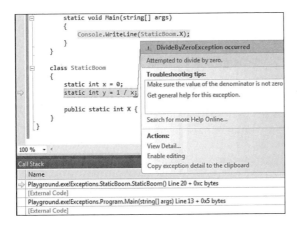

FIGURE 23.15   A static constructor blowing up.

The InnerException of the TypeInitializationException contains the original exception object (in our case, a DivideByZeroException caused by the initialization of the static field y). To see the source of the exception with your own eyes, enable first-chance exceptions and observe the exception being thrown on the line that initializes y. The call stack at this point is most interesting, as shown in Figure 23.16.

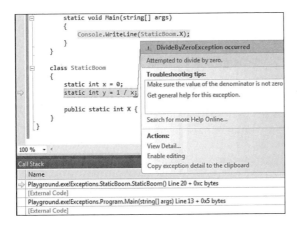

FIGURE 23.16   The place where the static constructor gets called.

The transitions back and forth between native and managed code indicate where the runtime is coming around to ensure the static constructor has been run before the first access to any of the type's static fields.

BEFOREFIELDINIT

When a type is marked with the `BeforeFieldInit` type attribute, which can be seen in ILDASM, the CLR is free to run the type initializer at or before the first access to a static field defined for the type. The C# compiler emits this attribute under certain circumstances, signaling the CLR it can be more relaxed about the timing of the static constructor call. When this attribute is emitted is rather subtle: When a custom static constructor is defined (even if it's empty), the attribute is present; otherwise (for example, if just static fields are being initialized), it's not.

This makes the timing of the discussed exception also more "relaxed," meaning you can expect it at unexpected times. To avoid confusion, just make sure your static constructors don't throw exceptions.

ObjectDisposedException

`ObjectDisposedException` typically indicates a bug in your program. Types implementing the `IDisposable` interface throw an exception of this type to signal use of the object after it has been disposed (for example, by use of a `using` statement):

```
FileStream fs = File.OpenRead(file);
using (fs) {
    // Do some stuff.
}

// This call will fail with an ObjectDisposedException as Dispose has been
// called when the using block was exited.
var more = fs.ReadByte();
```

Correct use of the `using` statement will prevent use of the acquired resource after the block has been left. The preceding exception wouldn't have been possible if the code had been written as follows instead:

```
using (FileStream fs = File.OpenRead(file)) {
    // Do some stuff.
}

// Now this line doesn't compile anymore since fs is not in scope.
var more = fs.ReadByte();
```

This is because the `using` statement used here was turned into the following form during compilation, introducing a new block to scope the `fs` variable:

```
{
    FileStream fs = File.OpenRead(file)
    try {
        // Do some stuff.
    }
    finally {
        if (fs != null)
            fs.Dispose();
    }
}

// Clearly, the fs variable above cannot be seen on the next line anymore:
var more = fs.ReadByte();
```

However, `IDisposable` objects are not always used in conjunction with the using statement because they might have to be maintained in an object's fields instead. In that case, the containing type itself most likely needs to implement `IDisposable` by itself so that all the resources on which it depends get properly disposed of, too. At that point, it becomes the responsibility of the developer of the containing type to protect it against improper use after disposal by using the `ObjectDisposedException`. The typical pattern for implementing `IDisposable` is shown here:

```
class MixedResource : IDisposable {
    // Native resource, e.g. a handle to a shared memory section
    private IntPtr _native = ...;

    // Managed resource, in practice a more specific type is used, e.g. Stream.
    private IDisposable _managed = ...;

    // Indicates whether we have been disposed.
    private bool _disposed = false;

    public void DoSomething() {
        if (_disposed)
            throw new ObjectDisposedException(/* add a message */);

        // Do real work here.
    }

    public void Dispose() {
        Dispose(true /* coming from Dispose */);
        // Avoid second disposal caused by the garbage collector calling the
        // finalizer method ~MixedResource.
```

```
        GC.SuppressFinalize(this);
    }

    ~MixedResource() {
        Dispose(false /* coming from finalizer */);
    }

    private void Dispose(bool disposing) {
        // Permit duplicate calls to Dispose without ObjectDisposedException.
        if (!_disposed) {
            // Managed resources get disposed on the spot when the containing
            // object's Dispose method is called. If we've gotten here through
            // the finalizer, we should not be touching other managed objects!
            if (disposing) {
                _managed.Dispose();
            }

            // Clean up native resources next, e.g. using Win32 CloseHandle.
            CloseHandle(_native);
            _native = IntPtr.Zero;

            // This flag will be used to throw ObjectDisposedException.
            _disposed = true;
        }
    }
}
```

OutOfMemoryException

When the managed heap becomes full, the garbage collector will ask the operating system for more virtual memory. When this request fails, the OutOfMemoryException is thrown. This exception cannot be caught by application code and will terminate your program on the spot. One reason you cannot catch the exception is that it takes immense powers to deal with such an exception without allocating more memory while doing so. In addition, no guarantees are made about the execution of finally blocks and finalizers in out-of-memory conditions because they may allocate memory on their own. Luckily, outstanding open handles to Win32 resources will be closed either way because the operating system takes care of this upon program termination.

CER, INSUFFICIENTMEMORYEXCEPTION, AND SO ON

The CLR provides super-specialized means to deal with memory management for applications that require the highest reliability imaginable. One large set of such mechanisms is found under System.Runtime.ConstrainedExecution (CER), which provides ways to create high-reliability code by constraining the actions that can be carried out in code. Writing CERs is a highly specialized task.

One closely related mechanism is the InsufficientMemoryException that's thrown by a MemoryFailPoint object. This object acts as a memory gate, allowing code to check whether enough memory will be available to carry out an operation. If not, the code can catch this exception and throttle down its needs or perform actions that will decrease the program's memory use.

Finally, there are the CLR hosting APIs that are used to run managed code in an otherwise native code process. A great example of this is SQL Server 2005 and later, where the database can be extended using managed code (for example, with stored procedures or user-defined functions). In such a setting, the host might want to have fine-grained control over memory management by the CLR to prevent the runtime from destabilizing the host process. With high reliability and performance guarantees made by SQL Server, having tight control over memory management is a key requirement addressed by the specialized CLR hosting APIs.

An exhaustive discussion of memory management at the operating system level is beyond the scope of this discussion. Just be aware that virtual memory differs from physical memory, and therefore this exception doesn't necessarily mean that the machine has run out of memory. All it means is that the application has exhausted its virtual memory address space. An example of such a mishap is shown here:

```
var lst = new List<byte[]>();
while (true) {
    lst.Add(new byte[1024 * 1024]);
}
```

Obviously, real-world issues will be more subtle than the preceding example. Nevertheless, the presence of a garbage collector makes memory leaks much less likely, and the occurrence of an OutOfMemoryException generally points to a design flaw in your program (for example, loading gigantic files all at once rather than piecemeal).

So that you understand the nonexistent relationship between the machine's total physical memory consumption and the virtual memory exhaustion by a single program, see Figure 23.17, which illustrates the memory situation at the point of the crash, broken in the debugger.

Notice how physical memory consumption is at 53% at the point the Exceptions.exe process crashes. Another piece of data that matters quite a bit here is the "bitness" of the process. Because the application was compiled as an x86-specific application, its user mode address space is (by default) limited to 2GB, which we're getting close to at the point of the crash. To show this, the Commit Size column was added to the Task Manager.

For more information about OS-level memory management techniques, virtual memory, and page files, refer to books covering general operating system design or (more specifically) Windows internals.

FIGURE 23.17   `OutOfMemoryException` does not refer to physical memory.

StackOverflowException

Besides the heap memory, there's another finite resource in an application: its stack used to keep track of local variables, method calls, and evaluation of expressions. When this resource gets exhausted, a `StackOverflowException` results. Again, this is one of the exception types that's uncatchable because properly dealing with such a circumstance is far from trivial. (You shouldn't cause any further stack usage doing so.)

Typically, a `StackOverflowException` indicates an unbounded recursive algorithm in your code (which is a bug) or the fact you're processing "deep" recursive data structures. Let's take a look at a few examples:

```
void BlowUp() {
    BlowUp();
}
```

Depending on the amount of state kept for every frame on the call stack (for example, the use of local variables), the number of recursive method calls that can be made will vary. In the preceding example, I managed to make about 16,000 calls before disaster struck.

Recognizing the source of a stack overflow is fairly straightforward: Look at the Call Stack window at the point of the crash and spot the repeating call pattern. From there, try to figure out why the recursion happens in the first place or why it doesn't finish properly. Figure 23.18 shows the Call Stack window revealing a stack overflow exception.

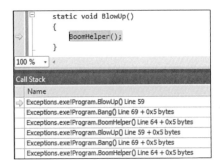

FIGURE 23.18   Repetitive method calling pattern leading to stack overflow.

Recursive algorithms are typically data-driven (for example, visiting a data structure to perform certain actions on individual parts of it). A good sample is a tree:

```
class TreeNode<T> {
    public TreeNode<T> Left { get; set; }
    public TreeNode<T> Right { get; set; }
    public T Value { get; set; }
}
```

A recursive algorithm can be written to visit every node in the tree (for example, using a "depth-first" traversal algorithm):

```
void Visit<T>(TreeNode<T> node) {
    if (node.Left != null)
        Visit(node.Left);
    if (node.Right != null)
        Visit(node.Right);
    Console.WriteLine(node.Value);
}
```

The following piece of code will then write 1, 2, and 3 to the screen:

```
Visit(
    new TreeNode<int> { Value = 3,
        Left  = new TreeNode<int> { Value = 1 },
        Right = new TreeNode<int> { Value = 2 }
    });
```

A deep tree may exhaust the evaluation stack due to the recursive Visit method diving deeper and deeper into the tree data structure:

```
var t = new TreeNode<int> { Value = 1 };
for (int i = 0; i < 100000; i++)
    t = new TreeNode<int> { Value = i, Left = t };

Visit(t);
```

The tree constructed iteratively here is shown in Figure 23.19. Empirically, I found out the maximum tree depth that the algorithm can deal with to be around 25,000 nodes.

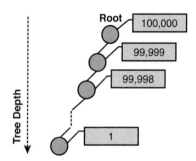

FIGURE 23.19   Deep tree data structure.

The main question to ask in situations such as these is whether such a big highly nested data structure is realistic. (Perhaps it indicates a bug in the code that generates the data structure in the first place.)

If it's realistic for your application to deal with such data structures for one reason or another, you might want to trade the recursive algorithm for one that emulates a stack by using a stack collection (like Stack<T>). We won't go into detail about this because it gets quite specialized and is really a subject for a class on data structures and algorithms.

TAIL CALLS

Some recursive methods are really *tail recursive*, which means that recursive calls happen all the way at the end of any execution path throughout the method. For example:

```
void CountUp(int n) {
    Console.WriteLine(n);
    CountUp(n + 1);
}
```

This piece of code will blow up on a stack overflow because of endless recursive calls to CountUp. As a C# developer, you'll say, "Why don't you write this as a loop in the first place?" That's right, but a functional programmer will more likely think in terms of recursion rather than imperative-style loops. In F#, the preceding code looks like this:

```
let rec countUp n =
    printf "%d\n" n;
    countUp (n + 1)
```

In F#, this recursion won't blow up because the compiler has detected the method to be tail recursive, emitting code as if you had written the following C#-style code:

```
void countUp(int n) {
    while (true) {
        printf("%d\n", n);
        n++;
    }
}
```

If you like reasoning in terms of recursion and want compiler intelligence to take care of figuring out how to make your recursive code work, F# is something for you to take a closer look at.

In fact, the concept of tail recursion is known by the runtime, as well, with a tail call instruction available. Tail calls work only when no further code needs to run after a recursive call is made, allowing the runtime to reuse the same stack frame for the call. The F# compiler can emit such calls when build settings allow it by means of a `tailcalls` compiler flag. Because (this kind of) recursion is rarely used in C# programs, the C# compiler never emits the tail call instruction.

ExecutionEngineException

Congratulations, you found a bug in the CLR. If you ever see this exception type pop up, make sure to let the CLR people at Microsoft know through channels like Connect. Not to discourage you, but I have not seen a single occurrence of this exception in my 10 years of experience with the platform.

Readers with a hacking mindset are invited to corrupt the process's memory through some native debugger to mimic an error condition in the execution engine. Chances are you'll cause it to throw this exception to acknowledge your disruptive interactions. Let's move on to something more realistic.

ArgumentException

Still in the proximity of the bug-indicating exceptions category, we've landed at exception types you should be throwing yourself as well to indicate *your* API users are doing something silly or unexpected. `ArgumentException` is such an exception, signaling a parameter has an unsupported value.

For example, the `File.OpenRead` method will throw this exception when:

```
path is a zero-length string, contains only white space, or contains one or more
invalid characters as defined by System.IO.Path.InvalidPathChars.
```

When accepting a path from some external source (such as the user), those requirements can be checked before calling the API. Alternatively, you could catch the exception to signal the mishap, but checks upfront are generally more desirable (for example, to reject user input with direct feedback in the UI before any operation is attempted). However, this depends, case by case. In most instances, I treat the occurrence of this type of exception as a bug in my code.

Notice that the list of documented exceptions shows up in IntelliSense as soon as you type the member name. Figure 23.20 shows this for the `File.OpenRead` method.

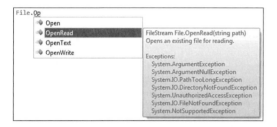

FIGURE 23.20   Documented exceptions for `File.OpenRead`.

The most commonly used constructor overload for `ArgumentException` looks as follows:

```
public ArgumentException(string message, string paramName);
```

For the second parameter, specify the name of the parameter that received an invalid value. This data can be retrieved again through the `ParamName` property.

ArgumentNullException

`ArgumentNullException` is the little, more specialized, brother of `ArgumentException` and is used to signal an unexpected null reference supplied for a parameter. Again, it pinpoints a missing null check in your code and should be treated seriously. Ask yourself how the null reference got to that very place in the code to begin with.

Extinguish the evil null reference as close to its root possible (for example, an entry point to the component you're developing). And the way to do it is by throwing exactly this exception. Constructors typically used for this purpose include the following:

```
public ArgumentNullException(string paramName);
public ArgumentNullException(string paramName, string message);
```

The first constructor often suffices because the meaning of a null argument doesn't need much more explanation other than its parameter.

THE API HALL OF SHAME AND FXCOP

If you choose to use the second overload, notice the little mess-up made by the framework designers back in the early .NET days: The paramName and message parameters are opposite compared to the ones on `ArgumentException`. As a band-aid, the FxCop rule "Microsoft.Usage CA2208" was introduced, which detects swapped arguments on the constructors of those exception types. It does so by inspecting the string passed to the paramName parameter against all the method's parameter names that are present.

EXTENSION METHODS

A question that comes up sometimes is what exception type to use when an extension method's this parameter receives a null reference. At the call site, it looks like an instance method call, so a `NullReferenceException` may be the most natural thing to expect:

```
var res = source.Where(n => n > 0); // LINQ's Where operator
```

However, `NullReferenceException` should really be reserved for real attempts to dereference a null reference, as detected by the runtime. This becomes especially apparent when the extension method is written as a regular static method call:

```
var res = Enumerable.Where(source, n => n > 0);
```

Here you don't expect a `NullReferenceException` at all.

ArgumentOutOfRangeException

Similar in spirit to the `IndexOutOfRangeException` for arrays, this exception type is used to signal a supplied argument is outside some range. Once more, it typically indicates sloppy input validation on the side of the caller, which should be avoidable in general.

Examples of the use of this exception type include the various collection data types in `System.Collections` and its sub-namespaces:

```
var lst = new List<int> { 1, 2, 3 };
int thereIsNoThirdElement = lst[3];
```

Use of the exception type for your own APIs is straightforward using constructors similar to the ones seen for `ArgumentException` (with the paramName coming first). As a little reminder, keep in mind that *argument* and *index* are distinct concepts. Use of this type of exception doesn't imply any particular member type (like an indexer) or a specific data type (like a numeric value) is to be used. It's equally valid for a method to throw an exception of this type to signal its string argument was outside a range of acceptable values.

InvalidOperationException

When an operation is carried out on an object that's not in a valid state to do so, this exception type is raised. Sometimes this is due to not following a certain "protocol" that may be documented informally in the documentation for the type. For example, an object might need some kind of Initialize call before any other members can be called. As a concrete example, consider the `SqlConnection` class from `System.Data.SqlClient`:

```
using (SqlConnection conn = new SqlConnection(connString)) {
    Console.WriteLine(conn.ServerVersion);
}
```

Here the ServerVersion property getter will throw the discussed exception because the connection hasn't been opened yet by calling conn.Open().

This exception is also commonly thrown when enumerating over a collection while it's being modified. This invalidates enumerator objects that are in use because all sorts of things could have happened to the collection underneath. Although you might think all collection change operations could be accounted for inside the enumerator, there are quite a few interesting situations that can arise. For example, MoveNext may already have said there's still an element to follow, but a change happening immediately thereafter might get rid of the element. This would break the contract that a MoveNext call returning true ensures that the subsequent call to the Current method will succeed. For reasons such as these, any further use of the enumerator after a collection modification is simply disallowed:

```
var lst = new List<int> { 1, 2, 3 };
foreach (var n in lst)
    lst.Add(n);
```

NotImplementedException

As the name pretty much implies, this exception results whenever a method or member is not implemented. This can indicate you're dealing with a stub for functionality that's not yet implemented. Visual Studio's code editor Implement Interface feature uses this exception type for the method stubs it generates, as shown in Figure 23.21.

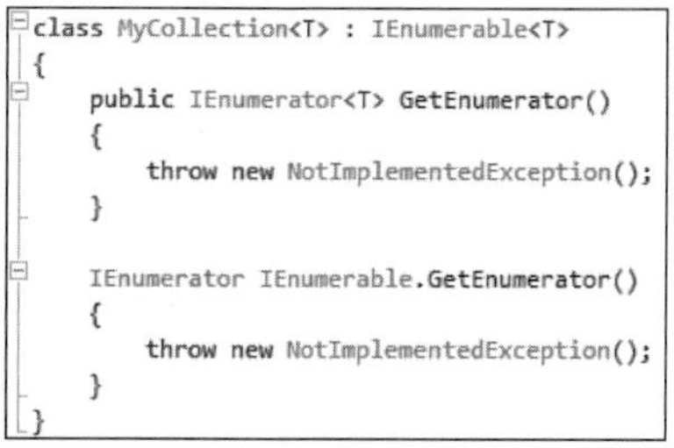

```
class MyCollection<T> : IEnumerable<T>
{
    public IEnumerator<T> GetEnumerator()
    {
        throw new NotImplementedException();
    }

    IEnumerator IEnumerable.GetEnumerator()
    {
        throw new NotImplementedException();
    }
}
```

FIGURE 23.21   Code generated by Visual Studio's Implement Interface feature.

From a code-generation point of view, this is very beneficial because throwing an exception makes the compiler's flow analysis happy as well: If a method has to return an object, throwing an exception instead is the simplest way to make the generated code compile.

The use of NotImplementedException should be reserved to indicate missing functionality as opposed to signaling an operation is not supported. The former exception type is more often used for stubs, whereas the use of NotSupportedException indicates that a certain interface member implementation doesn't make sense in the context of the type that implements it. We come back to this in a second.

NotSupportedException

NotSupportedException doesn't indicate an implementation of an operation is not present; instead, it means the operation *doesn't make sense* to implement. You might wonder why the operation isn't just omitted in such a case, but often you don't have a choice but to provide it when an interface is implemented or a base class has to be used.

Examples of the use of this exception type can be found in the System.IO namespace when dealing with Stream objects that do not support certain operations, such as Seek. It's not uncommon for custom derived stream objects to support only a fraction of the base class's functionality, hence warranting the use of NotSupportedException to indicate the missing functionality.

Another place where NotSupportedException occurs is in the code that gets emitted by the C# compiler for the implementation of an iterator. As you remember from our discussion about LINQ, iterators implement the IEnumerator<T> interface, which has a Reset method on it. However, this method gets a stock implementation that throws this exception:

```
static IEnumerator<int> GetNumbers() {
    int i = 0;
    while (true)
        yield return i++;
}

static void Main() {
    var nums = GetNumbers();
    if (nums.MoveNext())
        Console.WriteLine(nums.Current);

    // Oops, we advanced the enumerator too far. Let's try to reset it...
    nums.Reset();                      // Throws a NotSupportedException.

    if (nums.MoveNext())
        Console.WriteLine(nums.Current);
}
```

The Reset method was a bit of overengineering back in the .NET 1.0 days, mainly present for COM interop purposes (compare the IEnumVARIANT COM interface). Because the interface specifies this method may throw the NotSupportedException, it's not much worth as an abstraction we can rely on in general. In addition, it never gets called by the code emitted for foreach loops.

Because of all those reasons, Reset is mostly unused, and the C# iterator feature doesn't bother to support it either. Iterators are one of the most complex language features in terms of code generation, so avoiding further complication for an additional marginally useful Reset method was a welcome simplification. And if you really want to reset an iterator, just request a new one (which is a cheap operation anyway):

```
static void Main() {
    var nums = GetNumbers();
    if (nums.MoveNext())
        Console.WriteLine(nums.Current);

    // Want to start with 0 again... Simply get a new iterator object.
    nums = GetNumbers();
    if (nums.MoveNext())
        Console.WriteLine(nums.Current);
}
```

In general, seeing a NotSupportedException means your code is calling something it shouldn't reach out to. However, when calling through an abstraction like a Stream object that's handed in from the outside, things are a bit more complicated: Should you just call the Seek method and be prepared to catch an exception, or what? It turns out the availability of the Seek method is paired with a CanSeek property one can check before attempting to make the call.

This sample from the System.IO space should give you a good idea of how to deal with API design that introduces an interface or base class with operations that are allowed to be unsupported by implementers or subtypes. In such a case, it's unreasonable for users of the API to catch a NotSupportedException simply to figure out what they can do with the object they received. Provide Can-prefixed properties instead, which should be implemented or overridden to signal an operation's availability.

FormatException

Quite often, string objects are used to accept inputs that have a certain structured form, like a number's string representation or a URI. In such a case, the String type does not support enough validation of input by itself, and additional checking will be carried out by the consumer of the string object. For example, a number consists of digits, possibly with a decimal separator character, a sign character, or an exponent used in scientific notation. If this form is not respected for the string-based input, a FormatException is raised.

An example can be found on the static Parse methods on numeric types:

```
int invalid = int.Parse("Hello");
```

Notice that those methods provide additional parameters to regulate accepted input formats (for example, when a hexadecimal format is used) and the culture to use. The latter is important when dealing with localized user input where different characters are used for various parts of a number (for example, for the decimal separator sign), depending on the culture:

```
var res = int.Parse("1A", NumberStyles.HexNumber,
                NumberFormatInfo.InvariantInfo);
```

FormatException can often be prevented by checking the input by using a TryParse method provided on the same types.

Throw an exception of this type to signal invalid string input. While you're at it, writing the validation and parsing code, it's often not much trouble to add a separate method that does only the validation:

```
public static bool TryParse(string input, out MyData data) {
    // Parse the input, e.g. using System.Text.RegularExpressions.
}

public static MyData Parse(string input) {
    MyData res;
    if (!TryParse(input, out res))
        throw new FormatException(...);
    return res;
}
```

AggregateException

Exceptions are dealt with on a per-thread basis. However, with an increased emphasis on parallel computing, the situation of having multiple exceptions flowing on different threads becomes a new challenge. When an API spawns parallel tasks and multiple exceptions are thrown from the different executing tasks, you don't want to be able to analyze all those from the outside, too.

A good example is the new System.Threading parallel constructs introduced in .NET 4, including parallel loop constructs exposed on the Parallel static class:

```
Parallel.For(0, 10, i => {
    if (i % 2 == 0)
        throw new Exception("Even number!");

    // Do meaningful work.
});
```

The preceding code spawns parallel tasks for each of the loop body executions, executing the specified lambda expression with the loop iteration value as the input. The For call by itself waits until all the parallel tasks finish. Inside the loop's body, an exception can occur, which needs to be surfaced somehow on the call to For. However, having parallel tasks going on, it's possible that any number of those fail.

Because only one exception can be thrown by the For method, all the tasks' exceptions are collected and thrown using a single AggregateException that exposes all of those using an InnerExceptions property:

```
public class AggregateException : Exception {
    ...
    public ReadOnlyCollection<Exception> InnerExceptions { get; }
}
```

When doing parallel programming, you'll get used to dealing with this type of exception if the individual parallel tasks may be throwing exceptions you are willing to handle from the outside. A useful Handle method is available to analyze all the exceptions and to handle them selectively:

```
public void Handle(Func<Exception, bool> predicate);
```

The predicate delegate gets called for all the exceptions in the AggregateException's InnerExceptions collection, one by one. If you answer true, indicating you did handle the exception, for all of them, the method simply returns. If any exception was left unhandled (that is, one or more of the delegate invocations returned false), the unhandled exceptions are collected in an AggregateException, which is thrown from Handle.

Besides Handle, a Flatten method is available to flatten AggregateExceptions that are contained in the InnerExceptions collection, into a single AggregateException. This comes in handy when dealing with nested parallel calls, like two Parallel.For calls. The inner Parallel.For call may throw an AggregateException, which will get wrapped in another AggregateException by the outer Parallel.For. To get rid of the intermediate aggregations, you can use Flatten.

Summary

In this chapter, you learned why exceptions are important and how to deal with them, both from a consumer and producer perspective. You saw how to catch exceptions with the try statement and learned about its associated catch and finally blocks. This chapter also covered several best practices related to when and why (or why not) to catch exceptions. With regard to producing exceptions, we discussed creating our own exception types.

We also covered some of the most essential often-used exception types that appear in the .NET Framework's BCL.

IN THIS CHAPTER

▶ Organizing Types in
  Namespaces 1213

▶ Declaring Namespaces 1219

▶ Importing Namespaces 1223

While proceeding with our study of the C# programming language and the .NET platform, we've been combining smaller constructs into larger ones. First, we studied what expressions can do for us, followed by a chapter on statements. Next, we grouped those code blocks into members that get organized into types.

Finally, we've arrived at the topmost constructs, which allow for the organization of types into a hierarchical naming scheme and act as containers for deployment. The first is a language construct known as namespaces, also supporting cross-language scenarios. The second is assemblies, which are the CLR's model for code, metadata, and resource containers.

In this chapter, you learn how to organize your types in namespaces and thus avoid name clashes and provide for a logical organization of functionality. Besides declaring namespaces, you also see how to import and use them, including some more tricky scenarios with aliases and extern aliases.

Organizing Types in Namespaces

Simply stated, namespaces provide a way to establish a hierarchical naming scheme for types in .NET libraries and applications. At the language level, it's possible to declare new namespaces containing various types. Besides providing namespaces, there's also the act of using them, which is based on the concept of importing them in code.

One level below the language, the runtime doesn't really know much about namespaces because types always are referred to by a fully qualified name. Where a full type name looks like `System.Collections.Generic.List<int>`, you can simply write `List<int>` if the containing namespace has been imported. In other words, using namespaces yields an abbreviation of type names.

Once Upon a Time

In the world of Win32 and COM, there's little support to organize code in logical units, resulting in a flat application programming interface (API). Although C++ has a notion of namespaces, lots of APIs originate from earlier times when the use of namespaces wasn't part of the design philosophy for those APIs.

For example, Win32 is basically an API consisting of functions and some data types, with no object-oriented aspirations. All those functions live in a single "namespace," and therefore it's perfectly possible to run into situations where two functions with the same name will clash. Such a problem manifests itself at compile time because the compiler (and in C/C++, we should also mention the linker) can't figure out what you mean. To reduce this problem a bit, you can use header files to establish some organization, although problems can still occur when multiple headers are included:

```
#include <windows.h>

void SaveData(__in LPCWSTR file)
{
    HANDLE hFile = CreateFile(file,
                        GENERIC_WRITE,
                        0,
                        NULL,
                        CREATE_ALWAYS,
                        FILE_ATTRIBUTE_NORMAL,
                        NULL);
```

Besides the potential for name clashes, other problems exist with a flat declaration space. One such problem has to do with discoverability of APIs. As you can imagine, the number of functions or data types available can explode very quickly, especially when meaty header files (such as windows.h) are included. Although various functions logically belong together (for example, the ones dealing with file I/O), nothing reflects this.

Figure 24.1 illustrates just a tiny subset of all the functions that start with `Create`, creating a huge search burden for developers unfamiliar with the APIs.

Although part of the issue stems from the lack of types to encapsulate state and bundle it with functions operating on that state, things are still quite messy in the world of COM, where interfaces provide a better logical organization. In some sense, all this buys us at the level of API structuring is reducing one level of clutter, while we're still faced with a challenge of finding interfaces and auxiliary types that typically live in one single flat namespace:

```
HRESULT hr;

// The following interface is declared in a flat namespace.
IBackgroundCopyJob* pJob = ...;

hr = pJob->AddFile(L"http://foo/bar.txt", L"c:\\temp\\bar.txt");
if (SUCCEEDED(hr))
{
    ...
}
```

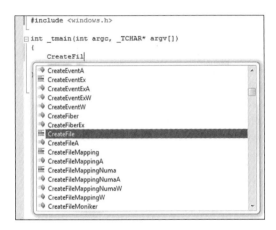

FIGURE 24.1   Win32 functions live in a flat namespace.

Figure 24.2 shows the use of a COM API, where this time all interfaces get lumped together in a flat declaration space, often improving on the situation a little bit by using some prefix scheme for interface names.

Furthermore, now that we've introduced some level of typing in APIs, we get a "nice" mix of top-level functions, interfaces, enums, and so on (all lumped together). This is similar to having folders in a file system but sticking a whole bunch of files in the root folder anyway.

Also notice the somewhat-related problems (elaborated on during our discussion of assemblies in Chapter 25, "Assemblies, and Application Domains") of versioning, creating cryptic type names with integer suffixes or Win32 functions with an Ex suffix (for extended).

FIGURE 24.2   COM interfaces push the declaration space problem one level up.

HEADER NIGHTMARES

The use of headers in C and C++ is a notorious source of headaches. Various reasons come to mind, including the problems with duplicate definitions (requiring use of preprocessor tricks), the order of inclusion, and the separate notion of lib files that have to be linked in for things to work.

In the world of .NET, assemblies are self-describing and also act as the means to refer to a library during development time. Although reference assemblies are dehydrated from a code perspective (hence they're somewhat like very rich headers, including type and member information), they don't suffer from the problems related to headers.

It's clear that the approaches taken by the C-influenced world of Win32, COM, and so on have various drawbacks, such as the following:

▶ Discoverability of APIs is quite painful because all functions and types live in a single flat namespace (which can also lead to name clashes).

▶ Tooling can't help much with finding APIs, and providing decent IntelliSense support is challenging.

▶ Building applications requires multiple references to libraries, including the use of headers and a link-time reference to a library file.

Assemblies and Namespaces

Because several of the previously mentioned problems are related, it's good to take a look at them collectively. One central issue has to do with tooling, where the requirement of headers describing binary libraries can be solved by bundling this metadata with the code of the library. This is precisely what assemblies do, as shown in Figure 24.3.

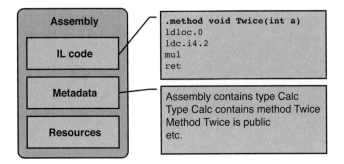

FIGURE 24.3   Assemblies contain code, metadata, and resources.

To solve the second issue, which involves avoidance of name clashes for types across multiple libraries, the concept of namespaces has been introduced. Notice that this problem does not directly affect methods because they are contained inside types. Although global methods are supported at the CLR level, they're not exposed by various managed code languages (including C#).

By coming up with a naming scheme consisting (by convention) of a company name, followed by a product name, and possibly a hierarchy of component names, you can avoid name clashes when composing such libraries in a larger context (such as an application). For example:

```
namespace Contoso.CashFlow.Client
{
    public sealed class Terminal
    {
        ...
    }
}
```

Here we have created a hierarchy of three nested namespaces, abbreviated using the dot notation to separate the parts. Now it's perfectly fine for another company like the sample company Fabrikam to have another class called Terminal or even to have a clash at a namespace below the company level.

Inside the CLR, namespaces are essentially part of type names, which just get a whole lot longer. At the language level, as you see later, you can avoid having to write those long type names by importing the namespace. If multiple such namespaces are imported and a type name is used that occurs in multiple of those (for example, Terminal, which was defined by both companies), you will have to disambiguate the name (for example, by using the full type name including the interface). Figure 24.4 shows the IL code emitted for a method that constructs a Terminal object from Contoso's CashFlow Client library. It does so from a different assembly, referencing the one containing the Terminal type.

```
using Contoso.CashFlow.Client;

class Program
{
    static void Main()
    {
        var t = new Terminal();
    }
}
```

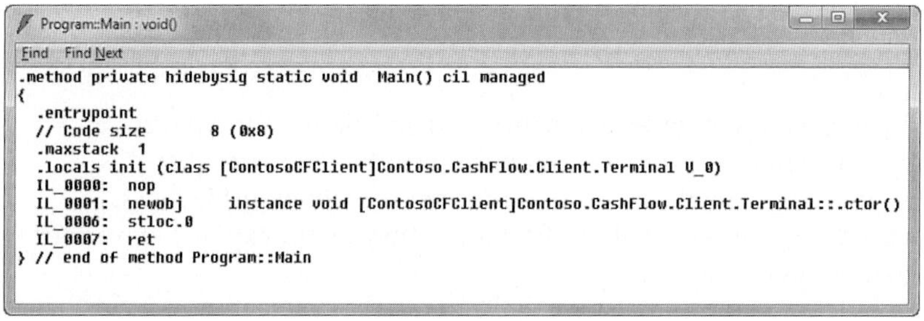

```
Program::Main : void()                                              [ _ ] [ □ ] [ X ]

Find   Find Next

.method private hidebysig static void  Main() cil managed
{
  .entrypoint
  // Code size       8 (0x8)
  .maxstack  1
  .locals init (class [ContosoCFClient]Contoso.CashFlow.Client.Terminal V_0)
  IL_0000:  nop
  IL_0001:  newobj      instance void [ContosoCFClient]Contoso.CashFlow.Client.Terminal::.ctor()
  IL_0006:  stloc.0
  IL_0007:  ret
} // end of method Program::Main
```

FIGURE 24.4   Namespaces are merely an illusion created by front-end languages.

On the first line of this C# fragment, we're importing the namespace, such that we can simply write Terminal rather than the long type name (including the namespace). At the IL level, though, the full type name is used.

In front of the fully qualified type name Contoso.CashFlow.Client.Terminal, another name is specified in between brackets. This corresponds to the name of the assembly defining the type. Here we've compiled the Terminal type into an assembly with the name ContosoCFClient. For the CLR to know where to find the type being referred to, it needs to know what assembly to look in.

This brings us to a discussion about the difference between namespaces and assemblies. In short, the two are mostly unrelated concepts. The name of an assembly doesn't dictate what namespaces can be defined inside it, nor does the name of a type (and its namespace) pose restrictions on which assembly it can be defined in. The only real relationship between both concepts is the fact that assemblies contain types and types live in namespaces, and therefore assemblies contain namespaces. In fact, the definition of a namespace can be spread across multiple assemblies, as exemplified by the framework assemblies System.dll (which, for instance, contains the System.Uri class) and mscorlib.dll (containing types like System.String).

MSCORLIB VERSUS SYSTEM

Why are there multiple assemblies defining types of the Framework's top-level System namespace? The answer is partly historical and partly technical.

One of the more technical arguments is that mscorlib.dll has quite a few types that aren't just managed but make so-called internal calls into functionality that's defined at the CLR level. A good example of such a type is `System.Object`, which has many runtime representations and relies on CLR code for some of its core operations (such as `GetType`, which talks to metadata services).

When building applications in languages like C#, mscorlib will always be included by default, and so will System.dll. You can easily get rid of the latter if you really want to for some obscure reason, by dropping it from the referenced assembly list in Visual Studio's Solution Explorer. To exclude mscorlib.dll, you must dig a little deeper in the Project properties, under Build, Advanced.

Declaring Namespaces

To declare a new namespace, use the `namespace` keyword in C#:

```
namespace Contoso.CashFlow.Client
{
    // Classes, structs, interfaces, enums, delegates, etc. can go in here
}
```

The default namespace chosen for new code files in a Visual Studio project is based on a setting specified for the project. This setting, shown in Figure 24.5, gets its default value from the name of the project upon creation. The output assembly name follows this default inferred value, too. It's considered good practice to reflect the top-level namespace for types defined in an assembly in the assembly's name. For example, the `System.Web` assembly (mostly) contains `System.Web` functionality.

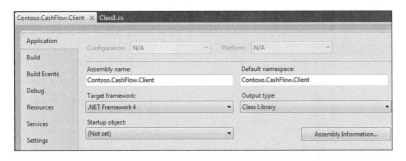

FIGURE 24.5   Default namespace configuration setting.

Namespaces can be nested in a variety of ways. One is using the dot-separated notation for namespace names, which really establishes a hierarchy of nested namespaces. As an alternative, you can physically nest namespace declarations in one another:

```
namespace Contoso
{
    namespace CashFlow
    {
        namespace Client
        {
            // Types could go here...
            // ...as well as other subnamespaces
        }

        // More types could go here...
        // ...as well as namespaces that are siblings to Client
    }

    // And so on...
}
```

The dot notation is usually preferred because it avoids large indentation levels in code files, and it is better to avoid declaring multiple sibling namespaces in the same file.

It's advisable to reflect the namespace and type structure in the project's directory name and filename structure. The root folder of the project corresponds to the top-level namespace, subfolders to nested namespaces, and files to type names.

Visual Studio will infer the namespace for a new code file based on the folder in which it's located, as shown in Figure 24.6. The namespace name can always be changed in the code itself, but following this folder and file pattern is usually beneficial in terms of finding declarations quickly (especially if you're doing so outside the IDE without the aid of tools such as Class View or Object Explorer).

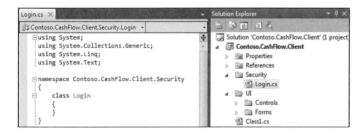

FIGURE 24.6   Visual Studio reflects folder structure in namespace names.

From a runtime and language compiler point of view, the physical location of a code file doesn't have any impact whatsoever. All that matters is what the code says about namespace and type names. What the runtime sees are types with unique names within an assembly.

THE DIFFERENT JAVA LANDSCAPE

In the world of Java, things work out quite differently because .class files (the binaries corresponding to type definitions) are structured in packages, whose hierarchical names are reflected in folder names and filenames. In .NET, the unit of deployment is an assembly rather than an individual type's compilation binary. You learn in Chapter 25 how the runtime locates assemblies and types therein.

Naming Conventions

Concerning naming, the convention is to use the company name for the top-level namespace name, followed by a product name, a series of (sub)component names, and finally the types within those components. You can find examples of this in the .NET Framework redistributable itself, where the Microsoft namespace is used for anything that isn't part of the core framework (see sidebar) (for example, Microsoft.Win32 for Win32 API wrappers, such as Registry access).

THE HOLY SYSTEM NAMESPACE

Core parts of the assemblies that ship with the .NET Framework redistributable collectively define the System namespace and its many subnamespaces. Use of this namespace is reserved for Microsoft and the companies participating in the definition the ECMA standard of the .NET Framework libraries.

Platform-specific APIs, such as Registry access, which only applies to the Microsoft Windows platform, are defined outside the platform-neutral System namespace and follow the Microsoft.* pattern.

The main reason to use the company name for the top-level namespace name is to avoid name clashes across components delivered by different companies. Since C# 2.0, such an ambiguity can also be resolved using extern aliases, as discussed later.

Visibility

Namespaces don't have a notion of visibility. In C# terms, you could say namespaces are implicitly declared as public because they can't be used to restrict visibility of the types defined within them. In other words, it's up to the types (and members therein) to declare their visibility.

Figure 24.7 illustrates how namespaces are totally compiled away into longer type names, which is what the CLR sees. In other words, there's no place in an assembly to put metadata (such as visibility) on a namespace declaration. What tools like ILDASM and .NET

Reflector do is show types in their namespaces by analyzing the dot-separated pattern followed for their naming. The fact there's no such thing as metadata associated with a namespace is *reflected* in the lack of a `NamespaceInfo` object in the reflection APIs.

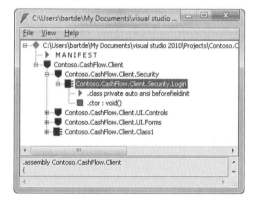

FIGURE 24.7   Namespaces don't survive compilation and become part of type names.

Name Clashes Within Namespaces

The "construct" on which the C# compiler operates when turning code into an assembly is called a compilation unit, which in practice maps to a code file. All of those units are processed together, almost as if it were one large file containing all the declarations made in the code.

Multiple occurrences of the same namespace are just fine. In more official terms, the language considers namespaces *open ended*. Other compilation units processed by the compiler are free to add more declarations to a namespace:

```
// File1.cs
namespace Contoso.CashFlow.Client
{
    class A { ... }
}


// File2.cs
namespace Contoso.CashFlow.Client
{
    class B { ... }
}
```

When multiple types with the same name are declared in the same namespace, it results in an error, as illustrated in Figure 24.8. One good way to avoid such name clashes is to adhere to a folder name and filename structure, as discussed earlier.

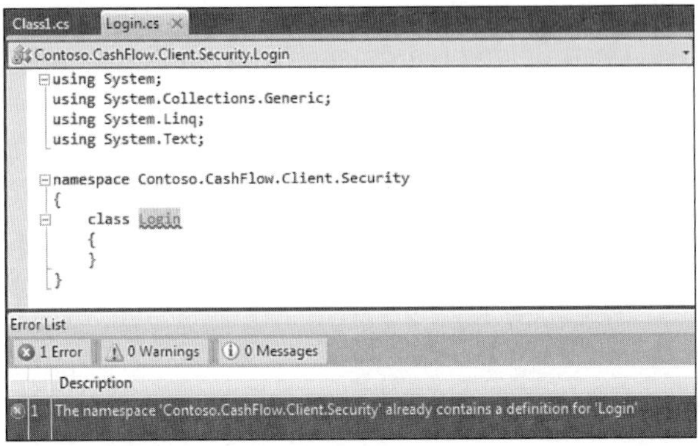

FIGURE 24.8   Name clashes across multiple files don't go unnoticed.

Importing Namespaces

In C#, the way to import namespaces is by means of the `using` directive. As a result, instead of having to use fully qualified type names, you can refer to types by a shorter name. Leveraging using directives simply affects the name resolution carried out by the compiler. At runtime, types are always referred to by fully qualified names, as you saw before in Figure 24.4.

Using directives are scoped to the immediately enclosing compilation unit (that is, code file) or the namespace declaration in which they're contained. For example, given the following code, you can refer to types in the `System` namespace directly:

```
using System;

namespace Contoso.CashFlow.Client
{
    class Program
    {
        static void Main()
        {
            DateTime d = DateTime.Now; // Instead of System.DateTime.
        }
    }
}
```

You can't apply the `using` directive to partial namespace names, based on what has been imported already. In other words, it's not possible to write the following:

```
using System;
using Collections; // Error: this won't refer to System.Collections
```

Because of this, the order of using directives doesn't matter semantically. They all stand by themselves, also allowing for tooling to clean up and reorder directives, as shown in Figure 24.9.

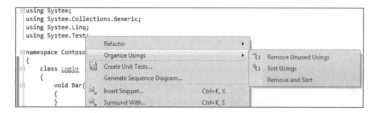

FIGURE 24.9   The Organize Usings feature in Visual Studio's code editor.

Similarly, you cannot abbreviate type names in piecemeal fashion. To fix the following problem, you must either import System.Collections and refer to Arraylist without any namespace name or use the fully qualified name in its entirety:

```
using System;

namespace Contoso.CashFlow.Client
{
    class Program
    {
        static void Main()
        {
            Collections.ArrayList lst = ...; // Error: can't find it
        }
    }
}
```

Within namespace declarations, it's possible to import namespaces, too. Within a namespace declaration, a bit more flexibility for imports exists, being able to refer to sibling or parent namespaces. For example

```
namespace Contoso.CashFlow.Client.Security
{
    using Client; // Refers to Contoso.CashFlow.Client parent
    using UI;     // Refers to Contoso.CashFlow.Client.UI sibling
    ...
}
```

Name Clashes Due to Imports

Because namespaces were invented to resolve name clashes in some flat global namespace (for example, as seen in Win32), they allow for types with the same (short) name to exist in different namespaces existing alongside each other. When multiple such namespaces containing a type with the same name are imported, a conflict will occur when trying to refer to that particular type.

For example, when adding references to both System.Drawing and WindowsBase (the former of which is used by Windows Forms and the latter by Windows Presentation Foundation [WPF]), multiple definitions of a Point type exist (among many others, such as Size). Figure 24.10 shows the Resolve feature in Visual Studio that can be used to resolve a type name if no using directive for a containing namespace has been specified (yet).

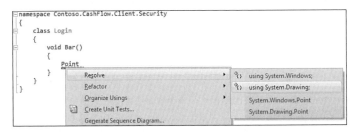

FIGURE 24.10   Resolving a type name in Visual Studio's code editor.

When carrying out the operation shown here, a using directive for System.Drawing will be added to the top of the file, allowing us to refer to the Windows Forms Point type immediately. However, if we also import the System.Windows namespace, we get a name clash when referring to Point, as illustrated in Figure 24.11.

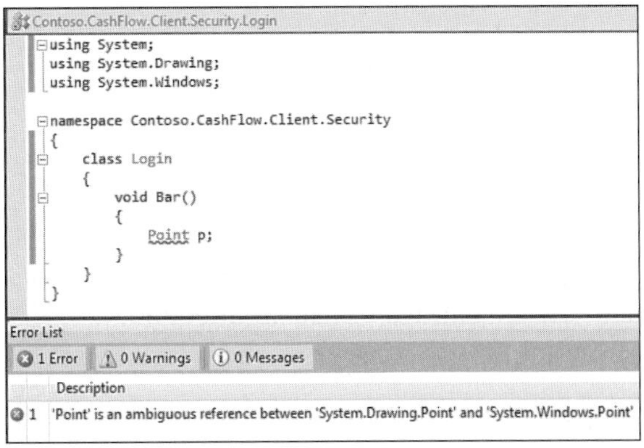

FIGURE 24.11   Ambiguous type name requiring manual resolution.

There are different ways to resolve this conflict, the most obvious of which is to refer to the intended type by its full name. This can be done in a case-by-case manner, only for those types that are subject to a conflict. In other words, there's no need to back out a namespace import because of a single issue:

```
var point = new System.Drawing.Point(3, 4);
```

Again, the Visual Studio feature to resolve names can help here. Other unambiguous names can stay abbreviated. For example

```
// Only in the System.Windows namespace (defined in the WindowsBase assembly).
var vector = new Vector(3, 4);
```

Use of those long type names can hinder code readability, though, especially if several such conflicts occur. To mitigate this issue, C# supports a way to define aliases for namespace imports.

Using Aliases

The using directive can be extended with the definition of a named alias, acting as an abbreviation for the namespace or type name on the right side. An example of this is shown in Chapter 22, "Dynamic Programming," when dealing with the Word and Excel automation APIs. In this context, the Application type exists in both namespaces used for Word and Excel interop. Use of an alias allowed us to abbreviate references to them:

```
using Word  = Microsoft.Office.Interop.Word;
using Excel = Microsoft.Office.Interop.Excel;
```

Now we can write the following two lines of code, disambiguating a reference to the Application interface:

```
var excel = new Excel.Application();
var word  = new Word.Application();
```

Defined aliases are scoped within the containing compilation unit or the immediately enclosing declaration of a namespace.

Aliases can also be used to refer to types, including generic ones as long as they're closed constructed types; that is, no generic parameters are omitted or remain unbound:

```
using WpfPoint = System.Windows.Point;
using IntList  = System.Collections.Generic.List<int>;
```

This feature tends to be used to a lesser extent. Some C++ savvy readers may draw a parallel with typedefs in some native languages. This analogy only holds to a limited degree. For example, it's not possible to have an alias defined in an assembly such that every user of the assembly gets it. This is simply because using directives are lexically scoped within source code files and have no representation at runtime whatsoever. Even though the IL assembler language has similar aliasing mechanisms, the runtime always operates on full type names.

Extern Aliases

Despite the fact naming conventions for namespaces and types exist, it's still possible to end up with ambiguities across different assemblies. One more or less common case is when multiple versions of an assembly need to be referenced (for example, for compatibility scenarios). Those assemblies might have the same namespace and type names, so a new ambiguity arises: Whose assembly's namespace or type is being referred to?

Figure 24.12 shows what happens if both those assemblies contain the following namespace and type, which we attempt to use from our code:

```
namespace Bar
{
    public class Foo
    {
    }
}
```

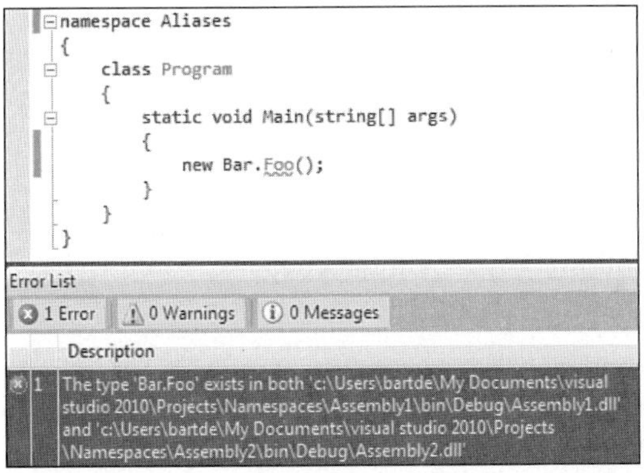

```
namespace Aliases
{
    class Program
    {
        static void Main(string[] args)
        {
            new Bar.Foo();
        }
    }
}
```

Error List

❌ 1 Error	⚠ 0 Warnings	ⓘ 0 Messages
	Description	
⊗ 1	The type 'Bar.Foo' exists in both 'c:\Users\bartde\My Documents\visual studio 2010\Projects\Namespaces\Assembly1\bin\Debug\Assembly1.dll' and 'c:\Users\bartde\My Documents\visual studio 2010\Projects\Namespaces\Assembly2\bin\Debug\Assembly2.dll'	

FIGURE 24.12   Referenced assemblies containing a conflicting type definition.

C# 2.0 introduced the concept of extern aliases to alleviate this problem. To understand this feature, it's important to understand how reference assemblies are passed to the compiler using the /reference flag. For example, compiling an assembly that's referring to System.Drawing and WindowsBase will result in a compiler invocation like this:

```
csc /r:System.Drawing.dll /r:WindowsBase.dll File1.cs File2.cs
```

Starting with C# 2.0, it's possible to specify an alias in front of an assembly passed to the /reference (shorthand /r) flag. This is known as an extern alias:

```
csc /r:X=Assembly1.dll /r:Y=Assembly2.dll File1.cs File2.cs
```

In the preceding example, referring to namespaces and types inside Assembly1.dll can be abbreviated using X, while those in Assembly2.dll are accessible using alias Y. Inside Visual Studio, you can specify extern aliases from the Properties pane for a selected referenced assembly. This is illustrated in Figure 24.13.

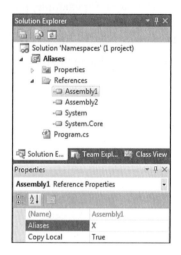

FIGURE 24.13   Configuring extern aliases.

The default value for the Alias property is global, which has a corresponding keyword allowing reference to it. To traverse an alias followed by a namespace name, you use the :: operator, as shown here:

```
global::System.Collections.Generic.IEnumerable<int> numbers = ...;
```

Obviously, the global alias specification can be omitted unless we're trying to resolve a conflict. In our preceding example, we're faced with a conflict for the Bar.Foo type across two assemblies. Assuming we've configured the aliases as X and Y, we can now import those aliases in a code file using the extern keyword:

```
extern alias X;
extern alias Y;
```

Given those two alias imports, we can write the following:

```
var fooFromX = new X::Bar.Foo();
var fooFromY = new Y::Bar.Foo();
```

Notice that assembly-qualified references to types are everyday business in IL code because the runtime requires this form to locate referenced types. Figure 24.14 shows the compiled IL code corresponding to the preceding fragment. All the extern alias feature in C# provides for is syntax to carry out this disambiguation across assemblies containing a type with the same name.

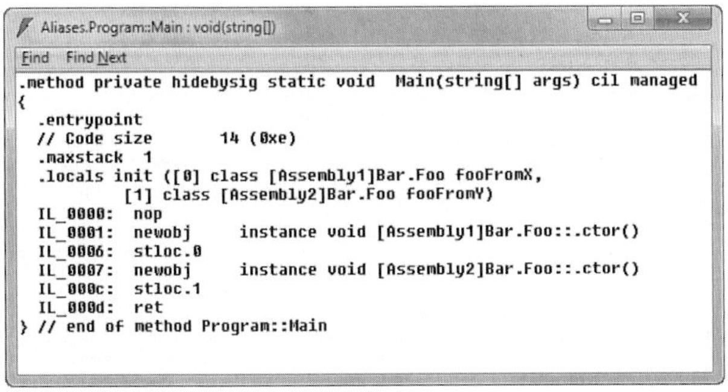

```
 Aliases.Program::Main : void(string[])
 Find   Find Next
.method private hidebysig static void  Main(string[] args) cil managed
{
  .entrypoint
  // Code size       14 (0xe)
  .maxstack  1
  .locals init ([0] class [Assembly1]Bar.Foo FooFromX,
           [1] class [Assembly2]Bar.Foo fooFromY)
  IL_0000:  nop
  IL_0001:  newobj      instance void [Assembly1]Bar.Foo::.ctor()
  IL_0006:  stloc.0
  IL_0007:  newobj      instance void [Assembly2]Bar.Foo::.ctor()
  IL_000c:  stloc.1
  IL_000d:  ret
} // end of method Program::Main
```

FIGURE 24.14   In IL code, types are always prefixed with the assembly in which they're defined.

Use of :: is officially known as namespace alias qualification and can also be used to write super-robust code in the face of potential future changes to code. For example, it's possible to have imported a namespace with an alias that starts to clash with a type name somewhere in the future:

```
// File1.cs
namespace Bar
{
    using Foo = System.Drawing;

    class Program
    {
        private Foo.Point point; // Refers to System.Drawing.Point
    }
}
```

If we now introduce a Bar.Foo type somewhere else, the preceding code will break:

```
// File2.cs
namespace Bar
{
    class Foo
    {
        ...
    }
}
```

The Foo.Point type specified for the field in the Program class now becomes a problem to resolve, as illustrated in Figure 24.15.

FIGURE 24.15   An alias conflicting with a type.

One way to resolve this is by changing the alias being used. Alternatively, the use of aliases can help here, too. In fact, the problem is of a syntactical nature, where the use of the . operator has different meanings. One is to dot off a type name (for example, into static members), whereas another is to dot into namespace hierarchies possibly using aliases. Replacing the . with a namespace alias qualifier using :: will resolve the issue:

```
class Program
{
    public Foo::Point point;
}
```

In short, namespaces help a lot with the logical organization of types in a hierarchical manner, but you should be prepared to resolve some remaining clashes using a variety of techniques as described here.

Extension Methods

As discussed in Chapter 10, "Methods," in the section, "Extension Methods," extension methods piggyback on the using directive to be brought into scope. This is quite special in the language because it makes the resolution of members depend on namespaces, where the using directive only influenced types in the pre-C# 3.0 era. A good example of the use of extension methods is found in LINQ:

```
using System.Linq;

class Program
```

```
{
    static void Main()
    {
        var rabbits = new[] { 1, 1, 2, 3, 5, 8, 13, 21, 34, 55 };
        var evenRes = rabbits.Where(x => x % 2 == 0);
        ...
    }
}
```

Again, the use of using directives is a compile-time thing only because the above is turned into a static Where method call, defined on the System.Linq.Enumerable static class, which lives in the System.Core assembly:

```
var evenRes = Enumerable.Where(rabbits, x => x % 2 == 0);
```

The Where method becomes available for resolution once the System.Linq namespace gets imported. Figure 24.16 illustrates that Visual Studio has special knowledge about the usage pattern of extension methods when using query comprehension syntax.

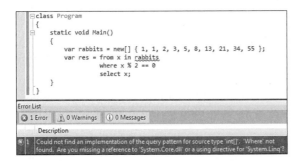

FIGURE 24.16   Visual Studio knows about the LINQ extension methods.

In System.Core, the Where method is defined as follows, highlighting the essential bits that comprise an extension method definition:

```
// Somewhere in System.Core
namespace System.Linq
{
    public static class Enumerable
    {
        public static IEnumerable<T> Where<T>(this IEnumerable<T> source,
                                              Func<T, bool> predicate) { ... }
    }
}
```

Extension methods are resolved by searching for them in enclosing as well as imported namespaces. Instance methods take precedence if an applicable overload is available, preventing the search for extension methods from ever happening. For the full set of rules applied to resolve (extension) methods, refer to the language specification.

Summary

Structuring applications into manageable pieces is a very important task for developers in today's world. As the complexity of applications and components grows, it's ever more important to be able to tame this complexity and find our way around code.

Those observations hold on different levels, ranging from structuring types in logical containers, to runtime aspects where multiple components have to play in concert while reducing risks to an application hosting them. In other words, we need facilities provided by languages and tools to organize and explore types and members, but the runtime also must participate, to realize goals of loading components and providing isolation when needed.

In the camp of languages and tools, we find the notion of namespaces, which are merely enlarged type names from the runtime's point of view. Using a dot-separated naming scheme, a type's name is divided into the type's "short name" and the namespace in which it's contained. When using types, you can import the namespace to abbreviate those long names. However, when many libraries are used, name clashes may occur. In such a case, you can fall back to the long name or introduce aliases. C#'s keywords exposing those principles are namespace, to create a namespace, and using, to import one.

Focusing on the runtime aspect of taming the complexity of large components and application, we explore the concept of assemblies and application domains in the next chapter.

CHAPTER 25

Assemblies and Application Domains

IN THIS CHAPTER

▶ Assemblies 1233

▶ Application Domains 1277

After covering namespaces in the previous chapter, this chapter covers assemblies in detail. We take a look at various types of assemblies you can build from Visual Studio and cover the various settings associated with them. In terms of deployment, we study naming and versioning, as well as the concept of strong names. This provides a segue into the world of the Global Assembly Cache (GAC) for centralized storage of assemblies and the native image generation (NGEN) technology to create native images for intermediate language (IL)-based assemblies. Finally, you'll see that assemblies are more than containers for IL code and can also contain resources and so on.

To wrap up the chapter, we change our focus from the deployment aspect of assemblies to runtime aspects. You'll see how assemblies get loaded and how the common language runtime (CLR) establishes isolation using application domains. We also briefly cover .NET Remoting, a low-level communication mechanism between application domains.

Assemblies

Assemblies are self-describing units of functionality, consisting of code and metadata defining types and their members. Figure 24.3 in Chapter 24, "Namespaces," illustrates what makes up an assembly. In this part of the chapter, we focus on a set of aspects associated with assemblies, ranging from build time to runtime. While exploring assemblies, we discuss their naming and versioning, the concept of strong naming and the Global Assembly Cache (GAC), how they get loaded, visibility aspects, and more.

Modules and Assemblies

Assemblies serve many roles, including the following:

▶ They serve as a typical unit for the deployment of code, associated metadata, and embedded resources.

▶ They act as a means to stimulate code reuse by building libraries that can be reused from different components or applications.

▶ They provide for a versioning story, resolving core issues that existed before in the world of COM with the "DLL hell."

▶ Scoping and visibility allow for "programming in the large," where aspects of an implementation can be hidden.

▶ Security decisions can be made based on an assembly's identity, location, and so on, as well as based on permissions configured on it.

From a deployment point of view, assemblies can consist of one or more files, although it's typical to use a single file nowadays. The parts that make up an assembly are known as *modules*, sometimes referred to as netmodules. In fact, when using .NET Reflector, you've already seen those modules. Figure 25.1 shows how the mscorlib and System assemblies consist of a single module.

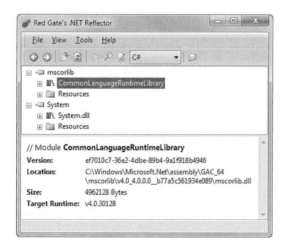

FIGURE 25.1   Modules are included by assemblies.

Although Visual Studio doesn't provide facilities to build and bundle modules, command-line compilers do. Here we'll create an assembly consisting of two modules, each of which is built using a different language.

```
// Compile using:  csc /t:module module1.cs
class CSharp
{
    public void Bar() {}
}

// Compile using:  vbc /t:module module2.vb
Class VisualBasic
    Public Sub Bar()
    End Sub
End Class
```

The preceding code will produce two files called module1.netmodule and module2.netmodule, which can be linked together using a tool called al.exe for Assembly Linker. Alternatively, both the C# and VB compilers have a flag called /addmodule that can be used to link in modules.

With the following command, a multifile assembly is created, including both modules that were created earlier. Figure 25.2 shows the resulting assembly in .NET Reflector:

```
al /target:library /out:sample.dll module1.netmodule module2.netmodule
```

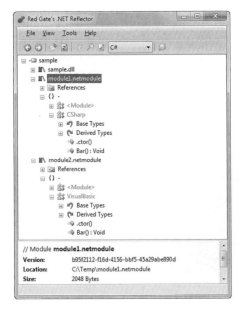

FIGURE 25.2   Multiple modules referred to by a multifile assembly.

Because assemblies typically consist of a single file, we won't cover multifile assemblies extensively in this book; see MSDN documentation for more information. It suffices to know that assemblies are not the smallest unit of deployment supported by the CLR, but the single-file assembly configuration is the most common case.

DO ASSEMBLIES NEED TO BE FILES?

Although most documentation mentions assemblies and (binary) files in the same breath, it's not the case that assemblies are tied to files. All that matters to the CLR is to be given a sequence of bytes that follow a grammar that's well specified in the Common Language Infrastructure (CLI) specification.

One example where assemblies are not physically stored in a separate file on disk is the CLR integration into SQL Server 2005 and later. Here, assemblies are stored in a table and read as a byte sequence to be loaded into the runtime.

Types of Assemblies

Different types of assembly files can be created, depending on their roles. Executable assemblies differentiate from others in that they have an entry-point method and are referred to as applications. Library assemblies contain components that are used by other libraries/applications.

On the Windows platform, executables are stored with an .exe extension and library binaries are stored with a .dll extension. To the CLR, the extension is of little relevance and isn't part of the assembly's name, as you see later. To make assemblies into proper code binaries on the platform, they're stored in Windows PE/COFF format, which stands for Portable Executable, Common Object File Format. Command-line language compilers reveal the output file types that can be generated, as specified through the /target flag, as shown in Figure 25.3.

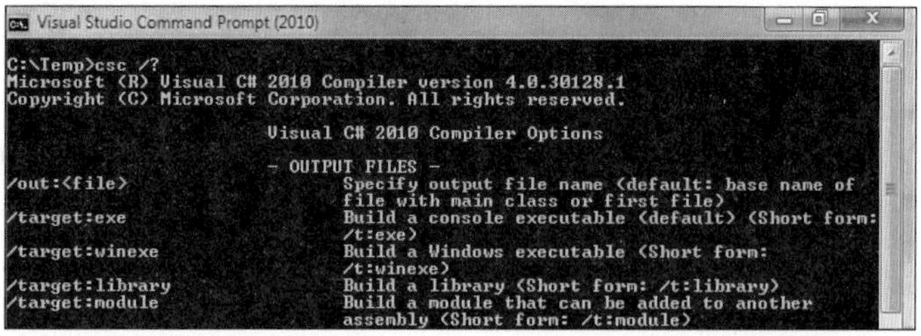

FIGURE 25.3   Output file types supported by the C# compiler.

Those types correspond to Visual Studio project types and a flag in the resulting binary PE/COFF file, indicating to the Windows loader how to treat the file:

▶ The exe target is used by console applications and marks the PE/COFF file to use the CUI or Console UI subsystem.

▶ The winexe target is used by Windows Forms and WPF applications and uses the GUI subsystem so that no console window is shown.

▶ The library target creates a .dll file and is used whenever some kind of Class Library project is used.

We saw the module target before and mentioned the fact that it's not directly supported through Visual Studio's project system. The binary file format is also a PE/COFF file.

SHOWING THE BINARY FILE HEADERS

Geeks might be interested in the underlying file format used by .NET assemblies. On the Visual Studio Command Prompt, use the dumpbin tool to inspect a binary file (for example, using the /headers flag to show the PE/COFF headers). In the output of executable file headers, you'll find an "optional header" called subsystem, revealing CUI or GUI.

Assembly Properties

The configuration of an assembly's properties is done through the project properties in Visual Studio. Figure 25.4 shows the Application tab, which contains most of the relevant properties.

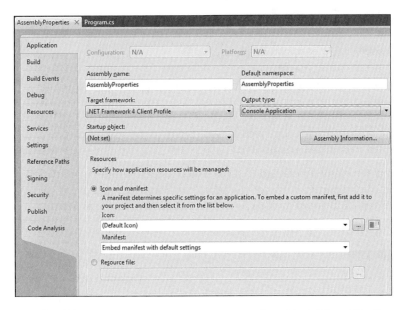

FIGURE 25.4   Some assembly properties configurable in Visual Studio.

Most settings should be self-explanatory. In the Startup Object drop-down, you can select an entry point function if multiple candidates exist, which triggers the use of the /main flag on the command-line compiler. The Resources section can be used to configure the application icon and a manifest, which contains additional information about the executable as used by Windows (for example, to trigger User Account Control). For more information about this feature, refer to the Visual Studio documentation and MSDN.

The Assembly Information button provides access to a bunch of other properties that are specified using assembly-level custom attributes carrying metadata. Figure 25.5 shows those properties.

Assembly Information	? ✕
Title:	AssemblyProperties
Description:	
Company:	Microsoft
Product:	AssemblyProperties
Copyright:	Copyright © Microsoft 2010
Trademark:	
Assembly version:	1 0 0 0
File version:	1 0 0 0
GUID:	0a78aa68-bd1d-468e-b660-f1bc815b3c51
Neutral language:	(None)
☐ Make assembly COM-Visible	
	OK Cancel

FIGURE 25.5   Various configurable assembly properties.

We discuss the naming and versioning of assemblies in the next section. One thing to notice, though, is the difference between an assembly version (which is what the CLR cares about) and a file version (used by Windows and installers). The GUID and COM-Visible settings near the bottom are for advanced scenarios where the managed code assembly needs to be used from COM components.

Behind the scenes, those settings get persisted in a file called AssemblyInfo.cs, which can be found by expanding the Properties entry for the project in Solution Explorer, as shown in Figure 25.6. Extra information about various settings can be found in the emitted comments in this code file.

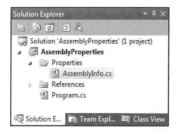

FIGURE 25.6   Assembly-level metadata is contained in AssemblyInfo.cs.

I'll leave it to you to inspect the assembly after compilation in a tool such as ILDASM or .NET Reflector, tracing back the assembly-level attributes that get set here.

Extra assembly-level settings can be found under the project properties Build tab. One setting of particular interest is the Platform target. This setting has historically proven to be confusing, and in the latest release has introduced a bit of controversy. First, let's explain what it's all about, with Figure 25.7 as a pointer to the location of the setting.

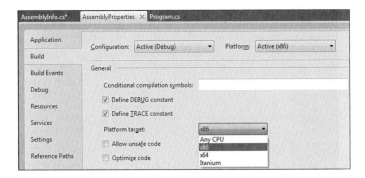

FIGURE 25.7   Platform target setting.

As you know by now, the CLR provides a hardware-independent virtual machine based on an intermediate language called IL. This means code can be turned into native code at runtime, a task performed by the Just-in-Time (JIT) compiler. .NET's JIT compiler supports to turn IL into x86, x64, or Itanium assembler.

The Platform target setting allows you to restrict what the emitted IL code can be turned into at runtime. Notice this doesn't by any means tell the compiler to go and emit native code. Assemblies *always* ship IL code; in fact, compilers like C#'s don't even know how to emit native code.

So if the setting is set to, say, x86, the IL can only be translated into x86 assembler at runtime. This doesn't mean the code can't run on an x64 platform, though, because 64-bit Windows has a facility called WOW (for Windows on Windows), which allows 32-bit code (which is referred to as x86 here) to run. However, if the Platform target were to be set to x64, the code would run on only an x64 machine (because, obviously, a 32-bit machine isn't capable of running the bigger x64 instruction set).

Now, what has changed in Visual Studio 2010 that caused quite some controversy in the beta days? In earlier versions, the default setting for the Platform target was Any CPU, which means the IL would be turned into whatever the target machine is capable of. Although this leverages most of the CLR's's flexibility, it has some drawbacks. Even though x64 is the future (by all means), a number of limitations still apply:

▶ 64-bit programs tend to be a bit slower due to larger pointer sizes, and therefore use more memory and have bigger impact on CPU caches.

▶ Interop with native code can be quite hard to get right when you must support different processor architectures, requiring quite a bit of additional testing.

▶ Some features on the CLR and Visual Studio don't fully support x64 yet (for example, historical debugging and edit-and-continue).

Also the benefits of x64 start to pay off once we're talking about applications that can really take advantage of a huge address space above the 2GB user mode address space limit (assuming a default machine configuration) posed by the 32-bit architecture. For all those reasons, Visual Studio 2010 projects default to x86 for executable assemblies (like console applications and Windows Forms or WPF applications).

It can't be overemphasized that this *doesn't* mean that executable assemblies configured to target x86 won't run on x64 platforms anymore. Figure 25.8 shows such an assembly running on a 64-bit system using WOW64.

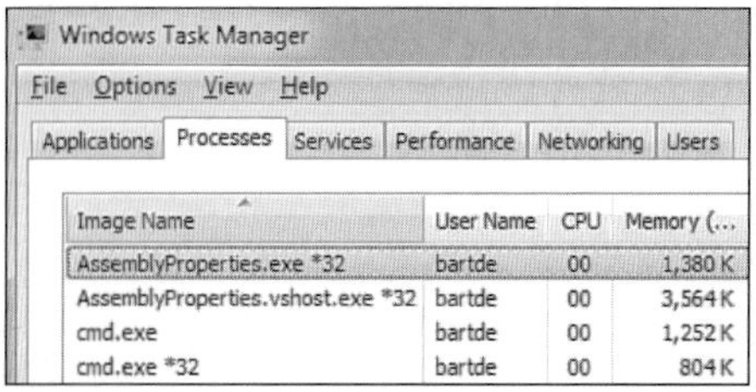

FIGURE 25.8   An x86-targeting assembly running on an x64 system.

In today's world, it's up to the developer to decide whether it makes sense for a managed application to take advantage of full-blown 64-bit, which may require a lot of additional testing in case native interop is used. (For example, COM interop, as discussed before, may cause some grief.)

Class Library projects still default to Any CPU because they're loaded in a process and have to adapt to whatever "bitness" that process is running under. In other words, it's up to the executable assembly to decide what architecture to target.

CHANGING THE TARGET PLATFORM OF AN ASSEMBLY

Besides reconfiguring the Platform target setting in Visual Studio and recompiling the assembly, there's another way to change the targeted architecture, even when the assembly has already been compiled.

Using corflags.exe, you can change the CLR header of an assembly. For example:

```
corflags /32bit- sample.exe
```

The preceding command will remove the x86-only flag, which will cause the assembly to be treated as Any CPU again.

Naming, Versioning, and Deployment

One of the key aspects of assemblies is found in their naming and versioning. Prior to the introduction of .NET, versioning was quite painful due to the so-called DLL hell. In the days of COM and use of "classic" DLLs, deployment of components involved registering them for use at runtime. However, when multiple versions of a component existed, they typically overwrote the binary/registrations, causing other programs to start using the new version. If the new version is not completely backward compatible, chances are high something breaks in other installed applications.

Early on in the design of .NET, it was determined that this problem had to be resolved. This called for a new naming and versioning story on the new units of deployment (that is, the assemblies). The first important change to the deployment story is the support for xcopy deployment, allowing (library) assemblies to sit alongside application assemblies, with no registration needed whatsoever. At the center of this feature lies the self-describing nature of assemblies, carrying all required metadata for type discovery with them.

To illustrate xcopy deployment in practice, let's create an application with an assembly on which it depends. You'll see how to declare such dependencies in a Visual Studio solution later, but for now we'll go with plain command-line compilation. First, we create the library consisting of the following C# code file:

```
// Calc.cs
public static class Calc
{
    public static int Add(int a, int b)
    {
        return a + b;
    }
}
```

To compile the library into a .dll assembly, invoke the following command:

```
csc /t:library calc.cs
```

Given the new calc.dll file, we now create an application that depends on it. To do so, enter the following code in a new file:

```
// Program.cs
class Program
{
    static void Main()
    {
        System.Console.WriteLine(Calc.Add(3, 4));
    }
}
```

To establish the dependency between both assemblies, the compiler needs an additional flag, as shown here. Notice that the default target type is exe, so we don't need a /t flag:

```
csc /r:calc.dll program.cs
```

The dependency of program.exe on calc.dll is declared in the executable assembly's manifest, as can be seen from ILDASM. Figure 25.9 illustrates the manifest for our program.exe assembly.

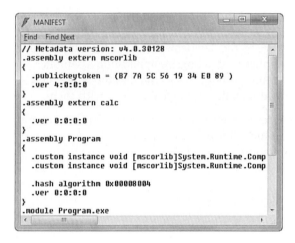

FIGURE 25.9   Reference to external assemblies the application depends on.

Two extern assemblies are referenced, one of which is mscorlib. You learn shortly what the magic word *publickeytoken* stands for. Right below the mscorlib reference we can see our calc assembly being referenced.

A few things should be pointed out. First, at the level of the CLR there's no such thing as an extension on assembly names. When trying to find a dependent assembly, the CLR will look in a variety of locations (as discussed later), appending .dll and .exe extensions when it browses around for files. Second, notice how every extern assembly carries a version number with it. Because we didn't specify a version for calc, it defaults to a 0.0.0.0 version. Assemblies declare dependencies in a precise manner, so no future version of a component can be loaded accidentally. You learn in the section called "The Global Assembly Cache (GAC)" when precisely the CLR enforces version numbers to match when loading dependencies.

REDIRECTING ASSEMBLY VERSION BINDING

You might wonder whether it's possible to cause a managed application to use a later version of a dependency without recompiling it against a later version of that assembly. The answer is yes, using something known as *publisher policy*. By sticking a configuration file alongside the executable, it's possible to redirect a "dependent assembly" to a new version.

It should be emphasized that the approach taken by the CLR is much the opposite of what was done in earlier days, where the latest version of a component would win and could affect existing applications on the machine.

To carry on with our xcopy deployment example, copy both calc.dll and program.exe to another folder. This suffices to make the application work, without requiring any kind of change to the Registry and whatnot. When the dependent assembly, calc.dll, gets dropped (or renamed to an extension other than .dll or .exe), the CLR will throw an exception when it tries to load the dependent assembly. Figure 25.10 illustrates the motions of xcopy deployment.

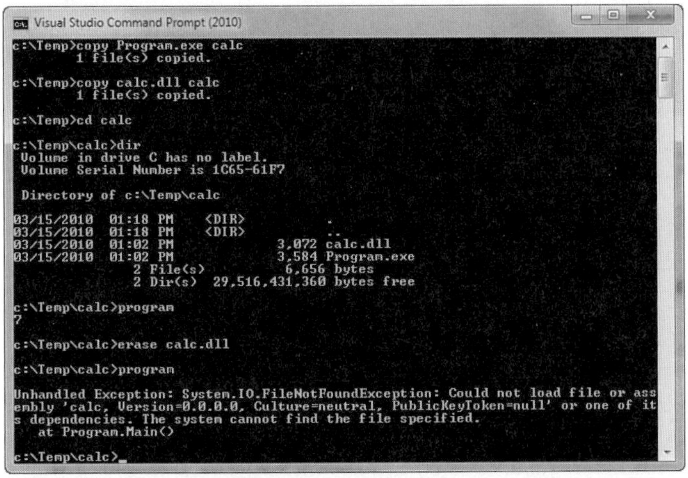

FIGURE 25.10   Using xcopy deployment in practice.

You learn how the CLR locates assemblies for loading in the section, "How Assemblies Get Loaded at Runtime." For now, let's focus on the naming and versioning aspect of assemblies. Starting with the latter, we've seen already how version numbers can be specified through a project's properties in Visual Studio. Behind the scenes, this is turned into an assembly-level attribute that specifies the version number. For our experiment, let's add that manually to calc.cs:

```
// Calc.cs
using System.Reflection;
[assembly: AssemblyVersion("1.0.0.0")]

public static class Calc
{
    public static int Add(int a, int b)
    {
        return a + b;
    }
}
```

When we recompile the library assembly and look in ILDASM, we now see that the assembly has a 1.0.0.0 version. At this point, we're still deploying dependent assemblies next to the application assembly, in which case versioning doesn't matter much. In fact, the CLR doesn't enforce versions to match in this case. You'll see that program.exe still runs fine, despite the fact calc.dll has boosted its version number.

In xcopy deployment scenarios, it's the application's responsibility to make sure the local application folder has a consistent mix of program and dependent assemblies. Because no other applications will use those "private binaries," matching up version numbers is not required. However, when assemblies start to be shared across different applications or other libraries, we're entering the danger zone that previously led to DLL hell. To mitigate this, strong naming was introduced, which is discussed next.

One final word on naming of assemblies: It's considered good practice to make the name of the assembly match the top-level (most-common prefix) namespace of the types contained inside it. For our quick-and-dirty calculator example, we didn't have such a namespace, but for our earlier examples of `Contoso.CashFlow.Client`, that would have been the perfect name for the assembly.

Strong Naming

Simple names like `calc` can lead to some ambiguity when assemblies are shared across different applications. This is precisely what has been a critical issue in times of the DLL hell, where components were overwritten by newer versions. For example, suppose that `SimpleCalc` is an application that relies on calc.dll version 1.0, which is registered so that it can be shared across programs. Later, `SuperCalc` comes around with version 2.0 of the calc.dll library, which it also registers centrally. At this point, the later version wins and overwrites the older one. Now things may go bad for `SimpleCalc` if the new version is not (fully) backward compatible with the older one.

Strong naming was invented to resolve this issue. By making a name stronger than just a simple name like `calc`, those ambiguities can be avoided. Strong names include the following parts:

- ▶ A simple textual name, such as `calc`. This is what gets configured through the Visual Studio project settings and in practice corresponds to the filename containing the managed code assembly.

- ▶ A version number, consisting of four parts (major, minor, build, revision) to indicate precisely which version of the assembly we're talking about. This gets specified using the `AssemblyVersion` attribute, as you saw before.

- ▶ A public key token, revealing the origin of the assembly. This corresponds to the company that signed (using the corresponding private key) and published the assembly. You learn more about signing (using various tools) later in the section, "Creating and Using Strong-Name Keys."

- ▶ An optional culture specification, indicating what user culture the assembly is meant to be used for. This proves particularly useful when creating localized and globalized applications.

So far, we've only seen the first two parts of assembly names. Let's take a look at the other ones now.

Understanding Strong-Name Signing Keys

To carry out strong-name signing, a key must be used to sign the assembly during build. In fact, there are two sides to this, so to be precise, we have to discuss a public and private key *pair*. Without going into much detail on cryptography, the private key is meant to be kept, well, private by the company signing the assembly, whereas the public key can be shared with the world. Based on the public key, which gets embedded in the signed assembly's manifest, the CLR can verify that the assembly hasn't been tampered with. From the public key, a smaller public key token is derived that becomes part of the assembly's strong name.

Figure 25.11 shows the signing process:

▶ First, the initial compilation of the assembly, emitting code and metadata, is carried out. This is the same as building weakly named assemblies.

▶ A hash is computed from the produced assembly's bytes, using a hashing algorithm such as SHA-1. This enables verification of the integrity of the assembly.

▶ The computed hash is signed using the RSA encryption algorithm, using the company's private key, producing a signature that gets embedded in the file.

▶ To allow the runtime to verify the signature, the public key gets embedded in the assembly's manifest.

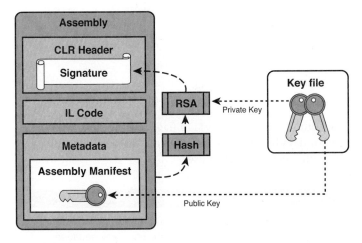

FIGURE 25.11   Strong-name signing.

In reality, things are a bit more complicated because the file being signed must change for the generated signature to be embedded inside it. Doing so within the range of bytes that got hashed would invalidate the hash, so the file format accommodates for a proper place to store a hash.

Creating and Using Strong-Name Keys

There are various ways to create a strong-name key, but the most convenient of all is to use Visual Studio directly. In a project's properties, go to the Signing tab and check the Sign the Assembly option, as shown in Figure 25.12. In the drop-down box, you can select an existing key file or create a new one. Because this key file also contains the private key, the file can be protected using a password, which is strongly recommended because the unauthorized use of the private key allows another party to sign an assembly in your company's name.

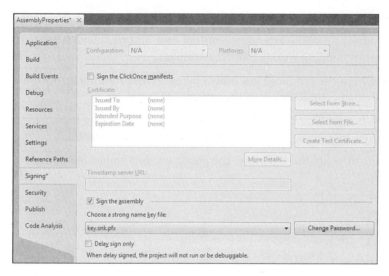

FIGURE 25.12   Specifying a strong-name key file for signing.

During build, the file is fed to the compiler using a /keyfile flag, causing the assembly to get signed as described previously. In days before .NET 2.0, the key was specified using an attribute called AssemblyKeyFile, which is no longer in use.

DELAYED SIGNING

Another option for signing is the use of delayed signing, which is useful in a few scenarios. Avoid sharing the private key with a lot of people inside your company because any leak of the key should be avoided at all costs. Using delay signing, you can sign an assembly using its public key only. We won't cover this feature in detail here; for more information, refer to the MSDN documentation.

Alternatively, a strong-name key can be created using the .NET Framework sn.exe tool, which has a whole bunch of parameters. One is the /k flag, which is used to create a new strong-name key, as shown in Figure 25.13. Using the /p flag, you can extract the public key out of a key file, which subsequently can be visualized using /tp. This also shows the public key token that will become part of the strong name of every assembly signed using the key.

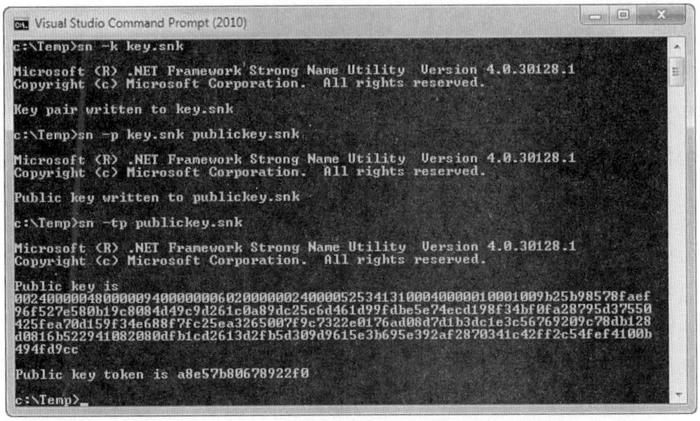

FIGURE 25.13   Using the Strong Name Utility sn.exe.

Using the created key.snk, we can now build and sign our calc.dll assembly as follows:

```
csc /t:library /keyfile:key.snk calc.cs
```

Inspecting a Strong-Named Assembly

The resulting assembly manifest, shown in Figure 25.14, is much larger because it includes the public key. In addition, the hash algorithm that was used to compute the assembly's hash is revealed (SHA-1 is used by the C# compiler).

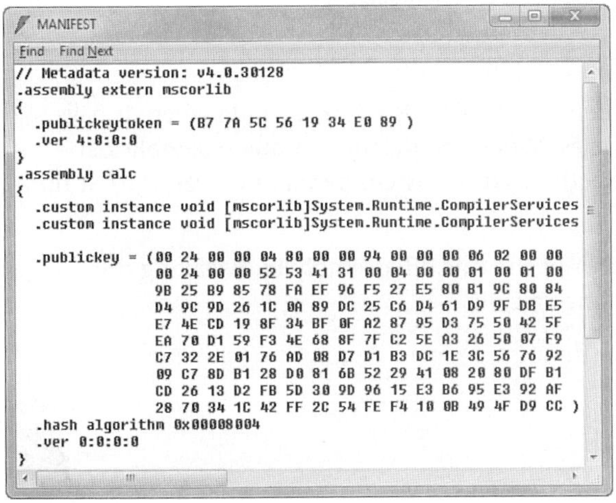

FIGURE 25.14   The public key embedded in the assembly manifest.

To continue our exploration, let's rebuild our program.exe assembly as well, again by refer-ring to the calc.dll as a referenced assembly:

```
csc /r:calc.dll program.cs
```

Notice that we're not strong-name signing the program.exe assembly, though we could. The philosophy of this example is that we are sharing the calc.dll library across multiple applications, requiring that one to be strong-named signed.

It's perfectly possible for a weakly named assembly (like program.exe) to refer to a strongly named one, but not the other way around. In other words, if calc.dll were to depend on other libraries, all of those would have to be strong-name signed, too. In some sense, this establishes a trust boundary around strongly named assemblies. Assume a strong-named assembly were able to refer to a weakly named one. In such a case, you'd be running into the situation where you're no longer provided with protection against DLL conflicts.

If we now look at the assembly manifest for program.exe, we see that not only the version number but also the referenced assembly's public key token is included in the .assembly extern metadata entry. Figure 25.15 shows this.

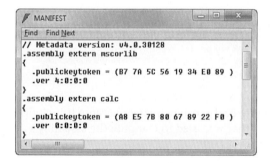

FIGURE 25.15   Metadata referring to strong-named assemblies.

Strong-Name Verification at Runtime

When strong-named assemblies are referenced, the CLR is put in a mode where it pays extra attention to integrity of dependencies. When the runtime locates assemblies, it makes sure the strong name matches exactly what the assembly manifest refers to. If not, an exception is triggered.

As an exercise, change the version number of the calc.dll assembly by tweaking the AssemblyVersion attribute and recompiling calc.dll:

```
// Calc.cs
using System.Reflection;
[assembly: AssemblyVersion("2.0.0.0")]

public static class Calc
{
```

```
    public static int Add(int a, int b)
    {
        return a + b;
    }
}
```

Don't recompile program.exe and try to run it with the newer version of calc.dll sitting next to it. Now the CLR will complain that the strong name of the referenced assembly (having .ver 0:0:0:0) doesn't match up with the actual calc.dll assembly's name (having .ver 1:0:0:0). Figure 25.16 shows the FileLoadException that indicates this mismatch.

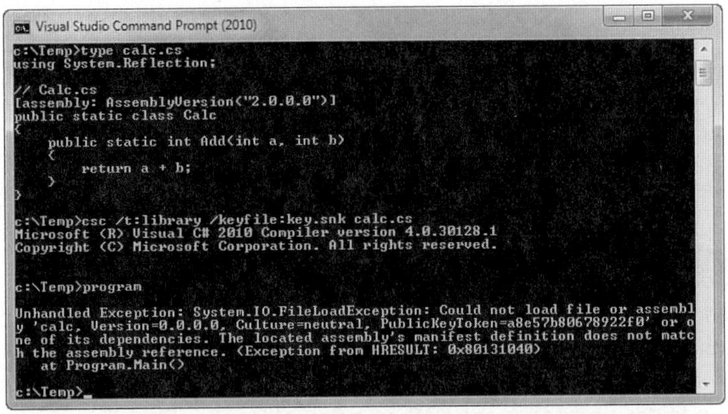

FIGURE 25.16   The CLR detects version mismatches for strong-named assemblies.

During development, it's possible to bypass such verifications by using sn.exe's /Vr switch. Use this with extreme caution; it poses a security threat on your machine.

The Global Assembly Cache

Loaded with knowledge of strong naming, we're ready to tackle the Global Assembly Cache (GAC), which provides a way to share assemblies across applications in a machine-wide manner (hence the world *global*). For assemblies to be stored in the GAC, they have to be strong name signed.

Up to now, we've always deployed assemblies privately in an application folder. As you will see later in the section, "How Assemblies Get Loaded at Runtime," there are different places where the CLR looks for a referenced assembly, one of which is the current folder. Both weak- and strong-named assemblies can be deployed privately, but only strong-named assemblies can go in the GAC.

Inspecting the GAC

A good starting point for our exploration of the GAC is looking at it. Essentially, the GAC is a central folder location where the CLR can go and look for assemblies. Prior to .NET 4, this was an "assembly" subfolder of the Windows installation directory. In the latest release, a new location has been introduced underneath the Microsoft.NET folder. The main reason for this so-called GAC splitting is the fact CLR 2.0 and 4.0 can exist side by side on the same machine, and the latter version should not pick up v2.0 targeting assemblies accidentally.

Figure 25.17 shows the top-level folder structure of the GAC used by .NET 4. The different folders correspond to target platform architectures, where MSIL is used for the architecture-neutral assemblies (Any CPU).

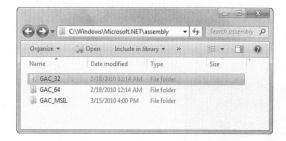

FIGURE 25.17   The .NET 4 GAC location.

VIEWING THE PRE-.NET 4 GAC

Prior to .NET 4, the GAC lived underneath %windir%\assembly. In fact, .NET 4 keeps native images (a concept explained later in the section "Native Image Generation (NGEN)") in there, too. Viewing this folder is slightly more difficult because a shell extension is registered for the folder, presenting the GAC as a flat folder structure. This shell extension can be disabled by adding a DWORD value called `DisableCacheViewer` to HKLM\Software\Microsoft\Fusion, set to 1. Fusion used to be the code name of assembly caching and loading features in the CLR.

Underneath those architecture folders, each shared assembly has a folder corresponding to its simple textual name. For example, the `System.Core` assembly exists underneath the GAC_MSIL folder. There's one more level of indirection, though, with intermediate folders containing the assembly version number and the public key token:

```
%windir%\Microsoft.NET\assembly
+ GAC_MSIL
  + System.Core
    + v4.0_4.0.0.0__b77a5c561934e089
      - System.Core.dll
```

This intermediate folder is prefixed with the targeted runtime's version. In case of the .NET Framework `System.Core` assembly, that's v4.0.

An alternative way to inspect the GAC is by using the gacutil.exe tool that can be used from the Visual Studio command prompt. The following command lists all the assemblies that are registered in the GAC. (On my machine, a total of 1,432 assemblies were found, spread across .NET 2.0 and .NET 4.)

```
gacutil /l
```

By specifying a partial assembly name (for example, System.Core) to the /l flag, the tool will show only matching entries, as illustrated in Figure 25.18.

FIGURE 25.18   Using gacutil.exe to list assemblies in the GAC.

The presence of .NET Framework assemblies in the GAC explains why there's no need (luckily!) to redistribute those alongside an application binary. Later, in the "How Assemblies Get Loaded at Runtime" section, you see how the CLR locates assemblies referenced by an application.

HOW INSTALLERS DEAL WITH GAC ASSEMBLIES

A more advanced gacutil.exe flag, /lr, displays references to GAC assemblies (for example, put there by installers like the .NET Framework Redistributable). Various installer technologies provide ways to install assemblies to the GAC, also putting guards in place against their removal.

Installing an Assembly in the GAC

To install an assembly in the GAC, you can use the gacutil.exe tool with the /i flag, specifying the filename of a strong-named assembly. This is illustrated in Figure 25.19. Let's give it a try on the calc.dll assembly we built before. To make this work, you need to run from an elevated Visual Studio command prompt because we're going to touch machine-global state. After we install the assembly, we use /l to observe the assembly being added to the GAC.

Based on the processor architecture of the assembly (which defaults to Any CPU or MSIL for class libraries in Visual Studio), the file will get copied to the appropriate folder in the GAC. After the installation has taken place, you should be able to locate the assembly file in the following folder; the public key token portion will vary:

```
%windir%\Microsoft.NET\assembly\GAC_MSIL\calc\v4.0_2.0.0.0_a8e57b80678922f0
```

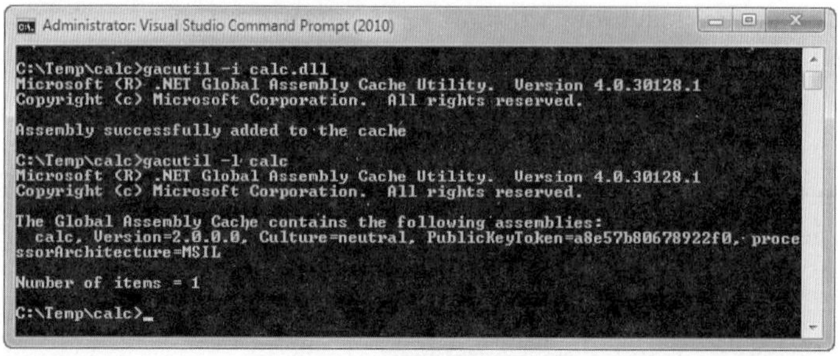

FIGURE 25.19   Installing an assembly to the GAC.

WHEN AND HOW TO PROPERLY INSTALL GAC ASSEMBLIES

Before asking how to install GAC assemblies that go with a product of yours, the first question to bring up is whether it's appropriate to use the GAC for some of your assemblies. In general, private deployment of assemblies is the way to go except when you either have to share assemblies (supporting versioning) across different applications or other components on the system must be able to load it by an assembly name. The latter situation can arise when you're writing add-ins for various technologies, such as Internet Information Services (IIS) modules.

To install assemblies to the GAC in some installer, refer to the documentation of the installer technology being used. For example, the Visual Studio Setup and Deployment Projects enable the creation of Windows Installer packages, where adding assemblies to the GAC is supported. One implication of choosing to use the GAC is that the installer will need to run elevated.

Finally, it should be emphasized that simply copying an assembly into a GAC folder is not a supported way to deploy assemblies to the GAC. Besides the folder structure consulted by the CLR, other registration locations play a role. Use of either gacutil.exe or one of the CLR "Fusion" APIs (as used by installers) is the way to go.

With the calc assembly deployed to the GAC, we can verify the CLR finds it there for use by the program.exe application. To fully test this claim, delete the calc.dll file that's still sitting next to the executable binary and try to run program.exe. Even without a privately deployed copy of calc.dll, the application works now. After removing the assembly from the GAC (using the /u flag, specifying the assembly name; that is, with no file extension), the application stops working. This is illustrated in Figure 25.20.

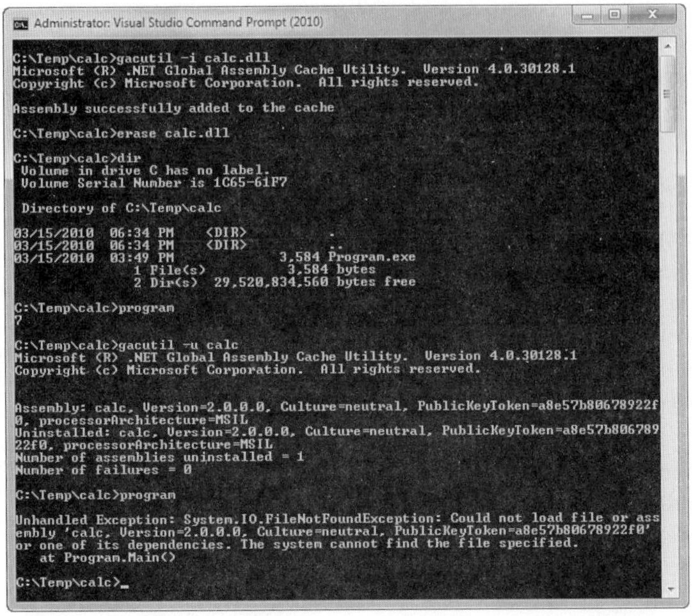

FIGURE 25.20   Illustration of an application loading a dependency from the GAC.

EASY TESTING OF GAC'ED ASSEMBLIES DURING DEVELOPMENT

When some application you're developing and testing requires certain assemblies to be deployed to the GAC, it can be a quite tedious to go through build, deploy, and debug cycles over and over again. This tedious process disturbs the convenient F5 debugging experience quite a bit. Luckily, there's an easy recipe to simplify life. On the Visual Studio project's property configuration, go to Build Events and add a post-build command:

```
<pathToTools>\gacutil.exe -i $(TargetPath)
```

Here, substitute <pathToTools> with the location of gacutil.exe. (Tip: Use the where gacutil command from a Visual Studio 2010 command prompt to find the full path.) Now every compilation cycle will automatically deploy the built assembly to the GAC.

Referencing Assemblies

Going back to the Visual Studio development environment, we now focus on creating and referencing assemblies. You've seen how this works plenty of times already, but some things deserve some further attention.

Solutions Consist of Projects

First, we should highlight the difference between solutions, projects, and the topic at hand: assemblies. The relationship between them is quite simple: Projects typically build a single assembly, and multiple projects are bundled into a solution.

Solutions don't have a runtime representation and are a Visual Studio-only concept, providing for a better development experience when building different assemblies in a group.

Depending on the type of the project, a different type of assembly will be built, such as a class library (.dll), a console application, or a Windows UI-based application (both with a .exe extension). Some projects have additional build logic beyond compilation; for example, to wrap the binaries in a deployment unit (for example, a CAB file for SharePoint extensions) or additional deployment manifests for things such as SQL Server .NET assemblies (requiring registration using a series of T-SQL statements).

References Between Assemblies

As you learned earlier, assemblies can refer to other assemblies to utilize other functionality. Various .NET Framework assemblies are typically referenced, but it's obviously also a good practice to factor your applications into different assemblies (for example, to separate the UI from business logic and data access). To establish references between assemblies, the Add Reference dialog is used, as shown in Figure 25.21. You can find this dialog by right-clicking a project or the References node underneath it.

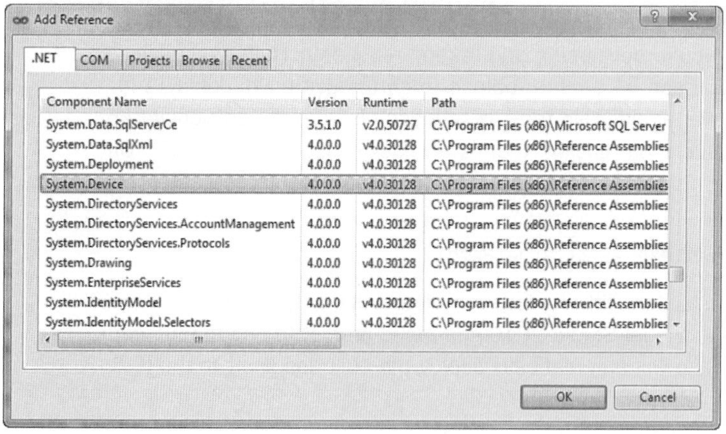

FIGURE 25.21   Add Reference dialog from the .NET tab.

The five tabs visible on the Add Reference dialog allow you to refer to different kinds of libraries, ranging from .NET assemblies to COM libraries (which result in the use of an interop assembly). In Figure 25.21, the .NET tab is active, showing a set of .NET assemblies that can be referenced, together with their versions, the runtime they target (which corresponds to the CLR version) and the path where the assembly lives on the developer's machine.

WHERE THE .NET TAB'S ASSEMBLIES COME FROM

A popular misconception is the origin of the assemblies in the .NET tab in Visual Studio. Some people believe this reflects the GAC on the developer's machine, but this isn't the case.

The .NET tab collects assemblies from a series of reference assembly paths that are specified in the Registry (search MSDN for details). Depending on the Visual Studio version, the Registry location varies, mainly due to the introduction of multitargeting in recent releases. Multitargeting allows the same Visual Studio tools to be used to write applications targeting different versions of the framework.

On the Projects tab, you can refer to another project in the solution, which has a couple of implications. First, it will result in the assembly having a runtime reference to the referenced assembly. Besides this, there are tool-level implications with respect to build:

- When building a project, MSBuild will traverse into projects being referenced, making sure the last built binary is not out of date with respect to the sources. If this is the case, the assembly will be built again. This traversal of project references continues until all dependencies are up to date.

- Executable projects will get a copy of the binaries built from referenced projects alongside the executable binary. If you inspect the bin\Debug or bin\Release folder of such a project with one or more references to other projects, you can notice this. By doing so, the application can be run from the build output folder because the runtime will locate dependent assemblies right next to the executable assembly.

DEVELOPMENT TIME VERSUS RUNTIME

Although the .NET tab of the Add Reference dialog mentions the assembly's location on the developer's machine, this doesn't have any impact on the runtime aspect of the application. If you inspect the path of the assemblies in the dialog carefully, you'll see the majority lives in a folder called Reference Assemblies (which indicates their use): for referencing during development. All that ends up in the built assembly are references to other assemblies *by their names*.

The assembly loader is responsible for finding assemblies from various search locations, such as the GAC or the current working folder, as you will see in the next section. In the case of reference assemblies, the corresponding runtime folder is usually the GAC. For cross-referencing projects, one typically deploys the application such that the referenced assemblies live in the same folder as the main executable, just as you can see in the bin\Debug or bin\Release build output folders.

How Assemblies Get Loaded at Runtime

Now that you've seen how assemblies get referenced at development time, we can take a look at how the runtime locates assemblies at runtime. Given an assembly that has references to other assemblies, how does the runtime find them (and when)?

Xcopy Deployment

One of the early goals of the .NET Framework was to simplify the deployment model for applications. This was known as the "xcopy deployment" vision, meaning one can just copy an application's binaries to some folder and run the application from that location as is, without requiring any registration or so on. In the world of COM, there was a much higher burden on installing and running applications because components typically required registration in the Registry for the runtime to find them.

To illustrate matters, let's create a new Visual Studio solution with two projects in it: a console application that will result in the application's main executable (containing the UI) and a class library containing the logic of a calculator. The former refers to the latter, using the Add Reference dialog's Projects tab. The result should look like Figure 25.22, highlighting the cross-project reference.

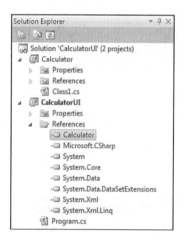

FIGURE 25.22   A project referring to another project.

Feel free to add some `Calculator` type to the `Calculator` class library project and use it from the CalculatorUI console application project. Because the default namespace for both projects will differ, you must add a namespace import to refer to the class library's `Calculator` class.

What matters more than the application assemblies' logic is the organization of the application in terms of the different binary files, which we can inspect after compiling the whole solution. Figure 25.23 shows the bin\Debug output folder for a debug build of the CalculatorUI project. Ignoring the `vshost` executable, which is used for debugging purposes when pressing F5 in Visual Studio, and debug symbol files (.PDBs), there are two assemblies here. One is the CalculatorUI.exe file itself, and the other is the class library Calculator.dll assembly it referred to.

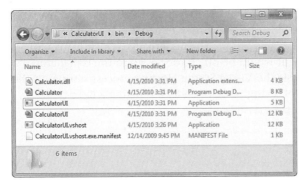

FIGURE 25.23   Build output for the console application referring to a class library project.

Just copying those two files to another folder will suffice to deploy the application and make it run from another folder. That's why this kind of deployment is referred to as xcopy deployment.

Loading Referenced Assemblies

The next question to ask ourselves is how referenced assemblies get loaded. As you've seen before in this chapter, references to assemblies live in an assembly's metadata, which is consulted by the runtime to locate types contained therein. Assuming you added some code to our calculator example, exercising the use of a type cross-project, a .extern directive will appear in the CalculatorUI's manifest. Figure 25.24 illustrates this.

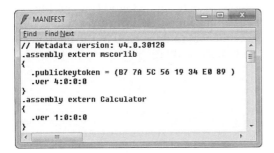

FIGURE 25.24   References to other assemblies.

Notice assemblies referenced by Visual Studio projects do not necessarily end up in the metadata of the compiled assembly. Compare Figure 25.22's list of references with the two assemblies referenced in Figure 25.24. Only when types from an assembly are being used will an .extern directive for the assembly appear in the resulting binary.

Given the information of referenced assemblies, when does the runtime trigger loading of them? Due to the just-in-time compiled nature of code, the runtime is in a position where it can discover used types (and the assemblies in which they are contained) in quite a lazy fashion, deferring loading of assemblies until the point they're needed. We can see this by using the debugger. First, we disable the Visual Studio hosting process, which loads more assemblies than needed so our experiment would be off. To do so, go to the CalculatorUI's project properties and uncheck the Enable the Visual Studio Hosting Process setting on the Debug tab. Now assume you have the following piece of code, leveraging a `Calc` type that's defined in the referenced `Calculator` class library:

```
static void Main(string[] args)
{
    Bar();
}

static void Bar()
{
    // Lives in the other assembly...
    Calculator.Calc.Add(1, 2);
}
```

The important bit here is the fact we're using the `Calc` type in the `Bar` method and not directly in the `Main` method. As long as we don't hit the `Bar` method during execution of the program, there's no need to load the assembly in which it's contained. To visualize that the runtime indeed defers loading of this assembly, set a breakpoint on the call to `Bar` and press F5.

As shown in Figure 25.25 using the Modules window (which can be found through the Debug, Windows menu), the referenced Calculator.dll file didn't get loaded yet before a call to `Bar` is made. However, once we enter `Bar`, references to types used in the method's code body need to be resolved. At that point, the Calculator.dll file gets loaded, which can be observed in the Modules window again.

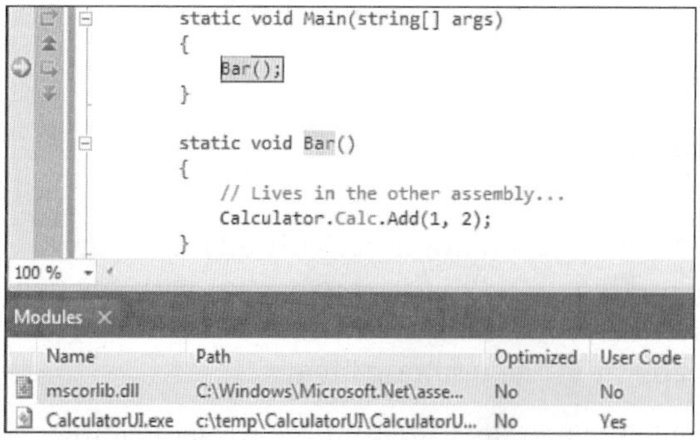

FIGURE 25.25   The referenced Calculator.dll assembly didn't get loaded yet.

How Assemblies Are Located

As shown in Figure 25.24, all a reference to an assembly consists of is its name (possibly more than just a short name; that is, also including version and optional strong-name info). In particular, there's no file path information included in the assembly. And because we are able to xcopy deploy the assemblies to some location on the file system, there's no such thing as a registration database that says "Hey, if you're looking for an assembly called Calculator, look for the file in that folder."

This brings us to the question of how the runtime finds assemblies. The task of locating and loading assemblies is what the loader is responsible for, otherwise known by its older code name Fusion. When asked to locate an assembly given a name, it goes ahead and searches a series of folders for a match. Folders considered in the search vary based on configuration and the nature of the assembly. In particular, for strong-named assemblies, it makes sense to look in the GAC, too.

For practical purposes, the most important bit to know is that assemblies can be found alongside the assembly referencing it. This is precisely the technique used in our case and illustrated in Figure 25.23: For CalculatorUI.exe to locate the Calculator assembly, the loader will start by searching the working directory and find a matching DLL file right next to the executable. One way to analyze assembly-loading failures is to use a tool called fuslogvw.exe, which stands for Fusion Log Viewer. From a Visual Studio command prompt, elevated using administrative credentials, launch the tool and go to Settings to configure the logging as shown in Figure 25.26.

FIGURE 25.26   Configuring the Fusion Log Viewer.

Locating and loading an assembly is referred to as binding. In Figure 25.26, we've enabled logging for all binds, though you could also enable to log only failures. To illustrate this tool in action, go to the bin\Debug folder we saw in Figure 25.23 and remove the required Calculator.dll assembly (assuming CalculatorUI.exe is using functionality from it; for example, as in our code fragment shown earlier). Now try to run the application, which

will result in a `FileNotFoundException` because the referenced Calculator assembly could
not be located. Figure 25.27 shows this issue.

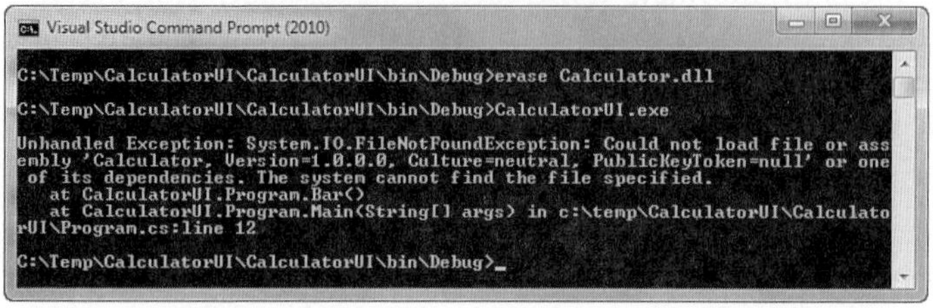

FIGURE 25.27   Failure to load a referenced assembly.

Notice once more the exception originates at the point the `Bar` method is entered as indicated by the call stack. When you refresh the logger, you should now see two entries with
information about the binds carried out by the application. One is just about loading the
executable assembly, and the other contains information about the failure to load its referenced Calculator assembly. Figure 25.28 shows those two entries.

FIGURE 25.28   Two log entries for assembly bindings.

By clicking View Log, details can be shown in a web page format, which is shown for the
second (failure) entry in Figure 25.29. After a dump of general information (or pre-bind
state) on where the application is running from and what's being loaded, the log continues with the bind logging information:

```
LOG: This bind starts in default load context.
LOG: No application configuration file found.
LOG: Using host configuration file:
LOG: Using machine configuration file from
 C:\Windows\Microsoft.NET\Framework\v4.0.30128\config\machine.config.
LOG: Policy not being applied to reference at this time.
LOG: Attempting download of new URL
 file:///C:/Temp/CalculatorUI/CalculatorUI/bin/Debug/Calculator.DLL.
LOG: Attempting download of new URL
 file:///C:/Temp/CalculatorUI/CalculatorUI/bin/Debug/Calculator/Calculator.DLL.
LOG: Attempting download of new URL
 file:///C:/Temp/CalculatorUI/CalculatorUI/bin/Debug/Calculator.EXE.
```

```
LOG: Attempting download of new URL
 file:///C:/Temp/CalculatorUI/CalculatorUI/bin/Debug/Calculator/Calculator.EXE.
LOG: All probing URLs attempted and failed.
```

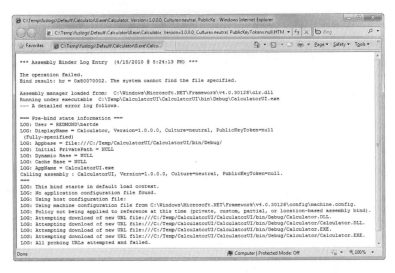

FIGURE 25.29   An assembly load failure log dump.

A few things can be noticed here. First, configuration files can influence the loading process. For more information about this, refer to MSDN documentation (because this is not used that often). Second, notice the search order for "download attempts" to locate assemblies. The CLR can load assemblies using a variety of protocols (including regular file lookup) and does so in a sequence of paths based on the calling assembly's location and the requested assembly's name. Also notice how the extension is not part of the assembly name but is appended for searches (where .dll takes precedence over .exe). The whole process of locating an assembly based on a name is called *probing*.

DIFFERENCE WITH JAVA

Readers familiar with Java will observe quite a few differences. In .NET, loading of a type is based on finding its containing assembly, not on finding a .class file based on a package name. Hence, there's no such thing as a CLASSPATH either.

Native Image Generation (NGEN)

As you know by now, the CLR uses a JIT compilation strategy to turn IL code into instructions executable on the CPU architecture of the machine where the application is running. This has several benefits, including code portability across different architectures. It also simplifies the act of code generation by various front-end language compilers because IL abstracts away from concrete machine aspects such as the use of registers. The JIT compiler takes on the burden of analyzing the IL code to turn it into efficient processor instructions.

DUMPING IL AND JIT-GENERATED CODE

Curious readers might wonder what processor assembly code generated by the JIT for a given method looks like. Using the SOS debugger extension, which you've seen on various occasions in other sidebars already, we can get to know this. In the following listing, a typical sequence of debugger commands is shown to trace this information back:

```
.load c:\Windows\Microsoft.NET\Framework\v4.0.30128\SOS.dll
extension c:\windows\microsoft.net\framework\v4.0.30128\sos.dll loaded

!name2ee Calculator.dll!Calculator.Calc.Add
Module:       001438dc
Assembly:     Calculator.dll
Token:        59acd57306000001
MethodDesc:   00143da8
Name:         Calculator.Calc.Add(Int32, Int32)
JITTED Code Address: 00300110

!dumpil 00143da8
ilAddr = 00312050
IL_0000: ldarg.0
IL_0001: ldarg.1
IL_0002: add
IL_0003: ret

!U 00143da8
Normal JIT generated code
Calculator.Calc.Add(Int32, Int32)
Begin 00300110, size 4f
00300110 55                  push        ebp
00300111 8BEC                mov         ebp,esp
// Omitted much more x86 instructions, one of which is an "add" instruction...
0030015D 5D                  pop         ebp
0030015E C3                  ret
```

Obviously, you don't have to know any of the JIT magic that's going on behind the scenes. However, if you want to satisfy your curiosity and can read x86 or x64 instructions fluently, looking at the JIT-produced code is a great new hobby.

The JIT terminology refers to the time when IL instructions are turned into architecture-specific instructions, namely when a method is first hit for execution. The mechanism that enables this technique is a so-called thunk that acts as a placeholder for not-yet-compiled methods. When a call is made to such a method, the thunk calls the JIT compiler, and the address of the compiled code is stored such that subsequent calls to the same method don't trigger recompilation. Note that all of this takes place in the memory of the running process, and no permanent storage (like the file system) is used to stow away compiled methods. In other words, when the process is restarted, JIT compilation takes place again for the methods that get executed. This whole mechanism is illustrated in Figure 25.30.

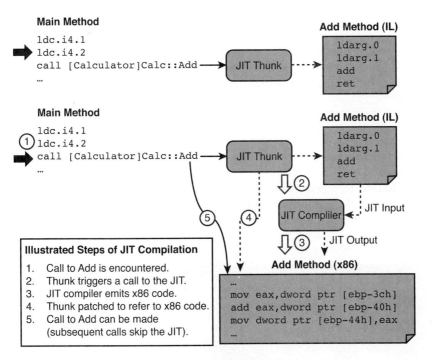

FIGURE 25.30   JIT compilation visualized.

Despite all advantages of JIT compiler, it should be obvious that the JIT compilation itself consumes CPU cycles, imposing an initial cost on the execution of IL code. For commonly used functionality (for example, in the framework libraries), it doesn't make sense to have JIT compilation going on for every single application using those methods. One could say that JIT compilation happens too late for those libraries. From a portability point of view, we can't ship x86 or x64 specific code, though. Putting all requirements together (that is, avoiding redundant JIT compilation costs but still retaining portability), we need a way to compile IL code into a processor-specific instruction set on the target machine but before applications run.

This is where native image generation, or NGEN, enters the picture. You can safely regard this runtime service as some kind of "offline JIT," which turns IL-containing assemblies into "native images," in a wholesale fashion (rather than on a per-method basis).

Typically, this service gets invoked during the installation of an application or a framework, which is exactly what the .NET Framework installer does for framework assemblies. Because of this, the framework can continue to redistribute architecture-independent assemblies while boosting runtime performance by compiling them into binaries with processor-specific instructions during installation.

NO SILVER PERFORMANCE BULLET

One has to keep in mind that use of NGEN for an assembly doesn't necessarily provide a speed-up because there are many factors to the performance equation. For one thing, native images tend to be larger, and hence load speeds differ from IL-based images.

To know when NGEN is right for your assemblies, performance measurements should be carried out. Our discussion about NGEN has as its main goal to raise awareness of the existence of the feature and not to provide exhaustive guidance for when it's appropriate to use. Plenty of online resources, such as MSDN, go into much more detail about using NGEN.

To create and install a native image for an assembly, you can use the ngen.exe tool that comes with the .NET Framework. Figure 25.31 shows the use of the tool to create and install a native image for our Calculator.dll assembly, followed by a display command to show the assembly's NGEN state. Feel free to experiment with the "ngen display" command applied to one of the framework assemblies, which produces a much more dense output with dependent assemblies.

FIGURE 25.31   Use of ngen.exe to install an assembly and show its state.

Beside synchronous installation of assemblies to the NGEN cache, there are command-line flags to queue up work at various priorities. A background service monitors the queue for work and executes it at a good point in time (for example, when the computer has gone idle for a while). This queuing option is usually used by installers to shorten the installation duration. An application's functionality won't be impaired by the lack of a native image for one or more of its assemblies; it might just run slower. Because the NGEN service (with executable name mscorsvw.exe) begins producing native images for queued up assemblies, applications pick those up when the assemblies get loaded.

The NGEN cache lives underneath the Windows installation folder in a subfolder called assembly\NativeImages_<version>_<architecture>. The version part matches the runtime version, and the architecture part is either 32 or 64. Each assembly with an NGEN image has a folder named after the assembly's name, containing an additional subfolder used for the cache's internal organization. Figure 25.32 illustrates the folder containing the native image for our assembly.

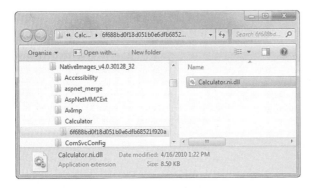

FIGURE 25.32   Native image for our Calculator assembly in the NGEN cache.

When loading our CalculatorUI.exe application assembly now, the loader will find the reference to the Calculator assembly and find a native image for it, which will get loaded. You can see this from inspecting the Modules list when running the application under the debugger, with unmanaged code debugging enabled. Doing so will show the native image, Calculcator.ni.dll, in the Modules list.

WHAT'S INSIDE A NATIVE IMAGE?

Native images contain the native code for an assembly. In addition to this, they contain all the metadata describing the types and members defined in it. In fact, you can simply use ILDASM to look inside an assembly in the NGEN cache.

Visibility Aspects

Assemblies are not just the typically used unit of deployment for .NET code, they also have a runtime impact with regard to protection. The internal visibility modifier embodies precisely this in the C# language, restricting access to types or members to the current assembly only.

REFLECTION AS AN ESCAPE VALVE?

Visibility is enforced by the runtime, as discussed later, such that it isn't possible for code to invoke methods or access members that it doesn't have access to. However, using reflection services, it's possible to bypass visibility checks. To prevent this from happening, other security measures have to be put in place with regard to partial trust applications. Refer to MSDN for more about these code security facilities.

Internal Visibility Revisited

To illustrate the internal visibility and how the runtime enforces access to types and members across assemblies, let's play around a little with our small example. Start by declaring the Calc type in the Calculator assembly as public and compile the whole solution. The consuming CalculatorUI assembly works just fine when trying to access the Calc type's Add method because both the class and the method are public:

```
namespace Calculator
{
    public class Calc
    {
        public static int Add(int a, int b)
        {
            return a + b;
        }
    }
}
```

Now let's do something a bit more sneaky and mark the Add method as internal, thus restricting access to the current assembly. Instead of recompiling the whole solution, just recompile the Calculator project. If you're attempting to recompile CalculatorUI, the compiler would detect you're trying to access the Add method, which has insufficient visibility to be called across assemblies.

However, let's see what the runtime thinks about it and put the updated Calculator.dll file alongside the application executable. Figure 25.33 shows this operation being carried out, followed by an invocation of the application. This triggers an invalid call to the Add method, which should not be accessed from outside its defining assembly. The runtime detects this pathological situation and throws a MethodAccessException in response to it. Having assemblies that are outdated work with each other can result in such situations, so it's important to recognize such exception types. Other examples include other AccessException types and the set of MissingException types.

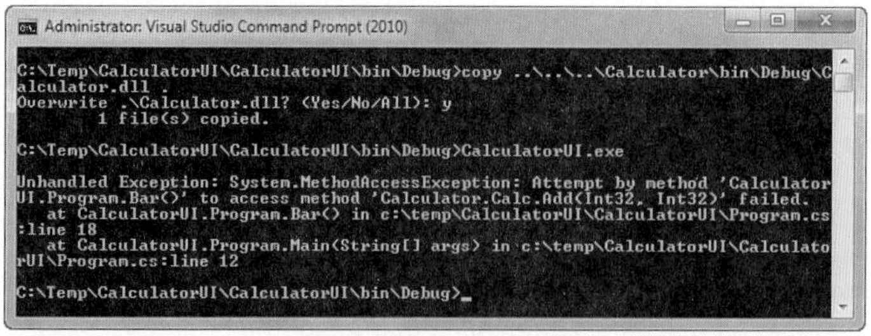

FIGURE 25.33 A MethodAccessException thrown for a method call visibility violation.

The InternalsVisibleTo Attribute

Sometimes it makes sense for two assemblies to have some access to internally marked types or members of another assembly. Doing so is a matter of trust and can be based on different needs. Maybe there are circumstances where it makes sense to factor an application component into multiple assemblies. Because the public access modifier means exposing something to the entire world, that might not be the optimal choice. As you will see, internal may help here. Another scenario has to do with testing, where test assemblies might need access to some of the internal state of an application's or library's assembly.

Introduced in .NET 2.0, the InternalsVisibleToAttribute custom attribute defined in the System.Runtime.CompilerServices namespace provides a way to declare the exposure of internal types and members to a trusted assembly. It's important to emphasize the fact that an assembly must declare *which* other assemblies it allows to have access to its internal state.

Here is an example of this attribute's use in the context of our Calculator example, where the Calculator class library assembly allows the CalculatorUI application executable assembly to access internal types and members:

```
[assembly: System.Runtime.CompilerServices.InternalsVisibleTo("CalculatorUI")]


namespace Calculator
{
    public class Calc
    {
        internal static int Add(int a, int b)
        {
            return a + b;
        }
    }
}
```

With this attribute in place, the application will work again, despite the fact the Add method is declared to be internal. Notice, though, we've been using the weakest of naming schemes to declare the friend assembly relationship. Any assembly that has the name CalculatorUI will be able to access internal state of our Calculator assembly now. Luckily, you can specify a stronger name by including the friend assembly's public key (that is, the full public key, not just the public key token).

Figure 25.34 illustrates how the language compilers are aware of this attribute, in this example signaling the fact that no public key was specified in the friend assembly identifier. To generate this error, strong-name sign the Calculator assembly using the project properties Signing tab. For more information about how to specify a public key in an InternalsVisibleTo attribute, refer to the MSDN documentation.

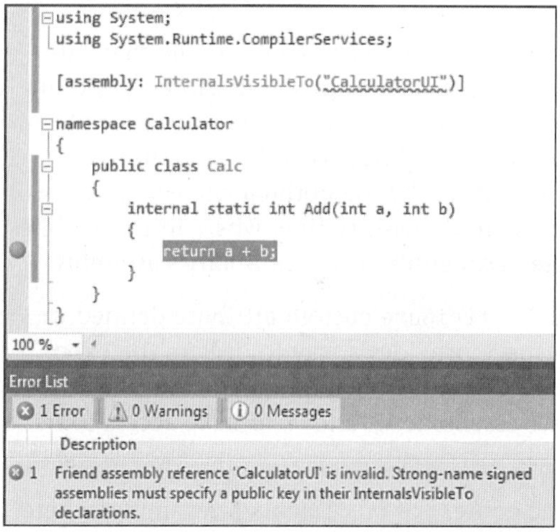

```
using System;
using System.Runtime.CompilerServices;

[assembly: InternalsVisibleTo("CalculatorUI")]

namespace Calculator
{
    public class Calc
    {
        internal static int Add(int a, int b)
        {
            return a + b;
        }
    }
}
```

```
100 %  ▼

Error List
🚫 1 Error    ⚠ 0 Warnings   ⓘ 0 Messages

      Description
🚫 1   Friend assembly reference 'CalculatorUI' is invalid. Strong-name signed
      assemblies must specify a public key in their InternalsVisibleTo
      declarations.
```

FIGURE 25.34 `InternalsVisibleTo` used on a strong-name-signed assembly.

USE WITH CARE

Because `InternalsVisibleTo` exposes all internal functionality to all the friend assemblies, it nearly moves one protection level for the entire assembly. When you now see something marked with an internal access modifier, you no longer know the reach of its visibility. In fact, internal by itself is already a bit of a hack that has no place in the object-oriented paradigm.

It's good to use this feature with extreme caution and consider carefully whether it's feasible to expose cross-assembly functionality really as public. The cross-assembly use of certain types perhaps indicates improper factoring of functionality.

Embedded Resources

Besides acting as containers for code and metadata, assemblies can also store resources for use at runtime. Visual Studio directly supports the creation of such assemblies by including files in the project and marking their build action as embedded resource. This is illustrated in Figure 25.35 for a file that was added to the project using the Add, Add Existing Item entry from the project's context menu in Solution Explorer.

Now this stream can be accessed using the `System.Reflection` APIs on the `Assembly` type, using the `GetManifestResourceStream` method. This method returns a `Stream` object, which can be used to access the data by various `Read` operations. In our sample code, we're a bit more sophisticated and use .NET 4's `CopyTo` method of the `Stream` class to copy the data from one stream to another. As the target of the copy operation, we use a newly created file:

```
using (var stream = typeof(Program).Assembly.GetManifestResourceStream(
                        "EmbeddedResourceSample.img0.jpg"))
using (var saveAs = File.Create("img0.jpg"))
{
    stream.CopyTo(saveAs);
}
```

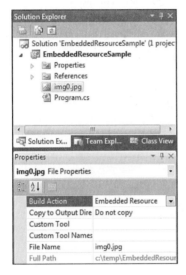

FIGURE 25.35   Marking a file to be included as an embedded resource in the assembly.

Notice the use of using blocks to properly dispose the streams after their use. One thing to be cleared out is the name of the embedded resource, which is prefixed with the name of the containing assembly (it seems). This can be observed by looking at the assembly in tools like .NET Reflector, as shown in Figure 25.36.

SATELLITE ASSEMBLIES AND MORE

This use of resources is only the tip of the iceberg of the .NET Framework's built-in capabilities to deal with resources at runtime. Besides binary streams, lots of other types of resources exist, such as strings. The picture of resources is also a lot bigger than simply accessing them; in real-world scenarios, the culture of the user must be taken into account. With this, we enter the fascinating world of localization and globalization of applications.

One notion related to resources has to do with the redistribution of assemblies that contain such resources for a particular culture, using a naming scheme that contains the culture name (for example, en-US, nl-BE, or fr-FR). Because it makes sense to have a separation between application logic and localizable resources (for example, to be able to redistribute other supported application cultures simply as additional files to a baseline installation), .NET came up with the notion of satellite assemblies.

A thorough discussion about satellite assemblies is beyond the scope of this book. In essence, they are resource-only assemblies that get stored in a culture-specific folder right next to the application's executable assembly. At runtime, when resources are queried for using APIs like System.Resources, the framework looks for the most applicable satellite assembly based on the user's culture and gets the requested resource objects from there.

Localization and globalization are topics that deserve books of their own. For more information, refer to MSDN.

FIGURE 25.36   An embedded resource's name as shown through .NET Reflector.

Type Forwarding

When designing and evolving nontrivial frameworks, it's often challenging to put types in the right assembly. Although a certain spot may make lots of sense in a certain version of the framework, that doesn't necessarily remain the case in future releases. For reasons such as architectural layering, it might be a good idea to relocate a type to some other assembly (for example, to avoid the need for excessive references between assemblies).

Such a situation arose in the move from .NET 3.5 to .NET 4. In the former release, generic delegate types such as System.Func<T, TResult> were introduced. Because this release of the framework was layered on top of .NET 2.0 baseline assemblies, it was chosen not to touch them for the addition of new types, and the set of Func and Action delegates ended up in a newly crafted System.Core assembly. Since things have evolved, those types are used more and more (for example, in the DLR introduced in .NET 4). It no longer made sense for all DLR libraries and users thereof to have to refer to this System.Core assembly to use things as trivial as Func and Action delegates. Their new and better home was mscorlib.

However, a move of types from one assembly to another requires all users of those types to recompile their assemblies, such that references to those types are patched up. Recall that on the runtime level, types are referred to by their full name, which not only includes the namespace and the type name but also the assembly. For example, use of the generic Func<int, int> delegate is represented as follows in IL:

[System.Core]System.Func<int, int>

It's clear that a move of the type to another assembly will result in a type not found exception when the runtime fails to locate it. This is where type forwarding comes in, to mitigate this very issue. Without the need for assemblies consuming the moved type to be recompiled, this feature tells the runtime where a type has moved to.

To carry out a type-forwarding operation, you use the TypeForwardedToAttribute, which lives in the System.Runtime.CompilerServices namespace. This assembly-level attribute simply points to a type (using a System.Type object) that now lives elsewhere. For example, the source code for System.Core in .NET 4 contains something like this:

```
[assembly: TypeForwardedTo(typeof(Func<,>))]
```

Recall the syntax to refer to an open generic type using typeof, omitting generic type parameters and leaving the commas in. In addition to the preceding code, the generic Func delegate's definition has been moved to the mscorlib assembly source code. When the System.Core assembly is compiled, the compiler finds the Func type in the referenced mscorlib assembly and the preceding type-forwarding attribute gets compiled into a metadata entry in System.Core's assembly manifest:

```
.class extern forwarder System.Func`2
{
   .assembly extern mscorlib
}
```

Figure 25.37 illustrates some of the type forwarders in System.Core version 4. By putting them in place, existing .NET applications that are retargeted to .NET 4 can continue to find the Func and Action delegate types, even though they refer to their old home, the System.Core assembly, internally.

In addition to TypeForwardedToAttribute, which is turned into an assembly-level metadata entry for use by the runtime, there's a type-level TypeForwardedFromAttribute, which (starting from .NET 4) has to be stuck on the type that has been moved:

```
[TypeForwardedFrom("System.Core, Version=3.5.0.0, ...")]
delegate TResult Func<T, TResult>(T arg);
```

This allows various other pieces of the framework and tools to reconstruct the entire picture of the move. One service that benefits from this information is the serialization infrastructure.

FIGURE 25.37   Type forwarders in `System.Core`.

WHEN COMPATIBILITY IS A CORE REQUIREMENT

As usual, the use of a feature gives rise to a balancing act with architectural purity on one side, compatibility on another side, and the burden of carrying out the fix to be considered too. Type forwarders are no different and provide some kind of last-resort fix when you have strong reasons to move a type and absolutely have to keep existing assemblies work (without recompiling them). So if you're working on something totally new with no compatibility story to take care of, there's no reason to complicate matters by using type forwarders.

Reflection Flashback

When we discussed reflection in Chapter 21, "Reflection," we focused on two main concepts of the technology: discovery of types and members and invocation or interaction with those (for example, to dynamically invoke a method). While we focused on types and their members, we mostly omitted a discussion of reflection on assemblies. Although you saw how to find types that belong to an assembly (a discovery feature), we didn't pay much attention to reflection operations targeting assemblies.

Earlier in this chapter, you saw one such assembly-level operation, which had to do with the loading of embedded resources. But there's more. In fact, we can load assemblies through the reflection APIs, too. So far, you've seen that assemblies get loaded by the runtime when a type or member is encountered that lives in an assembly that hasn't yet been loaded. In certain scenarios, such as add-ins, referenced assemblies are no longer a known fact at compile time. Based on application configuration settings, we need to discover and load assemblies *dynamically*.

What's Running?

Before delving into the functionality that enables us to load assemblies dynamically at runtime, we first explore some other functionality exposed on the Assembly class, allowing us to discover what's running:

▶ GetEntryAssembly retrieves the Assembly object representing the entry-point assembly that started executing the application. As you see in the "Application Domains" section later in this chapter, this correlates with the notion of application domains. One typical use for this is to detect version information (using GetName().Version on the Assembly object) for the entry-point assembly (for example, to display it in some Help, About menu).

▶ GetExecutingAssembly will return an Assembly object for the assembly that's currently running. Called from a method, this will correspond to the assembly in which that method was defined. This can be useful for diagnostic purposes, when writing logging entries, or so on. Beyond just retrieving information about the currently executing assembly, you can use things such as StackTrace in the System.Diagnostics namespace.

▶ GetCallingAssembly figures out where the caller of the current method originates from in terms of the defining assembly. For publicly visible methods, this can come in handy to make decisions based on the context of the caller, although you should use such trickery with care. One reason for this warning is that the name of an assembly is easily spoofed, especially when no strong naming is used.

▶ GetAssembly correlates a given Type object to its containing assembly, just like the Assembly property on the Type object will do. A commonly used trick to retrieve all types defined in an assembly is to start from a type that's known to be defined in that assembly and get to its declaring assembly through the reflection APIs. Once you're there, it's easy to call GetTypes to inspect the assembly.

When calling the first three methods from the Main method of an assembly, you should get the same result back. One caveat applies, though, when doing debugging with the default configuration in Visual Studio. When you press F5, your main assembly isn't just started regularly; instead, it gets loaded through a hosting process. Consider the following piece of code to illustrate this:

```
namespace Hosting
{
    class Program
    {
        static void Main()
        {
            Console.WriteLine(Assembly.GetCallingAssembly());
            Console.WriteLine(Assembly.GetEntryAssembly());
```

```
            Console.WriteLine(Assembly.GetExecutingAssembly());
            Console.WriteLine(Assembly.GetAssembly(typeof(Program)));
        }
    }
}
```

Figure 25.38 shows the setting that enables the use of the hosting process. When turned on, starting a debugging session will check whether such a hosting process is already running. You can recognize this process by its vshost name before the .exe file extension. If needed, the process is started. Either way, when the process is found, the debugger attaches to it, and your application's assembly gets loaded in that process. By doing so, various debugging scenarios can be optimized. However, a few API calls, such as the first one shown in the preceding code fragment, will be off:

Microsoft.VisualStudio.HostingProcess.Utilities, Version=10.0.0.0,
Culture=neutral, PublicKeyToken=b03f5f7f11d50a3a
Hosting, Version=1.0.0.0, Culture=neutral, PublicKeyToken=null
Hosting, Version=1.0.0.0, Culture=neutral, PublicKeyToken=null
Hosting, Version=1.0.0.0, Culture=neutral, PublicKeyToken=null

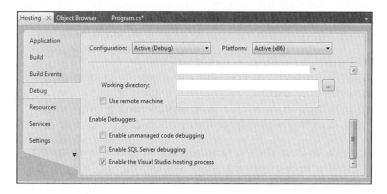

FIGURE 25.38   Setting enabling the Visual Studio hosting process (the default value is on).

Loading Assemblies

Besides having a static reference to an assembly, introduced through the use of either the /r compiler flag or the References node in a Visual Studio project, you can load assemblies dynamically at runtime. To do this, several static methods on the Assembly class can be used.

Assembly.Load is the first method that's available to carry out this job. Various overloads are available, including the following:

▶ Accepting a byte[] containing the raw byte sequence of an assembly based on the executable COFF format. In other words, if you were to stuff an assembly into a byte array (for example, using System.IO functionality), you could use this method to load it as an assembly. To the runtime, there's no need for an assembly to live on disk. In fact, other CLR hosts, such as SQL Server, can abstract over the loading process for assemblies (for example, loading them from a database).

▶ Taking in an `AssemblyName` object that describes the assembly's name, which includes the short name as well as version info and a public key token. The loader searches for the assembly in locations starting from the local folder and continues its merry way, probing other locations based on the name. For strong-named assemblies, this includes the GAC.

▶ Using a string rather than an `AssemblyName` to specify the assembly's full name (that is, including the version, public key token, and the culture). The logic used to find the assembly is the same as for the previous overload.

An example is shown here, using a hard-coded string literal. In more typical scenarios, you will discover the assembly that needs to be loaded through configuration settings or so on, truly emphasizing the dynamic nature of the assembly load. By showing the name in the code, we can illustrate the format of an assembly's full name.

```
var addIn = "AddIn, Version=1.2.3456.0, Culture=neutral, " +
            "PublicKeyToken=0123456789abcdef";
var asm = Assembly.Load(addIn);
```

Additional overloads exist, some of which can be used to specify debugging symbols, whereas others deal with security evidence used for Code Access Security (CAS). Since .NET 4, the notion of CAS policy has been deprecated and so are the overloads. If you still have code relying on those, it's time to revisit your code.

Because the `Load` family of methods carries out an assembly load based on a name, using the loader's search logic to locate the assembly, there's no room for a string-based overload that will load an assembly given a file path. For this purpose, the `LoadFile` method exists:

```
var path = @"c:\temp\addin.dll";
var asm = Assembly.LoadFile(path);
```

In reality, there are some deeper intricacies on the behavior of different load methods, with respect to so-called load contexts. We won't elaborate on this point; instead, refer to MSDN for more thorough coverage. In addition to `LoadFile`, there's `LoadFrom`, which can perform loads based on a URI. It has several disadvantages over using `Load` but has some applications; you can find more information at MSDN.

Finally, there's the distinct scenario of loading assemblies just because you want to use reflection APIs over their contents (for example, to write tools such as .NET Reflector). In such a case, it doesn't make sense to trigger the invocation of certain pieces of code contained in the assembly. For this, there are two sister methods to `Load` and `LoadFrom`, called `ReflectionOnlyLoad` and `ReflectionOnlyLoadFrom`, respectively. As an example, the following code displays types in a given assembly but fails to instantiate a type:

```
var asm = Assembly.ReflectionOnlyLoadFrom(\temp\calc.dll");

// Reflection is permitted.
foreach (var type in asm.GetTypes())
    Console.WriteLine(type);

// But invoking operations, such as instantiation of types, is not.
try
{
    dynamic calc = asm.CreateInstance("Calc");
    Console.WriteLine(calc.Add(1, 2));
}
catch (ArgumentException)
{
    Console.WriteLine("Thrown due to reflection-only load.");
}

var asm2 = Assembly.LoadFrom(\temp\calc.dll");
foreach (var type in asm2.GetTypes())
    Console.WriteLine(type);

// In the regular LoadFrom context, instantiation and invocation is permitted.
dynamic calc2 = asm2.CreateInstance("Calc");
Console.WriteLine(calc2.Add(1, 2));
```

One critical piece of knowledge about assembly loads, whether they are reflection only or not, is that they cannot be undone. In other words, there's no such thing as an Unload method on an Assembly object that causes the assembly to disappear from memory. There are many reasons for this. For example, other assemblies might have been loaded that depend on the presence of another assembly. Or delegates might exist that refer to functionality defined in an assembly.

Based on the previous statements, you will wonder whether the only way to get rid of an assembly is to completely shut down the process. Luckily, that's not the case; the CLR has an intermediate notion of isolation called application domains. They can be loaded and unloaded, as you see in the "Application Domains" section late.

In addition to application domains, the .NET 4 runtime's System.Reflection.Emit APIs enable you to create a dynamic assembly that's marked as RunAndCollect. Subject to some restrictions, those collectible assemblies can be unloaded without having to unload the application domain in which they were created. The MSDN documentation outlines those restrictions in an article titled "Collectible Assemblies for Dynamic Type Generation."

Application Domains

Modern operating systems, runtimes, server software, and so on spend a lot of their efforts on providing meaningful isolation boundaries between various users. At the operating system level, such isolation doesn't exist just to establish walls between user accounts, but also exists at a much more fundamental level. In particular, processes provide an isolation boundary between applications, ensuring that code running in one process cannot affect code running in another one. Another point of view is to say that all the interaction patterns between processes, to overcome the fundamental isolation provided by the operating system, have to be done very explicitly (for example, by making use of cross-process communication facilities or shared memory sections).

The .NET runtime is no different in its desire to provide a foundation offering ways to establish isolation boundaries. Such boundaries provide various benefits ranging from reliability (for example, no accidental stepping on someone else's memory) over security (for example, one container for code execution is less trusted than another one) to control over the loading and unloading of code. In the world of .NET, those isolated containers are called application domains. Figure 25.39 shows the relationship between a process hosting the CLR, containing one or more application domains, which act as containers for loaded assemblies.

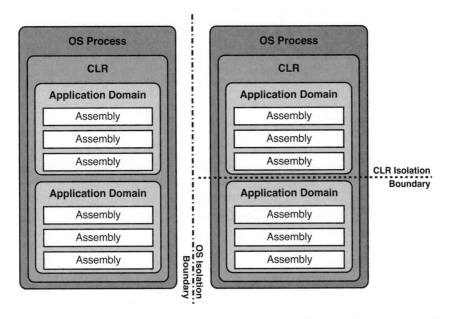

FIGURE 25.39   Operating system processes, application domains, and assemblies.

Starting from .NET 4, multiple versions of the CLR can also be loaded in the same process, also providing isolation between them. We won't elaborate on this aspect because it's quite a specialized topic aimed at CLR host implementers. You can find more information in the MSDN documentation.

Creating Application Domains

Every .NET application has at least one application domain, known as the default domain. Additional domains can be created, either through managed code or from within hosting code in case you're writing a CLR host. We focus on the former scenario, where we want to use application domains to isolate certain pieces of code from other pieces. Examples of such use include loading of assemblies containing add-in code into a separate application domain. This allows the hosting process to stay in control because it can unload the whole add-in domain and all of its assemblies (for example, if the add-in functionality is misbehaving). In addition, only certain communication patterns will be allowed such that the loaded add-in cannot access data structures it shouldn't have access to or invoke code that's privileged to be run by the add-in host only.

To create a new application domain, you use the `CreateDomain` factory method on the `AppDomain` class. Different overloads exist, some of which deal with providing security evidence. We don't get in a thorough discussion about those security aspects and instead focus on the aspects of creating application domains and running code in them. The following code fragment creates a new domain and starts a .NET executable assembly (that is, with a `Main` method entry point) inside it. Overloads of `ExecuteAssembly` allow for specifying string arguments and retrieving the exit code.

```
var ad = AppDomain.CreateDomain("App1");
Console.WriteLine(ad.Id + " " + ad.FriendlyName);
ad.ExecuteAssembly(\temp\app1.exe");
AppDomain.Unload(ad);
```

Under the debugger, we can clearly see the app1.exe assembly getting loaded when the call to `ExecuteAssembly` is made. To see this, break under the debugger while the executable is running. Once we unload the domain by calling `AppDomain.Unload`, all the contained assemblies get unloaded, too. Figure 25.40 illustrates this by showing the Modules list before and after the call to `Unload`.

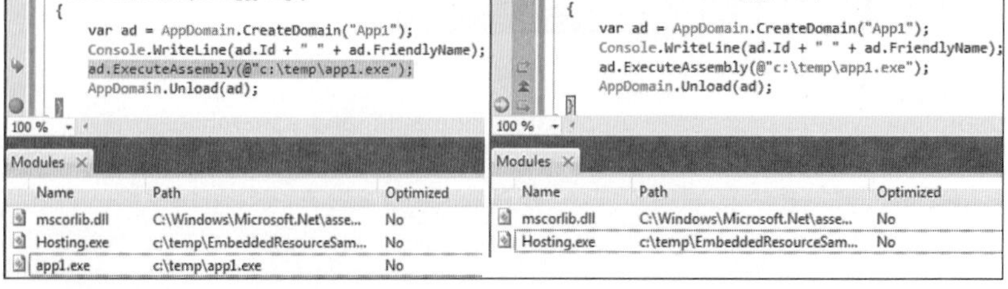

FIGURE 25.40   Loading and unloading of assemblies is tied to an application domain.

Using the AppDomain.CurrentDomain static get-only property, you can inspect the currently executing application domain. Various instance properties and methods exist that give access to the list of assemblies in the domain, different search paths used when assemblies are loaded or references are resolved, as well as various security-related settings. To illustrate this property, put the following bit of code in the app1's Main method and observe how it sees the information about the domain in which it's running. When invoking the app1 program directly, it will print different information because it will be running in the default domain.

```
var ad = AppDomain.CurrentDomain;
Console.WriteLine(ad.Id + " " + ad.FriendlyName);
```

The use of whole executable assemblies simply to invoke some code in an application domain is often overkill. We often just want to load one or more assemblies and instantiate types defined in those assemblies. To load assemblies into an application domain, the Load method can be used, which looks an awful lot like the Assembly's Load method.

Searching for assemblies will proceed from the application's base folder. Additional paths can be searched based on the application domain's setup, which can be specified as an AppDomainSetup-typed parameter passed to the CreateDomain call. In particular, properties like ApplicationBase are of use.

Cross-Domain Communication

The ability to load assemblies in a domain is nice but not quite the functionality we need to enable bigger scenarios. Of more use is the capability to create an object instance in the target domain and invoke operations on it. To achieve this, some form of cross-domain communication needs to be provided. As you might expect, all this is built in to the CLR. In fact, different mechanisms exist, as you will see, but first we should take a look at the APIs that allow us to create an object instance in a specified target application domain.

Creating Object Instances

To load an assembly and create an instance of one of the assembly's types in a target application domain, four methods exist. All of them start with the CreateInstance prefix and vary in two orthogonal ways. First, there's a distinction in the way the specified assembly is located, analogous to Assembly's Load and LoadFrom methods. Second, there's a variation in the behavior of how the instance is returned:

▶ CreateInstance looks for an assembly by its name and returns an ObjectHandle to refer to the returned object.

▶ CreateInstanceAndUnwrap performs the same lookup for an assembly by name but unwraps the object into a System.Object instance.

▶ CreateInstanceFrom locates an assembly by a given file path and returns an ObjectHandle to refer to the returned object.

▶ CreateInstanceFromAndUnwrap also finds an assembly by its file path but unwraps the object into a System.Object instance.

So what's this mysterious ObjectHandle about? Basically, they are a communication primitive used to refer to an object that has been created across domains. We ignore the intricacies of them and use the Unwrap methods to avoid them altogether.

To illustrate the technique of creating an instance of a type in an application domain, we start by creating a separate library assembly that will be what we load. To keep things simple, let's go for a calculator example once more:

```
using System;

public class Calc
{
    public int Add(int a, int b)
    {
        Console.WriteLine(AppDomain.CurrentDomain);
        return a + b;
    }
}
```

Compile the preceding into a .dll assembly (for example, using a Class Library project). Use calc.dll as the assembly's name. To proceed, we create the host application, which loads the assembly through CreateInstanceFromAndUnwrap:

```
class Program
{
    static void Main()
    {
        var ad = AppDomain.CreateDomain("AddIn");

        dynamic calc = ad.CreateInstanceFromAndUnwrap("Calc.dll", "Calc");
        Console.WriteLine(calc.Add(1, 2));

        AppDomain.Unload(ad);

        foreach (var asm in AppDomain.CurrentDomain.GetAssemblies())
            Console.WriteLine(asm);
    }
}
```

Note a few things about this example. First, CreateInstanceFromAndUnwrap returns an object typed as System.Object. Because our host application doesn't have a Calc type handy to cast the returned object to, we need to apply other tricks to call the functionality exposed by the object. For simplicity, we use C# 4.0's dynamic feature here, but later, in the section "Use of an Interface Contract," you see how to structure a host and an add-in properly, using a common interface to represent the contract. Second, after unloading the application domain of the add-in, we're printing all the assemblies in the default domain.

To run the host application, make sure to stick the calc.dll file next to the host's executable assembly such that the add-in assembly can be found. However, when you try to run the host with the add-in at this point, an exception results, as shown in Figure 25.41. This provides us with a great starting point to explain the requirements on types that are used across different application domains.

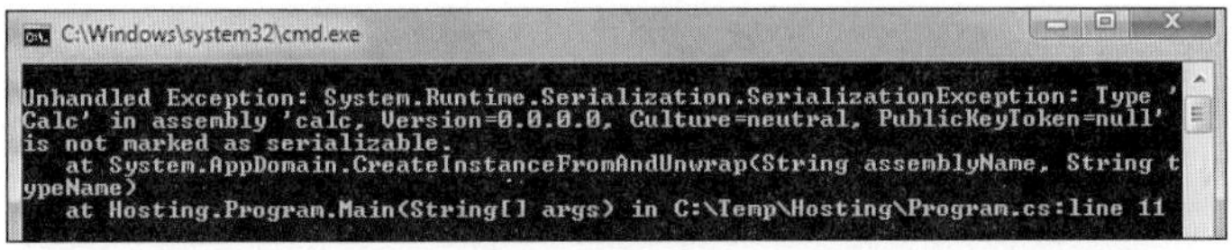

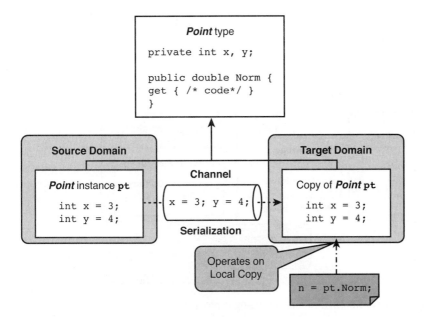

FIGURE 25.41   Failed to establish communication between application domains.

Before remedying this issue, we need to examine remoting facilities a bit more, to really understand what the SerializationException is all about. Because those topics deserve whole books by themselves, we limit ourselves to the essentials.

Flavors of Remoting

Passing objects across a boundary (in this case, an application domain) can be carried out in two different ways. Either you pass them by value, through a mechanism called *serialization*, or by reference. Figure 25.42 depicts the first mechanism, whereby an object gets copied by value. When the target domain tries to obtain a point instance from the first domain, the object's data gets copied into the target domain. Obviously, both domains need to know the structure of the Point type to accommodate this.

FIGURE 25.42   Copy-by-value realization using serialization.

Of critical importance in this whole story is how calls made on the `Point` object operate against the local copy of the object. In this example, we're simply computing the norm (distance to origin), which happens entirely by running code in the target domain on the local copy. The same would hold for mutating calls (for example, changing the value in any of the fields): Changes would be applied only locally. To realize serialization semantics for cross-domain use of objects, mark the type using the `Serializable` attribute:

```
[Serializable]
public class Point
{
    ...
}
```

Notice that the use of serialization can be applied to a reference type, such as our `Point`, which is defined as a class. The main thing the attribute affects is how the object gets marshaled across domain boundaries. Within the same domain, the object retains its reference type properties.

The alternative means to deal with objects across domain boundaries is to share and access them by a cross-domain reference. as shown in Figure 25.43. Here, we have a `Person` type that gets marshaled by reference (you see how in a minute) across the domain boundaries.

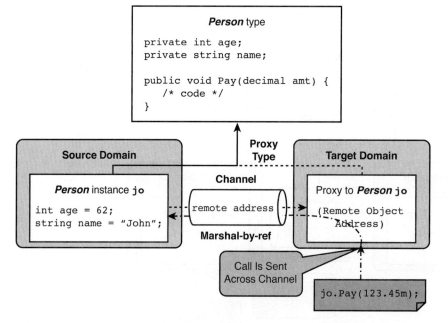

FIGURE 25.43   Marshal-by-reference realization using a proxy object.

In the target domain, we now don't obtain a copy of the original object that lives in our domain; instead, we get a (transparent) proxy object that looks just like the original object from a member's point of view. However, when we make a call on the object, the call gets remoted to the target instance in the originating domain. The runtime takes care of constructing this remoting proxy type on-the-fly, essentially capturing the data required to make a call back to the original object. Various remoting channel types exist, some dealing with communication between domains within the same process, while others allow a call to be remoted over, for example, a TCP/IP network. That's right, cross-application domain communication can stretch multiple processes or even multiple machines.

A thorough discussion about .NET Remoting is beyond the scope of this book, and nowadays many other ways to communicate across domains exist, such as Windows Communication Foundation (WCF). Suffice to say that one derives from MarshalByRefObject to mark a type as marshal by ref:

```
public class Person : MarshalByRefObject
{
    ...
}
```

Notice that the creation of such a type imposes a big tax on the (single) inheritance axis of the type because you must derive from a base class. In fact, this turns out to be a good thing, as alluded to in the following sidebar.

A MUCH-NEEDED WARNING ABOUT LOCATION TRANSPARENCY

The use of marshal-by-ref objects realizes so-called *location transparency*, a wonderful piece of technology leveraging one of the most fundamental computer scientist's tools: abstraction. Many frameworks have implemented such a means to establish remote procedure calls (RPCs), such as Microsoft's COM.

In all of those frameworks, many layers of abstraction *hide* all the technicalities associated with the creation of proxy objects (in fact, in .NET Remoting this is a whole runtime service of its own), management of lifetimes (using the concept of a lease in .NET Remoting), abstraction of networking layers (so-called channels), and serialization formats (binary, XML, and so on).

However, with this huge amount of abstraction comes a big issue: The expense of network calls is no longer made obvious in types and their operations. Consider our Person example again. We already saw how the call to Pay got marshaled to the remote object, which seems just fine. But imagine what happens if we had a bunch of properties, such as Name and Age, exposed on the object. Without even knowing the object is remote, you could simply "dot into" those properties from a remote domain, causing network calls to happen for every single such operation. This if often referred to as "chatty communication."

For this reason (among others, such as access coordination to remote objects), the industry has moved on to more service-oriented styles of programming, as exemplified by technologies like web services. In such a setting, one makes calls to operations defined on a (stateless) web service "façade," serializing objects or unique identifiers across. For example, paying our John person would be done by making some `Pay(8491, 123.45m)` call, where 8491 is John's unique identifier. The use of (static) web service façade methods gives rise to a more chunky form of communication. Now the transparency is limited to the operations defined on a web service proxy object and doesn't get entangled with whole object graphs.

A `MarshalByRefObject` Calculator Add-In

To continue our exploration of cross-domain communication between objects, let's fix our `Calc` type by making it marshal by ref. You should feel free to experiment with a serializable object, as well, as explained before. Here is the adapted code that makes our `Calc` type amenable for use across application domains:

```
using System;

public class Calc : MarshalByRefObject
{
    public int Add(int a, int b)
    {
        Console.WriteLine(AppDomain.CurrentDomain);
        return a + b;
    }
}
```

Using our existing hosting code shown before, we can now get the calculator to work without the exception displayed in Figure 25.41. The use of .NET Remoting becomes apparent if we hover over the `calc` object and see its type, which reflects the use of a transparent proxy. Figure 25.44 shows how the remote object's type name is buried in a series of indirections put in place by the .NET Remoting infrastructure.

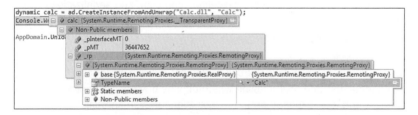

FIGURE 25.44   Transparent proxy type introduced by .NET Remoting.

Because our calculator's `Add` method prints the application domain in which it's executing, we can see the call is taking place in the `AddIn` domain. Try executing the same host but with the `Calc` type marked as `Serializable` and observe how the call will now be made within the host's application domain, as the object got *copied* by value.

If you take a while during the debugging session shown in Figure 25.44, you might get to see the error shown in Figure 25.45. This indicates an expired lifetime lease for the remote object. Without going into much more detail, the concept of a lease allows the runtime's remoting infrastructure to collect remote objects after a certain amount of inactivity. In a distributed world where connections can fail, it makes a lot of sense to be able to collect an unused object. To override the default lifetime control, you can override the `MarshalByRefObject`'s `InitializeLifetimeService` method. Returning a null reference will cause leases not to expire at all. You can find more information in the MSDN documentation.

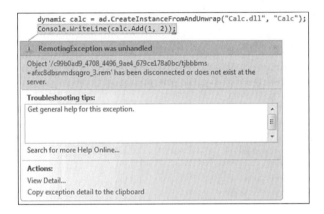

FIGURE 25.45   A remoting lease has expired, revealing the object's remote address.

Use of an Interface Contract

So far, we've been using C# 4.0's dynamic feature to invoke the calculator object's `Add` method because we don't want to refer to the add-in assembly statically, and therefore we don't have a type to cast the created remote object to. This decoupling between an add-in host and the various add-ins is precisely our goal when creating extensible applications.

Instead of using `dynamic`, it makes sense to establish a firm contract between a host and the add-ins by means of an interface. To illustrate this, we revamp our example by introducing an interface for an add-in operation:

```
public interface IBinaryOperation
{
    int Compute(int a, int b);
    string Name { get; }
}
```

With this interface in place, everyone can write a binary operator for the extensible calculator host application. For example:

```csharp
public class Pythagorean : MarshalByRefObject, IBinaryOperation
{
    public int Compute(int a, int b)
    {
        return (int)Math.Sqrt(a * a + b * b);
    }

    public string Name { get { return "Pythagorean"; } }
}
```

To make things as loosely coupled as possible, we introduce different assemblies for the host, the contract interfaces, and any of the add-ins. Although the host and add-ins all refer to the assembly containing the contract interfaces, there's no direct connection between the add-ins and the host. Figure 25.46 illustrates a typical organization in terms of Visual Studio projects in a solution, revealing cross-project references.

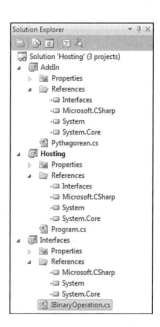

FIGURE 25.46   Establishing a shared contract between host and add-ins.

Now we can adapt our host's code to cast the instantiated add-in object to the common interface, instead of relying on `dynamic`:

```
var ad = AppDomain.CreateDomain("AddIn");

var calc = (IBinaryOperation)ad.CreateInstanceFromAndUnwrap(
    "AddIn.dll",
    "Pythagorean"
);

Console.WriteLine(calc.Compute(3, 4));
```

In a more realistic extensible application, both the assembly name and type name of the add-in will be loaded from some kind of configuration store.

With this separation between host and add-in put in place, we also see that unloading the AddIn domain becomes very effective, causing the loaded add-in assembly to get unloaded properly. The only remains of loading the add-in will be the shared interface assembly, which belongs to our host's circle of trust. In other words, it's now possible to get rid of a misbehaving add-in altogether by unloading the corresponding domain. This point is proven in Figure 25.47.

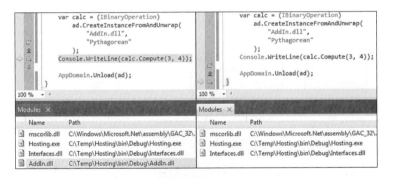

FIGURE 25.47   Unloading of the add-in domain.

The Managed Add-In Framework

Although .NET Remoting as a communication mechanism for distributed computing has been largely superseded by service-oriented architecture (SOA) patterns (using either classic web services in ASP.NET or the WCF stack), it still pays off in scenarios where the most basic form of cross-domain communication is required. In particular, add-ins typically require strong isolation properties, which can be realized using application domains, as we saw before.

Use of application domains doesn't provide a silver bullet, though. Certain behaviors can still have fatal consequences, such as an out-of-memory, stack-overflow, or other exceptions that corrupt the process state. To provide protection against those kinds of misbehavior caused by an add-in, a separate add-in process is required.

Setting up this entire infrastructure is a rather tedious and repetitive task, with lots of caveats related to providing resilience against various problems in configuration and runtime behavior, as well as lifetime management. Moreover, complicating matters further, add-in-driven applications are often plagued by versioning issues. Those arise when either the host or an add-in has to evolve and can't continue to obey to the shared contract interface between them. Finally, there's also a lot to worry about proper add-in discovery.

To take away all of this manual plumbing, the .NET Framework has a managed add-in framework in the System.AddIn set of namespaces. Essentially, it abstracts away lots of the complexities mentioned previously. Because of its general-purpose nature, the initial cost in terms of different projects for an extensible application can be a bit overwhelming. Nonetheless, having sufficient layers of abstraction in place allows you to develop an add-in application that has proper add-in discovery, isolation, versioning, and so on.

Figure 25.48 shows the add-in framework architecture, which has a beautiful symmetry between the host side and the add-in side. In the middle, we recognize the concept of a contract, which again is realized using an interface that acts as the single shared notion between both sides. Instead of connecting directly between both parties, the add-in framework introduces the notion of views and adapters, which provide a versioning-capable mapping between the host or add-in to the shared contracts.

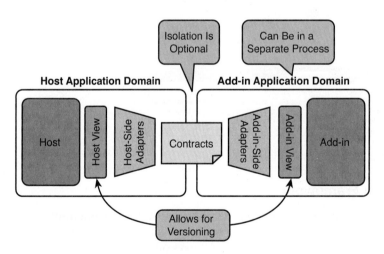

FIGURE 25.48   Overall architecture of the add-in framework.

Besides the pipeline facilities sketched here, the add-in framework also provides APIs to discover add-ins and build up a so-called store. We don't have the room to build up a complete add-in framework example here; so, refer to the MSDN library for a sample solution.

WHAT ABOUT MEF?

Starting from .NET 4, the Managed Extensibility Framework (MEF) ships out of the box with the framework redistribution. At first sight, there's quite a bit of overlap with the goals of the add-in framework (because both deal with extensible applications). The main difference lies in MEF's focus on *composition* (wiring up add-in objects with their consumers), whereas add-ins focus more on the *isolation and versioning* aspects (using the architecture shown earlier).

From this point of view, both technologies can be thought as complementary. In fact, both can be combined to leverage benefits of both frameworks.

Summary

In the previous chapter, we learned how to structure applications into manageable pieces from a language point of view, using the concept of namespaces. Separate from this, the runtime plays a role, too, to realize goals of loading components and providing isolation when needed.

On the boundary between runtime, languages, and tools, we find the unit of deployment for code and metadata on the .NET platform. Referred to as assemblies, they act as the container for types, all metadata describing those types and their members, as well as embedded resources. Visual Studio provides various project templates to create those assemblies for different goals, such as a console or GUI application (an .exe file) or a class library (a .dll file). Assemblies can refer to other assemblies they want to use. At runtime, the CLR locates and loads assemblies from various locations. No registration is needed to install or use an assembly, which is referred to as xcopy deployment. For general-purpose assemblies, however, it's not uncommon to register them to the GAC.

Various auxiliary services are provided to deal with assemblies and code they contain. One is the capability to turn code into native instructions after deploying the assembly to a user's machine. This facility is called NGEN. Other services deal with naming (using strong-name keys), loading assemblies at runtime through various APIs, the ability to expose internal types and members to friend assemblies, and forwarding of relocated types to another assembly.

Finally, during execution of an application, assemblies are tightly related to application domains, which provide the basic unit of isolation in the runtime. Although assemblies can be loaded into an application domain, they cannot be unloaded unless the containing domain gets unloaded as a whole. Security-related settings can be used to influence the behavior of the application domain when loading and executing code. To communicate between those isolation units, you typically need to pinch a hole between application domains to invoke operations on objects in a different domain. The .NET Remoting and type serialization infrastructure built in to the runtime helps out with this. Abstractions over those APIs are provided for scenarios such as building extensible add-in-driven applications.

CHAPTER 26

Base Class Library Essentials

IN THIS CHAPTER

▶ The BCL: What, Where, and How? 1293

▶ The Holy System Root Namespace 1301

▶ Facilities to Work with Text 1346

Now that you've been introduced to most of the day-to-day C# language features used, we should say a word or two about the Base Class Library (BCL) provided by .NET. Rarely, other than for academic examples, can a program be written without the use of a significant number of application programming interfaces (APIs) and libraries. And that's a good thing, really. The relationship between the runtime, various languages that build on it, and all the libraries provided by the .NET Framework should be such that the same language-level skills can be reused to reach out to many of the libraries that are available.

Unless certain library-intensive patterns become very common, there's no good justification to taint the language with new features that give a false impression of "integration" and cannot be taken out without breaking existing code. Only the compelling scenarios that truly benefit from language integration tend to make it, such as LINQ. One common characteristic of such features is their generic nature, allowing them to be used with wide range of libraries. For example, LINQ's query expressions can be used to target any kind of data source, ranging from in-memory object graphs, hierarchical data, and relational storage to various other data models and stores.

As a result, the pace at which different layers of the framework tend to evolve differs with many levels of magnitude. Over the years, the set of APIs provided by the framework has grown in quite a spectacular manner. All of this could be achieved without making huge changes to the languages or the framework. This observation becomes clear when looking at various releases of the framework. For example, all the 2.0, 3.0, and 3.5 "waves" were built on the same CLR

2.0 runtime. And while certain versions of programming languages are in use, many more framework libraries appear, some of which as part of out-of-band releases. For example, the Managed Extensibility Framework (MEF) could do everything it had to without requiring changes to the runtime, any of the languages, or even essential base class libraries.

Figure 26.1 shows a conceptual diagram of layering of runtimes, languages, and libraries. Obviously, applications are written to make use of all of those, but the amount of library features used significantly outnumbers the language features. This book tends to focus on the two bottom layers of the diagram: mastering the C# programming language and knowing fundamentals about the runtime that underpins language features (for example, generics, DLR, reflection).

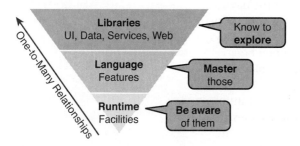

FIGURE 26.1   Runtimes, languages, and libraries.

Good layers of abstraction supported by language features such as code patterns (for example, `foreach` loops, `using` blocks, query syntax), object orientation, namespaces, and so on provide a win-win situation in this jungle of libraries. From the library writer's point of view, an API can be given, by obeying good design principles, a natural feeling for users in various languages. At the same time, users' skill sets can be reused to target all those libraries. Language design principles, such as static typing, together with runtime facilities, such as rich metadata support, tend to aid users in exploring APIs. A good example of tooling features leveraging this can be found in IntelliSense and the Object Browser (which should really be called Type Browser).

Doing justice to all the framework libraries just by reviewing them in a shallow manner is nearly impossible, so refer to specialized titles for deep coverage of things such as UI programming (for example, using Windows Presentation Foundation [WPF]), targeting the Web (for example, using ASP.NET and Silverlight), communication and services (for example, using WCF), and so forth. Often, the number of auxiliary concepts introduced by those technology pillars is way too high to familiarize you within a limited space. Examples of this include configuration and installation aspects (for example, deploying a web application), various designer tools (for example, designing a WPF application), and specialized debugging (for example, when using T-SQL stored procedures in a database).

Instead, we focus on a common set of foundational libraries that can truly be regarded as base class libraries and emphasize a couple of essential patterns that will help you explore various libraries.

The BCL: What, Where, and How?

Our main goal in this chapter is to introduce you to the essential libraries that come with the .NET Framework and tend to be used in a wide variety of scenarios. No matter whether you're writing a UI application, a web application, services, or even some kind of cloud-based application, having a clue about libraries turns out to be very beneficial. Although the term *Base Class Library* (BCL) has become harder to define over the years, I'll piggyback on this widely used acronym to introduce what I believe to be essential.

What Is Covered?

A significant number of namespaces that are part of the BCL are not covered here because they've gotten attention already in the context of language feature discussion. For example, while talking about generics, we covered the main uses of the feature, namely collections. Similarly, the discussion about LINQ put us in a great spot to discuss essential interfaces such as IEnumerable<T> and some APIs that are used to deal with specific data models. During our dynamic programming exploration, things such as System.Reflection and the DLR were covered in quite some detail as well.

Highlights of this chapter include coverage of namespaces (for example, the root System namespace) and various children (for example, Diagnostics, IO, Text, and Threading). So that you get a feel for the components and their installation, we'll work through a simple Windows Service example, covering System.ServiceProcess and System.Configuration. From a scenario point of view, our emphasis is on themes, such as working with text, doing I/O, and so on, instead of tackling specific domains like UI programming. To set realistic expectations, don't expect to master the covered namespaces in an end-to-end manner: Lots of those APIs have different levels of complexity, ranging from the very simple to the more involved scenarios that require tight control. Most of the time, we focus on the basics and call out areas that may require deeper exploration if you're interested.

Things I consider too specialized for meaningful coverage in the limited number of pages available include APIs like DirectoryServices (to interact with Active Directory and LDAP-based directory services), Messaging (exposing MSMQ message queuing to managed code), Transactions (to deal with things such as distributed transactions), COM+ support in ComponentServices, and many more hidden gems throughout the rich .NET Framework set of APIs.

Default Project References

The assemblies that get referenced upon creation of a new project serve as a good starting point for exploration of the BCL and commonly used APIs. Depending on the project type, a different set of references is present. It should be obvious that building a Windows Presentation Foundation (WPF) application requires different dependencies than the creation of a WCF service library.

The most primitive set of references is likely to be found in our much beloved Console Application template, so let's take a look at it. Figure 26.2 shows the default set of references displayed for such a project, targeting .NET Framework 4.

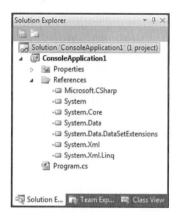

FIGURE 26.2   Default set of references added for a .NET 4 Console Application.

This set of references might be a little surprising at first. Some functionality, like XML and Data, doesn't seem to be needed for a lot of scenarios. That's a good observation; all the default project templates do is introduce some commonly used functionality to ease their discovery. Over the years, those default references have grown quite a bit. For example, the .NET 3.5 tooling introduced references to LINQ assemblies.

REFERENCES ARE LOADED LAZILY

Despite the presence of references in the References section of a project in the Solution Explorer, this doesn't imply that all those assemblies will effectively get loaded. Only the ones that are used at runtime, which can obviously depend on the code path taken during execution, will get loaded. It's the Just-in-Time (JIT) compiler's role to invoke the loader when a reference has to be chased to be able to run a certain piece of code.

You are welcome to take a look at the references through the lenses of ILDASM as well. In short, references specified in Visual Studio get propagated to the build system, based on MSBuild nowadays, which invokes the C# compiler using the /r flag to pass in references. Those references end up in the metadata of the compiled assembly as extern references. For framework assemblies, a strong name is used to refer to them. At runtime, the assembly will be found from the Global Assembly Cache (GAC, as discussed Chapter 25, "Assemblies and Application Domains"), when it's required for execution.

Namespaces Versus Assemblies

An important distinction we drew in Chapter 25 is that between namespaces and assemblies. One way to approach this is by stating that namespaces provide a means to do logical partitioning of functionality, whereas assemblies are physical containers for types and members. A many-to-many mapping exists between both concepts: A single assembly may contain different namespaces, and a single namespace may be spread across different assemblies.

This configuration can sometimes lead to some confusion where one wonders what happened to his or her favorite type. In such a circumstance, two things should be checked. First of all, a using directive for the namespace containing the type might be missing. This can easily be rectified using the Visual Studio's "smart tag tip" that pops up as shown in Figure 26.3. Ctrl+. (dot) can be used to make the menu appear if you don't like to use the mouse.

FIGURE 26.3   Visual Studio editor support to resolve a namespace.

If the name of the type cannot be found in any of the referenced assemblies, this way of adding a namespace import won't help you. To track down the missing reference, a couple of options exist. One is to use the Object Browser—just enter the type's name and have the tool search through a set of .NET Framework reference assemblies it knows about. Figure 26.4 shows this in action.

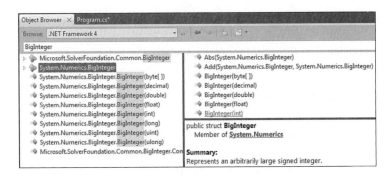

FIGURE 26.4   Using the Object Browser to find a type.

After the type has been found in Object Browser, the Member Of link in the details pane can be used to navigate to the corresponding namespace in the tree view, which will also reveal the assembly the type is defined in. Figure 26.5 shows this.

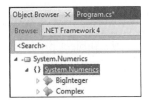

FIGURE 26.5   Navigating assemblies, namespaces, and types in Object Browser.

An alternative path to hunt for the assembly defining the required type is to look in MSDN documentation. Each type's documentation entry includes the namespace and assembly, as shown in Figure 26.6.

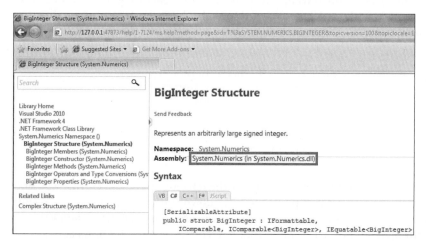

FIGURE 26.6   Finding the assembly a type is defined in MSDN documentation.

After the type has been found, the next step is to add a reference to the assembly if it's not there yet. The Add Reference dialog was discussed in Chapter 25 and shows all the .NET assemblies that have been registered in file system locations where the IDE goes and looks for reference assemblies.

The System and mscorlib Assemblies

Two of the most important assemblies for the majority of managed applications are mscorlib and System. Rarely does any application not touch functionality defined in one of those assemblies. The distinction between both is mostly a matter of logistics, reflecting how the framework and runtime designers decided to split up things.

Notice that mscorlib doesn't appear in the References section in Visual Studio, even though it's being referenced by the compiler. The philosophy behind this is that a whole bunch of types defined in the System namespace live in mscorlib and are required to write C# applications. For example, because System.Object is used as the base class for every type, the compiler needs to be able to reference it in the generated intermediate language (IL). And as you can guess, System.Object lives in mscorlib.dll.

If for some advanced reason you want to omit a reference to mscorlib and define your own System namespace (including things like Object, ValueType, Array, and so on) for the compiler to target, there's a truly advanced option to do so. Go to the project properties, click through to Build, and click the Advanced button. This allows you to enable the Do Not Reference mscorlib.dll setting as shown in Figure 26.7.

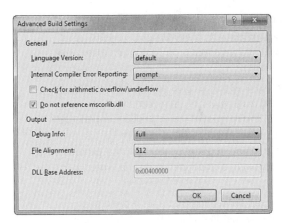

FIGURE 26.7   Disabling the much-needed reference to mscorlib.dll.

As soon as you do this, the compiler will complain about essential types missing, in a way similar to what's shown in Figure 26.8. Now you're responsible for defining a System namespace with types such as Object and some 30 more. If you pass this challenge, you'll have an assembly that doesn't depend on mscorlib.dll. In practice, though, there are very few compelling scenarios where this comes in handy, so you can always rely on mscorlib.dll being referenced. Visual Basic has a similar feature called *runtime agility*, which allows the frequently used runtime library for the language to be dropped.

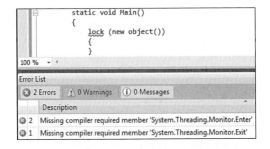

FIGURE 26.8   Life without mscorlib.dll is painful but reveals language dependencies.

OTHER LANGUAGE DEPENDENCIES

Over the years, the C# language has become dependent on more framework APIs against which to emit code. In C# 1.0, most dependencies were found in mscorlib and included things such as System.IDisposable, System.Threading.Monitor, and so on. I leave it as an exercise for you to relate those two example types to some of the discussed C# language features.

New features introduced in C# 2.0 required more functionality to be present at the framework API level. For example, iterators leverage the IEnumerable<T> and IEnumerator<T> interfaces. The use of nullable types relies on methods defined by the Nullable<T> struct (for example, HasValue).

Going one version further to C# 3.0, a few more dependencies were added to support the set of LINQ-related language features, although most of them simply rely on method signatures and names. For example, the language doesn't take a dependency on System.Linq.Enumerable or System.Linq.Queryable but simply binds against methods such as Where and Select when translating query syntax. For the expression tree representation of lambda expressions, though, a dependency on the types in System.Linq.Expressions exists.

The latest version of C#, version 4.0, introduced something that hadn't been seen before for C#: a language-specific runtime library, just like Visual Basic had since its very early days. This design decision was made to support the dynamic typing feature, where a runtime library is needed to carry out overload resolution that follows the rules of the C# language (but deferred until runtime rather than implemented by the compiler).

One implication of those dependencies is that certain language features can simply be disabled by dropping references to certain framework assemblies. For example, if you inexplicably dislike LINQ to Objects or IQuerable<T> forms of LINQ, it's just a matter of dropping System.Core or (less invasive) dropping the using directive for System.Linq. To disable C# 4.0 dynamic, it suffices to omit a reference to Microsoft.CSharp.dll. Whether those tricks will continue to work in the future (because other functionality might and likely will end up in those assemblies) is something I prefer not to make any judgment about.

It's a good exercise to relate language features back to some of the framework APIs on which they depend. Again, ILDASM is your best friend to uncover them. In fact, we've done so for a whole bunch of language features discussed throughout the book. Innocent-looking keywords such as lock, using, switch, and so on all rely (sometimes, for example, for switch) on certain framework types.

In summary, both mscorlib.dll and System.dll are your best friends to find a whole set of frequently used APIs that define a significant portion of what we refer to as the BCL. However, in .NET 3.5 (and hence, in the world of sub-obvious versioning schemes, C# 3.0), another player entered the scene: System.Core.dll.

System.Core's Story of Red Bits and Green Bits

After the initial release of the .NET Framework, the runtime, libraries, languages, and tools started to evolve at quite a different pace. This confirms the observations we made at the start of this chapter, with CLR 2.0 staying at the heart of the releases that immediately followed it. In particular, .NET 3.0 and .NET 3.5 leveraged the same runtime. At the same time, those releases brought service packs to lower layers of the system, including the CLR and BCL libraries. Figure 26.9 attempts to bring some structure to this picture.

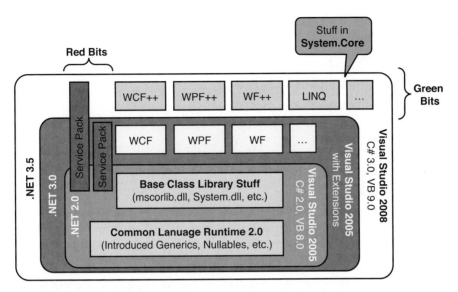

FIGURE 26.9   Versioning of runtime, libraries, and tools.

One challenge faced in the .NET 3.5 era was how to ship service packs to the layers underneath while introducing new functionality. It's not until a user installs a service pack to .NET 3.0 or .NET 2.0 components that all of a sudden a whole bunch of new functionality needs to become available. The reasoning behind this is just that service packs should simply be containers for patches to existing functionality, also giving a maximum level of backward compatibility.

The solution one came up with was to bucketize features and fixes into green bits and red bits. The former category contains new functionality and should therefore not slip into a user's configuration if a service pack is applied to, say, .NET 2.0. As a result, those new pieces of functionality must end up in a new assembly that didn't exist before. This became the role of System.Core.dll, which contains "new stuff" that could have been BCL functionality if it had been introduced in an earlier version. In that respect, it can be seen as a natural extension to System and mscorlib. Figure 26.10 shows that lots of functionality was added to various "core" System namespaces. The most notable examples are the HashSet<T> collection type, support for named pipes, and the whole LINQ feature set.

Other green bits assemblies exist, such as System.Windows.Presentation.dll for some of the enhancements made to WPF, which weren't just fixes. On the other hand, red bits simply denote prior framework versions' assemblies that have been subject to changes in the .NET 3.5 release and were simply patched in-place.

This technique of separating out fixes from new functionality using physical separation of assemblies, while keeping the logical structure of namespaces intact, illustrates why the distinction between both concepts actually has a value. Other variables sometimes factor into the decision of whether a new assembly has to be introduced. Examples include performance concerns associated with loading big assemblies from the disk, if only a tiny subset of the assembly's functionality is leveraged by end users.

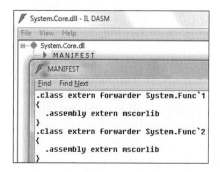

▲ ┈▭ System.Core [3.5.0.0]
  ▷ {} Microsoft.Win32.SafeHandles
  ▷ {} System
  ▷ {} System.Collections.Generic
  ▷ {} System.Diagnostics
  ▷ {} System.Diagnostics.Eventing
  ▷ {} System.Diagnostics.Eventing.Reader
  ▷ {} System.Diagnostics.PerformanceData
  ▷ {} System.IO
  ▷ {} System.IO.Pipes
  ▷ {} System.Linq
  ▷ {} System.Linq.Expressions
  ▷ {} System.Management.Instrumentation
  ▷ {} System.Runtime.CompilerServices
  ▷ {} System.Security
  ▷ {} System.Security.Cryptography
  ▷ {} System.Security.Cryptography.X509Certificates
  ▷ {} System.Threading

FIGURE 26.10   `System.Core`'s framework enrichment.

In .NET 4.0, the `System.Core` assembly was kept even though this latest version of the framework supports a complete side-by-side installation alongside earlier versions of the runtime and the libraries. Strictly speaking, the functionality in `System.Core` could have been merged into traditional and historical BCL containers like the `mscorlib` and `System` assemblies. For reasons of discovery of features (people have gotten used to associating, say, LINQ with `System.Core`) and performance (size of core assemblies that are loaded by every application), `System.Core` was kept.

A few commonly used types were relocated, though (for example, the `Func` delegate types), as shown in Figure 26.11. This use of forwarding allows applications compiled against the .NET 3.5 `System.Core` assembly to continue working even though some of the types have been moved to `mscorlib`. Such a refactoring was deemed useful to avoid having to load `System.Core` for other portions of the framework that depend on those commonly used types.

```
 System.Core.dll - IL DASM
File  View  Help
⊟┈◆ System.Core.dll
      ▶ MANIFEST
    MANIFEST
    Find  Find Next
    .class extern forwarder System.Func`1
    {
      .assembly extern mscorlib
    }
    .class extern forwarder System.Func`2
    {
      .assembly extern mscorlib
    }
```

FIGURE 26.11   Types forwarded from `System.Core` to `mscorlib` in .NET 4.

In summary, when targeting .NET 3.5 or later, `System.Core` is the third big member of the BCL assembly triad, alongside `mscorlib` and `System`. When looking for commonly used functionality, include this assembly in your search. It should be no surprise that all project templates targeting the latest versions of the .NET Framework include references to all of those assemblies.

REFERENCE ASSEMBLIES

The installation of the .NET Framework and Visual Studio tools include so-called reference assemblies that live in the Program Files folder. Those are the ones that are used by various tools. However, they've been stripped down and contain just the metadata needed by those tools. In particular, the executable (IL) code has been removed from them. At runtime, assemblies in the GAC are picked up by the loader.

The Holy System Root Namespace

From now on, we'll ignore the diverse physical locations of BCL functionality and start with the assumption all types can be found. The default configuration of references in a newly created .NET 4 project will suffice. In places where it does not (for instance, an assembly other than the ones referenced is needed), I mention this explicitly.

The framework's core namespace is System. In this first section, we explore the root namespace, looking at some of the types and members we skipped over in the preceding chapters. This allows us to discuss some related concerns, such as dealing with formatting of particular data types and so on.

Primitive Value Types

We have already seen all of the primitive value types supported by the C# language, using suffixes for literals (for example, 123L for a long) and various operations defined on them. However, some operations require use of static or instance members on those types. Let's take a look.

Parsing Strings

One rather common operation used to obtain a primitive value is to parse external input, for example, coming from a database, directly from the user, or text-based stores such as XML files. In such a case, parsing a textual representation of a value into a proper value is needed.

Two methods exist on most primitive types that allow for precisely this: Parse and TryParse. Their behavior differs in whether an exception gets thrown when parsing fails. In fact, before .NET 2.0, the only available methods were Parse, requiring the user to write exception-handling code for something that isn't really an exceptional kind of failure. An example of TryParse, which is more commonly used nowadays, is shown here. Use of the Parse method is still a good idea if you don't expect input to be malformed, hence making a failure to parse truly exceptional:

```
string ageString;
int age;
do
{
    Console.Write("Enter your age: ");
    ageString = Console.ReadLine();
}
while (!int.TryParse(ageString, out age));

Console.WriteLine("Your age is {0}.", age);
```

In this piece of code, we're also using the notion of format strings to print the obtained age to the screen. We discuss this framework feature in much more detail later in the "Formatting Text" section. For now, simply think of {0} as a place holder for the first params array element passed to WriteLine.

Because today's software landscape is subject to globalization, parsing values from text is not something that will work in a uniform manner throughout the world. Textual forms of values such as numbers, dates, and so on highly depend on the culture of the user. Proper globalization of software is a topic of its own, with whole books devoted to the subject, so we'll restrict ourselves to a basic example of dealing with different numeric styles. The core enumeration that's used to work with numbers is called NumberStyles and is defined in the System.Globalization namespace. It's an enum that supports the use of flags, so composite styles are possible. Figure 26.12 shows the enum's values.

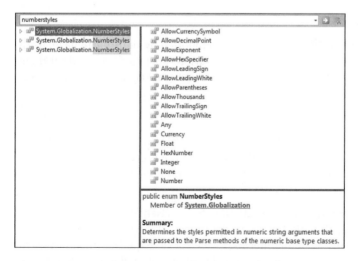

FIGURE 26.12   Values of the NumberStyles enum.

An example is the AllowThousands flag, which specifies that thousand separators can be used. In conjunction with AllowDecimalPoint, the string 87,654.32 is a valid numeric string in English. Some of the values in the enum simply combine flags into a handy shortcut. For example, the Numer style contains both flags that we've discussed here as well as flags for leading and trailing signs and whitespace.

If you *parsed* the preceding paragraph carefully, it should be clear that one piece of the puzzle is missing: How's the target culture determined? In the example described previously, the string 87,654.32 will parse fine for English, but in the author's native culture (Belgian Dutch), the decimal point is written as a comma, and optional thousand group separators use a point. The same number is now written as 87.654,32. This is where another parameter to Parse and TryParse comes in.

Using the IFormatProvider parameter, you can specify the culture-specific formatting that's desired. Luckily, you don't have to implement this interface to make use of this feature: The CultureInfo class, also defined in System.Globalization, does so already. So the remaining question is where to get such CultureInfo objects. Besides the ability to new up such objects, static members on the class are often very useful. Figure 26.13 shows the use of decimal.TryParse with a specific culture.

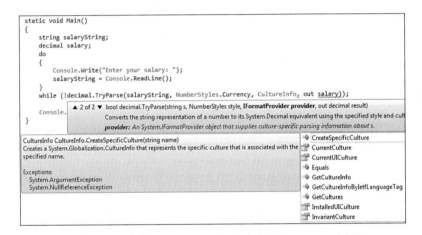

FIGURE 26.13   Using a culture to perform decimal string parsing.

Some cultures are readily available, such as the current (UI) culture, which can be set in a number of ways or can be obtained from the user's profile settings (the default). The so-called invariant culture is useful for storing and retrieving data in a culture that's the same on every machine, also regardless of specific settings. If left unspecified, the current info is used, which can also be obtained from NumberFormatInfo.CurrentInfo, which is another way to obtain an IFormatProvider. An example using cultures is shown here:

```
Console.Write("Enter your culture: ");
string culture = Console.ReadLine();

string salaryString;
decimal salary;
do {
```

```
    Console.Write("Enter your salary: ");
    salaryString = Console.ReadLine();
}
while (!decimal.TryParse(salaryString, NumberStyles.Currency,
                        new CultureInfo(culture), out salary));

Console.WriteLine("Your salary is {0}.", salary);
```

Here is some sample input and output, clearly revealing failure to parse our input, depending on the culture:

```
Enter your culture: en-US
Enter your salary: 87,654.32
Your salary is 87654.32.

Enter your culture: en-US
Enter your salary: 87.654,32
Enter your salary:

Enter your culture: nl-BE
Enter your salary: 87.654,32
Your salary is 87654.32.
```

Notice how the output of all the WriteLine calls is the same. Later, you'll see how we can influence string formatting to follow specific culture settings. In fact, both parsing and formatting can be considered more or less as inverse functions.

Special Values

Most primitive types have some special values intrinsically tied to the domain of the type. For example, integer data types have a certain range whose boundaries can be retrieved using constant fields like MinValue and MaxValue:

```
Console.WriteLine("32-bit signed integers range from {0} to {1}.",
                  int.MinValue, int.MaxValue);
```

For floating-point numbers, other characteristic values exist, such as the NaN (not-a-number) values that result from things such as division by zero, and the infinity values as defined in the IEEE specification of floating-point numbers:

Obviously, those fields are read-only or constant and filled in by the BCL and runtime. Refer to the discussion about fields in Chapter 11, "Fields, Properties, and Indexers" for more information about the distinction between const (for example, used for int.MaxValue) and read-only (for example, used for DateTime.MinValue).

USE OF KEYWORDS OR TYPE NAMES?

In the preceding examples, we've been using the C# keywords for primitive types, like int and decimal, to dot into static members. Alternatively, we could have used the type names that correspond with them, such as Int32 and Decimal in the System namespace. Which style to use is nothing more than a matter of user preference, and both mean exactly the same thing.

This can be confusing at first for developers with a Java background, where int and Integer have a different meaning: The former indicates a primitive value, whereas the latter is used to refer to a "boxed" reference type wrapping such a value. In .NET, the act of boxing is tied to the use of the values in relation to the object base type.

Working with Arrays

A commonly used family of types consists of arrays, which really are a form of type constructors: given any type, you can construct an array type out of it. To facilitate certain common operations, the System.Array type exists. All arrays derive from this type, giving them some useful instance-level members and properties. For example, the rank of an array denotes the number of dimensions:

```
var xs = new int[10];
var ys = new int[3,4];
var zs = new int[3][];
```

For the first array, the rank will be 1 because there's only one dimension. The second one has a rank of 2 because of the use of the multidimensional array feature. For the last one, a jagged array, the rank of zs is still 1:

```
Console.WriteLine(xs.Rank); // 1
Console.WriteLine(ys.Rank); // 2
Console.WriteLine(zs.Rank); // 1
```

To find the range of valid indexes along the different dimensions of an array, methods such as GetLowerBound and GetUpperBound can be used. In practice, they are rarely used, in favor of for loops generating a range from zero to the array's length minus one, or a foreach loop that takes care of all the heavy lifting.

The static members on System.Array are of more interest in various circumstances. A couple of examples are shown in the following code:

```
var rnd = new Random();
var xs = new int[20];
for (int i = 0; i < 10; i++)
    xs[i] = rnd.Next(10);
```

```
Array.Resize(ref xs, 10); // drop last ten, like LINQ's Take
Array.Sort(xs); // in-place quicksort, like LINQ's OrderBy
Array.Reverse(xs); // in-place reversal, like LINQ's Reverse

var ys = new int[10];
Array.Copy(xs, ys, xs.Length); // more overloads available
Array.ForEach(ys, Console.WriteLine); // like a foreach-loop

int fiveAt = Array.BinarySearch(ys, 5); // -1 if not found
bool anyEven = Array.Exists(ys, i => i % 2 == 0); // like LINQ's Any

// Other operations include:
// - TrueForAll (like LINQ's All operator)
// - Find and FindAll (like LINQ's Select operator)
// - Ways to find indexes for an element
```

Notice the high number of "like LINQ" remarks made in the code comments here. A historical perspective definitely helps here because arrays have been in the framework since the early days, whereas LINQ's generalization of sequence operators was introduced in .NET 3.5. For some of those operations, there's quite a difference between using the Array type's static method and use of LINQ operators. In particular, lots of Array methods operate on the data in an in-place manner, whereas LINQ to Objects produces new sequences (based on IEnumerable<T>) without mutating the underlying data. It's also the case that the Array methods are heavily optimized based on the array-specific characteristics, such as the capability to index efficiently and upfront knowledge of the array's bounds. Things such as BinarySearch and Sort can leverage those properties to provide very efficient implementations.

Segments

A relatively little-known type related to arrays is ArraySegment<T>, which was added to the framework in .NET 2.0. It basically allows bundling an array together with an offset and a length. Users of the struct can consult this information (for example, to figure out the part of an array they're allowed to operate on):

```
var xs = new[] { 3, 7, 2, 5, 1, 4, 0, 9, 6, 8 };
//                     ^^^^^^^^^^^^^^
var ys = new ArraySegment<int>(xs, 3, 5);

// Retrieving start and end elements in the segment
var fst = ys.Array[ys.Offset]; // 5
var lst = ys.Array[ys.Offset + ys.Count - 1]; // 9
```

A good exercise for readers interested in algorithms is to implement some recursive sort algorithm where the bounds of a sort operation are communicated using an ArraySegment value.

Buffers

Arrays are represented as contiguous blocks of memory that the CLR knows, based on the array's element type, how to index into. For example, an array holding Int32 values will occupy 4 bytes per element. To access the fifth element, an offset of 16 bytes must be skipped into the array's memory to land on the element.

In the world of native code, developers often manipulate arrays in a low-level manner by calculating offsets into the array's memory. Such manipulations tend to cause lots of bugs and can actually violate memory and type safety (for example, when reaching out of the bounds of the array). To restore some of those lower-level manipulation techniques, the Buffer type can be used, while preserving various forms of safety. For example, it's not possible to use Buffer operations over an array holding references because twiddling with references is a dangerous act that should be kept to the garbage collector.

An example of a simple operation is to ask for an array's byte size:

```
var xs = new[] { 3, 7, 2, 5, 1, 4, 0, 9, 6, 8 };
var len1 = Buffer.ByteLength(xs); // xs.Length * sizeof(int)
var len2 = xs.Length * sizeof(int);
```

Armed with such knowledge, you can do various kinds of manipulations on bytes that fall within the bounds of the array. Obviously, this is a rather specialized task that requires the user's knowledge about how primitive types are laid out in memory. One such piece of knowledge is the little-endian ordering of bytes. The following example plays a bit with the bytes of a 32-bit signed integer stored in an array:

```
var xs = new[] { 3, 7, 2, 5, 1, 4, 0, 9, 6, 8 };


byte b1 = Buffer.GetByte(xs, 0); // 3 due to little-endian architecture
byte b2 = Buffer.GetByte(xs, 1); // 0
byte b3 = Buffer.GetByte(xs, 2); // 0
byte b4 = Buffer.GetByte(xs, 3); // 0

Console.WriteLine("0x{0:X}", xs[0]);  // 0x00000003
Buffer.SetByte(xs, 1, 0x42);          //         ^^
Buffer.SetByte(xs, 3, 0x17);          //     ^^
Console.WriteLine("0x{0:X}", xs[0]);  // 0x17004203
```

Here, the first 4 bytes on the array's memory used for elements are occupied by the bytes that comprise the 32-bit integer value of 3 used for the first element. By means of the GetByte method, we can actually see those bytes in their raw form. The SetByte method touches those bytes, making the manipulations highlighted on the right in the comments. Notice the use of the {0:X} format string, which dumps the first params array argument to WriteLine in hexadecimal format. Later, we'll see the richness of string formatting illustrated more broadly. Suffice to say that formatting of strings offers lots of flexibility beyond just punching and filling "holes" in strings.

One more possible manipulation allowed by the `Buffer` class is to do a block-copy of one array to another, possibly of another primitive data type. For example, in the preceding, we have an array of 32-bit integers, all of which would actually fit in single byte values. Using the `Buffer`'s `BlockCopy` method, we can copy elements into such an array:

```
var xs = new[] { 3, 7, 2, 5, 1, 4, 0, 9, 6, 8 };
```

```
// 3 0 0 0 7 0 0 0 ...
var ys = new byte[Buffer.ByteLength(xs)];
Buffer.BlockCopy(xs, 0, ys, 0, xs.Length);
```

In some circumstances, this can prove useful to convert an array of primitive types in a very effective way, reducing user burden and runtime overhead that would come from manual copying.

WHAT ABOUT UNSAFE CODE?

One thing I've deliberately omitted from this book altogether is C#'s capability to write unsafe code, allowing manipulation of pointers and so on. As the name implies, this kind of code is inherently unsafe with regard to type safety and usually is used only in advanced interoperability scenarios. Often, it's just better to use other languages, such as C++/CLI, for such tasks.

The Math Class

Every self-respecting foundational API has facilities to deal with math. The BCL is no different in this respect with the `System.Math` static class that provides a plethora of handy mathematical operations on various numeric types. We don't cover all of them in detail, so let's highlight the most important aspects.

Constants

Anyone with any background in math knows two of the most important constants used in various applications. Those are e (2.71828...) and pi (3.14269...). Both of them are available as constants on the `Math` class, with double precision:

```
Console.WriteLine(Math.Pow(Math.E, Math.Log(5)));
Console.WriteLine(Math.PI * r * r);
```

In the first example, we're taking the natural logarithm (`Log`) of 5 and using it as the exponent with base e, which is the reverse power (`Pow`) operation. The result should be 5 again. The second example shows one of the typical uses of pi to compute the surface of a circle with radius equal to `r`.

Simple and Discrete Math

In the preceding examples, we've already seen a couple of interesting functions like `Pow` and `Log`. Other such functions exist, briefly summarized here:

▶ Exp is the same as using Pow with the base equal to constant e. Log and Log10 compute the natural and 10-based logarithm, respectively. Sqrt takes the square root of a number.

▶ Sign returns a value's sign using negative or positive one (for example, -1 for int). Abs computes the absolute value of a given number.

▶ Ceiling produces the smallest integral value larger than or equal to a fractional number. Obviously, floor does exactly the opposite. Round rounds to the nearest integral value. Truncate drops the nonintegral part of a fractional number.

▶ Max and Min speak for themselves. It's worth pointing out all overloads for these methods take only two parameters. LINQ operators on arrays, and more generally sequences using IEnumerable<T>, can be used to compute minimum and maximum over longer sequences.

Examples of those functions are listed here:

```
Console.WriteLine(Math.Sqrt(2));            // 1.4142135623731
Console.WriteLine(Math.Log10(1000));        // 3
Console.WriteLine(Math.Abs(-5));            // 5
Console.WriteLine(Math.Sign(-5));           // -1
Console.WriteLine(Math.Ceiling(Math.PI));   // 4
Console.WriteLine(Math.Floor(Math.E));      // 2
Console.WriteLine(Math.Round(Math.PI));     // 3
Console.WriteLine(Math.Round(Math.E));      // 3
Console.WriteLine(Math.Truncate(Math.PI));  // 3
Console.WriteLine(Math.Truncate(Math.E));   // 2
```

Another family of related functions deals with multiplication and division of integral values beyond the regular capabilities provided by built-in operators. For example, the multiplication of two 32-bit integers does fit in a 64-bit integer, but the built-in operator for multiplication of those values produces an Int32:

```
int x = int.MaxValue;
int y = int.MaxValue;
var z = x * y;
Console.WriteLine(z);
```

This piece of code produces, to the surprise of many, the value 1. If you hover over the var keyword used for implicit typing of variable z, you see the result of the multiplication is typed to be an Int32 and the multiplication was carried out as a 32-bit one. Due to overflow, the seemingly incorrect result is produced, which can be guarded against (at the expense of runtime checks) using the checked keyword:

```
int x = int.MaxValue;
int y = int.MaxValue;
var z = checked(x * y);
Console.WriteLine(z);
```

One solution is to widen any of the two 32-bit integer values into a 64-bit long one (for example, by using casting syntax on x or y). Alternatively, the Math.BigMul method can be used:

```
int x = int.MaxValue;
int y = int.MaxValue;
var z = Math.BigMul(x, y); // Now z is an Int64 (or long)
Console.WriteLine(z);
```

To compute an integral division's quotient as well as the remainder (as taught in elementary school math), the DivRem method can be used. It uses an output parameter to communicate the remainder to the caller:

```
int num = 17;
int den = 5;

int rem;
int div = Math.DivRem(num, den, out rem);
Console.WriteLine("{0} * {1} + {2} = {3}", div, den, rem, num);
```

Trigonometry

One thing that cannot be missing from a basic math library is support for trigonometry using functions like sine, cosine, tangent, and their hyperbolic brothers. Math's set of methods has all of those aboard, based on radian double-precision values for their input:

```
double angle = 45 * Math.PI / 180;
Console.WriteLine(Math.Sin(angle)); // Should be Math.Sqrt(2) / 2
Console.WriteLine(Math.Cos(angle)); // Should be Math.Sqrt(2) / 2, too
Console.WriteLine(Math.Tan(angle)); // Hence the division of those is 1
```

BigInteger: Beyond 32-bit and 64-bit Integers

Introduced in .NET 4 to support various functional and dynamic languages, the BigInteger type provides unlimited-precision integral value math. Internally, it's based on bit-vectors on which operations are done by turning those into basic math operations that the processor supports, including 32-bit and 64-bit arithmetic as well as bit-level operations. Luckily, all of this plumbing is nicely abstracted away from the user, and thanks to rich operator overloading the use of BigInteger is quite simple.

First of all, note that BigInteger lives outside the triad of BCL assemblies, namely in the System.Numerics assembly. The namespace listening to the same name as this assembly will have to be imported, too, for unqualified use of the struct's name.

To create a new BigInteger value, numerous paths can be taken. One is to invoke a constructor that can take a whole bunch of primitive numeric types, or a byte array that contains the bytes that make up a big integer if you love to deal with low-level representations right from the start. Alternatively, implicit conversions can be used to turn numeric values of primitive types into a BigInteger:

```
BigInteger x = new BigInteger(uint.MaxValue); // 2^32 - 1
BigInteger y = ulong.MaxValue; // 2^64 - 1
```

All expected math-related operators have been overloaded, allowing easy use of the created big integer values. For example, we can simply multiply the preceding:

```
BigInteger z = x * y;
Console.WriteLine(z);
Console.WriteLine(BigInteger.Log(z, 2)); // 95.999 ~= 2^(32 + 64)
```

The use of BigInteger.Log illustrates the availability of Math-alike static methods for various operations on big integer values. The reason they haven't been moved to the Math class is due to framework assembly layering. Adding a BigInteger overload to, say, the Math.Log method would make Math's assembly (mscorlib) dependent on the newly introduced System.Numerics assembly. It would also be the case that references to the new assembly are needed for compilers to have all the information needed to do proper overload resolution.

To illustrate a few other operators available, consider the following implementation of an unlimited-precision factorial computation:

```
BigInteger n = 10000;
BigInteger fac = 1;
for (BigInteger i = 2; i < n; i++)
    fac *= i;

Console.WriteLine(fac);
```

This produces a number of no fewer than 35,656 digits that one couldn't even dream of computing efficiently before .NET 4 without external libraries or a custom (and likely error-prone) implementation of large integer arithmetic. It's left as an exercise for you to spot all the overloaded BigInteger operators used in the preceding code. (Tip: There is more than a handful.)

Static methods on BigInteger include typical Parse and TryParse methods, as well as functions similar to those on the Math class (except for things such as trigonometry). One slightly unexpected method is GreatestCommonDivisor, which should speak for itself.

NO C# LITERAL (YET?)

Unfortunately, it's not possible to create a BigInteger value by writing a literal in C# code unless it fits in a 64-bit integral, in which case you're merely creating some primitive value (for example, an Int32) that can be implicitly converted to BigInteger. I would definitely love to see literal support for BigInteger values, which on the flip side would obviously add another dependency to the language, needing a reference to the System.Numerics assembly.

Without this support, you can either use the BigInteger.Parse method to write down the value as a string literal or turn the big integer value into a byte array, which would be more efficient (though, as usual, let measurements be your guide in deciding what to optimize). If you want to go for the latter option, simply use the Parse method once, call ToByteArray on the produced BigInteger value, and turn that byte array in a piece of C# array initializer code:

```
var bs = BigInteger.Parse("12345678901234567890").ToByteArray();
Console.WriteLine("new byte[] { " + string.Join(",", bs) + " }");
```

This would be precisely the kind of code the C# compiler could generate (during compile time) for the use of a BigInteger literal, passing the byte array to one of the BigInteger constructors. For the output of the preceding, this would look like the following:

```
var x = new BigInteger(new byte[] { 210, 10, 31, 235, 140, 169, 84, 171, 0 });
Console.WriteLine(x); // 12345678901234567890
```

If BigIntegers become popular in the C# community, maybe we'll see direct support for them in a future version of the language. Languages that aim more at the scientific computation community, such as F#, do provide direct support today.

Complex Numbers

While the BCL teams were at it, adding System.Numerics with the BigInteger type, they also added a complex number struct. Because most readers won't have to deal with complex numbers on a day-to-day basis, we restrict ourselves to a small refresher on the concept of complex number in Figure 26.14, as well as a simple code fragment.

Creation of a Complex value can be done in a number of ways. One is to specify real and imaginary parts of the number to the constructor, both of which are typed using double floating-point precision values. Math-savvy readers will recall there's another representation of complex numbers, though, based on polar coordinates. Because this also involves two doubles, one for the radius and one for the angle (in radians), it wasn't possible to provide another constructor because it would end up having the same signature. In lieu of this, a static method called FromPolarCoordinates is provided. Besides those two ways of constructing new complex values, three public read-only fields are provided with commonly used complex numbers:

```
var c1 = new Complex(3.0, 4.0);
var c2 = Complex.FromPolarCoordinates(1.0, Math.PI / 3 /* 60 degrees */);
var c3 = Complex.Zero;
var c4 = Complex.One;
var c5 = Complex.ImaginaryOne;
```

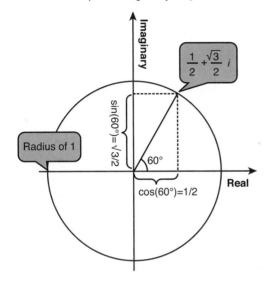

FIGURE 26.14   Brief recap of complex number theory.

The ToString representation simply prints the real and imaginary parts as the default textual form, also known as the Cartesian coordinates:

```
Console.WriteLine(c1); // (3, 4)
Console.WriteLine(c2); // (0.5, 0.866025403784439) - see Figure 26.14
Console.WriteLine(c3); // (0, 0)
Console.WriteLine(c4); // (1, 0)
Console.WriteLine(c5); // (0, 1)
```

Four instance-level properties are available on Complex values, allowing the two parts of both representations to be queried. For example, the first complex number we wrote down has a radius of five (known as the magnitude) and an angle (known as the phase) that can be derived from the real and imaginary parts using the Atan function:

```
// Magnitude = Math.Sqrt(3.0 * 3.0 + 4.0 * 4.0)   Phase = Math.Atan(4.0 / 3.0)
Console.WriteLine("({0}, {1})", c1.Magnitude, c1.Phase);
```

All sorts of calculations can be done with `Complex` values, thanks to a whole lot of over-loaded operators. Conversions exist from primitive number values (and even the `BigInteger` struct) to complex numbers whose imaginary part will be set to zero. We won't go into detail on all those operations; instead, I encourage you to consult some standard works on number theory if your knowledge of complex numbers has become a bit dusty. Here are a few examples of working with complex numbers:

```
Console.WriteLine(c1);
Console.WriteLine(c2.Real);       // Cosine of angle
Console.WriteLine(c3.Imaginary); // Sine of angle
Console.WriteLine(c4.Magnitude); // Radius of circle
Console.WriteLine(c5.Phase);      // Angle in radians


Console.WriteLine(c1 + c2 * c3 - c4 / c5); // Standard arithmetic
Console.WriteLine(Complex.Pow(c1, c2));     // Refer to theory :-)
Console.WriteLine(Complex.Reciprocal(c3)); // 1 + 0i divided by c
Console.WriteLine(Complex.Negate(c4));      // Flip both signs
Console.WriteLine(Complex.Conjugate(c5));   // Flip imaginary sign
```

With this, we wrap up our discussion about complex numbers. One thing that's worth mentioning is that the introduction of those numbers as part of the BCL allows for true interoperability between languages that provide them natively and others, like C#, that want to consume such values.

Generating Random Numbers

A fairly common task is to generate random numbers (for example, to create a random permutation of objects in a collection, to write a lottery application, to generate test input sequences). The `System` namespace contains a `Random` class that's designed for this purpose, producing what's known as a *pseudo-random sequence*.

SECURITY, SECURITY, SECURITY

It can't be emphasized enough that the `Random` class is not well suited for use in a security-critical context (for example, to provide cryptographic strength random numbers) in part due to its pseudo-random (and hence predictable) nature.

For such uses, the `System.Security.Cryptography` namespace should be put into action, with its `RandomNumberGenerator` base class and derive types. However, when you find yourself creating such random numbers, it's good to ask why you're doing it in the first place. If you happen to be implementing some kind of cryptographic algorithm yourself, immediately stop doing so unless you're a world authority in that field (in that case, I'm incredibly pleased you're reading this book).

Security and cryptography are things everyone should use when appropriate for the task at hand. At the same time, it's no good trying to implement such low-level facili-ties yourself. You'll find that the `System.Security` namespace and all of its children contain plenty of well-tested and massively reviewed facilities you can readily leverage.

To generate random numbers, instantiate a new Random object, optionally with a generator seed. If left unspecified, the system picks a seed, which is currently chosen from the Environment.TickCount static property. Once a random number generator has been created, any of its Next* methods can be used to return the next random number:

```
var r = new Random();

for (int i = 0; i < 5; i++)
    Console.WriteLine(r.Next(0, 100)); // Within range [0, 100[

for (int i = 0; i < 5; i++)
    Console.WriteLine(r.NextDouble()); // Always between 0.0 and 1.0

var bs = new byte[5];
r.NextBytes(bs);                        // Fills the given array with bytes
foreach (byte b in bs)
    Console.WriteLine(b);
```

Following is a popular example of approximating the value of Pi by generating random numbers and computing the number of them that fall within the unit circle. Obviously, such a technique has only limited mileage, but nonetheless it's an interesting curiosum. Figure 26.15 shows the approach we're taking. Basically, we generate random points in a one-by-one square. Of those, we count the number that fall within the unit circle with radius one. The proportion of hits and the total number of "shots" approximates one-quarter of Pi.

The code performing this computation a number of times is shown here:

```
const int TOTAL = 1000000; // Number of shots per turn
var random = new Random();

for (int t = 0; t < 10; t++)
{
    int within = 0;
    for (int i = 0; i < TOTAL; i++)
    {
        double x = random.NextDouble();
        double y = random.NextDouble();

        double r = Math.Sqrt(x * x + y * y);
        if (r < 1.0) // Within the circle
            within++;
    }

    var approx = (double)within * 4 / TOTAL;
    Console.WriteLine(approx);
}
```

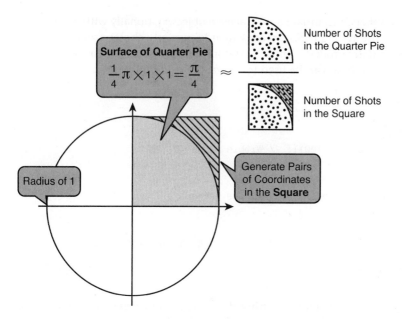

FIGURE 26.15   Approximating Pi using random numbers.

On my machine, the run of 10 approximations resulted in the following value approximations of Pi:

3.142252
3.140372
3.143872
3.143084
3.142656
3.143024
3.13976
3.139144
3.14488
3.141488

Don't expect to see much better precision, though. Various factors influence how good of an approximation we can get, and far better algorithms exist to compute Pi (contests even exist for this popular math theme).

ONE AND ONLY ONE RANDOM NUMBER GENERATOR

A common mistake made by users encountering the Random class for the first time is the creation of multiple instances without specifying a custom seed. If those creations follow each other closely, the chosen seed value will be the same because it's taken from Environment.TickCount, which has only millisecond precision. In such a setting, all the created random number generators will produce the same sequence. Often, it's just better to have a single random number generator stuffed somewhere in a static field for reuse throughout various components.

Working with Date and Time

Date and time values are notoriously hard to work with for a variety of reasons, most of which have to do with globalization. Different calendar systems exist, people live in different time zones, representation of dates can be done in a number of ways, and so on. The designers of the .NET Framework tried hard to accommodate all those needs using just a handful of types. And quite frankly, they did quite a good job of it, with only one introduction of a new type in .NET 2.0 to compensate for the lack of a good solution to time offsets relative to UTC time.

Absolute Time and `DateTime`

The first notion we need is that of absolute time. `DateTime` is the struct that's used to represent such values, which consist of date and time information. At the same time, it allows for various kinds of computations and conversions.

Here are some basic examples of creating a `DateTime` value using the constructor and the `DateTime.Now` static property:

```
// January, 1st of 1 AC at midnight
var start = new DateTime();
Console.WriteLine(start);


// Ticks are measured in 100 nanoseconds, starting from 01/01/2001 12:00:00 AM
// Hence, the below corresponds to February, 1st of 1 AC at midnight
var fromTicks = new DateTime(
    10L * 1000 * 1000 * // from 100ns to microsecond, millisecond and second
    60 * 60 * 24 *      // from second to minute, hour and day
    31);                // 31 days in January
Console.WriteLine(fromTicks);


// From year, month and day, at midnight
var birthday = new DateTime(1983, 2, 11);
Console.WriteLine(birthday);


// Month, day, hour, minute and second are all set to 11
var elfelfelf = new DateTime(2011, 11, 11, 11, 11, 11);
Console.WriteLine(elfelfelf);


// DateTime.Now gets the current time, up to tick precision
var now = DateTime.Now;
Console.WriteLine(now);
```

It should be no surprise that all the components of a DateTime value can be accessed using instance-level properties with predictable names. Of those, Ticks contains the total number of ticks that represent the instance, and properties like Day and Hour are used to access a particular component of the value.

Internally, a DateTime value is stored as a single ulong value that corresponds to the number of ticks since .NET's beginning. Access to various component value properties involves quite some arithmetic to compute the requested value, taking things such as leap years into account. Luckily, all of this complex arithmetic is hidden from the end user:

```
var now = DateTime.Now;
Console.WriteLine(now.Year);
Console.WriteLine(now.Month);
Console.WriteLine(now.Day);
Console.WriteLine(now.Hour);
Console.WriteLine(now.Minute);
Console.WriteLine(now.Second);
Console.WriteLine(now.Millisecond);
```

Later, we'll see how to format DateTime values using format strings, which makes "pretty printing" easier. Besides the components shown previously, other interesting data of the value can be retrieved, such as the day of the week:

```
var birthday = new DateTime(1983, 2, 11);
Console.WriteLine(birthday.DayOfWeek);   // Friday (a DayOfWeek enum value)
Console.WriteLine(birthday.DayOfYear);   // 42 (31 days in January + 11)
```

It's also possible to obtain the Date component of a DateTime value by using the Date property. Similarly, the time of day can be retrieved using TimeOfDay, returning a TimeSpan value (which is discussed later).

LEAP YEARS AND DAYS IN A MONTH

As you can imagine, the existence of leap years complicates all sorts of arithmetic that has to be done with dates. Because the fact whether a year is a leap year can be computed (divisible by four, modulo some exceptions to compensate for Mother Earth's true cycle around the sun), an IsLeapYear static method has been exposed to the users, as well. Furthermore, the DaysInMonth method can be used to find the number of days in a specified month of a given year.

Conversions

Historically, date and time values have had various representations. For example, a bunch of Win32 APIs use a so-called FILETIME value. In that system, the timeline starts at 1 January 1601 rather than the year 1. Similar to .NET's representation of time, the precision of measurements is in 100ns.

Given a `FILETIME` value, you can create a `DateTime` value using the `FromFileTime` and `FromFileTimeUtc` static methods. Conversely, a `DateTime` value can be turned into `FILETIME` by means of the `ToFileTime` and `ToFileTimeUtc` instance methods:

```
var now = DateTime.Now;
long fileTime = now.ToFileTimeUtc();
DateTime aWhileAgo = DateTime.FromFileTimeUtc(fileTime);
```

Another representation is so-called binary, which can be used to restore a `DateTime` value in an exact manner. This is not quite the same as just a tick count because date and time values also contain a `Kind` flag. This flag is used to indicate whether the value is measured based on UTC (universal coordinated time, so it ought to be spelled UCT) time or represents a local time that's offset by a time zone. We discuss time zones and the `DateTimeOffset` struct in the section "What about Time Zones?" and beyond. For now, I just want to draw attention to the use of the binary representation and associated conversions:

```
var now = DateTime.Now;  // Note: the Kind of DateTime.Now is "Local".
long binary = now.ToBinary();
DateTime aWhileAgo = DateTime.FromBinary(binary);
```

One more foreign representation of `DateTime` values is as OLE Automation dates, which are abbreviated OADate. We'll ignore this representation here.

String Representations of `DateTime` Values

An obvious other representation of `DateTime` values is as a string. Conversions from and to a string are supported through static `Parse` methods and various `ToString`-alike methods, respectively.

Starting with the former one, a string can be converted to a `DateTime` using the `Parse` method, optionally specifying a format provider (such as a `CultureInfo` object) or a flag's value of type `DateTimeStyles`. We omit a discussion about the various flags that are available and refer you to MSDN documentation for more information. Notice how the parameters of all `Parse` methods on built-in essential value types follow the same kind of pattern.

The following example shows how a Belgian Dutch representation of my date of birth is turned into a `DateTime` value. In my humble opinion, the order of the day in front of the month is more logical than the en-US representation anyway:

```
var birthday = DateTime.Parse("11/02/1983", new CultureInfo("nl-BE"));
Console.WriteLine(birthday);
```

Other string representations of the same date can be fed to the `Parse` method; for example, using a textual form of the month (for example, februari in Dutch).

Besides just the `Parse` method, the framework also provides a `ParseExact` method that works based on format strings. An array of format strings can be given to denote the acceptable shapes of the input. If an exact match is found, the corresponding value is returned. If there isn't a single exact match, an exception results:

```
var formats = new[] {
    "dd/MM/yyyy", "dd/M/yyyy", "d/MM/yyyy", "d/M/yyyy",
    "dd/MM/yy", "dd/M/yy", "d/MM/yy", "d/M/yy"
};
var culture = new CultureInfo("nl-BE");
var birthday = DateTime.ParseExact("11/2/83", formats, culture,
                                DateTimeStyles.None);
Console.WriteLine(birthday);
```

In the preceding code, the sixth format string did produce a match for the given input, which has two digits to denote the day, one for the month, and two for the year (which is projected in the 20th century, resulting in 1983). This method can prove useful to deal with systems where the storage format of a `DateTime` value follows a number of patterns and you want to avoid random behavior when multiple formats match. Format strings are discussed in more detail later when we talk about text in general (see the section titled "Formatting Text").

Besides the `Parse` and `ParseExact` methods, Boolean-returning variants prefixed with the word `Try` exist. Instead of throwing an exception on invalid or ambiguous input, those methods will return false or true to indicate success. Use of both methods is totally analogous to similar methods on primitive types like Int32.

For the opposite direction of `DateTime` conversion (that is, to a string), various `To` methods exist. `ToString` takes an optional format string or a format provider, but a few stock conversion methods are provided out of the box as well:

```
// 11/02/1983
Console.WriteLine(birthday.ToString("dd/MM/yyyy"));
```

```
// 11/02/1983 0:00:00 with 24-hour notation (no AM/PM designator)
Console.WriteLine(birthday.ToString(new CultureInfo("nl-BE")));
```

```
// Friday, February 11, 1983 - a similar method exists for time
Console.WriteLine(birthday.ToLongDateString());
```

```
// 2/11/1983 - a similar method exists for time
Console.WriteLine(birthday.ToShortDateString());
```

Calendar Systems

So far, we've ignored an important detail. While various examples have shown how to deal with culture-specific string representations, there's another axis to globalization treatment of date and time, namely the use of different calendar systems. In fact, the `DateTime` struct uses a representation that's described as follows at MSDN:

*Time values are measured in 100-nanosecond units called ticks, and a particular date is the number of ticks since 12:00 midnight, January 1, 0001 Anno Domini (Common Era) in the **GregorianCalendar** calendar.*

The key takeaway from the preceding description is that a `DateTime` value's representation is based on the Gregorian calendar because it's in much of the world. However, this doesn't imply that .NET can't support other calendars. In fact, it does, and a glance at the `System.Globalization` namespace immediately reveals the support for a whole series of calendar systems (most of which I honestly have never heard about).

To be politically correct, we can either show all of them or none of them. Because we've already mentioned the GregorianCalendar, we feel obliged to give the full list (as of .NET 4) here:

- ChineseLunisolarCalendar
- EastAsianLunisolarCalendar
- GregorianCalendar
- HebrewCalendar
- HijriCalendar
- JapaneseCalendar
- JapaneseLunisolarCalendar
- JulianCalendar
- KoreanCalendar
- KoreanLunisolarCalendar
- PersianCalendar
- TaiwanCalendar
- TaiwanLunisolarCalendar
- ThaiBuddhistCalendar
- UmAlQuraCalendar

When creating a `DateTime` using any of the constructors, overloads exist that take in a `Calendar` object. At that point, values passed for the components (like day and hour) are subject to the calendar's rules. Various methods exist on `Calendar` objects to obtain parts of a `DateTime` value using the calendar's rules and calendar-specific notions. For example, the Chinese lunisolar system has notions of sexagenary year cycles (using a 60-year based system) and leap days and months.

Because the art of writing correct globalized software is a specialist domain of its own, we don't go into further detail on it and refer you to books devoted to the subject, as well as the MSDN documentation.

What About Time Zones?

Yes, another complication in date and time notions is the concept of time zones. .NET's BCL provides intrinsic support for this, too. Two classes are available to work with time zones: `TimeZone` and `TimeZoneInfo`. The latter is the most modern and flexible container of time zone functionality, with support for multiple adjustment rules.

An adjustment rule basically reflects oddities associated with the time zone in question, such as the daylight saving time period on a year-to-year basis (which could change over time, making the use of a single adjustment rule inappropriate). Because there are a whole bunch of complications when dealing with time zones (such as the notion of ambiguous time, when `DateTime` values can be mapped to multiple UTC values), we'll skim over the `TimeZone` facilities by just giving a little taste:

```
var here = TimeZone.CurrentTimeZone;
Console.WriteLine(here.StandardName); // Pacific Standard Time
Console.WriteLine(here.GetUtcOffset(DateTime.Now)); // -07:00:00
Console.WriteLine(here.IsDaylightSavingTime(DateTime.Now));
```

The preceding code uses the classic `TimeZone` class to retrieve the computer's current time zone and print a few pieces of information about that zone.

Using the `TimeZoneInfo` class, we get more flexibility with regard to adjustment rules, and for that reason it's the recommended way to deal with time zones whenever your scenario permits. Here I show how to enumerate all the time zones that deal with daylight savings time and print some information associated with them:

```
var res = from zone in TimeZoneInfo.GetSystemTimeZones()
          where zone.SupportsDaylightSavingTime
          select new { zone.Id, zone.DisplayName,
                       Adjustments = zone.GetAdjustmentRules().Length };

foreach (var zoneInfo in res)
   Console.WriteLine(zoneInfo);
```

To find a specific time zone (for example, based on its name), static methods exist. Analogous to the `TimeZone` class, a static property called `Local` returns the object for the local time zone. Using other static methods, conversions of `DateTime` values between zones or with regard to UTC time are possible:

```
var brussels = TimeZoneInfo.FindSystemTimeZoneById("Romance Standard Time");
Console.WriteLine(TimeZoneInfo.ConvertTime(DateTime.Now, brussels));
Console.WriteLine(TimeZoneInfo.ConvertTimeToUtc(DateTime.Now));
Console.WriteLine(DateTime.UtcNow);
```

In this example, we obtain the time zone for Brussels (shared with Copenhagen, Madrid, and Paris) and convert our local time, obtained using `DateTime.Now`, to the local time in

Brussels. Using `ConvertTimeToUtc`, you can convert time to UTC time. This also allows us to illustrate the `UtcNow` static property on `DateTime`, which returns a `DateTime` value with its `Kind` property set to `Utc` as opposed to `Local`.

After a brief detour through the notion of `TimeSpan` values, we'll see how a `DateTime` can be bundled with an offset, resulting in a `DateTimeOffset` value. When developing robust globalized applications, the `DateTimeOffset` struct provides various advantages over the classic `DateTime` struct.

Relative Time and TimeSpan

While `DateTime` is the primary notion of absolute time, `TimeSpan` acts as the primary representation of relative time. It goes without saying that this has to be taken with a grain of salt because, as you saw before, even `DateTime` is kept relative to a starting point on the time axis (that is, January 1 of the year 1).

`TimeSpan` basically acts as a difference between date/time values. The creation of such a value can be achieved in many ways, using constructors and various static methods. On the constructor menu is one that's based on ticks (again in 100 nanosecond units) and a series of constructors that take in hours, minutes, and seconds, with optionally a number of days/milliseconds too. For example

```
var bestTime = new TimeSpan(2, 3, 59);  // 2 hours, 3 minutes and 59 seconds
var hundredDays = new TimeSpan(100, 0, 0, 0);  // overload with days, h, m, s
```

The excessive number of zeros that must be passed to certain constructor overloads can be grueling. To make such code look clearer, a number of `From*` static methods exist, too, as shown here:

```
var hundredDays = TimeSpan.FromDays(100);
```

In fact, those static methods take in double values rather than integers and therefore can be used to express code in a more natural way from time to time (for example, 0.5 days). Because the `TimeSpan` struct provides overloads for additive operators (as well as comparisons), we can also write things as follows:

```
var bestTime =   TimeSpan.FromHours(2) + TimeSpan.FromMinutes(3)
                + TimeSpan.FromSeconds(59);
```

Because relative time is merely a difference between absolute `DateTime` values, use of the subtraction operator on such values also yields a `TimeSpan`. Conversely, the addition of a `DateTime` and a `TimeSpan` results in a `DateTime`:

```
var startTime = new DateTime(2008, 9, 28, 8, 40, 25);
var endTime = new DateTime(2008, 9, 28, 10, 44, 24);
var elapsed = endTime - startTime;
Console.WriteLine(elapsed);
```

```
var endTime2 = startTime + elapsed;
Console.WriteLine(endTime == endTime2);
```

Different metrics can be obtained from a `TimeSpan` value, including the components of the value (milliseconds, seconds, minutes, hours, and days), as well as totals. Examples of both are shown in the next example:

```
Console.WriteLine(elapsed.Hours + ":" + elapsed.Minutes);
Console.WriteLine(elapsed.TotalSeconds);
```

Nicer formatting can be obtained by using format strings. The default result produced by the `ToString` method writes down hours, minutes, and seconds, each represented by two digits and separated by colons. If nontrivial days or milliseconds values are stored by the `TimeSpan` value, those are printed, as well. For example:

```
42.12:34:56.789  // 42 days, 12 hours, 34 minutes, 56 seconds, 789 milliseconds
```

`Parse` and `TryParse` methods are available, as well as their `Exact` variants, completely analogous to the static methods on `DateTime`.

PERFORMANCE MEASUREMENTS

Certain people are keen on performance measurements of all sorts. Others are rather skeptical about excessive practice of those when no red flags have been raised on an application's or library's performance (yet). Either way, if you have to carry out such measurements, do it in a correct way. Subtracting `DateTime` values doesn't cut it due to limited precision. Use of the `Stopwatch` class is the way to go, as you will see when we discuss the `System.Diagnostics` namespace in Chapter 27, "Diagnostics and Instrumentation."

Arithmetic with `DateTime` Values

In the discussion about `TimeSpan`, you learned how the difference between two `DateTime` values produces a `TimeSpan`. Adding a `DateTime` and a `TimeSpan`, on the other hand, returns another `DateTime` value. For convenience, the `DateTime` struct also has a series of `Add` methods that avoid the need to create a `TimeSpan` value first:

```
var hundredDaysFestival = DateTime.Now.AddDays(100);
```

A single `Subtract` method is provided to subtract a `TimeSpan` from a `DateTime` value, mainly for use by languages that don't have operator overloading support. This shows how good API design accommodates for languages that may be missing some of the conveniences that are present in C#. In fact, operator overloading support is not in the list of Common Language Specification (CLS) compliance rules.

DateTimeOffset

With knowledge of `DateTime` and `TimeSpan` under our belt, we can wonder what it would mean to combine both in a single value. This is precisely what `DateTimeOffset` does as a way to overcome certain issues that existed with the `DateTime`'s simplistic approach to local versus UTC time, as indicated by the `Kind` property.

`DateTimeOffset` contains both a `DateTime` and an offset of type `TimeSpan`. The offset is meant to indicate the difference between the `DateTime` value and UTC time. This is not completely the same as the use of time zones, though, because the latter also have a notion of daylight saving time and adjustment rules.

Nowadays, use of `DateTimeOffset` is recommended over the use of plain old `DateTime` because of various advantages. One big advantage is that date/time values represented by the type unambiguously define a point in time. We don't go into further detail about when it's appropriate to use a `DateTimeOffset` rather than `DateTime`. Instead, refer to MSDN for more documentation on the subject. From a usage point of view, both structs have a similar public contract, so you should immediately feel at ease in both worlds.

GUID Values

During the COM era, identification and mapping of interfaces was driven by unique identification numbers, known as GUIDs. Although this is just one of the many uses of globally unique identifiers, COM definitely is the one that jumps immediately to mind.

For COM interoperability as well as other uses, the .NET Framework has a struct to represent such identifiers: `System.Guid`. A GUID is basically nothing more than a "very random" 128-bit integer that has a global uniqueness property. Global in this context means that there's a very low likelihood of two generated GUIDs (no matter where and when that happens) being the same. For that reason, it's safe to generate a GUID for some use (for example, to identify a COM interface) and assume it won't clash with other such identifiers generated by other parties.

While a GUID can be used for other purposes than COM-related programming, one should ask the question whether the globally unique property is needed for the problem being solved. If that isn't the case, a much smaller, say 32-bit, identifier is likely a better choice. Not only does it have the advantage of being cheaper in terms of storage, it's often possible to generate those numbers in an incremental fashion, making identifiers easier to memorize. For example, the cashier will be glad that tomatoes have an identifier of 42 rather than {5b8a5333-1bfd-494a-b73a-8812d254d89b}.

Creating a GUID from a known value can be done in many ways, using constructors as well as `Parse` and `TryParse` methods. Because of the different textual representations used for GUIDs, a family of `Exact` parse methods is provided as well. One of those string forms of a GUID was just shown and can readily be used to create a new `Guid` value, as follows:

```
var myId = new Guid("5b8a5333-1bfd-494a-b73a-8812d254d89b");
```

Whether curly braces are used around the GUID doesn't matter here, and case does not influence the outcome. The seemingly weird form of a GUID consisting of four unequal segments is due to the typical internal representation of the identifier, which is also apparent from other constructor overloads:

```
public Guid(int a, short b, short c, byte[] d);
public Guid(int a, short b, short c, byte d, byte e, byte f, byte g, byte h,
            byte i, byte j, byte k);
public Guid(uint a, ushort b, ushort c, byte d, byte e, byte f, byte g, byte h,
            byte i, byte j, byte k);
```

We won't go into detail about the history behind GUIDs and their various byte-level representations. Instead, refer to Win32 and COM documentation (if you're interested).

In quite a few cases, you don't have a predefined value of GUID to begin with, and you need to generate one on the spot. That's what the NewGuid static method can be used for, which internally simply uses the CoCreateGuid COM API to generate such a new identifier:

```
Console.WriteLine(Guid.NewGuid());
```

If a specific textual output is needed, the ToString method can be used to pass in a format string to influence the shape of the output. We discuss the concept of format strings separately when talking about working with text, in particular in the section "Formatting Text."

LET THE SYSTEM DO ITS JOB

Some methods seem like pure magic. Guid.NewGuid certainly seems to be uttermost magic, providing guarantees about providing globally unique values (with a very, very low probability of failing at it).

Messing with the result of such an API is likely not a good idea because you might end up defeating the function's guarantees. There are true stories of people using the GUID-creation APIs to generate what they believed to be unique identifiers. Turns out those people took only part of the GUID's 128 bits, thinking part of the GUID would still have the same uniqueness guarantees of the GUID as a whole. Because some parts of a generated GUID value are derived from the machine's identity, you might end up picking a part that doesn't exhibit global uniqueness properties. Be warned!

In quite a few scenarios, generating a new GUID is not a runtime thing but must be done at development time (for example, to expose a .NET assembly and its types to the world of COM). While the Guid.NewGuid method can be used for this purpose, tools that come with various SDKs can be used as well. In particular, the uuidgen.exe tool comes in handy. Inside Visual Studio, a UI-based version (known as guidgen.exe) is available through the Tools menu's Create GUID entry, shown in Figure 26.16.

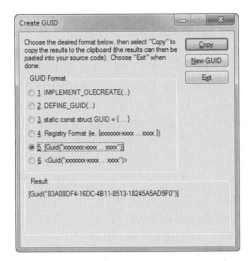

FIGURE 26.16   Pick your GUID representation form.

Compared to previous versions, the guidgen.exe tool now has two new options (5 and 6) to generate `GuidAttribute` notations in either C# or Visual Basic syntax. One uses this attribute in COM interoperability scenarios.

Nullability Revisited Briefly

During our discussion about nullable value types, introduced in .NET 2.0, we mentioned the syntactical sugar in C# to be an abbreviation for use of the `Nullable<T>` struct:

```
int? x = 42;
Nullable<int> y = null;
```

Both the `int?` and `Nullable<int>` types in the preceding example are therefore the same. A few more things can be told about nullable types.

First of all, don't forget the instance-level members available on any `Nullable<T>` object. C# conveniently provides a more natural syntax to express those constructs, but it's good to know about their existence:

```
bool b = x.HasValue;              // Same as:     bool b = x == null;
int c = y.GetValueOrDefault(25);  // Similar to:  int c = y ?? 25;
int d = x.Value;                  // int d = (int)x;
```

Furthermore, a couple of static methods exist to deal with nullables. One used in combo with reflection scenarios is `GetUnderlyingType`, which basically gets the `Nullable<T>` generic argument T; for example, `int?` maps onto `int`.

Two other handy static methods are `Equals` and `Compare`, which can be used to carry out equality checks and comparisons (à la `IComparable`, returning an integer value to indicate relative order) on any two nullable values of the same underlying type. This takes into account the possibility for any of the two values to be null (`HasValue` set to false). Examples of truths implemented by those methods include the following:

▶ null < non-null (for example, `Nullable.Compare<int>(null, 42) < 0`)

▶ null = null (for example, `Nullable.Equal<int>(null, null) == 0`)

▶ non-null > null (for example, `Nullable.Compare<int>(42, null) > 0`)

The `Uri` Type

In the world of massively connected systems, addressing of endpoints is quite common, so it makes sense to have a built-in primitive for uniform resource identifiers (URIs). The `Uri` class provided for this purpose supports both absolute and relative URIs and has a bunch of properties to query the various parts of a URI. A basic example is shown here:

```
var url = new Uri("http://bar:8080/foo/quz?answer=42");
Console.WriteLine(url.Host);          // bar
Console.WriteLine(url.Port);          // 8080
Console.WriteLine(url.AbsolutePath);  // /foo/quz
Console.WriteLine(url.Query);         // ?answer=42
```

Lots of complexities exist with regard to escaping, security of hostnames, and so forth. This is one of the reasons why `Uri` is an immutable type, so you can't go and tweak parts of it by touching the various properties. To create new `Uri` objects from parts, don't use techniques like string concatenation (which has many traps); use the `UriBuilder` class instead:

```
var builder = new UriBuilder();
builder.Scheme = Uri.UriSchemeFtp; // or use "ftp"
builder.Host = "localhost";
builder.Port = 21;                 // this is the default and will be omitted
builder.Path = "downloads";
builder.UserName = "bartde";
Console.WriteLine(builder.Uri);    // ftp://bartde@localhost/downloads
```

For security reasons, never trust input that's coming from users blindly. If you're dealing with a URI, this is no different. Use the `Uri` class and its facilities to make sure you've been handed valid input.

Interacting with the Environment

Today's programs don't stand on their own. They often have to interact with the outside world in a variety of ways. While we explore I/O in Chapter 28, "Working with I/O," one form of interaction is covered here: talking to "the environment."

The concept of an environment is hardwired in the operating system. Every program has access to it, containing both global information as well as some information that's specific to the program's invocation (such as the command line used). In .NET, all this information is made available through the (static) class Environment.

Instead of giving a dump of what can be read in MSDN documentation, let's limit ourselves to a few examples. First of all, here's some general information about both the physical and virtual (as in CLR) machine we're executing on:

```
Console.WriteLine("Machine name:    " + Environment.MachineName);
Console.WriteLine("Processor #:     " + Environment.ProcessorCount);
Console.WriteLine("OS version:      " + Environment.OSVersion);
Console.WriteLine("64-bit OS:       " + Environment.Is64BitOperatingSystem);
Console.WriteLine("64-bit process:  " + Environment.Is64BitProcess);
Console.WriteLine("Working set:     " + Environment.WorkingSet / 1024 + "MB");
Console.WriteLine("CLR version:     " + Environment.Version);
Console.WriteLine("System32 at:     " + Environment.SystemDirectory);
Console.WriteLine("Not a service:   " + Environment.UserInteractive);
Console.WriteLine("User info:       " + Environment.UserDomainName + "\\"
                                      + Environment.UserName);
Console.WriteLine("Boot time:       " + (DateTime.Now -
                                      TimeSpan.FromMilliseconds(
                                          Environment.TickCount)));
```

Some of those properties return primitive values, others provide richer information. For example, the OSVersion property really returns an OperatingSystem instance that can be queried for version numbers, service pack levels, and so forth. The CLR version property (which simply reads Version), returns an object of type Version containing the four parts such a number is composed from.

64-BIT ODDITIES

On my machine, the queried 64-bit flags return True for the OS but False for the process. If you have been paying attention in previous chapters, you will recall that the default architecture for managed code executables has been set to 32-bit starting from Visual Studio 2010. As a result, the process is running in "Windows on Windows" (WOW) 32-bit emulation mode.

Changing the flag to AnyCPU on the Build properties tab of the project settings will cause the process to run 64-bit on a 64-bit machine, thus with both properties returning True. Whether that's an appropriate thing to do for your program depends on various factors. When dealing with interoperability, you might shoot yourself in the foot quickly if testing for any of the architectures isn't carried out properly. After all, this was one of the main reasons to toggle the 32-bit flag in the latest release of Visual Studio.

Besides machine-specific and user-specific information, we can also get information that's closer to our process. This includes environment variables (which our process in fact can influence and will get inherited by child processes), the command-line that was used to start the process, and so on.

Tales About the Command Line

You might wonder why the `Environment` class even deals with providing command-line access; isn't that something `Main` already does? That's true, but there are a variety of circumstances where passing the array of arguments through the program is just too inconvenient or even impossible (if you're a component loaded in some process). That said, some care has to be taken with command-line arguments. The various ways to obtain them differ in subtle ways. An example

```
using System;

class Cmdline
{
    static void Main(string[] args)
    {
        Console.WriteLine("CommandLine:");
        Console.WriteLine("  " + Environment.CommandLine);

        Console.WriteLine("Main:");
        foreach (var arg in args)
            Console.WriteLine("  " + arg);

        Console.WriteLine("CommandLineArgs:");
        foreach (var arg in Environment.GetCommandLineArgs())
            Console.WriteLine("  " + arg);
    }
}
```

From the three forms, the second one is the most meaningful in most cases. The first and third differ from the second in that they include the (path to the) executable that's used to start the program. For example

```
C:\Windows> c:\temp\CmdLine.ExE "Hello, world!" 42
CommandLine:
  c:\temp\CmdLine.ExE  "Hello, world!" 42
Main:
  Hello, world!
  42
CommandLineArgs:
  c:\temp\CmdLine.ExE
  Hello, world!
  42
```

The inclusion of this first entry in the command-line arguments may be unexpected and stems from the way the underlying Win32 API behaves.

WHERE DOES MY APPLICATION RUN FROM?

Recently, a friend asked me this exact question. It turns out it isn't quite as easy as one might think. Using the "working directory" clearly isn't a good idea because that can change, and shortcuts can influence it, too. One of my first reactions was to use the GetCommandLineArgs first element; however, that doesn't necessarily contain the full path because the user may simply be in the right directory, allowing the application to be started without a qualified path.

The correct way to answer this question is by using the Assembly class and its CodeBase property, which returns a URI in a string, typically with the file:// scheme. Using the Uri class, this can be mapped back to a local path. The remaining question is which assembly to use. The static GetEntryAssembly method on the Assembly class is precisely what we need:

```
var from = new Uri(Assembly.GetEntryAssembly().CodeBase);
Console.WriteLine(from.LocalPath);
```

That same Assembly object can be used to query the version of the application, which can come in handy to show command-line help or an About dialog.

Environment Variables

One of the simplest ways to communicate settings and machine or user characteristics between applications is to use environment variables. Using the Environment class, they can be read and modified easily. While lots of those environment variables are wrapped one way or another, sometimes you must query the environment directly, given the name of a variable:

```
var proc = Environment.GetEnvironmentVariable("PROCESSOR_IDENTIFIER");
```

A target enum value can be specified as an additional parameter to limit the search to the user or machine environment or the environment block associated with the current process. Other methods exist to enumerate the whole environment.

In some cases, one wants to expand environment variables, just like command-line processors do. For example, given the string "%WINDIR%\notepad.exe", you might want to get the expanded path. Notice though some I/O APIs can work with strings that haven't been expanded upfront, so this might not be needed depending on your scenario. Nonetheless, here's how to achieve expansion:

```
var notepad = Environment.ExpandEnvironmentVariables(@"%WINDIR%\notepad.exe");
```

On my machine, this returns C:\Windows\notepad.exe. Notice, though, that code can write to environment variables, too. Depending on the target, this setting gets persisted in the process's environment block, the user's Registry hive, or the machine hive. Windows-level security protection mechanisms are in place to prevent tampering with the machine settings if the user isn't eligible to do so. However, because the process environment block shadows settings that come from the user profile or the machine level, you must be careful:

```
Environment.SetEnvironmentVariable("WINDIR", "oops");
```

The preceding creates a WINDIR environment variable in the process environment block, so unqualified access to the variable without an environment target flag will cause this setting to take precedence:

```
// Prints oops
Console.WriteLine(Environment.GetEnvironmentVariable("WINDIR"));
```

To avoid this, qualification can be used:

```
Console.WriteLine(Environment.GetEnvironmentVariable("WINDIR",
                    EnvironmentVariableTarget.Machine));
```

One more thing to notice is that child processes inherit the process environment block from their parent. Setting environment variables can be a handy way to influence a child process that gets spawned by your application (for example, when creating automation for installations). An example of this technique is shown here:

```
Environment.SetEnvironmentVariable("MSG", "Hello");
System.Diagnostics.Process.Start("cmd.exe");
```

Figure 26.17 shows how the cmd.exe child process (which can outlive its parent but still have the inherited environment block) sees the MSG variable that has been set.

FIGURE 26.17   Inheritance of the environment block.

Special Folders and Drives

Another piece of data exposed by the Environment class is path information for special folders that deserve a special status by the shell. For example, the Start Menu is known as a special folder, among many others. The SpecialFolder enumeration can be used to specify such a folder and to retrieve its path by calling the GetFolderPath method:

```
var start = Environment.GetFolderPath(Environment.SpecialFolder.StartMenu);
```

To get an idea about the system drives available on the machine, you can use the GetLogicalDrives method.

Exiting the Program

When it's time to quit the application for some reason, different options exist to achieve this task. One is to simply return from the Main method, with or without an exit code, depending on the signature chosen. Sometimes it's not convenient to get all the way back to Main, though, and instead, termination needs to happen on the spot. Different options are available for that case. Excluding an unhandled exception, we discuss those now.

One is to use Environment.Exit, passing in an exit code. Zero is usually used to mean success. One thing to be aware of is that this is quite an abrupt way to exit the program because things such as finally blocks won't run. After all, the stack doesn't get unwound. For this reason, it might not be the best option. Notice, though, that various Win32 resources use handles to track down usage and detect when a resource can be reclaimed. When a program quits, the operating system takes care of cleaning up the orphaned resources. The following code shows the use of Exit, annotating its behavior:

```
try
{
    Console.WriteLine("About to exit...");
    Environment.Exit(0);
    Console.WriteLine("Can't get here!");
}
finally
{
    Console.WriteLine("Doesn't happen either...");
}
```

Another method is called FailFast and does precisely what you expect it to do. It causes the process to be terminated immediately due to a failure, passing it a string as well as an optional Exception object. The failure will be logged in the event log, and the error reporting service will be invoked (if no debuggers are configured, in which case the dialog from Figure 26.18 shows up). Just like the Exit method, finally blocks won't run, which is the best thing to do in "panic mode" when the state of the application has been jeopardized.

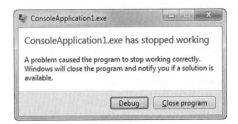

FIGURE 26.18   A fatal error reported by FailFast.

Leave the GC Alone (Most of the Time)

Automatic memory management has been one of the biggest features of the managed code execution engine, relieving developers of the burden of writing error-prone pieces of code to deal with proper cleanup of resources. That said, in some cases the garbage collector (GC) needs a bit of your cooperation to do the right thing. But let's not go too fast. Dealing with the GC directly should be more of an exception than a rule. In fact, the collector exhibits its best performance if it's left alone to determine when and what to do by itself.

Philosophy of Generations

As discussed previously on various occasions, the managed memory heap maintained by the CLR is divided into three generations, numbered 0 through 2. Objects start their lifetime in the smallest generation, generation 0. Upon a collection of objects in some generation, objects that survive the collection are promoted to the next generation. This process continues until an object ends up in generation 2, the largest of all of them, where it stays until it ultimately dies.

The philosophy of generations is that lots of objects in today's programs tend to be short-lived. Keeping the first generation, where objects start their life, small is a natural design choice if this property holds. When that generation becomes full, a large number of objects will be available for collection because they're not in use anymore.

To trace down the objects that can be collected, the GC starts from a set of roots, which are object references from certain locations, such as the stack, static fields, and thread-local storage. From those roots, object references are followed recursively, to mark all the objects that can still be reached. After this mark phase, a sweep phase is started, which reclaims all the objects that haven't been marked. Finally, the holes in the heap can be cleaned up by compacting the heap.

WHY TYPE SAFETY IS ESSENTIAL

It can't be emphasized enough that types and the various safety guarantees that go with them are the bread and butter of managed code execution. Lots of runtime services rely heavily on this type information being available. The GC is one such service. When tracing objects during the mark phase, the collector has to figure out where it can find references to other objects.

It all starts with roots. Assume we're looking at stack locations. At any point in time, the runtime needs to know exactly what type of object is occupied in what location on the stack. This information is needed to determine which locations contain a reference into the heap (everything but unboxed structs essentially) and which don't. Those objects are alive for sure and need to be marked. From the roots, the GC now needs to find heap-allocated objects that are referenced by those objects. To do so, it needs to know the field layout of the type on the heap. For example, given that the location contains a Person, we know that the field at offset 12 contains a 4-byte reference to a string.

Other services in the runtime depend heavily on type information being available at runtime. Obviously, the JIT has interest in this to emit correct code, and so do things like interoperability layers. You gotta love static types!

In the first couple of chapters, we illustrated in a slightly simplified manner the way the GC operates. We won't revisit this here. If you want more information about memory management in the world of managed code, you can find several CLR-centric works on the subject.

Now let's take a look at some statistics kept by the GC with regard to generations. Those statistics are used for a variety of purposes, one of which is to tune the behavior of the GC dynamically at runtime. Depending on the usage patterns of the managed heaps, the collector tries to find an optimal strategy to perform its duties (for example, by dynamically expanding certain generations). Because the CLR is a multilanguage platform, a wide range of allocation patterns is not unheard of. For example, functional languages like F# that promote immutable objects will see many more allocations because of the need to create a new instance instead of mutating one that already exists. In C# and Visual Basic, on the other hand, mutation of objects is common business. The following code shows how many generations there are, how much memory has been allocated, and what the collection count for different generations looks like:

```
static void Main()
{
    long total = GC.GetTotalMemory(false /* don't trigger collection */);
    Console.WriteLine(total);   // Some 60KB

    int generations = GC.MaxGeneration + 1;
    Console.WriteLine(generations);   // 3 for 0 through 2

    for (int i = 0; i < generations; i++) // most likely all print 0
        Console.WriteLine("Gen {0} = {1}", i, GC.CollectionCount(i));
}
```

For a program as trivial as this one, it's probably the case that no generations have happened yet. It's hard to imagine there's enough code in the startup path, before our Main method gets called, that causes generation 0 to be full. Nonetheless, this could definitely happen (for example, when static constructors are present). The following example simply adds a static constructor to the Program class (containing Main), growing generation 0 with 2048 1KB arrays. Results may vary, but on my PC, this was sufficient to trigger a single collection of generation 0:

```
static Program()
{
    for (int i = 0; i < 2 * 1024; i++)
    {
        byte[] b = new byte[1024];
    }
}
```

To give you some feel for more detailed and empirical studies of the behavior of the GC, let's modify the simple fragment a bit by allocation memory from main after the user presses Enter, using a straightforward loop. Notice that just like the preceding code, none of the created objects survive a collection of generation 0 because they get abandoned immediately after being allocated. To be really precise, one object allocated in the loop may survive because a reference to it will be held by a local variable slot on the stack while the allocation of a new array is triggering the collector to come in:

```
static void Main()
{
    while (true)
    {
        long total = GC.GetTotalMemory(false);
        Console.WriteLine(total);

        for (int i = 0; i < 3; i++)
            Console.WriteLine("Gen {0} = {1}", i, GC.CollectionCount(i));

        Console.WriteLine("Press ENTER to allocate more");
        Console.ReadLine();

        for (int i = 0; i < 2 * 1024; i++)
        {
            byte[] b = new byte[1024];
        }
    }
}
```

In the output, you will see the amount of memory grow, also due to the way the CLR (pre)allocates memory from the operating system when it notices more memory usage. The amount of memory allocated is large enough to trigger quite a few generation 0 collections. With a bit of luck, you'll also see a generation 1 collection coming in and total memory shrinking. Figure 26.19 shows some of this behavior.

Don't forget that other objects, besides our allocated arrays, will be alive because various framework components have been loaded. Those add some memory pressure, too.

Instrumenting your code to gather statistics works only for small examples and doesn't really apply very well to production systems. Luckily, the CLR provides a whole lot of performance counters that can be used to visualize the state of the runtime (such as the GC) for any given process. Figure 26.20 shows some of the counters related to garbage collection in the Performance Monitor MMC snap-in, which can be loaded from Start, Run as perfmon.msc.

Analyzing those statistics often provides a good insight as to why your application has certain issues. Hopefully, you won't have to look at those statistics often, but in case you do, you now know where to find them.

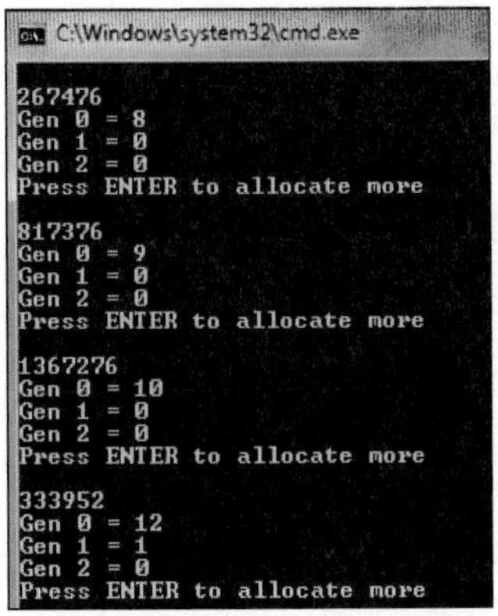

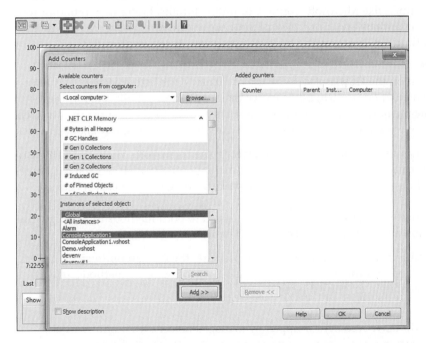

FIGURE 26.19   Memory growth and shrinkage.

FIGURE 26.20   Some performance counters related to CLR memory management.

STATIC THINGS DON'T MOVE

Beware of everything that's static. From the explanation on the past few pages, it should be clear that their treatment as GC roots makes static fields a common source of managed memory leaks. Make sure to clear static fields that keep (large) object graphs alive at an appropriate time (if permitted by your program).

When Collections Take Place

As discussed earlier, collections take place when memory allocation fails due to a lack of space on the heap. The GC does its best job to grow and shrink generations such that the overhead of collection goes down. For completeness, we have to mention the fact that the GC static class has a `Collect` method that can be used to trigger a garbage collection for any (or all) of the generations on the spot.

We won't give an example of using this method. If you ever have to use this method, there's likely some other problem in your program. Manually triggering a collection should be done only as a last resort because it disturbs the GC's regular rhythm of operation, where it decides on its own when it's good to perform a collection. Because running a collection requires a suspension of the execution engine, no user code can run, and your program comes to a halt.

In short, use of the `Collect` method should be received with lots of skepticism. If you believe you have a legitimate reason to call it, I strongly recommend talking to the CLR folks through channels like Microsoft Connect or online forums. Either they pinpoint root causes of your program's behavior or welcome your suggestion to improve the GC, as it's one of those runtime services everyone benefits from when it gets improved.

Memory Pressure

The more information the GC has about the use of memory, the better. Most of this information it can figure out on its own, but if native memory buffers get allocated in the process space, the memory manager doesn't have a crystal ball to get to know this. In such a case, methods on the GC class can be used (with care) to let the GC know about this fact.

At the time of this writing, I am aware of one place in the framework where this facility is used. When WPF calls into native APIs to allocate memory for media, it lets the GC know there's additional memory pressure added to the process, using the `AddMemoryPressure` method. The opposite, `RemoveMemoryPressure`, gets called when this memory is released. It's absolutely critical to balance out the amounts passed to both methods to avoid giving a wrong impression about memory usage to the memory manager.

Given the information about additional memory pressure, the GC can optimize its collection strategy. For more information about when and how to use those methods, refer to the MSDN documentation on the subject.

Finalization

When dealing with native resources wrapped by managed objects, it's quintessential to properly dispose of those resources when no longer needed. We studied before how to use the `IDisposable` pattern to allow deterministic cleanup of resources on the spot, which is usually done with C#'s `using` statement (merely a wrapper around the use of `try` and `finally` blocks). However, when the user is sloppy and forgets to properly call the `Dispose` method when the object is no longer needed, the only possible rescue path is having the GC take care of the cleanup. This is what finalizers were invented for, exposed to C# programmers using (improperly named) destructor methods. For typical Win32 handle-based resource wrapping, it's recommended to use techniques like `SafeHandle` to avoid implementation mishaps.

The use of finalizers puts quite a bit of pressure on the GC because it cannot reclaim memory occupied by the managed object immediately. Instead, the object first must be put on a finalization queue, which contains objects that need to have their Finalize method called before being deallocated. Because the execution engine has come to a halt for user code during a collection, those finalizer methods cannot be called as part of the GC's operation and have to be deferred until a next opportunity. Not only does this enlarge the object's lifetime further, it also makes the GC's life harder. This is a cost you don't want to pay when the user has properly called the Dispose method, in which case the finalization can be suppressed, allowing the GC to bypass this step:

```csharp
public class WrappedResource : IDisposable
{
    private IntPtr _handle;
    private bool _disposed = false;

    public WrappedResource(IntPtr handle)
    {
        _handle = handle;
    }

    public void Dispose()
    {
        Dispose(true);
        GC.SuppressFinalize(this);
    }

    private void Dispose(bool disposing)
    {
        if (!_disposed) {
            CloseHandle(_handle);
            _handle = IntPtr.Zero;
        }
        _disposed = true;
    }

    ~WrappedResource()
    {
        Dispose(false);
    }

    [System.Runtime.InteropServices.DllImport("kernel32")]
    private extern static bool CloseHandle(IntPtr handle);
}
```

Other methods on the GC class exist to deal with finalization. One such method is called ReRegisterForFinalization to undo the effect of the SuppressFinalize call. This and other methods that impact finalization have pretty narrow and rather specialized usage scenarios. Once more, MSDN is your best landing place to find out more.

Weak References

One directly visible garbage collection feature we haven't touched on yet is support for what's known as weak references. Up to this point, we've always said that objects are kept alive by means of existent references to them, originating from other objects that are alive. The mark phase of collection utilizes the property and principle to track down objects that cannot be reclaimed during the sweep phase following it. To be more precise, we should have said that those references are strong references.

Weak references, on the other hand, don't keep an object alive. If no strong references to an object exist, an object that only has weak references to it can be reclaimed during the next GC cycle. In some sense, it's a zombie object that still can be used, but nothing is keeping the GC from taking it away.

Creation of a weak reference is done through the WeakReference class, which benefits from special treatment by the runtime because of its use of GCHandle structs. The following code shows how a weak reference is constructed:

```
var zombie = new WeakReference(person);
```

Assuming no strong references exist to the person object passed to the constructor, the collector can take away that object when it sees fit to do so. However, while the object hasn't been collected yet, it can still be accessed through the Target property of the weak reference:

```
var reborn = (Person)zombie.Target;
```

If the preceding code returns null, the object targeted by the weak reference has been reclaimed and is gone for good. The IsAlive property on the WeakReference instance can be used to detect this fact too.

BE CAREFUL WITH POWERFUL WEAPONS

Some people believe weak references to be the best thing since sliced bread if you're faced with a memory management issue. Although it has a certain appeal to it, use extreme caution. Misuse of the feature may lead to the false impression a memory leakage problem has been solved. In some cases, a bad bug has been covered up badly by use of weak references where sudden disappearance of an object struck at times the code wasn't expecting it.

Certain portions of the .NET Framework (such as WPF) make heavy use of the concept of weak references, for good reasons. Nonetheless, the introduction of new uses of the technique should always raise some questions. For example, would you rather implement a data cache using weak references (as shown in the MSDN documentation for the WeakReference class) or craft some cache policy mechanism yourself? No matter what you choose, memory management-related business requires proper testing under various load conditions.

Native Interop with `IntPtr`

The notion of references in managed code is morally equivalent to pointers, as known from native code programming. There are a whole series of differences, though, which have to do with type safety, the presence of a garbage collector, and the desire to build a platform-independent runtime. The implications brought to us by type safety and the use of a GC are closely related, as can be seen from the way the collector traces objects by following references, requiring access to type information. But there's more, the fact objects can move in memory means that the object address captured in a reference can and will change during the program's lifetime.

Our previous discussion should be enough to understand already that there's quite a world of difference between pointers and managed references. Another difference comes from managed code's capability to target different platforms, where addressable memory differs (for example, between x86 32-bit and x64 64-bit). Hence, native pointers must have the right number of bits to allow correct addressing. For that reason, they can't use the notion of, say, an integer number (int) in C#. If you recall correctly, a C# int does correspond to an Int32 struct underneath, which reveals the fixed length, regardless of the platform the code happens to run on.

For managed code applications to interoperate with native components, it's important that there's some notion of a "native pointer" that follows the addressing width used by the platform on which the code is running. Notice this is a slight simplification due to the existence of WOW64 32-bit emulation of a 64-bit operating system, where 32-bit addressing can still occur if running in emulation mode (for example, when the platform target of a managed executable is set to x86 as opposed to AnyCPU).

This need for a native pointer representation in managed code is filled in by the IntPtr struct in the System namespace. In pure managed code, you should never see this type being used. However, when interoperability enters the picture, an IntPtr is the correct way to let the CLR talk to native code and vice versa. The closest "type" for an IntPtr in C/C++ code is void*. Being a weakly typed reference that can point at an object that's implemented in native code, there's no business for the GC to deal with such objects. Memory management of native resources is at the sole discretion of the underlying libraries, possibly (and typically) requiring you to make certain API calls to trigger the cleanup manually.

An example of the use of an `IntPtr` can be seen in the definition of `SafeFileHandle`:

```
public sealed class SafeFileHandle : SafeHandleZeroOrMinusOneIsInvalid
{
    private SafeFileHandle() { ... }
    public SafeFileHandle(IntPtr preexistingHandle, bool ownsHandle) { ... }
    protected override bool ReleaseHandle() { ... }
}
```

Here, a Win32 handle (which merely is an index into some table maintained by the operating system for your process) is represented by an `IntPtr` value. Nowadays, several of the unmanaged resources, such as file handles, have been wrapped in specialized types for interoperability. For example, `SafeHandleZeroOrMinusOneIsInvalid` acts as a base class for handles that originate from certain APIs that signal failure using zero or minus one values.

SWISS CHEESE HEAPS

Notice it's also possible to share managed objects out to native code. In such a case, it's important to make sure the GC doesn't move the object in memory while native code can manipulate it. Because of the opaque nature of an `IntPtr`, there's no way the GC can figure out an object is shared with some other world.

To prevent the collector from moving the object in memory, a mechanism called *pinning* exists. Basically, the managed object gets marked as pinned, which prevents the collector from moving it in memory during a collection cycle. As all the readers who've been involved in a furniture move know, working around some object that's unmovable can be quite hard and annoying. This is no different for the GC; pinned objects pose a challenge when the GC has to fit moving objects around the unmovable object.

When pinned objects don't get unpinned properly, heap fragmentation can ensue, which hampers performance because of harder collection cycles and can cause allocation failures even though enough memory seems to be available. This is due to the heap starting to look like Swiss cheese, full of holes, where no objects can be fit into anymore during collection.

It's clear that premature unpinning should never be done because it endangers the most important property of your program: correctness. Also, you need to know what the native API does with the object reference you're handing it. It's possible it doesn't hold on to it after an outgoing method call, making it possible to delimit the code area for pinning quite nicely. But if the native code keeps the object it's given in some table, you're in deeper waters. In short, interoperability can be tricky business. Luckily, lots of standard native APIs, such as popular Win32 and COM functionality, have been wrapped already.

Any more discussion about interoperability is beyond the scope of this book. For more information about it, refer to various bibles on the subject, such as Adam Nathan's interop guide.

Lazy Initialization Using Lazy<T>

 Introduced in .NET 4, the generic Lazy<T> class allows delayed initialization of some data that might not be required during a program's lifetime. If that's the case, it would be wasteful to precompute such a value in all circumstances.

The Lazy<T> class can be used in a number of ways, all of which require you to tell it how to create a new instance of type T. One is by giving it a Func<T> delegate that acts as the instance factory:

```
private Lazy<double> _pi = new Lazy<double>(() => {
                              return /* long running computation of PI */;
                });
```

If you must obtain the value of the expensive computation, a simple call to the get-only Value property or to the ToString method suffices. This will trigger the object's initialization and store the obtained value for future reuse. That is, the factory can be run only once:

```
double area = _pi.Value * radius * radius;  // Triggers computation of PI
double circumference = _pi.Value * 2 * radius;  // Precomputed  value of PI
```

However, to be precise, I should point out that parameters can be passed to control multi-threaded behavior of lazy initialization values. In such cases, it might be that multiple threads try to obtain the value, both triggering the invocation of a factory at the same time. A LazyThreadSafetyMode enum value can be passed to specify the desired behavior if this happens. We don't detail this aspect here.

Other constructors to Lazy<T> exist that allow a different kind of factory to be used. If no function delegate is specified, a default constructor in T is looked for, which will be called through the Activator.CreateInstance<T> API behind the scenes. This overload is useful when expensive logic exists in a constructor of an object that's not always needed for the program's execution:

```
class Expensive
{
    public Expensive()
    {
        /* lots of work goes in here */
    }
}

...

var costly = new Lazy<Expensive>();
var expensive = costly.Value;  // Will trigger execution
```

If you can live without a lazily constructed object but you'd benefit from having it around, the IsValueCreated property can be inspected to make a decision about what to do in your code. In other words, if someone has already invested enough to make the object, we'll use it. However, if no one has bothered to do so, we could decide to go without it:

```
// Lots of other code could run here...
if (costly.IsValueCreated)
{
    // Great, let's use it; we won't trigger expensive initialization here!
    var expensive = costly.Value;
    ...
}
else
{
    // Live without costly.Value here; we don't want to pay the price!
}
```

Tuple Types

Some languages provide a loosely structured way to combine multiple objects (for example, to pass them around in an all-in-one fashion). This comes in handy to over-come the typical single output channel of a method. Output parameters can be used as an alternative to deal with such cases, but they're more invasive at the method's call site. When using output parameters, you must introduce local variables and need to specify the out keyword on all such parameters, which can be quite distracting when reading the code:

```
int res;
if (int.TryParse("42", out res))
    ...
```

Tuple types allow multiple objects to be passed around by just wrapping them in an object with multiple (readonly) fields, exposed through properties. For example, with a two-tuple (or pair if you will), the TryParse method could return a Tuple<bool, int>:

```
return new Tuple<bool, int>(true /* success */, 42);
```

Now the consumer can inspect the result by decomposing the tuple using properties giving strongly typed access to the parts of it:

```
var res = FancyInt.TryParse("42");
if (res.Item1)  // the Boolean success part
{
    int value = res.Item2;  // the int vaue part
    ...
}
```

You could say the preceding code is less convenient or uglier, and there's truth in that. However, languages with first-class tuple support offer pattern-matching capabilities to obtain a tuple's components using cleaner syntax. For example, in F#-alike syntax

```
(success, value) = FancyInt.TryParse("42")
```

SYNTACTICAL CONVENIENCE?

C# doesn't have built-in syntax for tuples. It might happen in a future release, although there are some challenges. Most likely, the feature would be considered incomplete if no pattern-matching capabilities are added to the language. At least, with the unification of tuple types across languages, tuple values can be constructed and consumed from any language.

Tuples support the `Equals`, `GetHashCode`, and `ToString` methods in straightforward and predictable ways. This takes away the burden of having to implement a separate class every time a compose value has to be returned. However, in C# and Visual Basic, with no decomposition syntax for tuples, usage is rather ugly with properties like `Item5`.

Because there are tuple types with up to seven values, you might think tuples with more values cannot be represented. Nothing is further from the truth; the eighth tuple type has a `TRest` generic parameter that can be used to do nesting. It's recommended to use that one to encode a tuple with arity higher than seven because overloads for methods like `ToString` know about the `TRest` special treatment and will provide more meaningful results:

```
var t = new Tuple<int, int, int, int, int, int, int, Tuple<int, int>>(
    1, 2, 3, 4, 5, 6, 7, new Tuple<int, int>(8, 9));
Console.WriteLine(t);  // (1, 2, 3, 4, 5, 6, 7, 8, 9)
```

What truly matters for tuples in the BCL is having a unified representation for many languages to talk about tuples.

CONVENIENCE OR LAZINESS?

The flip side of tuples is they can encourage laziness because you don't have to declare classes to wrap multiple values, also requiring overrides for methods like `Equals` and `GetHashCode`.

Their ugly use in classic .NET languages like C# and Visual Basic should make you think about API design. Personally, I see them as nothing but a cross-language interoperability story, with the occasional use within method bodies as wrappers around related state. Even in that case, anonymous types are likely a better choice because they provide meaningful names for their properties.

As soon as a tuple is publicly exposed, it's almost certainly a better idea to create a specific wrapper type with meaningful property names. That said, nothing should prevent developers from implementing them using a single tuple field inside, also forwarding `Equals` and `GetHashCode` calls to the tuple underneath. However, think about the maintainability of that class's code, too. If the use of properties with names `Item1` to `Item7` is sprinkled throughout your code, it will be hard to maintain a solid understanding of the code. Even worse, chained accesses like `Rest.Rest.Item5` for deeply nested tuples might be needed. This is code obfuscation at its best. In such cases, it's better to just go through the burden of defining a custom type with `Equals` and `GetHashCode` implementations yourself.

I personally hope to see the "ceremony" required to declare immutable objects with a constructor, property getters, `Equals`, `GetHashCode`, and `ToString` overrides decrease in the future. Wouldn't it be great if the language allowed us to write things such as the following?

```
class Person(string Name, int Age) { }
```

One can hope!

Facilities to Work with Text

Use of text is everywhere. It's what the user often enters in input fields, what gets read from files and various other data sources, and so on. Having means to convert back and forth between text and other values is an essential API capability. In addition, rich formatting capabilities are most welcome, too, helping with localization of your applications. In this section, we look at all of this, as well as at various other means to deal with text, such as regular expressions and encoding schemes.

Formatting Text

One common operation is to represent objects in a textual form. By now, the first thought that should come to mind is to use `ToString`. In the light of localization and the fact that many types of objects can have different textual representations, the simple method provided by `System.Object` does not always suffice, though:

```
public virtual string ToString();
```

In particular, the lack of one or more parameters to control the desired result makes this overload not always applicable. MSDN defines the `ToString` method as follows:

> This method returns a human-readable string that is culture-sensitive.

The IFormattable Interface

Also, the documentation states that other `ToString` methods can be provided through an interface called `IFormattable`:

```
public interface IFormattable
{
    string ToString(string format, IFormatProvider formatProvider);
}
```

In fact, we've been looking at such methods on a number of occasions already when we were covering lots of primitive types such as numeric values and DateTime. During this discussion, we learned how the IFormatProvider interface is implemented by the CultureInfo class in System.Globalization, allowing us to control the culture used for the formatting of an object's textual representation. For example:

```
Console.WriteLine(123.45.ToString(new CultureInfo("en-US")));
Console.WriteLine(123.45.ToString(new CultureInfo("nl-BE")));
```

In the preceding example, the first line prints 123.45, whereas the second one uses a comma for the decimal separator character (printing 123,45). Notice this ToString overload doesn't come from the IFormattable implementation but is a one-parameter shortcut that omits the format parameter we talk about next.

Format Strings

Text formatting has been a traditional domain for mini-languages embedded in larger general-purpose languages such as C, C++, C#, and Visual Basic. For example, developers with a native code background will know printf's format string syntax:

```
printf("The value is %d", 42);
```

.NET is no different in this respect, defining the concept of format strings that can be used to control text formatting in value-to-text conversions. Let's take a look at those features by touching on some of the most commonly used formatting specifiers.

First of all, it's important to realize every data type can define its own formatting styles, which nicely align with the domain of the data. For example, for numeric fractional values, it makes sense to define the concept of a decimal-point notation, while date and time values can define formatting in terms of the value's components (such as year and minute). Because numbers are frequently used specimens in programs, we take a look at them first. The following code shows the same number being formatted in a variety of ways:

```
var enUS = new CultureInfo("en-US");
var nlBE = new CultureInfo("nl-BE");
var jaJP = new CultureInfo("ja-JP");

double d = 123.456;
int i = 1234;
long l = 123456789;
```

```
// Currency, usable for all numeric values
// Number of decimal digits determined from culture or explicitly
Console.WriteLine(d.ToString("C", enUS));  // $ 123.46
Console.WriteLine(d.ToString("C", nlBE));  // &euro; 123,46
Console.WriteLine(d.ToString("C", jaJP));  // ¥ 123
Console.WriteLine(d.ToString("C3", enUS)); // $ 123.456
Console.WriteLine(d.ToString("C0", nlBE)); // &euro; 123
Console.WriteLine(d.ToString("C2", jaJP)); // ¥ 123.46

// Decimal, usable for integral values only
// Number of digits controls left padding with zeros
Console.WriteLine(i.ToString("D", enUS));  // 1234
Console.WriteLine(i.ToString("D5", nlBE)); // 01234

// Scientific notation with exponent
// Default decimal precision is 6 but can be controlled
Console.WriteLine(l.ToString("E", enUS));  // 1.234568E+008
Console.WriteLine(l.ToString("E3", enUS)); // 1.235E+008
```

This should give you the hang of it. Lots of other numeric format strings exist, which are richly documented on MSDN. A short overview is given here:

- C for currency

- D for decimal, used for integral values only

- E for scientific exponential notation

- F for fixed-point notation

- G for general; that is, the most compact notation (scientific or fixed point)

- N for number, with use of (thousand) group separators, decimal points, and so forth

- P for percent, which multiplies a number by hundred and adds a % sign

- R for round-trip, allowing back-and-forth conversion of a number to a string

- X for hexadecimal representation of integral values only

Standard format strings are not the only option, though. One can dine à la carte, too, by using so-called custom format strings. Such strings allow very tight control over the value being formatted, with things such as zero and digit placeholders, the ability to use group and decimal separators, scaling, exponents, use of literal text, and so on. The following code illustrates a few uses:

```
// Digit placeholders
// Doesn't insert zeros if no digit appears at the given position
Console.WriteLine(i.ToString("#####", enUS)); // 1234
```

```
// Zero placeholders
// Inserts zeros if no digit appears at the given position
Console.WriteLine(i.ToString("00000", enUS)); // 01234

// Decimal point
// Here mixed used with trailing zero padding
Console.WriteLine(d.ToString("0###.##", enUS)); // 0123.46
```

Other custom specifiers are available, whose documentation can be found on MSDN. Some of them are very powerful, but as a result sometimes have rather cryptic syntax.

MINI-LANGUAGES

Unfortunately, format strings are one of those leftover mini-languages that tend to invade frameworks. An unfortunate implication of this is the need for developers to learn them separately from the programming languages being used. Also, the language doesn't care about those opaque strings and doesn't perform any kind of compile-time checking for them.

It has been a good trend to eliminate such magic strings; for example, by language features such as LINQ (instead of using, say, T-SQL) and even C# 4.0 dynamic (instead of specifying, say, a method as a string). First-class format specifiers would likely be quite complicated but could work.

Until further notice, format strings are a necessary evil that can result in signaling of runtime errors if unsupported specifiers are used, or when they're used in an improper fashion (for example, use of D on a fractional number).

Formatting doesn't only apply to numbers. Lots of other types have a formatting story as well. A few examples are shown here:

```
// Date patterns without time
// Others include date/time, UTC, year/month, roundtrip, etc.
var bd = new DateTime(1983, 2, 11);
Console.WriteLine(bd.ToString("d", nlBE)); // 11/02/1983
Console.WriteLine(bd.ToString("D", nlBE)); // vrijdag 11 februari 1983

// Custom date/time specifiers
// ddd = short day of week; dd = day of month; MM = month
Console.WriteLine(bd.ToString("ddd dd/MM", enUS)); // Fri 11/02
```

There's no use in cloning the MSDN documentation here. What matters most is to have gotten some familiarity with the richness of formatting, enough to encourage you to explore format strings in more detail.

One more thing we have to look at is the capability to format multiple values in one string, at one time. This is known as composite formatting. On various occasions earlier in this book, we skimmed over this when using one of the more advanced overloads of the `Console.WriteLine` method:

```
Console.WriteLine("{0} costs {1}", product, price);
```

As you can guess, the {0} and {1} substrings act as placeholders for the values passed in the subsequent arguments. The first argument here acts as a composite format string, followed by a single params array:

```
public static void WriteLine(string format, params object[] arg) { ... }
```

Composite format strings can be used in a number of places, of which the `WriteLine` method is just one. Likely, the most general purpose one is the static `Format` method on the `System.String` class itself, with a signature similar to the one just shown.

LOCALIZABLE APPLICATIONS

Use of format strings should be in every self-respecting .NET developer's genes because it's the main way to achieve localizability of applications. Simple string concat won't cut it because the order of words in a sentence often varies across different languages.

Obviously, one doesn't keep the format strings in the compiled binary if they need to be translated. Instead, localization tables are used, which can be loaded and queried through BCL facilities we don't elaborate on here. Make sure to check this out if you need to write localizable software (who doesn't nowadays?).

There's more you can do beyond just filling in placeholders of a composite format string. In addition, each so-called format item can have an optional format string to format the corresponding argument value, as well as an optional alignment. Format items have the following grammar:

```
{index[ ,alignment][ :formatString] }
```

Of those, we've already seen the `index` (which is zero-based) and some of the format strings that can be used for various objects. For example, combining the use of an index with the C (for currency) format string, we can write the following:

```
Console.WriteLine("{0} costs {1:C}", "Chai", 123.45m);
```

This prints the output shown here, relying on the current user's culture (which can in fact be tweaked programmatically through `System.Globalization` features):

```
Chai costs $123.45
```

The `Format` method on `System.String` supports an extra `IFormatProvider` argument (passed in as the first argument due to the use of a params array, which has to come at the end), which, as we know, can be filled in by a `CultureInfo` object:

```
var description = string.Format(nlBE, "{0} costs {1:C}", "Chai", 123.45m);
```

Obviously, the preceding code picks up the Dutch Belgian notation for a price, which uses the euro currency symbol rather than dollars.

MAGIC STRINGS REQUIRE ESCAPES

Whenever some extraordinary characters enter a string literal, people want a way to be able to escape them. For example, in regular string literals, we need a means to escape double quotes using the \ character. Due to the special status of \ in so-called verbatim string literals (with the @ prefix), we need another escape for ", simply by doubling them. Format strings are no different in this respect, requiring a way to escape the special-purpose curly braces. The way to do this is by, again, doubling them. For example, `"{{ {0} + ({1} * {2}) }}"`, where the outermost curly braces are escaped and the inner three pairs of two curly braces denote format items.

Notice that the same index of a format item can occur multiple times in a format string if the argument with that index has to be printed more than once. Each occurrence can have a different format string or alignment option, though. It's also the case that the order of format items doesn't have to follow the order of argument (after all, that's what the use of indexes is for):

```
var musicGroup = string.Format("{1}{0}{0}{1}", "B", 'A');  // Returns ABBA
```

What we haven't discussed yet is the ability to specify an alignment to a format item. This comes in handy when printing multiple rows of data, consisting of parts with a varying length. In such a setting, numbers are typically right-aligned while texts are left-aligned. In combination with standard numeric format strings that insert zeros in places where digits are zero, this can produce some good-looking output.

The basic idea is this: An alignment specification is simply an integer number that's used to control the width occupied by the value inserted in the place of the format item. If the text representation of that value exceeds the specified alignment width, it won't truncate the string but will instead ignore the alignment width. If truncation is desired, you can use `String` methods to achieve this effect. Furthermore, the alignment width's sign indicates the alignment; negative indicates left alignment, positive for right alignment. Here is an example printing a price list:

```
Console.WriteLine("{0,-30} {1,8:C}", "Product name", "Price");
Console.WriteLine("{0,-30} {1,8:C}", new string('-', 30), new string('-', 8));
```

```
foreach (var product in products)
    Console.WriteLine("{0,-30} {1,8:C}", product.Name, product.Price);
```

In the preceding example, we're using 30 characters for the width of product names, which get printed in a left-aligned manner. The price gets right-aligned with a maximum width of eight characters (enough to fit a currency symbol, four digits for the nonfractional part of the price, a decimal point separator, and two more digits for the cents.). On the first two lines, we also print a header with the same alignments and use the string constructor to repeat a dash character a number of times. Consider the following input:

```
var products = new[] {
    new { Name = "Chai", Price = 1.25m },
    new { Name = "Expensive lawn mower", Price = 495.95m },
    new { Name = "Chang", Price = 5m },
};
```

With this products collection, the following is printed:

```
Product name                     Price
-----------------------------    --------
Chai                              $1.25
Expensive lawn mower             $495.95
Chang                             $5.00
```

This shows rich format items at work using the mandatory index, an alignment, and (for the price) a format string. As you can see, a lot of formatting work can be done by the framework on your behalf, while allowing for easier localization.

Parsing Text to Objects

Converting objects to a textual representation is one thing, dealing with user (or text file and so on) input and turning it into rich objects is another thing. You've already seen a whole set of Parse, TryParse, and Exact variants, but there are a few more things to note.

Sometimes going back and forth between objects and text is not a lossless conversion. In such cases, the framework often provides a format string named R to emit a text representation that will restore the original value when using a Parse method. A good example is floating-point numbers, whose decimal representation is not exact:

```
double value = 1.0 / 3.0;

string text = value.ToString();
Console.WriteLine(text);            // 0.333333333333333
double res1 = double.Parse(text);
Console.WriteLine(res1);
Console.WriteLine(value == res1);   // False
```

```
string precise = value.ToString("R");
Console.WriteLine(precise);              // 0.33333333333333331
double res2 = double.Parse(precise);
Console.WriteLine(res2);
Console.WriteLine(value == res2);        // True
```

As you can see from the output for the preceding fragment, the precise ToString text does contain additional digits that the default ToString output doesn't have. Because of this, round-tripping doesn't produce the precise same value for the first example. When using the R style, though, things work just fine. Whenever you need to persist data (in particular, floating-point numbers or a BigInteger) as text and expect to be able to read it back, use the round-trip style.

Regular Expressions

Parsing of text into a primitive value is easy enough using the various kinds of Parse methods. However, a more complex parsing task often needs to be accomplished. In that case, the BCL's support for regular expressions enters the picture. Because regular expressions are a language of their own, we just touch on some of the capabilities, deferring a thorough discussion to MSDN once more.

The first thing to make sure when working with regular expression facilities is to have a using directive to import the System.Text.RegularExpressions namespace. When this is done, you have unqualified access to the Regex class, which is the entry point of the API. First, you create a new instance of this class, specifying the regular expression pattern and an optional set of RegexOptions flags. Let's ignore this detail for now and go with a plain regular expression without special options:

```
var regex = new Regex("0¦([1-9][0-9]*)");

while (true)
{
    Console.Write("> ");
    string input = Console.ReadLine();
    Match match = regex.Match(input);
    if (match.Success)
        Console.WriteLine(match.Value);
}
```

This read-eval-print loop (REPL) takes in a user input string and matches it against the specified pattern. Upon success, the first match found within the user input string is printed. Notice a match is the longest sequence in the input string that conforms to the specified pattern. In this case, the pattern states that valid input is either 0 or (using a vertical bar) a digit in the range 1 through 9 ([1-9]) followed by any number of digits in the range 0 through 9 ([0-9]*).

Here is sample output for a series of user input strings. Notice how Match simply returns the first match and doesn't require the whole input to be a match:

```
> 0
0
> 123a456
123
> abba123
123
```

Besides the Success and Value properties on the Match object, you can query for the index of the match's occurrence as well as its length. If multiple matches are searched for, you can use the NextMatch method on the returned Match object or make use of the Matches method instead:

```
var regex = new Regex("0¦([1-9][0-9]*)");

while (true)
{
    Console.Write("> ");
    string input = Console.ReadLine();
    foreach (Match match in regex.Matches(input))
        Console.WriteLine("{0} @ {1}", match.Value, match.Index);
}
```

For the same input as shown next, we now find two matches for the "123a456" string, including the match indices:

```
> 0
0 @ 0
> 123a456
123 @ 0
456 @ 4
> abba123
123 @ 4
```

Finally, for simple matching scenarios, the IsMatch method can be used as well. This method returns a Boolean indicating whether the start of the input string produces a valid match. If the full input string needs to produce a match, you can carry out some simple tricks like using Match and checking the length of the Value property to match the length of the input.

WHEN PERFORMANCE NEEDS IMPROVEMENT

Regular expressions lend themselves very well for precompilation. In fact, compiler theory starts with this very fact, covering principles of lexing and parsing, which makes heavy use of finite automata. A regular expression is nothing more than some kind of textual representation of such an automaton. Using the `Compiled` flag on the `Regex` constructor, you can ask the API to "compile" the regular expression such that it performs very well.

Under the hood, the regular expression compiler emits code that gets turned into an assembly that's loaded into the current application domain. I leave it to your imagination to think about the infrastructure used to achieve this. Real geeks may even have an attempt at using lightweight code generation or even the `System.Linq.Expressions` namespace to build such a compiler themselves.

Obviously, a cost is associated with such a compilation phase, so its benefits likely only outweigh the cost if you're going to reuse the `Regex` object over and over again (for example, when parsing a large input set of data).

Regular expressions can do more than just find matches for a given pattern; they can also be used to capture what's known as groups. A group is simply a part of a bigger regular expression pattern that can be extracted from the match. For example, assume you expect the user to enter a numeric range using the hyphen as a separator symbol. In that case, you really want to capture both the from and to parts of the range during regular expression matching. That's where groups come in handy:

```
var regex = new Regex(@"(?<from>0¦([1-9][0-9]*))\-(?<to>0¦([1-9][0-9]*))");

while (true)
{
    Console.Write("> ");
    string input = Console.ReadLine();
    Match match = regex.Match(input);
    if (match.Success)
        Console.WriteLine("from {0} to {1}",
                          match.Groups["from"].Value,
                          match.Groups["to"].Value);
}
```

In the pattern used for the example, two groups are specified using the rather cryptic (as not unusual for regular expressions) (?<group>pattern) syntax. The group part is a friendly name for the group, which can be omitted, allowing access to it by index. The pattern part speaks for itself and is a regular expression by itself. In this case, we use the same integer number matching pattern for both the from and to groups we want to extract. Here is a sample session, illustrating the extraction of matches groups in action:

```
> 1-5
from 1 to 5
> 123-987
from 123 to 987
> 0-
> -9
```

With this, we conclude our journey through regular expressions and leave further research to you. It should be mentioned that MSDN has plenty of content on the regular expression language and all its capabilities. Because crafting powerful and reusable regular expressions can be an art, some people felt inspired to create whole websites with commonly used ones (for example, for email addresses). Web searches can be of great help when you're in need of a regular expression that's up to the task at hand.

VERBATIM STRINGS

In the preceding example, notice how the - symbol got escaped using a backslash. If C# didn't have the concept of verbatim string (you know, the ones prefixed with an @ sign), all regular expression escapes would need to be doubled. In fact, the syntax of regular expressions and their escape characters was the main driver to introduce the concept of verbatim string literals.

Commonly Used String Methods

Throughout this exploration of the framework's rich functionality to deal with text, we have barely spoken about the type it's all about: System.String. Let's spend a minute or two pinpointing a few useful methods of this class.

STRINGS ARE CHARACTER SEQUENCES...

And because sequences are implemented using the IEnumerable<T> interface, guess what? The whole set of query operators defined over IEnumerable<T>, here with T substituted for char, shows up in the IntelliSense on a string object. This can be perceived as annoying at times. In fact, prior to Visual Studio 2010, for some reason I don't understand, IntelliSense on string objects never showed the extension methods.

Obviously, this behavior can be suppressed by commenting out the System.Linq using directive. Nonetheless, I still believe it'd be great for the Visual Studio tools to provide an option to suppress display of extension methods or have a means of toggling between both modes easily.

Various Checks

One often wants to check whether a string object obeys to certain expectations. Apart from string equality, things such as StartsWith and EndsWith are useful means to analyze a string for a certain structure. Those two methods could be regarded as a way to do a wildcard search, but `Contains` can, too. The following observations hold:

```
s.StartsWith("B")   ~   s matches B*
s.EndsWith("t")     ~   s matches *t
s.Contains("a")     ~   s matches *a*
```

Other ways to achieve similar effects exist (for example, by leveraging `IndexOf` kind of methods). Those return an index of the first (or last, for `LastIndexOf`) occurrence of a given fragment in the string. A negative return value denotes failure and therefore can be interpreted as a "doesn't contain" condition. For tasks more sophisticated than the ones discussed here, regular expressions likely provide a good angle of attack.

Mutation? Not So Much

You might recall the immutable nature of strings from our first encounter with this data type. Contrary to a lot of unmanaged or native languages, managed strings do not permit in-place mutation of the value (for example, by changing characters). Despite this intrinsic limitation, lots of instance methods exist on `System.String` that seem to hint at possible mutation. This isn't the case, though, because all of those methods return an entirely new string object.

A few examples are shown here:

```
string s = "world.";
s.Insert(0, "Hello ");
s.Replace('.', '!');
Console.WriteLine(s);  // Contrary to what you may expect, this prints "world."
```

Why does this code print `"world."` as opposed to `"Hello world!"`? If we had looked more closely at the IntelliSense for `Insert` and `Replace` (or other methods, like `Remove`, for that matter), we would have seen them return a `System.String` object themselves. That's the new object that contains the modified *copy* of the original string value. So to achieve the expected effect, you would write the following:

```
string s = "world.";
s = s.Insert(0, "Hello ");
s = s.Replace('.', '!');
Console.WriteLine(s);  // Prints "Hello world!"
```

Notice, though, that this little piece of code has created no less than three copies of the string value, all of which could be very large if we were dealing with input coming from some file or another source that tends to be lengthy. It should be clear that this excessive use of copying puts quite a bit of pressure on the GC. If this turns out to be a problem for your application's performance, a `StringBuilder` should be used (as discussed next).

WHAT ABOUT +=?

Some people believe the += operator on strings to be magical. They think it's using secret tricks to append a value to an existing string without creating copies. This simply is not the case either. The following fragment really deals with a total of three string objects:

```
string s = "Hello";
s += " world!";
Console.WriteLine(s);
```

The two literals will be embedded in the assembly and loaded from there, using the ldstr instruction. The += operation is roughly turned into the following:

```
s = s + " world!";
```

This in its turn gets compiled into a String.Concat static method call, which will indeed produce a third string object containing the concatenation of both. Now because the two parts of the concatenation are known at compile time, you might think the compiler is smart enough to perform the concatenation by itself. This isn't the case, though, for this particular example. However, for some uses of the + operator involving string literals, the compiler can be smarter and perform such simple and straightforward optimizations. If we had written the following, such a trick would be carried out, only having to load a single string object:

```
string s = "Hello" + " world!";
Console.WriteLine(s);
```

This may be surprising because the compiler is dealing with constants that can be folded at compile time. Similarly, when using lots of + operators to perform concatenations, the knowledge of associativity of the operator can be leveraged to concatenate the constant parts at compile time. A trip to ILDASM can be a good learning experience from time to time.

Trimming and Padding

Two common operations are to rip off excessive or introduce desired padding. The Trim and Pad methods are precisely what's needed to achieve those goals. Similar to the methods discussed earlier, they don't mutate the string object in-place but create whole new copies. As stated earlier, if this hurts performance because a lot of such operations are done or big strings are involved, the StringBuilder methods can be a good alternative. Having said that, the following code shows a few uses of those methods:

```
Console.Write("Enter your name: ");
string input = Console.ReadLine();
string name = input.Trim(' ', '\t');
Console.WriteLine("Welcome {0}!", name);
```

Here, the Trim method takes away any space or tab characters (specified using a params array parameter) at the start or the end of the given string. If only one side of the string

should be sanitized, the `TrimStart` and `TrimEnd` methods can be used. If no trim characters are specified, all whitespace characters are considered (defined in terms of the
`char.IsWhiteSpace` check).

The opposite operation of trimming is padding, where padding characters (typically plain
old spaces) are inserted either at the start or at the end of the string. The amount of
padding is computed from the desired total width of the string after padding takes place.
This effect is comparable to the use of the alignment specification in format items as
seen earlier:

```
string price = "$123.45";
Console.WriteLine(price.PadLeft(10));  // Prints "   $123.45"
Console.WriteLine("{0,10}");           // Prints "   $123.45" as well
```

Splitting and Joining

Another set of related operations is splitting and concatenation. The former takes a string
apart into pieces, based on a separator to look for, resulting in an array of strings. For the
latter operation, two variants exist. One is plain old concatenation, which glues a given
sequence of strings together without a separator in between adjacent parts. The join operation allows specification of a separator character, though:

```
Console.Write("Enter a comma-separated list of entries: ");
string input = Console.ReadLine();
string[] parts = input.Split(',');
string result = string.Join("; ", parts);
Console.WriteLine(result);
```

Overloads exist to influence the behavior of splitting, in particular what to do when an
empty group is found (that is, due to two consecutive separator characters). For the `Join`
method, starting from .NET 4, you can specify `IEnumerable` sequences of objects to be
joined together, using their `ToString` method results. This allows LINQ to Objects to be
used in conjunction with joining or concatenating strings, something I use quite often.

The `StringBuilder` Class

As stated numerous times already, the immutable nature of strings can be a blessing and a
curse. The latter is especially true if lots of string manipulations have to be made, which
effectively results in the creation of lots of intermediary string objects. Although short-
lived objects are cleaned up pretty effectively by the garbage collector, having a lot of
those, each of which can be substantially big, is suboptimal too. This can often be avoided
by making use of the `System.Text.StringBuilder` class.

DEFAULT USING DIRECTIVES

A few releases of Visual Studio ago, a using directive for the System.Text namespace was added to the default template for newly created code files. An obvious reason for its inclusion is the frequent use of StringBuilder as a highly recommended best practice. Notice that the presence of more using directives doesn't have any impact whatsoever on the application's performance, contrary to what some people believe. This same remark holds for the default presence of various referenced assemblies, which will get loaded only if functionality inside them is truly accessed from code being executed.

Introducing new default namespace imports is something the Visual Studio team doesn't go over too lightly. Each such addition might introduce naming conflicts. Avoiding such conflicts is one of the main reasons why namespaces were invented in the first place. In the limit, importing each and every namespace would bring us back to the state of affairs in languages that lack namespaces. Luckily, lots of namespaces that ship with the BCL have very few such conflicts.

One handy tip is the ability to customize default templates (and in fact, build your own if you want). Take a look at the Visual Studio installation folder and browse to Common7\IDE\ProjectTemplates\CSharp\Windows\1033 to locate a whole set of templates that appear in the New Project dialog for C# applications targeting the Windows platform. The Zip files you find here simply contain the blueprint of new projects being created. You can find more information about templates and ways to create those (in fact from within Visual Studio) on MSDN.

Creation of a new StringBuilder is simply done using any of the class's constructors. If you happen to know a good estimate of the capacity required to fit the string being created or manipulated, it's beneficial to pass this to the capacity parameter. Doing so will avoid the expense of reallocating the internal array used to store the string when its capacity is exceeded (remember realloc from C?).

The operations on a StringBuilder object are fairly simple. Using various overloads of Append, stuff can be added to the end of the current string that's being represented by the builder. The AppendLine method speaks for itself. AppendFormat can be used to leverage format strings as part of an append operation, which is more efficient than using string.Format first (which would require intermediate allocations). For example, the C# compiler generates code that uses the Append methods for the implementation of an anonymous type's ToString method.

Manipulations of the string contained by the builder are provided through methods like Insert, Replace, and Remove, which work similarly to the corresponding methods on the System.String class. The big difference is the in-place modification of the data that defines the string.

Talking about the representation of a string in a StringBuilder, it shouldn't come as a surprise that a builder is essentially a wrapper around an array of characters. The presence of an indexer (with a getter as well as a setter) is direct evidence of this.

STRING REPRESENTATION FOR INTEROP

Being effectively a mutable string, it should come as no surprise that the use of `StringBuilder` is commonly seen in interoperability code. Because native code often likes to modify strings in place, this type is the ideal candidate. More background on those kinds of interoperability can be obtained from various online sources as well as books devoted to the subject.

Finally, to get data out of a string builder, you use the `ToString` method. A common use of those kinds of builder objects is to concatenate numerous data entries in an efficient manner:

```
var sb = new StringBuilder();
foreach (var person in people)
    sb.AppendFormat("{0}\t{1}\r\n", person.Name, person.Age);
return sb.ToString();
```

In addition, complex formatting tasks can benefit from the use of string builders. Often, one single call to `string.Format` doesn't suffice because conditional logic might be required to omit optional parts of a textual representation. In such a situation, use of imperative code to make decisions and perform calls to `Append` or `AppendFormat` is appropriate.

That said, always ask a few questions. One is whether the computed string is really needed in its full form. For example, when visualizing data to the user, it might suffice to show data in chunks or use UI controls that can show separate entries in some kind of listbox. Another question is what you're about to do with the resulting string. If the answer is to write it to a file or any other kind of I/O system, you're likely better off using `Write` or `WriteLine` methods on `TextWriter` objects that are exposed by such I/O systems. We talk about I/O next.

Text Encoding

One final important aspect of working with text is the plethora of representations that exist out there when it comes to sending text across different (sub)systems. Although the .NET platform as a whole—including languages, frameworks, runtime, and tools—has standardized on Unicode as the representation of strings, plenty of systems deal with other formats such as ASCII or different UTF representations.

The `System.Text` namespace supports various encoding schemes that can be used from the `Encoding` class's static properties. Including Unicode, ASCII, UTF7, and a few others, those return objects of `Encoding` derivatives. Through those objects, you get access to encoder and decoder objects, among various other encoding-related properties and facilities.

For example, to turn a string into a byte sequence representation for a given encoding scheme, the GetBytes method can be used. In the opposite direction, a byte array can be passed to the GetString method to obtain a .NET string representation back:

```
var bytes = Encoding.ASCII.GetBytes("Hello ASCII!");
var hello = Encoding.ASCII.GetString(bytes);
Console.WriteLine(hello);
```

This trivial piece of code shows the round-tripping of a simple string through the ASCII encoding scheme. For more complicated examples, refer to MSDN. The fact that some people have made a living out of the creation of text stacks and all the intricacies is good evidence of the depth of the topic. (I have seen plenty of text specialists within Microsoft using Unicode books for their monitor stands.)

Summary

This chapter introduced essential capabilities offered by the BCL that ships with the .NET Framework. This includes working with various primitive types, ranging from numerical representations, dates, times and GUIDs, all the way to text. Because the BCL is a huge collection of useful tools, it should come as no surprise that chapters covering the BCL's features feel a bit like potpourri. Nonetheless, we've tried hard to keep this chapter related to working with simple data values and objects.

In the next chapters, we explore other facilities of the BCL, including diagnostics and quality assurance for code, I/O mechanisms, and more.

CHAPTER 27

Diagnostics and Instrumentation

IN THIS CHAPTER

▶ Ensuring Code Quality 1364

▶ Instrumentation 1378

▶ Controlling Processes 1386

W riting high-quality software should be a no-brainer. It's also common wisdom that catching bugs early during development is beneficial to reduce cost and user frustration. Luckily, .NET comes armed with a whole series of tools, built in to the framework and otherwise, that help the developer achieve those goals.

In this chapter, we focus on code quality from different angles. To start, we look at various development-time tools and techniques that help keep up a high-quality standard. Those include code analysis and FxCop, various Visual Studio tools, and simple but effective techniques such as writing code with asserts. Starting from .NET 4, code contracts extend upon such tools, allowing developers to write down, analyze, and enforce conditions the code should obey.

One thing we don't cover here is the extended tooling available in Visual Studio to do test-driven development (TDD). Although I'm a firm believer in taking such an approach, having some continuous monitoring of potential code regressions and code coverage, we simply don't have the space to do the subject justice. (You can find any numbers of books devoted to TDD and the use of Visual Studio tools to achieve this.)

Being able to catch problems early is one thing, but there will always be cases where deployed and running software needs to be checked for mishaps and debugged accordingly. Various classes that can be found in the `System.Diagnostics` namespace help to build better code that's instrumented to make such production analysis easier to accomplish. In particular, we talk about event logging, use of the performance counter infrastructure in Windows, and various ways to interact with a debugger from code.

Finally, as a little extra, we cover the `Process` class, which can be used to spawn processes and query them for various properties. The common thread between this class and most of the other topics covered in this chapter is the `System.Diagnostics` namespace, which we consider to be an integral part of the Base Class Library (BCL).

Ensuring Code Quality

Getting code quality to high levels right from the start of development is a very valuable thing to do. Issues uncovered later in the development cycle of a product tend to have exponentially higher costs compared to issues discovered early on. Different tools can be leveraged to ensure high levels of code quality.

Focusing on facilities in the BCL, our exposition of code quality tools and techniques doesn't include a praise of unit testing virtues, a good development process, and so on. I strongly recommend enterprise-class developers invest their time in learning about those aspects, too. Keywords such as *test driven development (TDD)* and *software development in teams* jump to mind immediately. Unfortunately, we don't have the room to dive into those aspects. Books dedicated to those subjects, also focusing on tools like Visual Studio Team System, are highly recommended.

Code Analysis

One of the biggest merits of good framework design is to have common patterns and conventions that make developers feel at home when discovering your application programming interface (API). It should be no surprise that tools have been written to enforce those goals by means of static, compile-time analysis of code. It turns out such tools can also be used to point out a plethora of common bugs or suboptimal development practices.

Collectively known as "code analysis" in Visual Studio, all those static compile-time checks provide a great means to be vigilant about certain aspects of code quality in a continuous manner. Starting with Visual Studio 2010, code analysis rules have been grouped in so-called rule sets, which control the amount of "noise" you can tolerate.

I recommend turning on code analysis as shown in Figure 27.1 early in the development cycle of an application, library, or whatnot. This is also the ideal time to study rule sets and determine which one is best for you. In addition to enabling the build-time code analysis, it also might be a good idea to check the `Build` flag to treat errors as warnings. If someone introduces a new violation, one is required to tackle the problem (either by fixing it or by suppressing it) before checking in code. In fact, such rules can be enforced in Team Foundation Server, as well.

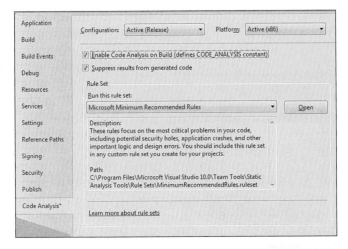

FIGURE 27.1   Enabling code analysis with the minimum recommended set of rules.

A thorough discussion of all the rules implemented in this feature is beyond the scope of this discussion. The best way to familiarize yourself with the rules is to just run the code analysis tools, with the maximum rule set, on a non-trivial-sized project that didn't have the feature turned on previously. Doing so will be an eye-opener and reveal a whole lot of potential defects you might want to examine.

HOW RULES ARE WRITTEN

Rules are basically implementations of some `IRule` interface that gets a chance to look at compiled code by means of an expression tree format. Those trees are built from the compiled intermediate language (IL) code and provided by a framework known as CCI, or the Common Compiler Infrastructure, which can be downloaded from CodePlex. One key difference with the `System.Linq.Expressions` trees is the origin of the trees. Whereas the LINQ ones are crafted at compile time, CCI extracts them from already compiled code.

Recommended corrective actions can be found by highlighting the warning in Visual Studio's Errors and Warnings pane and pressing F1 to open Help. After studying this guidance, you may still decide the error is a false positive or you have good reasons to dismiss the advice. In such a case, errors can be suppressed, as shown in Figure 27.2.

Suppressions should be used with care and be based on good justification. All a suppression does is insert a custom attribute from the `System.Diagnostics.CodeAnalysis` namespace in the place you indicate, either on top of the member or in a GlobalSuppressions.cs file. Tools use this information to suppress messages in subsequent runs.

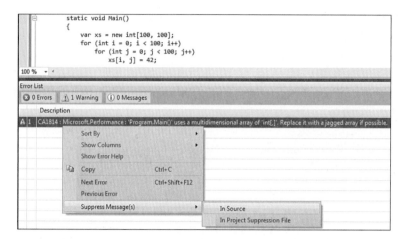

```
static void Main()
{
    var xs = new int[100, 100];
    for (int i = 0; i < 100; i++)
        for (int j = 0; j < 100; j++)
            xs[i, j] = 42;
}
```

FIGURE 27.2   Use of suppressions to disable a warning.

Asserts and Contracts

Statically discovering typical code defects is a big convenience, but it isn't a silver bullet. Lots of conditions are intrinsic to the algorithms you're coding up and simply cannot be detected by tools without particular knowledge of the developer's intent.

To communicate intent, various mechanisms have been created over the years. The oldest and simplest one is to use asserts, which are pieces of code that perform a logical check, typically only in special builds of your software. If the check fails, the developer is notified and invited to break in the debugger to analyze what's going wrong. Maybe the condition makes a false assumption about code invariants, or you've just caught a problem on the spot before it can do further damage.

Code contracts were introduced in .NET 4 based on a Microsoft Research project that was run in the years before the release. Contracts allow a more declarative approach to stating the code's intent, also communicating various conditions and expected code invariants to tools. Examples include pre- and post-conditions of methods, exception behavior, and assumed absence of null references. Based on this knowledge, tools can try to detect problems statically, by theorem provers that reason about your code. Alternatively, runtime checks can be generated.

Before we delve into both of those approaches, it's useful to contrast both models and relate them to the use of runtime checks. First of all, asserts are typically used as a tool to be leveraged at (extended) development time only. The reason we mention extended in this definition is that so-called checked builds may be used in tests or sometimes even in preproduction to uncover issues. Nonetheless, the excessive number of checks that could arise from asserts is likely not a price you want to pay at runtime, especially if you're dealing with internal implementation details that should never be violated unless a bug exists in your code. This is different from issues that can arise from unexpected or even malicious user input, which should always be checked at runtime.

This choice between development time and runtime checking of conditions has been quite black and white in the past. Runtime checks use exceptions, while asserts get compiled away in release builds and trigger developer alerts when violated during debugging. With the advent of code contracts, this choice can be controlled more tightly. In fact, you can balance between compile-time checks and runtime checks by leveraging post-build tools that essentially rewrite assemblies to omit or insert runtime checks.

Developing with Asserts

Asserts are a code-driven way to document invariants that should hold in your code (for example, the fact a reference should not be null in nonpublic code or an integer denoting an index should be within valid bounds). Formulating an assert is simply done using a Boolean-valued expression passed to the Debug.Assert method, which is defined in the System.Diagnostics namespace. For example:

```
private static void Sort<T>(T[] values, int from, int to)
{
    Debug.Assert(from <= to, "Expected from to be less than to.");
    ...
}
```

I'll leave it to you to implement a sort algorithm that divides the input array in two halves and recursively calls the Sort method to sort the halves. Doing so implies the need to compute indices in preparation of a recursive call. Those kinds of calculations are prone to subtle off-by-one errors and such. The goal of the assert is to catch such issues. Also when implementing the Sort method, think of other assumptions you're making with regard to the input (and that therefore warrant the declaration of additional asserts).

A publicly exposed Sort method will simply wrap this, passing in the bounds of the entire array, effectively causing the whole array to be sorted if the private recursive Sort method is implemented correctly:

```
public static void Sort<T>(this T[] values)
{
    if (values == null)
        throw new ArgumentNullException("values");

    Sort(values, 0, values.Length - 1);
}
```

You should observe that for private calls, we don't use exceptions here to signal invalid inputs. Instead, asserts are used to catch issues where asserts are broken. Because the private Sort method with sorting bounds is really an implementation detail, it's our sole responsibility to ensure we're calling the method in an appropriate manner. Using exceptions is an option but introduces an unnecessary runtime checking cost simply to guard for mistakes that we should have caught during development.

Instead of doing nothing to check valid input, an assert helps you understand the intent of the code and will signal a problem earlier. Assume, for example, that you end up with some piece of code that iterates over the chunk of the array to sort based on the `from` and `to` parameter values. It shouldn't be difficult to see that such a loop would silently break if `from` is larger than `to`:

```
for (int i = from; i < to; i++)
    ...
```

An assert would spot the discrepancy in the input, whereas blindly going with the input tends to lead to much more fragile code where a fatal mistake could go unnoticed for a while (maybe parts of the array could remain unsorted). Therefore, it's a good practice to document assertions by means of `Debug.Assert`, which should hold in your code.

So what happens if an assert fails? The answer depends on the flavor of the build of the code. If you're building `"Debug"`, the asserts will be left in place and wired up to produce a dialog box as shown in Figure 27.3. If you're building `"Release"`, the calls to `Assert` are compiled away completely, thanks to the conditional attribute that's put on top of it. You can see this by pressing F12, for Go to Definition, with the cursor on the `Assert` method:

```
[Conditional("DEBUG")]
public static void Assert(bool condition, string message);
```

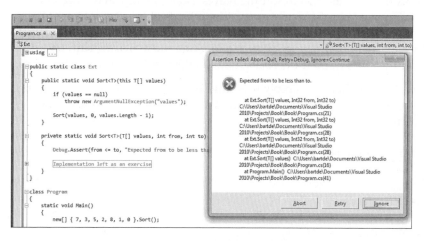

FIGURE 27.3   An assert failure dialog during debugging.

In other words, if you're building without `DEBUG` defined (which is done through the build settings for the "Debug" flavor in Visual Studio), calls to `Assert` are simply stripped out, and you don't pay any runtime price whatsoever. This is what makes an assert quite different from an `if` check followed by an exception, which isn't compiled away in a conditional manner unless you use `#if` yourself. You will agree this is much more invasive in the code than the use of a simple call to `Assert`:

```
private static void Sort<T>(T[] values, int from, int to)
{
#if DEBUG
    if (from <= to)
        throw new ArgumentException("Expected from to be less than to.");
#endif
    ...
}
```

The failure dialog, as shown in Figure 27.3, has three buttons in the title bar. In particular, the Retry button is (somewhat counterintuitively) hooked up to break in the debugger, allowing investigation of the failure. When no debugger is attached, the developer gets a chance to attach a debugger at this point. We look at the ways you can communicate with the debugger from code in the next sections titled "Diagnostic Debugger Output" and "Controlling the Debugger".

To summarize asserts, they're a very simple yet effective way to identify problems in your code on the spot, instead of having to figure out why something fails much further down in a call stack. Programming with asserts takes some training, but always ask yourself whether you're making assumptions about state in your code. If so, that spot might be a good candidate to inject an assert call.

A Primer to Using Code Contracts

Asserts and exceptions are a world of difference with regard to their behavior and their impact on the compiled code. Previously, we emphasized when to use which technique. With the introduction of code contracts in .NET 4, the world has become less black and white. Code contracts allow you to state invariants that can either remain in the code and act as runtime checks (throwing exceptions on violations) or be stripped out.

Furthermore, the expressiveness of code contracts is much higher than a plain Boolean expression. This also allows tools to reason about code (for example, to generate tests in an automated fashion; search for Microsoft Research Pex on the Web).

The API for code contracts also lives under the System.Diagnostics namespace but in a dedicated subnamespace called Contracts. The Contract static class acts as the one-stop shop to express contracts in code. This is shown in Figure 27.4, highlighting just one of the methods that's quite different from a simple Debug.Assert call. The Ensures method basically formulates a post-condition, which is a condition that should hold true after the containing method exits. In case of an exceptional return, there may still be conditions that should hold true (for example, proper cleanup of state), which can be stated as a contract using EnsuresOnThrow.

Similarly, preconditions can be formulated. Using the Exists and ForAll methods, you can express predicates that should hold (for example, for any or all of an array's elements). Other useful tidbits include the ability to refer to an old value of some variable (for instance, before a piece of code runs) and express conditions that should hold by comparing it to the new value. All of this goes far beyond what the Debug class has to offer and enables you to take a declarative approach to state a lot of invariants (that is, without having to resort to a bunch of #if conditional imperative code). For more information about the expressive power of code contracts, refer to MSDN.

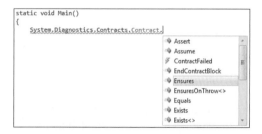

FIGURE 27.4   Code contracts methods to express various conditions.

The interesting thing about code contracts is they don't get enforced by default, and the use of separate tools is required to rewrite the code, injecting checks in all the places needed. This shouldn't come as a big surprise because code contracts look like plain old method calls to the compiler but often express something of a global nature:

```
public int Count
{
    get
    {
        Contract.Ensures(Contract.Result<int>() >= 0);
        // Implementation goes here...
    }
}
```

In the preceding snippet, a contract is used to state that the getter ensures that the int values result is larger than or equal to zero. However, how can those calls perform checks to see this is really the case? In fact, there might even be multiple paths in the implementation of the getter that do return a value to the caller. What really needs to happen is that the code gets checked statically, using advanced tools like theorem provers, to ensure there cannot be a single code path that violates the formulated constraints. Alternatively, this piece of code needs to be rewritten such that prior to any return, a check is carried out to ensure the contract holds.

Logic to rewrite contract method calls into advanced checks is not built in to compilers like C#'s and Visual Basic's. It was chosen to implement code contracts as a library rather than an extension to all the .NET language compilers, such that any language that's capable of making method calls (which one isn't?) can benefit from contracts. To perform analysis based on contracts, or to inject runtime checks, separate tools can be downloaded from MSDN DevLabs at http://msdn.microsoft.com/en-us/devlabs. Those tools integrate with Visual Studio 2010 and allow for a smooth integration with your product's build.

To wrap up our primer to code contracts, I highly recommend that you check out the code contracts API and it's very expressive nature. Samples that can be found on the aforementioned website should be a good guide to understand code contracts. By adding more information about your code's intent, rich tooling can be enabled to check whether the stated invariants hold true under all circumstances. If static checking at build time is not possible, you can resort to runtime checks that ensure contracts do not get violated, signaling exceptions otherwise.

Diagnostic Debugger Output

Another capability of the System.Diagnostics namespace is to interact with a debugger from inside your code. Samples include emitting diagnostic information about what your code is doing, which can be visualized in a debugger's output window. Let's take a look at some of those capabilities.

Revisiting the Debug class, notice the presence of Write and WriteLine methods. Using them, you can write information to the debugger. Just as with Assert calls, the calls to those methods are omitted from the assembly if it isn't built using the DEBUG flag, so there's no runtime overhead in release build binaries. An example is shown here:

```
private void ContactPaymentService(string account, decimal amount)
{
    Debug.WriteLine("Connecting to payment service");
    try
    {
        // More code goes here...
    }
    catch (IOException ex)
    {
        Debug.WriteLine("Failure to communicate: " + ex.Message);
        // Production code to handle the exception...
    }
}
```

CONDITIONAL DEBUGGER OUTPUT

Variants on Write and WriteLine exist, with an If suffix. Besides the message to be emitted, they also take a Boolean-valued condition that controls whether output is written to the debugger.

This is different from using an if statement together with a Write or WriteLine call, due to the conditional compiled nature. You don't want the if check to remain in the release build's assembly code but the Write(Line) call to be omitted from the resulting assembly code. Combining both the condition and the output in one single call allows all the effects of the check and the output to be stripped away in case of a non-debug build.

In fact, this is the ideal place to point out some of the dangers of conditionally compiled code in imperative languages like C#, where side effects are part of common programming practice. Consider the following code fragment:

```
[Conditional("DEBUG")]
static void Bar(int i) { }

static void Main()
{
    int i = 0;
    Bar(i++);
    Console.WriteLine(i);
}
```

Bar is much like Debug.WriteLine in that it gets omitted from the compiled code if the DEBUG symbol is not defined. What do you think the code prints in Debug versus Release mode? Let me tell you: 1 versus 0. The reason is because the compiler takes away the whole call site to Bar, including evaluation of parameters (here using the post-increment operator on i) in case DEBUG is not defined. To make a long story short: Don't have side effects in calls to methods such as Debug.WriteLine!

Figure 27.5 shows the output of a Debug.WriteLine call in the Output window in the Visual Studio 2010 IDE. If this window doesn't show up, go to Debug, Windows to enable it.

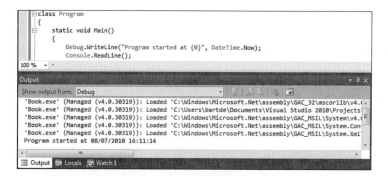

FIGURE 27.5   Debugger's Output window showing output from Debug.WriteLine.

Other features exposed by the Debug class include the ability to control the indentation of output, which is useful to emit a tree-shape debug output trace. The indentation can be used to reveal the depth of a call. Using the following code, you will see the WriteLine calls made inside the Bar call to be indented relative to the part stack frame. Obviously, you should make sure the Indent and Unindent calls are balanced properly. Notice that an exception in the commented-out section will spoil the indentation level, so ideally a finally block is used to make sure the Unindent call happens:

```
static void Bar()
{
    Debug.Indent();
    Debug.WriteLine("Bar - Begin");
```

```
    // Code goes here

    Debug.WriteLine("Bar - End");
    Debug.Unindent();
}
```

Debugger output can be sent to many listeners, known as trace listeners, which are simply objects derived from the `TraceListener` class in `System.Diagnostics`. Code used to emit debugger output can be kept in place, but its underlying trace listeners can be switched out for others (for example, in a preproduction scenario). By doing so, you gain an easy mechanism to analyze what code is doing if problems arise, without the need to even attach a debugger. This can be done through the use of configuration files, as shown here; more information can be found on MSDN:

```
<configuration>
  <system.diagnostics>
    <trace autoflush="false" indentsize="4">
      <listeners>
        <add name="myListener"
             type="System.Diagnostics.TextWriterTraceListener"
             initializeData="TextWriterOutput.log" />
        <remove name="Default" />
      </listeners>
    </trace>
  </system.diagnostics>
</configuration>
```

Finally, the `Debug.Fail` method is pretty much the same as a failed assert triggered by a call to `Debug.Assert(false)`, but it also prints a message—including the stack trace of the point of failure—to the trace listeners. For all those diagnostic debugger output logging mechanisms, keep in mind their conditionally compiled nature. If you need to provide diagnostics that are available in production, other mechanisms, such as direct use of the Windows event log, come in handy. We discuss them later in this chapter in the "Using Event Logs" section.

Controlling the Debugger

Besides the `Debug` class, the `System.Diagnostics` namespace has a `Debugger` class, whose static methods are used to control the debugger. Arguably, the most useful of all its methods is `Break`, which causes the code to break in the debugger at the point of the call. This functionality is often used to debug a program's startup path, in cases where it's rather inconvenient to have a debugger attached already. For example, some other process may launch your program without leaving you a chance to attach a debugger.

IMAGE FILE EXECUTION OPTIONS

In fact, the problem of debugging a startup path has been around since the early days of Windows. It's not really a problem, though. The designers of the loader that is used to run executables on Windows envisioned this problem (or likely hit the difficulty themselves plenty of times).

To make such debugger scenarios more appealing, they put in a grand hack called Image File Execution Options, which is a Registry-based setting that can be specified on a per-program basis. You can find it under the Local Machine hive of the Registry at HKLM\SOFTWARE\Microsoft\Windows NT\CurrentVersion\Image File Execution Options. Each executable whose process creation should be subject to tweaks applied by the loader has a subkey that specifies such options. For example, settings affecting process creation for notepad.exe executable images live under a subkey called notepad.exe.

The Debugger setting enables you to cause the loader to start a specified program rather than the original executable. The original executable's path is passed to the "debugger" executable as the first command-line argument. This way, a debugger can be configured to intercept any creation of a process for a given executable.

An example of the use of Break is shown here:

```
static void Main()
{
    Debugger.Break();
    // More code goes here...
}
```

The code's behavior depends on the presence of an attached debugger. If that's the case, our call to Break simply causes us to break into the debugger at the line of the call. If no debugger is attached yet, a dialog displays, as shown in Figure 27.6.

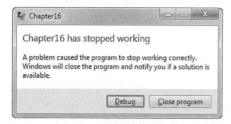

FIGURE 27.6   Result of a call to Debugger.Break without a debugger attached.

Depending on the machine's configuration (that is, whether a debugger has been set up), the dialog's look will vary. In any case, you can now attach a debugger to the process that has triggered a Break call, and doing so puts you straight on the line where the

`Break` call was made. From that point, state can be analyzed and, if desired, execution can be resumed.

One key difference with the `Debug` class's methods lies in the fact that the `Debugger` methods are not conditionally compiled. In other words, things such as `Debugger.Break` also causes a "release" binary to break at the point of the call.

THE CASE OF DEBUGGER-DEPENDENT BEHAVIOR

Some people love to use the `Debugger.IsAttached` get-only property to check for the presence of an attached debugger and make code exhibit different behavior based on this condition. Uses of this trick exist in UI frameworks (for example, to be peskier about cross-thread violations in user code during development). The presence of a debugger is a good indication of "development."

Although this conditional execution of logic may be justified in certain cases to ease the use of a library during development time, it should be clear that it can also be the utmost source of frustration when debugging the library itself. (I have personally experienced this.)

Logging Stack Traces

From a debugging developer's point of view, the most precious treasure to tackle a problem is most likely a stack trace. Having this information available answers the question about what the code is doing at a certain point in time. While this piece of information is readily available in a debugger, it's sometimes useful to log a stack trace in code.

Here the `StackTrace` class in `System.Diagnostics` comes up as the hero of the day. The creation of a new instance of this class captures the stack trace of the current thread. A few constructor overloads exist to extract a stack trace from an `Exception` object, to skip a specified number of frames, and so forth. A silly example is shown here:

```
static void Bar()
{
    var trace = new StackTrace();
    Console.WriteLine(trace);
}

static void Main()
{
    Bar();
}
```

The StackTrace object can be printed by means of its ToString method (here implicitly called by the use of WriteLine) or can be decomposed into individual stack frames by using the GetFrame and GetFrames methods. The preceding snippet prints this:

```
at Program.Bar()
at Program.Main()
```

SEEING A LARGER STACK TRACE?

It's possible, and in fact very likely, that you'll see a larger stack trace when trying to run this example. This is due to the Visual Studio hosting process, which is used to enable certain debugging scenarios and by itself is a managed application that sits higher up the call stack.

You can recognize such a call stack by the presence of a frame that reveals a call to RunUsersAssembly in Microsoft.VisualStudio.HostingProcess.HostProc. While the hosting process has certain well-documented benefits, it sometimes can be considered harmful because some global properties differ. For example, inspection of things such as the application domains, the native command line, and so forth will differ.

By passing true to the constructor, file info can be obtained as well, given a symbol file (with extension .pdb) is found. Note that this process is rather slow, so use of stack trace logging is better avoided in performance-critical code paths. Also keep in mind that exceptions do have a stack trace out of the box, so there's no need to have explicit code to capture such a trace. You can still use the StackTrace class to inspect the stack trace in more detail from code (for example, on the level of individual frames).

Measuring Performance Using StopWatch

Performance measurement of pieces of code should be done using a precise-enough time to have any value whatsoever. Just subtracting DateTime values doesn't cut it because of the relatively low resolution of DateTime values. To prove this point, enter the following piece of code, which computes 50 factorial a number of times:

```
for (int j = 0; j < 10; j++)
{
    var start = DateTime.Now;

    var n = 1L;
    for (int i = 2; i < 50; i++)
        n *= i;

    var end = DateTime.Now;
    Console.WriteLine(end - start);
}
```

Feel free to increase the outer loop's iteration count. In any case, the output shouldn't make much sense because some of the factorial calculations turn out to take no time (that is, printing 00:00:00), whereas others take 1 or more milliseconds. Obviously, there's always a chance of having some noise (for example, because of triggering a lazy initialization code path in the framework that takes time on the first call, or because of the garbage collector pausing your code temporarily). Nonetheless, a zero-time calculation doesn't make sense. Instead of dumping the raw `TimeSpan` value computed from subtracting the two `DateTime` values, try to print its `Ticks` value:

```
for (int j = 0; j < 10; j++)
{
    var start = DateTime.Now;
    ...
    var end = DateTime.Now;
    Console.WriteLine((end - start).Ticks);
}
```

Again, zero values come up. If you recall correctly from our discussion about `DateTime` values, their maximum precision is 100 nanoseconds. This can obviously explain the zero values, as we might be below this threshold value, so the two `DateTime.Now` evaluations resulted in the same value even though time has elapsed. It's also good to put things in perspective a bit. With today's processors ticking at several gigahertz, the order of magnitude for a single instruction's execution is 10 power –9 seconds. Count down in orders of three: milli, micro, nano.

Luckily, Windows has provided means to get more accurate timing values through an API known as `QueryPerformanceFrequency` and `QueryPerformanceCounter`. Both of those are wrapped by the managed code `StopWatch` class. Lots of little caveats apply because this functionality relies on the goodwill of the processor itself, the BIOS, as well as the Hardware Abstraction Layer (HAL), some of which have issues on older systems. In any case, `StopWatch` is your best friend if you need high-precision measurements of performance:

```
for (int j = 0; j < 10; j++)
{
    var sw = new Stopwatch();
    sw.Start();

    var n = 1L;
    for (int i = 2; i < 50; i++)
        n *= i;

    sw.Stop();
    Console.WriteLine(sw.Elapsed);
}
```

As shown here, its use is fairly straightforward with `Start` and `Stop` methods and a property called `Elapsed` to return the measurement. Other methods exist that enable you to reset or restart the stopwatch. Read-only fields called `Frequency` and `IsHighResolution` can be used to reveal what can be expected from the stopwatch with regard to its overall precision.

With the preceding change made to our code, meaningful results show up. On my machine, each computation of the factorial of 50 took a few elapsed ticks, with a very low degree of variance among the measurements.

PERFORMANCE ANALYSIS WISDOM

It can't be stressed enough that performance measurements should be taken with a grain of salt, especially the micro-benchmarking kind. While you might be able to beat the hell out of a particular code path's performance, all that matters is whether that code has true impact on the application's or library's overall performance.

Always make sure to start by identifying the "hot path" of your code (that is, the one that's the least performing in certain important user scenarios) using performance analysis tools as found in higher-end Visual Studio editions. Only after you've done your work on identifying a possible culprit should you undertake further detailed measurements to narrow down your search for a performance killer.

It should also be clear that performance responsibilities vary a lot based on the usage scenarios of the code. Libraries with essential functionality such as math operations or collections have a huge impact on a lot of consumers and should be designed with lots of care. For example, the BCL's collection types have a good amount of documentation on the algorithmic complexity (expressed in so-called big-O notation) of various operations such as element insertion, retrieval, and so on.

Finally, be sure not to optimize your code beyond the point of correctness. It should be obvious this is the case, but far too often this happens in practice. A solid set of unit tests and regression tests can help a lot, but thoughtless code changes should be avoided at all costs.

Instrumentation

In the `System.Diagnostics` namespace's functionality discussed thus far, we've concerned ourselves with development-time utilities. Examples included the ability to log diagnostic debugger output, develop with asserts, and so on. An equally important aspect to high-quality software is maintainability. It's the (sad) truth that software tends to fail in production at the most inconvenient times. Asking the IT administration department to attach a debugger to a server that's producing revenue for your company usually will not be well received. Instead, having diagnostic logging, and more generally other kinds of instrumentation, built in will do a lot to help you figure out what's going on.

Although a whole realm of manageability techniques can be built in to software, we just discuss a few common ones that in fact have been supported by the framework since the early days. In particular, we discuss how to write to Windows event logs and how to provide performance counters to trace statistics of the running code.

Using Event Logs

Event logs are a centralized means in the Windows platform to keep track of diagnostic information about running software components in the system. Both the operating system and its services and third-party applications can plug in to it. The designers of the .NET Framework deemed it useful to have a managed wrapper around the APIs used to communicate with the event logging component of Win32.

The EventLog class in System.Diagnostics is the wrapper class for event logs exposed to managed code. Various static methods are available to create what's known as an event source, basically an identifier to correlate an event log entry with its origin. In addition, methods such as WriteEntry and WriteEvent are available to write to a specified event log. To limit the need to specify an event log's name as well as a source, you can create an instance of the EventLog class and use instance members to perform various actions. This includes the ability to query an event log for various properties such as its size, retention policies, overflow action when the log reaches it capacity, and so forth.

Log entries need to have a source, which is a distinct identifier for the origin of the log entry. Creating such a source requires administrative privileges and can be carried out in a configuration utility used to configure your application, thus avoiding the need (and general bad practice) to run your application as an administrator all the time. The following code shows how to check for the existence of a source, followed by the creation thereof in case it's found to be missing:

```
const string SOURCE = "Chapter27";
const string APPLICATION = "Application";

if (!EventLog.SourceExists(SOURCE))
    EventLog.CreateEventSource(SOURCE, APPLICATION);
```

Once a unique event source has been established for our application, we can use it to write to the log file. Various flags can be passed to a log entry, including the type of the entry (informational message, warning, error, security audit record, and so on), numeric identifiers to denote application-specific states, as well as a byte array for "raw data" with more information about the entry (for instance, the serialized form of an object). Use of unique status codes has various advantages as it makes searching for corrective actions easier (for example, "Source Chapter27 error code 1234"), while message strings can be subject to localization. The following code shows how to log an informational message with a few application-defined status codes. The dot (.) parameter to the EventLog constructor is used to refer to the local computer.

```
const int STARTED = 1001;
const short LIFECYCLE = 1;
```

```
using (var log = new EventLog(APPLICATION, ".", SOURCE))
{
    log.WriteEntry("Application started.", EventLogEntryType.Information,
                   STARTED, LIFECYCLE);
}
```

Because the `EventLog` class implements `IDisposable`, use of a using block is highly recommended to ensure proper cleanup of the native resources it holds on to. Figure 27.7 shows the Application log (shown through Event Viewer, an MMC snap-in available from Administrative Tools or by running eventvwr.msc) after the call to `WriteEntry`.

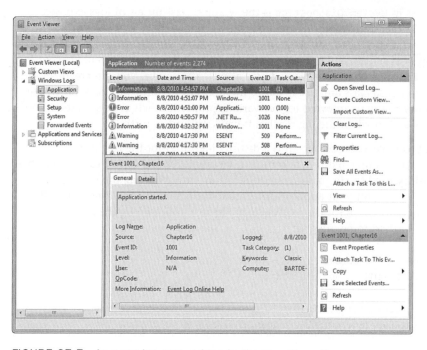

FIGURE 27.7   An event log entry written by the `EventLog` class.

Another way to deal with event logs is to create a component, as shown in Figure 27.8.

Components are just classes that derive from a common component base class, which provides a few benefits. One is the ability to remote such objects through .NET Remoting; another is the design-time story in the Visual Studio IDE. We'll ignore the first aspect and just show the use of the component designer in Figure 27.9.

Using the log can be done now by exposing the private field created for the `EventLog` instance (for example, through a property) or by providing specialized wrappers. Other parts of your application leverage the component (which can be remoted, allowing it to support more-complex application architectures) to do all sorts of instrumentation actions, such as logging. Various settings of the `EventLog` component object can be configured with the Properties window, as shown in Figure 27.9.

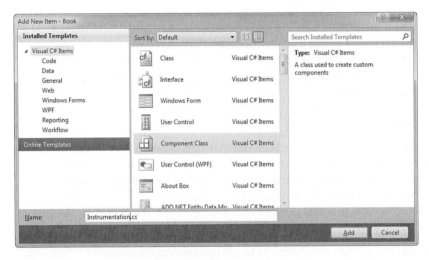

FIGURE 27.8   Creating a new component class.

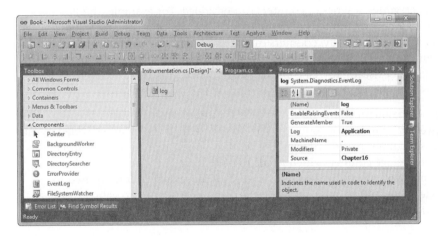

FIGURE 27.9   An event log in the designer of a component.

With regard to what we've discussed here, we've assumed the use of the local computer's event log, despite the fact that the API has support to communicate with logs on other machines. Notice that event logs are subject to various security settings and policies, so this kind of communication with another machine can have certain complications. Running in a Windows domain avoids some of those complexities, for sure.

Also notice that the event log facilities in Windows do have rich capabilities from an administrator's point of view, including the ability to view logs remotely, associate tasks with entries, and so forth. If you end up using event logs heavily, make sure you are aware of all the features they support. This will prevent you from cloning features that are natively supported by the system and allow you to benefit from the many man-years of development, debugging, and tuning.

Monitoring with Performance Counters

Using event logs is a great way to log discrete messages that can be used to trace the flow of execution for a given application or its individual components. However, in many cases, it's more valuable to monitor the dynamism of an application, which typically has a numeric nature. Examples include tracing the number of user requests a service is handling, object allocation rates, resource pool utilization, and so on. For such scenarios, the use of performance counters comes in handy.

Just like event logging, the concept of performance counters is rooted in the operating system's facilities. A whole bunch of counter types exist, which indicate their numeric nature. Examples include time-based counters (for example, elapsed times for some operation), increment-based counters (for example, number of requests), fractional values (for example, for some utilization percentage), and many more. A full discussion of all those types would be a waste of paper, so let's move on and discuss the essentials.

The first thing to do, just as with event logs, is to set up counters by means of a "counter category." For those of you who've looked into performance counters through Performance Monitor before, examples of such categories are Processor, Memory, and so on. Within such categories, a series of counters can be added. For example, the Processor category built in to Windows has tens of counters that log idle time, user time, power state transitions, and so on. Finally, counters can be single instance or multiple instance. In the case of our running Processor counter category example, on a multiprocessor machine counters will exist for any CPU in the system. For CLR-related counters, one instance can exist per managed application running on the machine.

The following code fragment shows how to create a counter category with a friendly description as well as a number of counters. The order in which the counters added to the category appear sometimes matters, depending on the counter type. In this example, this is the case for the average counter, which needs to be followed by a base counter. The reason for this shouldn't be too hard to see. Because an individual counter is used to represent a single value, and because an average is computed out of two values (using a numerator and denominator), two such counters are needed:

```
const string SOURCE = "Chapter27";
const string DESCRIPTION = "Sample counters";

const string TXCOUNT = "# of transactions";
const string PROCRATE = "Processing rate";
const string PROCRATEBASE = "Processing rate base";

if (!PerformanceCounterCategory.Exists(SOURCE))
{
    PerformanceCounterCategory.Create(SOURCE, DESCRIPTION,
        PerformanceCounterCategoryType.SingleInstance,
        new CounterCreationDataCollection
        {
```

```
        new CounterCreationData(TXCOUNT,
                                "Keeps track of number of bank transfers",
                                PerformanceCounterType.NumberOfItems32),
        new CounterCreationData(PROCRATE,
                                "Average transaction processing rate",
                                PerformanceCounterType.AverageCount64),
        new CounterCreationData(PROCRATEBASE,
                                "Denominator for processing rate counter",
                                PerformanceCounterType.AverageBase),
    }
  );
}
```

In this example, we settle for a single instance counter, assuming there will only be one "Chapter27 server application" running at a time. From the vocab used to name the different counters, you can infer we're mimicking a (bank) transaction processor. While you're at it, explore the other static methods on PerformanceCounterCategory, such as Delete.

Next, assuming the counters are set up, let's write a piece of code that obtains all the counter objects. The false parameter passed to the constructor disables read-only use, allowing us to modify the counter's value from our code:

```
var txCount = new PerformanceCounter(SOURCE, TXCOUNT, false);
var procRate = new PerformanceCounter(SOURCE, PROCRATE, false);
var procRateBase = new PerformanceCounter(SOURCE, PROCRATEBASE, false);
```

Given those three counter objects, we can now cook up some simple sample program that queues up transaction requests, monitored by the txCount counter. Another part of the program dequeues those requests and processes them. To demonstrate this queuing and processing behavior, we'll use two threads and .NET 4's ConcurrentQueue<T> generic collection type. In Chapter 29, "Threading and Synchronization," and Chapter 30, "Task Parallelism and Data Parallelism," we cover the notion of concurrency in more detail.

```
Console.WriteLine("Press ENTER to start processing...");
Console.ReadLine();

var rand = new Random();
var queue = new ConcurrentQueue<int>();

new Thread(() =>
{
    while (true)
    {
        Thread.Sleep(rand.Next(1000, 5000));
```

```
        int n = 0;
        int tx;
        while (queue.TryDequeue(out tx))
        {
            Console.WriteLine("Processing transaction {0}", tx);
            Thread.Sleep(rand.Next(0, 100));
            txCount.Decrement();
            n++;
        }

        procRate.IncrementBy(n);
        procRateBase.Increment();
    }
}).Start();

for (int tx = 0; true; tx++)
{
    Console.WriteLine("Requesting transaction {0}", tx);
    queue.Enqueue(tx);
    txCount.Increment();

    Thread.Sleep(rand.Next(0, 200));
}
```

The background thread basically wakes up every 1 to 5 seconds, based on a random sleep duration value. At that point, it continues dequeuing all the transactions that are waiting to be processed. Processing is mimicked by small delays of 0 to 100 milliseconds. Finally, the rate counter is incremented with the number of transactions that have been processed, and the base counter is incremented by one, indicating a batch has been processed. The performance counter infrastructure will only expose the former counter to the user, computing an average based on the delta of the procRate counter between two successive increments of the corresponding base. In our case, this simply acts as a measure for the amount of work done per iteration of the processor thread.

In the main thread, we enqueue work with an arrival rate throttled between 0 and 200 milliseconds per request. To see the behavior of the application through performance counters, start the program and wait for the Console.WriteLine-based prompt to come up. At that point, open the performance counters MMC snap-in from Administrative Tools (or by using perfmon.msc in Start, Run) and add the Chapter27 counters as shown in Figure 27.10.

I encourage you to experiment with multi-instance counters, as well, which will reveal a nontrivial value in the Instance column for each instance. The managed API to work with multiple instances is pretty straightforward. Examples of such use include the case where multiple instances of a service are running and each of them benefits from individual statistics. Notice that the Performance Counters snap-in has support to aggregate values from multiple instances by selecting a fake instance called Total. If you have a multicore machine, the Processor counters reveal this capability nicely, allowing a processor utilization breakdown on a per-CPU basis (the instances) and a roll-up value across all CPUs.

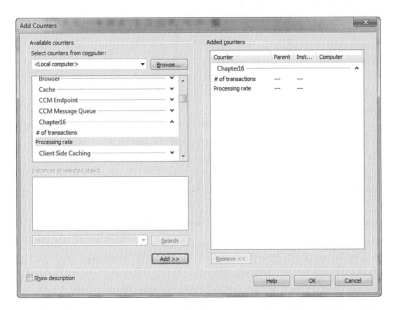

FIGURE 27.10   Adding our performance counters to the display.

Once the counters are added to the display, press Enter in the running transaction processing sample application to start its work. Figure 27.11 shows the program, which has been running for a few minutes. The red line indicates the queue depth as logged by the txCount counter's Increment and Decrement calls. Periodically, a green spike appears, which indicates a batch has been processed as logged by procRateBase and its numerator value counter procRate. Based on this information, queuing theory savvy developers can draw conclusions about the processing speed of transactions and the impact it has on users (for example, how long it takes for a transaction to be processed). Much more sophisticated counters could be devised to permit the analysis of a running transaction processor system, but this should give you a good idea about the possibilities to code up such support.

Other Manageability Frameworks

Other manageability techniques vary in difficulty and are often used only in specialized scenarios. For example, full-blown server products likely want rich instrumentation that can be used to analyze a running system but also to send commands to it. The Windows platform has built-in facilities for this in the form of Windows Management Instrumentation (WMI) and, more recently, Windows PowerShell.

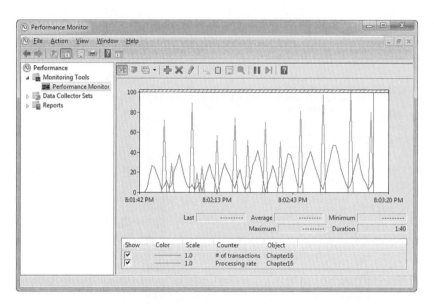

FIGURE 27.11   Analyzing runtime behavior of our sample application.

Writing providers for those technologies is a specialized task for which we refer to online documentation and books devoted to the subject. Suffice to say, a managed code story for them exists, so as a C# developer you shouldn't feel left out. Whether you need to spend time and money learning about them depends quite a bit on the kind of applications you're building. Typically, servers and services benefit quite a bit from such investments, allowing IT administrators to perform maintenance routines without developer intervention.

Controlling Processes

It's not uncommon for an application to need to interact with other programs on the same machine. This includes spawning other processes, monitoring them, and so on. The `System.Diagnostics` namespace contains functionality that enables those scenarios from managed code.

Querying Process Information

The `Process` class is the central abstraction to deal with processes. A series of static methods enables you to obtain `Process` instances by name, process ID, or unfiltered. We used this capability earlier in this book when discussing LINQ because the process list is a nice nontrivial data source that speaks to the imagination of many readers (at least, I think so). The following code shows this, also emphasizing the availability of many properties on `Process` objects:

```
var memoryHogs = from p in Process.GetProcesses()
                 where p.WorkingSet64 > 50 * 1024 * 1024 /* 50 MB */
                 select p;

foreach (var memoryHog in memoryHogs)
    Console.WriteLine(memoryHog);
```

The WorkingSet64 property exposes the memory working set size as an Int64 (long) value (and hence the 64 suffix). Many other properties are available on instances of the Process class, including processor utilization time, information about loaded modules (such as DLL files), threads running in the process, and so on. I leave it to you to explore this data, maybe by building a little Task Manager (or Process Explorer) clone based on it.

Starting Processes

Spawning another process is simple using the Process.Start method. The easiest way to achieve the task at hand is to specify an executable filename. Overloads exist that take in more information, such as arguments and/or user credentials, to perform a "run as" execution. Let's keep things simple and start cmd.exe as shown here. Notice that we don't specify a full path and rely on the environment settings to resolve the path automatically:

```
var cmd = Process.Start("cmd.exe");
```

SHELL EXECUTE BEHAVIOR

The managed Process API is a wrapper around the CreateProcess Win32 API as well as the ShellExecute API provided by the Windows Shell. Depending on the use of the API, either of the two is chosen. For example, when passing an HTTP address to the Process.Start method, ShellExecute will launch a browser.

The returned object is a Process instance that can be used to monitor the process. Because starting a process is an asynchronous act, we can continue execution while the process is running. One common task is to synchronize with another process's termination and grab its exit code. This can be done using the WaitForExit method:

```
cmd.WaitForExit();
```

When this blocking method returns, the target process will have terminated, and the exit status will be available through the HasExited, ExitCode, and ExitTime properties. For example, write down the following piece of code and run it:

```
var cmd = Process.Start("cmd.exe");
Console.WriteLine("We're not blocked while cmd.exe is running...");
cmd.WaitForExit();
Console.WriteLine(cmd.ExitCode);
```

In the command prompt instance that shows up, enter **exit 5** to exit the prompt with exit code 5. Our application should observe this through the `ExitCode` property. In some cases, you can't afford to block the parent process while waiting for the child process to terminate. Instead, the use of an event seems more appealing. This too is possible, as shown here:

```
var cmd = new Process
{
    EnableRaisingEvents = true,
    StartInfo = new ProcessStartInfo("cmd.exe")
};
cmd.Exited += (o, e) => Console.WriteLine(cmd.ExitCode);
cmd.Start();

while (true)
{
    Thread.Sleep(500);
    Console.Write(".");
}
```

Here we're using the `ProcessStartInfo` object in conjunction with the `Process` class's constructor. This is done to avoid a race condition that would exist if we were to use `Process.Start`, in which case it's possible the process exits before we get a chance to attach an event handler to the Exited event. Running the preceding code prints dots to the screen, even while the child process is running. If the child process terminates, the event handler code (here specified using a lambda expression) is executed. Although printing dots is not the most appealing application, it clearly shows the asynchronous nature that's realized through the use of an event.

`ProcessStartInfo` has plenty of other rich capabilities, such as the capability to control how the spawn process's window looks or even to hide it to avoid distracting pop-ups seen by the user. The following example shows a useful trick to redirect a process's "standard output" to our process (for example, to log what another process is doing in a UI of ours). Similarly, we could interact with the process's standard input or error output:

```
var tlist = new Process
{
    StartInfo = new ProcessStartInfo("tasklist.exe")
    {
        RedirectStandardOutput = true,
        UseShellExecute = false
    }
};
tlist.Start();
Console.WriteLine(tlist.StandardOutput.ReadToEnd());
```

In the next chapter, you learn more about I/O types such as StreamReader, which is used here as the type of StandardOutput. An important aspect to point out is the required setting of UseShellExecute to false to guide the Process class to use the CreateProcess Win32 API, rather than ShellExecute, which doesn't support redirection of input/output. This piece of code simply blocks until the StandardOutput is completely read into a string object, printing it to the screen. As a result, it prints the process listing in a text format as received by the tasklist.exe command.

Summary

In this chapter, we briefly looked at the System.Diagnostics namespace, highlighting its main features. Those include ways to instrument code to ease debugging as well as the monitoring of production software. We also learned about the introduction of the code contracts API in .NET 4, which allows you to go beyond the expressiveness of simple debug asserts by expressing more invariants about your code.

Finally, we also examined a common operation for programs: the ability to interact with other processes on the system. This functionality, too, finds its home in the same System.Diagnostics namespace.

CHAPTER 28

Working with I/O

IN THIS CHAPTER

▶ Files and Directories 1392

▶ Monitoring File System
Activity 1400

▶ Readers and Writers 1401

▶ Streams: The Bread and
Butter of I/O 1408

▶ A Primer to (Named)
Pipes 1423

▶ Memory-Mapped Files in a
Nutshell 1426

▶ Overview of Other I/O
Capabilities 1429

Almost every application must deal with input and output. I/O is an incredibly broad term that could apply to user interaction all the way to making calls over a network. From a narrower point of view, file operations are commonly referred to as I/O operations.

In this chapter, we look at what the Base Class Library (BCL) classifies as I/O by means of the System.IO namespace, which mostly deals with operations on files and directories. This chapter also introduces the notions of streams, readers, and writers, which are used by other parts of the framework to expose I/O. We also cover the essential operations on those types to achieve synchronous and asynchronous I/O operations.

Other System.IO capabilities are discussed as well, ranging from file system watchers to more recent features, including the use of named pipes to establish communication between processes or different components of a system. Finally, memory-mapped I/O was introduced in .NET 4 and is touched on briefly in this chapter.

The key takeaway of this chapter isn't to understand all the I/O capabilities in the framework. Such an exhaustive understanding would require us to cover things such as networking sockets as well, for which we don't have room. Instead, we focus on the key concepts that can be applied over and over again to deal with I/O in various application programming interfaces (APIs).

Files and Directories

Probably the most obvious I/O capability is to interact with the file system. Before getting into details about creating or modifying a file, we discuss the API surface to list files and directories. This will also include macroscopic file- and directory-level operations, such as making copies or deleting files. The main classes exposing this kind of functionality are `DriveInfo`, `DirectoryInfo`, and `FileInfo`, all of which live in the `System.IO` namespace.

Listing Drives

Querying the computer's drive letters and related information is achieved through the use of the `DriveInfo` class. To create instances of this type, either use the constructor that takes a drive letter (such as A, B:, or C:\), or use the `GetDrives` static method to get an array of all the drives on the machine.

Each `DriveInfo` object provides access to information about the drive represented by the object. This includes things such as the drive type (fixed disk, DVD, and so on), volume labels, free space, and so forth. The following example shows some of this information for all the drives on the machine:

```
static void Main()
{
    foreach (var drive in DriveInfo.GetDrives())
    {
        Console.WriteLine("{0} - {1}", drive.Name, drive.DriveType);
        if (drive.IsReady)
        {
            Console.WriteLine(drive.DriveFormat);
            Console.WriteLine(string.IsNullOrEmpty(drive.VolumeLabel)
                            ? "(no label)"
                            : drive.VolumeLabel);
            Console.WriteLine("{0} free of {1}",
                            GetSize(drive.TotalFreeSpace),
                            GetSize(drive.TotalSize));
        }
        else
        {
            Console.WriteLine("(No disk present)");
        }

        Console.WriteLine();
    }
}


static string GetSize(double size)
{
    var prefixes = new[] { "bytes", "KB", "MB", "GB", "TB", "PB", "EB" };
```

```
    int i;
    for (i = 0; size > 1000; i++)
    {
        size /= 1024;
    }

    return string.Format("{0:##0.##} {1}", size, prefixes[i]);
}
```

ASTRONOMIC STORAGE SIZES

Readers with an eye for detail may remark that the GetSize method can hit an array out-of-bounds exception when exceeding the exabyte range. Although this is unlikely, I encourage you to compute the number of bytes that fit in 1024 exabytes and compare this with the range of a signed long integer.

This piece of code prints the following on my laptop:

```
C:\ - Fixed
NTFS
(no label)
0.99 GB free of 74.43 GB

D:\ - Fixed
NTFS
Backup
215.29 GB free of 465.76 GB

E:\ - CDRom
UDF
HET_EILAND_DVD_2
0 bytes free of 6.24 GB

Y:\ - CDRom
(No disk present)
```

Other drive types can show up, such as connected network drives, removable storage, and RAM disks. Be aware that some operations on a DriveInfo object can signal errors by throwing an exception when access is denied, the drive is not ready, and so on. Refer to the MSDN documentation for more information about the types of exceptions than can be thrown under various circumstances.

THE SUBST COMMAND

Multiple drives can show up for the same underlying storage volume because of the way the operating system allows mapping different letters to the same storage. This can occur if you use the Disk Management MMC snap-in or even the command-line subst command. For example, running subst T: C:\temp will map drive letter T: to the C:\temp folder. The .NET DriveInfo API will actually see the T: drive with exactly the same information as the C: drive that holds the data.

The ideal bridge to our subsequent discussion of DirectoryInfo objects is DriveInfo's RootDirectory property. This property gives access to the root directory of a ready drive (for example, C:\ for the C: drive). As you may already expect, this allows us to enumerate the file system on the drive. Finally, notice the DriveInfo object does not expose any kind of lifecycle operations, such as creating drive letters.

Working with Directories

As you know, directories are containers for files and other directories and thus provide a hierarchical means of organizing data. This is almost accurate because there are ways to create cycles on a file system. Ignoring this detail, you should already have an idea about what the DirectoryInfo will expose. Let's take a look by means of an example:

```
Console.Write("Enter path: ");
var path = Console.ReadLine();
Console.WriteLine();

var folder = new DirectoryInfo(path);
if (folder.Exists)
{
    Console.WriteLine("Full name: " + folder.FullName);
    Console.WriteLine("Name: " + folder.Name);
    Console.WriteLine("Created: " + folder.CreationTime);
    Console.WriteLine("Parent: " + folder.Parent.FullName);
    Console.WriteLine("Root: " + folder.Root);
}
```

This little piece of code shows a few interesting properties of directories, including a way to navigate to a folder's parent and (drive) root folder DirectoryInfo object. An example of the output looks like this:

```
Enter path: c:\windows\system32

Full name: c:\windows\system32
Name: system32
Created: 7/13/2009 8:20:14 PM
Parent: c:\windows
Root: c:\
```

Richer navigation can obviously be achieved, using various methods. Two approaches exist, both of which we cover now. The first is to use the Get methods that enable you to retrieve files and directories immediately contained by the directory. Three of those methods exist: GetFiles, GetDirectories, and GetFileSystemInfos. The last one may be surprising but reveals a common base class for both DirectoryInfo and FileInfo, with common properties such as name, attributes, time stamps, and so on. An example of a simple dir command is shown here:

```
var folder = new DirectoryInfo(path);
if (folder.Exists)
{
    foreach (var child in folder.GetFileSystemInfos())
        Console.WriteLine("{0} {1}", child is FileInfo ? " " : "D", child);
}
```

Here we use a type check to determine whether a child object is a directory or a file.

Another way to enumerate directories and files is to use the Enumerate methods. The difference is that these methods allow the specification of a search pattern as well as a search scope (for example, to search all subdirectories). An example is shown here:

```
var folder = new DirectoryInfo(path);
if (folder.Exists)
{
    foreach (var exe in folder.EnumerateFiles("*.exe",
                                        SearchOption.AllDirectories))
        Console.WriteLine(exe.FullName);
}
```

Exceptions can occur because of unauthorized access, so be sure to handle this condition appropriately (for example, if the search path is taken from some [user] input).

JUNCTIONS IN THE SEARCH ROAD

Enumerating files and folders recursively is always a dangerous business because cycles can occur due to the operating system's support for so-called junctions. For example, a cycle can be created as follows:

```
C:\Temp>mklink /J Self C:\Temp
Junction created for Self <<===>> C:\Temp
```

Now enumerating the C:\Temp folder recursively will actually result in an infinite loop because the C:\Temp\Self junction refers to its parent. Unfortunately, the built-in APIs traverse such junctions, which can lead to this kind of pathological scenario.

I encourage you to create a recursive enumeration that's not prone to this kind of issue. This is harder than you might think because state needs to be kept and comparison of paths is also not very easy. In the end, I suggest that you not use in-depth enumeration methods if the target path is an unknown nontrusted location (for instance, coming from user input). Lucky for us, for a lot of scenarios it suffices to descend a single folder level at a time (for example, in directory browsing dialogs).

Retrieving properties of directories is one thing; in lots of cases, you also want to carry out manipulations of directories. Methods to accomplish those operations exist, too, on the `DirectoryInfo` class. A few examples are shown here:

```
var folder = new DirectoryInfo(path);
if (!folder.Exists)
    folder.Create();

var subfolder = folder.CreateSubdirectory("Bar");
Console.WriteLine(subfolder.CreationTime);

subfolder.Delete(/* can specify to recurse into subdirectories */);
Console.WriteLine(subfolder.Exists);
subfolder.Refresh();
Console.WriteLine(subfolder.Exists);
```

Most of these are self-explanatory, but `Refresh` may need some explanation. The various classes in `System.IO` that represent files and directories don't always hit the operating system APIs to retrieve data, which speeds up operations. In the preceding code, calling `Exists` returns false even though the folder has been deleted already. Beware of this quirk (which is by design, no need to file bugs), and use the `Refresh` method if you're keeping those info objects around for requerying.

IF IT EXISTS, IT MIGHT BE GONE

The use of properties such as `Exists` has limited value. In the world of multitasking and multithreading, it may be the case that others are changing the (file) system's state without your knowledge, invalidating your existence check:

```
if (file.Exists)
{   // What if other code is scheduled here, removing the file?
    file.Delete();
}
```

Only one reliable way exists to check for a shared object's existence, including files and directories: Don't perform a check at all! Instead, just take an action on the object. In other words, even if you have lots of `Exists` checks, always be prepared for code operating under such an assumption to fail. That is, exception handling (of course, without swallowing caught exceptions) is the way forward.

Finally, if you really need lots of file-related operations to fail or succeed together in a transactional manner, you might want to look at Windows Vista's (and later) support for Transactional NTFS, abbreviated TxF. At this point, there are no built-in wrappers in .NET to support this, but people have had successes at building such wrappers using (lots of) P/Invoke.

A few operations we haven't mentioned include the capability to move whole directories using MoveTo and means to deal with the directory object's security descriptor. The latter is a rather specialized undertaking, benefiting from an intimate knowledge of the Windows NT security subsystem and access control lists (ACLs) in particular. To get or set the ACL, the GetAccesControl and SetAccesControl methods are provided, using types from the System.Security.AccessControl namespace. I leave an exploration of those APIs to you and recommend that you study MSDN thoroughly before tackling security-related business.

Working with Paths

In the previous examples, we've been dealing with user input to specify a path. If a path contains invalid characters, constructors like DirectoryInfo's will throw an exception to signal such an issue.

Often, developers need to go beyond just taking a prepared path. While paths are just string values, manipulating them as such (for example, using plain old concatenation) isn't a particularly good idea, especially when user input is involved. The chance of building an invalid path exists, so it's better to let specialized functions do the job. For this purpose, the static methods on the Path class were introduced as wrappers around a set of APIs available in Win32.

One set of methods deals with breaking up a path in its constituents, such as the file or directory name, the extension, and so on. Other methods that deal with analyzing paths enable you to detect invalid characters, check whether a path is absolute or relative, and so on. Examples of some of those methods are shown here:

```
var path = @"c:\temp\test.txt";

Console.WriteLine("Absolute:  " + Path.IsPathRooted(path));
Console.WriteLine("Root:      " + Path.GetPathRoot(path));
Console.WriteLine("Directory: " + Path.GetDirectoryName(path));

Console.WriteLine("File name: " + Path.GetFileName(path));
if (Path.HasExtension(path))
    Console.WriteLine("Extension: " + Path.GetExtension(path));

Console.WriteLine("Full path: " + Path.GetFullPath("test.txt"));
```

Output of all methods should be predictable, maybe with the exception of the last. The use of GetFullPath allows a relative path to be turned into an absolute one, using the current working directory.

Other methods on the Path API allow modification and manipulation of paths, such as changing an extension or combining path fragments with path separators (typically a \ character). For example:

```
var path = Path.Combine(\", "temp", "test.txt");
var back = Path.ChangeExtension(path, ".bak");
Console.WriteLine(back);
```

Finally, some handy methods exist to obtain the temporary folder, generate a random file-name, and physically create a temporary file. This last capability is the sole API on the Path class that creates a file, while the others only perform string manipulations:

```
Console.WriteLine(Path.GetTempPath());
Console.WriteLine(Path.GetRandomFileName());

// Creates an empty file on disk under the %TEMP% location.
Console.WriteLine(Path.GetTempFileName());
```

This piece of code produces the following output on my machine. As mentioned earlier, the last line contains the full path to a (zero-byte) temporary file that can be used by the application as a scratchpad and whatnot. It's considered polite to remove such a tempo-rary file when you're done with it, using methods like File.Delete:

```
C:\Users\bartde\AppData\Local\Temp\
noqh02b4.yik
C:\Users\bartde\AppData\Local\Temp\tmp4A41.tmp
```

The FileInfo Class

To top off the set of Info classes, there's FileInfo. This is most likely the one you'll be dealing with quite often if you want to pass around an object representing a file, its loca-tion, and its various attributes. The members on the type shouldn't come as a big surprise because we all know common file-level operations.

One thing that sets it apart from the discussed Info classes so far is the capability to get to and manipulate the contents of an individual file. We ignore this aspect right now and come back to it later when discussing file I/O.

A few examples illustrating the properties of a FileInfo object are shown here:

```
Console.Write("Enter path: ");
var path = Console.ReadLine();
Console.WriteLine();
```

```
var file = new FileInfo(path);
if (file.Exists)
{
    Console.WriteLine("Created:   " + file.CreationTime);
    Console.WriteLine("Accessed:  " + file.LastAccessTime);  // Bogus...
    Console.WriteLine("Modified:  " + file.LastWriteTime);
    Console.WriteLine("Directory: " + file.Directory.FullName);
    Console.WriteLine("Read-only: " + file.IsReadOnly);
    Console.WriteLine("Attributes: " + file.Attributes);
    Console.WriteLine("Size:      " + GetSize(file.Length));
}
```

In this example, we're using the GetSize "pretty printing" helper defined earlier in the example of drive information listing. The Attributes property returns a flags enum that enables you to check for flags such as hidden, system, compression, encryption, read-only, and so on. Because checking for read-only is a fairly common operation, a dedicated property for the task was introduced.

LAST ACCESS TIME

Notice our polite comment on the LastAccessTime property in the preceding example. This property doesn't provide much meaningful information because the file system delays the update of this time stamp (for NTFS up to one hour). In fact, in recent versions of the operating system, such as Windows 7, updating the last access time is disabled by default, which increases performance. You can check this setting by running fsutil query DisableLastAccess.

Just as for the DirectoryInfo class, various file-level operations are exposed on this class as instance methods. Examples include MoveTo to move a file to another location (also allowing a rename operation), Replace to overwrite it with another file, and Delete for obvious purposes.

Access control methods are present too but require the reader's further self-study of Windows NT security, as mentioned earlier. One security-related easy-to-use pair of methods is Encrypt and Decrypt, available on NTFS volumes. They leverage the EFS (Encrypting File System) feature of the file system. When encrypting a file using this mechanism, it will only be decryptable by the account that encrypted it originally, ignoring the existence of recovery agents. (Refer to TechNet for more information about the configuration and management of EFS.)

Monitoring File System Activity

Before getting into ways to create and manipulate files, let's look at how we can monitor file system activity. Such activity includes the creation, removal, renaming, and modification of files by any party using the file system. Far too often, people resort to polling techniques to check for the presence of a file instead of using some kind of monitoring API to observe file creation. Polling the file system isn't cheap and involves excessive I/O.

Luckily, .NET exposes low-level file system APIs that enable you to watch activity. The component class used for this purpose is called `FileSystemWatcher`. Because this class is defined as a component (as discussed briefly in the preceding chapter), we can use it from the Toolbox and drag it onto a designer, such as a Component designer, as shown in Figure 28.1.

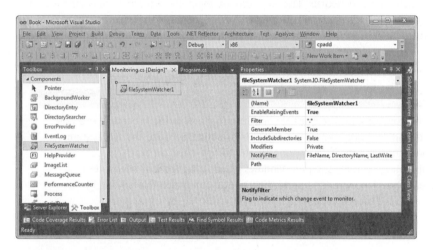

FIGURE 28.1   Using the `FileSystemWatcher` component.

To observe any changes through the events exposed by the object, it's essential for the `EnableRaisingEvents` property to be enabled. Other configuration settings to be supplied include a filter (by default set to `*.*`), the path to monitor for changes, and whether subdirectories should be monitored (defaults to `false`). The flags set on the `NotifyFilter` property allow specification of what changes will trigger a `Changed` event. Other events, such as `Created`, `Deleted`, and `Renamed`, are not impacted by those flags. To hook up event handlers, go to the events display in the Properties window and double-click the events you're interested in. This generates event handler methods on your behalf, as shown in Figure 28.2.

In the event handler, the event arguments can be inspected to obtain the full path to the file that was affected. For the `Changed` event, the type of the change can be checked as well. Instead of showing the use of a component class with a designer (which is easy to get working), we use the `FileSystemWatcher` directly from code to illustrate its power:

```
using (var watcher = new FileSystemWatcher(Path.GetTempPath(), "*.*"))
{
    watcher.Created += (o, e) =>
    {
        Console.WriteLine("Created: " + e.FullPath);
    };

    watcher.EnableRaisingEvents = true;

    Console.WriteLine("Monitoring... Press ENTER to exit.");
    Console.Read();
}
```

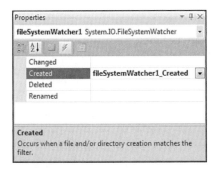

FIGURE 28.2   Configuring an event handler for a `FileSystemWatcher` object.

To see the event handler getting called, opening an instance of Internet Explorer or an Office tool such as Word should do the trick because those programs write files to %TEMP%, using APIs similar to `Path.GetTempFileName`.

Readers and Writers

At the heart of .NET's input/output model sits the concept of streams. Before we go there, let's look at the layer right above them. There we find the concept of readers (for the *I* in I/O) and writers (the *O* in I/O), both of which make use of streams easier. In fact, the file and directory APIs directly exposed those.

The File Class

Alongside the `FileInfo` class, the `System.IO` namespace provides a home for a static class called `File`. Whereas one typically uses a `FileInfo` to pass around information about a file as an object, the `File` class provides a series of static methods that expose file system functionality. In fact, some of `FileInfo`'s instance methods simply call into some of the static methods provided on file.

A first set of methods that deal with files on a wholesale basis is omitted from our discussion here because we've seen similar methods like Delete on FileInfo. Instead, we focus on methods that provide access to the contents of a file, which brings us to the concept of readers and writers quite directly.

DIRECTORY VERSUS DIRECTORYINFO

As you might expect by now, the DirectoryInfo class also has a sibling called Directory, which is a static class exposing various directory-level operations. The philosophy is similar: The static class provides a flat API that's close to Win32 functions with similar functionality. The DirectoryInfo class, on the other hand, represents a single directory and has instance-level methods.

Convenient File Read Methods

Let's start by showing how to read a whole text file, as shown here:

```
using System;
using System.IO;

class Program
{
    static void Main()
    {
        string[] lines = File.ReadAllLines(@"..\..\Program.cs");
        foreach (var line in lines)
            Console.WriteLine(line);
    }
}
```

Assuming this code is written in a typical Console Application project, a simple press of Ctrl+F5 starts the program from the compilation target folder bin\Debug. The use of a relative path two levels up brings us to the folder containing the source files, referring to Program.cs. In summary, the preceding, when executed from Visual Studio, will print itself.

The ReadAllLines method is nothing but a convenience method around lower-level functionality. In fact, initial versions of the .NET Framework omitted such methods, being one of the main customer feedback items for the BCL team. A similar method called ReadAllText exists, which doesn't return a string array but rather one string containing all the file's text (hence containing \r\n or \n characters). Both of them have overloads that take in an Encoding object to guide the read operation and the conversion to text.

Another similar method is ReadAllBytes, returning a byte array. Although all of them are helpful methods, they should be used with some care when potentially big files are involved. For one thing, all the methods are synchronous and therefore block until the whole file is read. You'll learn in the section "Asynchronous Read and Write Operations" how to do asynchronous file I/O operations. It's also the case that you don't often need the whole file contents, allowing for more fine-grained access patterns, as discussed in the section "Working with Files: Take Two."

Convenient File Write Methods

Mirror images of the ReadAll methods exist to allow similar write operations. It speaks for itself that they are prefixed with WriteAll. These methods create a new file, write the specified contents to it, and close the file.

For example, the following code combines the ReadLines and WriteAllLines methods, using an overload for the latter method that takes in an IEnumerable<string>. Before .NET 4, only overloads taking in an array of strings existed, which made the use of LINQ on conjunction with the API a rather suboptimal experience. In this little example, we copy a file but remove leading whitespace:

```
using System;
using System.Linq;
using System.IO;

class Program
{
    static void Main()
    {
        File.WriteAllLines(
            @"..\..\Program.bak",
            from line in File.ReadLines(@"..\..\Program.cs")
            where !string.IsNullOrWhiteSpace(line)
            select line.TrimStart()
        );
    }
}
```

Besides the WriteAll methods, there's also AppendAllLines and AppendAllText, which allow appending to an existing file (or creating one if the file doesn't exist yet). In contrast, the WriteAll methods create a new file, possibly overwriting existing ones.

You might have noticed this example uses a method called ReadLines rather than the ReadAllLines method discussed earlier. What's the difference? The answer lies in the return type, with ReadLines returning an IEnumerable<string>. Internally, this method is implemented as an iterator, and therefore a single line can be read at a time in response to a MoveNext call on an acquired enumerator. For example, because of the lazy nature of the various LINQ query operators, the following has to read only the first three lines of input:

```
using System;
using System.Linq;
using System.IO;
```

```
class Program
{
    static void Main()
    {
        File.WriteAllLines(
            @"..\..\Program.bak",
            File.ReadLines(@"..\..\Program.cs").Take(3)
        );
    }
}
```

In contrast, the use of `ReadAllLines` would drain the whole file contents into an in-memory array. If you'd be enumerating that array and break from the loop before reaching the end (which is more or less what `Take` does), you'd have (pre)fetched way too much useless data from the file.

Exposing Files with Readers and Writers

The set of `Read`, `Write`, and `Append` methods we've discussed thus far all rely on lower-level constructs in the I/O APIs to achieve their goals. It's quite obvious that you can use those primitives directly as well (for example, using other methods exposed by the `File` class).

Methods such as `AppendText`, `CreateText`, and `OpenText` are precisely what I'm referring to here. Instead of consuming or exposing string sequences such as arrays, the concept of `StreamReader` and `StreamWriter` objects is used. For example, using `CreateText`, you obtain a `StreamWriter`, which can be used to write to the underlying file:

```
using (StreamWriter sw = File.CreateText("log.txt"))
{
    sw.WriteLine("{0} - Started", DateTime.Now);
    // Do work
    sw.WriteLine("{0} - Stopped", DateTime.Now);
}
```

As mentioned before, the `Create` method differs from `Append` in the way it deals with existing files, so the preceding code will overwrite a log.txt file (in the working directory) if it already exists. Notice the use of a `using` block to close the file under all circumstances, including the possibility of an exception occurring. If you don't do so, a file handle will remain open, causing the file to appear locked, as shown in Figure 28.3, where an attempt to delete the file is made while the file is still opened.

Notice the size of the file is also still 0 bytes. Indeed, when opening the file before it gets closed, there's no guarantee about the contents you'll be able to see. The reason this manifests itself is because of the lack of automatic flushing in the default configuration, which enables you to improve performance of file I/O. If you really need and want such flushing behavior (despite the impact it has on the file system), you can set the `AutoFlush` property on the `StreamWriter`:

```
using (StreamWriter sw = File.CreateText("log.txt"))
{
    sw.AutoFlush = true;

    sw.WriteLine("{0} - Started", DateTime.Now);
    // Do work
    sw.WriteLine("{0} - Stopped", DateTime.Now);
}
```

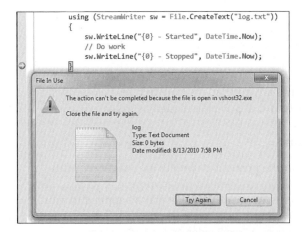

FIGURE 28.3   Improper disposal can cause grief.

Doing so will cause every write call on the writer to cause a flush operation. A better approach is to call the Flush method manually in places where you absolutely want the data to be flushed to disk (for instance, because you need readers to be able to see the contents of a file immediately after some critical work has been performed).

Besides the WriteLine method, a Write method with a whole bunch of overloads exists, allowing values of primitive types to be written. As the name implies, they don't get followed by a newline character. Speaking of which, the newline character used by the stream writer can be configured through the NewLine property. It really isn't a single character but rather a string, which defaults to "\r\n".

The opposite of writing is reading, as accommodated by the StreamReader class. In the following example, we basically do what ReadAllLines does internally:

```
using (StreamReader sr = File.OpenText(@"..\..\Program.cs"))
{
    while (!sr.EndOfStream)
        Console.WriteLine(sr.ReadLine());
}
```

Other loops are often seen to read text, such as one that repeatedly calls the ReadLine method and checks for null to detect whether the end of the file has been reached. As expected, other methods, such as Read, ReadToEnd, and ReadBlock, can be found, all of which allow reading at different levels of granularity. For example, the Read method has two overloads, one of which returns a single character, whereas another takes in an array of characters to be populated:

```
using (StreamReader sr = File.OpenText(@"..\..\Program.cs"))
{
    var buffer = new char[1024];
    int read = sr.Read(buffer, 0, buffer.Length);
    Console.WriteLine("{0} characters read", read);
}
```

Before studying the File class's capabilities any further, it's time to take a closer look at the concept of readers and writers, which find use outside file I/O as well.

TextReader and TextWriter

The two classes we briefly encountered in the previous examples are subclasses of the TextReader and TextWriter classes. Using object-oriented programming at its best, these base classes offer virtual methods for a series of operations that can be applied in more than just the context of file I/O. In fact, on our much beloved Console class, you can find static properties called In and Out that expose a TextReader and a TextWriter:

```
string line = Console.In.ReadLine();
Console.Out.WriteLine(line);
```

Console directly offers access to those common operations by providing shortcut methods on the class itself, but in reality a pair of reader and writer objects provides access to the Win32 console. In fact, those readers and writers can be substituted by means of Set methods, such as SetIn. This is quite handy when you're writing a console application that can receive input directly from the console (through user interaction) or from a file (for example, as specified through a command-line flag). Using the SetIn method, you can simply continue writing code against methods like Console.ReadLine while input is being redirected from another reader:

```
static void Main(string[] args)
{
    if (args.Length == 1)
    {
        Console.SetIn(File.OpenText(args[0]));
    }

    string line;
    while ((line = Console.ReadLine()) != null)
```

```
    {
        // Process input
    }
}
```

As you can see, the abstraction level introduced by TextReader is quite handy. As an example of a place where a TextWriter object is used, take a look at the LINQ to SQL base class for data contexts, known as DataContext. To log generated T-SQL statements that are sent to the server in response to enumerating over a LINQ query, the Log property on DataContext enables you to set a TextWriter. Although a file could be used, one often assigns Console.Out to it:

```
var ctx = new NorthwindDataContext();
ctx.Log = Console.Out;

var res = from p in ctx.Products where p.UnitPrice > 100m select p;
foreach (var p in res /* here a T-SQL statement will be built and logged */)
    Console.WriteLine(p.ProductName);
```

StringReader and StringWriter

Besides StreamReader and StreamWriter deriving from the TextReader and TextWriter base classes, other derived types exist. StringReader and StringWriter are such classes, allowing reading from and writing to string objects. Because strings are immutable, this is a bit of a lie because the StringWriter uses a StringBuilder to write (and append) to.

An example of the use of these two types is shown here:

```
StringBuilder sb = new StringBuilder();
TextWriter writer = new StringWriter(sb);

string input = Console.ReadLine();
writer.WriteLine(input);

TextReader reader = new StringReader(sb.ToString());
string line = reader.ReadLine();
Console.WriteLine(line);
```

This is just a very roundabout way of taking input and writing it back to the console, but it shows the typing relationships of the various classes involved and how the StringBuilder acts as an intermediary StringWriter target.

On to Streams

Our discussion of StreamReader and StreamWriter classes is the ideal way to transition to the subject of streams. In fact, StreamReader and StreamWriter are slight misnomers because they operate with textual data, whereas a stream is more general. What a stream really represents is a stream of bytes allowing read, write, and seek operations.

The StreamReader and StreamWriter classes clearly operate on streams but expose them as characters or strings, which is quite logical given their base classes but rather illogical given their naming. Without skipping too much ahead, suffice to say the Base Class Library (BCL) has readers and writers for streams that operate on binary data as well. They are called BinaryReader and BinaryWriter. We discuss those two types as part of our discussion of streams in the next section.

Streams: The Bread and Butter of I/O

The notion of a stream is the lowest you can go in terms of .NET's managed code I/O system. Figure 28.4 shows an overview of the members of the Stream class.

```
BeginRead(byte[ ], int, int, System.AsyncCallback, object)
BeginWrite(byte[ ], int, int, System.AsyncCallback, object)
Close()
CreateWaitHandle()
Dispose()
Dispose(bool)
EndRead(System.IAsyncResult)
EndWrite(System.IAsyncResult)
Flush()
Read(byte[ ], int, int)
ReadByte()
Seek(long, System.IO.SeekOrigin)
SetLength(long)
Stream()
Synchronized(System.IO.Stream)
Write(byte[ ], int, int)
WriteByte(byte)
CanRead
CanSeek
CanTimeout
CanWrite
Length
Position
ReadTimeout
WriteTimeout
Null
```

FIGURE 28.4   The Stream class seen through Object Browser.

First of all, let's discuss a stream's potentially supported capabilities, which include the capability to read from and write to a stream and also the capability to seek. A seek operation basically moves a cursor—as seen through the Position property—that indicates where the next read or write operation will take place. Another capability is whether an operation on a stream is subject to timeout.

Capabilities are queryable through a set of Is* properties, which is of importance if you deal directly with Stream objects. Because a Stream acts as the base class for a wide range of data streams, some operations might not be supported by all of them. For example, the Null stream (exposed through the public read-only Null field on Stream) doesn't support timeout, so don't expect settings like ReadTimeout to have effect. To prevent exceptions from being thrown in highly polymorphic code operating on a wide range of possible streams, check those Is* properties before carrying out certain operations.

As you can see from the Read and Write methods, stream objects deal directly with byte values rather than characters, numbers, and so on. Let's take a look at a couple of stream object examples.

Memory Streams

To emphasize I/O is much more than just files, let's start by using streams to look at in-memory data. The following code uses a byte array as an in-memory storage for data that gets surfaced through two memory streams. Each stream has an offset in the array and can be marked as read-only. In some sense, a stream acts as a "view" of the underlying raw data.

```
var bs = new byte[20];

var ms1 = new MemoryStream(bs, index:  5, count: 10, writable: true);
var ms2 = new MemoryStream(bs, index: 10, count: 10, writable: false);

ms1.Seek(5, SeekOrigin.Begin);      //      @ relative =  5, absolute = 15
ms1.Write(new byte[] { 9, 8, 7 }, 0, 3);

Console.WriteLine(bs[10]);          // 0x09 @                absolute = 10
Console.WriteLine(ms2.ReadByte()); // 0x09 @ relative =  0, absolute = 10
Console.WriteLine(ms2.ReadByte()); // 0x08 @ relative =  1, absolute = 11
Console.WriteLine(ms2.ReadByte()); // 0x07 @ relative =  2, absolute = 12

bs[18] = 1;                         // 0x01 @                absolute = 18
ms2.Seek(5, SeekOrigin.Current);
Console.WriteLine(ms2.ReadByte()); // 0x01 @ relative =  8, absolute = 18
```

Figure 28.5 shows how things are laid out in memory. Each stream has a position that is automatically updated by operations, such as ReadByte. Because of this, you can see subsequent calls to ms2 print values from consecutive cells of array memory. Various Seek operations are used to move the position in the stream, either relative to the start of the stream or to the current position. The three ReadByte calls on ms2 have moved the cursor by three positions, so adding another 5 relative from the current position (as seen on the second to last line) puts us at a total of 8 bytes away from the start of the stream. That's precisely where 0x01 was written to the underlying array, and thus we see that value being surfaced by the next ReadByte call.

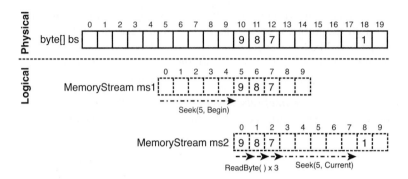

FIGURE 28.5   Physical storage with logical views using `MemoryStream` objects.

The use of `MemoryStream` can prove handy when different subsystems need to work together in populating or reading data stored in in-memory data structures. Each such system has a view on the area of data it's responsible for or can read from. This kind of in-memory stream can also be used as an offline "composition surface" for data that's subsequently written to another stream using the `WriteTo` method.

Working with Files: Take Two

Where the use of `StreamReader` and `StreamWriter` are great to deal with text files, they fall short in providing byte-level access to a file. Other methods on the `File` class used to open or create files expose `FileStream` objects, which allow for richer manipulation of the data contained in a file. For example:

```
using (FileStream fs = File.OpenRead(\windows\system32\notepad.exe"))
{
    var m = (char)fs.ReadByte();
    var z = (char)fs.ReadByte();
    Console.WriteLine("{0}{1}", m, z);
}
```

This trivial example shows how to obtain a `FileStream` object that can read from the specified file. It uses the `ReadByte` method two times to read the first 2 bytes of an executable file, which are always MZ, after the creator of the executable file format, Mark Zbikowski. Although this is plain old ASCII text, you can see we're simply reading the data as bytes and interpreting them as characters. Looking further in the file, you would obviously see data that doesn't look very meaningful when interpreted as textual data (such as the executable's assembly code).

The `OpenRead` method is just one of the many `Open` methods available. It controls the operations allowed on the obtained `FileStream`, in the case of `OpenRead` being set to read-only. The most generic method is Open, which can be passed a number of flags, including the file mode, file access, and file sharing:

▶ FileMode indicates the actions implied by opening a file. This includes the capability to create a file with or without overwriting behavior, to append to an existing file, and so on.

▶ FileAccess is simply read, write, or a combination of both. The flags enum has a convenient ReadWrite combo available.

▶ FileShare controls what others can do with the file while the FileStream is used. For example, you can allow others to read the file while it's in use but disallow simultaneous writes.

File.Create and File.OpenRead are shortcuts into this most generic Open method. An example of using the Open method is shown here:

```
using (var fs = File.Open(path, FileMode.Open, FileAccess.Read,
                          FileShare.ReadWrite))
```

With those specified flags, the file specified by path will be opened for read access, throwing an exception when the file does not exist. The ReadWrite sharing allows any other party to open the file allowing those actions. Therefore, this is one of the most permissive opening modes.

BinaryReader and BinaryWriter

To go beyond raw byte sequences when dealing with I/O data, the BCL designers invented the BinaryReader and BinaryWriter classes. Just as StreamReader and StreamWriter can be constructed by passing in a Stream object to a constructor, this abstraction simplifies the use of streams by providing additional methods. For example, where StreamReader concerns itself with the notion of textual data and provides a ReadLine method, the BinaryReader class exposes Read methods for various primitive multibyte data types.

Let's look at an example, again using binary files:

```
using (var fs = File.OpenRead(\windows\system32\notepad.exe"))
using (var br = new BinaryReader(fs))
{
    br.BaseStream.Position = 0x3c;
    int offset = br.ReadInt32();

    br.BaseStream.Position = offset;
    char[] signature = br.ReadChars(2);
    Console.WriteLine(new string(signature));
}
```

First of all, notice the use of `using` blocks to ensure proper disposal of the reader that's sitting on top of a stream, as well as the stream itself. It's considered good practice to make sure all such `IDisposable`-capable I/O resources are cleaned up deterministically using this pattern.

The create `BinaryReader` is just a view over the underlying file stream object, which can now be consumed more easily. A binary reader object by itself doesn't have ways to change the position in the stream but does expose the underlying stream through the `BaseStream` property. In our example, we use the stream's `Position` property to jump to the position at offset 0x3c in the executable file.

Reading data from the selected position using some primitive type is where the use of a `BinaryReader` comes in handy. For example, to get an Int32 value from the current stream's position, we can use `ReadInt32`. This reads 4 bytes and stuffs them into a signed 32-bit integer in a little-endian format.

BIG OR LITTLE ENDIAN?

Windows is one of the operating systems that chose the use of "little-endian" byte ordering within larger words (such as a 32-bit, 4-byte integer). The endian-ness concept was introduced in a paper by Danny Cohen titled "On Holy Wars and a Plea for Peace," in which he was inspired by *Gulliver's Travels* (Jonathan Swift). In Swift's book, religious sects called the Lilliputians had a dispute about how to crack open boiled eggs. One camp said to start from the "little end," whereas the opponents said to start from the "big end." Cohen used this for an analogy with byte ordering: Should the representation of words in memory start with the little end (that is, least significant byte) or the other way around?

In a little-endian architecture, as used by Windows and therefore .NET's BCL sitting on top of it, the least significant bytes of a (quad, double, single) word come first. For example, the double word (or a 32-bit integer) with value 0x12345678 is really stored as the sequence 0x78, 0x56, 0x34, 0x12. `ReadInt32` applies this rule when computing a 32-bit integer value out of the 4 bytes it acquired from the stream (that is, it "reverses" the bytes to build up the 4-byte 32-bit integer).

Now that we've read the signed 32-bit integer representing some kind of offset (see the next sidebar to reveal the mystery of this magic offset), we set the underlying stream's position to the retrieved value. In fact, it's worth pointing out that the call to `ReadInt32` by itself caused the `BaseStream`'s position to have increased by 4 as it read that many bytes from the stream. We're disregarding this automatic position update, which would allow us to continue calling `ReadInt32` to read consecutive groups of 4 bytes, each of which denotes a 32-bit integer. Instead, we just use the setter of `Position` to advance the cursor to where we want.

At the new position, we use yet another specialized `Read` method on `BinaryReader`, this time to read a specified number of characters into an array. The two characters read are finally printed to the console by using one of the System.String constructor overloads that constructs a string out of a character array. The result of this piece of code should read PE, no matter what executable file you give it.

PE/COFF FILES

So what's all the magic in this example about? Executable files on Windows are known as Portable Executable files, or PE files. The acronym COFF is mentioned quite often, too. It stands for Common Object File Format. You can download the specification of those files' layout from the Microsoft website (search for PE/COFF).

If you're a true geek and decide to look up this specification, you'll find that executable files exist of a DOS header, which nowadays prints "This program cannot be run in DOS mode" if you try to run a modern application on, say, MS-DOS or some emulator. However, the old DOS stub is still used by the loader because it does contain a file offset pointing at the location where the "modern" PE/COFF header lives. All of this bit-twiddling is a matter of maintaining compatibility. As you can guess by now, this offset lives at location 0x3c.

After we adjust the position in the file stream object to 0x3c, we can read the PE/COFF header, which starts with 4 bytes containing P, E, \0, \0. In our example, we simply read the first two of those. The bit-twiddling type of readers are most welcome to take the PE/COFF specification and implement a C#-based tool to extract much more information from an executable (up to and including the executable code byte sequences in there).

Asynchronous Read and Write Operations

All the I/O operations explained in the previous sections have been of the synchronous kind, meaning the caller is blocked until the data becomes available. Sometimes it's more appropriate to read or write data asynchronously and get notified when the action has been completed. The Stream class has intrinsic support for this modus operandi.

The essence of this feature is found in Begin/End method pairs, such as BeginRead and EndRead. Where Read is a blocking operation waiting for data to be read and bubbled up to the application, the BeginRead method immediately returns. However, it doesn't have the requested data available right away. Instead, it will call you back after it has completed. To do so, a callback procedure is passed to the BeginRead method. As we all know, passing around a reference to a method is accomplished with a delegate.

Let's explore this asynchronous method pattern and start by looking at the BeginRead method signature:

```
IAsyncResult BeginRead(byte[] array, int offset, int numBytes,
                AsyncCallback userCallback, object stateObject);
```

This signature is pretty much the same as Read apart from the return type and the two additional parameters at the end. Those are what make the operation asynchronous. On to the AsyncCallback parameter type, which (as the name implies) is a delegate type:

```
delegate void AsyncCallback(IAsyncResult ar);
```

The role of this delegate is to point at a method that accepts the result of the operation, as represented by an IAsyncResult. Such an object by itself doesn't contain the data that has been received. Instead, upon the completion callback, you should feed the object to the corresponding EndRead method to gain access to the information computed asynchronously.

An example of calling the Begin method is shown here, using a lambda expression to declare the callback procedure. Notice we pass null for the stateObject for a reason explained later:

```
using (var fs = File.OpenRead(\windows\system32\write.exe"))
{
    var buffer = new byte[1024 * 1024]; // 1 MB buffer
    IAsyncResult iar = fs.BeginRead(buffer, 0, buffer.Length, result =>
    {
        // This code will be called upon completion.
        int count = fs.EndRead(result);
        Console.WriteLine("{0} bytes read", count);
    }, null);

    Console.Write("Read operation started");
    while (!iar.IsCompleted)
    {
        Console.Write(".");   // Here we could be doing other useful work.
    }

    Console.ReadLine();
}
```

The result of running this code will immediately show "Read operation started" while the I/O operation is in progress in the background. This proves the BeginRead method returned immediately. At some point in the future, the callback procedure (specified here using a lambda expression) is called. In the meantime, the main thread's code can continue to execute, in this case for the very useful purpose of printing dots while the I/O is in flight. If we want to, we can also check for completion state using the IsCompleted property on IAsyncResult.

Figure 28.6 shows the background worker thread calling the callback procedure, which happens while the main thread is doing its job. In this case, the main thread has already reached the end of the dot-printing loop where it checked for completion. In many cases though, the main thread will still be ticking away, doing other useful stuff (for example, pumping messages for a user interface framework such as Windows Forms or Windows Presentation Foundation [WPF]).

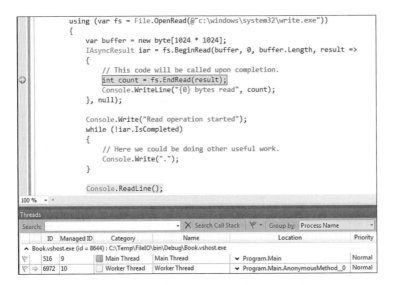

```
using (var fs = File.OpenRead(@"c:\windows\system32\write.exe"))
{
    var buffer = new byte[1024 * 1024];
    IAsyncResult iar = fs.BeginRead(buffer, 0, buffer.Length, result =>
    {
        // This code will be called upon completion.
        int count = fs.EndRead(result);
        Console.WriteLine("{0} bytes read", count);
    }, null);

    Console.Write("Read operation started");
    while (!iar.IsCompleted)
    {
        // Here we could be doing other useful work.
        Console.Write(".");
    }

    Console.ReadLine();
```

100 %

Threads

Search: X Search Call Stack   ▼ ▾ Group by: Process Name

	ID	Managed ID	Category	Name	Location	Priority
∧ Book.vshost.exe (id = 8644) : C:\Temp\FileIO\bin\Debug\Book.vshost.exe						
▽	516	9	Main Thread	Main Thread	▾ Program.Main	Normal
▽ ⇨	6972	10	Worker Thread	Worker Thread	▾ Program.Main.AnonymousMethod_0	Normal

FIGURE 28.6   Asynchronous completion on a worker thread.

BEWARE OF CACHING

Running this example multiple times could produce quite different timing behavior, due to the operating system's caching of data retrieved through I/O operations and even hardware-level caches.

Notice what the EndRead method on FileStreams looks like. It basically accepts the asynchronous result object and returns the operation's result, which in the case of file read is the number of bytes read and written to the buffer. Figure 28.7 shows how this pair of Begin/End methods corresponds to the synchronous counterpart. The bold text indicates portions of signatures that are introduced by the asynchronous pattern.

```
IAsyncResult BeginRead(byte[] array, int offset, int numBytes,
                       AsyncCallback userCallback, object stateObject);

        int EndRead(IAsyncResult asyncResult);
+ ────────────────────────────────────────────────────────────
        int Read(byte[] array, int offset, int numBytes);
```

FIGURE 28.7   The asynchronous method pattern adds a few intermediaries.

There are various ways to receive the data, but all of them involve calling the EndRead method with the IAsyncResult object retrieved. Often this is done inside the callback procedure using its parameter, but sometimes you use the BeginRead's return value for this particular purpose, often combined with a null callback:

```
IAsyncResult iar = fs.BeginRead(buffer, 0, buffer.Length, null, null);

// Do some work for which the data is not needed yet...
// But at some point we need it, so we call EndRead to block till we got it:
int count = fs.EndRead(iar);
```

In this particular sample code fragment, EndRead immediately returns if the data became available while we were doing other work after calling BeginRead. If that's not the case, though, EndRead will block until the data eventually arrives.

How Asynchronous Methods Work

To summarize the operational nature of asynchronous methods, callback procedures and the use of worker threads, look at Figure 28.8. At some point at time 0, some thread (say, the main thread) decides to start an asynchronous call for a file I/O read operation. It does so by preparing an empty buffer and an AsyncCallback delegate, which it passes to BeginRead. This causes the FileStream class to prepare a "ticket" of type IAsyncResult that represents the operation that will be run. Before it returns this to the caller, it spawns a worker thread that will do the I/O.

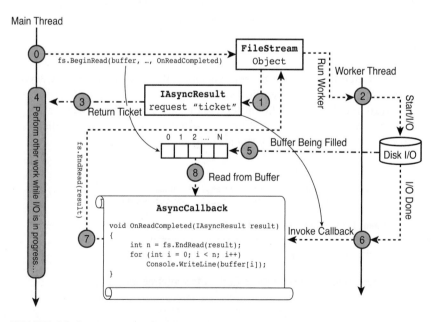

FIGURE 28.8   Summary of asynchronous method calls.

From this time on, the main thread is free to do whatever it wants while the file read is being taken care of by the worker thread, using interop with the operating system's I/O subsystem. The main thread's freedom is indicated by the rectangular area on the main thread. This code could also use the `IAsyncResult` ticket to poll for completion status or even decide to block for the data to become available as mentioned before. We assume the main thread doesn't perform such an action.

While the main thread is plowing along happily, the worker thread in collaboration with the operating system is filling the buffer. At some point, the worker thread will be notified by the operating system about the I/O completion. In response to this, the worker invokes the callback function specified by the user during the `BeginRead` call. For the callback to be able to correlate the completion with the request that was made, the `IAsyncResult` object is passed to it. (Contrast this with the `AsyncCallback` delegate signature as illustrated in the figure.) This allows a call to `EndRead` to look up the return value of the operation, in this case the number of bytes read. We haven't shown where this value is stored and how it's retrieved by `EndRead`, but that's the beauty of interfaces and the encapsulation provided by object-oriented frameworks.

Finally, the callback procedure can use the retrieved byte count to read from the buffer it passed in initially, now populated with the requested data. All of this happens while the main thread can continue its other activities. As you will see in Chapter 29, "Threading and Synchronization," use of worker threads (and more generally the notion of concurrency) brings with it some responsibilities. For example, it wouldn't be safe for the main thread to read from (or write to, Heaven forbid) the buffer before the worker thread has done its job.

What About the State Parameter?

As touched on briefly in our example, the `Begin` method of an asynchronous method pattern pair takes in an `AsyncCallback` as well as a state object. What's that for? Because asynchronous methods were introduced as early as .NET 1.0, there wasn't a rich way to work with delegates yet in languages such as C#. Recall that anonymous methods were added in C# 2.0, followed by the shorter lambda expression syntax in C# 3.0. So in the early days, you had to write the following:

```
void Bar(string path)
{
    using (FileStream fs = File.OpenRead(path))
    {
        byte[] buffer = new byte[1024 * 1024];
        IAsyncResult iar = fs.BeginRead(buffer, 0, buffer.Length,
            new AsyncCallback(OnReadCompleted), null);

        // Here we could be doing other useful work.
    }
}
```

```
void OnReadCompleted(IAsyncResult result)
{
    // Where to get the FileStream from? What about the byte[] buffer?
}
```

In this setting, the OnReadCompleted callback method requires a way to gain access to the FileStream object to call EndRead on it, passing the IAsyncResult object in. Furthermore, the buffer will need to be consulted, as well, for the written bytes to be read in.

Although it's quite typical for resources like the FileStream object to be owned by some object encapsulating it, putting the byte[] in a field as well solely for the purpose of sharing it between two methods seems kind of dangerous. Other parts of the class's code could touch this unexpectedly (for example, while an asynchronous operation is in flight), causing threading issues. This is where the state parameter comes in, allowing some object to be passed between the BeginRead and EndRead call. For example:

```
class LogAnalyzer : IDisposable
{
    private FileStream _fs;

    public LogAnalyzer(string path)
    {
        _fs = File.OpenRead(path);
    }

    public void StartRead()
    {
        byte[] buffer = new byte[1024 * 1024];
        IAsyncResult iar = _fs.BeginRead(buffer, 0, buffer.Length,
            new AsyncCallback(OnReadCompleted), buffer);
    }

    private void OnReadCompleted(IAsyncResult result)
    {
        int n = _fs.EndRead(result);
        byte[] buffer = (byte[])result.AsyncState;

        // Do something with the populated buffer contents
    }

    public void Dispose()
    {
        // Left as an exercise. Think about what you want to clean up here, and
        // what effects this may have (tip: stuff is going on in the background).
    }
}
```

The state parameter is accessible inside the callback method through the `AsyncState` property exposed by `IAsyncResult`. Obviously, if you want to share more than just a single object, an object array or a wrapping class could be created (or, in .NET 4 and later, the `Tuple` types could be leveraged).

However, due to the introduction of anonymous methods and lambda expressions in later stages of the framework's and languages' development, the use of such a "state-threading" mechanism has become largely redundant. Recall how we wrote the initial asynchronous file read example earlier:

```
using (var fs = File.OpenRead(path))
{
    var buffer = new byte[1024 * 1024];
    IAsyncResult iar = fs.BeginRead(buffer, 0, buffer.Length, result =>
    {
        int count = fs.EndRead(result);
        for (int i = 0; i < count; i++)
            Console.WriteLine(buffer[i]);
    }, null);

    ...

}
```

As you will recall, anonymous methods and their shorthand lambda expression syntax allow capturing variables from the enclosing scope. In this case, the lambda expression used for the callback "closes over" both the `fs` and `buffer` variables. This causes the compiler to cook up so-called display classes containing fields to hold those objects for them to be shared across the declaring method and the callback lambda. This is illustrated in Figure 28.9 through .NET Reflector.

As you can see, the lambda expression gave rise to an anonymous method referred to by the `AsyncCallback` delegate passed to `BeginRead`. The `<Main>b__0` method is what you had to write manually prior to C# 2.0 and 3.0. Inside this method, access to `fs` and `buffer` variables that were declared in the `Main` method is achieved by using fields on what's known as a "display class." In fact, two of them have been generated, one per captured outer variable, all of them chained together. Both the `Main` method and the callback method use them to share information between each other.

We conclude our detour through anonymous methods and closures here and refer to Chapter 17, "Delegates," for more information. Suffice to say that C# makes the use of asynchronous method calls slightly easier thanks to the availability of closures on anonymous methods. This effectively makes the original intended use of the state parameter on asynchronous method calls redundant in most (if not all) cases.

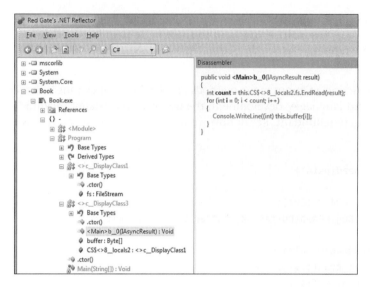

FIGURE 28.9   Summary of asynchronous method calls.

ASYNCHRONOUS DELEGATE INVOCATION

Remember that it's possible to invoke any delegate asynchronously using the BeginInvoke method. To retrieve the result of the computation, you use the corresponding EndInvoke method, which obviously takes in an IAsyncResult. For example:

```
Func<int, int> twice = x => x * 2;


int n = 21;
twice.BeginInvoke(n, iar =>
{
    int res = twice.EndInvoke(iar);
    Console.WriteLine("And the answer to ({0} * 2) is {1}!", n, res);
}, null /* the dreaded state parameter */);


Console.WriteLine("Please wait while we're computing ({0} * 2)...", n);
```

Although this is a contrived example, it clearly shows the use of asynchronous methods in a context other than (file) I/O. Nothing here should come as a surprise because the pattern that's followed is exactly the same as the one you learned about on the FileStream API. As you explore the .NET Framework BCL, you'll find many more places where this pattern is applied.

Beware of Lifetime Issues

Performing work asynchronously implies the introduction of concurrency. After all, if the initiator of an asynchronous operation wants to continue work without being blocked for the result to come, clearly some other unit of execution needs to take on the task of computing the result in the meantime. This is where the use of worker threads enters the picture (refer to Figure 28.8).

We discuss threading in more detail in Chapter 29, but I want to warn you now about some potential complications. In particular, when writing code, keep in mind the lifetime of objects required by the callback procedure. Based on our original example of an asynchronous file read, can you spot a flaw in the following piece of code?

```
using (var fs = File.OpenRead(\windows\system32\write.exe"))
{
    var buffer = new byte[1024 * 1024];
    fs.BeginRead(buffer, 0, buffer.Length, result =>
    {
        int count = fs.EndRead(result);
        for (int i = 0; i < count; i++)
            Console.WriteLine(buffer[i]);
    }, null);
}


Console.ReadLine();
```

Figure 28.10 shows what happens if you try to execute this code. So what's going on here? Notice the gray background on which Console.ReadLine() is rendered, which is indicative of where the main thread is right now, while the callback is happening on a worker thread. But wait a second; hasn't the main thread already left the using block? Indeed, because the FileStream resource was disposed already by the main thread, the worker thread hits an exception when it tries to use the FileStream object to call the EndRead method on it. The fix is to make sure not to dispose the FileStream so early. One suitable spot may be the callback procedure itself, after the call to EndRead.

This kind of resource lifetime management can be quite a challenge to get right under all circumstances. It's the unfortunate nature of parallel code that one has to keep such issues in mind. Making sure that objects have a proper owner and do not leak between boundaries of abstraction is always a good practice. For example, imagine how much worse things could get if the FileStream object could be accessed by other code as well (for example, disposing it at unpredictable times)?

REACTIVE EXTENSIONS FOR .NET

Very recently, I have been involved in the development of the Reactive Extensions (Rx) for .NET, which is a framework to help simplify asynchronous programming. You can find more information about it on the Web by searching for "DevLabs Reactive Extensions." One of the things it does is provide a wrapper around asynchronous method pairs, exposing them as IObservable<T> objects. Because of the abstraction provided by IObservable<T>, a rich set of operators can be used on them. Also, dealing with error cases becomes easier.

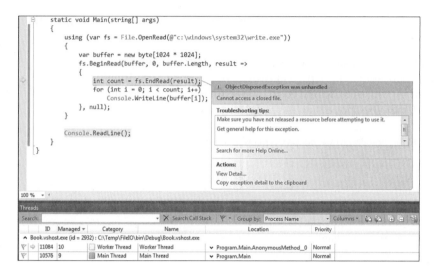

FIGURE 28.10   Make sure not to dispose of objects too early.

Streams Are Everywhere

Streams are a very useful abstraction that's used far beyond just file I/O operations. As you explore the .NET Framework, you'll find plenty of places where streams are used. Examples include the NetworkStream class in System.Net.Sockets, which represents the data coming from or being sent to a socket, using protocols such as TCP or UDP. Yet another place where sockets are used is in low-level data access (for example, for what's known as file streams in SQL Server 2008 and later). Exposing them to managed code uses the concept of a SqlFileStream, which encapsulates the communication with the server over the Tabular Data Stream (TDS) protocol.

Often, streams are also used "over" other streams. An example is compression, as seen in the System.IO.Compression namespace. Given any stream (for example, coming from a file), you can wrap it in a compression stream such as GZipStream. An example of this is shown here, reading the Program.cs itself (using a relative path "trick" explained earlier) and copying it to a compressed stream that writes to another file:

```
const string SRC = @"..\..\Program.cs";
const string TGT = @"..\..\Program.gz";

using (var zipped = File.Create(TGT))
using (var compress = new GZipStream(zipped, CompressionMode.Compress))
using (var source = File.OpenRead(SRC))
{
    source.CopyTo(compress);
}
```

```
Console.WriteLine("Source length = " + new FileInfo(SRC).Length);
Console.WriteLine("Zipped length = " + new FileInfo(TGT).Length);
```

Notice how the GZipStream object is constructed to sit on top of a destination stream to write the compressed data to. The source file stream is then copied using CopyTo method, which causes the GZipStream to write the data through to the underlying target stream after compressing the data. Figure 28.11 shows this.

FIGURE 28.11   GZipStream operates on other streams.

I leave it to you to cook up the opposite composition of GZipStream to achieve decompression. In that case, the .gz file needs to become the input, and the GZipStream needs to be written to the uncompressed destination file. Essentially, this is just the mirror image of what's shown in Figure 28.11.

A Primer to (Named) Pipes

To reinforce your knowledge of streams acquired in the previous section, let's explore another System.IO capability that was added a few .NET Framework versions ago: (named) pipes. The concept of a named pipe is to provide an efficient interprocess communication mechanism that's natively supported by the operating system. Although you won't likely use such a low-level mechanism—in favor of higher abstraction levels as provided by Windows Communication Foundation (WCF), for example—it acts as a good sample of working with streams.

A total of five Stream subclasses exist in the System.IO.Pipes namespace, one of which acts as an intermediate base class for the other four. Let's not go into too much detail about the additional facilities provided by this PipeStream class over its base class. Figure 28.12 shows a class diagram of the relevant types in this namespace.

Two different communication mechanisms can be used that are collectively referred to as *pipes*. One is a named pipe, which is more flexible in its functionality compared to the concept of an anonymous pipe. For example, the former supports communication over a network to another computer, whereas the latter typically is used to exchange data between parent and child processes.

The simple application we'll write here does nothing but send a single text message from a server to a client using a named pipe. To do so, we'll write just one executable that can operate as a client or a server depending on the command-line input. Inside the implementation, we use the NamedPipeClientStream and NamedPipeServerStream classes, touching briefly on the concept of connecting pipes. To make our lives easier with regard to

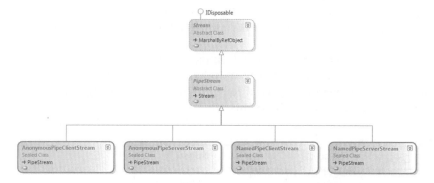

FIGURE 28.12   `PipeStream` and derived classes.

sending and receiving information to and from the pipe, we use the `StreamReader` and `StreamWriter` classes. In short, everything we learned thus far is used in concert here. Let's take a look at the code now:

```
const string PIPE = "PipeSample";

static void Main(string[] args)
{
    if (args.Length == 1)
        Client(args[0]);
    else
        Server();
}

private static void Client(string server)
{
    using (var client = new NamedPipeClientStream(server, PIPE,
                                                  PipeDirection.In))
    {
        Console.Write("Connecting to {0}... ", server);
        client.Connect();
        Console.WriteLine("Connected");

        using (var reader = new StreamReader(client))
        {
            var message = reader.ReadLine();
            Console.WriteLine("Received message: " + message);
        }
    }
}

private static void Server()
```

```
{
    using (var server = new NamedPipeServerStream(PIPE, PipeDirection.Out))
    {
        Console.Write("Waiting for connection... ");
        server.WaitForConnection();
        Console.WriteLine("Connected");

        using (var writer = new StreamWriter(server))
        {
            Console.Write("Enter message: ");
            var message = Console.ReadLine();
            writer.WriteLine(message);
        }
    }
}
```

The Client method takes in a computer name where the named pipe server lives and uses the NamedPipeClient stream to set up communication. Although pipes can be set up for bidirectional communication, we make the client read-only using PipeDirection.In. To connect to the server, we call the Connect method, which could also take in a timeout value. Note also that more advanced constructor overloads exist, which allow control over pipe options, security aspects, and so on.

Once the client is connected, we establish a StreamReader over the stream to receive a single line of text. It's worth thinking for a moment about how the general-purpose stream reader can read a line of text from any kind of stream, keeping in mind that streams only have byte-level read and write operations.

The server is a mirror image to the client and differs in that no computer name has to be specified (after all, the machine itself is the server) on the NamedPipeServerStream constructor. As data is sent to the client, we configure the pipe direction for outbound traffic only. Another difference is the way we establish a connection, which now waits for a client to arrive. Overloads to the constructor of NamedPipeServerStream allow you to specify how many connections can be established, but we assume just one here. I leave it to you to discover asynchronous methods that can be used to spawn a worker thread as a client connects to the server (tip: it starts with Begin...).

How we write data from the server to the client should be obvious given the mirrored nature of both parts. This time we use a StreamWriter and its WriteLine method to send data across the pipe. Figure 28.13 shows two command prompt instances running the server and client component of this application.

Again, I leave it to you to envision a true chat application using named pipes, although easier techniques through WCF exist. One typically uses pipes to interact with existing software components that leverage them already. Notice that communication stacks such as .NET Remoting and WCF can leverage (named) pipes themselves in one of their "channel" implementations. Pipes provide an efficient way to send data across two or more Windows processes and are a good choice in such a setting. What frameworks like .NET Remoting and WCF give you is a higher level of abstraction where whole objects can be sent, method calls can be made, and so on.

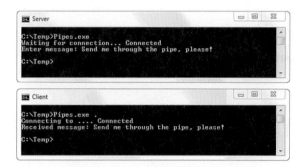

FIGURE 28.13   Messaging through named pipes in action.

Memory-Mapped Files in a Nutshell

Introduced in .NET 4, memory-mapped files is yet another exposure of Win32 power to managed code developers. With memory-mapped files, you can achieve a number of things. One is to set up interprocess communication once more, this time using shared memory that's identified with a "map name." Multiple processes can read from and write to the shared memory. For this to work properly, some kind of synchronization will be needed, which goes beyond what we can cover in this book.

Another capability is closer to everyday development, though: the ability to work with extremely large files by mapping them into the memory address space and accessing them as if it were in-memory data. This includes the ability to do random accesses (without a need to seek through a file; for example, by means of a stream), create views over the file, and so on. For a thorough description of memory-mapped I/O capabilities, refer to MSDN. We have a little sampler here, though.

Consider again an executable file that we somehow want to inspect for data. You've seen before how to retrieve the PE/COFF header magic string using regular stream-based operations. This time around we try to achieve the same (and a bit more) using memory-mapped files:

```
using (var file = MemoryMappedFile.CreateFromFile(\Temp\Notepad.exe"))
{
    using (var accessor = file.CreateViewAccessor())
    {
        int offset = accessor.ReadInt32(0x3c);

        Header header;
        accessor.Read<Header>(offset + 4, out header);
```

```
        // Print header fields of interest
    }
}
```

Here two essential notions are shown. The first is the creation of a memory-mapped file object from a path. Lots of options can be specified, but `CreateFromFile` is always used to refer to a physical file. Other factory methods exist that can be used to create shared memory sections. We're operating on a copy of Notepad.exe because the file will be opened for read/write access when using this factory method with a minimal number of parameters. Typically, mapping a file is used to manipulate the file anyway, so this makes sense.

The second key aspect is that of a view accessor. This is a way to obtain a view over a part of the file or the entire file. Here we go for the latter, but you can imagine using a multigigabyte file and only mapping a few bytes at an offset several megabytes away from the start. This would never need to load the entire file from disk because the operating system keeps track of the "mapping" between the view's address space and the part of the underlying file that's being mapped. This is what sets memory-mapped files apart from dealing with regular file streams.

Using the obtained accessor we now retrieve, as explained in an earlier example, the offset value stored at location 0x3c. After that, we do something very nice and neat. We use the generic `Read` method to map a portion of the view's data into a struct that we have defined, as follows:

```
[StructLayout(LayoutKind.Explicit)]
struct Header
{
    [FieldOffset(0)]
    public Machine Machine;

    [FieldOffset(2)]
    public ushort NumberOfSections;

    [FieldOffset(18)]
    public Characteristics Characteristics;
}
```

This corresponds to (parts of) a table that can be found in the PE/COFF spec referred to earlier. Figure 28.14 shows an excerpt from this specification.

The reason we jump 4 bytes ahead of the offset we read in before is to skip over the magic "PE\0\0" string of 4 bytes. Next, we map the data using `Read<Header>` into a struct value where explicit layout is used to specify offsets conform the table. For both the `Machine` and `Characteristics` fields, we define an enum (only part of the values is shown here to conserve space, see the specification for the full list):

```
enum Machine : ushort
{
    Amd64 = 0x8664,
    I386 = 0x14c,
    IA64 = 0x200,
    // Most other documented machine architectures are extinct (e.g. MIPS16)
}


[Flags]
enum Characteristics : ushort
{
    ExecutableImage = 0x2,
    LargeAddressAware = 0x20,
    Machine32Bit = 0x100,
    // Lots of other flags exist, see specification.
}
```

3.3. COFF File Header (Object and Image)

At the beginning of an object file, or immediately after the signature of an image file, is a standard COFF file header in the following format. Note that the Windows loader limits the number of sections to 96.

Offset	Size	Field	Description
0	2	Machine	The number that identifies the type of target machine. For more information, see section 3.3.1, "Machine Types."
2	2	NumberOfSections	The number of sections. This indicates the size of the section table, which immediately follows the headers.
4	4	TimeDateStamp	The low 32 bits of the number of seconds since 00:00 January 1, 1970 (a C run-time time_t value), that indicates when the file was created.
8	4	PointerToSymbolTable	The file offset of the COFF symbol table, or zero if no COFF symbol table is present. This value should be zero for an image because COFF debugging information is deprecated.
12	4	NumberOfSymbols	The number of entries in the symbol table. This data can be used to locate the string table, which immediately follows the symbol table. This value should be zero for an image because COFF debugging information is deprecated.
16	2	SizeOfOptionalHeader	The size of the optional header, which is required for executable files but not for object files. This value should be zero for an object file. For a description of the header format, see section 3.4, "Optional Header (Image Only)."
18	2	Characteristics	The flags that indicate the attributes of the file. For specific flag values, see section 3.3.2, "Characteristics."

FIGURE 28.14   COFF header of an executable file.

On my 64-bit machine, the 64-bit version of Notepad returns the values shown in Figure 28.15 after reading the COFF header using the mapped file APIs. You can compare those values to the output of dumpbin.exe /headers notepad.exe, running from a Visual Studio command prompt. The dumpbin.exe tool is an SDK tool that does precisely this, albeit from native code.

Although I haven't shown the true power of memory-mapped files to deal with large files or shared memory sections, you've seen how random access can be achieved using views.

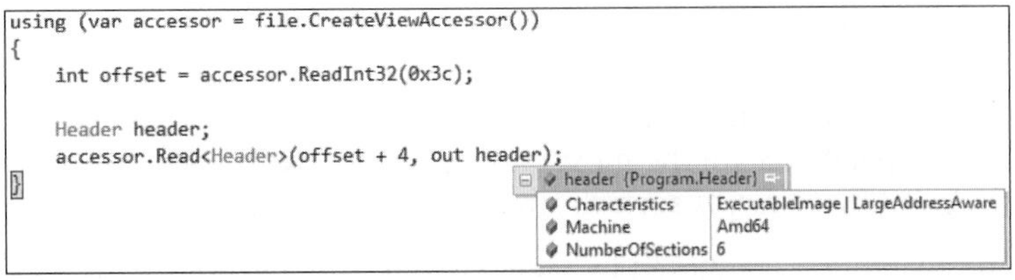

```
using (var accessor = file.CreateViewAccessor())
{
    int offset = accessor.ReadInt32(0x3c);

    Header header;
    accessor.Read<Header>(offset + 4, out header);
}
```

header {Program.Header}	
🔧 Characteristics	ExecutableImage | LargeAddressAware
🔧 Machine	Amd64
🔧 NumberOfSections	6

FIGURE 28.15   Some executable header values for 64-bit Notepad.exe on Windows 7.

Note that this mechanism is pretty similar to our use of MemoryStream objects before, as shown in Figure 28.5. The difference is we're now looking at a file through virtual memory addresses, nicely abstracted away by the new .NET 4 APIs for managed code developers. If you ever need to deal with large files and can't afford to load them completely from disk, have lots of seeks, and so on, this is something to look into.

Overview of Other I/O Capabilities

The .NET Framework has a rich I/O story, of which you saw only the tip of the iceberg here. Other capabilities not discussed here include the following:

▶ Isolated storage, a way to store data in a sandbox where it's associated with an application, typically running in partial trust. Examples include web downloads that are isolated for use by the application (and user) that downloaded it. By erecting an isolation boundary, potentially malicious partial trust applications can do very little harm and can't disturb other applications' data. Look at the System.IO.IsolatedStoreage namespace if this sounds interesting.

▶ Support for packaging of multiple files in a single container, based on the Open Packaging Convention (OPC) standard as used by various file formats, including XPS and the new XML-based Office formats. Containers for such packages are typically ZIP files and consist of what's referred to as "parts." See the System.IO.Packaging namespace for more information.

▶ Serial port communication is available through System.IO.Ports's SerialPort class. Simple Read and Write methods are all that's needed to communicate with other hardware connected to a serial port. The constructor of the class has support for a variety of settings, such as baud rate, parity bits, and so on. Because the class is implemented as a component, it can be dragged to designer surfaces.

▶ For very specialized use, the .NET Framework has a wrapper around the Common Log File System (CLFS) that was introduced in Windows Vista and Windows Server 2008. This can be used to implement specialized components such as transaction processors. You can find more information in the MSDN documentation for System.IO.Logging.

Summary

In this chapter, you learned about the rich I/O capabilities offered through the `System.IO` namespace. Although file I/O operations are the most common kind, we focused on the generic functionality introduced by concepts such as streams, readers, and writers.

With regard to file system capabilities, we started by taking a look at the various `Info` classes that provide information about drives, directory hierarchies, and files. Leaving the macroscopic world of files as black boxes, we dove into various ways to read from and write to files. Such facilities span a wide gamma of techniques that balances ease of use with low-level control. For example, methods such as `ReadToEnd` are of incredible convenience, while `BinaryReader`-based I/O offers significant flexibility.

While discussing the functionality exposed by `Stream` objects, we also introduced the notion of asynchronous methods with a couple of concrete samples. This technique is useful to avoid blocking an application's capability to do useful work while I/O is performed in the background. Using this pattern requires a good understanding of delegates and, to a lesser extent, threading infrastructure. The latter is discussed more thoroughly in the next chapter.

Finally, we looked at some recent additions to `System.IO`, including interprocess communication using pipes and memory-mapped I/O.

IN THIS CHAPTER

▶ Using Threads 1432

▶ Thread Pools 1463

▶ Synchronization
  Primitives 1471

Today's computers have tremendous processing power. Not only does this get reflected in clock speeds (which seem to have reached a ceiling due to heat dissipation challenges), but the number of processing cores in machines is ever increasing too. This trend toward many-core machines poses an ongoing challenge as to how to write software that can take advantage of these computing resources.

Writing concurrent programs isn't anything new, though. Operating systems, such as Windows NT, introduced scheduling mechanisms that allowed programs to run multiple threads of execution at the same time. While such parallel execution wasn't truly achievable on single-processor machines, preemptive scheduling certainly gave programs (and hence users) the impression they could accomplish multiple tasks at the same time.

Unfortunately, the use of constructs like threads is a necessary evil in relation to certain frameworks, in particular the user interface (UI) kind, where a dedicated thread of execution is responsible for dispatching messages. Because of this historical fact, lots of readers will have encountered multithreading the hard way, as illustrated in Figure 29.1.

Nonetheless, mastering the art of writing scalable but correct code that keeps on performing better as computing resources are being added is a tremendous asset in today's developer's mindset. Although this art can be quite hard to master due to the inherent complexities of synchronization and such, this chapter introduces core notions and things to be aware of.

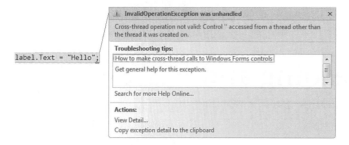

FIGURE 29.1   Cross-threading violations are an inconvenient truth in UI programming.

As a quick overview, let's start by exploring threading as it's known to the operating system and the CLR built on top of it. We then explore CLR-specific notions associated with threads and introduce the `Thread` and `ThreadPool` classes. From there, we enter the minefield of synchronization worries and explore the various primitives that help us out. Finally, we dive into the .NET 4 aspects of parallel programming using the Task Parallel Library (TPL) and its related technologies, such as PLINQ.

Using Threads

Before we delve into specifics of multithreaded programming in managed code, we should spend a few minutes talking about the general notion of threading and how it's achieved at the operating system and CLR level.

Explaining the Concept of Threads

Processes executing on Windows can have multiple threads inside them. Threads are where code is executed, and multiple threads can carry out different tasks at the same time. This is achieved by running code on different cores or creating a multicore illusion using (preemptive) operating system scheduling. The operating system kernel is responsible for scheduling threads according to a policy that consists of various factors. For example, threads can have relative priorities, causing the scheduler to favor one thread over another. Threads can get boosted when certain events occur; for example, when clunky user interaction is to be avoided. Furthermore, threads can get blocked because they're waiting for resources to become available, thus allowing the scheduler to let another thread run and make progress.

From this slightly simplified description, it should be clear that processes are merely some collection of threads and some associated data structures, but threads are really what gets scheduled and run by the operating system. Scheduling involves a number of low-level techniques, such as swapping out the processor registers such that threads can resume where they left off. That is, when the scheduler decides to take away a thread from a processor on which it's running, it stores away the thread's state so that it can be rehydrated when the thread is assigned to a processor for execution again. Figure 29.2 shows this mechanism in a conceptual manner.

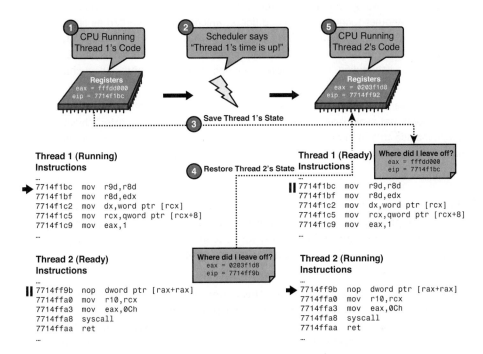

FIGURE 29.2   Context switching carried out by the scheduler to give threads a turn.

Note that in a preemptive operating system like (modern) Windows, a single thread (and hence the process to which it belongs) cannot monopolize the system. Each thread gets a "quantum" of CPU clock ticks it can consume before being taken away from the processor forcefully by the kernel's scheduler, in favor of another thread (if such a thread that's ready to execute exists). The length of the quantum varies based on Windows configuration settings (in particular, whether you're running a client or server workload). In other words, threads get their turns to execute. Threads should really be thought of as "virtual processors" that can act as if they have a processor of their own. However, because one can have more threads than physical processors, a third party—the operating system and its scheduler—needs to coordinate use of the physical resource.

CONTEXT SWITCHES, FIBERS, AND USER MODE SCHEDULING

The mechanism of storing one thread's state and restoring another one's to give the latter a chance to execute is known as a context switch. These are fairly expensive, and for highly scalable systems you try to avoid this cost by means of various techniques.

One is to avoid getting the kernel's scheduler involved, which is where most of the cost comes from. This led to the invention of things such as "user mode scheduling," first exercised by the SQL Server operating system (a low-level layer that sits immediately on top of the real operating system) and later introduced in Windows 7 and Windows Server 2008 R2. Another technique is to use fibers, which can be regarded as lightweight threads but suffer from quite a few limitations (for example, thread-local storage becomes problematic). In fact, at some point an attempt was made to make the CLR support fiber mode scheduling, but this never materialized because of technical challenges encountered.

As you will see, even in the world of managed code there are synchronization primitives and other notions that avoid taking large performance hits by doing "smarter" things. Such things include thread pooling, use of "slim" versions of wait events, and so on. Stay tuned to learn more.

Prior to the introduction of multiprocessor or multicore systems, there was only a single CPU, and therefore preemptive scheduling was the only way to mimic simultaneous execution of different programs and their threads. The idea of preemption is that the scheduler can preempt a thread's execution in favor of another one, as explained earlier and illustrated in Figure 29.2.

Today, true parallel execution is pretty much the standard with the omnipresence of multicore machines. Although this allows for higher throughput when using well-written software, it also unveils lots of potential problems with regard to synchronization when shared resources are being used by multiple threads truly at the same time (from different CPUs). Figure 29.3 shows this pictorially.

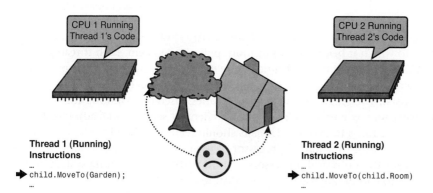

FIGURE 29.3   Race condition for two threads accessing shared state.

The Managed Code Story

Processes running managed code are no different with respect to execution and can have multiple threads. In fact, the common language runtime itself creates a number of threads (for example, for finalization and garbage collection). Threads running managed code are typically referred to as managed threads, while others are called native threads. Not only can the CLR create native threads; often interoperability with native libraries within a managed code process is responsible for the creation of new threads as well. In fact, some .NET Framework libraries do so, and hybrid managed/native applications, such as Visual Studio 2010, have a rich collection of threads plowing away.

Managed threads happen to be backed by native threads on which the CLR piggybacks, allowing the operating system's threading facilities to offer their benefits. However, the CLR adds a bunch of facilities on top of raw native threads. The essential thing here to realize is that each (native or managed) thread has its own call stack. To support features like exception handling, the CLR controls certain data that's kept on the stack for it to be able to find managed method call frames and so on. Garbage collection, too, needs support from CLR-specific notions interwoven with a managed thread's state. Recall one of the phases of garbage collection needs to scan for "roots" on all thread stacks.

All in all, the CLR is just another native component that leverages native threads. It just turns out that the managed code runtime does a lot of bookkeeping to allow managed code to run on those native threads. In summary, you could state that the CLR adds its own policies and some mechanisms to the underlying threading infrastructure on which it relies. This can go as far as reusing native threads for multiple pieces of work that are executed by managed code, a mechanism known as thread pooling. And as soon as managed components keep their own list of work to be executed, it's fair to say that component is also taking over part of the scheduling.

Figure 29.4 shows a simplified picture of this. Native applications have only native threads, which are totally managed by the operating system scheduler. The managed application shown on the right has plenty of native threads, some of which are solely used by the CLR's execution engine itself. Others are used as a managed thread running user code, with the CLR's involvement for various aspects of state management. Finally, thread pools can exist that use a limited number of native threads but allow user code to post work to a queue. This realizes a kind of multiplexing mechanism by which the CLR reduces the number of native threads and performs its own kind of scheduling policies (for example, by draining the work item queue and assigning a thread to do the work). We return to many of the points made here later.

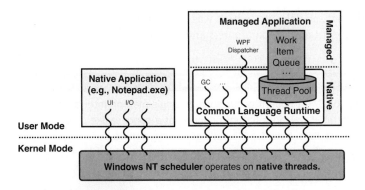

FIGURE 29.4   Native and managed threads coexisting.

.NET Framework 4 adds another level of abstraction to the notion of running work in a parallel manner. This is realized by the Task Parallel Library (TPL), exposed through additions to the System.Threading namespace. This new library has its own notion of task schedulers, which employ interesting techniques to make sure multiple cores are leveraged in an optimized manner. We discuss some of this as well, focusing on the Task<T> class and explaining how this new scheduling infrastructures does something known as work stealing.

Where It All Starts: The Thread Class

The closest you can get to a "raw thread" is using the Thread class, which lives in the System.Threading namespace that will be the topic of this chapter. By "raw thread" we mean a native (as all of them ultimately are) thread that can run managed code but isn't subject to lots of additional management by the CLR or any library. In particular, no techniques such as pooling or specialized scheduling are employed.

Creating Threads

Use of the Thread class is pretty simple. We start by looking at the instance members defined on the Thread class, so we need to create an instance first. All a thread object needs to know about is what code it has to run. As you should infer by now, the idea of delegating execution of code is where delegates enter the picture. It shouldn't come as a surprise that the constructors of Thread take in delegate-typed objects:

```
public Thread(ParameterizedThreadStart start);
public Thread(ThreadStart start);
```

Overloads exist that can control the maximum stack size the newly created thread can use, but we omit this detail from our discussion. From the two constructors, we can pick one with the most convenient delegate type. Let's start by looking at the second one, which is the simpler of the two:

```
public delegate void ThreadStart();
```

In fact, this is nothing but the Action delegate (which was introduced at a later point, hence the apparent duplication): It takes no parameters and doesn't return anything.

SINGLE-METHOD INTERFACES AND JAVA'S RUNNABLE

As mentioned earlier in this book, the frequent occurrence of single-method interfaces in lots of frameworks is exactly what warrants the introduction of a concept like delegates. Other frameworks, such as Java, have traditionally gone with a more pure object-oriented approach, where the act of passing a single piece of code around involves implementing an interface.

For the creation of a thread in Java, one therefore uses the Runnable interface, which has exactly one method called run. To reduce the burden of having to go and declare a class implementing the interface, the Java language introduced the notion of anonymous inner classes, allowing inline implementation of an interface. Although such a feature could come in handy from time to time, it mostly covers up for the lack of delegates. I don't really miss the days of implementing a plethora of "listener" interfaces to perform simple event-handling tasks.

The simplest example of creating a thread using this constructor overload is shown here, using lambda expression syntax to declare the thread's code:

```
var work = new Thread(() => {
    Console.WriteLine("Doing work!");
});
```

Obviously, we explore more useful thread jobs in a while. Notice at this point that the thread isn't running yet. In a few moments, we start talking about a thread's life cycle, including the ability to start it (which is pretty much the only thing you should ever do with a thread).

Besides the constructor taking in a ThreadStart, there's also one that allows passing a parameter to the thread's code body using a ParameterizedThreadStart:

```
public delegate void ParameterizedThreadStart(object obj);
```

The sole difference with the ThreadStart delegate is the presence of the object-typed parameter. The fact both ThreadStart delegates return void shouldn't come as a surprise. After all, the act of starting a thread will introduce asynchrony, where another piece of code starts running in the background. Waiting for that code's result would imply some kind of blocking. In Chapter 30, "Task Parallelism and Data Parallelism," you see how the .NET 4 class Task<T> can produce a value. Using the constructor with the ParameterizedThreadStart looks as follows:

```
var processRequest = new Thread(req => {
    var request = (WebRequest)req;
    // Process the request, e.g. by loading a file from the disk and sending
    // it back to the client over an HTTP/TCP socket.
});
```

Because the parameter is statically typed to be of type System.Object, you must use a cast to view the object through the expected type. If generics had been part of the first version of the .NET Framework, most likely the Thread class would have been generic in the type of the input parameter. And similarly, the ParameterizedThreadStart delegate could be replaced by an Action<T> delegate, such that the parameter would be strongly typed. Where the thread's parameter comes from (that is, how it gets passed to the lambda expression) will be answered in the next section, "Starting Threads," when we meet the `Start` method.

CLOSURES STRIKE AGAIN

Today, all this API bloat for thread parameterization is mostly a redundant historical arti-fact. Ever since C# 2.0 introduced closures, it has been possible to capture one or more outer variables for use within the thread. Be careful, though:

```
var user = "Alice";
var work = new Thread(() => {
    // The variable user is really an implicit parameter to the thread...
    Console.WriteLine("Processing user " + user);
});
user = "Bob";
work.Start();    // See later, but what will the thread print?
user = "Carol";
```

Closures effectively introduce shared state between the thread creator and the thread itself. The preceding code definitely won't print Alice because the user variable gets assigned Bob before the thread starts. However, depending on the timing of the birth of the new thread, it might or might not see Carol being assigned to user. Whether you're using closures or not, any kind of shared state should be treated carefully.

Whether to use anonymous methods or lambda expressions to declare the body of a thread's code inline depends mostly on stylistic factors. If the thread's body tends to be large (and typically it is; for example, running a request processing loop or so), it's often better to declare a separate worker method and have the `ThreadStart` delegate refer to that one:

```
void OnRequestReceived(WebRequest request)
{
    var processRequest = new Thread(ProcessRequest);
    processRequest.Start();  // See later
}

void ProcessRequest(object req)
{
    var request = (WebRequest)req;
    // Process the request, e.g. by loading a file from the disk and sending
    // it back to the client over an HTTP/TCP socket.
}
```

Starting Threads

Now that you've seen how `Thread` objects can be created, let's look at the life cycle of threads. Instantiation of the `Thread` class doesn't cause a thread to start its execution immediately; instead, you must trigger the thread's start manually by calling the `Start` method on it. At that point, the thread can be scheduled for execution, which obviously involves running the code inside it. Let's show a complete but still trivial example of creating and starting a thread:

```csharp
using System;
using System.Threading;

class Program
{
    static void Main()
    {
        var worker = new Thread(() =>
        {
            Console.WriteLine("Worker thread - Hello!");
        });

        Console.WriteLine("Main thread - Press ENTER to start worker");
        Console.ReadLine();
        worker.Start();

        Console.WriteLine("Main thread - Worker started");
        Console.WriteLine("Main thread - Press ENTER to quit");
        Console.ReadLine();
    }
}
```

Some explanation of behavior is required here. Because the thread we designate as a worker isn't started immediately, the main thread will first print the message that prompts the user to press Enter to start the worker thread. Until that very point, the output of the program should be quite predictable. However, after the thread is started, things can vary from run to run. Figure 29.5 shows possible interleaving of both threads that are now competing to be scheduled.

SHARED STATE LURKING AROUND MANY CORNERS

Readers with an eye for detail will notice that our code could be prone to shared-state issues because the console output is really used by both threads, potentially at the same time. This could very well cause issues, depending on how the console I/O subsystem treats the situation of simultaneous access by multiple threads. We don't digress here, and instead save this concept for later coverage in the section titled "Synchronization Primitives," named after the constructs used to safeguard shared access.

This figure simplifies matters a lot and omits several possible relative orders of the threads executing code. For one thing, on multicore machines (as most of them are today) it's perfectly possible for multiple threads to be truly doing stuff at the same time. Figure 29.5 shows only two possible execution orders, with only one single thread active at a time. We've also omitted a number of possible states that threads can be in. For example,

`Console.ReadLine` really blocks the thread somehow until user input becomes available. We haven't indicated such a special "waiting for I/O to complete" state in the figure.

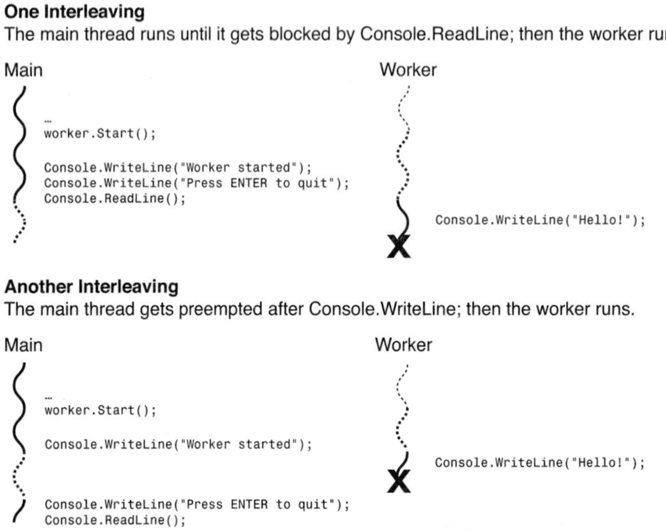

One Interleaving
The main thread runs until it gets blocked by Console.ReadLine; then the worker runs.

Main   Worker

```
...
worker.Start();

Console.WriteLine("Worker started");
Console.WriteLine("Press ENTER to quit");
Console.ReadLine();
                          Console.WriteLine("Hello!");
                     X
```

Another Interleaving
The main thread gets preempted after Console.WriteLine; then the worker runs.

Main   Worker

```
...
worker.Start();

Console.WriteLine("Worker started");
                          Console.WriteLine("Hello!");
                     X
Console.WriteLine("Press ENTER to quit");
Console.ReadLine();
```

FIGURE 29.5   Threads can run independently from each other with different interleaving.

Parameterized threads are also started using the `Start` method, albeit with an overload that accepts the parameter object that's to be passed to the thread's code. The little code example here should make this clear immediately:

```
var worker = new Thread(message =>
{
    Console.WriteLine("Worker thread - {0}", message);
});

Console.Write("Main thread - Enter message to send to worker: ");
var input = Console.ReadLine();
worker.Start(input);
```

As stated before, the use of the `ParameterizedThreadStart` can often be replaced by the use of closures with anonymous methods or lambda expressions. Even for simple scenarios, this can prove beneficial, in particular when multiple parameters have to be passed to the thread's code. Without closures, you would have to declare a class to wrap all the parameters to be passed or use one of the Tuple types in .NET 4. The use of closures doesn't preclude factoring out the thread's body into a separate method though, as shown here:

```
string message = ...;
int repeat = ...;
var worker = new Thread(() => PrintMessage(message, repeat));
worker.Start();
```

Here, we capture both the message and repeat variables in the lambda expression body, causing the creation of a closure. The compiler is really taking over the burden of creating a wrapper class with fields for message and repeat values to be passed from the main thread to the worker. If we were to use a `ParameterizedThreadStart` delegate, we'd be responsible for parameter packing and unpacking, typically with ugly casts and whatnot, ourselves. An example is using arrays, here fully expanded in C# 1.0 code:

```
string message = ...;
int repeat = ...;
Thread worker = new Thread(new ParameterizedThreadStart(PrintMessage));
worker.Start(new object[] { message, repeat });
```

The `PrintMessage` method now would have to conform the delegate with its weakly typed parameter:

```
void PrintMessage(object args)
{
    string message = (string)((object[])args)[0];   // Magic indexes
    int repeat = (int)((object[])args)[1];          // Casts and (un)boxing
    ...
```

More About a Thread's Life Cycle

So far, we've seen three states a thread can be in. You should be able to recite at least two of them. First of all, each new `Thread` instance represents a thread in a state where it hasn't been started yet. Upon calling the `Start` method, the thread can enter the running state, where it's executing code. A third state might not be immediately obvious because we haven't talked about it much: A thread can be waiting for some operation to be completed, which is often referred to as being blocked.

BLOCKING IS HARD

True blocking of threads is quite uncommon in the world of managed code. Because of the deep support for COM interoperability, the managed runtime has to make sure that threads can continue to dispatch messages required by the COM runtime. We don't have the room to explain all the intricacies of this here, but suffice to say a thread being blocked can be quite an overstatement in the context of managed code. However, it is the case that certain operations that deal with I/O can appear as blocking the thread waiting for the operation to complete. Recall, though, that the CLR ultimately manages a lot of the thread's behavior and is always free to create certain illusions to managed code running. This is just some manifestation of the powerful concept of layering and abstraction.

Besides those states that are pretty much under the control of the developer, a bunch of other internal states exist that are managed by the runtime. We don't talk much about them because they're merely implementation details. One that should sound familiar is the suspended state, where the CLR has decided a thread cannot continue to execute managed code because a garbage collection has to take place. Because such a collection requires patching up references because of objects moving around, it is unsafe for threads to continue running while memory is changing underneath them. This is just one example where the runtime enforces its own policy about thread life cycles that goes beyond what the operating system natively knows about.

Let's ignore the internal states and move on to the ones that can be influenced directly by writing code against the Thread application programming interface (API).

How to Stop a Thread

A logical question is how to stop a thread. There are a number of ways to do so, but the most convenient one by far is to let the thread exit by itself. That is, when the thread returns from its entry-point method (which is what gets passed by means of a delegate), it ultimately dies. This is merely a sketch of the managed story for threads because the CLR performs cleanup work after a thread quits. In case of thread pool threads, which are covered in the "Thread Pools" section, the underlying native thread doesn't necessarily die; instead, it can be returned to the pool to run other work in the future.

Letting a thread die by natural causes (that is, exiting from its entry-point method) is by far the most humane thing to do. This also means that to stop a thread it's a good practice to make a thread check for some "request to stop" flag and let it perform necessary cleanup by itself, granting the stop request as soon as it sees fit. An example of this common technique is shown here:

```
var stopped = false;

var clock = new Thread(() =>
{
    while (!stopped)
    {
        Console.WriteLine("Tick - " + DateTime.Now);
        Thread.Sleep(1000);
    }
});

clock.Start();

Console.WriteLine("Press ENTER to stop the clock...");
Console.ReadLine();

stopped = true;
clock.Join();
```

There's quite a bit of magic waiting to be explained. What should be well understood by now is the creation of a new thread, here using a lambda expression for syntactical convenience. Also, the closure over the stopped variable creates a piece of shared state that will be read by the thread to check for a request to stop doing work.

Inside the thread's logic, we use Thread.Sleep to suspend the thread for a specified time, which is passed in milliseconds. As a result, the thread prints a time message every 1 second.

DRIFTING TIMERS

This is a bad way to create a timer because the 1,000 milliseconds is not a firm number that can always be granted by the operating system. Because it might take several more milliseconds to see the thread being resumed, and because the thread itself is doing nontrivial work (that is, a WriteLine call) that takes time, too, we can and will see the timer drifting over time.

A much better way to build this kind of clock is by using specialized timers, one of which is defined in System.Threading and appropriately called Timer. Although the interval might not be granted precisely (because the underlying operating system is not a real-time one), drift is being taken care of. For our explanation of stopping a thread, this sample is fine.

When the main thread decides the block thread is no longer needed and can stop doing its duties, it sets the stopped flag to true. At some point in the future, the clock thread will pick this up and quit the loop, causing it to stop. To wait for this to happen, the main thread calls Join on the clock thread. As a result, the main thread gets blocked until the clock thread quits. Figure 29.6 shows the life cycle of both threads.

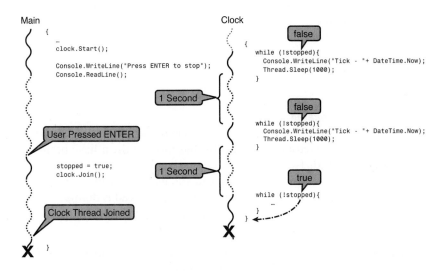

FIGURE 29.6   Threads waiting, sleeping, and joining.

In the "Synchronization Primitives" section you learn how events (not as in "C# event" but as in "some synchronization primitive") can be used to block and wake up a thread in an imperative manner.

NEVER ABORT THREADS

Let's try to be crystal clear about this: Although the Thread class has an instance method called Abort, you should never use it. (I was tempted to write "unless..." but was able to resist.) But why is this?

First, the behavior of Abort should be explained. Upon calling Abort, the CLR will throw a ThreadAbortException in the target thread. This is often referred to as an asynchronous exception because it can occur at any point in the target thread. Every chance the CLR sees to throw the exception can be used (for example, before any method call is made; yes, even on a nop instruction).

Although this all seems fine, lots of bad things can happen (more than I care to list here). In short, because of the possibility of dealing with corrupt state, give up on the application domain that ran the thread being aborted. Instead, to stop a thread, make sure you can do so in a cooperative manner using a flag or some other technique.

Waiting for a Thread to Complete

As you can see from Figure 29.6, it's possible for the main thread to be waiting a while for the join to occur because the other thread can't immediately grant the stop request. In this particular case, it can take up to a second for the clock thread to wake up, observe the stopped flag being set, break from the loop, and ultimately quit the thread's method.

We could also use a Join overload that accepts a timeout duration, which returns a Boolean to indicate whether the thread joined within the timeframe allotted. In some cases, such a strategy is worthwhile (for example, to interleave some useful work with waits for other threads to terminate):

```
while (!clock.Join(250))
    Console.WriteLine("Waiting for clock to stop...");
```

Why Suspend and Resume Are Deprecated

Besides start and stop, one would expect to find other life cycle management methods on the Thread class. In fact, some such methods indeed exist, but most of them have been deprecated or their use is discouraged. Two particular ones are Suspend and Resume. The reason for the deprecation (as early as .NET 2.0) of Suspend and Resume lies in the inability for code requesting a thread's suspension to know what that target thread is doing. Because of this, one could easily deadlock the entire program in a variety of ways. Such bugs are notoriously hard to track down and resolve.

In short, never use Suspend or Resume on threads. Instead, to synchronize threads, use primitives such as events, mutexes, semaphores, monitors, and so on (as discussed later in this chapter; see the section titled "Synchronization Primitives").

Yielding to Others

When a thread has run out of juice, it can voluntarily yield its turn for code execution to others. This is most likely the closest you can get to native thread control from the .NET Framework, because this function corresponds closely to an equivalent Win32 API with the same purpose.

As you can guess, the method to realize a yield is called Yield. Like most methods for threading, it's a static method that applies to the current thread. In other words, you can yield your own turn to execute code but not some other thread's:

```
// Have done some work, but can take a nap now...
Thread.Yield();
// At some point, we'll be scheduled again and end up here...
```

When a yield operation occurs, another thread that's ready to execute will be picked by the operating system scheduler to run. It should be emphasized that yielding is an act that's carried out explicitly by a thread.

Threads can be switched out in favor of others for multiple reasons that are beyond the direct control of the thread. For example, a thread can become blocked waiting for I/O to complete, or a thread's quantum can be expired. Context switches as a result of such situations are under the control of the OS scheduler directly (although one can argue that issuing an I/O operation is more or less "asking" to be scheduled away in case of the occurrence of blocking).

COOPERATIVE SCHEDULING

Yielding is a weak form of cooperative scheduling. Today's common operating systems employ preemptive scheduling to switch out a thread if the thread's quantum expires. The operating system scheduler plays the role of a big brother that's watching everything that happens on the system and always has the power, by piggybacking on clock interrupts, to switch between threads.

Prior to preemptive scheduling, applications had to be well behaved to yield execution time to one another in an explicit manner. It goes without saying that relying on the kindness of others is not evident. More often than not, a single program could run away and monopolize the system for itself. That said, some systems still employ cooperative scheduling for good reasons. One example is the SQL Server OS, where the user mode scheduler relies on the cooperation of various parts of the system to avoid blocking and expensive context switching.

Thread.Yield could be argued to be a weak form of cooperative scheduling in that a thread can decide not to use its full quantum, which gets enforced by the OS's preemptive scheduler. Although a thread can yield, it doesn't pose any problem if it doesn't because the preemptive scheduler is there to pause a thread if it has run for long enough.

Interrupting a Blocked Thread

Another life cycle method available for the control of threads is Interrupt, which is an instance method. It can be used to interrupt a thread that's in a so-called WaitSleepJoin state. This state characterized being blocked because of a wait due to the use of the lock keyword (or the underlying Monitor class), a thread sleep, or the use of the Join method discussed before.

When calling Interrupt on a thread that's currently in any of the aforementioned states, a ThreadInterruptedException will occur in the target thread. As usual, if the exception goes unhandled, the target thread will die. Working with this interrupt mechanism therefore requires threads to be prepared to be interrupted, which can work well in a controlled environment.

As with the Abort method, the occurrence of an exception in a target thread at some unexpected point of execution is quite unnatural. Personally, I use Interrupt rarely. If its goal is to wake up threads from a blocked state to shut down an application in its entirety, gentler techniques are often available. Although we haven't talked about (synchronization) events yet, you should have no trouble understanding that waking up a thread that's waiting for an event can be accomplished by signaling that event. However, a signal typically indicates a resource being available for use, which won't be the case if the event is signaled simply to unblock the thread:

```
sharedFile.WaitOne();  // See later for a discussion of WaitOne.
// When some thread sets the sharedFile event, we'll execute this code.
```

A similar example could be given using the lock keyword. Possible ways to discover why the event was signaled include a check for some "stopping" flag (that's set before signaling the event in case of setting the event to unblock the thread) or the use of multiple events and the WaitAny construct (discussed in the section, "Synchronization Primitives"). In short, Interrupt has its use (although rather seldom).

Managed Thread Characteristics

Being layered on top of native threads, managed threads are in some sense richer than just native threads. For example, the state a managed thread can be in introduces a number of managed code–specific states, such as WaitSleepJoin discussed in the previous section. Besides those differences, a whole lot of properties on Thread reveal a lot of useful information about threads. Some of those thread settings can also be set to control their behavior.

Background Versus Foreground

A first useful property of managed threads is whether they are foreground threads or background threads. The difference between both concepts is minimal. The only altered behavior of a background thread is that it won't keep the process from being terminated after all foreground threads have quit. In other words, a foreground thread can keep a process alive until it exits, whereas a background thread can't. For example, consider the following fragment of code where two threads are running, one of which has been configured as a background thread. The other thread uses the default setting for IsBackground, which is set to false:

```
static void Main()
{
    var t1 = new Thread(() =>
    {
        for (int i = 0; i < 10; i++)
        {
            Console.WriteLine("Background says {0}", i);
            Thread.Sleep(500);
        }
    }) { IsBackground = true };

    var t2 = new Thread(() =>
    {
        for (int i = 0; i < 10; i++)
        {
            Console.WriteLine("Foreground says {0}", i);
            Thread.Sleep(100);
        }
    });

    t1.Start();
    t2.Start();
}
```

This code prints all the messages from the foreground thread, which is keeping the process alive. However, when the foreground thread completes in about 1 second, the background thread won't have a chance to execute further because the sole thread that kept the process alive has exited.

Notice there are three threads in this example: the two that have been created using our code, and one for the main thread. Can you infer whether the main thread is foreground or background? Observe how the Main method can finish without taking down the process. Why is that? Because some foreground thread keeps the process alive.

What happens if the main thread is still going but all other threads in the program have finished? Clearly, you don't want your program's main thread to be terminated abruptly because some of your other threads have finished their duties. In other words, the main thread needs to keep the process alive as well, having a chance to reach its end. That's exactly what it means to be a foreground thread:

```
static void Main(string[] args)
{
    // Prints false
    Console.WriteLine(Thread.CurrentThread.IsBackground);
}
```

Typically, background threads are used to monitor the state of some component or other process. Such activities don't need to keep the program alive and are typically just meant to support the rest of the program. Marking such threads as background is a good practice.

You learn later, in the "Thread Pools" section, that thread pool threads are background threads. Similarly, advanced scenarios where native code creates threads will also cause them to be marked as background threads right from the start. Concerning exception behavior, no difference exists between background and foreground threads: Unhandled exceptions in either of them terminate the entire process. We cover exceptions in the "Dealing with Exceptions" section.

Giving Threads a Name

Debugging applications with a lot of threads can be a painful undertaking, especially if a lot of those threads are doing similar activities (for instance, processing user requests coming in from the network). Giving threads a friendly name definitely helps you see the forest for the trees. For this purpose, the string-valued Name property can be used:

```
var monitor1 = new Thread(() =>
{
    while (true)
    {
        Console.WriteLine("Monitor 1 heartbeat");
        // Do something more useful every second...
        Thread.Sleep(1000);
    }
}) { IsBackground = true, Name = "Monitoring thread 1" };

// ...
monitor1.Start();

// Prevent the main thread from exiting for the sample...
Console.ReadLine();
```

The preceding example shows how to tag the monitoring thread with a friendly name. This name shows up in the Threads window in Visual Studio, as shown in Figure 29.7. The additional threads that show up in this display are due to the use of the Visual Studio hosting process for debugging. Feel free to compare the outcome with and without the hosting process enabled. To disable the hosting process, see the project properties Debug tab.

Also notice how the code window marks where a thread currently is by using a gray background. In this particular snapshot of the process execution, one of the monitoring threads is in the Thread.Sleep call, as indicated in gray.

To make threads more explicit in the debugger, you can right-click anywhere in the Threads window and enable the Show Threads in Source option. Figure 29.8 shows threads being identified in the source by a threads icon in the margin.

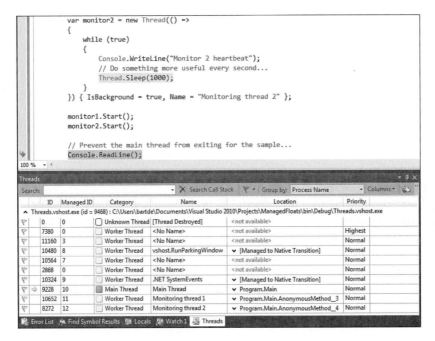

```
            var monitor2 = new Thread(() =>
            {
                while (true)
                {
                    Console.WriteLine("Monitor 2 heartbeat");
                    // Do something more useful every second...
                    Thread.Sleep(1000);
                }
            }) { IsBackground = true, Name = "Monitoring thread 2" };

            monitor1.Start();
            monitor2.Start();

            // Prevent the main thread from exiting for the sample...
            Console.ReadLine();
```

FIGURE 29.7   Threads with friendly names.

```
            var monitor2 = new Thread(() =>
            {
                while (true)
                {
                    Console.WriteLine("Monitor 2 heartbeat");
                    // Do something more useful every second...
                    Thread.Sleep(1000);
                }
            Thread(s) at Location:
                [10216] Monitoring thread 2 round = true, Name = "Monitoring thread 2" };

            monitor1.Start();
            monitor2.Start();
```

FIGURE 29.8   Thread identification in the code window.

Notice the text of the tooltip accommodating for the plural of *thread*. It's obviously possible for more than one thread to be executing in the same method at the same time. The call stack for both threads may differ in many ways, though. For example, multiple user requests may be executing the same authentication method at the same time, likely with different parameters. To switch focus of the debugger view to a particular thread, double-click the thread's entry in the Threads window. Observe how the Call Stack window (among others) changes to reflect the selected thread's state.

Thread IDs

Threads have multiple identities. Figure 29.7 shows two of those identities: the native thread ID (in the ID column) and the managed thread ID (in the Managed ID column).

The native thread ID is assigned by the operating system and is primarily of interest for hardcore debugging where a mix of managed and native code is executing in an application. Managed thread IDs are under control of the common language runtime and do not vary over time. Using this ID can come in handy for purposes of logging:

```
s_log.WriteLine("{0} @ {1} - Diagnostic message",
                Thread.CurrentThread.ManagedThreadId,
                DateTime.Now);
```

A Quick Look at Threading Apartments

The concept of threading apartments is an inheritance from the (good) old days of COM. We don't detail this aspect of managed threads because it's mostly relevant for users who have to deal with COM components, but illustrate the notion of threading apartments based on some common manifestations of the feature.

Those who've been using .NET for a while might have seen Main entry-point methods with the custom STAThread attribute applied to it, as shown here:

```
class Program
{
    [STAThread]
    static void Main()
    {
        ...
```

In fact, if you create a new Windows Forms project and check out the Program.cs file, you'll see an entry-point declared as shown here. This attribute causes the application to use COM with a single-threaded apartment, which affects COM components.

The same use of the STAThread attribute can be found (albeit with some more effort) for Windows Presentation Foundation (WPF) applications. To do so, enable the Show All Files option in Solution Explorer and look for the App.g.i.cs file in the obj\x86\Debug folder. You might need to build the solution for this file to show up because it get generated by the WPF build system and the XAML compiler. Figure 29.9 shows a WPF application's Main method decorated with the STAThread attribute.

If you try to create a WPF application from scratch, manually creating an Application instance and one or more Window instances, you might forget to specify the attribute on the Main method, resulting in the error shown in Figure 29.10. This error message also reveals why this attribute is required, but further discussion requires a thorough explanation of the COM runtime and its intricacies.

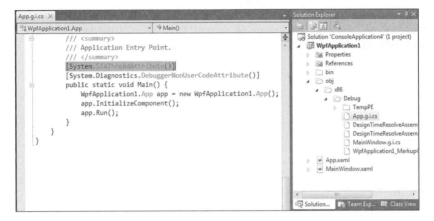

FIGURE 29.9   The STAThread attribute emitted on the Main entry-point method for WPF.

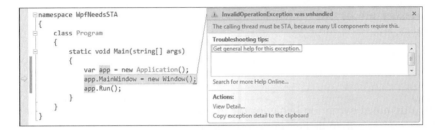

FIGURE 29.10   Many UI components require a single-threaded apartment.

Other than using the STAThread and MTAThread attributes on entry-point methods, you can also specify the apartment state using the SetApartmentState method on a Thread instance. For further information, consult the MSDN documentation.

Dealing with Exceptions

Unhandled exceptions occurring on any thread cause the application to be terminated by the common language runtime. Because of this, it's essential to guard your thread entry-point methods against unhandled exceptions if specific types of exceptions are tolerable. For example, threads handling user requests should not be able to take down the entire web or application server unless something really exceptional happens (such as memory corruption, out-of-memory situations, stack overflows, and so on).

This does not imply you should use the "catch-all" technique because this could silence way too many exceptions that could cause damage later during the application's execution (for example, because of broken invariants). In other words, one should know what's safe to catch rather than be lazy. Also, if you decide to put in place a last-resort top-level catch in a thread's entry-point method, it's generally a good idea to put logging in place as well, so you can analyze failure modes you might need to address in a more disciplined way.

The following example illustrates an application that will be terminated after approximately 1 second due to an unhandled exception in some thread. Obviously, the call stack where the exception originates in the failing thread may be much deeper:

```
class Program
{
    static void Main()
    {
        new Thread(() =>
        {
            Thread.Sleep(1000);
            throw new InvalidOperationException("Oops!");
        }).Start();

        while (true)
        {
            Console.Write(".");
            Thread.Sleep(100);
        }
    }
}
```

Prior to .NET 2.0, unhandled exception behavior for threads was quite different. In lieu of terminating the process, an unhandled exception simply resulted in a printout of the exception stack trace on the console. For thread pool threads, the worker thread was simply returned to the pool. Regular threads simply terminated without taking down the rest of the process. Finally, exceptions on the finalizer thread also got silently muted.

If an application needs to restore the .NET 1.0 and 1.1 behavior for compatibility reasons, you can add a setting to the application configuration file. This should be a last-resort option, for use while porting applications to .NET 2.0 or later:

```
<legacyUnhandledExceptionPolicy enabled="1"/>
```

Thread-Specific State

We already know that each thread has its own call stack; hence, stack-allocated data is state-specific to a particular thread (for example, local variables and parameters that are being passed to methods). In the "Synchronization Primitives" section we discuss how to share state between threads, preferably in a safe manner. For now, let's focus on other forms of thread-specific state.

The ThreadStatic Attribute

Static state is isolated on a per-application domain basis. Because multiple threads can be executing in the same application domain, such static state is shared across those threads. This behavior can be changed by applying the ThreadStatic attribute to a static field. First, let's show multiple threads accessing a static field without marking it as thread specific:

```
class Program
{
    static int s_i;

    static void Main()
    {
        new Thread(() =>
        {
            while (true)
            {
                s_i++;
            }
        }).Start();

        while (true)
        {
            Thread.Sleep(1000);
            Console.WriteLine(s_i);
        }
    }
}
```

In this program, the main thread acts as a reader while the other thread acts as a writer and updates the static field. It's evident that both operate on the same state because the printed value of s_i varies every time the main thread polls it.

THE POWER OF ESTIMATING

Although the preceding example is trivial, it's a good exercise to learn making estimates of processing power. On my PC, the deltas between consecutive s_i values that get printed to the console are about 700 million. Although this reflects the number of increment operations done in 1 second, don't forget about the loop's cost itself. Feel free to do some hardcore debugging on a fragment as simple as the one shown and analyze the generated native code. Doing so provides good insights in Just-in-Time (JIT) compilation and more.

By marking the s_i static field as ThreadStatic, we see that each thread has its own copy of the field. Because of this, you won't see the increments made by the writer (to its own copy). Therefore, the reader will print zero values all the time:

```
class Program
{
    [ThreadStatic]
    static int s_i;
```

```
static void Main()
{
    new Thread(() =>
    {
        while (true)
        {
            s_i++;
        }
    }).Start();

    while (true)
    {
        Thread.Sleep(1000);
        Console.WriteLine(s_i);
    }
}
}
```

The ThreadStatic attribute comes in handy when you want to avoid static state being shared across threads (for example, if multiple workers need to have their own copy of this state).

One caveat should be pointed out: Initialization of a field marked as thread static is not a good idea because the initialization code that assigns to the field lives in the (static) class constructor, which runs only once per application domain. The following code prints 42 and 0 because the static constructor for the class was executed on the main thread. The same initialization code wasn't run for the other thread.

```
class Program
{
    [ThreadStatic]
    static int s_i = 42;

    static void Main()
    {
        Console.WriteLine(s_i);                            // Prints 42 :-)
        new Thread(() => Console.WriteLine(s_i)).Start();  // Prints 0   :-(
        Console.ReadLine();
    }
}
```

Instead of relying on initialization code, which behaves in a flaky manner (as shown here), you should rely on the default value being set to the static field. Code can check against this value to perform one-time initialization. An example of a use of thread-static fields I've used recently is the allocation of thread-specific loggers. In such a case, synchronization is unnecessary when doing diagnostic logging because each thread gets its dedicated logger instance:

```csharp
class Program
{
    [ThreadStatic]
    static TextWriter s_logger;

    static void Main()
    {
        new Thread(() =>
        {
            EnsureLog();

            // Some thread that's responsible for some I/O operation.
            // At various times, it writes to the log, as shown here:
            s_logger.WriteLine("{0} - Performed some action", DateTime.Now);

            // Much more code is executed on this thread...
        }) { Name = "Lazy writer" }
        .Start();

        // Others threads could be created, each of which has to call
        // the EnsureLog method to have its s_logger field set up properly.
    }

    static void EnsureLog()
    {
        string name = Thread.CurrentThread.Name
            ?? Thread.CurrentThread.ManagedThreadId.ToString();

        // More complicated initialization logic could be dreamed up.
        // What matters is the fact this method will run multiple times
        // on different threads, initializing that thread's logger.
        s_logger = File.CreateText(name + ".log");
    }
}
```

Notice the use of the Name property of the current thread to initialize the log filename. From the code in Main, it might not be obvious this value gets set before the thread can see it. After all, we're using an object initializer that sets the thread's Name before the code (here specified in the lambda expression body) is run due to the call to Start. Once more, this reflects the nature of delegates in facilitating lazy execution of code in places other than where it's specified.

The ThreadLocal<T> Class

Closely related to the Lazy<T> class, the ThreadLocal<T> class was introduced in .NET 4. Essentially, this type addresses the shortcomings of the ThreadStatic attribute when initialization code is required for the per-thread state. The ThreadLocal<T> class acts as a factory for per-thread state, using a Func<T> delegate that's invoked once per thread upon calling the Value property. This pattern should be familiar; after all, the same pattern is used for Lazy<T>.

For instance, consider the code example from the previous section. Rewriting this example using the ThreadLocal<T> type (with T substituted for TextWriter) results in the following code:

```
class Program
{
    static void Main()
    {
        new Thread(() =>
        {
            // Some thread that's responsible for some I/O operation.
            // At various times, it writes to the log, as shown here:
            s_log.Value.WriteLine("{0} - Performed some action", DateTime.Now);

            // Much more code is executed on this thread...
        }) { Name = "Lazy writer" }
        .Start();

        // Others threads could be created
        Console.ReadLine();
    }

    static ThreadLocal<TextWriter> s_log = new ThreadLocal<TextWriter>(() =>
    {
        string name = Thread.CurrentThread.Name
            ?? Thread.CurrentThread.ManagedThreadId.ToString();

        // More complicated initialization logic could be dreamed up.
        // What matters is the fact this method will run multiple times
        // on different threads, initializing that thread's logger.
        return File.CreateText(name + ".log");
    });
}
```

Two key differences are the absence of the ThreadStatic attribute on the s_log field and the use of the Value property to retrieve the thread-local state. In addition, an IsValueCreated property exists to check whether the initialization delegate (or factory, if you like) has been run for the current thread already. This, too, follows the pattern seen on Lazy<T> before.

One advantage of the ThreadLocal<T> type is the ability to use it without the need for fields to tag the ThreadLocal attribute to. This proves particularly useful if you don't have control over such fields yourself (for example, when using closures). As you learned during our discussion of delegates, closures over local variables result in fields created on a "display class," which is totally under the control of the compiler. For example, look at the following code. To remind you about closures, Figure 29.11 shows the result of compiling this example.

```
static void Main()
{
    int i = 0;
    new Thread(() =>
    {
        while (true)
            i++;
    }).Start();

    while (true)
    {
        Thread.Sleep(1000);
        Console.WriteLine(i);
    }
}
```

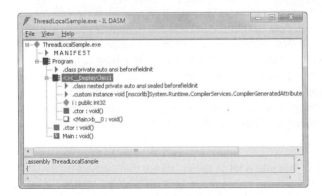

FIGURE 29.11   A closure over local variable i results in a field.

This is pretty much the same code as our multithreaded reader/writer counter example shown before, the sole difference being the use of a local variable for the counter rather than using a field ourselves. Because there's no syntactical way in C# to apply attributes to local variables, we can't use ThreadStatic here. In other words, the field generated due to the closure over the local variable cannot be influenced by the user.

However, `ThreadLocal<T>` can be used without any problem. As the use of lambda expressions (and hence closures) becomes more common, this is a great gift brought to us in .NET 4. In Chapter 30, you see uses of other .NET 4 constructs, such as `Parallel.For`, where the use of lambdas is very convenient. The introduction of those made the need for a `ThreadLocal<T>` construct more pressing. The following code shows how to make the counter variable thread local, just as we did before for the similar example with the `ThreadStatic` attribute. Recall this changes the behavior of the code, causing the reader to print its own private copy of the i, always set zero:

```
static void Main()
{
    var i = new ThreadLocal<int>();
    new Thread(() =>
    {
        while (true)
            i.Value++;
    }).Start();

    while (true)
    {
        Thread.Sleep(1000);
        Console.WriteLine(i.Value);
    }
}
```

A WORD ON THREAD SAFETY

Thus far, we haven't mentioned thread safety (something we discuss more fully as we cover synchronization primitives later in this chapter). In particular, we avoided a discussion about thread safety in the context of both our counter examples by having only one writer thread. However, if multiple parties were to attempt to write to a shared (that is, nonthread-local) counter, we'd need to stand still and think about ensuring thread safety. In the last counter example using `ThreadLocal<T>`, a pretty clear multithreading issue exists if there would be multiple writers. Take a look at the following line of code:

```
i.Value++;
```

This seemingly innocent line of code does quite a lot of things, things that cause the increment operation not to be atomic. First, the `Value` property is read using a getter call. Then the local copy of the retrieved value is incremented. Finally, the incremented value is assigned by using the `Value` setter. This is far from thread safe if multiple writers are updating the counter. More on this in a moment.

Thread-Local Storage

We've kept the "most native" way of establishing thread-local state for last because `ThreadStatic` and `ThreadLocal<T>` are the recommended ways to achieve this effect. Nonetheless, there is a third way to do thread-local storage.

The managed code abstraction that sits the closest to operating system primitives for thread-local storage is known as *data slots*. Management of data slots is done in a way that feels quite native, due to the `Allocate`/`Free` methods that are used:

```
var slot = Thread.AllocateNamedDataSlot("logger");

// Use the slot throughout the program with GetData and SetData calls.

Thread.FreeNamedDataSlot("logger");
```

As a result of calling `AllocateNamedDataSlot`, we get a `LocalDataStoreSlot` object that acts as a handle to access the data contained in the slot. This is achieved by means of the static `GetData` and `SetData` methods on the `Thread` class. Instead of holding on to the slot object, it can also be retrieved by means of its name:

```
// Initialization code.
var slot = Thread.AllocateNamedDataSlot("logger");
Thread.SetData(slot, new Logger() /* type definition omitted for brevity */);
```

Assuming the slot was allocated here, we can now use the `GetData` method to obtain the logger object. Each thread will have its own slot (requiring per-thread initialization as shown earlier), resulting in a separate logger per thread. This technique is typically used to avoid synchronization code for fundamental activities such as logging:

```
var slot = Thread.GetNamedDataSlot("logger");
var logger = (Logger)Thread.GetData(slot);
logger.WriteLine("Diagnostic message");
```

With this, we conclude our discussion of techniques that can be used to allocate per-thread state.

SHALLOW VERSUS DEEP

Beware of a false sense of security when using thread-local storage techniques. It's not because you're differentiating state on a per-thread basis (for example, to avoid synchronization issues) that all the associated state is partitioned as well.

For example, you might have multiple threads, each of which has its own logger object. But if those logger instances happen to contain a reference to the same underlying resource (by means of aliasing of object references), you're still in trouble. All you've done is segregated state on a shallow basis (such as the top-level logger), forgetting about the deep object graph underneath.

Moral of the story: Beware of any kind of shared state. If multiple parties need to access that state, you better read up on synchronization primitives.

Essential Threading Debugging Techniques

Debugging multithreaded programs can be a true challenge. After all, different parts of the program are running simultaneously, each of which can be changing state. The lack of proper synchronization around shared resources will make things go really bad, posing a true debugging challenge.

When Threads Are Frozen

Debuggers pause a program's threads when you're inspecting program state from the debugger, and resuming the program unfreezes all threads again. The notion of resuming should be understood in the broadest sense possible, including single-stepping (using F10). To illustrate this effect, consider the following piece of code:

```
class Program
{
    static void Main()
    {
        // Background thread.
        new Thread(() =>
        {
            while (true)
            {
                Thread.Sleep(30);
                Console.WriteLine("{0} - {1:hh:mm:ss:fff}",
                            Thread.CurrentThread.ManagedThreadId,
                            DateTime.Now);
            }
        }).Start();

        // Main thread's code.
        while (true)
        {
            Thread.Sleep(100);
            Console.WriteLine("{0} - {1:hh:mm:ss:fff}",
                        Thread.CurrentThread.ManagedThreadId,
                        DateTime.Now);
        }
    }
}
```

Set a breakpoint on the main thread's Console.WriteLine call. By the time we hit this breakpoint, the background thread will (likely) have printed some messages already. Once you're broken in the debugger, notice how all threads have been frozen. The background thread doesn't get a chance to make progress at this point. This is a good thing. Think about what would happen when you're analyzing state in the debugger while other threads can still modify things.

To see the effect of resuming execution, press F10 to single-step from the point where we hit the breakpoint. This moves the main thread to the closing curly brace on its `for` loop. Notice, though, the background thread also got unfrozen, and there's a chance (because you're dealing with timing, there are no certainties) the background thread made progress while execution was resumed for the very short time it took to single-step over the `Console.WriteLine` call. Figure 29.12 shows this effect, where it's clear the background thread made progress during the single-stepping we've done.

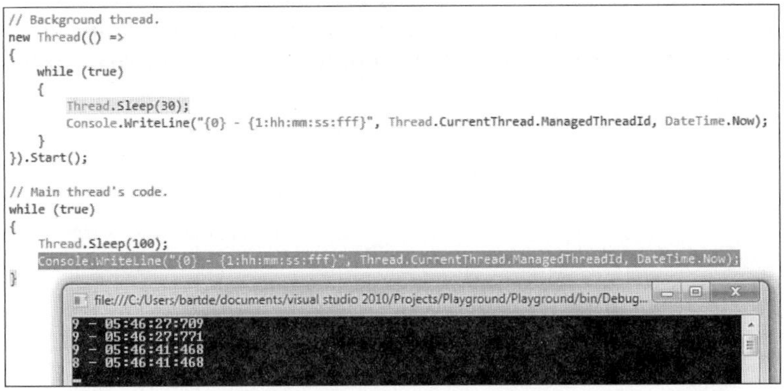

```
// Background thread.
new Thread(() =>
{
    while (true)
    {
        Thread.Sleep(30);
        Console.WriteLine("{0} - {1:hh:mm:ss:fff}", Thread.CurrentThread.ManagedThreadId, DateTime.Now);
    }
}).Start();

// Main thread's code.
while (true)
{
    Thread.Sleep(100);
    Console.WriteLine("{0} - {1:hh:mm:ss:fff}", Thread.CurrentThread.ManagedThreadId, DateTime.Now);
}
```

```
file:///C:/Users/bartde/documents/visual studio 2010/Projects/Playground/Playground/bin/Debug...
9 - 05:46:27:709
9 - 05:46:27:771
9 - 05:46:41:468
8 - 05:46:41:468
```

FIGURE 29.12   Analyzing debugger behavior with regard to thread execution.

Why do I consider this to clearly be the case? Just look at the time deltas in the output for the thread with ID 9. From this, you can see that I stayed in the debugger for about 14 seconds after hitting the breakpoint. During that time, the background thread didn't make any progress. However, upon hitting F10, this background thread had a chance to run and printed another message. This all happened while the debugger was waiting for the main thread (with ID 8) to complete the single-stepping, which took us beyond the `Console.WriteLine` call, explaining the last message.

Freeze and Thaw

While debugging multithreaded issues, you often want to do some "what if" analysis to get to the bottom of the observed behavior. Suppose, for example, that a whole bunch of threads are dealing with the same underlying resource and you observe that resource going bad one way or another. To pinpoint the source of the problem, you want to narrow down the problem to the thread that's improperly doing its synchronization duties.

Although there's no perfect way to do such analysis, I want to point out some tools that can help. One is the debugger's capability to freeze and thaw threads. When you freeze a thread, it remains suspended until you issue the thaw command on the thread, which enables you to eliminate a thread from the global picture you're trying to get of the misbehaving program. If the problem you're debugging suddenly disappears, that can be a pretty good indication of the frozen thread being at fault.

Another reason to freeze a thread is to reduce debugging noise. For example, if you have some thread sitting around to perform periodic maintenance activities, you might want to freeze that thread temporarily while you're performing your analysis. This is especially true if you've set a breakpoint in code that's run by multiple threads but you want to break into the debugger only when a relevant thread hits that code path. Although alternative techniques exist (for example, using a conditional breakpoint based on the thread ID property), the use of freeze and thaw can be appropriate here.

Figure 29.13 shows the use of the Freeze option from the context menu in the Threads window. Using the example from the previous section, we're about to freeze the thread that prints a message every 30 milliseconds. Pressing F10 to single-step the main thread will no longer permit the background thread from making progress, as long as Thaw isn't used on it to "unfreeze" it.

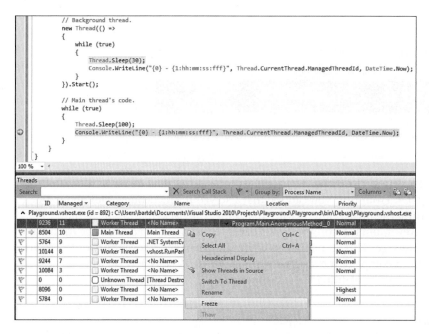

FIGURE 29.13   Freeze and Thaw options for a thread.

Yet another scenario is when you want to freeze a thread that will only make matters worse. Basically, you might want to prevent the program from accepting more work that causes more concurrency, thus making the analysis of program state harder. As usual, debugging a minimum repro of an issue is much more convenient than having to dissect a more complex problem state—for example, due to many concurrent users in the system. An example of this scenario is to block the thread that runs a procedure to receive work, such as a listener, to accept incoming calls from the network. Freezing that thread prevents more request workers (typically run on separate threads) from entering the picture.

Thread Pools

Creation of new threads is a fairly expensive operation. The reason for this goes all the way down to the operating system tasks that have to be performed to make the creation of a new thread happen. This includes the allocation of the thread's stack and various data structures (such as KTHREAD at the kernel mode level) to maintain the thread's state. Also, the thread needs to become eligible for scheduling, requiring the scheduler database to be updated to gain knowledge about the thread's existence.

KERNEL MODE VERSUS USER MODE

Threads are the unit of code execution on the Windows operating system. This means that threads get scheduled and can deal with synchronization. Because the concept of preemptive scheduling requires low-level support from the hardware (based on timer-based interrupts and whatnot), it shouldn't come as a surprise that threads are kernel-mode constructs. After all, the kernel's role is to provide an abstraction over the hardware and mimic a machine that can run lots of stuff in parallel, even though the hardware might have limited parallelism.

The cost of the kernel being involved in the creation of threads has resulted in the creation of abstractions higher up the software stack. A good example includes the concept of user mode scheduling (UMS) used by Microsoft's SQL Server to reduce context switching between threads. Windows 7 also includes a UMS mechanism.

Conceptually, such UMS mechanisms play pretty much the same abstraction role the kernel plays for the hardware. The kernel abstracts away certain limitations of the hardware: Although you might have only a handful of processor cores, it enables you to run thousands of threads. User mode schedulers, however, limit the parallelism created at the kernel level (to reduce costs associated with it), while allowing applications to create much more work under the impression it can and will be run concurrently.

Essentially, the layered cake formed by the user mode, kernel mode, virtualization technologies (such as Hyper-V's hypervisor), and hardware is nothing but a fancy multiplexing organization. Higher layers of the stack provide the impression that lower layers have more capabilities than they really have.

.NET's thread pool could be seen as a user mode scheduler. It accepts units of work that will be multiplexed onto real operating system threads, the number of which is controlled to reduce costs. Nothing beyond some engineering challenges prevents the common language runtime from leveraging things such as Windows 7's UMS in the future.

Whenever the creation of a resource is deemed expensive, the technique of pooling quickly enters the picture. Another example outside the realm of threading is the use of a connection pool to a database server, reducing the cost that would result from going over the network to set up a connection with the server.

The concept of a resource pool involves pre-allocating a set of resources that will be reused throughout an application's lifetime. This pool of resources can grow or shrink dynamically based on demand of resources.

.NET's Thread Pool

In the case of threading, pools have been created to reuse operating system threads. This observation holds at different levels; the operating system itself has this notion for various of its components. Of more interest to us is the concept of the .NET thread pool.

Typical use of the thread pool is to deal with relatively short-lived work items that need to execute in the background. For example, suppose you got a user request on a web service coming in. On the Web, you shouldn't be taking tens of seconds to provide a response for a web request. Users simply won't buy it and will navigate away from your website. In other words, the logic to provide a response for the user's request should be relatively short-lived. It should also be clear that processing the user request shouldn't prevent the server from accepting new requests in the meantime. In other words, you need to introduce concurrency for multiple simultaneous requests.

Adding up the two constraints posed by the preceding example, we should have each request run in parallel, but each such request should take only a small amount of time. Spawning a whole new thread to handle the request would be inefficient. There's not just the cost of creating and disposing (upon its completion) of the thread. Overall stress put on the system should be accounted for as well. To reduce the impact of thread creation, use of the thread pool is recommended in such a scenario.

In summary, thread pools typically come in handy when relatively short units of work have to be run, reusing physical operating system threads. Another good indicator for the use of thread pools is when the amount of work to be carried out is dependent on dynamic factors (for example, based on requests coming in to a web server).

Figure 29.14 shows the .NET thread pool in a slightly simplified manner.

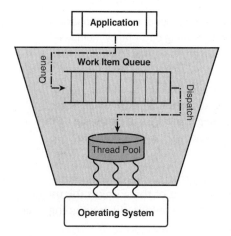

FIGURE 29.14   The .NET thread pool multiplexes work items onto system threads.

The `QueueUserWorkItem` Method

An exhaustive coverage of the ins and outs of the .NET thread pool is beyond the scope of this book. In what follows, we simply consider it to be a service provided by the runtime that allocates a number of threads within certain (configurable) boundaries.

Work items in the form of delegates are queued by library and application code to be executed sometime in the future, asynchronously from the caller's point of view. The method that enables this queuing is called `QueueUserWorkItem` and lives on the `ThreadPool` class in `System.Threading`. Both overloads accept a `WaitCallback` delegate object, optionally specifying a piece of state to be passed between the caller and the work item. As explained earlier in this chapter, use of such a state object has become largely redundant thanks to the introduction of closures in C# 2.0.

An example of queuing work is shown here. Notice the call to `ReadLine` to prevent the program from quitting prematurely. Thread pool threads don't keep the process alive; they are background threads, as explained earlier in this chapter:

```
static void Main()
{
    ThreadPool.QueueUserWorkItem(_ /* state object we don't care about */ =>
    {
        Console.WriteLine("Work item executed.");
    });

    Console.ReadLine();
}
```

Basically, there isn't much more to the thread pool's usage than what is shown here. Instead of creating a new thread, just use `QueueUserWorkItem` instead. To illustrate the huge difference in terms of the number of threads required to execute work items, let's write a simple test:

```
static void Main()
{
    Console.Write("Press ENTER to start... ");
    Console.ReadLine();

    Console.WriteLine("Scheduling work...");
    for (int i = 0; i < 1000; i++)
    {
        ThreadPool.QueueUserWorkItem(_ =>
        {
            Thread.Sleep(100);
        });
    }
}
```

```
    }

    Console.ReadLine();
}
```

This piece of code executes 1,000 units of work, each of which simply performs a sleep of one tenth of a second. Don't forget the act of scheduling is asynchronous, so we won't see the program block until all work is carried out.

Figure 29.15 reveals how many threads are running in the process (from the operating system's point of view, that is). The number can vary slightly, but you should definitely see far fewer than 1,000 threads being run.

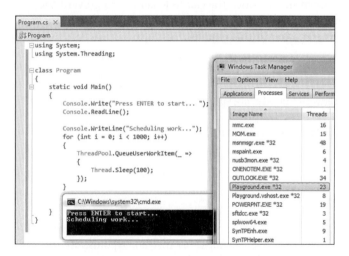

FIGURE 29.15   The thread pool's use of threads.

The minimum and maximum number of threads used by the thread pool can be tweaked through various methods on the ThreadPool class. We won't elaborate on this, and instead I refer you to the MSDN documentation for more information (look for SetMinThreads and SetMaxThreads).

Repeat the exercise, substituting the QueueUserWorkItem call for the code to create and start a new thread. This time, you see many more threads being allocated:

```
new Thread(_ =>
{
    Thread.Sleep(100);
}).Start();
```

You can also play with the sleep duration to emphasize the difference. The higher you make this number, the more visible the difference will be in Task Manager. Why is this? In case of raw use of thread objects, we allocate as many threads as we can cope with, each of which will be blocked for the sleep duration. Literally thousands of threads can be sleeping at the same time. When using the thread pool, we're merely blocking the threads from the pool, which are limited in their number. In other words, not all work items get a chance to start sleeping at the same time.

Performance Characteristics

This brings us to another important point: Use of the thread pool reduces the stress put on the operating system, but in doing so the degree of parallelism is reduced. In the example discussed here, quite a difference exists in behavior between use of the thread pool versus use of plain threads. When using the thread pool for our thousand parallel sleeping actions, they are not overlapped because only a limited number of work items is assigned to a physical thread at the same time. As a result, sleeping for 100 milliseconds in parallel will take much longer than 100 milliseconds in total. However, when using plain threads, the thousand sleeps can be going on at the same time, depending on the mood of the operating system scheduler.

Using the CountdownEvent synchronization primitive introduced in .NET 4, we can illustrate this behavior. We discuss such primitives later in the "Synchronization Primitives" section.

```
static void Main()
{
    const int N = 1000;
    var evt = new CountdownEvent(N);

    Console.WriteLine("Scheduling work...");

    var sw = new Stopwatch();
    sw.Start();

    for (int i = 0; i < N; i++)
    {
        new Thread(_ =>
        {
            Thread.Sleep(100);
            evt.Signal();
        }).Start();
    }

    evt.Wait();
    sw.Stop();

    Console.WriteLine(sw.ElapsedMilliseconds);
}
```

What's going on here? The main thread allocates a countdown event that starts with an initial value of 1000. A stopwatch is used to measure the time it will take for this counter to go down to 0. Each of the workers running in parallel (here using plain old threads) performs its sleep first and then signals the counter, which makes it go down with one. The main thread is blocked waiting for the event to drop to the zero state, caused by all workers having signaled the event. Then the stopwatch is stopped and the elapsed time is printed to the console.

If you run this experiment with plain thread-creation calls, the total time for all workers to complete will be around the same order of magnitude as 100 milliseconds. On my machine, the result was about 400 milliseconds. Although this is still four times more than the sleep of each parallel thread, it's not a world of difference. The delta is due to the cost of creating the threads themselves (this takes time, too!), overhead induced by scheduling, and possible competition of our threads with other applications running on the machine at the same time.

But what if you run the code using the thread pool instead? This time it will take much longer for the counter to reach zero because only a limited number of worker threads is sleeping at the same time. Stated otherwise, the sleeps are serialized to some extent. If the maximum number of threads in the pool were to be set to just one, the total time would be no less than 100 seconds (1,000 times 100 milliseconds). When running the test on my machine, it took about 10 seconds to complete all the sleeps. A quick calculation shows that the number of parallel threads performing the work should have been around 10. We sometimes call this number the degree of parallelism.

Figure 29.16 contrasts the use of the thread pool with the use of dedicated threads.

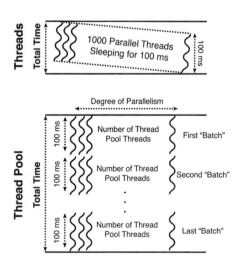

FIGURE 29.16   Effects of the thread pool's degree of parallelism.

Although this behavior might sound undesirable at first, don't forget about the contrived nature of the example shown here. For one thing, relying on firm timing is never a good idea, especially when dealing with concurrency. You're not running on a real-time operating system after all. Second, work items as simple as performing some sleep are not realistic either. In a real application, work items will be processing useful work, such as reading from files or interacting with web services. This typically results in blocking while waiting for resources (for example, I/O) to become available.

What the thread pool is really good at is making sure a potentially unbounded amount of work entered in the system doesn't crash the system. It does so by taking care of the mapping of logical work onto physical workers (in this case, threads). So when you're building some kind of service accepting user requests, consider using the thread pool to be a good citizen for the application, the runtime, the operating system, and the machine as a whole.

ABSTRACTING CONCURRENCY AND SCHEDULING

The framework contains many ways to introduce concurrency. In this section, we've seen two of them: starting "raw" threads and using the thread pool. Plenty of others exist, such as the WPF dispatcher used in UI programming.

But what does concurrency really mean? Concurrency is all about *where* things run. For the thread pool, this is any of the threads in the pool. When using the concept of a dispatcher in WPF or Windows Forms, this is some dedicated thread that pumps window messages.

A related notion is scheduling. This concept is all about the act of adding work to the system, which could give rise to the creation of additional concurrency or the reuse of existing concurrency. For example, a new thread could be started, but when using things such as dispatchers, work will be scheduled on an existing thread.

What would it mean to abstract over both those notions? How could we establish some kind of interface that can be shared across all kinds of schedulers? Let's look at one common piece across all the scheduling mechanisms we've covered thus far. No matter whether we want to run work on a new thread or we want to use the thread pool, we must pass the unit of work (the "work item") around one way or another. For threads, this is done using the ThreadStart delegate, while the ThreadPool's QueueUserWorkItem uses a WaitCallback delegate. Both have a similar signature in fact. If we ignore the state parameter (which is largely redundant due to the existence of closures, as mentioned already), all that remains is pretty much an Action delegate.

The Reactive Extensions for .NET library contains the abstraction of a scheduler based on this observation. IScheduler looks like this (slightly simplified):

```
interface IScheduler
{
    IDisposable Schedule(Action action);
}
```

This interface is really just about receiving work in the form of an action and running it at some point in the future, subject to the implementation's underlying resources (such as a pool of threads). The returned IDisposable is used to cancel out work if it hasn't been started yet.

Beware of Per-Thread State

When using the thread pool, beware of the notion of per-thread state being just what it is: state kept on a per-thread basis. However, because threads are reused across different work items, such state will appear to all the work items that happen to run on that thread. An example to illustrate this behavior is shown here:

```
static void Main()
{
    var state = new ThreadLocal<int>();
    for (int i = 0; i < 100; i++)
    {
        ThreadPool.QueueUserWorkItem(_ =>
        {
            Console.WriteLine("{0} @ {1}",
                state.Value++,
                Thread.CurrentThread.ManagedThreadId
            );
        });
    }

    Console.ReadLine();
}
```

Here, we use the ThreadLocal<T> class introduced in .NET 4 and explained earlier in this chapter. If every scheduled work item were to run on its own thread, we would expect the printed state to be equal to zero every time around. However, because the underlying threads from the pool are getting reused, we see things like this instead:

```
0 @ 5
0 @ 4
0 @ 3
0 @ 6
0 @ 9
1 @ 9
2 @ 9
```

Results vary, but you should see different threads being used and reused to run the work items that have been queued up.

Despite this caveat, thread-local state has its value even when using thread pools. In most cases, people use this technique to reduce the need for synchronization by having a per-thread resource. A good example is logging, having a dedicated logger for each thread. This technique still applies in combination with the thread pool. Because threads are where concurrent execution takes place, having an exclusive resource on a per-thread basis will do the trick. However, logging output of multiple work items will end up in the same log file. So although the physical use of the resource is properly protected, it might not be the right thing to do from a logical point of view. If you truly want each and every work item (for example, corresponding to processing for a user request) to have its own dedicated logger, you have to pass one around through the work item code being scheduled.

Synchronization Primitives

In daily life, there's a lot of concurrency. Everyone is doing his or her own thing at a personal pace. Although this provides absolute freedom, sometimes different parties need to work together to accomplish something. To do so, rules must be established to prevent the participating individuals from stepping on each other's toes.

Examples of this abound. Just think of traffic. Although lots of people can drive vehicles at the same time, traffic signs are put in place to prevent bad things (such as collisions) from happening. Thus, the degree of concurrency of all the parties involved might have to be decreased. For example, a road intersection is a shared resource used for vehicles coming from different directions. To make sure no two conflicting cars share the intersection at the same time, concurrency is reduced by allowing only nonconflicting uses of the resource.

Figure 29.17 shows two uses of a road intersection as a shared resource. This figure contrasts one good use with a bad use. Preventing the bad case requires reducing the amount of concurrent traffic by blocking cars from one direction.

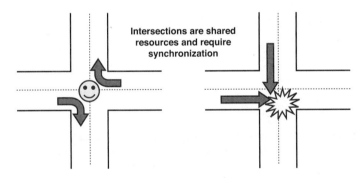

Intersections are shared resources and require synchronization

FIGURE 29.17   Synchronization of shared resource use is critical.

Notice, however, that it might be possible to devise a finer-grained synchronization scheme that still allows for a good amount of concurrency while mishaps are still prevented in all circumstances. This is where the art of synchronization comes in. Surely, prevention of car collisions in an intersection could be done by allowing only one car to cross the intersection at any given time. In other words, we're serializing access to the shared resource, which can be seen as a reduction of the degree of parallelism to one.

However, this slows down traffic immensely and, in fact, unnecessarily. Can't we just make the intersection safe but still allow for a good degree of parallelism? Surely, more intelligent synchronization is possible, as shown in Figure 29.17 on the left. Here two car directions are allowed to be exercised simultaneously, while still being safe. Devising an efficient yet safe use of shared resources is the art of synchronization.

Atomicity (or Lack Thereof) Illustrated

To give a programming-related example of the need for synchronization, let's keep things as simple as we can and take a look at a shared counter. None of the following code should be hard to understand at this point. We simply create and start a new thread to increment the counter repeatedly. In the meantime, the main thread performs its duties, decrementing the same counter value. Finally, we join the incrementing thread (called up) with the main thread and print the result.

```
static void Main()
{
    int n = 0;

    var up = new Thread(() =>
    {
        for (int i = 0; i < 1000000; i++)
            n++;
    });

    up.Start();

    for (int i = 0; i < 1000000; i++)
        n—;

    up.Join();
    Console.WriteLine(n);
}
```

The obvious question is what the preceding code fragment prints. In fact, I don't know, and you shouldn't be able to tell either. Why? Because serious synchronization issues are going on here. Running the code over and over again, you get different values, probably all of which are different from zero. Yet both threads perform an equal number of increments and decrements. What's going on?

To answer this question, we need to analyze how the shared resource is being used. But what's the shared resource in the first place? It's none other than local variable n, which is being "closed over" by the incrementing thread. Through the powers of C# closures, this variable got "hoisted" into a heap-allocated object. It's really as if we wrote a little class containing a single integer field:

```
class Closure
{
    public int n;

    public void ThreadProc()
```

```
    {
        for (int i = 0; i < 1000000; i++)
            this.n = this.n + 1;
    }
}
```

Now we can rewrite the Main method as follows:

```
static void Main()
{
    var c = new Closure();

    var up = new Thread(c.ThreadProc);
    up.Start();

    for (int i = 0; i < 1000000; i++)
        c.n = c.n - 1;

    up.Join();
    Console.WriteLine(n);
}
```

Did you see what went on here? Seemingly simple code, such as n++ and n−, just got turned into the lookup of a field, performing a computation on the obtained value and storing the updated value back into the field. Don't just take my word for it; take a look in ILDASM or .NET Reflector to see this is the case.

Figure 29.18 shows the code that corresponds to the post-increment operation in the second thread. Finding the post-decrement operation's code used in the main thread is left as an exercise but differs only in the use of a subinstruction rather than add.

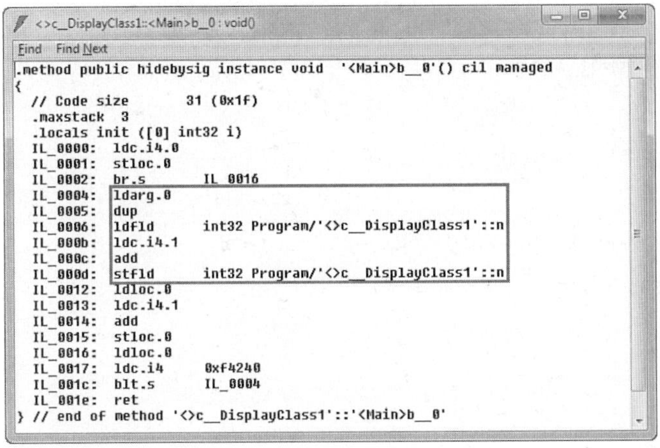

```
 <>c_DisplayClass1::<Main>b_0 : void()

Find   Find Next
.method public hidebysig instance void   '<Main>b_0'() cil managed
{
    // Code size       31 (0x1F)
    .maxstack  3
    .locals init ([0] int32 i)
    IL_0000:  ldc.i4.0
    IL_0001:  stloc.0
    IL_0002:  br.s        IL_0016
    IL_0004:  ldarg.0
    IL_0005:  dup
    IL_0006:  ldfld       int32 Program/'<>c__DisplayClass1'::n
    IL_000b:  ldc.i4.1
    IL_000c:  add
    IL_000d:  stfld       int32 Program/'<>c__DisplayClass1'::n
    IL_0012:  ldloc.0
    IL_0013:  ldc.i4.1
    IL_0014:  add
    IL_0015:  stloc.0
    IL_0016:  ldloc.0
    IL_0017:  ldc.i4      0xF4240
    IL_001c:  blt.s       IL_0004
    IL_001e:  ret
} // end of method '<>c__DisplayClass1'::'<Main>b_0'
```

FIGURE 29.18   Innocent-looking post-increment code decompiled.

Slightly simplified, both threads are really performing three actions, each of which can be run in parallel. So although it looks like n++ and n— are each done in a single step, there's really much more machinery going on to read a field, do a computation, and store the result. To be really precise, we should continue our analysis down the path of generated native code instructions, but that'd be quite a detour. What we focus on instead is our observation of the lack of atomic updates and how to remedy this.

Figure 29.19 shows two different execution interleaving schemes for the three steps taken by both threads that update the shared counter.

Recall the interleaving of threads is largely beyond the developer's control because of the way the operating system scheduler works. Obviously, our task is to prevent mistakes by taming the possible interleaving schemes by using synchronization mechanisms. In this particular case, we want to make sure the update operation of the shared state, n, is done atomically. That is, no partial updates should be visible by other threads. (In some sense, this is all about isolation, too.)

Monitors and the `lock` Keyword

One fundamental synchronization primitive is the concept of a monitor, as exposed through the Monitor class in System.Threading. In most cases, the use of a monitor is hidden because of the use of the lock keyword in C#, which leverages this primitive under the covers.

For our running example of a shared counter, we can make the following changes to prevent the two threads from updating the state simultaneously:

```
static void Main()
{
    object gate = new object();
    int n = 0;

    var up = new Thread(() =>
    {
        for (int i = 0; i < 1000000; i++)
            lock (gate)
                n++;
    });

    up.Start();

    for (int i = 0; i < 1000000; i++)
        lock (gate)
            n—;

    up.Join();
    Console.WriteLine(n);
}
```

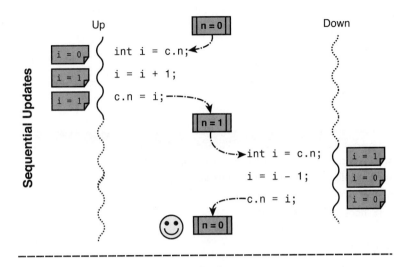

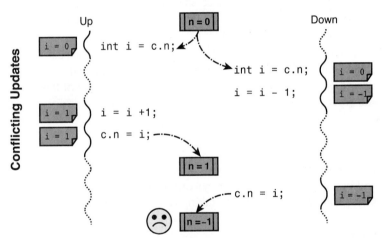

FIGURE 29.19   Different relative execution orders yield different results.

No matter how many times you run this code, the outcome should always be zero (as we expected in the first place). The way this works is by the monitor's guarantee that no two threads can be operating under the lock at the same time.

Monitors use an object as the "cookie" to perform the synchronization with, which relates to the way the common language runtime provides this service. (Objects have a SyncBlock associated with them.) It's typical to simply allocate a dummy object and use it around the code blocks that shouldn't run at the same time from different threads.

Use of the lock keyword turns into a try-finally statement, where the try block contains the code to enter the monitor and the finally block takes care of exiting the monitor. For example, consider the following piece of code:

```
object gate = new object();
lock (gate)
{
    // Do stuff...
}
```

Visual Studio comes with a code snippet for a "lock block." By default, this lock is taken on the `this` object, highlighted for substitution by some other object. You should really make this substitution because locking on `this` is considered evil:

```
// Don't do this at home!
lock (this)
    // Do work under the lock
```

Why? When you lock on an instance of your class that's shared with other code, someone else can take a lock on the object without you knowing about it. This can easily cause your program to become locked endlessly.

The core of this issue is sharing state—in this case `this` or the object itself—associated with an implementation detail (locking to make the code behave well), which should always be considered evil. Check out vssnippets.codeplex.com, a project of this book's reviewer, for some great code snippets to help you deal with concurrent programming (and more).

This is roughly turned into the following piece of code. Notice, however, that you shouldn't write this code by hand but should use the `lock` keyword instead. Over the years, the C# compiler has tweaked the code emitted for locks, taking care of tricky edge cases.

```
object gate = new object();
bool __lockTaken = false;
try
{
    Monitor.Enter(gate, ref __lockTaken);
    // Do stuff...
}
finally
{
    if (__lockTaken)
        Monitor.Exit(gate);
}
```

The overload passing a Boolean "lock taken" flag by reference was added in .NET 4 and is what the C# compiler emits code against. Ignore this flag for now, though. The basic idea of a monitor's `Enter` method is to block until no more (other) threads are inside the lock.

When the method returns, the code can proceed to run code that won't be influenced by other code using the same lock object. In summary, this means that the acquired lock is exclusive: Only one thread can be operating under the lock at any given point in time.

BEWARE OF BOXING

Don't use a value for the object to lock on because this results in boxing. Each time you use the lock keyword with a value (even if it's the same), a different (heap-allocated) boxed object is created. Because the monitor deals with objects on the heap, different boxed objects result in different locks. So you would end up with different nonexclusive locks, voiding the protection you thought you created.

Use of the Boolean flag to determine whether the lock was taken was introduced in the latest version of the .NET Framework to protect against certain exceptional cases. The lock should only be released, by calling Monitor.Exit, if the lock was acquired. If an exception occurred while attempting to acquire the lock, we would end up in the finally block, and the check for the "lock taken" flag reveals the lock shouldn't be released. Such a situation can happen when Interrupt is called on the blocked thread, which causes a ThreadInterruptedException to be thrown from the Enter call.

More functionality is defined on the Monitor class through static methods. For more information, refer to the MSDN documentation.

Mutexes

Mutual exclusion of code executing simultaneously is the essential idea to tame the concurrency monster. In fact, the concept of a mutex got its name from it. Semaphores are the generalization of mutexes and are discussed in the next section.

Using a mutex, we could make our running example thread safe as follows. This piece of code illustrates the two main operations invoked with a mutex.

```
static void Main()
{
    var mutex = new Mutex();
    int n = 0;

    var up = new Thread(() =>
    {
        for (int i = 0; i < 1000000; i++)
        {
            mutex.WaitOne();
            n++;
            mutex.ReleaseMutex();
        }
    });
```

```
    up.Start();

    for (int i = 0; i < 1000000; i++)
    {
        mutex.WaitOne();
        n--;
        mutex.ReleaseMutex();
    }

    up.Join();
    Console.WriteLine(n);
}
```

Again, the code will be guaranteed to print zero as a result. The basic idea is to use the WaitOne method to wait for the mutex to be released by another thread. When this call returns, we've grabbed the mutex and can run with it. When we're done, we release the mutex, allowing another thread to grab it. No two threads can have acquired the mutex at the same time. This technique is often used in real life, too. For example, if trains have to share the same track in opposite directions, a driver's protocol may be set up to avoid crashes. One such protocol is to require a driver to carry a stick before he or she is allowed to drive over the shared track. Figure 29.20 shows this in practice with train drivers carrying a flag (the mutex).

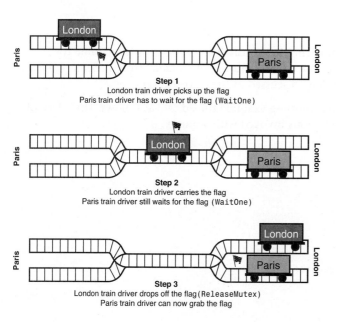

FIGURE 29.20   Mutexes applied in railway traffic.

So why would we use mutexes instead of taking the lock-based approach? Although the concept of a monitor sits at the level of the common language runtime, mutexes are a lower-level operating system primitive. Different constructors and static methods on the `Mutex` class illustrate this fact. In particular, mutexes can be named and used from different processes. This allows coordination of resource access across a set of different components of a bigger system.

As an example, consider the following code fragment. Here, the `Main` method takes in a name of an event to wait on. The application then tries to grab the mutex by calling `WaitOne`, after which it blocks waiting for user input to release the mutex. Running two instances of the application will clearly show how both instances can be waiting for one another:

```
static void Main(string[] args)
{
    var createdNew = false;
    var mutex = new Mutex(/* start as owned */ false, args[0], out createdNew);
    Console.WriteLine("Mutex {0} - Created = {1}", args[0], createdNew);

    Console.Write("Waiting... ");
    mutex.WaitOne();
    Console.WriteLine("Acquired.", DateTime.Now);

    Console.Write("Press ENTER to release... ");
    Console.ReadLine();
    mutex.ReleaseMutex();
}
```

Figure 29.21 shows this example in practice, where one instance of the application is waiting for the other instance to release the shared mutex. All we had to do to obtain the mutex is create an instance of `Mutex` passing in the common mutex name. The output parameter `createdNew` reveals whether an existing mutex was found. Alternatively, the `Mutex.OpenExisting` method can be used.

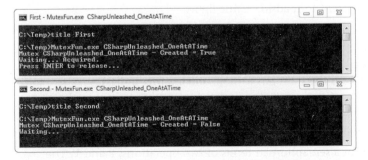

FIGURE 29.21   Mutexes coordinating resource access across processes.

One caveat to point out is this: If you try to morph the lock-based counter solution into the form using mutexes, you see a significant performance difference that favors the use of locks. The difference can be as large as a 100x factor.

The reason for the weaker performance of mutexes is their very low-level nature by which a thread becomes blocked at the operating system scheduler level, causing the thread to transition into another state and causing context switches. Monitors, on the other hand, are a common language runtime facility that sits much higher on the stack and are not as costly.

On the flip side, mutexes are the way to go if you need cross-process synchronization, where the use of monitors falls short. To prove that mutexes are low-level primitives, you can use the SysInternals Process Explorer tool and look at a process's resources, as shown in Figure 29.22. Mutexes are known as "mutants" in the operating system, and therefore they appear as such in the tool.

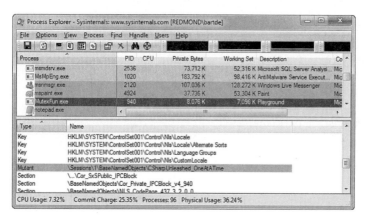

FIGURE 29.22   Mutexes are an operating system-level facility, known as mutants.

Semaphores

Semaphores are a generalization of mutexes. Maybe it's better to state the opposite: Mutexes are a special case of the semaphore primitive invented by the Dutch computer scientist Dijkstra. The name *semaphore* was inspired by synchronization mechanisms used in railways; they are the equivalent to roadside traffic lights.

Before getting into details about the Semaphore class and its properties, let's take a look at a railway semaphore. Figure 29.23 shows states a semaphore can be in, which are used to communicate actions to train drivers. I'm not an expert in railway design, but the basic idea is simple. One sign indicates the train has to stop, and another indicates it's safe to pass. An intermediate state sometimes exists, too, indicating another train is in the next segment, allowing the driver to proceed with caution. Nowadays, such signs have largely been replaced with traffic lights.

Dijkstra defined the concept of a semaphore in terms of two operations, P and V. The former stands for *prolaag*, a made-up Dutch word of *probeer verlaag* or "try to decrease." V, on the other hand, stands for the existing Dutch word *verhoog*, which means "to increase."

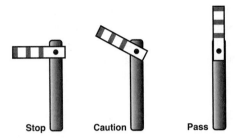

FIGURE 29.23   Railway semaphores synchronize access to a railway.

From a managed code point of view, semaphores are exposed through the Semaphore class, which is constructed with two integer values, one for an initial count and one for the maximum count. The idea is this: The maximum count indicates the number of concurrent entries that are possible to code protected by the semaphore. Using the railway semaphore as an analogy, this count would be two because two trains can be on the railway segment at the same time (one of which has to proceed with caution):

```
var railwaySemaphore = new Semaphore(2, 2);
```

The first parameter for initial count indicates how many parties are initially allowed to "run with" the semaphore. In the preceding, we set this number to 2, which means the railway semaphore was erected when no trains were on the segment that the device is about to protect. In other words, two trains are allowed to pass the semaphore right after it's taken in use by the railway company.

Two key operations exist on a semaphore (ignoring overloads), as shown here. The Release methods are used to decrement the value of the semaphore, either by one or by the specified count. The WaitOne methods are inherited from a WaitHandle base class (which is discussed in the "Signaling with Events" section) and increment the semaphore's value. If the semaphore has reached its maximum count, the WaitOne method blocks until the value gets decreased by Release calls:

```
public int Release();
public int Release(int releaseCount);

public virtual bool WaitOne();
// More WaitOne method overloads...
```

Multiple threads can be waiting on the semaphore at the same time. Which thread will get a chance to run after the WaitOne operation succeeds is unpredictable and depends on the operating system scheduler's mood. Unless the release count is more than one, no two threads will be able to return from the WaitOne operation. After all, primitives such as semaphores provide firm guarantees about their protection facilities. In case of a semaphore, it should never be possible to have more than the specified maximum uses of the semaphore at the same time.

An example with trains is shown here. Obviously, this simple example doesn't protect a shared resource for real (just an imaginary railway segment). True use of semaphores includes protecting a shared resource pool with an upper bound on the number of uses that are permitted simultaneously. Such an example is shown on MSDN.

```
var rnd = new Random();

var railwaySemaphore = new Semaphore(2, 2);
for (int i = 0; i < 10; i++)
{
    new Thread(() =>
    {
        // Time to leave the railway station.
        Thread.Sleep(rnd.Next(500, 8000));
        Console.WriteLine(Thread.CurrentThread.Name + " departing.");

        // Time to reach the semaphore next to the track.
        Thread.Sleep(rnd.Next(100, 5000));
        Console.WriteLine(Thread.CurrentThread.Name + " at signal.");

        // Waiting for the first signal.
        // The train is allowed to pass if no two trains are in the segment.
        railwaySemaphore.WaitOne();
        Console.WriteLine(Thread.CurrentThread.Name + " passed signal.");

        // Time to reach the end of the protected railway segment.
        Thread.Sleep(rnd.Next(2000, 4000));
        Console.WriteLine(Thread.CurrentThread.Name + " exited segment.");
        railwaySemaphore.Release();
    }) { Name = "Train " + i }.Start();
}
```

If the semaphore works correctly (it does), you shouldn't see more than two messages about a train passing the signal without a train exiting the segment first. It's left as an exercise for UI-savvy readers to implement a graphical visualization of the track, the signal, and the different trains driving over the railway.

Just like mutexes, semaphores are a built-in operating system primitives exposed to managed code. In the code shown here, we've been using a local semaphore without a name. However, constructor overloads exist, as well as a static OpenExisting method, to work with named semaphores. Such semaphore objects can be used across several processes to coordinate use of a shared resource pool, for instance.

Because of their impact on the scheduling of operating system threads (putting them in a waiting blocked state while acquiring the semaphore through WaitOne), you need to account for a certain overhead. To reduce this overhead in particular scenarios, a new type has been introduced in .NET 4 called `SemaphoreSlim`. This one doesn't rely on the operating system-level concept of a semaphore and is less expensive. It's especially well suited when only a single process needs protection for a shared resource because this class supports only local unnamed semaphores. In other words, it's a feature that sits at the common language runtime level without the operating system's knowledge of it.

One API-level difference is the `Wait` method rather than the `WaitOne` method. In fact, `WaitOne` is an inheritance (literally) from the `WaitHandle` base class used for various operating system-level synchronization primitive wrappers. The `SemaphoreSlim` not being such a primitive, it doesn't derive from this class. However, if a wait operation using a `WaitHandle` is desirable, the `AvailableWaitHandle` property can be used. We don't elaborate on the concept of wait handles just yet; they're discussed in more detail during our discussion in the "Signaling with Events" section.

Finally, where the `Semaphore` class doesn't expose the current count of the semaphore, the `SemaphoreSlim` class does through a `CurrentCount` property.

More Advanced Locks

Added in .NET 3.5 and .NET 4, respectively, the `ReaderWriterLockSlim` and `SpinLock` primitives are often useful, too. Their use is fairly specialized, so we'll limit ourselves to a basic discussion.

ReaderWriterLock(Slim)

The essential problem of various concurrency and synchronization problems boils down to simultaneous reader and writer accesses on a shared resource. Often, the presence of multiple readers is allowed, while writers should be protected from one another to prevent harm. Therefore, the classic monitor-based lock is often too coarse-grained because it can't differentiate from reader and writer accesses.

`ReaderWriterLock` and `ReaderWriterLockSlim` accommodate for such scenarios. The latter was introduced in .NET 3.5 and is recommended. Use of reader/writer locks is restricted to the current process only, and the lock doesn't wrap functionality provided by the operating system. In such a case, the slogan "the slimmer, the better" definitely holds, hence the advice to use `ReaderWriterLockSlim` nowadays. We only talk about this class to give you an idea about the lock's use.

In its very essence, `ReaderWriterLockSlim` exposes pairs of `Enter` and `Exit` methods for different kinds of accesses, as follows:

- ▶ **Read mode:** Any number of threads can be reading at the same time; in other words, sharing is allowed.

- ▶ **Write mode:** Only one thread can have this exclusive write access. Being in this mode prevents others from entering the lock due to its exclusive nature.

- ▶ **Upgradeable mode is a special read mode:** At some point in the future, the reader thread may decide to upgrade the lock to gain writer access.

The precise behavior of attempts to acquire the lock depends on the current state the lock is in. This is detailed in a table on MSDN. In short, the idea is to allow for many readers and to prevent writers from messing up state. To do so, writers block everyone else who attempts to access the lock in any mode. Readers, on the other hand, permit more readers to enter, unless a writer is waiting to gain access. An attempt to gain write access blocks until everyone else has left the lock.

It should be mentioned that two families of enter methods exist. One set of methods is of the form Enter followed by the desired access level. Those methods block until the requested access is permitted. The TryEnter set of methods returns a Boolean value to indicate whether the request (with an optional timeout) to enter the lock succeeded.

A trivial example of reader/writer locks is shown in the following code fragment:

```
var @lock = new ReaderWriterLockSlim();

int counter = 0;
new Thread(() =>
{
    while (true)
    {
        @lock.EnterWriteLock();
        counter++;
        counter--;
        @lock.ExitWriteLock();
    }
}).Start();

while (true)
{
    Thread.Sleep(100);

    @lock.EnterReadLock();
    Console.WriteLine(counter);
    @lock.ExitReadLock();
}
```

The main thread here acts as a monitor of some counter. Many such monitors could be observing the counter value simultaneously without doing any harm. However, some background thread is updating the counter constantly. Such updates should never be observable in an intermediate nonatomic state. Because of this, we need locks.

Try taking out any of the locks to see the counter invariant being broken. In particular, the counter should never read a value other than zero because the increment and decrement operations should remain balanced. You're also encouraged to add more reader and writer threads to the mix to show the reader/writer lock properly protects read and write accesses to the counter. Messing up the access level associated with a piece of code (for example, requesting read access but yet performing an update) should be sufficient to illustrate thread-safety issues by means of a nonzero counter value.

For further information about the meaning of upgradeable locks and so-called lock recursion policy, refer to the MSDN documentation on the subject. More realistic examples of protecting collections against update conflicts are also shown there.

THE DANGER OF EXPOSED LOCKS

Locks of any kind have quite a few drawbacks but are often a necessary evil to enable proper synchronization. One of the main issues with locks is their lack of composition and the need for careful acquisition of locks. For example, if locks are not acquired in a consistent order across different components in the system, it's possible to run into (hard-to-debug) deadlocks. Such deadlocks occur when multiple parties are in a deadly embrace, waiting for one another to release some lock. The simplest case is shown here:

```
// Thread 1              // Thread 2
lock (a)                 lock (b)
lock (b)                 lock (a)
    /* Do stuff */           /* Do other stuff */
```

If the first thread moves beyond acquiring the lock on a, and the second thread then moves on to acquire the lock on b, we're set up for disaster. Thread 1 now has to wait for the lock on b, while thread 2 is stuck waiting for the lock on a. This deadly embrace cannot be resolved, and both threads are stuck forever (ignoring the use of Interrupt or Abort).

When lock objects are publicly exposed, it's clear that all parties that make use of the locks must coordinate among themselves to agree on a proper locking scheme. This is where composition of software components breaks down quickly in the presence of locks.

Therefore, it's best to keep locks as implementation details properly encapsulated within classes or larger components with a good internal organization. Historically, sharing of locks has been done in a number of scenarios, often resulting in people shooting themselves in the foot. A good example is the nongeneric collections in .NET, such as ArrayList, which expose a SyncRoot object. It suffices for one sole party to hold on to a lock on the object to prevent others from making enumeration progress:

```
var lst = new ArrayList { 1, 2, 3 };

// Some bad guy got access to lst's SyncRoot object :-(
new Thread(() =>
{
    Monitor.Enter(lst.SyncRoot);
    Thread.Sleep(Timeout.Infinite);
}).Start();
```

```
foreach (int x in lst) // Stuck forever!
    Console.WriteLine(x);
```

This is just one example of a denial-of-service attack using locks. Other issues can arise when multiple resources are used improperly, causing deadlocks. Imagine the debugging nightmare this can get you into. Hopefully, horror stories like these suffice to motivate you to keep care of your locks!

SpinLock

The SpinLock struct was added in .NET 4 to facilitate high-performance scenarios where use of classic locks using the Monitor class is infeasible. Drawbacks related to classic locks include the need to allocate an object on the heap, adding more garbage collector and memory pressure. It should be clear that cases where this is a concern are highly specialized and shouldn't be considered the default.

Spinlocks operate by spinning in a tight loop until the lock becomes available. In other words, a spinlock simply burns CPU cycles while waiting for the lock to be freed to be entered by the requester. Such spinning is expensive unless it takes only a little while, so it's mainly suited for small locks. In other words, there's a point at which the cost of a spinlock outweighs the cost of a classic lock. To make a decision on which lock to use, performance measurement should be your guide.

The pattern for using a spinlock is totally analogous to using a classic lock, using a try...finally statement to ensure the lock is properly exited:

```
var @lock = new SpinLock();
var lockTaken = false;
@lock.Enter(ref lockTaken);
try
{
    // Do work...
}
finally
{
    if (lockTaken)
        @lock.Exit();
}
```

For more information and guidance about using spinlocks, take a look at MSDN. The documentation also includes advice as to how to decide between a classic lock and a spinlock, including the use of profiling tools in Visual Studio 2010.

Signaling with Events

Coordination of access to shared resources is just one (data-centric) concern of writing multithreaded applications. Another is to coordinate different pieces of an algorithm or a set of components to coordinate among themselves. This is where events (in the threading sense of the word, not as in the C# construct) enter the picture.

The primitive operations associated with an event are setting (or signaling) the event or waiting on it. You can compare this to a symphonic orchestra, where different players can be waiting for the orchestra conductor to give a signal to start playing their part of the symphony. No wonder that the word *orchestration* is often used in this context.

Two kinds of events exist. They differ in the way they react upon succeeding a wait operation. This deserves a bit more explanation. The example of the orchestra is analogous to a manual reset event. Multiple players, say the violinists, are waiting for a signal from the conductor. When the signal is given, they all start playing until the conductor resets the event. This operation is a manual action; it's not because a single player started playing upon the signal being given that the others still have to wait. In other words, multiple players can wake up as a result of the event being set. This is shown in Figure 29.24. Notice the orchestra conductor is named the "orchestrator" in this figure, using more common computer science terminology.

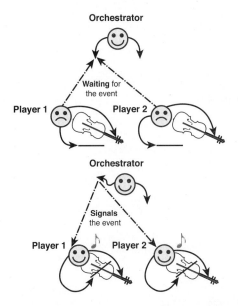

FIGURE 29.24   Use of manual reset events in a symphonic orchestra.

Autoreset events, on the other hand, allow only one thread that's waiting for the event to be awakened and start running. In other words, an effect of a thread succeeding its wait operation is to atomically reset the event. Real-life examples of this signaling use are harder to find.

Because events are typically used to signal the availability of some state produced by a thread, the difference between both kinds of events impacts the consuming threads that are waiting for the state to become available. In case of the manual reset event, all the consuming threads waiting for the resource can proceed as soon as the event gets signaled. In case of the autoreset event, a single thread wakes up and performs its duties with the available state.

Both kinds of events explained here are directly built atop Win32 primitives and have an effect on a thread's scheduling due to the low-level blocking that occurs. To reduce costs associated with this, the manual reset event has a slim variant introduced since .NET 4, called ManualResetEventSlim.

Running an Orchestra with ManualResetEvent

To illustrate the use of ManualResetEvent signaling, we build a larger version of the orchestra shown in Figure 29.24 in code now:

```
var conductorSignalsViolins = new ManualResetEvent(false);
var conductorSignalsTrumpetists = new ManualResetEvent(false);

for (int i = 0; i < 5; i++)
{
    new Thread(() =>
    {
        conductorSignalsViolins.WaitOne();
        for (int j = 0; j < 20; j++)
        {
            Console.Write(Thread.CurrentThread.Name + " ");
            Thread.Sleep(100);
        }
    }) { Name = "V" + i }.Start();
}

for (int i = 0; i < 3; i++)
{
    new Thread(() =>
    {
        conductorSignalsTrumpetists.WaitOne();
        for (int j = 0; j < 20; j++)
        {
            Console.Write(Thread.CurrentThread.Name + " ");
            Thread.Sleep(150);
        }
    }) { Name = "T" + i }.Start();
}

Thread.Sleep(1000); // Time for the trumpets
conductorSignalsTrumpetists.Set();

Thread.Sleep(2000); // Time for the violins
conductorSignalsViolins.Set();
```

In this example, two events are used to signal multiple parties in the play. All the violins wait for their event, while all the trumpets do the same on their event. Once the conductor sets the event at the time he wants them to start, they can proceed with their work.

Music-savvy readers will notice there are a couple of things missing here. How does the conductor know that all the players are ready to receive the event? Most likely, all of the players will be ready by the time the event gets set because their respective threads have been started for a while already. However, proper synchronization might need to be crafted more carefully, which we discuss in just a moment.

The CountDownEvent

Introduced in .NET 4, the countdown event allows for multiple parties to synchronize among themselves based on a count. That is, the event becomes set only if the total count reaches zero. Each call to Signal decrements the value by one or a specified amount. Upon construction, an initial count can be set. When the count reaches zero, a thread waiting for the event can continue from its Wait call.

In case of our orchestra, this mechanism could be used as an initial handshake. To limit the size of the code listing, we simplify things a bit and show just the handshake part, where the conductor is waiting for all players to signal they're ready:

```
var start = new CountdownEvent(8);
var conductorSignalsViolins = new ManualResetEvent(false);
var conductorSignalsTrumpetists = new ManualResetEvent(false);

for (int i = 0; i < 5; i++)
{
    new Thread(() =>
    {
        Console.WriteLine(Thread.CurrentThread.Name + " takes a seat.");
        start.Signal();
        conductorSignalsViolins.WaitOne();
        // Code to play my part...
    }) { Name = "V" + i }.Start();
}

for (int i = 0; i < 3; i++)
{
    new Thread(() =>
    {
        Console.WriteLine(Thread.CurrentThread.Name + " takes a seat.");
        start.Signal();
        conductorSignalsTrumpetists.WaitOne();
        // Code to play my part...
    }) { Name = "T" + i }.Start();
```

```
}

start.Wait();
// Orchestrator logic to set various events...
```

Now all the players have to move beyond the phase of taking a seat before the conductor can continue to send signals for them to play their parts at the desired times. A series of other methods exist to manipulate the count.

Dealing with `WaitHandle`

Thus far, we've only been dealing with simple waits for a single event. In the preceding discussion, we mentioned (in passing) the `WaitHandle` base type. This class acts as the base class for a plethora of synchronization primitives. Figure 29.25 shows the class hierarchy of `WaitHandle`.

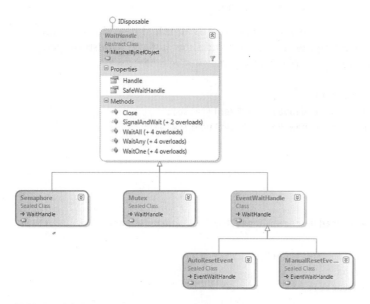

FIGURE 29.25   The `WaitHandle` class hierarchy.

`WaitHandle` instances represent the encapsulation of the operating system-level concept of a wait handle. This explains its properties with the word *Handle* in the name. It should also be obvious why the "slim" set of synchronization primitives doesn't derive from this class because the operating system is not involved in the operation of those slim primitives. As a result, those slim variants cannot be used across processes but have a better performance characteristic in scenarios where they're applicable.

In our presentation of the various synchronization primitives, we've focused on the use of the derived `WaitOne` method to perform a blocking wait. Various overloads of this method exist, which allow the specification of timeout values and whatnot.

What's equally interesting, though, is the existence of two groups of static methods, called WaitAny and WaitAll. Their role is to provide for synchronization involving multiple wait handles. In our orchestra example, all the players are waiting for the single conductor to tell them to start playing. However, imagine what would happen if the conductor never signals them to start playing? They would be stuck forever. Such a situation can arise when the fire alarm in the theater goes off. Clearly, you don't want the players to be stuck.

How do we fix issues such as the one described in the preceding paragraph? What we want to do here is to wait for *any* of two events to occur: One is the orchestra conductor, and another is the emergency "run for your life" case. In a more programming-related example, such a technique could be used to wait for an event or a cancellation signal. It should be clear that depending on which wait handle made the wait operation succeed, a different action should be taken. Let's zoom in on the code of an individual violinist to show how to perform a WaitAny:

```
var conductorSignalsViolins = new ManualResetEvent(false);
var emergencyAlarm = new ManualResetEvent(false);

for (int i = 0; i < 5; i++)
{
    new Thread(() =>
    {
        int res = WaitHandle.WaitAny(new[] { conductorSignalsViolins,
                                             emergencyAlarm });
        if (res == 0)
            // Code to play my part...
        else
            // Just quitting from the thread would suffice, but let's be
            // a bit more illustrative here...
            Environment.FailFast("Run for your life!");
    }) { Name = "V" + i }.Start();
}

// The orchestra conductor could signal to start playing - or -
// someone could set off the fire alarm.
```

The WaitAny method returns the array index of the wait handle that caused the wait operation to succeed. Based on this value, different code can be executed.

We omit the WaitAll method from our exploration of wait handles, but the operation is similar: An array of handles is passed in, but this time the wait succeeds only if all the handles have been signaled. This comes in handy when multiple parties have to signal readiness before another party can move on with its work.

Behind the scenes, those methods use the Win32 [Msg]WaitForMultipleObjects[Ex] functions. This explains why operating system handles are required to perform those advanced wait operations; that's all the operating system knows about. Some of the slim variants include the capability to still acquire a `WaitHandle` by "upgrading" the object to have a Win32 handle. In doing so, however, they lose part of their "slim" nature.

Interlocked Helpers

Looking back at our counter example, recall the core issue that made synchronization required to produce the right result. Some essential operations, such as increment and decrement of an integer value, didn't run atomically, which might have surprised many readers. Why is it that those simple operations can cause tremendous grief? The answer lies in their definition from a C# language point of view.

In particular, `i++` is merely a shortcut for `i += 1`, which on its turn is shorthand syntax for `i = i + 1`. Notice how we ignore the capability of such an increment expression to be used, well, as an expression. But the fundamental fact remains that such expressions are shorthand syntax for a sequence of mutation operations. This is where the runtime and the operating system get their flexibility to interleave different threads at places that are undesirable, leading to the problems we discussed.

Increment and Decrement

But does it have to be the case that fundamental operations like increment by one aren't atomic? It turns out the answer is no, thanks to the instruction set of platforms the code is running on (or better, JIT compiled to). Such instructions are exposed to managed code developers through the `Interlocked` class. Using static methods on `Interlocked`, we could rewrite our counter example as follows:

```
static void Main()
{
    int n = 0;

    var up = new Thread(() =>
    {
        for (int i = 0; i < 1000000; i++)
            Interlocked.Increment(ref n);
    });

    up.Start();

    for (int i = 0; i < 1000000; i++)
        Interlocked.Decrement(ref n);

    up.Join();
    Console.WriteLine(n);
}
```

The `Increment` and `Decrement` methods take in the value to be mutated using a `ref`- parameter. The guarantee provided by those methods is that the operation is done in an atomic fashion, so no other thread can observe intermediate states. The solution to the counter synchronization issue presented here is by far the most efficient one.

In some sense, this is a pathological case of mutual exclusion of code executing on multiple threads, where we're very lucky the operations can be done in an interlocked manner. If this isn't the case, a lock or a mutex will have to be used. Some other simple operations have an interlocked equivalent, such as adding (or subtracting) a value, as exposed through the Add method. However, calling whole methods from different threads in a mutual exclusive manner requires use of locks.

(Compare and) Exchange

Lots of performance-critical multithreaded code (as can be found in operating system kernels and whatnot) can take advantage of a few specialized interlocked operations. A common operation is to swap the contents of two memory locations atomically, with or without a condition associated with it.

Let's take a look at the simpler of the two first: the "interlocked exchange" operation exposed through Interlocked.Exchange method overloads. The overload used with 32-bit integer values is shown here:

```
public static int Exchange(ref int location1, int value);
```

Here, the location1 parameter refers to the value to be mutated by assigning it the value specified in the second parameter. The original value read from location1 is returned from the method:

```
int value = 24;
Console.WriteLine(value);  // Prints 24
Console.WriteLine(Interlocked.Exchange(ref value, 42));  // Prints 24
Console.WriteLine(value);  // Now prints 42
```

This primitive operation comes in handy in a variety of circumstances. In the MSDN documentation, a simple lock implemented using the Exchange method is shown. Refer to this documentation for more information.

A related operation is called "compare and exchange" and does slightly more work than the exchange operation we just looked at. One overload for use with integer values is shown:

```
public static int CompareExchange(ref int location1, int value, int comparand);
```

The idea is this: Before exchanging the value in location1 with the value specified in the second parameter, the original value in location1 is compared to the comparand. If both are equal, the exchange operation is performed; if not, nothing happens. Either way, the method returns the original value read from location1.

One place where this method proves to be useful is when we want to perform exchange of values when the state is what we expect it to be. The idea is that when another thread gets a chance to mutate the state before our thread gets a chance to perform the exchange, we want to do a check and the exchange operation atomically. Use of an if statement won't work here because other threads can tweak state in between the check and the `if` statement's body:

```
int value = 24;
if (value == 24)
    // If another thread can see "value", it could have changed here.
    Interlocked.Exchange(ref value, 42);
```

In fact, a simple counter example using `CompareExchange` is shown on MSDN for the documentation of this method. I kindly refer you to this example.

UNEXPECTED LIMITS OF 64-BIT ADDRESSING

Here's a story for you: 64-bit addressing by modern processors gives access to a huge address space of no less than 16 petabytes. Although this should suffice for a long time to come (but never say *never* when it comes to memory use), it's been a theoretical limit because of various practical issues.

One thing to keep in mind is that 64-bit addressing requires each reference, such as the address of a reference object, to be 64 bits, which obviously takes twice the space compared to a 32-bit address. Use of 64-bit architectures therefore boosts the memory usage by itself.

A rather unexpected limitation Windows had to deal with in the early days of 64-bit architectures was the lack of a compare-and-exchange instruction that could deal with two 64-bit addresses (for the original value and the target value). Obviously, such an instruction requires 128 bits of operands (two 64-bit addresses), which wasn't supported by all targeted architectures for a while. Primitive kernel data structures, such as a linked list (KLIST), rely on this operation for safe manipulation from different CPUs running code simultaneously.

Because of the limitations on the maximum operand size for this instruction, Windows had to reduce its maximum addressable space to be less than the full 64 bits promised by the architecture of the machine. This wasn't much of a problem, though, because the amount of RAM that fits in machines is way below the amount a 64-bit machine could theoretically address.

More Synchronization Mechanisms

A number of other synchronization mechanisms, which have yet to be discussed, exist in the .NET Framework. We limit ourselves to a brief overview of those constructs and their uses, referring to MSDN for more thorough coverage:

▸ Barriers have been added in .NET 4 and allow a number of parallel tasks to work hand in hand through some algorithm. The idea is that each such task signals arrival at a phase, at which point all the tasks block until each of them has arrived at the same phase. When that condition is met, they can all proceed from there, making their way to the next phase.

▶ `SynchronizationContext` is a concept mainly added for proper synchronization on UI threads, as seen in Windows Forms and WPF. However, other providers of synchronization models can be built, deriving from this base class. The idea is that a synchronization context can accept work by means of `Send` or `Post` calls that take in a delegate. This delegate then gets run in the right context as encapsulated by the `SynchronizationContext` object (for example, a message loop for the UI thread).

Choosing the right tool for the synchronization job at hand is a matter of learning. Start by identifying different parties that have to work with one another. Next, figure out how those parties depend on each other, requiring signals to be sent between them. When different actors have to manipulate the same data, locks might be required.

BackgroundWorker

Before concluding this chapter, we explore one more concept that's closely related to synchronization and leverages the thread pool: the `BackgroundWorker`. What makes it different from the other mechanisms we've explored up to now is its place outside the `System.Threading` namespace. Instead, it's defined in `System.ComponentModel`. One of the reasons for this is to reflect its use, typically related to UI programming.

The goal of `BackgroundWorker` is to make asynchrony easier to deal with. In many cases, background work has to be carried out without blocking the party that requested the work to be done in the first place. The requester and the worker move at their own paces, and therefore asynchrony results. However, this shouldn't preclude the requester from being able to receive progress updates of the background work or even to cancel it if there's no further interest in the result.

To set the scene for our brief exploration of the `BackgroundWorker`, look at Figure 29.26, where a Windows Forms application form is shown with this component added to it. Notice properties that have changed from their default values, indicated in bold. Those include `WorkerReportsProgress` and `WorkerSupportsCancellation`.

FIGURE 29.26   A `BackgroundWorker` component used in Windows Forms.

To make the worker do some useful job, events have to be implemented. There are three such events in total, as shown in Figure 29.27. We implement all three of them, serving the following roles:

▶ DoWork is triggered when someone calls RunWorkerAsync. The DoWork event handler will be run on a thread different from the one that called the RunWorkerAsync method, resulting in asynchrony.

▶ ProgressChanged is called every time the worker updates its progress from code running under the DoWork handler. This event handler is invoked on the synchronization context of the requester, in this case the UI thread. In other words, one can safely update the user interface from this handler.

▶ RunWorkerCompleted is similar to the ProgressChanged event with regard to where it gets run. It's triggered by the worker thread signaling completion.

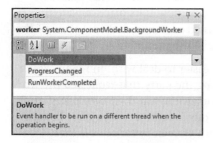

FIGURE 29.27   Events on a BackgroundWorker component.

Using the BackgroundWorker component, we now create an asynchronous block-based file copy tool. It simply uses two FileStream objects to read from and write to the source and destination files, respectively. All the copying logic is done from the DoWork event handler, which takes place in the background, relative to the UI thread where the user triggers the copy command. We omit a discussion of UI design and refer to Figure 29.28 for a possible interface including a few labels, text boxes, buttons, a numeric up/down control, and a progress bar.

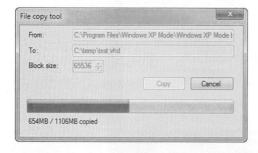

FIGURE 29.28   Our asynchronous file copy tool in action.

In the `Click` handler of the button used to start the copy operation, we put the following piece of code (ignoring obligatory input handling, left as an exercise):

```
private void btnCopy_Click(object sender, EventArgs e)
{
    // TODO: Disable parts of the UI while the copy is in progress.

    worker.RunWorkerAsync(new CopyInfo
    {
        From = txtFrom.Text,
        To = txtTo.Text,
        BlockSize = (int)blockSize.Value
    });
}
```

The definition of `CopyInfo` isn't rocket science; it consiss of three properties to hold the `From` and `To` paths and the block size. We use such an object to pass the copy operation info between the UI thread and the worker because the `DoWork` handler should not touch any UI control. Doing so would result in a cross-thread violation.

Calling `RunWorkerAsync` causes the `DoWork` handler of the worker component to be executed on a background thread:

```
private void worker_DoWork(object sender, DoWorkEventArgs e)
{
    var info = (CopyInfo)e.Argument;
    using (FileStream from = File.OpenRead(info.From))
    using (FileStream to = File.OpenWrite(info.To))
    {
        byte[] buffer = new byte[info.BlockSize];
        long total = from.Length, current = 0;
        while (!worker.CancellationPending)
        {
            int n = from.Read(buffer, 0, buffer.Length);
            to.Write(buffer, 0, n);

            current += n;
            worker.ReportProgress(
                (int)(current / (total / 100)), // Trick to avoid overflow...
                string.Format("{0}MB / {1}MB copied", current / MB, total / MB)
            );

            if (n < buffer.Length)
                break;
        }
    }
}
```

```
        if (worker.CancellationPending)
        {
            e.Cancel = true;
            // TODO: clean-up, e.g. deleting the target file.
        }
    }
}
```

Here we run a loop reading the source file in blocks of the specified size and writing those blocks to the destination file. We check for cancellation requests each time around the loop using the CancellationPending property on the worker. If no request to cancel exists, we move on and report progress using ReportProgress using a progress percentage value and an (optional) user state object (here a simple message string).

Progress reports are presented to the UI thread through the worker's ProgressChanged event, where we can update the interface by touching controls safely. This is shown in the following fragment:

```
private void worker_ProgressChanged(object sender, ProgressChangedEventArgs e)
{
    progressBar.Value = e.ProgressPercentage;
    lblProgress.Text = (string)e.UserState;
}


private void worker_RunWorkerCompleted(object sender,
                                    RunWorkerCompletedEventArgs e)
{
    if (e.Cancelled)
        MessageBox.Show("File copy cancelled.", this.Text,
                    MessageBoxButtons.OK, MessageBoxIcon.Warning);
    else if (e.Error != null)
        MessageBox.Show(e.Error.Message, this.Text,
                    MessageBoxButtons.OK, MessageBoxIcon.Error);
    else
        MessageBox.Show("File copy completed.", this.Text,
                    MessageBoxButtons.OK, MessageBoxIcon.Information);

    // TODO: restore UI controls, or close dialog, or ...?
}
```

The second method shown here handles the RunWorkerCompleted event, which gets triggered when DoWork reaches the end. This could also be due to an exception, which gets propagated through the event arguments as the Error property. Cancellation is also communicated across the background worker and the UI thread. With this, we finish up our brief exploration of the BackgroundWorker component.

Summary

Writing concurrent applications is becoming the standard because of the increased number of processor cores in today's machines. Having a solid understanding of mechanisms to run multiple units of work in parallel and to synchronize between them is an essential piece of knowledge for the modern programmer.

In this chapter, we learned about threads and thread pools to run work in parallel. We also explored how to use various locking and synchronization primitives to coordinate among those workers. In the next chapter, we look at task and data parallelism.

CHAPTER 30

Task Parallelism and Data Parallelism

IN THIS CHAPTER

▶ Pros and Cons of
Threads 1502

▶ The Task Parallel Library 1503

▶ Task Parallelism 1508

▶ Data Parallelism 1529

In Chapter 29, "Threading and Synchronization," we looked at parallel programming from a rather low level, focusing on the concept of threads and a whole set of synchronization primitives. We also learned about the cost of various operating system facilities, giving rise to the creation of thread pools and lightweight synchronization tools for managed code.

Today's computing landscape has radically shifted toward a higher need for parallel programming to speed up programs. In the previous decades, a slow-running program or library wasn't too big of a deal. It was only a matter of time for processor clock speeds to increase enough to make the program run sufficiently faster. Things have changed, though. Although the density of transistors that fit on a chip is still growing at a rapid pace (conforming to Moore's law), we've hit a wall with regard to clock speeds. Instead of getting faster and faster processors, we get more such processor "cores" on a single chip.

Because of this change at the hardware level, we as software folks need to adapt to the standard being multicore machines. It should be clear that this kind of programming requires different tools and (more important) a different mindset to "reason concurrently."

This chapter presents some of the recent work done in the field of parallel programming, starting with the .NET 4 BCL. You learn how low-level concepts such as threads fall short in the changing landscape for a few reasons. During our discussion, we introduce two ways to think about parallel programming: task-oriented versus data-oriented.

Pros and Cons of Threads

As you learned in Chapter 29, threads are the scheduling unit known by the Windows operating system kernel. Processes can have multiple threads which allow the process to process many of its tasks in parallel. Examples include running a message pump for a UI thread while background threads are used for computations or I/O operations that shouldn't block the UI.

Cutting Costs

The best way to think about threads is as virtual processors. They provide a level of abstraction on top of physical processors, and it's the operating system's task to switch between different threads such that all of them can make progress. The mechanism by which a thread is swapped out for another one to run is known as a *context switch*.

Context switches are expensive, and so is thread creation. So why would one create a plethora of threads as a means to run things in parallel? This question was exactly the motivation for introducing pools of threads. This way, the number of threads can be limited, reducing context switching. Pooling also allows for reuse of threads to carry out different work items drawn from a work item queue.

So is there anything good about threads, per se? The truth is, we can't live without them because they form the main mechanism to do work in parallel. Other such mechanisms exist, but they all have their own pros and cons. Examples include fibers (which the CLR doesn't support) and User Mode Scheduling, or UMS (which is more complicated to deal with).

An Ideal Number of Threads?

Based on those observations, what is an ideal number of threads? If we have too many threads competing for processor time, we face the costs of swapping back and forth between them. If we have too few, we're underutilizing the cores we have at our service. Figure 30.1 shows how a well-tuned parallel program could go about optimizing the number of threads by having work queues associated with each processor core available.

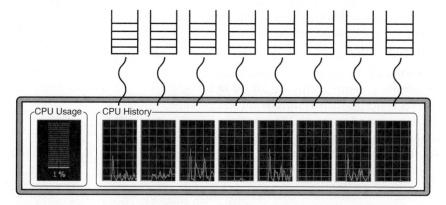

FIGURE 30.1   Keeping processors busy with an ideal number of threads.

In fact, this is pretty close to various pooling architectures, one of which we look at in this chapter. Now a key question becomes how to properly divide work into chunks that can run on different "worker threads."

The Task Parallel Library

.NET Framework 4 introduces the Task Parallel Library (TPL) as the new way to go about writing parallel programs. Key benefits of the TPL include the following:

▶ Efficient utilization of the cores available in the machine

▶ Intuitive programming model, leveraging lambda expressions and generics

▶ Support for task-oriented parallelism based on the notion of Task<T>

▶ Data-oriented parallelism with parallel iteration and PLINQ queries

▶ Composition of asynchronous computations

So you might wonder why we bothered talking about classic threading in Chapter 29 at all, if the TPL is all you need. There are a couple of answers to this question. First, it's good to know about the primitives that underpin higher levels of abstraction, such as the one provided by the TPL. Second, you'll most likely encounter existing code bases you have to maintain using classic threading. And finally, a lot of the facts pointed out in the preceding chapter hold true for every kind of parallel programming. For example, touching shared mutable state is fine as long as you have a proper and well-thought-out synchronization scheme in place.

Architecture

The architecture of the .NET 4 parallel programming facilities is shown in Figure 30.2, which can also be found on MSDN. It clearly pinpoints the layering of the individual components out of which the framework is built.

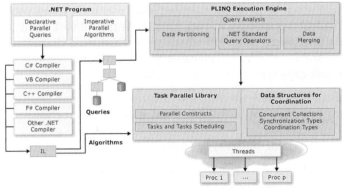

Source: MSDN Documentation on "Parallel Programming in the .NET Framework"

FIGURE 30.2   Keeping processors busy with an ideal number of threads.

Notice how the TPL is only a small building block of a bigger story. In our coverage of task and data parallelism in this chapter, we focus on the TPL but also PLINQ, which, strictly speaking, is a different component. Let's talk about the layering a bit more.

At the bottom of the diagram, you can see a number of threads that correspond to the processors (or cores) in the machine. The allocation of those threads follows the ideas pointed out before and illustrated in Figure 30.2. In other words, the framework tries its best to avoid introducing more concurrency than the machine can handle, but also tries to provide as much concurrency as is tolerable. Obviously, the introduction of concurrency is primarily triggered by components higher up the stack requesting more computation resources.

One level higher up, we find two parallel components: the Task Parallel Library and the Data Structures for Coordination. The former of those is where the notion of tasks is defined. We detail this concept in a moment, but for now simply think of a task as a unit of work that can be run in parallel with other such tasks. The latter of the two embodies all sorts of data structures used in a parallel computing context. This ranges from concurrency-safe collection types in `System.Collections.Concurrent` to synchronization primitives, some of which were discussed in the Chapter 29. We don't go into detail on those data structures here. In what follows, we abbreviate this component as CDS to stand for coordination data structures.

The bottom layers of the architecture form a fabric for computation on which a lot of applications can build. This is illustrated in the diagram by the arrow denoted with the word *Algorithms*. Any application can use the publicly exposed application programming interfaces (APIs) to do parallel programming, no matter what .NET language the developer prefers. However, it turns out the parallel programming libraries in .NET 4 can make direct use of the TPL and CDS. One prominent example is the PLINQ Execution Engine, which allows LINQ to Objects (and hence LINQ to XML) queries to be parallelized in an easy declarative manner. We look briefly at PLINQ, assuming prior knowledge of LINQ gained earlier in this book.

Declarative Versus Imperative

An important aspect to point out about parallel programming is the way you express your intent in code. Historically, parallel programming has been mostly in the ballpark of an imperative approach. Most popular languages have imperative roots, including the C# language, which derives from C and C++. In those languages, you basically have to hold the hand of the machine and state explicitly what you want it to do.

Imperative languages are all about how you want things to be carried out. Essentially, you're sitting pretty close to the bare metal of the machine, manipulating instruction pointers through control flow, manipulating memory through assignment, and so on. As a result, there's little the machine, some runtime, or a language compiler can do to magically improve your code. There's little room to wiggle with the code you wrote. For example, consider the following loop:

```
foreach (var x in xs)
    ProcessItem(x);
```

Agreed, a smart compiler will do its best to make the loop go as efficiently as possible, but it won't violate some essential assumptions of the programming language in which you've written this code. One such assumption has a small syntactical footprint in the code, but has far-reaching implications. What I'm talking about is the single semicolon inside the loop body. You should read this innocent token in the code as sequencing. Boiling this down to its very essence, look at the following code:

```
A();
B();
```

All this means is to call A, and *then* call B. Similarly, for the foreach loop shown just a moment ago, the assumption is that ProcessItem is called for the elements of the sequence in the order over which they are iterated. That is, there's no room for parallel evaluation here.

FUNDAMENTALIST FUNCTIONAL PROGRAMMING

One reason automatic parallelization of code is a red herring in today's programming languages and runtimes is the lack of "purity." Side-effects pop up around every corner in programs, including the slightest bits of I/O. Let's illustrate this with an innocent example:

```
var now = new Tuple<DateTime, DateTime>(DateTime.Now, DateTime.Now);
```

Here, we create a tuple with both components set to the same DateTime.Now value. Or not? Reading the clock is an I/O operation that costs time, too. Hence, between evaluating the first DateTime.Now call and evaluating the second one, time will have elapsed. Both components of the tuple won't be the same!

Optimizing this code to eliminate the duplicate evaluation of DateTime.Now will produce different results. Now the two components of the tuple will always be the same. Because of the change in the code's semantics, such optimizations simply cannot be made. Even evaluating both DateTime.Now expressions *in parallel* is a big no-no. What if the two evaluations run on different processors, really at the same time? (Remember, clocks do have limited precision.)

As can be seen from the example shown here, imperative programming ties together the hands of the compiler, runtime, and machine, disallowing it from making certain optimizations. Although this can be said to be a contrived scenario, just imagine what would happen if DateTime.Now were not just about input but also about output. Any optimization would eliminate the duplicate output operation.

Unfortunately, this also leaves out any room for legitimate safe optimizations. An example of such code is shown next:

```
var zeroes = new Tuple<double, double>(Math.Sin(0), Math.Sin(0));
```

The sine of zero isn't going to change. Now we could perfectly eliminate the common `Math.Sin(0)` subexpression and prevent wasting computation time, but there's nothing telling the compiler or the runtime this is okay to do.

In the world of fundamentalist pure functional programming, all side effects must be made explicit in types using so-called monads. As a result, evaluation order of a side effect–free portion of code can be done in any way the compiler or runtime sees fit. Imperative languages still have to learn a lot.

In a declarative world, things are quite different. In such a world, you just state what you want the code to produce as a result. The way the language, runtime, libraries, and ultimately the machine make this happen is irrelevant to you. All you care about are the results to be produced by the code. LINQ queries are a perfect example of declarative constructs:

```
var xs = Enumerable.Range(0, 1000);
var res = from x in xs
          where x % 2 == 0
          select x + 1;


foreach (var x in res)
    Console.WriteLine(x);
```

Nothing here prevents the query processor from splitting up the input sequence xs into multiple portions to run the filtering and projection code in parallel over them, merging results afterward. It turns out this is an almost true statement because you have to decorate the query with a little hint to make it run in parallel using PLINQ. We discussed this in Chapter 20, "Language Integrated Query Internals," in the section, "Parallel LINQ."

Parallel APIs in .NET 4 facilitate both ways of writing parallel programs. Primitives provided by the TPL are closer to imperative programming, whereas frameworks like PLINQ definitely are far more declarative. Some constructs are in the center of both approaches, making imperative constructs a bit more declarative. For example:

```
Parallel.ForEach(xs, x =>
    ProcessItem(x)
);
```

In this piece of code, we're still writing what looks like an imperative foreach loop, but now we're giving the framework a bit more flexibility. By using the Parallel class to formulate a foreach loop, we give the framework the freedom to run the loop body in parallel for each of the iterations. Notice the use of C# lambda expressions here, which make the code look as if there were a "parallel `foreach`" construct in the language.

SYNCHRONIZE, SYNCHRONIZE, SYNCHRONIZE!

You might be tempted to sprinkle the parallel loop shown in our discussion all around your existing code base. Extreme caution should be taken, though. First, you don't have any guarantee anymore about the order in which things will run. Because of this, results might appear in an order you don't expect. For example, if the loop writes to a file or makes calls to a web service, those output operations will be shuffled around because of the parallel execution.

Second, our discussion about output-order complications pinpoints a potentially bigger problem. By now, whenever you hear the words *input*, *output*, or *state* mentioned in the same sentence as *parallel* or *concurrent*, a red flag should be raised. Our parallel `foreach` loop may run much faster, but why would you care if it no longer produces correct and safe results?

The important word is *synchronization* once more. Constructs introduced in .NET 4's parallel programming libraries don't have a crystal ball that allows them to inspect your code and see it's thread safe. Proper synchronization continues to be your responsibility.

What Are Tasks?

You can think about tasks in a variety of ways. One is to start from the notion of a thread and state that tasks are like lightweight threads, running on top of a pool of low-level operating system threads. This is quite an implementation-oriented definition that starts from machine-level mechanics and builds an abstraction out of it.

A better way to think about tasks is to see them as representations of future values that get computed by means of a function. As such, tasks are sources of asynchrony in your code: While the task is running, you can do other useful work, until the point you want to await the task's result. Furthermore, tasks can be composed in a variety of ways.

In the definition in the preceding paragraph, the word *future* is used intentionally: Computer science literature often refers to this mechanism as *futures* ("in the future, there will be a value") or promises ("the tasks promise to compute a value"). Contrast the data-oriented nature of tasks with regular threads to see the difference:

```
// Using threads, there's no convenient way to return data.
var a = 42;
new Thread(() => {
    var res = ComputeResult(a); // Using a closure, see Chapter 17, "Delegates"
    // How can we return res?
}).Start();
```

```
// Using tasks, data just flows.
var t = Task<int>.Factory.StartNew(() => ComputeResult(a));
// Do other work...
Console.WriteLine(t.Result);
```

We detail how to work with tasks in the next section, "Task Parallelism," but suffice to say that tasks provide a much nicer abstraction to perform computation in the background, allowing the result to be obtained in a variety of manners at a later point in time.

TASK IS THE NEW THREAD (POOL)

Tasks should really be thought of as the new threads. Chapter 29 mentioned a number of disadvantages inherent to threads, including their cost to create. You also learned how the thread pool is used to reduce such costs and even to avoid excessive context switching by multiplexing multiple units of work onto the same physical operating system threads that get reused.

The introduction of tasks makes direct use of threads largely obsolete because they can be used for both long-running work and for short-lived operations. The latter case clearly is where you would have been using the thread pool before, although it suffers from limitations such as the ability to return values and compose operations. Tasks are a much better abstraction.

Using the thread pool for long-running work used to be problematic because you were stealing away a worker in the thread pool for a long time. The engineering done to the task infrastructure (and the underlying revamped thread pool on top of which it's built) means that tasks can now be used for long-running work, too.

Task Parallelism

Two specific types of parallelism can be distinguished: task versus data parallelism. The former concentrates on ways to run parallel tasks, or units of work, to process some operation. This is the closest to the notion of threads. Data parallelism creates parallel units of work by means of applying operations to chunks of data, which can originate from a partitioning operation of a sequence. We first cover task parallelism.

Creating and Starting Tasks

The Task Parallel Library (TPL) lives in the System.Threading.Tasks namespace, and we'll assume this namespace to be imported in the code examples that follow. To create a new task, first think about the work you want to run and whether it returns a value. If so, your goal is to create a Task<TResult> instance. Here, the generic parameter is substituted for the return type of the operation. If no data has to be returned, a nongeneric Task object can be created.

Using the Task Constructor

One way to create a new task is by using the `Task<TResult>` or `Task` constructor, where you pass in a delegate to the operation that has to be carried out. (Obviously, anonymous method expressions or lambda expressions can be used for this very purpose.)

```
var task = new Task<int>(() => {
    // Do lots of work here, computing int value "res".
    return res;
});
```

Notice how a `Task<TResult>` is conceptually similar to a `Func<TResult>`. The main difference between them is the invocation of the function taking place somewhere else, from a concurrency point of view. This is where a task's asynchrony comes into play.

The way we instantiated a task here doesn't trigger its immediate execution. Just like threads, tasks have a life cycle of different states they can go through. When created using the constructor, the task is in the `Created` state. For it to start running, you call the `Start` method on it, which causes it to go into the `WaitingForActivation` state, where it can get picked up by the scheduler to start running (after going through the `WaitingToRun` state, to be precise).

```
task.Start();
```

Ultimately, the task can run to completion (indicated by the `RanToCompletion` status) or terminate in another way, such as an error or due to cancellation.

We detail some of the constructor parameters in the "Task Creation Options" section, later in this chapter.

Using the Task Factory

Quite often, though, the first thing you're going to do with a task is to start it anyway. In such a case, it's highly recommended to create the task and start it immediately by using the `StartNew` method on a `TaskFactory`. The pattern to do this is shown here:

```
var task = Task<int>.Factory.StartNew(() => {
    // Do lots of work here, computing int value "res".
    return res;
});
```

Notice the generic parameter on `Task` can be omitted because it can be inferred from the lambda expression's return value. I've left it in for clarity, though.

THE EXTENDED ROLE OF TASKFACTORY

The `TaskFactory` class has many more methods than just `StartNew`. For most of them, refer to the MSDN documentation. One series of methods I want to point out explicitly, however, is called `FromAsync`. They enable you to bridge with the `Begin/End` asynchronous method pair pattern that occurs in quite a few places of the .NET Framework. An example of its use is shown here:

```
var file = File.OpenRead("c:\\temp\\demo.txt");
var buff = new byte[1024];
var task = Task.Factory.FromAsync<byte[], int, int, int>(
            file.BeginRead, file.EndRead, buff, 0, buff.Length, null);
```

The `FromAsync` factory method overloads take in generic parameters that match the `Begin` method parameter types and the `End` method return type. From this, the `AsyncCallback` and state parameters are omitted because they're always the same in this well-known pattern.

As a result, we get a `Task<TResult>`, where `TResult` matches the result type of the imported `End` method in the asynchronous method pair. The parameters passed to the `FromAsync` method include delegates to `Begin` and `End` methods and the parameters passed to the `Begin` method. From this point on, the invocation to the asynchronous method is represented as `Task<TResult>`, which means it can be used in any way the TPL allows.

Task-Creation Options

Some of the task's constructor overloads and factory's `StartNew` overloads take in a flags enumeration value of type `TaskCreationOptions`. Three nontrivial options exist:

▶ `LongRunning` acts as a hint to the scheduler that the task will be long running. Based on this hint, the scheduler can decide to allocate more worker threads for ad hoc parallelism because the long-running task is there to stay anyway. If this hint is not specified, it takes the scheduler some time to figure out the long-running nature of your task.

▶ `AttachedToParent` allows for the creation of hierarchical tasks where a parent task can't complete until all of its attached child tasks also complete.

▶ `PreferFairness` influences scheduling, such that tasks scheduled sooner execute sooner and tasks scheduled later execute later (which is said to be fairer).

Let's focus on the `AttachedToParent` option for a moment. Here's an example of how a child task can spawn from inside another parent task:

```
var t = Task.Factory.StartNew(() => {
    var s = Task.Factory.StartNew(() => {
        Console.Write("Task " + Task.CurrentId + " waiting for input... ");
        return Console.ReadLine();
```

```
    }, TaskCreationOptions.AttachedToParent);

    // Do work and return.
});
```

When we wait for task t to complete (see the "Retrieving a Task's Result" section) or use another means to specify a continuation (see the "Continuations" section), we cannot continue to execute until all of its attached children complete. In other words, a hierarchy of tasks has been created. In the example shown here, the child task is blocked for user input (just for the sake of illustration), and it will take until the user enters the requested input before the task completes. Because of the child task's AttachedToParent option, the parent task cannot complete until this happens, too.

Retrieving a Task's Result

Because tasks can return a value as the result of background computation, an obvious question is how to retrieve the result. This section examines one way, which leaves the Task<TResult>-based world of asynchrony and blocks until the result is available. Later in this chapter, we discuss how to schedule more work based on a task's result, using the concept of continuations (see the "Continuations" section).

Here's how to retrieve a task's result: Just call the Result property. This causes the receiving thread to block until the result is available:

```
var task = new Task<int>(() => {
    // Do lots of work here, computing int value "res".
    return res;
});

// Do other useful work until you can't but wait and block for the task's
// result to become available.

Console.WriteLine(task.Result);
```

The most important part of the sample code shown here is, likely, the comment before we call the Result property. Because you introduced the task to run asynchronously from the caller's point of view in the first place, it doesn't make sense to sit and wait for the task to complete right after creating it. Waiting for a task's completion is a synchronous act that you should do only if you absolutely need the value.

Different ways to wait for a task exist. Because tasks can also be nonvalues (using an Action delegate to specify the work they represent), the Result property makes sense only for the Task<TResult> kind. However, Task<TResult> also derives from the nongeneric Task base class, which also has a Wait method to wait for the task to run to completion. One benefit of using Wait is that you can specify a timeout:

```
var task = new Task<int>(() => {
    // Do lots of work here, computing int value "res".
    return res;
});

// Do other useful work until you can't but wait and block for the task's
// result to become available. However, while waiting using Wait, we can still
// report some progress.

while (!task.Wait(1000)) // Could also use task.IsCompleted
    Console.Write(".");

Console.WriteLine(" Done!");
Console.WriteLine(task.Result);
```

In this example, we print progress dots while waiting for the task to complete for just 1 second at a time. The Boolean return value of Wait on the timeout-based overload indicates whether the task completed. Now, the task.Result call won't block because we do it after we succeeded a wait operation on the task.

Other overloads to Wait take in a so-called CancellationToken. This concept is explained in the "Cancellation of Tasks" section, later in this chapter. The basic idea of such a token is to unify all the cancellation needs in the framework, especially in context of parallel and asynchronous programming. A simple example of this is shown here:

```
var task = new Task<int>(() => {
    // Do lots of work here, computing int value "res".
    return res;
});

Console.Write("Waiting for task result...");
var cts = new CancellationTokenSource();
try
{
    task.Wait(cts.Token);
    Console.WriteLine(task.Result);
}
catch (OperationCanceledException)
{
    Console.WriteLine("Cancelled!");
}
```

The only piece missing from the preceding code is a call to cts.Cancel based on user input that can be processed during the wait operation (for example, on a UI thread). Such a call causes the OperationCanceledException to be thrown from Wait.

Dealing with Errors

Tasks can execute arbitrary code, which obviously can also fail. How do exceptions thrown on tasks manifest themselves if they remain unhandled? Before discussing that, let's review what happens when regular threads are used:

```
new Thread(() => {
    throw new InvalidOperationException("Oops!");
}).Start();
```

This causes the process to terminate because of the unhandled exception, ignoring the behavior in .NET 1.0 where this wasn't the case. When working with threads, you must protect your threads against unhandled exceptions right inside the thread's logic (of course, subject to the desired scrutiny): Don't handle what you can't deal with!

What you should remember from this is where a thread's exceptions can be caught: only on the inside. In other words, there's no way to observe the exception from the outside or to declare what must continue to happen in response to such an exception. (To understand the phrase *continue to* used here, see the "Continuations" section, later in this chapter.)

With tasks, the situation differs significantly. Although you can still harden your task's code against catchable exceptions from the inside (and you should if it makes sense), such an exception can also be observed on the outside. One such place where a task's exception pops out is when calling the Result property or the Wait method:

```
var t = Task<int>.Factory.StartNew(() => {
    throw new InvalidOperationException("Oops!");
});

var res = t.Result; // Oops, this will throw
```

What might be unexpected at first is the type of exception that results from such a wait operation. The original exception got wrapped in an AggregateException, as shown in Figure 30.3. What's up with this?

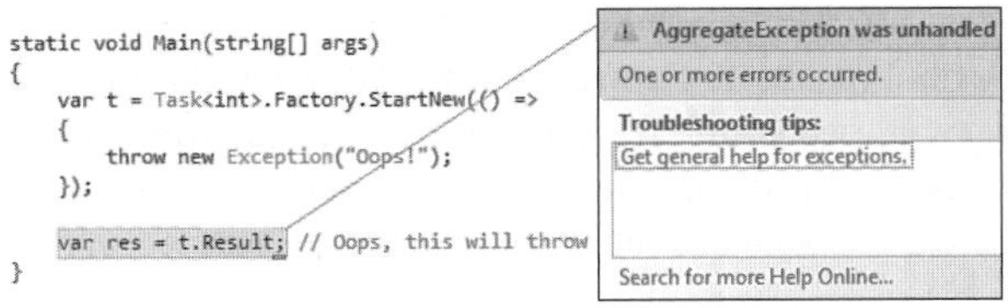

FIGURE 30.3   An AggregateException when waiting for a failed task.

Because tasks can be attached to a parent, it might be the case that multiple child tasks threw an exception. When waiting for the parent task, you should have a way to see all of the child tasks' exceptions. This is where the AggregateException type comes in.

Exploring `AggregateException`

There isn't much to the `AggregateException` type. Basically, it's an exception type whose instances can wrap multiple exceptions in a property called `InnerExceptions`, exposed as a `ReadOnlyCollection<Exception>`.

Even though you can simply inspect the collection's elements to handle exceptions you know how to handle, there's a more convenient way to go about this using a method called `Handle`. This method takes in a function mapping each inner exception onto a Boolean to indicate whether it got handled. Think of this as the equivalent of LINQ's `Where` query operator method, filtering out the inner exceptions that got handled:

```
try
{
    var res = t.Result; // Oops, this will throw
}
catch (AggregateException ae)
{
    ae.Handle(ex => {
        var ioe = ex as InvalidOperationException;
        if (ioe != null)
        {
            // Handle the exception here and return true when succeeded.
            return true;
        }
        return false;
    });
}
```

Inside the `Handle` lambda parameter, you typically perform a type-based switch on the exception object received. If you successfully handle the exception, return `true`. If not, `false` has to be returned. Upon completion of the `Handle` call, nothing happens if all the exceptions got handled. If some exceptions remain unhandled (as indicated by a `false` return value), a new `AggregateException` is thrown with the remaining exceptions wrapped inside it.

The astute reader will think of one more case, though: What if an `AggregateException` contains another such `AggregateException` inside it? Do we need to type-switch on this type and recursively handle exceptions wrapped inside it? Lucky for us, the answer is no when using the `Flatten` method. This method unwraps nested `AggregateException` (at any depth in the tree of exceptions) into a flat `AggregateException` with all exceptions directly inside its `InnerExceptions`:

```
try
{
    var res = t.Result; // Oops, this will throw
}
catch (AggregateException ae)
```

```
{
    ae.Flatten().Handle(ex => /* handler logic here  */);
}
```

A First Taste of Exception Continuations

Continuations, explained in the suitably named "Continuations" section later in this chapter, allow a declarative specification of work to do upon completion of a task. We discuss the ContinueWith method in all its glory in the aforementioned section, but here's a simple example:

```
var t = Task<int>.Factory.StartNew(() => {
    throw new InvalidOperationException("Oops!");
});

t.ContinueWith(t_ => {
    var ex = t_.Exception;
    // Handle the AggregateException here (using Handle).
}, TaskContinuationOptions.OnlyOnFaulted);

// A success continuation (using OnlyOnNotFaulted) could be specified too.
```

A continuation is a piece of work done after completion of a task, receiving the task as the parameter to the lambda expression. Different TaskContinuationOptions flags can be used to control the behavior of the continuation (for example, to call it only upon a failure case). Similarly, cancellation and success cases can have their own continuation. We explore this concept in the "Continuations" section.

(Truly) Unhandled Exceptions

What if we never obtain the Result property of a valued task, never call Wait on a void-resulting task, or never execute a continuation function upon the task's (erroneous) completion? Where does the exception go then? Clearly, unhandled exceptions should never be dropped on the floor. Invariants in your code might no longer hold, making further work a dangerous business.

In short, the best thing to do is never to abandon a task object without ever observing its result or taking appropriate error handling measures. After all, why did you start a task if you are never going to look at its result? Nonetheless, cases exist where a task gets abandoned or just exists to cause a side-effect (especially in case of nongeneric tasks that lack a result value).

When a faulted task is abandoned, the TPL does the best thing it can do to surface the exception, although (admittedly) it's not the prettiest thing: Exceptions come out on the finalizer of the task. As you recall from Chapter 12, "Constructors and Finalizers," it's the garbage collector's responsibility to call a finalizer before it reclaims memory for a dead object that implements such a method. Here's a simple example to reproduce this behavior:

```
Task.Factory.StartNew(() => { throw new Exception("Oops!"); });

Console.ReadLine();
GC.Collect(); // Don't try this at home!
```

In the preceding code, the exception comes out when the GC.Collect method is called, here only used for illustrative purposes. (You should call this method only as a last resort.) An alternative sample is shown next, emphasizing the timing when the exception pops out and takes down your application:

```
Task.Factory.StartNew(() => { throw new Exception("Oops!"); });

int i = 0;
while (true) {
    var bs = new byte[1024 * 1024]; // Stressing the GC for our own education.
    Console.WriteLine(i++);
}
```

Figure 30.4 shows the result of running this code, which allocates 1MB arrays that get abandoned instantaneously, causing the garbage collector to kick in at some point when a new allocation fails because of a full generation.

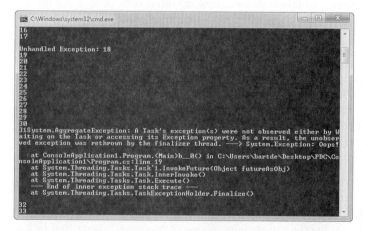

FIGURE 30.4   The finalizer of an abandoned task propagates its exception.

As you know from Chapter 12, the finalizer thread kicks in after the garbage collector has resumed execution of the virtual machine, because finalizers run managed code. So at some point after the garbage collector detected the task object as being dead (hence no one can ever observe its exception using TPL APIs), it gets dequeued from the finalization queue and the finalizer is invoked. At that point, the TPL surfaces the exception that was unhandled. Figure 30.4 clearly shows the exception message, which explains this design. Quite soon after this happens, the application is torn down as a whole. Clearly, the best thing to do is to ensure you set up a good exception-handling strategy where applicable, avoiding these kinds of sudden crashes.

To emphasize the point we're making here, this behavior occurs only when the task object is abandoned and no user code can ever observe the faulted state of the task. A simple change to the sample code illustrates this behavior clearly:

```
var t = Task.Factory.StartNew(() => { throw new Exception("Oops!"); });

int i = 0;
while (true) {
    var bs = new byte[1024 * 1024]; // Stressing the GC for our own education.
    Console.WriteLine(i++);
}
```

You might wonder how assigning the task to a temporary variable changes matters quite substantially in our sample. The answer is simple: As long as the task is assigned to a local variable (in a live stackframe), the garbage collector sees it as reachable, and hence the object never ends up on the finalization queue. Of course, if we assign null to variable t, or quit from the method without retaining the reference to the task (either by returning, assigning it to a field, or whatnot), the task is unreachable again, and the behavior from Figure 30.4 comes back.

In short, if you can handle exceptions meaningfully, never forget to put in place code that does so, either by waiting for the task or setting up a continuation.

UNOBSERVEDTASKEXCEPTION

In fact, there's another way to deal with unhandled task exceptions at a global level. The TaskScheduler type, which represents the default scheduler used by the TPL, exposes a static event called UnobservedTaskException, where you can still handle such exceptions as a last resort:

```
TaskScheduler.UnobservedTaskException += (sender, e) => {
    e.Exception.Flatten().Handle(ex => {
        // Try to handle the exception, returning true or false.
    });

    // If we get here, we can tell the TPL not to "escalate" on the finalizer.
    e.SetObserved();
};
```

Personally, I believe it's rather unlikely and superhuman if you can meaningfully recover from unhandled exceptions without knowing the bigger context of from where the error originates. If you think you can, this event might prove useful, though.

Continuations

One advantage of using tasks is their better composition compared to lower-level constructs such as threads. As mentioned at the beginning of the "Task Parallelism" section, earlier in this chapter, tasks can produce a result of some type. Taking some further action based on the result (which also could be an error or even a cancellation) is a common thing to do. This is where continuations come in.

The Basic Concept

Although they sound scary, continuations are really simple constructs. Before going into the specifics of their use in conjunction with tasks, let's explore them from a conceptual point of view. Consider the following piece of imperative sequential synchronous code:

```
int c = Add(a, b);
Console.WriteLine(c);
```

This piece of code calls a method Add, which at some point returns the sum of a and b, which we receive and can use to continue to use (for example, to print it to the screen). Let's examine a few things about this code.

First, notice how sequencing plays an important role in the code: The call to the Console.WriteLine method cannot take place until Add returns. The semicolon syntax in languages such as C# makes the sequential execution nature explicit syntactically.

Second, and related to the previous point, this code is inherently synchronous: You can't do anything but sit and wait for Add to come back before other work can be done. Although this seems tied to the notion of sequencing, we can still have sequencing without being synchronous. This is where continuations come in.

In continuation passing style (CPS), the preceding code fragment is rewritten in the following style, which at first might look a little weird:

```
Add(a, b, c => {
    Console.WriteLine(c);
});
```

Now we call some method Add, which not only takes in its two inputs, it also accepts a callback parameter that receives the result of the computation. This is where execution *continues* after Add's computation finishes (and hence the name continuation). Here's how the Add method is implemented:

```
static void Add(int a, int b, Action<int> continueWith)
{
    continueWith(a + b);
}
```

Notice we still have sequencing of operations going on: First, a and b are added together to be fed into the continuation function, which then runs after the addition takes place. Those operations are still sequential in nature. However, this is no longer the semicolon kind of sequencing we're used to from languages such as C#. Now all the remaining code to execute after the addition sits in a lambda expression.

One essential difference that's become visible after making this transformation is the change in Add's return type. Now, the Add method returns void. It's not that we have lost the result of the addition, though; the result will be fed into the continuation.

So far, we haven't done anything truly different from the synchrony point of view. This code is still intrinsically synchronous: Calling Add computes the sum of its first two arguments, followed by a call to the continuation function. However, now we could easily introduce concurrency in the Add method to compute the sum of a and b without blocking the caller to Add. As soon as that value is available, the continuation function can be called, still on a different thread. In the world of CPS, the introduction of asynchrony becomes quite easy:

```
static void Add(int a, int b, Action<int> continueWith)
{
    new Thread(() => continueWith(a + b)).Start();
}
```

Now the Add method is an asynchronous method from the caller's point of view. At the point this method returns, work is going on in the background without blocking the caller. When the sum value is available, the continuation will be called in the *future*.

Hidden Continuations in the .NET Framework

Continuations have been prominent in the .NET Framework without them being called such. Probably the best example of them is the asynchronous method invocation pattern, which we can illustrate using BeginInvoke and EndInvoke on delegates:

```
Func<int, int, int> add = (a, b) => a + b;
add.BeginInvoke(3, 4, iar => {
    int c = add.EndInvoke(iar);
    Console.WriteLine(c);
}, /* state */ null);

// The main thread can continue asynchronous while the delegate is being
// invoked. At some point the AsyncCallback continuation will be called.
```

This is nothing but CPS entrenched in the .NET Framework, with some noise due to the BeginInvoke and EndInvoke methods, the IAsyncResult dragon, the AsyncCallback delegate, and a largely redundant state parameter. Other than this, we're dealing with a continuation here.

Continuations on Tasks

The concept of continuations is exposed on Task and Task<TResult> in the form of the ContinueWith method. The function passed to this method gets called when the task completes. Typically, the continuation function results in the creation of a new task that runs the continuation code. All of this allows sequencing of asynchronous operations in a one-at-a-time fashion. Here's an example:

```
Task<int> first = new Task<int>(() => {
    // Do lots of work here. For simplicity's sake, let's return 42 verbatim.
    return 42;
});

Task<string> second = first.ContinueWith(t => {
    // Compute based on the first task's result. By trivial example:
    return t.Result.ToString();
});

Console.WriteLine(second.Result);
```

Notice how a continuation gives rise to a new Task or Task<TResult>, where the type of the returned data can differ from the original task. In fact, ContinueWith is a form of function composition on steroids, in the context of asynchronous computation.

The previous code fragment is rather incomplete, though. It assumes the first task did complete successfully because it just dots into the Result property to do its work. To be more robust against failures, various properties on the "antecedent task" (which is the previous task that was run before the continuation is invoked) can be used to inspect the situation we're dealing with. For example, the IsFaulted property will reveal there was an exception, which in turn can be retrieved from the Exception property.

Specifying Continuation Options

There are different ways to define continuations, reducing a lot of the typical clutter inside the ContinueWith lambda expression to deal with checking for faulted state or cancellation (explained in the section "Cancellation of Tasks"). Enter TaskContinuationOptions.

Before we list those options, it should be mentioned that a task can have more than just a single continuation:

```
var answer = Task<int>.Factory.StartNew(() => 42);
answer.ContinueWith(t => Console.WriteLine("C1 " + t.Result));
answer.ContinueWith(t => Console.WriteLine("C2 " + t.Result));
Console.ReadLine();
```

If there's just a single continuation, as shown in the preceding section's example, it's quite common to use a fluent interface pattern of dotting sequenced continuations together as a long chain:

```
Task<int>.Factory.StartNew(() => 42)
    .ContinueWith(t => t.Result / 2)
    .ContinueWith(t => t.Result.ToString())
    .ContinueWith(t => Console.WriteLine("42 / 2 = " + t.Result));
```

This works nicely if you put all error-handling or cancellation-handling logic inside the continuation functions. However, if you want to take distinct continuation actions for the different states a task can complete in, you must use the first style of assigning tasks to temporary variables to specify multiple continuations. Those two styles are contrasted in Figure 30.5.

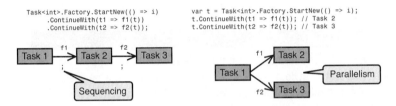

FIGURE 30.5   Sequencing versus parallel continuations.

So here are some of the continuation option flags that can be specified when creating a new continuation:

- ▶ NotOn* flags prevent the continuation from running if the specified state is true for the antecedent task. Suffixes for this family of flags include Faulted, Canceled, and RanToCompletion.

- ▶ OnlyOn* flags, for the same three states as specified in the previous bullet point, cause the continuation to be called only if the antecedent task finished in the specified state.

- ▶ ExecuteSynchronously causes the continuation to run synchronously on the thread where the antecedent task completed. This option should be used only when the continuation is short running.

Other continuation options are the same as for the TaskCreationOptions, allowing for the specification of fairness preference, the long-running hint, or to attach the task to its parent.

An example of a task with two continuations, one for success and one for failure, is shown in the following code fragment:

```
var answer = Task<int>.Factory.StartNew(() => {
    // Left to the reader: Compute a value "res"; may throw.
```

```
    return res;
});


answer.ContinueWith(t => {
    // Will only be called in success cases.
    Console.WriteLine(t.Result);
}, TaskContinuationOptions.OnlyOnRanToCompletion);


answer.ContinueWith(t => {
    // Will only be called in error cases. Handle any exception we can handle.
    t.Exception.Flatten().Handle(ex => {
        // See section "Exploring AggregateException" for more information.
        return false;
    });
}, TaskContinuationOptions.OnlyOnFaulted);
```

THE FUTURE OF C# (AND VISUAL BASIC)

One feature that's most likely going to end up in a future release of C# is support for writing sequential-looking imperative-style asynchronous code. Continuations on tasks form the low-level machinery that allows chaining together asynchronous calls. Due to their low-level nature based on callbacks, code tends to be turned inside out, ending up in continuation lambdas with lots of error-checking code.

The new proposed async feature in C# 5.0 and VB 11.0 allows writing imperative-looking code based on a new expression called await:

```
public async Task<int> CountWords(string url)
{
    string text = await DownloadStringAsync(url);
    return text.Split().Length;
}
```

Here, the DownloadStringAsync method is assumed to return a Task<string>. By performing an await operation on this task, the compiler turns the remainder code in the method into a continuation on this task. This just shows the tip of the iceberg of what's possible: All imperative constructs, such as branching and loops, can be used in an asynchronous method. Under the hood, the compiler generates a state machine of continuations, much like iterators do in C# 2.0 and later.

For more information, search the Web for "Visual Studio Async CTP."

In summary, continuations are used to chain together asynchronous computations. As discussed in the next section, it's also possible to cancel continuations. Given this option, and the ability to handle exceptions, continuations provide for sequencing points in chains of asynchronous computations.

Cancellation of Tasks

One thing that has been notoriously difficult in the world of asynchronous code (among other things, such as other threading and synchronization constructs) is the means to cancel an operation. Starting with .NET 4, cancellation has been unified in terms of two concepts: `CancellationToken` and `CancellationTokenSource`.

We don't elaborate on the intricacies of the mechanism here but instead focus on the essentials of the feature. Figure 30.6 summarizes the basic interactions with constructs for cancellation.

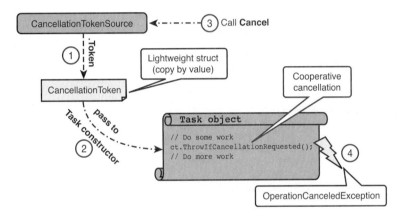

FIGURE 30.6 Cancellation of a task.

The first key notion is that of a `CancellationTokenSource`. This class is where a request for cancellation comes in by means of a call to `Cancel`. The operation being cancelled can check for this situation through a so-called `CancellationToken` struct, which can be obtained from the token source using the `Token` get-only property. This lightweight object can be passed in a variety of places across the TPL and `System.Threading` APIs starting from .NET 4. In the section "Retrieving a Task's Result," earlier in this chapter, you saw how the `Wait` method on a `Task` accepts a `CancellationToken`, allowing for cancellation of this operation.

Note that cancellation for tasks is done in a cooperative manner. In contrast to the `Thread.Abort` method, which throws an asynchronous `ThreadAbortException`, a cancellation token merely represents a flag the task should check periodically to quit the task's code when it sees a request for cancellation. It can do so either by using the `IsCancellationRequested` property or by invoking `ThrowIfCancellationRequested`, both on the token value. The latter method throws an `OperationCanceledException` that takes down the task. Obviously, this error can be observed when waiting for the task or from within continuation functions.

When wait operations occur in a task, the same token should be passed to those such that the cancellation can also unblock such wait operations. Because of the cooperative nature of cancellation, it can take a while before a cancellation is granted. This also assumes the task's code checks for cancellation on a regular-enough basis.

An example of cancellation support in tasks is shown here:

```
var cts = new CancellationTokenSource();
var ct = cts.Token;

Task.Factory.StartNew(() =>
{
    while (true)
    {
        // Alternatively, ThrowIfCancellationRequested could be used,
        // requiring the caller to handle this case.
        if (ct.IsCancellationRequested)
            return;

        Console.WriteLine(DateTime.Now);
        Thread.Sleep(1000);
    }
}, ct);

Console.WriteLine("Press ENTER to stop the clock...");
Console.ReadLine();
cts.Cancel();

Console.WriteLine("Clock stopped");
Console.ReadLine();
```

In this piece of code, we use the IsCancellationRequested property to check for such a request, which we handle by stopping the task. Using this technique, the task's status doesn't transition into Canceled but ends up in RanToCompletion because it terminated gracefully. This often suffices. However, if it makes sense for the owner of the task or for continuations to check the canceled state, an OperationCanceledException is the way to go. An example of this pattern is shown here:

```
if (ct.IsCancellationRequested)
{
    // Do cleanup if necessary (if none, the if-check can be omitted).
    ct.ThrowIfCancellationRequested();
}
```

Parallel Invocation

Invoking a single task suffices in many cases, but it often makes sense to achieve parallelism by running multiple tasks. Although we can simply create multiple tasks, some higher levels of abstraction exist in the TPL. One such abstraction is `Parallel.Invoke`, which takes an array of `Action` delegates to invoke in parallel. You can think of each such action resulting in a task being created. Only when all the tasks complete, the `Parallel.Invoke` call returns. This said, `Parallel.Invoke` makes no guarantees that the actions really run in parallel because of the way scheduling works. (The same worker might pick up all the actions, causing them to run sequentially.)

A sample of `Parallel.Invoke` is shown here:

```
Parallel.Invoke(
    () => Console.WriteLine("First task"),
    () => Console.WriteLine("Second task"),
    () => Console.WriteLine("Third task")
);
```

Another overload to the `Invoke` method takes in a first `ParallelOptions` parameter, which can be used to specify a number of flags. One is the degree of parallelism, used to limit the maximum number of parallel workers that get spawn to run the work. Yet another flag is a cancellation token, whose role should be self-explanatory.

In fact, the `Parallel` class is where task and data parallelism meet. This section covers only the `Invoke` method, which is much closer to task parallelism than it is to data parallelism. In the "Data Parallelism" section, later in this chapter, we examine parallel loop constructs exposed as static methods on the `Parallel` class.

Concerning the case of errors occurring in one or more tasks, you can probably guess how those errors get surfaced to the caller of `Parallel.Invoke`. `AggregateException` is your best friend once more. Similarly, cancellation of parallel invocation work can result in an `OperationCanceledException` wrapped inside an `AggregateException`.

Waiting for Multiple Tasks

The `Parallel.Invoke` method shown in the preceding section brings us to an interesting facility in the TPL. Did you see the one single most important difference compared to regular tasks? Here it is: Although the individual pieces of work passed to `Parallel.Invoke` can run in parallel using asynchronous tasks, the sum of the parts is synchronous. That is, `Parallel.Invoke` doesn't return until all of its actions have been executed (or some error or cancellation has occurred).

If you read Chapter 29 carefully, you might immediately think of a way to achieve this kind of synchronizing behavior across multiple parallel actions. What about using events such as `ManualResetEvent` or even the (new in .NET 4) concept of a `CountDownEvent`?

Although such a technique will work, it's rather difficult to get right (in particular when errors and cancellation enter the mix). Moreover, if not done carefully, you might induce expensive context switches because of the low-level nature of some of those wait primitives layered on top of Win32 synchronization facilities.

Luckily, the TPL provides for `WaitAll` and `WaitAny` constructs that enable us to wait for the completion of many tasks (either waiting for all of them to complete or for at least one to complete). An example of a simple `Parallel.Invoke` clone is shown here:

```
static void Main()
{
    var cts = new CancellationTokenSource();
    ParallelInvoke(cts.Token,
        () => Console.WriteLine("First task"),
        () => Console.WriteLine("Second task"),
        () => Console.WriteLine("Third task")
    );
}

static void ParallelInvoke(CancellationToken ct, params Action[] actions)
{
    var tasks = (from action in actions
                 select Task.Factory.StartNew(action, ct))
                .ToArray();

    Task.WaitAll(tasks, ct);
}
```

For fun, I've included a means to thread a cancellation token throughout the `WaitAll` call and all the `StartNew` calls that spawn the tasks. This shows one of the overloads of the `WaitAll` method on `Task`.

Other overloads of `WaitAll` allow specification of a timeout, and use of a cancellation token is optional (as usual). Errors in any of the child tasks appear collectively in an `AggregateException` thrown from the `WaitAll` call.

The `WaitAny` methods should be quite self-explanatory, as well, especially if you've had prior exposure to the equivalent method on `WaitHandle`. Those methods return an integer value indicating the index of the task in the array that completed. Overloads exist that accept a timeout value or a cancellation token. The presence of the cancellation tokens throughout the TPL API is one of the key differences with classic means to synchronize using `WaitHandle` objects. It was not uncommon before to see dummy events being passed to `Wait` methods to allow them to be unblocked:

```
WaitHandle cancel = new ManualResetEvent(false);
// Assume other events exist
```

```
int i = WaitHandle.WaitAny(new[] { cancel, event1, event2 });
if (i == 0)
    // Indicates the cancellation event was signaled.
```

Although this pattern works well in practice, it adds unnecessary burden to your code. In other places where cancellation was desired (for instance, cooperatively inside a thread), yet a different mechanism was needed (for example, using a cancellation Boolean flag). In the world of TPL, all cancellation scenarios are unified using cancellation tokens.

How the Task Scheduler Works

A thorough discussion of scheduling is beyond the scope of this discussion, but a basic understanding of task scheduling in the TPL is good to have. For more in-depth information, refer to MSDN documentation.

First, note that scheduling in the TPL is extensible because you can create your own subtype of TaskScheduler. In fact, a scheduler is fairly easy to create by implementing just three methods. Figure 30.7 shows the class diagram for the abstract base class used to implement schedulers. Italicized methods indicate abstract ones. The QueueTask method is the most essential one, allowing a new Task object to be scheduled for execution. TPL abstractions call into this method to spawn work.

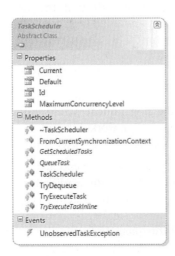

FIGURE 30.7   Custom TaskScheduler implementations can be provided.

We do not cover how to go about such a scheduler implementation, but we do continue to sketch how the default TPL scheduler does its work.

.NET 4 Thread Pool Essentials

The default TaskScheduler in the TPL gets passed to all sorts of APIs (including task creation, Parallel methods, among others) if no custom scheduler is specified. The way this scheduler works is by queuing work on the .NET thread pool, which we already discussed from a user's point of view in Chapter 29.

Compared to earlier versions of .NET and the CLR, the thread pool has been improved a lot to enable higher scalability and throughput. In particular, the thread pool's queue of work items is now implemented using a data structure known as a ConcurrentQueue, also available in the System.Collections.Concurrent namespace. This queue uses lock-free algorithms to reduce the time needed to enqueue and dequeue work items. This benefits all users of the ThreadPool class, as well. So even if you don't upgrade your code to use the TPL just yet, existing .NET code that uses the QueueUserWorkItem method to schedule background work automatically becomes faster when running it on the .NET 4 platform.

Thus far, we've referred to the thread pool as if there's only one such pool. Nothing is further from the truth, for a couple of reasons. First, each application domain has its own thread pool for reasons of isolation: It shouldn't be possible to leak delegates across application domains where they can do harm to other parts of the system.

Second, and more relevant to our discussion, local queues associated with each worker thread are used to run queued work items. Those queues are used to schedule child tasks created in the context of another (parent) task. By doing so, thread locality is preferred to execute those child tasks whenever possible. This tends to have positive effects all the way down to increased processor cache hits. One reason is that parent and child tasks typically manipulate the shared data structures (mutable or not). The technical argument that running related work on the same thread has this positive effect is based on the reasoning that the operating system scheduler tries to avoid migrating a thread across CPUs, thus increasing the likelihood of CPU cache hits when accessing memory.

Figure 30.8 shows how top-level tasks (step 1) get queued in the global queue, while child tasks (step 3) get queued in the local queue of their parent. In step 2, a worker thread that's currently idle is woken up to grab work from the global queue and start executing it.

If local queues of workers have work in it, but another worker is sitting idle, the scheduling infrastructure can employ work stealing. This mechanism enables an idle worker to steal work from another worker's queue to maximize the throughput of the system ("keep your many cores busy"). Heuristics are applied to determine whether stealing work from another queue is worth it, and if so the work gets stolen from the queue in first-in, first-out (FIFO) order.

You can find more information about work stealing and more advanced concepts such as task inlining in the MSDN documentation related to TPL.

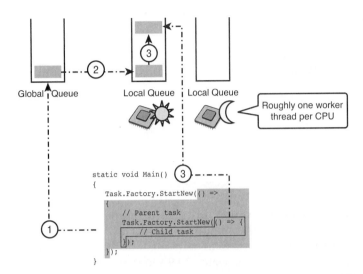

FIGURE 30.8   Global and local queues used to schedule and execute tasks.

Data Parallelism

We're now ready to look at data parallelism. This means of achieving parallel computing exploits the capability to process large data sets by partitioning them into chunks, each of which gets processed in parallel. Such techniques have existed for a long time in database query processor engines but apply equally well in the context of a general-purpose programming language. This is where TPL's data parallelism comes in, which can be found in the `System.Threading.Tasks.Parallel` class.

Parallel For Loops

One first form of data parallelism is exposed by the `Parallel.For` set of methods, which provide a parallel `for` loop. The idea of a parallel `for` loop is to run the iterations of the loop in parallel, followed by a wait operation for all the iterations to complete. This is similar to the `Parallel.Invoke` construct we looked at in the "Parallel Invocation" section, earlier in this chapter.

An example of one of the simplest overloads of `Parallel.For` is shown here. Notice how similar this loop looks to a regular C# `for` loop, thanks to the concise syntax of lambda expressions:

```
double[,] xs = GetMatrix(300, 400);
double[,] ys = GetMatrix(400, 500);
double[,] zs = new double[300, 500];

var sw = Stopwatch.StartNew();
Parallel.For(0, zs.GetLength(0), i =>
{
```

```
    for (int j = 0; j < zs.GetLength(1); j++)
    {
        zs[i, j] = 0.0;
        for (int k = 0; k < xs.GetLength(1); k++)
        {
            zs[i, j] += xs[i, k] * ys[k, j];
        }
    }
});
sw.Stop();
Console.WriteLine(sw.Elapsed);
```

This typical example of the parallel for loop is used to perform a matrix multiplication where each of the rows in the resulting matrix is computed in parallel. Although we're dealing with a shared result array, there are no clashes in accessing it because each of the cells can be computed independently of each other. Figure 30.9 shows the parallel partitioning of work in a schematic way.

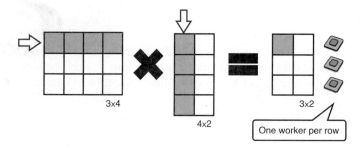

FIGURE 30.9   Data parallelism for matrix multiplication.

The use of the Stopwatch class from the System.Diagnostics namespace enables us to measure the time it takes to perform this operation using data parallelism. Testing the same code with a regular sequential for loop is equally simple:

```
sw.Restart();
for (int i = 0; i < zs.GetLength(0); i++)
{
    for (int j = 0; j < zs.GetLength(1); j++)
    {
        zs[i, j] = 0.0;
        for (int k = 0; k < xs.GetLength(1); k++)
        {
            zs[i, j] += xs[i, k] * ys[k, j];
        }
    }
}
```

```
}
sw.Stop();
Console.WriteLine(sw.Elapsed);
```

On my machine, the parallel code completed in 751 milliseconds, whereas the sequential code took a stunning 2364 milliseconds, about three times slower. This run was done on an eight-core machine. Although there's a substantial speedup going on here, don't expect a linear scaling in terms of the number of cores available. There's still overhead associated with spawning and scheduling work, too.

WHAT ABOUT USING THREADS?

It's a good exercise to try to parallelize the matrix multiplication using plain old threads, using one thread for each resulting row. In our example, this allocates no fewer than 300 threads. The cost of creating (in terms of CPU cycles and the memory impact due to allocations of each thread's stack) and starting those threads and all the context switching will be nontrivial.

Simple Overloads

The simplest of overloads to For take in three parameters: an inclusive lower bound, an exclusive upper bound, and a delegate representing the loop body. Two families of For loop methods exist, one based on Int32 (C# int) values and another based on Int64 (C# long) values:

```
static ParallelLoopResult For(int fromInclusive, int toExclusive,
                              Action<int> body);
static ParallelLoopResult For(long fromInclusive, long toExclusive,
                              Action<long> body);
```

The resulting ParallelLoopResult struct is explained in the next section. In many cases, this value is simply disregarded.

Using ParallelLoopState

A second group of overloads just extends the loop body delegate with an additional parameter of type ParallelLoopState:

```
static ParallelLoopResult For(int fromInclusive, int toExclusive,
                              Action<int, ParallelLoopState> body);
static ParallelLoopResult For(long fromInclusive, long toExclusive,
                              Action<long, ParallelLoopState> body);
```

The use case for a ParallelLoopState is to break prematurely from the loop in a variety of ways. To see why this has to be done this way, consider the following regular for loop constructor first:

```
for (int i = 0; i < 1000; i++)
{
    if (shouldStop(i))
        break;
    // Do work otherwise.
}
```

Here the `break` statement is used to quit from the loop based on some condition that can (but doesn't have to) depend on the loop iteration variable. The way `break` statements work is by emitting a branch instruction to jump beyond the entire `for` loop. This kind of control flow doesn't work in the same way inside lambda expressions, though. Although you can break outside a loop contained inside such a function, you can't jump out of the lambda expression, which after all is nothing more than an anonymous method. We say that a *nonlocal jump* is not possible using a break statement.

To alleviate this, the `ParallelLoopState` class was introduced. It's used to communicate from inside the loop that a stop of the loop is requested:

```
Parallel.For(0, 1000, (i, state) =>
{
    if (shouldStop(i))
    {
        state.Break();
        return;
    }
    // Do work otherwise.
});
```

By calling `Break`, the `Parallel.For` code ceases to spawn new tasks for the iterations beyond the current point where the break was requested. For example, if `shouldStop` evaluates `true` in iteration 10, the call to `Break` will cause no iterations beyond the 10th to get scheduled. This said, it might be the case (due to the parallel execution nature) that iterations beyond the current iteration are already in flight. Those can't be prevented from running anymore, so breaking is a best-effort service.

One invariant that `Break` ensures is that all the iterations before the point the `Break` call is issued will get executed. In the running example of breaking from the loop at the 10th iteration, this ensures that the iterations before the 10th are scheduled and get run. This mimics the behavior of a C# `break` statement as closely as possible: All iterations before the break call can execute, but iterations beyond the point are (to the extent possible) prevented from running.

An alternative way to stop a parallel loop is by calling `Stop` on the `ParallelLoopState` object. The sole difference compared to `Break` is that there's no guarantee that work before the current iteration will get run. In our example, calling `Stop` during the 10th iteration provides no guarantees that the preceding 9 iterations get executed.

The `ParallelLoopState` class contains a few other instance members that occasionally come in handy. They include properties to check whether a stop is requested and which iteration this happened in. For example, `ShouldExitCurrentIteration` can be checked to return from the loop iteration code prematurely because a request to terminate the loop was issued. Similarly, the `IsStopped` property can be checked for a stop request. You can find more information on MSDN.

One final thing we should mention is the role of the return type on the `For` methods, which is `ParallelLoopResult`. This class exposes two instance properties that enable the caller to check whether the loop completed in its entirety (`IsCompleted`) and what the lowest break iteration was if the loop didn't run to completion (`LowestBreakIteration`).

Use of `ParallelOptions`

Other overloads to `Parallel.For` take in a `ParallelOptions` object, which can configure up to three settings:

```
public class ParallelOptions
{
    public CancellationToken CancellationToken { get; set; }
    public int MaxDegreeOfParallelism { get; set; }
    public TaskScheduler TaskScheduler { get; set; }
}
```

The first one allows the specification of a cancellation token that can be used to cancel the loop from executing further, causing an `OperationCanceledException` to be thrown from the `Parallel.For` code.

Using the `MaxDegreeOfParallelism` property, the number of parallel workers used to process the loop iterations can be limited. You should exercise caution when using this flag because you might be needlessly reducing the scalability of your application, especially if you use magic constant values here. This flag can be used when you happen to know about competing resources and want to divide parallel resources in one way or another. Typically, such calculations depend on the number of cores, which can be obtained through the `System.Environment` class.

Finally, the `TaskScheduler` property can be used to pass in your own scheduler. The MSDN documentation shows how to implement such a beast if you really have to (if the default scheduler lets you down for some reason).

Using Thread-Local Data

One final set of overloads provides for thread-local data that can be manipulated safely inside the loop body. (Only one thread can be accessing the data at a time.) A separate action is invoked to aggregate the thread-local states (manipulated by the workers from the loop's iterations) into a global result. An example will make this clearer, but let's show one of the overloads first:

```
static ParallelLoopResult For<TLocal>(int fromInclusive, int toExclusive,
    Func<TLocal> localInit,
    Func<int, ParallelLoopState, TLocal, TLocal> body,
    Action<TLocal> localFinally);
```

The first function parameter, called `localInit`, is used to initialize thread-local state. Each body invocation receives the loop variable and the `ParallelLoopState` (explained in the preceding section) and the current thread-local value. In those overloads, the body is no longer an action but has become a function that returns the updated thread-local state because of the iteration's execution. The final parameter is executed once for every thread-local that was initialized during the execution of the loop and is used to aggregate those results when the loop completes.

Here's an example, also shown on MSDN:

```
var xs = Enumerable.Range(0, 1000000).ToArray();
long total = 0;

Parallel.For<long>(0, xs.Length,
    () => 0,
    (j, loop, subtotal) => {
        subtotal += xs[j];
        return subtotal;
    },
    subtotal => Interlocked.Add(ref total, subtotal)
);

Console.WriteLine("The total is {0}", total);
```

For each unique worker thread that's involved in executing the parallel `for` loop, the function for local state initialization (here simply returning `0`) will be called. From this point on, the initialized data is stored in thread-local storage that's fed to the loop body function every time the worker processes a new iteration. The updated subtotal is then returned from the loop body, to be stored in the worker thread's thread-local storage again. When all the workers have completed all their work for the loop, the aggregation function is called, where we sum up (in a thread-safe manner) the subtotals into a global total.

I recommend carrying out the debugger experiment illustrated in Figure 30.10. First, you'll see a relatively small number of calls to the initialization function, more or less proportional to the number of processor cores (or the degree of parallelism if specified) available. This is due to the initialization happening only once per worker, which is nothing but a thread that gets reused across multiple work items.

After all the loop bodies have executed on the active workers, the subtotals that live in the workers' thread-local state will be aggregated through the `finally` function that will get called once per worker.

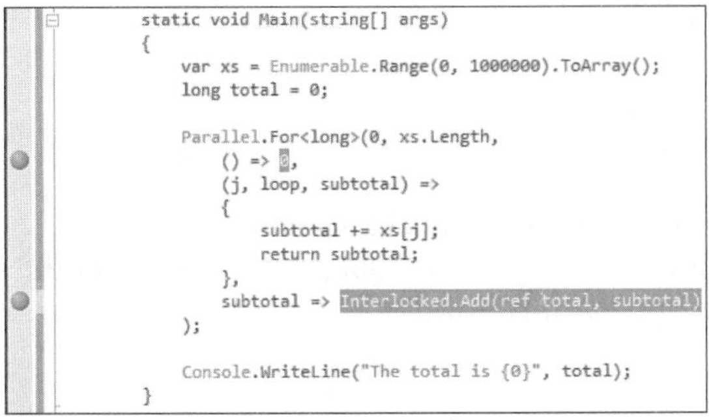

```
        static void Main(string[] args)
        {
            var xs = Enumerable.Range(0, 1000000).ToArray();
            long total = 0;

            Parallel.For<long>(0, xs.Length,
                () => 0,
                (j, loop, subtotal) =>
                {
                    subtotal += xs[j];
                    return subtotal;
                },
                subtotal => Interlocked.Add(ref total, subtotal)
            );

            Console.WriteLine("The total is {0}", total);
        }
```

FIGURE 30.10   Observing function calls during a parallel loop with thread-local state.

Using the thread-local state option of a parallel for loop means that you don't have to manage such state yourself (which can be rather error-prone otherwise). Typically, this technique is used when the resulting loop has to compute some kind of aggregation value.

AggregateException Strikes Again

It should be quite obvious that all the overloads of parallel loop constructs (and the Parallel.Invoke method discussed in the "Parallel Invocation" section) can throw an AggregateException that collects all the exceptions that happened on the parallel tasks that got spawned by the data parallel construct.

Parallel Foreach Loops

Just as the Parallel.For method resembles a C# for loop, the Parallel.ForEach method is designed to mirror the C# foreach loop. Given an enumerable sequence, the ForEach method allows for the parallel execution of a loop body for each of the elements in the given sequence.

Most of the concepts discussed in our coverage of For carry over to the ForEach case as well, including the use of ParallelLoopOptions, the ParallelLoopState with Break and Stop methods, and the ParallelLoopResult. Similarly, thread-local state can be associated with the workers that carry out the loop's work.

In what follows, we focus on the additional concepts introduced for the Foreach loop that are unique to this kind of loop. But first, let's consider a simple example of the use of this data parallel operation with one of the most extensive overloads:

```
var xs = Enumerable.Range(0, 1000000);
long total = 0;

Parallel.ForEach(xs,
    () => 0L,
    (x, loop, subtotal) => {
        subtotal += x;
        return subtotal;
    },
```

```
    subtotal => Interlocked.Add(ref total, subtotal)
);
```

```
Console.WriteLine("The total is {0}", total);
```

Here we're iterating over the enumerable sequence with parallel loop body executions. Again, we're using a long-valued thread-local state to compute subtotals of the sum of the sequence's elements, which get aggregated into the final sum.

The Role of Partitioners

To run operations on the elements of a sequence in parallel, the sequence needs to be partitioned into chunks of work. This is where the concept of partitioners enters the picture. They play a crucial role in the PLINQ implementation, too (see the section "Parallel LINQ" in Chapter 20).

The idea of a partitioner is to let the workers that execute the loop body process more than just individual elements one at a time. For example, if you have 100 elements and four cores, it makes sense to have each core take care of the work for 25 elements. Such a common partitioning scheme is called *range partitioning*, where the input sequence size has to be known upfront to create index-based ranges for each worker. This scheme has a disadvantage, though: If one worker completes way before other workers are done with their part of the work, the idle worker cannot steal work.

Another way to partition a sequence is *chunk partitioning*, where chunks of a given size are processed by workers. This differs from range partitioning in that the split-up of the work is not statically based on the number of workers. For example, given 100 elements and a chunk size of 5, we get 20 units of work. If there are, say, four cores with a worker allocated for each core, they will on average execute five chunks each. This isn't static allocation of chunks to workers, though; if a worker is presented with a chunk, it can process much faster than another worker can process its chunk, and it can readily move on to the next chunk. Overall, the throughput of the system is higher. *Load-balancing partitioning* is another name for the use of dynamic chunk-based partitioning.

You can create a partitioner by using the `Partitioner.Create` factory methods. A set of overloads is based on from and to bounds, combined with range sizes, creating a partitioner that employs *range partitioning*. Other overloads can take in an array or an IList<T> object, whose length is known immediately. Depending on a Boolean flag named loadBalance, the resulting partitioner uses range partitioning or *load-balancing chunk partitioning*.

For more information about the use of partitioners and the creation of custom partitioners, refer to the MSDN documentation about the subject.

Summary

Taking advantage of multicore machines is becoming increasingly important. From a programmer's point of view, the new features in .NET 4's System.Threading libraries make it easier to do so.

In this chapter, we explored the notion of task parallelism centered around the Task and Task<TResult> types. We discussed how to create tasks, await their results, work with continues, and deal with various aspects such as errors and cancellation. In summary, tasks are the new means to perform work asynchronously, whether it's long running (where you'd have used threads before) or more ad hoc short-lived computations (using thread pools before). We also discussed how the task scheduler works, layered atop of the improved thread pool, employing techniques such as work stealing.

We finished our discussion of modern .NET 4 approaches to parallelism with a tour through data parallelism, exposed through the Parallel class's loop methods. During our discussion, you learned about loop state, parallelization options, partitioning schemes, and more.

Index

SYMBOLS

. (period), 335

; (semicolons), 217

#region directive, 497

$exception, applying, 1182

+ operator, 260

, (commas), trailing, 558

- operator, 260

. (dot) parameter, 1379

; (semicolons), 355

| operator, 565

~ == operator, overloading, 624-626

NUMERICS

64-bit

    addressing, 1494

    environments, 1329

    programs, 1239

A

aborting threads, 1444

absolute time, 1317-1318

abstract classes, 683-685

abstract keyword, 656

abstract syntax trees. *See* ASTs

abstraction

    concurrency, 1469

    levels, 6

    stacks, 644

Accept method, 1094

access control lists. *See* ACLs

AccessException types, 1266

accessing

    CAS, 1275

    control systems, 488

    cross-thread, 884

    elements, 347-349

    fields, 335, 546-549

    generics, 336-337

    indexers, 349

    late-bound property, 1073

    members, 335-338, 486, 1097

    protected accessibility, 669-670

    static members, 549

    types, 24

accessors

    add, 847-851

    get, 573, 649

    properties, 571

    remove, 847-851

    set, 573, 649

accumulation, types, 1011

accuracy of timers, 839

ACID (atomicity, consistency, isolation, and durability), 461-462

ACLs (access control lists), 1397

Action delegate, 856

actions, ForAll, 1034-1035

Activator.CreateInstance<T> method, 728

Active Server Pages. *See* ASPs

Active Template Library, 7

add accessor, 847-851

add function, 73

add keyword, overflow, 262

Add method, 28, 334, 340, 516, 701, 780, 1266

Add New Item dialog box, 532

add.ovf instruction, 263

Add Reference dialog box, 1312

adding

    libraries, 102

    members, 1051

    performance counters, 1385

add-ins

    MarshalByRefObject calculator, 1284-1285

    .NET Framework, 1287-1289

addition on the binary level, 260

addressing, 64-bit, 1494

ADO.NET, 161-163

advanced locks, 1483-1486

agents, isolation of state, 97

Aggregate operator, 267, 1009

AggregateException, 1211-1212, 1513-1515

aggregation

    GroupBy method, 1016

    operators, 1008-1017

AJAX, 888, 897

algorithms

    parallel, 96

    recursive, 1203

aliases, 208-209, 326, 506

    BCL, 1117

    conflicts, 1230

    namespaces, 1226-1227

    reference types, 185

All operator, 1017

allocating

    heaps, 792

    memory, 43, 470, 475

    objects, 44

ambiguous type names, 1225

analysis

    code, 117, 543-544, 1364-1365

    memory leaks, 857

    performance, 1378

    runtime behavior, 1386

    threads, debugging, 1461

AND operator, 274, 276

anonymous function expressions, 789-790

anonymous iterators, 983

anonymous methods, 344-346

anonymous types, 66, 386

    generics, 739

    object initializers, 930-933

Any operator, 1017

apartments, threads, 1450-921

APIs (application programming interfaces), 6, 60, 1291

    Delegate, 826

    discoverability of, 1216

    exception handling, 415

    expression trees, 1093-1104

    generics, 699

    inheritance, blocking, 665

    LINQ, 64, 901

    namespaces, 1214

    .NET Framework versions, 100

    parallelism, 1506

    parameters, renaming, 800

    string concatenation, 269

    System.Data.SqlClient, 904

    System.Xml.Linq, 917

APL, 15

Append method, 1404

application programming interfaces. *See* **APIs**

ApplicationException, 1193

applications

    ASP.NET, 124

    automation, 1159

    building, 1216

    with COM interop, 1154-1165

    compiling, 175-176

    Console Application, 124

    deployment, 10

    domains, 37-39, 1233, 1277-1289, 1278-1279

    entry points, 171-172

    extensibility, 1059-1070

    ExtensiCalc, 1059

    Hello World, 110

    localizing, 1350-1352

    native, 1435

    .NET, 109-116

    reactive, 835-843, 888-900

    running, 175-176

    types, 10

    Visual Studio 2010, 124-169

    Windows Forms Application, 124

    WPF, 124

applying

    arrays, 1305-1310

    attributes, 1077-1078

    delegates, 836-839

    directories, 1394-1397

    dynamic keyword, 1119-1127

    event logs, 1379-1381

    ExpressionTreeVisitor, 1105-1107

    extensions, 527-528, 1059

    gacutil.exe, 1251

    generic types, 708-709

    lightweight code generation, 1104

    mutexes, 1477-1480

    paths, 1397-1398

properties, 569-572

semaphores, 1480-1483

strong-name keys, 1246-1247

task constructor, 1509

TaskFactory, 1509-1510

thread-local data, 1533-1535

threads, 1432-1462

approximating Pi, 1316

arbitrary precision arithmetic, 187

architecture

add-ins, 1288

DLR, 1148-1150

TPL, 1503-1504

ArgumentException, 412, 1185, 1205

ArgumentNullException, 240, 419, 983, 1185, 1206

ArgumentOutOfRangeException, 1207

arguments, 505

command-line, debugging, 421

passing, 506-507

arithmetic

with DateTime values, 1324

expressions, compilers, 1084-1091

operators, 253, 255-265

characters, 259

decimals, 258

floating-point, 255-257

integers, 255-256

nullables, 265

arity of operators, 248

ArrayList, 754

arrays, 228-236, 333

applying, 1305-1310

element access, 348

initializers, 231-233

internal representation, 228

jagged, 233-235

LINQ, 1306

manual array indexing, 295

multidimensional, 235-236

parameters, 510-512

single-dimensional, 229-231

types, covariance, 741-744

ArrayTypeMismatchException, 1196

as keyword, 631

as operator, 311-315

ascending keyword, 936

AsEnumerable operator, 1022-1024

AsOrdered operator, 1032-1033

AsParallel method, 1028-1031

ASP.NET, 10, 39, 124, 151-154, 1292

ASPs (Active Server Pages), 8

assemblers

IL code, 291

languages, 778

assemblies, 1217, 1233-1276, 1277

application domains, 38

BCL, 1294-1298

bindings, 1260

collections, 1083

default values, 514

deployment, 1240-1244

files, 1236

GACs, 36, 108, 1233, 1242, 1249-1253. *See also* GACs

inspecting, 112-116

installing, 36

loading, 35-36, 1274-1276, 1278

locating, 1259-1261

manifests, 26-27

modules, 1234-1236

mscorlib, 1296-1298

naming, 1240-1244

navigating, 1295

.NET, 15-17

NGEN, 42

properties, 1237-1240

references, 1253-1255, 1301

reflection, flashback, 1272-1274

resources, embedding, 1268-1270

runtime, loading, 1255-1261

satellite, 1269

saving, 1091

searching, 1255, 1296

services, loading, 11

strong naming, 1244-1249

System, 1296-1298

System.Interactive, 1016

testing, 1253

types, 1236-1237

   definitions, 1227

   forwarding, 1270-1272

unloading, 37, 1278

versioning, 1240-1244

visibility, 1265-1268

Assembly property, 1055

AssemblyInfo.cs file, 1238

AssemblyName object, 1275

AssemblyQualifiedName property, 1055

AssemblyVersion attribute, 1248

asserts, 1366-1365, 1367-1369

assignment

   compound, 287-290, 611

   constants to variables, 252

   definite, 290-294

   local variables, 212-213

   operators, 285-297

   redundancy, 293

   simple, declaration versus, 285-287

   statements, 354-355

values

   to members, 559-560

   parameters, 507

associations, statements, 360

associativity

   binary operators, 250

   null-coalescing operators, 283

   operators, 248-250

   result types, 282

   simple assignment, 286

ASTs (abstract syntax trees), 1038

AsyncCallback delegate, 816

asynchronous

   computation of Fibonacci numbers, 818

   distributed computing, 889

   invocation, 811-824

   methods, 1416

   programming, 95

   read and write operations, 1413-1421

atomicity, 458, 1472-1474

attacks, injection, 906

attributes

   AssemblyVersion, 1248

   AttributeUsage, 1118

   BeforeFieldInit type, 1198

   customizing, 1075-1081

   InternalsVisibleTo, 1267-1268

   serialization, 1282

   STAThread, 885

   StructLayout, 596

   ThreadStatic, 1452

AttributeUsage attribute, 1118

authentication, Windows integrated authentication (-E), 913

auto-completion, 738

   event handlers, naming, 864

auto-implemented properties, 74-75, 572-573, 873-875

automation

memory management, 43-46

numbering, 559

Office, 1159

parallelization, 1505. *See also* parallelism

Average aggregation, 960

Average operator, 1013

Axum, 97

B

backgrounds

mode, NGEN, 42

threads, 1446-1448

BackgroundWorker component, 1495-1498

backing fields, 571

backward compatibility, 6, 59

Bag dynamic object, 1145

Bar method, 480, 508, 645, 1260

base calls, 682

Base Class Library. *See* BCL

base classes

constraints, 723-724

constructors, 659

Expression, 1093-1094

members, hiding, 666-669

base keyword, 656, 659

BaseType property, 1055

BASIC, 7

BCL (Base Class Library), 10, 14, 30, 51-53

Activator.CreateInstance<T> method, 728

aliases, 1117

assemblies, 1294-1298

default project references, 1293-1294

exception types, 1193-1212

GACs, 36

interfaces, 871

join clause, 950

multiple interfaces, 664

namespaces, 1293

output parameters, 508-510

overview of, 1291

references, 1294-1298

statements, 353

System root namespace, 1301-1346

System.Core.dll, 1298-1301

text, 1346-1362

WeakReference, 715

BeforeFieldInit type attribute, 1198

BeginInvoke method, 816

behavior

CLR, 39

debugger-dependent, 1375

methods, refactoring, 540

runtime analysis, 1386

shell execution, 1387

big endians, 1412-1413

Big O notation, 754-755

BigInteger type, 1310-1312

binary

expressions, 1095-1096

notation, 188

operators, 248. *See also* operators

associativity, 250

as lifted operators, 607

BinaryReader class, 1411-1412

BinaryWriter class, 1411-1412

Bind operation, 1137

binders, 1128-1134, 1138

BindingFlags, 1075

bindings

assemblies, 1260

assembly versions, redirecting, 1242-1244

dynamic keyword, 1110

let clauses, 961-964

bits, floating-point numbers, 193

black boxes, 92

BlockExpression statement, 1101

blocking

inheritance, 665-666

message loops, 823

threads, 1441, 1446

blocks, 351

catch, 414

finally, executing, 1175

protected, 1178

statements, 356-357

switch statements, 371

try, 414

using, 597

Body property, 73

Boolean

expressions, 358

logical operators, 275-277

values, 196-197, 353

Boolean expressions, 1107

bootstrapping at runtime, 33-35

boxing, 700

conversions, 631

equality operators, implementing, 616

generic types, 710-712

types, 478-479

branching operations, 362

break statements, 366, 378-380

breakOuter method, 379

breakpoints, debugging, 137

Breakpoints window, 137

broken arrow covariance, 630-631

buffers, 1307-1308

build support, 130-135

building applications, 1216

built-in

conversions, 627-631

operations, 1061-1062

types

languages, 185-209

reserved words, 197

C

c

control flow/stack maintenance abstractions, 644

runtime, heaps, 44

Win32 programming in, 6

C-style function pointers, 783

C++, 10

abstraction levels, 6

classes, 590

caches, 1415

GACs, 36, 108, 1233, 1242, 1249-1253. See also GACs

polymorphism, 1136

Calculate method, 22, 1039

calculateFib method, 823

calculating

code metrics, 538

integral type precision, 187

CalculatorUI.exe, 1259

calendar systems, 1320-1321

Call Information mode, 1183

Call Stack pane, 136

Call Stack window, 1183

calls

asynchronous methods, 1416

base, 682

constructors, 328

Debugger.Break, 1374

delegates, 342

dynamic

call sites, 1128-1134

languages, 81-83

optimization, 1051

finalizers, 592

generic methods, 733

instance members, 491

methods, 340, 353-354, 1042

nonvirtual, 679

OrderByDescending, 936

reverse extension method, 529

stacks, 254, 406, 416, 471

Standard Query Operator method, 934

virtual, 679

callvirt method, 340

camel casing, 546

cancellation of tasks, 1523

CancellationPending property, 1498

CanReduce property, 1094

captured outer variables, 790-793

Cartesian coordinates, 632, 634

CAS (Code Access Security), 11, 47-49, 254, 1075, 1275

case sensitivity, 172, 189

cast expressions, 300-306

Cast operator, 997

Cast<T> operator, 968

catch blocks, 414

catching exceptions, 428, 1174, 1184-1187

causes of exceptions, 412-415

CCI (Common Compiler Infrastructure), 1365

CCR (Concurrency Coordination Runtime), 97

CDS (Coordination Data Structures), 96

cells, nonblocking, 95

CER (System.Runtime.ConstrainedExecution), 1200

chaining

method calls, 1042

query expressions, 956

ChangeIt method, 472

char parameter, 326

characters

arithmetic operators, 259

literals, 189-190

sequences, 1356

Unicode, 189, 327

checked contexts, 352

checked exceptions, 422, 1171. *See also* exceptions

checked keyword, 628

checking

enumeration flags, 275

for flags, 566-567

overflow, 260-265

query statements, 905

timestamps, 135

types, 286, 767

violations, 783

Church, Alonzo, 70, 347

CIL (Common Intermediate Language), 12, 16

CKHR macro, 1170

Class Library, 124

classes, 465

abstract, 683-685

base, constraints, 723-724

BCL. *See* BCL

BinaryReader, 1411-1412

BinaryWriter, 1411-1412

C++, 590

Counter, 649

Debug, 1371

declaring, 393

derived, designing events for use by, 869-871

Directory, 1402

DirectoryInfo, 1402

Environment, 1329

File, 1401

FileInfo, 1398-1399

functions, 781. *See also* functions

hierarchies, 864

inheritance for, 657-669

instances, 579. *See also* instances

languages, 184-185

Lazy<T>, 1343-1344

mapping, 913

Math, 1308

.NET, 19-20

OOP, 656

ParallelLoopState, 1533

PipeStream, 1424

single inheritance for, 661-663

static, 589

Stream, 1408

StringBuilder, 1359-1361

StringReader, 1407

StringWriter, 1407

structs, comparing, 466-486

System.Console, 291

System.Exception base, 1191

System.GC, 713

TextReader, 1406-1407

TextWriter, 1406-1407

Thread, 791, 1436-1441

ThreadLocal<T>, 1456-1458

WaitHandle, 1490

clauses

finally, 432-433

from, 923, 1029

group by, 942-949

into, 955-961

join, 949-954

let, 918, 961-964

orderby, translation, 941

Select, 924, 927-933, 955

WHERE, 534

where, 71, 933-936, 1029

cleanup, deterministic resource, 438-447

CLFS (Common Log File System), 1429

CLI (Common Language Infrastructure), 12-14, 56, 112, 1178

single inheritance for classes, 661

zero-initialization, 585

Click handler, 1497

Client Profile (.NET 3.5), 106

cloning, deep, 762

Close methods, 434

closures, local variables, 1457

CLR (Common Language Runtime), 11, 16, 30, 1233

array type covariance, 744

behavior, 39

entry points, 33, 176-177

errors, 18

exception handling, 431

fields, 550

hosts, 39

managed code, 1435

memory

allocating, 43

management, 292

multilanguage usability, 1049

namespaces, 1217

.NET Framework, 102

overview of, 32-51

processes, 1278

protected accessibility, 670

runtime, shims, 106

strong-named assemblies, 1249

types, 17-24

CLS (Common Language Specification), 13

compliance, 202-208

compliant types, 19

generics, 727-729

multilanguage usability, 1049

role of, 23-24

co- and contravariance, generic, 786

COBOL, 12, 15

code

analysis, 117, 543-544, 1364-1365

binders, 1138

compiling, 59

contracts, 1369-1371

cross-language interoperability, 12

defects, 412-415

dynamic call sites, 1129

editors, 128-130

hash, 755-758

IL, 24, 27-29, 72. *See also* IL code

insight features, 139-143

interoperability, 11, 1240

IronPython, 1122

iterator, 977

Just My Code, 424

lightweight generation, 1082-1091

lock statements, 456-458

managed, 24-32, 1434-1436

manipulation, 93

metrics, calculating, 538

navigating, 116

.NET

compiling, 111-112

running, 112

writing, 110-111

NGEN, 42-43

paths, 503

quality, 1364-1378

return statements, 407

reuse, 649

Show External Code, 1115

snippets, 490

exceptions, 1192

writing, 1192

types, 180-182

Windows Forms designer, 879

wrappers, 595

writing, 1052-1053

Code Access Security. *See* **CAS**

Code Analysis, 311, 354

Code Document Object Model (CodeDOM), 93, 1100-1101

Code Metrics, 539

CodePlex, 77, 169, 1365

co-evolution of languages, 878

collections, 1338

assemblies, 1083

generic types, 61

initializers, 333-335, 701-702

in-memory, 902

syntax, 766, 770-771

types, 389, 753, 775

generic, 762-775

generics, 697-699

nongeneric, 753-762

COM (Component Object Model), 7, 10, 50
   exceptions, 1169-1170
   interfaces, 1164
   interoperability, 83-86, 1150-1165
   managed code, 1152-1154
   namespaces, 1216
   overview of, 1152
   tabs, 1155
Combine method, 826, 845
combining delegates, 824-830
COMEFROM, 403
command-line, 109, 1330-1331
   arguments, debugging, 421
   MSBuild, 135
commands. *See also* functions
   Dec, 648
   GCRoot, 856
   Inc, 648
   prompts, Visual Studio 2010, 121
   SOS, 1182-1188
   subst, 1394
commas (,), trailing, 558
comments
   delimited, 223-224
   documentation, 224-228
   single-line, 220-221
Common Compiler Infrastructure (CCI), 1365
Common Intermediate Language. *See* CIL
Common Language Infrastructure. *See* CLI
Common Language Runtime. *See* CLR
Common Language Specification. *See* CLS
Common Log File System. *See* CLFS
Common Object Runtime. *See* COR
Common Type System. *See* CTS

communication
   cross-domain, 1279-1287
   serial port, 1429
   WCF, 1283
commutativity, 619
Compact Framework, 10
compacting heaps, 45
Compare method, 771, 1493
CompareTo method, 719
comparison operators, 271
compatibility
   backward, 6, 59
   forwarders, 1272
   types, 18
Compile method, 1087-1091
compilers, 25
   arithmetic expressions, 1084-1091
   base class members, hiding, 667
   expression trees, 1092-1093
   extension methods, 529-532
   as services, 92-94
compiling
   applications, 175-176
   code, 59
   compile-time participation, 94
   .dll assemblies, 1241
   generic constraints, 720
   IL code, 31
   iterators, 984-989
   JIT, 39-41, 1263
   .NET, 111-112
   query statements, checking, 905
   regular expressions, 1355
complex numbers, 1312-1314
complexity, 778
compliance, CLS, 202-208
Component Object Model. *See* COM

Component Object Runtime Execution Engine, 33

Component Object Runtime Workstation, 34

components
    BackgroundWorker, 1495-1498
    event logs, 1381
    FileSystemWatcher, 1400

compound assignments, 267, 287-290, 611

compound keys, 945-949

computed keys, 945

computing prime numbers, 394

Concat method, 737

Concat operator, 1019

concatenation
    LINQ, 920
    strings, 266-270

concrete types, 324-325

ConcRT, 96

concurrency, 91, 94-97
    abstracting, 1469
    loops, 400-401

Concurrency Coordination Runtime. See CCR

conditional debugger output, 1371-1373

conditional operators, 278-281, 611-615

conditions, code contracts, 1370

configuring
    assembly properties, 1237-1240
    event handlers, 1401
    extern aliases, 1228
    Fusion Log Viewers, 1259
    IDEs, 121
    IntelliTrace, 1183
    platform targets, 1239
    post-build events, 1067
    strong-name keys, 1246-1247
    Windows settings, 1433

conflicts, aliases, 1230

Console Application, 124

console user interfaces. See CUIs

Console.WriteLine method, 291

const keyword, 213, 358

constants, 1308
    concatenation, 267
    fields, 555-557
    floating-point, 194
    local variables, 213-214
    variables, assigning, 252

constituent types, 572

constraints
    base classes, 723-724
    default constructor, 724-731
    generics, 716-732
    interfaces, 717-723

constructing
    generic types, 702, 708
    objects, 702

constructors, 22, 324, 325-328, 579
    abstract representations of, 182
    base class, 659
    default constraints, 724-731
    fields, initializing, 552
    inheritance, 658
    initializers, 585-586
    instances, 579-580
    naming, 581
    state, 1066
    static, 586-589, 1197
    structs, implementing on, 583
    tasks, applying, 1509

constructs, loops, 400

contagious properties, dynamic typing, 1112-1114

containers, types, 1131

Contains operator, 1017

ContainsGenericParameters property, **1056**

Content property, **305**

context

   grammar, 925

   keywords, 59, 178-179

   switching, 1433-1434

continuation

   after grouping, 958

   into clauses, 955-961

   exceptions, 1515

   options, 1520-1522

   tasks, 1518-1522

continuation passing style (CPS), **1518**

continue statements, 379

ContinueWith method, **1520**

contracts

   code, 1366-1365, 1369-1371

   interfaces, 689, 1285-1287

contravariance, **87-89, 740-751**

   delegates, 866

   generics, 746-749, 893

controlling

   debuggers, 1373-1375

   processes, 1386-1389

controls, flow, **644**

conventions. *See* naming, conventions

conversions, **603, 628-641**

   boxing, 631

   built-in, 627-631

   dates and time, 1318

   enumerations, 628

   explicit, 628, 632

   implicit, 299-317, 520, 628, 632

   integral values, 563

   MSDN documentation, 638-641

   narrowing, 628

   nullable, 628

   numeric, 627-628

   references, 629-630

   strings to enum values, 563-564

   unboxing, 631

   user-defined, 631-637

   widening, 628

cooperative scheduling, **1445**

coordinates

   Cartesian, 632, 634

   X-coordinate, 634

Coordination Data Structures (CDS), **96**

copy tool, **1496**

   deployment, 1256-1257

copy-by-value realization, **1281**

CopyTo method, **1268, 1423**

COR (Common Object Runtime), **1151**

_CorExeMain function, **33**

costs

   of exceptions, 1174

   of threads, 1502

Count get-only property, **648**

Count operator, **1012**

Count property, **669**

CountDownEvent, **1467, 1489**

countdowns

   GUIs, 882-888

   mechanisms, 835

Counter class, **649**

counters, monitoring performance, **1337, 1382-1386**

covariance, **87-89, 740-751**

   broken arrow, 630-631

   delegates, 866

   generics, 705, 746-749, 893

   safety, 744-745

CPS (continuation passing style), **1518**

crashes, debugging, **1184**

Create method, 1404

CreateDomain method, 1278

CreateInstance method, 724

CreateInstance<T> method, 728

CreateJobObject method, 596

creating. *See* formatting

cross-domain communication, 1279-1287

cross-language

    inheritance, 31

    interoperability, 12, 1127, 1137

    use, generic constraints, 727

cross-thread access, 884

cryptography, 1245

CTS (Common Type System), 13, 56

    multilanguage usability, 1049

CUIs (console user interfaces), 176

curly braces, 357, 361

    exception handling, 424

Current property, 974

currying, 796

customizing

    accessors, 851

    attributes, reflection, 1075-1081

    interfaces, 123

    ordering, 941

D

data binding, WPF, 875-876

data filtering, 401

data parallelism, 1529-1536

Data property, 1190

data representations, dynamic typing, 337

data structures, 704, 720

Data Structures for Coordination, 1504

data types, 180-182

databases

    mappers, 157-163

    relational, 61

        LINQ, 903-907, 911-917

        reflection, 1073

DataSet, 157-159

dates, 1317-1325

DateTime type, 19, 1317-1318

DateTime.Now static property, 1317

DCOM (Distributed COM), 7

DDE (Dynamic Data Exchange), 1137

deallocation

    memory, 470, 476

    objects, 444

Debug class, 1371

Debug toolbar, 137

Debug.Assert method, 1367

Debug.Fail method, 1373

debuggers, controlling, 1373-1375

debugging

    anonymous function expressions, 790

    asserts, 1368

    command-line arguments, 421

    diagnostics, 1371-1373

    exception handling, 417

    extensions, 1067

    history, 1184

    IntelliTrace, 1183-1184

    MDAs, 1181

    support, 134, 136-138

    threads, 1460-1462

    types, 18

    visualizers, 1104

    Visual Studio 2010, 117

DebugView, 1103

Dec command, 648

decimals
  arithmetic operators, 258
  types, 194-196
declaration statements, 351, 357-358
declarative languages, 90, 1504-1507
declarative programming, 92
declaring
  classes, 393
  events, 877
  extern methods, 536-538
  fields, 546
  generic types, 703-708, 732
  handlers, 427
  implicitly typed local variables, 215-220
  instance constructors, 580
  local variables, 209
  Main method, 490
  namespaces, 1219-1223
  pairwise declaration, 615
  properties, 569-572
  versus simple assignment, 285-287
  types, 933
  values, 555
  variables, 285
  virtual members, 675-676
DeclaringType property, 1055
decomposing types, 465
Decrement method, 1493
decrement operators, 294-297, 355, 610-611
deep cloning, 762
deep tree data structures, 1204
DefaultIfEmpty source generator, 992
defaults
  constructor constraints, 724-731
  keyword, 714
  namespace configuration settings, 1219
  project references, 1293-1294

(T) expression, 715
values
  expressions, 320-323
  optional parameters, 514
  type parameters, 714-716
defects, code, 412-415
deferred overload resolution, 1114-1117
DefineOperation method, 342
defining
  classes with constructors, 580
  custom attributes, 1076-1077
  exception types, 1190-1193
  extension methods, 524-526
  finalizers, 591
  flags enum values, 565
  indexers, 575-576
  interfaces, 686-688, 1060-1061
  methods, 501-502, 517-518
  operators, 604-605
  private instance constructors, 525
definite assignment, 290-294, 510
delayed signing, 1246
delegates, 777
  Action, 856
  anonymous function expressions, 789-790
  applying, 836-839
  AsyncCallback, 816
  asynchronous invocation, 811-824, 1420
  captured outer variables, 790-793
  combining, 824-830
  contravariance, 866
  covariance, 866
  events, 834-835
  expression trees, 797-799
  extensible calculators, creating, 802-807
  functional programming, 777-782
  generics, mapping, 1133

instances, 343-344, 787-797

invoking, 341-344, 799-803, 1098

keywords, 341, 797

lambda expressions, 795-797, 825

limitations of, 839-840

method groups, 518

MultiCastDelegate, 784

.NET, 21-22

optional parameters, 801

overview of, 782

Target, 1135, 1142

types, 782-786

    Func<int, int>, 1271

    Func<TResult>, 816

Update, 1137

used in LINQ to objects, 807-811

delete operator, 591

delimited comments, 223-224

Delphi, 15

denial-of-service attacks, locks, 1486

denominators, checking, 256

dependencies

    assemblies, 1241

    languages, 1297-1298

    tracking, 135

    types, 348

deployment

    applications, 10

    assemblies, 1240-1244

    copy, 1256-1257

    extensions, 1066-1068

    .NET assemblies, 16

    xcopy, 1241, 1243

derived classes, 1424

    events, designing for use by, 869-871

design

    APIs, 60

    evolution of C#, 58

    interfaces, 688-690

    nullable types, 61-62

    runtime, 24

designers

    Visual Studio 2010, 144-155

    Windows Forms, 498

destructors, 589-601, 853

    IDisposable interface, 595-601

detecting typos, 130

deterministic ordering, 250. See also precedence

deterministic resource cleanup, 438-447

development

    asserts, 1367-1369

    code in multiple languages, 32

    managed code, 56-58

    team, 167-169

    usage-first, 496

Diagnostic Events mode, 1183

diagnostics, 1363

    debugging, 1371-1373

dialog boxes

    Add New Item, 532

    Add Reference, 1312

    New Project, 124-125

diamond problem, 661

dictionaries, 897-900

Dictionary<TKey, TValue> type, 766

Dijkstra, Edsger, 402

directives

    .extern, 1257

    .maxstack, 115

    #pragma, 405

    preprocessing, 221-222

#region, 497

using, 1223, 1231, 1295

directories

I/O, 1392-1399

navigating, 1394-1397

Directory class, 1402

DirectoryInfo class, 1394, 1402

DirectoryNotFoundException, 1185

disabling

Just My Code, 424

mscorlib.dll, 1297

warnings, 1366

disassembler tool (ildasm.exe), IL, 25

disassembling Main methods, 114

Disassembly window, 137

disasters, runtime, 412, 415-418

discovery

of APIs, 1216

custom attributes, 1079

extensions, 1064-1066

types, 1056-1057

discrete math, 1308-1310

dispatching

dynamic, 1134-1140

operators, 623

disposal objects, 439-441

Dispose method, 440, 599, 686, 1176

_disposed field, 445

Distance method, 665

Distinct operator, 993

Distributed COM. See DCOM

DivideByZeroException, 255, 1193

division

floating-point arithmetic operators, 256

by zeros, 255

.dll assemblies, compiling, 1241

DLLs (dynamic-link libraries), 7, 16, 27

DLR (Dynamic Language Runtime), 338

architecture, 1148-1150

dynamic call sites and binders, 1128-1134

dynamic dispatch, 1134-1140

dynamic operations, 1147-1149

DynamicMetaObject, 1144-1147

DynamicObject, 1140-1144

internals, 1127-1150

DNA (Windows Distributed interNet Applications Architecture), 8

do...while statements, 380-381

docking panels, 123

documents

comments, 224-228

MSDN, 1296

XML, 907. See also XML

domain-specific languages (DSLs), 92

domains

applications, 37-39, 1233, 1277-1289, 1278-1279

cross-domain communication, 1279-1287

isolation of state, 97

reasoning, 503

dot (.) parameter, 1379

DotGNU, 12

downloading IronPython, 1119-1120

DownloadStringAsync method, 1522

DoWork event handler, 1496

doWork parameter, 791

drives

listing, 1392-1393

special, 1332

DSLs (domain-specific languages), 92

dumping IL code, 1262-1264

dynamic calls

optimization, 1051

sites, 1128-1134

Dynamic Data Exchange (DDE), **1137**

dynamic dispatch, **1134-1140**

dynamic keyword, **80-81, 1109-1127**

    deferred overload resolution, 1114-1117

    dynamic typing, 1112-1114

    IronPython, 1119-1127

    System.Dynamic type, 1117-1119

    types, 1111-1112

Dynamic Language Runtime. *See* DLR

dynamic languages, **16, 76-89.** *See also*
  languages

    calls, 81-83

dynamic late-bound operations, **1098**

dynamic-link libraries. *See* DLLs

dynamic operations, **1147-1149**

dynamic parameters, **1128**

dynamic programming, **1109**

dynamic typing, **201-202, 310, 337-338**

DynamicMetaObject, **1144-1147**

DynamicObject, **1140-1144**

E

editions, Visual Studio 2010, **117-118.** *See also*
  versions

editors

    code, 128-130

    XML, 133

effects

    quadratic, 1019

    side, 353

    while statements, 376-380

efficiency

    as operators, 311

    of query generation, 917

EFS (Encrypting File System), **1399**

elements

    access, 347-349

    Import, 133

embedding

    metadata, 33

    PIAs, 1163-1165

    resources, 1268-1270

Empty source generator, **991**

empty statements, **355-356**

EnableRaisingEvents property, **1400**

enabling

    Code Analysis, 312, 1365

    first-chance exceptions, 425

    MDAs, 1181

    No PIA feature, 1164

encapsulation, OOP, **647-648**

encoding text, **1361**

Encrypting File System. *See* EFS

endians, big/little, **1412-1413**

EndInvoke method, **816**

Ensures method, **1369**

entry points

    CLR, 33

    languages, 171-177

enumerables, **387**

enumerations, **387**

    conversions, 628

    .NET, 19-20

    NodeType, 317

    operators, 274-275

    switch statements, 369

_enum.MoveNext() method, **989**

enums, **558-569**

    flags, 564-567

    overview of, 558

    string conversions, 563-564

    switch statements, 568

System.Enum type, 561-564

underlying types, 559

Environment class, 1329

Environment.TickCount static property, 1315

environments

error conditions, 418-422

interacting with, 1328-1333

variables, 1331-1332

EPROM (erasable programmable read-only memory) chip, 807

epsilon-delta definitions, 256-257

equality operators, 272-273, 607

implementation, 615-626

pairwise declaration, 615

EqualityComparer<T> type, 769

Equals method, 273, 547, 616, 756

overriding, 617-619

properties, 619

on System.Object, 622-624

erasable programmable read-only memory (EPROM) chip, 807

Erlang, 90

Error List pane, 132

errors, 410. *See also* exceptions

abstract classes, 684

CLR, 18

environment conditions, 418-422

tasks, 1513-1518

Treat Warnings as Errors, 404

Win32, 1168

estimating processing power, 1453

Evaluate method, 614

evaluating

Boolean expressions, 358

expressions, 251

lazy, 915, 956

left-to-right, 353

LINQ, 981-984

REPL, 1121, 1353

stacks, 28, 251-254, 471

subexpressions, 250

switch statements, 371-376

EventArgs, 862-869

EventHandler, 862-869

Eventhandler<T>, 867-869

events, 22, 336, 833

add/remove accessors, 847-851

countdown GUI, 882-888

declaring, 877

delegates, 834-835

derived classes, designing for use by, 869-871

extensions, 530

Finished, 838

garbage collection, 853-856

handlers, configuring, 1401

handling, 834, 852-861

INotifyProperty interface case study, 871-882

logs, 1379-1381

manual reset, 1487

multithreading, 845, 846

.NET, 840-843

overview of, 843-845

patterns, 861-871

properties, symmetry between, 427

queries, 891

raising, 842, 845-847

reactive applications, 835-843, 888-900

reflection, 1074

signaling with, 1486-1492

sources, 895

Tick, 838

in UI frameworks, 876-882

Excel with COM interop, 1154-1165. *See also* applications

Except operator, 1019

exceptions, 409, 1167, 1170-1172

AggregateException, 1211-1212, 1513-1515

ApplicationException, 1193

ArgumentException, 412, 1185, 1205

ArgumentNullException, 240, 419, 983, 1185, 1206

ArgumentOutOfRangeException, 1207

ArrayTypeMismatchException, 1196

catching, 428, 1174, 1184-1187

causes of, 412-415

checked, 422

code snippet, 1192

COM, 1169-1170

continuations, 1515

DirectoryNotFoundException, 1185

DivideByZeroException, 255, 1193

ExecutionEngineException, 415, 1205

File.ReadAllLines, 419

FileNotFoundException, 420, 1185, 1260

first-chance, 425, 1178-1182

FormatException, 413, 1210-1211

handling, 11, 46-47, 409-437, 1172-1188

filters, 431-432

foreach loops, 987

statements, 352

IndexOutOfRangeException, 412, 1195

inner, 437

InsufficientMemoryException, 1200

IntelliTrace, 1183-1184

InvalidCastException, 304, 315, 630, 699, 755, 1195

InvalidOperationException, 629, 886, 1207

MethodAccessException, 1266

NotImplementedException, 1208

NotSupportedException, 1185, 1208

NullReferenceException, 239, 315, 412, 802, 1180, 1194

ObjectDisposedException, 1198

as objects, 411

OutOfMemoryException, 412, 415, 418, 1188

OverflowException, 263, 628, 1194

PathTooLongException, 1185

PrintException, 1182

propagating, 49

properties, 572

rethrowing, 429-431

RuntimeWrappedException, 429, 1188-1190

StackOverflowException, 415, 1202

StopOnException, 1182

System.Exception base class, 1191

tasks, 1513

ThreadAbortException, 412, 457

threads, 1451-1452

throwing, 423, 1188-1190, 1208

TypeInitializationException, 588, 1196

types, 1190-1193, 1212

UnauthorizedAccessException, 1185

unhandled, 1515-1517

UnobservedTaskException, 1517

Win32, 1168-1170

Exchange method, 1493

exclusive OR (XOR) operator, 274

ExCop, 517

exe targets, 1236

executable projects, 1255

ExecuteAssembly, 1278

ExecuteSynchronously flag, **1521**

executing. *See also* starting

  filters, 935

  finally blocks, 1175

  flow with finally clauses, 436

  IL code, 28

  image files, 1374

  iterators, 976

  managed code, 24-32

  ordering, 938

  parallel execution, 1434

  simultaneous, 452

  threads, 451

ExecutionEngineException, **415, 1205**

ExitCode property, **1388**

exiting programs, **1333**

expando objects, **531-532, 1143-1144**

experimentation, **110**

explicit conversions, **299-317, 628, 632**

explicit interface implementation, **691**

explicit types, **66**

explicitly typed iteration variables, **385**

exposing files with readers and writers, **1404-1406**

Expression base class, **1093-1094**

Expression Blend, **498**

expressions, **247**

  anonymous function, 789-790

  arithmetic compilers, 1084-1091

  binary, 1095-1096

  Boolean, 358, 1107

  cast, 300-306

  compound assignment, 288

  default (T), 715

  default values, 320-323

  dynamic keywords, 1113

  evaluating, 251

  initializers, 67-68

  invocation, 339-347

  lambda, 22, 70-71, 346-347, 1098

    anonymous function syntax, 963

    delegates, 795-797, 825

    IL code, 1039

    operators, 267

    recursive, 859

    threads, 1438

  object initializers, 329

  overview of, 247-250

  queries, 330, 796

    chaining, 956

    into clauses, 955-961

    overloading syntax, 1025-1027

    syntax, 920-964, 1001

    translation, 1036-1038

  regular, 1353-1356

  statements, 351, 353-355

  trees, 71-74, 797-799, 1036-1046, 1139-1140

    APIs, 1093-1104

    compilers, 1092-1093

    leaf nodes, 1095

    object models for, 1085-1087

    for query expressions, 1041-1046

    reflection, 1091-1107

  unary, 1095-1096

  Visual Studio 2010, 119

ExpressionTreeVisitor, applying, **1105-1107**

Ext method, **342**

extenders, **24**

extensibility, **72, 117, 538**

  applications, 1059-1070

  MEF, 1059, 1067-1070, 1289, 1292

extensible calculators, creating, 802-807

Extensible Markup Language. *See* XML

ExtensiCalc, 1059

ExtensionAttribute, 529

extensions
    applying, 1059
    debugging, 1067
    deployment, 1066-1068
    discovery, 1064-1066
    loading, 1059, 1064-1066
    members, 531-532
    methods, 68-69, 336, 522-532, 1207
        applying, 527-528
        compilers, 529-532
        LINQ objects, 970-974
        namespaces, 1231-1232
    OOP, 656
    writing, 1066-1068

extern aliases, namespaces, 1227-1230

.extern directive, 1257

extern methods, 536-538

external assembly references, 1242

extracting methods, 541

F

F#, 15, 78, 90
    type safety, 18

factory methods, 183, 365

failures
    asserts, 1368
    Debug.Fail method, 1373

false operators, 614

features, languages, 59-63

fibers, 1433-1434

Fibonacci numbers
    asynchronous computation of, 818
    functions, 812

fields, 22, 336, 545-558
    accessing, 335, 546-549
    backing, 571
    constants, 555-557
    declaring, 546
    _disposed, 445
    extensions, 530
    initializing, 549-553
    naming conventions, 546
    non-atomic post-increment on, 450
    properties, 332
    reflection, 1075
    volatile, 558

FIFO (first-in, first-out), 758

File class, 1401

file systems, monitoring, 1400-1401

File.ReadAllLines exceptions, 419

FileInfo class, 1398-1399

FileNotFoundException, 420, 1185, 1260

files
    assemblies, 16, 1236. *See also* assemblies
    AssemblyInfo.cs, 1238
    Hello.cs, 110
    I/O, 1392-1399
    image execution options, 1374
    marking, 1269
    memory-mapped, 1426-1429
    MSBuild, 132
    multiple, packaging, 1429
    PDB, 134, 214
    PE/COFF, 33, 1236, 1413, 1426
    project definition, 132
    read methods, 1402-1403
    streams, 1410-1411

write methods, 1403-1404

XML documentation, 227

FileSystemWatcher component, 1400

filter function, 921

Filter type, 518

FilterBool struct, 613

filtering

    data, 401

    exception handling, 431-432

    queries, 807

    where clauses, 933-936

finalization, 1338

Finalize method, 594

finalizers, 22, 579

    defining, 591

    implementation, 594

    running, 591-594

finally blocks, executing, 1175

finally clauses, 432-433

finally keyword, 389

finding operators, 605-606

Finished event, 838

First operator, 994

first-chance exceptions, 425, 1178-1182

first-in, first-out (FIFO), 758

FirstOrDefault operator, 994

fixed-point combinators, 860

flags

    checking for, 566-567

    enumerations, 275

    enums, 564-567

    event logs, 1379

    ExecuteSynchronously, 1521

    /keyfile, 1246

    __lockTaken, 458

    NotOn*, 1521

OnlyOn*, 1521

x86, 1240

flashback, reflection, 1272-1274

floating-point

    arithmetic operators, 255-257

    numbers, 272, 632

    types, 190-194

flow control, 644

folders

    projects, 496

    special, 1332

    Visual Studio namespaces, 1220

folds left, 1010

Foo method, 508

for loops, parallelism, 1529-1535

for statements, 381-383

ForAll action, 1034-1035

foreach keyword, 755, 915

foreach loops, 295, 483, 926, 935, 1292, 1505

    exception handling, 987

    ForAll method, 1034-1035

    grouping, 944

    LINQ, 974

    parallelism, 1535-1536

foreach statements, 384-393, 830

foreground threads, 1446-1448

foreign languages, 375

FormatException, 413, 1210-1211

formatting, 1394-1397

    application domains, 1278-1279

    generics, 699-703

    instances, 1279-1281

    objects, 323-335

    paths, 1397-1398

    strings, 1347-1350

    tasks, 1508-1511

text, 1346-1352

threads, 1436-1438

forms, Windows Forms Application, **124**

forwarding types, **1270-1272, 1300**

Framework (.NET)

add-ins, 1287-1289

continuations, 1519

frameworks, **24**

manageability, 1385

MEF, 100, 1059, 1067-1070, 1289, 1292

nontrivial, 1270

System.Core.dll, 1300

versions, 27

FreeBSD, **12**

Freeze option, **1462**

from clauses, **923, 1029**

FromAsync factory method, **1510**

FullName property, **1055**

Func<int, int> delegate type, **1271**

Func<T1, TResult> delegate type, **797**

Func<TResult> delegate type, **816**

functional programming, **90**

functionality, **464**

delegates, 777-782

history of, 778-779

functions

add, 73

anonymous function expressions, 789-790

C-style function pointers, 783

_CorExeMain, 33

Fibonacci, 812

filter, 921

GetLastError, 1168

Hypotenuse, 346

identity key selector, 936

Lightweight Function, 1115, 1142

pointers, 344

programming with, 779-782

projection, 736

SetLastError, 1169

WIN32 namespaces, 1215

Fusion, **1259**

FxCop, **93, 361, 1206**

naming, 869

G

GACs (Global Assembly Caches), **36, 108, 1233, 1242, 1249-1253, 1294**

testing, 1253

gacutil.exe, **1251**

garbage collection, **438-439**

destructors, 589. See also destructors

events, 853-856

finalizers, 592. See also finalizers

generic types, 714

garbage collectors. See GCs

GCRoot command, **856**

GCs (garbage collectors), **11, 34, 43-46, 268, 1334-1341**

heap allocation, 476

managed code, 1435

generating

lightweight code, 1082-1091

random numbers, 1314-1317

XML documentation files, 226

generators, sources, **990-992**

GenericParameterPosition property, **1056**

generics, **60-61**

access, 336-337

anonymous types, 739

APIs, 699

CLS, 727-729

co- and contravariance, 786

conditional operators, 280

constraints, 716-732

contravariance, 746-749, 893

covariance, 705, 746-749, 893

creating, 699-703

data structures, 720

delegates, mapping, 1133

LINQ, 740-741

methods, 502, 521, 732-739

.NET, 23

overview of, 697-700

performance, 699

System.Object, 699

types, 304-306, 320-322, 483

    applying, 708-709

    boxing, 710-712

    checking, 767

    collection, 697-699, 762-775

    declaring, 703-708

    delegates, 802

    garbage collection, 714

    instantiation, 700

    methods, 697

    modifiers, 705-708

    performance, 709-714

    templates, 705

    typeof, 320

get accessors, 573, 649

GetAlternativeDefault() method, 283

GetAssembly, 1273

GetCallingAssembly, 1273

GetDefault() methods, 283

GetDefaultValue method, 283

GetEntryAssembly, 1273

GetEnumerator method, 390, 392

GetExecuteAssembly, 1273

GetExtensions method, 1065

GetHandler method, 851

GetHashCode method, 619, 757

GetLastError function, 1168

GetLowerBound method, 1305

GetPrint method, 793

getters, 348

GetType method, 672, 1050

GetUpperBound method, 1305

Global Assembly Caches. *See* GACs

global queues, 1529

globally unique identifiers. *See* GUIDs

Golde, Peter, 57

goto statements, 378, 380, 402-405, 1168

GotoExpression statement, 1101

grammar, contextual, 925

graphical user interfaces. *See* GUIs

green bits, 101

group by clause, 942-949

GroupBy method, aggregation, 1016

GroupBy operator, 1003

grouping, 942-949

    continuation after, 958

    foreach loops, 944

    methods, 518-519, 787-788

    objects, 960

    operators, 1003-1008

    partitioning, 942

GroupJoin operator, 1006

growth, memory, 1337

GUIDs (globally unique identifiers) values, 1325-1327

GUIs (graphical user interfaces), 6, 176

    countdown, 882-888

    .NET tools, 109

Gunnerson, Eric, 57

Gyro, 60, 702-703

GZipStream object, 1423

H

HAL (Hardware Abstraction Layer), 1377

handle.exe, 433-436

handlers

    declaring, 427

    events, configuring, 1401

_handlers dictionary, 850

handling

    events, 834, 852-861

    exceptions, 11, 46-47, 409-437, 1172-1188. *See also* exceptions

        filters, 431-432

        foreach loops, 987

        statements, 352

hard casts, 308-310

Hardware Abstraction Layer. *See* HAL

hash tables, 755-758

HashSet<T>, 772-774

Haskell, 90, 780, 921-922

Haskell's call-by-need semantics, 281

headers

    methods, 502

    PE/COFF, 34

heaps, 44, 326, 580, 1342

    allocation, 792

    LOH, 478

    memory allocation, 475

    .NET, 507

    stacks, comparing, 470-478, 584

Hejlsberg, Anders, 57

Hello World application, 110

Hello.cs file, 110

help, Manage Help Settings utility, 144

Help Library (Visual Studio 2010), 120

HelpLink property, 1191

hexidecimal display for variables, 271

hiding base class members, 666-669

hierarchies

    classes, 864

    GAC, 36

    nested namespaces, 1217

    polymorphism, 655

    result types, 281

    types, 199, 309

highlighting syntax, 179-180

history, 5-9

    of COM interop, 1137

    debugging, 1184

    of functional programming, 778-779

    of OOP, 643-647

holes, 705

homoiconicity, 73, 1038-1041

horizontal partitioning, 936

hosting

    CLR, 39

    IronPython in C#, 1121-1123

hot paths of code, 1378

HRESULT, 264-265, 410, 1169

HResult property, 1191

Huginin, Jim, 76

Hungarian notation, 209, 883

Hyper-V, 1463

Hypotenuse function, 346

I

IAsyncResult-pattern, 815

ICalculation interface, 1060

ICollection interface, 766

IComparable<T> interface, 771

IComparer interface, 87

IComparer<T> interface, 747

icons, 1103

identifiers

   naming, 358

   ranges, 925, 957

   transparent, 962-964

identity

   key selector function, 936

   projection, 927-928

IDEs (integrated development environments), 7, 116, 121

IDisposable interface, 440, 595-601, 663, 686

IDisposable types, implementation, 443-447

IDs, threads, 1449

IEnumerable interfaces, 387, 390, 393

IEnumerable<T> interfaces, 69, 87, 335, 390, 525, 693, 968-970, 1293

   generic types, 705

   iterators, 979-981

IEnumerable<T> types, 932

IEnumerator<T> interfaces, 968-970

IEnumerator<T> types, 388

IEqualityComparer<T> interfaces, 622-623

IEquatable<T> types, 770

IExtensionProvider implementation, 1066

if statements, 197, 311, 356, 358-363, 503

IFormattable interface, 1346

IIS (Internet Information Services), 39

IL (intermediate language) code, 24, 27-29, 72, 1233

   assemblers, 291

   COM interop, 1151

   constants, 555

   constructed generic types, 708

   direct method invocation, 340

   disassembler tool (ildasm.exe), 25

   dumping, 1262-1264

   evaluation stacks, 251-254

   exception handling, 427

   floating-point constants, 194

   generic constraints, 721

   if statements, 361

   indexers, accessing, 349

   JIT compilation, 39-41

   lambda expressions, 1039

   LCG, 93

   lock statements, 458

   OOP, 645

   .s suffix, 363

   stacks, 471

   try statements, 1177

   types, defining, 1229

   virtual dispatch, 678

ILASM tool, 26

ILDASM, 214

   custom attributes, 1079

   generic types, 704

   nullable value types, 243

ildasm.exe, 121

IList<T> interface, 687

Image type dependency, 365

images

   accessibility in, 670

   file execution options, 1374

   NGEN, 42-43

   types in, 656-657

Immediate window, 137

immutability, 95, 486, 626

imperative languages, 1504-1507

imperative-style programming, 808

Implement Interface feature, 1208

implementation

   abstract members, 685

   auto-implemented properties, 572-573, 873-875

   constructors on structs, 583

equality operators, 615-626

Fibonacci, 812

finalizers, 594

GetHashCode method, 619

IDisposable types, 443-447

IExtensionProvider, 1066

indexers, 577-578

interfaces, 690-694

monads, 999

types, 464

virtual members, overriding, 673

implicit conversions, 299-317, 520, 628, 632

implicit interface implementation, 691

implicitly typed local variables, 215-220, 768-769

Import element, 133

importing

namespaces, 130, 386, 528, 1223-1232

Office PIAs, 1155

in keyword, 747

inappropriate use of IDisposable, 446-447

Inc command, 648

Increment method, 1493

increment operators, 294-297, 355, 610-611

indexers, 22, 545, 574-578

access, 349

ArrayList, 754

defining, 575-576

element access, 348

extensions, 530

hash tables, 758

implementation, 577-578

manual array indexing, 295

reflection, 1072-1073

types, 304

IndexOutOfRangeException, 412, 1195

inferences

grouping, 943

range variables, 923

types, 66, 734, 737

let clauses, 962

local variables, 357

infix ?? operator, 283

infoof operator, 1073

inheritance, 14

blocking, 665-666

for classes, 657-669

constructors, 658

cross-language, 31

members, 660

OOP, 648-653

single, 656

structs, 664

initializers

anonymous types, 930-933

arrays, 231-233

collections, 333-335, 701-702, 766, 770-771

constructors, 585-586

expressions, 67-68

objects, 67, 328-332

initializing

fields, 549-553

zeros, 585

injection attacks, 906

inline caches, polymorphism, 1136

in-memory, 902-903, 909-911, 952

InnerException property, 1191

inner exceptions, 437

InnerScope method, 210

INotifyProperty interface case study, 871-882

input/output. See I/O

input validation, 412-415

inspecting

    assemblies, 112-116

    GACs, 1249-1251

    strong-named assemblies, 1247

    transparent identifiers, 962-964

installers

    GAC assemblies, 1251

    .NET, running, 106

installing

    assemblies, 36, 1249-1253

    .NET Framework, 99-109

    Visual Studio 2010, 119-120

instances

    constructors, 579-580

    delegates, 343-344, 787-797

    objects, creating, 1279-1281

    references, accessing static members, 549

    reflection information, retrieving, 319

    types, 182-183, 490-496

instantiation

    Excel application objects, 1156

    generic types, 700

    IntelliSense, delegates, 787

    objects, 1096-1097

    references, 327

    types, 1057-1058

instrumentation, 1363, 1378-1386

InsufficientMemoryException, 1200

int operands, 607

Int32

    operands, 252

    values, 711

integers

    arithmetic operators, 255-256

    BigInteger type, 1310-1312

    nullable, 242

integral

    literals, 187

    numbers, 466

    types, 186-190

    value conversions, 563

integral bitwise logical operators, 273-274

integrated development environments. *See* **IDEs**

integration

    LINQ, 901. *See also* LINQ

    operating systems, 100

    Windows integrated authentication (-E), 913

    WPF, 123

intellectual property. *See* **IP**

IntelliSense, 16, 329

    auto-completion, 738

    code, 129

    delegate instantiation, 787

    dynamic typing, 1112

    extension methods, 525

    generic constraints, 719

    initializer lists, 332

    in-memory data, 910

    member access, 336

    methods, defining overloads, 517

    named parameters, 515

    optional parameters, 514

    parameters, naming, 706

    polymorphism, 676

    static typing, 337

IntelliTrace, 1183-1184

interacting with environments, 1328-1333

interactive mode, NGEN, 42

interactive programming, 814

interface keyword, 686

interfaces

    APIs, 6, 60, 415

    BCL, 871

COM, 10, 1164, 1216

constraints, 717-723

contracts, 689, 1285-1287

countdown, 835, 882-888

CUIs, 176

customizing, 123

defining, 686-688, 1060-1061

design, 688-690

ExtensiCalc, 1062-1064

generic constraints, 722

GUIs, 6, 176

ICalculation, 1060

ICollection, 766

IComparable<T>, 771

IComparer, 87

IComparer<T>, 747

IDisposable, 440, 595-601, 663, 686

IEnumerable, 387, 390, 393

IEnumerable<T>, 69, 87, 335, 390, 525, 693, 968-970, 1293

generic types, 705

iterators, 979-981

IEnumerator<T>, 968-970

IEqualityComparer<T>, 622-623

IFormattable, 1346

IList<T>, 687

implementing, 690-694

IObservable<T>, 890, 894-897

IObserver<T>, 894-897

IQueryable<T>, 69

multiple inheritance, 663-665

.NET, 20

Object Browser, 139

OOP, 656, 686-694

Runnable, 1437

single-method, 688, 1436

versions, 688

Visual Studio 2010, 123

zero-method, 688

interleaving threads, 1474

intermediate language. See IL code

internal representation

arrays, 228

floating-point types, 191-192

nullable value types, 242

internals

DLR, 1127-1150

GAC, 36

LINQ, 967

visibility, 1266

InternalsVisibleTo attribute, 1267-1268

Internet Information Services. See IIS

interning strings, 626

interoperability, 10, 49-51, 1435

code, 11, 12

COM, 83-86, 1150-1165

cross-language, 1127, 1137

dynamic object, 1145

with Excel and Word, 1154-1165

IntPtr, 1341-1342

native code, 1240

interrupting blocked threads, 1446

Intersect operator, 1018

into clauses, 955-961

IntPtr, 1341-1342

InvalidCastException, 304, 315, 630, 699, 755, 1195

InvalidOperationException, 629, 886, 1207

Invoke method, 342, 784, 816, 886

invoking

asynchronous delegates, 1420

asynchronous invocation, 811-824

delegates, 341-344, 799-803, 834, 1098

expressions, 339-347

members, 1051, 1097

methods, 339-340

parallelism, 1525

I/O (input/output), **1391**

directories, 1392-1399

file systems, monitoring, 1400-1401

files, 1392-1399

memory-mapped files, 1426-1429

overview of capabilities, 1429

pipes, 1424

readers, 1401-1408

streams, 1407-1423

writers, 1401-1408

IObservable<T> interface, 890, 894-897

IObserver<T> interface, 894-897

IP (intellectual property), 29

IQueryable<T> interface, 69, 1043-1046

IronPython, 15, 1145

dynamic keyword, 1119-1127

IronRuby, 15, 77, 1127

is keyword, 631

is operator, 306-307, 311

IsAbstract property, 1055

IsArray property, 1056

IsClass property, 1056

IsCOMObject property, 1056

IsCompleted property, 822

IsDefined method, 563

IsEnum property, 1056

IsEvenAndPrint method, 953

IsGenericType property, 1056

IsGenericTypeDefintion property, 1056

isinst instruction, 307

IsInterface property, 1055-1056

IsNested property, 1055

IsNonPublic property, 1055

isolation, 1060

application domains, 39

of state, 97

storage, 1429

IsPointer property, 1056

IsPrimitive property, 1056

IsPublic property, 1055

IsSealed property, 1055

IsValidOperator method, 806

IsValueType property, 1056

IsVisibile property, 1055

ItemGroups, 133

iteration

statements, 352, 376-392

variables, read-only treatment of, 391

iterators, 62-63, 392-400

anonymous, 983

compiling, 984-989

IEnumerable<T> interface, 979-981

LINQ, 974-981

queries, 399

while loops, 976

J

J++, 8

jagged arrays, 233-235

Java, 8, 478

assemblies, 1261

namespaces, 1221

Java Virtual Machines. *See* **JVMs**

JavaScript, 201

JIT (Just-in-Time), 708

assemblies, 1239

compilation, 11, 39-41, 254

compiling, 1263

dumping, 1262-1264

OOP, 645

join clause, 949-954

Join operator, 1007

joining, 1359

   operators, 1003-1008

   threads, 1443

jumps

   instructions, 33

   labels, 366-368

junctions, directories, 1395

Just My Code, 424

Just-in-Time. *See* JIT

JVMs (Java Virtual Machines), 8, 76

K

Kennedy, Andrew, 60, 703

kernels, threads, 1463

/keyfile flags, 1246

keys

   compound, 945-949

   computed, 945

   public

      assemblies, 1247

      tokens, 1244

   simple key selectors, 945

   sources, joining, 952

   strong-name, 1245-1247

Keys property, 384

keywords, 1305

   abstract, 656

   add, overflow, 262

   as, 631

   ascending, 936

   base, 656, 659

   checked, 628

   const, 213, 358

   contextual, 59, 178-179

   default, 714

   delegate, 341, 797

   dynamic, 80-81, 1109-1127. *See also* dynamic keywords

   extern, 537

   finally, 389

   foreach, 755, 915

   in, 747

   interface, 686

   is, 631

   languages, 177-180

   let, 962

   lock, 1474-1477

   new, 182, 493, 647, 656, 668

   Of, 703

   operator, 604, 633

   orderby, 935-941

   override, 594, 656, 673

   public, 647

   ref, 508

   return, 346, 502

   reuse of, 732

   sealed, 656, 665, 676

   select, 330

   Shared, 490

   static, 493, 586, 647

   this, 210, 524, 546, 660, 732

   try, 389

   unchecked, 264-265

   using, 528

   value, 59, 570

   var, 66, 77, 324, 385

   virtual, 655, 672

   where, 59, 397, 739

   yield, 63, 810

   yield return, 974

Kleene closer operators, 243

Knuth, Donald, 402

L

LabelExpression statement, 1101

labels, jump, 366-368

lambda expressions, 22, 70-71, 346-347, 1098

anonymous function syntax, 963

delegates, 795-797, 825

IL code, 1039

operators, 267

recursive, 859

threads, 1438

Language Integrated Query. *See* LINQ

language-shaping forces, 91-92

languages, 171, 220-175, 1292

arrays, 228-236

assembler, 778

built-in types, 185-209

classes, 184-185

co-evolution, 878

comments, 220-228

cross-language interoperability, 1127, 1137

declarative, 90, 1504-1507

defaults, 652

dependencies, 1297-1298

dynamic, 76-89. *See also* dynamic languages

dynamic typing, 201-202

entry points, 171-177

features, 59-63

foreign, 375

Haskell, 780

identity projection, 928

imperative, 1504-1507

instances, 182-183

keywords, 177-180

local variables, 209-220

mixing, 30-32

multilanguage aspect of .NET, 14-15

null references, 237-240

nullable value types, 240-246

objects, 182-183, 198-201

relationships between, 14

specification, 290

types, 180-185

variables, 183-184

whitespace sensitivity, 361

Large Object Heap. *See* LOH

Last operator, 995

last-in, first-out (LIFO), 759

LastOrDefault operator, 995

late-bound

methods, 1071

property access, 1073

lazy evaluation, 915, 956

LINQ, 981-984

Lazy<T> class, 1343-1344

Lazy<T>.Value property, 571

LCG (Lightweight Code Generation), 93, 1082-1084

ldc, 253

ldnull instruction, 788

ldstr instruction, 267

leaf nodes, 1095

leaks, tracing, 855-860

leap years, 1318

left folds, 1010

left outer joins, 1008

left-to-right evaluation, 353

let clauses, 918, 961-964

lexical scoping, 210. *See also* scope

libraries, 1292

Class Library, 124

COM, 50

Help Library (Visual Studio 2010), 120

managed code development, 56

runtime, 93

statements, 353

TPL, 96, 1503-1508

versioning, 1299

life cycles, threads, 1441-1446

lifetime issues, avoiding, 1420-1421

LIFO (last-in, first-out), 759

lifted operators, 273, 606-609

Lightning, 9. *See also* .NET

Lightweight Code Generation. *See* LCG

Lightweight Function, 1115, 1142

limitations

of 64-bit addressing, 1494

of delegates, 839-840

LinkedList<T> type, 764

LINQ (Language Integrated Query), 22, 27, 64-66, 102

arrays, 1306

collection types, generics, 763-775

Concat method, 737

dictionaries, 897-900

examples of, 909-920

expression trees, 797

extension methods, 522, 530, 1231

foreach loops, 974

generics, 740-741

in-memory data, 902-903, 909-911

internals, 967

iterators, 396, 974-981

lazy evaluation, 981-984

mapping, 912

MinLINQ, 1022

object initializer expressions, 330, 334

objects, 967-990

delegates used in, 807-811

extension methods, 970-974

operators, 973

partial methods, 532

PLINQ. *See* PLINQ

providers, 72

queries

code translation, 541

expression syntax, 920-964

relational databases, 903-907, 911-917

Reverse operator, 525

to SQL, 159-161

standard query operators, 990-1024

translation, 915

XML, 907-908, 917-920

to XSD, 919

List<int> type, 333

List<T> type, 762

collections, 68

parameters, 304, 320

listing drives, 1392-1393

literals, 1312

characters, 189-190

concatenation, 267

integral, 187

null, 237, 630

runtime conversions, 301

strings, 197

little endians, 1412-1413

live objects, 477

Load method, 918, 1275

loading

assemblies, 35-36, 1255-1261, 1274-1276, 1278

extensions, 1059, 1064-1066

floating-point constants, 194

referenced assemblies, 1257

references, 1294

runtime, versions, 34

local queues, 1529

local storage, threads, 1458-1459

local variables, 209-220

closures, 1457

implicitly typed, 768-769

type inferences, 66, 259, 357

localizing applications, 1350-1352

Locals pane, 136

locating

assemblies, 1259-1261

streams, 1422-1423

Location property, 467

lock keyword, 1474-1477

locks, 352, 1436-1494

advanced, 1483-1486

interlocked helpers, 1492-1494

objects, 447-462

statements, 452-456

__lockTaken flag, 458

logging

events, 1379-1381

SELECT statements, 915

stack traces, 1375-1376

logic programming, 90

logical operators, 273-278, 611-615

Log Viewers (Fusion), 1259

LOH (Large Object Heap), 46, 478

LongCount operator, 1012

LoopExpression statement, 1101

loops

concurrency, 400-401

for, parallelism, 1529-1535

foreach, 295, 483, 926, 935, 1292, 1505

exception handling, 987

ForAll method, 1034-1035

grouping, 944

LINQ, 974

parallelism, 1535-1536

goto statements, 380

messages, blocking, 823

parallel, 401, 1507

REPL, 1121, 1353

while, iterators, 976

wrapping, 823

low-level manipulation, 644

lval-capturing semantics, 792

M

macros

CKHR, 1170

Word, 1151

Main method, 25, 111, 490, 501

disassembling, 114

maintenance

dynamic languages, 78

OOP, 644

manageability frameworks, 1385

Managed Debugging Assistants. *See* **MDAs**

Managed Extensibility Framework. *See* **MEF**

managing

automatic memory, 43-46

EFS, 1399

heaps, 44

managed code, 1434-1436

COM (Component Object Model), 1152-1154

development, 56-58

executing, 24-32

wrappers, 595

managed threads, 1446-1451

memory, 292

projects, 117

resource, 352, 409

types in namespaces, 1213-1219

mandatory lists of operators, 610

manifests, assemblies, 26-27

manipulating code, 93

manual

array indexing, 295

parallelization, 65

reset events, 1487

resolution, 521

ManualResetEvent, 1488

mappers, databases, 157-163

mapping

classes, 913

generic delegates, 1133

LINQ, 912

memory-mapped files, 1426-1429

O/X, 908

tables, 913

marking

files, 1269

objects, 477

marshal-by-reference realization, 1282

MarshalByRefObject calculator add-in, 1284-1285

Math class, 1308

Math.Abs method, 519

matrix multiplication, 1530

Max methods, 1114

Max operator, 1015

MaxBy operator, 1016

.maxstack directive, 115

MDAs (Managed Debugging Assistants), 1181

Measure method, 712

measuring

performance, 712-714, 1376-1377

PLINQ, 1031

MEF (Managed Extensibility Framework), 100, 1059, 1067-1070, 1289, 1292

members

accessing, 335-338, 486, 549, 1097

adding, 1051

base class, hiding, 666-669

discovery, 1051

encapsulation, 647

extensions, 531-532

inheritance, 660

invoking, 1051, 1097

.NET, 22

types, 486-499

values, assigning, 559-560

virtual

declaring, 675-676

overriding, 673-675

polymorphism, 670-682

visibility, 488-489

memory

allocation, 470, 475

automatic memory management, 43-46

CLR, allocating, 43

deallocation, 476

floating-point numbers, 193

foreach statements, 387

growth and shrinkage, 1337

heaps, 326, 583

in-memory data, 902-903, 909-911

join clauses, 951

leaks, 857

management, 292

pressure, 1338

reducing, 37

STM, 95, 461

streams, 1409-1410

string concatenation, 268

Memory window, 137

memory-mapped files, 1426-1429

Message property, 1191

messages

loops, blocking, 823

pipes, 1426

pumps, 819

metadata, 29-30, 33, 115, 464, 1217

assemblies, 1238

DynamicMetaObject, 1144-1147

embedding, 33

events, 844. *See also* events

operators, 626 ·

properties, 573

reflection, 1048-1053

strong-named assemblies, 1248

TypeForwardedToAttribute, 1271

Metadata Exchange, 689

meta-programming, 73, 91, 93

Method property, 1107

MethodAccessException, 1266

methods, 18, 336, 501

Accept, 1094

Activator.CreateInstance<T>, 728

Add, 28, 334, 340, 516, 701, 780, 1266

anonymous, 344-346

Append, 1404

AsParallel, 1028-1031

Bar, 480, 508, 645, 1260

BeginInvoke, 816

breakOuter, 379

Calculate, 22, 1039

calculateFib, 823

calls, 340, 353-354

callvirt, 340

chaining, 1042

ChangeIt, 472

Close, 434

code analysis, 543-544

Combine, 826, 845

Compare, 771, 1493

CompareTo, 719

Compile, 1087-1091

Concat, 737

Console.WriteLine, 291

constructors, 579. *See also* constructors

ContinueWith, 1520

CopyTo, 1268, 1423

Create, 1404

CreateDomain, 1278

CreateInstance, 724

CreateInstance<T>, 728

CreateJobObject, 596

Debug.Assert, 1367

Debug.Fail, 1373

Decrement, 1493

DefineOperation, 342

defining, 501-502

Dispose, 440, 599, 686, 1176

Distance, 665

DownloadStringAsync, 1522

EndInvoke, 816

Ensures, 1369

_enum.MoveNext(), 989

enums, 562. *See also* enums

Equals, 273, 547, 616, 756

overriding, 617-619

properties, 619

on System.Object, 622-624

error codes, 410

Evaluate, 614

Exchange, 1493

Ext, 342

extension, 336

extensions, 68-69, 522-532, 1207

    applying, 527-528

    compilers, 529-532

    LINQ objects, 970-974

    namespaces, 1231-1232

extern, 536-538

extracting, 541

factory, 183, 365

Finalize, 594

Foo, 508

ForAll, 1034-1035

FromAsync factory, 1510

generics, 502, 697, 732-739

GetAlternativeDefault(), 283

GetDefault(), 283

GetDefaultValue, 283

GetEnumerator, 390, 392

GetExtensions, 1065

GetHandler, 851

GetHashCode, 619

GetLowerBound, 1305

GetPrint, 793

GetType, 672, 1050

GetUpperBound, 1305

GroupBy, 1016

groups, 518-519, 787-788

headers, 502

IL code, 28

Increment, 1493

InnerScope, 210

invocation, 339-340

Invoke, 342, 784, 816, 886

IsDefined, 563

IsEvenAndPrint, 953

IsValidOperator, 806

Load, 918, 1275

Main, 25, 111, 114, 490, 501

Math.Abs, 519

Max, 1114

Measure, 712

MoveNext, 920, 968

naming, 517

Object.ReferenceEquals, 273

On*, 870

OnCompleted, 893

OnError, 893

OpenRead, 1411

op_Explicit, 634

op_Implicit, 636

OrderBy, 940

overloading, 512, 516-522

parameters, 504-516

Parse, 918

partial, 499, 532-536

Partitioner.Create factory, 1536

Peek, 759

PLINQ, 1033

Pop, 759

precedence, 526

PrintFile, 424

PrintGCStats, 713

PrintMessage, 1441

Push, 759

query operators, 1024-1025

QueueUserWorkItem, 1465-1467

Read, 1404

ReadAllLines, 424, 1402

ReadByte, 1410

ReadLine, 413

Reduce, 1094

ReduceAndCheck, 1094

ReduceExtensions, 1094

refactoring, 537-543

ReferenceEquals, 622-624

reflection, 1070-1071

Remove, 845

Reset, 322, 1209

results, 353

Resume, 1444

return type, 502-504

Reverse, 68, 522

SayHello, 1083

Select, 1042

signatures, 172-173, 540

single-method interfaces, 1436

Sort, 1367

Start, 837

StartWith, 985

static, 69

strings, 1356-1361

SuppressFinalize, 601

Suspend, 1444

ThenBy, 940

ToString, 340, 671, 674, 1094

TryParse, 509, 517, 1186

Update, 331

UserBlackListed, 277

virtual, 1048-1049

VisitChildren, 1094

void-returning, 407

WaitAny, 1491

WaitForExit, 1387

Where, 781, 1042

where, 397

Write, 129, 1371, 1404

WriteLine, 111, 517, 678, 1371

metrics, calculating, **538**

MFCs (Microsoft Foundation Classes), **6**

Microsoft Foundation Classes. *See* MFCs

Microsoft Research, **60**

Min operator, **1015**

MinBy operator, **1016**

MinLINQ, **1022**

mixing languages, **30-32**

model-driven software, **93**

models

    objects, 1085

    pipeline, 964

modes

    NGEN, 42

    Release, 214

modifiers

    generic types, 705-708

    variance, 750

modifying target platforms, **1240**

Module property, **1055**

modules, assemblies, **1234-1236**

monads, **999**

monitoring

    collection count, 594

    file systems, 1400-1401

    performance counters, 1382-1386

Mono, **12**

months, leap years, **1318**

Moonlight, **12**

Moore, Gordon E., **94**

MoveNext method, **920, 968**

MSBuild, **112, 132**

    command line, 135

    projects, 1255

mscoree.dll (Component Object Runtime Execution Engine), **33**

mscorlib, **37, 1218-1219, 1296-1298**

mscorwks.dll (Component Object Runtime Workstation), 34

MSDN documentation, 638-641, 1296

MultiCastDelegate, 784, 824

multicasting, 863

multidimensional arrays, 235-236

multihandling, 863

multilanguage
   aspect of .NET, 14-15
   usability, 1049-1052

multiparadigms, 89-91

multiple files, packaging, 1429

multiple inheritance, 14. *See also* inheritance
   for interfaces, 663-665

multiple language support, 10

multiple modules, 1235

multiple sources, 926

multiple tasks, 1525-984

multithreading, 845, 846

mutable value types, 483-486

mutation, 1357

mutexes, 1477-1480

N

n-ary orderings, 938-940

Name property, 582, 1055

named parameters, 512-516, 566, 762-763, 1078

Namespace property, 1055

namespaces, 1213
   aliases, 1226-1227
   BCL, 51, 1293
   CLR, 1217
   COM interfaces, 1216
   declaring, 1219-1223

extern aliases, 1227-1230

hierarchies, 1217

importing, 130, 386, 528, 1223-1232

Java, 1221

method extensions, 1230-1232

name clashes within, 1222, 1225-1226

naming conventions, 1221

nested, 1219

System, 110, 1223

System root, 1301-1346

System.Collections, 333

System.Collections.Generic, 61

System.ComponentModel, 871

System.Diagnostics, 1391

System.IO, 275, 418

System.IO.Pipes, 1423

System.Linq, 922

System.Threading, 456, 469

System.Threading.Tasks, 1508

System.Xml, 907

tools, 1216

types, managing, 1213-1219

visibility, 1221

Visual Studio, 1220

WIN32 functions, 1215

naming
   aliasing. *See* aliases
   assemblies, 1240-1244
   case sensitivity, 172
   constructors, 581
   conventions
      fields, 546
      methods, 517
      namespaces, 1221
      properties, 573
   event handlers, 863-866
   FxCop, 869

identifiers, 358

methods, 517

parameters, 331-332, 1162

strong naming, 1244-1249

styles, 209

threads, 1448-1449

type parameters, 706

types, 1225, 1305

variables, 115

NaN (not a number), 256

narrowing conversions, 628

Nathan, Adam, 596

native applications, 1435

native code interoperability, 1240, 1341-1342

native image generation. See NGEN

navigating

assemblies, 1295

code, 116

directories, 1394-1397

paths, 1397-1398

Visual Studio 2010, 120-123

nested namespaces, 1217, 1219

nesting

types, 488

UI controls, 498

.NET, 6

Add Reference dialog box, 1312

applications, 109-116

array type covariance, 742

assemblies, 15-17, 1237. See also assemblies

CLI, 12-14

code

compiling, 111-112

running, 112

writing, 110-111

delegates, 21-22, 782

events, 840-843

Framework

4.0, 103-106

add-ins, 1287-1289

continuations, 1519

installing, 99-109

source code, 139

type hierarchies, 199

version history, 27

versions, 99-106

GAC locations, 1250

generics, 23

heaps, 507

IAsyncResult-pattern, 815

installers, running, 106

interfaces, 20

members, 22

multilanguage aspect of, 14-15

overview of, 9-12

Reflector, inspecting assemblies, 112-116

remoting, 1283

thread pools, 1436-1467

tools, 109

types, 17-24

new keyword, 182, 493, 647, 656, 668

new operator, 323-335, 590

New Project dialog box, 124-125

newobj instruction, 327, 581

NGEN (native image generation), 42-43, 1233, 1250, 1261-1265

No PIA feature, enabling, 1164

nodes

leaf, 1095

Team Explorer tree, 167

NodeType
enumeration, 317
property, 1094
nominal equivalence, 785, 803
non-atomic post-increment on fields, 450
nonblocking cells, 95
non-case-sensitive suffixes, 189
nongeneric collection types, 753-762
nonprivate visibility, 546
non-short-circuiting logical operators, 614
nontrivial frameworks, 1270
nontrivial orderings, 937-938
nontrivial projections, 929-930
not a number (NaN), 256
notation
Big O, 754-755
binary, 188
Hungarian, 209, 883
octal, 188
Notepad, 109
Notepad, writing code, 110-112
NotImplementedException, 1208
NotOn* flag, 1521
NotSupportedException, 1185, 1208
null, 272
checks, 622
literals, 630
references, 237-240
null-coalescing operators, 282-285
nullability, 606-609, 1327-1328
nullables
arithmetic operators, 265
Boolean logic, 277
conversions, 628
types, 61-62
value types, 177-246
Nullable<T>, 245

NullReferenceException, 239, 315, 802, 1180, 1194
NullReferenceExceptions, 412
numbers
automatic numbering, 559
BigInteger type, 1310-1312
complex, 1312-1314
Fibonacci, 812
floating-point, 272, 632
integral, 466
prime, computing, 394
random, generating, 1314-1317
numeric conversions, 627-628

O

Object Browser, 139, 1295
Object Linking and Embedding. *See* OLE
object-oriented programming. *See* OOP
Object.ReferenceEquals method, 273
object/relational (O/R), 91
object/XML (O/X) mapping, 908
ObjectDisposedException, 1198
objects, 198-201, 299
allocating, 44, 439
AssemblyName, 1275
constructing, 702
COR, 1151
creating, 323-335
deallocation, 444
disposal, 439-441
dynamic keywords, 1113
dynamic typing, 337
DynamicMetaObject, 1144-1147
DynamicObject, 1140-1144
exceptions as, 411
expando, 1143-1144

finalizers, 593

grouping, 960

initializers, 67, 328-332, 930-933

instances, creating, 1279-1281

instantiation, 1096-1097

LINQ, 967-990

   delegates used in, 807-811

   extension methods, 970-974

live, 477

locking, 447-462

marking, 477

models, 1085

orientation, 1055

ParallelOptions, 1533

proxy, transparent, 1283

references, 45

reflection, 1054. *See also* reflection

SafeHandle, 601

strings, 1027

Table<T>, 1042

text, parsing, 1352

types, 182-183, 463, 716. *See also* types

octal notation, 188

Of keyword, 703

Office. *See also* **applications**

   automation, 1159

   COM interop, 1150-1165

   PIAs, importing, 1155

OfType operator, 996

OLE (object linking and embedding), 7, 1137

On* method, 870

on-the-fly construct types, 66

OnCompleted method, 893

OnError method, 893

OnlyOn* flag, 1521

OOP (object-oriented programming), 6, 10, 90, 199, 469, 502, 643, 755

abstract classes, 683-685

classes, inheritance for, 657-669

encapsulation, 647-648

history of, 643-647

inheritance, 648-653

interfaces, 686-694

overview of, 643-657

polymorphism, 654-656, 670-682

protected accessibility, 669-670

types in pictures, 656-657

op_Explicit method, 634

op_Implicit method, 636

open types, reflection, 320

OpenRead method, 1411

operands

   expressions. *See* expressions

   int, 607

   Int32, 252

operating systems

   integration, 100

   processes, 1277

operations

   dynamic late-bound, 1098

   on type parameters, 714-716

operator keyword, 604, 633

operators, 247

   AND, 274, 276

   as, 311-315

   +, 260

   -, 260

   Aggregate, 267, 1009

   aggregation, 1008-1017

   All, 1017

   Any, 1017

   arithmetic, 253, 255-265. *See also* arithmetic operators

   arity of, 248

AsEnumerable, 1022-1024

AsOrdered, 1032-1033

assignment, 285-297

associativity, 248-250

Average, 1013

binary, 607

Boolean logical, 275-277

Cast, 997

Cast<T>, 968

comparison, 271

compound assignment, 611

Concat, 1019

conditional, 278-281, 611-615

Contains, 1017

Count, 1012

decrement, 294-297, 355, 610-611

defining, 604-605

delete, 591

dispatching, 623

Distinct, 993

enumerations, 274-275

equality, 272-273, 607, 615-626

Except, 1019

expressions. *See* expressions

false, 614

finding, 605-606

First, 994

FirstOrDefault, 994

GroupBy, 1003

grouping, 1003-1008

GroupJoin, 1006

increment, 294-297, 355, 610-611

infix ??, 283

infoof, 1073

integral bitwise logical, 273-274

Intersect, 1018

is, 306-307, 311

Join, 1007

joining, 1003-1008

Kleene closer, 243

Last, 995

LastOrDefault, 995

lifted, 273, 606-609

LINQ, 973

logical, 273-278, 611-615

LongCount, 1012

Max, 1015

MaxBy, 1016

Min, 1015

MinBy, 1016

new, 323-335, 590

non-short-circuiting logical, 614

null-coalescing, 282-285

OfType, 996

optimization, 252-254

OR, 274, 276

OrDefault, 996

OrderBy, 1002

OrderByDescending, 1002

ordering, 1002-1003

overflow checking, 260-265

overloading, 603-627, 609-616, 722, 1138

postfix, 294-297

precedence, 248-250

predicates, 1017-1018

prefix, 294-297

projection, 997-1002

queries, 807

relational, 271-273

result types, 281-282

Reverse, 525, 1020

Select, 997

SelectMany, 998

SequenceEqual, 1018

sequences, 1018-1022

set theoretical, 1018-1020

shift, 270-271

Single, 995

SingleOrDefault, 995

Skip, 993

SkipWhile, 993

standard query, 990-1024

subexpressions, 250

Sum, 1013

Take, 994

TakeWhile, 994

ThenBy, 1003

ThenByDescending, 1003

ToArray, 1021

ToList, 1021

translating, 626-627

true, 614

typeof, 317-320

unary, 260, 607

Union, 1019

Where, 992-993

XOR, 274, 621, 757

Zip, 562, 1000

_ops field, 805

optimizing

binding operations, 1110

code quality, 1364-1378

conditional operators, 279

dynamic calls, 1051

join clauses, 953

operators, 252-254

PLINQ, 1028-1031

queries, 1020

optional parameters, 512-516

options

continuations, 1520-1522

Freeze, 1462

ParallelOptions object, 1533

Thaw, 1462

Visual Studio 2010 installation, 119

O/R (object/relational), 91

OR operators, 274, 276

OrDefault operators, 996

orderby clauses, translation, 941

orderby keyword, 935-941

OrderBy method, 940

OrderBy operator, 1002

OrderByDescending operator, 936, 1002

OrderedList<T> type, 718

ordering, 250. See also precedence

from clause, 924

customizing, 941

evaluation, 254

exception handlers, 428, 1173

generic constraints, 721-723

lock acquisitions, 460

n-ary, 938-940

nontrivial, 937-938

operators, 1002-1003

orderby keyword, 935-941

secondary, 938-940

syntax, 738

Organize Usings feature, 1224

orientation, objects, 1055

out modifier, 705

out-of-order delivery of asynchronous responses, 898

outer joins, left, 1008

OutOfMemoryException, 412, 415, 418, 1188

How can we make this index more useful? Email us at indexes@samspublishing.com

output

   debugging, 1371-1373

   parameters, 508-510

Output window, 1180

overflow

   checking, 260-265

   stacks, 609, 1203

OverflowException, 263, 628, 1194

overloading

   constructors, 329

   deferred resolution, 1114-1117

   for loops, 1529, 1531-1533

   methods, 512, 516-522, 526-527

   operators, 603-627, 722, 1138

      ==, 624-626

      identifying operators that can be
         overloaded, 609-616

   query expression syntax, 1025-1027

   task constructors, 1510

override keyword, 594, 656, 673

overriding

   Equals method, 617-619

   v-tables, 681

   virtual members, 673-675

O/X (object/XML) mapping, 908

P

packaging multiple files, 1429

padding, 1358

pairwise declaration, 615

panels, docking, 123

Parallel LINQ. *See* **PLINQ**

parallel stacks, 452

parallelism, 65, 1501

   algorithms, 96

   data, 1529-1536

effects of thread pools on, 1468

execution, 1434

for loops, 1529-1535

foreach loops, 1535-1536

invoking, 1525

stacks, 452

threads, 1502-1503

TPL, 1503-1508

parallelization, 90, 95, 401

ParallelLoopState class, 1533

ParallelOptions object, 1533

ParallelQuery<T>, 1032

parameterization, 916

parameters

   arrays, 510-512

   char, 326

   COM interop, 1160

   dot (.), 1379

   doWork, 791

   dynamic, 1128

   methods, 504-516

   named, 512-516, 566, 762-763, 1078

   naming, 331-332, 1162

   output, 508-510

   references, 508

   renaming, 800

   state, 1417-1420

   threads, 1438

   types, 714-716

      generics, 699

      naming, 706

   values, 505-508

Parse method, 918

parsing

   strings, 1301-1304

   text to objects, 1352

partial methods, 499, 532-536

partial types, 496-499

Partitioner.Create factory methods, 1536

partitioners, 1536

partitioning

    grouping, 942

    horizontal, 936

    vertical, 933. *See also* projection

Pascal, 15, 546

passing

    arguments, 506, 507

    reference-typed objects, 506

    values, 473

paths

    code, 503

    navigating, 1397-1398

    return statements, 407

PathTooLongException, 1185

patterns

    events, 861-871

    queries, 941, 949, 954, 1024-1027

PDB (Program Database) files, 134, 214

PE/COFF (Portable Executable, Common Object File Format), 33, 1236, 1413, 1426

Peek method, 759

performance

    analysis, 1378

    Code Analysis, 313

    code quality, 1364-1378

    counters, 1337

    dynamic languages, 78

    generics, 699, 709-714

    late-bound calls, 1071

    measurements, 1376-1377

    measuring, 712-714

    monitoring, 1382-1386

    NGEN, 1264-1265

    regular expressions, 1355

    threads, 1467-1469

period (.), 335

persistence, sequences, 1020-1022

Pex (Program Exploration), 166

philosophy of generations, 1334-1337

Pi

    approximating, 1316

    value of, 556

PIAs (primary interop assemblies), 50, 86

    embedding, 1163-1165

    Office, importing, 1155

pictures

    accessibility in, 670

    types in, 656-657

pinning, 327

P/Invoke, 49, 269, 536, 1397

    signatures, 596

pipeline models, 964

pipes, 1423-1426

PipeStream class, 1424

placeholders, 705

platform version history, .NET, 100

platforms, configuring targets, 1239

PLINQ (Parallel LINQ), 96, 1027-1035

    measurements, 1031

    methods, 1033

    optimization, 1028-1031

    overview of, 1031-1033

Point type, 467

Point value, 583

pointers

    C-style function, 783

    functions, 344

policies, CAS, 1275

polling, 822

polymorphism, 663, 702-703

    inline caches, 1136

    OOP, 654-656, 670-682

pools, threads, 1463-1471, 1528

Pop method, 759

populating .NET Reflector assembly lists, 113

portability of NGEN, 1263

Portable Executable, Common Object File Format. *See* PE/COFF

ports, serial communication, 1429

post-build event configuration, 1067

postfix operators, 294-297

#pragma directive, 405

precedence
methods, 526
operators, 248-250

predicates, operators, 1017-1018

preemptive scheduling, 1445

prefixes
naming conventions, 546
operators, 294-297

preprocessing directives, 221-222

pressure, memory, 1338

primary interop assemblies. *See* PIAs

prime numbers, 63

primitives
immutability, 486
synchronization, 65, 1471-1498, 1504
types, 19
value types, 1301-1305

PrintException, 1182

PrintFile method, 424

PrintFile.exe, 433

PrintGCStats method, 713

printing, REPL, 1121, 1353

PrintMessage method, 1441

private access modifier, 489

private fields, 546. *See also* fields

procedural programming, 90

processes, 38
controlling, 1386-1389
information queries, 1386
operating systems, 1277
SIPs, 38
starting, 1387-1389

processing power, estimating, 1453

profiles, Client Profile (.NET 3.5), 106

Program Database files. *See* PDB files

Program Exploration. *See* Pex

Program.Main, 1142

programming. *See also* code
asynchronous, 95
COM, 50
declarative, 92
dynamic, 1109. *See also* dynamic programming
functional, 90, 777-782
with functions, 779-782
GUIs, 6
imperative-style, 808
interactive, 814
logic, 90
meta-programming, 73, 91, 93
OOP, 6, 90, 199, 469, 502. *See also* OOP
procedural, 90
reactive, 814
reactive applications, 888-900
Show External Code, 1115
side-effect-free, 95
UI, 871-882
Win32 in C, 6

programs
causes of termination, 413
exiting, 1333

ProgressChanged event handler, 1496

Project tag, 132

projection

continuation after, 955

functions, 736

identity, 927-928

nontrivial, 929-930

operators, 997-1002

Select clause, 927-933

projects, 1254

default project references, 1293-1294

folders, 496

management, 117

MSBuild, 1255

properties, 127

Projects tab, 1255

propagating exceptions, 49, 1172

properties, 22, 336, 545, 569-574

accessors, 571

assemblies, 1237-1240

auto-implemented, 74-75, 572-573, 873-875

Body, 73

Content, 305

Count, 669

Count get-only, 648

Current, 974

declaring, 569-572

Equals method, 619

events, symmetry between, 427

ExitCode, 1388

expression trees, 1041

extensions, 530

fields, 332

indexers, 578. *See also* indexers

IsCompleted, 822

Keys, 384

late-bound property access, 1073

Location, 467

Method, 1107

Name, 582

projects, 127

reflection, 1072-1073

Service, 493

System.DateTime, 319

trivial, 74

types, 1055-1056

Visible, 331

PropertyGroups, 132

protected accessibility, 669-670

protecting. *See also* **security**

blocks, 1178

IP (intellectual property), 29

prototyping, 110

providers, LINQ, 72

proxy objects, transparent, 1283

public constants, 555. *See also* **constants**

public keys

assemblies, 1247

tokens, 1244

public keywords, 647

pumps, messages, 819

Push method, 759

Python, 76, 201, 337

types, 1123-1127

Q

quadratic effects, 1019

quality, code, 1364-1378

quantification, universal, 702-703

queries

events, 891

expressions, 330, 796

chaining, 956

into clauses, 955-961

overloading syntax, 1025-1027

syntax, 920-964, 1001

translation, 1036-1038

filters, 807

iterators, 399

LINQ, 65, 901. *See also* LINQ

operators, 807

optimization, 1020

patterns, 941, 949, 954, 1024-1027

process information, 1386

standard query operators, 990-1024

statements, checking, 905

Queue<T>, 774

queues, 758-759, 1529

QueueUserWorkItem method, 1465-1467

quotations, 73, 1098

R

RAD (Rapid Application Development), 7

raising events, 842, 845-847. *See also* **events**

random numbers, generating, 1314-1317

Random object, 1315

Range source generator, 991

ranges

identifiers, 925, 957

variables, inferences, 923

Rapid Application Development. *See* **RAD**

reachable objects, finding, 45

reactive applications, 835-843, 888-900

Reactive Extensions (Rx), 890, 1469

reactive programming, 814

Read method, 1404

Read mode, 1483

read-eval-print-loop. *See* **REPLs**

read-only fields, 547, 553-555. *See also* **fields**

read-only treatment of iteration variables, 391

ReadAllLines method, 424, 1402

ReadByte method, 1410

readers, I/O, 1401-1408

ReaderWriterLockSlim, 1468

ReadLine method, 413

real values, literals, 194

realization, marshal-by-reference, 1282

recursion, 472

algorithms, 1203

Fibonacci implementations, 813

lambda expressions, 859

red bits, 101

Red Gate, 112

redirecting assembly version binding, 1242-1244

Reduce method, 1094

ReduceAndCheck method, 1094

ReduceExtensions method, 1094

reducing memory, 37

redundancy

assignments, 293

cast expressions, 301

ref keyword, 508

refactoring

engines, 93

methods, 537-543

support, 116

ReferenceEquals method, 622

on System.Object, 622-624

references

assemblies, 1253-1255, 1301

BCL, 1294-1298

conversions, 629-630

default project, 1293-1294

external assemblies, 1242

generic collection types, 765

IronPython, hosting, 1121

loading, 1294

null, 237-240

NullReferenceException, 1180

objects, 45

output parameters, 509

parameters, 508

types, 470, 731-732

aliasing, 185

instantiation, 327

values, comparing, 466-470

weak, 715-716, 1340-1341

reflection, 317-320, 1047, 1054-1081

arithmetic expressions, 1084-1091

custom attributes, 1075-1081

events, 1074

expression trees, 1091-1107

extensions

applying, 1059

loading, 1059

fields, 1075

flashback, 1272-1274

indexers, 1072-1073

late-bound property access, 1073

lightweight code generation, 1082-1091

MEF, 1067-1070

metadata, 1048-1053

methods, 1070-1071

multilanguage usability, 1049-1052

properties, 1072-1073

relational databases, 1073

System.Type, 1054-1055

types, 479-483, 716

visibility, 1265

Reflector, 486, 664

binding, 1110

.NET, inspecting assemblies, 112-116

Reflector (.NET), compiler-generated expression trees, 1092

reflexivity, 619

Refractor, 539

regions, 497

regular expressions, 1353-1356

relational databases, 61

LINQ, 903-907, 911-917

reflection, 1073

relational operators, 271-273

pairwise declaration, 615

relationships

joining, 949-954

between languages, 14

types, 464

relative time, 1323-1324

Release build, 363

Release mode, 214

releases. *See* versions

remote procedure calls. *See* RPCs

remoting, 1281-1285

remove accessor, 847-851

Remove method, 845

renaming parameters, 800

Repeat source generator, 991

repeating disposal, 599

REPLs (read-eval-print-loops), 78, 93, 1121, 1353

reporting, 822

representations, strings, 561-562

reserved words, 1117

   aliasing, 208

   built-in types, 197

Reset method, 322, 1209

resolution

   deferred overload, 1114-1117

   method overloads, 519-522

resolving

   namespaces, 1295

   type names, 1225

resources, 1217

   deterministic cleanup, 438-447

   embedding, 1268-1270

   management, 352, 409

   synchronization, 1471

restrictions

   query operators, 992-996

   types, 731-732

Result property, 1515

results

   methods, 353

   tasks, retrieving, 1511-1512

   types, operators, 281-282

Resume method, 1444

rethrowing exceptions, 429-431

retrieving task results, 1511-1512

return keyword, 346, 502

Return source generator, 991

return statements, 406-407, 503

return type, 502-504

reuse

   code, 649

   of keywords, 732

   tools, 103

reverse extension method call, 529

Reverse method, 68, 522

Reverse operator, 1020

   LINQ, 525

rewriting contract method calls, 1370

rich type information, 767

right side (rhs), 285

robustness of dynamic languages, 78

roles

   of assemblies, 1234-1236

   of CLS, 23-24

   of metadata, 1048-1053

   of partitioners, 1536

Rotor, 12

RPCs (remote procedure calls), 1283

Ruby, 201, 337

Ruby on Rails, 15, 76

rules

   CLS, 24

   code analysis, 544

   for code analysis, 1365

   types, 17-18. See also types

Runnable interface, 1437

running

   applications, 175-176

   finalizers, 591-594

   .NET

      code, 112

      installers, 106

runtime, 1292. See also CLR

   assemblies, loading, 1255-1261

   behavior analysis, 1386

   binders, 1110

   bootstrapping, 33-35

   cast expressions, 300-306

   CCR, 97

   checks, 1367

   concatenation, 267

   COR, 1151

   design, 24

disasters, 412, 415-418

dynamic languages, 81-83

extension methods, 529

extern methods, 538

is operator, 306-307

LCG, 93

libraries, 93

LINQ translation, 915

members, adding, 1051

read-only fields, 556

shims, 106

strong named assemblies, verifying, 1248

versioning, 34, 1299

RuntimeWrappedException, 429, 1188-1190

RunWorkerCompleted event handler, 1496

Rx (Reactive Extensions), 890

S

s_ prefix, 494

.s suffix, 363

SafeHandle objects, 601

safety

covariance, 744-745

multithreading, 847

threads, 651, 1458

types, 17-18, 1334

satellite assemblies, 1269

saving assemblies, 1091

SayHello method, 1083

scalability, 78

scheduling

abstracting, 1469

cooperative, 1445

preemptive, 1445

Task Schedulers, 1527-1528

UMS, 1463

user mode, 1433-1434

Schonfinkel, Haskell Curry, 796

scope, 1234

local variables, 210-212

SDKs (software development kits), 14

sealed keyword, 656, 665, 676

searching

assemblies, 1255, 1259-1261, 1296

junctions, 1395

streams, 1422-1423

types, 1295

wildcard searches, 1357

secondary orderings, 938-940

security

assemblies, 1234

CAS, 47-49, 254, 1075, 1275

injection attacks, 906

IP (intellectual property), 29

.NET, 11

tokens, 11

segments, 1306

SEH (Structured Exception Handling), 1167, 1189

Select Case, 375

select clauses, 924

projection, 927-933, 955

select keyword, 330

Select method, 1042

Select operator, 997

SELECT statements, 904, 911, 915

selection

sources, 923-927

statements, 352, 358-376

SelectMany operator, 998

semantics

   binding, 1110

   lval-capturing, 792

   operators, 613

semaphores, 1480-1483

semicolons (;), 217, 355

sensitivity, whitespace, 361

SequenceEqual operator, 1018

sequences

   characters, 1356

   expressions. See expressions

   foreach loops, 944

   operators, 1018-1020

   versus parallel continuations, 1521

   partitioning, 1536

   persistence, 1020-1022

   service pools, 726

serial port communication, 1429

serialization

   attributes, 1282

   copy-by-value realization, 1281

Server Explorer, 155-157

servers, SQL Server, 1434

ServerVersion property, 1207

Service property, 493

service-oriented architecture. See SOA

ServicePool<T> type, 725

services

   compilers as, 92-94

   pools, sequences, 726

   Web services, 11

set accessors, 573, 649

set theoretical operators, 1018-1020

SetLastError function, 1169

setters, 348

Shared keyword, 490

Shared Source CLI. See SSCLI

shared-state, troubleshooting, 1439

sharing resources, synchronization, 1471

shells

   execution behavior, 1387

   Visual Studio 2010, 118

shift operators, 270-271

shims

   runtime, 106

   sizing, 34

short-circuiting operators, 611-615. See also operators

Show External Code, 1115

shrinkage, memory, 1337

side effects, 353

   side-effect-free programming, 95

   while statements, 376-380

signaling with events, 1486-1492

signatures

   entry points, 173-175

   methods, 172-173, 540

   P/Invoke, 596

signing

   processes, assemblies, 1245

   strong-name, 1245

Silverlight, 10, 12, 112, 498, 1292

simple assignment, declaration versus, 285-287

simple key selectors, 945

simple math, 1308-1310

Simple Object Access Protocol. See SOAP

simultaneous execution, 452

single inheritance, 656. See also inheritance

   for classes, 661-663

Single operator, 995

single-dimensional arrays, 229-231

single-line comments, 220-221

single-method interfaces, 688, 1436

SingleOrDefault operator, **995**

singularity, **38**

SIPs (software isolated processes), **38**

sizing shims, **34**

Skip operator, **993**

SkipWhile operator, **993**

sleeping, threads, **1443**

Smalltalk, **15**

snippets, code, **490**

    exceptions, 1192

    writing, 1192

Snow White effect, **822**

SOA (service-oriented architecture), **1287**

SOAP (Simple Object Access Protocol), **11**

soft casts, **308-310**

software development kits. *See* SDKs

software isolated processes. *See* SIPs

software transactional memory. *See* STM

Sollich, Peter, **57**

Solution Explorer, **126-127**

solutions, **1254**

SomeException type, **1189**

Son of Strike. *See* SOS

Sort method, **1367**

SortedList<T>, **721**

SortedSet<T>, **774**

SOS (Son of Strike), **417**

    commands, 1182-1188

    leaks, tracing, 855-860

source code, **116**. *See also* code

    .NET Framework, 139

Source property, **1192**

sources

    control, Visual Studio 2010, 169

    events, 895

    generators, 990-992

keys, joining, 952

multiple, 926

selection, 923-927

special drives, 1332

special folders, 1332

special values, 1304-1305

specifying strong names, 1246

SpinLock struct, 1486

splash screens, Visual Studio 2010

splitting, 108, 1359

SQL (Structured Query Language)

    expression trees, 797

    injection attacks, 906

    LINQ to, 159-161

    relational databases, 903-907, 911-917

    SQL Server, 39, 1434

SSCLI (Shared Source CLI), 12

Stack<T>, 774

StackOverflowException, 415, 1202

stacks, 759-761

    abstraction, OOP, 644

    calls, 254, 406, 471

    evaluation, 251-254, 471

    heaps, comparing, 470-478, 584

    overflow, 609, 1203

    overflowing, 416

    software, 38-39

    traces, logging, 1375-1376

    transitions, evaluating, 28

    unwinding, 1175

    walking, 49

Stacktrace property, 1192

stand-alone identity projections, 929

Standard Query Operator method call, 934

standard query operators, 990-1024

standardization, CLI, 12

Start method, 837

starting

processes, 1387-1389

tasks, 1508-1511

threads, 1438-1441

Startup Object, 1238

StartWith method, 985

state

constructors, 1066

isolation of, 97

parameters, 1417-1420

per-thread state, 1470-1471

threads, 1452-1458

statements, 89

assignments, 354-355

blocks, 356-357

break, 366, 378-380

continue, 379

declaration, 351, 357-358

do...while, 380-381

empty, 355-356

expressions, 351, 353-355

for, 381-383

foreach, 384-393, 830

goto, 378, 380, 402-405, 1168

if, 197, 311, 356, 358-363, 503

iteration, 352, 376-392

lock, 452-456

overview of, 351-353

queries, checking, 905

return, 406-407, 503

SELECT, 904, 911, 915

selection, 352, 358-376

switch, 315-317, 363-376, 568, 1101

trees, 1101-1104

try, 1176-1179

try-catch, 1171

try-catch-finally, 1172

try-finally, 1172

UPDATE, 534

using, 435, 441-443, 1172

while, 376-380

STAThread attribute, 885

static

classes, 589

constructors, 586-589, 1197

helper methods, creating, 68

keyword, 493, 586, 647

members, 337, 549. *See also* members

method, 69

modifiers, 490-496

types

checking, 701

dynamic keywords, 1116-1117

typing, 61, 914

stitching expression trees, 1045

stloc, 253

STM (software transactional memory), 95, 461

StopOnException, 1182

stopping threads, 1442-1444

StopWatch, 1376-1377

storage

custom attributes, 1068

isolation, 1429

local storage, threads, 1458-1459

Stream class, 1408

streams

asynchronous read and write operations, 1413-1421

files, 1410-1411

I/O, 1407-1423

memory, 1409-1410

searching, 1422-1423

String type, 19

StringBuilder class, 1359-1361

StringReader class, 1407

strings

concatenation, 266-270

DateTime values, 1319-1320

enum conversions, 563-564

formatting, 1347-1350

interning, 626

literals, 197

methods, 1356-1361

objects, 1027

parsing, 1301-1304

representation, 561-562

types, 197-198

verbatim, 1356

StringWriter class, 1407

Strong Name Utility sn.exe, 1247

strong naming, assemblies, 1244-1249

StructLayout attribute, 596

structs, 465, 583

classes, comparing, 466-486

FilterBool, 613

inheritance, 664

values, nullability, 606

structural typing, 1015

Structured Exception Handling. *See* SEH

structures

data, 704

generics. *See also* generics

.NET, 19-20

StyleCop, 362, 517

styles, naming, 209

subexpressions. *See also* expressions

evaluating, 250

left-to-right evaluation, 353

subst command, 1394

subtypes, 680

suffixes

decimal types, 196

non-case-sensitive, 189

.s, 363

Sum operator, 1013

supersets, 102

support

build, 130-135

debugging, 134, 136-138

multiple languages, 10

refactoring, 116

tools, 11, 78

Suppress Warnings list, 405

SuppressFinalize method, 601

suppressions, disabling warnings, 1366

Suspend method, 1444

sweeping heaps, 45

switch statements, 315-317, 363-376, 1101

enums, 568

evaluation, 371-376

SwitchExpression statement, 1101

switching context, 1433-1434

Syme, Don, 60, 703

synchronization, 1431

primitives, 65, 1471-1498, 1504

TPL, 1507

SynchronizationContext, 1495

syntax

ASTs, 1038

cast expressions, 301-304

collection initializers, 766, 770-771

contextual grammar, 925

delegates, combining, 827-829

highlighting, 179-180

IDisposable types, 444

named parameters, 1078

operators, 613

ordering, 738

query expressions, 920-964, 1001, 1025-1027

Visual Basic, generic types, 703-705

System assembly, 1296-1298

System namespace, 110, 1223

System root namespace, 1301-1346

System.Collections namespace, 333

System.Collections.Concurrent, 775

System.Collections.Generic namespace, 61

System.Collections.ObjectModel, 775

System.Collections.Specialized, 775

System.ComponentModel namespace, 871

System.Console class, 291

System.Core, 1271

System.Core assemblies, 1250

System.Core.dll, 1298-1301

System.Data.SqlClient API, 904

System.DateTime, 318

System.Delegate, 829, 887

System.Diagnostics, 712, 1391

System.Dynamic type, 1117-1119

System.Enum type, 561-564

System.Exception base class, 1191

System.GC class, 713

System.Interactive assembly, 1016

System.IO namespace, 275, 418

System.IO.Pipes namespace, 1423

System.Linq namespace, 922

System.Object, 201. *See also* objects

Equals method on, 622-624

generics, 699

ReferenceEquals method on, 622-624

reflection, 1050

System.Reflection, 319

System.Runtime.ConstrainedExecution (CER), 1200

System.String type, 69

System.Text.StringBuilder, 269

System.Threading namespace, 456, 469

System.Threading.Parallel, 400

System.Threading.Tasks namespace, 1508

System.Type, 318, 1054-1055

System.ValueType, 664

System.Xml.Linq APIs, 917

System.Xml namespace, 907

T

Table<T> object, 1042

tables

hash, 755-758

joining, 949-954

mapping, 913

relational databases, 903

tabs

COM, 1155

.NET assemblies, 1255

Projects, 1255

Tabular Data Stream. *See* TDS

Take operator, 994

TakeWhile operator, 994

Target delegate, 1135, 1142

targets, 82

platforms, configuring, 1239

types of assemblies, 1236

TargetSite property, 1192

Task Parallel Library. *See* TPL

Task Schedulers, 1527-1528

TaskFactory, applying, 1509-1510

tasks, 1507-1508

  cancellation of, 1523

  constructors, applying, 1509

  continuations, 1518-1522

  errors, 1513-1518

  formatting, 1508-1511

  multiple, 1525-984

  results, retrieving, 1511-1512

  starting, 1508-1511

TDD (test driven development), 1364

TDS (Tabular Data Stream), 1422

team development, 167-169

Team Foundation Server. *See* TFS

TechNet, 1399

templates, generic types, 705

ternary operators, 248. *See also* operators

test driven development (TDD), 1364

testing

  assemblies, 1253

  unit, 163-167

text, 1346-1362

  encoding, 1361

  formatting, 1346-1352

  objects, parsing, 1352

  string methods, 1356-1361

TextReader class, 1406-1407

TextWriter class, 1406-1407

TFS (Team Foundation Server), 11, 118, 134, 167

Thaw option, 1462

ThenBy method, 940

ThenBy operator, 1003

ThenByDescending operator, 1003

theories, complex numbers, 1313

this keyword, 210, 524, 546, 660, 732

ThreadAbortException, 412, 457

Thread class, 791, 1436-1441

Thread.CurrentThread.ManagedThreadId, 986

thread-local data, applying, 1533-1535

ThreadLocal<T> class, 1456-1458

threads, 1431

  aborting, 1444

  apartments, 1450

  applying, 1432-1462

  background, 1446-1448

  blocking, 1441, 1446

  concepts of, 1432-1434

  costs of, 1502

  cross-thread access, 884

  debugging, 1460-1462

  exceptions, 1451-1452

  execution, 451

  foreground, 1446-1448

  formatting, 1436-1438

  ideal number of, 1502-1503

  IDs, 1449

  interleaving, 1474

  kernels, 1463

  life cycles, 1441-1446

  local storage, 1458-1459

  managed, 1446-1451

  multithreading, 845-846

  naming, 1448-1449

  parallelism, 1502-1503

  parameters, 1438

  performance, 1467-1469

  per-thread state, 1470-1471

  pools, 1463-1471, 1528

  safety, 651, 1458

  starting, 1438-1441

  state, 1452-1458

  stopping, 1442-1444

  user mode, 1463

  waiting, 1444

  yielding, 1445

How can we make this index more useful? Email us at indexes@samspublishing.com

Threads window, 138

ThreadStatic attribute, 1452

throwing

exceptions, 47, 423, 1188-1190, 1208.
   See also exceptions

tasks, 1513

Tick event, 838

time, 1317-1325

absolute, 1317-1318

relative, 1323-1324

zones, 1322-1323

timers

accuracy of, 839

threads, 1443

TimeSpan, 1323-1324

timestamps, checking, 135

ToArray operator, 1021

tokens

public key, 1244

security, 11

ToList operator, 1021

tools

Code Analysis, 311

copy, 1496

debugging, 138

disassembler (ildasm.exe), 25

FileSystemWatcher component, 1400

gacutil.exe, 1251

ILASM, 26

Manage Help Settings utility, 144

namespaces, 1216

.NET, 109

NGEN, 42. See also NGEN

Object Browser, 1295

P/Invoke Interop Assistant, 49

Reflector, 486

reuse, 103

Strong Name Utility sn.exe, 1247

support, 11, 78

versioning, 1299

Visual Studio, 16, 120

ToString method, 340, 671, 1094

virtual dispatch of, 674

TPL (Task Parallel Library), 96, 1503-1508

architecture, 1503-1504

tracing

leaks, 855-860

stacks, logging, 1375-1376

tracking dependencies, 135

trailing commas, 558

transfers, unboxing, 482

transitions, evaluating stacks, 28

transitivity, 619

translating

LINQ, 915

operators, 626-627

orderby clauses, 941

query expressions, 1036-1038, 1045

where clauses, 934

transparency

identifiers, 962-964

proxy objects, 1283

traversing junctions, 1395

Treat Warnings as Errors, 404

trees

ASTs, 1038

deep tree data structures, 1204

expressions, 71-74, 797-799, 1036-1046

APIs, 1093-1104

compilers, 1092-1093

leaf nodes, 1095

object models for, 1085-1087

for query expressions, 1041-1046

reflection, 1091-1107

statements, 1101-1104

trigonometry, **1310**

trimming, **1358**

trivial properties, **74**

troubleshooting

asserts, 1368

debugging, 1184

injection attacks, 906

Manage Help Settings utility, 144

tasks, 1513-1518

true operators, **614**

truth tables, nullable Boolean logic, **277**

try blocks, **414**

try keyword, **389**

try statements, **1176-1179**

try-catch statements, **1171**

try-catch-finally statements, **1172**

try-finally statements, **1172**

TryExpression statement, **1102**

TryParse method, **509, 517, 1186**

Tuple types, **320**

tuples, **1344-1346**

Type Library Exporter (tblexp.exe), **50**

Type Library Importer (tblimp.exe), **50**

Type property, **1094**

TypeInitializationException, **588, 1196**

typeof operator, **317-320**

types, **299, 463**

accessing, 24

accumulation, 1011

anonymous, 66, 386

generics, 739

object initializers, 930-933

applications, 10

arrays, covariance, 741-744

assemblies, 1236-1237

BigInteger, 1310-1312

Boolean values, 196-197

boxing, 478-479

built-in, 185-209

checking, 286, 767

classes versus structs, 466-486

CLR, 17-24

code, 180-182

collection, 389, 753. *See also* collection
    types

concrete, 324-325

constituent, 572

containers, 1131

data, 180-182

decimals, 194-196

declaring, 933

decomposing, 465

delegates, 782-786

Func<int, int>, 1271

Func<TResult>, 816

dependent, 348

Dictionary<TKey, TValue>, 766

discovery, 1051, 1056-1057

dynamic keyword, 1111-1112

EqualityComparer<T>, 769

exceptions, 1190-1193, 1212

explicit, 66

Filter, 518

floating-point, 190-194

forwarding, 1270-1272, 1300

generics, 304-306, 320-322, 483

applying, 708-709

~0-712
~ion, 61
~laring, 703-708
delegates, 802
garbage collection, 714
instantiation, 700
LINQ, 740-741
methods, 697
modifiers, 705-708
performance, 709-714
templates, 705
typeof, 320
hierarchies, 199
identifiers, ranges, 925
IDisposable implementation, 443-447
IEnumerable<T>, 932
IEnumerator<T>, 388
IEquatable<T>, 770
implicitly typed local variable declarations, 215-220
implicit versus explicit conversions, 299-317
inferences, 66, 734, 737
    let clauses, 962
    local variables, 357
instances, 182-183, 490-496
instantiation, 1057-1058
integral, 186-190
of joins, 1009
languages, 180-185
LinkedList<T>, 764
List<int>, 333
List<T>, 762
members, 486-499
of members, 336
MulticastDelegate, 824
mutable value, 483-486

namespaces, managing, 1213-1219
naming, 1225, 1305
nesting, 488
nullables, 61-62, 240-246
objects, 182-183
of operators, 249
on-the-fly construct, 66
overview of, 463-465
parameters, 714-716
    generics, 699
    naming, 706
partial, 496-499
in pictures, 656-657
primitive, 19, 1301-1305
properties, 1055-1056
Python, 1123-1127
references, 470, 731-732
    aliasing, 185
    instantiation, 327
reflection, 479-483, 716
relationships, 464
reserved words, 197
result, operators, 281-282
return, 502-504
safety, 17-18, 1334
searching, 1295
ServicePool<T>, 725
SomeException, 1189
static
    dynamic keywords, 1116-1117
    modifiers, 490-496
strings, 197-198
System.Delegate, 887
System.Dynamic, 1117-1119
System.Enum, 561-564
System.String, 69
tuples, 1344-1346

underlying, 559

union, 241

Uri, 1328

v-tables, 680

values, 325, 470-471, 731-732

visibility, 486-488

typing, 1015

typos, detecting, 130

U

UI (user interface)

controls, nesting, 498

ExtensiCalc, 1062-1064

frameworks, 876-882

programming, 871-882

Visual Studio 2010, 123

UMS (user mode scheduling), 1463

unary expressions, 1095-1096

unary operators, 260

as lifted operators, 607

UnauthorizedAccessException, 1185

unboxing, 483, 700. *See also* boxing

conversions, 631

unchecked contexts, 352

unchecked keyword, 264-265

underlying types, 559

unhandled exceptions, 1515-1517

Unicode characters, 189, 259, 327. *See also* characters

unified runtime infrastructures, 10

uniform resource identifiers. *See* URIs

Union operator, 1019

union types, 241

unit testing, 163-167

universal quantification, 702-703

unloading assemblies, 37, 1278

UnobservedTaskException, 1517

unwinding stacks, 1175

Update delegate, 1137

Update method, 331

UPDATE statement, 534

Upgradeable mode, 1483

URIs (uniform resource identifiers), 1328

Uri type, 1328

usage-first development, 496

User Account Control, 1238

user mode

scheduling, 1433-1434

threads, 1463

user-defined conversions, 631-637

UserBlackListed method, 277

using block, 597

using directive, 1223, 1231, 1295

using keyword, 528

using statements, 435, 441-443, 1172

V

v-tables, 680

validation, input, 412-415

values

BigInteger type, 1311

Boolean, 196-197, 353

constants, 556

declaring, 555

default

expressions, 320-323

type parameters, 714-716

GUIDs, 1325-1327

Int32, 711

...ions, 563

..9, 570

..., assigning, 559-560

...51

...llable value types, 240-246

parameters, 505-508

passing, 473

Pi, approximating, 1316

Point, 583

primitive types, 1301-1305

references, comparing, 466-470

special, 1304-1305

structs, nullability, 606

types, 325, 470-471, 731-732

unboxing, 482

var keyword, 66, 77, 324, 385

variables

captured outer, 790-793

constants, assigning, 252

declaration, 285

dynamic keywords, 1113

environments, 1331-1332

explicitly typed iteration, 385

hexidecimal display for, 271

iteration, read-only treatment of, 391

languages, 183-184

local, 209-220

closures, 1457

implicitly typed, 768-769

type inferences, 66, 259, 357

naming, 115

range inferences, 923

variance modifiers, 750

VBA (Visual Basic for Applications), 1137

Vector object, 348

vectors, zero-length, 609

verbatim strings, 1356

verifying strong named assemblies, 1248

versions

assemblies, 1240-1244

extension methods, 527

frameworks, 27

GAC, 36

interfaces, 688

.NET Framework, 99-106

runtime, 34, 267, 1299

vertical partitioning, 933. *See also* **projection**

VES (Virtual Execution System), 12

viewing

event sources, 895

first-chance exceptions, 1180

LINQ operators, 973

Object Browser, 139

pre-.NET 4 GACs, 1250

Show External Code, 1115

Visual Studio 2010 installation components, 120

views, DebugView, 1103

violations

checking, 783

covariant-safe use of generic type parameters, 747

default constructor constraints, 725

virtual dispatch, 678-681

Virtual Execution System. *See* **VES**

virtual keyword, 655, 672

virtual members

declaring, 675-676

overriding, 673-675

polymorphism, 670-682

virtual methods, 1048-1049

virtualization, 1463

visibility, 486-489, 1234

assemblies, 1265-1268

constituent types, 572

fields, naming conventions, 546

members, 488-489

namespaces, 1221

types, 486-488

Visible property, 331

VisitChildren method, 1094

Visual Basic, 7, 10, 13, 15

generic types, 703-705

Visual Basic for Applications. *See* **VBA**

Visual Blend, 498

Visual Studio, 11

assembly properties, configuring, 1237-1240

Code Analysis, 311, 354

constructed generic types, 708

delegates, 787

generics, 738

methods

defining overloads, 517

extensions, 1231

namespaces, 1220

.NET assemblies, 16

optional parameters, 514

Organize Usings feature, 1224

syntax highlighting, 179-180

types, resolving names, 1225

usage-first development, 496

Visual Studio 2010, 116-123

applications, 124-169

designers, 144-155

expressions, 119

installing, 119-120

interfaces, 123

Manage Help Settings utility, 144

navigating, 120-123

Solution Explorer, 126-127

source control, 169

Visual Studio for Applications. *See* **VSTA**

Visual Studio Team System. *See* **VSTS**

Visual Studio Tools for Office. *See* **VSTO**

void

return type, 504

void-returning methods, 407

volatile fields, 558

von Neumann machine model, 342

vshost.exe, 433-436

VSTA (Visual Studio for Applications), 118

VSTO (Visual Studio Tools for Office), 118, 154-155

VSTS (Visual Studio Team System), 167

W

Wadler, Philip, 999

WaitAny method, 1491

WaitForExit method, 1387

WaitHandle class, 1490

waiting, threads, 1443-1444

walking stacks, 49

warnings, 404

code analysis, 543

disabling, 1366

WCF (Windows Communication Foundation), 10, 27, 53, 689, 1283, 1423

weak references, 715-716, 1340-1341

Web services, 11

WF (Windows Workflow Foundation), 27, 53

WFCs (Windows Foundation Classes), 8

WHERE clause, 534

where clauses, 71, 933-936, 1029

where keyword, 59, 397, 739

Where method, 397, 781, 1042

Where operator, 992-993

loops, iterators

ors, 976

ts, 376-380

, sensitivity, 361

g conversions, 628

ard searches, 1357

Viltamuth, Scott, 57

Win32

    C, programming in, 6

    exceptions, 1168-1170

    function namespaces, 1215

WinDbg, 417

windows '

    Call Stack, 1183

    Output, 1180

Windows Communication Foundation. *See* WCF

Windows Distributed interNet Applications Architecture. *See* DNA

Windows Forms, 10, 124, 144-147, 1495

    countdown clocks, 882

    designer, 498

Windows Foundation Classes. *See* WFCs

Windows Management Instrumentation. *See* WMI

Windows on Windows (WOW), 1239

Windows operating system

    configuration settings, 1433

    integrated authentication (-E), 913

Windows Presentation Foundation. *See* WPF

Windows Workflow Foundation. *See* WF; WWF

winexe, 176, 1237

WMI (Windows Management Instrumentation), 1385

Word. *See also* applications

    with COM interop, 1154-1165

    macros, 1151

words, reserved, 1117

WOW (Windows on Windows), 1239

WPF (Windows Presentation Foundation), 10, 53, 147-150, 305, 498, 775, 1187, 1292

    applications, 124

    data binding, 875-876

    integration, 123

    Visual Studio 2010, 119

wrappers, code, 595

wrapping, loops, 823

Write method, 129, 1371, 1404

Write mode, 1483

WriteLine method, 111, 517, 678, 1371

writers, I/O, 1401-1408

writing

    code, 1052-1053

        .NET, 110-111

        snippets, 1192

    contract method calls, 1370

    documentation comments, 225

    event logs, 1380

    extensions, 1066-1068

WWF (Windows Workflow Foundation), 150-100

X

X-coordinate, 634

x64 platforms, 1240

x86 platforms, 1240

XAML, 497-499

xcopy, deployment, 1241, 1243

XML (Extensible Markup Language), 11

    documentation files, 227

    editors, 133

    LINQ, 907-908, 917-920

XOR (exclusive OR) operator, 274, 621, 757

XPath, 908

XSD, LINQ to, 919

Y

Y combinators, 860-861

years, leap, 1318

yield keyword, 63, 810

yield return keyword, 974

yielding to other threads, 1445

Z

zeros

   division by, 255

   heap memory, 580

   initialization, 585

   zero-length vectors, 609

   zero-method interfaces, 688

Zip operator, 562, 1000

zones, time, 1322-1323